Y0-EDQ-848

Current Biography Yearbook

1995

EDITOR
Judith Graham

SENIOR EDITOR
Elizabeth A. Schick

MANAGING EDITOR
Gray Young

ASSOCIATE EDITORS
Hilary D. Claggett
Miriam Helbok
Cliff Thompson
Eve Nagler

ASSISTANT EDITOR
Maureen Eastwood

CONSULTING EDITOR
Charles Moritz

THE H. W. WILSON COMPANY
NEW YORK

FIFTY-SIXTH ANNUAL CUMULATION—1995

PRINTED IN THE UNITED STATES OF AMERICA

International Standard Serial No. (0084-9499)

International Standard Book No. (8424-0884-6)

Library of Congress Catalog Card No. (40-27432)

Table of Contents

PREFACE

The aim of *Current Biography Yearbook 1995,* like that of the preceding volumes in this series of annual dictionaries of contemporary biography, now in its sixth decade of publication, is to provide the reference librarian, the student, or any researcher with objective, accurate, and well-documented biographical articles about living leaders in all fields of human accomplishment the world over. Whenever feasible, obituary notices appear for persons whose biographies have been published in *Current Biography,* and every attempt is made to pick up obituaries that have inadvertently been omitted in previous years.

Current Biography Yearbook 1995 carries on the policy of including new and updated biographical profiles that supersede earlier, outdated articles. Profiles have been made as accurate and objective as possible through careful researching of newspapers, magazines, authoritative reference books, and news releases of both government and private agencies. Immediately after they are published in the eleven monthly issues, articles are submitted to biographees to give them an opportunity to suggest additions and corrections in time for publication of the *Current Biography Yearbook.* To take account of major changes in the careers of biographees, articles are revised before they are included in the yearbook. With the exception of occasional interviews, the questionnaire filled out by the biographee remains the primary source of direct information.

The pages immediately following contain *Explanations, Key to Reference Abbreviations,* and *Key to Abbreviations.* The indexes at the end of the volume are *Biographical References, Periodicals and Newspapers Consulted, Classification by Profession,* and *Cumulated Index—1991-1995.* Some persons who are not professional writers but who have written books are included under *Nonfiction* in addition to their vocational fields. *Current Biography Cumulated Index 1940-1995* cumulates and supersedes all previous indexes, and the reader will need to consult only that index in order to locate a name within that period of time.

For their assistance in preparing *Current Biography Yearbook 1995,* I should like to thank the senior, associate, and assistant editors, and former associate editor Kieran Dugan, who writes the obituaries.

Current Biography welcomes comments and suggestions. Please send your comments to: *Current Biography,* H. W. Wilson, 950 University Ave., Bronx, NY 10452; Fax: 718-590-4566; email: cbmail@wlb.hwwilson.com

Judith Graham

Explanations

Authorities for biographees' full names, with some exceptions, are the bibliographical publications of The H. W. Wilson Company. The biographee's preferred or professional name form is given in the heading of the article, with the full name supplied in the article itself.

The heading of each article includes the phonetic pronunciation of the name if it is unusual, date of birth (if obtainable), and occupation. The article is supplemented by a list of references to selected sources of biographical information, in two alphabets: (1) newspapers and periodicals and (2) books. (See the section *Biographical References,* found in the back of this volume.)

Key to Reference Abbreviations

References to some newspapers and periodicals are listed in abbreviated form; for example, "Pub W 234:36 Jl 8 '88 por" means *Publishers Weekly* volume 234, page 36, July 8, 1988, with portrait. (For full names, see the section *Periodicals and Newspapers Consulted,* found in the back of this volume.)

January—Ja	July—Jl	Journal—J
February—F	August—Ag	Magazine—Mag
March—Mr	September—S	Monthly—Mo
April—Ap	October—O	News—N
May—My	November—N	Portrait—por
June—Je	December—D	Quarterly—Q
		Review—R
		Weekly—W

Key to Abbreviations

AAAA	Amateur Athletic Association of America
AARP	American Association of Retired Persons
AAUP	American Association of University Professors
A.B.	Bachelor of Arts
ABA	American Bar Association
ABC	American Broadcasting Company
ACA	Americans for Constitutional Action
ACLU	American Civil Liberties Union
ADA	Americans for Democratic Action
AEC	Atomic Energy Commission
AFC	American Football Conference
AFL-CIO	American Federation of Labor and Congress of Industrial Organizations
AID	Agency for International Development
ALA	American Library Association
A.M.	Master of Arts
AMA	American Medical Association
ANC	African National Congress
AP	Associated Press
ASCAP	American Society of Composers, Authors and Publishers
ASEAN	Association of Southeast Asian Nations
ASPCA	American Society for the Prevention of Cruelty to Animals
B.A.	Bachelor of Arts
BBC	British Broadcasting Corporation
B.D.	Bachelor of Divinity
B.F.A.	Bachelor of Fine Arts
B.L.S.	Bachelor of Library Science
B.S.	Bachelor of Science
CAB	Civil Aeronautics Board
CBC	Canadian Broadcasting Corporation
C.B.E.	Commander of (the Order of) the British Empire
CBO	Congressional Budget Office
CBS	Columbia Broadcasting System
CEA	Council of Economic Advisers
CIA	Central Intelligence Agency
CIS	Commonwealth of Independent States
CNN	Cable News Network
CORE	Congress of Racial Equality
CPB	Corporation for Public Broadcasting
D.C.L.	Doctor of Civil Law
D.D.	Doctor of Divinity
DEA	Drug Enforcement Administraton
D.Eng.	Doctor of Engineering
DH	Designated hitter
D.J.	Doctor of Jurisprudence
D.Litt.	Doctor of Literature
D.Mus.	Doctor of Music
D.Pol.Sc.	Doctor of Political Science
D.Sc.	Doctor of Science
EC	European Community
ECOSOC	Economic and Social Council (of the United Nations)
ECU	European Currency Unit
Ed.D.	Doctor of Education
EEC	European Economic Community
EEOC	Equal Employment Opportunity Commission
EMS	European Monetary System
EPA	Environmental Protection Agency
ERA	Equal Rights Amendment
E.R.A.	Earned-run average
ESPN	Entertainment and Sports Programming Network
EU	European Union
FAA	Federal Aviation Administration
FAO	Food and Agriculture Organization (of the United Nations)
FBI	Federal Bureau of Investigation
FCC	Federal Communications Commission
FDA	Food and Drug Administration
FEMA	Federal Emergency Management Agency
FHA	Federal Housing Administration
FPC	Federal Power Commission
FRB	Federal Reserve Board
FTC	Federal Trade Commission
GAO	General Accounting Office
GATT	General Agreement on Tariffs and Trade
GOP	Grand Old Party (Republican)
GSA	General Services Administration
HBO	Home Box Office
HEW	Department of Health, Education, and Welfare
HHS	Department of Health and Human Services
H.M.	His Majesty; Her Majesty
HUD	Department of Housing and Urban Development
ICC	Interstate Commerce Commission
IGY	International Geophysical Year
IMF	International Monetary Fund
IRA	Irish Republican Army
IRS	Internal Revenue Service
J.D.	Doctor of Jurisprudence
KGB	Committee of State Security (Soviet secret police)
L.H.D.	Doctor of Humane Letters
Litt.D.	Doctor of Literature
LL.B.	Bachelor of Laws
LL.D.	Doctor of Laws

LL.M.	Master of Laws
M.A.	Master of Arts
M.B.A.	Master of Business Administration
M.B.E.	Member of (the Order of) the British Empire
M.D.	Doctor of Medicine
M.E.	Master of Engineering
M.E.P.	Member of the European Parliment
METO	Middle East Treaty Organization
M.F.A.	Master of Fine Arts
MGM	Metro-Goldwyn-Mayer
M.Litt.	Master of Literature
M.L.S.	Master of Library Science
M.P.	Member of Parliament
M.Sc.	Master of Science
MSW	Master of Social Work
MTV	Music Television
NAACP	National Association for the Advancement of Colored People
NAB	National Association of Broadcasters
NAFTA	North American Free Trade Agreement
NASA	National Aeronautics and Space Administration
NATO	North Atlantic Treaty Organization
NBA	National Basketball Association
NBC	National Broadcasting Company
NCAA	National Collegiate Athletic Association
NEA	National Endowment for the Arts
NEH	National Endowment for the Humanities
NFC	National Football Conference
NFL	National Football League
NHL	National Hockey League
NIH	National Institutes of Health
NIMH	National Institute of Mental Health
NLRB	National Labor Relations Board
NOAA	National Oceanographic and Atmospheric Administration
NOW	National Organization for Women
NPR	National Public Radio
NSA	National Security Agency
NSC	National Security Council
NYSE	New York Stock Exchange
OAS	Organization of American States
O.B.E.	Officer of (the Order of) the British Empire
OECD	Organization for Economic Cooperation and Development
OMB	Office of Management and Budget
OPEC	Organization of Petroleum Exporting Countries
OSHA	Occupational Safety and Health Administration
PAC	Political action committee
PBS	Public Broadcasting Service
PEN	Poets, Playwrights, Editors, Essayists and Novelists (International Association)
Ph.B.	Bachelor of Philosophy
Ph.D.	Doctor of Philosophy
PLC	Public limited company
PLO	Palestine Liberation Organization
PTA	Parent-Teacher Association
RAF	Royal Air Force
RCA	Radio Corporation of America
RKO	Radio-Keith-Orpheum
ROTC	Reserve Officers' Training Corps
SAC	Strategic Air Command
SALT	Strategic Arms Limitation Talks
SDI	Strategic Defense Initiative ("Star Wars")
SEATO	Southeast Asia Treaty Organization
SEC	Securities and Exchange Commission
S.J.	Society of Jesus (Jesuit)
S.J.D.	Doctor of Juridical Science
START	Strategic Arms Reduction Treaty
S.T.B.	Bachelor of Sacred Theology
S.T.D.	Doctor of Sacred Theology
TNT	Turner Network Television
TBS	Turner Broadcasting System
UAR	United Arab Republic
UK	United Kingdom
UN	United Nations
UNESCO	United Nations Educational, Scientific, and Cultural Organization
UNICEF	United Nations Children's Fund
UNRWA	United Nations Relief and Works Agency
UPI	United Press and International News Service
U.S.	United States
USDA	United States Department of Agriculture
USFL	United States Football League
USIA	United States Information Agency
USSR	Union of Soviet Socialist Republics
VA	Veterans Administration
VFW	Veterans of Foreign Wars
VISTA	Volunteers in Service to America
WHO	World Health Organization
WPA	Works Progress Administration
YMCA	Young Men's Christian Association
YMHA	Young Men's Hebrew Association
YWCA	Young Women's Christian Association
YWHA	Young Women's Hebrew Association

List of Biographical Sketches

Current Biography Yearbook

1995

Current Biography Yearbook 1995

Abbott, Jim

Sep. 19, 1967– Baseball player. Address: California Angels, Anaheim Stadium, Anaheim, CA 92806

Jim Abbott is one of an elite group of major-league pitchers to have thrown a no-hitter, a feat he accomplished while he was a New York Yankee in 1993. Abbott, who began the 1995 season as a member of the Chicago White Sox and ended it as a California Angel, is also among the few hurlers whose fastballs have been clocked at over ninety miles an hour. What makes his success all the more remarkable is the fact that he plays ball without a right hand. He was born with a rounded stub at the end of his right arm, with one small, finger-like protrusion where his right hand should be. He pitches with his left hand, with the palm of his glove resting on the stub. After each pitch, he quickly switches the glove to his left hand, so that he can catch or field balls thrown or hit back. Prior to becoming a major-league pitcher, Abbott was an Olympic gold medalist, a collegiate baseball all-star, and a high-school standout in three sports.

Joe Picciolo/AP/Wide World Photos

Abbott's athletic achievements have amazed sports fans and inspired countless numbers of Americans with disabilities, who flock to ballparks to see him pitch. He receives hundreds of letters a week, many of them from handicapped children and their parents, and he tries to answer as many as he can, even though he has never considered himself to be disabled. "I just don't think all of this about me playing with one hand is as big an issue as everyone wants to make it," he told Ira Berkow of the *New York Times* (December 25, 1992). "I don't try to run from the attention about it; I just accept it." Abbott maintains that the toughest thing he faces is not his disability but major-league hitters. The feeling is apparently mutual. "He's got the hand that counts," Larry Sheets of the Baltimore Orioles told a reporter for the *Washington Post* (April 26, 1989) after facing Abbott's power pitching for the first time.

James Anthony Abbott was born on September 19, 1967 in Flint, Michigan, to Mike and Kathy Abbott, who were both eighteen years old and barely out of high school. Both parents managed to attend college while he was growing up, with his father eventually becoming a sales manager for a beer distributor, and his mother becoming a lawyer specializing in educational issues. Abbott has said that his parents never tried to make too much of his missing hand, especially after he refused, at the age of five, to wear the fiberglass and steel prosthesis with which he had been fitted. "My parents kept me in the mainstream," he told Berkow. "They never shielded me. When we moved to a new neighborhood, my father said, 'Jim, go out and meet the kids. Say, I'm Jim Abbott. Ask to play in their game.' . . . I will always be thankful . . . for how they dealt with it. They were young. They were alone. There were no support groups. Really, I look back with admiration."

Recognizing their son's natural athleticism, Abbott's parents tried to steer him into soccer, a sport where the use of hands is not necessary, but the boy loved baseball. So, at a local park, his father taught him to throw a baseball and then move the glove from his right wrist to his left hand in order to catch a quick throw back. Abbott repeated that maneuver thousands of times by himself, throwing a ball against the brick wall of the family's house, and switching the glove to his left hand to catch it, again and again, at closer and closer range to the wall, until the transfer became second nature. Many observers of Abbott's career believe that childhood practice was probably the key to his success in baseball, where his pitching skill was not in doubt but his fielding ability usually was. At every stage of his career, he had to prove that he could throw runners out. By the time he got to the major leagues, where line drives up the middle travel at dangerous speeds, and slow bunts require quick fielding, Abbott's split-second glove-switch technique was described in *Time* (March 20, 1989) as "legerdemain."

Abbott made his first start as a pitcher at the age of eleven, in a Little League game. After he threw a no-hitter, he became a local celebrity and found encouragement from family members and friends. "If someone had said, 'No, Jim, with that arm maybe you should sit this out and keep score,' I might have been crushed and never gone on," Abbott told Hank Hersch of *Sports Illustrated* (May 25, 1987). When he started playing for Flint Central High School, batters quickly challenged his fielding ability. In an early game, eight straight batters attempted to bunt. The first reached base, but Abbott threw the next seven out. During his senior year at Flint Central, he averaged two strikeouts and two hits allowed per game. He also batted .427. (To take his cuts at the plate, Abbott rested the bat handle on his right wrist, then grasped the wrist and the bat with his left hand.) Abbott was successful in other sports as well: he was the leading scorer in the Flint Central intramural basketball league, and he quarterbacked his football team to the state semifinals with four touchdown passes in one game. After his senior year in 1985, he was drafted by the Toronto Blue Jays in the thirty-sixth round, but he turned down the team's offer and instead accepted a baseball scholarship at the University of Michigan.

In three years as a pitcher for the Michigan Wolverines, Abbott had a 26–8 record and a 3.03 ERA, hurling thirteen complete games and six shutouts, racking up 186 strikeouts in 234 innings pitched, and committing only three errors. He led the team to two regular-season Big-Ten titles, in 1986 and 1987. Along the way he won a host of honors, including the Most Courageous Athlete Award in 1986, from the Philadelphia Sportswriters Association, and the 1987 Golden Spikes Award, which is presented annually to the outstanding amateur baseball player in the country by the U.S. Baseball Federation. His most prestigious honor was the 1987 James E. Sullivan Memorial Award, presented to the best American amateur athlete in any sport by the Amateur Athletic Union of the United States. Abbott was the first baseball player to win the Sullivan, and when he got to the podium to accept it, and saw the track-and-field star Jackie Joyner-Kersee and the diving champion Greg Louganis, both of whom had won Olympic gold medals, on the dais, he modestly joked: "I think they picked the worst athlete up here."

Following his sophomore season with the Wolverines, Abbott was selected to the baseball team representing the United States at the 1987 Pan American Games. Before the games began, the United States squad traveled to Cuba for an exhibition series. Abbott pitched in the third game in Havana, thrilling the local crowd when he threw out leadoff hitter Victor Mesa on a tough grounder down the third-base line. The United States went on to win that game over the heavily favored Cubans. It was the first American baseball victory over Cuba in twenty-five years, and Cuban president Fidel Castro made a point of personally congratulating Abbott. Another stop on the tune-up tour preceding the Pan American Games was Japan, where Abbott learned a little more about life with a disability. "They said in their country a little boy with one hand wouldn't be allowed to play, wouldn't be allowed to even get this far. And that just made me hope my playing has opened some eyes," he told Johnette Howard of *Sport* (March 1989). Abbott was chosen by the United States contingent to carry the American flag during the opening ceremonies of the Pan Am Games in Indianapolis. He had a 2–0 record with a 0.00 ERA in the competition, as the American team finished second.

After his third year at the University of Michigan, Abbott was picked as the first-round draft choice of the California Angels; he was the eighth player chosen overall. He decided to defer signing with the Angels in order to participate in the 1988 Summer Olympics. (Baseball was a demonstration sport in the 1988 games, in Seoul, South Korea.) In pre-Olympics games with the American team, Abbott was 7–1 with a 2.59 ERA. In the Olympic tournament itself, the United States team defeated South Korea, Australia, and Puerto Rico on the way to the final against Japan. Abbott, who got the start, allowed only seven hits and retired eleven of the final twelve batters as the United States won the gold medal, the nation's first international baseball title since 1974, with a 5–3 victory. At the end of the game, Abbott was at the bottom of the celebratory pile of players on the pitcher's mound.

Reporting to the Angels spring training camp before the 1989 season, Abbott drew international attention. Over the course of the season, he would be featured in dozens of newspapers and magazines, as well as on television and radio programs. The idea of a "disabled" person playing major-league ball was stirring to many people. Abbott tried to take it all in stride. "All I'm trying to do is pitch the best I can," he told Bruce Anderson for *Sports Illustrated* (March 13, 1989). In his first professional game, an exhibition contest against the San Diego Padres in Yuma, Arizona, he worked three scoreless innings, striking out four, walking none, and giving up just two hits. "He probably has as strong an arm as any lefthander I've caught," California catcher Lance Parrish told Tom Callahan of *Time* (March, 20, 1989). "His motion is so fluid, the ball just kind of explodes." A strong spring led the Angels to name Abbott to their starting rotation. He was only the tenth pitcher since 1965 to jump directly to the majors without any minor-league experience.

In his professional debut, on April 8, 1989 in Anaheim, California against the Seattle Mariners, Abbott pitched only four and two-thirds innings; he was hit hard and took the 7–0 loss. He also lost his second outing, five days later. Then, on April 24, he registered his first major league win, a 3–2 victory over the Baltimore Orioles. "That night I had the most incredible euphoria," Abbott told Rob Brofman for *Life* (June 1989). "I just wanted to hold onto it. I'd say there's nothing better than pitching a game and doing well. Nothing." His record for the season was 12–12, with a 3.92 ERA and 115 strikeouts in 181 innings pitched. The Angels scored only twenty-three runs in his twelve losses. In Abbott's second pro season, he dipped to 10–14, with a 4.51 ERA, and he lead the American League in hits allowed, with 246. The Angels provided Abbott with the sixth-worst run support in the league, scoring just ninety-six runs in all his starts and a total of only fifteen runs in his fourteen losses.

The 1991 season was a turning point for Abbott. He got off to a slow start and soon found himself with a 0–4 record and a 6.00 ERA. "It was the toughest thing I've gone through, baseball-wise, in a long time," he told Hank Hersch of *Sports Illustrated* (September 9, 1991). "In the back of your mind you think, maybe I just don't have it." For the first time in his life, he began to get bad publicity. But after listening to talk-radio commentators berating his pitching, he was actually pleased, because nobody blamed the losses on his lack of a hand. "It was all about pitching—this guy stinks. I thought, 'There it is. Finally, I've arrived,'" he told Hersch.

Hoping to turn his performance around, Abbott practiced his mechanics. Angels manager Doug Rader and pitching coach Marcel Lachemann advised him to rely more on his power pitches, use less off-speed stuff, and work the inside of the plate more. Team psychologist Ken Ravizza taught him to relax by talking to himself on the mound. Abbott also received encouragement from his teammates, his parents, and his fiancée, Dana Douty. He soon found his confidence again, as well as his throwing rhythm, and went on a 14–4 tear, with a 2.95 ERA, from May through September, becoming one of baseball's top pitchers. "It's been a renewal for me, it really has," he told Hersch. "There's so much more confidence. I like to go home and read the statistics now that I'm not ashamed of my own." Abbott finished up the 1991 season with an 18–11 record, a 2.89 ERA, and 158 strikeouts in 222 innings pitched. He was named to the American League All-Star team, and he finished third in the Cy Young Award voting.

The object of intense media scrutiny, Abbott turned down offers for the film or book rights to his life story. He was often compared to the one-armed outfielder Pete Gray, who had played for the St. Louis Browns for a single season, in 1945, but he tried to discourage the comparison, telling Ira Berkow, "I didn't grow up wanting to be another Pete Gray. I grew up wanting to be another Nolan Ryan." The young pitcher worked hard to keep up with the thousands of letters, mostly from young fans, that poured into club offices. Wherever the Angels played, he was asked to speak to or meet with disabled people. "It's a difficult spot, because I know what they're going through and I know how far a little help can go. I answer a lot of letters, but baseball has got to be my priority," he told Rob Brofman.

Abbott was often touched, however, by the children who came to see him. A seven-year-old boy with only parts of two fingers on one hand met him in the Angels' clubhouse during the 1991 season. "He asks me, 'Did kids ever tease you?' Abbott recalled in his 1991 interview with Hersch. "And it takes me back, because they did. People said to me, 'Aw, your hand looks like a foot.' And he said to me, 'They called me Crab at camp.' A vicious thing that is. So I said, 'Yeah, they teased me, too. Do you think it's a problem?' And he says, 'No.' And I said, 'Well, I don't think so either.' And for the first time I said to somebody, 'Look at me, I'm playing with these guys. There's Dave Winfield and Dave Parker and Wally Joyner. I'm playing with them and I'm just like you.' And I don't know if it helps or not. I don't know if it strikes any deep nerve. I don't even know if that's the point of it. But maybe it's just the fact he has someone to relate to. I think that's what mattered most."

In 1992 Abbott pitched well: he was fifth in the American League in ERA, with a 2.77 mark; allowed a career-low twelve home runs; went error-free in forty-six chances; and pitched seven or more innings in twenty-two of his twenty-nine starts. Yet his record was a mediocre 7–15, largely because the Angels gave him only 2.55 runs per game, the lowest mark in the league in twenty-two years. "He pitches his heart out every time," Rod Carew, the Hall of Famer and the Angels' batting coach, told Berkow. "But he pitched with incredibly bad luck. He could win twenty games for the Yankees, easy."

Abbott soon got the chance to prove Carew right. Following a contract dispute with the Angels, he was traded to the Yankees after the 1992 season for three minor-league players. He told Berkow that he was surprised by the trade. "I just thought I'd spend my whole career with the Angels," he said. "It's kind of easy to get it into your head that you're indispensable. And then suddenly I was traded and felt a real sense of rejection." Abbott also said he was concerned about how the move to New York would affect his wife, Dana, a native of Southern California, whom he had married in December 1991. Abbott was pleased, however, to play for a better team. "I'm excited to play for a club that wants to win," he told Joe Sexton of the *New York Times* (December 8, 1992).

On April 12, 1993 Abbott pitched the home opener at Yankee Stadium, against the Kansas City Royals, and put together a winning performance that an Associated Press reporter described as one to "cheer and cherish." In the 4–1 complete-game victory, he threw only eighty-five pitches, giving up eight hits, striking out four batters, and walking none. "I couldn't ask for more," Abbott said in a postgame interview. "It was a tremendous rush, one I will remember for a long time." Even the pitcher he defeated, Royals ace David Cone, was impressed. "How about Jim Abbott? He was great," Cone told reporters after the game. The rest of Abbott's season was mixed: he finished 1993 with an 11–14 record, an ERA of 4.37, and a career-low ninety-five strikeouts. But one of his late-season wins went into the record books, when, on September 4, he pitched a no-hitter against the Cleveland

Indians, becoming only the ninth player in the ninety-year history of the Yankees to achieve that goal. The ninth inning of the 4–0 game was particularly exciting, with the crowd of 27,225 standing and cheering as he retired Kenny Lofton on a ground ball, Felix Fermin on a long drive to center, and Carlos Baerga on an easy roller to short. "The last couple of innings, I had these huge goose bumps on my forearms, and the hair on the back of my head was standing up," Yankee first baseman Don Mattingly told *Sports Illustrated* (September 13, 1993). Buck Showalter, the Yankees' manager, told reporters that he had been afraid to go to the bathroom during the last four innings, fearing that it would jinx Abbott, who walked five batters but never allowed a runner past first base. Yankee reliever Paul Gibson summed up the night by saying, "He's done something only a select group of people have ever done in the history of the game, and he did it by overcoming the kind of physical challenge that would make most kids quit Little League."

Embroiled in a contract dispute with the Yankees following the 1993 season, Abbott was awarded in arbitration the $2.35 million the team had offered, rather than the $3.5 million he sought. In the strike-shortened 1994 season, he was 9–8 with a 4.55 ERA. His 20–22 career record with the Yankees did not live up to the team's expectations, or his own, despite his moments of glory, and in 1995 Abbott became a free agent. He signed a one-year contract with the Chicago White Sox in April 1995. In what turned out to be a brief career with the team, he was easily the best pitcher on a generally disappointing staff, posting a 6–4 record and a 3.36 ERA. On July 27 the fourth-place White Sox traded Abbott and the reliever Tim Fortugno to the Angels for four minor-league prospects: the outfielder McKay Christensen and the pitchers Andrew Lorraine, Bill Simas, and John Snyder.

Surprised by the trade, Abbott said he was sorry to leave Chicago, where he enjoyed playing, but was excited to be a part of the California Angels team again, which at the time was in first place. "How many times do you get a chance to be in a pennant race, to have a chance to fulfill a dream?" he asked Paul Sullivan of the *Chicago Tribune* (August 14, 1995). The Angels' fortunes collapsed in late summer, as the club blew the biggest lead in the shortest time in baseball history—ten and a half games in thirty-five days—and lost the American League Western Division championship to the Seattle Mariners in a tie-breaking game on the final day of the regular season. Abbott pitched fairly well during his second stint as an Angel, however, winning five and losing three. His complete record for the strike-shortened year was 11–8, with an ERA of 3.70.

Jim Abbott stands six feet, three inches tall and weighs 210 pounds, and he has a tall and powerful physique tailor-made for pitching. He lives in southern California with his wife, Dana. In a recent interview with Jack Curry of the *New York Times* (January 17, 1994), Abbott said that he was trying to work on developing a more easygoing approach to his career. He is aware that he has a reputation for being very hard on himself. He also realizes that he is a role model for many handicapped youngsters, but, as he told Steve Marantz in an interview for the *Sporting News* (July 19, 1993), he feels "a little empty" from all the "most courageous athlete" awards he has received over the years. "Courage is so much more than playing baseball with one hand," Abbott said. "That's not courage. Courage is fighting a war; being a parent of a child who is very sick, facing death. That's much more courageous than earning a lot of money playing baseball."

Selected Biographical References: Life 121:118+ Je '89 pors; N Y Times B p7+ D 25 '92 por; Newsweek 113:60 Je 12 '89 por; Sport 80:26+ Mr '89 pors, 82:56 Jl '91 por; Sporting N p12+ Jl 19 '93 pors; Sports Illus 70:27 Mr 13 '89 por, 71:64 Jl 24 '89 por, 75:22+ S 9 '91 pors, 79:62+ S 13 '93 pors; Time 133:78 Mr 20 '89 por

---

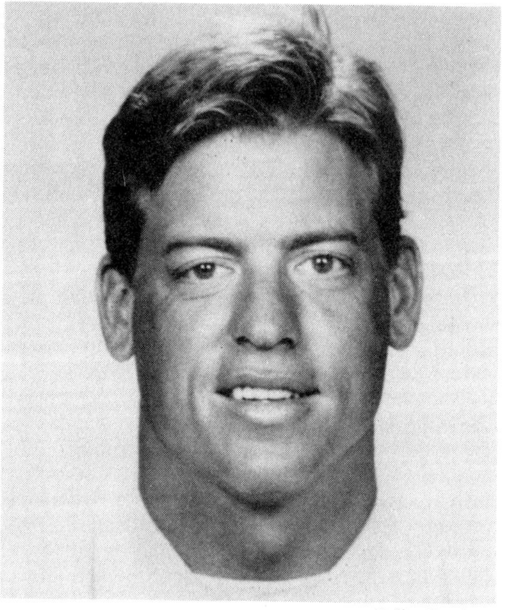

Dallas Cowboys

Aikman, Troy

Nov. 21, 1966– Football player. Address: c/o Dallas Cowboys, One Cowboys Parkway, Irving, TX 75063

When the Dallas Cowboys made Troy Aikman the first selection in the 1989 National Football League draft, the All-American quarterback from the University of California at Los Angeles joined a proud franchise that had fallen on hard times. In his rookie season with the team, the Cowboys lost fifteen times in sixteen outings, their only victory coming against the Washington Redskins when Aikman, who was injured, was out of the lineup. Mistrustful of Dallas coach Jimmy Johnson and prone to injury, the newcomer seemed unlikely to ever replace the Hall of Fame quarterback Roger Staubach in the hearts of Cowboys' fans, but during the 1992–93 season, a healthy Aikman emerged as one of the league's premier signal callers, and in a dramatic resurrection from the ashes of 1989's 1–15 record, Dallas claimed the first of its back-to-back Super Bowl victories. Proclaimed "the best quarterback in the NFL" by no less an authority than Roger Staubach himself, in 1993 Aikman signed a fifty million dollar contract that made him the highest-paid player in professional football history.

With his movie-star good looks, his genuine humility, and his championship rings, Aikman would appear to be a dream come true for Madison Avenue marketeers, who would like to package and sell him as an urban cowboy for the masses, an iconic heartthrob from the heartland clad in blue jeans and boots. The quarterback, however, is uncomfortable with the adulation he receives and wary of the merchandising that currently accompanies fame in professional sports. "You know, I wish there was a switch I could flip, where no one knows me," he confessed to Jill Lieber in an interview for *Sports Illustrated* (February 15, 1993). "And then, when I'm ready to make a splash, I'd flip the switch and say, 'Hey, I'm ready now.' Unfortunately, that doesn't happen."

Born in West Covina, California on November 21, 1966 and reared in Cerritos, a suburb of Los Angeles, Troy Kenneth Aikman was the youngest of Kenneth and Charlyn Aikman's three children. "I've gone through tough times . . . ," Aikman said to Jill Lieber. "People have this misconception that everything has been handed to me on a silver spoon. Nothing is given to anybody in life." As Jill Lieber noted, Aikman's "struggle began at the very beginning." He was born with a deformity of both feet that required the use of corrective orthopedic shoes, which he wore from the age of fourteen months, when he began walking, until he was three years old. The courage and toughness that Aikman has displayed as a football player was inspired by the example set by his father, a gritty, stoic pipeline construction worker and rancher. "Part of the reason I play the way that I play, and don't fear getting hit—people say I take unnecessary hits—I think that stems from back when I was younger and seeing how hard [my father] worked and how tough he was and wanting to prove to him that I was tough too," he said in a conversation with Jeff Weinstock of *Sport* (July 1993). "I think that deep down, I always wanted to prove that I was as tough as he was and that I could take anything that he had to give. And I think that through football I was able to prove that to him."

In 1979 the Aikman family moved from Cerritos to Henryetta, a small town in rural Oklahoma with a population of six thousand. Having exchanged the suburbs of Los Angeles for a 172-acre ranch, on which his family raised cattle, pigs, and chickens, the teenaged Troy experienced considerable culture shock, as Jill Lieber, for one, pointed out. "We had no neighbors," Aikman recalled. "I didn't like Oklahoma at all." Over time, however, he developed an appreciation for traditional small-town values and an abiding love of country music. (He has since come to call Henryetta his hometown, even though he spent his childhood in southern California and later attended the University of California at Los Angeles.) Although the rangy, strong-armed Aikman shone at quarterback for the Henryetta High School Hens, he was, by his own admission, a "real dorky kid." In an interview with Tom Friend of the *New York Times* (February 2, 1993), Aikman's high school principal, Rick Enis, recalled: "He took a typing class with thirty-eight girls, and I remember they went to a contest at Okmulgee State Tech. . . . At a lunch assembly, they announced the third-place winner, some little girl. Then second place was a little girl, and then the winner was—Troy. I kind of dropped my fork, although it was kind of embarrassing for him."

The object of a recruiting war between the University of Oklahoma and Oklahoma State University, Aikman gave an oral commitment to Jimmy Johnson, who was then the Oklahoma State head coach, but changed his mind and enrolled at Oklahoma. Barry Switzer, Oklahoma's head coach at the time, had restored the Sooners to national prominence by installing the wishbone formation, in which the quarterback is required to be a skilled runner rather than a passer. But because he had also recruited the gifted running back Marcus Dupree, whose abilities he wanted to showcase in an I-formation scheme, Switzer promised Aikman the chance to play in an offense with an opened-up passing attack. When Dupree dropped out of school, Switzer revived the wishbone, for which Aikman, a pocket passer, was unsuited. Early in the 1985 campaign, Aikman was sidelined for the season after he broke his leg in a game against the Miami Hurricanes, then coached by Jimmy Johnson. Led by Aikman's backup, Jamelle Holieway, a true wishbone quarterback, the Sooners went on to win the national championship with a 25–10 victory over Penn State in the Orange Bowl.

"He lied to me, no question about that, when he recruited me," Aikman said of Switzer in an interview with Randy Galloway of *Sport* (January 1991). "He tells me he's going to a passing game, and four days into workouts, he's back to the wishbone. But I will say this for the man—he was very up front about everything after that. I liked him, actually. Still do. He was as happy as a coach can possibly be the day I told him I was transferring." Jimmy Johnson tried to persuade the quarterback to attend the University of Miami, but Aikman "didn't like the city," as he put it. On the advice of Switzer, who, in Aikman's words, "went out and made sure" that his former recruit "ended up at the right place," Aikman enrolled as a sociology major at UCLA, where he could run a pro-style offense designed by coach Terry Donahue. Ineligible to play in 1986 because he was a transfer student, Aikman started at quarterback for the Bruins in 1987 and 1988. In his two years at the helm, he completed 64.8 percent of his passes for 5,298 yards and forty-one touchdowns while throwing only seventeen interceptions and led UCLA to consecutive 10–2 records. His victories included a 20–16 win over Florida in the 1987 Aloha Bowl and a 17–3 victory over Arkansas in the 1989 Cotton Bowl.

In April 1989 the Dallas Cowboys made Aikman the first player selected in the NFL draft, and Jimmy Johnson finally landed the quarterback he had been courting since Troy was a sophomore at Henryetta High. The Cowboys were a team in transition. Just two months before the draft, the oil millionaire Jerry Jones had purchased the Cowboys and installed Jimmy Johnson as head coach. To hire Johnson, his football teammate at the University of Arkansas, the new owner unceremoniously fired Tom Landry, the legendary coach who had been the squad's guiding force since the Cowboys joined the NFL in 1960. Although Landry had led Dallas to victory in two Super Bowls in the 1970s, his team had since become the league's doormat, enduring three straight losing seasons and finishing the 1988 campaign with a 3–13 record, the worst in the NFL. In the supplemental draft that was held in July 1989, Johnson spent the Cowboys' first-round draft pick for 1990 to acquire Steve Walsh, who had won twenty-three of twenty-four games at the University of Miami and was the starting quarterback on Johnson's 1987 national championship team.

Having signed the most lucrative rookie contract in NFL history, a six-year deal worth eleven million dollars, Aikman felt threatened and somewhat betrayed by Johnson's acquisition of Walsh. "I thought Jimmy had a natural allegiance to Steve, but the fact that he didn't make that clear or who he wanted for the future made the situation very tense," Aikman recalled when he spoke to Thomas George of the *New York Times* (January 31, 1993). "I wasn't close to Jimmy at all that first year and I was not happy." Although Aikman bested Walsh in head-to-head competition, he played behind a porous offensive line and took what one reporter described as "an ungodly pounding every week."

After missing five midseason games with a broken left index finger, Aikman returned to the starting lineup for the season finale against the Phoenix Cardinals. He threw for a rookie-record 379 yards and completed a pass for the go-ahead score with less than two minutes to go. Knocked unconscious on that play and carried from the field with blood flowing from his ear, Aikman watched groggily from the sidelines as Phoenix won in the final seconds of the game. "That was probably as low as I got," he recalled when he spoke to Jeff Weinstock. "I knew it couldn't get worse." Aikman was 0–11 as the Dallas starter, and the Cowboys once again finished the season with the league's worst record. For the year, he completed 155 of 293 passes (52.9 percent) for 1,749 yards and threw twice as many interceptions (eighteen) as touchdown passes (nine).

Aikman became the team's undisputed offensive leader after Walsh was traded to the New Orleans Saints in late September 1990. Getting off to a poor start, the Cowboys lost seven of their first ten games, but as Aikman gained confidence in his ability to read defenses and rookie Emmitt Smith developed into a game-breaking runner, Dallas reeled off four straight victories. In a crucial late-season game against the Philadelphia Eagles, however, Aikman sustained a separated shoulder in the first quarter, and with backup quarterback Babe Laufenberg unable to ignite the offense, the Cowboys finished out of the play-offs with a record of seven wins and nine losses. Although Aikman improved his rate of completion to 56.6 percent (226 passes out of 399 attempts for 2,579 yards), he once again threw more interceptions (eighteen) than touchdowns (eleven). "Even after losing the final two games," Jimmy Johnson wrote in his memoir *Turning the Thing Around* (1993), "we came out of 1990 with a lot of positive feelings, because we'd won four games in a row and felt that without the injury to Troy we'd have made the play-offs."

In the 1991 off-season, Johnson mended his strained relationship with Aikman by replacing offensive coordinator David Shula, whom Aikman disliked, with Norv Turner, a devotee of the "Air Coryell" passing attack that Don Coryell perfected when he coached the San Diego Chargers from 1978 through 1985. "We hit it off from day one . . . ," Aikman said to Brad Buchholz for *Inside Sports* (July 1992). "[Norv] was a guy I could relate to, be open with. He likes country music, he's down to earth." In addition to gaining Aikman's trust, Turner implemented a ball-control, quick-release passing game that exploited the quarterback's strengths—his compact throwing motion and his ability to find secondary receivers underneath the defensive coverage. "We sped up Troy, his motion, his footwork," Turner explained to Thomas George. "Obviously, when you do that, you've got to speed up everything else—the receivers have to change the style of routes they run for quicker throws and timing throws."

With Turner calling the plays, Aikman was enjoying a banner year when he suffered a knee injury in game twelve that knocked him out of the lineup for the remainder of the 1991 regular season. His backup, Steve Beuerlein, led the team to four straight victories, and the Cowboys finished the season with a record of eleven wins and five losses, making the play-offs for the first time since 1985. With Beuerlein calling the signals, Dallas bested the Bears 17–13 but fell to the Detroit Lions in a 38–6 rout in the second round. For the year, Aikman completed 237 of 363 passes (65.3 percent) for 2,754 yards and eleven touchdowns; he also managed to lower the number of his interceptions, to ten.

In 1992 Aikman played injury-free football for the first time in his NFL career. Guiding the Cowboys to a first-place finish in the NFC East with a record of thirteen wins and three losses, he completed 302 of 473 passes (63.8 percent) for 3,445 yards and threw for twenty-three scores against only fourteen interceptions. Aikman was the NFC's third-ranked passer during the regular season, and in the play-offs he performed at a record-setting pace. He completed fifteen of twenty-five for 200 yards in the Cowboys' 34–10 demolition of Philadelphia, and in the NFC championship game against the favored 49ers at Candlestick Park in San Francisco, he threw for 322 yards on twenty-four-of-thirty-four passing, including a seventy-yard bomb to wideout Alvin Harper in the fourth quarter that clinched the Cowboys' 30–20 victory. In Super Bowl XXVII, Aikman confounded the Buffalo Bills' secondary, completing twenty-two of thirty attempts for 273 yards and four touchdowns in a 52–17 blowout that earned him the game's most-valuable-player award and gave Dallas its first world championship in fifteen years. Aikman compiled a dazzling quarterback rating of 116.7 in the postseason, and in making eighty-nine pass attempts (sixty-one of them completed) without an interception, he broke Joe Montana's five-year-old play-off record.

Aikman began the 1993 season ranked twenty-fifth in salary among the league's twenty-eight starting quarterbacks. "There are some backups who get paid more than I do," Aikman told Jeff Weinstock. "But I signed the contract back in '89 and was happy with it. I will not sit out of camp forcing anybody to renegotiate my contract. I've always felt that if you sign a contract, then you fulfill it." Recovering from back-to-back losses at the beginning of the season, the Cowboys had won ten of fourteen games when, in late December, Aikman signed an eight-year, $50 million contract that made him the highest-paid player in professional football history. Dallas subsequently recorded two more regular-season wins, including a road victory over the New York Giants that gave the Cowboys the NFC East title and the home-field advantage throughout the play-offs.

After dismissing the Green Bay Packers in the conference semifinals, Dallas humbled the San Francisco 49ers by the score of 38–21 to set up a Super Bowl rematch with the Buffalo Bills. Aikman had completed fourteen of eighteen passes for 177 yards and two touchdowns when he was forced to leave the NFC championship game in the third quarter, after suffering a concussion. Returning to the lineup in time for Super Bowl XXVIII, he directed the Cowboys to a 30–13 triumph over the Bills. The win made him the fifth quarterback to win back-to-back Super Bowls—Bart Starr, Bob Griese, Terry Bradshaw, and Joe Montana have also notched consecutive Super Bowl victories—and it matched the pair of world championships that Roger Staubach recorded as the Cowboys' signal caller in the 1970s.

Aikman threw just six interceptions in 392 attempts during the 1993 regular season, completing 271 passes (69.1 percent) for 3,100 yards and fifteen touchdowns and recording a quarterback rating of 99.0, a mark exceeded in club history only by Staubach's 1971 rating of 104.8. In an interview with Richard Justice of the *Washington Post* (January 21, 1994), Norv Turner called Aikman the "most accurate passer [he had] ever seen" and he praised his pupil's "ability to eliminate almost all distractions," a quality that enables Aikman to maintain his composure whether he is, as Turner said, "on a roll or struggling, which he doesn't do very often." When he spoke with Richard Justice, Aikman said that he invests regular-season contests with the same intensity he puts forth in play-off games. "The thing I try to do in bigger games is prepare as best I can mentally, so I can go out and play, not try to do too much," he explained. "I try to be conscious of that when I'm on the field. I think when you try to play outside your abilities that's when you get in trouble. You get caught up in the magnitude of a particular game and end up hurting your team."

Aikman did not blanch at making an eight-year commitment to the the Cowboys, because, as he explained at a press conference on December 23, 1993, "the entire Dallas Cowboys organization" had shown that it "will do what has to be done to be competitive." Aikman's leadership of the team he has joined for what is likely to be his entire professional career was tested in 1994. Before the season began, in addition to the departure via free agency of key players from their defensive unit, Dallas lost both Norv Turner, who became the Washington Redskins' head coach, and Jimmy Johnson, who left the team in the aftermath of a clash of wills with Jerry Jones. Johnson's successor was Barry Switzer, who had no previous professional football experience and had not coached since 1989, when he resigned under a cloud from a scandal-ridden Oklahoma program that was placed on probation by the NCAA.

Although Aikman missed two games in 1994 due to injuries, Dallas won their division with a 12–4 record, which was second in the AFC, behind a resurgent San Francisco. In a divisional play-off contest against the Green Bay Packers, he turned in another superlative performance, racking up twenty-five pass completions for 337 yards and two touchdowns, even though he played the entire game with a brace on his sprained left knee. One of those touchdowns came on a ninety-four yarder to wideout Alvin Harper, the longest pass play in NFL play-off history. But Aikman was thwarted in his efforts to lead the injury-riddled Cowboys to a third consecutive Super Bowl by Steve Young and the San Francisco 49ers, who took advantage of three Dallas turnovers in the first eight minutes of the conference championship game to take a 21–0 lead and went on to capture the NFC title, 38–28.

"Friends say [Aikman is] pretty much what he appears to be," Richard Justice noted in the *Washington Post* (January 28, 1993). "He's soft-spoken and shy, a private man in a public position." Belying the notion that he is, in the words of his agent, Leigh Steinberg, "a marketing dream," Aikman has maintained an attitude of wary skepticism towards the merchandising of athletes. In an interview he gave to Don Pierson of the *Chicago Tribune* (February 4, 1993) after winning the Super Bowl MVP award, he declared: "So many players, once they get into a situation like this, they take it too far and lose focus as to what actually got them to that position. I won't do anything that's going to take away from preparing for the upcoming season. I'm not playing football for the endorsements."

With his blond hair, sky-blue eyes, and leading-man features, the six-foot four-inch, 222-pound Aikman may be the most eligible bachelor in Dallas, but he has steadfastly refused to succumb to the lure of celebrity. When asked his reaction to being named one of *People* magazine's "fifty most beautiful people," he quipped, "Well, they must not know very many people." Aikman likes to relax by listening to country music, working on his computer, and socializing with longtime friends and family members who have moved to the Dallas area. He recently appeared in the video for the song "Long Time Comin'," which was recorded by the country group Shenandoah, whose members are among his closest friends, and he also sang in a star-studded chorus as part of the fund-raiser Farm Aid V. The Troy Aikman Foundation, which he established in 1991, benefits children's charities in the Dallas–Fort Worth area. The quarterback is also an active supporter of a number of other charitable organizations. In 1991 and 1992 he was among the five finalists for NFL Man of the Year, an award bestowed annually to honor players for their contributions to their communities.

Selected Biographical References: Chicago Tribune IV p1+ Ja 15 '93; GQ p268+ S '93 por; Inside Sports 14:22+ Jl '92 pors; N Y Times C p7 D 27 '93 por, B p7+ Ja 26 '94 por; Sport 82:25+ Ja '91 pors, 84:38+ Jl '93 pors; Sports Illus 71:30+ Ag 21 '89 pors, 78:24+ F 15 '93 pors, 79:30+ O 25 '93 pors; Washington Post C p4 Ja 21 '94 por; Bayless, Skip. The Boys (1993); Johnson, Jimmy. Turning the Thing Around (1993)

U.S. Mission to the UN

Albright, Madeleine Korbel
(AHL-brite, MAD-eh-lin KOR-bel)

May 15, 1937– United States permanent representative to the United Nations; political scientist; educator. Address: c/o United States Mission to the UN, 799 United Nations Plaza, New York, NY 10017-3505

A naturalized American citizen who was born in Czechoslovakia and came to the United States at the age of eleven, Madeleine Korbel Albright has served as the country's permanent representative to the United Nations since the beginning of Bill Clinton's presidency, in 1993. Unlike most, if not all, of the eighteen men and one woman who preceded her at the UN post—among them Henry Cabot Lodge Jr., Adlai E. Stevenson, George W. Ball, George Bush, Daniel Patrick Moynihan, Andrew Young, and Jeane J. Kirkpatrick—Albright has acted not merely as a spokesperson for the executive arm of the American government but as a key behind-the-scenes strategist and policy-maker. "She already wields power and influence unprecedented for an American envoy to the UN," Richard Z. Chesnoff, a journalist who specializes in foreign affairs, observed in February 1995.

Often identified as a Washington insider, Albright made her debut on the political scene in 1975, as a fund-raiser for then-senator Edmund S. Muskie during his bid for the Democratic presidential nomination. A fiercely loyal Democrat, she served as an adviser on foreign policy during the presidential campaigns of Walter F. Mondale, Michael S. Dukakis, and Bill Clinton. Her experience in government includes stints as Muskie's chief legislative assistant and as a staff member of the National Security Council. Respected for her expertise in Soviet and Eastern European affairs, for eleven years she was on the faculty of Georgetown University, where she also directed the Women in Foreign Service Program. She was the vice-chairperson of the National Democratic Institute for International Affairs for nearly a decade, and she has headed the Center for National Policy for the past half-dozen years. A "political deal-maker by instinct," as she has been described, Albright is said to bring a "natural internationalism" to her job at the UN. She has been applauded for her forthrightness, her grasp of complex issues and skill at zeroing in on essentials, and her ability to both listen to and command the attention of others. Regarded by the Clinton administration as a "voice for action and forcefulness," she has also been praised for "knowing when to be tough." "At this stage in world history, practically every foreign policy issue has something to do with the UN," Albright has said. "It puts me in the wonderful position of being there at the takeoff, during flight, and at the landing."

Madeleine Korbel Albright was born on May 15, 1937 in Prague, Czechoslovakia to Josef Korbel and Anna (Speeglova) Korbel. She has one sister, Anna Katherine Korbel Silva, who is called Kathy, and one brother, John Joseph Korbel. According to one source, she was christened Madeleine Jana; others reported variously that she was originally named Maria Jana or Marie Jana, that one of her grandmothers nicknamed her Madeleine, and that her name was legally changed during her adolescence.

Albright's father was a member of the Czech diplomatic service, and between 1937 and 1948 the Korbel family lived successively in Belgrade, London, Prague, and then—during the three years that Josef Korbel served as the ambassador to Yugoslavia—Belgrade again. Being uprooted time and again apparently did not faze the young Madeleine. "I made friends very easily," she told Molly Sinclair, who profiled her for the *Washington Post* (January 6, 1991). "I think it has to do with the fact that I lived in a lot of different countries, went to a lot of different schools, and was always being put into situations where I had to relate to the people around me." On many occasions during her childhood, Albright has recalled, her father would enlist her to present bouquets to visiting dignitaries during welcoming ceremonies. She became fluent in English during World War II, when the Korbels lived in London. Beginning when she was seven or eight, for a year or two during the family's second stay in Belgrade, she was tutored by governesses, because her father, who staunchly opposed totalitarianism, wanted to avoid exposing her to the influence of Communists. At age ten she was sent to a boarding school in Switzerland, where she learned French.

At the beginning of 1948, Josef Korbel assumed the job of representing Czechoslovakia on the UN Commission for India and Pakistan, and he began working on the Indian subcontinent. In February 1948 the Czech government was overthrown in a Communist coup, and at some point in that year or early in 1949, Korbel learned that the ruling Communists had charged him in absentia with crimes against the state and sentenced him to death. Shortly thereafter he and his family (who had been living in New York for some months) were granted political asylum in the United States. In 1949 the Korbels settled in Colorado, where Josef Korbel had secured a position as a professor of international relations at the University of Denver. The author of many books on foreign affairs, he eventually became the dean of the university's Graduate School of International Studies and gained wide renown in his field. Albright has often mentioned her father and his scholarly writings in her speeches, and during interviews she has placed his name at the top of her list of mentors. By her own account, her worldview consists largely of ideas he "implanted" in her, as Jacob Heilbrunn quoted her as saying in a *New Republic* (August 22 and 29, 1994) profile of her. She often heard her father sharing his ideas with University of Denver students who visited the Korbel home. "My mother provided the ambiance and did palm reading, and my father was a great intellectual humanist," Albright told Molly Sinclair.

Despite her objections during the only heated confrontation she has recalled ever having with him, Josef Korbel insisted that Albright enroll at an extremely small private high school that had offered her a scholarship. "[The school] did give me a tremendous education," she acknowledged to Molly Sinclair. In *U.S. News & World Report* (February 13, 1995), Richard Z. Chesnoff wrote that "as a teenager, Albright set about becoming Thoroughly American Madeleine," and that by the time she graduated from high school, in 1955, she spoke English with no trace of a foreign accent. At Wellesley College, in Wellesley, Massachusetts, which she entered on a scholarship, she "indulged her twin passions"— journalism and politics—both inside and outside the classroom, Jacob Heilbrunn reported. A political science major, she campaigned for Adlai Stevenson in the 1956 presidential race, and for at least one year, she edited the campus newspaper. She earned a B.A. degree with honors from Wellesley in 1959.

Three days after her graduation, Madeleine Korbel married Joseph Albright, a scion of the Robert R. McCormick-Alicia Patterson newspaper dynasty, whom she had met during the summer of 1957, while both were interning at the *Denver Post*. The couple settled in Chicago, where Joseph Albright had begun working as a reporter with the Chicago *Sun-Times*. Madeleine Albright abandoned her own journalistic ambitions soon after their move, as the result of an interview she had with a *Sun-Times* editor. Addressing her as "Honey," the editor told her that neither the *Sun-Times* nor its competitors would hire a spouse of a *Sun-Times* reporter, and he advised her to pursue another career. "As it turns out, it was very lucky, because I would have been a lousy reporter, and I think I am pretty good at what I do now," Albright observed to Molly Sinclair. For a brief period in 1960, she held a job in public relations in the Chicago offices of *Encyclopaedia Britannica*.

In 1961 Joseph Albright took a job as a reporter and executive with *Newsday*, the Long Island, New York newspaper founded by Alicia Patterson, and the Albrights moved to Long Island. Between 1961 and 1967 Madeleine Albright gave birth to three daughters, including a set of twins. During that period, having employed a full-time housekeeper to share child-care duties, she enrolled in the graduate program in public law and government at Columbia University, in New York City. She studied under, among others, Zbigniew Brzezinski, who at that time directed Columbia's Institute on Communist Affairs. In 1968 she earned both an M.A. degree and a certificate in Russian studies from Columbia. She then began doing research for her doctoral dissertation, the subject of which was to be the part played by the press in the abortive attempt by Czech dissidents in 1968 to loosen the grip of Communism in their country through democratic reforms. In the course of her research, she interviewed many of the dissidents who had participated in those events. Albright has said that in order to write the dissertation—which she described as "the hardest thing [she] ever did"—she had to arise every morning at 4:30.

Meanwhile, in 1968, with Joseph Albright's promotion to Washington bureau chief of *Newsday*, Albright and her family had moved to the nation's capital. Among other volunteer activities in which she engaged after that move, she served on the board of directors of the Beauvoir School, a private school that her twin daughters attended. In the early 1970s, at the suggestion of a parent who had noted her skill at soliciting donations to the school, Albright helped to raise funds for Edmund S. Muskie's ultimately unsuccessful bid for the 1972 presidential nomination. (Several sources identified Muskie as an Albright family friend.) In 1976 Muskie, a senator from Maine, put Albright on his payroll as his chief legislative assistant. "I had just received my Ph.D.," she told Molly Sinclair. "That made it possible for Senator Muskie to introduce me as Dr. Albright, instead of Madeleine Albright, little housewife." Muskie was a member of the Senate Foreign Relations Committee, and Albright spent a substantial portion of her time dealing with foreign affairs.

In 1978 Albright joined the staff of the National Security Council, where, working under Zbigniew Brzezinski, who was then President Jimmy Carter's national security adviser, she served as a congressional liaison, with a focus on foreign policy legislation. With the advent of the administration of President Ronald Reagan, in 1981, she temporarily left government service. From 1981 to 1982 she was a senior fellow in Soviet and Eastern European affairs at the Center for Strategic and International Studies. Also in 1981 she was awarded a Woodrow Wilson Fellowship at the Smithsonian Institution's Woodrow Wilson Center for Scholars. As a fellow at the center until 1982, she wrote *Poland: The Role of the Press in Political Change*, which was published in 1983.

In 1982 the School of Foreign Service at Georgetown University, in Washington, D.C., appointed Albright to the dual positions of research professor of international affairs and director of the Women in Foreign Service Program. By 1993, when she left Georgetown, she had won four "teacher of the year" awards—a record number for that university, according to Jacob Heilbrunn, who attributed her success as an educator to her "approachability and knack for presenting complicated issues in plain language." At about the same time that she entered academia, she began hosting in her home what has been referred to as a high-powered foreign policy salon, at which she and her guests—who through the years included hundreds of Democratic politicians, professors, and theoreticians, among them Bill Clinton when he was the governor of Arkansas—analyzed and debated current issues over dinner. "These were not mere social gatherings, but sessions aimed at laying the groundwork for a Democratic return to power," Jacob Heilbrunn reported.

During the 1984 presidential race, Albright served as the foreign policy coordinator for Walter F. Mondale, the Democratic candidate, as well as for Mondale's running mate, Geraldine A. Ferraro. Also in that year she was named vice-chairman of the National Democratic Institute for International Affairs, a nonprofit corporation that conducts nonpartisan international programs to help promote and strengthen democratic institutions. In 1987 she became Michael S. Dukakis's senior foreign policy adviser in the then-Massachusetts governor's campaign for the presidency. During an interview that she had with Elaine Sciolino of the *New York Times* (July 26, 1988) a few days after Dukakis's nomination at the 1988 Democratic National Convention, Albright described her role in his campaign. "The most important thing is not that [Dukakis] has my views but that he has information and I serve as the honest broker and a good conduit to make sure he has what he needs," she said. "I have a lot of contacts of my own," she explained, "and a lot of people, once they read my name in the paper, started sending me their papers. There's a whole network of people in think tanks and academia who like to give their ideas to presidential candidates." Albright, who worked for Dukakis as a volunteer, reportedly wrote many of his speeches, and she apparently became so important to him that, according to Molly Sinclair, "virtually anyone who wanted to see him about a foreign policy issue had to go through her."

In 1989 Albright took over as president of the Center for National Policy, a nonprofit Democratic interdisciplinary research institute, and her prominence in Democratic circles grew significantly. Among other leading Democrats, Edmund Muskie expressed the opinion that, were the party to regain control of the White House, Albright should be considered for the position of national security adviser or even secretary of state. "If we're going to make these things unisexual, then Madeleine ought to be at the head of the line," he said to Molly Sinclair. "She has the ability. She is as credible, as on top of emerging foreign policy, as anyone I know."

Albright's influence on Capitol Hill was also increasing. A spokesperson for the Senate Foreign Relations Committee told Molly Sinclair in 1991 that Albright was "one of the people we turn to for advice and perspective" and that she conducted meetings at the Capitol at which leaders of Eastern European countries and other nations met with members of Congress and their senior aides. One of those leaders, the Czech playwright and human-rights campaigner Vaclav Havel, recruited her to serve as his interpreter and adviser during his first state visit to the United States, which he made in early 1990, shortly after being elected president of Czechoslovakia by his nation's parliament. He and Albright soon became close friends.

Albright helped the Democratic National Committee formulate the party's platform in 1992, and, in collaboration with Warren Christopher, Anthony Lake, and Samuel R. Berger, she developed foreign policy position papers for Bill Clinton after Clinton won the Democratic nomination for president that summer. At a press conference held on December 22, 1992, President-elect Clinton introduced Albright as his choice for delegate to the UN. (He named Christopher, Lake, and Berger to his foreign policy team as well.) "As a result of the generous spirit of the American people, our family had the privilege of growing up as free Americans," Albright said at the press conference, as quoted by Dan Balz in the *Washington Post* (December 23, 1992). "You can therefore understand how proud I will be to sit at the United Nations behind the nameplate that says 'United States of America.'" Commenting on Clinton's selection of Albright in the *Washington Post* (December 29, 1992), the columnist Mary McGrory described her as "an intellectual . . . with a heart" and added, "She is precisely the kind of woman everyone wished could have been in the room when the men were making their disastrous decisions about Vietnam."

At her confirmation hearing before the Senate Foreign Relations Committee on January 21, 1993, Albright said, "History will record that the end of the Cold War has marked a new beginning for the United Nations. . . . I am firmly convinced that, today, we are witnessing the best chance for fulfilling the United Nations' original mission." The mission statement of the UN charter, she reminded the senators at the hearing, calls upon the peoples of the United Nations "to save succeeding generations from the scourge of war, to reaffirm faith in fundamental human rights, to establish conditions under which justice and respect for international law can be maintained, and to promote social progress and better standards of life in larger freedom." "We not only need to fulfill their dreams but also to make this international organization face the challenges of the next century," she said. "And if we do not do it today, we may not have another opportunity."

The Senate unanimously confirmed Albright's nomination on January 27, 1993, and the next day she was sworn into office. In giving her the rank of cabinet officer, President Clinton returned to the precedent set when Jeane J. Kirkpatrick served as the United States' UN representative, during the administration of President Ronald Reagan. (President George Bush stripped the ambassadorship of cabinet rank when, in 1989, he appointed Thomas R. Pickering—Albright's immediate predecessor—to the position.) Albright also holds the rank and status of ambassador extraordinary and plenipotentiary, and she is a member of the National Security Council. As a key presidential adviser on foreign policy, she attends a biweekly conclave known as the "principals meeting," along with the director of the CIA, secretaries of defense and state, and national security adviser. Albright shuttles between UN headquarters in New York City and Washington as often as five times a week. "The people I work with appreciate the fact that I'm plugged into Washington," Kevin Fedarko quoted her as saying in *Time* (October 31, 1994). "I'm in the inner circle. I'm involved in everything."

Since presenting her credentials at the UN on February 1, 1993, Albright has inspected peacekeeping operations and other UN initiatives in more than a dozen countries overseas, including the former Yugoslav republics of Bosnia, Croatia, and Slovenia; the former Soviet republics of Moldova, Georgia, Armenia, and Azerbaijan; the African nations of Somalia, Ethiopia, Mozambique, and the Sudan; Cambodia, in Asia; in Central America, El Salvador; and in the Caribbean, Haiti. Among the matters that have required the greatest portion of her attention are the ethnic conflicts in the former Yugoslavia; the civil wars in Somalia and Rwanda; the reinstallation of the democratically elected government of Jean-Bertrand Aristide in Haiti; and the continuing use of economic sanctions as a means of pressuring Iraq to abandon its terrorist activities, aggressive actions toward Kuwait, and other behavior deemed unacceptable by the United States.

"I do not believe I can fulfill my mission to the UN unless I am also able to persuade the American people of the importance of that mission," Albright said on April 1, 1993, in one of the first of many speeches that she has given in the past two years in a number of different venues, in an effort to build support among Americans for the activities of the UN (and also for an increase in the United States' financial contribution to UN peacekeeping operations and other programs, which currently totals less than two-tenths of one percent of the federal budget). Generating enthusiasm among Americans for UN projects has never been easy, because, as Albright has observed, "Americans have always been ambivalent about activism abroad." But, as she declared in her April 1, 1993 speech, which she presented at the Town Hall of California, in Los Angeles, "neither our history, nor our character, nor our self-interest will allow us to withdraw from the center stage of global political and economic life." "It is the responsibility of leaders not simply to parrot public opinion, but also to shape it," she continued. "And we have a responsibility now to convey the fact that in today's world, domestic policy and foreign policy are no longer separable things. Yes, it costs money to help keep peace around the world. But by any measure, the most expensive peacekeeping mission is a bargain compared to the least expensive war—not just because it costs fewer dollars, but because it costs fewer lives [and] creates fewer refugees and orphans, and because it plants the seeds of future reconciliation, not future revenge."

Albright has retreated somewhat from her emphasis, early on in her ambassadorship, on the superiority of "assertive multilateralism" over unilateral responses in thwarting the ambitions of what she has called "petty tyrants and defiant warlords." In an address to State Department employees that she gave at the secretary of state's Open Forum on October 28, 1994, she said that "in seeking to further the full range of our interests, we will need—and we should use—every available foreign policy tool. . . . We should not be boxed into rigid choices between force and diplomacy, economic and political, unilateral and multilateral. Nor should we be lured by what [Ralph Waldo] Emerson called 'foolish consistencies'—a foreign policy that responds in the same way regardless of circumstance will be consistent only in its failure. Foreign policy is not auto mechanics; it is an art. The tools we select must be weighed against a matrix of past commitments, present capabilities, future hopes, and constant values. In each instance, we should seek to combine principle with pragmatism—to do the right thing and to do the thing right. . . . American military power and the credibility of its possible use remains the most potent force for international order in the world today."

According to Mary McGrory, Madeleine Albright is kind and hospitable, has a "strong strain of maternal solicitude," and is "universally known as a good soul." "What I've always found striking about Madeleine is her humanity, her true concern for individuals and their welfare," Kirk O'Donnell, a former president of the Center for National Policy, told Dan Balz. A diplomat interviewed by Barbara Crossette for the *New York Times* (November 25, 1994) described her as "a person of passionate temper." "Fiercely, emotionally proud" to be representing the United States at the UN, according to Crossette, Albright has said that she "love[s] every minute" of her job. Renowned for her outspokenness and for "her willingness to wield the big stick whenever the president needs to make a point," as Kevin Fedarko put it, she is also "a quintessential team player who hates to improvise and rarely says anything that isn't thoroughly vetted first in Washington," Julia Preston wrote in the *Washington Post* (October 14, 1994). Preston quoted a senior delegate from a developing nation as saying of Albright, "There's no pussyfooting around with her; you know exactly where you stand. She's tough—so what?"

Four years ago, at a talk Albright gave for a group of Georgetown University women students, she recalled that as a staff member of the National Security Council in the late 1970s, she "had to learn to speak out" for herself. "I would be in a White House meeting, and I would think of something and not say anything because I wasn't sure that it would add to the discussion. Then some man would say what I had been thinking, and it would be hailed as a great idea." Albright has worked to forge closer ties among the few women (seven as of October 1995) among the 185 permanent representatives at the UN and has expressed her determination to try to increase their numbers.

In addition to three books, among them *The Soviet Diplomatic Service: Profile of an Elite*, Albright has written book chapters and articles for professional journals. Her activities have included service as a trustee of the Black Student Fund, the Democratic Forum, and Wellesley College and as a member of the boards of directors of the Washington Urban League and the Atlantic Council. She is a member of the Council on Foreign Relations, the Czechoslovak Society for Arts and Sciences, the American Association for the Advancement of Slavic Studies, the executive committee of D.C. Citizens for Better Public Education, and several other groups. In addition to English, French, and Czech, she speaks and reads Russian and Polish. She received a W. Averell Harriman Democracy Award, from the National Democratic Institute for International Affairs, in 1995. Albright lives in a townhouse in the Georgetown section of Washington and owns a farm in Virginia. Her daughters Anne and Alice were born in 1961; her daughter Katharine, called Katie, was born in 1967. Her marriage to Joseph Albright ended in divorce in 1983.

Selected Biographical References: N Y Times A p16 Jl 26 '88 por, A p1+ N 25 '94 pors; New Repub 211:19+ Ag 22–29 '94; U S News 118:60+ F 13 '95 por; Washington Post F p1+ Ja 6 '91 pors, A p10 D 23 '92; Who's Who in America, 1995

Allen, Tim

June 13, 1953– Comedian; actor, writer. Address: c/o Marleah Leslie and Associates, 292 S. La Cienega Blvd., Suite 202, Beverly Hills, CA 90211; c/o Walt Disney Studios, 500 S. Buena Vista St., Burbank, CA 91521; c/o Hyperion, 114 Fifth Ave., New York, NY 10011

There are few personalities in today's entertainment world who have enjoyed such a seemingly meteoric rise to celebrity as Tim Allen, the hardware-wielding star of the top-rated television sitcom *Home Improvement*. Contrary to appearances, Allen's success was attained only after years spent in obscurity in the nightclubs of the comedy circuit. The comedic stock-in-trade of Allen's stand-up routines, which in turn became source material for his television series, has been his observations—always unabashed, often poignant, and usually punctuated with an audible grunt—about the nature of masculinity and the differences between the sexes. It is Allen's ability to take chances with his remarks, all the while admitting his own fallibility, that makes him seem "so right for these postfeminist times," according to Gerri Hirshey, writing in GQ (March 1994). "There's no antiseptic reek of correctness about this sitcom Modern Guy—just motor oil and Lava soap," she continued. "In his live performances," Ken Tucker

ABC, Inc.

Tim Allen

wrote in *Entertainment Weekly* (October 25, 1991), "Allen's bestial punch line became his trademark; it worked because it simultaneously symbolized and criticized the stand-up misogyny of many male comics." Since the debut of his television show, Allen has starred in a top-grossing movie, *The Santa Clause*, making him one of the most sought-after players in the crowded field of comedians-turned-actors, and written a best-selling autobiography, *Don't Stand Too Close to a Naked Man* (1994).

Tim Allen was born Timothy Allen Dick on June 13, 1953 in Denver, Colorado, one of the six children (five boys and one girl) of Gerald Dick, a real-estate salesman, and Martha Dick, a community-service worker. Allen's typical middle-class suburban childhood—replete with neighborhood gangs, BB guns, and the seeming omniscience of big brothers and older boys, as Allen recounted it in his autobiography—was marred by the constant teasing of other children about the slang connotations of his surname. "I believe my name created my life," Allen wrote in his book. His use of self-deprecatory humor as a defense mechanism against such barbs helped form his first comic sensibilities. "Dealing from childhood with people's reactions," he wrote, "helped form the basis of my humor about men and the differences between men and women. . . . What I learned growing up is that we have power over words, not the other way around. People made fun of my name every day, but I learned to cope. I numbed myself." He eventually trimmed his name upon entering the nightclub circuit, after the producers of a television talk show on which he was to appear refused to flash his surname onscreen.

The baiting and bullying notwithstanding, Allen's childhood was, by all accounts, normal until November 23, 1964, when his father was killed in a car accident involving a drunk driver who crashed into the Dicks' car as they were on their way home from a college football game. Allen, then eleven years old, and his sister were the only members of the family who did not attend the game. "This loss stretched every boundary I knew," he recalled in his book. "I wasn't king of my universe anymore. In fact, I felt helpless, useless, pathetic. I had no control, and my scramble to regain some made me grow up very quickly." Two years later his mother married a telex executive who had been her high-school sweetheart. A widower whose wife had also died in an auto accident, he had three children of his own. In 1967 the couple moved with their children to Birmingham, Michigan, a suburb of Detroit, where Allen completed high school. Following his graduation, he enrolled at Western Michigan University, in Kalamazoo, from which he received a degree in television production in 1976.

Allen began doing stand-up routines at Detroit's Comedy Castle in 1980, when, challenged by his close friend Bill Ludwig, he attempted to tell a few jokes onstage. Beginning in 1983 he developed his comedy routine at night, supporting himself by appearing in television commercials, including ones for Ford, Chevrolet, and Kmart. Before long, he signed with an agent in Los Angeles and began to break into top-tier comedy clubs. Comedy Castle owner Mark Ridley told Richard Zoglin of *Time* (December 12, 1994) that he had seen the difference between Allen and other fledgling comics in his first performance. "He was a bundle of nerves, shaking his hands and pacing himself into a frenzy," Ridley said, "but boom, once he was up there, he was in control."

In its nascent phase, Allen's routine relied heavily on sexual and scatological references. "It was like turning your guitar up real loud," he told Zoglin. Eventually, he began integrating anecdotes about communication between the sexes into his act. The origin of his would-be-macho handyman persona was a 1984 show in Akron, Ohio, in front of a room filled with Goodyear salesmen. After failing to elicit much response from the predominantly male audience with his usual one-liners, Allen shifted the emphasis of his routine that night to a subject to which he thought the crowd might relate, and he began to list the various tools one would find in a hardware store. "They started screaming," he told Jefferson Graham of *USA Today* (August 16, 1991). "I realized I was onto something."

When Allen realized that women also could relate to this newer material through their experiences with their husbands, he tied all of his themes together into a routine called "Men Are Pigs," complete with sequences of grunts meant to represent men's primal expressions of elation about their tools being extensions of themselves. The entire act caught on quickly, inciting a debate about whether the noises represented pigs' oinking or apes' grunting. In her article for *GQ*, Hirshey compared Allen's stand-up routine with that of one of his contemporaries who had attempted to capitalize on a different strain of the same topic, noting that "top wart hog Andrew Dice Clay self-destructed with his obscene misogynist buffoonery." In contrast, she continued, "Allen's stage persona is . . . surprisingly intelligent. Affectionate. Easily housebroken. With the exception of a few bluish bits in the stand-up act, Allen's piggy stuff is just honest, clean dirt—much of it at his own expense." After appearing in 1988 in the cable-television special *Showtime Comedy Club All-Stars II* and in the film *Comedy's Dirtiest Dozen*, Allen packaged his routine into a one-hour Showtime television special, *Men Are Pigs*, in 1990, for which he won a cable television ACE award in the same year.

It was at this time, in 1990, that Tim Allen came to the attention of Walt Disney Studios chairman Jeffrey Katzenberg, who had reviewed a tape of the comedian's Showtime special at a development meeting for new television series. "He set the room on fire," Katzenberg recalled to Richard Zoglin of *Time*. "It was like everyone had touched a raw electric wire." Katzenberg (who resigned from Disney in 1994 to form a new studio) and Michael D. Eisner, the chairman of the Walt Disney Company, attended one of Allen's live performances at the Improv comedy club in Los Angeles and approached the comedian backstage. Allen was subsequently offered the starring role in several situation comedies that were under development, including television versions of the movies *Turner & Hootch*, in which he would costar with a dog, and *Dead Poets Society*, in which he would play the part created by Robin Williams in the film. He declined both. It was not until he was introduced to Matt Williams, who had produced *Roseanne* and who had an ongoing development deal with Disney, that Allen was able to persuade the studio to develop a show for Disney's Touchstone Television division based upon the "Men Are Pigs" routine.

Addressing the comedian's theme of the confusion experienced by contemporary men, *Home Improvement* incorporates ideas from two books of popular psychology: the poet Robert Bly's *Iron John: A Book About Men* (1990), about male identity, and the linguist Deborah Tannen's *You Just Don't Understand: Women and Men in Conversation* (1990), about miscommunication between the sexes. The pilot introduced Allen as Tim Taylor, the host of a *This Old House*-style home-repair show called *Tool Time*. At home Taylor is a voltage-happy klutz, a perpetually bemused husband, and a helpless father of three boys. Patricia Richardson took the part of Taylor's independent, level-headed wife, Jill, a full-time mother attempting to return to the work force. In between mishaps at work and at home, Taylor imbibes words of wisdom (often derived from the pages of Bly or Tannen) from his next-door neighbor, Wilson (Earl Hindman), whose face is always half-obscured by the picket fence that divides their property. Because Matt Williams, David McFadzean, and Carmen Finestra, the show's co-executive producers, wrote the script for the pilot, they were credited with "cocreator" titles, as the Writers' Guild of America rules require, but the show's credits indicated that it was based on the stand-up comedy of Tim Allen. "I developed the whole show," Allen told Jefferson Graham of *USA Today* (August 26, 1992). "They made the characters come alive."

During the intense media coverage that preceded *Home Improvement*'s premiere on ABC, on September 17, 1991, a revelation about Allen's past threatened to come to light. Anticipating reports in the tabloids, Allen admitted to network executives, and then to the general public, that he had served a federal prison term from 1980 to 1983. After graduating in 1976 from college and finding himself essentially directionless, Allen had begun selling cocaine. "I knew I was wrong," he acknowledged in an interview with Rita Kempley of the *Washington Post* (November 20, 1994). "Immediately I wanted out of this so bad, but it's like the CIA in those old spy movies—it's real easy to get into, and it's really hard to get out." In 1979, as the result of an undercover operation conducted by Michigan police, Allen and twenty others were arrested. It was during the period between his arraignment, at which he pled guilty to charges of possession and distribution of narcotics, and his sentencing, in November 1980, to eight years in prison (he ultimately served twenty-eight months at a minimum-security federal facility in Minnesota), that Allen had first dabbled in stand-up comedy at the Comedy Castle. "Even today," Allen noted in his book, "it's a big shock to people that I spent any time behind bars. They say, 'You're not that kind of guy.' Well, yes, I was that kind of guy. Half model citizen, half hooligan."

Humor proved to be a critical element for Allen in surviving prison, for he was able to defuse potentially violent flare-ups by making his would-be attacker laugh uncontrollably at his dead-on Elmer Fudd imitations. "Being funny saved my life—on the inside, in *my* inside, and, as I was soon to discover, on the outside," he wrote in his autobiography. "Plus I had a few uninterrupted years with no responsibilities to work on my material." Aided emotionally during this time by the steadfast support of Laura Deibel, whom he had dated in college and whom he married in 1984, Allen has indicated that he actually benefited from his incarceration, because it enabled him to focus and redirect his energy. "In a hideous way, aside from the pain it put my family and friends through, getting caught probably saved my life, because it had no direction," Allen said in his interview with Jefferson Graham for the August 16, 1991 *USA Today* article. When the story of Allen's conviction was made public, ABC executives demonstrated absolute commitment to the success of *Home Improvement*. "As far as we're concerned," Robert Iger, the president of ABC Entertainment, told Graham, "this is something in Tim's past that he's taken care of. It will not, in any way, diminish our enthusiasm for the show or for Tim Allen. We don't view it as a problem and don't think a big deal should be made out of it."

When *Home Improvement* debuted in the fall of 1991, most critics focused strictly on the show itself, which initially garnered mainly lukewarm praise. A reviewer for *Rolling Stone* (October 3, 1991) felt that "*Home Improvement* breaks its bit when Allen gets home [from hosting *Tool Time*] and tries to have a sitcom: his wife and sons are relatively bland and colorless." "Allen's sitcom may well work," John J. O'Connor wrote in the *New York Times* (September 17, 1991), "although by the second episode it already shows uneasy signs of cuteness bloat." On a more positive note, Marvin Kitman characterized the show in *New York Newsday* (September 16, 1991) as "a comedy of substance about the male spirit and how it impacts on people and things around him. . . . The show is well-conceived, well-written, and very funny." He also found in Allen "a likeable performer, a real fresh talent, . . . [and] the most wonderful example of a stand-up comedian crossing over to acting since Richard Lewis of *Anything but Love* and Jerry Seinfeld of *Seinfeld*."

Although its critical reception was decidedly mixed, *Home Improvement* became an instant favorite of television viewers, nudging its way into the Nielsen top ten by the middle of its first season. By the summer of 1992, the show had become that season's highest-rated new series, standing at the number-five position overall. Less than a year later, Carla Hills reported in *TV Guide* (April 24, 1993) that since early February 1993, the show had been viewed by an average of thirty million people, most of whom, according to Hills, were women. "It's astounding," co-executive producer David McFadzean told Hills. "I believe the numbers we're getting are because we've created almost an alternative to other sitcoms. It has a lot of hard edges, but the characters love each other." As the seasons wore on, the show's characters developed fuller personalities and greater credibility, and the themes evolved from mishaps with power tools into more sophisticated areas like miscommunication between spouses.

At the end of the show's first season, Allen cohosted (with Kirstie Alley and Dennis Miller) the 1992 Emmy Awards ceremony, "an unprecedented achievement for such a newcomer to Hollywood," according to Jefferson Graham of *USA Today*, and during the summer hiatus between the first and second seasons, he embarked on a thirty-city stand-up concert tour. In the interview with Graham, Allen attributed his ability to handle his fame to the lessons he learned behind bars. "Had I not made that mistake and learned from it," he said, "I wouldn't have the strength or the peace of mind to do this now and not let it affect me." He added, "I still think I'm much better as a comedian than I am on the show." Allen's modesty notwithstanding, he won a People's Choice Award in 1994 for best male television performer and a Golden Globe Award in 1995 for best actor in a musical or comedy series. Although in 1994 *Home Improvement* was nominated for an Emmy Award as outstanding comedy series, the show failed to garner an Emmy nomination in 1995, an oversight that Allen has taken as a deliberate snub.

By the autumn of 1994, building upon *Home Improvement's* extraordinary success, Tim Allen's career had expanded in scope to include writing and film acting. His triumphs in these two arenas were both immediate and simultaneous, to such an extent that by the first week of December he was able to make a claim unprecedented in the annals of entertainment: he was the star of the highest-rated television series, the author of a best-selling book, and in his feature-film debut, the central figure in a top-earning motion picture. *Don't Stand Too Close to a Naked Man*, the most successful work yet to be published by Disney's four-year-old Hyperion book division, reached number one on the *New York Times* best-seller list for nonfiction in October 1994. "The humor is a strange amalgam of the callow and the sophisticated," according to a reviewer for *Publishers Weekly* (August 15, 1994), "and the result is only intermittently funny, and then only mildly so." "What Disney wanted was pretty much a yukfest," Allen told Tim Appelo for *Entertainment Weekly* (November 18, 1994), "but I was not prepared to do that—and I came back with a renewed sense of where I'm coming from. It helped me blow out my motors and defoul my spark plugs." In apparent agreement, Appelo referred to the book as "certainly the most ambitiously revelatory of the TV comics' tomes now inundating bookstores."

Like his television ratings, Tim Allen's financial benefit to Disney studios has been unprecedented. In addition to the estimated $400 million that *Home Improvement* had earned by December 1994 in the sale of reruns alone, his first movie, *The Santa Clause*, was a runaway hit, earning $84 million at the box office in its first four weeks of release and becoming the fourth-highest-grossing film of 1994. Directed by former *Home Improvement* director John Pasquin for Walt Disney Pictures and cowritten by Leo Benvenuti and Steve Rudnick, *The Santa Clause* features Allen as Scott Calvin, a divorced father who reluctantly assumes Santa Claus's gift-delivering duties when the real Saint Nick falls off Calvin's roof on Christmas Eve. When this new occupation becomes permanent, Calvin uncontrollably begins to metamorphose into character, growing whiskers and gaining an immense belly, and he is soon transformed spiritually as well. In his review for *Newsweek* (November 21, 1994), Jeff Giles called *The Santa Clause* "clunky and ramshackle," but Ralph Novak of *People* (November 21, 1994) proclaimed the movie "the most playfully amusing, inventive new cinematic Christmas fable in several decades. . . . Everything is accomplished with sweetness and reverence for the institution it addresses."

Nineteen ninety-five proved to be a banner year for Allen, who in May was reportedly earning $250,000 per episode of *Home Improvement*, which went into syndication on the Fox Television

Network in September. According to a report published in *TV Guide* in the spring of that year, he was the most powerful television star in Hollywood, in terms of possessing hiring and firing authority and having the freedom to launch new ventures. In the autumn, he introduced a signature hammer he had designed for the Hart Tool Company; if successful, the hammer may inaugurate a series of designer tools, profits from which would be donated to charity. Building on the success of *The Santa Clause*, Allen provided the voice of Buzz Lightyear, an astronaut doll, in Disney's forthcoming animated movie *Toy Story*. In the spring of 1996 he is scheduled to begin filming "Indian in the City," in which he will star as a man who discovers he has a child who was reared in the Amazon by his estranged wife.

Tim Allen spends his increasingly scarce leisure time with his wife, Laura Deibel, who manages his business affairs, and their five-year-old daughter, Katherine ("Kady" or "K.D.") Dick, with whom he shares a home in California's San Fernando Valley and a lake house in northern Michigan, next door to Laura's parents' home. His hobbies include reading about the universe, bicycling, driving race cars, playing golf, and collecting automobiles—including a 1966 Ferrari, a Porsche (a gift from Disney), and a pair of Mustangs—and, of course, power tools.

Selected Biographical References: Entertainment W 89:62+ O 25 '91 pors, 249:20+ N 18 '94 pors; GQ 64:92+ Mr '94 por; N Y Times H p31+ S 22 '91 por; People 38:105+ Jl 6 '92 pors; Time 144:76+ D 12 '94 pors; Allen, Tim. Don't Stand Too Close to a Naked Man (1994); Contemporary Theatre, Film, and Television vol 12 (1994); Who's Who in America, 1995

Rosica, Mulhern & Associates Inc.

Amos, Wally

July 1, 1936– Entrepreneur; theatrical agent; social activist. Address: P.O. Box 897, Kailua, HI 96734

In 1980 the Smithsonian Institution's National Museum of American History acquired for its "Business Americana" collection two symbols of the Famous Amos Chocolate Chip Cookie Corporation and its founder, Wally Amos: the straw hat and embroidered cotton shirt that Amos had made his trademarks after opening the first store in the nation devoted to the sale of homemade-style chocolate-chip cookies. Debuting in Hollywood in 1975, Amos's business launched what grew into the immensely lucrative gourmet cookie industry in the United States. A "classic American entrepreneur, a man with a dream and no money" and the hero of a celebrated success story—his portrait appeared on the cover of *Time* in 1977—Amos promoted his product with the same gusto that had marked his previous careers as the first black talent agent at the prestigious William Morris Agency and as an independent theatrical manager. "I don't sell cookies, I *am* the cookie," he has said. "My personality is part of that cookie; the cookie is an extension of my personality."

Exploiting his fame and popularity for the benefit of others, since the late 1970s Amos has devoted countless hours to national literacy and dropout-prevention programs, and, since his "spiritual awakening" in around 1978, he has given hundreds of inspirational and motivational lectures at universities and elsewhere. He continued those activities after losing control of the Famous Amos company, in the mid-1980s, terminating his association with it completely, in 1989, and, in 1991, establishing another company, Wally Amos Presents: Chip & Cookie, which he closed the next year during a legal battle with the owners of Famous Amos. He started the Uncle Noname Cookie Company, his current business, in 1992. Amos is the coauthor, with Leroy Robinson, of *The Famous Amos Story: The Face That Launched a Thousand Chips* (1983). He has also written, with Gregory Amos and Camilla Denton, respectively, two semiautobiographical books: *The Power in You: Ten Secret Ingredients for Inner Strength* (1988) and *Man with No Name: Turn Lemons into Lemonade* (1994). He won the Horatio Alger Award in 1987 and the National Literacy Honors Award in 1990.

The only child of Wallace Amos Sr. and Ruby Amos, Wallace Amos Jr. was born on July 1, 1936, in his parents' tiny house in a black community in

Tallahassee, Florida. His older half brother, his mother's first son, did not live with the Amos family. Wally Amos has described his father as "a good person" who "always remained true to himself" and did "the best he knew how to do with what he had to work with." A laborer at the local gasworks who, like his wife, could neither read nor write, Wallace Sr. was seldom home even when he was not at his job. Similarly, Ruby Amos spent less time at home than the average mother in their community, but not because she was socializing elsewhere; rather, her outstanding qualities as a domestic kept her in great demand. According to Amos, his mother "willingly took on all of life's challenges and never complained."

Unlike his father, Amos's mother was an uncompromising disciplinarian, and she whipped young Wally whenever he deviated in any way from her strict code of behavior. When neither of his parents was home, various neighbors looked after him, and they often reminded him that "Ruby's commandments should not be broken," in his words. Another person of influence during his early years was his paternal grandmother, who treated him with what he has described as "a very tender and understanding kind of love." His parents, by contrast, seldom displayed any affection toward him, and they rarely laughed. Conscientious churchgoers, they regarded as a sin "anything that appeared to be fun, like dancing," as he recalled in *The Famous Amos Story*.

Wally usually walked the four miles to and from the combination primary and secondary school where his formal education began. When he was about ten, he transferred to a small school that had just been established in his mother's church. "We were made to *think*, to be curious about why things were the way they were, to seek solutions, and not to add to the problems," he has written of the instruction that he received there. By his own admission, as a youngster he developed an obsessive desire to earn money, and he built up a successful shoeshine business and also delivered newspapers.

In 1948 Amos's parents separated. (They later divorced.) Soon afterward Wally moved to the New York City borough of Manhattan to live with his mother's sister Della, Della's husband, Fred, and Fred's son Joe in a three-room apartment where the living room doubled as his and Joe's bedroom. "Jovial and happy all the time," as he has described her, Della loved to cook and bake. One of her specialties was chocolate-chip cookies. "A thrill of expectation would course through me when she began gathering the ingredients to bake a batch," Amos has recalled in *Man with No Name*. "The experience included many sensory pleasures besides the taste of the cookies: the soft touch of the dough and the exquisite trespass of snitching some before it was baked; the sweet smell that came from the oven as the cookies turned brown; the heat of a fresh-baked cookie melting in your mouth; the oozy softness of a little pool of chocolate before it had time to cool; the warmth of the kitchen on a snowy New York day. All of this culminated in the great cookie ritual: the licking of the bowl." "For me, chocolate-chip cookies have always been an expression of *love*," Amos wrote in *The Power in You*.

In Manhattan Amos entered a public junior high school and attended integrated classes for the first time. "A bit of a showoff," as he has labeled himself as an adolescent, he soon made friends and organized a social club. Despite his popularity, he harbored the feeling that he was "not as good as the next guy," as he has said, and feared rejection. For awhile he awoke each morning at 5:00 o'clock to deliver newspapers before going to school. He later earned spending money by delivering groceries and, subsequently, ice.

In 1951, at around the time of his graduation from junior high school, Amos's mother and maternal grandmother settled in Manhattan, and he moved in with them. Enticed by a school recruiter's assertion that "cooks make a lot of money," he enrolled at Food Trades Vocational High School. In a program of on-the-job training, he spent every other week preparing pancakes, salads, and desserts in the kitchen of a large Manhattan hotel. After failing for the third or fourth time to gain a promised position among the hotel's entrée chefs, he quit school. Inspired by the example of his best friend, whose appearance in military uniform he much admired, he joined the United States Air Force. During his four years of service, which began in late 1953, he learned to repair radar and radio equipment and earned a high school equivalency diploma.

After his military discharge Amos returned to New York City, where, under the GI Bill, he enrolled at the Collegiate Secretarial Institute. The school's administrators, Sadie Brown and Lee Myers, who became his mentors, repeatedly urged him to "strive for excellence" and expressed their confidence in his abilities and potential. He continued to attend afternoon classes after he began working, mornings and nights, as a stockroom clerk at Saks Fifth Avenue, a department store, in 1957. In part, as he has said, to "disprove the myth that black people were lazy and lacking in ambition" and also to live up to the faith that Sadie Brown and Lee Myers had in him, Amos performed his duties at Saks with uncommon diligence and enthusiasm. Guided by his supervisor, Ernie Riccio, another of his mentors, he became knowledgeable not only about his department but also about warehouse operations in general. When, after fifteen months, Riccio was promoted, Amos—although he was the youngest worker in the stockroom—succeeded him as supervisor. Acting on the suggestion of the store's assistant general manager, he enrolled in a class in merchandising at New York University, but, discouraged by the heavy emphasis on math, he soon dropped out. He quit his job at Saks in mid-1961, after being denied a salary increase that he had requested.

Shortly thereafter Lee Myers set up an interview for Amos at the William Morris Agency, a leading theatrical booking agency, and he was hired to work in the mailroom. In addition to sorting and delivering mail, he served as a receptionist or secretary when needed and even fulfilled such tasks as replacing toilet paper in the company's men's rooms. "Working in the mailroom was a job that required you to listen, be observant, have initiative, plenty of patience, and do what you were told to do as quickly and efficiently as possible," he observed in *The Famous Amos Story*. "It was also the perfect place to be to see how the agency functioned; you could literally see the business from the ground up." After only about two months—a remarkably short time in the annals of the company—he was promoted to substitute secretary, and a few months later he was made secretary to Howard Hausman, a senior vice-president. Hausman immediately began grooming him for advancement, by such means as having Amos listen in on his phone calls and attend meetings. When William Morris formed a music department, Amos, on Hausman's recommendation, became the secretary to Jerry Brandt, a supervising agent. Because Brandt delegated many aspects of his job to him, Amos gained, as he has said, "both insight and experience in the day-to-day activities of an agent." Within a few months he started working as an assistant agent, and, not long afterward, in 1962, he was named a full-fledged William Morris talent agent.

"I decided that I would operate in an honest, open, and aboveboard manner, and that I would not patronize my associates or clients . . . ," Amos has said, in describing the "ground rules" that he adopted in his new position. "It was also my decision to build a reputation based on integrity, dignity, trust, ability, and hard work. Agents, I realized, had shady, underhanded images, and I wanted to clearly establish that that was not the manner in which I operated." He soon demonstrated that he could recognize extraordinary talent in as-yet little-known entertainers. Among the people in that category whom he booked were the singer/songwriter Paul Simon and his partner, Art Garfunkel. He also represented such established vocalists as the Supremes (Diana Ross, Mary Wilson, and Florence Ballard), Dionne Warwick, Sam Cooke, and Marvin Gaye.

By his own account, after half a dozen years at the William Morris Agency, Amos began to feel both "burned out" and "stagnant." Assigned to handle primarily rock-'n'-roll artists, he had become increasingly discontented since the emergence of hard rock. Adding to his unhappiness were two rebuffs, both of which he has attributed to his race: his failure, despite his seniority, to be named to the top position in the music department when it became vacant and the rejection of his request to be transferred to the agency's television or film department. In 1967 he left William Morris and moved to Los Angeles, with the idea, as he has recalled, that he would "build a self-contained, musically oriented entertainment company handling recording, music publishing, and personal management."

Amos's first project as an independent personal manager was arranging a concert in Philharmonic Hall (now Avery Fisher Hall), in New York City, for the South African trumpeter Hugh Masakela. Within months of the concert, without warning and while owing Amos thousands of dollars, Masakela terminated their business relationship. That painful rupture was followed by a six-year-long series of disappointments and frustrations for Amos. "I would put all my hopes in my clients, and then nothing would happen . . . ," he recalled in *The Famous Amos Story*. "I grew tired of never having any money and never knowing how I was going to get money to pay my expenses." To lift his spirits, Amos started baking chocolate-chip cookies, which he would hand out at meetings with producers and others in the entertainment field. His aunt Della, who had since died, had not revealed her recipe to him, so he followed the directions on packages of Nestle's chocolate chips. "The cookies' reputation began to grow as my contacts multiplied," he recalled in *The Power in You*. "People looked forward to those friendly, edible calling cards. . . . The cookies always opened doors and got rave reviews."

Amos has traced his decision to extricate himself from personal management and start a cookie business to a conversation he had in October 1974 with B.J. Gilmore, who was then a secretary to the musician Quincy Jones, during which she suggested that he open a store to sell his cookies. Although many other people had assured him that his cookies were good enough to sell, Gilmore "pushed him through that invisible barrier that separates us from *maybe* to *I will*," he has said. While continuing to represent his few remaining clients, he sought prospective investors, with the aim of raising twenty-five thousand dollars to buy baking equipment and ingredients, rent and furnish a store, and cover other anticipated expenses. He reached that goal with investments from the singers Marvin Gaye and Helen Reddy, the theatrical business manager Jeff Wald, who was then Reddy's husband, and Artie Mogull, a film company executive. On March 9, 1975, just five months after his crucial conversation with B.J. Gilmore, thanks to what he has described as "huge donations of sweat equity" from many of his friends, he hosted a pre-opening-day party outside his store, on the corner of Sunset Boulevard and Formosa Avenue in Hollywood, to which he had invited some twenty-five hundred guests. When the store opened for business the next day, customers were already lined up outside.

"When I decided to open a store selling only chocolate-chip cookies, I also decided to sell the best-tasting, highest quality, cutest, most adorable chocolate-chip cookies that I possibly could," Amos wrote in *The Power in You*. "I made a conscious commitment to excellence and quality. I refused to use second-rate chocolate simply because everybody else did. . . . My goal was to make a homemade-tasting cookie, which would be different from anything that was currently being sold." It took him about a year and a half to work out what he judged to be the perfect cookie recipe. By that time, following his lead, a bevy of "new cookiemongers," as Elin Schoen called them in *New York* (August 15, 1977), had started marketing their own versions of the "new breed of chocolate-chip cookies, the you-could-swear-it's-homemade variety," as she wrote. In a gustatory survey of the products of Amos and seven of his competitors, Schoen reported that Amos's cookies were "not just happy cookies" (a reference to Amos's sales pitch) but "delirious—light and airy, redolent of pecans, with a whisper of coconut. . . . As with salted peanuts, one is not enough."

Meanwhile, in the summer of 1975, the Famous Amos Chocolate Chip Cookie Corporation entered the wholesale market, with sales to Jurgensen's, a gourmet grocery concern based in Pasadena, California, and the San Francisco branch of Macy's department store chain. Within two years the upscale department stores Bloomingdale's and Nieman Marcus and other outlets had also begun carrying the cookies, which were packaged in brown bags decorated with pictures of a bearded Amos smiling at a cookie. According to Elin Schoen, "upon their arrival at Bloomingdale's in New York City . . . , they caused a stir in Upper East Side culinary circles unrivaled by anything since the advent of the Cuisinart. *The* chocolate-chip cookie had arrived." And by mid-1977, she reported, "Famous Amos paraphernalia," including T-shirts, duffel bags, umbrellas, and jewelry, filled a substantial portion of Bloomingdale's delicacies department, making it look like, as she put it, "a monument to Wally Amos."

"I wish we had Amos in every department," the food buyer for the Manhattan branch of Macy's told Elin Schoen, in describing the opening day, in 1977, of that store's Famous Amos section. "It's 'Here I am, I'm Wally Amos, and if I tell you these cookies are great, ladies, they are!' He kisses the women, autographs his bags, . . . and he even played the kazoo." Indeed, Amos had adopted the kazoo as the "official instrument of The Cookie," as he wrote in *The Power in You*, as a way of making people laugh and also having fun himself. In line with his "emphasis on comedy," in his words, he had abandoned his business suits in favor of boldly patterned Hawaiian shirts and Panama hats and adopted the role of manager of "The Cookie." "My cookies and I became a duo, and we put on a show together," he explained in *Man with No Name*. The star of the show was "the chocolate-chip cookie with pecans, with the other cookies being 'guest stars.'"

In the process of promoting his "client," Amos himself became a star of sorts on the American scene. For four years beginning in 1977, he rode on a float in Macy's Thanksgiving Day parade. He was interviewed on dozens of television and radio shows and was the subject of many newspaper and magazine articles, among them "The Hot New Rich," the cover story of the June 13, 1977 issue of *Time*. According to that article, Amos's two factories (one on the West Coast and the other in Nutley, New Jersey) were then producing six tons of cookies weekly for several Famous Amos retail stores as well as department stores and gourmet food shops, and in the previous twelve months his company's gross earnings had reached a million dollars.

In May 1977 Amos had moved to Honolulu, having been drawn to the city's beautiful beaches and weather and friendly inhabitants. "I'm having a ball!" he told Elin Schoen a few weeks after his move, which he had made, as he later acknowledged, in the mistaken belief that his performance as head of Famous Amos would remain unchanged despite Hawaii's distance from his factories and other operations. Always somewhat slack, Amos's hold on the reins of authority began to loosen even more. With relatively inexperienced friends of his, rather than professional managers, handling day-to-day affairs, the company's chronic shortage of available funds began to worsen. In 1985, Gail Buchalter reported in *Forbes* (March 10, 1986), because of both inept management and increasing competition, the Famous Amos company "lost three hundred thousand dollars on sales of more than ten million dollars."

Desperate for cash, Amos decided to solicit investments from outsiders. Although sources do not agree on the identities of the series of investors who bought into the company, it has consistently been reported that between 1985 and 1989, the Famous Amos corporation changed hands four times, and Amos's personal equity in it dropped from a 48 percent stake to zero. With his responsibilities reduced to promotion and publicity exclusively, he was paid a fixed salary for work that occupied him only part of each week. In 1989, feeling that he had become trapped in what he has labeled "an owner/slave relationship" and seemed destined to be, at best, a puppet of the newest owners (whom he suspected no longer wanted his services at all), Amos left the company. (Of the more than sixty million dollars that the owners realized when, in 1992, they sold the Famous Amos company to a Taiwanese corporation, he received nothing.)

"I take responsibility for what happened to me," Amos told Michael Ryan, who profiled him for *Parade* (May 22, 1994). In *Man with No Name* Amos recalled, "When my company rejected me and gave me lemons, I decided to turn those lemons into lemonade. I remembered that doors had slammed in my face before, yet others had always opened to more brilliant prospects. . . . I knew that the proper use of this period in my life was to benefit people in need." He had begun devoting a substantial portion of his time to charitable causes (or "vehicles for giving," as he prefers to call them) a decade before, about a year after he had joined the Unity Church in Hawaii and had started "to get in touch with [his] inner self and view life from a spiritual perspective." In 1979 he became the national spokesperson for Literacy Volunteers of America, a program in which nonprofessional volunteers help teenagers and adults learn to read or improve their reading skills, and later he became active in Cities in Schools, a national dropout-prevention program, the National Center for Family Literacy, and other organizations. While still employed by Famous Amos, he had also begun giving lectures on the powers of positive thinking, among other inspirational topics, at colleges and elsewhere, and after he severed his connection with Famous Amos, his schedule of speaking engagements became heavier. After attending one of his talks, Dorothy Gilliam wrote in the *Washington Post* (October 31, 1988) that "Amos fairly resonated with enthusiasm—cajoling, encouraging, and stroking his audience with humor, poetry, and homespun wit." During fallow periods, he supported himself and his family by borrowing from his retirement savings.

After losing majority control of his company, Amos had signed a legal document specifying that, if and when his contract were terminated, he would refrain for two years from "conducting business on behalf of any other organization engaged in the production or marketing of cookies." In 1991, two years after his termination, he and his wife launched a new company—Wally Amos Presents: Chip & Cookie—to market dolls, books, and other products as well as cookies. A year later the owners of the Famous Amos company obtained a court order enjoining him from using either his name, his likeness, or even his voice in conjunction with any food-related business—a prohibition to which he had agreed in writing some years before. According to the terms of the settlement that the owners and Amos reached after a protracted legal battle, the Famous Amos company "owns the trademark rights to the name 'Wally Amos' for any business that involves food," while Amos "owns the name Wally Amos for any non-food endeavor" and can use "his name, likeness, and reputation" for publicity purposes, even for marketing cookies. The Famous Amos owners, moreover, may not claim on their cookie packages that they are using Amos's original recipe. Amos plans to donate to Cities in Schools a portion of the profits generated by his latest business venture, the Uncle Noname (pronounced No-NAH-may) Cookie Company, which he started in 1992 after ending the operations of Chip & Cookie. As of early 1995 the Noname company, which specializes in pecan chocolate-chip cookies made with chocolate as the main ingredient and real vanilla extract, had not yet produced a profit.

Wally Amos, who is six feet, one inch tall and no longer has a beard, is renowned for his charm, friendliness, joie de vivre, and wide smile. His first marriage, to the former Maria La Forey in 1958, produced two sons, Michael and Gregory. From his second marriage, to the former Shirlee Ellis in 1966, he has one son, Shawn. Both those marriages ended in divorce. Amos lives in Kailua, Hawaii with his third wife, Christine, an artist, whom he married in 1979, and their eleven-year-old daughter, Sarah. He has appeared in television sitcoms and advertisements and has hosted *Learn to Read, Another Page*, and *GED on TV*, public-television series aimed at eliminating illiteracy. In addition to the Horatio Alger Award and the National Literacy Honors Award, the latter of which was presented to him at the White House by President Goerge Bush and First Lady Barbara Bush, his honors include the President's Award for Entrepreneurial Excellence (1986), an honorary doctorate from Johnson & Wales University, and induction into the Babson College Academy of Distinguished Entrepreneurs. "I am in the people business, not the cookie business . . . ," Amos, who recites several prayers every morning and meditates daily, has said. "I deal in *love*."

Selected Biographical References: Boston Globe p49+ O 3 '94 por; Parade p4+ My 22 '94 pors; People 37:101 F 17 '92 por; Philadelphia Inquirer G p1+ Jl 21 '94 pors; Wall St J B p2 Ag 16 '94 por; Amos, Wally and Leroy Robinson. The Famous Amos Story (1983); Amos, Wally and Camilla Denton. Man with No Name (1994)

U.S. House of Representatives

Armey, Richard K.

July 7, 1940– United States Representative from Texas; educator; writer. Address: 301 Cannon House Office Bldg., Washington, DC 20515

When the Republicans swept the Senate and the House of Representatives in the midterm elections of 1994, Dick Armey, the man whom *The Almanac of American Politics* once deemed "hardly likely to be a power" in Congress, became the first Republican majority leader in the House since the 1950s. A former professor of economics, Armey had virtually no political experience when he won an upset victory over the popular incumbent Tom Vandergriff in 1984 and claimed the seat representing Texas's Twenty-Sixth Congressional District, in the Dallas-Fort Worth area. By most accounts, Armey's early days in the House were marked more by brazenness and ideological zeal than by political finesse. While his penchant for making outrageous remarks has not changed noticeably in recent years, his approach to lawmaking has, as the alliances with Democrats and moderate Republicans he has occasionally formed in order to introduce legislation demonstrate. He nonetheless remains an archconservative, as evidenced by his antiabortion stance, his coauthorship, with Newt Gingrich, of the Republicans' so-called Contract with America, his desire to repeal the 1994 ban on assault weapons, and his continued criticism of the administration of President Bill Clinton.

The fourth of the seven children of Glen Forest Armey, a farmer and grain dealer, and Marion (Gutschlog) Armey, a bookkeeper, Richard Keith Armey was born on July 7, 1940 in Cando (pronounced "can do"), North Dakota. Information about his early life is scarce. As a young man, he worked for a time as a grain-elevator operator and also as a telephone lineman. In *U. S. News & World Report* (December 12, 1994), Gloria Borger reported that Armey made the decision to attend college (and become the first in his family to do so) in November 1958, as he was working atop a thirty-foot pole in sub-zero weather at three o'clock in the morning, attempting to fix a power line.

Armey enrolled at Jamestown College, in Jamestown, North Dakota, obtaining his B.A. degree in 1963. In the following year he received his master's degree from the University of North Dakota, in Grand Forks. He taught economics at the University of Montana, in Missoula, and at West Texas State University, in Canyon, before earning his Ph.D. at the University of Oklahoma, in Norman, in 1968. For four years beginning in 1968, he was an assistant professor at Austin College, in Sherman, Texas, and in 1972 he became an associate professor at North Texas State University, in Denton, where in 1977 he was named chairman of the economics department, a position he held until 1983.

Aside from having served in 1982 as a volunteer for Jim Bradshaw, an unsuccessful Republican candidate for the Twenty-Sixth Congressional District seat, Armey had no experience in politics prior to 1984. One evening during that year, however—in an incident that has since become political legend—Armey, turning to his wife as they watched coverage of congressional proceedings on the cable network C-SPAN, said, "Honey, those people sound like a bunch of darn fools." His wife replied, "Yeah, you could do that." Motivated by that exchange and by the fact that he had grown weary of being part of a conservative minority in his academic circle, Armey mounted a campaign against the Democratic Congressman Tom Vandergriff.

At the outset Armey's chances of winning seemed slim. He ran unopposed for the Republican nomination, mainly because other members of his party considered the incumbent to be virtually unbeatable. Vandergriff was a veritable fixture in the Dallas-Fort Worth region. Before his election to Congress, he had been the mayor of the nearby city of Arlington for a quarter-century and had vastly improved that city's economy by attracting industry and encouraging tourism. By contrast, Armey was a political unknown. Almost as crippling a factor as his obscurity was his tendency to make incendiary statements. For example, his platform called for the elimination of Social Security, and in one stump speech he said that he was "embarrassed" to have been a university professor, citing black studies courses as examples of the "pure junk" he felt was being taught on college campuses.

Working in Armey's favor, however, was the continuing popularity of the conservative icon Ronald Reagan, who was coasting toward his second presidential term and whose policies Armey strongly supported. But the outcome of the race may have been determined by a combination of Vandergriff's apparent complacency and Armey's relentlessness. While Vandergriff eschewed television and radio spots in favor of personal appearances and purchased newspaper ads only in the last two weeks of the campaign, Armey missed no opportunity to publicize his conservative views on the economy, particularly his belief in the free market and in cuts in federal spending. He criticized his opponent for having voted to limit Reagan's tax-cut plan and even distributed comic books portraying Vandergriff as a flunky of the Democratic House Speaker Thomas P. ("Tip") O'Neill, an unabashed liberal and a chief critic of the tax cuts. On Election Day, Armey defeated Vandergriff with 51 percent of the vote.

Once he arrived at Washington, it did not take the freshman legislator long to establish his conservative credentials. Among his earliest votes were those in 1985 in favor of the production of the MX missile and in support of cuts in government subsidies for water projects. In the same year, he attracted considerable media coverage when, in order to make the case for ending federal funding of the National Endowment for the Arts, he passed out samples of what he considered to be obscene works by poets supported by the organization. The ploy was only the first of the many offbeat tactics for which he would become known. He again displayed an eccentric streak, and provided fodder for the press, by sleeping in the House gymnasium to save on housing expenses while Congress was in session—and, after he was ordered to leave the gym, by spending nights on the sofa in his office.

In 1986 Armey came out in favor of less-stringent gun-control laws, aid to the Contras in Nicaragua, and a reduction in public-housing construction. He voted against overriding President Reagan's veto of economic sanctions against South Africa, which at the time operated under a system of racial apartheid, and he withheld support from a movement to stop the manufacture of chemical weapons. From all appearances, his stands on those and other issues met with approval in his home district, for he trounced two opponents to claim the 1986 Republican nomination and easily beat Democrat George Richardson in that year's general election. In each of his reelection bids since then, he has been returned to office with more than two-thirds of the ballots.

The overwhelming support from his constituents notwithstanding, Armey began his second term with a reputation among his House colleagues as someone better at drawing attention to himself than at passing legislation. Describing himself as a "budget commando," he worked with a small group of other likeminded legislators to reduce the spending proposed in numerous bills in the House, but most of his amendments "went down in flames," as a writer for the *Wall Street Journal* (June 2, 1988) phrased it.

Eventually, however, Armey made what a fellow Texas Republican, Senator Phil Gramm, called "the transition from the realm of being a protester to the realm of governing." The first sign of that transition came after Frank C. Carlucci, the secretary of defense under President Reagan, urged Congress to take the necessary steps to shut down unneeded military bases, contending that billions of dollars could be saved by such an action. Although the closing of bases had proven to be a politically sensitive issue in the past, typically provoking protests from the representatives in whose districts the targeted bases were located, Armey rose to Carlucci's challenge. He tried to attach to a 1987 defense authorization bill a proposal to entrust the selection of those bases to an independent commission, thereby taking the matter out of Congress's hands and depoliticizing the process. His measure was defeated in a close vote. In 1988 he tried again, this time with a compromise proposal that gave Congress limited authority to disapprove lists of bases drawn up by the commission. When that amendment passed by a vote of 223 to 186, Armey had achieved his first significant legislative victory.

Of the lesson he learned from that legislative victory and from other experiences he had had in the House, Armey said to Jeffrey H. Birnbaum of the *Wall Street Journal* (June 2, 1988), "You can be so ideologically hidebound you can cut yourself out of the process. This is an institution of trade-offs." In that spirit of cooperation, Armey worked with the liberal California Democrat Barbara Boxer, then a Congresswoman, to earmark $220 million to be used by the Coast Guard for enforcement of drug laws, and as a member of the Budget Committee, he helped produce a rare bipartisan budget agreement. But while he had displayed a willingness to form partnerships with ideological adversaries to achieve some goals, his stands on other issues in 1988 left little doubt about his conservative bent. He voted to bar federal funds for abortions in cases of rape or incest, opposed the seven-day waiting period for the purchase of handguns, and declined to oppose Reagan's veto of the civil rights restoration bill. His voting record in that year earned him a 100 percent approval rating from the American Conservative Union and, not surprisingly, a rating of zero from the liberal Americans for Democratic Action.

In 1989 Armey voted against halting the production of the B-2 stealth bomber. He also opposed overriding President George Bush's veto of the Democrats' minimum-wage bill. Again showing support for Bush, he refused to join the House members who came out against lowering the capital-gains tax. In the following year Armey allied himself with those seeking a constitutional amendment to outlaw the desecration of the American flag, and he refused to help pass the family and medical leave bill over Bush's veto. Echoing the stands he had taken in previous years, he voted against the civil rights bill and against allowing abortions in military facilities overseas. He was part of the majority who voted to authorize the use of force to expel Iraq from Kuwait in the Persian Gulf war.

Meanwhile, joining forces with the liberal Democratic congressman Charles E. Schumer of New York, in the summer of 1990 Armey had once again sought to curb government spending, on this occasion by taking on the House Agriculture Committee. Learning that a disproportionately high percentage of federal farm subsidies was being given to the small minority of wealthy farmers, Armey, who referred to that group collectively as "a 350-pound man on a life-support system," coauthored an amendment to deny government support to farmers whose net incomes exceeded one hundred thousand dollars per year. The measure was rejected by a vote of 263 to 159.

Still, by the early 1990s Armey had gained the respect of many of his colleagues and a reputation as a serious legislator. He had steadily moved up in the hierarchies of the Budget Committee and the Education and Labor Committee, and in 1991 he became the ranking Republican on the Joint Economic Committee. He proved himself once and for all to be a powerful force in Congress when, late in 1992, he won the chairmanship of the Republican Conference, defeating Jerry Lewis of California in close balloting. Armey's new position made him the third-ranking Republican in the House, subordinate only to Robert H. Michel of Illinois, at that time the House minority leader, and Newt Gingrich of Georgia, then the minority whip. Unlike Michel and Lewis, who were often eager to compromise with Democrats, Armey shared with Gingrich an unyielding stance on those issues that split members of Congress along party lines. "I see confrontation as a tool," Armey was quoted as saying by the *New York Times* (December 8, 1992).

Confrontation has been perhaps the key element in Armey's relations with Bill Clinton since the latter won the 1992 presidential election. During a meeting at the White House in early 1993, Armey told Clinton that he would be a one-term president if he pursued the budget he had proposed. It was under Armey's name that House Republicans issued a 1993 report attacking Clinton's plan to reform health care, warning that the plan would result in many new taxes and regulations and would lead to losses of jobs in small businesses. Armey also derided the president's national service program as "welfare" for "aspiring yuppies." His criticism of the Clinton administration has more than once taken on a personal tone. Upon meeting First Lady Hillary Rodham Clinton, the leader of the president's task force on health-care reform, he said, "The reports on your charm are overstated, and the reports on your wit are understated." He angered even members of his own party when, referring to Clinton, he declared to Democrats on the House floor, "Your president is just not important to us."

In 1994 Armey made his ideological opposition to the Clinton administration official when he and Newt Gingrich coauthored the Contract with America, a package of legislation the Republicans promised to introduce in Congress within the first one hundred days of the next session should voters grant the party a majority in the House of Representatives in the November elections. Among the items listed were measures intended to pass a balanced-budget amendment, set term limits for members of Congress, reform the welfare system, require a three-fifths majority in both houses of Congress to raise taxes, and cut the capital gains tax. Whether or not as a result of the promises offered by the Contract with America, in November voters sent large numbers of Republicans to the House and Senate, resulting in the first GOP-controlled Congress in forty years. With the retirement of Robert Michel at the end of 1994, Gingrich ascended, with considerable fanfare, to the position of Speaker of the House, and Armey became House majority leader.

"We didn't win power; we gained responsibility," Armey told participants at the Conservative Leadership Conference in December 1994, as quoted by the *New York Times* (December 6, 1994). In the period following the elections, Armey claimed that his party's minority status had in the past forced him to assume a more combative attitude than he would otherwise have displayed and that, as the new majority leader, his focus would be on furthering the interests of the country rather than on settling old political scores. His new position left him free to be his "natural, easygoing self," as he told Michael Isikoff for *Newsweek* (November 28, 1994).

"Easygoing" was not, however, among the adjectives used to characterize Armey in the wake of comments he made during an interview with radio broadcasters on January 27, 1995. When the discussion turned to the money he was paid for writing a book scheduled for publication later in the year, he recalled the accusations of unethical behavior that had been made against Newt Gingrich over a lucrative book deal, and he expressed his wish to avoid the same situation. In saying that he did not want Barney Frank, an openly gay Congressman, "haranguing in [his] ear because [he] made a few bucks off a book," Armey referred to his colleague as "Barney Fag." He immediately insisted that the remark was a simple mispronunciation and had not been intended as a slur, and after failing to persuade reporters not to publicize the incident, he apologized to Frank privately and on the House floor.

Not everyone was satisfied with Armey's explanation and apology. "I don't think [the slur] was on the tip of his tongue, but I do believe it was in the back of his mind," Frank said, as quoted in the *New York Times* (January 28, 1995). "There are a lot of ways to mispronounce my name. That is the least common." In the judgment of the *New Republic* (February 20, 1995), Armey's claim that he had said "fag" as a result of conflating the words "Frank" and "harangue" was, "to put it mildly, unconvincing." An editorial in the *New York Times* (January 29, 1995) titled "Hate Speech Comes to Congress" declared that Armey had "spoken in a formal setting with bigotry aforethought" and had "won a permanent place in the annals of congressional disrepute." For his part, Armey blamed the media for depicting his remark as an intended epithet, and he said it was "regrettable that the mangling of a name in a way that would be clearly offensive had it been intended should shift the public debate away from issues like balancing the budget, cutting taxes, and reforming our failed welfare system."

In April 1995, nearly one hundred days after the commencement of the 104th Congress, Armey, Gingrich, and a host of other Republicans gathered outside the Capitol to celebrate the passage in the House of many of the bills proposed in the Contract with America. Among the legislation Armey has sought to enact in recent months is a flat-tax rate, under which each American would be taxed 17 percent of his or her income—with no credits or deductions except allowances for low-income earners and children. Under such a system, he has said, "You could pay your taxes on a form the size of a postcard."

Armey is the author of *Price Theory*, which was published in 1977, and he contributed chapters to *Global Free Trade* and *The Privatization Revolution*, titles in the Champions of Freedom series published by Hillsdale College Press. His essay "The Road Away from Serfdom" appeared in Hillsdale's monthly monthly digest of speeches. His most recent work is *The Freedom Revolution: The New Republican House Majority Leader Tells Why Big Government Failed, Why Freedom Works, and How We Will Rebuild America* (1995).

Dick Armey, a former marathon runner, stands six feet, three inches tall. The liberal congressman Charles Schumer told Michael Isikoff for the *Newsweek* article that Armey is "not a mean conservative," and the moderate Republican representative Jim Leach described him as "not anger-driven" and as having "a cheerful, almost impish sense of humor." Armey has stated that he is "officially Presbyterian" but that he "probably [enjoys] the Baptist church more." He drives a red pickup truck with a bumper sticker that reads "Jimmy Buffet for President," a reference to the singer and songwriter. One of his main avocations is fishing, a sport he sometimes enjoys in the company of the Supreme Court justice Clarence Thomas, whose wife, Virginia, is on Armey's staff. Armey and his wife, Susan, are the parents of five grown children, from their previous marriages.

Selected Biographical References: N Y Times B p9 D 9 '94 por; Newsweek 124:26+ N 28 '94 por; U S News 117:52+ D 12 '94 pors; Wall St J p56 Je 2 '88 por; Washington Post A p27 F 21 '94 por; Almanac of American Politics, 1994; Politics in America, 1986, 1994; Who's Who in America, 1995

Agence France Presse

Armstrong, Gillian

(JIL-ee-an)

Dec. 18, 1950– Australian filmmaker. Address: c/o William Morris Agency, 151 El Camino Drive, Beverly Hills, CA 90212

Gillian Armstrong burst onto the international filmmaking scene in 1979 with her widely acclaimed debut feature film, *My Brilliant Career*, which was also the first feature made by an Australian woman since the 1930s. According to Gary Arnold of the *Washington Post* (March 12, 1980), the film, about a young woman in turn-of-the-century Australia who feels compelled to choose between romance and career, "establishe[d] her instantly as the most sensitive and accomplished woman director in the English-speaking world." Since then, Armstrong has made several other motion pictures, including the much-acclaimed *The Last Days of Chez Nous* and *Little Women*, that have solidified her reputation as a world-class filmmaker with a special talent for portraying headstrong, complex women whose dreams and desires are out of sync with traditional expectations of the role of women in society. As Molly Haskell observed in *Film Comment* (March 1993), "Armstrong cuts closer to the core of women's divided yearnings than any other director."

The second of three children, Gillian May Armstrong was born December 18, 1950 in Melbourne, Australia, into a middle-class, suburban family. Her father worked in real estate, and her mother was a schoolteacher. She first became interested in the arts (though not in cinema) during primary school, when she took part in several of her school's theatrical productions. "The teacher told my mother I had a talent in that area," Armstrong recalled to Kristine McKenna, who interviewed her for the *Los Angeles Times* (March 21, 1993), "so, when I was eleven my mother got me involved with some local drama groups where I helped paint the scenery." Having decided to become a set designer, upon completing secondary school she entered Swinbourne College, an art school in Melbourne. Fortuitously, as it turned out, her costume and theatrical design classes were offered by the school's film department, for it was as a result of her contact with the department that she became interested in cinema. "I started seeing all the classics—by Welles, Fellini, Bergman, De Sica—and I was smitten," she told McKenna. By the time she graduated, she had made a few short films, though she did not yet envision herself as a director.

Armstrong was "lucky," as she has put it, to have graduated from art school at the very time that the Australian government had committed itself to helping to establish the country's nascent film industry. The director Fred Schepisi was among those who received government funds to make films, including the short called *Libido*, and to assist him on the film he recruited Armstrong, whose schoolwork had impressed him. Schepisi also encouraged her to seek a career as a filmmaker.

Good jobs in the film industry were hard to come by, however, and after moving to Sydney, Armstrong worked as a waitress for several months before finding a position as an assistant editor on industrial and educational films. In Sydney she also became involved in the Women's Film Group, an advocacy group for female filmmakers and television producers that, among other initiatives, successfully lobbied the government to set up a fund to support female filmmakers. Then, in 1973, Armstrong got her first big break, when she became one of the twelve applicants, out of a total of 750, to be accepted into the first class of the newly established Australian Film and Television School.

At the time Armstrong attended the school, each student was given enough money to make three short films using professional casts and crews. (The school has since discontinued the practice.) Her first project, a ten-minute short entitled *One Hundred a Day*, dealt with a young woman working in a boot factory in the 1930s who has an illegal abortion. Next came a documentary concerning loneliness and sex called *Satdee Night*, which she intended to be shown in schools. Her third film school effort, *Gretel*, an adaption of a Hal Porter story, was screened at a short-film festival in Grenoble, France.

Following her graduation from the film school, Armstrong worked as an art director and prop mistress on various motion pictures. She then made *Smokes and Lollies* (1975), the first of a trio of documentaries chronicling the lives of three working-class girls from Adelaide, and a short feature, *The Singer and the Dancer* (1976), which turned out to be the last film for which she wrote her own screenplay. Although Armstrong does not think of herself as a particularly gifted screenwriter, *The Singer and the Dancer* not only won the Australian Film Institute award for best short but drew the attention of the producer Margaret Fink, who in 1977 hired Armstrong to direct *My Brilliant Career*. Armstrong thus became the first Australian woman to direct a full-length feature film since the 1930s.

Based on a turn-of-the-century autobiographical novel by a woman named Miles Franklin, *My Brilliant Career* (1979) centers on Sybylla (Judy Davis), a high-spirited teenage girl from a poor farming family whose ambition is to become a great writer. Sybylla's plans are complicated by her involvement in a buoyant relationship with a handsome property owner; because of the prevailing expectations of a woman's role in society, she feels that she cannot both accept his proposal of marriage and realize her professional goals. To the dismay of many viewers, she chooses to pursue the latter. "They should have had a great affair, and she could have gone on and written her books," Armstrong said to Mark Mordue in an interview for *Sight & Sound* (Autumn 1989). "It was a tragedy of their time that it couldn't happen."

To Armstrong's surprise, *My Brilliant Career* became an international hit. "We thought we would be lucky if three people came to see it and not all of them were relatives," she joked to Jamie Wolf for a profile in *American Film* (January/February 1985). In addition to having the honor of being screened at the 1979 Cannes Film Festival, it received several awards in Australia, England, and the United States. Jack Kroll of *Newsweek* (October 22, 1979) expressed the view of many when he described *My Brilliant Career* as "a universally appealing story told with an integrity, humanity, warmth, and humor you can taste."

The flood of offers that Armstrong subsequently received from Hollywood studios also took her by surprise. "It wasn't something I had thought of doing, films with Sally Field, Dustin Hoffman," she has said. "I mean, it was all a bit of a shock." She also felt uneasy about the prospect of working in a foreign country among people she had never worked with before. "I know that making a film is a team effort, and it was only my second film," she explained to Ruth Reichl in an interview for the *New York Times* (March 8, 1995). "Why would I want the stress and strain with a whole lot of strangers?"

Lacking a compelling reason to accept any of the Hollywood offers, Armstrong opted to remain in Australia, at least for the time being, and to make two documentaries, one about Tasmanian wood craftsmen and the other about the potter Harold Hughan. Similarly, for her second feature she chose a script that was markedly different from that of her debut film: *Starstruck*, a new wave musical comedy about two Sydney teenagers searching for stardom. "It's totally frivolous," she said of the 1982 release, as quoted in the *Washington Post* (April 15, 1983). "But there was something that touched me about the people. When I was interviewing actors, I knew some of the very heavy ones would ask why on earth I was doing this frivolous film, so I prepared an answer for them: It's in praise of free spirits. That shut them up." While some critics, like the "heavy" actors, were taken aback by the lighthearted nature of *Starstruck* many others agreed with Alex Keneas, who in *New York Newsday* (November 11, 1982) hailed the film as "irresistible fluff."

Armstrong finally answered Hollywood's call when she agreed to direct *Mrs. Soffel* (1984). A fact-based narrative set in turn-of-the-century Pittsburgh, the film concerns the eponymous heroine, a prison warden's wife (Diane Keaton), who falls in love with Ed Biddle, a convicted murderer on death row (Mel Gibson), and helps him and his brother escape, fleeing with them. "How could two people from such extreme walks of life fall in love?" Armstrong asked during an interview with Steve Ginsberg for *Women's Wear Daily* (February 5, 1986). "That's what intrigued me about this story. What was it about this man that made a woman risk so much and leave her own children? It's a story that arouses your curiosity about human nature."

A number of critics were enthralled by *Mrs. Soffel*, among them, Jamie Wolf, who rhapsodized, "'Magisterial' is the word that comes to mind. . . . From the lovely stately calm of the opening sequence, [the film] moves with assured, inexorable force through the prison material toward the feverish, desperate intensity of the climactic scenes in the snow, and these have a terrible beauty that stays palpably in your bones long after you leave the theatre. Particularly in its second half, the film is visually stunning, and not merely in a pictorial sense: Its whole look, with its thematic contrasts between darkness and light, serves the theoretical underpinnings and advances the story in a way that would do credit to a silent film director's work." Others similarly found it to be "vital" and "authentic," though some concluded that it was "bewilderingly monotonous" and that the relationship between Mrs. Soffel and Ed Biddle was entirely unbelievable.

After completing her next project, *Hard to Handle*, a movie about Bob Dylan, for HBO, Armstrong returned to Australia to work on her fourth feature film, *High Tide* (1987). She drew her inspiration for the film from a change in Australia's adoption laws that allowed children to contact their natural parents. "I saw a picture in the paper, of a sixty-year-old daughter sitting with the ninety-year-old mother she'd just rediscovered," Armstrong told Molly Haskell. "I couldn't get over it. I realized this primitive bond was so strong that a woman went looking for her mother at the age of sixty."

As originally conceived, *High Tide* was to focus on a father who abandons his fourteen-year-old daughter, but Armstrong eventually concluded that the story would be more potent if it was the mother who leaves her child. "We realized it would make for a tougher, more original film," she told Myra Forsberg in an interview for the *New York Times* (March 6, 1988). "We had all seen stories about the lonely, alienated eighties man who is touched by a relationship with a child . . . And we thought it would be great to create a modern woman who was a drifter, because the behavior of a mother who deserts her child is still not condoned by society. It's much more accepted that a man will walk out on his child." This line of reasoning led to the creation of the film's protagonist, Lilli (Judy Davis), a washed-up singer who becomes stranded in a dreary trailer park when her car breaks down. There, she rediscovers her daughter, whom she abandoned after the death of her husband years before, an encounter that forces her to reexamine her life.

In bringing the script to the screen, Armstrong realized that her greatest challenge would be to present Lilli in a sympathetic light. "We always knew it was a difficult character and that the audience would have a disposition against her," she explained to Myra Forsberg. "Since our story enters many areas that could be considered sentimental, we wanted to create a character that had an edge, and in a lot of cases her behavior is not likable—even before you know that she's a mother who's deserted her child. We hoped that an audience would finally see there were reasons behind her behavior, and that you could truly care about her, but it was a fine line we were treading." According to a number of critics, Armstrong achieved her goal. Michael Wilmington, writing in the *Los Angeles Times* (December 18, 1987), found himself to be alternately "charmed and repelled" by Lilli, while Steve Warrick observed in his *Film Quarterly* (Summer 1989) review of the movie that it "has one of the most completely realized female sensibilities ever captured on film."

Armstrong returned to Hollywood for *Fires Within* (1991), a love story with a Cuban political backdrop starring Greta Scacchi and Jimmy Smits. To her dismay, her collaboration with MGM Studios turned out to be, in her words, "absolutely the worst experience of [her] life," mainly because the film was taken from her control during postproduction and completely reedited. "My mistake was previewing the film too early, but I naïvely thought we were working as a team and had this idea of 'let's see what we have so far and sort out what we should do,'" she explained to Kristine McKenna. "That threw everyone into a state of panic and opened the film to committee reworking."

Following this disaster, Armstrong retreated to Australia to make *The Last Days of Chez Nous* (1993), which in the opinion of some is one of her most accomplished films. Set in a suburban house in Sydney, *Chez Nous* focuses principally on Beth (Lisa Harrow), a successful, fortysomething novelist, and her relationships with her French husband, her teenage daughter from a previous marriage, and her much younger sister Vicki, who, upon her return from an extended trip to Europe, becomes the catalyst for slowly surfacing resentments and betrayals. As with *High Tide*, one of the challenges Armstrong faced in making this film was figuring out how to make the audience empathize with, if not like, Beth, who is not a particularly appealing character, as the director has acknowledged. "Helen [Garner, the screenwriter] is very tough on her main character and really believes that women of Beth's generation had to push so hard for their rights that their softer side was lost," Armstrong told Peter Brunette of the *Washington Post* (April 4, 1993). "And when I say 'softness' I don't mean being all coy and sweet, but just making more time for yourself, maybe becoming more selfish, and not trying to be super-everything." Most critics did indeed find much to admire in Beth ("This woman will be true to herself, we realize, and to anyone who needs her," Anthony Lane observed in the *New Yorker* [March 1, 1993]), and they were captivated by the film as a whole. In a representative review for *Sight and Sound* (March 1993), Lizzie Francke described *The Last Days of Chez Nous* as "a poignantly observed and dry-humored account of emotional blundering and bruising." The film was nominated for eleven Australian Film Institute awards and was warmly received at the Berlin and London film festivals.

Armstrong's most recent screen credit is her adaptation of the novel *Little Women*, Louisa May Alcott's classic Civil War-era story about four daughters in a New England family, which centers on the high-spirited, tomboyish Jo, whose ambition is to become a writer. When first offered the project, Armstrong "had a lot of doubts," as she was quoted as saying in *Sight and Sound* (April 1995), "because [she] felt that it touched on many of the concerns of *My Brilliant Career*." But she eventually concluded that sufficient time had elapsed since the earlier film. Moreover, as she explained to Ruth Reichl, she thought that "it would be nice to make a film that [her] daughters could go to. . . . They want to see characters they can identify with, and there's a real shortage of girls' stories." Saturated with glowing detail, warmth, and conviviality, Armstrong's cinematic rendering of the novel became a surprise hit of the 1994 Christmas season. Georgia Brown, who reviewed the movie for the

Village Voice (December 27, 1994), proclaimed it "a new classic."

In addition to making feature films, Armstrong has produced several documentaries, the best-known of which is the trilogy of films that began with *Smokes and Lollies*. Collectively, they follow the lives of three working-class girls from Adelaide, Australia, as they pass from adolescence to young adulthood. In the first installment, which was commissioned by the South Australian Film Commission in 1975, three fourteen-year-olds are seen discussing themselves, their lives, and their aspirations. Armstrong revisited the girls four years later to make the second film, *Fourteen's Good, Eighteen's Better* (1980). In that span of time, one of the young women had become a divorced mother of two children, another had married a man who had had several brushes with the law, and the third had taken a job in an office and was trying to save money to buy a used car. By the time she made the third film, *Bingo, Bridesmaids and Braces* (1988), the women were twenty-six. "Following them for that amount of time has almost mirrored the effect of the women's movement on working-class women," Armstrong told Ruth Reichl. "Their ideas and aspirations were so horrifyingly low. They became much greater believers in education and careers for their daughters than they were for themselves. So I'm interested to see how it affects their daughters." The films, for which Armstrong is said to be better known in Australia than for any of her other works, have been shown widely in the country's schools and have won an award from the Victorian Teachers' Federation.

During an interview with Rosemary Neill for the *Bulletin* of Sydney, which was reprinted in *World Press Review* (November 1988), Armstrong tried to account for the keen interest in the series: "I once went to Canberra to lobby for the film industry, and I had dinner with some members of the opposition, . . . and they wanted to talk to me more about *Fourteen's Good, Eighteen's Better* than anything I had made before. . . . I thought, that is the film's real use: if it can help people who are actually making the laws, if it can help break down clichéd ideas." She also believes the film has enabled Australians to look at their compatriots anew. "Seeing people and their lives, the decisions that they've made, their hopes and dreams is the most effective kind of lesson," she was quoted as saying in *Cinema Papers* (November 1988). "You can see what happens to people through lack of choice, fate, coincidence." Armstrong hopes to continue the series by tracing the lives of the women's daughters.

Although most of Armstrong's colleagues find her to be full of humor and spirit, she has nevertheless acquired a reputation for being prickly and brusque. Armstrong has attributed this image to her refusal to compromise her artistic vision. "If my reputation is 'she's a bit difficult,' the best I can say is that I fight for quality," she told Margot Dougherty, who profiled her for *Premiere* (May 1993). "And when I came back to Australia and had total control, I made what many people consider my best film in years," she added, referring to *Chez Nous*. Armstrong's commitment to her own vision of what a film ought to be extends to the types of projects that she agrees to take on. Indeed, she is notoriously selective about the films she directs, having turned down *Ghost*, *Working Girl*, and *Mermaids* because she believed the screenplays were inferior. "I have no interest in making films just to make money," she told Kristine McKenna. "And that makes it easier for me to wait for the ones I really want to do." Armstrong lives in Sydney with film the editor John Pffefer and their two daughters.

Selected Biographical References: Am Film 10:20+ Ja/F '85 pors; Chicago Tribune XIII p8+ Ap 11 '93 por; Los Angeles Times p19+ Mr 21 '93 por; N Y Times C p1+ Mr 8 '95 pors; Premiere 6:44+ My '93 por; Sight & Sound 58:270+ Autumn '89 por; 5:28+ Ap '95; Washington Post C p1+ Ap 15 '83 pors, G p3 Ap 4 '93 por

---

Mary Kay Cosmetics

Ash, Mary Kay

May 12, 1918– Cosmetics company executive. Address: c/o Mary Kay Cosmetics, 8787 N. Stemmons Frwy., Dallas, TX 75247

In 1963, using her life savings of five thousand dollars, the expertise that she gained during a twenty-five-year career in direct sales, and her insights into effective management, Mary Kay Ash emerged from an early retirement to launch a business in skin-care products and cosmetics. What began as a tiny storefront operation with nine saleswomen has become, as of 1995, the largest direct seller of skin-care products and cosmetics in the United States. With more than $1.5 billion in annual retail sales to nearly twenty-three million customers, it has also become the nation's best-selling brand of those commodities, having captured 10 percent of the skin-care market and 8.5 percent of the market for cosmetics. Each year since 1992, Mary Kay Cosmetics has appeared on *Fortune* magazine's list of the five hundred largest industrial corporations in the United States.

"My interest in starting Mary Kay Cosmetics was to offer women opportunities that didn't exist anywhere else," Mary Kay Ash, the long-time chairperson of the company, has said. In building what she envisioned as her "dream company," she adhered to a philosophy based on what she has labeled "three beautiful and simple ideas": the golden rule—"Do unto others as you would have them do unto you"; her belief that, in setting their priorities, people should place "God first, family second, and career third"; and her conviction that "with lots of praise and encouragement, everyone can be successful." Her personal success and that of the hundreds of thousands of women who, as independent businesspeople, sell Mary Kay products in twenty-four countries worldwide attest to the soundness of her approach. Mary Kay Cosmetics was featured in both editions of the book *The 100 Best Companies to Work for in America*, which also listed it as one of the ten best companies for which women can work.

Although she adopted the surname of her third husband on their marriage in 1966, Mary Kay Ash has long been known universally as simply Mary Kay. The youngest child of Edward Alexander Wagner and Lula Vember (Hastings) Wagner, she was born Mary Kathlyn Wagner on May 12, 1918 in Hot Wells, Texas. Around the time of her birth, Jon Anderson reported in the *Chicago Tribune* (February 14, 1991), her parents owned a hotel near Houston. When she was two or three, her father entered a sanatorium for tuberculosis patients. By the time of his discharge, about four years later, Mary Kay and her mother had moved to Houston, where her mother, a trained nurse, had become the manager of a restaurant—a job for which she was paid far less than her male counterparts but significantly more than she could have earned as a nurse. On workdays she left the house before Mary Kay awakened and often did not return until after her daughter had gone to bed. Beginning at the age of about seven, Mary Kay assumed responsibility for many household tasks when her mother was at work, as well as for ministering to her father, who had become a virtual invalid. (Her brother and two sisters had already moved away from home.) "It never occurred to me that things should be any different," Mary Kay has recalled. "I would come home from school and clean the house. Then I would do my homework. But I accepted this, and what's more, I enjoyed it." Sometimes she would telephone her mother at work to get instructions for preparing supper. After giving Mary Kay step-by-step directions, her mother would invariably say, "Honey, you can do it."

Her mother also repeatedly told Mary Kay, "Anything anyone else can do, you can do better"—words that reinforced the girl's inborn competitive spirit. "It became necessary for me to excel in anything I did," Mary Kay has said, in describing how she always strived to get the highest grades, type faster than anybody else in her typing class, and sell the most boxes of Girl Scout cookies. "I never thought in terms of *beating* the other children . . . ," she explained in *Mary Kay* (1994), her autobiography, which was originally published in 1981. "I concentrated upon competing with myself." On the few occasions when she failed to meet her goals, her mother helped her to deal with defeat by encouraging her "to look to the future: to do better the next time—to try harder," as she has recalled. She has credited her fifth-grade teacher with teaching her how to "think on [her] feet" and "for much of the people motivation that has been so important in [her] life," in her words. In junior high school she won second place in a statewide contest in extemporaneous speaking, and in high school, where she was a member of the debating team, she earned honors in formal debate. She completed high school in just three years.

Because her mother's income was so limited and few scholarships were available, Mary Kay did not apply to any colleges, despite her excellent academic record. By her own account, when one of her best friends and others among her schoolmates began their undergraduate studies, she felt envy for the first time. In an attempt to outshine them, the seventeen-year-old Mary Kay married J. Ben Rogers, whom she has described as "a very big radio star" in Houston then. "I thought he was a tremendous catch—sort of the Elvis Presley of the time," she has written of Rogers, who sang with a musical group at night and pumped gas during the day. Within a few years Mary Kay gave birth to a daughter and a son.

Mary Kay's introduction to direct sales occurred in the latter half of the 1930s, when a door-to-door saleswoman peddling a set of books called the *Child Psychology Bookshelf* made a bargain with her: if Mary Kay succeeded in selling ten sets, she would be given a set free of charge. Simply by transmitting her genuine enthusiasm for the books in telephone calls to friends and parishioners of her church, Mary Kay snared ten customers in a day and a half. She then began selling the books part-time, and at the end of nine months, she had earned more than $7,500 on sales of $25,000 worth of books. She had also incurred the displeasure of many of her friends, who accused her of persuading them to spend a lot of money for something they seldom used. "Well, what good are books that aren't read?" Mary Kay reflected in her autobiography. "[The buyers'] laziness was certainly not my fault. Still, I learned that the customer must be *taught* how to successfully use the product."

Around the time that Mary Kay stopped selling books, her husband lost his filling-station job.

Working as a team, the couple tried to earn a livelihood through direct sales of expensive pressure cookers and frying pans at get-togethers, called "parties" in the parlance of the trade, in people's homes. While her husband would extol the assets of the cookware in a host's living room, Mary Kay would make a similar pitch in the kitchen, where she would be using the pots and pans to prepare a dinner. Because of the Depression, many of their potential customers were in straitened financial circumstances, and only rarely did the couple's sales prowess and the cookware's demonstrably high quality overcome a reluctance to replace serviceable pots and pans with something so costly. "Besides, selling it took what I considered a hard sell, and I was never very good at that," Mary Kay has pointed out.

In 1939 Mary Kay got another job in direct sales, as a representative for the Houston-based Stanley Home Products Company, which manufactured such things as floor brushes and cleaning agents. She has often recounted how, soon after joining the concern, she attended a Stanley convention at which she watched the most successful of Stanley's salespeople crowned "queen of sales" and rewarded with an alligator-skin handbag. "I was so impressed with the crown, the alligator bag, and most of all the recognition bestowed upon the queen that I vowed, on the spot, the next year I would be queen," Mary Kay has recalled. She actually voiced her intention to Stanley's president, who responded by saying, "You know, somehow I think you will." "Those few words literally changed my life . . . ," she wrote in her autobiography. "The president of the company thought I could do it. After that, I could not let him down."

Meanwhile, heeding advice offered to convention participants, including such suggestions as "Hitch your wagon to a star" and "Get a railroad track to run on," Mary Kay had persuaded the "queen of sales" to hold a demonstration party one night during the convention. While the woman gave her sales talk, Mary Kay transcribed her words in nineteen pages of notes. "That sales demonstration became my railroad track, and those notes became my springboard to success," she has said. Almost immediately after the convention, she quadrupled her sales, and the next year she was named Stanley's queen of sales. But to her disappointment, she received not an alligator handbag but a light used for nighttime fishing. "Bag or not, I had become queen of sales by setting a goal, breaking it down into small realistic tasks, and broadcasting it to the world," she has observed.

During World War II Ben Rogers served in the armed forces, and Mary Kay became her family's primary breadwinner. In 1942, eager to pursue her dream of becoming a doctor, she enrolled at the University of Houston. A year or so later, exhausted from a daily routine that now entailed hours of classes and homework in addition to hours of selling, homemaking, and child care, she took an aptitude test that indicated her uncommon talents in such areas as persuasion. After pondering the advice of a university dean, who reminded her that she had ten years of training ahead of her before she could open a medical practice, she quit college to concentrate fully on building her career in sales.

When Mary Kay's husband returned to civilian life, he announced that he wanted a divorce. After the dissolution of the marriage, Mary Kay assumed full responsibility for supporting herself and her three children (her second son had been born in 1943). "I had a very hard time accepting the divorce . . . ," she has acknowledged. "For almost a year, I felt that I had failed as a woman, as a wife, and as a person." During that year she developed symptoms of what several doctors diagnosed as rheumatoid arthritis. The symptoms grew so severe that she was warned she would soon be totally incapacitated. Horrified at the thought of burdening her mother with her care and that of her children, she resolved to improve her Stanley sales record by hiding her unhappiness behind a cheerful demeanor at her home demonstrations. Her strategy resulted not only in an increase in her income but also in the disappearance of all signs of arthritis. Her earnings grew still further after she hired a full-time housekeeper, which allowed her to devote substantially more time to her job.

In 1952 Mary Kay resigned from Stanley, where she had been given the title of manager, and began working as the national training director for the World Gift Company, a Dallas-based direct-sales firm. "In truth, I was acting as the national *sales manager*—and for a salary much less than the job was worth," she has said. Many times during the years that she worked for World Gift, upon presenting to male colleagues what she believed was a promising marketing plan, she would be told, "Mary Kay, you're thinking just like a woman"—a remark that invariably enraged her. In 1963, after a man whom she had trained was named her supervisor and given a salary twice as high as hers—something that had happened to her at least once before—she quit the job. Although she was only in her mid-forties, she decided to retire. (She had remarried in about 1960 and presumably no longer had to rely entirely on herself for support.)

Immediately after her retirement, Mary Kay began to write down her ideas for a career guide that might help women avoid some of the pitfalls she had encountered as a woman in the business world. She embarked on that project not merely to keep herself busy but also to rid herself of some of the anger she felt about the mistreatment she had experienced and about the opportunities that had been closed to her because of her sex. She also harbored resentments about incidents in which both male and female workers had been treated with disrespect and about company rules and procedures that completely disregarded workers' normal concerns as human beings. As she compiled an inventory of what she viewed as positive corporate policies and another enumerating negative ones, she realized that the first list "defined the 'dream company,'" in her words. "I asked myself, 'Why are you *theorizing* about a dream company? Why don't you just start one?'" Setting aside her writing project, she thought about what product she might sell. It had to be something that women "could believe in, could use and recommend with all their hearts," she explained to Letha Mills for *Active Years* (August 1994). "And in direct sales, it's very important to have a product that will be used up, so there are several sales to be made." She decided to try to market skin-care products.

With part of her life savings of five thousand dollars, Mary Kay obtained the rights to the formulas for the homemade skin-care creams and lotions that she had been using since being introduced to them at a Stanley party a decade before. Prepared and bottled by the woman who had hosted the party, they were the woman's pleasantly scented reformulations of various malodorous substances that her father had used in tanning leather and that had evidently kept his hands remarkably soft throughout his working life. Mary Kay used the balance of her savings to buy the requisite chemical substances and containers, a few furnishings, and some used office equipment and to lease a five-hundred-square-foot storefront in a large office-building complex in Dallas. She also hired a chemical manufacturer to produce her five-product basic skin-care set. While her husband dealt with legal and financial matters related to her embryonic business, Mary Kay recruited a sales force of nine of her friends.

One month before the scheduled opening of Beauty by Mary Kay, as the company was originally named, Mary Kay's husband died of a heart attack while eating breakfast one morning. When she informed her lawyer and her accountant of his death, both of them immediately advised her to abandon her entrepreneurial plans. Her lawyer even showed her a pamphlet about the large number of cosmetics companies that failed each year. Mary Kay's children, on the other hand, encouraged her to proceed. Her older son, Ben, told her she could have all the money in his savings account if she needed it. Her son Richard, who was then twenty years old, quit a job that paid him nearly twice as much as his mother could offer him and became her partner. (Five years later the American Marketing Association was to name him "man of the year.")

With its entire inventory of skin-care sets and a few cosmetics displayed on inexpensive Sears Roebuck shelving, Beauty by Mary Kay opened its doors on September 13, 1963. The nine saleswomen, whom Mary Kay christened "consultants," gave facials and showed off the company's products in the storefront as well as in people's homes. (Mary Kay did so as well, until she realized how uneasy customers felt about a company whose manager performed the same functions as the sales personnel.) Instructed by Mary Kay never to use high-pressure salesmanship, the consultants held "classes" at which they taught women how to use Mary Kay products—a sales technique that, according to Mary Kay, no company had ever tried before. "Your role is not to sell cosmetics," the saleswomen were told. "Your role is [to ask yourself] . . . 'What can I do to send these women home feeling more beautiful on the outside, knowing full well that they'll become more beautiful on the inside as a result?'" To help her consultants sharpen their teaching skills, Mary Kay wrote a four-page instruction manual, and she also began producing a mimeographed newsletter for them. (The current edition of the *Mary Kay Consultants Guide* is more than two hundred pages long. The company also produces *Applause*, a monthly magazine, and various other publications for its sales force.)

Within three and a half months, sales of Mary Kay products totaled $34,000. Mary Kay and Richard Rogers soon had to rent a second space in which to store sufficient inventory to supply their rapidly growing sales crew and meet demand. After eight months her older son came to Dallas to manage the warehouse and to assist his mother and brother with filling and packing orders. "Our hard work paid off . . . ," Mary Kay reported in her autobiography, in recalling their sixteen- to eighteen-hour workdays. "The first calendar year brought us $198,000 in wholesale sales, and at the end of the second year, we had reached the unbelievable total of $800,000!" By that time Beauty by Mary Kay had become Mary Kay Cosmetics, the sales force had grown to more than three thousand, and the company had moved into a building that accommodated, in addition to offices and a room for training consultants, a warehouse measuring five thousand square feet. Mary Kay Cosmetics' corporate headquarters is now housed in a nine-building complex in Dallas. Mary Kay products sold in the United States and Canada are manufactured nearby at a state-of-the-art facility the size of three football fields. Five huge regional centers handle distribution of the company's line of two hundred skin-care, cosmetic, and fragrance products. In 1989 the company declared a moratorium on animal testing of all its products and their ingredients, and it has collaborated in efforts to develop alternatives to such testing.

"At Mary Kay, you're in business for yourself, but never by yourself," a company leaflet asserts. After an initial investment of about a hundred dollars for a kit containing demonstration items and educational materials, a consultant may stock as little or as much as she wants and may work as few or as many hours each week as she desires. Her profit on each sale may be as high as 100 percent. Through an intricate system of incentives related to the number of new consultants that an established consultant recruits and their volume of sales, the company pays salespeople commissions of up to 13 percent on wholesale orders. Sales directors at various levels of the Mary Kay "consultant career path," whose duties include training, guiding, and motivating salespeople, may receive bonuses and all-expenses-paid vacations as well as commissions. According to Mary Kay publicity handouts, the company gives away six million dollars' worth of diamond jewelry and other gifts and prizes annually. The more than seven thousand cars—including Cadillacs painted "Mary Kay pink"—that consultants and directors have received in recent years for outstanding sales and recruiting have been valued at more than $116 million. Winners of the cars are recognized at "Seminar," Mary Kay's annual convention, which in 1994 drew some forty thousand consultants and directors to Dallas for four consecutive three-day sessions. Mary Kay has called Seminar "the ultimate expression of a very simple concept—'praise people to success.'"

"Praise people to success" is a key aspect of Mary Kay's approach to supervision and administration, which she spelled out in her book *Mary Kay on People Management* (1984) and which is studied in the business schools of many universities. Dedicated to "all 'people managers' who still believe that *people* and *pride* are the two foremost assets in building a successful business," *Mary Kay on People Management* describes what Mary Kay characterizes as "a unique managerial concept that allows fairness to flourish in business." Her philosophy rests not only on the golden rule but on such precepts as "Sandwich every bit of criticism between two heavy layers of praise," "People will support that which they help to create," and "Help other people get what they want—and you'll get what you want."

The success of Mary Kay Cosmetics and of many of the more than 375,000 Mary Kay consultants (the vast majority of whom are women) provides evidence of the wisdom of Mary Kay's managerial philosophy. According to the company's literature, 80 percent of the 3 percent of American women who earn more than one hundred thousand dollars annually are associated with Mary Kay; the average annual income of the more than ninety Mary Kay national sales directors is "well into six figures"; hundreds of the seven thousand Mary Kay directors earn more than fifty thousand dollars a year and many others earn more than one hundred thousand; and "it is estimated that more women have earned over one million dollars from their Mary Kay careers than at any other company in the world." Mary Kay herself became a millionaire in 1968, when her company went public. (It returned to private ownership in 1985, when she and her family bought back all outstanding public shares for $315 million.) Mary Kay's current personal worth has been estimated to be more than $320 million.

"As sweet as a magnolia blossom, Mary Kay comes in a softly rounded package with an ice-cream complexion," Kristin McMurran wrote in *People* (July 29, 1985). In *Women's Enterprise* (November/December 1994), Marjie Mugno Acheson described the five-foot three-inch Mary Kay as "extremely approachable." In adherence with her conviction that "no matter how busy you are, you must make the other person feel important," in her words, she unfailingly gives whoever addresses her her complete attention, and she reportedly never refuses to listen to the personal as well as the professional problems of consultants or any of the more than twenty-two hundred Mary Kay corporate employees. By her own account, she is "blessed with natural enthusiasm" and has always had a great deal of energy. Still actively involved in company affairs since becoming chairperson emeritus in 1987, she has continued her long-held habits of making a list each night of the six most important things she must do the next day and of awakening at 5:00 A.M. to attend to business-related paperwork before breakfast. While dressing, cooking, and traveling, she listens to motivational tape-recordings. She is a long-time member of, and major fund-raiser for, the Prestonwood Baptist Church, in Dallas. A self-described workaholic, she occasionally relaxes by painting in acrylics. Mary Kay's third husband, Melville Jerome Ash, died in 1980; her daughter, Marylyn Rogers Theard, died in about 1990. Her son Richard is currently chairman of the board of Mary Kay Cosmetics; her son Ben left the company some years ago to become a developer in Dallas. As of 1994 she had sixteen grandchildren and twenty-four great-grandchildren.

The many honors Mary Kay has received include the Dale Carnegie Leadership Award and the Horatio Alger Distinguished American Citizen Award (both in 1978), the first annual National Sales Hall of Fame Award (1989), the Kupfer Distinguished Executive Award from Texas A&M University (1993), and the Pathfinder Award of the National Association of Women Business Owners (1995). In 1993 the UN Environment Program recognized Mary Kay Cosmetics for "its commitment to the cause of the environment" and "its exemplary leadership in promoting sound environmental policies within the cosmetic industry." The Mary Kay Foundation gives hundreds of thousands of dollars annually to social-service programs and medical research and treatment facilities, prominent among them the Mary Kay Ash Cancer Research Laboratory at the Saint Paul Medical Center in Dallas, which was dedicated in 1993. In addition to her autobiography, which has sold more than a million copies, and her book on management, which remained on the *New York Times* best-seller list for eleven weeks in 1984, Mary Kay is the author of *From My Heart*, a collection of brief inspirational essays that she wrote to "help women realize how great they really are," and *Mary Kay: You Can Have It All* (1995), which is subtitled "Lifetime Wisdom from America's Foremost Woman Entrepreneur."

Selected Biographical References: Chicago Tribune V p1+ F 14 '91 por; Fortune 128:68+ S 20 '93 pors; People 24:57+ Jl 29 '85 pors; Robb Report 8:28+ Jl '84 pors; Who's Who in America, 1995

Bakker, Robert T.

(BAH-ker)

1945(?)-Paleontologist; writer. Address: 1447 Sumac Ave., Boulder, CO 80304

Robert T. Bakker is possibly the best-known dinosaur paleontologist alive today. With his trademark cowboy hat, waist-length hair, and long beard, he is instantly recognizable to dinosaur enthusiasts, who can be counted on to turn out in large numbers to hear him lecture, in his booming voice, on the many virtues of the long-extinct animals. To some, he is even something of a hero, for Bakker has devoted virtually his entire career to setting the record straight about dinosaur lifestyles, physiology, and behavior. Indeed, more than any other paleontologist, Bakker is responsible for popularizing the notion that dinosaurs were not the pea-brained, dull-colored, swamp-dwelling sluggards they were once thought to be but were rather enormously successful animals that dominated Mesozoic Earth by dint of their agility, cunning, and fast metabolism.

While the general outlines of Bakker's theories are consistent with current scientific thought, few of the specifics have been unreservedly embraced by his fellow paleontologists, who regard him as something of a loose cannon, given on the one hand to drawing sweeping, oversimplified conclusions and on the other to proclaiming outlandish theories that are unsubstantiated by the notoriously poor fossil record. (His theory that the extinction of dinosaurs was caused by the spread of disease is a case in point. "This is a leap off the cliff of knowledge into the abyss of speculation," Peter Dodson, a paleontologist at the University of Pennsylvania, told Don Lessem for Lessem's 1992 book *Kings of Creation*.) Yet Bakker is also regarded by some of his colleagues (among them no less a figure than Stephen Jay Gould, the curator of Harvard University's Museum of Comparative Zoology) as a brilliant thinker, and they have conceded that many of his conclusions, while initially suspect, have later proved to be fundamentally correct. "These Bakkerian extrapolations!" Dale Russell, a Canadian dinosaur paleontologist, said of Bakker's insistence that dinosaurs were warm-blooded, during an interview with Virginia Morell for *Discover* (March 1987). "How many times have we dismissed his ideas and then had to reconsider them in the light of new evidence?"

Robert Bakker was born in about 1945 in Ridgewood, New Jersey, the younger of the two sons of an electrical engineer and his wife. His parents, both of whom are conservative Christians, are now retired and live in Florida, and his brother, Donald, is a high school teacher in Massachusetts. Bakker thinks he may have inherited his iconoclastic spirit from his maternal grandmother, who was from "the part of Holland where free-thinkers, antipapists, Jews, smugglers, and counterfeiters went and were hanged as criminals," he told Vicki Lindner, who interviewed him for *Omni* (March 1992). "The family agreed she was a little loony, but interesting. And more than once it's been said I take after Grandma Meyer. I don't back down." Whatever the source of his rebellious streak, Bakker began bucking convention at an early age. Although his family members have always pronounced their surname "baker," he pronounces it "bocker," because, when he was in high school, he delved into his family's history and learned that this was how his Dutch forebears pronounced it.

Bakker became hooked on dinosaurs as a young boy. The pivotal moment occurred, he has recalled, in 1955, when he read a *Life* magazine article that featured an artist's rendering of one of the great beasts slogging through the mud. He was so enchanted by the pictures—he has likened the experience to "Saul's conversion on the road to Damascus"—that he decided to spend the rest of his life learning about these creatures. Even the fact that dinosaurs were then considered to be "evolutionary flops," as he put it, failed to dissuade him from pursuing that goal.

This less-than-flattering image of dinosaurs can be traced in part to ideas advanced by Sir Richard Owen, a nineteenth-century British anatomist whose studies led him to conclude that the animals were closely related to lizards. (It was Owen who coined the term "dinosauria," meaning "terrible lizard.") It also derives from the fact that dinosaurs became extinct sixty-five million years ago, while mammals—their evolutionarily superior rivals, according to popular thinking—went on to dominate Earth. The supposed dinosaur-lizard connection, combined with the dinosaurs' demise as a class of animals, helped establish the notion that dinosaurs lost the evolutionary race to mammals because they were slow-moving, dim-witted—in short, inferior—animals.

While this view of dinosaurs was periodically challenged by some researchers, it tended to dominate both popular and scientific thinking until the 1960s, the decade when Bakker entered Yale University, in New Haven, Connecticut. Among the challengers was John Ostrom, one of Bakker's professors at Yale. As a result of his study of a fossil dinosaur claw he had discovered in 1964, Ostrom came to believe that the animal could not possibly have led a stereotypically reptilian existence. Because the foot, with its scythe-like claw, was supremely well adapted for killing prey, the animal to which it belonged, Ostrom explained to Virginia Morell, "must have been a fleet-footed, highly predaceous, extremely agile, and very active animal."

Recognizing Ostrom was on to something, Bakker decided to launch his own investigation of dinosaur lifestyles. He began by analyzing the dinosaur specimens on display at Yale's Peabody Museum of Natural History. Before long, he grew troubled by the decidedly reptilian postures of the specimens: they were mounted just like lizards, with their forelimbs splayed out to the side and their stomachs dragging along the ground. By the time he completed his two-year-long study of dinosaur anatomy, Bakker had become convinced that this scenario was dead wrong. Dinosaurs were not built so much like lizards, he concluded, as they were like elephants and other large mammals. Extrapolating from this observation, he further concluded that dinosaurs, like mammals, were energetic, swift creatures that were capable of regulating their internal body temperatures. Bakker has attributed what he believes to be his colleagues' wrongheadedness to what he calls their "pretzel," or twisted, logic. "Because everyone assumed they were lizards," he told Virginia Morell, "they made them look and act like lizards."

Never one to keep his opinions to himself, Bakker detailed his findings and interpretations in a paper that appeared in *Discovery*, the quarterly magazine of the Peabody Museum of Natural History, in 1968, the year in which he earned his B.A. degree from Yale. "If dinosaurs were really slow-moving mountains of cold-blooded flesh," he wrote, "how did they manage to suppress speedy, warm-blooded mammals for millions of years?" In challenging the widely held assumption that dinosaurs were cold-blooded—in other words, dependent on their external environment to raise their body temperatures and therefore to spur them to action—Bakker sparked what was to become the ongoing debate over whether dinosaurs were cold-blooded or warm-blooded.

In retrospect, the *Discovery* paper was significant not only because of its content but because it was reported on by several major newspapers, thus marking the beginning of the media's fixation with Bakker's often controversial ideas about dinosaurs. Also, it was less than enthusiastically received by his colleagues—like much of his later work. Indeed, in those days Bakker's insistence that dinosaurs were warm-blooded, or endothermic, placed him squarely in the minority. "I think he's got some good points," Edwin H. Colbert, a former curator of fossil reptiles at New York City's American Museum of Natural History, said of Bakker's paper during an interview with a reporter for the *New York Times* (June 2, 1968), "but I'm not sure you can be as positive about them as he seems to be."

Notwithstanding his colleagues' reluctance to accept his ideas, or perhaps partly because of it, Bakker forged ahead with his effort to come up with compelling evidence that dinosaurs led active lifestyles. It was this mission, in fact, that preoccupied him throughout the three years he worked at the Peabody Museum following his graduation from college, and then over the course of his doctoral studies at Harvard University, beginning in 1971, and during his tenure at Johns Hopkins University, on whose faculty he served from 1976 until 1984.

One of the arguments that Bakker came up with to support his theory that dinosaurs were warm-blooded involves fossil trackways—fossilized dinosaur footprints. According to him, they showed that dinosaurs moved at a pace so rapid that it could be sustained only if they were capable of maintaining a constant internal body temperature. The fact that dinosaurs had large rib cages also suggested to Bakker that the animals were warm-blooded, for it meant that they possessed large hearts—a prerequisite for a fast metabolism. Yet another piece of evidence was his discovery that the ratio of predatory dinosaurs to prey in fossil-rich localities is comparable to that of predatory warm-blooded animals to their prey in modern animal populations. (Because the energy requirements of warm-blooded animals are greater than those of cold-blooded ones, animal populations can support fewer warm-blooded predators than cold-blooded ones.)

The warm-blooded dinosaur scenario was further bolstered, in Bakker's view, by evidence that the dinosaurs' habitat during the Jurassic period (which lasted from about 213 million to 146 million years ago) was not swampy, as had been previously thought, but rather seasonally arid, and therefore not unlike the grassland environment of the Serengeti in Africa today, where rainy seasons alternate with dry seasons. "[The dinosaurs] had to follow the rains—like the elephants in East Africa today—to find the new green shoots. But you can't be cold-blooded and migrate," he explained to Virginia Morell. "Reptiles don't have the sustained capacity for exercise. Lizards can sprint short distances, but they can't cruise. You need a high metabolism for that."

While Bakker's colleagues considered some of his arguments compelling, few found them persuasive enough to conclude, as Bakker apparently had, that dinosaurs were in fact endothermic. "I didn't," Jack Horner, one of the world's leading dinosaur paleontologists, told Morell. "Not based on the evidence he had. I argued and argued with him about the dinosaurs being warm-blooded. I didn't think any of his arguments really held up. Take the predator-to-prey thing: you can have a real bias in what animals are preserved in the fossil record. I didn't buy his paleo-latitudes either. But the stuff that [the French scientist] Armand de Ricqlès was doing looked like something you might be able to work with, only you needed the right material, a growth series."

Horner was referring to Ricqlès's studies on the microstructure of dinosaur fossil bones, which, the latter had found, bore striking similarities to the bones of such fast-growing (and endothermic) animals as modern birds and mammals. This finding caught the attention not only of Horner but of many researchers, who felt compelled to concede that Bakker might, after all, have been on to something all along. Still, even the most enthusiastic supporters of the warm-blooded dinosaur scenario (Bakker excluded) prefer to state that *some* dinosaurs *may* have been warm-blooded and to emphasize that the physiology of any extinct animal will always remain a subject of speculation.

For his part, Bakker is impatient with his more conservative colleagues' reluctance to embrace the notion that dinosaurs were warm-blooded. He even seems to attribute their equivocation to a kind of intellectual weakness or a fear of abandoning traditional ideas about dinosaurs—"the party line," as he has somewhat uncharitably called it. "I've often heard the statement, 'Well, there are flaws in the warm-blooded theory,'" he told Vicki Lindner. "Anyone saying that is missing the point. The real question is, Which theory is stronger? Slow, cold-blooded, stupid? Or fast, warm-blooded, smart? Not one dinosaur bone that's been cut looks like an alligator bone. Every single one has shown the animal grew fast. If you take these dinosaurs apart, no matter how you cut them, they sure look like big birds. . . . Yet people cling to the central dogma, 'Oh, dinosaurs were all big, and it was a warm climate, so they didn't have to be warm-blooded.' It doesn't wash; we should be beyond this."

As might be imagined, Bakker's combativeness, his apparent certitude about the correctness of his ideas, and his seeming disdain for those scientists who adhere to the "central dogma" have contributed to his reputation as the enfant terrible of the paleontological establishment. As a result, his pronouncements are at best respectfully considered and at worst dismissed as impossible to prove. One of the more evenhanded assessments of Bakker's contribution to the field was offered by John S. McIntosh, a retired Yale physics professor, during an interview with Terence Monmaney for the *New Yorker* (May 31, 1993): "I've always had deep respect for [Bakker's] ideas, though I don't go as far as he goes. He certainly got people thinking. He was very largely responsible for getting dinosaurs back into the mainstream of paleontology."

Indeed, in large measure thanks to Bakker—who has disseminated his ideas to the general public through lectures, appearances in television documentaries, and his book *The Dinosaur Heresies: Unlocking the Mystery of the Dinosaurs and Their Extinction* (1986)—dinosaurs are no longer objects of derision but are considered to be intelligent creatures that thundered across the dry floodplains of the Mesozoic Era, from 230 million to 65 million years ago. Bakker's ideas about dinosaurs are even said to have informed the blockbuster film *Jurassic Park*, one of whose most memorable scenes depicts a cunning *Velociraptor* trying to make a lunch of two of the film's human protagonists.

The question of whether or not dinosaurs were warm-blooded, which was the most hotly contested debate among dinosaur paleontologists during the 1970s, was supplanted in the following decade by the debate over why dinosaurs became extinct sixty-five million years ago. Not surprisingly, Bakker did not hesitate to offer his views on the subject. The debate was sparked by the discovery in 1978 of a layer of iridium in rock strata dated to be sixty-five million years old. Because iridium is rare in Earth's crust and comparatively more common in celestial objects, the discoverers of the iridium layer, Walter Alvarez, a geologist, and his father, Luis Alvarez, a physicist, postulated that an asteroid or large meteorite had crashed into Earth sixty-five million years ago. The impact, they further speculated, would have caused a thick dust cloud to envelop the planet—so thick that no sunlight would have reached Earth, which would have both caused the temperature to drop and interrupted photosynthesis. This, in turn, would have precipitated the demise of many plant species and the animals that fed on them, including large herbivorous sauropods like *Barosaurus*, as well as, ultimately, the animals at the top of the food chain, among them the carnivorous theropods *Tyrannosaurus rex* and *Allosaurus*. The asteroid-impact theory was further strengthened by the discovery of an impact crater of the expected size and age off the coast of the Yucatan in 1991.

Somewhat surprisingly, perhaps, given his obvious penchant for melodrama, Bakker has dismissed as pure nonsense the notion that the dinosaurs died out as the result of some kind of extraterrestrial cataclysm. He found the explanation inconvincing at least partly because of evidence that many dinosaur species had gone extinct long before the end of the Cretaceous. "When Alvarez published his theories, people snapped them up because they explained everything in one great iridium zap," Bakker told Jim Robbins in an interview for *Discover* (March 1991). "But the work was incomplete. We were looking at the possibility of at least eight such die-offs [during the Mesozoic Era], and explaining just the last one—and resorting to a cosmic cataclysm to do it—seemed a bit naïve."

Also casting doubt on the asteroid-impact theory, according not only to Bakker but to most paleontologists, is the fact that frogs, crocodiles, and other temperature-sensitive creatures managed to survive the Cretaceous extinction, which is the opposite of what one would expect. "The asteroid partisans have this great theory that explains why everything on Earth should die at the end of the Cretaceous," Bakker told Jim Robbins. "But everything on Earth doesn't die. At the Cretaceous . . .

and the other extinction events the pattern appears to be the same: large and medium-size animals are eliminated, and small animals—the overwhelming majority—are free to range out and evolve."

In place of the asteroid-impact theory, Bakker has come up with an explanation of his own—one that, incidentally, most of his colleagues consider to be both far-fetched and impossible to prove. Citing both the appearance of many land bridges at the end of the Cretaceous (as a result of continental drift) and the likelihood that dinosaurs would have begun to explore new migration routes, he has argued that as different dinosaur populations came into contact with one another, they would have brought with them diseases to which some populations would not have been immune. "The animals that would move fastest across land bridges are big . . . ," he explained to Terence Monmaney. "What would happen if you had fifty species of land animal suddenly meeting one another? You're mixing thousands of diseases."

While Bakker has been particularly outspoken on the debates over thermoregulation in dinosaurs and their extinction, he has also taken a stand on several other issues as well. He has contended, for instance, that the evolution of flowering plants was tied to that of certain herbivorous dinosaurs—a notion that few scientists have taken seriously. He is also in the minority in maintaining that dinosaurs were brightly colored. On the other hand, Bakker has long been an ardent proponent of the theory that dinosaurs as a class of animals never actually became extinct, but that they survive today as birds—a view that is now accepted by a majority of paleontologists.

In 1984 Bakker left his position at Johns Hopkins University and moved to Boulder, Colorado, where he lives with his wife, Constance Clark, and his dog. (Three earlier marriages ended in divorce.) Since moving West, Bakker has written two books for popular audiences, *Dinosaur Heresies*, in which he discusses his controversial theories, and *Raptor Red*, a novel published in 1995, as well as several articles for the magazine *Discover*, and he has continued to be a big draw on the lecture circuit. He has also worked as a consultant to Dinamation, a California-based company that produces robotic dinosaurs, and to Sega, a Japanese video-game company, and he somehow manages to find time to lead fossil-hunting expeditions.

For all his outspokenness and his confidence in the validity of his theories, Bakker has no interest in seeing his ideas being embraced uncritically. "God, no. Then I'd be the new orthodoxy!" he told Vicki Lindner. Nevertheless, he appears to be quite pleased that many of his ideas have helped shape the public's understanding of dinosaurs. "The battle is mostly won. *The Golden Book of Dinosaurs*—the most widely distributed book on dinosaurs—is totally different than the one I grew up with. Brontosaur is out of the swamps; it's no longer green; dinosaurs are evolving into birds . . . That means a hundred million kids worldwide have been correctly informed. The genie is out of the bottle and will never go back in."

Selected Biographical References: Discover 8:26+ Mr '87 por, 12:52+ Mr '91 pors; New Yorker 69:42+ My 31 '93; Omni 14:64+ Mr '92 pors; Bakker, Robert T. The Dinosaur Heresies: New Theories Unlocking the Mystery of the Dinosaurs and Their Extinction (1986).

AP/Wide World Photos

Barad, Jill E.

(bah-RAHD)

May 23, 1951– Business executive. Address: Mattel Inc., 33 Continental Blvd., El Segundo, CA 90245-5012

Jill E. Barad, the president and chief operating officer of Mattel Inc. since 1992, is one of the few women at the helm of a Fortune 500 company, or any publicly traded firm. Barad, who joined the toy-manufacturing company as a product manager in 1981, proved herself to be an unusually capable executive in several divisions at Mattel, but she owes her reputation in the industry in large part to her rejuvenation of the Barbie doll, the "anatomically impossible, age-indeterminable fashion doll," in the words of one writer, that has been a favorite playtime companion of little girls (and an increasingly popular collectible) since 1959. Named marketing director of the Barbie line in 1982, she expanded the collection to include a variety of "career" and "play" Barbies and about 250 accessory items, ranging from furniture to cosmetics. Under her guidance, sales of Barbie dolls climbed from $485 million in 1988 to over $1 billion in 1994. "Maybe it's too obvious to compare Jill Elikann Barad to her star product, Barbie," Kim Masters observed in her profile of the executive for *Working Woman* (May 1990). "But it's tempting. After all, Barad has a pretty face, a knockout wardrobe—and a great career. . . . She has risen through the ranks so quickly that in 1988 *USA Today* dubbed her 'the toy industry's Princess of Power,'" a reference to the action doll for girls that Barad developed and launched in 1985.

Over the course of her career at Mattel, Barad has also been credited with expanding the Hot Wheels miniature-car line; introducing a number of new dolls, including the popular Li'l Miss Makeup; negotiating lucrative financial arrangements with the Walt Disney Company and McDonald's, among others; and teaming up with Mattel's chairman and chief executive officer, John W. Amerman, to acquire the rival toy makers Fisher-Price and Kransco—deals that, according to at least one market analyst, made Mattel the largest toy manufacturer in the world. "Jill always comes through with the big idea," Amerman said, as quoted in *Business Week* (June 8, 1992).

Barad was born Jill Elikann in New York City on May 23, 1951, the youngest daughter of Corinne (Schuman) Elikann, a pianist and artist, and Lawrence (Larry) Stanley Elikann, an Emmy Award-winning television and film director. From her earliest years Barad was encouraged by her parents "to be anything [she] wanted to be," as she recalled to Divina Infusino in an interview for *Harper's Bazaar* (March 1990). "They didn't put confines around that idea. But I was also brought up with the sense that no one was going to give you anything. What you wanted for yourself—respect, money—you had to earn. If you had to be dependent, you were in a vulnerable position." As a teenager growing up in New York City, Barad dreamed of becoming an actress, and she became adept at imitating the mod look then in vogue. By the age of sixteen, she told a reporter for *People* (May 9, 1994), she "never left the house without lipstick or eye makeup. It was the time of Twiggy, when you did patent-leather liner and false eyelashes."

Barad parlayed her expertise with makeup into a part-time job as a beauty consultant for Love Cosmetics while she was attending Queens College, in the New York City borough of Queens. After receiving a B.A. degree in English and psychology in 1973, she worked briefly as an assistant to the film producer Dino De Laurentiis. Her desire to pursue an acting career apparently faded after a single day in front of the cameras, in the nonspeaking role of Miss Italian-America in the producer's 1973 gangster movie *Crazy Joe*. Shortly thereafter, she was hired by Coty Cosmetics to train department-store cosmeticians in the art of makeup application. Enterprising and ambitious, Barad soon began sending unsolicited product-marketing proposals to Coty executives. Her initiative won her a quick promotion to the management ranks. Within three years of joining the company, she was brand manager for Coty's entire line, a post she held until shortly before her marriage to Thomas Kenneth Barad, a film executive, on January 28, 1979.

Moving to Los Angeles, where her husband was based, she quickly landed a job as an account executive in the Los Angeles advertising agency Wells, Rich, Greene. Her assignments there included the Max Factor cosmetics account. She left the agency before the end of the year, just prior to the birth of her first child. She spent the next two years at home, caring for her son, an experience she has since described as "a real learning time" for her. When she reentered the job market in 1981, she was hired by Mattel Inc. as a product manager in the boys' toys division. Among her first projects was a new toy called A Bad Case of Worms, a gelatinous blob that was designed to slither down walls. The toy flopped, but Barad apparently was not blamed for its disappointing sales. "I think everyone thought I managed *out* of that well," she told Anne B. Fisher of *Fortune* (September 21, 1992). In 1982 Barad asked Tom Kalinske, a senior vice-president at Mattel, for a bigger challenge. He responded by naming her marketing director for Barbie dolls. She was promoted to vice-president of marketing in 1983, senior vice-president in 1985, and executive vice-president in 1986.

Throughout the early to mid-1980s, one of Mattel's biggest sellers was its Masters of the Universe toy line, a collection of action-hero figures designed for boys. Inspired by a conversation she had with her sister, Barad decided to add the first super hero action doll for girls—She-Ra, the Princess of Power—to the Masters of the Universe line. "We were talking about how boys had all these powerful and aggressive toys," Barad said, in recalling that conversation to Kim Masters, "and it seemed time to offer little girls a role model who also had strength and power." The market for the Masters of the Universe collapsed by the mid-1980s, and although She-Ra was a successful product, it survived for only two years. "She wasn't very popular with moms," Barad has said of the doll.

Mattel, which had expanded its operations on the basis of the strong sales of the Masters of the Universe toys, was left with an overloaded inventory and an overstaffed work force. The ensuing company retrenchment caused considerable turmoil among employees. Barad herself accepted a lateral transfer in 1986, from the marketing division to product development. In an interview for *Savvy Woman* (May 1989), she admitted to Ann Hornaday that the move was a little traumatic at the time, but that it turned out to be "a wonderful benefit" in the long run. "I think a lot of us don't allow ourselves to go off course because of the fear that it's going to take something away, versus expanding the horizons we have," she said. According to Kim Masters, Barad was criticized by some of her former colleagues for having switched alliances in the company too easily, as a way to protect herself, a charge she has strongly denied.

In the late 1980s Barad launched several new doll lines, including Rainbow Brite, the Heart Family, P.J. Sparkles, and perhaps most important, Li'l Miss Makeup. She had wanted to introduce a makeup doll for several years, but she had always been deterred by the messiness of cosmetics application. The solution came to her when she saw the innovative color changing process created for Mattel's Hot Wheels Color Racers. Drawing on that process, she developed a technique whereby the color on Li'l Miss Makeup's face could be activated by the touch of a wand filled with cold water; application of a warm-water wand makes the color disappear. The method effectively eliminated the need for real makeup. When Mattel executives decided to feature the doll at the annual new-product toy fair in 1988, Barad pushed her staff to get it ready in six months, rather the nine to twelve months it usually takes to finish a new product. "Jill expects miracles from us," Diana Troup, Mattel's executive vice-president of product design and packaging told Clint Willis for an article in *Working Woman* (December 1993) "And she gets them. She makes us believe we can do it." The doll was a big hit, grossing an estimated fifty million dollars in its first year. In 1989 Li'l Miss Dress Up was added to the line, and in the following year, Li'l Miss Magic Hair.

It was, however, Barad's management of the three-decades-old Barbie doll line that became her claim to fame at Mattel and in the toy industry as a whole. Her strategy was to expand the collection, so that little girls would want to own multiple versions of the doll. "It's not just putting another dress on another little doll," Barad has said, as quoted in the *Business Week* article, "but how do you bring that doll to life?" Under her direction. Mattel came out with "play patterns" of Barbie, such as Barbie on skis and Barbie on Rollerblades. The dolls were sold with accompanying sports outfits and equipment. Noting that the girls who took part in the company's focus play groups often pretended to be going to work, Barad decided to offer career versions of the doll as well. But because she also knew that girls regularly chose to play with the frilliest clothes, she designed Day-to-Night Barbie, a career woman whose conservative business suit could be converted into a dressy evening outfit. The concept was a big success, and other day-to-night versions followed, among them Doctor Barbie, whose lab coat turned into an evening gown, and Flight Time Barbie, who doubled as a pilot and flight attendant and came with a party dress inspired by the flamboyant designs of the French couturier Christian Lacroix. Barad told Hornaday that Mattel's customers were pleased to see that "Barbie *does* have talent and skills, and does go to work and make money, and *that's* how she affords her car!" The "new" Barbies were heavily promoted in television commercials, including a dramatic sixty-second spot with the slogan "We Girls Can Do Anything," which eventually became the centerpiece of the advertising campaign.

Barad has often said that she considers Barbie to be a worthy role model for girls. "I'm very conscious of showing that Barbie's been an astronaut or that she's a doctor," she told a writer for *People* (May 5, 1995). "It's what we do in the world, not what we look like, that will be remembered." What Barad did was help to send sales of Barbie dolls through the roof. Over $1 billion of Mattel's $2.7 billion in sales in 1993 came from the Barbie division. By that time company surveys were showing that the average Barbie owner had seven versions of the doll. In 1994 there were some ninety different Barbie dolls from which to choose. Seth Lubove, writing in *Forbes* (September 26, 1994), listed some of them: "kidsize Barbies that come in wearable wedding dresses that retail at $140; adult collector Barbies that wear Nicole Miller-designed clothes and are priced at $65; a limited-edition Gold Jubilee anniversary Barbie expected to sell at $300 that now retails for as much as $1,000." There were also Barbie dollhouses, Barbie sports cars, Barbie games, Barbie backpacks, and Barbie-inspired bedding, clothing, and accessories.

The idea is to continue expanding the avenues of fantasy, Barad explained in the interview for the May 1990 *Working Woman* profile, because "little girls like change." One change that is unlikely, however, is an official "marriage" between Barbie and her steady boyfriend, Ken. "Little girls are marrying and unmarrying her all the time," Barad said. "If we were to officially set it, it would cut off some of the fantasy." The resurgence in the sales of Barbie dolls and Barbie-related merchandise has not been without problems. A talking version of the doll whose vocabulary included the phrase "math is tough" was roundly criticized when it was introduced in 1992, for reinforcing the gender stereotype that girls do not do well in math. The offending computer chip was quickly replaced.

After demonstrating with the Barbie collection how a new approach can expand and invigorate an established line of toys, Barad put that strategy to work on other Mattel staples. One of Mattel's more popular product lines is Hot Wheels, a toy-car series that has been on the market for over twenty-five years. Hot Wheels had traditionally featured only the miniature scale models of cars, but Barad expanded its purview to include "anything that flies, rolls, or floats," as she once out it. Sales of Hot Wheels jumped 32 percent in 1992, after she took responsibility for the line. Barad has credited some of her success to her time in the field, for she has made a point of finding out what retailers and children want. "Jill has a keen awareness of what the marketplace wants and how to give it to them," Gary Jacobson, a toy-industry analyst for the investment firm Kidder, Peabody & Co., Incorporated, told Clint Willis. She has also earned a reputation for maintaining the goodwill of retailers. "Barad really knows the business and her product line, so if there is a problem with a line at the store, she addresses it immediately," Michael Goldstein, the vice-chairman of Toys "R" Us, told Willis. "A few months ago, some Barbie dolls, like Hollywood Hair and Earring Magic Barbie, weren't selling. Jill came up with a 'buy one, give one to your friend' promotion that promised a second, identical doll free to anyone who bought one. That got them out of the stores. She realizes problems, reacts, and solves them quickly."

In recent years Barad has devoted a considerable amount of her time to enlarging Mattel's share of the marketplace. She was part of the management team that strengthened the firm's franchise ties to the Walt Disney Company, boosting sales of Mattel's Disney toys to about $275 million a year by the end of 1993. Barad also formed alliances with McDonald's and with the children's cable television network Nickelodeon that generated an estimated $100 million in sales for Mattel in the first two years of the agreements alone. In 1993 Barad and Mattel CEO John Amerman negotiated the acquisition of Fisher-Price, Inc., the leading manufacturer of preschool and infant toys, for a reported $1 billion in stock. The following year they paid $260 million in cash for Kransco Manufacturing Inc., which makes Frisbees and Hula Hoops. By the end of 1994, according to Seth Lubove of *Forbes*, Mattel was poised to push past Hasbro Inc. as the world's largest toy company. Asserting that "Mattel is not a doll company anymore," Barad told Lubove that the company's goals for the future included expansion into the electronic entertainment market, beginning with talking Barbie dolls and Barbie video games.

Unlike the majority of women executives in the highest echelons of American corporations, Barad has made her climb to the top while raising a family. A survey of eight top female executives published in *Business Month* (April 1990) found only two of the eight had children; one of the two was Barad, who has two sons. Throughout her career, Barad has steadfastly rejected the notion that corporate success and motherhood are incompatible. In the interview with Ann Hornaday for *Savvy Woman*, she recalled: "People had said to me, 'Jill, you know you can't have it all, make your choices, decide what you want. Do you want a career, do you want a family, do you want children? But no, you can't have it all.'" She realized the naysayers were wrong when she was promoted to vice-president of Mattel's girls' toys division when she was five months pregnant with her second child. "It really said to me, 'That's not true! That's someone else's truth, not mine,'" she told Hornaday. The most difficult aspect of her job, she has said on more than one occasion, is the fact that she must travel frequently, including trips to Asia six times a year to check on new technology for toys. "There are realities to the fact that I cannot be everywhere," she explained to Masters. "I've accepted that. I try to put my priorities in order—and it works out better some times than others."

In April 1993 Barad was deemed one of the ten smartest women in America by the editors of *Ladies Home Journal*, and in the following year she was numbered among the world's fifty most beautiful people by the staff of *People* magazine. Barad, who stands five feet, five inches tall and weighs 120 pounds, is a strikingly photogenic woman with dark eyes, long dark hair, and an infectious smile. "There's a flamboyance about her," Paul Fireman, the chairman of Reebok International, Ltd., on whose board Barad sits, has said, as quoted in *People*. "She's got an intriguing look." Barad lives in California with her husband, Tom, who is now an independent film producer, and her sons, Alexander David and Justin Harris. The two boys have often been pressed into service as toy testers. When asked to describe her professional philosophy for *Harper's Bazaar*, Barad told Divina Infusino that she had "no particular formula" for success. "I'm willing to take some risks. I don't believe you have to do things the way they've always been done . . . . When people ask, 'Why are you successful?' they don't realize that 'you' is multiple. There are always so many others involved. If I can take any credit, it's that somehow I inspire those I work with to be as good as they are. My role is really to lead people to achieve the results I'm obliged to deliver."

Selected Biographical References: Forbes 154:84+ S 26 '94 por; Fortune 126:56 S 21 '92 por; Harper's Bazaar 123:184+ Mr '90 pors; Working Woman 15:88+ My '90 pors, 18:46+ D '93 pors; Who's Who in America, 1995

Remy de La/AP/Wide World Photos

Baulieu, Etienne-Emile

(boh-LYUH, et-YEN-ay-MEEL)

Dec. 12, 1926– French biochemist; physician; abortion rights activist. Address: c/o Laboratoire des hormones, Hôpital de Bicêtre, 94270 Le Kremlin-Bicêtre, France

The French biochemist Etienne-Emile Baulieu, who has described himself as "a medical doctor who practices science," is best known as a key figure in the development of RU-486, a steroid that interrupts early pregnancy and offers an alternative to surgical abortion. Baulieu gained an international reputation among steroid-hormone researchers at the age of thirty-three, when he discovered a hormone secreted by the adrenal gland. In the 1960s he turned his attention to fertility control because he wanted to enable women to gain control over their reproductive lives and to help stabilize Earth's rapidly growing human population, which, at present rates of increase, may reach ten billion during the next century.

For the past three decades, Baulieu has worked as a French government researcher and as a consultant to the pharmaceutical company Roussel-Uclaf, and since the invention of RU-486 by the Roussel-Uclaf chemist Georges Teutsch in 1980, he has crusaded for its use internationally. Condemned as a "death pill" by some opponents of abortion, widely referred to as the "abortion pill," and dubbed a "contragestive" (meaning contragestation) by Baulieu, RU-486 is expected to win FDA approval in 1996. Baulieu maintains that he is not, in his words, "for abortion" but, rather, is "for women." "Two hundred thousand women die in botched abortions every year," he has repeatedly pointed out. "RU-486 can save them." In 1989 Baulieu received the Albert Lasker Clinical Medical Research Award, one of the highest honors in medicine, for his contributions to the field of steroid hormone biosynthesis, metabolism, and receptors and for his role in developing RU-486, "the first safe, effective contragestive medication."

The first of three children, Etienne-Emile Baulieu was born Etienne-Emile Blum on December 12, 1926 in Strasbourg, in the region of Alsace, in northeastern France. His father, Léon Blum (who was not related to the French socialist leader Léon Blum), a physician, won the Legion of Honor from France for his heroism during World War I, when, through an ingenious ruse that he carried out while serving in the German army as a citizen of German-occupied Alsace, he obtained information about German troop movements that he passed along to French intelligence agents. He later served as a professor at the Faculty of Medicine of Strasbourg and as the head of a Strasbourg medical clinic. He did pioneering, independent research in the treatment of diabetes, and in the early 1920s, as a Rockefeller Foundation fellow, he became one of the first doctors to conduct clinical trials of insulin. Baulieu's mother, the former Thérèse Lion, whom Baulieu has described as "brilliant as well as beautiful," was a conservatory-trained pianist who held both an advanced degree in English and a law degree. Before her marriage she participated in the fight for women's suffrage in England.

When Baulieu was four years old, his father died, and his mother moved with her son and two daughters to Paris. "She made us work extremely hard" in athletics as well as academics, Baulieu has recalled of his upbringing. He began his secondary school education at the Lycée Pasteur, in the Paris suburb of Neuilly-sur-Seine. In 1940, after Germany invaded France in World War II, the Blums left Paris to live in Grenoble, which was not yet occupied by the Germans, and Baulieu enrolled at the Lycée Champollion. When his activities as a member of a Communist-controlled group attracted the notice of the Gestapo, the family moved again, to Annecy, in the department of Haute-Savoie. In 1942, in an attempt to deflect attention from himself and his family and hide the fact that his father was Jewish, Etienne-Emile Blum secured false identification papers on which his surname appeared as Baulieu, a name that he chose himself and that he has used ever since. He collaborated with the French underground in the countryside, and after the liberation of Haute-Savoie and until the end of 1944, when the Germans were expelled from France, he served in the French army. His activities with Communist and other leftist organizations continued for the next dozen years.

In 1945 Baulieu began his study of medicine, at the Faculty of Medicine of Paris. To please his mother, who he has said was "very ambitious" for him, he also entered a doctoral program in science at the Faculty of Sciences. While in that program, where he concentrated first on chemistry and then on biochemistry, he "fell under the spell," as he has put it, of one of his professors, the biochemist Max-Fernand Jayle. He assisted Jayle with research on haptoglobin, a protein that Jayle had discovered in 1941. Jayle "took [him] into his family, offering warmth as well as knowledge," Baulieu recalled in *The "Abortion Pill": RU-486—A Woman's Choice* (1990), which he wrote with Mort Rosenblum, a senior correspondent for the Associated Press in Paris.

After earning his medical degree and, very soon afterward, his doctorate in science, Baulieu spent four years (1951–55) as an intern in Paris hospitals. Some of his most vivid memories of those years are of women who had gotten massive infections or badly injured themselves internally after their attempts to self-induce an abortion. Most of them had to undergo a uterine scraping (commonly known as a D & C, for dilatation and curettage), a painful procedure that many physicians in France would perform without administering anesthesia, because, as Baulieu learned, they felt such women should be punished. "Teach her a lesson she will remember," he heard one of them say.

Upon completing his residency, Baulieu, with a scholarship that he won with Jayle's assistance, spent some time in England to study the recently developed technique of paper chromatography, a tool that, in his words, "started [him] on a double career, in the clinic and the laboratory." In 1956, Baulieu reported in *The "Abortion Pill"*, Jayle, the newly installed chairman of the biochemistry department at the Faculty of Medicine of Paris, hired him as a tenured professor, thus freeing him from university politics. (According to another source, he served as a professor of biochemistry at the schools of medicine in Reims and in Rouen before joining the Faculty of Medicine of Paris in 1961.) In any event, in the mid-1950s Baulieu began conducting research on steroid hormones, an area that he thought would bring him greater satisfaction than would further investigations of haptoglobin. He threw himself into his work with greater vigor after the Soviet Union's invasion of Hungary in 1956, an act of aggression that led him to end his affiliation with the Communist Party. "The best way to help society, I felt, was at the level of the individual," he wrote in his book. "That was how doctors helped."

While treating people who suffered from adrenal cancer, Baulieu began to study secretions of the adrenal gland. In 1959 he discovered dehydroepiandrosterone sulfate, a water-soluble hormone whose existence had eluded the many other chemists (including two Nobel Prize laureates) whose research also centered on adrenal secretions. His success hinged on his idea of looking for the substance in urine; the other scientists had assumed that the hormone was soluble only in fat and thus had not searched for it in urine. Baulieu's discovery, which shed new light on mechanisms of hormone transport, "caught the attention of everyone in the field," he has recalled. One of those scientists was the American biochemist Seymour Lieberman, who used Baulieu's findings to overcome a serious problem that he had encountered in his own research on steroids. In 1959 Lieberman invited Baulieu to work for a year in his laboratory at Columbia University, in New York City, but because of Baulieu's past involvement in militant leftist organizations, officials in the United States Department of State refused to grant him a visa. Despite the repeated entreaties of Lieberman and others, it was not until early 1961, a few weeks after the inauguration of John F. Kennedy as president, that Baulieu's visa came through and he went to Columbia, where he was named a visiting lecturer in biochemistry.

In New York City Baulieu almost immediately fell in with a group of artists, among them Frank Stella, Jasper Johns, Andy Warhol, and Richard Rauschenberg. He felt strongly drawn to them because, in his view, their working lives resembled his as a research scientist: "a life of pure imagination and intuition," as Megan Rosenfeld paraphrased him as saying in the *Washington Post* (December 18, 1986). "I realized from my artist friends the similarity of creation in science and art," Baulieu wrote in *The "Abortion Pill"*. "Like them, I was adding form to a blank space with only vague notions of where it would lead me. . . . We recognized a common spirit, and we were all confident of heading somewhere important."

Seymour Lieberman shared Baulieu's belief, and he "took every opportunity to promote the work of the young French protégé on his team," in Baulieu's words. "More than a mentor, Lieberman . . . was both a big brother and the father I never got to know," he has said. While in the United States, Baulieu gave a talk at the Worcester Foundation for Experimental Biology, in Shrewsbury, Massachusetts, at the invitation of the biologist Gregory Pincus, the foundation's director of research. During the 1950s Pincus, along with the gynecologist and obstetrician John Rock and the biologist Min Chueh Chang, had developed the first practical oral contraceptive pill. Apparently with the hope that Baulieu would be tempted to switch his research focus to the field of birth control, Pincus bought Baulieu a plane ticket so that he could visit a San Juan, Puerto Rico medical facility where clinical trials of the Pill, as it became known, were being conducted. "One look at the clinical data suggested how the Pill could change women's existence," Baulieu has recalled of his visit, before which, by his own account, he had known next to nothing about contraception. (All contraceptive devices except the condom had been outlawed in France in 1920.) "From that Puerto Rican experience, I realized the impact on human life that the product of birth control research could have. I was hooked, although I didn't know it yet."

In 1963 Baulieu was named head of U-33, a semiautonomous research unit of INSERM (the acronym for the name in French of the National Institute of Health and Medical Research), which is analogous to the National Institutes of Health in the United States. At around the same time, he became a permanent, independent research consultant for Roussel-Uclaf, one of the largest pharmaceutical companies in France. In exchange for suggestions for potentially productive avenues of research that he would present only to Roussel-Uclaf, Baulieu gained another workforce—highly trained Roussel-Uclaf chemists, who could test his hypotheses in the company's laboratories—and a way of getting, for his projects at INSERM, materials that would otherwise have been difficult to obtain. According to the terms of his consultancy, he would be paid only a set remuneration for his services; thus, he has never collected any royalties on sales of RU-486.

In 1965 Baulieu concluded that he had come to a dead end, at least temporarily, with his research into dehydroepiandrosterone sulfate. He felt eager to contribute to molecular biology, which in the mid-1960s was considered the "new biology," and to the "new endocrinology" that was developing around the study of receptors, the components of cells that transmit messages from hormones to the cells. Motivated also by a desire to advance the science of birth control, he decided to focus on the sex steroid receptors. "Pincus's enthusiasm had infected me, and I wanted to keep working in the directions pioneered by his work," he has recalled. "Where Pincus had worked in physiology, we would now do molecular endocrinology."

Some months before reaching that decision, Baulieu, at Pincus's instigation, had become a member of a World Health Organization panel of experts that convened regularly in Geneva, Switzerland to grapple with issues surrounding overpopulation and reproduction, including the high mortality rates associated with abortion in countries where such procedures are illegal. "At the Geneva meetings I was steeped in reports citing the desperation over the lack of contraception in poor countries," he wrote in *The "Abortion Pill"*. "I dreamed of developing new methods with original research in my own laboratory." A trip to India in 1970, during which, in Calcutta and other cities, he witnessed human misery on a scale that he had only read or heard about until then, reinforced his determination to try to alleviate the suffering that stemmed from uncontrolled fertility. France had taken a major step in that direction a few years before, when, on the recommendation of a committee appointed by the minister of health on which Baulieu served as one of thirteen "wise men," as they were dubbed, the government lifted the ban on contraceptive devices.

With the additional support of a long-term, virtually condition-free grant of $750,000 that he received from the Ford Foundation in around 1965, Baulieu and his team began what proved to be a many-pronged study that expanded scientists' understanding not only of hormone receptors but also of sex hormones themselves. Among other accomplishments, he and his coworkers pinpointed the location of progesterone receptors in the uterus and discovered that steroid receptors lie not only within cell nuclei but also, in some cases, on surface membranes. With the help of several outside scientists, they also discovered the existence on steroid receptors of so-called heat-shock proteins. When the receptors are capped by the heat-shock proteins, they are inactive; they are activated only when hormone molecules bind with them and the protein cap is released.

By the mid-1970s research by various scientists had demonstrated that, early on in pregnancy, progesterone performs several vitally important functions. Among them is helping to prepare the lining of the uterus for implantation of the fertilized egg, which, by the time it reaches the uterus, has developed into a pinhead-sized, one-hundred-cell embryo known as the blastocyst. In addition, by relaxing uterine muscles and tightening the cervix, progesterone helps to prevent the uterus from expelling the blastocyst. Since the effectiveness of progesterone hinges on its binding with its receptors, Baulieu realized that if it were possible to "decrease the activity of progesterone receptors with a drug and prevent the effect of the hormone," the reproductive process could be interrupted. "My association with Roussel-Uclaf was crucial to finding the right compound," he has noted. "Biologists might find a purpose for synthesizing new molecules, but chemists must actually make them." He knew that Roussel-Uclaf executives did not want to commit substantial resources to developing an antiprogesterone, which they believed would generate little profit. But he also knew that progesterone is closely related to cortisone and that therefore an antiglucocorticosteroid—a substance that counteracts the activity of cortisone—might also function as an antiprogesterone, so he suggested that Roussel-Uclaf invest in a search for an antiglucocorticosteroid that would be useful in the treatment of burns and wounds.

In 1980 Georges Teutsch, Roussel-Uclaf's top chemist, synthesized RU-486, an antiglucocorticosteroid that was officially identified as RU-38486, for Roussel-Uclaf and the total number of molecules that had been synthesized in the company's laboratories in Roumainville, France since 1949. A derivative of the organic chemical norethindrone, its generic name is mifepristone. Anticipating that the substance would also be effective as an antiprogesterone, Baulieu and his colleagues designed experiments to test it in animals. After huge doses of RU-486 triggered symptoms of acute adrenal insufficiency in three monkeys, Roussel-Uclaf officials ruled the compound a failure. Baulieu thereupon succeeded in convincing them that the experiment had proven only RU-486's potency as an antiglucocorticosteroid and not its toxicity. "I insisted on this point, and was able to rescue RU-486 from an early demise," he wrote in his book. That rescue, he has said, entitled him to the sobriquet "godfather of RU-486."

Baulieu presented the results of the animal testing and the first clinical test of RU-486, which showed that the drug was 80 percent effective in ending early pregnancies, at a meeting of the French Academy of Sciences on April 19, 1982 and in an article that appeared at around that time in *Comptes Rendus*, the academy's official journal, in which he gave full credit to his collaborators. In what Steven Greenhouse, in the *New York Times Magazine* (February 12, 1989), described as "an extraordinary move for a corporate chairman," Edouard Sakiz, the chairman of Roussel-Uclaf, "joined Baulieu in signing the landmark scientific paper." Subsequently, extensive clinical trials confirmed both the safety and the effectiveness of the drug, which is used in pregnancies that have progressed no farther than seven weeks.

RU-486 acts by usurping the place of progesterone; although it binds with progesterone receptors, it is a "false key," in Baulieu's words, and thus fails to trigger the release of the heat-shock proteins and, ultimately, prevents the implantation of the blastocyst in the uterus. The addition of a small dose of prostaglandin two days after the administration of RU-486, Baulieu discovered in the early 1980s, increases the drug's effectiveness to 95 percent. Because the fertilized egg lodges in a fallopian tube or in the peritoneal cavity in a small percentage of pregnancies (so-called ectopic pregnancies)—a potentially fatal circumstance—Baulieu has insisted that RU-486 must be made available only in settings where the recipients can be examined and monitored by medical personnel.

In 1988 Claude Evin, then France's minister of health, approved the sale of RU-486 in France. A month later, alarmed by the public condemnation of the pill by the Roman Catholic archbishop of Paris, a swelling chorus of protests by anti-abortionists, and threats of boycotts of Roussel-Uclaf and even of personal violence to company officers, Roussel-Uclaf announced that it would not market the drug. But two days later it reversed its decision, after Evin warned the company that unless it did so, the government, as French law allowed, would transfer ownership of the patent for RU-486 to another company. "I could not permit the abortion debate to deprive women of a product that represents medical progress," Evin declared. "From the moment government approval for the drug was granted, RU-486 became the moral property of women, not just the property of the drug company."

Baulieu has campaigned tirelessly around the world for approval of RU-486. "It takes someone of his knowledge and personality and energy to carry this crusade on," Seymour Lieberman observed to Charles Kaiser for *Vanity Fair* (November 1989). Despite the efforts of Baulieu and other leaders in the fertility- and population-control movements, only the United Kingdom and Sweden, to date, have followed France's example in legalizing the drug. A synthetic compound virtually identical to RU-486 has been produced in China and is being used there. In 1994 Roussel-Uclaf donated the United States patent rights for RU-486 to the New York City-based Population Council, a nongovernmental organization that, among other activities, conducts biomedical research to develop and improve contraceptive technology. Clinical trials of the drug in the United States began soon afterward and ended in mid-1995. The Population Council plans to submit a "new drug" application to the FDA within the next few months and anticipates FDA approval in 1996. Baulieu has often pointed out that RU-486 has been shown to have value in areas beyond reproduction, among them the treatment of certain breast cancers, Cushing's syndrome, and some inoperable brain tumors, and it has shown promise in alleviating stress disorders, healing severe burns and wounds, controlling glaucoma, and treating endometriosis. In *RU 486: The Science and the Politics* (1989), which was published by the Alan Guttmacher Institute, Michael Klitsch reported that the drug may also be used "to soften the cervix before inducing labor or prior to performing a surgical abortion."

An autobiographical as well as a scientific and historical account, *The "Abortion Pill"* was originally published in France in 1990, with the title *Génération Pilule*. The three-part epigraph that Baulieu chose for the book reflects his philosophy as a scientist and humanist: "Science has an essential virtue; it respects what is" (Primo Levi); "[Margaret Sanger] launched a movement that is obeying a higher law to preserve human life under human conditions" (Martin Luther King Jr.); "Woman is the future of man" (Louis Aragon).

In a speech given at Baulieu's induction into the French Academy of Sciences, in 1982, Seymour Lieberman characterized Baulieu as "optimistic, enthusiastic, high-spirited, open-minded, cultured, serious but always aware of the comedy, philosophic but never ponderous." "Baulieu is an informal, expansive man whose laboratory office reflects his creativity and complexity," Steven Greenhouse wrote. Said to be witty and charming, Baulieu is, by his own account, a workaholic. "One works because one is afraid of doing nothing, and then becoming obsessed with metaphysical problems," he told Charles Kaiser. "People who know me would say I am very optimistic and smiling, but really I am very anxious," he admitted to Megan Rosenfeld. "I am afraid of the human destiny, which of course leads to nothing." Baulieu and his wife, the former Yolande Compagnon, who have been married since 1947, have three adult children—a daughter, Catherine, and two sons, Laurent and Frédérique—and eight grandchildren. In his leisure time Baulieu enjoys skiing, wind-surfing, and cooking "for people [he] loves," in his words. The recipient of many honors and awards in France and abroad, he is a commander of the French Legion of Honor and a chevalier of the French National Order of Merit. For the past several years, Baulieu's main research interest has been the production of steroid hormones in the brain and their potential for awakening people who are in comas.

Baulieu has said that he believes it is important for scientists to be "as famous as painters or writers." "You have to personalize things a little, because people have the impression that science is a cold profession," he told Charles Kaiser. "But it is something that you do with your heart. Intelligence is very important, but you also need the will, the heart, passion, and persistence. Being a public figure is interesting because you are responsible for explaining the significance of science, not just treating sickness, but explaining how science is done—so that young people will not imagine that we are computers."

Selected Biographical References: Am Health 9:80+ Mr '90 por; Omni 13:75+ S '91 pors; People 33:121+ Ap 9 '90 pors; Science 245:1323+ S 22 '89 por; Vanity Fair 52:90+ N '89 pors; Washington Post C p1 D 18 '86 por, p14 O 3 '89 por; Baulieu, Etienne-Emile and Mort Rosenblum. The "Abortion Pill" (1990); International Who's Who, 1995–96

Bell Burnell, Jocelyn

(JOS-lin)

July 15, 1943– British astronomer; educator.
Address: c/o Physics Department, The Open University, Walton Hall, Milton Keynes, England MK7 6AA

The discovery of pulsating radio stars, or pulsars, by the British astronomer Jocelyn Bell Burnell in 1967 ranks as one of the most exciting events in the history of astrophysics. In what has been described as an outstanding example of serendipity, Bell Burnell made the discovery of what proved to be a new class of celestial objects when she was a twenty-four-year-old Cambridge University graduate student engaged in a search not for pulsars but for

The Open University

Jocelyn Bell Burnell

quasars. Known then as S. J. Bell, she was working under the supervision of the radio astronomer Antony Hewish. Her discovery, which opened the door to new ways of studying superdense matter and which has helped to elucidate the evolution of stars, earned Hewish a Nobel Prize in physics in 1974.

Shaped to a significant degree, until a few years ago, by geographical limitations imposed by her husband's job transfers, Bell Burnell's career in astronomy has been unusually varied. In addition to radioastronomy, she has made contributions to gamma-ray, X-ray, infrared, and submillimeter astronomy and has carried out research not only with ground-based telescopes but with instruments carried on satellites, launched on rockets, or flown in high-altitude balloons. One of only two women in Great Britain to hold the position of full professor of physics, she currently chairs the Physics Department at the Open University, the largest institution of higher learning in the United Kingdom. Bell Burnell has received several of the most prestigious awards in the field of astronomy, including, most recently, the Herschel Medal from the Royal Astronomical Society of London.

The first of four children, Jocelyn Bell Burnell was born Susan Jocelyn Bell on July 15, 1943 in Belfast, Northern Ireland to G(eorge) Philip Bell and M(argaret) Allison (Kennedy) Bell. Her brother, Adrian Bell, is a civil engineer; her sister Sarah Hillman is a sales manager, and her sister Deborah Evelyn is a computer systems analyst. Bell Burnell grew up in a rural part of County Armagh, Northern Ireland, in a many-roomed house that had been in her family for about two hundred years. The house, called "Solitude," was situated on a sizable piece of property, which her father farmed during World War II; before and after the war, he worked as an architect. Because their house was a considerable distance from other dwellings, the Bell children relied mostly on one another for companionship. One of Jocelyn's favorite solitary activities was constructing complex houses for her dolls, using her several building sets. Along with the rest of her family, she attended meetings of the Religious Society of Friends (commonly known as Quakers) each Sunday and went sailing every summer.

Bell Burnell's formal education began at a small school in a nearby town. In part because of what she has described as the mediocre teaching that prevailed there, she failed the eleven-plus, a compulsory nationwide exam on the basis of which students entering secondary school were placed either on a college-preparatory or a vocational-training track. In a conversation with Sharon Bertsch McGrayne, who profiled Bell Burnell for her book *Nobel Prize Women in Science* (1993), she attributed her failing grade additionally to her comparative immaturity—she had taken the exam at the relatively early age of eleven—and a scoring system that demanded a better performance from younger test takers than older ones. Because her parents planned to send her to boarding school in a few years, the local secondary school overlooked her poor exam results and allowed her to join other college-bound students.

At around this time Jocelyn began to develop a fascination with astronomy. Her father was designing an extension for the Armagh Observatory, and, on visits with him to the site, she became acquainted with the observatory's staff. Impressed by her enthusiasm and intelligent questions, they suggested that she consider making astronomy her career. Also as an adolescent, she systematically read books in her family's library by the British astronomer Fred Hoyle and other popularizers of astronomy. She was pleased to learn that radioastronomy can be a daytime occupation, unlike optical astronomy (the traditional branch of the discipline), which requires long nighttime sessions at a telescope.

In 1956, spurred by the conviction that Jocelyn needed and deserved a broader and richer curriculum than that offered by her school, Philip and Allison Bell enrolled their thirteen-year-old daughter at the Mount School, a Quaker boarding school for girls in York, England. Although it turned out that the school's science departments lacked adequate equipment, and some of the science teachers exhibited only a limited expertise in their subject areas, Bell Burnell has said that she considered her transfer to the Mount School a "good idea." "Going to boarding school gave me a new start . . . ," she told Sharon Bertsch McGrayne, "and I did very well." An active member of the school community, she served as the stage manager for student dramatic and operatic productions and as the captain of a field-hockey team. With other members of the campus archaeological society, which she founded, she went on digs to investigate the route of one of the Roman-built roads into York.

During Bell Burnell's five years at the Mount, the first manmade satellites were set in orbit by the United States and the Soviet Union, and lively arguments among scientists regarding the merits of the Big Bang versus the Steady State theory in explaining the origins of the universe spilled into the public arena. Those events and discussions fueled Bell Burnell's determination to become an astronomer. Nevertheless, when, in 1961, she enrolled at the University of Glasgow, in Scotland, she chose physics as her area of concentration, with minors in geology, math, and chemistry. In light of the fierce competition for jobs that faced fledgling astronomers, she had decided, majoring in astronomy would have amounted to "burning [her] boats a little too soon," in her words.

Bell Burnell had joined nearly three hundred other University of Glasgow freshmen in choosing to "read physics," in British parlance, but at the end of four years, only fifty physics majors remained. As the only woman in her physics classes after the first year, Bell Burnell endured a substantial amount of teasing, not all of it benign. "I had to learn not to blush, because Glasgow students could really be quite tough with a lone woman," Glyn Jones quoted her as saying in *New Scientist* (July 18, 1992). She escaped such harassment as well as the pressures of her academic load through her activities with Quaker groups and as a member of the stage crew of the campus drama society, a player on a university hockey team, and, one year, an organizer of "rag day" (an event during which students raise money for charity). In 1963 she received both the Cowie Book Prize and the Joseph Black Medal for her outstanding achievements in geology. She earned a B.Sc. degree with honors in physics in 1965.

In the fall of that year, Bell Burnell began graduate studies in astronomy at Cambridge University. Her arrival at Cambridge coincided with the start of construction there of a large radio telescope designed by Antony Hewish. Hewish, who agreed to serve as Bell Burnell's thesis adviser, had conceived of the telescope as a means of distinguishing ordinary radio galaxies from quasars (also known as quasi-stellar objects), which had been discovered only two years before. His design, to which Bell Burnell contributed after she joined Hewish's team, was based on the observation that quasars, which are compact radio sources, scintillate, or twinkle, more than extended radio sources. Working steadily for two years, Bell Burnell and several other students installed a thousand nine-foot-tall posts on a four-and-a-half-acre plot (an area the size of fifty-seven tennis courts). "Though slight in stature, she could swing a twenty-pound sledgehammer by the time she left Cambridge," Nicholas Wade noted in *Science* (August 1975). The team also constructed two hundred transformers, strung more than two thousand dipole antennas between the posts, and connected everything with 120 miles of wire and cable. Sheltered even on the coldest days only by a canvas "workroom," Bell Burnell cut and shaped the cable herself.

The radio telescope began operating in July 1967. Functioning simultaneously, four beams scanned the sky, finishing one complete scan in four days. The results of the scan—known as the output—were transcribed on four three-track pen recorders. Ninety-six feet of data-filled paper emerged from the recorders daily; each complete coverage of a targeted portion of the sky, therefore, produced nearly four hundred feet of paper. Hewish assigned to Bell Burnell the exacting, time-consuming job of interpreting the data on the chart paper, which she accomplished by visual examination. Complicating the analysis was a problem unavoidable in radioastronomy: In addition to cosmic signals, the radio telescope was sensitive to radio interference from passing automobiles, refrigerator motors, television broadcasts, and aircraft altimeters, and consequently the pen recorders indicated the presence of those and other sources of interference along with that of twinkling sources. Bell Burnell learned to distinguish between interference and scintillating sources after analyzing a few hundred feet of chart paper.

Although computers, despite their severe limitations at that time, would have aided analysis, she and Hewish decided against their use, at least until they had gained a sufficient degree of familiarity with the behavior of the telescope and receivers. "A human can recognize signals of different character, whereas it is difficult to program a computer to do so," she explained in a talk that she delivered to members of the New York Academy of Sciences and that appears in the academy's 1977 *Annals*. So enormous was the task of analysis that, despite her unwavering dedication to its execution, by October 1967 a thousand feet of unanalyzed chart paper had piled up, and by the end of November, a third of a mile of it still awaited her attention. "The temptation to cut corners on the analysis must have been considerable," Nicholas Wade observed.

One day in October Bell Burnell noticed what she called a "bit of scruff"—small ink marks covering less than half an inch on one four-hundred-foot section of chart paper—that looked slightly different from the signals from either twinkling sources or manmade objects. "I began to remember that I had seen this particular bit of scruff before, and from the same part of the sky," she has recalled. ("Unclassifiable things are too disturbing to be easily forgotten," she has said.) Furthermore, she soon determined, "it seemed to be keeping pace with twenty-three hours, fifty-six minutes." In other words, whatever was causing the scruff was keeping what is known as sidereal time rather than terrestrial time—it "reappeared with each revolution of the stars, not with each rotation of the earth," and it took twenty-three hours and fifty-six minutes to return to the same position in the sky.

Bell Burnell and Hewish decided that, to get a more revealing image, they would document the signal on the observatory's fast recorder. For several weeks after the fast recorder became available for their research, the mysterious source did not reveal itself. ("Pulsars rarely perform to order," Bell Burnell has explained.) Suspecting that it might have been a flare star, Hewish remarked to her, "It has died and gone, and you've missed it." Then, on November 28, 1967, as she worked in the observatory, Bell Burnell saw the long-sought signal being recorded. "As the chart flowed under the pen, I could see that the signal was a series of pulses," she has recalled. When she presented Hewish with measurements showing that the pulses were almost precisely one and one-third seconds apart, he concluded that the signals must be manmade. Within a short time, however, that idea was ruled out. Hewish and other members of his team then considered the possibility that the signals were being transmitted by what they referred to as "little green men"—creatures from another solar system in the Milky Way Galaxy. "Although they don't take it very seriously," Bell Burnell remarked to Nicholas Wade, "radioastronomers are aware that they would probably be the first people to come into contact with other civilizations." Bell Burnell herself harbored the notion that a star was generating the signals. With remarkable prescience, in a logbook entry dated December 19, 1967, she called the source a "Belisha beacon"—a reference to the flashing signal used for the protection of pedestrians at street crossings in British cities.

All the while, as part of the research for her doctoral dissertation, Bell Burnell had continued to examine every inch of the chart-paper recordings for evidence of interplanetary scintillation of compact radio sources. Just before Christmas she noticed some scruff on a recording of signals from a part of the sky far from the place where the first scruff-producing signals had emanated, and that very night another recording was made of the "new" scruff, which proved to be a series of pulses 1.2 seconds apart. "That removed the worry about little green men, since there wouldn't be two lots signaling us at different frequencies," she told Nicholas Wade. In January 1968 she confirmed the existence of two additional sources of scruff. She thus became the discoverer of the first four pulsars, as the sources of the pulses were soon dubbed. To date, more than 660 pulsars have been identified.

In February 1968, at a seminar held at Cambridge University, Antony Hewish announced the discovery of pulsars. "Every astronomer in Cambridge, so it seemed, came to that seminar, and their interest and excitement gave me a first appreciation of the revolution we had started," Bell Burnell has recalled. An article describing the discovery was published a few days later, in the February 24, 1968 issue of *Nature*, with Bell Burnell's name—as S. J. Bell—appearing second, after Hewish's, among the list of five authors. The disclosure in the article that Hewish's team had for a while speculatively placed responsibility for the pulses with an extraterrestrial civilization created a small sensation in the British press. The revelation that one of the Cambridge astronomers was a woman sparked an even greater stir. "I had my photograph taken standing on a bank, sitting on a bank, standing on a bank examining bogus records, sitting on a bank examining bogus records . . . ," Bell Burnell said during her New York Academy of Sciences talk. "Meanwhile the journalists were asking relevant questions like was I taller than or not quite as tall as Princess Margaret . . . and how many boyfriends did I have at a time?"

After her confirmation of the existence of the third and fourth known pulsars, Bell Burnell ended her analysis of the telescope's output and concentrated on writing her doctoral dissertation, which she entitled "The Measurement of Radio Source Diameters Using a Diffraction Method." On Hewish's recommendation she included information about the discovery of pulsars only in an appendix. After receiving a Ph.D. degree from Cambridge, in 1968, she joined the faculty of the University of Southampton, having sought a job in the part of England where her soon-to-be husband was working. "That move was the first of several that proved to be quite difficult," she told Sharon Bertsch McGrayne. "A lot of the moves I've made and the equally drastic changes of field within astronomy have been because I've moved as my husband moved around the country as a local government officer." At Southampton she taught atomic and nuclear physics to undergraduates and the university's first course in quantum mechanics. In addition, as the recipient of two fellowships, she worked with a team involved with research in gamma-ray astronomy. Among other projects, she investigated the mid-latitude electron density trough in the upper ionosphere and assisted in the design and development of the first 1-10 megaelectronvolt gamma-ray telescope. In 1973 she resigned her position at the university, to devote herself to the care of her newborn son.

The next year, having realized that full-time motherhood did not provide her with enough intellectual stimulation, Bell Burnell got a part-time position as a graduate programmer at the Mullard Space Science Laboratory, at University College, London; she later worked there half-time as an associate research fellow. At Mullard she became an expert in X-ray astronomy. Because the earth's atmosphere absorbs X-rays, astronomers use satellites or rockets to study X-ray-emitting celestial objects. Bell Burnell supervised a group of researchers charged with analyzing data gathered by Ariel V, a satellite that she has described as "enormously successful." "We kept tripping over discoveries," she told Sharon Bertsch McGrayne. "Before we finished with one discovery, there'd be another one. It was tremendous fun." With Ariel V's X-ray spectrometer, she and her coworkers observed galactic sources of X-rays, including transient X-ray sources and binary star systems, as well as active galaxies and clusters of galaxies.

On October 15, 1974, the day that Ariel V was launched, the Nobel Prize awards committee announced that Antony Hewish had won the Nobel Prize in physics for his "pioneering research in astrophysics." (Hewish won jointly with Sir Martin

Ryle, the leader of the Cambridge radioastronomy research team, who was praised for his "observations and inventions." They were the first astronomers to win the prize.) In citing Hewish for "his decisive role in the discovery of pulsars," the Nobel committee acknowledged the fact that Hewish had not himself discovered them. It did not specifically credit Bell Burnell's contribution, however. The year before, by contrast, the Franklin Institute of Philadelphia had awarded its famed Albert A. Michelson Medal to both Bell Burnell and Hewish. Although the institute did not divulge its reasons for giving a joint award, one of its prize-committee officials said, as quoted by Nicholas Wade, that it was "probably recognizing the recipients for equal efforts."

There is no record of public controversy regarding the awarding of the Nobel Prize to Hewish and not Bell Burnell until March 1975, when the London *Times* reported that Fred Hoyle had condemned the action of the Nobel committee as scandalous and had accused Bell Burnell's superiors at Cambridge of "pinching the discovery from [her]" ("or that was what it amounted to," he was quoted as saying). When she was questioned about Hoyle's charge by a *Times* reporter, Bell Burnell responded, "It's a bit preposterous, and he has overstated the case so as to be incorrect."

In an attempt to clarify his position, Hoyle wrote a letter to the *Times* (April 8, 1975) in which he contended that "the discovery of the signals by Burnell, and her finding that the source of the signals changed position with the stars, was what constituted the crucial step," as Nicholas Wade paraphrased his words. "Once this step had been taken, nothing that happened from there on could have made any difference to the eventual outcome," Hoyle wrote. Moreover, he explained, "there has been a tendency to misunderstand the magnitude of Miss Bell's achievement, because it sounds so simple—just to search and search through a great mass of records. The achievement came from a willingness to contemplate as a serious possibility a phenomenon that all past experience suggested was impossible. I have to go back in my mind to the discovery of radioactivity by Henri Becquerel for a comparable example of a scientific bolt from the blue." The theoretical astronomer Thomas Gold, whose name is associated with the generally accepted theory that pulsars are spinning neutron stars, concurred. According to Gold, Bell Burnell's recognition that the pulsar was keeping sidereal time represented the "true moment of discovery." In her 1977 speech at the New York Academy of Sciences, however, Bell Burnell expressed the view that since the supervisor of a research project must take responsibility if it fails, "it seems only fair . . . that he should benefit from the successes." "I believe it would demean Nobel Prizes if they were awarded to research students, except in very exceptional cases, and I do not believe this is one of them," she said.

In 1982, because of another of her husband's work-related relocations, Bell Burnell left the Mullard laboratory and began what became a nine-year association with the Royal Observatory, in Edinburgh, Scotland. During four years as a senior research fellow there, she coordinated infrared observations of active galaxies with radio, optical, ultraviolet, and X-ray observations. Concurrently, for one year, she was in charge of the observatory's visitor center. From 1986 to 1990 she served as the manager of the James Clerk Maxwell Telescope project. Owned by Great Britain, Canada, and the Netherlands and operated by the Royal Observatory, the telescope is located in Hawaii atop a fourteen thousand-foot volcanic mountain, where the unusually dry, clear air facilitates the detection of submillimeter radio waves. Directing the project required Bell Burnell to travel periodically not only to Hawaii but to the owner nations and to manage a budget of more than a million British pounds.

Feeling, in her words, "grossly overloaded" by her administrative responsibilities, Bell Burnell resigned her position in 1991 to become the manager of a project for a new, radioactively cooled, orbiting infrared space observatory known as EDISON. Later that year she ended her employment with the Royal Observatory to become a professor of physics at the Open University, in Milton Keynes, a city located about fifty miles northwest of London that was founded only within the last quarter-century. Established in 1969, the Open University provides home-study courses for adults living anywhere in Great Britain or continental Europe. In 1994 the extraordinary total of some twelve hundred students took the astronomy course that Bell Burnell's department created. For the past three years, Bell Burnell has chaired the Open University's Physics Department. Her current research projects include investigations of Cygnus X-3, the physics of plerions (synchrotron nebulae) around pulsars, and the surface temperature of pulsars.

Bell Burnell has written scientific articles for such journals as *Nature*, *Astronomy and Astrophysics*, and the *Journal of Geophysics*. Her professional activities have included service on many scientific panels and committees and efforts to promote the advancement of women in science and to popularize astronomy. For the past few years, she has helped to plan the Edinburgh International Science Festival, which attracts two hundred thousand visitors a year, and she frequently lectures and makes presentations for public broadcast. In addition to the Herschel Medal, which she received in 1989, and the Michelson Medal, her awards include the J. Robert Oppenheimer Memorial Prize from the Center for Theoretical Studies in Miami, Florida (1978), the Rennie Taylor Award, from the American Tentative Society (1978), and two honorary doctoral degrees. In 1987 she became the first recipient of the American Astronomical Society's Beatrice M. Tinsley Prize.

According to Glyn Jones, Jocelyn Bell Burnell is "resilient and affable." "For all her celestial research, [she] is the reverse of the remote don," Jones wrote. As quoted by Jones, one of Bell Burnell's younger colleagues at the Royal Observatory described her as "a lovely person to work with." "She was very honest and willing to give you well-considered advice," the colleague said. "If I had a problem, personal or scientific, she was very approachable." Bell Burnell lives in Milton Keynes and, in her leisure time, enjoys swimming, walking, learning foreign languages, knitting, sewing, and listening to choral music. For many years she has been deeply involved in Quaker and ecumenical activities. She has served as one of two Quaker representatives on both the British Council of Churches (1978–90) and the Scottish Churches Council (1987–90). In 1989 she presented the Swarthmore Lecture at the annual meeting of British Quakers. The lecture, which was published by the Quaker Home Service of London in 1989 as a book entitled *Broken for Life*, examined "the role of those with unhealed hurts," in her words, and was inspired, in part, by the discovery in 1983 that her son, Gavin, had juvenile diabetes. Gavin Burnell, who is in his early twenties, is currently studying material science. Jocelyn Bell Burnell's marriage to Martin Burnell ended in divorce in 1989.

Selected Biographical References: Annals of N Y Academy of Sciences 302:685+ '77; New Scientist 135:36+ Jl 18 '92; Science 189:358+ Ag '75; Shell Times no. 73 '90; McGrayne, Sharon Bertsch. Nobel Prize Women in Science (1993); Shapiro, Gilbert. A Skeleton in the Darkroom (1986); Who's Who, 1995

AP/Wide World Photos

Belushi, James
(buh-LOO-shee)

June 15, 1954- Actor. Address: Creative Artists Agency, 9830 Wilshire Blvd., Beverly Hills, CA 90212-1825

It is perhaps fitting that the films of the actor James Belushi often enjoy greater success as rental videos, which viewers can watch in the comfort of their own homes, than as big-screen entertainment: since the late 1970s Belushi has built a persona as an "average guy" whom one might sooner expect to find living next door than to see starring in a major motion picture. Belushi's film roles have fallen largely into two categories: that of the wise-cracking sidekick, in such movies as *About Last Night . . .* and *Red Heat*, and that of the ordinary man thrust into an extraordinary situation, as in *The Principal* and *Mr. Destiny*.

Beginning as a performer with the famous Second City troupe in Chicago and later becoming a cast member of the long-running television show *Saturday Night Live*, Belushi seemed for a time to pattern his career after that of his brother, the comic actor John Belushi, and some critics were relentless in comparing James with his superstar sibling. Over the years, however, James Belushi has emerged as a star in his own right, at least partly because of his pursuit of dramatic as well as comic roles. "There's a hole in the line of scrimmage for a person who can do comedy and drama at the same time," Belushi has said. "And I can do that."

The third of four children, James Belushi was born on June 15, 1954 in Chicago and grew up in the suburb of Wheaton. His father, Adam Belushi, an Albanian immigrant, was a bar and restaurant owner; his mother, Agnes (Samaras) Belushi, also of Albanian descent, was a homemaker who later became a real-estate agent and a bit-part film actress. He has an older sister, Marion, and a younger brother, Bill. His older brother, John, who rose to fame via *Saturday Night Live* and such feature films as *Animal House* and *The Blues Brothers*, died from a drug overdose in 1982. In an interview for *New York Newsday* (June 29, 1986), James Belushi discussed his parents' contribution to his and his older brother's show business success: "My father had the presence, my mother had the humor. The combination of those two elements . . . helped both of us out." As a boy, Belushi often worked after school in his father's restaurants, an activity that, he has said, formed the basis for their relationship.

While James Belushi was proud of his older brother's accomplishments (John was captain of the Central High School football team and acted in high school before going on to perform with the Second City troupe), he also felt somewhat diminished by them. He was, in his words, a "troublemaker" as a teenager, in what he has since recognized as an effort to attract attention. He found a more constructive outlet for his considerable energy in 1969, when he was assigned by one of his teachers at Central High School to give a speech about the Vietnam War. At first unsure of how to proceed, he eventually decided to deliver his address in the guise of an antiwar protestor. Belushi's teacher was sufficiently impressed by his impersonation to encourage him to try out for the upcoming school play. Following his teacher's advice, Belushi auditioned for and landed the lead role in the play, and he continued to be active in student theatre throughout his high school years. "All John's speech and drama teachers had left [the school] when he did," Belushi was quoted as saying in *New York Newsday* (August 8, 1982). "The new ones didn't know his work. It made me feel like it was something I did on my own."

Following his graduation from high school, in 1972, James Belushi pursued his interest in theatre at the College of Du Page, a nearby junior college, and at Southern Illinois University (SIU), in Carbondale, from which he received a bachelor's degree in speech. In 1977, while he was still attending SIU, he joined the Second City touring group. He later appeared with the troupe's home acting company, in 1978 and again in 1980. At Second City, Belushi first began to make a name for himself with a skit he cowrote and performed with Will Aldis. In that sketch, set in the White Horse Tavern—the New York City bar frequented by the poet Dylan Thomas during his American tours—two brothers drink shots of liquor while musing on poetry, sex, and death, among other topics. Eventually the two salute such self-destructive literary greats as Thomas, Ernest Hemingway, and Sylvia Plath. In the *Chicago Tribune* (August 9, 1992), Will Aldis recalled the sketch, which was partly based on an actual conversation between James and John Belushi, as the one that signified Belushi's coming-of-age as an artist—or, as Aldis phrased it, the one that "turned Jimmy Belushi into James Belushi" and "tapped into his roots." In 1984, the year that marked Second City's twenty-fifth anniversary, the Belushi-Aldis skit was recognized by the *Chicago Tribune* as one of the troupe's ten best pieces.

In the audience for one performance of the sketch was the television producer Garry Marshall, whose credits include the hit series *Happy Days* and *Laverne and Shirley*. Impressed by what he had seen, Marshall was instrumental in Belushi's landing his first television role, on the short-lived 1978 sitcom *Who's Watching the Kids?* In the following year Marshall helped the actor to get an assignment costarring with Michael Keaton in the new CBS sitcom *Working Stiffs*, which followed the trials of a pair of bumbling janitors in a Chicago office building. Despite some affectionate reviews, Belushi's second television series ultimately fared no better with viewers than had his first, and it was canceled after only four episodes.

The year 1979 also saw Belushi star in David Mamet's play *Sexual Perversity in Chicago*, about a couple's failed attempt to sustain a romantic relationship, at the Apollo Theater Center in Chicago. Belushi's performance won a rave review from Richard Christiansen in the *Chicago Tribune* (January 24, 1979): "As Bernie, the sexual braggart and emotional coward, Jim Belushi gives such an intense, full-scale, knockout comic performance that he threatens to run away with the show." In 1980 Belushi played the title role in *Baal in the Twenty-First Century*, Richard Nelson's adaptation of a play by Bertolt Brecht, which was produced in Chicago at the prestigious Goodman Theatre. He made his feature film debut in the same year, in Michael Mann's *Thief* (1981), a gritty, unflinching portrait of a hardened safecracker, played by James Caan. Belushi's portrayal of the thief's loyal accomplice inspired Gary Arnold of the *Washington Post* (March 27, 1981) to write, "Belushi . . . has a sleepy-eyed, beefy charm and physical authority, rather like the young Robert Mitchum crossed with the young Rod Steiger."

Tapped to play the Pirate King in the New York Shakespeare Festival's national touring production of Gilbert and Sullivan's comic opera *The Pirates of Penzance*, Belushi joined the company in Los Angeles in September 1981. When the production arrived in Chicago a few months later, Richard Christiansen of the *Chicago Tribune* (January 12, 1982) applauded the actor for delivering a "buoyant, solidly professional, on-target performance that sweeps the show forward and gives it some of its most rousing moments. Raising his arms in exultation every time he scores a high note or completes an artful slash of the sword, Belushi embodies the vigor and joy of performance that makes this *Pirates* so pleasing."

It was in March 1982, while Belushi was touring in *Pirates*, that he received a telephone call informing him that his brother John had died. In spite of the jarring news, he went ahead with the performance that had been scheduled for that night, publicly acknowledging his loss only by changing the color of his headband from blue to black. "I decided to do it for John," he was quoted as saying in *New York Newsday* (August 8, 1982). "When it came time to do the show, he was always there. I saw him go on one night at a little club on the South Side after he'd been in a fight in the alley and the side of his face was all swelled up. That gave me the strength to go through it."

The fortitude that enabled him to continue performing in *Pirates* notwithstanding, Belushi entered a turbulent period after his brother's death. "I hit rock bottom," he admitted to David Prescott for a *Chicago Tribune* (July 2, 1986) profile. "I was swimming, not sure where I was going." After he replaced John Malkovich as the star of Sam Shepard's play *True West*, produced Off-Broadway at the Cherry Lane Theater in 1983, Belushi began drinking during performances. Later in the same year, he won a place on the long-running comedy show *Saturday Night Live*, but within a couple of seasons his drinking and his quarrels with the show's executives and with other cast members led to his being fired. In addition, his marriage to Sandy Davenport, a former Second City actress, was unraveling. "I created my own problems," Belushi told Abe Peck in an interview for *Rolling Stone* (June 30, 1988). "I was the same way I was at Second City—very aggressive. It was a self-destructive drive, and I was on the same path as John. I had every reason in the world to hate myself, and I made sure that it stayed that way."

Belushi has credited his second wife, Marjorie Bransfield, whom he met in 1984, with helping him end his self-destructive behavior. He stopped drinking in 1985 and asked to rejoin the cast of *Saturday Night Live*. Although that request was turned down, he continued to find steady work in films. In 1985 he appeared in Stan Dragoti's comedy *The Man with One Red Shoe*, starring Tom Hanks. Paul Attanasio, in an otherwise negative review of that film for the *Washington Post* (July 23, 1985), pronounced Belushi to be "solid" as the lead character's best friend. The controversial director Oliver Stone, who had been taken with Belushi's work in a *Saturday Night Live* skit called "White Guys' Rap," cast him as Dr. Rock, the deejay who is the sidekick of the reporter played by James Woods, in the 1986 film *Salvador*.

In 1986 Belushi reprised his role as the womanizer Bernie Litko in the film version of *Sexual Perversity in Chicago*—Edward Zwick's *About Last Night . . .* To appeal to mainstream tastes, the film was less hard-edged than Mamet's stage play, and, perhaps as a result, it was not well received by critics. Belushi, however, came in for considerable praise. "The film's best performance is given by Jim Belushi," Vincent Canby wrote in the *New York Times* (July 1, 1986), in a representative review. "Mr. Belushi . . . is exceptionally funny as the sexist, lower middle-class King Kong of the singles scene, a fellow who confidently stalks the singles bars without any idea that he's an ape." Commenting on Belushi's contribution to the film, Rob Lowe, who played the male lead, was quoted in *Rolling Stone* (June 30, 1988) as saying, "He was great. He learned to trust himself and other people around him. He's no longer his own worst enemy."

Whereas *Salvador*, *About Last Night . . .*, and *The Man with One Red Shoe* had all featured Belushi in the role of the sidekick/best friend, his next two projects, "Birthday Boy" and *The Principal*, gave him a chance to showcase his talents in leading roles. Inspired by a sketch Belushi had created for Second City, "Birthday Boy," a half-hour comedy-drama about a salesman who experiences a series of mishaps on the day he turns thirty, was first aired in 1986 as a segment of Cinemax's *Comedy Experiment* series. Stephen Holden of the *New York Times* (August 14, 1986) felt that Belushi, who also wrote and coproduced "Birthday Boy," had made his character "genuinely sympathetic." In Christopher Cain's film *The Principal* (1987), the actor starred as a hotheaded, slovenly teacher given the task of shaping up a high school overrun by teenage thugs.

In the same year, Belushi appeared with John Ritter in Dennis Feldman's poorly received spy comedy *Real Men*. More successfully, he costarred in Walter Hill's action-packed *Red Heat* (1988) as the rumpled, wisecracking Chicago cop who teams up with a stern, uncompromising Soviet officer (Arnold Schwarzenegger) to catch a Moscow drug dealer on the loose in the United States. A reviewer for *Time* (June 20, 1988) declared that Belushi "mine[d] quick charm out of his surly role." None of the films in which he was seen over the next few years approached *Red Heat*'s popularity at the box office, although most of them would do well as rental videos. He appeared opposite Whoopie Goldberg in *Homer and Eddie* (1989); as a police officer whose partner is a German shepherd in *K-9* (1989); as a likable escaped convict who assumes the identity of a strait-laced ad executive (played by Charles Grodin) in the comedy *Taking Care of Business* (1990); as the partner of a police officer (John Candy) in the romance *Only the Lonely* (1991); and as a down-and-out con man rearing the young title character in John Hughes's sentimental comedy *Curly Sue* (1991).

During that period Belushi also headed the casts of two movies. *Mr. Destiny* (1990), directed by James Orr, found him portraying a bored business executive diverted from a midlife crisis by a man (Michael Caine) with the ability to change the past. While less than impressed by the film as a whole, a reviewer for *People* (November 5, 1990) declared that Belushi exhibited a "natural, muttish quality" that would make viewers "like him without even thinking about it." In *The Palermo Connection* (1991), a drama about the illegal narcotics trade, Belushi took the part of a New York City mayoral candidate calling for the legalization of drugs. His film credits for 1992 included a minor role in Roy London's *Diary of a Hitman*; a part in Eugene Levy's star-studded but otherwise unremarkable *Once Upon a Crime*, in which he gave what a reviewer for the *Washington Post* (March 27, 1992) called one of the "least objectionable" performances; and the central character in Andy Wolk's steamy *Traces of Red*. In the last-named film, Belushi played a Florida detective who suspects one of his lovers of having murdered the other. Although some critics dismissed *Traces of Red* altogether, others pronounced it to be solid—if, in the end, forgettable—entertainment.

Oliver Stone, who had directed Belushi in *Salvador*, cast him in the lead role in the ABC miniseries *Wild Palms*, which was first telecast in the spring of 1993. In that offbeat, futuristic, complexly plotted story, Belushi was Harry Wycoff, a Los Angeles lawyer duped into working for Tony Kreutzer (Robert Loggia), a United States senator, television mogul, and political/religious cult leader. Wycoff fights to thwart Kreutzer after learning of his plans to reshape society through the use of hallucinogenic drugs and holographic imagery. Belushi's interpretation elicited sharply contrasting assessments from the critics. Some reviewers, among them James Walcott of the *New Yorker* (May 17, 1993), thought that the actor had been miscast—that he, as Walcott put it, lacked "the sensitivity meter to portray innocence lost in a maze" and looked as if "he'd rather be knocking back a few Buds." Others agreed with Brian Lowry of *Variety* (May 10, 1993), who felt that Belushi "provide[d] a strong central presence."

Returning to the stage for the first time since the mid-1980s, in early 1993 Belushi replaced Judd Hirsch as Eddie Goldberg, the role for which Hirsch had won a Tony Award, in the Broadway production of Herb Gardner's play *Conversations with My Father*, about a man's relationship with his two sons. To prepare for his role as a Russian-Jewish bar owner in New York City, Belushi drew on his boyhood memories of working alongside his own immigrant father in a bar. "If I hadn't worked with my father, I wouldn't have had a relationship with him," Belushi was quoted as saying in *New York Newsday* (February 24, 1993). Not long after the end of his Broadway engagement, Belushi was back before the cameras for his role in the 1994 Showtime television film *Royce*, an action comedy in which he played a CIA agent bent on foiling a plot by fellow agents to steal a trainload of Russian nuclear weapons.

The actor's projects for 1995 have included *The Pebble and the Penguin*, an animated film for children, in which he supplied the voice of a penguin name Rocko; Jack Baran's unsuccessful dark comedy *Destiny Turns On the Radio*; and *Sahara*, a made-for-cable remake of the 1943 movie starring Humphrey Bogart. With regard to the last-named film, John J. O'Connor wrote in the *New York Times* (July 29, 1995); "Television remakes of Hollywood classics are usually disastrous. A stunning exception can be found . . . in Showtime's *Sahara*. . . . Now the Bogart character, Sergeant Joe Gunn, is played by James Belushi, who, less Bogey than Gene Hackman, delivers a terrific performance with stunning authority." In an interview for the *Chicago Tribune* (August 9, 1992), Belushi mused on his efforts to play comedic and dramatic parts: "It's OK if people think I'm funny. I think my problem is they don't know how to slot me, which shows versatility, but it doesn't show something they can count on. You know: 'He does this, let's get him, he *is* this guy.' So I'm always having to prove myself to get the roles."

While James Belushi's pursuit of serious roles has distinguished him from John Belushi, Mike McGrady observed in *New York Newsday* (June 29, 1986) that James "shares one great quality with his brother: He dominates every scene he's in. So strong is his presence that even when he's off camera, there's a kind of afterimage, a lingering effect enabling him to steal not just scenes but entire movies." Belushi has credited his brother, to whom he was extremely close, with passing on a bit of advice about theatrical performing that he has applied to his work in other media as well: "Always go on stage like a bull charging into a bull ring." Belushi is a recipient of the Spirit of Chicago Award, given by the Chicago Convention and Tourism Bureau. The actor stands five feet, eleven inches tall and has a stocky build and dark hair. He has been described as a ham for whom "life truly is a stage" but also as one whose "surface jocularity" coexists with a "dark, angry side and a short fuse." Belushi has a son, Robert, from his marriage to Sandy Davenport; that union, as well as his second marriage, to Marjorie Bransfield, ended in divorce. He makes his home in Los Angeles.

Selected Biographical References: Chicago Tribune mag p16+ Ag 9 '92 pors; Rolling Stone p36+ Je 30 '88 por; N Y Newsday II p3 Je 29 '86 por, II p4+ Ag 8 '92 pors, II p47+ F 24 '93 por; N Y Times C p13+ F 17 '93 por; People 12:104+ O 1 '79 pors; Contemporary Newsmakers, 1986; Contemporary Theatre, Film, and Television vol 3 (1986); Who's Who in America, 1995

Reed Saxon/AP/Wide World Photos

Bennett, Tony

Aug. 3, 1926– Singer. Address: Tony Bennett Enterprises, 101 W. 55th St., New York, NY 10019-5343

NOTE: This biography supersedes the article that appeared in *Current Biography* in 1965.

About half a century ago, Tony Bennett began his emergence as, in the words of the music critic Stephen Holden, "a male ballad singer . . . in the romantic Italian-American bel canto tradition" of Frank Sinatra and Vic Damone. In 1965, when the halcyon days of American popular song had not yet faded into history, Sinatra called Bennett "the best in the business . . . , the singer who gets across what the composer has in mind and probably a little more." After Sinatra, Bennett is the foremost surviving singer of the classics from what he has referred to as "the great American songbook," and while Sinatra—Bennett's senior by eleven years—has become less active, Bennett is enjoying a grand resurgence among young as well as old listeners. After signing with Columbia Records in 1950, Bennett made the charts with a string of hits, including the million-selling singles "Because of You," "Cold, Cold Heart," "Rags to Riches," and "Stranger in Paradise." He reached the height of his first round of popularity in 1962, with "I Left My Heart in San Francisco," which won two Grammy awards and became his signature song.

With the hegemony of rock 'n' roll and the demographics and marketing that came with it, which he resisted, Bennett's popularity waned, and during a hiatus from Columbia Records from 1971 to 1986 he did only a limited amount of jazz-oriented recording on his own label, Improv. Rebounding under the management of his son Danny, he won his third and fourth Grammy awards for the albums *Perfectly Frank* (1992) and *Steppin' Out* (1993) and crossed over into the lucrative alternative market, to the point of starring in 1994 in his own special, *Tony Bennett Unplugged*, on MTV. The soundtrack of *Tony Bennett Unplugged*, which was released on compact disc and cassette late in 1994, earned Bennett his fifth and sixth Grammy awards, for album of the year and best traditional vocal recording.

At the very beginning of his career, Bennett was a tenor, and dissatisfied with his range. "I didn't realize that the higher you sing the more it communicates—like Michael Jackson," he recounted to Jeff Giles for *Interview* (May 1990). "I was always trying to get deeper and deeper. But now-thank God for age—I have another five notes at the bottom of my register. I have a bigger range now, so I can sing in a baritone fashion or go up to a tenor." In his entry on Bennett in the *New Grove Dictionary of American Music* (1986), Stephen Holden wrote: "In the early 1950s Bennett . . . had a lyric baritone with a distinctively husky edge, which served him well as he developed into an increasingly jazz-oriented saloon singer. An admirer of classic jazz, he claims to have modeled his breathing and phrasing on the jazz pianist Art Tatum and his relaxed delivery on that of the singer Mildred Bailey." Bennett's best jazz album, *Tony Bennett: Jazz*, includes collaborations with the likes of Count Basie, Art Blakey, Herbie Hancock, and Stan Getz. Among his scores of other recordings are the album of golden oldies *Tony Bennett Sings His All-Time Hall of Fame* and the definitive boxed set of compact discs, *Forty Years: The Artistry of Tony Bennett*.

Tony Bennett was born Anthony Dominick Benedetto in the New York City borough of Queens on August 3, 1926. With his older brother and sister, he grew up in the Astoria neighborhood in Queens. After his father, John Benedetto, an Italian immigrant tailor and grocery store proprietor, died, when Bennett was eight or nine, his mother, Anna (Suraci) Benedetto, supported the family by working at home as a seamstress for the garment industry. "She would get angry if she was given a bad dress to work on," Bennett recalled in an interview with Claire Carter for a profile in *Parade Magazine* (February 16, 1992). "I discovered subliminally that stuck. I don't want to sing a song unless it's great." Anna Benedetto lived to enjoy for several decades her younger son's popular success as a singer.

In the performance-minded Benedetto family, the vocal talent was apparently passed on to the children through the father, who had a "beautiful voice," as Bennett told Claire Carter. Among the children, the talent was initially observed and encouraged in Bennett's older brother, John, who was a member of the Metropolitan Opera's children's chorus. Perhaps intimidated by his brother's shadow, Bennett tended to be facetious in his early singing, doing comic impersonations of the likes of Eddie Cantor, Al Jolson, and Jimmy Durante when performing with his siblings for parents and relatives in family musicales on Sundays. "The reason I'm in the business," he once said, "is when I was fourteen I saw Clayton, Jackson, and Durante [a vaudeville trio] at the Copa [the Copacabana nightclub], and the energy that came off that stage was like a three-ring circus." Concurrently, he was drawn to the graphic arts, beginning at age five with drawing, especially the creation of chalk murals on sidewalks, and later advancing to painting with watercolors.

After attending junior high school in Astoria, Bennett studied commercial art at the High School of Industrial Art (now the High School of Art and Design) in Manhattan. "I got my education by playing hooky and listening to Sinatra at the Paramount," he recalled to Howard Reich, who profiled him for the *Chicago Tribune* (July 15, 1990). "He opened up a whole new bag with the microphone, the artful use of intimate singing to show psychology, real thinking." Louis Armstrong was also an early hero of his. Among the other influences on him musically, then or later, were the big bands of Woody Herman, Count Basie, Benny Goodman, and Gene Krupa, the jazz playing of Miles Davis, Charlie Parker, and Stan Getz, and the singing of Bing Crosby, Billie Holiday, Sarah Vaughan, Mildred Bailey, Billy Eckstine, and Nat "King" Cole. Following his graduation from high school, Bennett served during the final months of World War II with the U.S. Army's 63d infantry division in Europe. According to some sources, he occasionally sang with army bands while in the service.

After the war, Bennett enrolled under the G.I. Bill at the American Theatre Wing's professional school, where he studied bel canto with Peter D'Andrea and contemporary vocal techniques with Miriam Spier, who, as he has recalled, advised him to "imitate the musicians," because if he "imitated the singers [he'd] just be one of the chorus." His first professional job, according to some sources, was that of a singing waiter at the Pheasant Tavern in Astoria. While struggling to build his career in singing, he also supported himself by working as an elevator operator in the Park Sheraton Hotel in Manhattan. "I came into the business at a tough time," Bennett told Howard Reich. "By the time the war was over, it was uneconomical for big bands to stay together. So I had to play the little lounges rather than the big dates with the big bands I had grown up listening to."

After several years of struggle, Bennett's first big break came when he won a spot as a competitor on the network television show *Arthur Godfrey's Talent Scouts*, on which he finished second to the singer Rosemary Clooney. Soon thereafter he and Clooney performed on Jan Murray's television program *Songs for Sale*. After seeing him on that show, Pearl Bailey recruited him for a revue she was headlining at the Greenwich Village Inn nightclub. Among those who saw the revue was the celebrated comedian Bob Hope, who was then, in 1950, in the midst of an engagement at the Paramount Theatre, the ultimate Manhattan showcase at the time. At Hope's invitation, Bennett joined the comedian in his show at the Paramount and subsequently accompanied him on a national tour. It was at Hope's suggestion that Anthony Benedetto, who had been using the stage name Joe Bari, changed his name to Tony Bennett. Hope also taught him how to walk onto the stage. "He told me, 'Come out smiling. Show the people you like them,'" Bennett told Claire Carter for *Parade*. "To this day, I still follow those rules."

In March 1950 Bennett was signed by Mitch Miller, then the head of Columbia Records' artists and repertoire department, on the basis of a demonstration cover recording of the old Russ Columbo hit "The Boulevard of Broken Dreams," which had modest sales but sparked some critical interest as a Columbia single. "Because of You," released in 1951, was the first of his recordings to make the national trade magazines' lists of the one hundred best-selling records. It was number one on the charts for eight weeks, and it remained in the top one hundred for thirty-one weeks, into 1952. In recognition of the single's sales of more than one million copies, Bennett was, as a matter of course, awarded a gold record by Columbia. Later in 1951 Columbia released Bennett's pop rendition of Hank Williams's country song "Cold, Cold Heart" (with "Be My Love" on the flip side), which also went gold. It was number one for six of the twenty-seven weeks it was on the charts in 1951 and 1952. Bennett's 1951 releases "I Won't Cry Anymore," "Blue Velvet" and "Solitaire" also made the charts.

Bennett was named male vocalist of the year 1951 by *Cashbox* magazine. He had moderate hits with the 1952 Columbia releases "Here in My Heart" and "Have a Good Time." In 1953 his third million-seller, "Rags to Riches," was the top-selling single for six of the twenty-four weeks it was on the charts. His fourth, "Stranger in Paradise," released late in 1953, was on the American charts for nineteen weeks, reaching number three, and it later became a best-seller in Britain as well. The music for many of Bennett's early Columbia releases, including those 1953 singles, was provided by the Percy Faith Orchestra. In 1954 Bennett made the charts with "There'll Be No Teardrops Tonight" and "Cinnamon Sinner."

From the beginning of rock 'n' roll's ascendancy in the mid-1950s, Bennett refused to adapt to the trend, sticking to his wonted "evergreen" ballads and rhythm numbers. "If Tony had embraced rock-'n'-roll, his career would have fizzled, because he had no feeling for it," Ralph Sharon, his longtime musical conductor and piano accompanist, explained to Claire Carter for *Parade*. Bennett had no recordings on the charts in 1955. The following year he was more successful with "Can You Find It in Your Heart," "Happiness Street," "From the Candy Store on the Corner to the Chapel on the Hill, "Just in Time," and "The Autumn Waltz," all achieving respectable sales figures. With the Ray Ellis Orchestra, Bennett recorded his fifth million-seller, "In the Middle of an Island," in 1957. That single was a best-seller for twenty-one weeks, reaching the number nine spot on the charts. Between 1957 and 1960 Bennett made the charts less spectacularly with the singles "One for My Baby," "I Am," "Ça, Ç'Est l'Amour," "Young and Warm and Wonderful," "Firefly," "Smile," and "Climb Every Mountain." On television, he was the summer replacement for Perry Como on Como's network show in 1956, and he later appeared on such network entertainment programs as *On Parade* and *Hollywood Palace*. In person, he became a major attraction in such nightclubs as the Copacabana in New York, the Dunes in Las Vegas, and the Fontainebleau in Miami.

As a recording artist, Bennett went hitless in 1960 and 1961. Early in 1962, while his career was still in the doldrums, he was booked into the Fairmont Hotel in San Francisco for the first time. Ralph Sharon, who was instrumental in introducing Bennett to almost every one of his hits, looked around for a song with local appeal and came up with a little-known number called "I Left My Heart in San Francisco," which had been written by Douglas Cross and George Cory in 1954. Bennett's recording of that song, released in July 1962, was on the charts in the United States for at least twenty-one weeks, peaking at number nineteen, and it was honored with two Grammy awards, for record of the year and best male vocal performance. In Britain it was a best-seller for at least eighteen weeks, climbing to number seventeen on the pop charts. Within two years its sales were running beyond 1.5 million copies. Bennett later presented his gold record of the single to the city of San Francisco.

"It really changed everything," Bennett said of the success of "I Left My Heart in San Francisco," as quoted by Claire Carter in *Parade*. "Ever since then, I've been sold out all over the world. . . . The first concert I ever did was at Carnegie Hall, as a result of 'San Francisco.' Before, I was always playing in clubs. We did a record of that night at Carnegie Hall. It was fantastic the way people cheered. . . . It was like going to heaven." Between 1963 and 1967 he was represented on the charts by such singles as "I Wanna Be Around," "The Good Life," "This Is All I Ask, "When Joanna Loved Me," "It's a Sin to Tell a Lie," "A Taste of Honey," "Who Can I Turn to?" "If I Ruled the World," "Fly Me to the Moon," "Love Theme from the Sandpiper," and "For Once in My Life."

By the late 1960s commercial demographics had become such that the major record companies were favoring young rock groups and pressing seasoned artists like Mel Tormé, Frank Sinatra, and Tony Bennett to record contemporary pop tunes often not in accord with their sensibilities and styles. When presented with some of the songs, Bennett was reminded of how his seamstress mother had felt when forced to work on cheap dresses. "Years ago there was a game to popular singing, and it was a *good* game," Bennett told Jeff Giles for *Interview* (May 1990). "There was an accent on individualism. Kay Starr had her style, Ray Charles had his style, Sinatra had his style. And each was an individual—a mini-monument. We were fans of one another, and there was a healthy competitiveness. But then record companies just got greedy. They said, 'Just do songs on the Top Forty.'. . . . They saw that there were more people of the Beatles' age group than any other age group. But I was trained as a performer before the Beatles. I was trained to play to the *whole* family, and common sense tells me that is better business." The changes in the music industry were dramatized when the mantle of leadership at Columbia Records passed from the classically trained Goddard Lieberson (who had counseled Bennett never to "sing anything you don't feel") to the more business-minded Clive Davis.

Bennett's bewilderment at music's having become "a media thing" and "all marketing," and his resistance to reaching rock audiences by changing his repertoire, to doing more albums like *Tony Sings the Great Hits of Today* (1970), and to promoting his recordings in stadium performances, all contributed to his departure from Columbia Records in 1971. By that time he had made eighty-eight Columbia albums, including *Tony Sings for Two, Tony Bennett Sings a String of Harold Arlen, Hometown, My Town, My Heart Sings, I Left My Heart in San Francisco, Tony Bennett at Carnegie, In Person* (with Count Basie), and *The Many Moods of Tony Bennett.* During the four years after his departure, Columbia Records released seven additional Tony Bennett albums, including *All-Time Greatest Hits.*

After leaving Columbia Records, Bennett never slackened as a live performer. "We were still packing houses all over the world," he told Greg Kot for a profile in the *Chicago Tribune* (May 12, 1989). "It felt good, but it also gave me more time to concentrate on my performing instead of having to worry about doing three albums a year." During his exile from Columbia Records, he also renewed and deepened his contact with jazz musicians, including Earl "Fatha" Hines and Charlie Byrd. On the Fantasy label, he recorded *The Tony Bennett-Bill Evans Album* (1975), consisting of voice-and-piano jazz duets. Subsequently, on his own, short-lived label, Improv, he recorded a second album with Evans, *Together Again*; an LP with the jazz pianist Marian McPartland, *Beautiful Music*; two albums with the guitarist George Barnes and the cornetist Ruby Braff, *Ten Rodgers and Hart Songs* and *More Great Rodgers and Hart*; and the Fred Astaire tribute *Life is Beautiful.* He also began turning his avocation, painting, into a lucrative second vocation, holding his first major show in Chicago in 1977 and his second in London in 1979.

Bennett's son Danny, a former rock guitarist, took over his management in 1979. (He would also produce his father's subsequent recordings). After several years of effort, Danny succeeded in reconciling his father and Columbia Records, whose management had also changed. "I sold them on the idea that here was a catalog artist, and there was gold in them thar hills," Danny recounted to John Marchese for the *New York Times* (May 1, 1994). "I told [Bennett], 'Look, marketing isn't a bad word.'" In 1986, after going nine years without a new release, Bennett signed again with Columbia Records. His first release under the new contract, and his first studio-recorded album in ten years, was the critically acclaimed *The Art of Excellence* (1986), dedicated to the singer Mabel Mercer, whom he admired for her way with lyrics and phrasing.

While that album included some numbers done with small swing combos as well as a spirited duet with Ray Charles on James Taylor's wry song "Everybody Has the Blues," the emphasis was on such lushly orchestrated ballads as "How Do You Keep the Music Playing?" and "Why Do People Fall in Love?" In discussing the album with Wayne Robbins of *New York Newsday* (May 9, 1986), Bennett said, "It was made for CD, which I consider the most promising thing for the kind of music, the philosophy that I've tried to adhere to since those days when the premise was to make a record that would last forever. . . . I think the compact disc and the laser disc have the potential for creating more solid-quality music, lasting music." Danny Bennett has said: "The CD made it possible for us to emphasize the voice, which is what made Tony a star to begin with."

Abetted on some tracks by cameo performances by the jazz soloists George Benson, Dizzy Gillespie, and Dexter Gordon, Bennett recorded the second release in his Columbia reincarnation, *Bennett/Berlin* (1987), featuring the "uptown" songs of Irving Berlin, including "They Say It's Wonderful," "The Song Is Ended," "When I Lost You," "Cheek to Cheek," and "White Christmas." Like *The Art of Excellence* and *Bennett/Berlin, Astoria: Portrait of an Artist* (1990) was a "concept" album. In this instance, the concept was autobiography—loosely speaking, because Bennett, as usual, wrote none of the songs, which ranged from vintage (including some reprises) to new, from snappy to affectionate, thoughtful, and poignant. On some of the songs Bennett was accompanied by his trio, including Ralph Sharon on piano, and on others, by the UK Orchestra Limited under the direction of the arranger Jorge Calandrelli. "While Bennett's trademark fondness for dramatic flourishes and finales sometimes gets the best of him . . . ," Mike Joyce wrote in his review of *Astoria* in the *Washington Post* (June 6, 1990), "it's a minor distraction on an album otherwise distinguished by sensitive and often stirring interpretations and arrangements. Fusing 'Weaver of Dreams' and 'There Will Never Be Another You' into a medley makes for a near-seamless match, and the subtle and often swinging liberties the singer and his trio take on 'Body and Soul' and other tunes are similarly effective."

In his review of *Astoria* in *Entertainment Weekly*, Greg Sandow (an avant-garde classical critic lately converted to rap and heavy-metal zealotry) dismissed Bennett's art as anachronistic and irrelevant to contemporary life. "All this music is written and sung in the style that dominated popular music before rock 'n' roll—which means before the '60s, before feminism, before what we've come to accept as the dawn of modern life." In the *Atlantic Monthly* (August 1990), Francis Davis countered: "Sandow is forgetting that music and the emotions it calls into play don't have to be raw in order to be real. He's also not giving Bennett—who is twice divorced and a product of the ethnic working class—credit for realizing that life doesn't always work out the way it did in the great old songs, and for knowing that that might be the best reason to go on singing them. . . . Why should it be necessary to choose between Tony Bennett and Bruce Springsteen? Bennett conveys as much urgency, although it's of a different sort. Often written about as though he were Sinatra's exact contemporary, he is eleven years younger, the difference of at least a generation in pop. The lost magic that Bennett mourns on *Astoria* was already vanishing by the time he began his career. . . . Forty years later he has become the best singer of his kind, but he must sometimes feel like an ambassador from a country that's fallen off the map."

"During the seventies," Davis continued, "Bennett developed what has become his most endearing vocal trait: bearing down on the key words of a lyric and sometimes deliberating them in what is practically a stage whisper or a shout, like a man thinking out loud while singing *con brio*. The effect is too fleeting—and too much Bennett's own—to be characterized as *sprechstimme* or *parlando*. In addition to making a virtue of the slight huskiness that has crept into his voice with age, it gives his performances an autobiographical depth comparable to that which Sinatra achieved in his late prime." The transformation of Bennett's vocal style can be traced in the 1991 Columbia release *Forty Years: The Artistry of Tony Bennett*, a four-CD boxed set consisting of hits culled from the record company's Tony Bennett library.

Meanwhile, discouraged over the relatively low sales of *Astoria*, Bennett was on the verge of leaving the Columbia label and perhaps even giving up recording altogether. Don Jenner, then newly installed as president of Columbia, begged the singer to stay and asked him to develop an album idea he could sell. The idea Bennett came back with was the turning point in his renewed career, resulting in *Perfectly Frank* (1992), consisting of covers of songs identified with Frank Sinatra, whom Bennett has described as "my best friend, professionally as well as personally." The album went gold, selling more than half a million copies, and brought Bennett his first Grammy award in three decades, for best traditional vocal performance. The following year Bennett won another Grammy, for best traditional pop vocal, with his next album, *Steppin' Out*, a collection of songs associated with Fred Astaire.

Meanwhile, Danny Bennett had been methodically implementing a ten-year plan for remarketing an old reliable singer in new packaging, beginning in the mid-1980s. Among the early results of Danny's efforts was adulatory coverage of Tony Bennett in *Spin*, the rock-oriented magazine. Soon Bennett found a hip ally in Paul Schaeffer, the music director of David Letterman's popular television show, who backed him musically in a series of performances on the show. Among his later television performances enhancing his youth culture imprimatur, one of the most effective was his singing the song "Capital City" on the cartoon situation comedy *The Simpsons* in 1991. (His voice was recorded in a studio and dubbed in sync with the cartoon character representing him on the show.) The director Martin Scorsese used Bennett's rendition of "Rags to Riches" over the opening credits of his 1990 film *GoodFellas*. The advertising firm of Wieden & Kennedy used Bennett in a commercial for Nike sneakers, and WordPerfect, the computer software company, sponsored a national tour by Bennett in 1993.

The final step was connecting Bennett with MTV, the youth-oriented cable television network, which had become the most important door to a mass pop music audience. That connection began in September 1993, when Bennett joined Anthony Kiedis and Flea of the Red Hot Chili Peppers in presenting an award at the MTV Video Music Awards. (They wore tuxedos; he wore a velvet top hat, sunglasses, a black T-shirt, and shorts.) Later, Bennett's video "Steppin' Out with My Baby," promoting his album *Steppin' Out*, ran regularly on MTV for a week. In the spring of 1994, the videotaped program *Tony Bennett Unplugged* (the source of the double Grammy-winning album of the same title) was presented on MTV as a special in the network's *MTV Unplugged* series. On that program Bennett, sang a score of the old standards in his repertoire, on some of which he was joined by various guest performers, among them K. D. Lang, Elvis Costello, and J. Mascis of Dinosaur Jr. In August 1994 Bennett was invited to perform at the twenty-fifth anniversary celebration of the Woodstock Festival, but a prior engagement in Cincinnati prevented him from accepting. In time for Christmas 1994, Columbia released *Snowfall: The Tony Bennett Christmas Album*. Among his other albums are *Tony Bennett: Jazz*, featuring collaborations with Count Basie, Art Blakey, Herbie Hancock, Zoot Sims, and others. The singer was given a lifetime achievement award at the World Music Awards ceremony in May 1995.

All the while, Bennett was on the road some two hundred days a year, fulfilling club, concert, and "industrial" engagements nationally and internationally. "Bennett sings straight from the heart, with a warmth that rings true—even when he delivers a torch song like 'Here's That Rainy Day' through his perpetually goofy smile," James Gavin wrote in the *New York Times* (September 27, 1992). "On stage at Radio City Music Hall, where he gave two recent concerts, Mr. Bennett exuded a boyish enthusiasm that belied his age. As ovations rose from the house, he held up his arms like a winning prizefighter, looking as if he wanted to embrace the whole audience."

Tony Bennett, who is of medium height, has a weathered face with a Roman nose, wide jaw, and skewed grin. His hair has gone, in the words of Richard Harrington in the *Washington Post* (June 30, 1991), "from curling blackness to brushy gray (and synthetics, perhaps)." In disposition, according to Harrington, he seems "always sunny," and he is "salt-of-the-earth friendly, courteous, low-key, just short of shy." In his article for the *New York Times*, James Gavin wrote: "He is still the kind of celebrity whom cabdrivers call by his first name and who answers gushy praise by clasping his forehead and murmuring, 'Ahh, geez, thanks.'" A sharp dresser, he is natty even when casual.

Bennett was married to Patricia Beach from 1952 until their divorce in 1971 and to Sandra Grant from 1971 until their divorce in 1984. By his first marriage he has two sons, D'Andrea, known as Danny, his manager, and Daegal, who, as the operator of a recording studio, has assisted in the renewal of his father's career. By his second marriage Bennett has two daughters, Joanna and Antonia. The singer lives in an apartment a short distance away from Radio City Music Hall (the venue of several of his sold-out concerts over the past ten years) in Manhattan. He does his painting both in the apartment and in the hotel and motel rooms in which he stays when on tour. (He insists on accommodations with copious natural light.) As a serious, widely exhibited graphic artist, he is a creator chiefly of landscapes and cityscapes done in oils, watercolors, and pastels and showing the influence of Monet, Cézanne, Renoir, ancient Egyptian artists, the Japanese printmaker Hokusai, and his friend David Hockney, among others. For recreation and exercise, Bennett plays tennis.

Selected Biographical References: Atlantic 226:85+ Ag '90 por; Chicago Tribune XIII p2+ Jl 13 '86 pors, V p3 My 12 '89 pors, XIII p8+ Jl 15 '90 pors; Entertainment W p22 Jl 26 '91 pors; Interview XX:56 My '90 pors; N Y Daily News Extra p33 S 17 '92 por; N Y Newsday Weekend III p1+ My 9 '86 pors; N Y Times II p30+ S 27 '92 pors; II p34+ My 1 '94 pors; New York 27:38+ Ag 22 '94 pors; New Yorker 70:37 Ap 25 '94; Parade p4+ F 16 '92 pors; New Grove Dictionary of American Music (1986); New Grove Dictionary of Jazz (1988); Nite, Norm N. Rock On (1974); Penguin Encyclopedia of Popular Music (1989); Who's Who in America, 1995

Liam White/Delacorte Press

Binchy, Maeve
(mayv)

May 28, 1940– Irish writer. Address: c/o Chris Green, 2 Barbon Close, Great Ormond St., London WC1 N3JX, England

"Plot has never been [Maeve] Binchy's strong suit or first love," John Kennedy Crane wrote in his *New York Times* (December 8, 1991) review of one of the Irish writer's novels. "It is, instead, her well-drawn characters and their dynamic interaction with one another in the most ordinary circumstances that characterize her fiction." Binchy's concentration on such "ordinary" topics as family life, long-term friendship, and small-town mores is perhaps what accounts for the universal appeal of her books, which are all set in Ireland or England but have become best-sellers on both sides of the Atlantic. A professional journalist who has spent most of her adult life as an editor, correspondent, and columnist for the *Irish Times*, Binchy achieved success as a fiction writer when she was in her forties, upon the publication of her first novel, *Light a Penny Candle*, in 1982. To date, she has written seven novels, five collections of short stories, several plays, and two collections of nonfiction.

Binchy has been faulted by some critics for her pedestrian use of language and her penchant for melodrama, but she has also won praise for her realistic plots, her eye for detail, and the affectionate tone with which she sculpts her tales. In an attempt to explain her books' wide following—as evidenced by their having been translated into several languages—Binchy told Nancy Mills of the *Chicago Tribune* (March 26, 1995), "I'm sure in Korea they must have possessive families, one-horse towns where they're dying to get to Seoul, drunken brothers, and love affairs that aren't reciprocated." Contributing to the popularity of her work in the United States was an announcement by then-First Lady Barbara Bush that Binchy is her favorite writer.

The eldest of the four children of Maureen (Blackmore) Binchy, a nurse, and William T. Binchy, a lawyer, Maeve Binchy was born on May 28, 1940, in Dublin, Ireland, and grew up in Dalkey, about ten miles to the south. She has characterized her family as being exceptionally close and has described her parents as having been loving and supportive. As a girl she attended the local convent school and was, like most people living in rural Ireland in the 1940s and 1950s, a devout Catholic. "You'd no more not think of going to Mass on Sundays than not serving Sunday lunch," the author recalled to Fred Newman for *Waterstone's Review* (September/October 1990).

Binchy graduated from University College Dublin in about 1961 with a degree in French and history. She then became a teacher at the Zion Schools in Dublin, a position she held until the age of twenty-three. As a parting gift, the parents of her students paid for her trip to Israel, where she worked on a kibbutz. Two events that transpired during her stay in Israel significantly shaped her adult life. She became a self-described "collapsed Catholic" when, while visiting the site of the Last Supper, she concluded, suddenly and without outward provocation, that the religious education she had received in her youth was built on a foundation of untruths. As she told Polly Toynbee for the *Guardian* (February 10, 1986), "One moment I believed the lot, angels with wings and a special Irish God, and the next I didn't believe a word of it." At roughly the same time, she inadvertently sowed the seeds of what would become her writing career. Her father found the letters she sent home, full of descriptions of her experiences in a foreign land, to be so insightful and engrossing that he sent one of them to the daily *Irish Independent*, where it was printed. Following its publication, Binchy thought she had "arrived," as she revealed to Katharine Weber for *Publishers Weekly* (October 26, 1992), for the payment she received was two pounds more than her weekly salary as a teacher.

When Binchy returned to Ireland, she sought work as a freelance writer rather than as a teacher—not only because of the boost in confidence she had received upon the publication of her letter but also because of the advice of other teachers. She wrote in an essay for the *Chicago Tribune* (March 17, 1991): "Teachers I regarded as elderly, who probably were younger than I am now, would say, 'Oh, I should have left [teaching]. I could have done this or that.' I thought, I must leave for a year, see what I can do, and then come back to teaching."

Binchy initially experienced difficulty in establishing herself as a writer. "I didn't understand that the reason that first article had been published was because it was unaffected; it was writing as I spoke," she remarked to Jean W. Ross in a 1989 interview for *Contemporary Authors*. "I thought you had to be sort of grown-up and have something terribly clever to write about, so I constantly kept putting on pretenses in my writing." Eventually a more seasoned journalist encouraged her to write about what concerned her most, and thereafter she found more success in the field. "I suddenly realized then that if you wrote about what was actually in your heart and expressed it as you would speak normally, it was quite easy to get published," she recalled.

In 1968 the *Irish Times* offered Binchy—who was without a day's newspaper experience—a full-time position as an editor covering "women's issues." "That was very unusual," she told Jean W. Ross. "I couldn't even type! But they still thought there was some hope there somewhere." Her mother died around the same time, and in 1972 her father passed away, leaving the thirty-two-year-old Binchy, who was still living in her parents' house, alone for the first time. She moved into her first apartment in Dublin, and soon thereafter, feeling lonely and unsettled, she moved to London and became a correspondent for the *Irish Times*. "I had thought going over to London as a features writer would be all Wimbledon and strawberries and cream and tennis and Ascot," she has written. "But it coincided with the IRA bombing campaign in Britain, so it was quite a different thing. I was standing out at night in a raincoat asking what size the bomb was, was there any warning, and that sort of thing."

In London, Binchy married Gordon Snell, a children's author and onetime BBC correspondent. It was with Snell's encouragement that Binchy, in her mid-thirties, began writing plays and short stories. The year 1976 saw the production in Dublin of her first play, the one-act *End of Term*, as well as the release of a compilation of her *Irish Times* articles, under the title *My First Book*. Two years later she published a book of short fiction, *The Central Line: Stories of Big City Life*, detailing the working and personal lives of young women living in London. The stories in that volume, along with those in her second book of short fiction, *Victoria Line*, were later issued together under the title *London Transports*. In 1979 her second play, *The Half Promised Land*, set on a kibbutz, was given a Dublin production, and a year later it was brought to the Society Hill Playhouse in Philadelphia. Her television screenplay *Deeply Regretted By* was produced by Radio Telefis Eireann, Ireland's state network, in 1979, the same year that the second collection of her newspaper writings, *Maeve's Diary*, was published.

Binchy was about to start on a third book of stories when her agent suggested that a longer work would gain more attention. "So I wrote an outline of a novel and a sample chapter," she told Jean W. Ross, "and because I was lucky enough to have had two books of stories . . . under my belt, the publishers thought it was worth commissioning." After a year of working on weekends and early mornings, she finished the novel. She was so unsure of herself that she informed only her husband of her efforts. Her modesty proved to be misplaced, for *Light a Penny Candle* became an almost immediate commercial hit. "I was totally unprepared for the huge success of it," Binchy told Jean W. Ross. Prepublication paperback rights for the book commanded the unheralded sum of fifty-three thousand pounds (about seventy-four thousand dollars), the highest price paid up to that time for a first novel in Britain.

Set in a small, fictitious Irish town, *Light a Penny Candle* traces the relationship between Elizabeth White and Aisling O'Connor, from girlhood through adulthood. Through the course of the novel, their friendship survives a host of trials, including physical separation, Aisling's affair with a former boyfriend of Elizabeth's, and the stress caused by both women's unsuccessful marriages. Following the book's publication in the United States, in 1983, a reviewer for *Harper's* (April 1983) found some of its drama "too heavy-handed and contrived," but Carol Sternhall, writing in the *Village Voice*, found the work "impressive" and proclaimed, "Binchy's strength is in her honesty: she refuses to trim all edges to get us drunk on easy answers."

The residents of the Irish resort town of Castlebay, the setting of Binchy's second novel, *Echoes* (1985), find their lives circumscribed by poverty and by the town's social strictures. The protagonist is Clare O'Brien, a shopkeeper's daughter determined to rise above her family's inferior social status. The novel was subsequently adapted for a British television movie.

According to Michelle Slung, writing in the *New York Times Book Review* (September 18, 1988), Binchy exhibited in *Firefly Summer* (1987), her third novel, a "firmer" command of the "moments of melodrama" than she had in her earlier novels. Calling it "the best Binchy yet," Slung lauded the author for doing "what she does best, which is to manufacture experience in which we fully share." The main character of the novel is Patrick O'Neill, an American of Irish descent who travels to the land of his ancestors to build a luxurious hotel on the site of a ruined manor in the small town of Mountfern, where he meets both encouragement and resistance from the townspeople. Binchy explained to Jean W. Ross that the novel grew out of her observation that many Irish-Americans go to Ireland with the belief that they are returning home, unaware of the gulf that exists between themselves and the Irish. "What Patrick O'Neill didn't understand," Binchy said, "was that, to the people of Mountfern, he was just as foreign as were the English lords of the soil who had gone. . . . I felt Patrick's whole return to Ireland was a misunderstanding. That's where the story came from."

"You can sense a remarkably gifted writer beginning to flex her muscles," Robert Plunket wrote in his assessment of Binchy's next novel, *Silver Wedding* (1988), for the *New York Times Book Review* (September 10, 1989). "Instead of a sprawling saga, she gives us an elegant literary construction, a comedy of manners as well as a soap opera." In this book, Binchy examined the personal conflicts of the members of one family and their circle of friends rather than those among the inhabitants of an entire town. Each chapter tells the tale of a single character, detailing his or her life in relation to the twenty-five-year marriage of Deirdre and Desmond Doyle. In the final chapter all of the characters come together for the Doyle's anniversary party. "Binchy . . . exhibits her gift for astute and loving characterization as she examines the way relationships and families work," a reviewer for *Publishers Weekly* (July 28, 1989) wrote. "She engagingly delineates the pressures, both stated and unstated, that repel or attract, the striving for approval from parents and lovers. At the silver wedding celebration, when the obligatory photograph is taken for the family album, the reader knows well what fears and doubts, secrets and achievements lie behind the happy smiles."

Circle of Friends (1990), which became the basis for Pat O'Connor's 1995 film of the same name, tells the story of three close friends, with contrasting personalities, who attend college together. At the center of the group is Benny Hogan, whom Binchy described to Fred Newman as being "a big girl like myself but very handsome, of course. That's the nice thing about writing, you can make someone that much nicer than yourself." She wrote about the novel in her *Chicago Tribune* essay: "I was ready to write a more autobiographical book. . . . It's about friendship and betrayal, and it's set in Ireland in the [1950s]. An editor in England said, ' . . . This book is all about sex, and yet nobody gets any.' That's the biggest compliment he could pay me because that is the way we were. We were obsessed by sex because it was so forbidden."

Evaluating *Circle of Friends*, the novelist Susan Isaacs wrote in the *New York Times Book Review* (December 30, 1990), "A cynical reader might reflect [that] this sort of fiction is so common that the characters will be completely fungible. Utterly predictable, they have been in a hundred novels. Sure, Maeve Binchy's . . . book takes place mainly at University College, Dublin, in 1957, but with this kind of pop bildungsroman, it could just as well be Mount Holyoke in 1943, Davenport College of Business in 1987—and it would be the same story. . . . So why bother reading *Circle of Friends*? Because it is a terrific tale, told by a master storyteller, comfortably predictable on the surface but full of nice, quiet surprises—those little astonishments we find in life, when our dearest friends do the unexpected."

The Lilac Bus, a collection of Binchy's short stories, was published in the United States the year after the appearance of *Circle of Friends*; its twelve tales had appeared earlier in Great Britain—eight of them collected in a 1984 volume called *The Lilac Bus* and the others published as *Dublin 4* in 1982. Referring to the twelve stories as "apprentice work," John Kennedy Crane nevertheless wrote in the *New York Times Book Review* (December 8, 1991), "Already the formal technique that characterizes her novels . . . is clearly evident."

Crane likened the first eight stories in *The Lilac Bus* to the interconnected tales of Sherwood Anderson's *Winesburg, Ohio* "in reverse": instead of wishing to leave their hometown of Rathdoon—as Anderson's George Willard desires to depart Winesburg—Binchy's characters return from Dublin every weekend on a lilac-colored bus, eager to escape the city and embrace the more familiar village. Each story is named for the central character of the piece, and all eight eventually work together to create "the cohesion of a novelette," a reviewer for *Publishers Weekly* (September 6, 1991) wrote, and "to portray the social order of Rathdoon." The final four stories in *The Lilac Bus*, which are connected only by their Dublin setting, proved to be, in the opinion of some reviewers, less successful than the eight preceding tales. The reviewer for *Publishers Weekly*, on the other hand, felt them to have "an equally engrossing cast," each focusing on "a woman who learns the strength of her mettle through adversity." The *Lilac Bus* was adapted for the screen and shown on British television.

The center of the action in Binchy's sixth novel, *The Copper Beech* (1992), is a village school, and the cast of characters includes the schoolchildren, their parents, the teachers, the town's priest, and the local doctor. *The Copper Beech*, like most of Binchy's novels, is character- rather than plot-driven, and like *The Lilac Bus* the novel unfolds through interconnected stories. Binchy's most recent novel, *The Glass Lake* (1995), is set in the Irish village of Lough Glass. After her mother disappears, an event that coincides with the discovery of the family's overturned boat on the lake, twelve-year-old Kit McMahon finds and burns what she assumes is her mother's suicide note. Kit carries the burden of her secret into adulthood, as the novel follows her relationships and her travels to Dublin and London. Paula Chin, writing in *People* (March 20, 1995), offered qualified praise for *The Glass Lake*: "Binchy . . . is in firm command of her craft—the writing solid, the details telling, the characters clearly drawn if stereotypical. . . . At 584 pages, *Lake* is comfort food—not great, but satisfying in its blandness and bulk—and just the kind of fare Binchy fans crave."

In her profile of the good-natured, six-foot-tall Maeve Binchy for *Publishers Weekly*, Katharine Weber wrote that her "conversation is an enthusiastic, generous flow of anecdotes and observations, punctuated by quips, queries, and conspiratorial asides." Polly Toynbee echoed that observation, stating that the novelist "talks like the fast-forward button on a video." She added that Binchy is physically "enormous, very tall and wide." Binchy explained to Toynbee, "I was miserable about being fat at school, but by the time I got to university I decided it didn't matter in the least, and I've never cared about it since." That attitude would appear to have influenced her approach to writing fiction, for, as she pointed out to Katharine Weber, "I don't have ugly ducklings turning into swans in my stories. I have ugly ducklings turning into confident ducks."

Binchy and Gordon Snell, who have been married since 1975, divide their time between homes in London and in Dalkey. The two writers work side by side at the same table, starting at 8:00 A.M. each day. "Anyone who sees this thinks we're mad," Binchy told Katharine Weber, "but the discipline of another writer sitting beside you *makes* you work." Beyond the purchase of the second house, in Dalkey, Binchy's lifestyle has changed little since she became a best-selling novelist. "I was lucky to be forty-three when I became successful," she told *People* (March 11, 1991). "I didn't want yachts or diamonds. To me money means I don't have to worry about the phone being cut off."

Binchy has continued to write a twice-weekly column and an occasional celebrity profile for the *Irish Times*. "I feel that I almost have to have a day job," she revealed to Jean W. Ross. "I'm afraid that if I just called myself Maeve Binchy, writer, I might stop writing or I might get nervous or self-conscious. But if I keep feeling that I can write in the time off from the newspaper, then it seems more honorable somehow." Currently in her mid-fifties, the novelist finds life "more and more interesting," as she wrote in the *Chicago Tribune* (March 17, 1991). "At this age, I suppose the only bad thing is that there's a feeling that it's not going to last forever."

Selected Biographical References: Chicago Tribune VI p3 Mr 17 '91 por; Guardian p20 F 10 '86 por; Pub W 239:42+ O 26 '92 por; Contemporary Authors vol 134 (1992)

Branson, Richard

July 18, 1950– British business executive. Address: c/o Virgin Group Ltd., 120 Campden Hill Road, London W8 7AR, England

Over the course of two decades, Richard Branson has expanded his tiny discount mail-order record operation, Virgin Records, into a loose-knit multinational, billion-dollar conglomerate of more than one hundred diverse businesses. Through a process that Branson calls organic expansion, in which Virgin grows by beginning new companies

Virgin Atlantic

Richard Branson

based on the needs and ideas spawned by the old ones instead of by acquiring existing businesses, the Virgin Group has become Britain's second-largest private company, employing more than seventy-five hundred people worldwide and comprising six independently run branches: the Virgin Retail Group, which oversees various retail operations, including Virgin Megastores, the fastest-growing record retailer in the world; Virgin Communications, with holdings in publishing, television post-production, and radio; Virgin Travel Group, which encompasses the award-winning Virgin Atlantic Airways; Virgin Interactive Entertainment, Plc., a publisher of computer entertainment products; Voyager Investments, which numbers among its many subsidiaries airship and ballooning operations and a modeling agency; and Virgin Hotels Group, which manages clubs and hotels. A seventh group, the Virgin Music Group, which was the seed of the empire, was sold to Thorn EMI in 1992.

Branson, who began his career by becoming a magazine publisher when he was a teenager, is not only Britain's most successful entrepreneur since War World II but perhaps the world's most charismatic businessperson. "I guess I chose [the name] Virgin because it reflected an inexperience in business . . . and also a freshness and slight outrageousness," he explained to Roger Cohen for a *New York Times* (February 28, 1993) profile. "I still like to think that people associate Virgin with something a bit different, something that has not been done before." With his tendency to enter into volatile industries and risky business ventures and his fondness for undertaking outrageous stunts in pursuit of free publicity (such feats have landed him in the *Guinness Book of World Records* three times), Branson has defied the staid conventions of big business. Although he was initially derided by critics as a "hippie businessman" with practically no chance for long-term success, virtually every one of his enterprises has prospered. He has managed to survive many of the pitfalls that beset other conglomerates, including a bout of expansion fever in the late 1980s and attacks from larger competitors, by holding firm to his formula for success: offering an original service at an affordable price.

One of the three children of Eve Branson, a former ballet instructor, glider pilot, and flight attendant, and Ted Branson, a lawyer, Richard Charles Nicholas Branson was born on July 18, 1950 in a suburb of London. "My parents brought me up with this philosophy," Branson has said, as quoted by Fred Goodman in *Vanity Fair* (May 1992): "'You must *do* things—you mustn't watch what other people are doing; you mustn't listen to what other people are doing.'" Taking that advice to heart, he spent much more time participating in sports than he did studying, until a knee injury limited his physical activity. "Having played sports since I was seven and never having looked at a book," he told Paul Mansfield for *Woman's Journal* (January 1985), "I realized I'd be hopeless at studying, so I quit to do something I knew I could do and which interested me." That something was *Student*, an "alternative culture" magazine that the fifteen-year-old Branson launched while he was a student at Stowe, an exclusive English boarding school. "I didn't like school, and I wanted to put the world right," he explained to Keith H. Hammonds for a *New York Times* (June 5, 1984) profile.

Branson's career as a journalist, however, was short-lived, for he soon became immersed in the role of publisher, handling the day-to-day operations of the magazine and selling advertising space. "I never had any interest in being a businessman," he told a reporter for *Business Week* (June 30, 1986). "I started out wanting to edit this magazine. But the business side became all-important, and I realized that if I didn't get all that sorted out I wouldn't be able to be an editor." With the combination of tenacity and informality that would become his trademark, Branson turned *Student* into a huge, albeit brief, success. From his makeshift office (a corner telephone booth), he sold ten thousand dollars in advertising space for the first issue; persuaded the writers Jean-Paul Sartre, Alice Walker, and John Le Carré to contribute articles; and finagled interviews from the likes of the actress Vanessa Redgrave and the novelist and essayist James Baldwin. The first issue of *Student* reportedly sold fifty thousand copies. Branson dropped out of Stowe when he was sixteen to commit himself full-time to the magazine.

When *Student* began to lose money in the late 1960s, Branson devised a plan to raise capital by selling discount records by mail. Christening the operation Virgin Records in 1970, he caught the country's retail-record industry off-guard with the success of his discount-record mail-order business, the first of its kind in Britain. *Student*, however, remained unprofitable, and in 1970, he was forced to cease publication. In the following year, when a postal strike threatened the mail-order operation, Branson responded by opening the country's first discount record store. He also purchased a recording studio. Strapped for cash to keep his growing enterprises afloat, he devised a number of innovative money-saving schemes. One illegal scheme—selling tax-exempt export records on the domestic market—landed him in jail for a night on charges of tax fraud, an experience that had a profound effect on the young entrepreneur. After his parents mortgaged their home to post his bail, Branson pleaded guilty, eventually paying some eighty-five thousand dollars in fines. "In one sense I'd recommend that everyone go through that experience," he told Echo Montgomery Garrett for an article in *Success* (November 1992). "One night in jail teaches you that sleeping well at night is the only thing that really matters. Every single decision since has been made completely by the book."

In 1973 Branson and his cousin and new business partner Simon Draper produced the first original album under the Virgin Records name, launching what would become the sixth largest record label in the world. *Tubular Bells*, a haunting instrumental album by the then-unknown artist Mike Oldfield, became one of the most popular records in Britain. It eventually sold more than 7 million copies worldwide and was used on the soundtrack of the hit movie *The Exorcist*. Branson capitalized on the unexpected success of his first album to hammer out lucrative worldwide distribution and marketing deals, earning the respect of many in the record business and attracting the attention of an apprehensive British financial community. "People thought that because we were twenty-one or twenty-two and had long hair, we were part of some grander ideal," Branson told Mick Brown for a London *Sunday Times* (June 8, 1986) profile. "But it was always 99.5 percent business."

Virgin Records experienced phenomenal growth over the next several years, as Branson earned a reputation for taking chances with unknown artists and developing raw talent. In 1977, for example, he signed the outrageous punk rock group the Sex Pistols, whose controversial BBC appearance had alarmed other record companies. The gamble paid off, for the Sex Pistols made two successful records on Virgin, firmly establishing the company's position as a hot new independent label. After a lull in the late 1970s and early 1980s, Virgin came roaring back in 1982, when Branson signed Boy George and Culture Club, a band unknown outside the London nightclub scene. The group became a major sensation on both sides of the Atlantic, selling millions of records. As Virgin Records' coffers bulged and its roster grew to include such artists as the Human League, UB40, and Phil Collins, Branson again looked to expand his empire.

In 1984 the California-based lawyer and businessman Randolph Fields contacted Branson to request financial backing for his planned airline, British Atlantic. Fields, who was having trouble persuading the British government to approve his proposed all-business-class London-to-New York route, asked Branson to finance the venture in return for a 75 percent stake in the operation. Uncomfortable with the idea of deviating from Virgin's successful strategy of expanding into related fields, Branson's advisers opposed the plan, fearing their fledgling empire could be destroyed by head-to-head competition with British Airways (BA), the most traveled international airline in the world. Branson, however, went with his instinct and agreed to the deal, reasoning that the volatile airline business was, in fact, closer in spirit to the entertainment industry than conventional wisdom allowed. "Obviously you've got to make sure you've got somebody running it who can safely get your airplane from A to B," Branson explained to Fred Goodman for *Vanity Fair*. "But once you've sorted that out, the airline business has everything to do with entertainment."

Industry observers, who criticized Branson's lack of experience in the field, and Britain's financial community, which felt he was spreading his empire too thin, predicted the quick demise of what many insiders referred to derisively as "the airline Boy George built." Branson's initial plan for the airline, renamed Virgin Atlantic Airways, was modest: to build the type of carrier that he would like to fly on and to offer an alternative to the high fares and burdensome restrictions imposed by the major airlines. Up and running in less than four months, Virgin Atlantic initially consisted of a single leased Boeing 747 flying round-trip daily between Gatwick Airport, just south of London, and Newark International Airport, in New Jersey. Branson distinguished his airline by offering perks that would be uneconomical for large carriers, including more leg room and a seat-back video screen for each passenger.

Lacking an advertising budget comparable to those of the large international carriers, Branson found himself in the unfamiliar position of serving as Virgin Atlantic's spokesperson. "Up until four or five months ago, I wouldn't do interviews," he told Paul Mansfield. "I wanted a completely private personal life. It was only when I decided to do the airline that I realized finally that we just had to go out there and sell it." To distance his airline from the often stodgy image of his larger competitors, Branson staged outrageous daredevil stunts to gain media coverage. In his first such foray, in 1985, he attempted to break the transatlantic speed record for powerboats; on schedule to surpass the record, his craft crashed and sank just 150 miles short of his goal. Undeterred, he attempted the stunt again the following year, and, on that occasion he succeeded in setting a world record.

Branson made headlines again in 1987, when he and the Swedish aeronaut Per Lindstrand became the first people to cross the Atlantic in a hot-air balloon. (It had been done in a helium balloon.) Although the thirty-four-hundred-mile voyage nearly ended in disaster when the pair overshot Ireland and crash-landed in the Irish Sea, the record-setting flight proved to be a major public relations success. In 1991 Branson and Lindstrand attempted a Pacific crossing, from Japan to California, in a record-size, 196-foot-tall balloon. Although they accomplished their goal of crossing the Pacific Ocean, they missed their destination by some eighteen hundred miles and landed instead on a frozen lake in the desolate Northwest Territories of arctic Canada, where they were stranded for six hours before rescue helicopters arrived. "It's a tremendous personal challenge and a wonderful distraction from running an empire," Branson said of his attention-getting exploits in an interview with Marc Frons for *Business Week* (June 30, 1986). "And it gives us millions of dollars of free publicity."

Encouraged by the phenomenal growth of the Virgin Group (as he had dubbed his empire), which had quadrupled in size in just four years, Branson set out in 1986 to expand his record label into the United States. To finance the venture, he decided to go public with Virgin's record-label and retail holdings. Although the sale was a success, several unforeseen events, including the October 1987 stock market crash and a lack of institutional support for Branson's brash style, took their toll on Virgin stock, prompting him to take his companies private again within two years with a vow to never again put himself at the mercy of "shortsighted" investors.

Eager to generate cash for a planned expansion of Virgin Atlantic, Branson focused on creating joint ventures and outside partnerships. Although the entire company had been valued at $440 million, within months of the stock buy-back he sold a 25 percent stake in his record label to Fujisankei Communications Group of Japan for $170 million. A year later he sold a 10 percent share in the airline to another Japanese company, Saibu Saison International, for $60 million. The deals with Japanese companies not only supplied Virgin with cash but also helped open the door to profitable Japanese markets. By 1989 Branson had created about twenty major partnerships and had sold outright several small chunks of his empire, fueling speculation that Virgin was in financial straits. Branson insisted that, on the contrary, he was restructuring his empire to shift his attention almost exclusively to the airline.

With Virgin Atlantic's original London–Newark and London–Miami routes operating at an industry-leading 80 percent capacity, Branson's first step in the planned expansion was to continue to compete on BA's most profitable routes. By 1991 he was well on his way to realizing his goal of flying to the world's twelve largest cities. The British government strengthened Virgin's competitive position by awarding the airline highly coveted spots at London's Heathrow Airport, approving new flights to New York's Kennedy Airport, and granting permission for a lucrative London–Tokyo route. By 1992 Virgin Atlantic had also gained routes to Singapore, Hong Kong, and Sydney as well as to Los Angeles and other American cities. Virgin's biggest coup came later in that same year, when the government awarded Virgin Atlantic a London–Johannesburg route, the world's most lucrative, ending British Airways' and South African Airways' long-held monopoly.

On the retail front, the enterprise that had begun in 1971 as an extension of Branson's discount record mail-order operation had matured into the Virgin Retail Group, which oversees Virgin Megastores—huge home-entertainment emporiums packed with music recordings, videotapes, and computer games. Intended to fuse shopping with entertainment, the megastores contain listening and viewing booths, condom vending machines, supervised play areas for children, and cafes, and they extend shopping hours beyond those typical of retail outlets. By 1992 there were more than thirty megastores in Britain, on the European continent, and in Australia and Japan, many of them funded by local partners. The Virgin retail operation entered the United States market in 1992, with the opening of a thirty-thousand-square-foot megastore on Hollywood's Sunset Boulevard. The Hollywood outlet is modeled after the huge Virgin Megastore on the Champs Elysées in Paris, which attracts more people each year (7 million) than the Eiffel Tower and which, with $130 million in annual sales, has the highest turnover of any record store in the world.

While the Virgin Megastores exhibited tremendous growth, in 1992 Branson's Virgin Atlantic fleet still consisted of only eight planes, compared to BA's 240. Nevertheless, Virgin Atlantic's successful blend of quality customer service and publicity-driven trendiness steadily lured hundreds of customers away from BA. With its popular Upper Class service, which features first-class perks for business-class fares, Virgin was costing BA an estimated $250 million a year in profits. For about half the price of BA's first-class service, Upper Class passengers are treated to first-class sleeper seats, on-board stand-up lounges, free neck massages and manicures, chair-arm videos, menus prepared by some of London's finest chefs, free standby transatlantic coach tickets, and, on certain routes, limousine service to and from the airport. Virgin Atlantic has been voted best airline in three consecutive years by *Executive Travel* magazine and has won numerous awards from a variety of travel publications for best business class. The astounding success of its Upper Class service has enabled Virgin Atlantic to offer competitive economy service as well. While Virgin's economy fares are about the same as those of its competitors, the amenities provided are comparable to those of other carriers' business-class accommodations.

Troubled by its dwindling market share, British Airways accused Virgin Atlantic of unfair business practices, citing its strategy of muscling in only on BA's prime routes. Branson, on the other hand, has regularly cited what he regards as BA's monopoly as an example of why small carriers have difficulty surviving. As the feud between the two airlines escalated, Branson responded with legal action. In his complaints to the European Commission and the Civil Aviation Authority, Branson contended that BA had waged an all-out "dirty-tricks campaign" to force Virgin Atlantic out of business. Among other things, he accused BA of instituting unfair pricing policies, flooding the market with discount tickets, overcharging Virgin Atlantic for maintenance services, and gaining access to its computerized booking system in a concerted effort to steal Upper Class customers. Claiming that BA had hired private detectives and a public relations firm whose task was not only to discredit Virgin but to defame him personally, Branson also filed a libel suit against the carrier.

Although BA initially dismissed Branson's allegations as a publicity stunt, the High Court ruled in his favor, awarding Virgin Atlantic nearly $1 million in damages as well as compensation for legal fees. Still not satisfied, Branson used the threat of further litigation—including an antitrust suit in the United States and action under the Data Protection Act—as leverage in his attempts to gain a formal public apology, a substantial cash settlement as compensation for commercial damage, prime take-off and landing slots at Heathrow Airport, and assurances that BA would not again engage in unfair practices. Although BA formally apologized and offered Virgin Atlantic a large sum of money to prevent further litigation, it balked at any other concessions and tried to persuade Branson to drop the subject forever. Unwilling to accept such an agreement, Branson initiated another round of lawsuits.

As the turf battle between the two airlines dragged on, Branson solidified his commitment to Virgin Atlantic in March 1992 by selling Virgin Music Group to Thorn EMI for $980 million. The sale of Virgin Records for the price that he had always contended the company was worth (analysts had maintained the price was too high) was considered a major coup for Branson. After the sale, which left him with nearly $700 million to pump into his airline, he made it clear that Virgin Atlantic intended to become a major player in international air travel. "British Airways has spent the last two years trying to push us into the abyss," Branson remarked in the interview for *Vanity Fair*. "Now it's time for them to accept that there'll be two British airlines for the next fifty years." With plans to increase his fleet to sixteen planes by the end of 1995, Branson finally had the resources to set up several new routes—including London to San Francisco, Chicago, and, eventually, Johannesburg—and the ability to compete with BA on more equal terms.

The proceeds from the sale of Virgin Records also enabled Branson to invest in other pet projects, among them a luxury Virgin train service, modeled after the airline, to compete with British Rail; a mini-airline, Vintage Air, that offers "nostalgia flights" on refurbished DC-3s between Orlando, Florida and the Florida Keys; and a partnership with Blockbuster Video that is expected to result in some fifty new Virgin Megastores in the United States alone. He has also discussed plans to create a Virgin Pacific and a Virgin Europe. "Air France deserves a run for its money at some stage, as does Lufthansa," he said, as quoted in the *Vanity Fair* article. "I think the same concept [as Virgin Atlantic] could be set up in other countries."

The sale of Virgin Music Group did not signify an abandonment of the entertainment industries by Branson. In June 1995 Virgin, which had sold its film distribution and production arm, Virgin Vision, several years earlier, reentered the film industry with the purchase of the 116-theatre MGM United Kingdom cinema chain. As is his wont, Branson moved into an old established industry with innovative new ideas. His concept for the chain is similar to the idea behind the Virgin Megastores, for Branson plans to turn the theatres into much more than just a place to watch movies by adding virtual reality arcades, CD and video shops, and restaurants such as Planet Hollywood. The purchase of the MGM chain also provides a ready-made market for the distribution of his new line of soft drinks.

Although Branson's carefully crafted image as a so-called adventure capitalist and his ability to maintain the Virgin mystique through his publicity stunts have contributed to the success of the Virgin empire, Branson has pointed to the attitude of his staff as the predominant factor. He has gone to unusual extremes to keep his employees happy, including sharing much of the proceeds from the BA settlement with Virgin Atlantic employees. "To get $400 each from British Airways is pleasant and also a great morale booster," he told Roger Cohen for the *New York Times* profile. Branson has boasted that he rarely has to fire a Virgin employee, that more than 85 percent of Virgin's new positions are filled internally, and that about twenty of Virgin's managing directors and presidents have become millionaires. "When people are put into positions slightly above what they would expect," he told Echo Montgomery Garrett for the *Success* article, "they're apt to excel."

In order to maintain a relaxed, creativity-inducing work environment, Branson keeps each of his companies small, reorganizing those that have grown unwieldy. As he explained to Garrett, "Once people start not knowing the people in the building, and it starts to become impersonal, it's time to break up a company." Branson takes pride in the personal relationships he has cultivated with his employees, who are encouraged to call him by his first name and to contact him directly whenever problems arise. He has also been known to offer moral support and financing to anyone who comes up with an original idea for a project. "We spend most of our lives working," he told Roger Cohen. "So why do so few people have a good time doing it? Virgin is the possibility of good times."

Richard Branson, who was described by Valerie Grove of the London *Sunday Times* (February 3,

1991) as a "gentle, uncomplicated soul whose boyish aura remains intact," is slim, with tousled, sand-colored hair and a beard that reveals a hint of gray. A casual dresser, he prefers sweaters, open-necked shirts, and faded blue jeans to suits and ties. Although he is almost always working, he tries to escape on weekends to his Oxfordshire country estate with his wife, Joan Templeman, and their two children, Holly and Sam. During the week, the Bransons make their home in the Holland Park section of London. In 1968 Richard Branson founded the Help Advisory Centre, which provides young people with counseling on birth control and sexually transmitted diseases. He established the Healthcare Foundation, a charity that concentrates on AIDS education, in 1987. During the Persian Gulf war, Branson donated the services of his Virgin Atlantic fleet to aid refugees, and he has lent his support to several other causes, such as Parents Against Tobacco. In the late 1980s Prime Minister Margaret Thatcher named Branson chairman of UK 2000, a partnership between the British government and private industry to clean up the country's environment by the end of the century.

Selected Biographical References: Bsns W p31+ Mr 23 '92 por; N Y Times III p8 Je 3 '84 por, IX p5 F 28 '93 por; Success p21+ N '92; Sunday Times p69 Ap 8 '84 por, p27 Je 8 '86; Vanity Fair 55:172+ My '92; Woman's J 6:32+ Ja '85 por; Brown, Nick. Richard Branson: The Inside Story (1988); International Who's Who, 1994–95; Who's Who, 1995

The Seagram Company Ltd.

Bronfman, Edgar M., Jr.

1955– Business executive; film producer. Address: c/o The Seagram Company Ltd., 1430 Peel St., Montreal, PQ Canada H3A 1S9; Joseph E. Seagram & Sons Inc., 375 Park Ave., New York, NY 10152-0002

The Seagram Company, the multibillion-dollar distilled-spirits concern, made a dramatic entrance into the entertainment and communications field in April 1995, when it agreed to purchase 80 percent of MCA, the Hollywood entertainment conglomerate, for $5.7 billion. The man behind the deal was Edgar Bronfman Jr., the grandson of Seagram's founder, and, since June 1994, its president and chief executive officer. Bronfman brought to the transaction both an insider's understanding of how the industry works, acquired from his experience as a Hollywood producer, and his business acumen, upon which he had drawn during his years working at Seagram, which he joined in 1982.

These advantages notwithstanding, some analysts were dubious about the wisdom of Bronfman's latest venture. Chief among their concerns was the fact that Bronfman chose to finance the purchase of MCA by selling Seagram's 25 percent stake in DuPont, the chemical company, which had accounted for a large percentage of the company's profits during the 1980s. For his part, Bronfman remains determined to prove the naysayers wrong, if for no other reason than his strong sense of pride in the family business. As he told Brenda Dalglish in an interview for *Maclean's* (June 13, 1994), "It is both a responsibility and a privilege to be able to continue the association between the company and the family."

Edgar Miles Bronfman Jr. was born in 1955, the second of the five children of Edgar M. Bronfman and Ann (Loeb) Bronfman. He has one sister, Holly, and three brothers, Samuel, Matthew, and Adam. Thanks to the success of the family business, he grew up in comfortable circumstances, first in Purchase, in New York State's Westchester County, then, from the age of eight, on Park Avenue in New York City, where he attended the upscale Collegiate School. He was a bright boy who performed well scholastically, notwithstanding his utter lack of interest in his studies. "From the time I was ten, I always knew, but always, that I would never go to college," he told Ken Auletta, who profiled him for the *New Yorker* (June 6, 1994). "School bored me to death." At the same time he was very mature for his age. He enjoyed the company of adults, and he held his own during discussions with his parents and their friends. "I remember having more mature conversations with Edgar than with almost any other member of the family," Bronfman's father told Auletta.

The family distilled-spirits business had been founded in Montreal in the 1920s by Bronfman's paternal grandfather, Samuel Bronfman. After Prohibition ended, the company successfully penetrated the huge market to Canada's south, and by the 1940s it had become the number-one distiller in the United States. Under the direction of Bronfman's father, who assumed full control of the company in 1971, Seagram expanded further and eventually grew into a multibillion-dollar firm. Although Edgar takes great pride in the accomplishments of his grandfather, father, and other family members who contributed to the success of the business, while growing up he had no interest in working for Seagram, preferring instead to make it on his own.

Bronfman's earliest ambition was to make a career for himself in the entertainment industry, which also held some interest for his father. In addition to running Seagram, the elder Bronfman invested in various film and theatrical projects, and from 1965 until 1967 he owned a large stake in MGM. The son soon came to share that fascination with Hollywood. When he was just fifteen, he became so excited by a screenplay he had read that he persuaded his father to finance its production. The resulting film, *Melody*, was produced by David Puttnam, who went on to become one of world's most successful film producers. Collaborating on the film was the young Bronfman himself, who managed to talk himself into a job as a production assistant. "He was very bright, incredibly tenacious and learned very fast—a very decent kid who has never been short with his opinions," Puttnam later said of him, as quoted in *Time* (May 16, 1994). "He was absolutely determined to do things on his own." The following summer Bronfman returned to England (where *Melody* had been shot) to work as a script reader for Puttnam. He eventually found one that he "fell in love with"—*The Blockhouse* (1973), a grim drama set in Poland during World War II—and he took time off from high school to complete it. Neither film was particularly successful.

After graduating from high school, Bronfman stood by his decision not to attend college and struck out on his own, apparently with intermittent financial assistance from his father. After working briefly in New York City, he moved to Hollywood, where, with the cachet of the family name, he was able to meet some of the industry's power brokers, including Barry Diller, then the head of Paramount Studios, who became a mentor to Bronfman. During his years in Hollywood, Bronfman worked mainly as a producer and was moderately successful. In the late 1970s he served as executive producer of CBS's *All Star Jazz Show*, and he won accolades for his skill in producing a musical, *Ladies of the Alamo*, which had a brief run on Broadway.

During this phase of his career, Bronfman continued to have, in his words, "no interest in getting into the Seagram business." Even if he had been interested, joining the company might have been a bit difficult since his relationship with his father had entered a rocky period. A conflict had developed between the two men when the younger Bronfman, to his father's chagrin, fell in love with Sherry Brewer, an African-American actress. "[My father] didn't want me to marry Sherry in the worst way," the son told Auletta. "I was too young to get married. He genuinely worried how difficult an interracial marriage was." The couple married in 1979, and father and son remained somewhat estranged as a result.

Bronfman's next project was to produce *The Border* (1982), which remains perhaps his most successful film. Directed by Tony Richardson and starring Jack Nicholson and Harvey Keitel, *The Border* is a socially conscious film focusing on the plight of illegal Mexican immigrants trying to enter the United States. Around the time of the film's release, Bronfman's father approached his son in a spirit of reconciliation and with a serious proposal. The elder Bronfman had long desired that one of his sons take over Seagram when he retired. He felt that Edgar was better suited for that role than his firstborn son, Samuel, despite the fact that the latter was already an executive with the firm, because he saw in Edgar many of the qualities that had enabled him to build Seagram into a thriving company. After the elder Bronfman formally proposed to Edgar Jr., that he join Seagram with a view to eventually taking the helm, the son weighed the pros and cons and accepted the offer. "There are a lot of parts to the answer," he told Auletta, in explaining what led him to join the company. "But the first part is family. There is an incredible pride in this company and in the family, in who we are and what our grandfather created, and what our father and uncle enlarged." He began working for Seagram in early 1982 as assistant to the office of the president.

After a few months, during which he got acquainted with Seagram's operations in New York, Bronfman requested a transfer to Seagram International. Edward Francis McDonnell, the division's president, was reluctant to have Bronfman join Seagram's European arm. Contrary to McDonnell's reportedly low expectations of Bronfman, the latter soon proved himself to be a great asset to the company. One of his accomplishments during his two years in Europe was Seagram's purchase of Oddbins, a retail chain of liquor stores. According to a cover story in *Business Week* (December 18, 1989), the chain soon grew into one of the most successful in England. He was also behind Seagram's acquisition of Matheus Müller, a sparkling-wine manufacturer that, as of 1989, according to the *Business Week* article, had become "the backbone of Seagram's business in West Germany."

In 1984 Bronfman returned to the United States to assume the presidency of the House of Seagram, which oversees the manufacturing, marketing, and sales end of the distilled-spirits operations of Joseph E. Seagram & Sons, Seagram's United States subsidiary. One of Bronfman's early initiatives was to revamp the marketing of wine coolers, in which

Seagram was faring poorly. In personally choosing the actor Bruce Willis, not then a household name, to star in the ad campaign, Bronfman pulled off an impressive marketing coup from which the company reaped huge profits for several years. "It was one of the great successes of all time," Bronfman's father told Ken Auletta. "We went from number five to number one. The only difference between Chivas Regal and something else is the creativity of the advertiser and the aura about it. That's what marketing is all about. And he knew how to do it." Wine coolers remained immensely popular until the late 1980s, when enthusiasm for them began to wane. Since then, analysts, and Bronfman himself, have questioned the wisdom of Seagram's having poured so much money—reportedly about $100 million—into the marketing of the beverages. "We would not have made the investment we did if we thought the category would decline the way it has," he was quoted as saying in *Business Week*.

When he joined Seagram, alcohol consumption in the United States was already in decline, mainly because of changes in the health consciousness of Americans, and Bronfman, who was acutely aware of the bottom line, realized he needed to cut costs wherever he could. To that end, he eliminated about one hundred jobs, cut loose several distributors, and got rid of four of the company's seven advertising agencies. He also focused on squeezing more profits out of the business. Concluding that Seagram's less-expensive brands, among them Wolfschmidt vodka and Calvert whiskey, had unacceptably low profit margins, he sold off a number of the low-end labels and devoted more of the company's resources to marketing its upscale products, such as Chivas Regal. This strategy eventually translated into increased profits: in 1993 Seagram posted record-high profits on its North American sales, despite the fact that the volume of sales was down.

Bronfman's decisiveness and business savvy at Seagram duly impressed his father, who in 1986 officially designated his second son as his eventual successor. In 1988 he was named executive vice-president both of the United States operations of the Seagram Company and of Joseph E. Seagram & Sons and was elected a member of Seagram's board of directors. He assumed full control of Seagram's operations in 1989, when he was named president and chief operating officer of the Seagram Company. His father retained ultimate control over the company's affairs in his role as chief executive officer.

During the late 1980s Bronfman resolved both to diversify the business beyond alcoholic beverages and to expand its existing liquor business into new markets. It was the first half of this two-pronged strategy that was behind Seagram's purchase of a small soft-drink maker, the American Natural Beverage Company, for about $15 million, which was sold at a loss in 1991 for $2 million. More successful, though it has yet to fulfill its promise, was Seagram's 1988 acquisition of Tropicana Products from Beatrice Foods for $1.2 billion. Bronfman's efforts to tap into the world liquor market include at least one decision "that wins unanimous approval" from financial analysts, according to the *Business Week* article: his decision to purchase Martell cognac for $732 million. With Martell, Bronfman had reasoned, Seagram would be well-positioned to gain a foothold in the growing liquor market in Asia, where cognac was (and remains) the drink of choice. With a view to further enhancing Seagram's global competitiveness, in 1993 Bronfman won for Seagram the right to distribute Absolut Vodka in the United States and in certain foreign markets. Both ventures, combined with Seagram's new emphasis on selling premium brands, led to increased profits. Indeed, a writer for *Business Week* (January 16, 1995) predicted that in 1995 Seagram's "liquor operating margins should top 15 percent, up from 12.6 percent in 1991."

While Bronfman's leadership of Seagram during the late 1980s and early 1990s was admirable, the company's strong performance was due not so much to improvements in Seagram's core beverage business, which was the main focus of his efforts, but to the dividends earned from Seagram's 25 percent stake in the DuPont Corporation, the giant chemical concern. Bronfman's father had invested in DuPont in 1981 in the belief that the chemical market would soon expand, a belief that proved to be correct. By late 1991 Bronfman was thinking about making the same kind of investment that his father had in DuPont—in other words, speculatively buying a stake in a company that was likely to do extremely well in the coming years. Bronfman turned to the burgeoning communications and entertainment industry, not only because he had experience, connections, and interest in the field but also because many analysts were predicting that the industry would soon undergo tremendous growth. After considering a number of possibilities, Bronfman set his sights on companies with Hollywood studios, and he ultimately decided upon Time Warner Inc.

Bronfman's strategy for gaining an interest in the media giant, which had no principal shareholder, was to buy its stock gradually, over a period of time. In February 1993 Seagram's board of directors paved the way for him to do so when it granted him permission to purchase up to 4.9 percent of Time Warner's stock. (The board settled on 4.9 percent because a higher percentage would require Seagram to publicly disclose its stake in Time Warner, and such an announcement would be certain to drive up the price per share.) Once Seagram had acquired 4.9 percent of Time Warner's stock, it became the corporation's largest shareholder. Later in 1993 Seagram's board increased the amount of Time Warner stock it would allow the company to buy to 15 percent.

When Time Warner officials learned of Seagram's activities, many of them feared that Bronfman was planning to launch a hostile takeover of the company, despite his assurances to the contrary. As a result, Time Warner went on the defense: in January 1994 it adopted a "poison pill" strategy to prevent anyone from acquiring more than 15 percent of Time Warner's stock. Time Warner's move had the desired effect—Seagram, which had acquired 14.9 percent of the company's stock by May 1994, refrained from buying any more shares—and thus successfully prevented Bronfman, whatever his ultimate intentions, from gaining a place on Time Warner's board.

Around the same time that Wall Street was abuzz with rumors of Seagram's alleged plans to wrest control of Time Warner, Bronfman's father was making plans of his own to announce his retirement from the Seagram Company. "I will tell the directors that I intend not to stand for reelection," he told Ken Auletta. "I will say this at the annual meeting. And then I will recommend—and they will do as they please—that my son be my successor." According to the elder Bronfman's wishes, at the June meeting in Montreal his son succeeded him as chief executive officer, completing the generational transition that had begun twelve years before.

By early 1995, with the Time Warner venture behind him, Bronfman had focused his attentions on another prize: MCA, the Hollywood conglomerate, whose major holdings include Universal Studios, recording and video companies, and publishing ventures. MCA had faltered under the ownership of the Japanese firm Matsushita Electric Industrial Company, which was in the market for a buyer. To raise cash for the purchase, Bronfman sold Seagram's interest in DuPont—a measure that did not sit well with investors, since DuPont had been fueling much of Seagram's growth for more than a decade. But Bronfman remained firm, and in April Seagram agreed to acquire 80 percent of MCA for about $5.7 billion. In his analysis of the purchase (which was concluded in June) for the *Financial Times* (April 8–9, 1995), Bernard Simon wrote, "MCA may be in a riskier business than DuPont. But as Mr Bronfman sees it, the explosion in North American popular culture and the innovative technologies being brought to television, music, and films make entertainment in the 1990s what oil and chemicals were in the 1940s and 1950s."

Bronfman's marriage to Sherry Brewer lasted until 1991, when they were divorced in a suit described as amicable. The marriage produced one son and two daughters. In 1994 he married Clarissa Alcock, the daughter of a Venezuelan oil company executive. According to the *Business Week* article, Bronfman has "a gentle manner not shared by many top executives. He speaks in a surprisingly hushed voice and possesses an easy, aristocratic grace." During his spare time, he writes lyrics for songs, a number of which have been recorded, among them Dionne Warwick's "Whisper in the Dark." In addition to a townhouse on Manhattan's Upper East Side, Bronfman has a weekend home in Pawling, New York.

Edgar Bronfman Jr. is a member of the board of trustees of the New York Public Library, the New York University Medical Center, and the New York City PBS affiliate WNET/Thirteen. He also is chairman of the board of governors of the Joseph H. Lauder Institute of Management and International Studies at the University of Pennsylvania. Bronfman was recently appointed to a newly created White House advisory group, the Export Council, by President Bill Clinton.

Selected Biographical References: Business W p90+ D 18 '89 por; Fortune 113:28+ Mr 17 '86 por; New Yorker 70:56+ Je 6 '94; Time 143:68+ My 16 '94 pors; Who's Who in America, 1995

AP/Wide World Photos

Burnett, Charles

1944– Filmmaker. Address: c/o Miramax Films, 375 Greenwich St., 4th Floor, New York, NY 10013

Nick Charles of the New York *Daily News* (January 5, 1995) summed up the plight of Charles Burnett when he called him "the most brilliant filmmaker you never heard of." Burnett began writing and directing movies in the early 1970s, and his works, although relatively few in number and cheaply made due to budget constraints, have won a number of prestigious awards as well as considerable critical acclaim and have been showcased in numerous festivals and retrospectives. Nonetheless, for most of the last two decades he has remained unknown to the average moviegoer. His thoughtful, nuanced film *To Sleep with Anger* (1990), the first of his works to feature professional actors, received praise from such high-profile publications as *Time* and the *New York Times* but performed poorly at the box office. Burnett may have at last found mainstream success, however, with his most recent release, *The Glass Shield* (1995), a study of police-department racism and corruption.

The thread that runs through most of Burnett's work is his evocation of the texture of African-American life. While he has devoted himself to making films that depict what is special in black culture, his characters nonetheless display the complexity of individuals rather than the predictability and one-dimensionality of racial stereotypes. "There's something unique about different peoples and what they've experienced," Burnett told David Sterritt of the *Christian Science Monitor* (October 2, 1990). "The thing is to not reduce it, not trivialize it, but show what it *is*, and show its universality."

Charles Burnett was born in 1944 in Vicksburg, Mississippi, the son of a career military man and a nurse's aide. He was three years old when his family moved to the predominantly black Watts section of Los Angeles. His parents separated when he was very young, and thereafter he and his brother were reared by their grandmother. The neighborhood in which he spent most of his formative years was made up largely of people who, like Burnett, had come from the South. While the older members of the community were models of stability, "it was the kids of [Burnett's] generation who had problems as they grew up," as the filmmaker explained to Michael Sragow for the *New York Times* (January 1, 1995). "Not all the kids, but the ones who dropped out or got into gangs." Burnett's stuttering, he has recalled, caused him to be ridiculed by such youngsters and kept him from joining in their activities. "That lack of involvement set a pattern of independence for me," he was quoted as saying by Jacqueline Trescott of the *Washington Post* (June 23, 1981).

"I was always interested in arts," Burnett told Trescott. "But my community wasn't interested in arts. You had to do something concrete, you had to make a living." As a consequence, Burnett enrolled at Los Angeles Community College with the aim of studying electronics. While he was there, however, he took a course in creative writing, which spurred his desire to become an artist of some kind. Also contributing to that desire was his discovery of the writers William Faulkner and Albert Camus and his growing love of films, among them Peter Glenville's *Becket* (1964) and Fred Zinnemann's *A Man for All Seasons* (1966). "I didn't know what to do with this passion," Burnett recalled to Michael Sragow. "I didn't know what to call it. I didn't know what cinematography was. But I thought: 'Cinematography. That's a nice word.'" In 1965 he left Los Angeles Community College to enroll at the University of California at Los Angeles (UCLA), where he earned a B.A. degree and an M.F.A. degree in film.

While he was at UCLA, Burnett won the Louis B. Mayer Award, and he used the cash prize to help finance *Killer of Sheep*, the project that served as his master's thesis. That film took five years to shoot, mainly because Burnett had reserved a role in the film for an actor-friend who was in prison and who continually failed to make parole. Burnett eventually decided to cast another actor in the part, but other problems—including personal disputes among the amateur performers and a lack of money—hindered his progress. The eighty-seven-minute, black-and-white movie was finally completed, for less than ten thousand dollars, in 1973.

Killer of Sheep is set in a poor neighborhood in South-Central Los Angeles and focuses on Stan (Henry Gayle Saunders), a slaughterhouse worker whose salary barely enables him to support his wife and two children and whose disenchantment with the tedium of his life causes him to distance himself emotionally from his family. Stan mirrors his surroundings, in that his gloomy demeanor is offset on occasion by glimpses of his tenderness and humanity. The open-ended film concentrates far less on plot than on character. In the opinion of Jacqueline Trescott, the "realism" projected by the cast members, all of whom were residents of Watts and friends of Burnett, "outweighed any lack of acting experience." Burnett explained to Trescott that his movie was in part a response to the projects of some of his fellow film students, who had attempted, without firsthand knowledge of their subject, to depict working-class life.

Killer of Sheep was not released commercially until 1978. Janet Maslin of the *New York Times* (November 14, 1978) felt that the film suffered from the absence of professional actors and that the amateur cast members delivered their lines "with either insufficient or excessive emphasis." She conceded that the movie was "beautifully photographed," but she also complained that while Burnett had "a keen eye for tiny moments," he failed to "demonstrate the kind of coherence that might give them larger meaning." In contrast, Janice Berman of *New York Newsday* (February 25, 1991) called the film "a diamond in the rough" and added, "Burnett works with the mental clarity of a documentarian, creating images that remain clear in the mind long after the film has ended." *Killer of Sheep* won the Critics' Prize at the 1981 Berlin Film Festival. In 1990, it was among the films designated "national treasures" by the National Film Registry of the Library of Congress.

Between the completion and release of *Killer of Sheep*, Burnett made a short film, *The Horse*, in the late 1970s. During that time, and for years afterward, he struggled to make ends meet and to obtain the money to shoot the films he envisioned. While applying for grants, he worked as a script-reader for a Los Angeles talent agency and as a messenger; he also wrote screenplays for friends' movies and mowed lawns. Because of the precarious state of his finances, his next film, *My Brother's Wedding*, was not released until 1983. The main character in that movie is Pierce (Everett Silas), a man in his early thirties who, while trying to figure out what to do with his life, lives with his parents and works in their Los Angeles dry-cleaning shop. Pierce's family, like Burnett's, has southern origins and old-fashioned values that include a strong work ethic. After his best friend, Soldier, is released from prison, Pierce is forced to choose between the lifestyle of his family—represented by his upwardly mobile brother and sister-in-law, who, in his opinion, have "sold out"—and Soldier's wilder ways.

Commenting on *My Brother's Wedding* some years after its release, Clifford Terry of the *Chicago Tribune* (January 11, 1991) wrote, "Burnett, who is one of the few directors to deal with the black middle and lower-middle class, has fashioned a fine, deceptively simple film." Terry went on to lament the "embarrassingly amateurish" acting of some of the nonprofessional cast, but he concluded, "Despite its rough edges, this is an impressive effort." At the time of the movie's initial distribution, a writer for *Variety* (September 21, 1983) noted: "Charles Burnett has come up with a well-observed, handsomely crafted human drama. . . . [He] has a strong feeling for his subject without having to hammer his points home. The picture has a facility for incorporating secondary characters, comic observations, and local color into the story and still maintaining the central focus."

Burnett wrote the screenplay for Billy Woodberry's *Bless Their Little Hearts* (1984), about an unemployed family man, Charlie Banks (Nate Hardman), who struggles to maintain his emotional stability and attempts to reaffirm his manhood through an extramarital affair. "*Bless Their Little Hearts* is so understated that at times it seems diffident, as if it were too shy to display its fury in more robust terms," Vincent Canby wrote in the *New York Times* (December 12, 1984). "This, however, is the style of the film that Woodberry, Burnett, and their splendid cast . . . have chosen to make, and it works beautifully."

As David Holmstrom reported in the *Christian Science Monitor* (March 8, 1993), when Burnett received a telephone call in 1988 from an inquisitive stranger, he at first thought he was talking to a representative of the Internal Revenue Service—until he discovered that he had been awarded a John D. and Catherine T. MacArthur Foundation grant in the amount of $275,000, to be paid over five years. The award, commonly referred to as the "genius" grant, is intended to free gifted individuals from financial worries, so that they can pursue projects of their own choosing. Burnett used the money to support himself while he completed his third full-length feature, *To Sleep with Anger*. The project attracted the interest of the well-known and highly regarded black actor Danny Glover, who not only accepted a leading role in the film (at less than his usual fee) but also invested in it. The movie came in at a cost of about $1.5 million, a paltry sum by Hollywood standards but much more than Burnett had spent on any of his previous projects. The filmmaker was also blessed for the first time with a cast of professional thespians that included, in addition to Glover, Mary Alice, Paul Butler, Richard Brooks, and Carl Lumbly.

The extended family at the center of *To Sleep with Anger* is headed by Gideon (Butler) and Suzie (Mary Alice), a couple who have reared their grown sons (Brooks and Lumbly) in California but whose own identities are rooted in their southern upbringing. Age-old customs are an integral part of their lives, as is revealed early in the film, when Gideon confides to Suzie that he has misplaced his "toby," or personal good-luck charm. As if conjured by that occurrence, an old acquaintance from the South, the charismatic but mysterious Harry Mention (Glover), unexpectedly appears on the scene and settles in for a long visit. Harry's arrival coincides with the onset of a variety of troubles that beset Gideon, Suzie, and their family.

"I wanted to make *To Sleep with Anger* for two reasons," Burnett told Derek Malcolm in an interview for the *Guardian* (February 14, 1991). "The first is that I think it is socially relevant—black people are being pulled in two different directions. They have their roots, but they are being asked to forget them in favor of the aspirations of a predominantly white-led society. The second is that the film allowed me to superimpose elements of an oral tradition of southern folklore that has been lost to generations on a dramatic situation that's totally contemporary and about ordinary black people. There's this terrible denial of our real culture going on. And the result of it is that young blacks know very little about it."

Vincent Canby of the *New York Times* (October 5, 1990) called *To Sleep with Anger* "a very entertaining, complex film, a comedy of unusual substance that also manages to keep the audience in suspense as to when the comedy might dissolve into some kind of vicious melodrama." He went on to pronounce the film Burnett's "most accomplished work to date." A writer for *Rolling Stone* (November 1, 1990) echoed that sentiment: "Burnett . . . has mixed past and present, poetry and realism, humor and terror, to make a unique and unforgettable film." *To Sleep with Anger* won the Special Jury Prize at the Sundance Film Festival in 1990, and it was shown in the same year to rapt audiences at both the Cannes Film Festival and the Toronto Film Festival. Like *Killer of Sheep*, it was named a national treasure by the Library of Congress.

Burnett received less acclaim for his made-for-television documentary, *America Becoming*. Financed by the Ford Foundation and written by Dai Sil Kim-Gibson and Virginia Kassel, *America Becoming* focuses on the experiences of recent immigrants from Asia, Central America, Eastern Europe, and the Middle East. Writing in the *Chicago Tribune* (December 8, 1991), Johanna Steinmetz referred to the documentary as a "curiously bland" work in which "no issues are engaged, no principals followed for longer than a few minutes." "It's rather like a video census-taking," she concluded, "a valuable document perhaps, but a film without any emotional or intellectual trajectory."

The filmmaker returned to drama with *The Glass Shield*, whose script, by Burnett, was inspired in part by a true story. The film's protagonist is J. J. Johnson (Michael Boatman), a recent police-academy graduate who is the only black deputy assigned to the Los Angeles County Sheriff's office. In his desire to fit in, J. J. turns a blind eye to, and eventually abets, the racism and corruption of his colleagues before taking a stand against such behavior. Although it is a police drama, *The Glass Shield* eschews the crowd-pleasing elements—such as shoot-outs and sex scenes—of more conventional offerings in the genre. At the same time, in tackling as explosive a subject as racism within the police department, Burnett made a conscious attempt to attract a larger audience than his films had previously enjoyed. His effort met with unqualified praise from Terrence Rafferty of the *New Yorker* (June 12, 1995): "This picture is one of the most penetrating explorations of institutional racism ever made. . . . Charles Burnett has made the most subversive American movie in years."

Perhaps inevitably, the artist with whom Burnett is most frequently compared is Spike Lee, whose movies, including *She's Gotta Have It*, *Do the Right Thing*, and *Malcolm X*, have made him the country's most prominent black filmmaker. As many observers have pointed out, however, the relaxed pace and subtle shadings of Burnett's works stand in sharp contrast to the "in-your-face," pounding style of Lee's often message-oriented films. While his movies, with the exception of *The Glass Shield*, tend not to be overtly political, Burnett himself is vocal about Hollywood's general unwillingness to deviate from racial stereotypes. "If I wanted to get immediate funding for another film," he told Derek Malcolm, "all I'd have to do is write a story about a black making an ass of himself, and I'd get four million dollars tomorrow." On the other hand, he explained to David Holmstrom of the *Christian Science Monitor*, "You've got to put it in perspective. You're not being shot at in Bosnia. You're making movies. You really can't complain."

Jacqueline Trescott described Charles Burnett as having a "small frame," a "soft, patient manner," and a "lean, serious face," and in his *New York Times* profile of the filmmaker, Michael Sragow reported that "some of [Burnett's] fiercest emotions surface with a rueful laugh or an exasperated shake of the head." In addition to the MacArthur Foundation grant, Burnett has been the recipient of grants from the Guggenheim Foundation, the Rockefeller Foundation, the National Endowment for the Arts, and the J. P. Getty Foundation. He lives in View Park, a predominantly black section of Los Angeles near Watts. He is married to Gaye Shannon-Burnett, who appeared in *My Brother's Wedding* and created the costumes for *To Sleep with Anger* and *The Glass Shield*. The couple have two sons, Jonathan and Steven.

Selected Biographical References: N Y Daily News p48 Ja 5 '95 por; N Y Times II p9+ Ja 1 '95 pors; Washington Post C p1+ Je 23 '81 por

Nancy Kaye/AP/Wide World Photos

Busch, Charles

Aug. 23, 1954– Actor; playwright. Address: c/o Theatre-in-Limbo, 123 West 3rd St., Suite C, New York, NY 10012

The actor and playwright Charles Busch may have acquired a rather conventional reputation as one of Off-Broadway's most entertaining performers, but he has done so by employing highly unconventional means: he is at his comic best when playing exceedingly offbeat female characters, complete with high heels, false eye lashes, and extravagant dresses—the flashier the better. Indeed, his more memorable roles include a two thousand-year-old lesbian vampire (in *Vampire Lesbians of Sodom*), a Norma Shearer-inspired concert pianist (in *The Lady in Question*), and a Gidget-like teenager who sometimes lapses into other personalities, including that of a tyrannical dominatrix (in *Psycho Beach Party*).

Busch's ability to cross gender lines while at the same time endearing himself to a broad spectrum of theatregoers can be attributed to the fact that, unlike other drag artists, he does not use his performances to promote a particular political view on homosexuality or to denigrate women. Instead, taking his cue from the old Hollywood movies he adores, Busch aims solely to entertain. "I'm a very old-fashioned entertainer, closer to Lucille Ball than some avant-garde, brutal satirist," Busch told Lisa Anderson in an interview for the *Chicago Tribune* (November 10, 1993). He has said that he was inspired to become a drag performer not by a desire to shock or to be different but by a need to be true to himself. By his own account, he has had a great affinity for such strong-willed female performers as Marlene Dietrich, Lauren Bacall, and Bette Davis since his childhood. "I thought maybe what's most disturbing about me is what is most unique: my theatrical sense, my androgyny, even identifying with old movie actresses," he explained to Alex Witchel, who profiled him for the *New York Times* (October 19, 1994). "The lesson I've learned is to be totally true to your origins and just go with it."

Charles Busch was born in New York City on August 23, 1954, and he grew up, with his two older sisters, Meg and Betsy, in Hartsdale, in Westchester County, New York. He was first exposed to the performing arts as a boy, when his father, a record store owner, took him to the opera, for which he had a special passion. A turning point in Busch's early life was the death of his mother, when he was seven. For the next seven years, he "sort of got lost in this world of old movies and trivia to block out the real world," as he told Lisa Anderson. "I had this completely overblown sense of the romantic," he said. "My favorite movie was *Marie Antoinette* with Norma Shearer." Busch soon came to idolize such feisty leading ladies as Bette Davis, an attraction that he later attributed to his homosexuality. Fortunately for him, his family was indulgent of his inclinations. "I mean, any child who wants to be Ida Lupino—get him to the psychiatrist quick . . . ," he told Anderson. "I was the androgynous child. What other role models did I have? You wonder why so many gay people love Bette Davis. Who else are they going to identify with? Bette Davis is battling the man's world as much as any little gay child does."

A second key event in Busch's early life was his move to New York City, where he lived with his Aunt Lillian, a former schoolteacher. In addition to encouraging the boy to pursue his artistic talents—she enrolled him at the High School of Music and Art and took him to the theatre—his aunt forced him to spend at least some of his waking hours in the real world, by requiring him to read the newspaper and helping him with his schoolwork. "Chuck was always special," the aunt recalled to Alex Witchel. "If I walked down the same street a thousand times, I never saw what he saw—the roof, the second story, the colors. But he was so shy it was almost pathological. I used to say to him, 'I can't have another Bobby Fischer [the notoriously reclusive chess player]', because that's what he would have been. He was such a lonely child. Before he moved in with me, I would pick him up in Hartsdale on a Friday afternoon, and he would be like a zombie. But the minute we crossed the river to New York, he was absolutely a new boy." His aunt's efforts paid off. After graduating from high school, Busch entered Northwestern University, in Evanston, Illinois, where he majored in drama.

Busch's experience at Northwestern turned out to be somewhat dissatisfying. Because he was considered to be, in his words, "too thin, too light, which is the euphemism for gay," he was never cast in any major theatrical roles. Yet his lack of success in mainstream productions proved to be a blessing in disguise, for it motivated him to begin to write his own material. One of his plays, *Sister Act*, caused a stir when it was mounted at the school in 1976. "My friend Ed and I played Siamese twin showgirls, Hester and Esther," Busch recalled to Lisa Anderson. "It made a big sensation at Northwestern. They'd never seen anything like it." He also found portraying female characters to be a liberating experience. "I never defined myself theatrically until I put on the lashes and heels," he told Patrick Pacheco in an interview for the *New York Times* (July 23, 1989). "It liberated within me a whole vocabulary of expression. It was less a political statement than an aesthetic one. I look kinda pretty in a dress."

Busch temporarily lost sight of that realization following his graduation from college. After moving back to New York City in 1978, he wrote and starred in a one-person show, *Alone With a Cast of Thousands*, in which he portrayed a number of characters, both male and female, but did not appear in drag. He at first had a measure of success with the show, for he and his director, Kenneth Elliott, whom he had met at Northwestern, managed to secure bookings for the show throughout the country. When he wasn't on tour, he would take whatever part-time jobs he could find, working variously as an office temp, an ice cream scooper, a receptionist, a sidewalk portrait artist, and an encyclopedia salesman. "I was afraid of getting a full-time job," he explained to Alex Witchel. "I thought it would kill my ambition."

For several years this formula worked well enough for Busch to earn a living, but in about 1984 he and Elliott had a stretch of bad luck. "For six months every theatre that was booking me either went bankrupt, burned down, or decided to hire Pat Carroll as Gertrude Stein," he recalled to Leslie Bennetts in an interview for the *New York Times* (August 13, 1987). "I found myself with no career. . . . It was pretty grim." Busch's circumstances became so bleak, in fact, that he eventually resolved to abandon his theatrical career altogether.

As a parting gesture to that phase of his life, Busch decided to put on "a little skit" for his friends, as he put it. "It was mostly cast as a party, rather than a play," he told Bennetts. That little skit, written by Busch and eventually entitled *Vampire Lesbians of Sodom*, was staged at the Limbo Lounge, a gay bar in Manhattan's East Village, with Busch appearing in drag. To his amazement, it was a hit among gay audiences, and before long he and his collaborators (who called themselves the Theatre-in-Limbo) decided to mount another, equally outrageous production, *Teodora, She-Bitch of Byzantium*, at the bar. The response was equally enthusiastic, as Busch recalled to Bennetts: "Here were these people screaming 'Diva! Diva!' I thought, 'They're even crazier than I am—they really buy it!'" Other plays written by Busch that were staged at the Limbo Lounge include *Pardon My Inquisition, or Kiss the Blood Off My Castenets* and *Times Square Angel*.

With his theatrical career revived, Busch next took on the challenge of staging *Vampire Lesbians* at a commercial venue. His chances of doing so were far from assured, for the material was anything but mainstream. One clue that it was not a run-of-the-mill production was the basic premise of the play: it concerns a two thousand-year feud between two lesbian vampires (Busch and Meghan Robinson, a frequent costar). The play also features a male vampire-hunter impersonating a female columnist and several young innocents who are preyed upon by the vampires, among others.

Many banks found the title of the play alone to be so off-putting that they were unwilling to open an account in its name. Theatres, too, considered *Vampire Lesbians* to be "wacko East Village-type entertainment only," as Ken Elliott, who directed the production, later recalled to an interviewer for *Variety* (December 9, 1987). Busch eventually succeeded in finding both a bank and a theatre; he then faced the problem of coming up with the resources to stage the show. He overcame that obstacle, too—by going "to every friend, family member, and ex-lover to raise the money," as he put it. Finally, *Vampire Lesbians*, which shared the billing with another of Busch's plays, *Sleeping Beauty, or Coma*, opened at the Provincetown Playhouse, in Manhattan's Greenwich Village, in June 1985.

Both plays, especially *Vampire Lesbians*, were enthusiastically received by theatre critics, including those at such staid publications as the *New York Times*. "'Impersonator' is too feeble a word for Mr. Busch," the *Times*'s reviewer, D. J. R. Bruckner, observed in the June 20, 1985 issue. "The female roles he creates are hilarious vamps, but also high comic characters. . . . The audience laughs at the first line and goes right on laughing at every line to the end, and even at some of the silences. That's no mean achievement." The positive notices attracted a diverse group of theatregoers that included yuppies, gays, and suburbanites, and before long *Vampire Lesbians* "gained cachet as a hip downtown novelty no more threatening than a Ken Russell musical," as Patrick Pacheco put it. In fact, the play went on to become the longest-running nonmusical in Off-Broadway history.

In addition to giving Busch (as well as his fellow male actors) the opportunity perform in drag, *Vampire Lesbians*, which was partly set in 1920s Hollywood, allowed him to spoof the movie conventions of that era. Lampooning old films, with which he was intimately familiar as a result of his childhood obsession, has since become a signature feature of his plays as well as the source of much of their humor. *Psycho Beach Party*, which opened at another Greenwich Village neighborhood theater in 1987, for instance, poked fun at the beach-party movies of the 1960s by subverting the traditional roles of male and female sexuality that those films assiduously promoted: many of the boys turn out to be gay, and many of the female characters were written with male actors in mind. Similarly, *The Lady in Question*, which opened in 1989 at the Orpheum Theatre, took aim at 1940s wartime dramas, particularly their often self-conscious glorification of the ideals of self-sacrifice and patriotism. Busch's 1991 production *Red Scare on Sunset* skewered the red-baiting that was rampant in Hollywood in the 1950s.

By the early 1990s, having established a solid reputation as New York City's best-loved drag performer, Busch began to apply his talents to other modes of entertainment. In 1993 he made his club debut at the Ballroom with his cabaret show *The Charles Busch Revue*, in which he turned his playfully satiric attentions from Hollywood to the television variety shows of the 1960s; appeared in the film *Addams Family Values*, in the role of Countess Aphasia, Gomez's cousin; made his debut in the legitimate theatre, as Solange in Jean Genet's *The Maids*; and wrote his first novel, *Whores of Lost Atlantis*.

Busch's foray into "serious" theatre was less than successful, according to Ben Brantley, who reviewed *The Maids* for the *New York Times* (September 30, 1993): "A large part of Mr. Busch's mainstream popularity as a man who portrays women can be attributed to an utter lack of polemical hostility in his comic characterizations. Placed in a drama that is fueled by hostility, and forced to squelch his urge to endear, he seems a shrunken presence, merely sly when he should be angry." Somewhat better received was Busch's first literary effort, a semiautobiographical novel about a gay playwright who, after years of struggling to make it in a straight world, wins acclaim by becoming a drag performer. Likening it to a children's tale about a group of outcasts who find meaning through committing themselves both to one another and to accomplishing a particular goal, Carolyn See, writing in the *Washington Post* (December 3, 1993), concluded that *Whores of Lost Atlantis* was "one of the most lovable, amiable, wholesome novels she had read in years."

Carolyn See was responding to an element that Busch consciously invests in much of his work—humanity. While his plays are most obviously zany and eccentric spoofs, they are also warm-hearted "morality plays," as Busch himself has described them. Even *Psycho Beach Party* "had a real resonance" for Busch; as he explained to Leslie Bennetts, he strongly identifies "with these people such as *Psycho*'s teenage surfers . . . who feel formless or vacant, who contrive a false persona but eventually find out who they really are." "Someone said the theme in all my plays was transformation and redemption," he said in his conversation with Patrick Pacheco. "That's probably true. . . . I may spoof the movies, but I don't spoof the message. I really believe in them. I think we're most affected by our earliest experiences, and mine was the opera. When I was a kid and went backstage and discovered that the glamorous diva onstage was really a fat schoolteacher, I wasn't disappointed at all. I thought it was pretty neat."

Of all of Busch's plays, the transformative element is perhaps most evident in *You Should Be So Lucky*, an "utterly winning new comedy," in the opinion of Ben Brantley of the *New York Times* (November 3, 1994), that opened in 1994 at the Off-Broadway theatre Primary Stages and went on to have a brief run on Broadway. *Lucky* is Busch's version of the Cinderella story, in which the leading character, Christopher (played by Busch), a lonely, pathologically self-conscious, and only occasionally employed gay electrologist is transformed into something of a media celebrity as a result of his friendship with Mr. Rosenberg (played by Stephen Pearlman), a wealthy Jewish businessman. Assuming the fairy godmother role, Rosenberg not only gets Christopher invited to a high-society charity ball (and picks up the tab for the rental of a tuxedo and a white Rolls-Royce limousine) but leaves the bulk of his vast fortune to him. *Lucky* "is an outlandish, corny, and magical tale of transformation that may not believe in itself but, boy, would it like to," Brantley concluded. "Like almost everything Mr. Busch has done, it's a hymn to the sanctuary of escapism. And Christopher's metamorphosis from nerdy agoraphobe to a vibrant pop-culture hero is, in a sense, a self-portrait of this particular artist."

You Should Be So Lucky was notable for another reason: it was the first play since his one-man show in which Busch did not appear in drag. "All these years, I've never thought it would be fun to play a boy," he told Lisa Anderson, in reflecting on his decision to portray Christopher. "Maybe at this late date I'm more at ease with myself and my identity." But Busch has been quick to point out that the notion that he has given up drag "is false." "I believe in drag . . . ," he told Alex Witchel. "Drag is being more, more than you can be. It's so much more fun to be big. Excess is thrilling to me. When I first started drag I wasn't this shy young man but a powerful woman. . . . Charles Ludlam [the founder of the Theater of the Ridiculous] once told me to play only female roles. And that's not a bad career, to end up at eighty years old creating an illusion on stage of a twenty-year-old beauty."

According to interviewers, Charles Busch is the antithesis of the glamorous, larger-than-life divas he is famous for portraying. "Busch is something of a shock in person," Lisa Anderson observed. "It is hard to reconcile this youthful, soft-spoken man with his tousle of chestnut hair, sweatshirt and jeans with some of his signature drag roles." The fact that he has achieved a measure of success by playing women seems to have come as a surprise to Busch himself. "It's really the idea, I guess," he told Alex Witchel, "of taking a weird hand of cards and trying to get away with winning the game." Busch lives in the Greenwich Village area of New York City.

Selected Biographical References: American Theatre p44+ D '93 pors; Chicago Tribune V p1+ N 10 '93 pors; N Y Times C p2 Je 13 '86, C p21 Ag 13 '87 por, II p5+ Jl 23 '89 por, C p1+ O 19 '94 pors; New York 22:44 Ag 7 '89; Contemporary Theatre, Film, and Television vol 6 (1989), vol 10 (1993)

Anthony Crickmay/Columbia

Bush, Kate

July 30, 1958– British rock singer; songwriter; musician; record producer; filmmaker. Address: c/o Columbia Records, 550 Madison Ave., New York, NY 10022

With her unusual voice, imaginative lyrics, and sometimes baroque musical arrangements, the British recording artist Kate Bush has for seventeen years been creating conceptually and technologically sophisticated art-rock albums. "Her songs display an antique English sensibility," according to Liam Lacey, writing in the Toronto *Globe and Mail* (November 25, 1985). "They're elaborate, mysterious affairs, like an Arthur Rackham illustration or an English country garden—filled with surprises, contrasts, and mood swings from the gnomic and foreboding to the childlike and fey." To Stephen Holden of the *New York Times* (November 1, 1989), her "high vibratoless voice and enraptured lyrics suggest a romantic English schoolgirl romping through the Jungian landscape of her own dreams."

Ever since she experienced overwhelming success with her first single, "Wuthering Heights," in the late 1970s, Bush's unique style has run counter to the prevailing norm, whether it be the primitive urges of the simultaneously emerging punk movement or the blatant self-promotion expected of a newly minted rock star. Fiercely independent, she was soon directing her own videos, producing her own albums, and virtually neglecting publicity. (She is much less well known in the United States, where she nonetheless has a devoted cult following, than in her native England.) Bush, who recently turned to filmmaking in conjunction with the release of her latest album, *The Red Shoes*, in 1993, has never ceased to develop her music, approaching it from a fresh angle each time she has entered her home recording studio. "The way I know I'm progressing is that things are a little disappointing to me each time," she told Tom Lanham in an interview for the *San Jose* (California) *Mercury News* (December 24, 1993), "and that means you're getting somewhere. And the positive thing is to let go of what you've done in the past and see everything as kind of a new adventure."

Catherine Bush was born on July 30, 1958 in Bexleyheath (one source says Welling), in the county of Kent, England, the daughter of Robert John Bush, a surgeon who played piano, and Hannah (Daly) Bush, an Irish dancer. Along with her parents and her two older brothers, Paddy and John, she often performed traditional English and Irish music at home. "From the earliest age I can remember," Bush told David Sinclair of *Rolling Stone* (February 24, 1994), "I was hearing the most beautiful tunes being made up." By the age of fourteen, Bush was composing her own material, having played piano since she was eleven; before then she had played violin. When she was a sixteen-year-old student at St. Joseph's Convent grammar school, a family friend, Ricky Hopper, introduced her to the guitarist David Gilmour, a member of the rock group Pink Floyd, who, after hearing several of her songs, arranged a recording session at London's Air studios to produce a demonstration tape. In 1974 Gilmour sent the demo tape to EMI Records and EMI Publishing, which signed Bush to her first recording and publishing contracts. A small inheritance from an aunt enabled her to begin voice training as well as studies in dance and mime, with, respectively, Lindsay Kemp and Adam Darius. To encourage her to develop her songwriting skills, in 1976 EMI gave her an advance of thirty-five hundred pounds. Around the same time, Bush performed locally with her brother Paddy and Del Palmer, her future boyfriend, bassist, and studio engineer, in the K. T. Bush Band.

Finally, in January 1978, at the age of nineteen, Kate Bush released her first single, "Wuthering Heights," whose lyrics were inspired by the novel by Emily Brontë. By March the song had reached the top of the British pop charts, where it stayed for four weeks, and in April Bush released her debut album, *The Kick Inside*, which included several of the songs that had been on the demo tape. Entering the British charts at number three, the album established Bush as a sensation in her home country, eventually selling more than one million copies there, and gained her a following in Europe, Australia, and parts of Asia as well. Another single from *The Kick Inside*, "The Man with the Child in His Eyes" (whose lyrics she had written at the age of fourteen), reached number six in Britain, although, like "Wuthering Heights" and the album in general, it did not fare as well in the United States, where it peaked at number eighty-five on the *Billboard* charts.

In December 1978 Bush followed up with *Lionheart*, which sounded to many critics like a rush job. Nevertheless, it ascended to number six in Britain, cementing her popularity there. The recipient of top newcomer, female singer, and songwriter awards from the British Phonographic Institute in 1978, Bush finished the year with a December appearance on the popular television variety show *Saturday Night Live*, her first live appearance in the United States. Fueled by EMI's ardent publicity campaign, Bush's image began to resemble that of a pin-up girl, much to the singer's dismay. "I had no control over the situation," she told Sheila Rogers of *Rolling Stone* (February 8, 1990). "It wasn't what I wanted. It was exactly not what I wanted."

In the spring of 1979, Bush launched the "Tour of Life" to promote her albums in twenty-eight cities in Britain and Europe. One of her meticulously choreographed shows, which typically lasted for nearly three hours and featured numerous costume changes, was a benefit concert at the Hammersmith Odeon, in west London, for the family of her lighting director, Billy Duffield, who had been killed in a stage accident. This concert, which included a performance by Peter Gabriel, the former lead singer of Genesis, became the source of several projects: a four-track EP, *Kate Bush on Stage* (1979), which went to number ten on the British charts; a thirty-minute television special directed by Bush for the BBC; and an hour-long video, *Live at the Hammersmith Odeon* (1981).

Despite the success of the tour—almost all of the dates were sold out—she resolved not to tour again. She had developed a fear of flying and had found herself exhausted by the rigors of traveling. "I suppose just after the tour I was at a point when I felt so exposed and so vulnerable," she explained to Terry Atkinson of the *Los Angeles Times* (January 28, 1990). "I needed to retreat and just make albums—be a songwriter again. That's how I started. I lost a lot of confidence as a performer during the tour—I get very nervous about the idea of performing live." Her fans have nevertheless remained important to her, as she told *Rolling Stone*'s David Sinclair. "It's very moving that a lot of people that I don't know are so supportive of what I do," she said. "I don't tour, I don't give them that much, really."

Bush was urged by EMI to begin making a third album almost immediately after she finished her tour. "They took me away from everything familiar and, four months later, wanted another record," she told Tom Moon of the *Philadelphia Inquirer* (January 9, 1994). "I figured out right then that music was [my] priority, not publicity. And that completely changed my life. I stopped doing all the things that were expected." Redefining her relationship with the label, she began to take hold of the reins of production herself. With Jon Kelly, Percy Edwards, and Rolf Harris, Bush produced *Never for Ever* (1980), whose first single, "Breathing," about nuclear fallout, reached number sixteen in Britain in May. Another single, "Babooshka," aided by a video directed by Keith

MacMillan, soared to number five in June. In September the album itself entered the British charts at the top, and it remained a best-seller for nearly six months. According to John Diliberto, writing in the 1993 holiday edition of *Pulse!*, *Never for Ever* demonstrated that Bush had come of age "with a song cycle that reveals a stylistic breadth and depth that few songwriters can match . . . . Multitracked and layered into choirs, her voice is now an instrument of orchestral scope."

Making extensive use of a Fairlight CMI computer-controlled digital synthesizer to imitate and alter sounds, including aboriginal rhythms, Bush produced her next collection, *The Dreaming* (1982), entirely on her own. Reviewing the album for the *New York Times* (April 17, 1983), John Rockwell wrote, "Her girlish voice is by now so augmented and clouded with filtering and overdubbing that much of the pure charm of her earlier albums is submerged. But in its place is a really fascinating textural density. If the digital process serves, at least at first, to mitigate against the multiple overdubbing that was possible with analogue recording, then perhaps *The Dreaming* will seem to future historians a final, baroque example of the possibilities of 'the recording studio as compositional tool,' as Brian Eno used to call it." Equally complex in its subject matter, *The Dreaming* featured a chameleonlike Bush singing, on various tracks, from the viewpoints of a burglar, a dope smuggler, Harry Houdini's lover, a guerrilla, and a well digger in the Australian outback. In his evaluation for *Stereo Review* (April 1983), Mark Peel commented, "In any one song you're apt to hear everything from an eerie, vaguely menacing whisper to an unnerving, animated shriek to a disembodied voice."

Although it reached number three in Britain, *The Dreaming* sold relatively few copies, and one of its singles, "There Goes a Tenner," failed to chart at all. The commercial failure of *The Dreaming* prompted EMI executives to inform Bush that she could no longer produce her own albums. Their decision motivated her to finish building her own forty-eight-track recording studio in her home south of London, a project that would consume her time and energy for the next two years. In the meantime EMI released the "mini-album" *Kate Bush*, a "best of" collection marketed only in the United States, and *The Single File*, a music video collection, both in 1983.

In 1985 Bush released the more accessible *Hounds of Love*, which immediately jumped to the number-one slot on the British charts and remained there for a month. The album's first single, "Running Up That Hill," her second-best-selling song, after "Wuthering Heights," proved to be her breakthrough hit in the United States, where it reached number thirty on the *Billboard* chart, the same position the album itself would reach by December of that year. Her first gold record in the United States, *Hounds of Love* is divided into two song cycles: the first side, also entitled "Hounds of Love," dwells upon the various negative emotions that can attend love, while the second side, "The Ninth Wave" (which Bush originally intended to use as the basis for a thirty-minute film), re-creates a drowning victim's penultimate and ultimate moments, including hallucinations and reminiscences. "All my musical motivations come from what the song is about—its subject, and the character who is singing the song . . . ," Bush told Liam Lacey. "Each song had a kind of shopping list of ideas that I wanted to be used. I'd work until every part was in place, adding more layering, and then stop." Replete with literary references, especially to Celtic mythology and the science fiction of Peter Reich, the album was recorded with Bush's trademark sophisticated technology complemented by Paddy Bush on the didgeridoo, balalaika, and fujare, among other "world music" instruments. In addition to "Running Up That Hill," *Hounds of Love* yielded "Cloudbusting" (with an accompanying video that starred Bush and the actor Donald Sutherland), "The Big Sky," "Experiment IV," and the title track, most of which made the charts in 1986.

The year 1986 also saw her duet with Peter Gabriel, "Don't Give Up," which appeared on his album *So*, reach number nine in Britain; in the United States, it eventually peaked at seventy-two. In 1987 Bush made a rare concert appearance, performing "Running Up That Hill" and "Let It Be" with David Gilmour and Peter Gabriel at the Secret Policeman's Third Ball, a benefit for Amnesty International, in London. In the same year, her greatest-hits anthology, *The Whole Story*, rose to the top of the British charts and became her best-selling album, and she was named Best British Female Artist at the sixth annual British Record Industry (BRIT) awards ceremony.

In making *The Sensual World* (1989), her debut release on Columbia Records, Bush again brought together an eclectic selection of instrumental and thematic sources. The album features Paddy Bush on some of the folk-instrumental tracks, which contain the sounds of the uilleann pipe, bouzouki, Celtic harp, mandolin, and tupan. Background vocals on three tracks were provided by Trio Bulgarka, three female folk singers from Bulgaria. "I've never worked with women on such an intense creative level, and it was strange to feel this very strong female energy in the studio . . . ," Bush informed Terry Atkinson. "It made me think of the words to 'The Sensual World.'" The title track was inspired by and loosely based upon the closing passage of James Joyce's *Ulysses*. "I came up with the idea of the word *yes*," she told Sheila Rogers, "and I suddenly thought, 'God, wouldn't it be interesting to play around with Molly Bloom's soliloquy?'" When the Joyce estate refused Bush permission to use the author's text in any way, she was compelled to either abandon or rework the concept. "I gradually rewrote it," she told Stephen Holden, "keeping the same rhythm of the words and the same sounds but turning it into its own story, which became the idea of Molly Bloom stepping out of the song into the beauty of nature." *The Sensual World* reached number two in Britain. In 1990 Bush's former label, EMI, released a boxed set, entitled *This Woman's Work*, of all her recordings to date.

Bush's most recent recording effort, *The Red Shoes* (1993), benefited from the talents of a plethora of guest musicians, including the guitarists Eric Clapton and Jeff Beck, Gary Brooker (the former Procol Harum pianist), and the singer formerly known as Prince, as well as Paddy Bush and Trio Bulgarka. The title track refers to Michael Powell's 1948 film, which was itself inspired by the Hans Christian Andersen fairy tale about a dancer driven mad after putting on a pair of red shoes that ultimately will not allow her to stop dancing. Bush also wrote, directed, and starred in the fifty-minute film *The Line, the Cross, the Curve*, which also featured Lindsay Kemp and the actress Miranda Richardson. Deriving its title from a line in the song "The Red Shoes"—"And this curve is your smile / And this cross is your heart / And this line is your path"—the film integrated six of the album's cuts into a surrealist fantasy. After being screened in selected cities in 1993, *The Line, the Cross, the Curve* was released on home video.

Secluding herself in her 350-year-old farmhouse south of London, where she enjoys gardening and entertaining friends, Kate Bush works hard to maintain her privacy. If she were unable to do so, she would "want to go completely mad," as she told Sheila Rogers, adding, "I don't see what my private life has got to do with my music. Although obviously there's a lot of me in my music. It's my music I feel I want to give to the world, and not myself." Referring to the handful of books that had been written about her as of 1990, she told Rogers, "There's not that much known about me, and what is known is so diverse . . . . It's a continual problem for me dealing with people's preconceptions of me. It's very difficult to get people to take me as I am. That's why I want my work to speak for me. Because that's what comes from my heart." Although she is appreciative of her fans' support, she has never been driven by the need to be popular. "I make music because I love making it," she explained to Terry Atkinson. "I do it for the sheer delight of watching it come together. I'm in love with the whole process. It's important to me to keep that kind of priority. If people want to hear it, that's a wonderful extra. But it's not something you should expect. You really have to do things for the love of doing them—and not for the reward afterwards."

Selected Biographical References: Los Angeles Times D p4+ Ja 28 '90 pors; Pulse! p58+ Holiday '93 pors; Rolling Stone p16 F 8 '90 pors, p13+ F 24 '94 pors; DeCurtis, Anthony and James Henke, eds. The Rolling Stone Album Guide (1992); Mack, Lorrie, ed. Encyclopedia of Rock (1987); Rees, Dafydd and Luke Crampton, eds. Rock Movers & Shakers (1991); Who's Who in America, 1995

Carroll, Jim

Aug. 1, 1951– Poet; singer; lyricist. Address: c/o Penguin USA, 375 Hudson Street, New York, NY 10014

As a poet and rock lyricist, Jim Carroll has translated New York City's rhythms and nuances into various mediums and has attracted comparison to the poetic songwriters Lou Reed and Bob Dylan as well as to the French Symbolist poet Arthur Rimbaud. Carroll's oeuvre, which includes prose and spoken-word recordings, has inspired several generations of young artists. Beginning at the age of twelve, when he and his friends spent most of their time playing basketball and wandering the streets, Carroll began chronicling his experiences in a journal that was published in 1978 as *The Basketball Diaries*. Jack Kerouac, who read some of the diary excerpts in the late 1960s, described Carroll's vigorous language as "better prose than 89 per cent of the novelists working today" were capable of producing. In 1995 *The Basketball Diaries* was made into a movie starring Leonardo DiCaprio. In his attempts to mirror New York City's harsh social conditions while revealing his own survivalist and escapist lifestyle, Carroll has suffused his "punk prose" and rock lyrics with images of death, leading Roy Trakin to postulate in the New York *Daily News* (November 23, 1980) that the poet's debut album, *Catholic Boy*, "could do for dying young what the Beach Boys did for surfing."

Tamela Glenn/Penguin Books

James Dennis ("from Dionysus," he has explained) Carroll was born on August 1, 1951 in New York City, the son of Thomas Joseph Carroll, a bartender and World War II veteran, and Agnes (Coyle) Carroll. He and his older brother, Thomas Joseph Carroll Jr., grew up in an Irish-Catholic household, first in the New York City borough of Manhattan on the East Side, then in the borough's northern section of Inwood, where Carroll's talent as a basketball player—and precocity as a writer—became apparent to his basketball coach, who arranged his admission to Trinity High School on an academic/athletic scholarship. While attending Trinity, an affluent prep school on the Upper West Side, Carroll honed his writing skills as the school newspaper's sports editor and began attending poetry readings at St. Mark's Church in the Greenwich Village area of Manhattan, where, at the age of fifteen, he first became acquainted with the works of such Beat writers as Allen Ginsberg, Frank O'Hara, and Jack Kerouac.

In 1967, at the age of sixteen, Carroll published his first book of poetry, a limited edition, seventeen-page collection entitled *Organic Trains*, which prompted the poet Ted Berrigan to declare him "the first truly new American poet" in a 1969 article for *Culture Hero*. Through Berrigan, Carroll gained entrée into the circle of poets who were involved with what had become known as the St. Mark's Project, including those he had previously known only through their work, such as Ginsberg, Anne Waldman, and John Ashbery. Meanwhile, excerpts of his prose had begun appearing in various small publications, including *Adventures in Poetry*, *Little Caesar*, and the *Ant's Forefoot*. The source of these pieces was a journal that Carroll had begun conscientiously keeping at the age of twelve and that would eventually be edited and published in toto as *The Basketball Diaries*, in 1978. Through these journals, Carroll's profound transformation from disaffected child into prematurely world-weary, heroin-addicted adolescent is traced in the uncompromising (although sometimes fictionally enhanced) detail that characterizes his mature art. Divided into broad sections, beginning with "Fall 63" and ending with "Summer 66," the journals, which quickly gained the author an underground following, would later be referred to by Steve Simels in *Stereo Review* (February 1981) as a "scary, mordantly funny odyssey along the dark underbelly of the sixties."

The first diary entry begins, "Today was my first Biddy League game and my first day in any organized basketball league. I'm enthused about life due to this exciting event." The last passage ends with the words, "I got to go in and puke. I just want to be pure." In an entry dated "Winter 64," he described his first encounter with heroin: "It was about two months back. The funny part is that I thought heroin was the NON-addictive stuff and marijuana was addictive. I only found out later what a dumb ass move it was. Funny, I can remember what vows I'd made never to touch any of that stuff when I was five or six. Now with all my friends doing it, all kinds of vows drop out from under me every day." Recalling that period of his life in an interview with Alex Williams for *New York* (April 24, 1995), Carroll mused, "I think the main reason I started using heroin was that everyone else was always going out drinking, and I hated drinking." Remarkably, Carroll was able to maintain his dual identity as street tough and standout athlete for at least a portion of high school, earning All-City status in basketball.

By 1970, when a selection of entries from what would become *The Basketball Diaries* appeared in George Plimpton's *Paris Review*, Carroll had become a celebrity in the underground New York literary scene. The excerpts earned him a Random House Young Writer's Award in 1970. After graduating from Trinity High School, Carroll briefly attended Wagner College in Staten Island "for a year, as far as the draft was concerned," he told Williams, but actually for only a few weeks. He then went to Columbia University for an even shorter period, dropping out to continue writing. He was soon hired as an assistant to New York artist Larry Rivers, for whom he stretched canvases and sharpened pencils. Occasionally, he even baby-sat the artist's children, even though he was still shooting heroin. "I was only getting off three or four times a day . . . ," he told Chet Flippo in an interview for *New York* (January 26, 1981), "just to write and to nod. At night, I'd go out and hustle, make some money." ("Nodding" refers to the dreamlike state achieved through the use of heroin.) He became further immersed in the city's art scene through Andy Warhol's Factory, a loose-knit gathering of artists, writers, and onlookers that had collected around Warhol's Union Square warehouse loft. In an article for the *Atlanta Journal* (March 13, 1981), Scott Cain indicated that Carroll even appeared in two Warhol-directed movies, though there is no other record of this.

In 1973 Carroll published *Living at the Movies*, his first full-length book of poetry, to critical acclaim. Five of the book's poems had previously been published in 1970 as *4 Ups and 1 Down*, a limited-edition (three hundred copies), eight-page pamphlet. In these poems, the writer's language began to move beyond the street slang that permeated his journal entries into a more structured, deliberate style. In the book's title poem, dedicated to Ted Berrigan, Carroll wrote: "So months of cool flowers close in these arms: / decay with their green obscenity. denial of everything / in an instant! / (how strange to be gone) (to be sure) / like Rene Magritte devouring an apple / (or two) / that's my language, divisions of words I know: / 'love:sky.'" "Carroll fully understands the nature of poetry because he perceives and follows the nature of his own life," Gerald Malanga wrote in his review of *Living at the Movies* for *Poetry* (December 1974). "He is original without being unique," Malanga continued. "His technique, however, is in advance of his maturity. At times he is capable of spoiling a good poem by a precious or very sentimental line or phrase."

A persistent myth associated with Jim Carroll is that *Living at the Movies* was nominated for a Pulitzer Prize. Chet Flippo, who recounted to Carroll that his own contact with the Pulitzer Prize committee revealed that no such nomination had been made, reported that Carroll responded that he had been informed that the book's publisher had intended to enter the book for competition. According to Flippo, nothing came of this. What was not a myth, however, was Carroll's escalating addiction to heroin. Like his artistic contemporaries Lou Reed and Iggy Pop, Carroll had allowed his life to become completely dominated by the drug. "I knew I was gonna kill myself if I stayed in New York," he told Flippo. In an interview with Bob Pfeiffer for the *Washington Post* (September 13, 1987), Carroll explained, "I was a total freak for being pulled in every different direction, wanting to take in every scene, . . . and I had to get rid of that ludicrous, vacuous obsession; I had to break away from that as much as being around drugs, because that's a drug too."

In an effort to simplify his life, Carroll left New York in 1973 for San Francisco. Shortly thereafter he made his way up the coast to the art colony of Bolinas, where a number of St. Mark's Project veterans had previously moved, and enrolled at a Marin County methadone clinic. Although he told Flippo that he had "kicked junk cold fifteen times," he found it infinitely harder to withdraw from methadone, saying that the symptoms of quitting heroin last about eight days whereas methadone withdrawal leads to a "month of physical torment, at the very least." "You can't get any sleep to escape it," he told Flippo. "I hate even thinking about it. But at any rate, I came out of it. And then I just became a recluse," he added, taking long walks and getting into a writer's routine of work and solitude. "In California," he told Bob Pfeiffer, "I learned how to be myself, and I lost completely that need to make the scene."

In Bolinas Carroll met Rosemary Klemfuss, whom he married in 1978 and who around the same time introduced him to the Bay Area nightclubs, which showcased a number of rock groups from New York City's burgeoning punk/new-wave movement, including Television, Blondie, and Talking Heads. Carroll also reconnected with the New York poet and songwriter Patti Smith, whom he had dated and who had been collaborating in poetry readings with guitarist Lenny Kaye. During a 1978 performance in San Diego as an opening act for Smith, in which her band played behind him, Carroll "talked-sang" his latest poetry/lyrics and immediately became fixed upon his career's new direction. "When I'd do readings, people would say, 'Mick Jagger reading poetry—you should do rock-'n'-roll,'" he recalled to Chet Flippo, citing Henry Miller as an additional influence on his thinking at the time. "Henry Miller's study of Rimbaud, which is really a study of Henry Miller, was the big factor for me going into rock—that was *it*. That whole thing about getting a heart quality out of work rather than just the intellectual quality."

Carroll's entry into rock music coincided with the 1980 mass-market publication of *The Basketball Diaries*, which had been released by a smaller publisher in 1978. The book's sudden availability garnered mainstream critical acclaim for Carroll and made the poet an instant favorite on college campuses throughout the country. In his evaluation for the *American Book Review* (February 1980), Jamie James wrote that the book "is a literary miracle; a description of the formation of an artistic sensibility written by the artist, not in retrospect, but in the process. . . . Despite the adolescent egoism and occasional tendency towards smart-aleckiness, the theme that reverberates through the whole, like the recurring melody of a jazz improv, is the struggle of a boy to hold on to his sense of himself." The book sold about five hundred thousand copies, in the estimation of its author, and Alex Williams asserted in his *New York* profile of Carroll that a study conducted by the publisher of *The Basketball Diaries* indicated that there were six readers of the book for each purchaser.

Later that year, after being signed to Rolling Stone Records by Mick Jagger, the Jim Carroll Band released *Catholic Boy*, produced by Earl McGrath and featuring, in addition to lyricist Carroll on vocals, Brian Linsley and Terrell Winn on guitar, Steve Linsley on bass, and Wayne Woods on drums. *Catholic Boy* yielded a nationwide college radio hit with the song "People Who Died," a nihilistic rock anthem with snarled, spoken lyrics against a chorus repeating the refrain "Those are people who died, died": "Teddy, sniffing glue, he was twelve years old. / He fell from the roof on East Two-Nine. / Cathy was eleven when she pulled the plug / On twenty-six reds and a bottle of wine. / Bobby got leukemia, fourteen years old. / He looked like sixty-five when he died. / He was a friend of mine." "People have been puttin' down the song for glorifyin' death," Carroll told Matt Damsker in an interview for the Philadelphia *Evening Bulletin* (December 17, 1980), "but it really celebrates lives. It's about people who got cut off without fulfillin' their potential." In a conversation with Barbara Graustark of *Newsweek* (September 8, 1980), Carroll clarified his intentions: "I don't want to glorify junk. Susan Sontag once told me that a junkie has a unique chance to rise up and start life over. But I want kids to know it's not hip to indulge yourself at the bottom unless you're planning on one helluva resurrection." Steve Simels called *Catholic Boy* "an extremely impressive debut album, flawed and pretentious at times, but also genuinely ambitious, gripping, and believable." Barbara Graustark remarked that although Carroll "isn't much of a singer," not since Lou Reed had "a rock singer so vividly evoked the casual brutality of New York City."

The Jim Carroll Band followed *Catholic Boy* with two more albums, *Dry Dreams* (1982) and *I Write Your Name* (1984), both of which were also produced by Earl McGrath and which featured guest appearances by Lenny Kaye of Patti Smith's band, among others. Comparing *Dry Dreams* to

Carroll's debut effort in a review for the *New York Times* (June 20, 1982), Robert Palmer wrote that the second album was an "improvement in several respects, . . . with some new songs that convey the sharpened perceptions and the sense of guilt and dread that are his principal subjects without sounding as pretentious as some of the more ambitious pieces on the earlier album." The notices that greeted *I Write Your Name* were generally more equivocal, with several writers commenting on Carroll's failure to develop a singing voice, an aspect of his music that was beginning to wear against the lyrical appeal of his albums. "The musical voice in which his rocklike poem-songs are presented is far less interesting . . . than his material demands," Bruce Pollock, an editor of *Guitar* magazine, wrote in the *Wilson Library Bulletin* (June 1984). "Though possibly necessary for the adequate performance of these works in concert, the typical rock scores provided for Carroll's lyrics lack the subtlety and power of his best material."

Resuming his literary efforts, Carroll next wrote *The Book of Nods* (1986), a collection of verse and prose poems. Some of the prose poems projected such diverse and hallucinatory imagery as an encounter with the painter Vincent Van Gogh ("With Van Gogh"), the death of a poet ("A Poet Dies"), and religious epiphany ("The Lakes of Sligo"), while other poems took on more personal themes, about his youth in New York City and his development as a writer in California. Noting in his review of the book for *Publishers Weekly* (April 4, 1986) that "Carroll would like to be poetry's renegade stepchild, an avant-gardist," John Mutter concluded, "This is a bad example of serious talent destroyed over the years by negligence and disregard for self-discipline." On a more positive note, Daniel L. Guillory wrote in his review for *Library Journal* (April 15, 1986) that "*The Book of Nods* is always interesting if sometimes uneven."

The next year saw, in addition to a reissue of *The Basketball Diaries*, the publication of a new batch of journals by Carroll entitled *Forced Entries: The Downtown Diaries: 1971–1973*, in which he chronicled his involvement with the Warhol Factory, his encounters with such Greenwich Village art community luminaries as Bob Dylan, Allen Ginsberg, W. H. Auden, and Terry Southern, his move to California, and his victory over heroin. "Carroll's peculiar aura of choirboy innocence transforms even the most decadent happenings into a good-natured romp," John Mutter wrote in *Publishers Weekly* (June 5, 1987), concluding that "his somewhat contrived verse works here to utterly charming effect." In his evaluation of both books for the *New York Times* (July 9, 1987), Christopher Lehmann-Haupt observed that "whether or not one believes Jim Carroll's redemption, his two diaries constitute a remarkable account of New York City's lower depths. At the very least, they should serve further to demystify the usefulness of drugs to writers."

In the late 1980s Carroll focused primarily upon writing and what had become known as the "spoken word" movement, which refers to the stylized, emotive recitation of one's writing. A contributor to a variety of spoken-word projects, Carroll has also worked in video and film. His work has been included on the extensive Giorno Poetry Systems albums (apparently named for the poet John Giorno), which combine spoken word, straight reading, and music. The series began in 1972 with the double album *The Dial-a-Poem Poets* and culminated in 1984 with *Better an Old Demon than a New God*. The Jim Carroll Band contributed music to the soundtrack of Fritz Kiersch's *Tuff Turf* (1985), in which the poet made a brief appearance as himself. Carroll also appeared in Ron Mann's 1984 movie *Listen to the City*. He has read from his work in the 1983 Giorno Poetry Systems video *Poetry in Motion*, which also contains performances and commentary by Charles Bukowski, Amiri Baraka, and Ntozake Shange, among others. MTV's *Cutting Edge* spoken-word video series also featured readings by Carroll.

More recently, Carroll released the album *Praying Mantis* (1992), his first solo full-length spoken-word effort, which contains selections from his diaries and poetry volumes as well as some unpublished poems. *Fear of Dreaming* (1993), the selected poems of Jim Carroll, comprises the complete *Living at the Movies* volume, much of *The Book of Nods*, and poems from the *Praying Mantis* album. *A World without Gravity: The Best of the Jim Carroll Band* was released in 1993 by Rhino Records. New interest in Carroll was sparked by Scott Calvert's cinematic adaptation of *The Basketball Diaries*, which premiered at the Sundance Festival in January 1995. Commenting on the movie, which starred Leonardo DiCaprio as the youthful Jim Carroll, the poet revealed only that "it moves well," telling Williams, "It's hard for me to really register on it because of the personal attachment."

Looking much the same as he did in his youth, according to interviewers, the six-foot two-inch former basketball star has thin red hair almost as pale as his smooth complexion. Some observers have compared his androgynous appearance to that of David Bowie. Amicably divorced from Rosemary Klemfuss, who remains his friend and lawyer, Jim Carroll has lived in the Inwood section of New York City for the past decade. He still performs with Lenny Kaye and delivers readings and spoken-word performances on college campuses. In the summers he teaches at Allen Ginsberg's Naropa Institute. He is currently working on two novels, one about the spiritual crisis of a young painter who abandons art and the other about a Vatican investigation of a miracle. "These are straight, linear novels in the third person," Carroll explained to Williams. "My editor was shocked. He was like, 'Jim! These are money books.' But if I don't get to work on these things, boy, I am betraying a gift; I mean, that's what *I* would define as a sin." Rising daily at 4:30 A.M. to write, he has kicked a television habit along with his addiction to drugs, although he told Williams that he doesn't "go for that complete abstinence thing" and that he indulges in an occasional margarita.

Selected Biographical References: Bulletin of Bibliography 47:81+ Je '90; Newsweek 96:80 S 8 '80 por; New York 14:32+ Ja 26 '81 pors, 28:64+ Ap 24 '95 pors; Washington Post G p1+ S 13 '87 pors; Contemporary Authors new rev vol 42 (1994); Contemporary Literary Criticism vol 35 (1985)

Agence France-Presse

Cédras, Raoul

(SEH-drahs, rah-OOL)

1950(?)- Haitian political leader; military officer. Address: Continental Riande Hotel, Panama City, Panama

In 1991 General Raoul Cédras became the most recent of a string of military leaders to launch a coup against the government in Haiti, which has the dubious distinction of being the poorest nation in the Western Hemisphere. What sets Cédras apart from his predecessors, however, is the fact that he toppled the government of Haiti's only popularly elected president, Jean-Bertrand Aristide, a former Roman Catholic priest and longtime advocate of the country's poverty-stricken masses. Following the coup Cédras, who served as Aristide's chief of security during the 1990 election that brought the latter to power, justified his act by arguing that Haiti was not ready to embrace democracy. "We need some *order* in this country first, so that people can work and feed themselves," he said. "Then we can put together some institutions working toward democracy."

Although Cédras might have been tolerated by the international community in an earlier era, with the demise of Communism he was viewed as an anachronism. During the Cold War, as Gaddis Smith observed in *Current History* (February 1995), "Cédras would have been embraced as precisely the sort of forceful leader needed to suppress international Communism and cooperate with the United States: a sensible no-nonsense fellow with good posture, a clear eye, and friends in the United States military. But in 1991 he was unacceptable." When sustained pressure from the United Nations and the Organization of American States, both of which imposed economic sanctions on Haiti, failed to persuade the general to relinquish power, the United States government issued orders to invade the country in September 1994. Just hours before American troops were due to enter the country, a delegation led by former president Jimmy Carter was holding talks with Cédras to persuade him to step down. At the eleventh hour Cédras agreed to do so, and in October he and his family went into exile in Panama. Aristide was restored to power on October 15, two days after Cédras left Haiti.

Little information exists in published sources in the United States about the origin of Raoul Cédras. He was born in about 1950, and according to the Haitian scholar Michel Laguerre, Cédras's father was black and his mother was either Syrian or Lebanese. Laguerre, who met Cédras in 1988 while working on his book *The Military and Society in Haiti* (1993), told *Current Biography* that at some point during the reign of François "Papa Doc" Duvalier, which began in 1957, Cédras's father served as the prefect of Jérémie, a seaport town on the Tiburon Peninsula, and that for a time he worked under Duvalier's son, Jean-Claude "Baby Doc" Duvalier, who was elected "president for life" following his father's death in 1971. As a form of compensation to Cédras's father, a place was made available for Raoul in the Haitian military academy, which he entered in the early 1970s. According to unidentified political opponents of Raoul Cédras's who were interviewed for *Time* (November 8, 1993), Cédras may at some time have undergone training with the United States Army at Fort Benning, Georgia. It has also been rumored that he developed ties with the Central Intelligence Agency.

Many of Haiti's economic and social troubles can be attributed to the rapacious dictatorships of François and Jean-Claude Duvalier. After the latter was driven from power in 1986, the country was ruled by a series of short-lived governments that did little to improve the living conditions of the country's poor. Aristide's victory in 1990, in Haiti's first democratic presidential election, was therefore greeted with tremendous hope not only by the vast majority of Haitians but by the international community as well. Notwithstanding his family's ties to the Duvalier dictatorships, during the 1990 campaign Brigadier General Cédras served as Aristide's chief of security, according to Ambrose Evans-Pritchard, writing in the *National Review*

(November 29, 1993). He performed his duties admirably, and following Aristide's election to the presidency, he became known as "Aristide's man," as Evans-Pritchard put it. After taking office, in February 1991, Aristide undertook a housecleaning of the military and named Cédras commander of Haiti's small, seven thousand-man army. In his book *Haiti's Bad Press* (1992), Robert Lawless reported that Cédras "was—ironically—regarded as a professional, nonpolitical officer of the type that would be needed to put down the inevitable coups against Aristide."

Early on in his term as president, Aristide began to take steps to reform Haiti's economy—steps that were welcomed by the Haitian masses but that were strenuously opposed by the tiny group of wealthy Haitians that had prospered during the Duvalier dynasty. Among other measures, Aristide planned to raise the minimum wage from about four dollars to seven dollars a day, redistribute land, freeze prices on basic goods, and mount an anticorruption drive. The Haitian elite feared that such reforms would erode the standard of living they had previously enjoyed. Early in his term, Aristide alienated members of the military, including Raoul Cédras, by ousting from the army some of its top officers. He also earned their distrust by inviting a group of Swiss police specialists to Haiti to help him train a police force that would be independent of the army. Like many other Haitians with positions of power to protect, Cédras became convinced that Aristide was intent on creating a dictatorship of the masses, whose hatred of the military was well known.

Tensions within the military officer corps, which mounted throughout the summer of 1991, were only exacerbated by Aristide's address to the United Nations on September 23, in which he called on the wealthy to share their riches with the poor. Upon his return to Haiti, Aristide learned that members of the military were planning to overthrow his government. Apparently in response to this news, he organized a rally at which he gave a speech in which he appeared to condone the practice of necklacing, which is a means of execution in which the victim is "necklaced" by a burning tire. Fearing that Aristide's supporters would be incited to violence, on September 30, 1991 soldiers launched what turned out to be a successful overthrow of his government. The coup, which had the support of a number of business and political leaders, was accompanied by a bout of bloodletting, with soldiers firing on citizens who attempted to assemble. Cédras served as the head of the army while the coup took shape.

In *The Uses of Haiti* (1994), Paul Farmer reported that after Aristide was arrested, he was handcuffed and taken to see Cédras, who said, "I'm the president now." In Cédras's recollection of that encounter, he asked Aristide to deliver a national radio address urging his countrymen to refrain from violence. Aristide refused, according to Cédras, on the grounds that the people would do what they felt they had to do. Concluding that he had little choice, Cédras ordered the military to take to the streets to restore law and order. He also, in his words, "made the decision that the safest way to save Aristide's life was to get him out of the country," and following several rounds of negotiations the deposed president was flown to Caracas, Venezuela, where he stayed briefly before going to the United States. On October 8, 1991 a committee of the parliament named a member of the supreme court, Joseph Nerette, as Haiti's new, provisional president. For his part, Cédras, as the leading figure in the military junta that masterminded the coup, emerged as the country's de facto leader.

International reaction to the overthrow of Aristide and Cédras's accession to power was swift. The Organization of American States immediately called for Aristide's return to office, sent a delegation to Haiti to open negotiations to that end, and placed on Haiti a hemispheric trade embargo. The United States also condemned the takeover, with Secretary of State James Baker calling the ruling junta "illegitimate" and President George Bush suspending foreign aid payments to Haiti and freezing Haitian assets held in American banks. In time, however, the Bush administration grew less enthusiastic about Aristide, and it soon backpedaled from its initial show of support, citing concerns about Aristide's human rights record and doubts about his ability to develop a harmonious working relationship with the military.

During an interview with Howard W. French of the *New York Times* (November 4, 1991), Cédras discussed his reasons for supporting the coup. Chief among them was his claim that in overthrowing Haiti's first popularly elected president he was in fact preserving the country's democratic institutions. Unnamed diplomats interviewed by French had difficulty accepting Cédras's explanation and expressed their doubts about his legitimacy as well as his intentions. "However impressive the edifice they are building, it resembles nothing so much as post facto excuse making," one diplomat told French.

Another of Cédras's justifications for the coup was somewhat more plausible. He contended that Aristide had violated the constitution by attempting to purge the military of certain individuals. As evidence, he presented French with what he said were blank, signed warrants that were used for politically motivated arrests. Cédras repeated these charges later during an interview with Bella Stumbo for *Vanity Fair* (February 1994): "Aristide's actions were unconstitutional and incorrect. . . . Although Aristide came to power by elections, he thought he came to power by revolution. By purging the military, he was violating the constitution from his first day in office." During his interview with French, Cédras also denied, despite evidence to the contrary, charges made by human rights groups that the military had rampantly murdered up to three hundred citizens in the course of the coup as a means of stifling dissent and showing power. And, although radio stations had been destroyed, Cédras denied any repression of the press.

In the weeks that followed the coup, Aristide undertook diplomatic maneuvers to orchestrate his return to power while Cédras consolidated his position as Haiti's de facto head of state. Although his government was not recognized as legitimate by any foreign power, the fact that Aristide had come to be regarded as a flawed leader somewhat enhanced its standing. Cédras's reputation was certainly not damaged by a July 1992 memo prepared by Brian Latell, a United States intelligence officer for Latin America, and submitted to the CIA. In his report, Latell characterized Cédras as a more reliable ally than Aristide, whom he regarded as potentially dangerous. "General Cédras impressed me as a conscientious military leader who genuinely wishes to minimize his role in politics, professionalize the armed services, and develop a separate and competent civilian police force," Latell wrote. "I believe he is relatively moderate and uncorrupt. . . . He compares especially favorably to nearly all past and most present senior military commanders." The contents of Latell's memo, which had been classified, was the subject of a December 19, 1993 article in the *Washington Post*.

During 1992 the Cédras regime remained determined to hold onto the reins of government. "We are on the right path," General Cédras maintained in May 1992, despite the fact that the nation had descended to new depths of violence, lawlessness, and economic disarray. While Cédras acknowledged that thousands of Haitians were attempting to leave the country by boat, he insisted that they were doing so as a result of the rapidly deteriorating economic conditions that were precipitated by the OAS trade embargo. "They [the OAS] say they want to save our country, but they have proceeded by destroying it," Cédras was quoted as saying in the *New York Times* (May 31, 1992). "A people has the sense of its own well-being. You cannot teach us what is good for us. Before imposing sanctions, why didn't they make an effort to understand the situation here?"

In January 1993 the Cédras regime held legislative elections, but they were seen by the international community as a ploy to pack the Haitian parliament with Aristide opponents. Cédras's government came under increased economic pressure in June, when the United Nations imposed stringent economic sanctions on Haiti. As it turned out, the sanctions had the desired effect. In July Cédras entered into talks with Aristide (although apparently the two men did not actually speak face to face) on Governors Island in New York City. After several days of negotiations, on July 3 they signed an agreement that would allow the deposed president to return to power in October 1993, by which time Cédras would have already stepped down. According to the terms of the agreement, in September Aristide swore in Robert Malval, a Haitian businessman, as the country's new prime minister, and the UN suspended (but did not formally lift) economic sanctions against Haiti.

To the consternation of many of the parties involved, General Cédras failed to surrender his post in October 1993, as stipulated by the so-called Governors Island agreement. After the deadline passed without Aristide's return to Haiti, the UN voted to put in place a naval blockade, to prevent oil and arms from entering the country. In addition, President Bill Clinton froze the American bank accounts and assets of General Cédras and others in his government. In the months that followed, Cédras emerged as the head of a troika that included Lt. Colonel Joseph Michel François, who headed the police, and Philippe Biamby, who served as the army chief of staff. An effort led by Prime Minister Malval to organize a conference of reconciliation broke down in December 1993, when Aristide came out against it and Haitian political leaders appeared to be uninterested in taking part.

Although Cédras sometimes appeared to realize that he could not retain power indefinitely, he at other times took steps suggesting that he had no intention of stepping down. For instance, when he appeared on NBC's *Meet the Press* in early May 1994, he spoke of his readiness to enter into negotiations, but he would not say whether he planned to leave Haiti if Aristide were to return, as he had once promised. Toward the end of that month, after the UN imposed stricter sanctions on his regime in an attempt to force him to turn over the government to Aristide, Cédras not only refused to do so but organized a new civilian government and named a provisional president, Emile Jonassaint. Yet in late June a high-ranking Haitian military officer, who spoke with a reporter for the *New York Times* (June 29, 1994) on the condition of anonymity, said that Cédras planned to step aside in October, when his term officially was to end.

The Cédras regime continued to send seemingly contradictory signals throughout the summer of 1994. In mid-July, in a move that was interpreted by the United States as a defiance of "the will of the international community," the military-backed government ordered the expulsion of a UN-OAS human rights team that had operated in Haiti since 1992. Not long after that, Cédras agreed to meet with a delegation from the United States. One of the members of the delegation, Bill Richardson, a liberal Democratic congressman from New Mexico, came away from his five-hour meeting with Cédras on July 18 with the impression that the military leader was "not as intransigent as everyone pictures him to be." But in mid-August Cédras was making public appearances throughout Haiti, leading some observers to speculate that he was planning to run for president in the upcoming elections. "Each day there is a new sign of the military's intention to stay," a supporter of Aristide was quoted as saying in the *New York Times* (August 18, 1994), in a reference to Cédras's public-relations campaign.

Meanwhile, the effects of the sanctions were clearly bringing pressure to bear on Cédras. Large numbers of factories had shut down, inflation was on the rise, and unemployment, always high in Haiti, had reached 80 percent. Added pressure came in August 1994, when United States government officials began to publicly discuss plans to invade Haiti to restore President Aristide to office. Cédras reportedly remained unmoved by the prospect of an American invasion. According to the president of the Haitian Senate, Bernard Sansaricq, Cédras was "very well aware than an invasion can happen. But if the United States thinks [he] is scared of them, they are making a big mistake."

On September 17, 1994 former president Jimmy Carter arrived in Haiti as the head of a delegation that included General Colin Powell, the former chairman of the Joint Chiefs of Staff, and Senator Sam Nunn of Georgia. Their mission was to come up with an arrangement that would enable Cédras to cede power without losing face—and thus render unnecessary the planned American invasion. On September 18, 1994, only hours after the Pentagon issued orders to launch the invasion and not long before American aircraft were scheduled to enter Haitian airspace, the delegation achieved its goal, by convincing Cédras that it was both an honor and a duty to resign.

After agreeing to leave office by October 15, 1994, General Cédras spent his remaining days in power negotiating the terms of his exile. The accord negotiated by Carter did not require Cédras to leave Haiti, but Cédras concluded it was in his and his family's best interest to do so, given that an amnesty bill passed by the parliament did not exclude the military from prosecution. He had not won the hearts and minds of the Haitian population, and in a ceremony during which he formally resigned his post, he was jeered by thousands of pro-Aristide demonstrators. "I will not be with you," he told a small coterie of his officers, as quoted by the *New York Times* (October 11, 1994). "I choose to leave our country for your protection, so that my presence will not be a motive for actions against the military establishment or a pretext for unjustified actions."

On October 13, 1994 Raoul Cédras, his wife, Yannick, and his two sons and one daughter arrived in Panama, whose government granted them asylum. The family moved into the Riande Continental Hotel in Panama City, where they occupied a two-bedroom suite. According to the terms of the exile agreement, the rent was to be paid by the United States for one year. At the same time, Cédras's financial assets in the United States were unfrozen. Soon after his arrival he reportedly acquired a personal computer and began writing his memoirs. During his leisure time he is said to enjoy skin diving.

Selected Biographical References: Nat R 45:24+ N 29 '93 por; Time 142:44+ N 8 '93 por; Vanity Fair 57:72+ F '94; Laguerre, Michel. The Military and Society in Haiti (1993)

Chihuly, Dale

(chi-HOO-lee)

Sept. 20, 1941- Artist. Address: c/o Chihuly Studio, 509 N.E. Northlake Way, Seattle, WA 98105

Jim Ball

"I call myself an artist for lack of a better word," Dale Chihuly, whose medium is glass, told an interviewer in 1995. "I'm an artist, a designer, a craftsman, interior designer, half-architect. There's no one name that fits me very well." The difficulty of categorizing him notwithstanding, Chihuly is universally labeled a glass artist, and in the domain of contemporary glass art, he is probably unsurpassed in his artistic and technical inventiveness and boldness, professional success, and influence. "An unquestioned genius," as Robert T. Buck, the director of the Brooklyn Museum, in New York City, has called him, he has become the most celebrated glassmaker in the United States since the turn of the century, when Louis Comfort Tiffany made stained glass a prominent feature of American interior design. Thanks in large measure to Chihuly, hand glassmaking, long considered a craft or decorative art, has gained recognition as a fine art, and the market for blown-glass objects, which was virtually nonexistent as recently as the mid-1970s, is thriving. Since 1976, when the Metropolitan Museum of Art, in New York City, purchased three of Chihuly's pieces, more than a hundred museums worldwide have acquired works by him for their permanent collections, and many major corporations and institutions have installed his creations in their public spaces. His work has been exhibited at dozens of museums and galleries, including the Louvre, in Paris, which honored him with one of its rare solo shows in 1986.

Trained in interior design and fine art at American universities, Chihuly was introduced to centuries-old techniques of team glassmaking when, in 1968–69, he served as an apprentice in Italy. Since the late 1970s, when the loss of his sight in one eye and a subsequent injury to a shoulder forced him to abandon glassblowing, he has led his own teams of artisans and thereby produced a body of work remarkable for both its size and its diversity. His collaborative approach revolutionized contemporary American glassmaking and is considered one of his most significant contributions to his field. With the imagination and intuition of a master choreographer, he has drawn on his teammates' talents and ideas to transform his artistic concepts into brilliantly colored, uniquely shaped creations that "dazzle the eye and tantalize the mind" and that, while firmly grounded in tradition, "push the edges of art glass beyond anything made anywhere in the world," as Marilynne S. Mason observed in the *Christian Science Monitor* (July 15, 1993). Chihuly, who taught at the Rhode Island School of Design for a dozen years, cofounded the Pilchuck Glass School, near Seattle, which in a quarter of a century has become what Jon Krakauer, writing in *Smithsonian* (February 1992), described as "the hub of the vast and continually expanding art-glass universe."

The grandson of immigrants from Czechoslovakia and Sweden, Dale Patrick Chihuly was born on September 20, 1941 in Tacoma, Washington. He was the second of the two children of George Chihuly, a meatcutter and union organizer, and Viola Chihuly, a homemaker, who worked as a barmaid after being widowed. In a profile of the artist for *ARTnews* (April 1993), Margaret Moorman described his mother as "industrious, encouraging, [and] progressive in her child-rearing" and as "perhaps the most important force" in his life in adulthood as well as childhood. Raised in a working-class neighborhood of Tacoma, as a teenager Chihuly fell in with a group of juvenile delinquents, but he refrained from participating in his friends' more egregious acts of lawlessness. After his brother was killed in a navy flight-training accident in 1956, and his father died of a heart attack a year later, his interest in school evaporated. Nevertheless, in 1959, following his graduation from high school, he enrolled at the University of Puget Sound, in Tacoma. "I only went to college because my mother told me I should," he admitted to Margaret Moorman.

In 1960 Chihuly transferred to the University of Washington, in Seattle, where, at least partly because he had enjoyed the process of decorating a basement rec room for his mother, he majored in interior design. He has attributed to his undergraduate education, which included courses in architecture, his habit of visualizing his glass creations "as part of a space," in his words. As a freshman and sophomore, he devoted much of his time to the activities of his fraternity. He took a leave from college in 1962–63 to travel about Europe and to work on a kibbutz in Israel. During his year abroad he befriended several people whom he has described as "older father figures," who he has said helped him to mature emotionally and from whom he learned some of the finer points of middle- and upper-class social behavior.

Chihuly returned to school determined to "do it right," as he recalled to Margaret Moorman, and he became, in his words, "a great student, kind of a workaholic." While studying weaving under Doris Brockway, he created tapestries in which he incorporated strands of copper wire that he had fused with melted strips of glass. His tapestries earned him the Seattle Weavers Guild Award in 1964. That summer, while traveling by train across Canada on the first leg of a trip to Ireland and the Soviet Union, he filled an album with thousands of painted color samples that he mixed from a complete set of Winsor & Newton watercolors. In 1965 he received highest honors from the American Institute (now Society) of Interior Designers and earned a B.A. degree in interior design.

After his college graduation Chihuly got a job as a designer with a major Seattle architectural concern, where he soon discovered that playing a small supporting role in large corporate undertakings did not suit him. By that time, moreover, he had become, as he has put it, "obsessed with glass." He has traced his fixation to an incident that had occurred one night a year or two earlier (and before he had ever seen anyone blow glass), when, while casually experimenting with glass in his basement apartment-cum-studio, he melted a few pounds of it in a makeshift kiln and then dipped into the hot liquid a pipe that he had found in the basement. When he blew into the pipe, a bubble formed. "It was kind of a miracle, because you have to get it at exactly the right moment," he told Margaret Moorman. "But it happened! Then I was hooked completely."

In 1966, after leaving the architectural firm, Chihuly worked for six months on a commercial fishing troller in Alaska. Then, with his savings from that job and a substantial scholarship, he entered the graduate program in glassblowing at the University of Wisconsin in Madison. He studied under Harvey K. Littleton, who is considered the founder of the contemporary studio-glass movement in the United States, having demonstrated in the early 1960s that glassmaking did not require large factorylike settings but, with the use of a new kind of furnace, could be blown by independent artists in small studios. After earning an M.S. degree in 1968, Chihuly enrolled in another master's degree program, at the Rhode Island School of Design (RISD), in Providence, where he began teaching undergraduates. He also began creating large environmental sculptures (so-called because each piece formed a mini-environment in space that potentially could literally surround the viewer). He received an M.F.A. degree in 1968. That summer and during the next three summers, he taught at the Haystack Mountain School of Crafts, in Maine.

Chihuly's first solo exhibition was mounted at the University of Wisconsin's Madison Art Center in 1968. Later that year, eager to expand his knowledge of glassblowing techniques and armed with both a Louis Comfort Tiffany Foundation grant and the first Fulbright fellowship to be awarded for glass studies, Chihuly went to Murano, an island near Venice that has been the center of the Venetian glass industry since the thirteenth century, to serve a year-long apprenticeship at the famed Venini glass factory. At Venini, which had never before allowed an American artisan to study its operations, Chihuly joined master craftsmen who worked as a precisely coordinated team.

Back in the United States in 1969, Chihuly established a glass department at RISD. (He subsequently helped to set up a glass program at the Snowbird Art School, a division of the University of Utah, and to build a glass studio at the Institute of American Indian Art, in Santa Fe, New Mexico.) One of his glass sculptures was included in the 1969 exhibition "Objects U.S.A.," which was organized for the Smithsonian Institution's National Collection of Fine Arts and traveled to museums in the United States and Europe. In 1970 Chihuly formed what was to become a four-year collaboration with the sculptor James Carpenter, who was then an RISD student. Their uncommon talents and imaginativeness were recognized immediately: in 1971 the American Craft Museum (then known as the Museum of Contemporary Crafts), in New York City, displayed their work in a solo show. For "20,000 Pounds of Neon and Ice," which premiered at RISD in 1971 and which is perhaps the best-known product of their collaboration, Chihuly and Carpenter embedded U-shaped, neon-filled glass tubing in huge blocks of ice, the slow melting of which was an intrinsic aspect of the work. The sculpture was later fabricated for Chihuly's enormously successful 1992 retrospective exhibition at the Seattle Art Museum. In 1993, working with his long-time studio assistant Charles Parriott and using five times as much ice and neon tubing as before, Chihuly recreated it indoors for the first time, on the ice floor of the Tacoma Dome.

In 1971, with two thousand dollars in startup money from the Union of Independent Colleges of Art, Chihuly cofounded, along with the art patrons John H. Hauberg and Anne Gould Hauberg, the Pilchuck Glass School. The Haubergs donated the land—sixty-four acres in the middle of a tree farm—for the school and also obtained additional funding. Currently, thirty faculty members, among them world-famous glass artists and people of note in other fields of art as well, ten gaffers (master glassblowers), fifty teaching assistants, and 250 students participate in Pilchuck's annual summer workshops. A dozen artists in residence work at the school year-round. "The impact of Pilchuck on the studio-glass movement, not just in the U.S. but around the world, is immeasurable, and Dale's contribution to that success is almost beyond description," the glass artist Benjamin Moore, who has served Chihuly as a gaffer for many years, told Margaret Moorman. "He has personally pushed glassblowing farther than anyone ever imagined it could be pushed, and his whole impulse is to share his knowledge with anyone and everyone he can bring together." Although Chihuly resigned his position as Pilchuck's artistic director several years ago, he remains an active member of the faculty. He also regularly gives talks and demonstrations at junior high schools, high schools, and colleges in the Seattle area and elsewhere.

In the mid-1970s, with the help of the first of the three National Endowment for the Arts grants that he received during that period, Chihuly produced a group of glass objects that he named the *Navajo Blanket Cylinders*. The cylinders were shown in 1975 in solo exhibits at the Utah Museum of Fine Arts, in Salt Lake City, and the Institute of American Indian Art. The next year Chihuly worked with Seaver Leslie to create his *Ulysses* and *Irish* cylinders, which were adorned with drawings that Chihuly merged with the glass by means of an innovative "pickup" technique that he had recently devised. The *Navajo Blanket*, *Ulysses*, and *Irish* cylinders initiated the succession of series in which, with what Carol Strickland, writing in the *Christian Science Monitor* (October 13, 1994), called "admit-no-limits bravado," Chihuly has explored the aesthetics and techniques of glassmaking. Many of the series constitute works in progress, because, after varying lengths of time, Chihuly has further developed them, often by increasing the sizes of individual pieces and making them more colorful or flamboyant. "Dale's real forte is in sensing the value of an idea and executing it in all its permutations," James Carpenter has observed.

During a lecture tour of Great Britain in 1976, the car in which Chihuly and Seaver Leslie were riding crashed, and Chihuly was thrown through the windshield. Critically injured, he spent about a year recuperating. The damage to his left eye, however, could not be repaired, and he emerged from his ordeal with sight in his right eye only. Despite his loss of depth perception (which requires binocular vision), he continued to blow glass. In 1979, after dislocating a shoulder while bodysurfing, he turned over to other glass artisans all the physical activities that are entailed in glassmaking. "I think maybe I was ready to give [hands-on labor] up anyway," he told Jon Krakauer for *Smithsonian* (February 1992). "You lose the big picture when you're sitting at the bench all day." In *People* (November 18, 1994), he was quoted as saying that he has "always [been] more interested in the product than in glassblowing itself." In any case, the idea of working alone has never held any appeal for him, and his apprenticeship at Venini had sparked in him a strong affinity for the team approach. "I love to work with people," he has said. "It inspires me to be working with a group of people on an idea. It's the way things happen for me."

By his own account, in the first decade or so of his career, Chihuly's total yearly income from sales of his artwork never topped a thousand dollars, and he supported himself on his earnings from teaching. Then, in 1976, the art historian Henry Geldzahler, who was at the time the curator of contemporary art at the Metropolitan Museum of Art, bought three of Chihuly's *Navajo Blanket* cylinders for the museum's permanent collection. Geldzahler's purchase attracted the attention of other museum curators, and Chihuly's professional fortunes quickly began to rise. By 1980, thanks to his steadily increasing sales, he felt secure enough financially to give up his position at RISD, where he had been named head of the glass department, and devote himself to his art.

Earlier, in the summer of 1977, he had begun working on another series of glass objects. His inspiration for it was the pile of Indian-made baskets that he had seen in a storeroom of the Washington State Historical Society in Tacoma. "I was struck by the grace of their slumped, sagging forms," he recalled in a quote that appears in *Chihuly: Form from Fire* (1993), by Walter Darby Bannard and Henry Geldzahler. "I wanted to capture this grace in glass. The breakthrough for me was recognizing that heat was the tool to be used with gravity to make these forms." The hundred or so baskets that Chihuly completed by mid-1977 were exhibited at the Seattle Art Museum that fall and at the Renwick Gallery of the Smithsonian Institution, in Washington, D.C., in the following year.

Chihuly's *Baskets* evolved into his *Sea Forms* series in 1980, when he began experimenting with ribbed molds and a traditional Venetian decorative technique in which he "trailed on," or spiraled around, the body of the baskets a thin thread of colored glass, giving them the appearance of seashells. "The inner structure produced by the ribbed molds allowed us to work with much thinner glass, and we pushed the blowing process as far as we possibly could . . . ," he explained in his book *Chihuly: Color, Glass and Form* (1986). "I felt I could make things with the blowpipe that had never been done before." Another of his projects in 1980 was the creation of large, acid-etched stained-glass windows for a synagogue in St. Louis, Missouri.

"As with the baskets, after a couple of years I felt I had pushed *Sea Forms* to their limits," Chihuly has said. He has traced the inception of the *Macchias* (1981), his next series, to his sudden desire to use all of the three hundred manufactured colors available to glassmakers and to create as many combinations and variations of them as possible. "I'm obsessed with color—never saw one I didn't like," he wrote in an article for *Southwest Art* (May 1994). Similar in shape to the undulant *Sea Forms*, each of the vessels in the *Macchias* series displays one color on its inner surface and a different one on its outer surface, the two hues separated and illuminated by "opaque white 'clouds,'" in Chihuly's words, which he applied by means of a new technique that he invented himself. "Blowing a piece that combines a range of colors is extremely difficult," he pointed out in *Southwest Art*, "because each color attracts and holds the heat differently." A "lip wrap"—a ribbon of glass in a third color that was laid on the mouth of each vessel—highlighted the waviness of the *Macchias*. "Each piece was another experiment," Chihuly recalled in *Southwest Art*. "When we unloaded the ovens in the morning, there was the rush of seeing something I had never seen before. . . . The unbelievable combinations of color—that was the driving force."

"Seen under bright light, [the *Macchias*' colors] look like nature caught on fire, nature in molten flux, nature in the process of being created," Robert Hobbs wrote in an essay for *Dale Chihuly: Objets de Verre*, the catalog that accompanied Chihuly's one-man show at the Louvre's Museum of Decorative Arts, in Paris. (Only two other Americans have had solo exhibitions at the Louvre.) Eventually, by solving various technical problems, he was able to increase the width of the *Macchias* to as much as four feet. "It turns out that size is extremely important to the *Macchias*, and with them I felt for the first time that a piece of my glass held its own in a room," he has said.

The *Persians* (1986), which Chihuly made in collaboration with Martin Blank and Robbie Miller, began, in Chihuly's words, as a "search for forms" that could be made naturally on the blowpipe. "Chihuly's control of his medium enables him to create undulating, organic forms that seem to be in motion . . . [and that] interact seductively with ambient light," Roberta Smith wrote in a *New York Times* (August 12, 1988) review of an exhibit of the *Persians*. Chihuly embarked on his next series, for which he collaborated with the Venetian master Lino Tagliapietra, by, in his words, "pretend[ing] to be a Venetian designer in the 1920s and see[ing] what [he] might come up with." Flamboyantly colored and ornamented vessels, the *Venetians* (1988) boldly developed the ideas of Venetian Art Deco designers. In his monograph *Venetians: Dale Chihuly* (1988), Ron Glowen wrote that the pieces "expand aggressively into space, like a living and growing thing. And like living things, each work of the *Venetians* has an individual character, . . . much more so than Chihuly's other series." "Exaggerated in size, color, and form, the *Venetians* surprise and astonish us—and even amuse us with their excessive splendor," Marilynne Mason reported in the *Christian Science Monitor* (July 15, 1993). With the addition of fanciful flowers created by Tagliapietra, the *Venetians* metamorphosed into the *Ikebanas* (1989), the design of which is reminiscent of Japanese flower arrangements.

Chihuly has worked in Seattle since 1983, and for the past five years in what he calls the Boathouse, a one-time racing-shell factory on Lake Union that he transformed into his residence as well as a glassblowing studio and shop. Functioning in his studio much like a film director who works with his own scripts, he leads a team of as many as eighteen people. According to various accounts, he has succeeded in securely maintaining artistic control while, at the same time, allowing his assistants to exercise their creativity. Many of his teammates—among them, for varying lengths of time, Flora Mace, Joey Kirkpatrick, William Morris, Richard Royal, Ginny Ruffner, Ann Gardner, Paul Marioni, and Curtiss Brock—studied at Pilchuck and have become respected glass artists in their own right. "I rely heavily on the intuition of my craftsmen . . . ," Chihuly told Jon Krakauer. "My job is to be a catalyst—to set the wheels in motion, keep the energy level high, and let things happen."

After getting an idea for a piece, Chihuly makes a large, very rough drawing of it, applying with his hands, a broom, a brush, or other tools whatever substance happens to be close by—coffee grounds or scouring powder, for example, in addition to paint. (Executed in minutes with vigorous, sweeping motions, some of the drawings have reportedly sold for as much as three thousand dollars apiece. The prices of the glass pieces themselves range from three thousand dollars for the smallest objects to twenty thousand dollars or more for a *Macchia* and a million dollars for an installation—a grouping of a dozen or more works.) Next, rather than proceeding to make a more precise painted rendition of the object, Chihuly discusses with his coworkers the ideas that he has suggested in his drawing. The discussion continues throughout the physically demanding, labor-intensive process of blowing and shaping the glass.

"The Boathouse shelters a rollicking, hyperkinetic hive of art in the making, a scene so charged with heat and noise and unbridled energy that it makes the average MTV video clip look soporific by comparison," Jon Krakauer observed. The work proceeds with a stereo blasting "to stimulate the flow of creative juices," Krakauer wrote, and with Chihuly offering guidance and encouragement. In rapid succession, one assistant or another builds a sufficiently large ball of glass on a blowpipe, blows the glass into a bubble, adds various colors (in the form of tinted glass dust) to the piece by rolling it across a steel plate, fuses the color to the glass, shapes the glass by spinning it and by other means, attaches ornamental elements to it, and otherwise manipulates the glass, which must be reheated in an oven every two minutes to a temperature of up to twenty-five hundred degrees Fahrenheit and repeatedly blown. "At times a dozen hands are flying over the piece at once," Jon Krakauer reported. "Each move is tightly choreographed, and the crew performs as smoothly as a crack team of cardiac surgeons." The artistry and technical skill of a dozen collaborators was needed for the creation of the *Niijima Floats* (1991), Chihuly's latest series. (The name refers to the floats that Japanese fishermen in years past attached to their nets.) Measuring up to forty inches in diameter and weighing as much as eighty pounds, the *Niijima Floats* are probably the largest blown-glass spheres ever made.

Chihuly's recent works include his critically acclaimed designs for the sets of the Seattle Opera's 1993 production of Claude Debussy's 1902 masterwork *Pelléas et Mélisande*, which were fabricated in special plastics from Chihuly's glass models, and huge, dazzlingly colored chandeliers that have struck many observers as over the top in their design. "The greatest obstacle to a universal appreciation of [Chihuly's] work is that he's inevitably ahead of his audience," Henry Geldzahler noted in *Chihuly: Form from Fire*. "Chihuly challenges taste by not being concerned with it. . . . His sole concerns are color, drawing, and form." Among the more than one hundred museums in the United States, Canada, Europe, Asia, and Australia that own works by Chihuly are the Whitney Museum of American Art and the Museum of Modern Art, in New York City; New York City's Cooper-Hewitt Museum and several other branches of the Smithsonian Institution; the Australian National Gallery, in Canberra; the Victoria and Albert Museum, in London; and the National Museum in Stockholm, Sweden. During a trip to Great Britain and Europe in 1994, President Bill Clinton presented Chihuly pieces to Queen Elizabeth II and French president François Mitterrand.

In *Northwest Design & Living* (Fall 1993), Dana Garrett described Dale Chihuly as "a frizzy-haired, eye-patched, swashbuckling bundle of kinetic energy." Jon Krakauer reported that he has a "Warholesque genius for self-promotion." "He's full of life and exciting to be around," Tracy Savage, one of his art dealers and his former production manager, told Dana Garrett. "People are drawn to him as well as to his work." Chihuly's honors include the American Council for the Arts Visual Artist's Award and, along with the Pilchuck school, the Governor's Art Award, from Washington State (both in 1984), the National Living Treasure Award, from the University of North Carolina at Wilmington (1992), the American Academy of Achievement Golden Plate Award (1994), and three honorary doctorates. He was named a University of Washington Alumni Legend in 1987. "What I like to do is work on my work more than anything else," Chihuly has said. "It's varied in such a way that I can work on a chandelier, do a drawing, . . . design a book, make some phone calls about an exhibition. It's all creative in some way that has to do with people seeing my work. That means a lot to me, being able to put it up in a nice way, and have a lot of people look at it, and really like it."

Selected Biographical References: ARTnews 92:110+ Ap '93 pors; Northwest Design & Living p28+ Fall '93 pors; Smithsonian 22:90+ F '92 pors; Chihuly, Dale. Chihuly: Color, Glass and Form (1986); Who's Who in America, 1995

Donna Covevey/MIT

Chomsky, Noam

(CHAHM-skee, nohm)

Dec. 7, 1928– Linguist; university professor; writer; political activist. Address: Massachusetts Institute of Technology, 77 Massachusetts Ave., Cambridge, MA 02139

NOTE: This biography supersedes the article that appeared in *Current Biography* in 1970.

"Noam Chomsky's position in the history of ideas is comparable to that of Darwin or Descartes," Neil Smith declared in *Nature* (February 10, 1994). "In this century his peers in influence are the unlikely trio of Einstein, Picasso, and Freud. . . . Like Darwin and Descartes, Chomsky has redefined our understanding of ourselves as humans; like Freud—but with added intellectual rigor—he has revolutionized our view of the mind; like Einstein, he blends intense scientific creativity with radical political activism; like Picasso, he has overturned and replaced his own established systems with startling frequency." Chomsky's work, most notably in *Syntactic Structures* (1957) and *Aspects of the Theory of Syntax* (1965), transformed the study of linguistics and influenced that of psychology, philosophy, and, to a lesser extent, anthropology, literary criticism, and education, among other subjects. In the 1960s he established the concept of generative-transformational grammar, and in the 1980s he developed the "principles and parameters" approach to language acquisition, which he summed up in the theory of a universal grammar.

In addition to his scholarship, Chomsky has earned a reputation as an eloquent and outspoken political dissident whose philosophy contains elements of libertarianism, socialism, and anarchism. An opponent of American involvement in the Vietnam War, he protested by helping draft resisters, refusing to pay his taxes, and speaking out on American foreign policy matters. In expounding his views, among which is that the United States dominates the developing world for its own national interests rather than in service to the democratic principles that government leaders use to explain international intervention to the American public, he has, over the years, built a loyal following abroad, where he is much in demand as a lecturer and writer, but his access to media outlets in the United States has been restricted. In the 1960s and early 1970s, he wrote for the journals *Liberation*, *Ramparts*, and the *New York Review*. His writings of the late 1970s were published in the leftist journals *New Politics* and *Socialist Review* as well as in the libertarian *Inquiry*, published by the Cato Institute, in Washington D.C. More recently, he has enjoyed more access to the American press, especially in the Boston-based political monthly *Z Magazine*, for which he has been writing regularly since the mid-1980s, the now-defunct *Lies of Our Times*, and *Covert Action Quarterly*, among other journals. The pieces he has written for American publications, however, are still vastly outnumbered by his output overseas, where his articles are frequently published in the mainstream daily newspapers and leading journals in England, Israel, Mexico, Argentina, and many of the nations of Europe, Asia, and the South Pacific.

Although most Americans are acquainted with neither his political commentary nor his work in linguistics, in other countries Chomsky is considered to be, as Charles M. Young wrote in *Rolling Stone* (May 28, 1992), "one of the most respected and influential intellectuals in the world." According to Ron Grossman of the *Chicago Tribune* (January 1, 1993), from 1980 to 1992 Chomsky was cited more often than any other living author in the scholarly journals indexed by the *Arts and Humanities Citation Index*, published by the Institute for Scientific Information, in Philadelphia. "Among intellectual luminaries of all eras," Grossman wrote, "Chomsky placed eighth, just behind Plato and Sigmund Freud," in the number of citations listed by that index over a seven-year period. For four decades Chomsky has been a member of the faculty of the Massachusetts Institute of Technology (MIT), in Cambridge, where, since 1976, he has held the position of Institute Professor of Modern Languages and Linguistics.

Avram Noam Chomsky was born on December 7, 1928 in Philadelphia, where he and his younger brother, David Eli, grew up. His father, William Chomsky, a renowned Hebrew scholar who had emigrated from Ukraine to the United States in 1913 to avoid being drafted into the army, taught at Gratz Teachers College and Dropsie College, both in Philadelphia. His mother, Elsie (Simonofsky) Chomsky, also a scholar of Hebrew, wrote children's books. Chomsky's precocity was nurtured at

Oak Lane Country Day School, an experimental elementary school. By the time he was ten, he was able to read the proofs of his father's edition of a thirteenth-century Hebrew grammar. At the same age, he wrote an editorial about the rise of fascism in Europe for his school's newspaper. As a teenager he would often take a train from Philadelphia to New York City to visit his uncle, an owner of a newspaper stand, whose political views Chomsky described in his interview with Ron Grossman: "First he was a follower of Trotsky, then an anti-Trotskyite. He also taught himself so much Freud he wound up as a lay psychoanalyst with a penthouse apartment."

After graduating in 1945 from Central High School in Philadelphia, Chomsky enrolled at the University of Pennsylvania, also in Philadelphia, where he met Zellig Harris, a politically active professor of linguistics who would become his mentor. Attracted to the prewar Zionist movement (although he preferred the concept of a binational, Jewish-Palestinian state to an all-Jewish homeland), Chomsky was so interested in the events leading up to the establishment of Israel that he considered leaving school to travel to the Middle East, but Harris persuaded him to finish his education. Pursuing a broad curriculum that included courses in linguistics, mathematics, and philosophy, Chomsky became a member of Phi Beta Kappa and in 1949 earned his bachelor's degree in linguistics. From 1950 to 1951 he was an assistant instructor in philosophy at the University of Pennsylvania, and from about 1946 he had been teaching Hebrew at the Mikve Israel School in Philadelphia. In 1951 he received his master's degree and was awarded a three-year junior fellowship from the Society of Fellows at Harvard University, which was renewed in 1954 for another year. In 1953, he lived for a few months on a kibbutz in Israel.

After defending his doctoral dissertation in 1955, Chomsky earned his Ph.D. from the University of Pennsylvania (even though the research had been done at Harvard) and began teaching at MIT as an assistant professor of modern languages, with a joint appointment in the Research Lab of Electronics. In 1958 he was promoted to associate professor, with a full professorship following three years later. Named Ferrari P. Ward Professor of Modern Languages and Linguistics in 1966, Chomsky was elevated to his current position of Institute Professor ten years later.

Chomsky was introduced to structural linguistics as an undergraduate, when Zellig Harris let him read the proofs of his then-forthcoming book *Methods in Structural Linguistics* (1951), which explained the inductive methods whereby information that would yield grammatical structures of a given language could be gathered and classified by analyzing the speech of a native speaker. On his own initiative Chomsky adapted some of Harris's methods, seeking to discover a set of rules by which one could generate linguistic structures. By 1955 he had completed a thousand-page manuscript that was widely distributed among graduate students and researchers; its ninth chapter, "Transformational Analysis," served as his dissertation. (Parts of the manuscript, which was partially revised in 1956, were eventually published in 1975 under the title *The Logical Structure of Linguistic Theory*.)

In 1956, at an MIT symposium on information theory, Chomsky presented his paper "Three Models for the Description of Language," in which he went beyond suggesting a generative grammar to actually positing some of its rules, in quasi-mathematical formulas. Among the audience was the psychologist George Miller, who recalled, as quoted in Howard Gardner's *The Mind's New Science* (1985), that "other linguists had said language has all the formal precision of mathematics, but Chomsky was the first linguist to make good on the claim. I think that is what excited all of us." This was so radical a departure that established linguists refused to concede its validity. It was not until the following year, with the publication of *Syntactic Structures*, which encapsulated some of the theories set forth in his thousand-page manuscript, that Chomsky's ideas gained widespread exposure within the linguistic community, aided by a book review written by the structural linguist Robert Lees in *Language*.

At the Ninth International Congress of Linguistics, at MIT in 1962, Chomsky presented an address called the "The Logical Basis of Linguistic Theory," which was published, in several versions, under the title "Current Issues in Linguistic Theory." In it he "explained in the first fully comprehensive way the difference between structural linguistics and generative grammar," as Michael C. Haley and Ronald F. Lunsford wrote in their book *Noam Chomsky* (1994). "The impact was apparently immediate and perhaps worldwide." Chomsky's reputation skyrocketed at this point, and sales of *Syntactic Structures* increased dramatically as his ideas began to gain acceptance. In 1965, he published his second seminal work, *Aspects of the Theory of Syntax*, in which he sought to formalize and elaborate upon the thoughts proposed in his earlier work. It was in this work that Chomsky firmly laid the basis of his beliefs in the cognitive nature of language acquisition, attacking the prevailing behaviorist model, which was based on the belief that language was acquired by imitation and conditioning. "Chomsky disagreed [with conventional wisdom] violently, arguing that language is based on broad structural principles, the knowledge of which is innate in human beings, part of our genetic endowment," Beth Horning wrote in *Technology Review* (October 1991). "What that means is that each of us develops language naturally in the normal course of events, much as we grow arms and legs."

In making these assertions, Chomsky was not only challenging the traditional field of linguistics but some of the most cherished tenets of psychology as well. From the outset of his career he has sought to link linguistics with psychology in an integral way. In 1959 he published a now-famous review attacking the premises of the eminent behavioral psychologist B. F. Skinner's book *Verbal Behavior*, in which Skinner attempted to figure out how to predict and control "verbal behavior" in a given environment by experimenting with stimuli and responses. "The only problem with behaviorist psychology is that it never discovered anything," Chomsky told Ron Grossman.

Proceeding from their view of the mind as a tabula rasa, behaviorists maintain that the only way to learn about the workings of the mind is by studying human behavior and drawing conclusions based only on what is observable; since mental functions cannot be observed directly, they are ignored. "Chomsky argues that the reluctance [of behaviorists] to appeal to the internal structure of the [mind] is simply dogma, with no scientific basis," Raphael Salkie wrote in *The Chomsky Update: Linguistics and Politics* (1990). In contrast, Chomsky believes that it is only in applying the traditions of scientific enquiry to the mind that any understanding of intelligence, knowledge, and language acquisition can be obtained. As for language's predictability, he told Ronald Lunsford in a 1989 interview that "language is appropriate to situations, but it's not caused by them."

In philosophy, Chomsky's ideas have also gone against the grain of modern empiricism, in many ways the dominant philosophy of the twentieth century, which holds that all knowledge is derived from experience. Chomsky's thought has more in common with the rationalists of previous centuries, including Descartes and Kant, who believed that the mind comprises a system of innate knowledge. Writing in *Language and Problems of Knowledge* (1988), Chomsky concluded, "Attention to the facts quickly demonstrates that these [empiricist] ideas are not simply in error but entirely beyond any hope of repair. They must be abandoned, as essentially worthless." Chomsky has further distanced himself from empiricists and behaviorists by drawing a distinction between "mysteries"—philosophical and psychological questions that, while intriguing, are by their nature beyond the ability of human science to uncover—and "problems," which are capable of being understood. In *Reflections on Language* (1975), Chomsky wrote: "Roughly, where we deal with cognitive structures, either in a mature state of knowledge and belief or in the initial state, we face problems, but not mysteries. When we ask how humans make use of these cognitive structures, how and why they make choices and behave as they do, although there is much we can say as human beings with intuition and insight, there is little, I believe, that we can say as scientists."

In Chomsky's rationalist view of knowledge, the mind is made up of distinct modules, each of which is responsible for a specific aspect of intelligence. "All the [modular] systems have their own properties and are independent of any basic learning mechanisms—if indeed such mechanisms exist, Chomsky hastens to add," Beth Horning explained, noting that "the very idea is anathema to legions of researchers who have spent their careers trying to define and assess general intelligence." Behavior, on the other hand, is a function of the workings of these various modules as they interact in the real world. Chomsky believes that it is the work of scientists to study the make-up of the modules and their function, leaving aside the infinite number of ways they are capable of interacting. Language is "a system that makes infinite use of finite means," he said in his interview with Lunsford, using the German philologist Wilhelm von Humboldt's phrase.

The excitement that had greeted Chomsky's initial postulation of a generative-transformational grammar was soon followed by the discovery, in the 1950s, "that little was known even about very simple constructions in well-studied languages (English, etc.)," as Chomsky explained to *Current Biography*. "To achieve 'descriptive adequacy' it seemed to be necessary to develop extremely rich and complex rule systems, differing considerably for different languages. But it was understood at once that that cannot be right. To achieve the more serious goal of 'explanatory adequacy' (which means, in effect, to account for language acquisition), it is necessary to show that all languages are cast to the same mold, with only slight variations at the margin; both the 'mold' and the permissible 'variations' must be part of common biological endowment, or no human languages could be acquired. The problem of how to resolve that tension was the main issue that drove research from about 1960 to 1980. . . . The end result . . . was an extension of the efforts begun around 1960 to resolve the conflict between the goals of descriptive and explanatory adequacy by finding principles that underlie all rules and constructions in all languages, so that actual descriptions can be much simplified. The tentative outcome is the (partially justified) speculation that there are no rules or constructions in the traditional sense at all, but only universal principles and restricted options of variation (parameters), possibly limited to lexical choices." Among Chomsky's more comprehensive later works on linguistics are *Lectures on Government and Binding* (1981), *Knowledge of Language* (1986), and *Language and Thought* (1993).

Chomsky's political writings have caused even more controversy than his linguistic theories. Of the nearly four dozen books he has written, almost half have concerned political or ethical issues in American foreign policy, its conduct, and its reportage. Although he has been interested in politics all of his life, he did not begin to speak publicly about the issues that moved him until 1964, when he joined the growing antiwar movement. He quickly became a popular campus speaker and participated in many protest activities. His first published work of dissent was his speech "The Responsibility of Intellectuals," a transcription of which was printed in the *New York Review of Books* in 1967 and in his collection of essays *American Power and the New Mandarins* in 1969.

A sharp condemnation of members of the liberal intellectual establishment, whom he characterized as apologists for American foreign policy, the essay, according to Charles Young of *Rolling Stone*, "defined the peace movement as much as any document and pushed the name Chomsky up there with Thoreau and Emerson in the literature of rebellion." Writing in the *Nation* (May 7, 1988), Brian Morton declared, "If only for the role he played during the Vietnam War, Noam Chomsky should be honored as a national hero." By the time the last American troops left Saigon, in 1975, much of the political activism that marked that era in American politics had subsided. But as Chomsky told Grossman, "I had a feeling that if I put a foot into the political water, it would be an endless sea of causes. Once the war was over, I knew I'd always find another issue I had to speak out on."

Among Chomsky's political works are *At War with Asia* (1970), *For Reasons of State* (1973), *Counterrevolutionary Violence* (written with Edward Herman, 1973), *Peace in the Middle East?* (1974), *Human Rights and American Foreign Policy* (1978), *The Political Economy of Human Rights* (written with Edward Herman, 1979), *Towards a New Cold War* (1982), *The Fateful Triangle* (1983), *Turning the Tide* (1985), *Pirates and Emperors* (1986), *Culture of Terrorism* (1988), *Manufacturing Consent* (written with Edward Herman, 1988) *Necessary Illusions* (1989), *Deterring Democracy* (1991), *Chronicles of Dissent* (1992), *What Uncle Sam Really Wants* (1992), *Year 501: The Conquest Continues* (1993), *Rethinking Camelot* (1993), *The Prosperous Few and the Restless Many* (1993), and *World Orders, Old and New* (1994).

A sampling of twenty years' worth of his political thought is collected in *The Chomsky Reader*, edited by James Peck. The pieces in that collection reflect the author's belief that the true nature of the United States' role in the world is distorted and hidden from the American people by the collusion of the corporate-owned media elite and the federal government representatives who protect business interests in order to get reelected or keep their jobs in the administration. Chomsky blames neither Republicans nor Democrats for this state of affairs, contending that both are "business parties" whose leaders, in cooperation with corporate executives, select presidential and congressional candidates. In that sense, he has argued, voters don't really have much of a choice, especially since "front-runners" are designated by the press more than a year before the actual election. By the same token, party platforms are hammered out by an elite group without broad public participation, and voters' only real remaining choice is to ratify (by voting) or not ratify (by abstaining) the options that have been preselected. True dissenters are either not heard from or are belittled, their views denigrated as being "outside the pale of intellectual responsibility," as Martin Peretz, the former editor of the *New Republic*, has said, in describing Chomsky's political beliefs.

Underlying Chomsky's brand of anarchistic libertarian socialism is a fundamental distrust of authority. "The basic anarchist idea," he told Paul Anderson and Kevin Davey of *New Statesman and Society* (June 3, 1994), "is that any system of authority has to prove its legitimacy: if it can't prove its legitimacy then it ought to be eliminated." Legitimacy "has to do with moral values and conceptions of human rights, which are not simply a matter of actions," Chomsky explained to *Current Biography*. "The actions of illegitimate authority may be benign; say a benign slave holder. It is slavery itself that is illegitimate, benign or not, popularly supported or not (even supported by slaves, as it sometimes was). It is illegitimate because it denies the fundamental human right to be free. Relations of authority and control that undermine this right might be legitimate anyway, but a justification has to be given; say, my keeping my grandchild from running into the street. The burden of proof is always on the structure of hierarchy and authority, and unless it can provide a justification, it is illegitimate. What is at stake is the nature of the relationship and some (admittedly imprecise and intuitive) conception of human rights and values; not the degree of support or even the morality of actions."

The likelihood of Chomsky's believing in governmental pursuit of a just cause is perhaps restricted by his belief in the evil capabilities of institutions per se. Addressing this paradox, Haley and Lunsford noted that Chomsky believes human beings are innately equipped with a knowledge faculty that enables them to recognize the difference between good and bad, and that when possible they will choose to do good. "[Chomsky] may see the [evildoer]," the authors wrote in *Noam Chomsky*, "but believe that [the evildoer] has gotten caught up in the web of a human institution that has taken arbitrary authority. Having been trapped in this institution, the [evildoer] has begun to act in the customary way for humans to act in such institutions. This line of thought would make Chomsky sound much more like a behaviorist than he . . . would like."

Although Chomsky has not shrunk from criticizing communist or fascist governments—indeed, be has said that the Cold War was maintained by both superpowers acting in their mutual interests in managing their respective spheres of influence—he has concentrated mainly on exposing the crimes against humanity allegedly committed by the United States, for example, in the course of supporting dictatorships in the Third World. "My view," he explained to Anderson and Davey, "is that solidarity means taking my country, where I have some responsibility and some influence, and compelling it to get its dirty hands out of other people's affairs. . . . The point is that the people of a country should be free to do what they want—and the main reason they're not is that we've got our boots on their necks. Once our boots are off their necks, it's up to them to figure out how to be free. If they're left with an oppressive government, then they can overthrow it—and maybe I'll help them."

In the interview with Anderson and Davey, Chomsky did not address the difficulties that might proceed from such a scenario, such as whether he would continue to support the new regime if it needed help in maintaining its authority, whose side he would take if "the people" were divided into equally legitimate camps, and so forth. According to Haley and Lunsford, this reluctance to spell out the logistics of various solutions is one of the weaknesses of Chomsky's line of thinking: "When Chomsky tells us that he favors a libertarian government that does not take for itself arbitrary authority and that respects the individual freedoms and creativity of its citizens, we can nod approvingly, but we cannot 'imagine' this government. It is not clear that Chomsky has a vision for what this government would look like."

One reason for the tremendous impact of Chomsky's thinking on the basic and social sciences is his willingness to share his ideas with others and to learn from his students, subordinating his ego to the advancement of knowledge. "I don't want any followers," Chomsky told Grossman. "My message, especially to students, is that they shouldn't be following anyone." Indeed, he encourages his students to question his teaching, to think for themselves rather than merely to absorb and regurgitate a closed set of conclusions; in this way his teaching is an integral part of his ongoing investigations into the material structure of the mind.

Chomsky has spent scattered semesters at other institutions around the world as a visiting professor, including Columbia University, in New York City (1957–58); the Institute for Advanced Study at Princeton, in New Jersey (1958–59); the University of California at Los Angeles (1966); the University of California at Berkeley (1966–67); and Oxford University, in England (1969). He also served as a research fellow at the Harvard Center for Cognitive Studies, in Cambridge, Massachusetts, from 1964 to 1965. Chomsky holds honorary doctorates from Cambridge University, the University of Chicago, the University of London, Loyola University, Swarthmore College, Bard College, Delhi University, the University of Massachusetts, the University of Maine, Gettysburg College, Visva-Bharati University, and the University of Pennsylvania.

Among the dozens of awards he has won are the Distinguished Scientific Contribution Award from the American Psychological Association (1984), the George Orwell Award for Distinguished Contribution to Honesty and Clarity in Public Language from the National Council of Teachers of English (1987 and 1989), the Kyoto Prize in Basic Sciences (1988), the James Killian Faculty Award from MIT (1992), the Lannan Literature Award for nonfiction (1992), the Joel Seldin Peace Award from Psychologists for Social Responsibility (1993), the Homer Smith Award from New York University's School of Medicine (1994), and the Loyola Mellon Humanities Award from Loyola University (1994). In 1990 his work served as the basis for the award-winning Canadian play *The Noam Chomsky Lectures*, and in 1992 a documentary film entitled *Manufacturing Consent: Noam Chomsky and the Media* was produced by the Canadian production company Necessary Illusions and the National Film Board of Canada.

Now in his sixties, Noam Chomsky has retained the wavy hair of his youth and maintained his serious, restrained manner in the hundreds of public appearances he makes every year. Although he can sometimes come across as bitter and despairing, according to some journalists, it is clear that the depth and breadth of his political thought stems from a commitment to revealing the truth in any given situation—an inherently idealistic endeavor. In some interviews he has displayed a wry sense of humor. When discussing his own work he is unfailingly modest, giving credit where credit is due and refusing to refer to any of his linguistic discoveries as a revolution, preferring the term "conceptual shift." Chomsky lives in Lexington, Massachusetts with his wife, the former Carol Doris Schatz, a linguist, whom he married on December 24, 1949 and with whom he has three children, Aviva, Diane, and Harry Alan.

Selected Biographical References: Maclean's p48+ Mr 22 '93 pors; Rolling Stone p42+ My 28 '92 pors; Haley, Michael C. and Ronald F. Lunsford. Noam Chomsky (1994); Salkie, Raphael. The Chomsky Update: Linguistics and Politics (1990); Who's Who in America, 1995

Chopra, Deepak

(CHOH-pruh, DEE-pahk)

1947(?)- Physician; lecturer; writer. Address: c/o Muriel Nellis, Literary and Creative Artists, 3543 Albemarle St. NW, Washington, DC 20008; c/o Crown/Harmony, 201 E. 50th St., 22d Floor, New York, NY 10022; c/o The Ford Group 872 La Jolla Rancho Rd. La Jolla, CA 92037

According to Deepak Chopra, awareness of the mind/body connection can facilitate healing, lead to inner peace, and even reverse the aging process. After working for fourteen years as an endocrinologist, Chopra resigned his position as chief of staff of a Boston-area hospital in 1985 to promote Ayurveda, an ancient Indian system of holistic healing that takes into account the integration of psychological and physical mechanisms. For his efforts in behalf of the Ayurvedic movement, in 1989 Chopra was christened the Dhanvantari of Heaven on Earth (also known as the Lord of Immortality, the mythical founder of Ayurveda) by Maharishi Mahesh Yogi, who taught transcendental meditation (TM) to the Beatles. Combining TM with the tenets of Ayurveda, Chopra's mind/body programs incorporate massage, yoga, meditation, herbal supplements, nutritional guidelines, and exercise regimens, all of which can be tailored to several mind/body types identified by a questionnaire or

Dana Fienman/Harmony Books

Deepak Chopra

a three-finger radial pulse diagnosis. The author of more than a dozen books that apply his strategies to various areas of health care, including his best-selling *Ageless Body, Timeless Mind: The Quantum Alternative to Growing Old* (1993) and his novel *The Return of Merlin* (1995), he has seen his writings translated into twenty-five languages. Since 1993 Chopra, who founded the American Association of Ayurvedic Medicine in Colorado Springs, has been the executive director of the Sharp Institute for Human Potential and Mind/Body Medicine in San Diego. "I don't see myself as an entrepreneur," he told Catherine Winters in an interview for *American Health* (January/February 1992). "I don't see myself as a doctor. I do see myself as a participant in the healing process of people and of a society that desperately needs to be healed."

Deepak Chopra was born in New Delhi in or around 1947 (he has said that he has forgotten exactly how old he is). His father, Krishan Chopra, was an Indian army physician who had fought the Japanese in the Burmese jungles during World War II and who later trained in London as a cardiologist. Chopra's younger brother, Sanjiv, a gastroenterologist and hepatic specialist, is an associate professor of medicine at Harvard University. Chopra attended an Irish Christian missionary high school in Delhi, where he wrote several award-winning short stories. "English literature was my forte," he told Dennis McLellan in an interview for *Publishers Weekly* (July 24, 1995). Chopra originally intended to study English literature and become a journalist, but then, while still in high school, he read a number of books featuring doctors as heroes, among them Sinclair Lewis's *Arrowsmith*, Lloyd C. Douglas's *The Magnificent Obsession*, and Arthur Conan Doyle's Sherlock Holmes detective stories. "I was fascinated by these doctors," Chopra recalled in his interview with McLellan, "and so I took my father by surprise and informed him that I wanted to go to medical school."

After graduating from the All-India Institute of Medical Sciences in New Delhi, he moved to the United States in 1970 with his wife, Rita, whom he had recently married. He completed an internship at Muhlenbert Hospital in Plainfield, New Jersey, where his introduction to professional medicine began with an autopsy. "My first American patient had been a dead man . . . ," he recalled in his memoir, *Return of the Rishi* (1988). "The machines were in the room and the family was outside the door. That seemed a little peculiar to me." In 1971 he moved to Boston, set up a successful practice in endocrinology, and held a string of teaching jobs at the medical schools affiliated with Tufts University, in Medford; Harvard University, in Cambridge; and Boston University. "I was very ambitious," he told McLellan. His medical career reached its apogee in 1985, when he was named chief of staff at New England Memorial Hospital (now Boston Regional Medical Center), in Stoneham, Massachusetts.

By the mid-1980s, however, Chopra had become disillusioned with traditional medicine, as he explained to Catherine Winters: "If you're in regular private practice and you're honest with yourself, you ask, 'What did I do today?' You find your time is spent writing prescriptions for antibiotics, tranquilizers, antiulcer pills, and sleeping pills. Medical training doesn't equip doctors to help patients make changes that will have a significant impact on their health." Moreover, his own health was impaired by his reliance on such toxin-producing substances as caffeine, tobacco, and alcohol. In *Return of the Rishi* he recalled that a fellow physician, Dr. Brihaspati Dev Triguna, after performing a pulse diagnosis on him, had told him to "slow down." "There are four important things to gain in life: fame, wealth, a happy family life, and spiritual attainment," Triguna had told him. "You are gaining all of them, but too fast. If you get them now, what will you do for the rest of your life? It is important that things come at the proper time."

Resolving to learn how to enhance his own vitality and that of his patients, Chopra read a book on TM in 1985. Within a week he had stopped drinking whiskey, and within three weeks he had quit smoking. Meanwhile, he had rediscovered the five-thousand-year-old Hindu tradition of Ayurveda (a Sanskrit term meaning "life science" or "knowledge of life"). According to Ayurveda, one's *prakriti*, or mind/body type, can be determined by a pulse reading or by one of the quizzes in some of Chopra's books. One's preeminent *dosha*, or physiological force, usually falls under one of three categories, although characteristics of all three may be present in varying combinations in an individual. *Vata*, which governs the nervous system and relates to movement, characterizes people who tend to be thin, sensitive, indecisive, and anxious and who have dry skin; *pitta*, the metabolic *dosha*, applies to those who are decisive, quick to anger, have a healthy appetite, and perspire easily; *kapha* predominates in those who are relaxed, have a tendency to gain weight, and suffer from allergies. The balance of each *dosha* or combination of *doshas* can be restored by beneficial foods, herbs, and exercises, according to Chopra.

After meeting with Maharishi Mahesh Yogi in Washington, D.C., later in 1985, Chopra resigned his position at the hospital and cofounded Maharishi Ayur-Veda Products International, Inc. (MAPI), which distributes a line of herbal supplements, teas, oils, incense, and auxiliary devices. The hyphen in Ayur-Veda, as Elise Pettus pointed out in an article for *New York* (August 14, 1995), rendered the name a TM trademark. In the same year, the maharishi appointed Chopra director of the Maharishi Ayur-Veda Health Center for Behavioral Medicine and Stress Management in Lancaster, Massachusetts (four other such centers were also opened in the United States). "Chopra was a huge asset from a marketing point of view," Curtis Mailloux, a former director of the Washington, D.C., TM center who "defected" from the movement in 1989, told Pettus. "Because he was so Western and had the good credibility, he was able to open up the clinic in Lancaster and get celebrities to go."

Guests at the Lancaster clinic, among them the actress Elizabeth Taylor, the fashion designer Donna Karan, and the investment banker Michael Milken, were given a variety of treatments for up to four thousand dollars per week. Instruction in TM was available for an additional fee. After their pulses were read, patients were prescribed daily enemas and warm-sesame-oil massages and baths and were advised about appropriate nutrition and exercise. Some of the less appealing Ayurvedic methods of *panchakarma*, or purification, among them vomiting and bloodletting, were omitted. Although Chopra has claimed, in some of his writings, that cancer can go into remission if a patient practices his mind/body awareness techniques, he has admitted that such a favorable outcome cannot always be assured. "Of course we lose patients," he told Catherine Winters. "Patients die at Harvard Medical School, the citadel of citadels. Our emphasis is on the quality of patients' lives. If we can get rid of someone's pain and make him feel emotionally secure and spiritually grounded, then more likely than not the quality of life will also be affected." Chopra has claimed to have treated more than ten thousand patients between 1985 and 1990.

In 1985 Chopra began writing books that complemented his clinical practice and spread the word about beneficial herbal products, many of which could be purchased through MAPI, of which he was the sole stockholder until 1987 and president, treasurer, and clerk until 1988. "Soon after MAPI started, I was advised to resign as a board member," he informed Catherine Winters, "since it would be perceived as a conflict of interest. But in what sense is it a conflict of interest? Who else but somebody who believes in Maharishi Ayur-Veda is going to talk about it? The conflict would arise if I gained some financial incentive, but all my earnings come from my lectures, my workshops, and my books."

Chopra self-published his first book, *Creating Health: The Psychophysiological Connection* (1985), after enduring numerous rejections of his manuscript. A slightly longer version was later published in England (in 1988) and in the United States (in 1987, with the subtitle *Beyond Prevention, Toward Perfection*, and in 1991, with the subtitle *How to Wake Up the Body's Intelligence*). The premise of that book, as of much of Chopra's subsequent work, was that "our thoughts tend to keep us healthy or make us ill," as he wrote in *Nation's Business* (October 1987). Crediting Hans Selye with being the first to apply the term "stress" to the human body, Chopra advised readers not only to minimize negative stress but also to maximize positive stress. Toward the latter goal, he recommended doing something that brings joy and concentrating fully on that activity while practicing it; reducing distractions at work; and finding inner satisfaction in daily tasks.

Chopra's second book, *Return of the Rishi*, received mixed reviews, perhaps because, according to reviewers, its subtitles—*A Doctor's Search for the Ultimate Healer* for the 1988 edition and *A Doctor's Story of Spiritual Transformation and Ayurvedic Healing* for the 1991 reprint—may have led readers to expect to learn more about Ayurveda. Instead, they were treated to a "reflective if self-infatuated autobiography," as a writer described it in a forecast for *Publishers Weekly* (December 18, 1987). In his next book, *Quantum Healing: Exploring the Frontiers of Mind/Body Medicine* (1989), Chopra asserted that "healthy people do not have to deteriorate automatically as they grow older." Citing a 1980 experiment in which a group of eighty-year-olds who were taught to meditate, relax, and play mind-sharpening word games lived longer, on average, than their counterparts who received no such instruction, Chopra concluded that "expanding your awareness is enough to extend your life." He enlarged upon his theories in *Perfect Health: The Complete Mind/Body Guide* (1990), which contains the quizzes to determine one's *dosha*, and *Unconditional Life: Mastering the Forces That Shape Personal Reality* (1991).

In 1991 a potentially serious blow was dealt to Chopra's credibility when the *Journal of the American Medical Association* (*JAMA*) published, in its October 2 issue, a rebuttal of an article by Chopra and two others that had appeared in the May 22–29 issue of the journal. In "Letter from New Delhi: Maharishi Ayur-Veda: Modern Insights into Ancient Medicine," Chopra and his coauthors, Hari M. Sharma and Brihaspati Dev Triguna, described the main principles of Ayurveda and the purported "metabolic changes" induced by TM but neglected to fully disclose their previous or current affiliations with Maharishi Ayur-Veda and failed to inform readers that the term referred to a specific product line. Instead, the authors identified Maharishi Ayur-Veda only as "a modern revival" of Ayurveda that "has taken place under the direction of Maharishi Mahesh Yogi in collaboration with leading Ayurvedic physicians." Another problem was the citation of studies of two MAPI herbal compounds, known as M-4 and M-5, involving the reduction of induced mammary cancer in laboratory animals, because the authors failed to identify the ingredients of the compounds, although they did provide footnotes to other sources that may have revealed the actual components. A number of angry letters to *JAMA* followed the publication of the article by Chopra and his coauthors, according to Robert Barnett and Cathy Sears, writing in *Science* (October 11, 1991). The vigilance of the journal's readers apparently surpassed that of the peer reviewers who had read the article before it was published. George Lundberg, the editor of *JAMA*, declared to the writers for *Science*, "I do believe that a different set of reviewers might have provided us with a very different outlook."

Preferring to correct the journal's error later rather than never, Lundberg assigned a thorough investigation of the matter to associate editor Andrew A. Skolnick, who charged in his rebuttal that Chopra's article was a thinly veiled advertisement for Maharishi Ayur-Veda products and that Chopra was still a consultant to MAPI. Chopra has said that he donated his services to MAPI, but, according to Skolnick, Chopra was making money from lectures and seminars that taught Maharishi's ideas. Skolnick wrote that the pulse diagnosis was described as "a variation of palm reading" by William Jarvis, the president of the National Council Against Health Fraud, who told Catherine Winters that Chopra was both a zealot and an entrepreneur. "Zealotry is more dangerous than fraud," he said. "Zealots don't know where to stop. They gather information that makes them look good and are blind to all the rest." Skolnick then detailed other cases of deception involving members of TM and the media. One such case involved an affidavit submitted in 1986 by the physicist Heinz R. Pagels on behalf of a litigious former TM member. Pagels, whose book *The Cosmic Code* (1982) was cited by Chopra in his *Perfect Health* as further reading for people who wanted to explore the connections between quantum physics and Maharishi Ayur-Veda, wrote in his affidavit, "There is no known connection between meditation states and states of matter in physics."

When interviewed by Catherine Winters just prior to publication of the *JAMA* rebuttal, Chopra said, "I've been called the worst things that you can be called—huckster, fraud. And I've been called the best things by my patients and by doctors. After a while it doesn't matter. You do what you have to do because you feel that it's important, that it's helping people and that it's making a difference in your life." But in a series of news releases that appeared in the wake of *JAMA*'s article, he was less sanguine about criticism of his efforts. "[Skolnick's] article in general distorts facts and is full of malice," he wrote. "This summer *JAMA* decided, for reasons I cannot fathom, to mount a witch hunt against me. . . . I tried repeatedly to reason with the editors, but it was clear to me that the journal had its agenda set in concrete from the start. This did not surprise me. *JAMA* speaks for the status quo in medicine. The American Medical Association has a long history of opposing medical alternatives that it perceives as a threat." In late 1992 Chopra and two TM groups sued Lundberg, Skolnick, and the AMA for $194 million for alleged defamation. In March 1993 the case was dismissed without prejudice.

In June 1993 Chopra left Lancaster and moved to La Jolla, California, where he became the executive director of the Sharp Institute for Human Potential and Mind/Body Medicine in southern California, under the auspices of the San Diego–based Sharp HealthCare, a network of seven hospitals, twenty-one clinics, and eight urgent-care facilities. Chopra also helmed the Center for Mind/Body Medicine at L'Auberge, a resort in Del Mar, California, where a week's stay can cost four thousand dollars. Guests have included former Beatle George Harrison, the actress Farrah Fawcett, and members of the singer Michael Jackson's family. (The center at L'Auberge closed abruptly in May 1995 and was scheduled to reopen in La Jolla in October 1995, according to Pettus.) Explaining his reasons for disassociating himself from TM in a letter to TM headquarters dated July 1993, Chopra wrote, "I had never felt comfortable in the role of a leader." TM headquarters subsequently made the break final, deleting all references to him in Ayur-Veda literature and directing regional TM centers to remove his books from their shelves and, as quoted by Pettus, "to ignore him and not try to contact him or promote him in any way. . . . This is extremely important for the purity of the teaching."

Judging by the success of Chopra's next book, *Ageless Body, Timeless Mind* (1993), the *JAMA* controversy had not hurt his reputation with the general public. *Ageless Body, Timeless Mind* landed on *Publishers Weekly*'s best-seller list on June 26, 1993 in the number-one position, which it held for nine consecutive weeks. More than a million hardcover copies of the book were sold, and Chopra's share of the profits from that work alone has reportedly surpassed four million dollars. Chopra's premise in *Ageless Body* is that the world has no independent, objective reality outside of the observer; it is merely a function of people's sensory perceptions, or "an induced fiction in which we have collectively agreed to participate."Asking his readers to suspend their belief in the material world, he invited them to accompany him on a "journey of discovery," during which he intended to explore a place "where youthful vigor, renewal, creativity, joy, fulfillment, and timelessness are the common experience of everyday life." Thoughts and emotions affect people's health on a chemical, cellular level, he argued, and therefore aging can be either facilitated, inhibited, or temporarily reversed through conscious processes.

In a chapter on longevity, Chopra enumerated "ten keys to active mastery," which included the following imperatives, shortened from the form in which they appear in the book: "Listen to your body's wisdom," "Live in the present," "Take time to be silent, to meditate, to quiet the internal dialogue," "Relinquish your need for external approval," "When you find yourself reacting with anger or opposition to any person or circumstance, realize that you are only struggling with yourself," "Know that the world 'out there' reflects your reality 'in here,'" "Shed the burden of judgment," "Don't contaminate your body with toxins," "Replace fear-motivated behavior with love-motivated behavior," and "Understand that the physical world is just a mirror of a deeper intelligence." These ideas were repeated and amplified by Chopra during a taped lecture called *Body, Mind, and Soul*, which brought in $150,000 in pledges when it was broadcast during a fund-raising drive by a PBS affiliate in Los Angeles in July 1995. The program was broadcast nationwide one month later, and has gone on to raise in excess of two million dollars for PBS affiliates. Two new PBS shows will air in 1996.

Chopra has frequently said that he expects to live well beyond the age of one hundred and that he is not afraid of dying. "If your internal reference point is eternity, then you transcend the fear of death by seeing your life and all of its events against a backdrop of awe and sacredness," he said in an interview with James Mauro of *Psychology Today* (November/December 1993), who asked Chopra what role religion played in that outlook. "Religion has had more devastating effects on civilization than anything else—more wars, more people have been killed," Chopra replied. "I personally think if you could remove religion from the face of the Earth, we would all be much happier people and really become spiritual in the true sense—where irrespective of the color of your skin and where you come from or which God you worship, I feel that I am connected to you, that I feel compassion and love for you. Religion may have said those things, but it never practiced those things, ever."

In the wake of the phenomenal success of *Ageless Body, Timeless Mind*, Chopra has churned out no fewer than eight more books, including *Creating Affluence: Wealth Consciousness in the Field of All Possibilities* (1993) and *The Seven Spiritual Laws of Success* (1994), which has sold more than a million copies and has been a best-seller for six months. In an interview with Elizabeth MacDonald for *Money* (December 1993), Chopra recommended twenty minutes of meditation a day and contended that affluence could be attained "by achieving wealth consciousness, a state of mind that involves creativity and joy. . . . If you are constantly concerned about money, then even if you have a billion dollars in the bank you are not rich." Three short volumes published in 1994 apply his concepts to specific problems: *Restful Sleep: The Complete Mind/Body Program for Overcoming Insomnia*; *Perfect Weight: The Complete Mind/Body Program for Achieving and Maintaining Your Ideal Weight*; and *Journey into Healing: Awakening the Wisdom Within You*, a book of aphorisms, many of them culled from his previous work. Two more books were scheduled for publication in October 1995: *Overcoming Chronic Fatigue: The Complete Mind/Body Program* and *Perfect Digestion: The Key to Balanced Living*.

Having conveyed his accumulated wisdom time and again in the nonfiction format, Chopra turned to fiction with *The Return of Merlin* (1995), a tale about "waking up the wizard that sleeps deep within all of us," as he wrote in the novel's introduction. "Nonfiction is arranging facts in a certain way to try and convince other people of your hypothesis," he observed in his interview with Dennis McLellan. "It's your best representation of what you think the truth is. But fiction tells the truth, because it reveals your innermost feelings and fantasies about situations, circumstances, people, and events. If you write fiction and you do it with intensity and passion, you reveal yourself—and you write the truth." The novel had its genesis in Chopra's reading, at the age of fourteen, Alfred, Lord Tennyson's *Idylls of the King*, twelve poems about the legend of King Arthur. In *The Return of Merlin*, Chopra transposes characters from the Arthurian legend into twentieth-century England, where they take part in a homicide investigation. "As the forces of good and evil do battle, Chopra, with sparkling wit, spiritual insight, and a light touch, weaves an inspirational parable imbued with the hope that trust, love, empathy, and awareness will one day supplant fear, hatred, and ignorance," wrote a reviewer for *Publishers Weekly* (May 8, 1995). Judith Dunford was less charitable in her review for *New York Newsday* (July 23, 1995): "The good news is that some moments are vividly imagined. The bad news is longer. Apart from its message—which will be appealing to some, repugnant to others—the novel lacks animation, in both senses. . . . It also lacks any of the whimsy, wit, or genius that, for example, raise the equally disjointed and episodic *Alice in Wonderland* to high art. The characters are about as differentiated as vegetables in canned soup. The dialogue and exposition are painfully clumsy and amateurish."

Chopra has also coproduced, with Time-Life video in 1994, a fifty-five-minute video called *Growing Younger*. Through his own Quantum Publications, he sells books, tapes, and herbal products and promotes his healing seminars and conferences. Writing projects on which he is currently working encompass three more novels, including an Indian romantic fantasy and a "spiritual thriller" about the escape of Satan from hell, and four more works of nonfiction, among them a mind/body textbook for physicians and a companion piece to his first novel entitled "The Wizard's

Way: A Step-by-Step Journey into the World of the Miraculous."

With his wife, Rita, Deepak Chopra lives in a split-level home nestled in the hills overlooking the ocean in La Jolla, California. Rising at 4:30 every morning, he meditates for an hour, works out in his home gym for an hour, then writes for at least three hours. "If all goes well I end up writing the whole day and into the night," he said when he spoke to McLellan. The Chopras have a son, Gautam, who is twenty, and a daughter, Mallika, who is twenty-four.

Selected Biographical References: American Health 11:43+ Ja/F '92 por; New York 28:28+ Ag 14 '95 pors; People 40:169+ N 15 '93 pors; Pub W 242:43+ Jl 24 '95 por; Who's Who in America, 1995

U.S. Department of State

Christopher, Warren M.

Oct. 27, 1925- United States Secretary of State. Address: State Department of the United States, Main State Bldg., 2201 C St. NW, Washington, DC 20520

NOTE: This biography supersedes the article that appeared in *Current Biography* in 1981.

Warren M. Christopher, who was appointed United States secretary of state in 1993, has had a distinguished career in international diplomacy. As deputy secretary of state under President Jimmy Carter from 1977 to 1981, he served both as the congressional point man for securing the passage of the Panama Canal treaties, which provided for the return of control of the canal to the government of Panama, and as the chief American negotiator for the release of the fifty-two Americans taken hostage by Iranian students in the aftermath of the revolution that toppled the repressive reign of Shah Mohammad Reza Pahlavi. On January 20, 1981, after 444 days in captivity, the hostages were released, just minutes after Carter's successor, Ronald Reagan, was sworn in as president of the United States. Christopher spent the following decade as a corporate lawyer in private practice with O'Melveny & Myers, one of Los Angeles's oldest and most prestigious law firms, with which he had been associated from the 1950s to the 1970s. He returned to public life in 1991, when he was appointed to head the independent commission that investigated widespread allegations of brutality and racism in the Los Angeles Police Department, which was roundly criticized in the wake of the videotaped beating by white police officers of Rodney G. King, a black motorist.

Following the 1992 election of President Bill Clinton, Christopher again found himself in the national spotlight, as leader of Clinton's transition team and then as his secretary of state. The choice of Christopher to guide the new administration's foreign policy was cheered in some quarters and jeered in others. Many observers agreed with Robert Reinhold of the *New York Times* (December 23, 1992), who declared that Christopher "brings an extraordinary attention to detail, infinite patience, poise, sure judgment, and an abiding conviction that most disputes can better be resolved through talking than fighting." Reinhold further described him, however, as lacking a geopolitical vision of the world, and Christopher has been frequently criticized for his reluctance to use military force. According to Jacob Heilbrunn, writing in the *New Republic* (February 1, 1993), "a scrutiny of his record [suggests that] Christopher is impelled by an uneasy blend of heady principle and exquisitely calibrated ambition. The result is a career marked by moral principles that are more often invoked than followed." There is no doubt that he has always weighed his options carefully before acting, a tendency that some have admired and others have derided. While touring the Yad Vashem Memorial, in Israel, which commemorates the six million Jews who died in the Holocaust, Christopher told Elaine Sciolino of the *New York Times* (February 28, 1993), "There is a heavy responsibility being secretary of state, and I worry about acquitting it well. It was brought home yesterday where I couldn't help but think, am I able to evaluate all the responsibilities? Am I able to sort out which of these things are possible situations like the Holocaust? You have a whole series of things that come across your plate. Is it Cambodia? Or is it Bosnia? Or is it Haiti? Can one possibly live up to those responsibilities?"

Warren Minor Christopher was born on October 27, 1925 in the small farming community of Scranton, North Dakota, the fourth of the five children of Ernest W. Christopher, a banker who suffered a stroke in 1937 following the collapse of his bank, and Catharine Anna (Lemen) Christopher, a homemaker who supported her children as a sales clerk after her husband's death in 1939. In that year the family moved to southern California, and Warren Christopher enrolled at Hollywood High School, where he was on the debating team. After attending the University of Redlands, in Redlands, California, in the 1942–43 academic year on a scholarship, he transferred to the University of Southern California, in University Park, Los Angeles, from which he graduated magna cum laude with a B.A. degree in 1945. On completing three years of service in the naval reserve, in 1946, he entered Stanford University Law School, in Palo Alto, California, where he was the founding editor of the *Stanford Law Review* and a member of the Order of the Coif, an honorary society. Equipped with his law degree, which he received in 1949, he clerked for a year in Washington, D.C., for Justice William O. Douglas of the United States Supreme Court.

Upon his return to Los Angeles in 1950, Christopher joined the prestigious and politically influential law firm O'Melveny & Myers, of which he was made a partner in 1958. According to Ninth Circuit judge Stephen Reinhardt, as quoted by Heilbrunn, O'Melveny & Myers was "a hotbed of racism into the late 1950s. . . . It was a very stiff, unimaginative place that didn't tolerate differences. Most people were very similar. It was hard to tell them apart. It was even hard to tell their wives apart." At the time, Christopher was a member of the California Club, whose charter refused membership to blacks, women, and Jews; he resigned from the club in 1976 to avoid embarrassing the Carter administration but renewed his association in 1981, after leaving the State Department. The conservative milieu in which he found himself in the 1950s did not prevent Christopher from initiating a letter-writing campaign to denounce Senator Joseph McCarthy for his anti-Communist witch hunts, nor did it stop him from serving, in 1959, as special counsel to California governor Edmund G. ("Pat") Brown, a Democrat, after having worked on his gubernatorial election campaign and writing his inaugural speech.

Perhaps Christopher's most prominent position in the California phase of his public-service career came in 1965, when he was appointed by Brown to the position of vice-chairman of the McCone Commission, chaired by former CIA director John McCone, which was established to look into the causes of urban rioting that year in the Watts section of Los Angeles. In the commission's exculpatory report, large portions of which were written by Christopher, according to Heilbrunn, the blame for the unrest fell neither on city or state governments nor on the police force but on local "riffraff." Christopher's experience on the McCone Commission proved valuable during the final two years of President Lyndon B. Johnson's administration, when he served as deputy attorney general under Ramsey Clark. In August 1967, after he was dispatched, along with Deputy Secretary of Defense Cyrus R. Vance, to Detroit following an eruption of rioting there, Christopher called for the president to send in the Eighty-second Airborne because the Michigan National Guard was allegedly inadequate to the task of quelling the violence. Then, in April 1968, when violence erupted in cities throughout the nation following the assassination of Martin Luther King Jr., Johnson put Christopher in charge of coordinating efforts by the United States Army and local authorities to control the disturbances in Chicago. A few months later Christopher prosecuted Chicago police officers for brutality during their efforts to control the crowd of antiwar protestors demonstrating outside the Democratic National Convention in that city.

In 1969 Christopher returned to O'Melveny & Myers in Los Angeles, where he sat out the administrations of Presidents Richard Nixon and Gerald R. Ford. In 1976 President-elect Jimmy Carter nominated Christopher as his deputy secretary of state under Cyrus Vance, the nominee for secretary of state. Although there was little opposition to the appointment, a small controversy erupted when Senator Jacob K. Javits, a liberal Republican from New York, alleged that while serving in Johnson's Justice Department, Christopher had known about and condoned illegal army surveillance of domestic dissident movements. Christopher denied the charges during his January 1977 confirmation hearings, and his nomination was approved by the full Senate on February 24, 1977. (These allegations resurfaced in 1993, along with documentation suggesting that in 1977 he had misled the Senate Committee on Foreign Relations regarding his awareness of military wrongdoing.)

In carrying out Carter's foreign policy, which was marked by an emphasis on human rights—in rhetoric if not always in deed—Vance and Christopher accumulated a mixed record. In 1978 Christopher denounced the Khmer Rouge's actions in Cambodia, where that group of Communist revolutionaries led by Pol Pot had been conducting a genocidal ruralization campaign that had resulted in hundreds of thousands of deaths since 1975. But he was silent on the issue of Indonesian violations of human rights in neighboring East Timor, which had lost an estimated one fifth of its population after being invaded and occupied by Indonesia in 1975. If Christopher had wanted to condemn Indonesia, whose troops had allegedly starved the Timorese people into submission, his options for doing so were apparently limited in light of Carter's appropriation of fifteen million dollars in military aid for that country in fiscal year 1978. In the autumn of 1979, however, the United States began an international relief effort in East Timor that lasted until December 1980, when Indonesian leaders decided the East Timorese had received enough from the outside world. In 1979 Christopher denounced the Nicaraguan dictator Anastasio Somoza, from whose regime the United States withdrew its support at that time. But evidently

Christopher did not publicly criticize Philippine leader Ferdinand Marcos, who had placed his country under martial law in 1972 (not to be lifted until 1981), and who continued to receive American support.

Christopher was more successful in the role of mediator and negotiator. Of particular concern during the Carter administration was the passage of the Panama Canal treaties, whereby the United States would honor its nearly century-old commitment to return control of the canal zone, and eventually of the canal itself, to the government of Panama. When the treaties, which had become a topic of intense public debate in 1977, ran into trouble in Congress in 1978, Christopher successfully defended the pacts, which were ratified by the Senate in March and April of that year. The first phase of the treaty, the return of the canal zone, went into effect on October 1, 1979; the final phase calls for the return of the canal to Panamanian jurisdiction by the year 2000.

Another area in which Christopher was particularly effective was in allieviating tensions between the United States and its allies. In 1978 he promised to end the arms embargo against Turkey, which had threatened to withdraw from NATO, and in 1979 he was dispatched to Taiwan to work out a framework of economic cooperation and security arrangements for the island nation after Carter's official recognition of the People's Republic of China, on December 31, 1978, had made state-to-state relations with Taiwan impossible. Christopher also became a key administration spokesman against the 1979 Soviet invasion of Afghanistan, and he defended to Congress the administration's decision to boycott the 1980 Summer Olympic Games in Moscow.

The most prominent role played by Christopher during the Carter administration came in its final year, when he emerged as chief negotiator in the Iranian hostage crisis, which began in November 1979 with the seizure by Iranian students of the American embassy, and its fifty-two officials and staffers, in Tehran. A botched helicopter rescue attempt in April 1980 led to Secretary of State Vance's resignation; Christopher's hopes of succeeding his mentor were dashed when Carter selected Senator Edmund S. Muskie of Maine, in what most observers characterized as an attempt to win favor with Congress. Christopher considered resigning because of the snub, but he stayed on to continue to work for the release of the hostages. He became the primary American negotiator in September 1980, when a high Iranian official made conciliatory remarks and spelled out conditions for the release of the hostages.

After Ronald Reagan was elected president two months later, Carter put pressure on Christopher to hurry the negotiations along, so that the hostages could be freed while he occupied the White House. On January 7, 1981 Christopher flew to Algeria for a final round of talks, which continued until a few minutes after Reagan was sworn into office, on January 20. Christopher was on hand in the Algerian capital of Algiers later that day to greet the planeload of former hostages on the first leg of their journey back to the United States. The meeting was an emotional one, even for the usually reserved Christopher, who later said, "There were very few people with dry eyes, and I was not among them." For his role in resolving the crisis, Christopher was awarded the Medal of Freedom by Carter. According to Jacob Heilbrunn, "though Christopher has been credited with the eventual release of the hostages, they were principally freed because the [Iranian] mullahs feared the military force that Reagan might unleash."

With a Republican back in the White House, Christopher returned to private practice in Los Angeles at O'Melveny & Myers, where he played a prominent role in increasing the already nationally renowned firm's stature and scope. He was named chairman of the firm's management committee, a position that gave him day-to-day operational control of the 550-lawyer firm, which has offices in New York City, Washington, D.C., Brussels, London, Tokyo, and San Francisco. During his tenure with the firm, it substantially increased its foreign-client base, especially in the Far East, where it signed up such industrial giants as Mitsui, Mitsubishi, Fuji Bank, Sumitomo Trust and Banking, Japan Airlines, and Hyundai. O'Melveny & Myers's domestic clients have included Southern California Edison, United Airlines, IBM, Occidental Petroleum, the city and county governments of Los Angeles, and the state of California. In 1981 Christopher was appointed to the board of directors of Southern California Edison, on which he had previously served from 1971 to 1977, and he was named to the board of the defense contractor Lockheed in 1987.

In 1991 Mayor Tom Bradley of Los Angeles called on Christopher to bring his reputation and his long history of deft political maneuvering to the investigation of the Los Angeles Police Department's conduct in the beating of Rodney King, on March 3, 1991. The Christopher Commission looked into the department's affairs for five months before presenting its findings. Writing in the *New York Times* (November 7, 1992), Robert Reinhold noted that " [Christopher's] report startled many [in Los Angeles] by eschewing compromise, forcefully detailing police misconduct and racism and calling for the replacement of the chief of police, Daryl F. Gates. Even the three commission members appointed by Mr. Gates joined in the report's recommendations, and it was Mr. Christopher's quiet lawyerly argumentation that brought them into the fold." John Spiegel, general counsel to the commission, was quoted by Reinhold in his December 1992 *New York Times* article as saying, "He was dealing with people from the community who had very strong feelings. It was very stressful. The meetings would go late into the evening and through all that, [Christopher's] patience and courtesy were just amazing. He really gave the people the sense that they were being listened to."

Within a few days of Bill Clinton's election as president, in 1992, Christopher was once again called on to serve at the national level, this time as the manager of Clinton's transition team. The president-elect chose Christopher because of the latter's long experience in government. Clinton had also evidently been pleased that Christopher, as head of his vice-presidential search committee, had recommended Tennessee senator Al Gore to be Clinton's running mate. Working out of the Little Rock, Arkansas transition office, Christopher shared duties with former National Urban League president Vernon Jordan, who headed another transition office in Washington, D.C. In announcing his appointment of Christopher to the cabinet post of secretary of state on December 22, 1992, Clinton said, "I have come to rely heavily on his judgment on a wide variety of areas, and I have come to know him as a friend I want nearby. With Warren Christopher as secretary of state, our country will be served by a person of keen intellect, clear vision, and deep values." Telling the press that the appointment was a "dream come true," Christopher vowed to continue to implement many of the initiatives of the George Bush administration, singling out the Middle East peace talks and the relief efforts in Somalia.

Because the Senate was controlled by Democrats, confirmation for most Clinton appointees was considered nearly guaranteed, but Christopher ran into some minor trouble. Senator Jesse Helms of North Carolina, the senior Republican on the Senate Foreign Relations Committee, probed the long-circulating accusations that, as deputy attorney general in the late 1960s, Christopher had known of or authorized an army intelligence plan to spy on domestic antiwar demonstrators. Although he had denied having such knowledge in 1977, a memo to Christopher uncovered in 1993 by the Associated Press at the Johnson presidential archives in Austin, Texas indicated that in 1968 Christopher had been informed of the illegal activity. Spokesmen for Christopher told reporters that although he may well have known, as his initials on the memo seemed to imply, he nonetheless did not remember. The matter ultimately caused only a slight ripple in an otherwise smooth confirmation process, which ended in Christopher's favor on January 20, 1993.

More substantive concerns have been raised by a statement by Zbigniew Brzezinski, Carter's national security adviser, who once pointed out that "Vance, and later Christopher, preferred to litigate endlessly, to shy away from the unavoidable ingredient of force in dealing with contemporary international realities, and to have an excessive faith that all issues can be resolved by compromise." Richard Haass, one of President Bush's National Security Council officers, criticized Christopher's modus operandi in an interview with J. F. O. McAllister of *Time* (June 7, 1993): "He's a mediator, used to a game with rules. He believes that if you look hard enough, you will find a common denominator out of which you can gradually construct some kind of edifice. It's very reactive. It's also easily overwhelmed by evil, and there is evil in this world." In his testimony to the Senate Foreign Relations Committee during his confirmation hearings on January 13 and 14, 1993, Christopher had tried to reassure critics who were worried about his ability to be decisive, especially on issues involving the military: "While there is no magic formula to guide such decisions, I do believe that the discreet and careful use of force in certain circumstances—and its credible threat in general—will be essential to the success of our diplomacy and foreign policy."

True to his stated intentions to continue some of the Bush administration's policies, Christopher toured the Middle East to promote peace talks on his first official trip abroad, in February 1993. Although he has scored some foreign-policy successes, most notably the relatively peaceful restoration of Haiti's democratically elected president, Jean-Bertrand Aristide, in October 1994, the aversion of a crisis over North Korea's potential nuclear capabilities, and the renewal and indefinite extension of the 1968 Nuclear Nonproliferation Treaty in May 1995, he has been widely criticized for perceived failures in Somalia and the former Yugoslavia. In famine-ravaged and war-torn Somalia, where a humanitarian-relief effort begun in December 1992 had by 1993 turned into an attempt to bring warring clan leaders to justice, eighteen American soldiers were killed before United States forces pulled out in March 1994.

In the former Yugoslavia, where independence movements of several of its six constituent republics had been violently resisted since 1991 by Serbs, who feared their new minority status in an independent Croatia and Bosnia and Herzegovina, the United States and its allies in NATO and the United Nations were severely criticized for repeatedly threatening the Bosnian Serbs with NATO air strikes (which were finally delivered in the summer of 1995) but failing to act when the Serbs violated various cease-fire agreements and overran areas designated by the United Nations as "safe havens" for Bosnian Muslim refugees. In September 1995 the warring parties in Bosnia signed an accord that was negotiated by Assistant Secretary of State Richard C. Holbrooke, who is the United States's special envoy to the Balkans. The prospect that the accord might lead to a peace agreement that would need to be enforced by the UN and/or NATO led the Clinton administration to reevaluate its two-year-old promise to send as many as twenty-five thousand troops to help NATO patrol new borders and protect humanitarian-relief workers. Faced with opposition from a Republican Congress, Clinton, national security adviser Anthony Lake, and chairman of the Joint Chiefs of Staff John Shalikashvili argued for deployment of a sizable military force. On the other hand, Christopher, according to Eric Schmitt of the *New York Times* (September 22, 1995), "has argued in private meetings that the United States can do its share with far fewer than twenty-five thousand forces."

Christopher's reluctance to offend allies by acting unilaterally in the Balkans drew fire from his detractors, but a writer for the *Economist* (February 13, 1993) declared that if his policy is "legalistic, cautious, and dependent above all on compromise, it is also basically sensible. If Mr. Christopher's handiwork can be said to be lacking in strategic sweep, so be it. For now in Bosnia, Marshallian vision is not only unnecessary, but probably undesirable." In a private meeting with Clinton in December 1994, Christopher reportedly offered to resign as secretary of state, but the president asked him to stay on and to capitalize on their foreign-policy successes.

Warren Christopher has often been depicted as dour and reserved. J.F.O. McAllister described him as a "natural introvert old enough to be Clinton's father, [who] glides into a room as silently as a monk. His gravelly monotone and wrinkled poker face give nothing away, his mobile eyes are friendly but curiously unreadable." Since December 21, 1956, Christopher has been married to Marie Josephine (Wyllis) Christopher, a former schoolteacher. They have three children: Scott, an investment banker in San Francisco; Thomas, a lawyer in Stockholm; and Kristen, who works in public relations in New York City. Lynn Collins, Christopher's daughter from a previous marriage, is a homemaker in the San Francisco Bay Area. He enjoys playing tennis, jogging, listening to jazz, and drinking a dry martini before dinner. Until he moved to Washington, D.C., in 1993, he divided his time between a traditionally furnished one-story home in the Beverly Hills section of Los Angeles and a beach house in nearby Santa Barbara.

Selected Biographical References: Am Spec 26:38+ F '93 por; Economist 326:30 F 13 '93 por; Interview 24:72+ N '94 por; N Y Times A p9 N 7 '92 por, A p1+ D 23 '92 por; New Repub 208:24+ F 1 '93 por; Newsweek 121:52 Mr 1 '93 por, 123:36+ Ap 4 '94 por, 125:31+ Je 26 '95 por; Time 142:48+ N 22 '93 por; U S News 115:24+ Jl 5 '93 por; Findling, John E. Dictionary of American Diplomatic History (1989); Who's Who in America, 1995

The Pushpin Group

Chwast, Seymour

(kwahst)

Aug. 18, 1931– Graphic designer; artist. Address: c/o Pushpin Group Inc., 215 Park Ave. S., New York, NY 10003

Self-described as "a designer who illustrates," Seymour Chwast is "a truly mythic figure in the annals of graphic design," in the words of Steven Heller, the art director of the *New York Times Book Review.* Chwast is a cofounder of the Push Pin Studios (known for the last decade as the Pushpin Group), whose approaches to graphic design since its formation in 1954 have indelibly influenced modes of visual communication throughout the world. In recognition of its extraordinary contribution to graphic design, in 1970 the Louvre, in Paris, mounted a retrospective exhibition of the work of Chwast and other Push Pin illustrators and designers. The exhibition, which included illustrations from the *Push Pin Almanack* and *Push Pin Graphic*, Push Pin's celebrated promotional publications, was called *The Push Pin Style.* According to Steven Heller, the Pushpin style may be characterized as a "distinctive, eclectic union of illustration and design" and as "a *spirit* based on humor, play, and surprise." As "style" is usually defined in art, Pushpin has never relied on a single style, and in the countless Pushpin assignments that he has completed individually, Chwast too has used a variety of styles as well as different media. Nevertheless, "his work is immediately identifiable, always marked by his personal design and color sense and his unique wit," as Lanny Sommese wrote in *Novum Gebrauchsgraphik* (June 1991).

Brilliantly adapting for contemporary audiences the "traditions, ideologies, forms, styles, idioms, and techniques" of centuries of art, and balancing image and type with consummate skill, Chwast has created thousands of designs and illustrations for magazines, newspapers, books, advertisements, posters, animated films, packaging, and record-album covers, among other vehicles, and graphics for corporations, institutions, and nonprofit organizations. "Chwast's longevity is remarkable," according to Lanny Sommese, "especially when one considers that graphic design chews up and spews out fresh talent at breathtaking speed. . . . There are few individuals who have remained on the cutting edge year after year. Chwast is one of that special group."

Chwast's huge body of work includes pen-and-ink and pencil drawings, acrylic paintings, monoprints, woodcuts, serigraphs, papier-mâché figures, galvanized-steel sculptures, and highly original typefaces. An acknowledged master of the art of the poster, he has produced antiwar and theatrical posters that have become icons of the genre and are represented in the permanent collections of major museums in the United States and overseas. He has also designed, illustrated, and/or coedited or written more than thirty books, including more than two dozen for children. His books for adults include *The Left-Handed Designer* (1985), a copiously illustrated survey of his work that he wrote in collaboration with Steven Heller. All of his creations, he has said, communicate his point of view. "What I do *is* my point of view," he told Heller during an interview that was transcribed for *The Left-Handed Designer*. "It pleases me that there is a bond with others that occurs when this happens. . . . I'm still amazed and get great satisfaction in seeing a drawing that I had done the day before printed in the *New York Times*. My work as a commercial artist, seen by millions, gives me joy and satisfaction."

An only child until the age of sixteen, Seymour Chwast was born on August 18, 1931 to Aaron Louis Chwast and Esther (Newman) Chwast in the New York City borough of the Bronx. His only sibling is his half-sister, Judith Chwast Manrique, who is a bank official. His father, a Veterans Administration file clerk, moonlighted as a waiter; his mother was a homemaker. At the age of five or six, Chwast began drawing cartoons. Inspired by newspaper comic strips, Walt Disney animated films, and the serial movies that were popular in the 1930s, he produced comic strips featuring characters of his own creation, among them heroic figures named Lucky Day and Jim Lightning. Beginning at the age of seven, he took art classes that were held under the auspices of the Work Projects Administration. In *Graphic Design USA* (1986), Steven Heller wrote that as a youngster Chwast "became profoundly aware of the difference between museum and street art and seemed to instinctively prefer the allure of billboards and advertisements to Picassos and Mondrians."

When Chwast was ten he moved with his parents from the Bronx to Saratoga Springs, New York, where the VA had transferred his father. He attended Saratoga Springs High School for two years. In 1945 his father received a job transfer back to New York City, and he and his parents settled in the Coney Island section of the borough of Brooklyn, where he enrolled at Abraham Lincoln High School. "On the outside this was an ordinary New York City public school," Steven Heller reported in *Graphic Design USA*, "but inside it was a hotbed of graphic design education." Chwast has described his graphic design teacher, Leon Friend, as "a charismatic father figure who gave [him] an appreciation of typography and graphic design and equated success in these areas with achieving nirvana." To have one's work printed constituted the height of success, Friend told his students, and he insisted that they enter as many art competitions as possible. Chwast complied, and when he was sixteen his first published illustration appeared, in a readers' column in *Seventeen* magazine. In Friend's classes Chwast was exposed to outstanding examples of poster art dating back several generations, and as a member of the Art Squad, a select group of the school's best art students, he made posters for school events. During summers he worked as a cashier at a Coney Island amusement-park concession.

After graduating from high school, in 1948, Chwast enrolled at the School of Art and Architecture at Cooper Union (formally known as the Cooper Union for the Advancement of Science and Art), a New York City institution that offers tuition-free instruction to students who perform sufficiently well on a qualifying examination. He majored in advertising art, having abandoned in high school his long-held plan to become a film animator. Chwast has said that he "owe[s his] life and career" to his experiences at Cooper Union. Among his instructors, he has singled out his drawing teacher, Sidney Delevante, as especially influential in his development as an artist and designer. During his interview with Steven Heller for *The Left-Handed Designer*, Chwast said, "Delevante . . . revolutionized my way of thinking by making me start everything from zero with nothing preconceived. I also learned from him that, while my work had a point of view, there were infinite ways of expressing it. He helped me find ways that were consistent with my personality." Chwast also learned a lot, he reported, from his fellow students Milton Glaser, Edward Sorel, and Reynold Ruffins. As undergraduates, Chwast, Glaser, and Ruffins formed a business that they called Design Plus, which, during its brief existence, executed two assignments: the illustrations and design for a children's book and a flyer for a theatrical performance.

Chwast was also strongly influenced by the work of such artists as Georges Rouault, Paul Klee, George Grosz, and Saul Steinberg, and as a self-described political activist who, in his words, "was sympathetic to radical and pacifist causes," he much admired prints by the artists Francisco de Goya and Honoré Daumier. "Theirs was a passion motivated by their beliefs about politics and society," he has said of Daumier and Goya. "Their work had bite. They expressed *feeling* you could only get through a print, and that approach conformed to the way I was thinking in those days." A Ben Shahn exhibition at the Museum of Modern Art, in New York City, also "proved to be a major influence" on him, he has said. "The power of [Shahn's] work emerged from the immediacy and directness of his style," he told Steven Heller. "It was awkward and decorative, like the work of the primitive artists, but the depth of his feeling and his humanity were always there." By around 1950, Chwast told Heller, he realized not only that he had no interest in fine art as a career but also that design—"how the type looked, how the spread looked, how the work was being used"—was "much more important to [him] than . . . illustration alone." "I found that I needed a message or literary reference to react to," he said. "Solving esthetic problems was either beyond me or seemed self-indulgent, considering my working-class background." A series of woodcuts with an antiwar theme that Chwast made as an undergraduate was privately printed as *The Book of Battles* in 1957.

During the three years that followed his graduation from Cooper Union with a diploma in 1951 (the college did not confer bachelor's degrees then), Chwast held a succession of jobs involving various aspects of graphic art. He worked first, for a year, as a junior designer in the promotion department of the *New York Times*, where his knowledge of typography broadened considerably under the guidance of George Krikorian, the department's art director. His inability to render comprehensive sketches (known familiarly as comps) soon led to his dismissal from a job at the design firm Sudler and Hennessey by its art director, the graphic designer and typographer Herb Lubalin. His stints at several other places, among them the art departments of *Esquire*, *House & Garden*, and *Glamour* magazines, did not last much longer.

Chwast was still employed by others when, in about 1953, he and Edward Sorel and Reynold Ruffins began soliciting freelance work as a team. To advertise their talents, they produced and mailed to prospective clients a bimonthly promotional piece, which they called the *Push Pin Almanack*. "While it had its own conventions, we were able to apply our own typographic ideas and do quaint drawings, consistent not only with almanacs but with the style of the times," Chwast has said of the *Almanack*. Encouraged by their success at getting a few assignments, in 1954 Chwast and Sorel teamed up with Milton Glaser to work for themselves full-time, as partners in what they christened the Push Pin Studios. When they had to communicate with clients, they used a pay phone outside the cold-water flat that served as their work space. "In those low-tech days . . . it took very little capital to go into business," Chwast has observed.

At first, a significant part of the Push Pin Studios' income (and the partners' earnings—twenty-five dollars apiece weekly) derived from sales of illustrations for a few educational slide presentations. Before long Chwast, Glaser, and Sorel began getting a variety of assignments, not only on the strength of their past work but through their newly incarnated promotional piece. Resembling a small magazine, the *Push Pin Graphic*, like its predecessor, contained in each issue text and pictures on a single theme, such as mothers, chickens, New Jersey, the South, the 1930s, good and evil, and the connection between crime and food. And like the *Almanack*, the *Graphic* provided Push Pin's partners with the opportunity to indulge in typographical experimentation and offered them a forum for their distinctive individual approaches to drawing. Proceeding "in the spirit of decorative illustration," as he has put it, Chwast devoted himself primarily to making monoprints, woodcuts, drawings with bold lines that he made with a Speedball pen, and drawings that he made on chipboard with colored pencils and acrylic paints. Chwast served as the editor and publisher of the *Push Pin Graphic* from 1976 until it ceased publication in 1981.

When Steven Heller remarked, during their conversation for *The Left-Handed Designer*, that whereas commercial art entails pleasing a client, the *Push Pin Graphic* required nobody's approval but the partners' own, Chwast said, "The art directors responded to that. They might not have been able to sell our approach to their clients, but selling it to *them* was half the battle. It proved that we could think, organize, and translate literary material into visual statements. But also, I think our work has always been accessible. It used to be called 'far out' in those days, but if our interpretation was right, the style was unimportant to the client. More importantly, we were *inventing* things." Two Push Pin "inventions"—Glaser and Chwast's idea of enclosing drawings in the *Graphic* in boxes with rounded corners, and Chwast's use of a broken line in some of his drawings—were almost immediately adopted by other designers.

Chwast has said that he "allow[ed] everything—old posters, rubber stamps, antiques, modern paintings"—to influence his work, and he freely "borrowed" from such sources as Victoriana, Art Nouveau, Art Deco, and primitive and folk art. "Surrealism also affected me: misplaced objects; the idea of doing fairly realistic situations that are confounded by odd relationships and strangely connected elements," he told Steven Heller. "Style in general is useful because it provides immediate clues to the message," he noted. "It might signal 'elegance' or 'modernity,' for instance. Putting an old style in a new context is surprising, because certain relationships may be ironic; others may fit perfectly well. But they allow a designer to make very graphic statements."

Edward Sorel ended his partnership in Push Pin in 1957, on the day that Chwast and Glaser moved their business from their original, low-rent quarters to a more upscale Manhattan space. In *Penrose Graphics Arts International Annual* (1976), Jerome Snyder described Chwast and Glaser as "distinct and divergent yet fully complementary personalities who came together in a creative collaboration of a kind rarely found [in the visual arts], and one which has proved a veritable cornucopia of the graphic arts." "If there is an untiring energy source in their individual and collective output," Snyder wrote, "it is the element of surprise, a delightful unpredictability of conceptual solution and artistic execution that never allows our interest to flag. . . . We are intellectually and visually indulged, and at least for that small viewing moment, the small world before us urges us on to larger spiritual satisfactions."

In 1975, a few months before Snyder's words appeared in the *Penrose* annual, Milton Glaser had left Push Pin. Chwast remained as director, with Phyllis Flood handling Push Pin's marketing and also managing the studio. In 1982, as a means of expanding the scope of the studio's assignments, he merged Push Pin with the design firm Lubalin, Peckolick and formed a partnership with its remaining principal, the graphic designer Alan Peckolick. The partnership ended in 1986, a year after the name of the studio was changed to the Pushpin Group. Such well-known illustrators and designers as Reynold Ruffins, Paul Davis, John Alcorn, George Stavrinos, James McMullan, Barry Zaid, and Sam Antupit have contributed to Pushpin projects and to the studio's renown. Earlier, in 1983, Chwast and Steven Heller cofounded Pushpin Editions, which has produced a wide range of books on graphic design and the arts.

In the late 1960s Chwast, independently of Push Pin, began designing and/or illustrating books for McGraw-Hill, Doubleday, Random House, and Delacorte Press, among other publishers. The first, *Connoisseur Book of the Cigar* (1967), was followed by a dozen children's books. "My only prerequisite for illustrating children's books is that they be fanciful or mysterious," he has said. Chwast wrote as well as designed and illustrated *Tall City, Wide Country* (1983), which is subtitled "A Book to Read Forward and Backward." His most recent solo-created books for children are *The Alphabet Parade* (1991) and *The Twelve Circus Rings* (1993). Most of his books for young readers, like much of his commercial art work, feature clearly contoured, simply drawn figures executed with stylograph, felt pen, or brush. Chwast favors a bright palette of acrylic colors in which pink, orange, delicate lilac, light blue, poison green, and canary yellow predominate. "There's nothing behind what I'm doing," he has said of such illustrations, which display, in his words, an "innocent, head-on style." "It's all laid out. There's no symbolism, no mystery."

Happy Birthday, Bach (1985), which Chwast designed and illustrated and which has captions by the musician and composer Peter Schickele, is a book for people of all ages. A celebration of the three-hundredth anniversary of Johann Sebastian Bach's birth, it contains three hundred images of Bach in guises ranging from court jester to civil-rights marcher. In *Graphic Design USA*, Steven Heller described the paintings, collages, drawings, and prints in *Happy Birthday, Bach* as "so stylistically rich and varied . . . that [the book] will serve the design historian as a complete record of Chwast's range." Chwast himself has said, "[*Happy Birthday, Bach*], more than any other work I've done, represents my involvement with concept and style."

Chwast designed and, with Steven Heller, coedited *Art Against War: 400 Years of Protest in Art* (1984). Written by D. J. R. Bruckner, it shows "the steady evolution in the vocabulary of art against war," in the words of Andrea Barnett, who observed in the *New York Times Book Review* (June 10, 1984) that *Art Against War* "is an eerie reminder of how often war has been the subject of art and [is] a timely exhortation too." Heller and Chwast are also the coauthors of *The Art of New York* (1984) and *Graphic Style, from Victorian to Post-Modern* (1988), the latter of which contains a brief text accompanied by more than seven hundred illustrations, ranging from examples of avant-garde typography and corporate logos to photos of furniture and shopping bags. "While Heller and Chwast provide us with the who, where, when, and how of style development, they also deal with the peripheral and reactionary trends, making the evolution of graphic styles more understandable," M. LaPorte wrote in *Choice* (April 1989), in a review that described *Graphic Style* as "a fascinating book for the casual reader" and predicted that it would "become a respected reference for the professional designer, artist, [and] craftsperson." Chwast and Heller's most recent book is *Jackets Required: An Illustrated History of American Book Jacket Design, 1920–1950* (1995).

"From early morning to well into the evening," Steven Heller reported, Seymour Chwast "sits on his turn-of-the-century wooden office chair, hunched over his drawing board. . . . As sirens and car horns from the street compete with the classical music from his radio, Chwast usually is intently drawing . . . drawing . . . drawing. From time to time he emerges from his office to consult on a job with an assistant or colleague, or to meet with a client, but for the most part, Chwast just works . . . works . . . works." By his own account, Chwast "always work[s] on half a dozen things simultaneously, in different states." "I observe the formal principles of design (proportion, harmony, dynamics, symmetry, line, mass, texture), while I am manipulating elements to suit my purposes . . . ," he has said of his approach to graphic design. "My drawing is weak. But I am not as interested in that as I am in making a graphic idea work. That's why I'm less concerned with *finish*. The concept has always been most to express the idea. Surface, neatness, rendering, and craft are things that interest me less." Chwast revealed to Heller that whenever he begins a new assignment, he thinks, "With the *last* drawing, I've had my *last* good idea," and he is consumed by the fear that he will never draw again. "It's a struggle, since everything's been done," he said.

Among the memorable illustrations that Chwast has produced for magazines and newspapers while engaged in that struggle are many caricatures of Richard M. Nixon that date from Nixon's presidency. The dozens of posters that he has created to publicize theatrical and television shows include his placards for the Mobil Oil Company–sponsored television productions of *I, Claudius* (1976), *Nicho-*

las Nickleby (1982), and *Five Stories by Noel Coward* (1987), the PBS *Mystery* series *Rumpole of the Bailey*, and the New York City Opera's 1983 productions of six Puccini operas. Among his most famous antiwar posters is one that bears the slogan "End Bad Breath." Created to protest the bombing of Hanoi by United States planes during the Vietnam War, it depicts Uncle Sam with a gaping mouth, inside which airplanes are dropping bombs over huts. In "War Is Madness," another of his antiwar posters, the eyes and mouth of a fierce male face are depicted as the silhouettes of bombs. "The poster—with its scale, visibility, immediacy, and its afterlife as 'art'—offers compelling possibilities," Chwast has said. Examples of Chwast's posters are in the permanent collections of the Museum of Modern Art and the Cooper-Hewitt Museum of the Smithsonian Institution, in New York City; the Library of Congress, in Washington, D.C.; the Gutenberg Museum, in Mainz, and the Stadtmuseum, in Munich, Germany; the Israel Museum, in Jerusalem; and the Suntory Art Museum, in Osaka, Japan.

The many book jackets that Chwast has illustrated include covers for editions of *The Death Ship*, by B. Traven, *Zorba the Greek*, by Nikos Kazantzakis, *Our Crowd*, by Stephen Birmingham, and a reissue of the novels of Dostoyevsky. A series of witty advertisements that he produced in the 1980s for *Forbes* magazine received wide distribution in periodicals and on billboards. (One ad shows a driver filling his roadster with gas from a pump that is portrayed as a huge copy of the magazine. The ad carries the message "*Forbes* fuels your drive.") In the arena of packaging, Chwast has designed a children's carton for McDonald's hamburgers, a box for a six-pack of an upscale beer, and a shopping bag for an elegant Paris boutique, among numerous other creations.

Chwast has taught classes in design at Cooper Union, the School of Visual Arts, and the Parsons School of Design and has frequently given lectures to student and professional groups on such subjects as design education, the social and ethical responsibilities of the designer, and the computer as a creative tool. In 1971–72, with Milton Glaser, he codesigned and served as art director of *Audience*, a hardcover magazine devoted to art and culture. In 1975 he was selected for membership in the Alliance Graphique Internationale. He has served on the board of directors of the American Institute of Graphic Arts and the New York Art Directors Club. His many design awards include the St. Gaudens Medal, from Cooper Union, in 1972, and a gold medal from the American Institute of Graphic Arts, in 1985. He was inducted into the New York Art Directors Club Hall of Fame in 1984, and he received an honorary doctorate from the Parsons School of Design, in New York City, in 1992. *IDEA*, Japan's leading graphic arts magazine, devoted an entire issue to his work, and he was the subject of a special feature in the *Frankfurter Allgemeine* magazine. Chwast has had solo shows—including ten exhibitions of his cut-out, galvanized-steel sculptures, which he began making in 1990—at museums and galleries in the United States, Germany, France, Switzerland, Ireland, Japan, Brazil, and the former Soviet Union. In 1986 Cooper Union held a thirty-five-year retrospective of his work. The Push Pin retrospective that was held for two months at the Louvre's Musée des Arts Décoratifs in 1970 marked the first time the Louvre so honored an American design studio. It subsequently appeared in museums throughout Europe as well as in Brazil and Japan.

Seymour Chwast has been described as "completely unassuming," reticent, soft-spoken, shy, unflappable, and, as Karen S. Chambers wrote in the graphic-arts magazine *U&lc* (Fall 1992), a mixture of "practicality and puckishness." In *Step-by-Step Graphics* (January 1990), Susan Davis reported that as he works, he "puff[s] on a pipe like an absent-minded professor." Chwast has been married since 1989 to the designer Paula Scher. Their previous, six-year marriage ended in divorce in 1979. Chwast's first marriage (1952–71), to the artist Jacqueline Weiner, and his third marriage (1980–82), to Barbara Wool, also ended in divorce. Chwast and his wife live in the Gramercy Park section of Manhattan, not far from his Pushpin studios. "I often have to run home to get a book I need for reference on an assignment," he told Lanny Sommese. From his marriage to Jacqueline Weiner, Chwast has two daughters: Eve, an artist with whom he has sometimes collaborated, and Pamela, a jewelry designer and bookkeeper. For relaxation, he watches old movies on television.

Selected Biographical References: Graphis 48:80+ Ja/F '92, 49:55+ S/O '93 por; N Y Times Mag p19+ Mr 6 '77; Novum Gebrauchsgraphik p61+ Je '90, p12+ Je '91; Chwast, Seymour and Steven Heller. The Left-Handed Designer (1985); Graphic Design USA, vol 7, 1986; Naylor, Colin, ed. Contemporary Designers (1990); Penrose Graphics Arts International Annual vol 68 (1975); Siegel, Rita Sue. American Graphic Designers (1984); Who's Who in America, 1995

Crumb, R.

Aug. 30, 1943– Cartoonist. Address: c/o Fantagraphics Books, 7563 Lake City Way, Seattle, WA 98115

For nearly three decades R. Crumb, the leading member of the group of "underground" cartoonists whose work revitalized comics in the late 1960s, has been one of the most influential figures working in his genre. His controversial strips, which have featured the antiheroes Mr. Natural, Angelfood McSpade, Whiteman, and Fritz the Cat, among a host of others, have satirized every aspect of American society from bourgeois values to the counterculture that he helped define. Crumb's

Self-Portrait/*Robert Crumb*

R. Crumb

comics are characterized by their lewd illustrations and their sexually explicit and sometimes violent content, phenomena all the more unsettling because his characters resemble in so many ways the cute heroes of "clean" comic strips. Although his work has attracted only a cult following in the United States, it has influenced many other American cartoonists, and Crumb enjoys mainstream success throughout Europe, where he currently resides.

The second of five children in a Roman Catholic family, Robert Crumb was born on August 30, 1943 in Philadelphia, Pennsylvania. He has a younger brother and two sisters; his older brother, Charles Crumb Jr., committed suicide in 1992. The Crumb family was what would later be termed dysfunctional. Charles Crumb Sr., a career marine, beat his children, breaking Robert's collarbone when the boy was five years old, and Robert's mother became addicted to amphetamines, which she used to control her weight in an effort to please her husband. Charles Crumb Jr. both mirrored and rebelled against his father's tyrannical behavior by forcing his brothers into an activity their father found loathsome: drawing cartoons.

In part, no doubt, because it provided a refuge from his chaotic family life, Robert Crumb developed a love for drawing. One of his favorite cartoon characters was Felix the Cat, and he and his older brother invented characters, such as Brombo the Panda, that were influenced by Felix and other animal heroes. Crumb's earliest efforts were not met with encouragement. He and his brother tried, and failed, to sell their comics door-to-door, and at Robert's high school in Milford, Delaware, where his family had moved when he was twelve, his teachers frowned on cartooning. "It was like sheer persistence that got me to where I am today," Crumb told Thomas Maremaa for a profile of the cartoonist in the *New York Times Magazine* (October 1, 1972). Crumb's adolescent years were a difficult period for him in other respects as well, for his extreme shyness and lack of athletic ability kept him from forming friendships with his peers. He has recalled that he "probably wouldn't have gotten that deeply into cartooning" had it not been for his loneliness and his need for a form of self-expression. "I can remember thinking when I was sixteen that one day when I was this great, recognized artist, I wouldn't be alienated any more," he told Maremaa.

After graduating from high school, Crumb lived with his parents for a year before moving to Cleveland, Ohio, where he accepted a job as a colorist at the American Greetings Corporation. Before long his boss, Tom Wilson, who later created the successful syndicated cartoon *Ziggy*, saw Crumb's sketchbooks and was so impressed that he had him draw humorous cards for the company. "The boss kept telling me my drawing was too grotesque," Crumb told Thomas Maremaa in 1972. "He got me to draw this cute stuff, which influenced my technique, and even now my work has this cuteness about it."

In his spare time, Crumb wrote and illustrated a 140-page cartoon novel, *R. Crumb's Yum-Yum Book*, in 1963 (Scrimshaw Press published it in the mid-1970s). A year or so later, he began drawing Fritz the Cat, who would become one of his most famous characters. A feline with human attributes, Fritz the Cat was, depending on the mood of his creator, a college student, con artist, lothario, or political revolutionary, and his adventures were serialized in *Cavalier* magazine before being published in book form in 1968. In the meantime, in 1965 Crumb had begun taking hallucinogenic drugs, an experience that he has credited with changing his attitude about many things, among them his drawing. "It made me stop taking cartooning so seriously," he told Thomas Maremaa. While he was visiting friends in Chicago in 1966, he "took some weird acid, and all of a sudden everything got real fuzzy." "I stayed that way for three months, and all this crazy stuff came out of my brain," he recalled. "That's how I invented [the characters] Mr. Natural, Angelfood McSpade, Mr. Snoid." Mr. Natural is the best-known of those creations. Bald, wearing a formless, ankle-length gown, with a long white beard and enormous feet (a Crumb trademark), he is part con man and part symbol for sexual liberation.

In January 1967, having quit his job at American Greetings Corporation, Crumb moved to the Haight-Ashbury section of San Francisco, then one of the rallying points for the counterculture. "I sat on Haight Street and got stoned with all the other hippies," Crumb told Peter Carlson of *People* (June 24, 1985). He also became one of a group of cartoonists whose work revived the subversive spirit of the earliest comics and defied the rigidly moralistic code that the industry had adopted, under governmental pressure, in the previous decade. (Among those artists was Art Spiegelman, who later gained fame for the two volumes of *Maus*, his cartoon novels about the Holocaust.) Crumb became the most prominent figure in that "underground" comics movement when the first issue of his comic book *Zap* appeared in February 1968.

Zap No. 1 featured Mr. Natural; Flakey Foont, a naïve young man who, with conflicting feelings about his carnal impulses, finds in Mr. Natural a mentor of sorts; and Whiteman, the most inhibited and among the most famous of Crumb's protagonists—a straitlaced representative of suburban America who represses his powerful sexual urges only to become more preoccupied by them. Since underground comics (or "comix," to the use the preferred spelling of the artists of the period) were generally denied mainstream distribution in stores and newsstands, Crumb himself, together with his publisher, Don Donahue, sold copies of *Zap* on the streets of San Francisco.

Indifference seems to have been the one response not provoked by Crumb's work. Some of his comics were banned or were the targets of police "busts" due to their alleged obscenity. In his profile of the cartoonist, Peter Carlson quoted a judge in Maryland as saying with regard to one cartoon, "To say this is art is ridiculous. It is a piece of trash." The legal challenges Crumb's work brought about seem not to have diminished its popularity, for within four years of *Zap*'s first appearance, his comic books were selling between eight thousand and ten thousand copies per month. While those numbers represented only a tiny fraction of the total sales in the comic-book industry, they were indicative of a significant following. *Zap* was also notable for reintroducing a saying, "Keep on Truckin'," that had been popular among blues artists of the 1930s. In its second incarnation, "Keep on Truckin'" became something of an unofficial national slogan, appearing with Crumb's illustration of a huge-footed pedestrian on tee-shirts and bumper stickers all over the United States. In addition to *Zap*, Crumb wrote and illustrated the magazine *Snatch*, and he contributed work to several other publications, including *Motor City Comics*, *Home Grown Funnies*, *East Village Other*, and *Bijou Funnies*. His work in those journals appeared under a multitude of pseudonyms, among them Crumbum, Crumski, and Little Bobby Scumbag.

Crumb's readership was made up largely of college students, intellectuals, and cultural critics, and his work consequently received no small amount of attention in the print media. Some observers compared the social commentary in Crumb's comics to that in the music of the folk-rock icon Bob Dylan. Among those was Jacob Brackman, who wrote in *Playboy* (December 1970), "Dylan and some others decimated cult 'n' brow divisions by showing that what seemed most common, what made kids scream, could be as good as any art produced in our time. Crumb's art is precisely that good. It compels us to disown the idea that comics are just simple-minded drawings with overhead balloons geared to people without enough upstairs to handle pictureless books."

Brackman went on to explain the nature of Crumb's appeal and the reason that he was ultimately an unsuitable, and unwilling, symbol for the counterculture: "Like Dylan, Crumb has acquired a cult of followers seeking clues to the proper conduct of their own lives. . . . Fans pore over his *oeuvres* for something like guidance; at least for an appropriate attitude, a posture toward all the *meshugaas* that's going down now. They play Flakey to Crumb's Mr. Natural. Hopeless. For he won't stop shifting his ground, shifting targets. Like all great fantasists, he's irresponsible. His worlds forever *suggest* the one we know but never bear any easy or explicit relation to it. Conditions are never quite the same, never quite the opposite."

The cartoonist's success "underground" translated into offers from mainstream publishers and others. Ballantine Books published two collections of his work, and he was commissioned to illustrate the cover of a Janis Joplin album. The year 1972 saw the release of the animated film *Fritz the Cat*, which represented, from Crumb's viewpoint, one of the disasters of his career. The agreement that he reluctantly signed with Ralph Bakshi guaranteed Crumb ten thousand dollars and a percentage of the profits realized by the project and gave Bakshi the right to animate the movie based on Crumb's comics from the 1960s. The end result was displeasing to the cartoonist. Insisting to Thomas Maremaa that Bakshi "put words into [Fritz's] mouth that [his creator] never would have had him say," Crumb declared, "It was *not* my movie. . . . A lot of people seemed to think I was involved. That bothers me." (In spite of Crumb's reaction to the finished product, the seventy-seven-minute, X-rated film, which chronicled the exploits—often sexual—of its central character, was well received by critics.)

His experience with that movie increased Crumb's reluctance to share creative control over any aspect of his work. Thus, when he was offered such potentially lucrative deals as a contract with *Playboy*, he turned them down. His distrust of the mainstream, which he associated with artistic compromise, extended even to his own comics: when *Zap* became too popular to suit Crumb, he titled his comics magazines *Despair* and *Uneeda* instead. Crumb "was not uncommercial," Tom Wilson told Peter Carlson for the *People* profile. "He was *anti*commercial."

While Crumb had rejected the various high-profile projects that had come his way, his mainstay—the underground comics market—was itself disappearing, due to its having become saturated with the work of inferior cartoonists and to the continual threat of police busts. Those lean years for the underground movement coincided with turmoil in Crumb's personal life. In the mid-1970s, at the same time that his first marriage, to Dana Morgan, was collapsing, the Internal Revenue Service informed him that he owed forty thousand dollars in back taxes.

Crumb has credited his second wife, the painter and underground cartoonist Aline Kominski, whom he had met in the early 1970s, with helping him to survive emotionally and financially during that period. Although the couple experienced some grueling poverty (Peter Carlson reported that at one point they lived in a "migrant-worker shack without plumbing"), together they were able to improve their situation. In 1978, the year that Crumb and Kominski married, the German company Zweitausendeeins printed one of the cartoonist's sketchbooks (the first of several it would publish), and Crumb was able to pay his debt to the IRS. Four years later he received an unexpected boon: a royalty check, from the producers of the movie *Fritz the Cat*, in the amount of thirty-one thousand dollars. (He and Kominski used the money to purchase the house in Winters, California that they had been renting.)

In the late 1970s and early 1980s, Crumb's work underwent changes. While it remained satirical and avant-garde—he founded the magazine *Weirdo* in 1981—it became considerably less concerned with sex. Gone were the likes of Mr. Natural, replaced by characters, including the yuppie Mode O'Day, more representative of the materialism of the period. Crumb also branched out into areas besides comic books. He had a highly successful show at an art gallery in San Francisco that featured his abstract paintings. He also provided the artwork for sets of boxed cards on American musicians, including *Heroes of the Blues* and *Early Jazz Greats*, and in 1985 he illustrated the tenth-anniversary edition of Edward Abbey's novel *The Monkey Wrench Gang*, a best-seller about four zealous environmentalists. Cartooning, however, remained Crumb's passion. After *Weirdo* ran out of funds in 1989, Crumb began writing and drawing *Hup*, a magazine published by Last Gasp, in San Francisco. In addition to featuring new characters, *Hup* reintroduced Mr. Natural and Flakey Foont and found Crumb once again indulging his penchant for lurid tales of sex.

That preoccupation has made Crumb, as Sharon Waxman phrased it in the *Chicago Tribune* (June 2, 1992), "the raw meat at many feminist barbecues." One story in a 1992 issue of *Hup*, for example, centered on Devil Girl, a woman whose head has been magically removed by Mr. Natural so that he can enjoy her body, unimpeded by her will or personality. "You know, I do this stuff, and then I'm horrified and embarrassed when I see it . . . but somehow I can't stop doing it," Crumb admitted to Sharon Waxman. He concluded that drawing such stories gets his darker impulses "out of [his] system" and keeps them "from getting worse." "I'd be in jail or a mental institution by now if I didn't draw that stuff," he declared. Among his defenders is Aline Kominski, who told Waxman, "He's acting out his fantasies. I think lots of women have masochistic fantasies, and that doesn't mean that they want to be raped." She added, "Anyone who takes the stuff literally is an idiot."

Evidence that Crumb's work has indeed been taken at face value was provided, however, in 1994, when two of his strips from *Weirdo*—"When the Niggers Take Over America" and "When the Goddamn Jews Take Over America"—were published without his knowledge in the Massachusetts-based, white supremacist magazine *Race & Reality*, whose editors apparently failed to grasp the ironic intent behind the cartoons. David Armstrong of the *San Francisco Examiner*, in an article reprinted in the *Chicago Tribune* (October 9, 1994), reported that Crumb "expressed surprise" at the appropriation of his work and quoted him as saying, "Some people don't get satire. To me, it shows how stupid those people are." Crumb added, "I was sweating when I was doing [the stories]. I thought, 'Some people are going to take it literally.' I always have gone close to that line. . . . I release all that stuff inside myself: taboo words, taboo ideas. It pours out of me as sick as possible. I wouldn't put it in a comic for children. But I don't work that mainstream audience."

In the last few years, the Seattle-based Fantagraphics Books has published several volumes of *The Complete Crumb Comics* as well as the cartoonist's sketchbooks. In successive years beginning in 1991, Last Gasp released *My Troubles with Women*, on which Crumb collaborated with Aline Kominski; *Weirdo Art of R. Crumb: His Early Period, 1981–1985*; and *R. Crumb Draws the Blues*. The year 1993 also saw the appearance of *Crumb's Complete Dirty Laundry Comics*, published by Last Gasp. The cartoonist and his parents and siblings are the subjects of Terry Zwigoff's 1994 film *Crumb*. Shown to acclaim at the Sundance Film Festival, the documentary was released commercially to enthusiastic reviews in the spring of 1995.

Describing Robert Crumb as "pale" and "frail," Sharon Waxman reported that his "skeletal frame is curved like a 'c'" and that he "wears glasses so thick that they distort his eyes—probably from years spent cross-hatching cartoons in bad light." In 1991 Crumb and Aline Kominski bought a house in a village outside Nîmes, in the south of France, where they live with their daughter, Sophie. From his marriage to Dana Morgan, which ended in divorce in 1977, Crumb has a son, Jesse. The cartoonist remains a shy man, and so he occasionally finds the attention that his work brings him to be a burden. By all accounts, he stopped taking drugs in the late 1970s, and Peter Carlson revealed that while "some authors ease the pain of public appearances with booze or dope," Crumb merely sketches to calm himself.

Crumb's chief avocation is music. He is an accomplished piano, banjo, and guitar player, and he has performed with a number of groups. His band R. Crumb and His Cheap Suit Serenaders released a self-titled album in 1974. When he lived in Winters, California, he was a member of the group Rural Sophisticates, and as of 1992 he was performing in France with the band Les Primitifs de Futur. He is an avid collector of old jazz recordings, with a collection estimated at three thousand discs, and even during the height of the hippie movement, he preferred a hairstyle and mode of dress popular in the big-band era of the 1930s. "He was like a kid whose parents had locked him in an attic full of old records and magazines," his friend Tom Wilson has recalled. "His taste in everything comes from a time when he did not exist."

Selected Biographical References: Chicago Tribune V p1+ Je 2 '92 pors; N Y Times II p1+ Ja 29 '95 por; N Y Times Mag p12+ O 1 '72 pors; People 23:75+ Je 24 '85 pors; Contemporary Authors vol 106 (1982); Contemporary Literary Criticism vol 17 (1981)

Anne Hall

Danto, Arthur C.

Jan. 1, 1924- Philosopher; art critic; writer; professor; scholar; essayist. Address: 708 Philosophy Hall, Columbia University, New York, NY 10027

Known for his breadth of knowledge, his original ideas, his lucid prose, and his willingness to jump into the cultural fray of the moment, Arthur C. Danto has taught philosophy at Columbia University for four decades. Since 1984 he has also written art criticism for the liberal weekly the *Nation*. Although the scope of his philosophy and his criticism has extended beyond subjects traditionally associated with either discipline, there are themes to which he repeatedly returns. The most controversial among them, perhaps, is his contention that the history of art—that is, the historical imperative to master appearances and to build upon previous styles through improvement or through the breaking of "rules" until none is left to be broken—had exhausted itself in 1964, when the pop artist Andy Warhol exhibited his silk-screened wooden replicas of Brillo soap pad shipping cartons. Because one cannot discern the difference between some of Warhol's creations and ordinary objects merely by inspecting them visually, Danto has argued, the distinction between art and nonart became at that time a conceptual, rather than a visual or empirical, question. "A problem is not genuinely a philosophical problem unless it is possible to imagine that its solution will consist of showing how appearance has been taken for reality," Danto wrote in his 1989 overview of philosophy, *Connections to the World: The Basic Concepts of Philosophy*.

In the 1992 collection *Beyond the Brillo Box: The Visual Arts in Post-Historical Perspective*, Danto explained that Warhol and other artists of his generation had indeed turned art into philosophy by raising the question of its own nature; in other words, by appearing to be so like actual Brillo boxes, Warhol's replicas asked the viewer to think rather than merely to perceive, and to engage in philosophical speculation or analysis to answer the question of what makes something a work of art if it cannot be differentiated visually from the real-world object that it represents. "Until the form of the question came from within art, philosophy was powerless to raise it," Danto wrote, "and once it was raised, art was powerless to resolve it. That point had been reached when art and reality were indiscernible." (In stating his belief that art history had ended, Danto was not implying that art itself had come to an end. On the contrary, he has noted, artists are freer than ever to create works of art in any particular style, or combination of styles, that they choose.) In addition to his twelve books of philosophy, three of which concern the philosophy of art, and three collections of essays in art criticism, Danto is the author of monographs on four individual artists: the photographers Cindy Sherman and Robert Mapplethorpe, the painter Mark Tansey, and the *New Yorker* cartoonist Saul Steinberg.

Arthur Coleman Danto, whose last name is of Sephardic origin, was born on January 1, 1924 in Ann Arbor, Michigan, the son of Samuel Budd Danto, a dentist, and Sylvia (Gittleman) Danto, a homemaker. His brother, Bruce, is a forensic psychiatrist practicing in California. Early in Danto's childhood his family resettled in Detroit, where he grew up. Unable as a teenager to "come to terms with life," as he told Elizabeth Frank, who interviewed him for the *New York Times Magazine* (November 19, 1989), he volunteered for the United States Army in 1942. "I think I erased the first eighteen years of my life," he told Frank. For the remaining three years of World War II, Danto served as a guard on trains running between Casablanca and Oran, in North Africa, and as a driver for the military postal service in Italy. By his own testimony, his years as a soldier helped release him from the constraints and confusions of his adolescence. "I had a really great time," he told Frank, "and although I was at various times in difficult situations—you know, air raids, et cetera—I was never at that time afraid. It was a great place to grow up, I think."

Shortly after his discharge from the army in 1945, Danto embarked upon his undergraduate education at Wayne University (now Wayne State University), in Detroit. Majoring in art and history, he excelled in his classes and graduated in only two years. Because he was entitled to two more years of study under the G.I. Bill, he decided to go to graduate school, putting on hold his plan to become a painter in New York City. "I tried to calculate what [academic subject] would give me the most time," he told Elizabeth Frank, "and I hit on the idea of philosophy." Enrolling in 1948 at Columbia University, in Manhattan, Danto earned a master's degree in philosophy a year later. He spent the following year studying philosophy on a Fulbright fellowship at the University of Paris. After he returned from France in 1950, he taught for a year at the University of Colorado while working on his doctorate, which he completed at Columbia in 1952.

In 1951 Danto had joined the Columbia faculty as an instructor in philosophy, a position he held until 1954, when he was made an assistant professor. He was promoted to associate professor in 1959 and to full professor in 1966. The year before, he had been a visiting lecturer in philosophy at Princeton University, in New Jersey, and at the University of California at Santa Barbara. In 1969 he chaired a student-faculty commission to redefine the mission of Columbia University's School of General Studies, a coeducational adult school caught between the demands of students who wanted a comfortable dormitory lifestyle and those who believed the needs of urban and working students should take priority. He was a visiting professor at Catholic University of America, in Washington, D.C., in 1972 and at the University of California at San Diego in 1973, and he was appointed a resident scholar at the Rockefeller Study Center in 1974. From 1975 until his retirement in 1992, he was Johnsonian Professor of Philosophy at Columbia University, where he is now a professor emeritus, having served as department chairman from 1978 through 1987.

Danto's career at Columbia was marked from the beginning by his devotion to the principles and methods of Anglo-American analytic philosophy, a tradition that approaches philosophical questions by closely analyzing the precise workings of everyday language. "I used to get this wonderful sense of thinking about a question and putting a lot of logical pressure on it and just having it open, like a starfish opening an oyster," Danto told Frank, adding that he used to think "that all the problems of philosophy, and maybe everything else, were going to yield to this very powerful method." While his passion for the discipline has endured, he acknowledged in his conversation with Frank that analytic philosophy has "become somewhat trivial now. I don't think anybody knows really what it is now. I think philosophy is sort of wandering in the dark."

In the past few decades, Danto has distinguished himself by applying analytic philosophy to a wide spectrum of inquiry, including the study of history, knowledge, ethics, and religion. *Philosophy of Science*, a volume of essays that he edited with a colleague at Columbia, Sidney Morgenbesser, appeared in 1960. Five years later Danto published *Analytical Philosophy of History*, in which he "convincingly shows," according to a reviewer for the *Times Literary Supplement* (November 25, 1965), "that any kind of narrative, even the simplest chronicle, involves arrangement, selection, and explanation, and goes on to a stimulating, if inconclusive, discussion of the crucial question of significance in history." In *Analytical Philosophy of Knowledge* (1968), Danto drew a distinction between descriptive and semantical concepts in an effort to clarify the nature of knowledge, one of the more persistent dilemmas faced by advanced students of philosophy. (*Narration and Knowledge*, published in 1985, is among the other works of philosophy Danto has written.) He illuminated the connections between action and cognition in *Analytical Philosophy of Action* (1973), arguing that, aside from mere physical movements, every action involves intention and context.

Whether analyzing a particular topic, the thought of individual philosophers, or entire philosophical traditions, Danto displays what many critics regard as a remarkable eloquence in his sustained, clearly thought-out arguments. Evaluating Danto's *Nietzsche as Philosopher* (1965) for the *New York Times Book Review* (January 23, 1966), Brand Blanshard noted, "Nietzsche was incapable of system in his writing or his thinking and Danto is systematic on his behalf. With skill and discernment he reveals the important strands of Nietzsche's wildly tangled skein and weaves them into a pattern."

Mysticism and Morality: Oriental Thought and Moral Philosophy (1972), a compact introduction to and assessment of the Eastern philosophies of Buddhism, Hinduism, and Taoism, was applauded by a reviewer for *Choice* (May 1973), who cited Danto's "urbane, lucid, nontechnical manner" of arguing against the "recurring hope of some Westerners that wisdom or salvation could be found in the teachings of the East." Elaborating on that theme in a preface to a later edition of the work, Danto wrote, "The factual beliefs [Indian and Chinese philosophers] take for granted are, I believe, too alien to our representation of the world to be grafted onto it, and in consequence their moral systems are unavailable to us."

Jean-Paul Sartre (1975), a comprehensive, advanced study of the French existentialist's oeuvre, was considered useful and provocative by some critics but was deemed flawed by Frederick Elliston, who wrote in *Library Journal* (September 15, 1975) that Danto "betrays his biases occasionally, e.g., misinterpreting the phenomenological doctrine of intentionality as a linguistic thesis and conflating eidetic and conceptual truths. . . . This book will interest those who are curious to discover what a well-known and sympathetic analytic philosopher makes of a major existentialist."

Danto's most recent philosophical work, *Connections to the World*, "grew out of and replaces," in the author's words, his first introductory book, *What Philosophy Is* (1968). Unlike most surveys of the history of philosophy, which trace the chronological development of philosophical thought by analyzing the concepts propounded by successive schools, Danto's book is divided into four sections: "The Singularity of Philosophical Thought," "Understanding," "Knowledge," and "The World." Each of these "ruthlessly condenses jungles of difference and detail," he wrote in the preface, adding that he hoped to provide "a guide to the heights and distances." Conjecturing in his book "that philosophy is just the effort to understand the relationships between subjects [selves], representations [appearances], and reality [the world]," he set out to explore the nuances of the cognitive connections between each of those categories. Writing for the *New York Times Book Review* (May 14, 1989), the philosopher Julia Annas reported "two large gaps in [his] argument": his exaggeration of "the self-contained nature of each philosophical theory and its rupture with the past," and his omission of a discussion of "ethical philosophy." But she concluded that "to write a book about philosophy that is both sophisticated and accessible is nonetheless a major feat, and greatly to be appreciated."

Art has been the subject of three of Danto's philosophical works. In *The Transfiguration of the Commonplace: A Philosophy of Art* (1981), a thoughtful account of modern art's transformation of ordinary objects into artistic artifacts that earned him the prestigious Lionel Trilling Book Prize, Danto sought to distinguish artistic theory from aesthetic theory. *The Transfiguration of the Commonplace* drew widespread attention from both philosophers and art theorists. "Seeing art as a mirror, an instrument of self-revelation," a reviewer for *Choice* (June 1981) noted, "Danto insightfully points to the transfiguring power of the artist's intentionality that externalizes not just what he sees, but his 'way of seeing the world.'" Broadening that discussion in *The Philosophical Disenfranchisement of Art* (1987), a collection of nine essays written for professionals and scholars, Danto posited his theory of the "end of art" in a single essay. Writing in the *Times Literary Supplement* (January 9, 1987), George Wilson argued that the book shared with *The Transfiguration of the Commonplace* "the wit and elegance of its writing, the breadth of reference, and the desire to force the recalcitrant discipline of aesthetics into significant conversation with contemporary art and criticism."

Danto's end-of-art theory received a full treatment in *Beyond the Brillo Box*, a collection of essays and lectures, including three William W. Cook Lectures on American Institutions delivered at the University of Michigan Law School, that examines the history of art after Warhol's Brillo box exhibit in 1964. Danto, who is virtually alone in arguing that the end of art has been attained, has been severely criticized for his views. Elizabeth Frank quoted Rosalind Krauss, the art historian and critic, as saying, "As for this *philosopher* talking to artists, spreading the pearls of philosophy before the swine of the art world—well, they're just pop-it beads."

Other chapters of *Beyond the Brillo Box* probe such contemporary controversies as the issue of censorship that arose when funding for the National Endowment for the Arts was up for renewal in 1990. "I have never fully understood the thesis that art is dangerous," Danto wrote in an especially provocative essay on "dangerous art." In it he noted that in "opposing art on grounds of content, one runs the risk of raising the artist's prices and turning him into a household word, as happened with Robert Mapplethorpe. So perhaps the most prudent course in dealing with dangerous art is to treat it as if it were after all innocuous, using the sanctity of art as a shield against its toxins, which has always been our tradition." In his interview with Frank, he distinguished between "disturbing" art, such as the highly unsettling paintings of Goya and Leon Golub, and "disturbational" art, which transcends the division between representation and life. "Reality must in some way then be an actual component of disturbational art," Frank quoted Danto as having written, "and usually reality of a kind itself disturbing: obscenity, frontal nudity, blood, excrement, mutilation, real danger, actual pain, possible death."

Danto's art criticism is no less controversial than his philosophy of art. In the early 1980s, impressed by the theories set forth in *The Transfiguration of the Commonplace*, Ben Sonnenberg, the founding editor of the literary magazine *Grand Street*, invited Danto to write for the journal and introduced his work to Elizabeth Pochoda, then the literary editor of the leftist weekly the *Nation*, who in 1984 invited Danto to be the magazine's resident art critic. In his *Nation* essays he eagerly explores an astonishingly wide range of artistic matters, from the works of such past masters as John Singer Sargent, Vincent Van Gogh, and Edgar Degas to more recent figures, among them the photographer Cindy Sherman. "The typical Danto column," Elizabeth Frank wrote, "is a potpourri of biography, history, and social and philosophical observations." Collected in three volumes to date, the first being *The State of the Art* (1987), the essays display a wide-ranging and unpredictable critical intelligence. "The main reason people read me," Danto explained to Frank, "is that they do not know what they will encounter. I do not predict my responses, and have no line to argue. I am looking to explain what I am talking about, and the explanations come from all over the place. . . . I depend a great deal upon inspiration for my hypotheses and normally don't write until I have it."

In an evaluation for the *New York Times Book Review* (August 5, 1990) of *Encounters & Reflections: Art in the Historical Present* (1990), Danto's second collection of art criticism, Marina Vaizey wrote, "Danto's insights are distinguished by his own broad frames of reference; an occasional and almost overwhelming attachment to, and description of, the sheer captivating sensuality of a particular work, from *The Kiss* by Gustav Klimt to Frank Stella's *Bijoux Indiscrets*; and a determination to make the reader, and the essayist, feel, see, and, above all, think. He has thus provided an invaluable vade mecum to the present art landscape." *Encounters & Reflections* earned Danto a 1990 National Book Critics Circle award for criticism.

In his third volume of essays previously published in the *Nation* and other mainstream journals, *Embodied Meanings: Critical Essays and Aesthetic Meditations* (1994), Danto addressed the changing role of the museum, the 1993 Whitney Biennial, and the Museum of Modern Art's much-maligned 1990 exhibition called "High & Low: Modern Art and Popular Culture." Reviewing the forty-one reviews and essays, a writer for *Publishers Weekly* (March 14, 1994) commented that "Danto's philosophically informed art criticism . . . bristles with erudition, eclectic taste, and keen intellect. He evinces fresh perspectives and generous sympathies whether he is discussing Old Masters like Titian and Velázquez; moderns such as Picasso, Seurat, and Kasimir Malevich; contemporary painters Francis Bacon and David Hockney; or sacred Tibetan art." A fourth collection of essays, "Contemporary Art and the Pale of History," based upon Danto's delivery of the Andrew Mellon Lectures in Fine Arts at the National Gallery in Washington, D.C., in the spring of 1995, is forthcoming.

Artists themselves have sometimes taken exception to Danto's writings on art. One prevalent complaint is that Danto assiduously neglects the strictly aesthetic or visual properties of a given work of art, refusing to analyze it without discussing its meaning. "He has no feeling for the guts of the work," an artist who preferred to remain anonymous told Frank. "He's skimming off the top and avoiding a deep emotional involvement." Another artist griped that Danto "regards [art criticism] as a *jeu d'esprit*—just to have a good time. He doesn't see the seriousness with which [art] affects other lives." When informed of those criticisms, Danto responded in his interview with Frank, "I don't think in the end, in terms of the structure of human agony, that art is that important. Against the framework of human suffering and need, it would be wrong to get that passionate about it."

In addition to his 1990 National Book Critics Circle award for criticism, Danto has been honored with two fellowships by the American Council of Learned Societies, in 1962 and 1969; a Guggenheim fellowship, in 1970; the Manufacturers Hanover/Art World prize for distinguished criticism, in 1985; the George S. Polk award for criticism, in 1986; and the ICP Infinity prize for writing in photography, in 1993. He has served as president of the American Philosophical Association and the American Society of Aesthetics, and he's a fellow of the American Academy of Arts and Sciences. A member of the board of directors of Amnesty International from 1970 to 1975 (and general secretary in 1973), he served from 1978 to 1993 as codirector of the Center for the Study of Human Rights, which is based at Columbia University's School of International and Public Affairs. Since 1965 he has edited Columbia University's *Journal of Philosophy*, of whose board he has been president since 1987.

The septuagenarian Arthur Danto is a fit, dapper man who is said to possess a reasonable, gracious, and cosmopolitan spirit. To many writers, his appearance, temper, and bearing have suggested "an Aristophanic version of Socrates," as Ben Sonnenberg has put it. On August 9, 1946 Danto married Shirley Rovetch, who died in July 1978 and with whom he had two daughters, Elizabeth Ann and Jane Nicole. He lives in New York City with his second wife, the artist Barbara Westman (whose work frequently graces covers of the *New Yorker*), whom he married on February 15, 1980.

Selected Biographical References: N Y Newsday p37 Ag 23 '92; N Y Times Mag p47+ N 19 '89 pors; Contemporary Authors vol 17-20 (1976); Rollins, Mark, ed. Danto and His Critics (1993); Who's Who in America, 1995

U.S. House of Representatives

Daschle, Tom
(DASH-uhl)

Dec. 9, 1947– United States Senator from South Dakota. Address: 509 Hart Senate Office Bldg., Washington, DC 20510

Senate Minority Leader Tom Daschle, a Democrat from South Dakota, was first elected to the United States Senate in 1986. He had previously been a member of the House of Representatives, to which he was elected in 1978, after serving his political apprenticeship as a legislative aide. Known for being a consensus builder with exemplary persuasive skills, he climbed the ladder in Congress rapidly but unobtrusively, alienating few colleagues while gaining the support of important allies in leadership positions. As a congressman and later as a senator, Daschle concentrated his efforts in the areas of agriculture, veterans' affairs, Native American concerns, and health care. Because he has never chaired a committee or shepherded a major piece of legislation through Congress, some of his Democratic colleagues have expressed concerns about whether he has what it takes to stand up to Senate Majority Leader Robert J. Dole, a Republican from Kansas. As the minority leader, Daschle must set a course for Democrats that is independent of Republicans and, to a lesser extent, of the Democratic administration of President Bill Clinton without seeming to unduly obstruct congressional action.

Thomas Andrew Daschle was born on December 9, 1947 in Aberdeen, South Dakota, the son of an auto-parts store owner and his wife. After graduating in 1969 with a B.A. degree from South Dakota State University in Brookings, where he was president of the SDSU Young Democrats, Daschle spent three years in the intelligence wing of the United States Air Force, rising to the rank of first lieutenant. His later assiduous attention to veterans' affairs has been attributed to "a certain guilt for never having served" in combat during the Vietnam War, according to Elaine S. Povich, who paraphrased the words of Daschle's friend Roger Andal in her profile of the senator for the *Chicago Tribune* (December 5, 1994). After working briefly as a financial investment representative, in 1973 Daschle went to Washington, D.C., to serve as a legislative aide for Democratic United States senator James Abourezk. Becoming the senator's field coordinator in late 1976, Daschle returned to South Dakota. Abourezk retired from politics at the end of his term in 1978, opting for a potentially more lucrative career as a lobbyist. For the remainder of Abourezk's term, Daschle served as a district aide. Meanwhile, in 1974 he had participated in the successful reelection campaign of South Dakota's other United States senator, the former Democratic presidential candidate George S. McGovern.

Having learned the ins and outs of legislative politics during his apprenticeship to Abourezk, Daschle launched his own campaign, for the United States House of Representatives, in 1978, when South Dakota's First Congressional District seat opened up with the decision of Larry Pressler, the Republican incumbent, to run for the United States Senate. Visiting more than forty thousand homes, Daschle and his first wife, Laurie Klinkel, poured all their energy into the campaign. After defeating the party favorite, Frank Denholm, in the primary election, Daschle barely squeaked by Leo Thorsness, his Republican opponent, in the general election, which was so close that when the recounts were finished a year later it was revealed that Daschle had won by a mere 110 votes. Handily reelected in 1980 with 66 percent of the vote to Republican Bart Kull's 34 percent, Daschle faced a more difficult race in 1982 against Republican Clint Roberts, the incumbent from the state's Second Congressional District, whose image was enhanced by his reputation as a model in ads for Marlboro cigarettes. Following the 1980 United States census, South Dakota's two districts were merged, and the incumbents squared off in the competition for representative at large, which pitted Daschle's eastern corn-belt territory against Roberts's western cattle ranches and Indian reservations. Each candidate carried his former district, and Daschle emerged the victor with 52 percent of the vote. A similar pattern prevailed in 1984, when Daschle beat Dale Bell with 57 percent of the vote by carrying 60 percent of his former district.

Throughout his eight years in the House, Daschle paid a lot of attention to such home-state issues as farm aid and gasohol (a grain alcohol-based automobile fuel), and he developed a solid record of good constituent relations, visiting many of the state's more isolated communities. In 1979 he joined the Veterans' Affairs Committee, where he immediately began trying to focus the committee's attention on the rights and needs of veterans of the Vietnam War. Previously, the committee had dealt primarily with the generation that had fought in World War II. Daschle advocated subsidizing the psychiatric treatment of Vietnam veterans who needed it, and he introduced a bill, passed by the House in 1981, that created a presumption of federal liability for veterans who were victims of exposure to the chemical defoliant Agent Orange. He continued to push ahead on that issue, having won the National Commander's Award from Disabled American Veterans in 1980, and a law to compensate veterans for such exposure was finally enacted in 1991. Another long-term pet issue has been the development of ethanol, or ethyl alcohol, which can be made from corn, rye, wheat, and potatoes, all of which grow in abundance in Daschle's district. In the late 1970s he was a vocal booster for gasohol, which is a cleaner-burning automobile fuel made up of 10 percent ethanol and 90 percent gasoline; he is still in favor of the development of ethanol as a fuel, a passion he shares with Senator Dole.

On social issues, Daschle is a moderate who leans slightly to the left of his conservative constituency. In fact, one reason the 1978 election was so close was Daschle's refusal to change his mind on abortion: he opposed congressional efforts to bar federal funding for abortions in cases that were not a result of rape or incest. He also lost support when he came out in favor of the national repeal of state right-to-work laws. In 1979 he voted to establish the Department of Education and opposed an antibusing amendment; in 1980 he voted for strengthening fair-housing laws and aiding the Sandinista government of Nicaragua and against approving registration for the military draft. Three years later he came out in favor of the Equal Rights Amendment and of raising the retirement age for Social Security to sixty-seven. In 1984 he voted to cut spending on education, to revise immigration laws, and to bar aid to anti-Sandinista forces in Nicaragua, and in 1985 he cast a vote against authorizing the procurement of twenty-one MX missiles.

As a member of the Agriculture Committee, Daschle consistently supported federal crop subsidies. His Farm Crisis Bill of 1981 would have boosted farm-product prices by taking one-sixth of American cropland out of production. President Ronald Reagan's agriculture secretary, John R. Block, called the bill, which died in committee on a tie vote, "misleading, self-defeating, and unwanted by farmers," and even Democrat Thomas S. Foley of Washington, a leading agriculture strategist in the House, refused to sponsor the bill. Such differences have long since been reconciled. One of Daschle's final and most popular acts on that committee was to sponsor a multibillion-dollar emergency farm-credit bill that passed both the House and the Senate before President Ronald Reagan vetoed it in 1985. Although he was unable to collect the votes necessary for an override, Daschle's efforts paid off handsomely later that year, when he started out as the favored candidate for the United States Senate in a run against Republican incumbent James Abdnor, who supported the administration's comprehensive farm bill instead.

Even before he announced his intention to run for the Senate, Daschle had been gathering the necessary behind-the-scenes support for a viable candidacy. In 1983 he joined the Steering and Policy Committee, which doles out assignments to Democratic representatives. Shortly after joining that committee, he helped put a close ally on farm policy, Byron L. Dorgan of North Dakota, on the powerful Ways and Means Committee, to whose chairman, Dan Rostenkowski of Illinois, Daschle had cultivated close ties. Other prominent Democrats with whom he made important connections were Morris K. Udall of Arizona, Richard A. Gephardt of Missouri, and Thomas P. ("Tip") O'Neill Jr. of Massachusetts. One measure of Daschle's popularity with the Democratic leadership was evident in February 1986, when he was chosen to give the party's response to Reagan's State of the Union address. In his speech, Daschle criticized the administration's failure to address the needs of farmers whose homes were being foreclosed on, whose crops were being priced out of the world market by an overvalued dollar, and whose equipment had been rendered more expensive due to higher interest rates.

The 1986 Senate race between Daschle and Abdnor was too close to call as late as three weeks before the election, when the lagging Abdnor had pulled even with his opponent in the polls. The surge in Abdnor's popularity was attributed to negative campaign ads that sought to link Daschle with the actress and health advocate Jane Fonda, whose antiwar activism had made her the bête noire of Vietnam veterans and who had been photographed with Daschle at a fund-raising event. Abdnor also implied that Daschle, the representative of a state whose economy runs on the meatpacking industry as well as on farming, was, like Fonda, a proponent of vegetarianism. "The race has gotten far too negative," Daschle charged in a televised debate with his opponent that took place in Washington, D.C., in mid-October. "It's cheated voters. Distorting the truth as badly as you have is inexcusable." Having recovered from the slump in his popularity by contending that Abdnor had voted to cut Social Security benefits, Daschle achieved a narrow victory in the November 1986 election, winning with 52 percent of the vote. Six years later, he easily won reelection by a two-to-one margin over Republican Charlene Haar, a former state party chairman and a schoolteacher.

Although Daschle never chaired a major committee or managed a bill on the floor, he distinguished himself in the Senate chiefly by tending to the issues he addressed in the House—agriculture and veterans' affairs—and by expressing a zealous desire to reform the way the Senate conducted business. "Simply to come here and work in a museum is not my idea of a modern legislative process," he said in 1987, as quoted in the 1990 edition of *Politics in America*. In the essay on Daschle in that edition, the senator was described as having "shown a genius not only for the right political issues, but also for the right mentors," and as possessing an "engaging, almost deferential personality" that belied his ambition. A few months before his election to the Senate, Daschle gave his endorsement to Robert C. Byrd of West Virginia, the incumbent Senate Majority Leader. After being reelected to that position, Byrd rewarded Daschle with a seat on the prestigious Finance Committee, as a member of which he added amendments to a trade bill to facilitate the exporting of agricultural products and to put in place retaliatory measures against countries that put up barriers to American farm-product imports. He also helped to repeal new taxes that had been levied on farmers for diesel fuel and heifers. On the Agriculture Committee, he continued to resist the efforts of the Reagan administration to cut farm subsidies. After he became chairman of the Agricultural Research and General Legislation Subcommittee in 1989, he stepped up his advocacy of federal assistance to the ethanol industry.

As cochair of Vietnam-Era Veterans in Congress, Daschle continued to fight for compensation for Agent Orange victims, ultimately winning a major battle in that area in 1991. He was also instrumental in the Veterans' Benefits Improvement Act of 1994, which authorized payment of disability compensation to Persian Gulf war veterans suffering from undiagnosed war-related illnesses. In the 1990s Daschle was a staunch supporter of Clinton's health-care reform efforts, which ultimately fizzled. He called weekly policy meetings of congressional leaders and administration officials and convened a two-day policy briefing for Congress members interested in those issues. "He's developed an unbelievable ability to boil discussion of health care into sound bites, basic language," Democratic senator John D. Rockefeller 4th of West Virginia said, as quoted by Janet Hook of *Congressional Quarterly* (June 11, 1994). He precluded any potentially negative consequences of his vote against the authorization of the use of force in the Persian Gulf in 1991 by directing his staff to help the families of troops from South Dakota who were sent to fight the Iraqis.

Throughout his career, Daschle has cultivated a reputation for being cautious, collegial, and careful not to offend colleagues or constituents. In 1991, for instance, he voted against a pay raise for senators. In 1988, having won over Finance Committee chairman Lloyd Bentsen of Texas, he was selected to give Bentsen's vice-presidential nominating speech at the Democratic National Convention, at which delegates nominated Michael S. Dukakis, then the governor of Massachusetts, for president. More important, Daschle backed Senator George J. Mitchell of Maine for Senate majority leader in 1988, after Byrd volunteered to step down. Mitchell, in turn, named Daschle the cochair of the Democratic Policy Committee in 1989. In that capacity, previously the sole province of the party leader, Daschle drafted the Democratic senators' agenda for the next two years.

In March 1994 Mitchell announced that he would not seek another term in the Senate. No sooner did Mitchell signal his intention to retire from Congress at the end of 1994 than Daschle began campaigning to succeed him as party leader, a position that would be chosen by Democratic senators on December 2, 1994. His opponent was Budget Committee chairman Jim Sasser of Tennessee, the only other senator who volunteered for the office, a thankless but high-profile job that requires long hours, much patience, and a lot of kowtowing to the other senators. "It's an impossible job," Senator Jim Exon of Nebraska told Janet Hook of *Congressional Quarterly* (April 16, 1994). "I decided I didn't want to do the job," Senator John B. Breaux of Louisiana told Hook. "I saw George Mitchell do it eighteen hours a day. That's fine for him—he's single. It's a good way to become single." If Daschle had any such qualms, he kept them well hidden. "He wants [the post]," Senator Rockefeller told Michael Wines of the *New York Times* (June 23, 1994), "and it's very obvious to people. And I think he'll win it relatively easily, because of his hard work, his intensity."

Senator Christopher J. Dodd of Connecticut entered the race in November, at the urging of colleagues, after Sasser, whom he had supported, lost his bid for reelection to the Senate. Both Dodd and Daschle, who have similar moderate-to-liberal voting records, favored reforming the Senate, especially by reducing the use of the filibuster, which Daschle referred to as "one of the most abused parliamentary tools of the Senate," as quoted by Adam Clymer of the *New York Times* (November 25, 1994). Although Dodd was only three and a half years older than his opponent, he had been a senator since 1981, and he enjoyed a higher level of public recognition. Therefore, more experienced senators lined up behind Dodd, who they thought possessed the combativeness needed to do battle with a Republican majority, while Daschle had the support of more reform-minded, junior senators.

On December 2, 1994 Daschle won the leadership of the Democratic Party by a vote of twenty-four to twenty-three; the tie had been broken by the lone proxy vote, cast by Ben Nighthorse Campbell of Colorado (who switched parties in March 1995, becoming a Republican). Carrol J. Doherty of *Congressional Quarterly* (December 3, 1994) attributed Daschle's victory to his tenacity and to his defiance of convention in releasing a list, prior to the secret balloting, of those who had promised to support him. "That made it hard for senators, who have been known to renege on private pledges in leadership races, to break their commitments," Doherty noted. Senator Wendell H. Ford of Kentucky was reelected without opposition as the assistant Democratic leader. At a news conference following his victory over Dodd, Daschle said, "To the extent that we can, we want very much to work with the White House. We will not be led by them; we will not view ourselves as an extension of them." He said that he would cooperate with Republicans to the extent necessary to avoid prolonged stalemates, but he added, "We stand ready to offer vigorous opposition to extreme proposals that threaten economic security or our nation's economic future. We will fight against proposals that are mean-spirited. . . . America's families need a thriving economy to produce the job security that is the heart of personal security."

In the early months of his leadership, Daschle faced challenges on several fronts. The first potential difficulty lay in the possibility of his being upstaged by more prominent Democrats with higher public profiles. On January 12, 1995 Clinton named Dodd chairman of the Democratic National Committee, which gave the senator from Connecticut his own launching pad from which to attack legislation proposed by Republicans in Congress. Another issue was Byrd's vocal role in opposing the Republicans' proposed balanced-budget amendment to the Constitution, which Daschle had supported in 1994, when it failed in the Senate, by four votes, to obtain the two-thirds majority required for passage. "Senator Byrd and Senator Dodd are articulate, highly respected advocates for our Democratic issues," Daschle said in an interview with Janet Hook of *Congressional Quarterly* (February 4, 1995). "Some would have it in some way as a problem and a competitive issue with me. It's just the opposite."

Indeed, Daschle needed all the help he could get in confronting Republican senators who wanted to balance the budget by cutting taxes and making deep cuts in government spending. Although he had previously voted for a balanced-budget amendment, in March 1995 Daschle changed his mind, helping to defeat the measure in the Senate, where it fell one vote short of passage. Contending that he still supported the idea of a constitutional amendment, Daschle indicated that he opposed the measure, which had been passed by the House in January, because he objected to a provision requiring that any tax increase be approved by an absolute majority of senators and representatives rather than by a majority of those present and voting. A week later he and Senator Exon sponsored legislation that would require the Senate to adopt a resolution to balance the federal budget by the year 2002.

The Democratic plan did not contain the details of the necessary spending cuts, but it did require the Republicans to do so, on the premise that they were in the majority and would resist any specific cuts proposed by the Democrats. On May 25, 1995 the Senate Budget Committee adopted a resolution on achieving a balanced budget by 2002, but only after defeating fifty amendments introduced by Democrats who wanted to compel the Republicans to defend their recommended cuts in such programs as Medicare and Medicaid and such areas as education and the earned-income tax credit. "Time after time," Daschle said, as quoted by George Hager in *Congressional Quarterly* (May 27, 1995), "on amendment after amendment, the wealthy won and the middle class lost."

Yet another difficulty that beset Daschle's efforts to concentrate on bolstering the morale of his party was the unfolding of an aviation scandal involving allegations of his going to inappropriate lengths—possibly intervening with federal officials—to aid a constituent. The suspicion that Daschle may have acted improperly was precipitated by news reports of the crash in February 1994 of a twin-engine Cessna operated by B & L Aviation of Rapid City, South Dakota. (The news did not seem to affect the voting for Senate minority leader, which adhered to patterns he had predicted earlier.) An investigation launched by the Inspector General's office in the Transportation Department revealed that the owner of B & L, Murl Bellew, a friend of Daschle who taught him how to fly, had been complaining about the wastefulness of multiple inspections of his charter company's aircraft by the Federal Aviation Administration (which is part of the Transportation Department) and the Forest Service (which operates under the auspices of the Agriculture Department and was at the time overseen by one of the Senate Agriculture Committee's subcommittees chaired by Daschle). Many of Bellew's planes that had passed FAA safety checks were cited for violations by Forest Service inspectors, who recommended that the company be barred from doing business with the government due to shoddy maintenance, pilots' neglect of routine preflight preparations, and other safety concerns. In June 1992 Daschle had begun to try to consolidate all inspections under the FAA, which would have stripped the Forest Service of its role in inspecting planes specifically for flight in the unfriendly terrain of the South Dakota back country.

When those revelations surfaced, Daschle denied that he was helping a friend, saying first that he had a duty to investigate his constituents' complaints, and later that his main objective had been to streamline government by eliminating duplication without compromising safety. But government investigators told Neil A. Lewis of the *New York Times* (May 7, 1995) that at least two FAA officials said that Linda Hall Daschle, the deputy administrator of the FAA, whom he married in 1984, had acted to halt a proposal to train Forest Service employees to conduct inspections for the FAA. If implemented, the program would have avoided duplication but still allowed the Forest Service to have some control over the safety of its charter flights. At the end of April 1995, the Forest Service announced it would no longer use B & L. Daschle, who has consistently denied any wrongdoing, issued a detailed report of his involvement with B & L. The report, prepared by his lawyer, Robert F. Bauer, and released in February 1995, concluded that Daschle had acted appropriately.

Tom Daschle has three children—Kelly, Nathan, and Lindsay—from his first marriage. He keeps fit by adhering to a strict regimen of daily jogging, which includes occasional outings with the president of the United States.

Selected Biographical References: Chicago Tribune I p4 D 5 '94 por; Congressional Q p1491+ Je 11 '94 pors; N Y Times A p10 D 3 '94 por; New Republic 210:20+ My 23 '94 por; Politics in America, 1996; Who's Who in America, 1995

Dees, Morris S., Jr.
(deez)

Dec. 16, 1936- Organization official; trial lawyer; civil rights activist; businessman; publisher. Address: b. c/o Southern Poverty Law Center, 400 Washington Ave., Montgomery, AL 36104; h. Rolling Hills Ranch, Mathews, AL 36052

"Remember me by my clients—they make my life worthwhile," the civil rights lawyer Morris S. Dees Jr. has said. For nearly a quarter of a century, as the chief trial counsel at the Southern Poverty Law Center (SPLC), Dees has fought to protect and advance the legal and civil rights of poor people and others of all races through litigation and education. Dees cofounded the SPLC, a nonprofit organization based in Montgomery, Alabama, in 1971, after building a highly successful career in direct marketing and publishing. He and his SPLC colleagues have handled, among many other suits, more than fifty major civil rights cases, some of which have involved appeals to the United States Supreme Court. Their courtroom victories have ended various government-sanctioned practices that discriminated against women, members of minority

Alice Hall

Morris S. Dees Jr.

groups, and the poor. The SPLC has also succeeded in getting death sentences overturned in many cases in which the defendants had been denied due process of law and, in two widely publicized trials, won a huge monetary judgment against the Ku Klux Klan and another against the neo-Nazi White Aryan Resistance. Neither the firebombing of SPLC's headquarters nor the death threats he has received from members of such hate groups have deterred Dees from his efforts to end racial and ethnic discrimination and violence in the United States. "I'll always be a trial lawyer," Dees has said. "No higher calling has come my way."

Known as "Bubba" to his family and friends during his youth in Montgomery County, Alabama, Morris Seligman Dees Jr. was born in Shorter, Alabama on December 16, 1936. According to an article by Bill Shaw in *People* (July 22, 1991), he is the eldest of the five children of Morris Seligman Dees Sr. and Annie Ruth (Frazer) Dees. In naming him for his father, his parents perpetuated the name of Morris Seligman, a Jewish merchant from Montgomery whom his paternal grandfather had admired. In about 1940 Morris Sr. left his job as an overseer on a cotton plantation to become a tenant farmer; later, in addition to growing cotton, he secured a partnership in a cotton-gin operation.

"My parents . . . weren't liberals or integrationists; they were just fair-minded folks," Dees told William Zinsser during an interview for *Smithsonian* (September 19, 1991). In his autobiographical book *A Season for Justice* (1991), which he wrote with Steve Fiffer, Dees reported that his mother, who "felt that her Christian faith demanded she act kindly to all God's children," often sat at the family breakfast table with black women from their community, helping them with bureaucratic paperwork. He has also recalled that when he was five, he received a rare whipping from his father for addressing one of the field hands with a racial slur. Dees grew up on intimate terms with the field hands and other blacks. From the age of ten, he was the only white member of his father's work crew, and, at a time when drinking fountains were segregated throughout the South, he, like his father, drank from the same water dippers used by the other laborers in the cotton fields.

Spurred by the knowledge that, although far from poor, his parents were often burdened by debt, from an early age Dees found opportunities to earn money. As a youngster he delivered newspapers and collected a penny apiece for the Coca-Cola bottles he found on roadsides. While he was in junior high school, he sold compost and fruits, and during his years at Sidney Lanier High School, in Montgomery, he farmed a small plot of cotton in addition to earning two cents a pound for picking his father's crop or chopping it for three dollars a day. Using the proceeds from such activities, he started his own herd of cattle. He also bought pigs, for five dollars a head, and then, after fattening them on scraps that he acquired (in exchange for cleaning the scrap bins) at his high school lunchroom, sold them for forty-five dollars each. A small-scale chicken farmer as well, he invented a device for plucking feathers, and he earned "a nice profit," in his words, by selling 250 dressed chickens a week to local stores. By the time he graduated from high school, in 1955, he had saved five thousand dollars, and that year he was named the star farmer of Alabama by the state chapter of Future Farmers of America.

Having abandoned, years earlier, his idea of training for the Baptist ministry, after his father had advised him to choose a more lucrative profession, Dees set aside his dream of owning a farm near his father's, because no land was available. Instead, he heeded his father's frequent exhortation that he become a lawyer and enrolled at the School of Business and Commerce at the University of Alabama, in Tuscaloosa. Shortly after his arrival, he heard news broadcasts about the murder in Mississippi of the fourteen-year-old black Chicagoan Emmett Till by two white men, allegedly for making lewd remarks to the wife of one of the men. Dees recalled in *A Season for Justice* that the horror of the crime "touched [him] so deeply that for the first time [he] seriously questioned the southern way of life," and it stirred him to protest publicly, with his first letter to a newspaper. "Maybe we believe in segregation," he wrote in the letter, which was published in a local paper. "But we also believe in justice. If this young man did something illegal, then he ought to be tried and convicted before he is punished, not lynched."

Dees had been only minimally aware of the Supreme Court's ruling, in *Brown v. Board of Education*, in 1954, that racial segregation in public school systems was unconstitutional. But in 1956 his attention was riveted by events surrounding the attempts of Autherine Lucy, a black woman, to enroll at the then all-white University of Alabama. Dees has recalled that he felt fright and disgust as, standing on the steps of a campus building, he watched thousands of white protesters shout epithets and throw rocks and bottles at Lucy. On the following Sunday, in an address to fellow members of the campus Baptist congregation in which he interwove a biblical text with remarks on the mob's behavior, he asked rhetorically, "How can we profess to be Christians and really hate our brothers?" A few days later he was informed that he would be replaced as superintendent of the congregation's Sunday school for married couples.

By his own admission, despite the sympathy he felt for Lucy, Dees retained "a traditional white southerner's feeling for segregation," and for much of the next few years, he was "remarkably oblivious" to the burgeoning civil rights movement. In addition to striving to maintain a high grade-point average, he concentrated primarily on supporting his growing family (he had married during his senior year in high school). During Dees's sophomore year, inspired by his mother's mailed gift of a cake for his birthday, he and his friend Millard Fuller began to solicit orders for cakes from the parents of other students. (According to Fuller's published reminiscences, he and Dees did not meet until several years later.) 'Bama Birthday Cake Service, their mail-order operation, was soon netting five hundred dollars monthly on sales of two hundred custom-made cakes produced at a local bakery. "The real bonanza was the education I got in direct mail . . . ," Dees recalled in *A Season for Justice*. "I learned to write sales copy, to design an offer, and to mail at the most opportune time."

In 1958, after receiving a B.S. degree, Dees entered the University of Alabama's School of Law. Meanwhile, he and Fuller had expanded their mail-order business to sales of holly wreaths and other items and had increased their clientele as well, by targeting organizations, for example, that would purchase their products for fund-raising purposes. They had also published a student directory and invested in real estate near the campus. By the time Dees earned an LL.B. degree, in 1960, he and Fuller had accumulated assets and equity of $250,000. During his college years Dees had also worked in several Alabama political campaigns, including, in 1958, George Wallace's unsuccessful gubernatorial race. (Wallace, according to Dees, was the "liberal" candidate, receiving endorsements from black groups.) Dees later aided the election campaigns of other office-seekers. As finance director for George S. McGovern during the then-senator's run for the presidency in 1972, he used his skills in direct-mail marketing to raise more than $24 million from nearly seven hundred thousand donors. He subsequently served as national finance director during Jimmy Carter's successful race for the presidency, in 1976, and during Senator Edward M. Kennedy's short-lived presidential campaign four years later.

Earlier, in 1960, having been admitted to the Alabama bar, Dees and Millard Fuller opened a law office in Montgomery, where they quickly established a flourishing practice made up mainly of what Dees has called "little bitty nothing cases." The weightier ones included a case connected with the bus trips that the Freedom Riders took throughout the South in 1961 to test the observance of Supreme Court rulings prohibiting racial segregation in bus terminals. As the legal representative of a neighbor who had been charged with taking part in the beating of a newsman reporting on the Freedom Riders, Dees sat at the defense table with, among others, Robert ("Bobby") Shelton, a Ku Klux Klan "imperial wizard" and the founder of United Klans of America. Upon leaving the courtroom on his last day in court, Dees was approached by a black Freedom Rider, who asked him, "How can you represent people like that? Don't you think that black people have rights?" "Yes, I do," Dees replied. "I agree with you a hundred percent." The encounter left him shaken. "Looking in the face of my accuser, I felt the anger of a black person for the first time . . . ," he confessed in *A Season for Justice*. "I vowed then and there that nobody would ever again doubt where I stood."

Concurrently with maintaining their legal practice, Dees and Fuller continued to build their mail-order business. Their profits increased markedly when they published, under the imprint Favorite Recipes Press, a series of cookbooks. A quarter of a million copies of the first book, *Favorite Recipes of Home Economics Teachers* (1963), were purchased within a few months of publication. During the next few years, their company became the largest publisher of cookbooks in the United States, with sales one year of 3.25 million books. Their phenomenal success prompted Dees and Fuller to give up their law practice and devote themselves full-time to their business. In his book *Love in the Mortar Joints* (1980), Fuller, who left the company in 1965 and later founded the charitable organization Habitat for Humanity, said, "Morris and I, from the first day of our partnership, shared the overriding purpose of making a pile of money. We were not particular *how* we did it; we just wanted to be independently rich. During the eight years we worked together, we never wavered in that resolve."

By his own admission, the deaths of four young black girls in the racially motivated bombing of the Sixteenth Street Baptist Church, in Birmingham, Alabama, in 1963, pushed Dees to "[come] to terms with [his] conscience." "In the months after Birmingham, I thought a lot more about civil rights and justice, trying to square what was happening in the streets with what I had been brought up to believe in church . . . ," he recalled in *A Season for Justice*. "[Millard Fuller and I] spent long hours sorting out our own feelings. There was a lot of baggage that had to be dumped, a lifetime of indoctrination that said giving black people their rights would destroy our cherished way of life. But the events surrounding us made us realize our way of life had to change."

In March 1965 Dees participated for the first time in an organized civil rights action. Along with Fuller, he drove some marchers to Selma, Alabama, where the group planned to join the walk, led by Martin Luther King Jr., to Montgomery to show their support for the legislation that later became the Voting Rights Act of 1965. Reports of his presence in Selma added to Dees's growing reputation within his community as a "nigger lover" (a view that had been reinforced when he and Fuller hosted a racially mixed Christmas party for their employees), and he and his family began to be ostracized. Feeling increasingly troubled by the segregationist stance of his church, he joined Montgomery's Unitarian Fellowship, which attracted him because, in his words, "they not only preached 'justice for all,' they practiced it."

In 1968, during a long layover that interrupted one of his business-related flights, Dees bought at an airport newsstand a copy of *The Story of My Life* (1932), by the crusading American lawyer Clarence Darrow. Identifying strongly with Darrow's feeling for the underdog, and deeply impressed by Darrow's commitment to helping the poor and the powerless and by his independence of thought and action, Dees resolved to "sell [his] company as soon as possible and specialize in civil rights law." "I was a good lawyer wasting my time trying to make a few more million dollars," he observed in *A Season for Justice*. During the next year, while absorbed in the preparation of an aerospace encyclopedia (which was published in conjunction with NASA and the Smithsonian Institution) and the marketing of a sex-education encyclopedia for children, he took on several lawsuits in behalf of the American Civil Liberties Union and represented the winning side in a case that ended racial segregation at the Montgomery YMCA.

In 1969 Dees accepted from the Times Mirror Company an offer of $6 million for his business. Within weeks of signing the buyout agreement, he formed a law partnership with Joseph J. Levin Jr. and opened an office in Montgomery. Dees and Levin agreed that they would bill only those clients who could afford to pay. In *pro bono* cases that they accepted early in their association, they won reinstatement for a teacher who had been fired for assigning Kurt Vonnegut's book *Welcome to the Monkey House* to her class, and they successfully argued a case that led to the landmark Supreme Court decision forcing the United States armed services to provide equal benefits for women. Although they lost a class-action suit involving a Montgomery newspaper's "separate but equal" scheme for printing the social announcements of blacks and whites, in the course of the trial the newspaper adopted a color-blind policy for such news.

In 1971, eager to "set important legal precedents," in Dees's words, regarding such issues as freedom of speech and the rights of women and members of minority groups, Dees and Levin established the Southern Poverty Law Center. "Our primary goal was to fight the effects of poverty with innovative lawsuits and education programs," Dees wrote in *A Season for Justice*. "We would target customs, practices, and laws that were used to keep low-income blacks and whites powerless." Dees explained to John Egerton that, because the center sought only suits that might provide "the models for new directions in the law," the SPLC was "not a public-interest law firm" or "a legal-aid society taking any case that [came] in off the street." "[We] basically only do cases that other lawyers can't do because of the complexity, expense, risk, or novelty," Dees told Robert E. Shapiro, who interviewed him for *Litigation* (Summer 1990).

To fill the SPLC's largely honorary position of president and provide what Dees has described as a "presence" that would "announce the center's values and promise," he and Levin enlisted the civil rights leader Julian Bond. Other prominent civil rights activists, among them Fannie Lou Hamer, Charles Evers, John Lewis, and Hodding Carter 3d, joined the SPLC advisory council. Their names appeared in Dees's first direct-mail solicitation for contributions, which drew donations from five hundred recipients, or 2.5 percent of those contacted—an unusually high rate of return. The contributions of more than three hundred thousand people currently support the SPLC, which, since its inception, has never billed any of its clients. To end the SPLC's reliance on fund-raising (which currently consumes 23 percent of its income from contributions annually), Dees is trying to amass an endowment fund of $100 million. By 1994 contributions to that fund had totaled $56 million.

Shortly before they founded the SPLC, Dees and Levin had taken on a case that subjected to judicial scrutiny Alabama's gerrymandered, multimember legislative districts. As a result of their success on behalf of the plaintiff, poor blacks and whites gained a greater voice in Alabama state politics. In one of the earliest actions that they handled under the rubric of the SPLC, the center won national publicity when Dees persuaded a federal judge to order the racial integration of the then all-white Alabama state police force. In other cases handled by the SPLC's lawyers (the center has often obtained the services of local counsel to augment its staff, which currently includes a half-dozen attorneys), courts banned the use of federal money for the sterilization of women without their fully informed consent and outlawed racial and gender discrimination in the selection of Montgomery juries.

The SPLC has often tackled cases involving crimes punishable by death. "The death penalty is a bad thing the way it operates in America today," Dees told Robert E. Shapiro, citing as one piece of evidence the fact that, as of 1990, four hundred of the approximately 450 people who had been executed for rape were black, and that with few exceptions each of those four hundred had been accused of raping a white woman. Moreover, Dees explained to Shapiro, because most of the lawyers assigned to capital-punishment cases do not have the specialized skills necessary to cope with them, the SPLC has sought what Dees described as "better and qualified lawyers . . . [who are] interested in this work." In a widely publicized case that came to trial in 1975, Dees and other SPLC attorneys represented Joan Little, a black woman who, while being held for burglary in a North Carolina county jail, had killed a white jailer who had attempted to rape her. The jury of seven whites and five blacks found that Little had acted in self-defense. With John L. Carroll and Dennis N. Balske, Dees has written three manuals (published in the early 1980s) for lawyers on the handling of capital cases.

In 1981, convinced that the Ku Klux Klan had begun making a strong comeback, Dees organized an SPLC project called Klanwatch, to monitor organized racist activity. The next year, after a newspaper article alerted Dees to Klan use of intimidation to prevent Vietnamese immigrants from plying their fishing boats in Texas gulf coast waters, the SPLC obtained a federal court injunction that stopped the Texas Knights of the Klan from harassing the fishermen and from operating a paramilitary camp. The Klanwatch project has developed legal strategies specifically designed to protect people from violence-prone hate groups. One tactic, which makes use of the common-law principle known as vicarious liability, involves holding the leadership of racist groups legally responsible for the consequences of their trafficking in hate. In 1987, using that approach, the SPLC won a $7 million, precedent-setting judgment against the United Klans of America on behalf of Beulah Mae Donald, the mother of a young black man lynched in Alabama by Klansmen who, Dees demonstrated, had been provoked to violence by their leaders' message of racial hatred. In the following year the SPLC won a $950,400 judgment against Klansmen who had attacked a group of blacks during a civil rights march in Georgia. "Financial damage suits against racially inspired violence will keep the Klan thinking they will be paying with their pocketbooks if they aren't careful what they do on a Saturday outing," Dees told Mark Curriden, who interviewed him for the *ABA Journal* (February 1989).

In another celebrated case, which went to trial in 1990, the SPLC won $12.5 million in damages against Tom Metzger, the founder of the White Aryan Resistance (WAR), and the WAR organization itself for their responsibility in the murder of an Ethiopian immigrant by several skinheads in Oregon. The case was the subject of *Hate on Trial*, a television special produced by Bill Moyers that aired on PBS in 1992, and of Dees's book *Hate on Trial: The Case Against America's Most Dangerous Neo-Nazi* (1993), which he wrote with Steve Fiffer. "Despite our success in destroying this dangerous demagogue [Metzger], our nation remains torn by racism and racial violence," Dees declared in that book, noting that in 1992, Klanwatch "identified 346 white supremacist groups in [the United States], a 27 percent increase over the number in 1990." "But even more alarming than the growth of these groups on society's fringe is the rising tension in mainstream America," he added. In 1991, in an effort to combat racial and ethnic divisiveness, SPLC launched an educational project called Teaching Tolerance. A semiannual magazine named for the project is sent free of charge in September and January to five hundred thousand schoolteachers; in 1994, fifty-two thousand schools ordered free copies of *America's Civil Rights Movement*, a new video-and-text teaching kit developed by the Teaching Tolerance project.

To provide the public with a powerful reminder of what Dees has called "the horrible price" many Americans have paid in the fight for civil rights, the SPLC commissioned the architect Maya Lin to design what has been named the Civil Rights Memorial. Inscribed on the black granite monument, which were dedicated in 1989, are the names of forty black people whose murders were racially motivated. According to Bill Shaw of *People*, Dees views the memorial as his "proudest achievement." "If people can look at those forty names . . . and say, 'God, they killed this man for using a restroom,' then we've accomplished something," Dees told Shaw. The monument stands in the plaza of the SPLC's headquarters, which were erected several years after a firebomb destroyed much of the organization's original building, in 1983, and which feature an expensive electronic security system.

According to William Zinsser, Morris Dees is "rangy" and has "curly blond hair and amused eyes"; Robert E. Shapiro described him as "earnest and soft-spoken" and wrote that, in speech marked by a "beguiling southern accent," he offers "story after story [about his life in the law], barely completing one before beginning the next." Dees lives in Mathews, Alabama on his twenty-five-hundred-acre ranch with his third wife, the former Elizabeth Breen. His previous marriages ended in divorce. From the first one, to the former Beverly Crum, he has two sons, Morris S. Dees 3d, a physician, and John Fuller Dees, a builder. From the second, to the former Maureene Buck, he has a daughter, Ellie, and two stepchildren. Dees gave up rodeo roping, a favorite leisure activity of his, after breaking a hand; his current avocational interests include vegetable gardening and reading aloud with his wife. He has taught at the John F. Kennedy School of Government, at Harvard University, and has been a guest lecturer at half a dozen law schools and many legal seminars.

Dees was named one of the ten outstanding young men of America by the United States Jaycees, in 1966, and trial lawyer of the year by the Trial Lawyers for Public Justice, in 1987. His many other honors include the Outstanding Service for Human Rights Award from Tuskegee Institute, in 1976, the Young Lawyers Distinguished Service Award from the American Bar Association, in 1987, the Roger Baldwin Award from the ACLU, in 1989, and the Martin Luther King Jr. Memorial Award from the National Education Association, in 1990. He was the subject of *Line of Fire: The Morris Dees Story* (1991), a made-for-television movie.

Selected Biographical References: People 36:50+ Jl 22 '91 pors; Progressive 52:14+ Jl '88; Dees, Morris, with Steve Fiffer. A Season for Justice: The Life and Times of Civil Rights Lawyer Morris Dees (1991); Who's Who in America, 1995; Who's Who in the South and Southwest, 1993-94

Brian Douglas

Delany, Bessie

Sept. 3, 1891-Sept. 25, 1995 Dentist; writer.

Delany, Sadie

Sept. 19, 1889- Educator; writer. Address: c/o Kodansha America Inc., 114 Fifth Ave., New York, NY 10011

In 1993, at the ages of 104 and 102, respectively, the black sisters Sadie and Bessie Delany published their memoir, *Having Our Say*, which became a runaway best-seller and made its authors the objects of a groundswell of public adoration. As witnesses to one hundred years of societal changes, the Delany sisters offered a view of America unique in its breadth. But more important for the readers of the nearly nine hundred thousand copies of the book sold to date, Sadie and Bessie Delany revealed themselves to be lovable, accomplished survivors, women who weathered a century of institutionalized racism as well as personal trials, emerging wise rather than bitter and with their senses of humor intact. The book also reveals the differences between the two women—Sadie Delany, a former high-school teacher in the New York City public schools, who is the soul of kindness and forbearance, and the far more outspoken Bessie, a retired dentist. "Sadie is the sugar, and I'm the spice," the younger sister wrote, and Sadie expressed a similar view: "The way I see it, there's room in the world for both me and Bessie. We kind of balance each other out."

Bessie Delany died in her sleep on September 25, 1995, and is survived by her sister. On the occasion of her death, First Lady Hillary Rodham Clinton wrote that she felt "blessed to have known" Bessie Delany, whose "life was an example for us all," and at her funeral the former New York City mayor David N. Dinkins referred to her life as one "filled with purpose and passion, with courage and daring, a life filled with joy, love, and giving." Before her death, Dr. Delany collaborated with her sister on a second book, *The Delany Sisters' Book of Everyday Wisdom* (1994), and *Having Our Say* was the inspiration for a hit Broadway play of the same name, which opened in March 1995.

Sarah Louise (Sadie) Delany was born on September 19, 1889 in Lynch's Station, Virginia. Two years later, on September 3, 1891, Annie Elizabeth (Bessie) Delany was born in Raleigh, North Carolina, where the family lived. The two women are the second and third, respectively, of the ten children born to Henry Beard Delany, a former slave who went on to become the nation's first black Episcopal bishop as well as the vice-principal of Saint Augustine's School in Raleigh, and Nanny James (Logan) Delany, the matron of Saint Augustine's School. The other Delany siblings were (in order of birth) Lemuel, Julia, Henry, Lucius, William, Hubert, Laura, and Samuel. Several of them led distinguished careers. Lemuel, for example, became a physician; Henry (known as Harry or Hap) became a dentist several years before his sister Bessie was to do so; and Hubert not only prosecuted five hundred cases—all but two successfully—as an assistant United States attorney for New York but also won a Republican congressional primary (he lost the general election) and eventually became a judge.

The siblings' accomplishments were rooted at least partly in the emphasis on education that formed an integral part of their upbringing. Saint Augustine's School (now Saint Augustine's College) was founded in 1867 under the auspices of the Episcopal Church as an institution for black students; the Delany family's house, which came to be called the Delany Cottage, was situated on the campus. "Growing up in this atmosphere, among three hundred or so college students, reading and writing and thinking was as natural for us as sleeping and eating," Sadie and Bessie Delany stated in *Having Our Say*. Each day the children attended morning church services ("It was religious faith that formed the backbone of the Delany family," Bessie Delany wrote) and then went to their classes, where their fellow students included adults who were learning to read and write. Other adults in the community included the destitute former slaves for whom Henry and Nanny Delany provided work and food when they could.

"I don't remember life without Bessie," Sadie Delany wrote about her younger sister in an early chapter of *Having Our Say*, and in a later section Bessie declared that she and Sadie had been "best friends from Day One." One activity in which the two participated was picking cotton, for money, on the farm run by the school. Each child in the family learned to play a musical instrument, and they often performed together for their own amusement, led by their father. That the girls socialized primarily with each other, and that their activities were limited to their house and its immediate environs, was due in part to the fact that, as the sisters observed, "things hadn't improved much since slavery days as far as the right of colored women and girls to be unmolested." "If something had been done to us, and our Papa had complained, they'd have hung *him* . . . ," they wrote. "We were not allowed to go off the campus without an escort. Matter of fact, we were not allowed to go to certain places *on* the campus without someone to go with us."

Sadie Delany is one of the last living Americans to remember the onset, in the 1890s, of the decades-long Jim Crow era, during which racial segregation in the United States was enforceable by law. Recalling the 1890s as the time when "everything changed," the sisters described being suddenly unable to do things that they had done "hundreds of times," such as drinking limeades at the local, white-owned drugstore. They were able to avoid feelings of bitterness toward all white people because of positive experiences with whites that "predated Jim Crow." At the same time they learned, from their father, to support their fellow blacks during those early years of segregation: although the family lived close to a white-run A & P grocery store, Henry Delany instructed family members to go out of their way to shop at a store owned by Mr. Jones, a black man, explaining, "Mr. Jones needs our money to live on, and the A & P does not. We are buying our economic freedom." Henry Delany "believed in individuality," his daughter Bessie wrote, "but at the same time, he was dedicated to the community."

When Sadie Delany graduated from Saint Augustine's School in 1910, her father told her, "You owe it to your nation, your race, and yourself to go [to college]." Although her family could not afford her tuition, and she was left to her own devices to come up with the funds to pay for her education, she heeded her father's advice that she refuse any scholarship and thus avoid being "beholden to the people who gave [her] the money." Sadie's degree from Saint Augustine's qualified her to teach secondary school, and so, in order to earn the money for her future studies, she took the post of Jeanes Supervisor for Wake County, North Carolina. Named for the person who had begun a fund for the improvement of black schools in the South, the position required her to travel to schools all over the county and either initiate or supervise domestic science programs. Sadie has recalled that many of the duties of school superintendent were thrust upon her, so that at the age of twenty-one, she was—in fact if not by official designation—"in charge of all the colored schools in Wake County." It was in that capacity that she conferred with Booker T. Washington, the black leader and founder of Tuskegee Institute, in Alabama, when he made visits to Raleigh.

It was also in that post that Sadie witnessed, for the first time, the conditions under which the majority of her fellow blacks in the South were forced to live—and came to understand how sheltered and privileged her own life had been by comparison. The revelation inspired her in what she felt was her "mission" to help people. "I know that I helped many people as Jeanes Supervisor," she wrote in *Having Our Say*, "and I am very proud of that. I inspired many people to get an education, and quite a few went on to Saint Aug's. A lot of the time, what those folks needed was inspiration, a little encouragement. That goes a long way."

In 1916 Sadie Delany enrolled in the two-year domestic science program at Pratt Institute, in New York City, and upon her graduation she entered Columbia University Teachers College. She has recalled that officials at the latter institution attempted to have her perform her student teaching at a Negro settlement school—where she had already taught while studying at Pratt—rather than in the New York City public schools, where she wanted to be assigned "with the other teachers," who were white. Nonconfrontational by nature, Sadie nonetheless made her wishes known. "I didn't fight them over it at Columbia," she has written, "I just kept reminding them about what I wanted, every chance I got. They gave in, finally." She graduated from Columbia in 1920 with a B.S. degree and obtained her master's degree from the same institution in 1925. Following a second, brief stint as Jeanes Supervisor in North Carolina, she returned to New York City to teach in the public schools. ("New York was no piece of cake for a colored person," she has written, "but it was an improvement over the South, child.") Her first assignment was at the predominantly black P.S. 119 elementary school in Harlem.

When it came to obtaining a position as a high-school teacher, which was considered more prestigious than a post in an elementary school, Sadie once again employed guile rather than confrontation to circumvent the "brick walls they set up for colored folks"—an approach she learned from her father. She applied for an assignment at a high school, and when, after three years, her name reached the top of the waiting list, she received a letter inviting her for an interview. "At the appointment, they would have seen I was colored and found some excuse to bounce me down the list," she wrote in *Having Our Say*. "So I skipped the appointment and sent them a letter, acting like there was a mix-up. Then I just showed up on the first day of classes. . . . Child, when I showed up that day—at Theodore Roosevelt High School, a white high school—they just about died when they saw me. A colored woman! But my name was on the list to teach there, and it was too late for them to send me someplace else." It was thus that Sadie Delany became the first black woman to teach domestic science at the high-school level in New York City. She continued to teach high school until her retirement.

Meanwhile, Bessie Delany had graduated from Saint Augustine's School in 1911. Taking from her father the same advice with regard to education that he had given to Sadie a year earlier, she went to work as a teacher, for a salary of forty dollars a month, in Boardman, North Carolina. She remained in that job until 1913, when she left to teach in Brunswick, Georgia. In 1919 she entered the dental school at Columbia University, becoming one of seven blacks—and the only black woman—in a class of 170. During that time, she shared an apartment in Harlem with Sadie and three of their siblings (in all, nine of the ten Delany children made their way to New York). By her own account as well as Sadie's, Bessie experienced more racial prejudice in those years than did her sister, a fact they have attributed to Bessie's being darker-skinned. After one of Bessie's dental-school assignments received a failing grade, one of her white classmates offered to test the professor's fairness by submitting the same work—and received a higher mark. In 1923, the year of her graduation, she was proud to have been selected as the marshal, or flag-bearer, at the commencement ceremony—until she learned that she was given the honor so that no white student would have to march beside her.

Bessie Delany became only the second black woman licensed to practice dentistry in New York. She shared offices in Harlem with her brother Hap and Dr. Chester Booth. Whereas she had suffered racial discrimination in dental school, she experienced gender discrimination at the hands of the blacks who were her patients. "Two times I remember that men patients of mine insisted that Hap come and pull their teeth," she wrote in *Having Our Say*. "I remember one man said to me, 'Can you pull teeth with those little hands?'. . . . But once a person had been my patient, they'd always come back. The word got out: That colored woman dentist has a gentle touch."

The services that Bessie Delany provided often went beyond her duties. At the time that she began her practice, children were required to undergo dental examinations before enrolling in the New York City public schools; because many black parents could not afford the procedure, Dr. Delany examined many children for free. For those patients who could pay her, she charged the same rates—"two dollars for a cleaning, two dollars for an extraction, five dollars for a silver filling, and ten dollars for a gold filling"—from the time she began her practice until her retirement, in 1950. "I never raised my rates because I was getting by O.K.," she wrote. "I was always very proud of my work, and that was enough for me."

One of Bessie Delany's patients was the writer James Weldon Johnson, who was the first executive secretary of the NAACP. Her office became a gathering place of sorts for Harlem's black activists and leaders—among them the sociologist E. Franklin Frazier—who met there to plan protests against unfair treatment of blacks. (Through their brother Hubert, among others, Sadie and Bessie Delany also became acquainted with other celebrities, notably the musical giants Duke Ellington and Cab Calloway.) During one such meeting, which coincided with the rerelease of D. W. Griffith's stylistically groundbreaking but openly racist 1915 film *The Birth of a Nation*, Bessie Delany said to Frazier, "How can y'all sit around here planning those silly sit-ins when they're showing *Birth of a Nation* at the Capitol [Theater in Manhattan]? . . . I'm going down there tonight and protest. And if you don't join me, well, shame on you!" As it turned out, Bessie left for the theatre late because of a dental emergency, and upon her arrival she was greeted by the sight of Frazier and several others, including the writer, scholar, and activist W. E. B. DuBois, being hauled into a police wagon. The next day, when those arrested chastised her for inspiring the protest and then failing to participate in it, Bessie told them, "Well, Hap and I did show up, it's just that y'all were too busy getting yourselves arrested to notice." As she recalled in *Having Our Say*, "They didn't think it was too funny."

For all their exposure to entertainers and activists in New York, Sadie and Bessie Delany retained, to a large extent, the innocence and modesty that had characterized them during their years in North Carolina. ("After all," Sadie has written, "we were Bishop Delany's daughters.") Following their father's death, in 1928, their mother moved to New York to live with them. The three women shared a number of apartments in Harlem before moving to a cottage in the New York City borough of the Bronx. When their mother began to need someone to care for her during the day, Bessie retired from her dental practice in order to do so. Nanny Delany died in June 1956. Her death was particularly hard on Sadie, who, despite the strong influence of her father on her life, had always been, in her words, a "mama's child." A year later, in part to help Sadie recover from her loss, the two sisters moved to a house in Mount Vernon, New York. "I had to think about the world in a completely different way," Sadie wrote. "Bessie says that for the first time in my life, I seemed to come into my own, as an individual person. I was sixty-seven years old." Upon Sadie's retirement from teaching, in 1960, she and her sister settled into the quiet life they would enjoy for the next three decades.

It was in 1991 that Amy Hill Hearth, a freelance journalist, was assigned to write a newspaper article about Sadie and Bessie Delany. At first the sisters were reluctant to cooperate, feeling that they were not "important enough," as Hearth told Roberta Hershenson for the *New York Times* (April 2, 1995). "I had to convince them and give this little impromptu speech—that I thought it was very important that people from their generation be represented, especially black women who hadn't had much opportunity. I guess my enthusiasm rubbed off." The story, published in the *New York Times* on September 22, 1991, prompted warm responses from readers and caught the eye of Minato Asakawa, the senior vice-president and general manager of Kodansha America Inc., a New York-based book company. Before long that company's representatives approached the Delany sisters with the idea of publishing a book about their experiences and opinions, and Hearth signed on as the cowriter.

Having Our Say: the Delany Sisters' First 100 Years alternates between chapters written in Sadie's voice, those narrated by Bessie, sections in which the sisters describe events together, and occasional, brief historical overviews penned by Hearth. The Delany sisters related the events of their own lives as well as details of their lineage (there are white and Native American ancestors on both sides of their family, and Nanny Delany's grandmother was the product of an affair between a black male slave and the wife of his white owner). In addition, they offered their views, formed over the course of the twentieth century, on such subjects as the current socioeconomic status of black Americans ("[What] slowed down the progress we made in the civil rights movement. . . . had a lot to do with lack of leadership after Martin Luther King [Jr.] died"), the unequal opportunities for blacks and whites ("Just look at [former vice-president] Dan Quayle. If that boy was colored he'd be washing dishes somewhere"), and economic policy ("That funny little white guy, Ross Perot, he is right about the deficit. . . . That deficit is a disgrace").

Having Our Say had an overwhelmingly positive critical reception. In a representative evaluation of the book, Jean-Claude Baker wrote in the *New York Times Book Review* (December 5, 1993) that it had made him feel "proud to be an American citizen" and added, "The combination of the two voices, beautifully blended by Ms. Hearth, evokes an epic history, often cruel and brutal, but always deeply humane in their spirited telling of it. But I am most struck by the hopeful tenor of their voices. 'I'll tell you something else, honey,' the Delany sisters declare. 'We were good citizens, good Americans! We loved our country, even though it didn't love us back.' The time has come to love them back.'" Readers and theatregoers seemed prepared to do just that, judging from the book's phenomenal sales and by the success—popular and critical—of the theatrical staging of *Having Our Say*. The Broadway production, which starred Gloria Foster as Sadie and Mary Alice as Bessie, was nominated for three Tony Awards.

In the meantime, the sisters' second book—*The Delany Sisters' Book of Everyday Wisdom*, also written with Amy Hill Hearth—was published in 1994. The Delanys explained in the prologue that after the publication of *Having Our Say* they had received letters from "a lot of folks, especially young ones," who didn't seem to "know how to live right." "We're as old as Moses," they wrote, "so maybe we have learned a few things along the way, and we'd like to pass them on." The book includes views and advice on such subjects as religious faith, discipline, self-reliance, frugality, and health. Rating the volume for the *New York Times Book Review* (December 11, 1994), Brooke Astor wrote, "In this complicated world, every reader will find something helpful, no matter what his background. The Delany sisters' philosophy and example create a standard for everyone."

While the sisters reportedly enjoyed the celebrity brought their way by the books and the play, it seemed to do little to alter the daily routine that they had developed over the years, which included prayer and yoga, an activity Sadie took up with her mother in the early 1950s ("I didn't know at that time that what we were actually doing was 'yoga.' We thought we were just exercising"). Sadie continued to cook, and Bessie to serve, their "big meal of the day," eaten at noon. Following milkshakes for dinner, they watched the *MacNeil/Lehrer NewsHour* on television. The one change effected by all the media attention seemed to concern the sisters' perception of life's possibilities. "Truth is, I never thought I'd see the day when people would be interested in hearing what two old Negro women have to say," Bessie Delany wrote. "Life still surprises me."

Sadie Delany continues to live at the house in Mount Vernon that she shared with her sister for thirty-eight years. Regarding the prospect of living without Bessie, Sadie said, as quoted in the *New York Times* (September 26, 1995), "I'll just do the best I can. I'll continue right on as if Bessie were here." Reflecting on her sister's life, she added, "Bessie lived to be 104, and she lived her life the way she wanted to. And especially the last couple of years, she has been having a ball. Between the play and the books, she has been having the time of her life. And she said you really couldn't ask for anything more."

Selected Biographical References: N Y Daily News p8 S 26 '95 por; Delany, Sarah and A. Elizabeth Delany, with Amy Hill Hearth. Having Our Say: The Delany Sisters' First 100 Years (1993)

Louise Erdrich/Henry Holt & Co.

Dorris, Michael

Jan. 30, 1945- Writer; anthropologist; educator. Address: c/o Charles Rembar, Rembar and Curtis, 19 W. 44th St., Rm. 711, New York, NY 10036

Thanks in no small part to the writer Michael Dorris, since 1990 federal law has required that the labels affixed to all bottles of wine or liquor sold in the United States carry this warning: "According to the surgeon general, women should not drink alcoholic beverages during pregnancy because of the risk of birth defects." Through his prizewinning book *The Broken Cord*, which was published in 1989, Dorris brought to widespread public attention the devastating impact even light or moderate consumption of alcohol by a pregnant woman can have on her baby during all stages of its development in the womb. *The Broken Cord* is a rich source of information on both fetal alcohol syndrome (FAS), which identifies a set of severe mental and physical handicaps, and fetal alcohol effects (FAE), the less damaging form of the disorder, which together afflict millions of people in many parts of world. The book is also the wrenchingly honest, deeply moving account of Dorris's struggles in raising his first adopted son, a Sioux child who was a victim of FAS, and, beginning when the boy was an adolescent, of the role played by his wife, the writer Louise Erdrich.

A mixed-blood Modoc who has strived through his writings and other forums to end the stereotyping of Native Americans, Michael Dorris began his professional life as an anthropologist. He has taught both anthropology and Native American studies at Dartmouth College for more than two decades. With the goal of reducing his academic responsibilities and thus gaining more time for his writing, he gave up his tenured position at Dartmouth in 1989 and assumed the title of adjunct full professor. In addition to works of nonfiction, among them dozens of essays on both personal matters and issues of social and political import, and books for children and young adults, he has written a best-selling novel, *A Yellow Raft in Blue Water*, and *Working Men*, a collection of short stories. He is also the coauthor, with Louise Erdrich, of the novel *The Crown of Columbus*. In what has been described as "a style of matrimonial collaboration that may well be unique," Dorris and Erdrich, whose books include *Love Medicine* and *The Beet Queen*, have cooperated closely on all facets of everything they have written, both as sole and as joint authors. "Basically, I think she and I have the same 'ear,' in the sense that as an artist has an 'eye,' a writer has an 'ear,'" Dorris has said.

An only child, Michael Anthony Dorris was born on January 30, 1945 in Louisville, Kentucky to Jim Leonard Dorris, many of whose ancestors were members of the Modoc tribe, and Mary Besy (Burkhardt) Dorris, who is part Irish. When Michael was two, his father, a United States Army career officer, was killed in a jeep accident in Germany. Soon afterward he and his mother left their quarters at a military base and, along with his maternal grandmother and his aunt Marion Burkhardt, moved into a small house in Louisville. In an essay for *Ladies' Home Journal* (May 1993), Dorris recalled, "My mother ran the house and devoted herself to the perfection of my childhood." Marion Burkhardt served not only as a second mother to him but also, in effect, as a proxy father, as he explained in a reminiscence for *Glamour* (June 1994). "My aunt was the one who pitched a baseball with me . . . , who took me horseback riding. . . . She helped me find my first jobs. . . . She gave me lessons in how to drive a stick shift." "It's often been observed that we're very much alike: stubborn, determined, softhearted, and righteous in our strongly held beliefs," he continued. "We argued often and passionately, and I honed my skills of rhetoric against her persistent but flexible skepticism. . . . She never failed to assure me that I could do anything with my life that I wanted, if I only tried hard enough." During summers and for a period during his teens, he lived with his father's relatives on reservations or in other places in Washington State and Montana.

As a youngster Dorris enjoyed reading Hardy Boys stories and Laura Ingalls Wilder's Little House series. A note to the local librarian from his aunt—"Please permit Michael to check out books for me"—enabled him, several years before he reached the required minimum age, to borrow books from the library's adult section. *Main Street*, by Sinclair Lewis, and a book by Karl Marx were among the first batch that he took home, he recalled in one interview. However, in an article published in the *Detroit News* (May 1991) that was subsequently reprinted in *Paper Trail* (1994), a collection of his essays, Dorris wrote that "the idea of consciously seeking out a special title" did not occur to him until he was fourteen, when a man whose lawn he mowed suggested, in what became an unspoken barter arrangement, that he borrow books from the man's personal library.

Dorris attended two secondary schools—St. Paul's Mission in Hays, Montana and St. Xavier High School in Louisville. At one or both, he edited the student newspaper and participated in debating-team activities. In 1963 he entered Georgetown University, in Washington, D.C., on a scholarship. He majored in English and classics. "For me, going to college was the most wonderful thing imaginable . . . ," Dorris, who was the first person among all his relatives to attend college, told Georgia Croft for the White River Junction, Vermont *Valley News* (April 28, 1987). "At last I was surrounded by other people who read in a place where people were expected to read. . . . I worked very hard. I wouldn't have dreamed of taking a year off to 'find' myself or even missing a class."

In addition to watching several movies each week, Dorris's extracurricular activities included working on the student newspaper and editing the campus literary magazine, where his first published story appeared. Although he "desperately wanted to be a fiction writer," as he told Georgia Croft, a student critic's assessment of his story as resembling an inferior installment of the comic strip "Mary Worth" embarrassed him so profoundly that for the next fifteen years he did not write fiction. In the summer of 1964, Dorris coordinated youth programs at the Fort Belknap Reservation, in Montana. During the next two summers, he worked as an office helper in New York City and as a clerk in a Paris bank. He graduated magna cum laude from Georgetown University in 1967 with a B.A. degree and as a member of Phi Beta Kappa.

With the aid of three fellowships, Dorris spent the next four years at Yale University, in New Haven, Connecticut, where he studied first theatre history and then anthropology. For three years he directed the Summer Urban Bus Program in New York City, which served between 160,000 and 500,000 people per summer. He spent a total of nineteen months in 1970 and 1971 in Alaska, investigating the effects of oil revenues on the inhabitants of Tyonek, a remote Indian fishing village, and learning Athapaskan, the villagers' language. "Doing ethnography in a small community is very much like puzzling out [fictional] characters . . . ," Dorris remarked to Sharon White and Glenda Burnside for the *Bloomsbury Review* (July/August 1988). As a field-worker, he explained, he was "constantly trying to figure out who was who and what was going on." In 1970 he earned a master's degree in theatre history and, in 1971, a master's of philosophy in anthropology, both from Yale.

One afternoon in 1970, Dorris was suddenly gripped by the idea of adopting a baby. So right did this notion seem that he "did not once question it . . . ," as he recalled in *The Broken Cord*. "My desire for a child was as clear and basic to me as instinct, and as undeniable and undissectable. It was pure *want*, not the shortcut to some other gratification or the tonic to a personal disappointment." A year later, although unmarried, he adopted a three-year-old Sioux boy. In 1974 he became the adoptive father of a second boy, a Sioux toddler, and in 1976 he adopted a Native American baby girl.

Meanwhile, Dorris had begun teaching. During the 1971–72 academic year, he taught anthropology as an assistant professor at Franconia College, an experimental institution in New Hampshire, and in 1972 he joined the faculty of Dartmouth College, in Hanover, New Hampshire. In his first year at Dartmouth, in addition to teaching anthropology, he established the college's Native American Studies Program. Through the program he met Louise Erdrich, a mixed-blood Turtle Mountain Chippewa who was then a student at Dartmouth. Dorris's first book, *Native Americans: Five Hundred Years After*, which featured photographs by Joseph Farber, was published in 1977. He next compiled an extensive bibliography of scholarly studies concerning Native Americans, a project that he completed in 1980. The bibliography, along with those of Arlene B. Hirschfelder and Mary Gloyne Byler, was published by the American Library Association in 1983 under the title *A Guide to Research on North American Indians*. The book was named one of the outstanding academic books of 1984–85 by the association's magazine *Choice*.

In 1980 Dorris took a sabbatical and went to New Zealand, to serve as a visiting senior lecturer in anthropology and Maori studies at the University of Auckland. While there, with the support of a Woodrow Wilson Faculty Development Fellowship, he researched the early relations between the British colonists and the Maoris. Concurrently, encouraged by the example of Erdrich, who regularly mailed to him poetry and fiction that she had written, he turned once again to creative writing. Reciprocally, he sent his newly produced poetry and short stories to Erdrich for her appraisal. "I went into writing fiction very much as Louise's student," Dorris told Charles Trueheart of the *Washington*

Post (October 19, 1988). In 1981 he and Erdrich again met at Dartmouth, to which she had returned as a visiting fellow. By the time they married, on October 10, 1981, the seeds of their literary collaboration had firmly taken root.

Dorris and Erdrich's earliest joint efforts include stories carrying the byline Milou North, a name that they created from the first syllables of their first names and the location of New Hampshire. "They're not terribly deep, but they're uplifting," Dorris has said. "[Each is] about a young woman in stress who resolves her issue affirmatively." The first North story, "Change of Light," appeared in *Redbook* in 1982. Written to please a particular audience, the story and two others in a similar vein were published in the British magazine *Woman* in 1983 and later reprinted in magazines in Europe and elsewhere.

In the meantime, Dorris had become involved in all aspects of the creation of works that bear only Erdrich's name as author, including her short stories "The World's Greatest Fisherman," which won the Nelson Algren Fiction Award in 1982, and her novels, among them the prize-winning *Love Medicine* (1984), for which Dorris served as agent, *The Beet Queen* (1986), and *Tracks* (1988). Similarly, Erdrich was participating in every facet of the creation of the works that carry Dorris's name as sole author. "As [each] book develops, we get so involved in the characters and the story that the last thing we think of is whose name is going to be on it," Dorris told Michael Schumacher for *Writer's Digest* (June 1991). "When the book comes out and we get reviews . . . , I think we read them with equally proprietary eyes."

For months before either of them begins writing any work of the imagination, Dorris and Erdrich discuss during their daily afternoon walks the appearance, personality, and other characteristics of possible characters, gradually bringing the people to life in their minds. They continue to flesh out their fictional creations in places like restaurants, where they speculate about what a character would wear when eating in such an establishment and what he or she might choose from the menu. Conversations about plot, dialogue, and all other aspects of the story continue virtually until the manuscript is published. After Dorris had written a substantial part of *A Yellow Raft in Blue Water*, for example, a discussion he had with Erdrich during a long car ride spurred him to change the protagonist from a boy to a girl, and, after subsequent talks, to add two more principal characters.

After their mental groundwork, Dorris told Michael Huey during an interview for the *Christian Science Monitor* (March 2, 1989), "whoever is going to be the primary author of the piece will sit down in isolation [and] confront the blank page." The writer gives a draft of a paragraph or as much as a chapter to the other person, who pencils in comments. Then the writer produces a second draft. That process is repeated half a dozen times or more and invariably leads to major rewrites. "The final say clearly rests with the person who wrote the piece initially, but we virtually reach consensus on all words before they go out," Dorris told Hertha D. Wong for the *North Dakota Quarterly* (Winter 1987).

In elaborating on their modus operandi, Dorris told Gail Caldwell of the *Boston Globe* (September 26, 1986) that the person serving in effect as editor "brutalizes [the draft] and tries to balance off the criticisms with little stars in the margin." "It's much stronger editing than we would tolerate from anybody else," he said. "We've gotten to the point of trusting that response, because in the beginning we had this agreement that we would never not say anything to spare the other person's feelings." "If the ['editor'] really objects strongly [to something], you know there's something wrong . . . ," he explained to Michael Schumacher. "You'll sulk . . . , but we've both concluded, after many, many such experiences, that the objecting person . . . is always right." "You can take risks with a trusted coworker that you couldn't otherwise," Dulcy Brainard quoted him as saying in *Publishers Weekly* (August 4, 1989). "I think I'd be a much more conservative writer if I didn't know Louise was there to read and catch me if I fall."

Dorris was inspired to write his first novel by a recollection of a chance encounter during his adolescence. One afternoon, after swimming to a raft, he had met a man who told him about his concentration camp experiences during World War II. When he recalled the incident many years later, the title "A Yellow Raft in Blue Water" immediately sprang into Dorris's mind. Set in the Pacific Northwest and on an Indian reservation in Montana and narrated in separate sections by a fifteen-year-old girl whose father is African-American, the girl's mother, who is an American Indian, and one of the mother's Native American aunts, *A Yellow Raft in Blue Water* (1987) presented "three portraits of remarkable psychological density," Michiko Kakutani declared in an admiring review for the *New York Times* (May 9, 1987). In describing some events from more than one point of view, Kakutani wrote, Dorris makes the reader "appreciate the nearly tragic results of family members being trapped within their own subjectivity, prisoners of their selfish anger and pain."

In similarly enthusiastic assessments, Anatole Broyard wrote in the *New York Times Book Review* (June 7, 1987) that, with *Yellow Raft*, Dorris had "realiz[ed] one of the extravagant dreams of anthropology—to describe a dying culture almost as if you were dying with it," and Cathi Edgerton, in *Voice of Youth Advocates* (August/September 1987), observed that he "fascinates us with the enigma of American Indian culture in its odd balance of patriotism and Red Power, ravaged by the inroads of Western ways. . . . Each thread of story binds the heart with the riddle of our common humanity and our insistence on separateness." *Booklist* and *Library Journal* named *Yellow Raft* an "Editor's Choice Book of 1987" in both the adult and the young adult categories. Editions of the novel have since been published in eight countries.

In speaking to Dulcy Brainard about *The Broken Cord* (1989), his next book, Dorris said, "I wouldn't have had the sense or the courage to write nonfiction this way without writing fiction first. I could never have written this book without having written *Yellow Raft*, and I couldn't have written *Yellow Raft* without having worked with Louise on *Love Medicine* and *The Beet Queen*." Dorris was unaware of the existence of fetal alcohol syndrome (FAS) until 1982, when, while visiting a reservation as a foundation consultant, he learned that, taken together, the multiple problems from which his first adopted child suffered—serious learning difficulties, poor judgment, inability to imagine future events (and thus to understand cause-and-effect relationships), and particular physical abnormalities and physiological maladies, including scoliosis and a severe seizure disorder—constituted a condition that, only a few years before, had been identified as FAS. Believing firmly in the "positive impact of environment," in his words, Dorris had showered his son with love and attention and had enlisted the services of many excellent medical, psychotherapeutic, and educational professionals, but the boy's problems had proved to be virtually intractable.

During the next three years, Dorris made many more visits to reservations where high rates of alcoholism had led to a high incidence of both FAS and FAE (the latter of which afflicts Dorris's two other adopted children). For a year in 1985–86, after getting a Rockefeller Foundation research fellowship and a leave of absence from Dartmouth, he gathered information for what he at first envisioned would be, in his words, "a footnoted study of the national implications" of FAS. Indeed, *The Broken Cord* presents a wealth of scientific information and statistics about FAS and the toll it has exacted in Native American communities. But it also became, as Dorris disclosed in the book, the "chronicle of a personal quest for understanding," because he had realized that "it would be hypocrisy to disguise in print [his] own family situation, [his] own motivations and biases." He had also decided to make *The Broken Cord* more readable for a general audience than the average scholarly text and to produce something that had "merit as literature, or at least . . . to aspire to that," as he explained to Rebecca Bailey for the *Valley News* (July 28, 1989).

The literary merits of *The Broken Cord* (1989) were among the outstanding features that inspired universal acclaim for the book. In a representative evaluation for the *Chicago Tribune* (July 23, 1989), Josh Greenfeld wrote, "Although the diagnoses and etiologies may differ when it comes to the mentally retarded and the developmentally disabled, the scenario is pretty much the same for the parents. And in chronicling his life with Adam [as Dorris's son, Reynold Abel Dorris, known as Abel, is called in the book], Dorris tells each familiar chapter—from denial through fuming rage to irate acceptance. What distinguishes this book is Dorris's relentless pursuit of the source of Adam's deviant behavior. The result is both an anthropological detective story and an impassioned warning that no thinking would-be parent can ignore." Among other honors, *The Broken Cord* was named the best nonfiction book of 1989 by the National Book Critics Circle, and it won both the Heartland Prize and a Christopher Award in 1990. *Audio World* named Dorris's reading of *The Broken Cord* the best audio recording of 1990 in which an author had read his or her own work. A prize-winning television adaptation of the book, for which Dorris acted as a consultant, aired in 1992. Less than a year before, in 1991, Abel Dorris had died, from injuries he sustained when he was struck by a car.

Dorris, who habitually works on more than one writing project at a time (and thereby, he has said, keeps writer's block completely at bay), and Erdrich had started collaborating on what would become their most recent novel, *The Crown of Columbus* (1991), in the early 1980s. One day, while crossing Saskatchewan by car, they sketched a five-page outline of the story. In 1985 the outline won them an advance of $1.5 million, a portion of which they used to establish a fund for FAS research. The product of extensive research (mostly by Erdrich), *The Crown of Columbus* consists of parts written separately by both Erdrich and Dorris. Most of the story is narrated alternately by Vivian Twostar, a Native American professor of anthropology at Dartmouth who has stumbled upon two pages from Christopher Columbus's lost diary, and Roger Williams, a Dartmouth classics professor and poet who fathered Vivian's second child. Embedded within their accounts of their adventures on a Caribbean island, where they have gone in hopes of getting what may be the rest of the diary, are examinations of their relationship and that of each of them with Vivian's teenaged son.

The Crown of Columbus received mixed reviews. In a positive assessment for the *Women's Review of Books* (October 1991), Carla Freccero described the novel as "a highly structured, complex, symbolic rewriting of American history in terms of Judeo-Christian and Native myths. . . . As it interweaves the public and historical with the personal and familial, [it] insists that the perspectives of European and Native, colonizer and colonized, cannot be reconciled without reenvisioning gender relations." In the *New York Times Book Review* (April 28, 1991), on the other hand, Robert Houston complained that "throughout, it strains credibility, and not only in matters of plot: a reader is left floundering to discover on just what level the authors want it to be read, or just how they want their characters to be taken," and David Finkle, writing in the *Voice Literary Supplement* (May 1991), called the book "brilliant hokum" and "beautifully spun cotton candy."

Dorris believes that many critics reacted unfavorably to *The Crown of Columbus* at least in part because it was published—merely by coincidence, he has insisted—just before the quincentennial of Columbus's arrival in the Western Hemisphere. "I would hope that some time from now . . . , it will be taken less topically and more as a novel of discovery . . . ," he told Allan Chavkin and Nancy Feyl Chavkin in a 1992 interview that appears in *Conversations with Louise Erdrich and Michael Dorris* (1994). "Another thing that I think disturbed some people is that *The Crown of Columbus* was fun to write. We enjoyed it thoroughly—the process of working together and being able to try a big expansive book that was full of information and populated with characters who were well-educated, who had at their disposal the lexicons of several traditions."

A generally favorable critical reception greeted the publication of *Working Men* (1993), a collection of fourteen of Dorris's short stories. "Whether set in an Alaskan fishing village, a rural Indiana cemetery, or an army PX in Vietnam, Dorris's remarkably varied stories are uniformly excellent," Albert E. Wilhelm wrote in *Library Journal* (September 1, 1993). After reading the collection for the *New York Times Book Review* (October 17, 1993), Tony Eprile found that the "inspired" stories in *Working Men* made those that were "merely well wrought" seem "disappointing." But as Eprile, who is himself a short-story writer, pointed out, "collections are rarely even," and, in this case, "the flaws are easily eclipsed by the overall strength of this sensitive and beautifully observed book. The description of pond building by the narrator of 'The Benchmark' could equally serve to describe Mr. Dorris's masterly attention to craft."

Dorris has written three books for children or adolescents and teenagers: the critically acclaimed *Morning Girl* (1992), which reached the top spot in *Publishers Weekly*'s list "Books for Younger Readers"; *Guests* (1994); and *Amory Goes Wild*, which was scheduled for publication in 1995. Some ninety of his essays and articles and two dozen of his short stories have been published in anthologies and in a wide variety of periodicals, among them *Mother Jones*, *Parents*, *Antaeus*, *Newsweek*, and the *New York Times*. Forty-three of his reminiscences and his essays on FAS and Native American issues and other social and political matters were reprinted in *Paper Trail*. Dorris's essays about the trip he made to Zimbabwe in 1992, as a board member of the Save the Children Foundation, won the 1992 Center for Anthropology and Journalism Award for Excellence; they appear in his book *Rooms in the House of Stone* (1993). He contributed the article "Fetal Alcohol Syndrome" to the *1994 Medical and Health Annual* of the *Encyclopaedia Britannica*. His novel *Cloud Chamber* is scheduled for publication in 1997.

Michael Dorris has been described as tall, rangy, and loquacious and as exuding "an air of quiet modesty and sadness, punctuated occasionally with a wry, self-deprecating humor," as Vince Passaro wrote in a *New York Times Magazine* (April 21, 1991) profile. "He seems truly surprised and slightly awestruck by his won success," Passaro observed. Dorris lives with Louise Erdrich and their children in what he has described as an isolated setting in Cornish, New Hampshire. In addition to their adopted children, Jeffrey Sava (called Sava) and Madeline, they have three daughters—Persia, Pallas, and Aza. A frequent lecturer, Dorris has been a consultant to many Indian groups and literary and governmental entities. His many honors include the 1985 Indian Achievement Award, the Dartmouth College Medal of Outstanding Leadership and Achievement (1991), and the World Conference on the Family International Pathfinder Award (1992).

Selected Biographical References: N Y Times Mag p35+ Ap 21 '91 pors; Pub W 236:73+ Ag 4 '89 por; Washington Post B p1+ O 19 '88 por; Chavkin, Allan and Chavkin, Nancy Feyl, eds. Conversations with Louise Erdrich and Michael Dorris (1994); Contemporary Authors new rev vol 19 (1987); Something About the Author vol 75 (1994); Who's Who in America, 1995

Herb Weitman

Early, Gerald

Apr. 21, 1952- Essayist; poet; educator. Address: Dept. of English, Washington University, Campus Box 1122, 1 Brookings Dr., St. Louis, MO 63130

"Gerald Early is one of the most exciting and provocative writers of his generation," the novelist and short-story writer Joyce Carol Oates has said, "and his prose is a continual delight." Under the umbrella of his principal subject, the relationship between black culture and the larger American society, Early has produced books and essays as accomplished and insightful as they are eclectic. *Tuxedo Junction: Essays on American Culture* (1990) and *The*

Culture of Bruising: Essays on Prizefighting, Literature, and Modern American Culture (1994), the collections of his own nonfiction pieces, reveal his impressive knowledge of, and unique takes on, such subjects as literature, jazz, and boxing. Among the books he has edited is the two-volume *Speech and Power: The African-American Essay and Its Cultural Content from Polemics to Pulpit* (1992), which contains articles by black writers ranging from Zora Neale Hurston and James Weldon Johnson to Charles Johnson and Henry Louis Gates. Early is a professor of English and director of African and Afro-American studies at Washington University, in St. Louis, Missouri. In addition to prose, he has written a book of poetry, *How the War in the Streets Is Won*, which was published in 1995, as was his most recent nonfiction work, *One Nation Under a Groove*.

Gerald Lyn Early was born on April 21, 1952 in Philadelphia, Pennsylvania, the youngest of the three children (and the only son) of Henry Early, a baker, and Florence Fernandez (Oglesby) Early, a preschool teacher. Henry Early died when his son was nine months old, and thereafter Florence Early reared her children in relative poverty in South Philadelphia. In his book *Daughters: On Family and Fatherhood* (1994), Early characterized his mother as a proud, stoic, and unsentimental woman who was "neither sympathetic nor affectionate" to him while he was growing up. "Whenever I would cry," he wrote, "she would always tell me to hush, that crying never solved anything." He also revealed, "When I was a boy, my mother never told me a single story about her childhood. . . . There was a great air of seriousness and purpose about my mother, and I think she thought that to indulge in such memory recitation was sentimental and childish. There was only the immediate concern of survival, of keeping her family together and out of trouble." Recalling his mother's "great skepticism, utter disdain, about the idea of needing other people, of having other people, whether black or white, think that they ever had done or ever could do anything for her," Early observed that he himself had "inherited something of that pride."

Although he has recalled being a "bookish" boy who displayed no particular athletic or fighting ability, Early befriended members of the Fifth and South Streets gang, one of many gangs in the city, and he witnessed many fistfights, one of which he described vividly in an essay in *Tuxedo Junction*. The environment in which he grew up, together with the fact that, as he has written, the South Philadelphia gangs of his generation produced such first-rate prizefighters as Jeff Chandler, Tyrone Everett, and Matthew Saad Muhammad, undoubtedly contributed to Early's fascination with boxing.

In *Daughters*, Early recounted describing to one of his children the moment he discovered that he wanted to be a writer. The revelation occurred one New Year's Day when he was a boy, while he watched a Mummers' parade with his mother. Periodically, as the costumed men proceeded down Broad Street, Florence Early took her son from their curbside street corner perch to a nearby jazz club so that he could get warm. Early was enchanted by the musicians. "I remember that I was amazed by this tenor saxophone," he wrote. "It was so shiny, golden, and it seemed monstrously big. I thought the thing was made out of pure gold. I thought it was something Arabian, something straight out of a fairy tale. . . . It seemed like the coolest thing on Earth." Asked by his daughter if he had wanted to play the instrument, Early responded, "No. . . . I wanted to describe it."

Early enrolled at the University of Pennsylvania, in Philadelphia, in the early 1970s. At some point during those years he read the book *Home: Social Essays*, by the poet and playwright Imamu Amiri Baraka, and he has credited that work with inspiring him to write essays, as it "stressed the doctrine of cultural nationalism, which enormously appealed to [his] puritan instincts of renovating the world through a covenant with one's own strength of character and one's sense of election." Early served his apprenticeship as a weekly columnist for his college newspaper, *The Daily Philadelphian*, beginning with a piece on the gang-related murder of his cousin. He received his B.A. degree in English literature, cum laude, in 1974.

During the mid-1970s Early worked for the Philadelphia city government. His job as a member of the Release on Own Recognizance Program, which he has described as "a monumental waste of [his] time and the taxpayers' money," was to interview people who had been arrested to determine whether they were eligible to be released without bail while they awaited trial. He also served a six-month stint as a communications supervisor with the Crisis Intervention Network, whose purpose was to monitor gang activity and control gang-related violence. Early eventually enrolled in the graduate program at Cornell University, in Ithaca, New York, where he earned his M.A. degree in English literature in 1980 and his doctorate in 1982. In the same year, Early, by then married and the father of two young daughters, became an assistant professor of Black Studies at Washington University. The summer of 1990 saw his promotion to full professor of English and African and Afro-American Studies, and in 1992 he became director of the African and Afro-American Studies program. In the meantime, he had begun publishing articles in *Antaeus*, *Callaloo*, *The Hudson Review*, and several other periodicals.

Twenty-one of those pieces were collected in Early's first book, *Tuxedo Junction*, which was published in 1990. The book's title, as Early explained in the introduction, is the name of a song that was recorded in 1939 by the black musician Erskine Hawkins and that became a "crossover" hit when the white bandleader Glenn Miller released a version of it in the following year. For Early, the song and its history are metaphors for "the doubleness of our American culture, the sense of something being there and being here, of being for 'them' and for 'us' and for all," the phenomenon that "generates the vital syncretism that makes [American culture] function."

Correspondingly, many of the subjects covered in *Tuxedo Junction* are those whose histories are inextricably intertwined with that of the African-American community but whose significance extends beyond it. In an essay about Vanessa Williams, the first black to win the Miss America pageant, Early acknowledged the positive effect of Williams's achievement on the morale of black women while declaring that "the very purpose and motivation of the Miss America contest [was] being called into question, and rightly so, by feminists of every stripe." Early stated in another piece, dedicated to the jazz pianists Thelonious Monk and Earl ("Fatha") Hines: "Hines is the forgotten great man of jazz, and his being forgotten is symbolic of the haphazard way that cultural tradition, black or white, gets passed along to another generation. Tradition in America is characterized by the most intense sort of alienation and by the most intense sense of longing; in the end, we are either hopelessly sentimental or crudely cynical."

The seriousness with which Early views boxing was demonstrated by the number of essays and articles devoted to it in *Tuxedo Junction* as well as by his declaration that "the three most important blacks of the twentieth century" are the heavyweight champions Jack Johnson, the first black to hold the title; Joe Louis, whose 1938 defeat of the German fighter Max Schmeling symbolized, for many, American fortitude in the face of the Depression and growing international tensions; and Muhammad Ali, who represented black defiance by joining the Nation of Islam and by deciding to relinquish his title and serve a prison term rather than fight in the Vietnam War.

In defense of boxing, a sport many have denounced as inhumane and have sought to ban, Early wrote in a piece reprinted in *Tuxedo Junction*, "This moralistic rage of the righteous misses a few major points. First, to ban boxing would not prevent the creation of boxers since *that* process, *that* world would remain intact. And what are we supposed to do with these men who know how to do nothing but fight? I suppose we can continue to lock them in our jails and in our ghettos, out of our sight and untouched by our regard. That, in the end, is precisely what those who wish to ban boxing really want to do: not to safeguard the lives of the men who must do this work but simply to sweep one excessively distasteful and inexplicable sin of bourgeois culture under the rug. Second, those who wish to ban boxing know that they will simply condemn those men to surer deaths by not legally recognizing the sport. Boxing banned will simply become . . . a very popular underground, *totally* unregulated sport. Finally, I think it is fitting to have professional boxing in America as a moral eyesore: the sport and symbol of human waste in a culture that worships its ability to squander."

Tuxedo Junction received very positive reviews. "[Early's] writing challenges, jokes, explains, and sympathizes, and he has a lucid, informal style," a writer for the *New Yorker* (May 21, 1990) observed. "The reader is frequently stimulated to argument and just as frequently excited by Mr. Early's originality." Gene Seymour, evaluating the book for the *Nation* (May 21, 1990), wrote: "The images [in Early's writing] come at you in a thick and heavy rush. At times, the sheer weight of his intelligence and virtuosity can wear you out. After moving from the myth of St. Nicholas and Black Peter to William Godwin's *Caleb Williams* in discussing [Herman Melville's] 'Benito Cereno,' you sense that it even wears Early out sometimes. But you're better off for the workout."

Early's next books, *My Soul's High Song: The Collected Writings of Countee Cullen* (1991), the two volumes of *Speech and Power*, and *Lure and Loathing: Essays on Race, Identity, and the Ambivalence of Assimilation* (1993), were collections that he edited and for which he wrote the introductions. The scholarship that Early brought to his treatment of Cullen, one of the leading poets of the Harlem Renaissance, was widely praised. Writing in *Library Journal* (January 1991), Ellen Kaufman called the introduction to *My Soul's High Song* "a moving portrait of a man whose biography has proven elusive," and in the *New Republic* (April 8, 1991), Jervis Anderson contended that the book "may be the best study of Cullen and his work that has yet appeared."

Citing such nonfiction works as James Baldwin's *The Fire Next Time* (1963), Eldridge Cleaver's *Soul on Ice* (1968), and Albert Murray's *The Omni-Americans* (1970), Early wrote in the introduction to the anthology *Speech and Power*: "Although there have been several outstanding black novels written in the twentieth century, black essays or essay collections have had generally as large, and in some cases an even larger impact on American life and letters than the most successful black novels. . . . We cannot fully understand black American literature, the black writer, or the course of black culture as an intellectual construct during the twentieth century without coming to grips with the meaning and function of the essay in the hands of the black American. It is on this simple yet vital premise that this collection is built."

The one hundred-plus works that make up *Speech and Power* date from the early part of the twentieth century to the 1990s. In order to make the collection comprehensive yet wieldy, Early published it in two volumes (the second appeared in 1993), each divided into several headings. The section labeled "On Being Black" includes pieces by the black activist and scholar W. E. B. Du Bois and the essayist Shelby Steele; "Boxing" contains essays by the novelist Richard Wright, the former heavyweight champion Floyd Patterson, and Early himself; and the poets Gwendolyn Brooks and Audre Lorde and the novelist Terry McMillan are among the contributors to the section, in the second volume, titled "Autobiography." A writer for the *Antioch Review* (Winter 1994) called *Speech and Power* "an important new collection."

In compiling *Lure and Loathing*, Early used as a "point of departure" the famous assertion made in *The Souls of Black Folk* (1903) by W. E. B. Du Bois: that every African-American feels his or her "twoness" as a result of being "an American, a Negro" with "two souls, two thoughts, two unreconciled strivings; two warring ideals in one dark body, whose dogged strength alone keeps it from being torn asunder," and that that "double consciousness" forces each black person to "see himself through the revelation of the other world." In *Lure and Loathing*, a wide array of contemporary black writers, including Toni Cade Bambara, Stephen Carter, Stanley Crouch, and Nikki Giovanni, addressed Du Bois's statement. A reviewer for *New York Newsday* (July 21, 1993) called the collection "engrossing" and "timely," and in the *Wall Street Journal* (May 20, 1993), Linda Chavez praised Early for assembling in one book such divergent points of view and thereby "demonstrat[-ing] that diversity within groups can be as wide as it sometimes is between them." Chavez pronounced *Lure and Loathing* "an especially impressive feat."

Daughters, a departure for Early, was written in a comparatively simple, straightforward style. In this brief work he offered a candid description of his relationship with his daughters, Linnet and Rosalind, and he discussed his coming to terms with the learning disability of Linnet, his older daughter; his and his wife's ambivalence over rearing their children in a predominantly white community; and his slow realization that his daughters, growing up in comfort and without the strict emphasis on emotional self-reliance that characterized his upbringing, are "as different from [him] as [he] was from [his] mother." The book's chapters are interspersed with poems that Early wrote for Linnet and Rosalind and with entries from the two girls' diaries. "Mr. Early has the benefit of modern American self-awareness, but . . . his gifts sometimes war with one another," Margo Jefferson wrote in the *New York Times* (December 2, 1994). "How well he describes lives and thoughts in progress. How jarring it is when he interrupts that progress with an elaborate poem or rhetorical flourish. But in the end, how satisfying it is to be in the company of a thoughtful writer and an honest father."

The Culture of Bruising, like *Tuxedo Junction*, is a collection of Early's own essays. As is true of the earlier book, *The Culture of Bruising* is concerned with the boxer as an abstract entity (symbolizing "the individual in mass society: marginalized, alone, and consumed by the very demands and acts of his consumption") as well as with specific figures in the sport, among them the fighters Sonny Liston, Floyd Patterson, Jake LaMotta, and Rocky Graziano. The book also includes an article titled "The Black Intellectual and the Sport of Prizefighting," and other chapters focus on literature, jazz, multiculturalism, baseball, and the slain black leader Malcolm X. The last section, comprising two essays, is titled "Life with Daughters." Reviewing *The Culture of Bruising* for the *Chicago Tribune* (October 9, 1994), Chris Petrakos wrote, "Perhaps what's most compelling about Early's writing is his dazzling flexibility of thought. There's no dogma, no rigidity of purpose other than the intellectual rigor of carefully examining whatever life in America throws into his path. That he shares his observations in such abundance is a gift that can be repaid by letting his words sink into our consciousness. . . . " *The Culture of Bruising* won the 1995 National Book Critics Circle Award.

The verses in *How the War in the Streets Is Won: Poems on the Quest of Love and Faith*, Early's first book of poetry, concern subjects—such as jazz and boxing—familiar to readers of his prose. The volume received mixed reviews. A representative assessment was that of a writer for *Library Journal* (June 1, 1995): "At his best, Early catches some hidden corner of an untold story. 'Cock-fight' and 'The Kings of Dead Box' rival the finest poems by many contemporary poets. Unfortunately, such gems are few. At his worst, he juggles adjectives, avoiding clichés by inches." Better received was *One Nation Under a Groove*, Early's brief book on Motown, the record company, founded by Berry Gordy Jr., that specialized in "crossover" music by black artists and thus came to symbolize the interrelatedness of black and white cultures. "Because he states straightaway that he comes not to theorize about Motown but simply to think about it, suggesting in his introduction that the book is a 'prelude and fugue to some deeper studies,' Early may be forgiven for certain historical omissions," Mary Elizabeth Williams wrote in the *Nation* (July 3, 1995). "The all-too-short *One Nation* skims the surface of Gerald Early's insights. If this is the prelude, the song is going to be something else."

Gerald Early has been the recipient of several honors, including the 1988 Whiting Writers' Award, which brought with it a cash prize of twenty-five thousand dollars, and the CCLM/General Electric Foundation Award for Younger Writers, also given to him in 1988. His writing was included in the 1991 and 1993 editions of *Best American Essays*. Among many other projects, Early served as a consultant for, and appeared in, Ken Burns's *Baseball*, the nine-part documentary that aired on PBS in 1994, and he was a contributor to Burns's book *Baseball: An Illustrated History*. He is currently completing a work on Fisk University. Early is an Episcopalian. Since August 27, 1977 he has been married to Ida Haynes Early, a college administrator. He and his family live in Webster Groves, Missouri.

Selected Biographical References: Contemporary Authors vol 133 (1991); Early, Gerald. Tuxedo Junction: Essays on American Culture (1990), Daughters: On Family and Fatherhood (1994); Who's Who Among Black Americans, 1994–95

Bachrach/The Scripps Research Institute

Edelman, Gerald M.

July 1, 1929- Biologist; educator. Address: Scripps Research Institute, Department of Neurobiology, SBR-14, 10666 N. Torrey Pines Rd., La Jolla, CA 92037

"I have a small romantic streak and a very definite belief that's coupled to it, which is that the asking of the question is the important thing," Gerald M. Edelman, a physician and physical chemist by training whose professional reputation rests on his contributions to the fields of immunology, developmental biology, and neurobiology, told Steven Levy in an interview for the *New Yorker* (May 2, 1994). "Anybody in science, if there are enough anybodies, can find the answer," he said. "It's an Easter-egg hunt. That isn't the idea. The idea is: Can you ask the question in such a way as to facilitate the answer?" While it remains to be seen whether his ideas on brain function, which has been the focus of his research since the late 1970s, will be upheld by future discoveries, there is little doubt that Edelman has made his mark on modern science by tackling some of the most challenging questions in the biological sciences. The first one occurred to him during the mid-1950s, when, during his free time, he was reading up on antibodies, the molecules without which humans and other higher organisms would succumb to the myriad foreign substances to which they are routinely exposed. Convinced that their antigen-fighting ability would remain a mystery until someone figured out what they looked like at the molecular level, he decided to try to decipher the molecular structure of one of them himself. In 1969 he and his colleagues did just that—an accomplishment that provided the first reliable molecular explanation of how the immune system works. The significance of his achievement was formally recognized in 1972, when he became one of the two corecipients of that year's Nobel Prize in Physiology or Medicine.

Contrary to what might be expected of a scientist who had "laid a firm foundation for truly rational research, something that was previously largely lacking in immunology," as Sweden's Karolinska Institute noted when it awarded him the Nobel prize, Edelman found the idea of spending the rest of his career working out the details of the immune system to be singularly unappealing. He wanted instead to solve a new problem, so in the mid-1970s he began to explore the phenomenon of morphogenesis, the process by which embryonic cells join to form functionally distinct groups of cells, or tissues. He switched fields again in the mid-1970s, when he began research on what he calls "that most complex object in the known universe" —the brain. "I would like at least to get a glimpse of how it is that we have come to be aware," he told Levy. Edelman's research on the subject has led him to conclude that the brain is a highly plastic organ that continually remakes itself throughout the life of the organism as it responds to the world. What many find deeply satisfying about his theory is that it both refutes the emotionally disquieting notion that the human brain is a computerlike entity that is "programmed" to "store" and "process" information, as has been proposed, and accounts for the sense of individuality that humans seem to need to believe they possess. For the time being, though, Edelman's theory of neuronal-group selection, unlike his previous work in immunology and developmental biology, remains hotly contested and will either be upheld or disproved by subsequent discoveries.

Gerald Maurice Edelman was born on July 1, 1929 in New York City, and he grew up in Queens, New York and the moderately well-to-do town of Long Beach, on Long Island, New York. His father, Edward Edelman, was a surgeon by training who practiced general medicine "among the poor," as his son put it, in the Ozone Park section of Queens. Though he would eventually follow in his father's footsteps, Edelman first aspired to become a violinist, having demonstrated some talent in playing the instrument as a boy. He was still toying with the idea of pursuing a career as a musician when he entered Ursinus College, a small school near Valley Forge, Pennsylvania that one of his two sisters attended.

During his first year or two in college, Edelman also took courses in science and chemistry. He quickly became bored with his school work, though—so much so that during his sophomore year he left college and moved with a friend to Miami Beach. At the urging of his mother, Anna, he eventually decided to return and complete his degree, but only on the condition that he not be required to attend lectures. To his surprise, the college administrators agreed, and he took only laboratory classes. At around the same time, Edelman concluded that he was not suited for a career as a performer and that he "had no talent for composition." Yet he was also adamantly opposed to pursuing a conventional career. "I said, 'Gee, where can I do something where I don't have to work?'" he recalled to Steven Levy. "Which seemed very important—the thought of doing a nine-to-five and having a career was horrifying to me."

The idea of devoting his life to research began to appeal to Edelman, for he had found that such work demanded a kind of creativity that was not unlike that required of an artist. To that end, after graduating from college in 1950 with a B.S. degree in chemistry, he enrolled at the University of Pennsylvania Medical School, where his suppositions about the nature of research were soon confirmed. "I . . . learned that to do it right required every bit as much skill as music, and then some," he told Levy. Upon receiving his M.D. degree in 1954, Edelman spent a year working as an intern at Massachusetts General Hospital, in Boston. Drafted into the army in 1955, he spent the next two years practicing medicine in Paris. "It formed a nice hinge interlude—what I call my F. Scott Fitz-Edelman period," he told Levy. "I fooled around in sports cars and made friends with a lot of the guys from the American Hospital. Lots of interest in night-clubbing and traveling. And that was where I first got interested in antibodies."

Indeed, by the time he completed his military service requirement, Edelman had become consumed by the problem of how an organism's immune system protects it against substances that it does not recognize as "self." Of particular interest to him was the fact that the body defends itself against foreign proteins that neither it nor its ancestors ever encountered before. "How can it be that so many possibilities [of future tissue invasion] are already realized in the lymphoid cells, with the possibilities of coupling with so infinitely many future events?" he asked an interviewer for the *New York Post* (October 14, 1972).

When Edelman first became interested in antibodies, it was known that the immune response is initiated by the production of millions of these molecules, which are structurally similar yet functionally different. In 1940 the chemist and future Nobel laureate Linus C. Pauling attempted to account for the diversity of antibodies by proposing that when a foreign substance enters the body, it is enveloped by a standardized antibody molecule that alters its shape to conform to the invader and then serves as a kind of "mold" from which vast numbers of similarly shaped antibody molecules are formed. According to this idea, the invader thus "instructs" the body to make a specific antibody. In the 1950s a competing theory was advanced that maintained that the body is genetically preprogrammed to produce a multitude of different antibody molecules. As a result of his reading on the subject in Paris, Edelman began to suspect that the latter theory, which had not gained general acceptance, was more likely than Pauling's to be correct, and following his return to the United States he decided to find out if it was. This became the focus of his work at Rockefeller Institute (now called Rockefeller University), in New York City, into whose graduate program he had been accepted.

To prepare himself for that decidedly ambitious task, Edelman arrived on campus three months before classes were scheduled to begin and used that time to master virtually all that was known at the time in the field of immunology. From the outset he was convinced that the answer lay in the chemistry of the antibody molecule itself. "Behind every key biological problem there is a chemical solution . . . ," he told Lawrence K. Altman in an interview for the *New York Times* (October 13, 1972). "The only way to understand how the antibody molecule could recognize foreign substances was to determine something about its chemical structure." In 1959 he published his first major finding: that immunoglobulins consist not of a single polypeptide chain but of two components—"heavy" chains and "light" chains—and are thus more complex than had been previously supposed.

After receiving his Ph.D. in physical chemistry, Edelman began what turned out to be a three-decade-long career at Rockefeller. Early on during his tenure there, he continued his research on immunoglobulins. (During this period he served as an assistant and associate dean as well as an assistant and associate professor and, from 1966 until 1974, as a professor.) Edelman's research was facilitated by new findings on multiple myeloma, a cancer of the bone marrow that is characterized by the mass production of a particular protein, called the Bence-Jones protein, after its discoverer, the nineteenth-century English physician Henry Bence Jones. Edelman realized that victims of the disease could aid him in his effort after it was discovered that the Bence-Jones protein is in fact the "light-chain" component of the myeloma globulin antibody.

Edelman and his colleagues were not the only scientists working on the problem. Their main competition came from a group of researchers in England headed by Rodney Porter, then a professor of biochemistry at Oxford University, that was reputed to be better equipped and staffed than Edelman's. Despite the odds against them, Edelman and his colleagues beat their rivals in the race to decipher the structure of the whole molecule. By analyzing large quantities of the myeloma globulin that his lab received from an individual afflicted with the disease, in 1969 Edelman and his colleagues became the first group to elucidate the structure of the myeloma globulin antibody itself. "Never before has a molecule approaching this complexity been deciphered," Walter Sullivan wrote of the feat in the *New York Times* (April 15, 1969). Porter's group accomplished the task some time later. The importance of Edelman's and Porter's work was recognized in 1972, when both men were jointly awarded the Nobel Prize for Physiology or Medicine, which carried a cash prize, to be split between them, of $101,000. In announcing the award, the Nobel Prize Committee stated that the two men had "incited a fervent research activity the whole world over, in all fields of immunologic science, yielding results and practical values for clinical diagnostics and therapy."

Knowledge of the structure of the myeloma globulin molecule in turn enabled scientists to infer the antibody's function. Since Edelman's analysis had confirmed that one end of the molecule is always the same, while the other is variable, scientists were able to conclude that, contrary to Pauling's theory, the body possesses a large pool of structurally similar but functionally different antibody molecules. The presence in the body of millions of slightly different molecules accounts for the organism's ability to defend itself against the myriad antigens that regularly enter it, for with so many antibodies prepared to spring into action, at least one is usually likely to be able to bind with the invader and precipitate the production of more antibodies. "There is an enormous storehouse of lymphoid cells which are locks but don't know they are locks—like a character in a Pirandello play—until the key finds them," Edelman explained in the interview for the *New York Post.*

This explanation was particularly compelling to scientists because it was consistent with the principle of natural selection, which had been conceived by the nineteenth-century naturalist Charles Darwin. In Darwin's formulation, those individuals in a given population that are better adapted to their environments are "selected" to survive and reproduce, while less well-adapted individuals are not. Similarly, Edelman's work showed that those antibodies that are equipped to combat a given antigen will be "selected" to proliferate. Edelman further proposed that each chain in a given antibody molecule is synthesized by combinations of genes, with the diversity of the molecules resulting from mutations that occur during the development stage of the antibody-producing cells.

After receiving the Nobel Prize, Edelman abandoned his immunological research. "I never was an immunologist," he told David Hellerstein in an interview for the *New York Times Magazine* (May 22, 1988), in explaining why he had relinquished such a promising field of research. "I solve problems." The problem Edelman decided to undertake next was in the completely different field of developmental biology. He wanted to find out what mechanisms governed morphogenesis, the process by which cells join to form tissues. And as he had done for immunology, he made a significant contribution to that area of research. At first, though, it was slow going. "He and his colleagues were trying all kinds of crazy ways to get cells to separate from each other and then reattach," Leif Finkel, a fellower researcher, told David Hellerstein. Then, in the mid- and late 1970s (by which time Edelman had been named Vincent Astor Distinguished Professor at Rockefeller), he and his colleagues discovered three different kinds of intercellular substances called cell adhesion molecules, or CAMs—molecules that "glue" cells together to form tissues. That finding transformed this branch of developmental biology into an intensely competitive field, according to Maxwell Cowan, the vice president and chief scientific officer of the Howard Hughes Medical Institute. "[It] was one of the major discoveries in developmental biology of the past two decades," he told Hellerstein.

Edelman's interest in embryology soon prompted him to investigate the development of the brain, which in turn led him to become preoccupied with another of the great unsolved mysteries of biology: What is it about the human brain (and those of higher animals, for that matter) that enables an individual to make sense of and deal effectively with a complex and ever-changing world? After all, writing a novel, enjoying a movie, or cooking a gourmet meal are not behaviors that were selected for at an earlier time in human evolutionary history. "There's no way evolution could have already given you all the answers," Edelman explained to Steven Levy. "Try a Shakespeare sonnet. Exactly what adaptation do you think adjusted your brain to the impact of a Shakespeare sonnet? There were no such things in *Homo habilis, Homo erectus,* even a Neanderthal. So it becomes clear that we have a problem here. Is it the case that your brain is a tabula-rasa device? Does your brain mirror the world?"

As Edelman pondered these questions, beginning in the mid-1970s, he became increasingly convinced that the brain, like the immune system, operates according to the Darwinian principle of natural selection. In about 1976 he came up with the first draft of his theory of brain function, which he calls the theory of neuronal-group selection. Since then, at the Neurosciences Institute, in La Jolla, California, which he has directed since 1981, he has tested his ideas on a series of machines (named Darwin I, Darwin II, Darwin III, and Darwin IV) that are programmed to simulate what he believes is happening in the brain. His results have to some extent lent support to his theory.

The theory itself is usually described as having three fundamental components. The first, which draws on Edelman's research in developmental biology, holds that during the prenatal stage of development, undifferentiated cells migrate throughout what will become the brain until, through the activity of CAMs, connections among neurons are established. This process results in the establishment of a unique pattern of neural pathways among both neurons and neuronal groups. In turn, sheets of neuronal groups, called "maps," form and become associated with a particular function, such as vision. It is at this stage of development, according to Edelman, that the brain's circuitry becomes fixed. If true, what this means is that the developmental process ensures that at birth the brain of every individual is unique. Even identical twins, with the same genetic endowment, possess brains with distinctive networks of interneural connections.

The next stage in the brain's development, according to Edelman's theory, begins after birth and continues throughout the life of the individual. During this phase connections among groups of cells and maps are either reinforced or weakened, depending on the stimuli the individual experiences. In other words, connections used in an activity that best enables the individual to cope with its environment will be strengthened, and the "less fit" connections will not.

The final aspect of Edelman's theory is that of "reentry," which can be described as the process by which neuronal groups in the various maps communicate with one another. No higher center is involved in reentry; instead, Edelman has explained, the various maps "talk" to one another in much the same way that members of a string quartet do to coordinate their playing. It is as a result of this process, Edelman believes, that the brain dynamically categorizes different stimuli. For instance, an individual is able to distinguish between various sounds—such as music being played in a neighboring room and a conversation in which he is engaged—because neuronal groups in specific maps are continually relaying sensory information back and forth to one another. If correct, Edelman's theory would invalidate the once-popular notion that memories and images are "stored" in the brain.

What some scientists find most appealing about the theory is that it is consistent with the Darwinian principle of natural selection: Darwin's populations of individuals are analogous to Edelman's connections among neuronal groups, with those connections that enable the individual to deal effectively with its environment being "selected," or strengthened. Edelman has discussed these ideas in three books written for a scientific audience: *Neural Darwinism: The Theory of Neuronal Group Selection* (1987), *Topobiology: An Introduction to Molecular Embryology* (1988), and *The Remembered Present: A Biological Theory of Consciousness* (1990). In 1992 he presented his theory in a book aimed at a lay audience, *Bright Air, Brilliant Fire*.

The scientific community remains divided over the validity of Edelman's theory of neuronal-group selection, and some scientists have been pointedly critical of it. His critics' chief complaint, though, is not that the theory is scientifically untenable but that Edelman's explanation of it is so saturated with jargon and rhetorical flourishes that even the most erudite of his colleagues cannot comprehend it. The comments of Gunther S. Stent, during an interview with David Hellerstein, are not atypical: "I consider myself not too dumb. I am a professor of molecular biology and chairman of the neurobiology section at the National Academy of Sciences, so I should understand it. But I don't." Edelman's admirers, on the other hand, are as enthusiastic in their praise as his detractors are resolute in their criticism. As Frederick Jones, one of Edelman's advocates and a scientist who works under Edelman in the Scripps Neurobiology Department, told Steven Levy, "I do think that what he has accomplished will not be recognized fully for a hundred years. After we're gone, people will discover him. What Freud was to psychology, Edelman will be to biology." In the meantime, the prospect that Edelman's theory may be correct provides humans with an opportunity to think of themselves in a new and provocative way. If his theory is valid, human thought and behavior are not governed by a computerlike entity, nor are they mediated by an unexplainable, supernatural force. Rather, the brain of each individual is from the earliest stages of its development a unique organ that has a built-in capacity to continually re-create itself as it encounters the world.

In 1992, after working for thirty-two years at Rockefeller, Edelman left that institution and moved to California to build the Neurosciences Institute and to assume the position of chairman of the neurobiology department at the Scripps Research Institute, in La Jolla. Additionally, he is a member of many professional organizations, including the American Philosophical Society, the National Academy of Sciences, the American Society of Biological Chemists, the American Association of Immunologists, the Genetics Society, the Society of Neuroscience, and the American Society of Cell Biologists. As of mid-1994 he had written five books, served as the editor of nine books, and was listed as either an author of or contributor to 424 articles.

Besides the Nobel Prize, Edelman has won numerous awards, including the Spencer Morris Award, from the University of Pennsylvania (1954); the Eli Lilly Prize in Biological Chemistry, from the American Chemical Society (1965); the Albert Einstein Commemorative Award, from Yeshiva University, in New York City (1974); the Buchman Memorial Award of the California Institute of Technology (1975); the Rabbi Shai Shacknai Memorial Prize in Immunology and Cancer Research, from the Hadassah Medical School at Hebrew University, in Jerusalem (1977); the Hans Neurath Prize, from the University of Washington (1986); the Cecile and Oskar Vogt Award, from the University of Dusseldorf, in Germany (1988); and the Warren Triennial Prize, from Massachusetts General Hospital (1992). A fellow of the New York Academy of Sciences, the American Academy of Arts and Sciences, and the New York Academy of Medicine, he has also received honorary degrees from Williams College, the University of Siena, Gustavus Adolphus College, and the University of Paris.

Journalists who have interviewed Edelman are invariably impressed by the tremendous breadth of his knowledge. Steven Levy reported that his conversation with Edelman, for instance, left him "aswirl in a maelstrom of observations on the mind-body conflict, scathing assessments of his competitors in the consciousness game, erudite literary citations, technical evaluations of issues in the world of high-end audio components, remarks on obscure but crucial organic molecules, a monologue on why Wagner marked the end of diatonic music, and an ominous description of what the future will be like when artifacts are conscious." Edelman has been married to the former Maxine Morrison since June 11, 1950. The couple have three grown children: Eric, David, and Judith.

Selected Biographical References: N Y Post p24 O 14 '72 por; N Y Rev of Bks 33:21+ O 9 '86; N Y Times p1+ Ap 15 '69 por, p32 Ap 15 '69, A p1+ O 13 '72, A p24 O 13 '72 por; N Y Times Mag p16+ My 22 '88 pors; New Yorker 70:62+ My 2 '94; Nobel Prize Winners (1987)

Sigrid Estrada/Farrar, Straus & Giroux

Ehrenreich, Barbara
(AIR-en-rike)

Aug. 26, 1941– Journalist; writer; social critic. Address: c/o Farrar, Straus & Giroux, 19 Union Square West, New York, NY 10003

A committed leftist and feminist, Barbara Ehrenreich has written extensively—in essays, conference papers, pamphlets, and books—about the economic and social status of women, with special emphasis on the history of women's health care and sexual freedom and oppression. In one of her books she delineated the history of men's widespread fear of commitment, blaming it on the pressure men faced in the 1950s to support a family. In another book she analyzed the anxieties among middle-class Americans, who live in a climate of unarticulated fear, according to Ehrenreich, of a decline in their standard of living. A recent novel of hers is part mystery, part science fiction, and part philosophical speculation. "People have sometimes thought I was a sociologist or a historian," Ehrenreich told Wendy Smith, who profiled her for *Publishers Weekly* (July 26, 1993), "but since I have no formal education in any of these things, I'm not tied to a discipline, so I can rampage through any kind of material I want."

Ehrenreich was born Barbara Alexander on August 26, 1941, in Butte, Montana to Ben Howes Alexander, a copper miner, and Isabelle (Oxley) Alexander, a homemaker who was active in the Democratic Party. She grew up with a longstanding heritage of atheism and independent thinking. Her father's maternal grandfather, according to family lore, gave up two opportunities to leave his job in the mines for better working conditions above ground. In the first instance, after having just been promoted to a driving job, he quit when the mine owner asked him to break in some horses for his wife's carriage. He then returned to mining, working underground for most of his life, until he had saved enough money to retire to a small farm. On his way there, the story goes, he encountered an indigent young Indian mother to whom he gave all his savings before turning around and heading back to the mines.

In recounting that tale in the introduction to her book *The Worst Years of Our Lives: Irreverent Notes from a Decade of Greed* (1990), Ehrenreich interpreted the story as follows: "I like to think that this was one more gesture of defiance of the mine owners who doled out their own dollars so grudgingly—a way of saying, perhaps, that whatever they had to offer, he didn't really need all that much." "So these were the values, sanctified by tradition and family loyalty, that I brought with me to adulthood," she continued. "Through much of my growing-up, I thought of them as some mutant strain of Americanism, an idiosyncrasy which seemed to grow rarer as we clambered into the middle class. Only in the sixties did I begin to learn that my family's militant skepticism and oddball rebelliousness were part of a much larger stream of American dissent."

Although she has made political activism and social commentary her life's work, Ehrenreich was trained in the sciences. In 1963 she received a bachelor of arts degree in chemical physics from Reed College, in Portland, Oregon, and in 1968 she completed a Ph.D. in cell biology at Rockefeller University, in New York City, where she had become politically active three years earlier, protesting the bombing of North Vietnam by United States forces. "I got swept up in the antiwar movement, as so many people did," she recalled in her interview with Wendy Smith. "I went into college as someone who loved the existentialists, had a soft spot in my heart for Ayn Rand, had no social or political views of any kind. Then I saw a little more of the world, read some newspapers—the war in Vietnam, the civil rights movement, those got me involved." Eventually, her interest in effecting change superseded her engagement with scientific progress.

During the 1960s Ehrenreich was involved in a plethora of progressive activities in New York City. She worked to improve the low-income housing situation, helped to expand educational opportunities for the underprivileged, organized union activists, advocated health-care reform, and helped to launch a student antiwar group, whose members soon began to galvanize peace activism off campus as well. Witnessing firsthand the student rebellions of 1968, at Columbia University, in New York City, and on European campuses, she and her husband, John Ehrenreich, a like-minded activist whom she had met while both were attending Rockefeller University (and whom she had married on August 6, 1966), combined their impressions and analyses of the student movement in their jointly written book, *Long March, Short Spring: The Student Uprising at Home and Abroad* (1969).

Ehrenreich's radicalization was facilitated by the experience of giving birth to her daughter, Rosa, in 1970. "I was the only white patient at the clinic, and I found out this was the health care women got," she told Judy Steed in an interview for the Toronto *Globe and Mail* (November 23, 1987). "They induced my labor because it was late in the evening and the doctor wanted to go home. I was enraged. The experience made me a feminist." With her husband John she coauthored *The American Health Empire: Power, Profits, and Politics* (1970), a report from the Health Policy Advisory Center in New York City, whose publications Ehrenreich edited from 1969 to 1971. While working as an assistant professor of health sciences at the State University of New York at Old Westbury, from 1971 to 1974, Ehrenreich coauthored with Deirdre English two pamphlets that explored male domination of women's health care: *Witches, Midwives, and Nurses: A History of Women Healers* (1972) and *Complaints and Disorders: The Sexual Politics of Sickness* (1973).

By 1974 Ehrenreich had divorced her husband and moved to Long Island, where she joined the local Nassau County chapter of the New American Movement (NAM), a socialist organization unaffiliated with but politically proximate to Michael Harrington's Democratic Socialist Organizing Committee (DSOC). "NAM came up with a vision of socialism that made sense to Americans," Ehrenreich explained to Judy Steed. "It was not communist or Marxist-Leninist—though we weren't bothered about communism—and it was not involved in electoral politics." In 1983 NAM merged with DSOC to form the Democratic Socialists of America, which Ehrenreich cochaired and in which she has remained active ever since.

In the meantime, journalism had turned into a full-time occupation for Ehrenreich, who became an editor of the biweekly news-feature magazine *Seven Days* in 1974. Health-care issues continued to be the subject of many—though by no means all—of her articles and essays. In a paper entitled "The Health Care Industry: A Theory of Industrial Medicine," presented at the International Conference on Women in Health in Washington, D.C., in June 1975, Ehrenreich argued that the American medical system was a microcosm that not only mirrored but institutionalized the sexism in society at large. Not only were women professionals consistently paid less than men, Ehrenreich found, but they also tended to occupy positions of "less power and prestige" than those of their male counterparts. Ehrenreich and English explored the ramifications for female patients of such discrimination in *For Her Own Good: One Hundred Fifty Years of the Experts' Advice to Women* (1978). "I was making the transition to being 'socially relevant,' as we called it in the sixties, and the obvious thing to write about was medical and public health issues," Ehrenreich recounted to Wendy Smith. "My background in biology meant I wasn't intimidated by doctors or their pronouncements about how the medical system should work."

In 1983, aided by a Ford Foundation Award for Humanistic Perspectives on Contemporary Society and by a fellowship from the New York Institute for the Humanities, Ehrenreich published her first solo effort, *The Hearts of Men: American Dreams and the Flight from Commitment*, a study of "the ideology that shaped the breadwinner ethic and how that ideology collapsed." In an effort to explain the antifeminist backlash of the 1980s, which blamed feminism for the erosion of "family values," Ehrenreich contended in *The Hearts of Men* that the weakening of the nuclear family was the result not of feminism but of male abdication of the breadwinner role. Furthermore, she argued that men began to rebel against that role as early as the 1950s, and not, as is commonly assumed, in response to the women's movement. Thus, according to Ehrenreich, the breakdown of the traditional family began with men, not with women.

As recently as the 1950s, men who were not married by the advent of their thirties often faced discrimination in the job market, because confirmed bachelors were widely suspected to be homosexual. Attempting to demonstrate that Hugh Hefner's *Playboy* ethic provided a much-longed-for heterosexual rationale for remaining single, Ehrenreich wrote that "the magazine's real message was not eroticism, but escape . . . from the bondage of breadwinning. Sex—or Hefner's Pepsi-clean version of it—was there to legitimize what was truly subversive about *Playboy*. In every issue, every month, there was a Playmate to prove that a playboy didn't have to be a husband to be a man." The freewheeling lifestyle of the single man was further legitimized in the minds of some men by doctors who blamed career-related stress for the high incidence of heart attacks among men. When representatives of the human potential movement added their voices to the chorus arguing for a guilt-free approach to sloughing off family responsibility in the name of "doing one's own thing," men joined the "flight from commitment" in ever-increasing numbers, Ehrenreich argued, without "overcoming the sexist attitudes that role has perpetuated: on the one hand, the expectation of female nurturance and submissive service as a matter of right; on the other hand, a misogynist contempt for women as 'parasites' and entrappers of men."

Most reviewers admired Ehrenreich's originality but found fault with her research methodology. For example, Eva Hoffman, evaluating *The Hearts of Men* for the *New York Times* (August 16, 1983), commented, "By her own admission Miss Ehrenreich is more interested in cultural imagery and ideas than in sociological proof; and to this reader, her narrative makes good, if sometimes unexpected, sense." "Barbara Ehrenreich . . . has written a witty, intelligent book based on intriguing source material . . . ," Judith Levine wrote in the *Village Voice* (August 23, 1983). "But I believe *The Hearts of Men* is wrong. When she claims that the glue of families is male volition and the breadwinner ideology—and that a change in that ideology caused the breakup of the family—I am doubtful. The ideology supporting men's abdication of family commitment is not new. It has coexisted belligerently with the breadwinner ethic throughout American history." Agreeing that "one may take issue with her cause-and-effect pairings," Lois Timnick wrote in the *Los Angeles Times* (July 24, 1983) that "Ehrenreich needs especially to be read by those who fear that 'women's libbers' will wrest away the values she shows men tossed out long ago, or who still cling to the notion that we could, if we wanted, go back to the mythical *Ozzie and Harriet* days."

In her next book, *Re-Making Love: The Feminization of Sex* (1986), which she coauthored with former *Seven Days* editors Elizabeth Hess and Gloria Jacobs, Ehrenreich dealt with the legacy of the sexual revolution—the change in national mores that began when the availability of the birth-control pill and the liberalization of abortion restrictions made it possible for women as well as men to have sex for pleasure alone, without the risk of an unwanted pregnancy. As Ehrenreich and her coauthors demonstrated, the potential for sexual equality that inhered in the sexual revolution has not yet been realized, because of the persistence of a double standard for men and women that rewards sexually active unmarried men for their virility but ostracizes unmarried women deemed to be promiscuous.

Anticipating by several years Susan Faludi's *Backlash*, which detailed the media-fueled negative perception of women who chose to remain single, Ehrenreich and her collaborators urged women to reject that message, to celebrate the choices that were made possible by the sexual revolution, and to recover their autonomy in the bedroom. The tone of *Re-Making Love* was deliberately optimistic, as Ehrenreich told Carla Hall of the *Washington Post* (October 19, 1986): "I get unhappy when I feel that we [feminists] just end up being the bearers of bad news. I think we have to emphasize more that there is a very positive affirmative side to the feminist experience, whether it's through reclaiming sexual identities and gaining sexual assertiveness or just the discovery of how wonderful women are."

Contending in her review of *Re-Making Love* for *Social Policy* (Spring 1987) that the book is "much more valuable for the questions it raises than for its answers," Frances La Barre complained that the authors overemphasized their "polar opposition to the conservative groundswell and its manifestation in the popular press. This opposition encourages them to draw the lines of debate around only one axis of human experience, namely, that of power—dominance and submission. They forget that the axis of attachment—connection and separation—is real too and not just an embarrassing romantic throwback." Evaluating the book for the *New York Times Book Review* (September 14, 1986), Judith Viorst wrote, "I find the authors persuasive when they claim that a broader view of the physical sex act is sexual progress. But I find myself resisting their wish to free sexual pleasure from larger meanings—not because such divestiture is immoral but because it is a gyp. There are plenty of pleasures around that can be savored with little emotional investment. . . . Linking erotic pleasure to genuine concern for one's sexual partner may be a better way of remaking love."

After collaborating with Fred Block, Richard Cloward, and Frances Fox Piven on *The Mean Season: An Attack on the Welfare State* (1987), Ehrenreich published *Fear of Falling: The Inner Life of the Middle Class* (1989), in which she probed the motivations and insecurities of America's middle class, by which she meant primarily white-collar professionals, as Joseph Nocera pointed out in his review for the *New Republic* (January 1, 1990). Commending Ehrenreich for perceiving the anxiety of former and subsequent generations of the middle class, Nocera faulted her analysis of her own generation's nervousness about slipping through the cracks of the middle class. In discussing the 1960s generation, she "invokes not insecurity, but treason," Nocera wrote. "She blames the sellouts of the glorious 1960s for the materialism around us. It's a lament distorted by anger, which obscures precisely what the rest of her analysis persuasively reveals: the powerful social, cultural, and economic consequences of anxiety." Among the more significant of those consequences is the decline of the public school system, as Ehrenreich noted in her book: "As the urban middle class withdraws from public spaces and services—schools, parks, mass transportation—it also withdraws political support for public spending designed to benefit the community as a whole." Snobbery within the middle class, abhorrence of the homeless, and rejection of affirmative action programs for women and minorities are among other consequences.

In 1990 Ehrenreich published what is virtually a companion piece to the 1980s, *The Worst Years of Our Lives: Irreverent Notes from a Decade of Greed*, a collection of fifty essays that previously appeared in *Mother Jones*, *Ms.*, the *Nation*, the *New Republic*, and *Atlantic Monthly*, among other periodicals. In her introduction to the book, Ehrenreich described the 1980s as an era when "the 'phonies' came to power on the strength . . . of a professional actor's finest performance. The 'dumb' were being led and abetted by low-life preachers and intellectuals with expensively squandered educations. And the rich . . . used the occasion to dip deep into the wallets of the desperate and the distracted." As Marcia Froelke Coburn wrote in her review for the Chicago *Sun Times* (May 13, 1990): "Ehrenreich takes the measure of a decade and finds it sadly, dismally lacking grace, dignity, and—most of all—compassion." While the author does not disguise her contempt for the Reagans, the religious right wing, and Republicans in general, she does manage to bring a more humorous touch to bear on such subjects as feminism, television, corporate women and the "mommy track," fast cars, and food, among other topics.

Around 1989 Ehrenreich felt compelled to begin writing a novel, as she explained to Wendy Smith: "It was escapism. I started the novel when we'd had two terms of Reagan, Bush had just been elected, and I was constantly grinding out columns and articles trying to make my good little moral points: don't fight, share things, all that stuff. I just felt that I had to go into another dimension for part of the time. . . . A lot of the ideas my characters explore are real thoughts I've had that could potentially have been expressed in a nonfiction way, if I could have figured out what *that* would have been," Ehrenreich told Wendy Smith. "We don't have a big market for metaphysical speculation, so you're almost forced to put it in another form."

The result was *Kipper's Game* (1993), set in a near-future dystopia plagued by multiple environmental and man-made disasters. The title refers to an addictive computer game invented by the eponymous missing son of the protagonist. Described by Sara Mosle in her assessment for *New York Newsday* (July 4, 1993) as "an ambitious and at times maddening biotechnological thriller, with elements of science fiction and social criticism," *Kipper's Game* received generally unfavorable reviews, primarily due to what was perceived as overreaching on the part of the author. "Part of the problem, one suspects," Evelyn Toynton wrote in the *Washington Post* (August 16, 1993), "is that there are just too many varieties of doom pending here. . . . The characters here are uniformly lifeless, and rather than narrating a series of exciting events, the book mostly consists of long-winded conversations interspersed with long-winded rumination." "You keep expecting Ehrenreich to pull all the strings of the narrative together, but she doesn't," Sara Mosle complained, adding, however, that "it's a testament to her storytelling powers that one believes she will for as long as one does. . . . Ehrenreich may not be the next [Aldous] Huxley or [George] Orwell—yet—but this is still a very impressive, formidable debut by an already accomplished writer."

In 1995 a collection of Ehrenreich's essays, previously published in the *Nation*, the *Guardian*, and *Time*, among other periodicals, was released in hardcover under the title *The Snarling Citizen*. In these pieces, Ehrenreich utilizes her sometimes scathing, sometimes gentle wit to unearth the truth, as she sees it, about breast implants, the history of the separation of church and state, housecleaning, Haiti, racist portrayals of the welfare system, and various sensationalized crimes, among other topics. Evaluating the essays for the *Chicago Tribune* (May 28, 1995), Penelope Mesic declared, "They startle and invigorate because those who espouse liberal causes—feminism, day care, and a strong labor movement—all too often write a granola of prose: a mild, beige substance that is, in a dull way, good for us. Ehrenreich is peppery and salacious, bitter with scorn, hotly lucid." Describing the author's point of view as "clear, compassionate, and entertaining" in an assessment of the same date for the *New York Times Book Review*, Claudia Ricci suggested that "even readers who take exception to Ms. Ehrenreich's leftist tilt can appreciate the depth of understanding she brings to make sense of our ever-changing world."

Barbara Ehrenreich has been a fellow at the Institute for Policy Studies, in Washington, D.C., and she received a Guggenheim Fellowship in 1987 as well as a National Magazine Award in 1980. She also has served on the National Organization for Women's Commission on Responsive Democracy. The author of a monthly *Time* magazine column, she has been a contributing editor of *Ms.* and *Mother Jones* magazines. Discussing with Wendy Smith the differences between journalism and writing books, Ehrenreich said, "I like to do both. They're completely different ways of thinking and living for me: journalism is a more frenetic lifestyle—I'm switching on CNN all the time and maybe going on television myself to argue with somebody—and writing books is more solitary, contemplative, reclusive, and obsessional." Ehrenreich and Gary Stevenson, a union organizer whom she married on December 10, 1983, live in the Long Island, New York town of Syosset. She has two grown children, Rosa and Benjamin, from her first marriage.

Selected Biographical References: Humanist p11+ Ja/F '92; Pub W p46+ Jl 26 '93; Toronto Globe and Mail A p7 N 23 '87; Contemporary Authors new rev ser vol 37 (1992); Who's Who in America, 1995

Elion, Gertrude B.

(EL-ee-uhn)

Jan. 23, 1918- Research scientist; chemist; pharmacologist; educator. Address: c/o Wellcome Research Laboratories, Burroughs Wellcome Co., 3030 Cornwallis Rd., Research Triangle Park, NC 27709-2700

Since the inception of the Nobel Prizes in 1901, the award for physiology or medicine has, with few ex-

Burroughs Wellcome

Gertrude B. Elion

ceptions, recognized the work of people who were engaged in noncommercial research at universities, medical centers, or other nonprofit institutions. In 1988, in one of its rare departures from that practice, the Nobel committee of the Karolinska Institute in Stockholm chose to honor three scientists who were employed by pharmaceutical companies when they did their pathbreaking work. One of the three was the Burroughs Wellcome Company chemist and pharmacologist Gertrude B. Elion, who won the prize, along with her colleague George H. Hitchings and the British scientist Sir James W. Black, for developing an array of novel drugs that, in the words of a Nobel committee member, "have stood the test of time" and remain "frontline agents for the treatment of a wide spectrum of illnesses."

"Rarely has scientific experimentation been so intimately linked to the reduction of human suffering," a writer for the 1988 *Nobel Prize Annual* observed about the work of Elion and Hitchings, which led to the synthesis of drugs that combat acute leukemia, gout, and malaria, among other diseases, and an immunosuppressant compound that made possible the successful transplantation of organs. Elion's development of acyclovir, the first effective treatment for herpes-virus infections, launched a new era in antiviral research. In 1986, three years after her nominal retirement, Burroughs Wellcome scientists who had worked under her used her methodology to develop AZT, the first drug approved by the Food and Drug Administration for use against AIDS.

Elion joined the staff of the Wellcome Research Laboratories in 1944. Until 1967, when she became the head of the Department of Experimental Therapy and thus gained a degree of autonomy, she served as Hitchings's right-hand researcher. Working primarily with the nucleic acid purine, Elion and Hitchings detected crucial differences in the biochemistry of bacteria, viruses, protozoa, and cancer cells, on the one hand, and normal cells, on the other. Based on their findings, they designed drugs that, while leaving healthy cells unharmed, interfered fatally with the nucleic acid metabolism of diseased cells. Their strategy revolutionized pharmacological research. "People often ask whether [the Nobel Prize] wasn't what I had been aiming for all my life," Elion has said. "Nothing could be farther from the truth. . . . My rewards had already come in seeing children with leukemia survive, meeting patients with long-term kidney transplants, and watching acyclovir save lives and reduce suffering."

The descendant, on her mother's side, of Russian Jews and, on her father's side, as records from European synagogues dating from as far back as the year 700 A.D. reveal, of a long line of rabbis, Gertrude Belle Elion was born on January 23, 1918 in New York City. Her father, who immigrated to the United States from Lithuania as a child, was a dentist. Other immigrants in his community thought of him as a wise as well as smart man and often solicited his advice. Elion's mother, the former Bertha Cohen, was a homemaker. "[She] had more common sense than anyone I have ever known," Elion wrote in an autobiographical article for the *Annual Review of Pharmacology and Toxicology* (Vol. 33, 1993). A prodigious reader, Bertha Elion had learned to speak English after arriving in the United States, at fourteen, from a part of Russia that is now Poland. "My father also loved to read," Gertrude Elion noted in her *Pharmacology and Toxicology* reminiscence, "and I can remember many evenings during my childhood when I was exposed to a variety of literature, poetry, history, biography, and fiction, being read aloud by my father."

In 1924, shortly after the birth of her only sibling—her brother, Herbert, who was an engineer and physicist—the Elion family moved from Manhattan to the Bronx, a New York City borough that was then semisuburban. By her own account, Gertrude Elion had a happy childhood. She liked playing with friends in the vacant lots that dotted her neighborhood and visiting the Bronx Zoo with her beloved maternal grandfather. Among her treasured memories are those of the Metropolitan Opera performances to which her father took her beginning when she was ten. A child with "an insatiable thirst for knowledge," as she described herself in *Les Prix Nobel* (1989), a Nobel Foundation publication, she loved school. "The mere acquisition of knowledge gave me excitement and pleasure," she has said. Passionately fond of reading both fiction and nonfiction and fascinated with "people who discovered things," in her words, she was deeply impressed by *Arrowsmith* (1925), Sinclair Lewis's novel about a physician who dedicates himself to bacteriological research, and *The Microbe Hunters* (1926), Paul de Kruif's account of the work of pioneering bacteriologists, and she was especially inspired by the scientists Marie Curie and Louis Pasteur and the medical missionary Albert Schweitzer.

Elion skipped four school terms before completing the ninth grade. She entered Walton High School, a public school for girls, at the age of twelve, and she was only fifteen when she graduated, in 1933. She and her parents had long assumed that she would go to college, and her mother as well as her father encouraged her to pursue a career. The 1929 stock market crash had wiped out her father's investments, and with them her chances of attending a private college, but thanks to her excellent grades, she gained admission to Hunter College, a tuition-free, academically rigorous, women-only institution in New York City.

Elion had always enjoyed all her school subjects nearly equally, and she completed high school with no clear idea about a vocation. Her uncertainty ended the summer following her graduation, when her grandfather died of stomach cancer. Devastated by his death and filled with a desire to help others escape the kind of suffering that he had endured, she resolved to dedicate herself to finding a cure for cancer. "I felt very strongly that I had a motive, a goal in life that I could try to do something about," she told Marguerite Holloway, who profiled her for *Scientific American* (October 1991). Reluctant to dissect animals, she majored in chemistry rather than biology. Her scientific education was enhanced considerably at the gatherings she attended at the home of one of her chemistry professors, where students who aspired to careers in science discussed articles in the latest issues of professional journals.

The United States was still in the grip of the Great Depression when, in 1937, Elion received an A.B. degree from Hunter College. Despite her superlative record—she graduated summa cum laude and as a member of Phi Beta Kappa—she failed to win a fellowship or graduate assistantship. Lacking the financial resources to embark on graduate studies, she made a thoroughgoing attempt to get work in a research laboratory. But her months-long quest proved fruitless, not only because of the nationwide shortage of jobs but also because of the refusal of many administrators to hire women chemists. One interviewer told her that the presence of a woman—particularly someone as attractive as the redheaded Elion—would distract male workers. "It surprises me to this day that I didn't get angry," Elion told Marguerite Holloway. "I got very discouraged. But how could I say, 'No, I won't be a distracting influence'?"

Desperate for employment, Elion enrolled in a secretarial course. She quit after six weeks, to take a three-month job teaching biochemistry at the New York Hospital School of Nursing. Some weeks after that assignment ended, she accepted an offer from Alexander Galat, a chemist whom she had met socially, to work without pay as his assistant at a small pharmaceutical company. She received her first paycheck—twelve dollars for a week's work—after six months. By the time she left, a year later, to enter the graduate program in chemistry at New York University, her first published paper (with Galat as principal author) had appeared, in the *Journal of the American Chemical Society*, and her salary had increased to twenty dollars weekly. To pay for her tuition, she supplemented her savings and the funds contributed by her parents by working as a doctor's receptionist and after earning the required license, as a substitute teacher of chemistry, physics, and general science in New York City secondary schools. She received an M.Sc. degree from NYU in 1941.

The drafting into military service of millions of men following the United States' entry into World War II resulted in a shortage of male chemists, and as a consequence, the resistance of laboratory directors to hiring women vanished. In 1942 Elion got work as a quality-control chemist for the Quaker Maid Company, where she performed such tasks as checking the freshness of vanilla beans and measuring the acidity of pickles and became proficient at handling many types of instruments previously unfamiliar to her. When, after a while, the opportunities for learning petered out, she grew dissatisfied with the work. In 1943 she landed a job as a research assistant in organic synthesis at Johnson & Johnson, which had recently launched a venture into pharmaceutical development. Six months later the company scrapped that project and offered her a position in which her sole responsibility would have been testing the tensile strength of sutures. "That was not quite what I had in mind for my future," Elion has recalled, in explaining why she decided to seek employment elsewhere.

In mid-1944, at the suggestion of her father, who noticed the company's logo on a medication sample, Elion went for an interview at the research laboratories of Burroughs Wellcome, in Tuckahoe, New York, about a dozen miles north of the Bronx. The Burroughs Wellcome Company was established in the late nineteenth century by two American pharmacists, primarily as a means of generating money for research that would lead to the discovery of cures for grave human diseases, and the company's researchers were encouraged to follow their scientific instincts wherever they might lead. Elion's interviewer was George H. Hitchings, who needed another assistant to help in his search for compounds for treating cancer and other serious diseases. "Instead of asking me a lot of questions about myself, Hitchings proceeded to tell me what he was doing," Elion has recalled.

To find a cure for a particular disease, most medical researchers at that time relied on a trial-and-error method, systematically examining the physiological effects of one substance after another on animals suffering from that ailment or a similar one. Hitchings's approach, by contrast, focused on cell growth and the mechanisms by which particular chemical compounds acted at the cellular level. He was studying purines and pyrimidines, the structural bases of DNA and RNA. The tack that he had chosen for his investigations immediately sparked Elion's interest. "I didn't understand half of what he was saying, but his description of his work so enthralled me that I knew then and there that I would lose no time finding out about it," Stephanie St. Pierre quoted her as saying in *Gertrude Elion: Master Chemist* (1993), a book for younger readers. Hitchings, in turn, was impressed by Elion's enthusiasm as well as her scholastic achievements and laboratory experience. Disregarding the advice of his assistant Elvira Falco, who warned him that Elion's attractive outfit indicated her unsuitability for hard work, within days of their meeting he hired her at the salary she had requested—fifty dollars a week.

The work in Hitchings's laboratory was guided by the antimetabolite theory, which was first proposed by the pharmacologists Donald Woods and Paul Fildes in about 1940. Success hinged on chemically disrupting nucleic acid metabolism in disease-causing organisms or cancer cells while leaving healthy cells unimpaired. Hitchings was focused on a bacterium called *Lactobacillus casei*. "We didn't know the pathways of nucleic acid synthesis, but we knew that bacteria knew how nucleic acids were formed, because they could take these building blocks, incorporate them into DNA, and live very happily," Elion explained during an interview for the 1988 *Nobel Prize Annual*. "The idea was to change the building blocks slightly, . . . to fool a cancer cell or a bacteria or a virus into taking them up and then find that it's stuck and it can't get rid of them or utilize them and so can't multiply."

Functioning at first solely as an organic chemist, Elion set to work synthesizing a particular purine, a task that required a series of complicated steps and often-constant monitoring of reactions. The difficulty of that project was compounded by onerous working conditions, which worsened with the onset of summer. Not only was her laboratory not air-conditioned, but, in addition, the operations of a baby-food dehydration oven directly below the lab often heated the floor to temperatures exceeding one hundred degrees Fahrenheit. Nevertheless, Elion completed her assignment in a surprisingly short time and proceeded to synthesize other purines and also pyrimidines and pteridines. "Some of these were actually compounds that had never been described before, and I felt the excitement of the inventor who creates a 'new composition of matter,'" she has recalled. Hitchings never restricted her to a narrowly defined set of duties, and her work soon branched out into other disciplines—such as microbiology, biochemistry, pharmacology, immunology, and virology—thus significantly boosting her job satisfaction.

Beginning in 1947, substances created by Elion and others in Hitchings's laboratory were sent to the Sloan-Kettering Institute (now called the Memorial Sloan-Kettering Cancer Center), in New York City, where they underwent antitumor testing in mice. A compound that Elion synthesized in 1948 was so successful in shrinking mouse tumors that Joseph H. Burchenal, a Sloan-Kettering physician, used it to treat several adult patients with leukemia. Although most patients could not tolerate the nausea and vomiting that it caused, the compound, 2,6-diaminopurine, freed one woman of symptoms for two years. But the woman died after a recurrence of the cancer, which failed to respond a second time to diaminopurine treatment. During a conversation with Katherine Bouton for a *New York Times Magazine* (January 29, 1989) profile of her, Elion said that she still wept for that patient, who, while in remission, had married and become a mother.

The problems associated with 2,6-diaminopurine notwithstanding, Elion and her coworkers believed that they were, in her words, "on the threshold of a 'breakthrough.'" Using the same chemical strategy, Elion synthesized and tested more than a hundred purine compounds. In 1950, having overcome several thorny methodological problems, she created two promising anticancer substances by substituting a sulfur atom for the oxygen atom in the purine molecules of each. One was thioguanine, or 6-TG, which Elion set aside for several years because it was so difficult to synthesize; it was ultimately used in treating acute myelocytic leukemia in adults. The second, 6-mercaptopurine, or 6-MP, proved to be so effective in inhibiting the growth of or completely shrinking mouse tumors that Joseph Burchenal quickly tested it in children with acute leukemia—a disease that, if untreated, results in death within an average of three months. Although 6-MP did not cure leukemia, by 1953 trials in many medical centers showed that by combining it with cortisone and methotrexate, the mean survival time of leukemic children could be extended by a year. At the end of 1953, the FDA, moving with remarkable rapidity, approved the use of 6-MP in treating acute childhood leukemia. In the following decades, other drugs were found to be more effective in fighting leukemic cells, but 6-MP is still prescribed for patients after they have gone into remission. Currently, after several years of maintenance therapy with 6-MP, about 80 percent of them are judged to be cured.

The knowledge that she had created such a beneficial compound helped to allay Elion's long-harbored misgivings about abandoning her pursuit of a Ph.D. degree. After joining the staff of Burroughs Wellcome, she had entered a doctoral program at Brooklyn Polytechnic Institute, the only local college at that time that offered graduate courses in chemistry at night. She was the only woman in the chemistry department. Her attendance had entailed a commute of an hour and a half to Brooklyn, a borough of New York City, several times a week at the end of her workday at Burroughs Wellcome, and an hour's subway ride from the college to her home in the Bronx late at night. She had completed two years of work toward her Ph.D. degree when—in what may have been another instance of gender discrimination—a Brooklyn Polytechnic dean had informed her that she could remain in the program only if she became a full-time student; part-time attendance, in his view, indicated a lack of serious intent. Rather than give up a job that she loved, Elion had turned her back on graduate work.

For many years after 6-MP received FDA approval, Elion studied its metabolism in humans, to determine why, after a symptom-free year or so following 6-MP chemotherapy, so many young victims of leukemia suffered a relapse and eventually died. "These were heartbreaking times," she has recalled. "We seemed to be so close to the solution and yet the ultimate goal eluded us." Her methodology involved producing and then elucidating the properties of various chemical derivatives of 6-MP (and also of 6-TG). Her work caught the attention of the immunologist Robert Schwartz of Tufts University Medical School, in Boston, who, based on Elion's descriptions of the biological effects of 6-MP and its derivatives, guessed that they would suppress the body's immune response to foreign tissue. Experiments conducted by Schwartz on animals showed that his hypothesis was correct. His lead was followed by others. In 1962, two years after the British surgeon Roy Yorke Calne successfully prevented the rejection of a transplanted kidney in a dog for more than eight months with the help of the 6-MP derivative azathioprine (marketed under the name Imuran), the American surgeon Joseph E. Murray administered azathioprine to achieve the first successful human kidney transplant in which the donor and the recipient were not related. (Murray received a Nobel Prize in 1990 for his work in organ transplantation.) Most of the more than one hundred thousand people who have received kidney transplants in the last three decades have undergone a regimen of azathioprine. The drug is also effective in relieving symptoms of rheumatoid arthritis and other autoimmune diseases.

Elion's metabolic studies of 6-MP had yet another valuable byproduct. The enzyme xanthine oxidase, she discovered, caused the breakdown of 6-MP. With the aim of prolonging the integrity of 6-MP in vivo, in the early 1960s she began researching the activity of the xanthine oxidase inhibitor allopurinol, a purine analogue. She thus learned that allopurinol reduces levels of uric acid in both blood and urine. That property made it an ideal treatment for gout, an excruciatingly painful and sometimes fatal condition that is characterized by an excess of uric acid. Subsequently, through what she has called an "excursion into the biochemistry of protozoa," Elion and other researchers demonstrated the efficacy of allopurinol (also called Zyloprim) in treating leishmaniasis and Chagas' disease, debilitating, potentially fatal protozoan-caused illnesses that are widespread in large areas of the world.

Meanwhile, Elion had received several promotions at Burroughs Wellcome: rising through the ranks in tandem with Hitchings, she had held the titles of biochemist (1944–50), senior research chemist (1950–55), assistant to the associate research director (1955–63), and assistant to the research director for chemotherapy (1963–67). In 1967, on the heels of Hitchings's advancement to vice-president in charge of research, she became the head of the company's newly created Department of Experimental Therapy. Three years later the Burroughs Wellcome research laboratories moved to much larger facilities in Research Triangle Park, North Carolina, and Elion settled in the nearby university town of Chapel Hill. Her department expanded into a sort of "mini-institute," with a tissue-culture laboratory and sections devoted to chemistry, enzymology, pharmacology, immunology, and virology.

Earlier, in 1968, Elion had heard about the discovery by other scientists that adenine arabinoside inhibited DNA viruses. "That rang a bell," she recalled in her *Pharmacology and Toxicology* reminiscence. Although she had discontinued her investigations of diaminopurine two decades before, she remembered that she had found that it is a close analogue of adenine. Perhaps 2,6-diaminopurine arabinoside too would have antiviral properties, she reasoned—correctly, as it turned out. Using an antiviral screen at the Burroughs Wellcome laboratories in the United Kingdom, the virologist John Bauer showed that the compound was active against both the herpes simplex virus, which causes blistering of the skin and mucous membranes of the mouth and genitals, and the herpes zoster virus, which causes shingles, a painful neurological disease. The intensive search for an effective antiviral compound that Elion then launched culminated, in 1974, in the synthesis by two members of the Burroughs Wellcome team—the organic chemists Howard Schaeffer and Lilia Beauchamp—of a guanine derivative that proved to be one hundred times as active as diaminopurine arabinoside. The derivative, an acyclic purine nucleoside, was named acyclovir.

During the next four years, maintaining total secrecy about their work, Elion and her team uncovered many of acyclovir's biological secrets. They determined that in a cell infected with a herpes virus, acyclovir was converted sequentially to three different metabolites, the last of which closely resembles a substance vital to the reproduction of the virus but which strongly inhibits the enzymes necessary to synthesize the viral DNA. The similarity is so great that the virus is tricked into incorporating the metabolite into its DNA, thus causing its own death. Elion's presentation of that and other findings regarding acyclovir at the Interscience Conference on Antimicrobial Agents and Chemotherapy, in Atlanta, Georgia, in 1978 created, in her words, "a major stir," and it immediately spurred other drug companies to develop antiviral acyclic nucleosides. "We had finally shown that antiviral drugs could be selective and that one could capitalize on the differences between the viral and cellular enzymes," she has said.

Marketed under the name Zovirax, acyclovir has been available in ointment and intravenous forms since 1982 and as an oral medication for the last decade. It is prescribed as a treatment for chicken pox and for genital herpes, herpes encephalitis, shingles, and other herpes infections. It is also effective in preventing the recurrence of herpes-virus infections in people undergoing cancer chemotherapy, the recipients of bone marrow or organ transplants, AIDS patients, and others whose immune systems have been suppressed. The best-seller among Burroughs Wellcome's products, it accounted for $838 million in worldwide sales in 1991.

In 1983, convinced that "with acyclovir now launched, . . . it might be a good time to retire as head of the department before a new drug turned up that [she] couldn't bear to leave," as she has explained, Elion resigned her position at Burroughs Wellcome. As scientist emeritus and consultant, however, she has maintained her association with the company and has taken an active part in discussions regarding ongoing research. Each year since 1983, she has also served as a mentor to a third-year medical student at the Duke University Medical Center, in Durham, North Carolina, where, for a dozen years before that, she had held the title of adjunct professor of pharmacology and medicine. She also lectures frequently, to audiences ranging from grade-school children to professional societies. (She has recalled as a singularly pleasurable moment in her career an argument that she had with a well-known scientist during her first presentation at a major professional conference. "I stood my ground," she told Katherine Bouton. "I knew I was right.") She has served as an adviser to many groups, prominent among them the National Cancer Institute, the American Cancer Society, and the tropical disease research division of the World Health Organization. Her bibliography lists some 230 journal articles and book chapters.

According to the biochemist Thomas A. Krenitsky, who succeeded her as head of the Department of Experimental Therapy, Gertrude Elion is "always the same person with everybody . . . , whether the other person is a student, a glassware washer, or the president of the company." Katherine Boutin described her as a "born teacher" who "seems to delight in the accomplishments of her junior associates." Called Trudy by those who know her, she regularly commutes from her townhouse in Chapel Hill to Metropolitan Opera performances. An avid photographer and world traveler, she also enjoys going to the ballet and the theatre and watching basketball games. After the death of her fiancé, in the late 1930s, she reportedly never again considered marrying. She has maintained a close relationship with her three nephews and one niece and their families (she took eleven family members with her to the Nobel ceremonies). In addition to the Nobel Prize, her dozens of honors include induction into the National Inventors' Hall of Fame (she was the first woman to become a member), the National Women's Hall of Fame, and the National Academy of Sciences, and twenty honorary doctoral degrees. "I still remember the feeling of pride when I received the first two, in 1969, from George Washington and Brown Universities," she has said. "They represented the Ph.D. I had never received and the vindication of my parents' faith in me."

Selected Biographical References: Annual R of Pharmacology and Toxicology 33:1+ '93 por; N Y Times A p1+ O 18 '88 por; N Y Times Mag p28+ Ja 29 '89 por; Sci Am 265:40+ O '92 por; Washington Post p10 O 25 '88 por; McGrayne, Sharon Bertsch. Nobel Prize Women in Science (1993); Nobel Prize Winners, Supplement 1987–1991 (1992); Who's Who in America, 1995

New York Jets

Esiason, Boomer

(uh-SIE-ah-suhn)

Apr. 17, 1961– Football player. Address: c/o New York Jets, 1000 Fulton Ave., Hempstead, NY 11550

Big and brash, Boomer Esiason of the New York Jets has played quarterback with an aggressive flair that has made him a standout. A star of two sports in high school, he became a football All-American while at the University of Maryland, where he led the Terrapins to back-to-back bowl appearances. Disappointed at not being a first-round National Football League draft pick in 1984, which sports observers blamed on his reputation for being undisciplined, Esiason proved his worth to the team that selected him in the second round, the Cincinnati Bengals. In his second professional season, he became the Bengals' starting quarterback and sparked an offensive explosion that led to a team record for total points scored. After coming under heavy criticism from Cincinnati fans in 1987, a year marred by a divisive players' strike and a disappointing 4–11 Bengals' season, Esiason went on to have a career year in 1988. He won the NFL's most-valuable-player award and led his team to Super Bowl XXIII, which the Bengals lost to the San Francisco 49ers in the final moments of the game. Over the next few seasons, the Bengals' fortunes plummeted, as age, injuries, and personnel changes weakened the team. By the end of the 1992 season, Esiason had been benched in favor of a rookie quarterback; he was subsequently traded to the Jets amid rumors that his arm strength had diminished irreparably. Although Esiason's arrival has not yet resulted in a turnaround for the Jets, the trade helped revive his career: he completed an impressive 60.9 percent of his passes in 1993 and 58 percent in 1994.

Nicknamed Boomer for the strong, incessant kicks he delivered inside his mother's womb, Norman Julius Esiason was born on April 17, 1961 to Norman and Irene Esiason in the Long Island town of East Islip, New York. When Esiason was five years old, his mother died of lymphoma, leaving his father, a safety engineer, to raise him and his two teenaged sisters. Describing his father's devotion to him, Esiason told Gerald Eskenazi of the *New York Times* (November 27, 1994): "He became my mother and my father. He gave up his social life for me." Avid fans of New York sports teams, father and son often went to Madison Square Garden to root for the Rangers. When brawls broke out on the ice between hockey players, young Esiason would become so emotionally involved that his father had to hold on to the back of his pants to keep him from jumping over the glass to join the fights. "Boomer was always intense about sports," Norman Esiason told Lonnie Wheeler in an interview for *Inside Sports* (October 1986).

An extrovert with a pronounced sense of right and wrong, Esiason took it upon himself to protect other children from bullies. In a profile of him for *Sports Illustrated* (October 4, 1993), Gary Smith described the strong and athletically gifted Esiason as the quarterback "of his block, of his friends as well as his teams." A frightening bout of juvenile arthritis sidelined Esiason for three months when he was fourteen years old, but after treatment the disease went into remission and has not returned. He played football and baseball at East Islip High School, and, in the winter of his senior year, he accepted a football scholarship from the only Division 1-A college to offer him one, the University of Maryland. The following spring, as a southpaw pitcher with a sizzling fastball, he had a 15–0 record, and in the final inning of a division-title game, he struck out the side on nine pitches to win the game for East Islip. That victory, he told Gerald Eskenazi, has remained his "greatest sports memory." His baseball success brought more offers of college scholarships and attracted the attention of a professional baseball scout, but Esiason stuck to his commitment to play football for Maryland. "I have no doubt that Boomer could have made it in any sport that he chose, but I really felt that he would end up in football," Sal Ciampi, one of Esiason's high-school coaches, told Lonnie Wheeler. "I could just picture him with that white hair being the quarterback. He has that charisma."

When Esiason arrived at Maryland for his freshman year, in 1979, there were three other quarterbacks on the Terrapins' team, and he saw little playing time. Not allowed to play baseball either, he became embittered and showed up out-of-shape for football in 1980. Terrapins coach Jerry Claiborne responded by redshirting him. "It was during that Claiborne period that Esiason first got the reputation as a player who was difficult to deal with, one who was more serious about partying than athletics," Lonnie Wheeler observed. In 1981, when Esiason rejoined the team, the Terrapins had their worst season in ten years. Claiborne was replaced by Bobby Ross, who installed a pro-style offense that utilized more passing and took advantage of Esiason's strong arm. "When I first came here, I heard rumors about this brash, blond-headed, cocky kid, but Boomer is just extremely competitive," Ross told Wheeler. The Terrapins, with Esiason as the starting quarterback, became the Cinderella team of the 1982 season, compiling an 8–3 record and earning a trip to the Aloha Bowl in Honolulu, where they lost, 21–20, to the Washington Huskies.

In his fifth year of eligibility at Maryland, Esiason passed for 2,322 yards, earned consensus All-America honors, and led the Terrapins to the Florida Citrus Bowl, where they were defeated by the Tennessee Volunteers, 30–23. Esiason had expected that he would be a first-round NFL draft pick in 1984, but he was not tapped until the second round, by the Cincinnati Bengals as the thirty-eighth player selected overall. When he arrived in Cincinnati, Esiason was on a mission to prove that the teams that had snubbed him had been wrong. In his rookie year, however, he served as a backup quarterback and had a limited role. For the 1984 season he completed 51 of 102 passes for 530 yards, making three touchdown throws and suffering three interceptions as the Bengals finished second in the AFC Central Division with an 8–8 record.

After the Bengals opened the 1985 season with back-to-back losses, coach Sam Wyche promoted Esiason to starting quarterback, and Esiason promptly revived the team's sagging offensive attack. In each of the next four games, the Bengals scored 37 points or more. By season's end, Esiason had thrown for 3,443 yards, completing 58 percent of his 431 passes for twenty-seven touchdowns with only twelve interceptions. Despite racking up a club record 441 points for the season, the Bengals finished 7–9, losing their last two games and the AFC Central Division crown. In 1986 Esiason, who started all sixteen games, completed 58 percent of his 469 passes for 3,959 yards. He connected for twenty-four touchdowns and had seventeen tosses picked off. His 8.44-yard average per pass attempt led all NFL quarterbacks and earned him his first appearance in the Pro Bowl. Improving their performance to 10-6, the Bengals finished second in their AFC division to the Cleveland Browns.

During the 1987 preseason Esiason signed a five-year deal with the Bengals for $1.2 million annually, which, at the time, was the most any NFL player earned in a season. The Bengals management had apparently decided that a long-term contract was the best way to keep Esiason, who spent a lot of time talking to the media, more focused on football. "They wanted to save me from me," he told Peter King, who profiled him for *New York Newsday* (December 29, 1988). "They were more concerned about me hurting them with my mouth than with my body." Just before the scheduled start of the regular season, the NFL players' union called a strike to protest the owners' refusal to grant free agency to players. Esiason, the team's player representative, voted against the strike, but once it began, he supported the union. When he learned that some of his teammates were financially strapped because of the strike, he lent them a reported total of almost three hundred thousand dollars. After NFL owners hired "replacement" players to start the season, Esiason led protests against the recruits who showed up at Cincinnati's Riverfront Stadium. The strike was especially divisive in Cincinnati, "one of the most antiunion cities in America," as Gary Smith pointed out, and the outspoken and well-paid Esiason became a "lightning rod for criticism." That criticism mushroomed after the strike ended, because the Bengals played badly, winning only four games in the shortened fifteen-game season. Although Esiason performed fairly well—he completed 54.5 percent of his 440 passes for 3,321 yards with sixteen touchdowns and nineteen interceptions—he received much of the blame. "I don't think I've ever seen one player take the full force of a fan reaction that bad," Cincinnati's general manager, Mike Brown, told Pete Axthelm in an interview for *People* (January 23, 1989).

Once the season was over, Esiason asked to be traded, but Brown turned him down. Esiason went on to have a storybook year in 1988, going from the villain of Cincinnati to the toast of the town. Named the NFL's most valuable player, he was the league's highest-rated passer, completing 57.5 percent of his 388 tosses for 3,572 yards, twenty-eight touchdowns, and only fourteen interceptions. He averaged a career-best 9.21 yards per throwing attempt, and he led the Bengals to a 12-4 record to win the AFC Central Division title. In his first postseason game, Esiason threw three first-half touchdowns against the Seattle Seahawks. Two speedy running backs—rookie Ickey Woods and veteran James Brooks—combined for 198 yards on the ground to help the Bengals win, 21-17. The Bengals then played the Buffalo Bills for the AFC Championship and triumphed, 21-10, as Esiason handed off twenty-nine times to Woods, who ran for 102 yards and scored two touchdowns.

The victory over the Bills sent the Bengals to Super Bowl XXIII, where they were pitted against the San Francisco 49ers, led by quarterback Joe Montana. Although Esiason was hampered by a bruised shoulder, the Bengals held a 16-13 lead late into the fourth quarter, having scored on two field goals and a 93-yard kickoff return by special-teams receiver Stanford Jennings. Then, with three minutes and twenty seconds left in the game, Montana began a 92-yard touchdown drive that ended with thirty-four seconds left and a 20-16 victory for the 49ers. Esiason finished the game completing eleven of twenty-five passes for 144 yards with one interception. "The Super Bowl is the pinnacle of success," Esiason told Hank Nuwer, reflecting on the game in an interview for *Inside Sports* (September 1989). "I've played in the Pro Bowl, and I'm fortunate to have won an MVP trophy, but at the Super Bowl you're there with your teammates. It's great two weeks prior to the Super Bowl. Then you lose and you're upset—it takes you two weeks to get over it—but in the long run you look back and think, 'Man, we've got to re-create the magic somehow.' "

The 1989 season saw the Bengals slip to an 8-8 record, in part because of defensive shortcomings and an injury to running star Woods. Despite the team's problems, Esiason was the highest-rated passer in the AFC, completing 56.7 percent of his 455 passes for 3,525 yards, twenty-eight scores, and eleven interceptions, and he made his third Pro Bowl appearance in four seasons. In 1990 the Bengals won the AFC Central title with a 9-7 record, but the team performed erratically. Esiason was once again the target of criticism from fans and the local media, even though he threw for 3,031 yards, making 1990 the sixth season in a row he had tallied over 3,000 yards. He completed 55.7 percent of his 402 passes and connected for twenty-four touchdowns, but he had a career-high twenty-two interceptions. In postseason play, the Bengals pounded the Houston Oilers, 41-14, before losing to the Los Angeles Raiders, 20-10.

The Bengals performed poorly during the 1991 season, winning just three games. Only a few players from the 1988 Super Bowl team were still with the team, and a frustrated Esiason, who played mid-season with a shoulder injury, lashed out at his new teammates. "We don't have very many strong personalities on this football team," he told Michael Knisley of the *Sporting News* (November 11, 1991). "In fact, personally, I think we have only one—me." Working behind a struggling offensive line, Esiason ended the year with more interceptions (sixteen) than touchdown passes (thirteen). He completed 56 percent of his 413 passes for 2,883 yards (6.98 yards per attempt). At the end of the season, a rookie head coach, David Shula, was hired to replace Wyche and turn the Bengals' fortunes around. After Cincinnati won just four times in eleven outings in 1992, Shula benched an ineffective Esiason in favor of rookie quarterback David Klingler, who had been the club's first-round draft choice that year. Esiason angrily denied league rumors that his arm was "shot," telling Chris Mortensen of the *Sporting News* (December 7, 1992), "There's nothing wrong with my arm that a great offensive line wouldn't cure." For the season,

Esiason completed 51 percent of his 144 passes for 1,407 yards, compiling a career-low mark of 5.1 yards per attempt and throwing for eleven touchdowns while being intercepted fifteen times. Over his last forty-one starts for Cincinnati, Esiason threw fifty-three interceptions; only one other quarterback, the Los Angeles Rams' Jim Everett, had more interceptions in the same time period.

In March of 1993 Esiason was traded by the Bengals to the New York Jets. "He hung up the phone after he found out, and he let out this whoop," Esiason's assistant, Tami Amaker, told Gary Smith of *Sports Illustrated.* "He shouted, 'Tami, I'm going *home*, I'm going *home!*' The way he said that word, *home* . . . , he said it like Dorothy in the *Wizard of Oz.*" The trade reunited Esiason with Jets head coach Bruce Coslet, who had been the Bengals' offensive coordinator during Esiason's best years. After signing a contract that made him the highest-paid Jet, at $2.7 million a year, Esiason set out to prove that the rumors about his arm were wrong. In his first three starts as a Jet, he threw five touchdown passes to lead the team to a 2–1 record, and he was named AFC player of the month for September. With an 8–6 record late in the season, the Jets seemed poised to go to the play-offs, but then the team lost their last two games to finish out of the running. For the season, Esiason completed an impressive 60.9 percent of his 463 attempts for 3,421 yards, with sixteen touchdowns and eleven interceptions.

Coslet had a postseason falling-out with the Jets' front office, and defensive coordinator Pete Carroll was hired to replace him. After compiling a respectable record of 7–4 in the early months of the 1994 season, the Jets went into a tailspin, losing their last five games. Esiason had another relatively strong season, chalking up 2,782 yards while completing 58 percent of 400 passes and throwing for seventeen touchdowns and thirteen interceptions. Dissatisfied with the team's performance, Jets owner Leon Hess fired Carroll. As the 1995 season began, Esiason was playing for his fifth head coach in five years, Rich Kotite, the former head coach of the Philadelphia Eagles.

Boomer Esiason, who stands six feet, five inches tall and weighs 220 pounds, has "just about the perfect makeup for a quarterback," as Sam Wyche told Lonnie Wheeler. During the years Esiason played for the Bengals, he was known for his love of the good life, often giving large parties for friends at his posh home in northern Kentucky. His wife, the former Cheryl Hyde, told Peter King in 1988 that her fun-loving, generous husband reminded her of the childlike character played by Tom Hanks in the movie *Big.* Life for the Esiasons was altered significantly, however, in 1993, when they were told that their two-year-old son, Gunnar, had cystic fibrosis, a genetic disorder that attacks the lungs and often shortens the lives of its victims. (Their daughter, Sydney, has tested negative for the disease.) A devastated Esiason considered quitting football to devote more time to his son but decided instead to continue playing and to use his celebrity to help in the fight against cystic fibrosis. "Football is therapy for the grieving parent, if you will," Esiason told Rich Cimini of the *Sporting News* (July 5, 1993).

Now living on Long Island with his wife and children, Esiason is busy off the field in the New York area. He owns a restaurant, Boomer's, on Manhattan's Upper West Side, and he does a weekly radio segment during the football season. After learning of his son's illness, Esiason and his wife created the Boomer Esiason Heroes Foundation to benefit cystic fibrosis research. The goal of the Heroes foundation is to create awareness while supporting research aimed at a cure for the disease. In May 1995 the Esiasons pledged $1.6 million to the National Cystic Fibrosis Foundation and dedicated the Gunnar H. Esiason Cystic Fibrosis and Lung Center at Cincinnati Children's Hospital. The center in Cincinnati is a leading institution for cystic fibrosis research and treatment. Esiason also participates in the Long Island Celebrity Golf Tournament, which benefits several charities, and he has been a spokesman for the National Arthritis Foundation. In Cincinnati, he helped raise funds for the Caring Program for Children, among other charities, including one he established in memory of his mother, the Irene Esiason Fund. While football remains important to him, Esiason told Gerald Eskenazi that his priorities have changed since he learned of his son's illness. "When you walk through the door at home, it doesn't matter that Daddy's somewhat of a celebrity," Esiason said. "You have a scary sense of reality."

Selected Biographical References: Inside Sports 8:54+ O '86 pors, 11:22+ S '89 pors; N Y Newsday p106+ D 29 '88 pors; N Y Times VIII p1+ N 27 '94 pors; People 31:43 Ja 23 '89 por; Sporting N p13 N 11 '91 por, p35 Jl 5 '93 pors; Sports Illus 79:16+ O'4 '93 pors; Who's Who in America, 1995

Estefan, Gloria

(ESS-teh-fahn)

Sep. 1, 1957– Singer; songwriter. Address: c/o Estefan Enterprises, 6205 Bird Rd., Miami, FL 33155; c/o Epic Records, Publicity Dept., 550 Madison Ave., 22d fl., New York, NY 10022

"My business is to try to evoke emotion," the Cuban-born singer and songwriter Gloria Estefan has said. Widely known as the "queen of Latin pop," Estefan is one of just a handful of Hispanic entertainers who have gained immense popularity not only in Latin America and in the Hispanic community in the United States but also among non-Spanish-speaking Americans—and, in Estefan's case, in Europe and Asia as well. "Everyone else's crossover dreams are the day-to-day details of Estefan's life," Wayne Robins observed in *New York Newsday* (February 27, 1991). "And at home in Miami, Estefan isn't just a star; she's an essential part

Estefan Enterprises

Gloria Estefan

of the social fabric and one of the few bridges between that city's predominant Cuban and Anglo cultures."

In 1975, when she was a college freshman, Estefan joined the Miami Sound Machine (MSM), which at that time was one of many indistinguishable Cuban-American bands that performed at parties in Miami. Exceedingly shy and unremarkable in both appearance and singing style, she originally served as an accompanist and occasional soloist. Under the guidance of the band's leader, Emilio Estefan, whom she married in 1978, she blossomed into a striking-looking, spirited, and polished performer with an ability to inspire concert audiences to rise to their feet to dance. Since the late 1980s she, rather than the band, has received top billing on tours and recordings. On such multimillion-seller albums as *Primitive Love, Let It Loose, Cuts Both Ways, Into the Light*, and *Mi Tierra*, which inventively interweave elements of pop, rock, disco, and Latin music, Estefan has offered what Richard Harrington, writing in the *Washington Post* (July 17, 1988), described as a "pop sensibility encompassing not only irresistible dance-floor workouts but aching ballads reminiscent of Karen Carpenter." Estefan was named songwriter of the year in 1989 by BMI (Broadcast Music, Incorporated), for her work on *Cuts Both Ways*, and she earned a Grammy Award for best Latin tropical album of 1993, for *Mi Tierra*.

Gloria Estefan was born Gloria María Fajardo on September 1, 1957 in Havana, Cuba to José Manuel Fajardo and Gloria (García) Fajardo. Her sister, Rebecca, was born in the early 1960s. According to Howell Llewellyn in *Billboard* (October 11, 1993), one or both sets of her grandparents immigrated to Cuba from a village in the Asturias region of Spain. Estefan's mother was a schoolteacher. Her father, who won a medal in volleyball at the Pan-American Games one year, worked in the security detail assigned to protect the family of the president of Cuba, General Fulgencio Batista. In early 1959, after Batista went into exile and Fidel Castro seized power, the Fajardos, along with thousands of other *batistianos*, as the opponents of Castro were called, fled Cuba and came to the United States. They lived briefly in Texas and South Carolina before settling in a Cuban enclave in Miami.

José Fajardo was one of the thirteen hundred Cuban refugees who, in 1961, as members of the CIA-trained and -equipped 2506 Brigade, took part in the Bay of Pigs invasion, the ill-fated attempt by the administration of President John F. Kennedy to overthrow Castro. After his capture Fajardo, along with most of his cohorts, spent a year and a half in a Cuban jail. After his release, in the hope that the United States would someday support another attempt to topple the Castro regime, he enlisted in the United States Army, where he attained the rank of captain. During the next few years, the Fajardos lived on a series of army bases in Texas and elsewhere. From 1966 to 1968 José Fajardo served in the Vietnam War. Not long after his return, he was discovered to be suffering from a degenerative muscular and neurological disease, which, according to three books for younger readers (all entitled *Gloria Estefan* and written, variously, by Rebecca Stefoff [1991], Grace Catalano [1991], and Fernando Gonzalez [1993]), his doctors suggested may have been caused by his exposure in Vietnam to the defoliant Agent Orange. Two of those books as well as some other sources identified his disorder as multiple sclerosis, but according to the National Multiple Sclerosis Society, no link has yet been established between multiple sclerosis and exposure to Agent Orange. José Fajardo's health rapidly worsened, and he soon became bedridden. In about 1974 he was admitted to a Veterans Administration Hospital, where he remained until his death in 1980.

For the last half-dozen years that her father lived at home, Gloria Estefan assumed responsibility after school for his care and that of her sister as well as for carrying out various household tasks. (Her mother worked during the day and took classes at night to enable her to earn certification to teach in Miami.) Although she felt both sorrowful and fearful about the deteriorating condition of her father and distress about the anguish and embarrassment that his nearly total reliance on her and others caused him, she never allowed herself to cry. As an outlet for her emotions and an escape from the oppressive feeling that she was, in her words, "carrying the weight of the whole world on [her] shoulders," she spent a lot of time alone in her room, singing and playing the guitar that her mother had given her when she was nine. She also liked to sing with her cousin Merci, with whom she became adept at harmonizing.

By her own account, Estefan had been steeped in music since infancy. Her relatives included a classical violinist, a salsa pianist, and two amateur singer/songwriters. As a child her mother won what Mary Beth McEvily, in *Shape* (March 1990), described as an international song-and-dance contest held to select a Spanish-speaking double for the young American film star Shirley Temple. (The elder Gloria never appeared in any films, however, because her father refused to allow her to go to Hollywood.) Gloria Estefan has recalled the thrill she felt when, as a six-year-old, she heard the British rock group Gerry and the Pacemakers sing "Ferry Across the Mersey" on a car radio. She learned traditional Cuban ballads from both her mother and her maternal grandmother and popular songs by listening, for countless hours, to records in her mother's large collection. She borrowed songbooks from her local library, and for a brief period, at the urging of her parents, she took lessons in classical guitar. (According to some sources, she is a self-taught guitarist.) As an adolescent and teenager, she also sang top-forty hits that she listened to on the radio. Her favorite singers included Johnny Mathis, Barbra Streisand, Diana Ross, and Karen Carpenter.

Estefan sometimes sang for her fellow students on the stage of the auditorium at the Lourdes Academy, the all-girls Roman Catholic high school that she attended. Such performances notwithstanding, during her high school years, she was so introverted and serious that, as she later learned, some of the nuns who taught her thought that she would probably become a nun herself. She had no such intention, however, and after her graduation from the academy, in 1975, she entered the University of Miami, where, on a partial scholarship, she majored in psychology. Although she never studied the Spanish language in school and her vocabulary in Spanish is quite limited, as an undergraduate she worked part-time as a translator for the United States Customs Service at Miami International Airport. She also taught guitar at a community center, and, for at least one summer, according to one source, she sang with a band that specialized in Latino music. To build her repertoire, she listened to recordings by the celebrated salsa singer Celia Cruz.

At a wedding reception that Gloria Estefan attended early in her first year at college, someone alerted the band leader to her talents as a vocalist. Acquiescing to his request that she perform, she sang two Cuban ballads, to which the wedding guests responded, as she has recalled, with a standing ovation. The band leader, who also played the accordion, was Emilio Estefan (sometimes identified as Emilio Estefan Jr.). Born in Lebanon into a Lebanese family that later settled in Cuba, Emilio Estefan had immigrated to the United States in the late 1960s, when he was in his mid-teens. Weekdays he worked at Bacardi Imports; evenings and on weekends, he and his band, the Miami Latin Boys, performed locally at private parties. Originally a three-member group, with, in addition to Estefan, the bass guitarist Juan Marcos Avila and the drummer Enrique ("Kiki") García, by 1975 it had nine instrumentalists. Like virtually all the other bands that had sprung up in Miami's Cuban community, it did not have a female vocal soloist.

Emilio Estefan had been trying for some time to come up with ways of distinguishing the Miami Latin Boys from its competitors. The warmth of Gloria Estefan's voice, the sincerity that she conveyed, and the enthusiasm with which the wedding guests greeted her performance convinced him that the addition of a singer like her might be exactly what the band needed. Because she thought that working with the Miami Latin Boys would interfere with her studies, Gloria Estefan rejected his offer of a job, but within a couple of weeks, his assurances that her responsibilities would not impinge upon her college schedule led her to change her mind. "I . . . joined . . . because I loved music, not because I wanted to perform," she has been quoted as saying. "I didn't want to be in the spotlight, didn't desire it. . . . It never crossed my mind that this is what I'd do the rest of my life. I wanted to be a psychologist." She debuted with the Miami Sound Machine, as the band was renamed, in the fall of 1975 at a party at a Miami hotel at which she sang one song: "What a Difference a Day Makes." Her cousin Merci began performing with MSM at the same time. (Merci remained with the band until the early 1980s.)

Repeatedly urged by Emilio Estefan, after they began dating in the summer of 1976, to try to improve herself "*noventa y cinco por ciento*"—that is, by 95 percent—the decidedly plump Gloria Estefan began dieting and exercising. (By the end of the next decade, she was reportedly doing as many as six hundred situps and running four miles daily.) Irked for a while because he seemed to be implying that he found only 5 percent of her pleasing, she eventually realized that his goal was to help her increase her self-confidence and whittle away at her extreme shyness. "Emilio saw a side of me that I didn't let people see, and he wanted that to come out," she explained during an interview with Daisann McLane for *Rolling Stone* (June 14, 1990). His approach produced striking results. Whereas at first Gloria Estefan, feeling "petrified," as she described herself to Bruce Dessau for the *Guardian* (September 15, 1989), remained mainly in the background during performances, playing maracas, as she got slimmer and more fit, she gradually assumed a more prominent role in the band, singing more often and with increasing assurance and animation. She also began adding simple dance routines to her performances. "When I was shy, I felt I had something in me I wanted to bring out, I just didn't know how to do it," she recalled to Richard Harrington for his *Washington Post* article. "It was a painful process, but I forced myself to do it, mostly by watching myself on videotape, which is the most horrendous experience there is. But it's the only way you can see what other people are seeing."

Estefan's continuing, extraordinary transformation coincided with—and undoubtedly contributed significantly to—MSM's growing popularity in Miami. The band began performing at dance clubs as well as at parties, choosing their music from an expanding repertoire that was designed to please diverse audiences, whether composed mainly of people from Cuba or Central or South America or mostly of black or white native-born, English-speaking Americans. To reach greater numbers of people, in the late 1970s MSM began to make recordings. They made one or two albums for a local record label that catered to Hispanic listeners and then another two on their own label. Cut in Spanish on one side and in English on the other, the albums offered a variety of music, including disco-style pop songs and ballads written by Gloria Estefan or other band members.

In 1978 Gloria Estefan earned a B.A. degree from the University of Miami. "My psychology degree helps me a lot in my career," she noted to Margaret Rooke and Ruby Millington for the London *Telegraph Magazine* (October 22, 1994). "I constantly auto-analyze myself." Within a few months of her graduation, she and Emilio Estefan got married. After their son was born, in 1980, the availability of several of their relatives to help care for him enabled her to continue pursuing her vocation with only minimal interruption. Also in 1980 MSM secured a contract for four Spanish-language albums with Discos CBS International, the Miami-based, Hispanic division of CBS Records. At around the same time, Emilio Estefan quit his job as head of Hispanic marketing at Bacardi Imports, so that he could devote all his energies to the creation of the contracted albums as well as to tasks associated with the increasingly heavy performance schedule of MSM, which at that point became a full-time band. (In the mid-1980s he ceased performing and added to his roles that of the band's manager.)

The albums that MSM made for Discos—*Renacer* (1981), *Otra Vez* (1981), *Rio* (1982), and *A Toda Máquina* (1984)—attracted large numbers of buyers in Latin America and became number-one hits in Panama, Honduras, Venezuela, Peru, and several other countries. They also sold reasonably well in Hispanic markets in the United States and also in Europe. MSM's renditions in Spanish of American pop songs were especially popular with Central and South American audiences, as the band discovered during their extensive, resoundingly successful 1981 concert tour. "We were always pretty much exactly pop, mixed in with some Latin rhythms," Gloria Estefan told Wayne Robins during an interview for his *New York Newsday* article. "The reason we were able to cross over in all the countries in Latin America was that we had a pop sound. Each one of these countries has their own folkloric sound. We were able to cross, because to them we were a North American group that sang in Spanish, but it was very much pop music."

In 1984 MSM released "Dr. Beat," with music and lyrics in English by Enrique García, on the B side of a single that, on its A side, offered a Spanish ballad. "Dr. Beat" has been described by one observer as "a silly but likable song with a brisk, Latin-style dance beat and a repetitive, jingly chorus." Indeed, "Dr. Beat" was evidently uncommonly likable. Its popularity soon spread beyond the listeners of the bilingual Miami radio station where it was first aired and the audiences of area pop stations, where it next got great exposure, to audiences as far away as Europe. For months it remained a favorite among disco patrons in England, and it climbed to the top spot in the dance-music market and reached the top five on European pop charts. In the United States, where CBS issued it as a twelve-inch dance single, "Dr. Beat" achieved the number-ten spot on the dance chart. Encouraged by the crossover appeal of "Dr. Beat," CBS decided to switch MSM to Epic Records, its international rock-music division.

The band's next album, *Eyes of Innocence* (1984), which generated only modest interest, was followed by the phenomenally successful *Primitive Love* (1985), some four million copies of which were sold worldwide. For their work on *Primitive Love*, MSM won American Music Awards in 1986 in two categories: best new pop artists and top pop singles artists. Three songs from the album—"Conga," "Bad Boy," and "Words Get in the Way"—became top-ten pop hits. "Conga," which was written by Enrique García, became the first single to appear concurrently on *Billboard*'s dance, Latin, black, and pop charts. The song inspired more than 11,000 people to form what was believed to be the world's longest conga line up to that time, at an MSM concert in Burlington, Vermont in mid-1986. Later, in 1988, an estimated 119,000 people danced the conga outdoors to MSM's music during Miami's Calle Ocho Festival—an event noted in the *Guinness Book of World Records*. "Conga" also won first prize at the 1986 Annual Tokyo Music Fair, where MSM represented the United States. "In Japan they had told us, 'Don't feel bad if you just hear polite applause because the Japanese are very reserved people, that's how they are,'" Estefan has recalled. "Then after the first song, they all jumped out of their seats and were dancing for the whole show. They even came up on the stage at the end of the show and danced with us."

The front of the jacket of *Primitive Love* featured a portrait of Gloria Estefan; a photo of the band was relegated to the back cover. The spines of the jackets of *Let It Loose* (1987) and *Cuts Both Ways* (1989), Estefan's next two albums, identified the performers as "Gloria Estefan and Miami Sound Machine." On *Into the Light* (1991), *Greatest Hits* (1992), *Mi Tierra* (1993), *Christmas Through Your Eyes* (1993), *Hold Me, Thrill Me, Kiss Me* (1994), and her most recent album, *Abriendo Puertas* (1995), only Gloria Estefan's name appears as the performing artist. Indeed, by the time *Cuts Both Ways* was produced, the band included no musicians who had played with MSM in its early years. (Its membership has continued to experience frequent turnovers.) Estefan, meanwhile, had emerged as a charismatic star in her own right, adulated as "nuestra Glorita" ("our little Gloria") in Miami's Cuban community, where she has served as what Jim Farber, in the *New York Daily News* (September 23, 1991), described as "a veritable one-woman advertisement for the endurance of the American dream." She also attracted huge numbers of admirers among other groups in the United States and overseas, for her lively performances of what Stephen Holden, in the *New York Times* (March 9, 1990), described as "danceable urban pop with a Latin accent," as well as for her renditions of deeply emotional ballads, sung in what Holden called "an appealing easy-listening voice that suggests a more rhythmically animated Karen Carpenter."

Estefan has also been recognized as a songwriter of uncommon skill. She herself has written or cowritten the music and lyrics of most of her nineteen top-ten hit singles. Among them are "Words Get in the Way," "Rhythm Is Gonna Get You," "Anything for You," "1-2-3" (cowritten by Enrique García), "Here We Are," "Don't Wanna Lose You," "Cuts Both Ways," "Coming Out of the Dark" (cowritten by Emilio Estefan and Jon Secada), "Live for Loving You" (cowritten by Emilio Estefan and Diane Warren), "Always Tomorrow," and "Mi Tierra." Seven of her songs reached the top of the pop, adult/contemporary, or Latin charts. To enhance her songwriting capabilities, in the late 1980s Estefan learned to play the piano. "Ballads are basically what I'm about," she has said. "I just feel you can express yourself more completely and eloquently in a ballad. It's easier to identify with someone else and form a bond with the audience."

In 1987 Estefan performed at the World Series, in St. Louis, and at the Pan-American Games, in Indianapolis. A film showing her entertaining American soldiers at the demilitarized zone between North and South Korea during the twenty-month world tour that followed the release of *Let It Loose* was televised in conjunction with the 1988 Summer Olympic Games, in Seoul, Korea. *Homecoming Concert* (1989), a video of Estefan and MSM's final concert on their *Let It Loose* tour, which was held before a standing-room-only crowd at the Miami Arena, was aired on the Showtime channel and won three Cable ACE awards. In 1988 Estefan participated with Sting, Peter Gabriel, and other performers in the five-continent Amnesty International "Human Rights Now!" concert tour, and that summer she sang a duet with the tenor Placido Domingo in a concert held in New York City's Central Park. She and Domingo later recorded "Hasta Amarte" (an adaptation in Spanish by Estefan of "Till I Loved You") for the album *Goya . . . A Life in Song* (1989).

In March 1990, midway through the world tour that she had undertaken after the release of *Cuts Both Ways*, Estefan suffered a cracked and dislocated vertebra as the result of a highway accident in Pennsylvania, and she underwent surgery in which steel rods were implanted permanently in her back to stabilize her spinal column. During her hospitalization and subsequent recuperation, which entailed months of intensive physical therapy at home, she reportedly received nearly fifty thousand get-well cards and letters, more than eleven thousand telegrams, and some four thousand bouquets. Inspired by her experience, a few months after the accident she began writing the first of the thirteen songs that were released in January 1991 on the album *Into the Light*. Her energetic performances during the world tour that followed its appearance and at such events as the benefit concert that she and her husband organized to aid victims of Hurricane Andrew, in 1992, provided evidence of her virtually complete recovery.

During a conversation with Enrique Fernández of the New York *Daily News* (June 27, 1993), Gloria Estefan remarked, "I feel Cuban-American. Cuban heart and American head." The five-foot two-inch, brown-eyed Estefan recently straightened her trademark mane of long, curly brown hair. According to Jan Moir of the *Guardian* (April 7, 1993), she has a "terrific, knuckle-cracking handshake." She is notable among celebrities for her completely down-to-earth manner and honesty and for never dramatizing any part of her personal history during interviews. Her unusually stable family life also sets her apart in the world of entertainment. She lives with her husband, their son, Nayib, and their daughter, Emily, who was born in 1994, on Star Island, an exclusive section of Miami. In addition to awards for her musical accomplishments, Gloria Estefan's honors include the Ellis Island Medal of Honor, an Hispanic Heritage Award for excellence in the arts, and an honorary doctorate in music from the University of Miami, all of which she received in 1993. In 1992 she served as a public member of the United States delegation to the UN General Assembly. She was named the Humanitarian of the Year by B'nai B'rith in 1992 and the Musicares Person of the Year in 1994 and was cited for outstanding philanthropy by the Alexis de Tocqueville Society in 1993. A statue of her was added to the "rock circus" exhibition at Madame Tussaud's wax museum, in London, in 1993. In the early 1980s Miami officials renamed the street where Gloria and Emilio Estefan lived when they were first married Miami Sound Machine Boulevard.

Selected Biographical References: N Y Daily News City Lights p27 Je 27 '93 por; N Y Newsday p4+ F 27 '91 pors; People 33:78+ Je 25 '90 pors; Rolling Stone p72+ Je 14 '90 pors; Sunday Times mag p32+ O 23 '94 por; Wash Post G p1+ Jl 17 '88 pors; Who's Who in America, 1995

John Gruen, courtesy Marlborough Gallery

Estes, Richard

(ES-tees)

May 14, 1932– Artist. Address: c/o Marlborough Gallery, 40 W. 57th St., 2d fl., New York, NY 10019; Northeast Harbor, ME 04662

Although the artist Richard Estes is universally identified as a leading exponent of what is known variously as photorealism, superrealism, or hyperrealism, he thinks of himself as "a good old-fashioned realist." "I don't see myself as doing anything particularly different from what one of the Old Masters might do if he were living in New York at this time," he told an interviewer in 1995. Meticulously detailed, painterly tours de force of verisimilitude, Estes's pictures, most of which focus on New York City streets or places in Venice, Rome, Barcelona, Paris, London, or Tokyo, have drawn comparisons with cityscapes by the eighteenth-century Venetian painters Bellotto and Canaletto and also to works by such acclaimed twentieth-century Americans as the artist Edward Hopper and the photographers Berenice Abbott and Walker Evans. "Like the cities that are his subject," John Updike wrote in his book *Just Looking: Essays on Art* (1989), Estes "feasts the eye to surfeit. . . . [He] renders with the coolly sensuous touch of a Vermeer what hitherto would have seemed too ugly to paint, too dreary to see. And behind his shoulder we stand, locked into his curious peace, simultaneously attentive to his art and face to face with our environment."

Estes gained international renown in the early 1970s, within a few years of his first group and solo shows. His paintings are based on but are not exact copies of photographs; he uses his photos, he has said, "the way Rembrandt or Velázquez would have used a sketchbook." "One of the reasons I like this kind of painting is not that it gives you all the reality," he told Laurie S. Hurwitz during an interview for *American Artist* (December 1991), "but that it gives you an organized sense of reality, a sort of ideal reality." "The work of this celebrated photorealist goes beyond the movement's characteristic slick coldness," Hurwitz declared; "it presents a personal and enigmatic vision of urban life. . . . Rather than being cold and photographic, in its cleanliness, its order, and its balance, his work reaches a poetry and perfection that few artists achieve." Paintings by Estes are included in the permanent collections of the Solomon R. Guggenheim Museum and the Museum of Modern Art, in New York City, the Smithsonian Institution and the Hirshhorn Museum, in Washington, D.C., the Art Institute of Chicago, and the Detroit Institute of Arts, among other public and private collections.

Richard Estes was born on May 14, 1932 in Kewanee, Illinois. In *Richard Estes: Paintings and Prints* (1993), his friend John Arthur, an independent art curator, reported that Estes grew up in Evanston, a suburb of Chicago. By his own account, however, Estes was raised "in the country," as he told Grace Glueck for *ARTnews* (November 1977). "The city to me is an alien, exciting environment," he said, in explaining why cityscapes interest him more than do rural scenes. In 1952 Estes entered the School of the Art Institute of Chicago, where, according to John Arthur, he did not distinguish himself artistically but "is remembered as earnest, hard-working, and highly disciplined." He especially enjoyed drawing and painting from models.

Estes graduated from art school in 1956. Except for the year 1962, when, while living on his savings, he painted in Spain, he spent the next decade unhappily employed as a commercial artist. He worked at publishing companies and advertising agencies, at times with the title of art director, in Chicago and then in New York City, where he moved in 1959. His responsibilities included doing pasteups, layouts, and illustrations, the last of which he also produced for occasional freelance assignments. Like other ad agency artists, he learned to take photographs to use as reference material for his illustrations. Pictures that he took in his leisure time of people in parks and cafeterias and on buses and trains served as subjects for his own paintings. In 1966, having apparently saved enough money to support himself for some time, he quit his job to become a full-time painter.

Meanwhile, Estes had grown increasingly dissatisfied with figurative painting, which he had come to regard as "much too literal," in his words. Each of his paintings "had too much story, as if it were trying to be an illustration," he told Linda Chase and Ted McBurnett for *Art in America* (November-December 1972). In nearly everything that he has painted since the late 1960s, people are either absent or present only peripherally. "A strong figure would be a distraction and make the painting look like an Edward Hopper—some sort of social commentary: 'Look at this poor man lost in the big city,'" he explained in an interview with Phil Patton for *Horizon* (June 1978). "You have to isolate a subject. That's one of the choices you make, and you say things just by those choices." Nevertheless, his oeuvre includes masterfully rendered depictions of men and women, such as the subway riders that appear in his painting *Williamsburg Bridge* (1987) and the equally individualized bus riders in *The Plaza* (1991), among other images of passengers on public conveyances, and such portraits as that of the French writer Marguerite Yourcenar (1985), which he painted on a commission from the Académie Française, in Paris.

In 1966 Estes participated in the first of the hundreds of group shows in which his work has been exhibited; in 1972 his paintings were included in three major international art exhibitions, in New York City, Venice, and Germany. The first of his seventeen solo exhibitions was mounted in 1968, at the Allan Stone Gallery, in New York City, which represented his work for the next twenty-five years. Some of the paintings shown at the gallery portrayed with photographic realism distorted reflections of trees, buildings, and other objects on the trunks, hoods, and windows of cars and buses. Inspired, at least in part, by pictures of shop windows taken by the French photographer Eugène Atget, during the late 1960s Estes began to paint closeup views of the windows of commercial establishments, in which images of such things as merchandise, interior fixtures, customers, signage, and reflections of buildings and street traffic mingle to form breathtakingly complex, almost abstract compositions. *The Candy Store* (1969), which is owned by the Whitney Museum of American Art, in New York City; *Cafeteria* (1970); *People's Flowers* (1971); *Alitalia* (1973), which is in the permanent collection of the Smithsonian Institution; and *Clothing Store* (1976) are examples of his facade paintings. Among the most frequently reproduced of such works is *Telephone Booths* (1968), a portion of which appeared on the cover of the magazine *New York* on December 16, 1968. *Telephone Booths* is in the world-renowned Baron H. H. Thyssen-Bornemisza Collection, in Switzerland.

In the late 1960s Estes began to paint frontal views of stores in nondescript commercial districts. In a *New York Times* (March 2, 1969) review of Estes's second solo exhibition at the Allan Stone Gallery, Peter Schjeldahl described the milieu of the artist's newest works—"street-level Manhattan in sunlight"—as "a strangely beautiful land of familiar vulgarities and unexpected splendors." "Light is the hero of these pictures," Schjeldahl wrote, "light that fires the city's latent colors and makes all its glass, aluminum, chrome, and ceramic surfaces swim with reciprocal reflections. . . . Perhaps the best tip-offs to Estes's tough, sentimental attitude are his head-on views of sleazy 42d Street movie houses in slanting sunlight—perfect gems of tawdriness possessed, in one case, of a nearly austere elegance and, in another, of an intimate warmth and charm." The exhibit led Schjeldahl to conclude that "the medium of paint and canvas" had not ceased "to give us fresh information about our world."

In the 1970s, in such paintings as *Woolworth's* (1974), *Chipp's* (1976), *Ansonia* (1977), *Gourmet Treats* (1977), *Baby Doll Lounge* (1978), and *Downtown* (1978), Estes offered broader New York cityscapes. In the past quarter-century, he has also produced large pictures of cities in Great Britain, continental Europe, and Japan. His first major Europe-sited painting, *Paris Street Scene* (1972), was followed by such works as *Café Express* (1975), in which a street is seen from within a Parisian eatery; *View Toward La Salute, Venice* (1980) and *Accademia* (1980), both of which are views from a boat; *Piazza di Spagna, Roma* (1986); *View of Barcelona* (1986); *Tower Bridge* (1989); *Shinjuku* (1989); and *View of Hiroshima* (1990). In an assessment for *Cover* (May 1995) of Estes's most recent solo show at the Marlborough Gallery, in New York City, which has represented his work since 1993, Michael McKenzie observed, "Estes has changed nothing. The same brilliance and purity of composition remains as intact as when some three decades ago he transcended the commercial world of advertising and forged into the art history books." The artist himself concurred: "The fact is that my work is still the same," he told McKenzie.

Estes has rejected the suggestions of some critics that, in light of the apparent indistinguishability, at least at first glance, of many of his paintings from photographs, he could accomplish his artistic goals just as well in color photos. "It's just simply impossible to look at slides," he explained to Linda Chase and Ted McBurnett. "They are too small, and if you project them, they lose [their] quality, and if you have prints made, they are too flat. . . . There's a lot of things in painting that you have more control over than you have in a photograph. You can't just ask the people to go away so you can take a picture, or move this car over there. In a painting you can make this line a little stronger, change the depth, things like that." Indeed, none of Estes's paintings are exact representations of their subjects. His panoramas, for example, invariably employ more than one or even many vanishing points and horizon lines; they may be lit by the morning sun on one side and by the afternoon sun on the other; buildings that are not part of the actual scene may be added, while structures that are there may be omitted; streets may be widened or narrowed, and things in the background enlarged; and, unlike the way the human eye or the camera records images, both near objects and those in the far distance are rendered in perfect focus.

"I don't try to change things," Estes has said. "I try to make it a little clearer, that's all—to show what's happening. . . . Sometimes a photograph, if you really examine it, can be not very realistic. It doesn't really explain the way things really are or how they really look." "I'm not trying to paint something different but something *more* like the place I've photographed . . . ," he told Laurie S. Hurwitz. "There is no such thing as a realistic painting. In reality, everything is constantly changing. A painting is just a selection of things. You can only take a few elements of reality—a few of the visual elements—never mind the noise, the smell, and the actual dimensions." "Estes is fond of quoting [the American painter James McNeill] Whistler's sentiment that nature copies art," Phil Patton reported. "He takes that pronouncement to mean that paintings such as his can introduce viewers to aspects of reality they never noticed before."

Estes takes photographs when vehicular and human street traffic is minimal, and only on sunny days, preferably when fluffy clouds dot a bright blue sky. He shoots dozens of close-up photos and distance shots at the same site, from different vantage points and with varying depths of field. He makes prints in the darkroom that he set up in the bathroom of his New York City apartment. A layered collage of prints that he creates and that he posts near his easel serves as what he calls his sketches for each painting. Unlike many other superrealist painters, he has never either projected images directly onto his canvas or, as John Arthur reported, "relied on mechanical means to transfer an image to the canvas." He begins each painting by blocking in major shapes with acrylic paints; next, still working in acrylics, he refines all parts of the picture. When the acrylic underpainting is complete in all details, he applies an overpainting in oil paints. His largest canvases, which exceed seven feet in width and three feet in height, may take him several months to complete. A number of Estes's paintings have been reproduced as silkscreen prints. In *Architectural Digest* (October 1982), John Arthur wrote that more than one hundred colors were used to create many of the prints—more than ten times as many colors as appear in most silk-screens—and that some of Estes's prints are "virtually indistinguishable" from the paintings on which they are based.

According to John Arthur, Richard Estes is "extremely private and somewhat reclusive," and he "has always been highly disciplined and methodical, habitually keeping regular hours in the studio." Estes paints both in New York City, where he converted one of the bedrooms of his apartment, which overlooks Central Park, into a studio, and in Maine, where, in his home on the coast, near Acadia National Park, a former ballroom serves as his studio. "I think the popular concept of the artist is [of] a person who has this great passion and enthusiasm and super emotion," Estes was quoted as saying in *World Artists, 1950–1980* (1984). "He first throws himself into this great masterpiece and collapses with exhaustion when it's finished. It's really not that way at all. Usually it's a pretty calculated, sustained, and slow process by which you develop something. . . . It's not done with the emotions; it's done with the head."

Selected Biographical References: Am Artist 55:28+ D '91; Art in America 60:73+ N/D '72; Horizon 21:66+ Je '78 por; Arthur, John. Richard Estes: Paintings & Prints (1993); Who's Who in America, 1995; World Artists, 1950–1980 (1984)

Jodi Wille

Etheridge, Melissa

May 29, 1961– Singer; songwriter; guitarist. Address: c/o Island Records, 825 Eighth Ave., 24th Floor, New York, NY 10019

"I come from the heartland, and that's the kind of music I make," the rock singer, songwriter, and guitarist Melissa Etheridge told David Wild in an interview for *US* (January 1994). "I'm not cutting-edge in that I don't make strange music. It's pretty straightforward rock-'n'-roll, in which it all comes from the soul. I'm not a trend." Accompanying herself on acoustic guitar, Etheridge sang in bars and small clubs in the Los Angeles area for six years before releasing her self-titled debut album in 1988. She expanded her fervent core following with her second and third albums, *Brave and Crazy* (1989) and *Never Enough* (1992), picking up a Grammy Award along the way. The title of her fourth album, *Yes I Am* (1993), was widely perceived to be an answer to the question of her sexual preference, because Etheridge had publicly declared her lesbianism earlier that year. The title track itself, however, is a love song about commitment and romantic obsession, subjects that her gender-neutral lyrics have addressed repeatedly. Etheridge's honesty in dealing with the darker side of love, her powerful, gritty voice, and her soulful performances have earned her frequent comparisons to two of her idols, Janis Joplin and Bruce Springsteen.

Melissa Lou Etheridge was born on May 29, 1961 in Leavenworth, Kansas, the daughter of John Etheridge, who taught psychology and government and coached basketball at Leavenworth High School, and Elizabeth Etheridge, a computer specialist employed by the United States Army. Although Melissa and her older sister, Jennifer, grew up just blocks away from a federal penitentiary, the proximity of the several prisons in Leavenworth didn't worry them, as Etheridge told Neil Strauss for the *New York Times* (December 14, 1994): "Because the prisons were in the town, when the prisoners escaped they always went to the neighboring towns."

Ever since she can remember, Etheridge has enjoyed popular music. Some of her earliest memories are of dancing to the music blaring from the family's radio when she was three years old. "I was hooked on radio," she told Patricia Smith of the *Chicago Sun Times* (August 5, 1990). "It was the middle of the sixties, so we're talking the Beatles, Tommy James and the Shondells, Steppenwolf. But the first music I ever really played was country and western, because that's what folks in Kansas wanted to hear." When she turned eight years old, her father presented her with her first six-string guitar, and she soon began lessons with a local jazz musician named Don Raymond. "He was real strict about timing," she recalled in an interview with Sue Carswell for *Out* (December/January 1994). "He tapped his foot really loud on an old wooden board. He's the reason I have really good rhythm."

At the age of ten, Etheridge wrote her first song, a folk tune entitled "Don't Let It Fly Away (It's Love)." Two years later she began performing on her own at teachers' conventions and local churches. Before long she was appearing at a wide variety of events and venues, including supermarket openings, bowling alleys, lounges, the local Knights of Columbus hall, and even the local jails. "Prisons have the most enthusiastic audiences," she told Carswell. "It's like playing for two thousand people who all want to be entertained." When she was thirteen years old, Etheridge began performing with her first group, a country-and-western outfit called the Wranglers, at neighborhood bars and at Parents without Partners dances. By then she had become proficient on the drums, saxophone, piano, clarinet, and twelve-string guitar.

Upon her graduation from Leavenworth High School, Etheridge enrolled at the rigorous Berklee College of Music, in Boston, which today proudly displays her picture in its brochures even though she dropped out after her second semester. "I just couldn't apply myself," she explained to James Sanford for the *Michigan Monthly Music Revue* (April 1994). "I was too caught up in the dream of being a rock star rather than being 'a musician.' The energy you spend studying for that, I would rather spend looking for jobs singing in bars and restaurants." Etheridge then took a part-time job as a security guard at Deaconess Hospital in Boston. During her off hours she performed at local clubs and coffeehouses and even in the city's Park Place subway station. After a year, no longer able to support herself, Etheridge returned to Leavenworth, where she worked in a local restaurant. After nine months she had saved enough money to buy a car.

In 1982, on her twenty-first birthday, Etheridge set off for Los Angeles, "the town of [her] dreams," as she has often referred to her new home. After initially experiencing difficulty in finding her niche in a city teeming with male heavy-metal musicians, glitter rockers, and new-wave acts, she eventually settled into the women's bar scene in Long Beach, California, where for the next four years she earned her living performing in lesbian clubs and at local women's music festivals alongside such folk veterans as Holly Near. It was then that she first heard the music of Joni Mitchell, Janis Joplin, and Joan Armatrading, all of whom were to influence her development. During that time she hired a manager and began incorporating more original music into her repertoire. "I had gone from a quiet sort of 'Hey, I'm just here in the corner and you don't have to listen to me' thing to standing up and doing a show, playing rock with an acoustic guitar and making people listen," Etheridge told Patricia Smith.

During a performance in late 1986 at a Long Beach club called Que Sera Sera, Etheridge received her first professional break when Chris Blackwell, the founder and chairman of Island Records and the person credited with discovering the reggae superstar Bob Marley and the Irish rock band U2, signed her to a recording contract after hearing four songs. Though she had been approached previously by several other recording executives, only Blackwell had expressed the commitment to produce her first album. "I was impressed by the passion she had for her performance," Blackwell told David Wild. "I thought at the time that potentially the next big rock-'n'-roll star like Bruce Springsteen would be a girl. I thought, and still think, that she's the most likely to fill that role." Blackwell's initial attempts to team Etheridge with Jim Gaines, who had produced albums for Eddie Money, Huey Lewis and the News, and Journey, resulted in a layered sound that was ultimately discarded for a leaner approach. Recorded live in the studio in four days, the final cuts featured Etheridge on electric guitar, Craig Krampf on drums, and Kevin McCormick on bass.

Released in 1988, *Melissa Etheridge* garnered strong reviews and solid, though not explosive, sales figures. Ralph Novak, evaluating the album for *People* (August 8, 1988), commented that "Etheridge's throaty, aggressively emotional, born-to-compete voice sounds like Bonnie Tyler. Her music has a rigorous vitality, and there's an edge to it." According to Hugh Wyatt of the New York *Daily News* (May 20, 1988), "Etheridge is a sensuous, dramatic vocalist with a countryish tinge who sounds convincing and honest as well. She is reminiscent of Janis Joplin and Kim Carnes, except she has more control and focus." Michael Segell, who reviewed the album for *Cosmopolitan* (March 1989), declared, "Rarely is a rock-song lyric as searing as Melissa Etheridge's evocation of a jilted lover's jealousy in 'Like the Way I Do': 'Does she stimulate you, attract and captivate you / Does she miss you, existing just to kiss you / Does she want you, infatuate and haunt you / Does she know just how to shock you, electrify and rock you / Does she inject you, seduce you, and affect you / The way I do?'"

The absence of "he" or "him" in Etheridge's lyrics enables both gay and straight listeners to relate to her music. "It's the way I've always written," the singer explained to Patricia Smith, "but it's not a conscious effort on my part. I didn't realize I was doing a genderless thing, but then I saw how it made my music accessible to almost everyone. . . . When I look at my audience, I . . . see that everyone has problems in love, everyone has pain they need to share. You don't have to slap a 'male' or 'female' label on that."

Writing in the *Boston Herald* (April 14, 1989), Larry Katz noted that for most of the forty-four weeks since its introduction, *Melissa Etheridge* had remained in the "lowest reaches" of the *Billboard* Top Two Hundred, but that it had recently climbed to number thirty-two. Katz attributed the album's ascent to Island Records' persistent support and to a performance she gave at the televised Grammy Awards show, which was seen by approximately forty million viewers in February 1989. That appearance helped the album to achieve certified gold-record sales of five hundred thousand copies; meanwhile, its first single, "Similar Features," entered the Top One Hundred pop chart.

Etheridge's second effort, *Brave and Crazy*, produced by Niko Bolas and recorded in just six days, was released in 1989. Her backing band on the album consisted of returning bassist Kevin McCormick (who also cowrote one song), drummer Mauricio Fritz Lewak, and guitarist Bernie Larsen. Reviews of the album covered the spectrum. Ron Givens, commenting in *Stereo Review* (January 1990), thought that "Etheridge's attitude [got] in the way of her music." "She moves back and forth between sensitive longing and headlong consummation without ever stopping in between . . . ," he complained. "Taken in small doses, Etheridge is quite effective. Over the course of an entire album, however, the repetitiveness and narrowness of her music get a little tiresome." For the hard-rocking, bluesy song "Bring Me Some Water," about the burning emotions that accompany the discovery that one's lover has been unfaithful, Etheridge was nominated for a Grammy Award.

The American concert tour that followed the release of *Brave and Crazy* yielded mostly favorable notices. Jon Bream of the *Minneapolis Star and Tribune* (February 12, 1990) declared Etheridge to be "a remarkable, emotionally charged singer of the caliber of Bruce Springsteen and Janis Joplin. She had the near-capacity crowd of twenty-five hundred hanging on her every word and saluting her like a pop icon." Comparing a recent performance to that of a year earlier, he found her to be "more confident, more controlled and less awed by her fawning fans. . . . Her material was stronger, the textures and arrangements more varied and her backup trio was more integral to the presentation." Within a few years of their releases, Etheridge's first two albums had gone platinum, that is, they had sold over a million copies each, for a combined worldwide total of 4.3 million units by April 1992.

Never Enough (1992), Etheridge's third album, was heavily promoted by Island Records, both in retail outlets and during the supporting tour. Even the compact disc's provocative cover, featuring a shirtless Etheridge with her back turned to the camera, her twelve-string Ovation guitar resting against her hip, was strategically designed with marketing in mind, according to Andy Allen, a senior vice-president and general manager at Island Records. The cover "forces you to make an opinion one way or the other" about the performer, Allen told Paul Verna of *Billboard* (April 4, 1992). The image was also intended to serve as an eye-catching device in an increasingly crowded market. "We live in a world of the vanishing album," Etheridge explained to Greg Baker of the *Miami New Times* (February 17–23, 1994). "Before, you could do complicated things in the artwork of vinyl albums. Now the configurations are tiny. I wanted a CD cover people could see all the way across the record store and notice. Also, I have a big problem with fashion. I'd prefer not to have to wear anything."

More experimental than her previous work, *Never Enough* was generally well received. Jim Cullen wrote in *Rolling Stone* (May 14, 1992) that although "there's nothing as arresting on this album as 'Bring Me Some Water,' . . . taken as a whole, *Never Enough* represents Etheridge's best work to date." The album "will surprise those who know [Etheridge] mainly as a high-octane rocker . . . ," Alanna Nash noted in her assessment for *Stereo Review* (June 1992). "She positively shines in her ballads about loneliness, emptiness, and desperation, hitting her stride in 'The Letting Go,' a mature and finely wrought song about recovering from the pain of romantic separation." Etheridge's first single from the album, "Ain't It Heavy," won her the 1993 Grammy Award for best female rock vocalist. In her acceptance speech, she dedicated the award to the memory of her father, who had died of liver cancer in 1991, and thanked her lover, Julie Cypher, for her support.

Had she won the award a year earlier, Etheridge would have caused a media sensation by publicly expressing her love for her girlfriend in that manner, because she did not "come out" until a spontaneous surge of pride overtook her at the first lesbian-and-gay inaugural celebration, which was held in January 1993 at the National Press Club in Washington, D.C., in honor of President Bill Clinton. Sponsored by the Human Rights Campaign Fund, the Triangle Ball provided the perfect opportunity for Etheridge to announce that she had been a lesbian all her life. "I had no plan to do it that night, no plan whatsoever," she explained to James Sanford. "It was the atmosphere." When asked by Rich Cohen of *Rolling Stone* (December 29, 1994–January 12, 1995) if her career had been affected by the announcement, Etheridge responded, "Only in a good way. . . . I think people appreciate openness and honesty. . . . I still get fan mail from guys that are really attracted to me, . . . and I think it's pretty cool that a guy can hear that someone's gay and can still feel that passion." Another career benefit that she derived from coming out was the freedom to cover certain favorite songs of her youth that happened to have a female subject, such as Rod Stewart's "Maggie May," which she performed to wild applause during her 1994 concerts.

A stir was created by the music press when Etheridge titled her next album *Yes I Am*. For fans who had not yet heard about her announcement at the Triangle Ball, the title was taken as confirmation of her sexual identity, even by those who had not previously thought to question it one way or the other, because the phrase presupposes an inquiry. But the title was also intended to be a general affirmation in an era when people tend to define themselves more by what they're not, as Etheridge explained to Rich Cohen: "You know, if someone asks you a question: 'Are you an Italian?' 'Yes, I am.' You are taking responsibility for that. You are acknowledging your history."

In the album's title song, the affirmation refers to the singer's confidence that she is the right partner for her lover. "'Yes I Am' is a love song that borders on the neurotic," Etheridge has explained. "It's saying, 'I don't want you to have any doubt that I am everything you need and want.' It's kind of that scary area of love. What is devotion and what is obsession?" The song "Talking to My Angel," about dealing with change and loss, refers to what the singer has described as her "angel complex," which derives from her having played her music in churches while she was growing up. "I was constantly around all these religious images," she has said, "and to me angels exist. . . . I feel we are definitely guided and helped, and I'm always referring to them in my work."

Yes I Am was engineered by the Grammy award-winning producer Hugh Padgham, who had previously overseen efforts by the Police, Sting, Genesis, and Phil Collins. Arranged by Etheridge in collaboration with bassist Kevin McCormick and drummer Fritz Lewak, the songs were recorded live in the studio. Other musicians who contributed to the album were Waddy Wachtel on lead guitar, Ian McLagan on organ, Scott Thurston on keyboards, Pino Palladino on bass, and James Fearnley of the Pogues on accordion. The album was originally recorded on analog and then mixed down to a digital format in order to get the sound of "real music slapping against tape," as Etheridge has said. Parke Puterbaugh wrote in *Stereo Review* (January 1994) that the album is "at times reminiscent of a good midperiod Stones album, its tunes building a steady head of steam as bluesy guitar figures curl with increasing fervor around Etheridge's mounting vocal attack." *Yes I Am* eventually went quadruple platinum and yielded two Top Ten singles, "Come to My Window" and "I'm the Only One." In November 1995 Ethridge released a fifth album, *Your Little Secret*. She has also performed on MTV's *Unplugged*.

Melissa Etheridge lives with her partner of five years, Julie Cypher, a music video director, in a Spanish-style house on a hill overlooking Hollywood. When they can find the time in between the demands of their respective careers, they retreat to a cabin in the San Bernardino mountains. In addition to having completed five albums, Etheridge has contributed songs to the soundtracks for the films *Weeds*, starring Nick Nolte; *Welcome Home, Roxy Carmichael*, featuring Winona Ryder ("I Will Never Be the Same," included by popular demand on *Yes I Am*); *Where the Day Takes You*, with Kyle MacLachlan and Dermot Mulroney; and Cypher's upcoming feature-film directorial debut, tentatively titled "Teresa's Tattoo." Politically active since she turned thirty, Etheridge is involved in the pro-choice movement and serves on the advisory board of Artists for a Hate-Free America, which raises funds to help communities fight antigay initiatives. She is a strict vegetarian. Her hobbies are collecting antique playing cards, art, and fast cars, including her "dream car," a black convertible Jaguar, and a 1995 BMW 740i; skiing; bowling, and spending time with her two cats, Gabrielle and Gwendolyn, a cockatoo named Boo, and a mixed Lhasa apso-terrier named Angel.

Selected Biographical References: Interview 24:168+ O '94 pors; Out p81+ D/Ja '94 pors; People 42:57+ S 5 '94 pors; Rolling Stone p110+ D 29 '94-Ja 12 '95, p38+ Je 1 '95 pors; Who's Who in America, 1995

Evers-Williams, Myrlie

(MUHR-lee)

Mar. 17, 1933 - Civil rights activist; organization official. Address: NAACP, 1072 W. Lynch St., Jackson, MS 39203

By a close vote on February 18, 1995, Myrlie Evers-Williams was elected chairperson of the National Association for the Advancement of Colored People, thus becoming the first female head of the 675,000-member civil rights organization founded in 1909. Prior to assuming her post, Evers-Williams was best known as the widow of Medgar Evers, the tireless civil rights worker and NAACP official murdered in 1963. In the time between her first husband's death and her taking the reins of the NAACP, however, Evers-Williams—who once claimed not to have "any desire to be a professional widow"—was active in fields as diverse as advertising, corporate philanthropy, and city government. She has accepted her new responsibilities at a time when the NAACP is suffering from internal strife, facing external challenges in an increasingly conservative political climate, and struggling to define its goals for the twenty-first century.

AP/Wide World Photos

Myrlie Evers-Williams

Myrlie Evers-Williams was born Myrlie Louise Beasley on March 17, 1933 in Vicksburg, Mississippi. Her parents separated when she was an infant, and thereafter she was reared by her grandmother, Annie McCain Beasley, and an aunt, Myrlie Beasley Polk, both of whom were teachers. Although she told Marilyn Marshall for *Ebony* (June 1988) that she led a "sheltered" existence as a child, she was not unaffected by racism, for the racial segregation of the region and era prevented her from attending the local white colleges. As a result, in 1950 she enrolled at Alcorn A & M College, in Lorman, Mississippi, as an education major and music minor. She met Medgar Evers on her first day at the school, and the two were married on Christmas Eve of the following year.

Evers-Williams left Alcorn without obtaining her degree; Medgar Evers completed his studies in 1952. Following his graduation the couple moved to Mound Bayou, in the Mississippi Delta, where Medgar found work as an insurance agent. He was so appalled by the squalor in which local black sharecroppers were forced to live that, in an effort to improve their living conditions, he became active in the NAACP. Appointed to the position of field secretary in 1954, he set up an office in Jackson, Mississippi, where his wife became his secretary.

As the civil rights movement of the 1950s and 1960s progressed, and resistance to integration became more entrenched, the couple received death threats. On occasion, Evers-Williams tried to persuade her husband to move their family, which by that time included three young children, to a safer environment, and they sometimes talked of living in California. The family nevertheless remained in Mississippi, where guarding against violence became a part of their daily existence. Marilyn Marshall reported that Medgar Evers trained his children to dive to the floor if they heard an unusual sound outside and that the entire family avoided the windows of their home at night. In the spring of 1963, their house was firebombed and Evers-Williams doused the flames with a garden hose. "We lived with death as a constant companion, twenty-four hours a day," she told Marshall. "Medgar knew what he was doing, and he knew what the risks were. He just decided that he had to do what he had to do. But I knew at some point in time he would be taken from me."

At 12:30 A.M. on June 12, 1963, Evers-Williams heard her husband, who was returning from an NAACP meeting, drive up to the house. Next, she heard the sound of gunfire, and she opened the door to find Medgar Evers collapsed on the porch steps. Less than an hour later, he died at the University of Mississippi Hospital. "Afterward, I remember thinking, 'I'm going to make whoever did this pay,'" Evers-Williams told Catherine S. Manegold of the *New York Times* (February 20, 1995). Byron De La Beckwith, an avowed segregationist and white supremacist, was put on trial for Medgar Evers's murder. "While I was testifying," Evers-Williams recalled to Claudia Dreifus of the *New York Times Magazine* (November 27, 1994), "the governor [of Mississippi], Ross Barnett, walked in . . . , and he paused and looked at me, turned, and went to Beckwith, shook his hand, slapped him on the shoulder, and sat down next to him. He was sending a clear signal to the jurors that his man was to be acquitted." After two all-male, all-white juries failed to reach a verdict, Beckwith was set free.

"For a moment," Evers-Williams has written, "I hated everybody with a white skin. But Medgar taught me not to hate anyone." She did, however, feel the need to relocate, telling Steven V. Roberts of the *New York Times* (March 26, 1970), "That house was a constant reminder. Every time I walked out of the front door, it was like seeing his body lying there. We had the same refrigerator with the bullet hole in it. It was just a little too much." Deciding that there was "nowhere in Mississippi [she] wanted to live," as she told one interviewer, in 1964 she moved with her family to Claremont, California, a suburb of Los Angeles. During that period she gave speeches for the NAACP, which, in exchange for her public appearances, continued to pay her husband's annual salary of sixty-one hundred dollars. She also continued her undergraduate education, at Pomona College, one of the Claremont Colleges, receiving her B.A. degree in sociology in 1968. Later in the same year, she took a job as the assistant director of the Claremont College system's Center for Educational Opportunity. In that capacity, she helped underprivileged high-school dropouts obtain their diplomas and go on to college.

In the meantime, in 1967 Evers-Williams published *For Us, the Living*, written with William Peters. A biography of her slain husband, the book details the growth of his conviction that "freedom

[had] to be won" and describes his work with the NAACP. "Evers . . . could have presented an emotional, slick history of the life and death of her husband," Fred Powledge wrote in the *New York Times Book Review* (November 19, 1967). Instead, he continued, "she chose to do a thorough job. She has written a book that is at the same time a beautiful story of the love between a man and a woman . . . , a textbook on how it is to be not white in Mississippi, and a self-searching essay on how it is to be a normal human being married to a man devoted to freedom." In 1983 the book was made into a television movie starring Howard Rollins and Irene Cara.

When the United States congressman Glenard P. Lipscomb, of California's Twenty-Fourth Congressional District, died in February 1970, Evers-Williams sought to fill the vacant seat. She wanted to run because she was "disturbed about what seemed to be the effects of polarization," as she told Steven V. Roberts in March 1970. She added, "We seem to be going backwards as a nation as far as human rights are concerned. As a nation we are dividing up into separate groups and pulling ourselves apart. . . . Those who say integration is not a realistic idea might be right, but I will hope and pray and work to show they are incorrect. I just don't see how this country can exist divided. The only way people can understand each other is through interaction. I simply don't see separatism working in this country." Her qualifications for elective office, she told a writer for *Newsweek* (March 30, 1970), included "a heritage of service, an abundance of concern, and a good ear."

Evers-Williams faced an uphill battle in the heavily Republican district. Of the nine people who declared their bids for Lipscomb's seat, she was the only Democrat, which proved to be an advantage only in that she won her party's primary unopposed. During the campaign, she received hate mail reminiscent of the threats made against her during her husband's lifetime. Her opponent in the general election was John Rousselot, a management consultant and former national officer in the ultraconservative John Birch Society. Among the areas of wide disagreement between the two candidates was the issue of federal spending: while Rousselot favored deep cuts in expenditures, Evers-Williams supported subsidies for what she called "people-oriented" programs. The two were somewhat more closely aligned in their views on the Vietnam War. Rousselot advocated a gradual withdrawal of United States troops, whereas Evers-Williams called for an immediate end to American participation in what she termed the "immoral and senseless" war. Although she lost the election, Evers-Williams came away with 36 percent of the vote (38 percent, according to one source), thus making a better showing than any other Democratic congressional candidate had made in the district in more than a decade.

Concurrent with her position at the Claremont Colleges, Evers-Williams was a contributing editor of *Ladies' Home Journal*, a post she held until 1974. Also during the early 1970s, she served for two years as a vice-president at Seligman & Lapz, a New York-based advertising firm. In 1975 she moved to Los Angeles to become director of corporate community affairs for the Atlantic Richfield Company (ARCO). She used her influence at ARCO to secure money for organizations that included the National Women's Education Fund and a group that supplied meals to poor and homeless people in the Watts section of Los Angeles. In the following decade Evers-Williams made another unsuccessful attempt at entering politics—this time as a candidate for the Los Angeles City Council—before becoming, in June 1987, the first black female commissioner of that city's Board of Public Works, appointed by Mayor Tom Bradley. As a member of the board, which is responsible for street maintenance, waste disposal, and other services, Evers-Williams oversaw approximately six thousand employees and a budget of hundreds of millions of dollars.

Meanwhile, in 1976 she had married Walter Williams, a civil rights worker, union activist, and onetime longshoreman whom she had met in 1968. As she explained to Sue Ellen Jares for *People* (June 19, 1978), she found in Williams a companion who did not feel threatened by Medgar Evers's legacy: "Others couldn't deal with the memory. Here was someone who cherished it." While Evers-Williams had fashioned a new life for herself, she remained as determined as she had been in 1963 to see that her first husband's killer was punished, and although she had long since left Mississippi, she continued to keep tabs on developments there, in case any proved useful in her pursuit of justice.

One such development occurred in 1989, when the Jackson, Mississippi *Clarion-Ledger* began to explore the possibility that the Mississippi Sovereignty Commission, a secret organization in operation during the 1960s, had engaged in jury tampering during Byron De La Beckwith's second murder trial. Learning of the investigation, Evers-Williams urged Mississippi authorities to hold a new trial. New witnesses came forward and testified that they had heard the defendant boast of killing Medgar Evers. On February 5, 1994, a racially mixed jury found Beckwith, then seventy-three years old, guilty of murder, and he was sentenced to life in prison. "I didn't realize how deeply implanted this need to clear everything up was," Evers-Williams told Claudia Dreifus. "I was reborn when that jury said, 'Guilty!'"

Evers-Williams had long been a member of the board of the NAACP, and had become one of its vice-chairs, when some of her fellow members urged her to seek the position of chairperson of the organization. She was initially reluctant to do so, mainly because such an undertaking would reduce the time that she could spend with her husband, who had developed cancer, but also, perhaps, because the NAACP was in a state of turmoil that many called the worst in its history. On August 20, 1994 Benjamin F. Chavis, the executive director, who was already at odds with more centrist members because of his ties with the controversial Nation of Islam leader Louis Farrakhan, was dismissed for using NAACP funds—without board approval—for an out-of-court settlement of a sexual harassment suit. In addition, in January 1995 a number of NAACP board members brought a federal suit against then-chairman William F. Gibson, charging that he had misused $1.4 million of the group's funds. As a result of the NAACP's troubles, many of its members and supporters withheld financial support. That situation, in turn, forced the organization to furlough much of its staff and left the board at a loss to pay off its debts, which were estimated at between three and four million dollars.

In spite of those daunting circumstances, on February 7, 1995 Evers-Williams announced her candidacy for the NAACP's chair, citing the organization's need for a "fresh start." During the previous summer, she had publicly urged the group to "address sexism within its operation" and change the composition of its sixty-four-member board, forty-eight members of which were men, to better reflect the membership, which was 65 percent female. Although, before the election, seven hundred NAACP delegates passed a motion of no confidence in the organization's leadership, the board remained almost evenly split between those supporting Gibson, who had alienated many through his friendly relations with Farrakhan, and Evers-Williams, who was seen as embodying the NAACP's traditionally mainstream ideology. In fact, the vote was as close as it could possibly have been, with thirty of the fifty-nine board members who participated in the election choosing Evers-Williams as the new chair. Evers-Williams took a symbolic step toward healing the divisions among her colleagues when, as the preface to her election-night speech, she blew her audience a kiss—a gesture greeted by enthusiastic applause.

Since assuming her post, Ever-Williams has vowed to fight what she has called attempts to counter the advances made by African-Americans—including efforts to eradicate affirmative action. She has also urged fellow blacks to improve their situation by means already at their disposal, and to that end she has organized a voter-registration drive in Jackson, Mississippi. "If we don't use what we have, then we deserve what we get," she said, as quoted by the *New York Times* (October 2, 1995). At the NAACP's eighty-sixth annual convention, held in Minneapolis in July 1995, she expressed her desire to attract more young people to membership in the NAACP (the median age of members is currently forty-nine).

"The gains that we have made are slowly but surely slipping away from us," Evers-Williams has declared, as quoted in Brian Lanker's book *I Dream a World: Portraits of Black Women Who Changed America* (1989). "I feel as though I should shout from mountain tops to valleys, 'Don't you see what's happening? Don't let history repeat itself!' I see the same challenges of the past with us, maybe cloaked a little differently. We are still plagued with racism. We still find discrimination in the job market, in education, and housing. There are still covenants to keep minorities out of certain geographical areas. I have faced discrimination, not only due to the color of my skin, but because I am female. I have had jobs that have been the same or equivalent to jobs of white males and have received anywhere from 15 to 30 percent less pay. But we keep a-coming. Strong as we've always been, more aware of ourselves, our strength, and power potential, willing to take more risks."

In her *New York Times Magazine* article, Claudia Dreifus described Myrlie Evers-Williams as "a handsome woman, tall, with a spark in her chestnut eyes." She lives in Bend, Oregon, where she moved in 1989 with her second husband, Walter Williams, who died on February 22, 1995. From her first marriage, Evers-Williams has two sons, Darrell and James, and a daughter, Reena. As she told Dreifus, she feels that she has succeeded in making a name for herself that is independent of that of Medgar Evers. "I know I wouldn't have had certain doors open to me if it hadn't been for Medgar," she has said. "I also know if I hadn't had the intellect, I wouldn't be able to use it."

Selected Biographical References: Ebony 43:108+ Je '88 pors; N Y Times A p1+ F 20 '95 pors; N Y Times Mag p69+ N 27 '94 pors; People 9:65+ Je 19 '78 pors; Washington Post B p1+ S 30 '74; Who's Who of American Women, 1995–96

Fassett, Kaffe

(FAS-et, kayf)

1937– Artist; needleworker. Address: c/o Ebury Press, Random House, 20 Vauxhall Bridge Rd., London SW1V 2SA, England

Self-described as "a painter with wools," Kaffe Fassett is one of the leading fiber artists of his generation. A native of California who settled in London in the mid-1960s, he is recognized among museum curators and private collectors worldwide for his dazzling creativity in both knitting and needlepoint. For several years after leaving the United States, Fassett struggled to build a career as a painter of portraits and still lifes. Aesthetically thrilled by the Shetland yarns that he discovered while visiting a fabric mill in Scotland as an assistant to the fashion designer Bill Gibb, he developed a consuming interest in hand-knitting virtually overnight. The hundreds of richly patterned and vibrantly colored garments—some incorporating as many as two hundred different yarns—that he has produced in the past quarter-century have "elevated knitting to an art form," in the words of Deborah Hoffmann of the *New York Times* (November 12, 1989). Fassett's needlepoints as well as his knitted works have been exhibited in museums in Great Britain and other parts of the world. In

The Westminster Trading Corp.

Kaffe Fassett

1988 he became the first textile artist to have a solo exhibition at the Victoria and Albert Museum, in London.

The "Pied Piper of knitting and needlepoint," as he has been called, Fassett has gained an enthusiastic following among hobbyists as well as art experts. Credited with revolutionizing needlework by "overthrowing the tyranny of complex techniques," he has written seven books—several of which have been best-sellers in the crafts category—for avocational needleworkers. According to Mary Colucci, a former executive director of the National Needlework Association, Fassett's "whole philosophy is one that encourages you to just pick up the needle, put aside your fears, and get into the beauty of the fiber." "I'm so moved when people tell me I've helped them unlock some inner creativity . . . ," he told an interviewer a few years ago. "If I can help them discover the same happiness and joy knitting has given me, that's great."

The second of five children, Kaffe Fassett was born in 1937 in San Francisco. His parents owned and managed a restaurant whose devotees included many artists and actors. His father also owned stables of saddle horses. In his book *Glorious Inspirations: Kaffe Fassett's Needlepoint Source Book* (1991), Fassett reported that he remembered very vividly the "decorative details in [his] early life." "Large shallow fish bowls are among my earliest memories," he wrote. "My mother was an ardent admirer of Oriental taste, and she gave us our meals on handpainted Chinese fish bowls in bold maroon and blue." At some point during his childhood, he and his family moved from near San Francisco's Chinatown to what he has referred to as the "wild coast"—the part of California known as Big Sur. He has recalled with pleasure his sightings of wildlife and discoveries of animal skeletons during his outdoor wanderings. In a photo taken when he was eighteen, he is seen standing in tall grass with the pelvic bone of a cow balanced on his head.

By his own account, as a youngster Fassett was a "precocious handful." He hated his original given name, which he has labeled "boring" and "dreadful," and at fifteen, inspired by a name in a children's book about an Egyptian boy, he began calling himself Kaffe. After attending a boarding school run by the disciples of Krishnamurti, an Indian guru, Fassett studied painting on a scholarship at the School of the Museum of Fine Arts in Boston. He left after less than a year. In his early twenties he traveled extensively in Turkey, Syria, and Afghanistan.

In a profile of him for the Canadian edition of *Reader's Digest* (June 1990), Deborah Cowley reported that when Fassett was in his mid-twenties, he met the British writer Christopher Isherwood. The descriptions of England in Isherwood's books, Cowley wrote, awakened in him a desire to see Great Britain. According to another source, however, what lured him to England was "the style and freedom of London during the heyday of the Beatles and [the fashion designer] Mary Quant." In any event, in 1964 Fassett went to England for what he thought would be a three-month voyage of discovery but that turned into a permanent stay. Not long after his arrival, the American Museum in Bath commissioned him to produce drawings for a guidebook. After working on that project in Bath for six months, he moved to London. For the next few years, he devoted himself to painting, but the income he earned from selling his portraits of children, still lifes, and renderings of gardens and houses barely enabled him to eke out a living. On many days he would spend hours sketching textiles, pottery, and other decoratively patterned objects at the Victoria and Albert Museum. (Many of them served as the inspiration for a large number of the 150 knitted works and needlepoints displayed in the exhibition of his work that the museum mounted in 1988. The show, which filled one of the museum's largest galleries and drew a quarter of a million visitors, later attracted record crowds in museums in Scandinavia.)

In around 1967 Fassett began designing knitwear for Bill Gibb, a successful Scottish clothing designer. The next year he accompanied Gibb on a visit to a wool mill in Inverness, Scotland, where Gibb intended to buy fabric. Stored in a section of the mill was a huge assortment of Shetland knitting wools, including many dyed in colors that evoked in Fassett's mind images of the Scottish countryside. In an interview with Melanie Falick for *Rowan Knitting Magazine* (Spring/Summer 1994), he explained that "what looks like a grass green in Shetland yarns has got lavenders, browns, and pink tones in it, too. The Shetlanders mix up colors in their yarns that are so subtle and beautiful that, if you look closely, you can see the landscape in them." As he gazed at the wools, he told Terry Trucco for the *New York Times* (May 20, 1987), he wondered, "What's the matter with people, running around in navy and beige?" Seized by the idea of creating a multicolored garment, he bought twenty skeins of yarn of different hues and a pair of knitting needles at the mill.

During the train trip back to London, Fassett realized that his plan to have someone knit his imagined garment according to his specifications would not be feasible, because there was little chance that he could successfully communicate to another person his vision of "striated sandstone and ancient biblical robes," as he has described it. Having concluded that he would have to make it himself, he asked one of his traveling companions to demonstrate to him the basics of knitting. "By the time I reached London, I was in full flood," he told Deborah Cowley. By spending most of his waking hours "just piling one amazing color on another," as he has put it, within a very short time he completed his first knitted work—a cardigan composed of narrow stripes. (Now dotted with what he has called "sweet little moth holes," it remains in his personal collection.) Years later his studio assistant Zoë Hunt, with whom he wrote *Family Album: More Glorious Knits for Children and Adults* (1989), taught him about "finish, shape, and beautifully balanced knitting," in his words.

The experience of juxtaposing colored yarns in knitted rows excited Fassett enormously. "It worked in a way that paint never did," he has said. During an interview with Deborah Norton for *American Craft* (December 1985/January 1986), he offered some of the reasons for his fascination with knitting. "When you paint you have an infinite range of colors which can be combined in any number of ways. You have to find your way in a forest of unlimitedness. But textiles impose immediate restrictions. Knitting is an incredible discipline—working row by row, combining units of color, while all the time anticipating what you're going to need. I enjoy bursting beyond the boundaries of these limitations."

After a subsequent trip to Scotland—made not long after he went there with Bill Gibb—Fassett stopped painting for many years. He had planned to paint landscapes while sheltered in a van during that trip, but continuous heavy rain reduced visibility to near zero. "Finally I just gave up . . . ," he recalled to Melanie Falick. "At every little mill we passed, we stopped and bought yarn, so I was building up quite a collection when I started to knit them. I knitted the landscape into a jacket instead of painting it. I think that's when I finally decided to put away the paints—that knitting was going to tell the story."

By then Fassett had begun producing sweaters of his own design at what Deborah Cowley described as "a staggering rate." He awakened at 6:00 A.M. every day to knit. "At that time you weren't considered a serious artist if you were involved with textiles," he observed to Terry Trucco. "But once I started, I couldn't give up. I thought if art doesn't allow you to get involved with something as creative as textiles, then fiddledeedee." Before long he began showing his creations to knitwear manufacturers, but for some months none expressed any interest in them. His luck turned when he mailed what he has called "a little waistcoat"—known as a vest in the United States—to Judy Brittain, the editor of the British magazine *Vogue Knitting*. "When I made it I was looking at illuminated manuscripts and thinking about Ireland and Scotland, and those incredible little shapes carved into medieval stones," he told Melanie Falick. Brittain was so impressed by the waistcoat that she included a story about it in the spring 1969 issue of *Vogue Knitting*. Intrigued by the article, the owners of Missoni, a prominent knitwear firm based in Milan, Italy, went to London to see Fassett's whole body of work, and they immediately hired him to design their collection. He remained in the Missonis' employ for the next two years. According to one source, during that period he created designs for a few other prestigious fashion houses as well. A knitted ensemble that he produced in collaboration with Bill Gibb was featured in *Vogue Knitting* around that time and was displayed in the Museum of Costume in Bath as the "outfit of the year."

In the 1970s Fassett began to attract a following among a coterie of fashion-conscious lions of society, who would commission him to knit one-of-a-kind garments for them. His early admirers included Princess Michael of Kent. Through the years he has also sold his custom-designed and -knitted apparel to such luminaries of the entertainment world as Lauren Bacall, Shirley MacLaine, Barbra Streisand, and Candace Bergen. Early on he knit all the garments himself; more recently, he has made only parts of them and has relied on his assistants to complete them according to his specifications. (He sometimes employs as many as half a dozen full-time helpers.) In the late 1980s some of his hand-knitted sweaters and coats sold for as much as five thousand dollars apiece. Westminster Trading Corporation, in Amherst, New Hampshire, markets Fassett's hand-knitted sweaters in the United States.

In around 1980 Fassett's designs began to reach a far wider audience, by means of knitting kits produced and distributed by Rowan Yarns, a company headquartered in Yorkshire, a county in northeastern England. Each of the kits, which he created in partnership with Stephen Sheard, the director of Rowan, offered hobbyists instructions for a simplified version of one of Fassett's designs together with the requisite yarns and a photograph of the finished garment. Despite its relatively high cost, the first kit, for a striped sweater with bat-wing sleeves, sold extremely well, as did the second, for a sweater patterned with triangles in twenty-one colors, and its successors. In the United States, retail prices for Fassett-Rowan kits currently range from about $150 to more than $300. As of 1990, more than a quarter of a million of Fassett's knitting and needlepoint kits had been purchased in fourteen countries.

Fassett's work in needlepoint dates from the mid- to late 1970s. "Before attempting needlepoint, I had the idea that it required a daunting amount of patience," Elizabeth H. Hunter quoted him as saying in *House Beautiful* (November 1988). "Luckily, my first canvas was medium-mesh worked in tent stitch. Imagine my amazement and delight when the work flowed so effortlessly that I was done in no time." Each of Fassett's needlepoint designs requires the use of only two simple stitches—the tent and the long—on a ten-mesh canvas, a relatively large lattice that facilitates speed. Fassett "believes you should do needlepoint the way you might paint—fast enough so the colors and design take shape before you weary of the project," Elizabeth Hunter wrote. The needlepoint kits that he began designing for Ehrmans, a British concern, in 1987 proved to be so popular that Ehrmans discontinued every other item in its catalog and switched to selling only needlepoints. In describing the two kits for pillow covers that were featured in her article for *House Beautiful*, Elizabeth Hunter observed that "with their lush colors and complex shadings, his pillows . . . only *look* difficult."

According to Fassett, the primary value of kits is their potential to "*unplug* people"—that is, to remove barriers to creativity. "The world is full of traumatized people who've been told, 'Leave design to the designers,' as if we were brain surgeons or something," he remarked to Dylan Landis of the *Chicago Tribune* (January 31, 1988). Designing a needlepoint cover for a cushion, he has suggested, may require nothing more than placing some leaves or cut-out pictures of fruits on the cushion and "arranging them until they click." Ideas for creating original knitted goods, he has advised, may be triggered by simply combining yarns of many different colors in a basket. "If that basket sings and makes you want to work out of it, you're halfway there." (According to Fassett, "even if you think you know what a color looks like, you can often find surprising new qualities by trying new combinations.") When you have found at least twenty colors that you like, "cast on and just roar along," and if you feel unsure about the course you have chosen, "add twenty more colors." "Everybody has a very personal color bias in their soul," he has maintained. "It's just a matter of letting it out. It's like a muscle; you develop it by using it, and the more you use it, the more you use it successfully." Fassett is convinced that, by experimenting with pattern and color and refusing to be bound by preconceived notions, almost anyone can create an original design. In an article for the *Spectator* (December 3, 1988), Tanya Harrod contended that few other artists would agree with him, because they are "infuriated by amateurism." "Fassett is above such a mean attitude," she wrote. "His only desire appears to be to spread happiness and color."

By his own account, the source of many of Fassett's design and color ideas is "the timeless world of ethnic decorative arts." Ancient mosaics and Islamic tiles and other styles of tilework have inspired him, as have such things as Japanese and European brocades, old English fabrics, Russian icons, old carpets, Turkish kilims, Indian silk embroideries, Oriental painted landscapes, Japanese kimonos, Chinese vases, Delft china, Spanish architecture, Victorian portraits, parquet floors, antique maps, duck decoys, and patchwork quilts. The fur of spotted cats and other animals, feathers, mosses and lichens, tree bark, grasses, flowers, leaves, weathered wood, old stone walls, aerial views of farmland, and other things found out-of-doors have also fired his imagination. He has even used such sights as litter and peeling paint as the basis for original designs. Many of his creations employ such classic geometric patterns as zigzags, interlocking crosses, six- and eight-pointed stars, diamonds, triangles, and tumbling blocks. According to Fassett, "good designing follows no rules; remaining open to the unexpected is paramount."

In *Fiberarts* (January/February 1990), Carol La Branche wrote that Fassett "admits to stitching badly, . . . letting stitches be backward and higgledy-piggledy." "I don't care a hang about technique," he told Deborah Cowley in the interview for her *Reader's Digest* profile of the artist. "Little mistakes don't bother me. It's the overall look and the play of the colors that matter." "I love it when things begin to go 'wrong,' and a kind of wild abandon creeps into my work," he has said. To enhance color, Fassett sometimes combines yarns of several types—most often wool, mohair, chenille, silk, or cotton—in the same garment. He uses no stitches except the rib and the standard stockinette—a row of knit stitches followed by a row of purl stitches. "There's so much to do with color in knitting—it's been neglected for so long—that I'm not interested in anything else," he told Deborah Norton. He recommends that knitters apply the "intarsia method," which calls for "using a separate length of yarn for each area of contrasting color and linking one color to the next by twisting them around each other where they meet on the wrong side to avoid holes."

In his *Chicago Tribune* article, Dylan Landis reported that Fassett does not plan his designs on paper before starting to knit. (When doing needlepoint, on the other hand, he draws the "bare bones of the design on paper so that the outlines can be easily transferred to a canvas," as he wrote in *Glorious Inspirations*.) After completing a few rows of knitting, he mounts the work-in-progress on a vertical surface and surveys what he has done before proceeding with the next few rows. For those of his designs that will appear in a book, one of his assistants translates his stitchery into diagrams and detailed instructions. While the patterns of color within Fassett's garments are often complex, his knitted wear generally features simple lines. "I'm not into fussy tailoring," he has said.

Glorious Knitting, Fassett's first book, was published in Great Britain in 1985. (It appeared in the United States in the same year with the title *Glorious Knits*.) "A grown-up book for knitters," in his words, it offered instructions for more than thirty of his designs, most of which incorporated more than twenty colors of yarn. In his conversation with

Terry Trucco, Fassett said that he anticipated that sales of the book would generate "a few nice little royalties" with which he could buy more yarn. To his surprise, *Glorious Knitting* became a best-seller in the "how-to" category, and within two years, around one hundred thousand copies had been sold. Knitters in the United States bought more than fifty thousand copies of *Glorious Knits* during the same time period.

So great was the appeal of Fassett's next book, *Glorious Needlepoint* (1987), among hobbyists and others that fifty thousand copies of it were sold before its official publication date. In an enthusiastic review of the book for *Threads* (June/July 1988), Lilo Markrich declared, "If you enjoy the relaxing rhythm and color play of canvas stitching but have ceased to be inspired by marketplace offerings, take heart, for help is at hand. If you've always hankered to try needlepoint but feared the skill was beyond you, you too will enjoy *Glorious Needlepoint*. Experienced and novice stitchers will benefit equally from the information and inspiration this book offers." Markrich also noted that the photographs in *Glorious Needlepoint* "enable the reader to see exactly what Fassett is talking about." "Together, the photographer Steve Lovi and Fassett have created the most tantalizing settings to draw the reader into a mix of reality and fantasy," she wrote. In preparing his books for knitters, Fassett has traveled extensively throughout the United Kingdom and elsewhere with Lovi and other photographers, looking for what he believes will be the best settings in which to photograph the people modeling his garments.

Usually accompanied by his assistant Brandon Mably, who is also a designer, Fassett spends a considerable amount of time each year lecturing and giving workshops in Great Britain, the United States, Canada, Australia, and the Scandinavian countries, among other places. "The enthusiasm he generates is incredible," the organizer of a Fassett knitting demonstration in Vancouver told Deborah Cowley. "After his visit, everyone wanted to dash home and knit!" "His influence is everywhere," Cowley quoted Judy Brittain of *Vogue Knitting* as saying. "Before Kaffe, British knitting design was deadly boring. Today's imaginative multicolored sweaters make you realize what a transformation he has achieved." *Glorious Color*, Fassett's six-part television series about knitting, aired in Great Britain in the late 1980s. His most recent book, *Glorious Interiors*, was published in 1995.

In the past two decades, Fassett has designed successful lines of upholstery fabrics and wallpapers in addition to knitted goods and needlepoints, and he has received many private commissions for designs of tablecloths and curtains as well as fabrics and wall coverings. Five large tapestries and a tufted rug that he designed for the Edinburgh Tapestry Weavers, in Scotland, appeared along with other samples of his work in an exhibit that has toured many countries. On a commission from the Northern Ballet Theatre, a British group, he designed a vibrantly colored set and equally colorful costumes for a new dance called *D'Ensemble*. His recent needlepoint commissions include two five-foot-long tapestries for the British department-store chain Marks and Spencer and two three-foot-long tapestries for a cruise ship. Owners of his tapestries include the artist Helen Frankenthaler and the writer Ruth Rendell.

For many years Fassett has lived and worked in a small apartment-cum-studio in a house in north London. Often working from dawn until dusk, he does most of his knitting or needlepoint while sitting cross-legged and barefoot on a long backless couch in a room that Deborah Cowley described as resembling "an Eastern bazaar." Lining one of its walls are floor-to-ceiling shelves filled with some five thousand spools or skeins of yarn. According to Cowley, its furnishings also include "overlapping Oriental carpets on the floor, needlepoint cushions strewn everywhere, checkerboard blankets draped over a chair, and multicolored tapestries covering three walls." "Whenever I lay a newly finished needlepoint or knitted garment on the floor to study, a cat invariably strolls up to place itself in the middle of the work, looking ravishing," Fassett wrote in *Glorious Inspirations*. His assistants work in an adjoining room.

Tall and youthful in appearance despite his graying hair, Kaffe Fassett has been described as having a gentle face and "boyish liveliness and zeal," and he is said to be friendly and unassuming. "His soft mid-Atlantic accent is the only evidence of his California origins," Deborah Cowley noted. According to Cowley, Fassett, who owns an old bicycle but not a car, "cares little about money and shuns any trappings of wealth." "I only need a humble way of living to be content," she quoted him as saying. He regularly runs and sometimes swims in Hampstead Heath, which is near his home. A few years ago he started painting again. "My painting is affected by the color I've learned from yarns . . . ," he told Melanie Falick when she interviewed him for *Rowan Knitting Magazine*. "I love playing with color in a more vibrant way."

"I always pack my knitting or needlepoint project first when traveling," Fassett revealed in *Kaffe's Classics: 25 Favorite Knitting Patterns for Sweaters, Jackets, Vests, and More* (1993). By all accounts, his needles seldom leave his hands, and he has even continued his work at dinner parties. He has maintained that during the countless occasions when he has knitted or done needlepoint in such public places as parks, trains, and buses, he has never been teased or harassed. "I've been in a train full of soccer players, drunk as lords, and they never said a thing," he told Dylan Landis. "Knitting still remains my most stimulating yet relaxing activity," he said recently, "and I thank the powers that be that I can make a living at it."

Selected Biographical References: Chicago Tribune XV p12 Ja 31 '88 por; N Y Times C p1+ My 20 '87 pors; Reader's Digest (Canadian edition) p88+ Je '90 por

AP/Wide World Photos

Feinstein, Dianne

(FINE-stine)

June 22, 1933- United States Senator from California. Address: 331 Hart Senate Office Bldg., Washington, DC 20510

NOTE: This biography supersedes the article that appeared in *Current Biography* in 1979.

In 1992 Dianne Feinstein, a Democrat, became the first woman to be sworn in as a United States senator from California. Overcoming devastating electoral defeats and personal tragedy, Feinstein has achieved a remarkable string of firsts for women in politics. In 1969 she became the first woman to be elected president of the San Francisco Board of Supervisors, the equivalent of a city council. Twice defeated in her bid to become the city's mayor, in 1978 she became the first woman to hold that position, when she ascended to the office upon the assassination of her predecessor. In 1984 she was among the first women to be considered for selection as a vice-presidential candidate on a major-party ticket, and in 1990 she became the first woman to be nominated by a major party to be governor of California.

A strong campaigner, Feinstein is a consensus builder, preferring the middle to either extreme, a characteristic she has attributed to her association with Robert F. Kennedy in 1968, on whose campaign for the Democratic presidential nomination she served. "Problems don't fit into neat ideological test bags," she told Jordan Bonfante of *Time* (June 18, 1990). "Some problems require 'right' solutions. Some require 'left' solutions. Some require commonsense solutions." Although she has often been the sole woman campaigning among a field of male candidates, Feinstein has focused on issues that transcend gender, among them crime prevention, environmental preservation, and education. Over the years her political philosophy has evolved, leading some critics to charge her with inconsistency in such areas as capital punishment, taxation, urban development, gay rights, and feminism. Discussing Feinstein's policy shifts in his biography of the senator, *Never Let Them See You Cry* (1994), Jerry Roberts concluded that "such points and counterpoints reflect her personality—earnest but calculating, ambitious but insecure, compassionate but peremptory, honest but manipulative, resolutely independent but preoccupied with law and order."

Dianne Feinstein was born Dianne Emiel Goldman on June 22, 1933 in San Francisco, the eldest of the three daughters of Leon and Betty (Rosenburg) Goldman. The spelling of her first name reflects a tribute to her maternal aunt Anne. She grew up in the comfortable surroundings of San Francisco's elite Presidio Terrace section. Her father, a nationally known surgeon and a professor at the University of California at San Francisco Medical School, was the son of Orthodox Jews who had immigrated to California from Poland near the end of the nineteenth century. Her Russian Orthodox mother, a former nurse and model who claimed she was born Pasha Pariskovia in St. Petersburg, Russia, suffered from what would, in the latter part of her life (and upon invention of the CAT scanner), be diagnosed as a brain disorder, which subjected her to extremes of temperament and a pronounced absence of reasoning capabilities. During her childhood, Dianne and her sisters, Yvonne and Lynn, were often the objects of their mother's sudden fury, which would erupt without warning. "We lived in a great deal of fear," she told biographer Jerry Roberts. "The part that was so hard was the unpredictability."

Nonetheless, there were good times in the Goldman household, as Feinstein recalled to Keith Love in an interview for the *Los Angeles Times Magazine* (February 25, 1990): "It was not always easy with my mother, but she was still a good mother. She took good care of me and my sisters. I think I can say I was happy growing up." In addition to the stabilizing presence of Leon Goldman, who was as well loved and highly respected by his colleagues as by his daughters, Feinstein benefited from exposure to her father's brother, Morris, a clothing manufacturer who took her to the Monday afternoon sessions of the San Francisco Board of Supervisors—which he would mockingly refer to as the "Board of Stupidvisors." According to Jerry Roberts, it was Morris Goldman who planted the seed of political ambition in his niece, telling her, "Dianne, you get an education and you can do this job."

After attending San Francisco public schools through the eighth grade, Feinstein became the only Jewish student at the Convent of the Sacred Heart, a very strict Catholic high school that catered to the daughters of the city's social elite. In 1951, she entered Stanford University, where, after earning a D in genetics, she switched her major from premedical studies to political science and history. In addition to studying, she modeled clothes on her uncle's television show, played golf, taught horseback riding, and joined the Young Democrats. In her senior year she ran for vice-president of the student body. In the middle of a campaign speech she was attempting to give at a fraternity house, one member of the jeering, heckling audience picked her up and carried her into a shower stall, where she was thoroughly drenched. Rather than protest the action, according to Roberts, Feinstein took it in stride and campaigned harder than ever. Once elected, she used her position to deny the fraternity a much-desired permit to hold an overnight party in celebration of an important football game.

Upon her graduation from Stanford in 1955 with a B.S. degree, Feinstein received an internship with the San Francisco-based Coro Foundation, which sought to provide young people with political experience. After working briefly on the Democrat George Reilly's unsuccessful mayoral campaign, she was assigned by the foundation in 1956 to the San Francisco district attorney's office, where she began working for a thirty-three-year-old prosecutor named Jack Berman. A whirlwind courtship between the two was followed quickly by marriage, on December 2, 1956. Three years later the marriage ended in divorce, leaving Feinstein on her own with an infant daughter, Katherine Anne, who had been born on July 31, 1957. During her marriage, she had become involved in several neighborhood political causes and had worked briefly with the California Industrial Relations Department to help determine a new minimum wage for women and minors in the state.

For the next several years, Feinstein divided her energies between caring for her daughter and exploring her career options, all the while attending occasional civil rights protests and, in 1960, volunteering to work on the presidential campaign of John F. Kennedy. She also developed her creative side, learning to play folk guitar and to sail on the San Francisco Bay. Having been well received by audiences as the male lead in several high school theatrical productions, as an adult she took lessons in the Stanislavsky method of acting, but her stage appearances were greeted less enthusiastically, and an exploratory trip to New York City ended in discouragement.

Confirmed in her belief that her true calling lay in politics, Feinstein in 1961 approached the governor of California, Edmund G. ("Pat") Brown, to inquire about the possibility of employment. She received an offer of membership on the Board of Trust of the California Institution for Women, later called the California Women's Board of Terms and Parole, which set prison terms and parole conditions for female convicts. During her five-year appointment to the board, Feinstein would form her initial views on such key issues as abortion, whose illegality meant that Feinstein had to set terms for the incarceration of abortionists. "Many times," she recalled, as quoted by Jerry Roberts, "the women that they performed an abortion on suffered greatly. . . . I had occasion to read the case histories and saw the morbidity and the mortality, and the suicides and the tragedies. And I think we can never go back to the way it was thirty years ago, because thousands of women are going to die unnecessarily."

Feinstein also had a strong opinion regarding the emotionally charged issue of capital punishment; she vehemently opposed the death penalty, which was not used in California from 1967 to 1992. According to Roberts, Feinstein in the 1960s wrote that "though you may owe it to your fellowman to put a criminal out of commission, there is no moral or religious ground that gives you the right to terminate the life of another human being." Decades later, having come to believe in the potential for capital punishment to deter some crimes, she was quoted by Roberts as saying, "In those days I saw the criminal justice arena very differently than I do now. The nature of the problem has changed. I think my perspective is very different. I was very young and what you see in the world plays a real role in how you come to view things." Some of her statements would seem to indicate a belief that in some cases convicted criminals deserve to die. "I began to look differently at the streets" in light of later experiences, she told Roberts. "I began to see that there are people who have no regard for other people's lives—and over time came to forge the view that by your acts you can abrogate your own right to life."

In 1966 Feinstein resigned from her position as vice-chairperson of the Los Angeles–based Board of Terms and Parole in order to spend more time in San Francisco with her daughter and her second husband, Bertram Feinstein, a neurosurgeon nineteen years her senior, whom she had married on November 11, 1962. It wasn't long, however, before she was once again fully involved in local politics. From 1966 to 1968 she chaired San Francisco's Advisory Committee for Adult Detention, a highly visible position from which she reported on the conditions of the city and county jails, and in 1968 Mayor Joseph Alioto appointed her to a blue-ribbon committee on crime. In 1969 she campaigned for a seat on the eleven-member board of supervisors, spurning suggestions that a woman could not be elected to that body (none had been elected—although a few had been appointed—in forty-eight years).

With her campaign financed in part by her father and her husband, in addition to her own fund-raising efforts, Feinstein outspent her rivals, who were vanquished in the 1969 election partly as a result of her charismatic performance in televised campaign ads, which were unprecedented in an election of that relatively limited scope. According to Roberts, Feinstein spent an estimated one hundred thousand dollars to win a part-time position that paid ninety-six hundred dollars per year in a race decided by about two hundred thousand voters. Of the eighteen candidates running for five open seats, five were incumbents. As the highest overall vote-getter, Feinstein was automatically elected to a two-year term as president of the board, thereby becoming the first woman ever to hold that position. In her nearly nine years on the board, she served as its president for a total of three terms, from 1970 to 1972, from 1974 to 1976, and in 1978.

Not burdened with having to earn a living, as she herself has pointed out, Feinstein became the board's first full-time supervisor, investing more time and energy in her work than did many of her colleagues. Setting the tone for her entire political career, she immediately hired a budget analyst and a think-tank of city planners to help her make decisions. By nature a hands-on manager with a deeply felt need to gather as much background information and first-hand knowledge as possible, she quickly gained a reputation for making her staff work long hours. Universally regarded as a demanding boss, she could sometimes be insensitive, according to Roberts, but she also demonstrated warmth and concern for her colleagues, assistants, and constituents that often went beyond the call of duty. "Dianne is almost unsuited to politics," a longtime ally, California State Assembly Speaker Willie Brown, told Keith Love during Feinstein's gubernatorial candidacy in 1990. "She's too candid, too direct, too incapable of game-playing. But I think that's why she'd make a good governor. She genuinely cares about issues; she's almost a Florence Nightingale. I mean, she once got out of her car and gave some bum in the Tenderloin [district] mouth-to-mouth resuscitation."

During her tenure on the board of supervisors, Feinstein urged an increase in the number of police officers on foot patrol and advocated reform of the city's criminal-justice system. One of her least-popular moves in her first term was her decision to raise or create taxes on employer payrolls, parking utilities, and businesses. In one of the nation's earliest pitched battles between advocates of free speech and those who would restrict pornography, she demonstrated a rather apolitical disregard for how her actions would be perceived by various interest groups when she opted instead to do what she felt was right. After paying a visit in 1970 with her staff to a local theatre featuring pornographic movies, Feinstein fought for tightened zoning restrictions that would limit or abolish adult nightclubs and movie theatres. "We have become a kind of smut capital of the United States," she told reporters at the time, as quoted by Roberts. "I didn't quite believe the real low this kind of activity had reached until I went to one of these theatres and witnessed firsthand some of the activities there. As a woman, I feel very strongly about it, because part of what is happening, what is shown on the screens, works to the basic denigration and humiliation of the female."

This issue would soon come into conflict with Feinstein's strong support of the gay rights movement, due to her expressed belief that pornographic movies also "promoted homosexual cruising." Feinstein did, in fact, play a major role in the advancement of rights for homosexuals. She conferred legitimacy on many gay activist groups by attending rallies during her campaign, authored and obtained passage of a measure to ban job and hiring discrimination against gays, and favored a state law that would legalize all private sexual conduct between or among consenting adults—legislation viewed by the gay and lesbian community as crucial in their fight against police harassment. She also fought to control the city's rapid growth by placing curbs on the height, color, and bulk of new buildings, blocked the construction of a new bridge, and passed a noise-pollution-control ordinance.

Feinstein's initial and stunning successes on the board of supervisors quickly propelled her into the spotlight of the San Francisco political field, inspiring her, in 1971, to launch the first of two unsuccessful attempts to be elected mayor of that city. After a last-minute decision to challenge the weakened incumbent, Joseph Alioto, Feinstein immediately found herself involved in a campaign that pitted a well-connected and seasoned politician against one who was not only a relative novice but also a woman in a landscape dominated by men. Even though the city's registered female voters outnumbered their male counterparts by about 7 percent, there were many questions, and some antagonism, from both genders as to Feinstein's ability to be the first woman to run the city's government. Her campaign was not helped by her unpopular support for busing as a method of integrating public schools, especially after her opponents brought to the public's attention her daughter's attendance at a private school, and she lost allies in the slow-growth movement when she opposed Proposition T, which limited the height of new buildings to six stories. Her city income-tax proposal also bombed. Coming in third behind Alioto and Harold Dobbs, a Republican attorney, Feinstein captured less than one-quarter of the vote.

After her 1973 reelection to the board of supervisors, Feinstein made another abortive attempt, in 1975, to become mayor of a city that had become significantly polarized due to strikes by municipal workers, including police officers, firefighters, bus drivers, sanitation workers, and nurses. Winning only 27 percent of the vote, she again finished third, trailing state senator George Moscone, who captured 40 percent, and John Barbagelata, a fellow supervisor who edged her out with 28 percent of the vote. After the city changed its model of representation from a general one to one in which supervisors were required to live within the voting districts they would represent, Feinstein won reelection in 1977 to become what was now called a district supervisor and president of the board once again.

By the mid-1970s San Francisco was in the throes of dynamic, and often violent, political upheaval characterized by rashes of kidnappings, shootings, robberies, and bombings carried out by such fringe groups as the Symbionese Liberation Army and the New World Liberation Front. An assassination attempt was made on then-President Gerald Ford during a 1975 visit, and Feinstein herself was the object of two bomb attacks, one of which took place in 1976 at her home, where a bomb made of explosive gel was discovered by her daughter after it failed to detonate. When the windows of her vacation home overlooking Monterey Bay were shot out in 1977, Feinstein began packing a .38-caliber pistol for self-defense. "In San Francisco," Sidney Blumenthal wrote in the *New Republic* (August 13, 1990), "the dream of the Diggers' utopia had turned rancid; it was the age of Altamont, the Black Panther Party, and Patty 'Tanya' Hearst." Feinstein's personal traumas were compounded by the deaths from cancer of her father, in 1975, and her second husband, in April 1978.

In no mood to enter another bruising mayoral race, Feinstein told a reporter on the morning of November 27, 1978 that she planned to retire from politics. Hours later, as president of the board, she automatically became mayor of San Francisco after a disgruntled former supervisor named Dan White fatally shot George Moscone and Harvey Milk, the first openly gay supervisor, in their offices after Moscone refused to reappoint White to the board, from which he had recently resigned. That afternoon Feinstein held a press conference as acting mayor at which she announced the deaths and ordered an immediate citywide state of mourning. She won high marks for her strength, grace, and presence of mind, as evidenced by an editorial that appeared at the time in the *San Francisco Chronicle*, as quoted by Blumenthal: "She was poised. She was eloquent. She was restrained. And she was reassuring and strong."

Feinstein's healing leadership helped imbed her image forever into the hearts and minds of San Franciscans during a particularly strife-ridden period of the city's history. Just nine days before the double assassination, nine hundred members of Jim Jones's People's Temple, most of whom were residents of the Bay Area, where Jones had only two years before been named city housing commissioner, had committed suicide in Guyana. Yet another trying episode occurred just a few months after her installment as mayor, which was formalized on December 4, 1978 by a vote of six to two by the remaining supervisors. On May 21, 1979, at the conclusion of his trial on two counts of first-degree murder, Dan White was instead found guilty of the lesser charge of voluntary manslaughter, for which he received a sentence of seven years and eight months. (Released after serving six years, he committed suicide upon returning to San Francisco.) The ensuing outrage on the part of the city's gay community culminated in a twenty-four-hour period of marches and riots that would later become known as "White Night," during which the mayor, separated physically and ideologically from the police chief, Charles Gain, failed to restore order before the riots produced significant damage in the area surrounding city hall.

After finishing out Moscone's term, Feinstein was reelected in 1979. In the November primary, she won 42 percent of the vote, while her opponent, supervisor Quentin Kopp, a conservative Democrat, won 40 percent. The rest of the votes went to a third candidate supported by gay voters, who subsequently provided Feinstein's margin of victory in the December runoff, which was mandated because no candidate had captured a clear majority. During her first full term as mayor, Feinstein worked to strengthen the city's services, increasing police presence and improving garbage pickup and public transportation. Near the end of the term, however, a fringe left-wing political group called the White Panthers waged a recall campaign against the mayor to protest her support of tighter handgun restrictions. The recall movement was not much of a threat, however, until her veto, in December 1982, of a domestic-partners law, which would have granted some benefits, such as insurance, to unmarried couples (straight or gay) who registered at city hall. Within a few weeks of the veto, the White Panthers had gathered thirty-five thousand petitions, more than enough to force a recall vote. She survived the April 1983 recall vote easily, taking over 80 percent of the ballots cast. The huge margin of victory had the added benefit of guaranteeing an easy victory in the general election later that year. In 1984 Walter F. Mondale, the Democratic presidential candidate, considered naming Feinstein as his running mate, but she was eventually passed over in favor of New York congresswoman Geraldine A. Ferraro.

During her second term as mayor, Feinstein grappled with San Francisco's rapid growth by obtaining federal money to overhaul the city's aging trolley car system and developing the "Downtown Plan" to restrict the areas in which skyscrapers could be built. But she also earned an increasingly conservative reputation on issues involving gays and women. Although the city's network of AIDS services, for which she had secured federal funding, was considered to be a model for other cities, Feinstein had angered many gay activists by shutting down the city's bathhouses. And despite her support of the Equal Rights Amendment, she opposed such concepts as comparable worth (pay equity for female city workers) and automatic job reinstatement after maternity leave. Although she declared that she was pro-choice, Feinstein refused to allow a routine street closing for an abortion rights rally, and she did not endorse a symbolic "Women's Reproductive Freedom Day" resolution. Defending herself in her interview with Jordan Bonfante, she contended, "I've lived a feminist life. I had to quit a job because there was no maternity leave. I raised a child as a single mother. I put together legislation. I haven't been a marcher, but I've lived it."

Compelled by San Francisco's two-term limit to relinquish the mayoralty, from which she departed in 1988 with high approval ratings, Feinstein next set her sights on the governorship of California after George Deukmejian announced that he would not seek a third term. In the primary in 1990, she won 52 percent of the vote, easily defeating Attorney General John Van de Kamp, who had waffled on capital punishment, but she ran into trouble in the general election. Campaigning on a pro-environment, abortion rights platform that also included a plank in favor of the death penalty, Feinstein found it difficult to differentiate herself from Republican United States senator Pete Wilson, whose positions were similar. That she had also left San Francisco with an estimated $172 million deficit weakened her claims of being a fiscal conservative, even though she tried hard to convey to voters the fact that every fiscal year closes with a projected shortfall, for which compensation is usually duly forthcoming in the actual budget.

With her campaign financed largely by her third husband, Richard C. Blum, a wealthy investment banker whom she had married on January 20, 1980, Feinstein came under intense scrutiny. (Both she and Wilson, according to the 1994 edition of *Politics in America*, would later be fined for spending irregularities.) "Technically, no woman married to an investment banker then could ever be in public life," Feinstein complained in an interview with Robin Toner for the *New York Times Magazine* (September 30, 1990). "This is all his business. I have nothing to do with it. It's his—and it was before we were married. . . . Clearly there's a strategy here that's really basically pretty sexist. It's sort of implicit that somehow the woman can't be doing all this by herself." Wilson's larger bank account and better party organization ultimately carried him to victory in November, although with less than a majority (49 percent to 46 percent).

Feinstein ran for the United States Senate in 1992, which was widely known as the "year of the woman" because of the unprecedented numbers of women running for and elected to local, state, and national office in the wake of their outrage over the treatment of alleged sexual-harassment victim Anita Hill during hearings held by the Senate Judiciary Committee in October 1991 on the nomination of Clarence Thomas to the Supreme Court. That Thomas was confirmed despite Hill's testimony galvanized female voters, lending new meaning to the often-bandied term "gender gap." When he vacated his Senate seat to assume the governorship, Wilson had appointed a political consultant named John Seymour in his place, and a special election was scheduled for 1992 to determine a permanent replacement for the remaining two years of the term. After trouncing state controller Gray Davis in the primary, capturing 58 percent of the vote, Feinstein easily defeated the little-known Seymour in November 1992. Because Feinstein's victory occurred in a special election, she was sworn in ahead of Barbara Boxer, another Democrat from northern California, on November 10, 1992. Two years later she was reelected to a full six-year term when she edged out Michael Huffington, a millionaire Republican congressman from Santa Barbara, 47 to 45 percent. Because the vote in the general election was so close (except in San Francisco, where Feinstein garnered 80 percent of the vote), Huffington refused to concede his loss until February 1995.

Since her election to the Senate in 1992, Feinstein has written legislation that initially was given little chance of passage but which subsequently won the approval of both houses of Congress and was signed into law by President Bill Clinton. Such legislation included a ban on the future manufacture, sale, and possession of semiautomatic military combat weapons and the California Desert Protection Act, which incorporates more than three million acres into two national parks, Joshua Tree and Death Valley, and one national preserve, the East Mojave. Feinstein serves on the Senate Judiciary, Foreign Relations, and Rules and Administration Committees. On the Foreign Relations Committee, she is the ranking member on the subcommittee that oversees the Middle East; she also serves on the subcommittees on African affairs and East Asian and Pacific affairs. Appointed to Judiciary's immigration subcommittee, she has proposed legislation aimed at stopping illegal immigration.

During her career, Feinstein has been named on numerous occasions to the United States Conference of Mayors, and she has served as a director of the Bank of California, cochair of the San Francisco Education Fund's Permanent Fund, and president of the Japan Society of northern California. She has received the President's Medal from the University of California at San Francisco and honorary degrees from, among other institutions, the University of San Francisco, Mills College, Antioch University, and Golden Gate University. She has also been the recipient of the United States Navy's Distinguished Civilian Award, the Episcopal Church's Award for Service, and the French Légion d'Honneur.

Since 1984 Dianne Feinstein has lived with her third husband, Richard Blum, in a Tudor house across the street from where she grew up. From her marriage to Blum, she has three stepchildren, Heidi, Annette, and Eileen. Her daughter from her first marriage, Katherine Feinstein Mariano, is a former assistant district attorney in San Francisco who is now in private practice. Her granddaughter, Eileen Feinstein Mariano, was born to Katherine and her husband, Rick, on September 18, 1992. While she has little time for hobbies, Dianne Feinstein enjoys reading, hiking with her husband, and painting.

Selected Biographical References: Los Angeles Times mag p11+ F 25 '90 pors; N Y Times Mag p28+ S 30 '90 pors; New Republic 203:23+ Ag 13 '90; People 34:66+ O 8 '90 pors; Time 135:24+ Je 18 '90 pors; Morris, Celia. Dianne Feinstein: Storming the Statehouse (1992); Politics in America, 1996; Roberts, Jerry. Never Let Them See You Cry (1994); Who's Who of American Women, 1993–94.

AP/Wide World Photos

Flanagan, Tommy

Mar. 16, 1930- Jazz pianist. Address: 139 W. 82nd St., New York, NY 10024

Lauded by one admiring critic as "a poet of jazz piano," for his exceptionally graceful melodic invention, Tommy Flanagan is perhaps the premier exponent of the single-note, improvised line, a style rooted in bebop. After decades of accompanying such major jazz figures as Miles Davis, John Coltrane, Sonny Rollins, and Ella Fitzgerald, with whom he was associated for more than twelve years, Flanagan now leads his own highly successful trio, which currently includes Peter Washington on bass and Lewis Nash on drums. Of the trio's many critically acclaimed recordings over the years, four have been nominated for Grammies. Flanagan himself was named top jazz pianist by *Jazztimes*, in 1990, and by the *Down Beat* readers' poll, in 1990 and 1993, and critics' poll, in 1992 and 1994. In 1993 he won the coveted Jazzpar prize, one of the world's most prestigious jazz awards, and in 1994 he was named to the American Jazz Hall of Fame, at Rutgers University's Institute of Jazz Studies.

Esteemed as a consummate craftsman, especially by his fellow musicians, Flanagan has played on over three hundred albums (more than one hundred between 1956 and 1968 alone) in the course of his career, working with a virtual who's who of jazz instrumentalists and singers, among them Milt Jackson, Paul Chambers, Donald Byrd, Coleman Hawkins, Kenny Dorham, Wes Montgomery, Gene Ammons, Pepper Adams, Phil Woods, Freddie Hubbard, Kenny Burrell, and Thad Jones. Since leaving Ella Fitzgerald in 1978 to go out on his own, as a soloist and in duo and trio settings, Flanagan has developed arrangements of increasing authority and fire from his immense store of standards, jazz classics, and his own compositions. On his recordings, he tends to feature the music of musicians with whom he feels an affinity, notably Duke Ellington, Billy Strayhorn, Thelonious Monk, Tadd Dameron, and Thad Jones. Many of his albums are tributes that focus on one composer. "I like to give a song a reading from my soul, especially if I'm connected to the writer and know what he meant," Flanagan explained to Leonard Lopate in an interview that was broadcast on the WNYC-AM radio program *New York and Company* on November 17, 1994. "I like to just keep adding what I feel he would like to hear in his music." The results of this organic process are creations of almost classical balance, alive with vivid melodic thrusts, unexpected accents, and spontaneous associations.

Tommy Lee Flanagan was born on March 16, 1930 in Conant Gardens, an entrenched black community in northeast Detroit. He was the youngest of the six children, five of them boys, of Johnson Alexander Flanagan and his wife, Ida, both of whom had migrated north from Georgia in search of a better life. His father was a letter carrier for the post office for thirty-five years, enabling the family to withstand the lean years of the Depression; his mother helped out by selling dresses for a mail-order company. A music lover who knew about and appreciated jazz, Mrs. Flanagan made sure there was always a piano in the house. One of Flanagan's earliest memories is of a player piano, which he has remembered watching intently, mesmerized by the movement of the keys. The player piano was succeeded by an upright, and by the time he was ten or so, he was able to pick out the pieces his oldest brother, Johnson Jr., was practicing. It wasn't long before Tommy was following Johnson and his sister, Ida, off to piano lessons with Gladys Dillard, a popular local teacher.

Flanagan's first instrument, however, was the clarinet, a Christmas gift when he was six years old. Each of his siblings also received a musical instrument for Christmas—a different one for each child—and they learned to play together. With the aid of a chart, Flanagan taught himself the correct clarinet fingering; by adolescence, he was proficient enough to join the band at Northern High School, but the clarinet never completely satisfied him. After hearing recordings by the pianists Art Tatum, Teddy Wilson, and Fats Waller, he was hooked. Eventually, playing the piano supplanted baseball as his favorite pastime. "Nobody had to keep after me to practice," he recalled to Ken Franckling in an interview for *Jazztimes* (August 1989). "They had to tell me to stop." Trained in the classical tradition of Bach and Chopin, Flanagan supplemented his formal studies by listening to such pathbreaking jazz pianists as Nat "King" Cole and to the new style of music being played by alto saxophonist Charlie Parker and pianist Bud Powell. By his midteens he was spending most of his free time jamming with other young jazz enthusiasts.

In the years immediately following World War II, Detroit was a bubbling cauldron of jazz talent, with plenty of places for musicians to get together and jam and several flourishing jazz clubs. Among the many well-known musicians who honed their skills in postwar Detroit were trumpeter Donald Byrd, tenor saxophonist Billy Mitchell, baritone saxophonist Pepper Adams, cornetist and flugelhornist Thad Jones, drummer Elvin Jones, bassist Major Holley, singers Betty Carter and Sheila Jordan, and pianists Barry Harris and Roland Hanna. The pianist Hank Jones, the eldest of the "Jones boys," was already established and was a pacesetter for some of his younger counterparts. "It was either be good at what you were doing or go to the factory, so we formed our own piano assembly line," Flanagan quipped to Leonard Lopate.

The presence of so many prodigiously gifted young players spurred Flanagan on. "It was a great time to be growing up [in Detroit] . . . ," he told Ken Franckling. "I met and heard everybody up close. I heard Tatum. I even had a chance to play with Bird [Charlie Parker] a few times as a teenager when he came to Detroit." He has not forgotten the impact of Tatum's visit to a club where he happened to be playing. He recalled that night to Bret Primack and Richard Dubin for *Contemporary Keyboard* (December 1979): "It scared me to death. . . . I met him, and he said he liked the way I played. He tried to encourage me, even though I knew I was stumbling all over myself. I played some things I heard him play—'Lullaby of the Leaves,' 'Sweet Lorraine,' stuff like that. That night after the gig, I went to an after-hours place to hear him. . . . He was amazing. It looked so effortless." Shortly thereafter, when Flanagan heard the revolutionary pianist Bud Powell perform with the Cootie Williams orchestra at a nightspot in Detroit and began playing closer attention to Powell's records, he told Franckling, "BAM! It was all summed up, right there. Everything started to come together."

Flanagan's early gigs in Detroit, in the late 1940s, were with vibraphonist Milt Jackson (who later became part of the Modern Jazz Quartet), saxophonist Lucky Thompson, and Billy Mitchell, whose band at the time included Thad and Elvin Jones. He eventually became the house pianist at a main jazz spot, the Bluebird, where he backed up visiting artists, including Miles Davis, the young trumpeter whose lyrical, slightly mournful tone would soon become a leading voice of jazz, and tenor saxophonist Sonny Stitt, among others. After serving a two-year hitch in the United States Army, including a stint in Korea, Flanagan returned to Detroit, where, in 1953, he joined guitarist Kenny Burrell's group. He moved to New York City when Burrell did, in February 1956. "We just kinda got fed up with Detroit," Flanagan explained to Wayne Enstice and Paul Rubin for their book *Jazz Spoken Here: Conversations with Twenty-two Musicians* (1992). "There was only the same jobs repeating themselves; we made all the cycles. We felt it was time for us to go to New York to see if Detroit jazz could stand up in New York. . . . And it did. We kinda knew it would if we just had a chance to play."

At a loft jam session in Manhattan shortly after his arrival, Flanagan met the bassist Oscar Pettiford. He sat in and played "Jack the Bear," an Ellington composition that features the bass. Impressed, Pettiford invited the newcomer to rehearse with his big band, and Flanagan wound up playing a concert at Town Hall with the group. "Right after the concert," he recalled to Lee Jeske for a *Down Beat* profile (July 1982), "Elvin [Jones] was looking for me because Bud Powell didn't show up that night at Birdland [the major Midtown jazz club at the time]. So I finished that two weeks at Birdland for Bud. It was a trio with Tommy Potter and Elvin, and after playing all those years in Detroit with Elvin, it was comfortable. I guess people knew I was in New York then."

It didn't take long for word about the latest Detroit pianist to spread. In early March 1956 Flanagan did his first recording sessions, with Thad Jones, Burrell, Mitchell, Pettiford, and others for the Blue Note label; one of those sessions was issued as *Detroit-New York Junction*. On March 16 he recorded some tracks with Miles Davis for the trumpeter's Prestige album *Collector's Items*. That summer he accompanied Ella Fitzgerald at the Newport Jazz Festival. He also added his dancing lines to Sonny Rollins's dark-toned tenor sax on the Prestige collection *Saxophone Colossus and More*, which has since come to be seen as a benchmark in Rollins's career. In the fall of that busy year, Flanagan embarked on a year-long tour with trombonist J. J. Johnson, during which he made his recording debut as a leader, in a session in Stockholm on August 15, 1957, fronting bassist Wilbur Little and drummer Elvin Jones. The resulting disc, *Tommy Flanagan Overseas*, was issued in the United States by Prestige.

Upon his return to New York, Flanagan cut several albums, including one called *The Cats*, with saxophonist John Coltrane, Burrell, and trumpeter Idries Sulieman. In late 1958 he played an engagement at the popular downtown Manhattan jazz club the Composer with his trio, then returned to work as a sideman, for trombonist Tyree Glenn and trumpeter Harry "Sweets" Edison. In the spring of 1959, Coltrane fired the opening volley of the musical revolution to come with the release of his album *Giant Steps*. Flanagan joined the sax player at the session, along with Paul Chambers on bass and Art Taylor on drums. The album (especially its title track, with its progressions of minor thirds and minor fifths that Coltrane had devised as an alternative to the standard circle of fifths) remains an important jazz document.

After touring throughout South America with an all-star band that included Coleman Hawkins on tenor sax, Roy Eldridge on trumpet, and Herbie Mann on flute, in 1961 Flanagan joined Hawkins's band, with whom he recorded several albums, including *Moonglow*, *Bean Bag*, and *Night Hawk*. It was during a British tour with Hawkins that

Flanagan once again crossed paths with Ella Fitzgerald, who was also performing in England. Taken by Flanagan's adeptness at accompanying, she asked him to join her backup group. He accepted, remaining with the singer for two and a half years. A stint with singer Tony Bennett, who shared Flanagan's affection for Ellington and Strayhorn ballads, followed. After an abortive attempt to gain a foothold in the cliquish local club scene in California in the mid-1960s, Flanagan returned to Fitzgerald's band in 1968. He spent the next decade concertizing, touring, and recording with her; between engagements he occasionally slipped into the studio with other leaders or on his own.

While he was Fitzgerald's pianist and musical director, Flanagan rarely unpacked his bags, for the notoriously hard-working singer habitually worked forty-eight weeks out of the year. He described those years to Whitney Balliett, the veteran jazz critic of the *New Yorker* (February 24, 1986): "Working for Ella was different from working for a lot of other singers, because she had such high standards. Her intonation was perfect. [Guitarist] Jim Hall once said that he could tune up to her voice." While Fitzgerald relied on Flanagan's lyrical introductions and sparkling harmonic settings, he got only occasional, brief solos. During one break, he recorded his only solo album to date, *Alone Too Long* (1977), for the Denon label, and on another he cut a trio album for Galaxy called *Something Borrowed, Something Blue* (1978) with Fitzgerald's bassist Keter Betts and drummer Jimmie Smith. Eventually, however, the wear of constant traveling, repeating the same material, and staying on top of current pop tunes began to take its toll on Flanagan, and in March 1978 he had a mild heart attack. After his recovery, he decided to strike out on his own. He had been, in his words, "toying with the idea" for some time. "There was no problem with me finding work . . . , and there were a lot of opportunities to record, but I just never felt prepared to do them because I was doing enough preparing to stay up on [Fitzgerald's] job," he explained to Lee Jeske. "It was a good time to leave, I think. Ella . . . told me shortly afterwards that I *should* be on my own, not always backing her up. She said I had too much talent to be in an accompanying role."

In the late 1970s and early 1980s, Flanagan appeared regularly at small clubs like Bradley's, the popular New York duo room, first with Red Mitchell on bass and then with the classically trained Czech bassist George Mraz, who played many of the trickiest bebop melodies in unison with the piano and tracked Flanagan's harmonic ideas like a shadow. As Flanagan told Ken Franckling, "He is one of the few bass players who doesn't worry so much about being heard as being felt. You can hear that pulse. And his intonation is just about as perfect as you can hear on any string instrument." To document their intertwined and vibrant music, Flanagan and Mraz recorded a duo album, *Ballads and Blues*, which was released by Inner City in 1979. Two years earlier, Inner City had issued *Eclypso*, a trio date on which Flanagan and Mraz were joined by Elvin Jones. *Eclypso* was nominated for a Grammy as best recording by a jazz group. That disc, along with two other albums, *The Tommy Flanagan Tokyo Recital* (1975), featuring the music of Ellington and Strayhorn, and *Montreux '77*, both on the Pablo label, had established Flanagan's identity as a premier trio player. Successful diversions from the trio format were two-piano sessions with Hank Jones, released by Galaxy in 1978 under the titles *Our Delights* and *More Delights* (a sequel called *I'm All Smiles* was issued in 1984), and with Kenny Barron, recorded by Denon as *Together*.

By the early 1980s Flanagan had solidified his reputation as the leader of an outstanding trio through the release of such acclaimed albums as *The Magnificent Tommy Flanagan* (Progressive) and *Giant Steps* (Enja), with George Mraz and the drummer Al Foster, both of which were nominated for Grammies, and *Super Session* (Inner City), with Red Mitchell and Elvin Jones. Lee Jeske assessed *The Magnificent Tommy Flanagan* and *Super Session* for *Down Beat*: "Flanagan has a prodigious but subtle technique. His style is rooted in bebop, but it reflects the whole jazz tradition, from gospel and blues through the romanticism of Bill Evans and into modernism. In his many years as a sideman and accompanist, he learned to listen and respond, aware of his musical surroundings. Consequently, his playing has the coherence and sense of musical purpose that mark the very finest jazz." Furthermore, Jeske wrote, Flanagan's introductions "are often striking—like a good lead on a story, they hook you into the material that follows. His arrangements are clear and straightforward but never commonplace. Most important, he is a very inventive soloist, never at a loss for a new harmonic angle on an old song."

Thelonica, a 1982 release on Enja, was a tribute to the pianist Thelonious Monk and Monk's friend Baroness Nica de Koenigswarter, a devoted jazz fan and supporter. For the collection, Flanagan worked up six Monk tunes, including "Off Minor" and "Ugly Beauty," easing his way around Monk's angular twists and turns without losing his upbeat flow. He composed the title tune, which combines the names of the two friends, himself, and stirred in nuances of Monk's "Brilliant Corners" and "Mysterioso." The tune both opens and closes the album, first as an extravagantly rich and varied piano solo, then as a trio number. Mraz and Art Taylor caught Flanagan's accents with panache on the up-tempo tracks and backed him with sensitivity on the ballads "Pannonica" and "Reflections." *Thelonica* was selected as one of the ten best records of the 1980s by the *Village Voice*, and it brought Flanagan a fourth Grammy nomination.

Nights at the Vanguard (Uptown), a live recording made before a packed house at the Village Vanguard in 1986, inspired a rave review from Chuck Berg, in the April 1988 issue of *Down Beat*: "Tommy Flanagan has been at the summit of pianistic creativity for decades. It's amazing, then, to observe that he has ascended to yet another level. . . . Flanagan is playing not just over, but beyond the rainbow. With superb, indeed, sublime backing from bassist George Mraz and Al Foster, Flanagan etches deceptively simple arabesques whose balance and form are of classical measure. Like the leanness found in the paintings of Pablo Picasso and Joan Miró, Flanagan doesn't waste a thing. Each note counts." Tracks include Thad Jones's "A Biddy Ditty," the punctuated, bluesy "Like Old Times," and Monk's wry "San Francisco Holiday (Worry Later)."

The 1989 collection *Jazz Poet*, on Timeless, presents an eclectic selection from Flanagan's extensive musical catalogue, with numbers by composers ranging from W. C. Handy to Rodgers and Hart. Backed by George Mraz and the young drummer Kenny Washington, who offered what David Grogan, writing in *People* (August 20, 1990), called "seemingly telepathic support," Flanagan turned Matt Dennis's "That Tired Routine Called Love" into "a restless romp" and brought "a lilting tenderness" to J. J. Johnson's "Lament," and he glided through the up-tempo tunes "with an ease that calls to mind the movements of Fred Astaire." "While avoiding pyrotechnics and clichés, Flanagan plays with such self-assurance that his harmonic and rhythmic choices seem constantly surprising, and perfect," Grogan concluded. "He makes it seem as if the piano were singing a song of itself." *Jazz Poet* was voted one of the ten best records of 1990 by *Billboard*.

On *Beyond the Bluebird* (Timeless, 1991), Flanagan revisited his Detroit roots, accompanied by guitarist Kenny Burrell, George Mraz, and Lewis Nash, who has been Flanagan's drummer since 1989. The group percolated through some Charlie Parker blues, Benny Carter's "Blues in My Heart," Thad Jones's "5021" (whose opening phrase Flanagan frequently quotes), two Flanagan originals, including the blues-saturated title tune, and the Jerome Kern standard "Yesterdays." In the view of *Village Voice* jazz critic Gary Giddins, writing in the January 14, 1992 edition of the weekly, the "superb" collection served as "a model of Flanagan's penchant for interacting with his musicians." Describing Flanagan and Burrell's nine-minute version of "Yesterdays," Giddins said, "The arrangement never relaxes its drama or interest yet never breaks the thread of constantly recapitulated melody. . . . It's the kind of true duet you don't often hear unless John Lewis and Milt Jackson [the pianist and vibraphonist, respectively, of the Modern Jazz Quartet] are on stage."

Two of Flanagan's most recent recordings are tributes. *Let's Play the Music of Thad Jones* (Enja, 1993) features eleven tunes by that flugelhornist and composer. The prevailing mood on the disc, on which Flanagan is supported by the Danish bassist Jesper Lundgaard and Lewis Nash, is live-wire, sinewy bebop, although there are some pensive moments. *Lady Be Good . . . for Ella* (Verve, 1994), an affectionate homage to the singer, includes a number of classics that he often played with her, among them "How High the Moon," "Angel Eyes," "Cherokee," and two versions of "Oh, Lady Be Good," long a vehicle for Fitzgerald's exuberant scat singing. *Down Beat*'s Jack Sohmer hailed the recording as "a performance drenched in feeling." In connection with winning the Jazzpar prize in 1993, Flanagan, Lundgaard, and Nash recorded *Flanagan's Shenanigans* for the Swedish label Storyville; the trio is augmented on some tracks by a small group of brass and woodwinds.

Highlights among Flanagan's many concert appearances in recent years include Lincoln Center's Classical Jazz series focusing on the music of Tadd Dameron (1988) and Bud Powell (1989); dates with his trio at the Montreux Jazz Festival (1990), Carnegie Hall (1991), and the Newport Jazz Festival (1991); two tours of Japan as a member of 100 Golden Fingers, a group of top American mainstream jazz pianists; and appearances at the Marciac Festival, in the south of France, the Pori Festival, in Finland, and the Playboy Festival, in Chicago.

Performing before huge audiences at festivals is part of the successful jazz musician's life, but for some listeners, the details that distinguish Flanagan's playing are most easily appreciated in more intimate settings. Whitney Balliett described the ambience the pianist creates in a club in his *New Yorker* profile: "Flanagan demands close listening. His single-note melodic lines move up and down, but, since he is also a percussive player, who likes to accent unlikely notes, his phrases tend to move constantly toward and away from the listener. The resulting dynamics are subtle and attractive. These horizontal-vertical melodic lines give the impression of being two lines, each of which Flanagan would like attention paid to. There are also interior movements within these lines: urgent double-time runs; clusters of flatted notes, like pretend stumbles; sudden backward-leaning half-time passages; dancing runs; and rests, which are both pauses and chambers for the preceding phrase to echo in. Flanagan is never less than first-rate. But once in a while . . . he becomes impassioned. Then he will play throughout the evening with inspiration and great heat, turning out stunning solo after stunning solo, making the listeners feel they had been at a godly event."

Flanagan himself explained his technique to Balliett in this way: "The fact is, I try to play like a horn player, like I'm blowing into the piano. The sound of a piece—its overall tonality—is what concerns me. If it's a blues in C, you play the whole thing like a circle. You have the sound of C in your head, your mind is clouded with the sound. The chords of a tune are not that important, and neither is the melody. But they are both there if you get lost." More recently, in the radio interview with Leonard Lopate, he said, "I think music should be made easy to listen to, not so crowded up that you can't separate the lines that you're playing. . . . If you can play something very clean, and it has a lot of technical difficulty, then that's good." He also aims for some of the qualities he admires in Art Tatum's playing. "When you're playing alone, you're really accompanying yourself, which was a beautiful way that Tatum played," he explained to Lopate. "He had so many tools to work with. He could play a melody in his right hand and accompany with the left hand in such a way it was on a melody of its own. I try to get close to that."

By Flanagan's own account, he rarely practices, although he occasionally takes out a Chopin waltz or some other classical piece and reads through it. And he sometimes tries out phrases that have lodged in his mind and might lead to a new composition. In his spare time, he often listens to the music of Duke Ellington and Billy Strayhorn, and he regularly attends friends' performances. After undergoing heart surgery in 1991 and 1992, Flanagan cut back on touring for a while, but he has since resumed a more active performance schedule, and he is planning to record a collection of Sonny Rollins tunes. His wife, Diana, whom he married in 1976 and who acts as his manager and record producer, accompanies him on tour. They make their home in an apartment on the Upper West Side of Manhattan, near Central Park, where he enjoys taking long, leisurely strolls. Flanagan has three children—Tommy Jr., Rachel, and Jennifer—from his first marriage, which ended in divorce.

A modest and self-deprecating man, Flanagan deflects compliments. "I just want to sit down to a good piano with my band and play as well as I can," he told Stanley Crouch, as quoted in the *Village Voice* (June 4, 1985). "You can't mess around. I found that out from people like Coleman Hawkins, who was an amazing musician and who was so committed to the art and the passion of the music that he always gave his best. As much as I can, I try to be like him. If I can do that, . . . every good thing and every bad thing can be put into perspective, and I can give the audience something complete, something well done, and something with real feeling."

Selected Biographical References: Contemporary Keyboard p12+ D '79 por; Down Beat 49:25+ Jl '82 por, 60:20+ Ja '93 por; Jazztimes p18+ Ag '89 pors; New Yorker 54:203+ N 20 '78; 62:80+ F 24 '86; New Grove Dictionary of Jazz (1988)

Ford, Richard

Feb. 16, 1944- Writer. Address: c/o Amanda Urban, International Creative Management, 40 W. 57th St., New York, NY 10019

"I'm probably never going to write out of one voice and don't wish that I could," Richard Ford once told an interviewer. While Ford's half-dozen works of fiction have in common male protagonists and often feature situations with the potential for violence, their locales have ranged all over and even outside the United States—from Ford's native Mississippi to Mexico to the suburban New Jersey setting of his third novel, *The Sportswriter* (1986), the work that won him a significant following. Ford, who himself has lived in an unusually large number of places, has been called perhaps the country's "most peripatetic fiction writer." His nomadic lifestyle, taken together with his body of work, has made him "a symbol of rootless America," in one journalist's words.

Although he identifies himself as a Mississippian, Ford rejects the label of southern writer. "What [the term] used to mean," he explained to Jane A. Mullen for the *Christian Science Monitor* (July 30, 1986), "was that you wrote like [William] Faulkner. That's mostly all it has ever meant, because before Faulkner there was no such thing as an important, isolable tradition of southern literature. And there is none now. There are just good writers and not-so-good writers." One of the "good" writers to whom he has often been compared is Ernest Hemingway, and, like that master of the novel and the short story, Ford has been ranked among the brightest literary lights of his generation. His most recent work is the novel *Independence Day* (1995).

John Foley/Knopf

Richard Ford was born on February 16, 1944 in Jackson, Mississippi, the only child of Parker Carrol Ford, a traveling starch salesman, and Edna (Akin) Ford. As a boy he suffered from dyslexia. He overcame the affliction with the help of his mother, who "stood over [him] and made [him] learn to read," as he told Dinitia Smith for the *New York Times* (August 22, 1995). Ford added about his condition, "It makes me pore over words, sound words out in my mind"—a practice that, as Smith observed, may have contributed to his prowess as a writer. It was through Edna Ford that the boy came to have a high regard for authors: the family's house was across the street from the house occupied at the time by the novelist and short-story writer Eudora Welty, and Ford's mother pointed the famous woman out to him. "I could tell from the tone of my mother's voice that being a writer was something estimable," he recalled to Dinitia Smith.

Because Parker Ford's occupation kept him on the road during the workweek, Richard Ford saw his father mainly on weekends or when he and his mother accompanied him on business trips. Ford has written that his "most enduring memories of childhood" are "mental snapshots not of [his] hometown streets or its summery lawns but of roads leading *out* of town. Highway 51 to New Orleans. Highway 80 to Vicksburg and darkest Alabama." When Ford was eight years old, his father suffered a heart attack (he would have a second, fatal one less than a decade later), and thereafter Edna Ford drove her husband to and from his business meetings. As a consequence, Richard Ford began living part of the time at the Marion, the hotel run by his grandparents in Little Rock, Arkansas.

In an autobiographical article originally printed in the San Francisco magazine *Trips* and republished in *Harper's* (June 1988), Ford wrote with affection about his grandparents, particularly his grandfather: "He was a fatty who played winter golf in pleated gabardines, shot pool and quail. He qualified as a sport, a Shriner, a wide, public man, a toddling character in a blue suit with change in his pockets and a money clip. To me, he was the exotic brought to common earth, and I loved him." Ford recalled that while "certain things *were* acknowledged lacking," such as children his own age and neighbors, there was a steady stream of guests, employees, "lobby lizards" ("older men with baffling nicknames like Spider, Goldie, Ish—men who lived out in town but showed up each day"), and others, spied by Ford from his window on the sixth floor, who were simply passing through town. "Was it lonely for me? No. Never," he wrote. "It is not bad or lonely to see that life goes on at all times, with you or without you. Home is finally a variable concept."

During his teen years Ford became a "petty troublemaker," in the words of Bruce Weber, who profiled the writer for the *New York Times Magazine* (April 10, 1988). His mother, who eventually moved to Little Rock, prevented him from landing in serious trouble, however, by telling him, "Don't call up here from jail. Because there won't be anybody home." Ford apparently heeded the lesson in personal responsibility; for a time after his father died and before he went to college, he lived on his own and worked for the Missouri Pacific Railroad, as a fireman on a train that sprayed the shoulders of railroad tracks with the insecticide DDT.

In 1962 Ford enrolled at Michigan State University, in East Lansing, intending—per his grandfather's advice—to study hotel management. Before long, however, he switched his major to English. As an undergraduate he composed some short stories, although he had not yet committed himself to a career as a writer. Following his graduation from college, in 1966, Ford made several ill-fated career choices: he taught for a year in Flint, Michigan; attempted to join the ranks of the Arkansas State Police, which rejected him, in part, because of his college degree; and enlisted in the United States Marine Corps, only to be discharged after contracting hepatitis. In 1967 he matriculated at Washington University Law School, in St. Louis, Missouri, where he spent one semester before realizing that he was dissatisfied with the direction his life was taking.

Ford thus moved to New York City to be with Kristina Hensley, the woman with whom he had fallen in love in college and from whom he had since become separated. Early in 1968, Ford has recalled, he decided to marry Hensley and to become a writer—"the two decisions that changed [his] life." Regarding the latter step, Ford told Bruce Weber, "That's just the spark of anyone's imagination. You think to yourself: 'Let's do something different.' And being a writer just seemed like a good idea. It was just casting off into the dark. But I think that's the way people make themselves into whatever they finally make themselves, good or otherwise."

Ford supported himself during his time in New York by working as the assistant science editor of *American Druggist* magazine. He and Hensley then undertook the first of the many moves they have made. During the late 1960s Ford remained in Irvine, California long enough to study writing and literature under the novelists E. L. Doctorow and Oakley Hall at the University of California, where he earned his M.F.A. degree in 1970. It was in the same year that he felt "ready to begin being a writer," as he phrased it in another article for *Harper's* magazine (August 1988). He submitted a number of his short stories to literary magazines, without the desired result. After more than a year had passed, two of Ford's stories were accepted for publication by a magazine based in New Zealand. His initial elation cooled after that success failed to lead to his being published in the United States.

Ford's response to that situation was to start work on a novel. "I needed to get better—much, much better at what I was doing, and in ways I don't even want to think about now," he wrote in the August 1988 *Harper's* piece. "A novel would take those years; I could go more slowly; there was more to work on, get better at. No demoralizing rejections would crash into my mailbox every morning. . . . And in trade for this easement, this slow-going, this sumptuous usage of my time and youth, I'd have a novel, maybe, when all was over—a not-inconsiderable achievement. It was a bargain I was only too happy to enter." From 1971 to 1974 Ford received a stipend as a member of the University of Michigan Society of Fellows. For two years beginning in 1974, he served as a lecturer at the University of Michigan, in Ann Arbor. Meanwhile, he labored over the novel that, as Bruce Weber reported, "used up everything he had learned in his life up to that point"; the book was published in 1976, under the title *A Piece of My Heart.*

The novel's narrative alternates between the points of view of two men, Robard Hewes and Sam Newel, whose separate quests lead them to a region on the Arkansas-Mississippi border. Hewes, a laborer, has abandoned his lover in Nevada, lured to his native South by letters from an old flame, who is now married to a minor-league pitcher; Newel, a law student and also a southerner, has come to test the appeal that the South holds for him before committing himself to a life in Chicago with the woman he loves. Through such passages as "The air smelled like piled newspapers and the city felt low-spirited and musty like an uncle," Ford evoked the southward journeys of the two men, who eventually meet and who both mirror and complement each other in their backgrounds and desires.

Several reviewers felt *A Piece of My Heart* to be the work of a gifted writer laboring unnecessarily under the burdens of one or more literary traditions. In a representative assessment, the novelist Larry McMurtry wrote in the *New York Times Book Review* (October 24, 1976), "The South—dadgummit—has struck again, marring what might have been an excellent first novel. *A Piece of My Heart* shows obvious promise, but it also exhibits all the characteristic vices of southern fiction . . . , starting with portentousness. One would hope that, in Mr. Ford's case, [those] vices won't prove incurable. His minor characters are vividly drawn, and his ear is first-rate. If he can weed his garden of some of the weeds and cockleburrs of his tradition, it might prove very fertile."

Facing what he described to Bruce Weber as "the dark night of [his] little soul," Ford wrote his second novel twice, changing its narrative during the revision from first-person to third-person. The protagonist of *The Ultimate Good Luck* (1981) is the Vietnam veteran Harry Quinn, who travels to Mexico to rescue his girlfriend's brother from prison. The reviews of the book were mixed, with several critics taking exception to the level of violence in the story. A writer for *Kirkus Reviews* (February 15, 1981), for example, attacked Ford's "dreadful macho/psychological prose, a syrup boiled down from the worst tendencies of everyone from Hemingway to Robert Stone," and declared that with his second novel Ford had "fulfill[ed] none of [the] promise" of *A Piece of My Heart,* "settling instead for dismal posturing and imitative melodrama." On the other hand, C. D. B. Bryan, writing in the *New York Times Book Review* (May 31, 1981), praised the novel's "taut cinematic quality" and found it to possess "a style that bathes [Ford's] story with the same hot, flat, mercilessly white light that scorches Mexico" and to capture "exactly that disquieting sense of menace one often feels lurking there just off the road."

During the period between the publication of *A Piece of My Heart* and that of *The Ultimate Good Luck,* Ford had made ends meet by securing grants from the Guggenheim Foundation and the National Endowment for the Arts and by teaching at Princeton University, in New Jersey, and at Williams College, in Williamstown, Massachusetts. *A Piece of My Heart,* despite praise from some corners, sold only a few thousand copies. After his second novel failed to find a larger readership than had his first, he put aside fiction for a time in favor of sportswriting, selling pieces on commission to *Inside Sports.* "That was a great job," he told Bruce Weber. "Unfortunately, the magazine had the audacity to go out of business." (It would later be revived.)

Turning again to fiction, Ford spent the next several years at work on his third novel, *The Sportswriter* (1986). That book is narrated by the thirty-eight-year-old Frank Bascombe, a divorced father mourning the death, in the recent past, of one of his children. The author of a well-received book of short stories, Bascombe has given up fiction to become a sportswriter, preferring to craft pieces about action rather than emotion. His career change is emblematic of his desire, since his son's death, to distance himself from other people and from his own feelings. In addition to its surface parallels to Ford's own career, *The Sportswriter* has a deeper connection to its author's life: shortly after he began work on the book, Edna Ford died, following a long illness. Kristina Hensley told Bruce Weber for the *New York Times Magazine* profile, "I was impressed with how [Ford] channeled his grief [over his mother's death] into Frank's grief over his son."

The Sportswriter solidified Ford's reputation as a gifted novelist and won him a wider readership. More than one critic compared the work to *The Moviegoer,* Walker Percy's celebrated novel about a genial man out of sync with the world around him. Michiko Kakutani of the *New York Times* (February 26, 1986) called *The Sportswriter* Ford's "finest book to date" and "a devastating chronicle of contemporary alienation," and in *Newsweek* (April 7, 1986), Walter Clemons wrote: "Ford is one of the best writers of his generation. . . . Each of his works, *The Sportswriter* most of all, shows an original fictional intelligence. He's crafty, subtle, and surprising."

Even some of the reviewers who found fault with the book's meandering style were impressed by the power of Ford's/Frank's observations. "*The Sportswriter* is . . . slow-paced and, like its protagonist, lacks a clear sense of direction; it arrives nowhere, so to speak," Robert Towers observed in the *New York Review of Books* (April 24, 1986). "The book is, instead, a reflective work that invites reflection, a novel that charms us with the freshness of its vision and touches us with the perplexities of a 'lost' narrator who for once is neither a drunkard nor a nihilist but a wistful, hopeful man adrift in his own humanity." *The Sportswriter* won a PEN/Faulkner citation for fiction, and *Time* chose it as one of the best books of 1986.

The short-story collection *Rock Springs*, Ford's next work, appeared the following year. Most of the book's ten tales are written in the first person; each is set in the American West and features a male protagonist whose life is defined by misfortune. The title story is narrated by a gentle, philosophical man who, having written some bad checks, is on the run in a stolen car with his girlfriend and young daughter. In "Great Falls," which begins, "This is not a happy story. I warn you," a man recalls the dissolution of his parents' marriage. The young narrator of "Optimists" watches as his father kills a man with a single punch. The book won wide acclaim. "The first thing that needs to be said about this collection of stories," John Edgar Wideman wrote in the *New York Times Book Review* (September 20, 1987), "is that the finest of them achieve luminous moments, moments with potential to change how the reader sees and thinks. . . . The stories of *Rock Springs* are extremely concentrated, so a reader who pays attention not only wants to turn pages but to prolong them, experience the supple, ironic, expanding and contracting medium Mr. Ford compounds from everyday speech."

For all the praise accorded Ford's stories, there were those who complained that the writer had given his narrators, most of whom are not highly educated, an eloquence they might not possess. "There is a drama inherent in people trying to find a language for their experiences, and even the most unlettered and unschooled can be moved to lyrical utterances," Ford explained to James Wood for the *Guardian* (July 17, 1989). "It's just that mostly, these outbursts of feeling go unrecorded, and it's literature's privilege to make these utterances useful beyond their own isolation in people's lives." As he phrased it in his conversation with Bruce Weber, "Human beings continue to surprise us. It is just a fact of life that people are always doing things they shouldn't be able to do. . . . People just say things that make you stare off, sometimes."

In contrast to *Rock Springs*, the writer's fourth novel, *Wildlife* (1990), received mixed notices. "Mr. Ford seems to have bitten off more than he can chew," Christopher Lehmann-Haupt wrote in the *New York Times* (June 1, 1990), in evaluating the story of the sensitive sixteen-year-old narrator, Joe Brinson, whose mother has an affair after her husband leaves the family to help fight a colossal forest fire. While Joseph Coates, writing in the *Chicago Tribune* (May 27, 1990), called *Wildlife* a "consistently fine novel," many critics agreed with Eliot Fremont-Smith, who declared in *USA Today* (June 15, 1990), "There is no moral edge to this tale, no spiritual dimension, no purpose connected to character. The passion, the fire, the humane and poignant truths—it all turns out to be kind of weightless, a slice of limbo."

Ford rebounded in 1995, with *Independence Day*, in which he picks up the story of Frank Bascombe. Beginning just before the Fourth of July in 1988 (*The Sportswriter* was set over Easter weekend in 1982), the plot of *Independence Day* finds Frank, now a realtor, angling tentatively to reunite with his wife; attempting to reach out to his troubled fifteen-year-old son; and still yearning for spiritual calm. "Richard Ford has created, and continues to develop in *Independence Day*, a character we know as well as we know our next-door neighbors," Charles Johnson wrote in the *New York Times Book Review* (June 18, 1995). "Frank Bascombe has earned himself a place beside [Arthur Miller's] Willy Loman and [John Updike's] Harry Angstrom in our literary landscape, but he has done so with a wry wit and a *fin de siècle* wisdom that is very much his own." Michiko Kakutani of the *New York Times* (June 13, 1995) agreed: "Mr. Ford has written a worthy sequel to *The Sportswriter* and galvanized his reputation as one of his generation's most eloquent voices."

In 1992 Ford wrote in the *Guardian* that he had changed residences "twenty times, probably, in twenty years." His reasons for staying on the move appear to be a mix of the practical and the spontaneous: "My wife got a better job, I got a better job. . . . I missed the West. I missed the South. I missed my pals. I got sick of their company. Longing's at the heart of it, I guess. Longing that overtakes me like a fast car on the freeway and makes me willing to withstand a feeling of personal temporariness." His lifestyle, he conceded, "has the effect of stressing life's, shall we say, transitory nature. But life *is* transitory. And with my plan, at least, you get the satisfying sensation that you're seeing more of it."

Richard Ford stands over six feet tall and has "sloping shoulders, taut features, . . . pale, severe eyes," and "a Southerner's instinctive solicitous manners," as Bruce Weber described him. In addition to his prose fiction, Ford has written a play, *American Tropical*, which was produced in 1983 at the Actors Theatre in Louisville, Kentucky, and a screenplay, *Bright Angel*, which was based on two of his short stories and was made into a 1991 film starring Sam Shepard. He was a contributor to *Fifty Great Years of Esquire Fiction* (1983), edited by L. Rust Hills, and he has placed numerous essays in magazines, on subjects ranging from motels to baseball. He has won awards from the Mississippi Academy of Arts and Letters, the New York Public Library, and the Echoing Green Foundation, among other institutions. His wife of more than a quarter-century, Kristina Ford, is a former model who holds a Ph.D. degree in urban and regional planning. Ford enlists his wife's aid in his work, sometimes reading aloud to her whole manuscripts of his novels. The couple currently lives in New Orleans, where Hensley is the executive director of the city planning commission.

Selected Biographical References: Harper's 276:38+ Je '88, 277:72+ Ag 88; N Y Times Mag p50+ Ap 10 '88 pors; People 34:71+ Jl 9 '90 pors; Contemporary Authors new rev ser vol 47 (1995)

AP/Wide World Photos

Foreman, George

Jan. 10, 1949- Boxer; minister. Address: George Foreman Youth and Community Center, 2202 Lone Oak Rd., Houston, TX 77093-3336

NOTE: This biography supersedes the article that appeared in *Current Biography* in 1974.

On November 5, 1994, at the age of forty-five, George Foreman defeated Michael Moorer to become the oldest heavyweight champion in boxing history, regaining the title he had lost twenty years earlier and completing a quest that, in the view of some observers, defied the laws of nature. In 1987, when he began his boxing comeback after a ten-year absence from the ring, Foreman was routinely dismissed as too old and out of shape to have a prayer of winning the heavyweight crown, and some boxing aficionados feared that he would not survive the attempt. But Foreman, who, when he first held the heavyweight title, was known for his mercilessness in the ring and his belligerent demeanor outside it, disarmed his critics with self-deprecating humor about his age and eating habits and with an ever-lengthening string of victories.

Foreman proved himself to be a legitimate contender and confirmed his status as the "people's champ" in 1991, when he went the distance in impressive—though not victorious—fashion against then-heavyweight champion Evander Holyfield. A minister who preaches in his own Church of the Lord Jesus Christ, in Houston, Texas, Foreman has used the large sums he has earned during his boxing comeback to endow his George Foreman Youth and Community Center, an athletic and recreational facility designed to steer troubled youngsters away from the streets.

George Edward Foreman was born on January 10, 1949 in Marshall, Texas, the fifth of the seven children of Nancy Ree (Nelson) Foreman. Foreman was twenty-seven years old when he discovered that his biological father was not J. D. Foreman, Nancy Foreman's husband, but Leroy Moorehead, whom the boxer eventually met and befriended. After J. D. Foreman left the family, Nancy Foreman raised her children in a slum in Houston's Fifth Ward, earning a meager income as a short-order cook. Foreman has cited, as an example of the poverty in which his family lived, the Saturday nights he and his siblings spent waiting for their mother to come home from work. "She'd buy a gigantic hamburger, big and round, and bring it home," he told Richard Hoffer for *Sports Illustrated* (July 17, 1989). "We're talking about seven children. And she'd give everybody a little piece. And I'd sit there and nurse that little piece, kiss it a little bit, smell it, and finally eat that little piece. There was nothing more I wanted in life than to be able to have enough food."

The values Foreman embraced as a youth were shaped by the crime- and drug-infested streets of his neighborhood. As he told Richard Hoffer, "I thought a hero was a guy with a big, long scar down his face, a guy who'd come back from prison, a guy maybe killed a man once. Can you imagine, my goal was to have a scar on my cheek?" During his ninth-grade year, he dropped out of E. O. Smith Junior High School, where he had received little attention apart from that accorded his participation in football. For the Hester House gang, one of a dozen teen gangs that operated in the Fifth Ward, he served as the "lead enforcer," in Hoffer's words, robbing and beating anyone who happened onto the group's turf.

It was at the age of fifteen that Foreman first resolved to change his behavior. While hiding from the police after participating in a robbery, he thought of a remark his cousin had made after he had tried to conceal an earlier misdeed: "Why you bothering to excuse yourself?" she had asked him. "You know nobody in this family is ever going to become anything anyway." The memory of her remark prodded Foreman to prove her wrong. He immediately ended his criminal activities. Soon afterward, through a television endorsement that featured the football great Jim Brown, he learned about the Job Corps, a federal program established to provide troubled youths with job skills and education. During his resulting two-year stay in the Corps, first in Grants Pass, Oregon and then in Pleasanton, California, Foreman was frequently disciplined for picking fights, but he escaped dismissal and took full advantage of the program's curriculum. He learned bricklaying, carpentry, and electronics and developed interests in anthropology, Latin, math, and literature, and by the time of his graduation, in 1967, he had earned his high school equivalency diploma.

In the meantime, Foreman had begun boxing under the tutelage of a Job Corps instructor, Charles ("Doc") Broadus. On January 26, 1967, in his first official amateur fight, in the San Francisco Golden Gloves tournament, Foreman knocked out his opponent in the first round. He went on to win another tournament, in Las Vegas, before losing a bout in Milwaukee. Following his graduation from the Job Corps, Foreman returned to Houston, where he was able to find only the most menial jobs. "We wrote to each other," Broadus has recalled. "I told myself, 'Doc, do something. Do it quick. Give up on this boy and he'll be in the penitentiary.'" Broadus arranged for Foreman to work as a physical education instructor in the Job Corps while he pursued his boxing career.

By winning the National Amateur Athletic Union boxing championship, Foreman qualified for the United States Olympic team. In October 1968, less than two years after he had begun boxing, he became the gold medalist in the heavyweight division at the Summer Olympics in Mexico City, scoring a technical knockout over the Soviet boxer Ionas Chepulis with left jabs that "packed trip-hammer power reminiscent of Joe Louis," in the view of one writer. After the match, Foreman presented his defeated rival with a dozen roses.

Following his victory, the new Olympic champion expressed new-found pride in his identity as an American by gesturing in the ring with a miniature American flag. His action provoked controversy in the black community, coming as it did in the wake of a protest against American racism by the African-American sprinters John Carlos and Tommie Smith, who gave black-power salutes on the victory stand after receiving their medals. Foreman returned to Houston expecting a hero's welcome, but he instead found himself being ostracized by African-Americans, some of whom labeled him an Uncle Tom. "What a homecoming," he recalled in *By George: The Autobiography of George Foreman* (1995), written with Joel Engel. "Imagine—the Olympic heavyweight champion, an outcast. There was no place to escape but into myself. That's when I began withdrawing. It wasn't long before I became the kind of man it was easy to root against."

Foreman turned professional a year after the Olympics; in his professional debut, in June 1969, he knocked out Donald Waldheim. "When you get hit by George, you feel like you've been pumped with Novocain," Waldheim has said. "The first time he hit me in the face, it went numb; I had no feeling in my cheeks or lips. It was like going to the dentist." Foreman knocked out thirty-two other opponents over the next two and a half years, but he was nonetheless frequently dismissed as someone who preyed on "tomato cans," or boxers of limited skill. Little was expected of him when he met the heavyweight champion, Joe Frazier, in Jamaica on January 22, 1973. Frazier had scheduled the match largely to busy himself until he and his arch-rival, Muhammad Ali, could fight again. As it turned out, however, Foreman destroyed Frazier, decking him six times before the fight was ended, in the second round.

As heavyweight champion, Foreman cultivated his newfound image for ferocity, modeling himself at this stage of his career after the former champion Sonny Liston, who was known for his murderous pre-bout stares at opponents and his demolition of most of the men he fought. Foreman successfully defended his title against challenges from Joe ("King") Roman in September 1973 and Ken Norton in March 1974; the latter contest, the longer of the two, ended with a second-round knockout. Foreman told Jon Saraceno of *USA Today* (December 21, 1990) that during this period he often thought of killing someone in the ring: "Then I knew I would have that respect. When I would stare across the ring before a fight, I would think, 'Maybe this is gonna be the lucky one.' When I looked him in the eye, I was really sizing him up as a trophy, like a deer hunter. You know, something to hang on the wall. Some guys were saying, 'I can stop Foreman,' but I knew I could stop them from thinking that by killing one of them."

When Foreman agreed to fight Muhammad Ali in the fall of 1974 in Zaire, Ali was the clear underdog, because Foreman was younger, possesed superior punching power, and had quickly dispatched two fighters—Frazier and Norton—to whom Ali had lost in protracted battles. Ali, however, attacked Foreman psychologically as well as physically, both before and during "The Rumble in the Jungle," as their fight was billed. He taunted Foreman publicly from the moment they arrived in Zaire, and it was not long before Foreman "was feeling bewitched," as Foreman's publicist, Bill Caplan, told Richard Hoffer. During the fight itself, Ali employed his now-famous "rope-a-dope" strategy: leaning against the ropes and shielding himself with his arms, he insulted the champion while Foreman threw punches that rarely found their mark. In the eighth round, Ali stepped away from the ropes and easily kayoed the exhausted Foreman.

Losing that fight "knocked me off my axis," Foreman said in *By George*. "The heavyweight title meant much more to me after I lost it than when I held it. Without it, I was nothing." Foreman sought to resuscitate his reputation in the following year by facing five opponents, for three rounds each, in a single exhibition in Canada, but the stunt was ridiculed by many. His first serious challenge after his loss of the heavyweight crown came on January 24, 1976, against Ron Lyle, who was also struggling to reestablish himself after a knockout loss to Muhammad Ali. The fact that neither boxer could afford a defeat contributed to the brutality of the fight. The ABC boxing analyst Alex Wallau was quoted as saying about the Foreman-Lyle bout, "I can't remember a fight with so many reversals of fortune." In the fourth round, after being sent to the canvas by his opponent, Foreman rose and knocked Lyle down in turn, only to be floored a second time before the bell. Foreman returned in the fifth round, however, to knock Lyle out with a virtually unanswered barrage of twenty-nine punches. The tenacity and mettle displayed by the two men, according to Jeff Ryan of *Sport* (March 1993), made the fight a "masterpiece."

On March 17, 1977 Foreman lost a twelve-round decision to Jimmy Young, despite having connected in the seventh round with a left hook that Young, as he told an interviewer in 1994, "can still feel." "I have never told George this," Young added, "but when he caught me with that punch, I was out cold. All he had to do was push me with his little finger. How I survived that round I will never know." Foreman told Jose Torres that he had refrained from dispatching Young in the early rounds on the advice of the boxing promoter Don King. The network televising the bout, King informed Foreman, wanted the contest to last longer than a typical Foreman fight so that more commercials could be broadcast. When Foreman finally attempted to knock Young out, he has recalled, he "didn't have the energy."

In his dressing room after the fight, Foreman experienced what some around him believed to be a hallucination brought on by dehydration but what he has called a religious revelation. As Richard Hoffer reported, Foreman thought to himself, "Who cares about a boxing match? I still got everything. If I wanted to, I could retire now, go to the country . . . , and die." With the thought of death, Foreman recalled, he felt himself falling into "a deep, dark nothing, like out in a sea, with nothing over your head or under your feet," and "a horrible smell came with it. . . . A smell of sorrow. . . . And then I looked around, and I was dead. . . . And then I said, I don't think this is death. I still believe in God. And I said that, and I was back alive in the dressing room. And I could feel the blood flowing through my veins."

After that experience, Foreman gave up boxing. He began attending church regularly and reading and discussing the Bible. In 1978 he was ordained a minister by the presiding ministers of the Church of the Lord Jesus Christ, in Houston. Churches throughout North America invited Foreman to "testify" at their services, and during an evangelical mission to Africa, he preached before sixty thousand people in Kinshasa, Zaire, the site of his loss to Muhammad Ali. "This time," he wrote in *By George*, "they cheered." Eventually, Foreman established his own Church of the Lord Jesus Christ, outside Houston. For ten years, he has said, he did not ball his fist. His only contact with boxing came through his George Foreman Youth and Community Center, a recreation facility and gymnasium, run by his brother Roy, which was created to give troubled youngsters an alternative to delinquency.

"I had [the center] going real good," Foreman told Hoffer, "but each month it was starting to eat into my principal a little more." Finally his accountant told him, "You're going to have to give up either your lifestyle or your youth center." Foreman at first attempted to raise extra money by accepting honorariums for speaking engagements before church congregations. He felt embarrassed, however, when, after a speaking engagement at an evangelical conference, the organizer pleaded with the audience for donations to Foreman's youth center. Foreman has recalled thinking: "I know how to get money. I'm going to be heavyweight champ of the world. Again."

Foreman returned to boxing in 1987, at the age of thirty-eight. He reduced his weight from 315 to 267 pounds for his first post-retirement fight, against Steve Zouski. Some sportswriters accused him of "plodding" about the ring, but Foreman seemed to have lost little of his punching power, and he won by a technical knockout. Although he went on to defeat twenty-three opponents in the next three years, only one—Gerry Cooney—was a ranked contender, and the boxing skills of many of the others were denigrated by sportswriters. The opponents, Hugh McIlvanney wrote in the London *Observer* (September 23, 1990), "could scarcely have been less dangerous if pulled from a mortuary drawer," and Foreman defeated them with punches that "you could time . . . with a sundial," as more than one observer put it. In the *New York Times Magazine* (March 24, 1991), Foreman explained his choice of adversaries: "I'd seen others, like Muhammad Ali and Joe Frazier, fail in their comebacks because they were looking for overnight success. I treated myself like a young man, a prospect."

In spite of the skepticism of sportswriters and others, sports fans became increasingly intrigued by Foreman, who unveiled a new, affable, self-deprecating public personality along with his newly shaved head. By offering frank, often humorous commentary on his age ("God bless all the people who know that being forty is not a death sentence"), his fighting weight, which was in the 250-to-260-pound range ("dieting interferes with my sense of contentment, which is worse than being heavy"), his opponents ("People say I won't fight anybody who is not on a respirator. That's a lie. They have to be off the respirator at least a week"), and his diet (he made a point of devouring cheeseburgers, chocolates, turkey legs, and other items in front of journalists), Foreman became a folk hero. "Foreman has captured the imagination of the multitude who dream of seeing a middle-aged fat man make nonsense of the natural laws of physical decline," Hugh McIlvanney noted in the London *Observer* (April 14, 1991).

Foreman, who served as his own manager (his trainer is the former light-heavyweight champion Archie Moore), became so popular that he was able to arrange to fight the heavyweight champion, Evander Holyfield, on April 19, 1991. Although this gave Foreman the opportunity to regain the title he had lost almost seventeen years earlier, the poor reputation of most of his previous twenty-four opponents led many to question his ability to present a serious challenge to Holyfield, who was twenty-eight years old and considered to be an almost perfect physical specimen. But while Holyfield won the twelve-round fight by decision, Foreman impressed observers by throwing a "sledgehammer" jab, hurting Holyfield several times during the bout, and fighting with a "skill and moxie" that "demolished the widespread notion that he was a sham," as Phil Berger wrote in the *New York Times* (December 5, 1991). "Holyfield had the points," Foreman said, "but I made a point."

In April 1992, while waiting for a rematch with Holyfield, Foreman defeated the twenty-seven-year-old British boxer Alex Stewart in a brutal ten-round battle that left Foreman's face so badly swollen that some feared that his jaw had been broken. Fighting again in June 1993, in Las Vegas, Foreman lost a twelve-round decision to a twenty-four-year-old, Tommy Morrison. After that bout he announced his intention to retire from boxing. In the offing was a television sitcom, in which Foreman would star as a retired boxer working with troubled youngsters. The series, *George*, was canceled after eight episodes. "Located in television's graveyard, Saturday night, *George* ranked too near the bottom of the ratings," Foreman wrote in *By George*. "[But] at least now I could put on my tombstone: PREACHER, BOXER, ACTOR."

Foreman returned to boxing a second time in a bout against World Boxing Association (WBA) and International Boxing Federation (IBF) champion Michael Moorer, who had dethroned Holyfield. The WBA initially refused to sanction the match, citing Foreman's age and fourteen-month layoff. In November 1994, however, the contest took place, with the forty-five-year-old Foreman, the underdog, wearing the same trunks he had worn twenty years earlier, in his fight with Ali. Moorer dominated most of the bout while, round after round, Foreman waited for his chance to land the right hand that was considered to be his best chance for victory. Seeing an opening in the tenth round, Foreman, as one writer described it, drove a right hand "downward with the shocking force of a hydraulic log-splitter and smack between the gloves of Moorer," knocking the champion out.

Defending his crown in April 1995, Foreman was awarded a decision over the German fighter Axel Schultz, in a bout that many thought the challenger had won. In fighting Schultz, Foreman had defied the wishes of the World Boxing Association, which had stipulated that Foreman make his first title defense against the number-one-ranked contender (then Tony Tucker) or be stripped of his title. Foreman lost his only remaining title—the International Boxing Federation championship—after refusing to comply with the IBF's order that he fight Schultz again in the fall of 1995. The former champion has said that he will fight perhaps once more before retiring again, no later than 1996.

The six-foot three-inch Foreman, in part to distinguish himself from the insecure, angry, threatening, womanizing spendthrift he admits to having been during his first reign as heavyweight champion, keeps his face and head shaved (the "old" Foreman sported sideburns, a mustache, and a full head of hair). He has "a handsome brown face with a smile complete with old—and new—mischief," Jose Torres has written. Davis Miller, reporting for *Sport* (May 1991), described Foreman's sermons as being "more energetic than evangelistic, unfocused yet pragmatic," delivered while he "prowls back and forth, much in the manner of the young lions he once kept as pets. His dominating presence is undeniable as he tells oblique stories about his years before having been saved and about his post-salvation life. He warns his congregation not to take that drink on Saturday night and not to lay down with that inviting stranger."

George Foreman lives in the Houston suburb of Humble, where his church and youth center are located. From two of his four previous marriages, all of which ended in divorce, and two other relationships, Foreman has four daughters—Michi, Freeda, Natalie, and Georgetta—and two sons, George Jr. and George 3rd. He is currently married to the former Mary Martelly, whom he calls Joan. The couple have three children: a girl, Leola, and two boys, George 4th and George 5th. Explaining his decision to name all his male offspring (who are distinguished from one another by their nicknames) after himself, Foreman told a writer for *Jet* (March 14, 1988), "One of the baddest feelings I had was that feeling of not knowing where I came from; what my roots were. I figured that with all of them having that name, they should know where they come from. It's never too late to get some roots."

Selected Biographical References: Chicago Tribune V p1+ Je 27 '95 pors; N Y Times Mag p41+ Mr 24 '91 pors; People 35:107+ Ap 22 '91 pors; Sports Illus 71:60+ Jl 17 '89 pors; Time 134:8+ Jl 24 '89 por; Foreman, George and Joel Engel: By George: The Autobiography of George Foreman (1995)

Frank, Barney

Mar. 31, 1940- United States Representative from Massachusetts. Address: 2404 Rayburn House Office Bldg., Washington, DC 20515-2104

"One of those natural politicians who has an instinct for how to frame an issue and how to get things done," as one observer described him, Barney Frank has served the exceedingly heterogeneous Fourth Congressional District of Massachusetts in the United States House of Representatives since 1980. Frank, a Democrat, has won wide respect on Capitol Hill for his brilliance, honesty, effectiveness as a deal-maker, and seemingly limitless capacity for hard work. He has also earned a reputation as "a sharp-tongued and quick-witted debater" and as "one of the most colorful and quotable figures in the Congress," as Jerry Gray reported in the *New York Times* (January 6, 1995). "He's one of the few members who, when he takes to the floor [of Congress], causes people all over the Capitol to turn up the volume on their TVs to see what he's saying," Congressman Edward J. Markey of Massachusetts has said, as quoted by

U.S. House of Representatives

Barney Frank

Weston Kosova in the *New Republic* (March 6, 1995). "In almost every speech there's a line that will get to the heart of the argument."

An outspoken and unabashed liberal, Frank has vigorously championed such traditionally liberal causes as economic fairness for workers, women, and minorities; increased government funding for education and health care; safer workplaces; affordable housing; a drastic reduction in military spending; and elimination of the death penalty. At the same time, he has avoided a rigid adherence to liberal orthodoxy or Democratic ideology, as is illustrated, for example, by his attempt in 1993 to broker a compromise on the issue of homosexuals in the armed services. By such means as his book-length essay *Speaking Frankly: What's Wrong with the Democrats and How to Fix It* (1992), he has also strived to make liberalism more attractive to voters. "My goal is to be a pragmatic zealot," he has said. "What's the point of having strong ideals if you don't pay a lot of attention to how to implement them?"

In the late 1960s and early 1970s, Frank worked as an assistant to Mayor Kevin White of Boston and then to Massachusetts congressman Michael J. Harrington. Between 1972 and 1980 he served four terms in the Massachusetts state legislature. By his own account, during his fourteen years in Congress he has devoted more of his time to the economic affairs of his district than to any other issue. Editorials that appeared in local Massachusetts newspapers in 1992 lauded him for working tirelessly for and genuinely caring about his constituents and for "time and again prov[ing] responsive to local needs and interests in a way few other politicians could match." His popularity in his district enabled him to win reelection after such potentially politically fatal events as his disclosure of his homosexuality in 1987 and his formal reprimand by the House of Representatives in 1990 for improperly using the power of his office in a matter involving one of his personal employees. Since January 1995, when the Republicans became the majority party in the House, Frank has assumed a leading role during floor debates. His job, he has said, is "to shine the light where the Republicans don't want it to be shone."

The son of Samuel and Elsie (Golush) Frank, Barney Frank was born in Bayonne, New Jersey on March 31, 1940. He has one brother, David Frank, and two sisters, Doris Breay and Ann F. Lewis, the latter of whom was a Democratic political consultant before becoming a vice-president of Planned Parenthood Federation of America. Among Frank's cherished early memories are those of the occasions when his mother took him to movies featuring such comedy teams as Laurel and Hardy, Abbott and Costello, and the Three Stooges. Along with a keen-edged sense of humor, as a youngster Barney Frank developed a "knack for nettling," as Jerry Gray wrote in the *New York Times* (January 6, 1995). "Barney's ability to point out other people's inconsistencies and hypocrisies in a humorous way was not always warmly received by people, especially when they were authority figures," his sister Ann recalled to Gray. Frank vividly remembers the fury he felt when, as a high school student in 1955, he read an article in *Life* magazine about the murder that year of Emmett Till in Mississippi after the fourteen-year-old black youth had allegedly whistled at a white woman. "It's probably bigotry that bothers me most," Frank said many years later. "Bigotry and undeserved poverty." During his teens he sometimes pumped gas at the truck stop that his father owned and managed.

Frank received an A.B. degree from Harvard University in 1962. He later enrolled in the university's graduate program in political science. Between 1963 and 1967 he worked at Harvard as a teaching fellow in government, and in 1966–67 he served as the assistant to the director of the Institute for Politics at Harvard's John F. Kennedy School of Government. In 1967 he abandoned his pursuit of a Ph.D. degree to assist in Kevin White's first, successful mayoralty race in Boston. As Mayor White's executive assistant from 1968 to 1971, he gained an intimate familiarity with Boston politics and made the acquaintance of many of its players. He then served briefly as an administrative assistant to Michael J. Harrington, a United States congressman from Massachusetts.

In 1972 Frank ran for election to the Massachusetts House of Representatives, to fill the seat held by the representative from Boston's Back Bay, who had decided to retire. The large number of Boston University students who voted for George S. McGovern in that year's presidential contest contributed significantly to Frank's victory. "I'm one of the few people in the country who can say he benefited from George McGovern's coattails," he has been quoted as saying. As a state legislator Frank concentrated on such areas as women's rights, homosexual rights, and social services. In compiling a boldly liberal record that attracted attention in national as well as Massachusetts liberal circles, he consistently ignored many political formalities and repeatedly wrangled with house leaders over issues. Despite his unorthodox behavior and conspicuously slipshod attire, he won three additional two-year terms as a state lawmaker. (One year his campaign posters featured a photo of him in a rumpled suit beneath the words "Neatness Isn't Everything.") According to a *New York Times* (September 16, 1980) article by Michael Oreskes, during his tenure in the Massachusetts house, Frank was named "legislator of the year" by several state and national organizations. In 1977 he earned a J.D. degree from Harvard University, and in 1979–80 he taught public policy at Harvard's Kennedy School of Government.

In 1980 the liberal congressman Robert F. Drinan, a Jesuit priest who had represented the Fourth Congressional District of Massachusetts for the previous decade, announced that, in light of Pope John Paul II's reaffirmation of a church ruling that prohibited Roman Catholic clergymen from seeking public office, he would not run for a sixth term. Frank, whom many observers regarded as Drinan's "philosophical heir," declared his candidacy for the seat soon afterward. To fulfill the constitutional residency requirement for congressmen, he moved from Back Bay to the town of Newton. During the primary campaign, Humberto Cardinal Medeiros, the archbishop of Boston, warned parishioners of the more than four hundred Roman Catholic churches in his diocese against voting for candidates who (like Frank) approved the legalization of abortion. Nevertheless, Frank, who was actively supported by Drinan, among others, and who received the endorsement of the *Boston Globe* (the largest-circulation newspaper in the state), defeated Mayor Arthur Clark of Waltham, his politically conservative, antiabortion challenger, with 52 percent of the vote. In the general election, in which he ran against the Republican Richard Jones, he won by a similar margin.

As a member of the Ninety-Sixth Congress, Frank was named to the Government Operations Committee; the Select Committee on Aging; the Banking, Finance, and Urban Affairs Committee, where in 1981 he sponsored a bill aimed at preventing new owners of low-income buildings from evicting current tenants; and the Judiciary Committee, where he strenuously fought attempts by Ronald Reagan's administration to dismantle the Legal Services Corporation. He argued against legislation that offered tax advantages to oil producers and attacked the administration's budgetary cuts in programs for the elderly. Summing up Frank's accomplishments during his freshman term, a writer for *Politics in America, 1984* noted that the congressman had "wad[ed] into the conservative tide with a combination of humor and conviction that left even ideological opponents paying him grudging respect."

As it existed in 1980, the Fourth Congressional District of Massachusetts was a politically complex "geographical oddity," with residents of great social, cultural, and economic diversity. Extending for nearly two hundred miles, it encompassed affluent suburbs, depressed factory towns, and farms. After the Massachusetts legislature redrew congressional district lines in 1982 (an action necessitated by a drop in the state's population), the district remained similarly heterogeneous but within radically different borders. Only 30 percent of the more than half a million people in the new Fourth Congressional District had been represented by Barney Frank, while 70 percent of them had been served by Representative Margaret M. Heckler, an eight-term Republican whom the redistricting had instantly cast as Frank's opponent in the upcoming election. "If you asked legislators to draw a map in which Barney Frank would never be a congressman again, this would be it," Frank was quoted as saying at the time.

Zeroing in on Heckler's major weakness, in his campaign Frank exploited the existence of considerable dissatisfaction among low-income, elderly, and blue-collar voters with Heckler's support of President Reagan's economic policies. Heckler was saddled as well with a reputation for indecisiveness, and despite being the odds-on favorite to win, she assumed a defensive posture early in the race. By attacking Frank for supposedly supporting prostitution because he had favored the establishment of a "vice zone" in Boston, she alienated many voters in the district's large politically liberal areas. After what ended as the nation's most expensive congressional race (Heckler spent close to a million dollars; Frank, close to a million and a half) and one of the most bitterly contested, Frank triumphed with 60 percent of the vote.

In the 1984 election Frank trounced his Republican opponent, Jim Forte, with 74 percent of the vote. His margin of victory in the 1986 contest, in which he ran against Thomas D. DeVisscher, a member of the American Party (the Republicans did not field a candidate), was even greater: he snared 89 percent of the vote. Two years before, he had transformed his appearance by losing approximately sixty pounds, getting a stylish haircut, and outfitting himself in a fashionable new wardrobe, but his manner and the political modus operandi for which he had become known in the halls of Congress had remained unchanged. According to a writer for *Politics in America, 1984*, he "somehow manage[d] to be cynical and idealistic, genial and argumentative, self-righteous and whimsical—all at the same time." In *Politics in America, 1986*, he was described as a congressman whom "nobody can ignore, and few can predict. . . . Frank adopts issues with a wide-ranging enthusiasm that has made him one of the most versatile legislators on [Capitol] Hill, able to shift from crime or housing legislation one day to an eloquent speech on agricultural marketing orders the next."

Under Frank's chairmanship, in 1985 the Government Operations Employment and Housing

Subcommittee produced a report that described as "grossly inadequate" the efforts by the Occupational Safety and Health Administration to protect workers who were responsible for cleaning up sites contaminated by toxic wastes. On another front that year, Frank vehemently protested the amount allocated for the Defense Department in Congress's $386.2 billion omnibus spending bill. As a member of the One Hundredth Congress, Frank relinquished his chairmanship of the Government Operations Committee subcommittee on manpower and became the chairman of the Judiciary Committee's Administrative Law and Governmental Relations Subcommittee.

Although Frank was prominent among lawmakers who pressed for such obviously liberal measures as a bill that would make it easier for the poor and the elderly to obtain low-cost, generic medications, he also espoused positions that most other congressional liberals opposed. He found himself in the minority among liberals, for example, in supporting the controversial Simpson-Mazzoli immigration reform bill (a measure that many Hispanic organizations denounced, for fear that it would make it more difficult for all aliens to obtain employment) and in pushing for a law that would give student religious groups equal access to school facilities available for use by nonreligious student groups. In another example of his consistent refusal to sidestep issues widely regarded among liberals as too touchy to confront, Frank pressed for the use of computers to uncover welfare fraud, maintaining that if liberals "don't deal with waste and fraud in a responsible way, conservatives will use it as an excuse to destroy the whole [welfare] program," as he put it.

In May 1987, during an interview with a *Boston Globe* reporter, Frank acknowledged that he was homosexual. "I don't think my sex life is relevant to my job," he was quoted as saying. "But on the other hand, I don't want to leave the impression that I'm embarrassed by my life." By his own account, his decision to "go public" stemmed both from his belief that he could not escape much longer the scrutiny to which the personal lives of American political figures were increasingly being subjected and from his desire to prevent the sort of speculation that had followed the recent death from AIDS of another House member. "I have no reason to expect anyone to be reading my obituary anytime soon," he told Linda Greenhouse for the *New York Times* (June 3, 1987), "but I do fly home on weekends, and we can all be hit by a truck, and I don't want the focus to be: Was he or wasn't he, did he or didn't he." Of the many letters that he received from his constituents in the first few days after his disclosure, Frank told Linda Greenhouse, about six out of seven supported him. The results of the 1988 election provided further evidence that a large majority of the voters in his district continued to regard him as worthy of representing them. Although Debra Tucker, his Republican opponent, tried to create an issue out of Frank's personal life, he won 70 percent of the more than 241,000 votes cast.

Frank's sexual orientation became a topic of public discussion again in June of 1989, as the result of the controversy that surrounded the circulation of a Republican National Committee memo to two hundred GOP leaders. By comparing the voting record of Thomas S. Foley, the newly elected speaker of the House, with that of Frank and by bearing the headline "Tom Foley: Out of the Liberal Closet," the memo attempted to portray Foley as an extreme liberal who might be gay. Frank denounced the memo as "obviously scurrilous and vicious." Convinced that, in his words, "if [the Democrats] did not threaten retaliation, [the Republicans] would continue unilateral shelling," he told reporters that if the GOP did not "cut the crap," as he put it, he would reveal the names of Republican congressmen and other well-known Republicans who he knew were homosexual. In the face of public condemnation of the memo by prominent Republicans, including President George Bush, as well as Democrats, Mark Goodin, who said he had written and distributed the memo, resigned from his position as communications director of the Republican National Committee. (Lee Atwater, the chairman of the committee and a recognized master of bare-knuckle politics, professed complete ignorance of the memo's preparation and distribution and refused to accede to the demands of some Democrats that he too resign.)

Less than three months later, a story published in the *Washington Times* catapulted Frank into a maelstrom of embarrassing publicity. The source of the story was Stephen L. Gobie, who had worked as Frank's housekeeper and driver for about two years, starting in 1985. A convicted felon, Gobie was on probation when Frank had met him through a personal ad. Among other claims, Gobie told a *Washington Times* reporter that he had run a prostitution business out of Frank's rented townhouse with the congressman's full knowledge. On April 25, 1989, the day the article appeared, Frank held a news conference at which he said that he had known Gobie was a prostitute but that he had hoped to help rehabilitate him. Although he acknowledged the truth of some of Gobie's assertions, he said that he had been unaware of Gobie's bisexual prostitution ring until his landlady had alerted him about Gobie's suspicious activities, at which point he had fired him. "Thinking I was going to be Henry Higgins and trying to turn him into Pygmalion was the biggest mistake I've made," Frank was quoted as saying by Tom Morganthau for *Newsweek* (September 25, 1989). "It turns out that I was being suckered." In the *Washington Post* (September 17, 1989), Maralee Schwartz reported that when he was asked why he had gotten involved with Gobie, he responded, "The answer is the pressures of antigay prejudice. In my case, it was compounded by low self-esteem."

Within a few weeks of the appearance of the *Washington Times* story, the *Boston Globe*, the Roman Catholic diocesan newspaper in Frank's district, and various journalists and other individuals and organizations urged Frank to relinquish his seat. Others sprang to his defense. House Speaker Foley issued a statement in which he asserted, "[Frank] has provided outstanding service to his constituency and the nation, and I am absolutely confident that he will continue to do so long after this matter has been forgotten." In the *New Republic* (October 9, 1989), the columnist Morton M. Kondracke dismissed as "nonsense" the arguments that Frank had become "a fatal political burden" for the Democratic Party and that "his legislative effectiveness has been destroyed." "I personally believe that a lot of Frank's ideas—especially on defense, foreign policy, and economics—would be disastrous if they were implemented," Kondracke wrote. "But Barney Frank is a national treasure, and he ought to be preserved." "His personal judgment was bad, but his political judgment on hundreds of issues, large and small, tactical and substantive, has never been needed more . . . ," an editorial in the *Nation* (October 9, 1989) declared. "What has been overlooked in all the to-do about his future is the true significance of his predicament, which is the predicament of all transgressors of our mythical sexual norms who desire to serve government. . . . Nothing gets said about the intolerance ingrained in our culture that makes life hell for those like Frank who discover they are different." In *New York* (October 9, 1989), the veteran journalist Joe Klein, after noting that "in recent months, it has become increasingly clear that [Senator Alfonse] D'Amato has operated his office as a candy store for campaign contributors," declared that "the D'Amato business—coming, as it does, in tandem with Congressman Barney Frank's imbroglio with a male prostitute—offers fresh evidence of the perverse set of values now passing for and misdescribed as 'ethics' in Washington." "I've known Barney Frank for twenty years, known him to be as honest and principled as any human I've met," Klein added.

Taking an action that Frank himself had called for, the House ethics committee launched an investigation into Gobie's accusations. In a report that was released on July 20, 1990, the committee stated that it had uncovered no evidence that Frank had known about the prostitution ring. It did find, however, that Frank had used his congressional privilege to get Gobie's parking tickets waived and that he had sent to two lawyers a misleading letter (which eventually reached the prosecutor handling Gobie's case) regarding the extension of Gobie's probation. Through those actions, the committee decided, Frank had "reflected discredit upon the House." On July 26 the House held an exceptionally emotional and raucous four-hour floor debate, during the course of which Frank accepted the committee's findings and apologized for his behavior. After rejecting the motion, made by the California Republican William Dannemeyer, that he be expelled or, as Representative Newt Gingrich of Georgia proposed, that he be censured, it voted 408 to 18 to reprimand him.

Three months before that event, Frank had announced that he would seek a sixth term. In the ensuing campaign the Republican nominee, John Soto, a little-known accountant and lawyer, hammered away at Frank for having "failed miserably," as he put it, to exercise good judgment with regard to Gobie and challenged Frank to submit to a test for the HIV virus and then to make public the results. As the election returns showed, Soto's tactics miscarried: two-thirds of the votes went to Frank. In 1992, despite the changes in his constituency caused by redistricting that year, Frank won by the same margin in a race in which he faced three opponents. The candidates who contested his seat in 1994, all of whom represented minor parties, offered so little competition that *Congressional Quarterly* did not even print their names in its election-coverage issue.

Although Frank maintained a lower profile in Congress for several years after Gobie's story hit the newsstands, within a few months he had returned to his party's "strategic fold," in the words of an article in *Politics in America, 1992.* The article described his maneuverings during one debate as "classic Frank," with the lawmaker negotiating on the sidelines with Republicans at whom "in public, he lobbed sarcastic grenades." One observer characterized Frank's comeback after the House reprimand as "a testament to his perseverance, intelligence, and hard work, qualities admired across the political spectrum, even by those who disagree with his views and lifestyle."

With his assignment to the Budget Committee in 1991, Frank gained a position of influence from which to agitate for reductions in defense spending. He had long held the view that even during the Cold War, maintaining the military superiority of the United States required far less than the amounts allocated to the armed services in the federal budget. In *Speaking Frankly*, which was published a year after the collapse of the Soviet Union, he wrote, "The Cold War is over. America has won. And as the winners, Americans are entitled to a victory dividend—the right to spend some of the vast sums that for forty-five years have gone toward containing communism instead of on our pressing domestic needs. We can save more than $150 billion every year from our current level of defense and intelligence spending without sacrificing our standing as by far the strongest nation in the world, or jeopardizing our ability to defend any vital national interest."

Frank played a prominent role in the 1993 debate concerning the prohibition on homosexuals in the United States armed forces. Convinced that Congress was not ready to lift the ban completely, Frank advocated a compromise whereby gay or lesbian servicepeople would be permitted to maintain an openly homosexual lifestyle off-base, when not on duty, but would be forbidden to reveal their homosexuality while on duty or in uniform—"a policy that says 'Don't ask, don't tell, and don't listen, and don't investigate,'" in his words. His approach, which subsequently became official policy, incurred the wrath not only of those in favor of maintaining a complete ban but also of homosexual groups, who accused him of betrayal. In an interview with Kenneth J. Cooper for the *Washington Post* (May 20, 1993), Frank said that he found himself "telling each side things they don't want to hear." "That's the tension in my job, to try to interpret the groups to each other," he explained. (On March 30, 1995, in a lawsuit, brought by six homosexual members of the armed forces, that is expected eventually to reach the Supreme Court, the "don't ask, don't tell" policy was ruled unconstitutional by United States district court judge Eugene H. Nickerson.)

According to the *Almanac of American Politics 1986*, Barney Frank "may very well have the deadliest—and politically most effective—wit in Congress." One of his most frequently quoted remarks was prompted by the opposition of people on the political far right to both abortion and child-nutrition programs. "Sure, they're pro-life," he said. "They believe that life begins at conception and ends at birth." In response to the Reagan administration's contention in 1985 that a rising economic tide would "lift all boats" and thus benefit poor Americans, he said, "If you don't have a boat and you are standing on tiptoes in the water, a rising tide is not a cause for jubilation." He conveyed his objections to a six billion dollar antidrug bill passed by the House in 1986 by calling the measure "the legislative equivalent of crack." "It yields a short-term high, but does long-term damage to the system, and it's expensive to boot," he explained. During the fourteen-hour-long floor debate in the House on the opening day of the 104th Congress, Frank observed to the Republican majority, "You told us you would be family friendly. You forgot to tell us it would be the Addams family." Barney Frank served as the national chairman of Americans for Democratic Action for two years beginning in mid-1985. He has lived with Herb Moses, an economist, since 1987.

Selected Biographical References: N Y Times A p24 Je 3 '87 pors, A p14 S 15 '89 por, A p21 Ja 6 '95 por; Newsweek 114:17+ S 25 '89 pors; Almanac of American Politics, 1994; Politics in America, 1996

Craig Sjodin/ABC

Franz, Dennis

Oct. 28, 1944– Actor. Address: c/o Cynthia Snyder Public Relations, 3518 Cahuenga Blvd. West, Ste. 304, Los Angeles, CA 90068

"My philosophy is that if everyone is going to be good in a show, I like to be the bad guy," the actor Dennis Franz has said. "That way, you get noticed." Numbered among his "bad guy" roles are some of the two-dozen-plus police officers he has portrayed on stage and screen over the course of his career. Some elements of those heavies can be found in the flawed, ill-mannered, yet oddly sympathetic detective Andy Sipowicz, his character on the popular weekly television program *NYPD Blue*, which debuted in the fall of 1993. His portrayal of Sipowicz has earned him an Emmy Award as best actor, among other awards.

Franz got his start as an actor on the Chicago stage before moving to the West Coast in the late 1970s to pursue movie and television work. In the 1980s he parlayed a guest-starring assignment on the highly successful television drama *Hill Street Blues* into a continuing role on the show, which, in turn, led to his being chosen to portray Sipowicz. "I'm a lot more passive than most of the guys I play," Franz has been quoted as saying. "But acting is a great outlet for me. Most of us in real life walk away from a situation wishing we had done or said something different. But my characters don't usually have that problem. They say and do exactly what they mean."

The son of Franz Schlachta, a German immigrant, and his wife, Eleanor, Dennis Franz was born Dennis Schlachta on October 28, 1944 in Maywood, Illinois, outside Chicago. He has two sisters. Franz attended Proviso East High School, which Bill Davidson, in a profile of the actor for *TV Guide* (August 30, 1986), described as "turbulent." There, his easygoing nature and large build enabled him to break up fights and other disturbances, which led to his receiving the nickname "Peacemaker." A good athlete, he earned letters as a quarterback on the school's football team and as a catcher on its baseball squad. When his high-school girlfriend became interested in acting,

Franz auditioned for a part in Proviso East's production of Arthur Miller's *The Crucible*. "The guys trying out were sort of meek," he recalled to Bernard Weinraub of the *New York Times* (May 12, 1994). "I used to sing when I was a kid, and my father's words to me were, 'Be loud.' So I got up and was loud. And I got one of the leads." He portrayed the Reverend Hale in *The Crucible* and subsequently appeared in other student theatrical productions, often as a villain.

After Franz Schlachta, a baker, developed an allergic reaction to flour and abandoned his trade, he went to work in the post office, where he helped his son to get a job as a mail carrier. "I may have been the worst postal worker in history," Franz admitted to a writer for *USA Weekend* (March 10–12, 1995). "I was easily distracted by puppies, doughnut shops. I'd take mail home and watch TV, then go finish. It would be dark, and people were waiting for me on their porches." He was, he said, "a bad example."

Franz eventually continued his education, first at Wright Junior College, in Chicago, and then at Southern Illinois University, in Carbondale, "to keep out of the draft," as he confessed to Bill Davidson. In college he played leading roles in stagings of Eugene O'Neill's *Long Day's Journey Into Night* and George Bernard Shaw's *Arms and the Man* before being expelled by the university for failing to obtain his degree within the required time limit. Having by then become, in his word, "curious" about military service, he enlisted in the United States Army and, as he told Davidson, "regretted his curiosity about two weeks after he was in." Franz served a year-long tour of duty during the Vietnam War, first as part of the 82d Airborne Division and then in the 101st Airborne. "I watched a lot of guys die and get wounded, but I was not one of them," he told one interviewer. As he revealed to Hilary De Vries for an article in the *Chicago Tribune Magazine* (January 23, 1994), the experience made him "a much more serious person."

After his military discharge, in 1970, Franz returned to Maywood, where he spent about a year living with his parents and "just letting off a lot of anger," as he put it, about the things he had endured in Vietnam. He then turned again to acting, which helped to buoy him emotionally. With fellow thespians from his college days, he founded first the Unexpected Company, a traveling dinner-theatre group, and then the American Touring Company. He then became a performer with the Old Orchard Country Club theatre, in Arlington Heights, Illinois. It was there, in about 1973, that Stuart Gordon discovered Franz and invited him to join the Organic Theatre Company, of which Gordon was the founding director. Among the members of the troupe whom Franz befriended was the future film star Joe Mantegna.

Over the next five years, Franz played a wide variety of parts in Organic productions, including the title role in Shakespeare's *Macbeth*. He and other of the company's actors wrote and appeared in *Bleacher Bums*, a play that won a local Emmy Award when it was televised in Chicago. Franz told Thomas D. Elias for the New York *Daily News* (June 10, 1990) that the story, about a group of Chicago Cubs baseball fans, was "based on real life." "I'm . . . one of those frustrated fans who lives to love the Cubs even though I know they're going to lose most of the time," he added. "I love 'em anyway." The play enjoyed a record-breaking run in Los Angeles, where it was staged years later, and Elias described it as "American theatre's most enduring ode to baseball fans."

The filmmaker Brian De Palma was in the audience for a performance of the Organic production of Terry Curtis Fox's play *Cops*, about a group of off-duty Chicago police officers who become involved in a hostage situation, that featured Franz and Mantegna, and he subsequently cast Franz in his movie *The Fury* (1978), a supernatural thriller starring Kirk Douglas. In the same year, Franz appeared in Robert Altman's satiric film *A Wedding*, whose large cast also included Carol Burnett and Mia Farrow. At about that time, Altman persuaded Franz to move to Los Angeles to pursue more film work, and Franz, together with Mantegna and two other fellow actors, left Chicago for Hollywood. He soon landed the part of the detective on the trail of the razor-wielding psychopath in De Palma's *Dressed to Kill* (1980), and he worked with the director a third time in *Blow Out* (1981). Other feature films in which Franz appeared in the 1980s include Richard Franklin's *Psycho II* (1983), a sequel to Alfred Hitchcock's 1960 horror classic; De Palma's thriller *Body Double* (1984); Blake Edwards's unsuccessful comedy *A Fine Mess* (1986); and *The Package* (1989), an action/suspense movie directed by Andrew Davis and starring Gene Hackman. Franz also turned up in the made-for-television offerings *Deadly Messages* (1985) and *Kiss Shot* (1989), the latter of which starred Whoopi Goldberg as a pool shark and Franz as her handler.

Meanwhile, Franz had appeared as a police officer in *Chicago Story*, a short-lived series about cops, lawyers, and doctors that debuted on NBC in March 1982. Not long afterward, he began his association with the creative team behind the award-winning *Hill Street Blues*, which, during its six seasons on NBC, from 1981 to 1987, was credited with setting a new standard for television police drama. According to one account, the series' creator, Steven Bochco, had seen Franz's work in Brian De Palma's films and decided to cast the actor as a crooked cop to be featured in two *Hill Street* episodes. As another source has it, Franz won the part after outperforming other actors at an open casting call. In any event, he turned up during *Hill Street Blues*'s 1982–83 season as the compellingly obnoxious, corrupt, and murderous detective Sal Benedetto. Bochco and others involved with the show were so taken with Franz's performance that they wrote his character into three additional episodes before deciding, as one staff member told Bill Davidson, that Benedetto was "so bad that the only logical thing to do . . . was to kill him off." *TV Guide* selected Franz's Benedetto as the television villain of the year.

Eager to maintain a professional relationship with Franz, Bochco immediately cast him as a coach in his 1983 program *Bay City Blues*, which focused on a minor-league baseball team. For a couple of years after that ill-fated show was canceled, Franz guest-starred in a number of television action dramas, including *The A-Team*, *Simon & Simon*, and *T. J. Hooker*, invariably playing "the psychopathic bad guy, as usual," as he has phrased it. One exception was his role as "a redneck schnook from the South," as he described the character he portrayed in an episode of *Hardcastle and McCormick*. That show's executive producer, Stephen J. Cannell, liked Franz's performance so much that he offered him the lead role in a pilot.

At about the same time, Jeffrey Lewis, who had taken over as executive producer of *Hill Street Blues* after Bochco's departure, was searching for an actor to play a new character on the continuing drama. "We felt we had to do something to shake up the show . . . ," Lewis told Bill Davidson. "Our cops were *too* good. We had buffoons and sleazebags, yes, but they all had integrity. We needed a rule-bender, a troublemaker, a survivor. . . . He couldn't be *all* bad, or we'd end up having to blow him away, as we did with Benedetto. He'd have to be tough, a guy who knew how to get the job done—but in his own way. At the same time, he'd have to have characteristics to make him sympathetic to the audience—bravery, an amusingly rebellious amorality, the capacity to land on his feet." In addition, Lewis admitted to Davidson, "We also felt we had to do something to get Dennis back, or we'd lose him to Cannell."

As a result, Franz returned to *Hill Street Blues* at the start of the 1985–86 season as a regular cast member, playing the gum-chewing, tackily dressed Lieutenant Norman Buntz. While Buntz had in common with Benedetto an abrasive manner, he differed from Franz's former character in his dedication to his work. He stood out from the show's other regulars, however, because of his capacity for genuine wrongdoing, and his pursuit of justice sometimes took the form of vigilantism, which put him at odds with the show's central character, the upright Captain Frank Furillo (played by Daniel J. Travanti). On the positive side, Buntz was intrepid and resourceful, and his plainspokenness provided some of the show's funnier moments. Those qualities apparently appealed to fans of the series, and Franz's character helped *Hill Street Blues* to maintain its high ratings.

After *Hill Street Blues* went off network prime time, in 1987, Franz portrayed Norman Buntz in a spin-off, *Beverly Hills Buntz*, whose story line had the character relocate to the city of the title and become a private investigator. Perhaps because, as Franz later reflected, the show's writers made Buntz less interesting by "smoothing the edges off" him, so that he would not offend viewers, *Beverly Hills Buntz* was quickly axed. A similar fate awaited the spring 1990 entry *Nasty Boys*, which found Franz playing a narcotics detective, and *NYPD Mounted*, a 1991 project. Following the cancellation of those shows, Franz guest-starred in a number of television programs and accepted minor roles in the films *Die Hard II* (1990), the second installment in the popular series of action movies starring Bruce Willis, and *The Player* (1992), the satire about Hollywood directed by Robert Altman.

By the time Steven Bochco offered him a starring role as a cop on *NYPD Blue*, Franz had had his fill of playing police officers, having done so, by his own estimation, twenty-five or twenty-six times. But he also saw the new show as an opportunity to rejuvenate his career, which had stalled since the cancellation of *Hill Street Blues*. The premiere episode of *NYPD Blue*, which aired on ABC in September 1993, introduced Franz in his incarnation as the foul-mouthed, hard-drinking Andy Sipowicz. Although he resembles Norman Buntz in some ways, Sipowicz has more meaningful relationships with the people around him than did Buntz, largely at Franz's urging. "Actors always make suggestions about their characters, but Dennis is one of the guys you actually listen to," David Milch, the coexecutive producer of *NYPD Blue*, told Hilary De Vries. "He is the kind of actor who is able to evoke all kinds of complications in supposedly simple characters."

As a result of Franz's input, some of the story lines on *NYPD Blue* focus on Sipowicz's relationship with his previously estranged son (Michael De Luise) and with Assistant District attorney Sylvia Costas (Sharon Lawrence), whom Sipowicz married at the end of the 1994–95 season. Franz carries more of a dramatic load as Sipowicz than he did as Buntz, for *Hill Street Blues* followed the lives of a large cast of characters, while *NYPD Blue*'s main focus is on Sipowicz and Detective Bobby Simone (played by Jimmy Smits, who replaced David Caruso as costar of the series in 1994). Despite some controversy over the violence and the occasionally steamy sex scenes, *NYPD Blue* has proven to be a hit with critics as well as viewers, and in 1994 it picked up a record twenty-six Emmy Award nominations, including one for Franz, as best actor in a dramatic series. The actor went on to win the Emmy, and in 1995 his work on the show earned him a Screen Actors' Guild Award and a Golden Globe Award.

Commenting on the similarity between the two kinds of characters—police officers and villains—he has most often played, Franz pointed out to Thomas D. Elias, "There's an awareness they seem to share. There's a sense of authority both . . . seem to flaunt, whether they're law-abiding or just strong on street sense." He told Hilary De Vries that he has "always had respect for policemen." Stuart Gordon, who recruited Franz for the Organic Theatre Company, traced the actor's ability to portray cops convincingly to his experience in the Vietnam War, explaining to De Vries, "Dennis saw combat, and that makes him different from most actors. When he plays policemen, guys who put themselves on the line, it is very real to him."

The five-foot eleven-inch Dennis Franz, who weighs between 210 and 220 pounds and has thinning hair and a sizeable paunch, was described by his former *NYPD Blue* costar David Caruso as "easily one of the most likable guys you'll ever want to meet." After observing Franz on the set of the show, Hilary De Vries reported, "Franz is not only not like the tough, cynical characters he plays but is that genuine Hollywood rarity—a mature, generous actor who . . . brings a refreshingly unneurotic attitude to his career. . . . Unlike his voluble screen persona, he has an inherent taciturnity, as if long ago he answered life's difficult questions. His acting style involves no hysterics but an almost effortless transformation." Among the actor's recent credits is the role of a colorful Texas attorney for the made-for-television movie *Texas Justice*, which aired in February 1995 and received mixed reviews. He has a starring role in the soon-to-be-released film version of David Mamet's play *American Buffalo*, which also features Dustin Hoffman. On April 1, 1995 Franz married his longtime companion, Joanie Zeck, the head of an executive recruiting agency. He lives in Bel Air, California with Zeck, whose two grown daughters, from a previous union, he helped to rear. In his free time, he is an avid golfer and enjoys cooking.

Selected Biographical References: Chicago Tribune mag X p12+ Ja 23 '94 pors; N Y Times C p1+ My 12 '94 pors; TV Guide p36+ Ag 30 '86 pors

---

The Canadian Stage Company

Fraser, Brad

June 28, 1959- Canadian playwright; theatrical director; screenwriter. Address: c/o Shain Jaffe, Great North Artist Management Inc., 350 Dupont Ave., Toronto, Ontario, M5R 1V9, Canada

Since he first appeared on the Canadian theatrical scene, in the early 1980s, the playwright Brad Fraser has often found himself at the center of controversy. North American theatre companies and producers have sometimes been reluctant to stage Fraser's witty, fast-paced dramatic works because of his frequent use of onstage nudity, simulated sex, and profanity—elements that some reviewers and theatre administrators have deemed gratuitous. The outspoken playwright has been equally unorthodox in his subject matter: his characters routinely reject traditional values, and he frequently sets his explorations of human emotions and sexuality against an unsettling backdrop of brutal violence. But despite the debate that has surrounded the productions of such works as *Unidentified Human Remains and the True Nature of Love* and *Poor Super Man*, whose world premiere was performed before an audience that included members of the Cincinnati vice squad, Fraser's plays have been consistent hits at the box office, particularly among young theatregoers, and they have earned the playwright numerous awards, including the prestigious Floyd S. Chalmers Award for best new Canadian play, for *Unidentified Human Remains*.

Critics have cited Fraser's hip dialogue, up-to-the-minute themes, and cinematic pacing as the major factors contributing to the appeal he holds for the MTV generation. For his part, Fraser has said that he strives to make live theatre more interesting for contemporary audiences by giving them "a jolt every fifteen to twenty seconds," a tactic that stems from his early experiences watching naturalistic plays with "one set and four characters, all of whom talk about things that happened in the past until they are led to some sort of internal character revelation," as he put it in a recent essay for the Toronto magazine *Shift*. "We don't think that way anymore," he explained to Vit Wagner, who interviewed him for the *Toronto Star* (March 7, 1992). "We don't have the attention span for that. We pick up information much more quickly visually. Our eyes have been trained to pick up stuff out of a thirty-second commercial. I'm trying to find a way to get that into the theatre. The only thing I really want to do is entertain." A five-time winner of the Alberta Culture Playwriting Competition, Fraser has recently broadened his scope to include screenwriting.

The eldest of four children, Brad Fraser was born on June 28, 1959 in the Canadian prairie city of Edmonton, Alberta. He grew up in a tough, working-class neighborhood, and his childhood was scarred by alcoholism, domestic violence, and sexual abuse. Describing his youth in an interview for the Canadian newsmagazine *Saturday Night* (May 1992), Fraser told Scot Morison that a male cousin sexually molested him for almost ten years, beginning when he was about three, and that his father, a heavy-equipment operator for a highway construction company, was a mentally and physically abusive man who subjected his wife and children to frequent beatings, one of which was so severe that it left Fraser with a concussion. Intimidated by his father for much of his boyhood, Fraser reached a turning point when, at the age of thirteen, he came home from school one day to find that his parents had reconciled after several months of separation. "My heart just dropped . . . ," he recalled to Scot Morison. "That was when I made the decision that I would never be mistreated by him or anyone else again." The father reacted to his son's determination by beating him once again. Fraser was unable to defend himself against his powerfully built father, but he refused to live in fear. "I had no choice," he told Morison. "It was either kill myself or kill my father or come to that decision. Of the three options, that one seemed the most feasible." A year later, the Frasers divorced, and Brad and his siblings remained with their mother, Sharon.

As a student at Victoria Composite High School in Edmonton, Fraser indulged his growing interest in the theatre by enrolling in the school's performing-arts program. By his own account an "abysmal actor," he soon began to concentrate on playwriting. At the suggestion of his drama teacher, he entered a high school playwriting competition sponsored by the Department of Culture of the province of Alberta. His entry, *Two Pariahs at a Bus Stop in a Large City Late at Night*, took first place. The prize included a trip to Banff, Alberta to participate in a playwriting workshop under the direction of the Canadian dramatist Sharon Pollock. "As young as he was, he seemed to have had a rich life experience," Pollock said when she spoke to Scot Morison for the *Saturday Night* profile of the playwright. "He struck me as being a lot more aware of the true nature of the world around him than many of the other playwrights who were there, all of them a good deal older."

Agreeing with Pollock's assessment of Fraser as a writer of considerable promise, Vivien Bosley, the artistic director of the Walterdale Playhouse, an amateur theatre in Edmonton, invited him to write and direct a play for the theatre. Fraser spent, by his own count, "eight or nine months" working independently on his play, *Mutants*, which he has since described as a "Brechtian *singspiel*" about a group of teenagers who escape from a correctional institution to protest ongoing sexual abuse there. Shortly before auditions were to begin, however, some members of the theatre's board of directors moved to cancel the production, because of its controversial subject matter and frank language. After several long and heated board meetings, *Mutants* opened as scheduled, and it became the second-highest-grossing production of the Walterdale Playhouse's 1980–81 season, despite a generally lukewarm critical reception. In his review for the *Edmonton Journal* (January 28, 1981), Keith Ashwell contended that the play was marred by "objectionable shrillness and unnecessary bleakness," but he nonetheless applauded the young playwright's skill. "Now that Fraser has let off this vast blast of superheated steam, perhaps he will sit down and write a substantive play," Ashwell wrote, "for there is no doubt about his talent, his maturity as a writer. *Mutants* proceeds with a craftsman's certainty. It characterizes people with bold strokes. It dramatizes situations with a surgeon's appreciation of the jugular. . . . The substance, of remarkable self-assurance and an equally remarkable sense of theatricality, is there."

Among *Mutants*' admirers was Andras Tahn of the Twenty-fifth Street Theatre in Saskatoon, Saskatchewan. Tahn commissioned Fraser, who was then working as a directory-assistance operator, to write a new piece for the company. The result was the unsettling *Wolfboy*, about a homosexual relationship that develops between two boys—one of whom thinks he is a werewolf—in a hospital psychiatric ward. The production, which opened in 1981 to mixed reviews, generated further attention for the playwright in Canadian theatrical circles. *Wolfboy* was subsequently staged to considerable acclaim in Edmonton and Vancouver.

Fraser's next effort was *Rude Noises (For a Blank Generation)*, which began as a collaboration with the Theatre Passe Muraille, an experimental theatre collective in Toronto. After three months of unproductive improvisational sessions, Fraser suggested that the group begin again under his direction. The group's artistic director, Paul Thompson, agreed, but he gave the playwright a time limit of two weeks. Drawing on the material he had written over the previous three months, Fraser created a collage of scenes that examined the world of aimless street kids in Toronto through a non-linear narrative. *Rude Noises* was dismissed by Ray Conlogue of the Toronto *Globe and Mail* (March 19, 1982), among others, as a work "of emphatic insignificance" with "a veneer of wit and a paucity of observation and honesty." The negative reviews notwithstanding, *Rude Noises* became a surprise hit for the Passe Muraille troupe.

Buoyed by the popular success of *Rude Noises*, Fraser moved to Toronto, where he spent the next two years honing his craft, supporting himself by waiting tables. Among the plays he completed during this period was *Young Art*, his version of the Arthurian legend. His optimism began to wane, however, when a Theatre Passe Muraille production of *Wolfboy*, starring Keanu Reeves, was pilloried by the Toronto critics. Fraser was so discouraged by the poor notices that he vowed never to write another play. Within months of his return to Edmonton, however, he changed his mind and resumed writing. Over the next two years, his efforts included two darkly comic plays that were produced by Workshop West at the 1985 Edmonton Fringe Theatre Festival: *Chainsaw Love* and *Re-*

turn of the Bride, neither of which received a positive response from critics.

The most ambitious of Fraser's projects from this period was *Unidentified Human Remains and the True Nature of Love*, the work that announced his arrival on the international theatrical scene. The provocative, erotically charged play, which had its genesis in an improvisational exercise at Workshop West during the summer of 1985, marked a departure for the playwright, in that he turned away from werewolves and other fantastical images to explore such profoundly human themes as love and loss. Set in Edmonton, where a serial killer is brutally murdering young women, the play centers around David, a wisecracking, cynical gay waiter; his roommate and former lover, Candy; and his best friend, Bernie, who often arrives at David's apartment in blood-stained clothes and is eventually revealed to be the killer.

In a program note for its first production, Fraser said that he had written the piece "in direct reaction" to the "changes" he had seen in his hometown and elsewhere over the years, citing in particular the AIDS epidemic, the increase in violent crime, environmental destruction, and "rampant materialism." "*Unidentified Human Remains* is about my life . . . and the lives of many people I know," he wrote. "It is about anyone who listens to the morning news and wonders how . . . they can face another day. It is about wanting to close your eyes and make all the bad things go away and not being able to do so. . . . It is about taking risks and questioning values and challenging oneself in a way that is both frightening and exhilarating. Mostly it is about love—in all its many forms."

Unidentified Human Remains unfolds through a series of short scenes, with crosscuts and simultaneous action giving it an almost cinematic look. "I was so sick of . . . static intellectual theatre . . . ," Fraser explained to Tony Chase in a conversation for *TheaterWeek* (July 11–17, 1994). "I think the fractured structure I use is based on rock video and comic books, and limited attention spans. I guess you could call it my voice, and it first came together with *Unidentified Human Remains*." Determined to attract and hold his audiences' interest, he deliberately included scenes that called for full frontal nudity and simulated sex. Because of the play's graphic nature, however, one theatre company after another returned the script to Fraser, saying it was unproducible. Finally, Alberta Theatre Projects in Calgary agreed to stage the play as part of its 1989 PlayRites! Festival, an influential annual showcase for new Canadian works. Critics and audiences alike agreed that it was the best of the four works featured at the festival.

When *Unidentified Human Remains* opened in Toronto a few months later, Robert Crew of the *Toronto Star* (January 29, 1990) added it to his list of plays "not to be missed," calling it "a clever and skillful work" that "resonates with the true nature of theatre." Equally impressed was the British director Derek Goldby, who used his connections in the United States to mount a production of the play at the Halsted Theater Center in Chicago, where it ran for four months despite negative reviews from some of the city's most influential critics, among them Richard Christiansen of the *Chicago Tribune*, who dismissed it as a "soft-porn thriller." A subsequent Off-Broadway production scored a similar success at the box office and found slightly more favor with critics. Perhaps its most ardent supporter was William A. Henry 3d, who, in his assessment for *Time* (September 30, 1991), characterized *Unidentified Human Remains* as an "MTV drama" whose plot, "like a music video, features casual nudity, simulated sex, and arrestingly etched violence." In his view, the play was "not only stylistically apt and journalistically observant about its rock-and-anomie world but also deeply felt and thought. It stunningly blends punk popular appeal and poetic power."

Such enthusiastic notices were the order of the day when *Unidentified Human Remains* opened in Britain, at the Traverse Theatre in Edinburgh in 1992. Leading the applause was Robert Hewison of the London *Sunday Times*. "It is simply bursting with promise and talent . . . ," Hewison wrote in his review of December 6, 1992. "The writing is edgy, lyrical, whiplash-bitter. Fraser's subject is desolation and emotional impotence, which he dissects like a compassionate surgeon." The production moved to the Hampstead Theatre Club, in north London, early in the following year. *Unidentified Human Remains* was chosen as the best new play of the 1992–93 London season by *Time Out* magazine, and Fraser himself was named the year's most promising playwright by the London *Evening Standard*. The work has since been staged in Italy and Japan, and a film version, retitled *Love and Human Remains* and directed by Denys Arcand from Fraser's screenplay, was released in Canada and Europe in 1993 and in the United States in 1995.

Meanwhile, Fraser continued to work with Alberta Theatre Projects on such productions as *Blood Buddies*, on which he collaborated with Jeffrey Hirschfield, and *Prom Night of the Living Dead*, which he conceived with Darrin Hagen. In 1992, under the auspices of the project's PlayRites! Festival, Fraser unveiled *The Ugly Man*, his black comedy adaptation of the Jacobean psychological tragedy *The Changeling*. Set on a ranch in the Canadian West in the twentieth century, Fraser's campy, B-movie retelling of the lurid and blood-drenched tale (Fraser has described it as "the kind of thing that might happen if Barbara Stanwyck and Tennessee Williams were to fall on top of William Faulkner") features four unscrupulous young men, a spoiled and manipulative virgin, her rich mother, a maid who dabbles in magic, and a hideously disfigured handyman, all of whom are intentionally one-dimensional and unabashedly amoral. During the course of the play, almost all of the characters die.

Because of its graphic violence and sadomasochism, *The Ugly Man* created a considerable stir, despite Fraser's assertion that he had purposely chosen a Jacobean classic as the basis for his play in order to demonstrate that there are historical precedents for his work. "I get so much flak about the sex and the violence and all that, so I wanted to show that it's been around the theatre for an awfully long time," he explained to Vit Wagner. Although most reviewers recognized the play's commercial appeal, some, including Liam Lacey of the Toronto *Globe and Mail*, questioned what Lacey called its "self-conscious outrageousness." Referring to the play as "a steady parade of blood, buggery, and bondage," Lacey observed in his evaluation of March 27, 1992, "For the rock video, horror film, and comic book generation that Fraser is bringing into the theatre, these naughty pleasures of bad taste are entertainment in a way that enlightened theatre can never be. . . . But it . . . leaves you wondering what the theatre, and the world, are coming to." After he saw *The Ugly Man*, in a staging by the Co-Active Theatre Factory in London, Antony Thorncroft noted in the *Financial Times* (November 11, 1994), "It is easier to accept a body-strewn stage when the characters are decked out as sixteenth-century Spaniards—but the piece does nothing to dispel the belief that Fraser is one of the most exciting writers working in North America."

Fraser described his next major work, *Poor Super Man*, about a relationship between two men—one ostensibly straight, one gay—and how that relationship affects the women in their lives, as "the real follow-through to *Human Remains.*" One of the creative catalysts for the piece was the playwright's three-year relationship with an actor who had considered himself strictly heterosexual before he became involved with Fraser. Unable to find a Canadian company willing to stage the play, Fraser showed *Poor Super Man* to the Ensemble Theatre of Cincinnati, an adventurous American regional theatre, which eventually agreed to produce the piece, marking the first time one of Fraser's plays was scheduled to receive its world premiere outside Canada. After reading the script, however, one member of the Ensemble Theatre's board of directors complained about its sexually explicit content. In the light of the recent passage of an antigay municipal ordinance, the twenty-eight-member board voted to withdraw the play from the season's lineup, fearing that it would be "used as a political football," to quote John Vissman, the company's managing director. The cancellation soon came to the attention of the Canadian press corps, some of whom accused the Ensemble Theatre of censorship. Meanwhile, Fraser had asked the artistic directors of several leading Canadian theatrical companies to write letters in his behalf. In the end, the board reversed its decision, and the show was rescheduled for the spring of 1994.

Representatives from the Cincinnati police department's vice squad attended the premiere of *Poor Super Man*, in April 1994, but did not interfere with the production on opening night or during its subsequent sold-out run. The critical response was enthusiastic and overwhelmingly favorable. Hailing Fraser as "a major new force in North American playwriting," Chris Jones of *Variety* (May 16, 1994) described the play as "more thoughtful and serious" than *Unidentified Human Remains*. "Shot through with such contemporary demons as AIDS, loneliness, economic struggle, and personal repression, Fraser's often cynical play has a lot to say about modern life and love . . . ," Jones said. "Fraser argues for personal truth and integrity in place of our typically unrealistic expectations."

Noting Fraser's uncommon popularity among young, hip theatregoers, Jones identified as possible reasons his "rapidfire" dialogue and highly cinematic style. But his "main strength," in Jones's view, was simple: "He never bores his audience for a moment." In *Poor Super Man*, Fraser introduced a new element—namely, projections of comic book-style captions that reveal the characters' thoughts and provide commentary about the action. When *Poor Super Man* opened in Canada, in October 1994, in a staging directed by the playwright himself, Liz Nicholls of the *Edmonton Journal* singled out the "snappy" captions, which gave the play the look of "a bold comic strip," as one of the production's strong points. "Fraser's theatre, designed to be as fragmented as the modern TV-shaped mind . . . , is not one in which scenes develop," she wrote in her review of October 18, 1994. "Staccato exchanges happen, and they stop. And they have a cumulative buzz—not least because the dialogue is faster than a speeding bullet, smartass, revealing, and genuinely funny." Resoundingly positive notices also greeted the Traverse Theatre's production of the play at the 1994 Edinburgh Fringe Festival and, later, in London.

Fraser's most recent projects include a musical adaptation of the 1977 Canadian cult film *Outrageous*, which proved to be a popular attraction as a workshop production at the Calgary PlayRites! festival in 1994. In mid-1994 he signed a contract with Disney's Touchstone Pictures to write the screen adaptation of Brian Damato's novel *Beauty*, which he has described as a science-fiction romance. He is also writing the script for Alliance Communications' proposed film *Our Man in Manila*, based on a *Saturday Night* article about a Canadian who runs a bar in the Philippines. "I just really need some new challenges," he told Scott Feschuk for the Toronto *Globe and Mail* (October 13, 1994). "The theatre is a little restricting for me right now. . . . Down the road I want to come up with some new ways of telling stories. I think theatre and film are both very tired. I know I can do some interesting stuff, but first I've got to get to know film as intimately as I do theatre."

Muscular and fit as a result of the strenuous workout regimen he has followed in recent years, Brad Fraser has close-cropped dark hair and a "Clark Gable moustache," to borrow Scot Morison's description. For most of his adult life, he made his home in Edmonton, in a house large enough to accommodate his sizable collections of books, videotapes, and comic books. (His comic book collection alone is said to exceed seven thousand items.) Since selling his house a few years ago, he has lived in various hotels or stayed with friends. Unafraid of controversy, Fraser has readily admitted that he enjoys the extreme reactions his works provoke. "My plays are there to promote discussion and debate, not to be universally accepted by everyone and especially our parents," he said in the interview for *TheaterWeek*. "I'm really encouraged by the fact that so many established critics like to jump on me, because it means that I'm doing something that's dangerous, and whether they have to dismiss it or rail against it, I'm sure they're at least thinking about it."

Selected Biographical References: Chicago Tribune Arts p14+ F 17 '94 por; Saturday Night p44+ My '92 pors; Toronto Star p1+ Mr 7 '92 por; Canadian Who's Who, 1994

New York Times

Friedman, Thomas L.

July 20, 1953- Journalist. Address: c/o The New York Times, 1627 I St. NW, Washington, DC 20006

The winner of two Pulitzer Prizes for international reporting before the age of thirty-five, *New York Times* columnist Thomas L. Friedman cut his eyeteeth as a journalist in the Middle East. He first became interested in that area, especially Israel, when he was a teenager in Minneapolis, and by the time he completed graduate school, he was well versed in the politics, history, and cultures of the region. Notwithstanding the extensive knowledge he had acquired, when he arrived in Beirut, Lebanon to cover the civil war there as a reporter for United Press International in 1979, he found the violence, bombings, and atrocities he witnessed to be a far cry from the academic descriptions in his textbooks. As he continued his assignment in the Middle East, he found that Israel, especially in light of its 1982 invasion of Lebanon, was a country less perfect than the one he had idolized as a youth. Friedman, who became the *New York Times*'s Beirut bureau chief in 1982 and its Jerusalem bureau chief two years later, described his experiences in Lebanon and Israel in a memoir called *From Beirut to Jerusalem*, for which he won the 1989 National Book Award for nonfiction. A personal as well as a historical account of events, the book "tells as much about the inner quest of a Jew from the American Middle West . . . as it does about the Middle East," Cathryn Donohoe noted in her profile of Friedman for *Insight* (September 4, 1989). Friedman took a year off to write the book, and after returning to the *New York Times* in 1989, he became, successively, the newspaper's chief diplomatic correspondent, chief White House correspondent, and chief economic correspondent. In January 1995 he began his current assignment, as the foreign-affairs columnist on the *Times*'s op-ed page, one of the most prestigious positions in journalism.

Thomas Loren Friedman was born on July 20, 1953 in Minneapolis into "a rather typical middle-class American Jewish family," as he has put it. His father, Harold Abraham Friedman, was a ball-bearings salesman, and his mother, Margaret (Philips) Friedman, was a homemaker and part-time bookkeeper. In 1968 his parents took him to Israel to visit his sister, Shelley, who was spending her junior year of college at Tel Aviv University. "That trip would change my life," Friedman wrote in *From Beirut to Jerusalem*. "I was only fifteen years old at the time and just waking up to the world. The flight to Jerusalem marked the first time I had traveled beyond the border of Wisconsin and the first time I had ridden on an airplane. I don't know if it was just the shock of the new, or a fascination waiting to be discovered, but something about Israel and the Middle East grabbed me in both heart and mind. I was totally taken with the place, its people and its conflicts. Since that moment, I have never really been interested in anything else." Friedman spent the rest of high school reading all he could about Israel and lecturing his classmates and teachers to show off his knowledge about the country. "In fact, high school for me, I am now embarrassed to say, was one big celebration of Israel's victory in the [1967] Six-Day War," he admitted in his book.

While summering in Israel following his high school graduation, in 1971, Friedman became friendly with Arabs from the town of Nazareth, an association that inspired him to buy an Arabic phrase book and read about the Arabic world. Upon his return to the United States in the fall of that year, he entered Brandeis University, in Waltham, Massachusetts, where he majored in Middle Eastern studies. He enrolled in an Arabic language course during his first semester, and he spent two weeks in Cairo in 1972, en route to Jerusalem for a semester at Hebrew University. In the summer of 1974, he returned to Egypt for a semester of Arabic language courses at the American University in Cairo. When he got back to Brandeis, he gave a lecture about Egypt for his fellow students and faculty. In the audience was a graduate student from Israel who heckled him, mocking him for being a Jew who admired Egyptians. "I learned two important lessons from the encounter," Friedman recalled in his memoir. "First, when it comes to discussing the Middle East, people go temporarily insane, so if you are planning to talk to an audience of more than two, you'd better have mastered the subject. Second, a Jew who wants to make a career working in or studying about the Middle East will always be a lonely man: he will never be fully accepted or trusted by the Arabs, and he will never be fully accepted or trusted by the Jews."

After taking his B.A. degree summa cum laude from Brandeis in 1975, Friedman, the recipient of a Marshall scholarship, entered St. Antony's College, at Oxford University, in England, from which he earned an M.Phil. degree in Modern Middle East studies in 1978. Meanwhile, in August 1976, he had begun his journalistic career, writing an op-ed piece about Democratic presidential candidate Jimmy Carter's promise to Jewish voters that, if elected, he would fire Secretary of State Henry Kissinger. Friedman's essay discussed the oddity of that promise, since Kissinger was the first Jewish secretary of state in American history. With the help of his girlfriend and future wife, Ann Louise Bucksbaum, who was then working as a copy editor at the *Des Moines Register*, Friedman was able to publish his article in that newspaper on August 23, 1976. Over the next two years, he wrote several other op-ed pieces for the *Register* and for the *Minneapolis Star*.

Shortly before he graduated from St. Antony's, Friedman took his small portfolio of op-ed articles to the London bureau of United Press International and applied for a job as a reporter, even though he had not covered a single news event. "He was obviously an exceptionally bright young man," Leon Daniel, who was then the London bureau chief of UPI, told a reporter for the *Village Voice* (March 27, 1990). "Ordinarily, in those days, we didn't hire too many people off the street, but he was the exception." In an interview with Sam Staggs for *Publishers Weekly* (July 14, 1989), Friedman said, "UPI taught me how to be a journalist. It was on-the-job training, and gradually I learned how to write a news story."

In the spring of 1979, after a UPI correspondent in Beirut who had been nicked in the ear by a stray bullet decided to leave Lebanon, Friedman was offered the job in the Lebanese capital. Although he was nervous about going to a country in the midst of a civil war, he immediately accepted. "My friends and family all thought I was insane," he wrote in *From Beirut to Jerusalem*. "A Jew? In Beirut? I didn't really have a response for them; I didn't really know what awaited me. All I knew was that this was my moment of truth. I had been studying about the Arab world and Israel for six years; if I didn't go now, I would never go. So I went." Friedman, who spoke Hebrew and Arabic fairly well by that time, arrived in Beirut in June 1979 with his wife, Ann, whom he had married on November 23, 1978.

On his first night in Beirut, Friedman heard gun shots for the first time in his life; there had been a shootout in the street outside the hotel where he and his wife were staying. "The thought that went through my mind was, 'No, Toto, this isn't Kansas,'" he recalled to Cathryn Donohoe. Moving into an apartment in Muslim West Beirut, the area where most foreign reporters lived, the Friedmans tried to maintain a normal lifestyle, as most Beirutis did, despite the occasional outbursts of violence. Friedman remained in Beirut until 1981, when he accepted a job with the *New York Times* at the newspaper's New York headquarters. Eleven months later he was back in Lebanon, as the *Times*'s Beirut bureau chief.

On June 6, 1982 the Israeli army invaded Lebanon, in an effort to drive out Palestinian guerrillas who had been shelling settlements on Israel's northern border. While Friedman was covering the invasion, several members of the family of his Lebanese assistant, Mohammad Kasrawi, moved into Friedman's apartment to keep a close watch on his possessions. A few days later, on June 11, the apartment building was completely destroyed by an explosive device. Local police said the bombing was the result of a feud between rival Palestinian refugee groups who were squabbling over the allocation of apartments. Kasrawi's wife and two of his daughters were among the nineteen people killed in the explosion. The day after the blast, editors at the *Times* took the unusual step of publishing the transcript of a conversation between Friedman and Craig R. Whitney, the foreign-news editor in New York. "I have lost all my possessions except for a suit and shirts, but that is not a concern now," Friedman told Whitney via teleprinter. "Mohammed has devoted his life to the *New York Times*. You don't have any idea the places he and I have been in the past week, and I am just devastated [by] what has happened to him."

The possibility of becoming a victim of random violence was a fact of life in Beirut, but Friedman, like most of the other journalists in Lebanon, also had to face the realization that he could become a deliberate target. "There wasn't a single reporter in West Beirut who did not feel intimidated, constrained, or worried at one time or another about something he had learned, considered writing, or had written involving the Syrians, the [Palestinian Liberation Organization], the Phalangists, or any of the forty-odd militias in Lebanon," Friedman recalled in his book. "Every reporter in Beirut was fully aware that for $1.98 and ten Green Stamps, anyone could have you killed." Fearing retaliation, journalists sometimes filed stories without a byline, he has said, or sent their articles to other news bureaus outside Lebanon, which then relayed the stories to their newspapers. Friedman himself had yet another reason to worry about his safety. As he observed in *From Beirut to Jerusalem*, "Being the only full-time American Jewish reporter in West Beirut in the early 1980s was a tricky task at times, particularly during the height of the Israeli invasion." If a Lebanese pressed him about his ethnic origin beyond his being an American, he would say that his ancestry was Romanian, which was true. Occasionally, however, someone in Beirut would find out about his religion, causing him some anxiety, although by his account he was never in any real danger.

In May 1982 Friedman traveled to Syria to report on the Syrian government's massacre of an estimated ten thousand to twenty-five thousand of its own citizens in order to quell a rebellion in the city of Hama. By the time he arrived in Hama, more than two months had passed since the killings, but as he noted in his memoir, not all the blood had been washed away: "Walking through the nearly deserted streets, my notebook in my back pocket so no one would know I was a journalist, I was too shocked at first to talk to anyone." His account of what he found in the city, which had been literally flattened, was printed on the front page of the *New York Times* on May 29, 1982. The brutality of what he has called "Hama Rules"—the propensity of rivals in the Middle East power struggle to use massive overkill in order to send messages to each other—was something he tried to understand for years after the Syrian massacre.

A few months later Friedman reported on the massacre of an estimated three hundred to one thousand people that occurred over a three-day period, September 16–18, 1982, at two Palestinian refugee camps in West Beirut called Sabra and Shatila. The killings were committed by Lebanese militiamen from the Christian Phalangist Party who were bent on avenging the murder of their leader, Bashir Gemayal, on September 14. The Phalangists were allies of Israel, which had secured the area around Sabra and Shatila after the June invasion of Lebanon. Although Israeli soldiers did not take part in the mass killings, the fact that some of them were aware of the slaughter of civilians but did nothing to stop it later caused an uproar around the world and in Israel itself.

"Sabra and Shatila was something of a personal crisis for me," Friedman admitted in his book. "The Israel I met on the outskirts of Beirut was not the heroic Israel I had been taught to identify with." Israel's role in the incident, Friedman wrote, made him "[boil] in anger—anger which [he] worked out by reporting with all the skill [he] could muster on exactly what happened in those camps." By his own account, he "worked day and night on that story, barely sleeping between sessions at [his] typewriter." The resulting article, which he has described as "an almost hour-by-hour reconstruction of the massacre," occupied four full pages in the *New York Times* on September 26, 1982. In 1983 Friedman was awarded the Pulitzer Prize for international reporting, in recognition of his coverage of "the Israeli invasion of Beirut and its tragic aftermath," in the words of the Pulitzer Prize board. Friedman himself has said that he believes he received the award for his piece about the Sabra and Shatila massacre.

One night in April 1984, Friedman was abruptly awakened by the sound of mortar fire. His apartment building seemed to be under attack. As the shelling intensified, he crawled to his phone to call the *New York Times* foreign editor in New York, but before anyone answered he put the phone down, having realized that such bombardments had been going on in Beirut for nine years and that the fact that the target happened to be his apartment house was not news. Taking shelter in his bathroom, the only windowless room in his flat, he waited for the cease-fire. "All I could think was: This is really crazy," he recalled. "I am the *New York Times* correspondent in Beirut. I am being shelled, and it's not news. It's time to leave."

Two months later Friedman was on his way to Israel, to begin his assignment as the *Times*'s new bureau chief in Jerusalem. During his three years in Israel, Friedman often reported on Israel's occupation of the West Bank and the Gaza Strip, which it had captured in the Six-Day War and where 1.7 million Palestinians lived. Friedman was fascinated by the undercurrent of tension in Israel, even though daily life for most citizens living outside the occupied territories was relatively quiet and violence-free. In *From Beirut to Jerusalem*, he wrote about a photograph of Israel that he brought back to the United States as a symbolic reminder of the country. The picture "shows a beautiful old almond tree, its limbs stretched wide, standing on the banks of the Sea of Galilee. The tree is alone, framed by the placid blue waters of the Galilee. By all rights it should be a picture of total serenity, except that in the shade of the tree, next to its base, is a steel drum set into the ground. On top of the drum is written in Hebrew: SECURITY HOLE. This is where police dump unexploded bombs; such drums are all over Israel."

Friedman's tenure in Jerusalem ended in early 1988, a few months after the *intifada*, a rebellion by Palestinian youths, began in the occupied territories. Just before leaving his post, Friedman, his wife, and their two daughters experienced a rock-throwing incident firsthand. Friedman and his family were driving to a restaurant in Israeli-occupied East Jerusalem when a Palestinian teenager suddenly threw a stone at their car, which had Israeli license plates. No one in the family was hurt, but all were badly shaken. "I had seen massacres and car bombings and heard snipers until they had almost become routine," Friedman observed in his book. "I had dodged them all for ten years, only to get hit by a stone. It was a rather fitting punctuation mark for my journey." In 1988 Friedman won a second Pulitzer Prize for international reporting, for "balanced and informed coverage of Israel," to quote the citation from the Pulitzer Prize board.

Taking a year's leave of absence from the *New York Times*, Friedman spent most of 1988 working on *From Beirut to Jerusalem*, which he wrote with the help of a Guggenheim Fellowship. The style of writing he adopted for the book was purposely different from his newswriting. "Working in daily journalism, you're in a straitjacket when you write news," Friedman explained Sam Staggs. "Certain words and phrases are banned; for example, you can't say 'allege' in the *Times*. So I decided that in my book I would let it rip. I had the freedom to write without an editor standing over my shoulder saying, 'You can't use that word' or 'That's too harsh,' 'That's too nice,' etc."

From Beirut to Jerusalem gained mostly favorable reviews and became a modest best-seller. In a review of the book for the February 1990 edition of *Current History*, Carol L. Thompson wrote, "This is journalism at its best—observant, objective and sensitive." Peter McGrath, who assessed the book for *Newsweek* (July 24, 1989), agreed: "Friedman provides one of the best accounts yet of the Middle East psychodrama." *From Beirut to Jerusalem* is divided into two parts: the first describes Friedman's experiences in Lebanon, and the second, his adventures in Israel. "In Jerusalem, Friedman's stories change character," McGrath noted. "His writing loses its playfulness as he confronts the moral ambiguities of today's Israel." The book was reissued in paperback in 1995, with an updated chapter that includes Friedman's own prescription for a solution to the Israeli-Palestinian conflict.

Upon returning to the *Times* after his leave, Friedman joined the newspaper's Washington, D.C., bureau, where he covered the State Department as chief diplomatic correspondent, and then President George Bush as chief White House correspondent. He made one more change, to economic reporting, before he was selected by the *Times*'s publisher, Arthur Ochs Sulzerberger Jr., as the newspaper's foreign-affairs columnist. In his first op-ed column, published on January 1, 1995, Friedman announced that he would focus on Asian affairs. "Let's face it," he wrote, "when the history of the late twentieth century is written, the most important event may not be the reconstruction of Europe, the Cold War, or the collapse of Communism, but rather the rapid modernization in one generation of two billion people from Japan to the border of India. Never have so many raised their standard of living so fast." Since then, his topics have included, in addition to Asian affairs, the economic upheavals in Mexico and Russia, the war in Bosnia, the role of the North Atlantic Treaty Organization in Bosnia, and the rocky road to peace in the Middle East. Although he has invariably discussed complex issues in his columns, Friedman has often included personal anecdotes to illustrate particular points.

Friedman and his wife, Ann, and their daughters, Orly and Natalie, live in a suburb of Washington, D.C. In addition to his two Pulitzer Prizes and the National Book Award, Friedman has won several other awards, including the Overseas Press Club Award (1980), the Livingston Award for Young Journalists (1982), the New York Newspaper Guild Page One Award (1984), the Marine Corps Historical Foundation's Colonel Robert D. Heinl Jr. Memorial Award (1984), and the New Israel Fund Award for Outstanding Reporting from Israel (1987). Friedman also wrote the text for *War Torn*, a 1984 collection of photographs taken in war zones all over the world.

Selected Biographical References: Cur Hist 89:77 F '90; Insight 5:58+ S 4 '89 por; Newsweek 114:57 Jl 24 '89 por; Pub W 236:54+ Jl 14 '89 por; Village Voice p31+ Mr 27 '90 por; Contemporary Authors new rev vol 38 (1993); Friedman, Thomas. From Beirut to Jerusalem (1989); Who's Who in American Jewry, 1987

Habitat for Humanity

Fuller, Millard

Jan. 3, 1935– President, Habitat for Humanity International; lawyer; entrepreneur; social activist. Address: c/o Habitat for Humanity International, 121 Habitat St., Americus, GA 31709-3498

Millard Fuller is the president of Habitat for Humanity International, a grassroots, ecumenical Christian ministry based in Americus, Georgia that was established to eliminate homelessness and what has been labeled "poverty housing" wherever they exist. A United Nations committee has estimated that as many as one and a half billion people, or one quarter of Earth's human population, lack adequate housing, and perhaps a hundred million have no shelter at all. Habitat for Humanity, according to Fuller, who founded the organization in 1976 with Linda Caldwell Fuller, his wife, aims "to make shelter a matter of conscience"—"to make it politically, socially, and religiously unacceptable to have people living in substandard housing." Using donated money and material and volunteer labor, to date Habitat has built or renovated dwellings in partnership with more than thirty-five thousand low-income families in forty-three foreign countries and eleven hundred cities in the United States. No-interest mortgage payments for the houses, which are sold without profit, finance a so-called Fund for Humanity, which is used to build additional houses. "Habitat does more than build homes; it builds families, neighborhoods, and communities by bringing people together in a spirit of friendship and teamwork," former United States secretary of housing and urban development Jack Kemp, a former Habitat board member, has observed. President Bill Clinton, one of the organization's hundreds of thousands of volunteers, has called Habitat for Humanity "arguably the most successful continuous community-service project in the history of the United States."

Before dedicating his life to helping "God's people in need," as he has put it, Fuller devoted himself obsessively to various commercial enterprises. As the cofounder and president of the Fuller and Dees Marketing Group, he became a millionaire by the age of twenty-nine. Soon after, spurred by the near-collapse of his marriage, he gave almost all his wealth to charity and went to live at Koinonia Farm, an integrated Christian community near Americus. Through his association with Clarence Jordan, who had helped to organize Koinonia, he gained, in his words, "an understanding of the servanthood concept of the gospel." The idea for Habitat for Humanity and the Fund for Humanity sprang from a housing partnership that Fuller and Jordan established at Koinonia in the late 1960s. Another inspiration was Fuller's experience in developing a housing program for poor families in Zaire from 1973 to 1976, which he described in his book *Bokotola* (1977). Fuller is also the author of four books about Habitat for Humanity: *Love in the Mortar Joints* (1980) and *No More Shacks!* (1986), both of which were cowritten by Diane Scott, *The Excitement Is Building* (1990), written with Linda Fuller, and *The Theology of the Hammer* (1994).

Millard Dean Fuller was born on January 3, 1935 in Lanett, a cotton-mill town in eastern Alabama on the border with Georgia. His mother, Estin (Cook) Fuller, died when he was about three; from the marriage of his father, Render Alexander Fuller, a grocery-store owner, and his stepmother, Eunice (Stephens) Fuller, a homemaker, he has two younger half-brothers, Render Nicholas Fuller, who is disabled, and James Doyle Fuller, a lawyer. Millard Fuller's career as an entrepreneur began when, at the age of six, he fattened and then sold a pig that his father had given him. He proceeded to buy and sell more pigs and then chickens and rabbits as well, and he also developed modest trades in worms, which he sold to fishermen, and in firecrackers. "I enjoyed the experience of being a successful businessman," he wrote in *Bokotola*.

When Fuller was about ten, his father bought four hundred acres of farmland. One of his father's first actions after that purchase was the repair of a tiny, tumbledown shack that an elderly married couple had long inhabited on the property. Fuller helped in the reconstruction, which included building interior walls and ceilings with wood gleaned from several packing crates used to transport coffins. He has recalled feeling thrilled upon seeing the couple's joy when the work was complete.

His father's acquisition of the farmland spurred young Millard to sell his small animals and start a business in beef cattle. The income generated by that business, which he maintained until he graduated from high school, enabled him to build up a nest egg large enough to cover all his anticipated college expenses. As a high school upperclassman, he tended not only to his academic work and farm chores but also to his duties as president of the youth organization of the Southeast Conference of Congregational Christian Churches (now the United Church of Christ), which entailed a lot of traveling throughout six states.

In 1953 Fuller enrolled at Auburn University, in Auburn, Alabama. During one of his years there, in an attempt to wrest control of the student government from sororities and fraternities, he campaigned for the presidency of the student body as the representative of a new party that he had formed with some friends. "It was a close race, but I lost," he told Mary Ellen Hendrix, who interviewed him for the *Auburn Alumnews* (October 1992). "I felt awful. It was terrible to lose." Fuller's other extracurricular activities included writing a column for the campus newspaper. During the summer of 1955, he worked in Michigan on a construction crew, tackling a variety of carpentry jobs and gaining experience in such skills as mixing mortar, pouring foundations, and laying bricks. In his junior year he served as a delegate to the 1956 Democratic National Convention, in Chicago.

After receiving a B.S. degree in economics, in 1957, Fuller entered the School of Law at the University of Alabama, in Tuscaloosa, where he soon became immersed in various moneymaking ventures in collaboration with Morris S. Dees Jr., a fellow law student whose entrepreneurial instincts and aspirations closely matched his own. (In his autobiographical book *A Season for Justice* [1991], Dees, who cofounded the Southern Poverty Law Conference in 1971, dated the inception of their partnership several years earlier.) One of their businesses was a direct-mail operation, through which they sold such items as holiday wreaths and rubber doormats to nonprofit organizations, which resold them to generate income. They also published a student directory and then—having discovered that each calendar day marked the birthday of at least a dozen students—established the 'Bama Cake Service, whereby they delivered birthday cakes, custom-made by a local bakery, to students whose parents had responded to their mailed solicitations for orders. In addition, they invested in real estate in the neighborhood surrounding the law school. They would buy or lease a ramshackle building, renovate it (doing all structural repairs, painting, plumbing, cleaning, and yard work themselves), and then rent rooms to students. In the 1959–60 academic year, Fuller and Dees's gross earnings amounted to nearly twenty thousand dollars from real estate rentals and property sales and thirty thousand dollars from their other businesses.

Fuller served briefly in the United States Army in 1960. That year, after each received an LL.B. degree and passed the Alabama bar examination, he and Dees opened a law office in Montgomery, Alabama. They focused most of their energies not on their law practice but on their commercial enterprises. In one lucrative endeavor, they cleared a profit of seventy-five thousand dollars on sales of sixty-five thousand locally produced tractor cushions to Future Farmers of America chapters in secondary schools throughout the United States. The phenomenal success of *Favorite Recipes of Home Economics Teachers* (1963), a cookbook that they compiled and published themselves and then sold to chapters of Future Homemakers of America, prompted Fuller and Dees to publish other cookbooks, under the imprint Favorite Recipes Press. Within two years, during which they abandoned their legal work, they became the largest publisher of cookbooks in the United States. By that time Fuller and Dees had also become millionaires. "Now we want ten million!" Fuller wrote in his journal at the beginning of 1964.

Shortly after Fuller made that journal entry, he began suffering from a variety of distressing aches and pains. As the year progressed he also developed a breathing disorder, which became so severe that on some days he repeatedly found himself struggling for breath. Despite his anxiety about those and other health problems, which his physician conjectured were stress-related, he continued to work nearly nonstop, devoting many evenings and weekends to his business and spending little time with his wife and children. (He had married in 1959 and by the mid-1960s had a son and a daughter.) One day in November 1964, distraught by Fuller's emotional as well as physical absences and his single-minded pursuit of wealth, Linda Fuller abruptly left for New York City, to decide, with the help of a pastor, whether to end her marriage.

"The long week that followed was the loneliest, most agonizing time of my life," Millard Fuller disclosed in *Love in the Mortar Joints*. He fully admitted to himself for the first time that for years he had carelessly disregarded many of the Christian values with which he had been raised. Although he had retained his ties to organized religion—he and his wife had even helped to start a new United Church of Christ congregation—he realized that he had merely wanted to "maintain a Christian image for business reasons," in his words. His contributions to the church had dwindled to only a tiny percentage of his earnings. Moreover, in conducting his business, on various occasions he had compromised his integrity.

At the end of seven days of soul-searching, Fuller traveled to New York, where he and his wife recommitted themselves to each other and to Christian principles. "We felt a strong sense of God's presence as we talked about the future," Fuller wrote in *Bokotola*. "We felt that God was calling us out of this situation to a new life." To prepare for "this new thing—whatever it was," as he put it, the Fullers decided to sell nearly all their possessions, including their large house, lakeside vacation cabin, hundreds of acres of land, speedboats, and fancy cars, and to give to Christian agencies and missions all but a few thousand dollars from the proceeds. Within weeks Fuller also sold his share of his business to Dees and arranged with Dees to give the money realized to various humanitarian charities. (Five years later Dees sold the business; in 1971, he cofounded the Southern Poverty Law Center.)

In the month following their reconciliation, the Fullers lived at Koinonia Farm. Koinonia (the name comes from the Greek word for "fellowship") had been founded in 1942 upon the ideals of nonviolence, racial equality, and common sharing of material goods, with the accumulation of only enough possessions to sustain a simple lifestyle. While helping with such farm enterprises as packing and mailing boxes of pecans and fruitcakes, Fuller had many long conversations with Clarence Jordan, who was a Bible scholar. Their discussions, which focused on the teachings of Jesus Christ and "what it means to be his disciple in our modern world" and also on the "daily discovery of God's plan and the living of it," as Fuller has written, impressed him deeply. "Clarence introduced me . . . to the concept of being God's partner and partners with one another to do God's work in the world," he wrote in *The Theology of the Hammer*. "He also introduced me to the clear imperative in the Gospels to act out our faith."

For about two and a half years beginning in 1966, Fuller worked as a fund-raiser for Tougaloo College, a small, church-supported, predominantly black institution in Tougaloo, Mississippi. From his base in New York City, he made frequent trips throughout the United States to drum up support for the school. He took a two-month leave of absence from the job to visit, as a representative of the National Stewardship Council of the United Church of Christ, church-sponsored schools, hospitals, and agricultural and other projects in several countries in Africa. One of his most disturbing memories of that trip was that of sprawling shantytowns in Mbandaka, Zaire, the population of which had skyrocketed in recent years with the influx of thousands of people from rural areas.

In 1968 the Fullers returned to Koinonia Farm. Because of harassment and even physical abuse from some of its neighbors, Koinonia's permanent population had dwindled to just a half-dozen people. Rather than sell the property and restart elsewhere, Clarence Jordan and Fuller resolved to formulate a new mission for the community. During a four-day conference to which they invited, in Fuller's words, "fifteen spiritually sensitive and socially aware Christians," they came up with the idea of creating a Fund for Humanity and various partnerships. The housing-partnership plan called for building simple houses on half-acre plots in a corner of Koinonia's eleven hundred acres, to be sold to poor rural families in accordance with the injunction imparted in Exodus 22:25: "If you lend money to any of My people who are poor among you, you shall not be like a moneylender to him; you shall not charge him interest." The Fund for Humanity would finance construction. Capital would come from farming and light-industry partnerships (Linda Fuller started a mail-order business in handmade goods crafted by local women, for example, as well as a small sewing "factory" that produced trousers), together with solicited contributions, no-interest loans from donors unable to afford outright gifts, and, eventually, the homeowners' mortgage payments. "What the poor need is not charity, but capital," Fuller has quoted Clarence Jordan as saying. "Not caseworkers, but coworkers."

With Fuller serving as president of Koinonia Partners and directing the farming and industries partnerships, supervising volunteers and work camps, and handling publicity, among other administrative tasks, building began in 1969. (Clarence Jordan died later that year.) By mid-1972 twenty-seven houses had been erected, and workers were poised to begin constructing another thirty-two homes at a second Koinonia site. "It's so good to live here," one home-buyer told Fuller after moving from a shack with a leaky roof into his new house. "When it rains, I love to sit by the window and see it raining outside, . . . and *it ain't raining on me!*" Another new home-owner said to Fuller, "Being in this house is like we was dead and buried, and got dug up!"—a comment that Fuller, in *Love in the Mortar Joints*, characterized as "a powerful symbolic expression of what the resurrected Christ is all about." "We Christians had better be getting out our shovels and digging," he wrote, "for we are called to bring light to places where there is darkness, and to bring the resurrection of Christ to that which is 'dead and buried.'"

The promising start of partnership housing at Koinonia awakened in Millard and Linda Fuller the desire to try to initiate a similar program in Zaire. In the summer of 1973, after a half-year of preparation that included three months in Paris to study French, Zaire's official language, they went to Mbandaka with their children (by that time they had four) under the auspices of the Christian Church (Disciples of Christ). As the church's director of development for the equatorial region of Zaire, Millard Fuller set up a Mbandaka Fund for Humanity, using start-up money of three thousand dollars contributed by Koinonia Partners. Taking advantage of the availability of locally produced sand-and-cement blocks, Fuller oversaw the construction of small cement-block houses. Despite their lack of both electricity and running water, the houses "seemed truly heaven-sent to families whose mud-brick, dirt-floored huts were literally crumbling around them," Fuller has said.

Although, as Fuller reported in *No More Shacks!*, he had to grapple with such problems as "thievery, a ludicrous bureaucracy, capricious arrests, and a perpetual shortage of funds and materials" and to learn patience "in a land where time means very little," he accomplished a great deal during the three years he and his family spent in Zaire. By the time they left, 114 houses had been completely or partially built, and plans were afoot for housing projects at two more sites. In addition, Fuller had initiated a program called Rise Up and Walk, which raised funds for the purchase of artificial limbs for people who had become beggars after losing a leg, and a project in which eyeglasses collected in churches in the United States were distributed at minimal cost to people in Mbandaka. (Sales of a thousand pairs of glasses raised enough money to finance the construction of another house.)

Fuller returned to Koinonia Farm in 1976 gripped by the feeling that he was at another turning point in his life. Seeking a new direction for himself, he hosted a second conference of friendly "advisers." Emerging from that meeting was the idea of forming a new organization modeled on the Koinonia housing partnership and the Zaire project but with far larger goals. Named Habitat for Humanity International, it would raise funds, recruit volunteers, and "provide procedures and expertise to develop around the world a better habitat for God's people in need," as Fuller wrote in *No More Shacks!* Builders and community-development workers would be trained by Koinonia Partners. Operating out of headquarters at Koinonia (and, beginning soon after, a building in Americus), the staff would serve as facilitators for affiliate groups that would be formed at other locations. Each of those groups would be financed by its own Fund for Humanity, supplemented if necessary by contributions from Koinonia partnerships, and each would be responsible for recruiting workers and developing projects in accordance with local conditions and needs. Habitat would accept government help with the acquisition of land and utilities and for infrastructure such as streets and sidewalks but would not accept government funds for the actual construction of houses.

By 1980 eleven affiliate groups had been organized in the United States; overseas, five projects had been started. By 1994 there were 1,108 affiliate groups and 331 college chapters in the United States and Canada and a total of more than 160 affiliates in Hungary, Poland, thirteen countries in Central and South America and the Caribbean, fourteen countries in Africa, and eleven countries in Asia and the Pacific region. (Overseas groups get some personnel and a substantial part of their funds from the parent organization.) Between 1976 and 1991 Habitat for Humanity built ten thousand houses. In the following two years, another ten thousand were constructed. The next ten thousand were built in just fourteen months. Habitat is currently the seventeenth-largest home-builder in the United States. Fuller has predicted that by 1998, it will put up forty-five thousand houses annually.

The design of Habitat houses as well as the materials and technology used depend upon local conditions. Through the use of locally produced rammed-earth building blocks, among other money-saving measures, the cost of a new home in developing countries ranged from about five hundred to three thousand dollars in 1994. The average cost of a simple three-bedroom, one-thousand-square-foot Habitat structure in the United States in 1993 was $34,300, with monthly mortgage payments averaging $215. (In contrast, in 1993 the median sales price of all new privately owned one-family houses in the United States was $126,500.)

To qualify as a Habitat home buyer, an applicant must be living in substandard housing and earning too little to gain approval for conventional mortgage financing but enough to produce the small down payment required for a Habitat house and to pay Habitat's low monthly mortgage. Mortgage charges never increase, even if an owner's financial situation improves substantially. Owners are encouraged to accelerate their payments if possible, however, and to contribute to the local Fund for Humanity a portion of the amount they would normally have had to pay in mortgage interest. All buyers are required to invest several hundred hours of their own labor—what Habitat calls "sweat equity"—helping to build or renovate their own and other houses or, alternatively, working at a local Habitat office. Applicants for housing are selected without regard to race, religion, country of origin, age, marital status, or sex.

Each Habitat house is built without profit, using, whenever possible, donated supplies and the donated services of professionals skilled in such areas as surveying, architectural design, and construction. Most of the work is done by volunteers who have no expertise, and often no previous experience, in construction. (According to Fuller, Habitat houses remained standing in areas devastated by Hurricane Andrew in 1992, the Los Angeles earthquake in 1993, and severe flooding in Georgia in 1994, because volunteer builders tend to use ten nails where a practiced carpenter would use two.) In recent years some two hundred thousand people annually have volunteered their time to work for Habitat. The most prominent of the organization's volunteers have been former president Jimmy Carter and his wife, Rosalynn Carter, who have been contributors, fund-raisers, and active project participants for more than a decade. The Carters' assistance in the renovation of a nineteen-unit apartment building in New York City in 1984 attracted national attention to Habitat for Humanity. Dubbed Jimmy Carter Work Projects, such week-long events have been held annually ever since, in a different city each year. In 1989, for example, the Carters joined a thousand volunteers, including professional roofers and builders, in Milwaukee, Wisconsin, to construct six new homes and renovate eight others in just seven days.

Fuller has said that when people ask him how much money is needed to begin a Habitat project, he always answers, "A dollar." Then, as he explained in *No More Shacks!*, he adds, "You must also have a core group of committed people who are serious about serving the Lord using the economics of Jesus and about helping His children find a decent place to live. If you have the dollar and the committed people, and you move on faith, the Lord will move with you." The "economics of Jesus" is part of a larger concept that Fuller has labeled the "theology of the hammer," which rests on many biblical principles and teachings in addition to the command against charging interest. Among them are the injunctions that "you shall not harden your heart nor shut your hand from your poor brother, but you shall open your hand wide to him and willingly lend him sufficient for his need, whatever he needs" (Deuteronomy 15:8) and that "you shall not . . . lend [a poor man] your food at a profit" (Leviticus 25:37). Another is that "he who has two tunics, let him give to him who has none" (Luke 2:11). Fuller's philosophy also encompasses the ideas that, in his words, "Jesus can multiply the minute to accomplish the gigantic" and that "the needs of people are paramount, and the response to those needs is not connected in any way with people's usefulness or productivity." The Judeo-Christian tradition, Fuller declared in *The Theology of the Hammer*, "mandates that we do more than just talk about faith and sing about love. We must put faith and love into action to make them real, to make them come alive for people."

In *Time* (January 16, 1989), Don Winbush described the six-foot four-inch Fuller as "an Ichabod Crane look-alike who is incessantly joking, cajoling, commoving, pressing, pleading for Habitat. He leans and swaggers, hunches his shoulders, pokes his head, and forms grandfather spiders with his lean hands, which are constantly aswirl." "Millard's southern gentility is authentic; his joy effervescent; his enthusiasm constant; his energy relentless," Karen Sue Smith wrote in *Commonweal* (November 2–16, 1984). Although Fuller has been a partner in a law firm in Americus for two decades, he spends virtually all his time engaged in fund-raising, publicity, and other activities on behalf of Habitat for Humanity. In his early years as head of the organization, he drew a salary of only seven thousand dollars; in 1992, a year after his salary more than doubled, to thirty-eight thousand dollars (he refused the Habitat board's offer of fifty thousand), *Money* magazine identified him as the lowest paid among the top executives of the country's one hundred largest charities. "I have everything I want, so I consider myself rich," Fuller told Mary Ellen Hendrix.

In addition to fifteen honorary doctoral degrees, Fuller's honors include the Council of State Housing Agencies Outstanding Achievement Award (1986), the Common Cause Public Service Achievement Award (1989), and the Martin Luther King Jr. Humanitarian Award, from both the King Center (1987) and the Georgia State Holiday Commission (1992). He received the 1994 Harry S. Truman Public Service Award jointly with his wife, the former Linda Caldwell, to whom he has been married since August 30, 1959 and who has served as his assistant since the founding of Habitat for Humanity. The Fullers live in a low-income neighborhood of Americus, in a modest house without air-conditioning that they bought for $12,400 nearly two decades ago. Their children, who range in age from twenty-four to thirty-five, are Christopher, Kimberly, Faith, and Georgia.

Selected Biographical References: Auburn Alumnews 47:6+ O '92 pors; Commonweal 111:610+ N 2-16 '84; Southern Living 25:128+ Je '90 por; Time 133:12+ Ja 16 '89 por; Fuller, Millard. Bokotola (1977), Love in the Mortar Joints (1980); Who's Who in America, 1995

Allan Altchech

Galdikas, Biruté M. F.

(GAHL-di-kuhs, bi-ROO-tay)

May 10, 1948- Primatologist; conservationist. Address: c/o Orangutan Research and Conservation Project, Tromol Pos 1, Pangkalan Bun, Kalimantan Tengah, Indonesia; Orangutan Foundation International, 822 S. Wellesley Ave., Los Angeles, CA 90049

Within the humid rain forests of the Southeast Asian islands of Borneo and Sumatra, high up in the trees, live "the people of the forest," which is how the Malays describe orangutans, widely considered to be the most reclusive and enigmatic of the great apes. In part because of their extreme shyness but also because of the extraordinarily difficult working conditions that prevail in Borneo's rain forests, orangutans remained little understood for years after information began to be collected about chimpanzees and gorillas, their closest living relatives. Indeed, the first researchers who attempted to study the animals did not catch more than a few fleeting glimpses of their subjects before the creatures vanished into the dense foliage. But unlike those scientists, who eventually abandoned their research, Biruté Galdikas, a Canadian primatologist of Lithuanian heritage who launched a study of her own—the Orangutan Research and Conservation Project—in Borneo's Tanjung Puting National Park in 1971, persevered. Twenty-four years later she is still there, gathering data about the apes' lifestyle, behavior, and society. "Nobody's been with orangutans as long as she has or knows as much about them," Dr. Gary Shapiro, a vice-president of Orangutan Foundation International, which Galdikas established in 1987, told Lucia Mouat in an interview for the *Christian Science Monitor* (January 13, 1992). "To do what she does takes tremendous grit and a willingness to put up with not just the uncomfortable aspects of living out in the tropics but the politics and logistics of it all. That's the whole reason there aren't more people doing these kinds of studies. It's extremely difficult to keep up that energy level, and she's done it."

In addition to confirming that orangutans are unusual among higher primates in that they are solitary animals, Galdikas has discovered that they nevertheless form lasting social bonds. She was also the first scientist to observe orangutans eating meat, to watch a wild female give birth in a tree, and to learn that male orangutans occasionally rape females. And she has painstakingly identified each of the hundreds of plants and insects that comprise the orangutan diet. Equally important, she has developed a finely tuned understanding of orangutan character. "They are incredibly gentle beneath their bluster and very easy to get along with," she explained to Don Lessem in an interview for *Omni* (July 1987). "They aren't devious or deceitful like chimpanzees. . . . You won't see much politics among orangutans, but you will find an incredible strength of character."

Galdikas's work ranks in importance with that of Jane Goodall, and Dian Fossey, who became famous for their research on chimpanzees and gorillas, respectively. The three women are collectively known as "Leakey's Angels," a reference to the legendary paleoanthropologist Louis Leakey, whose support made their work possible. Galdikas has been sustained through the years not only by her intellectual fascination with orangutan behavior but also by her appreciation of and empathy for the animals themselves. As Sy Montgomery observed in *World Magazine* (October 1992), "The deeply personal relationships Biruté has formed with individual orangutans . . . are the crucible in which her science has been forged—informing her data, transforming her understanding, and inspiring a depth of commitment that few other scientists would choose." Galdikas has written about her life among orangutans in *Reflections of Eden: My Years with the Orangutans of Borneo* (1995).

Biruté Marija Filomena Galdikas, the oldest of the four children of Anatanas and Filomena Galdikas, was born on May 10, 1948 in Wiesbaden, in what was then West Germany. She has been fascinated by the natural world from her earliest years, and while growing up in Toronto, Canada, where her family settled when Biruté was two, she enjoyed wandering through a nearby city park in search of salamanders and tadpoles. She also enjoyed reading stories about apes and jungles; the first book she borrowed from the library, she has recalled, was *Curious George*, the classic children's story featuring a monkey as its title character. "I was fascinated by prehistory," she told Sy Montgomery in an interview for her book *Walking with the Great Apes: Jane Goodall, Dian Fossey, Biruté Galdikas* (1991). "Not just the written history, but all of it. Human history and beyond. . . . I remember thinking that if we understood our closest human relatives we'd understand our origins . . . maybe our own behavior." She soon developed a special interest in orangutans, partly because their eyes, unlike those of gorillas and chimps, resemble those of humans, for their irises are surrounded by whites. "There's something about their eyes, which are very similar to our own, and about the way they behave," Galdikas told Lucia Mouat. "They're very gentle, noble animals—and incredibly intelligent."

The Galdikas family later moved to Los Angeles, where Biruté would attend college, at the University of California at Los Angeles (UCLA), from which she received her B.A. degree, summa cum laude, in 1966. (She also attended the University of British Columbia.) By the time she was working toward her M.A. degree in anthropology at UCLA, she had already made it her goal to initiate a long-term study of orangutans in Indonesian rain forests, home to the last remaining wild populations of orangutans. She was thus well prepared for her first meeting with Louis Leakey, who, though best known for the breathtaking discoveries he and his wife, Mary Leakey, made of ancient hominid fossils at Olduvai Gorge, in Tanzania, was also involved in the study of man's closest living relatives, in that he was principally responsible for launching Jane Goodall's and Dian Fossey's long-term field studies of primates. His interest in studying the behavior of the great apes was rooted in his conviction that such knowledge would shed light on the behavior of man's earliest ancestors, a conviction that Galdikas, coincidentally, shared.

Even before Galdikas approached Leakey following a lecture he delivered at the UCLA campus in 1969, she "knew" that he would help her realize her dream of studying the most elusive of the great apes. "As soon as I heard him talk about primates and great ape studies, and sending Jane and Dian into the field, I knew this was it," she recalled to Sy Montgomery. "I knew I'd be going." Her first hurdle, though, was convincing him that she deserved his support, and to do that, she soon discovered, she had to pass a series of "weird little intelligence tests like you see in magazines," she has recalled. For instance, Leakey presented her with playing cards, placed face down, and asked her to tell him which were red and which were black. "I hadn't the faintest idea which were which, but I noticed some were slightly bent," she told Mark Starowicz, who profiled her for the *New York Times Magazine* (August 16, 1992). "I told him, and he was absolutely delighted." Leakey was delighted because he believed the ability to make detailed observations was crucial to the study of animal behavior. Leakey was also impressed by her determination. "Leakey didn't care about formal education," Galdikas explained to Don Lessem. "He wanted enthusiasm, belief in what you were doing." So he agreed to sponsor her, and by 1971 he had raised nine thousand dollars—not a lot of money but enough to get the project off the ground.

The reasons for Leakey's demand that his protégée be unwavering in her commitment to the study of orangutans became abundantly clear after Galdikas and her first husband, Rod Brindamour, arrived in Tanjung Puting National Park, a humid, swampy forest in southern Borneo. "It was filthy and filled with all sorts of vermin," Galdikas said of the old hut that was to be their home, as quoted in *People* (January 16, 1989). "Rod later told me he fully expected me to turn around and demand to be taken back." What lay beyond their camp, which she christened Camp Leakey, was no more inviting. Descriptions of the Indonesian rain forest often include tales of encounters with wild pigs, pythons, crocodiles, pit vipers, and king cobras. But as Galdikas wrote in her book *Reflections of Eden*, "The true hazards of the rain forest were little nagging things like viruses, parasites, insects, and plant toxins. The leeches were so abundant that we lost track of how many we took off our bodies during the course of any one day. Bloated with our blood, leeches fell out of our socks, dropped off our necks, and squirmed out of our underwear." Once, she noticed a large black spot on her buttocks that, in her words, looked "like the skin of an overly toasted marshmallow." It was so painful she could not sit down. She later realized she had gotten the burn when she sat on a fallen log that had been oozing toxic sap. Other hardships included wearing perpetually damp clothing; subsisting on a diet of rice, tinned sardines, canned pigs' feet, and bananas; and being unable to prevent her books from succumbing to the effects of mildew and termite infestation.

The difficulty of simply living on Borneo was matched by the enormous challenge Galdikas faced in trying to locate the animals she had been commissioned to study. Indeed, for the first several weeks in Tanjung Puting, she observed plenty of nests, high up in the trees, that the animals had constructed each night before going to sleep, but frustratingly few orangutans. Shy animals, they invariably vanished into the foliage as soon they detected her presence. More than a week passed before she set eyes on her first two orangutans. To follow them, she would have had to wade through the neck-deep water. "That's when I thought, 'Gee, this is going to be really hard,'" she told Virginia Morell in an interview for *Science* (April 16, 1993). As it turned out, slogging through the swampy forest became part of her daily routine. "I'd leave camp at 5:30 A.M. and find myself in pitch-black water up to my armpits," Galdikas was quoted as saying in *People*. On those occasions when she did chance upon orangutans, they often tried to obstruct her efforts to observe them by hurling dead trees and fruit at her and even defecating on her.

Yet another problem Galdikas encountered was that even when she succeeded in following one or more orangutans for several days, "nothing happened." Unlike chimps and gorillas, which, being highly social animals, are continually interacting with other members of their species, orangutans typically spend their days alone, and they often do nothing more exciting than travel from tree to tree in search of food. Moreover, when they do band together to form groups, they give little indication that they are aware of others' presence. Galdikas often saw one orangutan travel past another without so much as a glance in the other's direction. "Compiling data on the animals was considerably tougher for Biruté than for me," Jane Goodall has said. "Chimps are very sociable. It might take her a year to see what I can observe in one lucky day."

In spite of these difficulties, in the twenty-four years since she arrived in Borneo, Galdikas has succeeded in amassing more information about the species than any previous researcher before her. She has learned that orangutans, whose life span, at about fifty-five or sixty years, is comparable to that of humans, are not completely antisocial. Adult females, which reach sexual maturity at about the age of ten, for instance, travel in the company of their offspring until the young reach seven or eight years of age, and adolescent females frequently forage together. And while adult males are inveterate bachelors, seeking out the company of females only for the purpose of mating, Galdikas found that they, like the females, communicate with other orangutans by vocalizing. She also observed rape among orangutans, noting that a female will emit what she has described as a "rape grunt" when a male forces her to mate with him and will bite her attacker whenever possible.

The fact that the animals did not require frequent contact with other orangutans was of particular interest to Galdikas, for a high level of sociability had long been thought to be a distinguishing characteristic of higher primates. For Galdikas, this aspect of orangutan behavior has shaped her own understanding of human nature. "Orangutans forced me to come to terms with my own human nature, with the 'weakness' of simply being human," she wrote in *Reflections of Eden*. "*Homo sapiens* is a sociable species. We need mates, children, loved ones, friends, acquaintances, even pets. Without intimate relationships, without communities, we are stranded. Orangutans reflect, to some degree, the innocence we humans left behind in Eden, before our social organization, bipedalism, and toolmaking gave us dominion over the planet. Thus, understanding orangutans gives us a clouded, partial glimpse into what we were before we became fully human."

Galdikas documented the first several years' worth of her findings in her thesis, which she completed in 1978 and which won high praise from her colleagues. She received her Ph.D. in anthropology from UCLA in the same year. During the first decade of her stay on Borneo, Galdikas's Orangutan Project was funded by such prestigious scientific organizations as the National Geographic Society, the World Wildlife Fund, the L. S. B. Leakey Foundation, the New York Zoological Society, and the Chicago Zoological Society. Since 1984 it has received the bulk of its funding from Earthwatch, a Massachusetts-based scientific organization, which supplies her with teams of volunteers who pay their own way to assist her in her research.

Galdikas's research has given her the opportunity to speculate on human origins, a subject that has long fascinated her. Analyses of the genetic material of each of the great apes has indicated that chimpanzees are man's closest living relatives, sharing with humans almost 99 percent of their DNA. Orangutans, on the other hand, share 97 percent of their DNA with humans and are thought to have diverged from the evolutionary line that led to modern man more than ten million years ago. At that time, man's ancestors left behind them in the rain forest those of the orangutan. "Gorillas and chimpanzees to a certain extent have left the tropical rain forest, but orangutans stayed in the top of the forest canopy," Galdikas told Mark Starowicz. "In a sense they never left the state from which we first emerged. They are the one great ape that truly never left the Garden of Eden." But despite man's close evolutionary relationship with orangutans, and despite the many behavioral patterns that the two species share, Galdikas's research has attuned her to the vast chasm that separates them. "We tend to think that the other creatures who share our planet inhabit the same reality as we do, especially if they resemble us, as monkeys and apes do," Galdikas wrote in *Reflections of Eden*. "But their senses, their needs, their perceptions are not the same as ours. Communing with a wild animal of another species means glimpsing another reality."

Since her arrival on Borneo, Galdikas has concerned herself not only with her study of orangutan behavior but also with rehabilitating ex-captive orangutans. Many of the ex-captives are former pets that Indonesian government officials brought to the camp after confiscating them from their owners. (Trade in orangutans is a lucrative enterprise, with the animals selling for about fifty thousand dollars apiece on the black market.) Camp Leakey thus came to be inhabited not only by Galdikas, her husband, and her research assistants but also by a growing population of orangutans that had been to varying degrees habituated to the presence of humans. "Sometimes, I felt as though I were surrounded by wild, unruly children in orange suits who had not yet learned their manners," Galdikas wrote in *National Geographic* in 1980.

Galdikas's goal, however, was not merely to nurse the animals back to health—many of them arrived with potentially fatal diseases—but to return them to life in the wild. Of the infant ex-captives, the fortunate ones are adopted by older orangutans, which then teach the youngsters how to build a nest, knowledge that is crucial to their survival in the rain forest. Thanks to the program, more than one hundred ex-captive orangutans have been reintroduced to the wild. While some scientists have expressed concern about the impact that the ex-captives might have on the ecology of the area to which they are reintroduced, Galdikas believes that at a time when world populations of orangutans are threatened, the program is crucial. "These individual orangutans have a right to survive and a right to return to the forest," she told Sy Montgomery in the *World Magazine* interview. The program has also helped raise awareness of the plight of orangutans, for many of the tourists who visit Camp Leakey come to see the ex-captives.

As a corollary to her work with ex-captive orangutans, Galdikas has become increasingly involved in the conservation of the animals, which had once ranged throughout Southeast Asia but which are now found only in the rain forests of the islands of Borneo and Sumatra. The decline in the world's orangutan populations is in part the result of the activities of poachers, who, in the process of trying to capture infant orangutans for sale abroad, end up killing their mothers. A more severe threat, though, has been the clearing of vast swaths of the rain forests by loggers, who earn much-needed hard currency by selling tropical hard woods, mainly to the industrialized world. The net result of these enterprises is that the worldwide orangutan population has been reduced to between thirty thousand and fifty thousand—about one-tenth of what it was a century ago. To raise funds for orangutan conservation, in 1987 Galdikas established the Orangutan Foundation International, a nonprofit organization headquartered in offices attached to her parents' home in Los Angeles.

Galdikas's commitment to conserving the world's remaining wild orangutan populations has required her to learn how to negotiate her way through the often shadowy politics of the Indonesian bureaucracy. That she has had some notable successes—such as persuading the Indonesian government to declare Tanjung Puting a national park and bringing an end to the trade in captive orangutans in her province—is a testament to her own diplomatic skills and her ability to cultivate good working relationships with influential Indonesian government officials. "She has earned the respect of almost everybody there," Gary Shapiro told Sy Montgomery in an interview for *Walking with the Great Apes*. "That's how you effect change over there; you work within the system, you need to know the importance of paying the right calls, observing the rituals. Everything she is doing is to consolidate her position." For her efforts to preserve wild orangutan populations, Galdikas has received many honors, including the Sierra Club's Chico Mendes Award (1992–93), the Chevron Conservation Award (1993), and the United Nations Global 500 Environmental Achievement Award (1993).

Because of her growing involvement in orangutan conservation and her work with ex-captives, Galdikas has had less time to devote to publishing the material she and her researchers have gathered on orangutan behavior and society. This, in turn, has disappointed and even annoyed some of her academic colleagues. "Here is someone who has this tremendous wealth of material," Peter S. Rodman, a professor of anthropology at the University of California at Davis, told Mark Starowicz. "It could answer questions that the rest of us can only speculate about and we can't get at it. There are some implicit rules about what we do. If we seek support from some agency, then we receive it, and other people don't. So you expect something more than *National Geographic* articles, and descriptions of one's personal life with apes." Galdikas has responded to such criticisms by saying, as quoted by Starowicz, "When a species is threatened with extinction, I don't understand how anyone can say it is more important to study than to save it."

Galdikas's dedication to her work took a toll on her marriage to Rod Brindamour, who in the late 1970s decided he wanted to return to Canada. In 1979, after Rod had left Borneo with their son, Binti's, baby-sitter, with whom he had fallen in love, he and Biruté divorced; Binti joined his father in Canada a year and a half later. Galdikas visits her son during her annual visits to Canada, which she has made since 1981, when she became a visiting professor at Simon Fraser University in Vancouver, British Colombia. (She has since been named full professor.) Galdikas also serves as Professor Extraordinaire in the Faculty of Biology at Universitas Nasional, in Jakarta, the capital of Indonesia.

In 1981 Galdikas married Pak Bohap bin Jalan, a Dayak tribesman who had been one of her employees and who now serves as codirector of her orangutan project. Their relationship is atypical by Western standards, for Bohap does not speak English and has never traveled outside of Indonesia. (Galdikas is fluent in Indonesian.) "He's as educated as I am, except he wasn't educated at a university. He was educated by experience," Birutė was quoted as saying in the *People* article. "He's a very smart and shrewd man—smarter than I am." The couple have two children—Frederick and Filomena Jane, whom Galdikas named after her mother and Jane Goodall—and they live in what Sy Montgomery described as "a spacious, welcoming home, decorated with handmade Indonesian tapestries and tall earthen jars" in the Dayak village of Pasir Panganj.

Selected Biographical References: Christian Sci Mon p14 Ja 13 '92 por; Discover 15:100+ D '94 pors; International Wildlife 20:34+ Mr/Ap '90 pors; Life 13:70+ Ag '90 pors; N Y Times Mag p28+ Ag 16 '92 pors; Omni 9:76+ Jl '87 por; People 31:102+ Ja 16 '89 pors; Science 260:420+ Ap 16 '93 pors; World Magazine p20+ O '92 pors; Galdikas, Birutė. Reflections of Eden: My Years With the Orangutans of Borneo (1995); Montgomery, Sy. Walking with the Great Apes: Jane Goodall, Dian Fossey, Birutė Galdikas (1991)

Garzarelli Capital Inc.

Garzarelli, Elaine

(gahr-zah-REL-ee)

Oct. 13, 1952- Financial analyst. Address: c/o Garzarelli Capital Inc., 16661 Echo Hollow Circle, Del Ray Beach, FL 33484

Known as much for being a flashy presence in the buttoned-down world of high finance as for her prescience, Elaine Garzarelli is one of Wall Street's most widely followed stock-market analysts. During the early 1980s, when computer-based market analysis was changing the way stocks and bonds were bought and sold, Garzarelli developed her own sophisticated set of economic indicators, which served as the basis for her predictions of market performance. Her most memorable hour came in October 1987, when, virtually alone in foreseeing a significant downturn on Wall Street, she issued a warning to a nationwide television audience. The accuracy of her forecast, proved by the stock-market crash of October 19, 1987, subsequently brought her widespread attention and scrutiny. Her monthly market forecasts have remained highly popular with clients, and each year for more than a decade she has been named the top quantitative analyst in an annual poll of money managers. In October 1994, however, reportedly as a cost-cutting measure, Lehman Brothers—which had paid Garzarelli an annual salary believed to be $1.5 million—laid off their most famous economic seer. Four months later Garzarelli announced her intention to form her own money-management firm, Garzarelli Capital Inc. At the same time, she continued to provide a monthly report for industry executives and institutional investors, as she had done while employed at Lehman Brothers.

Elaine Marie Garzarelli was born on October 13, 1952 in Springfield, Pennsylvania, the second of the three children—and the only daughter—of Ralph J. Garzarelli, a loan officer and bank administrator who eventually became an executive vice-president of Continental Bank, and Ida M. (Pierantozzi) Garzarelli. It was Ida Garzarelli who encouraged her daughter's competitiveness and urged Elaine to enter what she called "a man's business." Garzarelli spent much of her youth competing, in academics and at such games as chess, with her older brother, Robert. "He was really the math brain in the family," she told Christine Hogan of Ms. (February 1988). "I had to work three times as hard just to keep up with him." In addition to excelling at activities that challenged her mind, Garzarelli was a good dancer, as she demonstrated by winning dance contests at Scenic Hills High School. For a profile that appeared in *Fortune* (January 4, 1988), Garzarelli said, "I stood out in school as being wilder than most, but on the other hand, I had very good grades."

At Drexel University, in Philadelphia, Garzarelli originally intended to study chemical engineering, but after taking a course in economics "by accident," she decided she had found a new calling. "Economics was for me," she told Polly Toynbee for the *Guardian* (November 22, 1987). "I just understood it at once. I found I knew it all without even studying." She told *Current Biography* that she found economics to be "just common sense." While she was still a student, she began working part-time for Roy E. Moor, then the chief economist for the Philadelphia investment firm Drexel Harriman Ripley. Moor, who was using computers to construct economic forecasts, enlisted Garzarelli's help, and in 1971 she followed him to a New York firm, A. G. Becker Paribas. After receiving her B.S. degree in 1973, she began working full-time for that company while continuing to attend Drexel part-time, at night, in pursuit of a master's degree, which she obtained in 1977. She has since received a doctorate.

During the mid-1970s, at A. G. Becker Paribas, Garzarelli again turned her attention to the development of a group of computer-aided indicators which, taken together, would provide a model of the general direction of the economy as well as a forecasting tool for specific sectors. She has recalled working nonstop from about 1973 until 1980 to fine-tune her system: "I never went out. I saw no one. I just worked, night and day for seven years." On a personal level, Garzarelli was profoundly affected by the death of her brother Robert in a car accident, in 1977, and the passing of her father, from a heart attack, two years later. In the interview for the *Ms.* profile, she discussed the effect of those traumas, telling Christine Hogan, "I feel in part that what I am doing now I am doing for them." She also cited the influence that her competitive relationship with Robert Garzarelli, in particular, had on her career: "When I went to work, I discovered that no one was as bright as Robert, which meant I was ahead of the game."

Garzarelli eventually offered forecasts produced by her system to a number of A. G. Becker's institutional clients. Due to the bewilderingly technical nature of her methods, Garzarelli was not immediately successful in persuading others of their usefulness, according to one Becker employee, who recalled Garzarelli's reports as having "twelve equations per model, R-squareds for everything, correlations coming out of our ears. It was beautiful, but it was just too much." In addition, as Garzarelli told Nancy Belliveau McConnell of *Institutional Investor* (July 1988), "When I went out on presentations, people fell asleep on me."

The situation changed in 1982, when the firm's new research director, John Hindelong, decided that Garzarelli's forecasts represented "one of the best-kept secrets of Wall Street." As McConnell reported, he "boiled [Garzarelli's] product down to its basics," then suggested that she share its findings—and her expertise—on television business programs. Garzarelli was, she has recalled, initially frightened by the prospect, but A. G. Becker helped her to conquer that fear by enrolling her in a course on public speaking, at which she eventually became adept. Within a couple of years she was making regular appearances on such programs as *Wall Street Week* and PBS's *Nightly Business Report*, and she also began offering her opinions to the business and financial press. She soon became well known for her personal charm and exuberance as well as for her efforts to market her product, and she worked assiduously at maintaining relations with even her smaller and less important institutional clients. She was named managing director of A.G. Becker Paribas in 1982, thus becoming the first woman to occupy that position. When the firm merged with Merrill Lynch, two years later, Garzarelli moved to Shearson Lehman Brothers.

Garzarelli's Sector Analysis Monthly Monitor, a fifty-page forecasting instrument, began to prove itself a solid performer during the early to mid-1980s. Coopers and Lybrand, the accounting firm employed to track its results, estimated that Garzarelli's advice would have been profitable if followed between 1982 and 1987, when (unlike most forecasters) she consistently identified those industries that outperformed the Dow Jones average. Her accomplishments were not lost on Wall Street. In 1984 Garzarelli made her debut in first place (she had been a runner-up the previous year) on *Institutional Investor*'s prestigious All-America Research Team—a list of professionals chosen through an annual poll—in the field of quantitative analysis. (She continued to occupy that position in every succeeding year through 1994.) So it was that in August 1987, in addition to compiling her financial reports, Garzarelli began to manage Shearson Lehman's Sector Analysis Portfolio, a mutual fund created especially for her, with an initial subscription of $440 million. (Investors in a mutual fund, rather than owning individual stocks, own shares in the fund itself, which is invested in a portfolio of different securities.) "I was finally persuaded [to manage the Sector Analysis fund]," Garzarelli told Polly Toynbee, "when I discovered that 85 percent—yes, 85 percent—of all mutual funds underperform the market average. I just couldn't believe people investing in them were getting such a bad deal. It's outrageous."

Over the years, Garzarelli had continued to fine-tune her set of thirteen economic indicators, adjusting them as necessary to changing market forces. Three of the measures—yearly shifts in profit of Fortune 500 companies, the gross national product, and the government's own economic dipsticks, such as unemployment—provided a reading of the general temperature of the economy. A group of seven indicators, including interest rates and the money supply, was related to monetary policy. Finally, three other yardsticks appraised the state of corporate finances, particularly the relation of companies' stock prices to profits earned and dividends paid. Weighing the three sets of indicators according to a sophisticated formula, Garzarelli found a final percentage figure that evoked a positive or negative signal in terms of buying and selling. The system she developed, as Polly Toynbee phrased it, was "sheer econometrics, shorn of hunch and guesswork." ("I'm an economist," Garzarelli has said, "not a gambler.")

In the early 1980s the stock market had begun a protracted and dizzying climb, and for nearly five years Garzarelli shared the optimism of Wall Street. Beginning in early 1987, however, Garzarelli's indicators—unlike the prognostics of most of her colleagues, who expected the bull market to continue—turned sour, suggesting that the market would lose steam by the end of the summer and remain low through the beginning of 1988. By August Garzarelli's analysis, particularly on account of rising Treasury bill rates, was offering an even gloomier set of statistics. Indeed, Garzarelli, who had invested half of her personal net worth in stocks, divested herself of them in favor of Treasury bonds. By late August she had sold half her stock portfolio, and by September 1 she was fully out of the market. "I was terrified by what the indicators showed," she has been quoted as saying. "I told my firm. I told my institutional clients. I told anyone who would listen. Something catastrophic was about to happen."

On October 13, 1987 Garzarelli appeared on CNN's *Moneyline*, predicting an imminent crash. Within a few days the market began to weaken, and on October 19—known ever since as Black Monday—the Dow Jones average plunged a record 508 points, with stocks losing a stunning 22.6 percent of their value overall. Garzarelli had pulled the Sector Analysis fund out of the market in time, and the value of her mutual fund actually grew by 5 percent in the wake of the crash. By contrast, those clients who had not heeded her advice telephoned her, sometimes in tears, to bemoan their losses. Garzarelli herself experienced a great deal of stress during the week of the crash—so much so that at one point, convinced that she was having a heart attack, she had a friend who was a nurse call for an ambulance. (As it turned out, she was merely suffering what her friend described as an anxiety attack.)

Following the crash, Garzarelli became a much-watched guru in the world of financial analysis—"the hottest Cassandra on the Street," according to *Fortune*, which also named her businesswoman of the year for 1987. She also had her detractors, who charged that her prediction of the crash had acted as a self-fulfilling prophecy. In her conversation with Christine Hogan, Garzarelli dismissed the accusation: "No one person has the power to move the market for more than an hour or two. It's ridiculous to think that one individual could cause such a crash. If the market had not been vulnerable, it would never have collapsed."

As Garzarelli's prognostications became much more widely followed, so did the performance of her new mutual fund. Within one month of the crash, the number of the fund's investors, who contributed a minimum of five hundred dollars each and an average of ten thousand dollars, had grown from fifty thousand to sixty-five thousand, and by January 1988 the fund itself had increased from $440 million to $670 million. One consequence of that growth, and the increased scrutiny that came with it, was that Garzarelli acted on a more conservative basis than she might have otherwise and did not recognize the market's fairly rapid recovery from the crash. Although her sector-analysis indicators pointed to an economic upsurge, in February 1988 her newfound caution, together with research into previous stock-market downturns, led her to counsel clients to shy away from the rising market. "It was the first time I'd ever seen a crash," she told a writer for *Changing Times* (May 1989), "and I wanted to make sure that the consumer wasn't going to stop spending and that everything was going to be all right." When it became clear that she had remained bearish for too long—her mutual fund lost about 13 percent of its value during 1988—she blamed herself for ignoring her own indicators and vowed never to do so again.

Over the next several years, Garzarelli made a number of well-timed predictions, especially with regard to the major moves of the stock market. In the fall of 1990, even as the stock market suffered the bearish period that she had predicted in July and Iraq's invasion of Kuwait led to further skittishness on Wall Street, Garzarelli turned bullish, foreseeing the market's rising from its gloom. To the surprise of many, the prediction proved to be correct. In the spring of 1991, Garzarelli was still high on the market, forecasting a consistent advance, and she has ever since remained generally bullish, explaining to a writer for *Fortune's Investor's Guide* (1993): "I think we are in a stretched-out bull market because of our slow economy and low interest rates. The reason the economy will remain sluggish in the 1990s . . . is that we have so much debt in so many sectors. The unwinding of this debt, which should take about four more years, will produce a lower rate of inflation. That type of environment is great for stocks and bonds."

Because of the flood of media attention accorded her, Garzarelli's controversial, unique—some would say bohemian—personal style was etched into investors' minds. She preferred to work not in her office but in her Greenwich Village apartment, spending half of each month compiling the Sector Analysis Monthly Monitor and the remainder of her working time meeting with and advising clients. Sandra McElwaine of *Cosmopolitan* (August 1988) described Garzarelli's at-home routine thusly: "Dressed in jeans, a T-shirt, and high heels, with the help of two assistants, she spends her days in front of a mammoth television set tuned to the financial network. . . . Curled up on a white sofa with two white telephones that ring incessantly, Garzarelli confers with colleagues and investors all over the globe."

Garzarelli remained with Lehman Brothers as director of sector analysis when the Shearson office merged with Smith Barney in July 1993. It was clear by that time, however, that the Sector Analysis fund, which Garzarelli had directed since 1987 in addition to providing her research and analysis, had not been as profitable as had been hoped. Each year since 1988 it had performed poorly compared with the average mutual fund, at least partly because the annual expense ratio on the fund was an exceptional 2.3 percent, which was higher than that of most funds. According to an article in *Business Week* (July 26, 1993), $1,000 invested in the fund in 1988 would have yielded $1,405 five and a half years later, compared to an average yield of $2,122. As a consequence, a number of investors deserted the Sector Analysis fund, and in August 1994 Smith Barney Shearson merged its holdings into its Strategic Investors Fund. Meanwhile, Lehman Brothers had been spun off by its parent, American Express, and sold to shareholders.

Lehman Brothers, like other Wall Street firms, took serious cost-cutting measures in the face of a strong decline in bond prices during 1994, laying off some eight hundred of its employees. Garzarelli became Wall Street's best-known casualty when she was let go from the firm. The timing of that action was ironic, inasmuch as her dismissal came soon after she had been named the top-rated quantitative analyst for the eleventh straight year in the annual poll conducted by *Institutional Investor*. The magazine noted that she had made prudent decisions on equities and that, "for the most part, Garzarelli's sector selections [had] been first-rate."

In February 1995 Garzarelli made public her plans to form a money-management firm, Garzarelli Capital Inc. In addition, she has also continued to produce her sector-analysis report, which is distributed through an arrangement with Zacks Investment Research, a Chicago-based firm specializing in econometrics forecasting. (Garzarelli has a longstanding relationship with Zacks based on materials they have provided for her sector analysis.) "Her work is exceptional," the company's president, Leonard Zacks, told *Current Biography*. "She has the best track record of any quantitative analyst."

"People say money can't make you happy," Garzarelli told Sandra McElwaine for *Cosmopolitan*, "but as soon as I felt comfortable, my whole life changed. I never have to worry anymore. I just always feel good." In order to share the fruits of her success, she has established a college fund for women majoring in economics. As for the role that her gender has played in her own career, she conceded to one interviewer that it had created some obstacles but that she has "tried to use sexism as an incentive to work harder, to prove [her]self." Among the few drawbacks to her career and the fame it has brought her are a loss of her privacy and restrictions on her mobility. As an example of the hazards of traveling by air during business hours, she has cited the story of a friend in her field, who was on an airplane on October 19, 1987 and consequently lost a fortune. "If only he had been able to see a screen, reach a phone," Garzarelli told Christine Hogan, with what Hogan described as a shudder. "He could have saved something."

The tall, red-haired Elaine Garzarelli has been married twice, both times to physicians; each union ended in divorce. Considered to be physically attractive, she has developed a glitzy image, leading Susan Antilla to comment in *Working Woman* (August 1991) that she "stands out like a Jackie Collins novel among the reference books." For the *Institutional Investor* article, Nancy Belliveau McConnell reported that the actress Sigourney Weaver used Garzarelli as a model for her role as an investment banker in the 1988 film *Working Girl*. Garzarelli later did some performing of her own: in 1993 she caused a stir among the more staid members of her profession when she starred in a group of television ads for No-Nonsense pantyhose. She donated her fifteen thousand-dollar fee to her college scholarship fund. In her limited free time, Garzarelli, who plays the piano, also listens to music, participates in sports, and enjoys comedy.

Selected Biographical References: Fortune 117:26+ Ja 4 '88 por; Ms 16:68+ F '88 por; N Y Times D p1 O 27 '94 por; Working Woman 16:48+ Ag '91 pors; Who's Who in America, 1994

ABC

Gifford, Frank

Aug. 16, 1930– Sportscaster; former football player. Address: ABC Sports, Monday Night Football, 47 W. 66th St., New York, NY 10023

NOTE: This biography supersedes the article that appeared in *Current Biography* in 1964.

In the history of prime-time television, few have proven to be more durable than Frank Gifford, the former star halfback who is the senior member of the trio of sportscasters on ABC's *Monday Night Football*, which celebrated its twenty-fifth year during the 1994 football season. As a player, Gifford made All America as both an offensive tailback and defensive back at the University of Southern California, and subsequently he was All Pro in eight of his twelve years with the New York Giants. Following his retirement from football in 1965, he served his apprenticeship in network television broadcasting with CBS Sports. He moved to ABC Sports to team up with Howard Cosell and Don Meredith on *Monday Night Football* in 1971, when the show was in its infancy. Since then, the weekly program, consisting of live coverage of a specially selected premium National Football League game beginning at 9:00 P.M. Eastern time on Mondays, has become television's longest-running prime-time attraction and a consistent finisher (over the past five years) in the top ten among 130 competing shows in national TV ratings. In the present *Monday Night Football* broadcast booth, Al Michaels does the play-by-play announcing, and Gifford adds his own relatively soft-spoken analysis to the more bombastic color commentary of Dan Dierdorf. "What I do is help blend the three of us together," he has explained. In private life Gifford is the husband of Kathie Lee Gifford, the cohost of the popular morning television talk show *Live with Regis and Kathie Lee.*

One of the three children of Weldon Gifford, an itinerant oil driller, and Lola Mae (Hawkins) Gifford, Frank Gifford was born Francis Newton Gifford in Santa Monica, California on August 16, 1930. He has a sister, Winona, who is several years his senior, and a brother, Waine, twenty months his senior. As Weldon Gifford went from oil field to oil field during the Depression, the Giffords moved from town to town, so that Frank never completed a full year in any one school during his elementary years. The repeatedly broken schooling confused him academically and exacerbated his apathy for scholarship. One positive interlude in Gifford's education came in his third-grade year, when the teacher, who had been trained in speech therapy, succeeded in helping him tame a noticeable lisp by keeping him after school every day and drilling him in exercises to cure what she called his "lazy tongue." (A trace of the lisp persisted into adulthood, and he took voice lessons to conquer it.) Regarding the lisp, Gifford observed in his autobiography, *The Whole Ten Yards* (1993), written with Harry Waters: "Maybe it was related to my shyness around strangers. . . . Or maybe it was my dawning realization that the Gifford kids weren't dressed so well. I think I was more aware of that than my brother, whose hand-me-downs I wore."

Because his family rarely stayed in one place for any length of time, Gifford has said that his older brother was his "only real friend." "He was like my dad: he picked up friends quickly, so I wound up playing with them, too," he recalled in *The Whole Ten Yards.* "My first football field was a beach, Hermosa Beach. I played a lot of touch football there with my brother and his pals, which meant I had to constantly compete with an older crowd. When they put together the teams, I always got picked first or second. That was the first time that I realized I could do things better than others athletically and look better doing them." Outside of sports, Gifford's chief interest during his boyhood was the outdoors, and his hero was a fictional character, Henry Ware, the protagonist of a series of adventure novels about the settling of the West called The Young Trailers. With his family, Gifford attended Pentecostal church services, including those ministered by the famous evangelist Aimee Semple McPherson in Los Angeles.

After sojourns in forty-seven oil towns, the Giffords settled in Bakersfield, California. At Bakersfield High School, Frank joined the football team as third-string end in his sophomore year, and the following season he became the passing and running tailback around whom the coach, Homer Beatty, built his offense. In his senior year, when Bakersfield High won the San Joaquin Valley championship, Gifford made the All-Conference team. He cocaptained the Bakersfield team that year with Bob Karpe, an offensive tackle who would go on to be named to the All-America team as a player for the University of California. Off the field, Gifford and Karpe were close buddies, double-dating on weekends and backpacking together in the Sierras, and they have remained in close contact ever since. During his senior season, Gifford fractured his left foot on the playing field, and the following summer one of his fingers was all but ripped off while he was working as a temporary roughneck on an oil rig.

Coach Homer Beatty turned Gifford's life around, not only guiding him athletically but persuading him to concentrate on his studies, partly to prepare him to qualify for a football scholarship at the University of Southern California (USC), Beatty's alma mater. Between his graduation from high school and his matriculation at USC, Gifford spent one semester at Bakersfield Junior College, acquiring additional credits. Playing football during that semester, he made Junior College All America. Because his scholarship at USC provided only for tuition, he did janitorial work in the university gymnasium throughout his college years to earn the money for room and board. During the summer following his freshman year, he worked as a roughneck in the Nevada oil fields.

Before the beginning of Gifford's sophomore year, USC's head coach, Jeff Cravath, told him: "For the upcoming season, we probably will use you on defense at first. But we will certainly include you in our plans for quarterback." In his autobiography, Gifford observed: "What Cravath actually meant, it soon became clear, was *fourth-string* quarterback. Jeff . . . simply didn't know what to do with a quarterback turned halfback who was also a good defensive back, punter, and placekicker. So he shunted me to safety and extra-point kicker, and that's where I basically languished for the next two years. It's a scenario that haunted my football career, first in high school, later even with the Giants. Though I was convinced I could run and pass better than the guys doing the running and passing, the coach saw me only on defense. . . . With no other option . . . , I learned patience."

After Gifford's junior season, Jess Hill succeeded Jeff Cravath as head coach at USC. "Just like Homer Beatty at Bakersfield High," Gifford recounted in his autobiography, "[Hill] switched us from the T formation to a combination of the wing T and the single wing and built his attack around me at tailback. Besides continuing to play defensive back, I ran and passed and blocked—and we won our first seven games." During that final college season, Gifford scored seven touchdowns, rushed for 841 yards, completed thirty-two of sixty-one passes, caught eleven passes for 178 yards, snared three interceptions, and kicked for twenty-six extra points and two field goals. He played in two All-Star bowl games, and *Collier's* magazine selected him as running back on its All-America team.

Frederick Exley, a lowly undergraduate at USC when Gifford was a football hero there, vented long-pent-up, ambiguous emotion in his quasi-fictional memoir *A Fan's Notes* (1988), in which Gifford is a major figure, an enormously admired/resented demigod. "Gifford's heroic image crisscrosses through Exley's pages like a broken-field runner, leaving a dazzling trail of envy and anger," David Behrens wrote in *New York Newsday* (August 5, 1984). "To narrator Exley, Gifford was the epitome of unattainable, infuriating perfection." The book, a cult classic, is on the reading lists of many college writing classes.

In 1952 Gifford, the number-one draft choice of the New York Giants, left USC. He did so without a degree, because the university would not accept his academic credits from Bakersfield Junior College, leaving him twelve units shy. Later, during his off-seasons with the Giants, he returned to classes at USC one night a week and finally received his B.S. degree in 1956. Meanwhile, beginning during his playing days at USC, he had been supplementing his income by working in films, initially as an extra. His first substantial job was kicking and otherwise doubling for Jerry Lewis in the football comedy *That's My Boy* (1951). In *The All American* (1953), he had two assignments: as a technical consultant, he taught Tony Curtis, the movie's star, how to handle a football, and as an actor, he played Stanley Pomeroy, a fraternity mate of the Curtis character. He did numerous stunt scenes in *Sign of the Pagan* (1954), and he had bit parts in two films starring James Garner, *Darby's Rangers* (1958) and *Up Periscope* (1959). During the same period he was cast in the leading roles—both undercover cops—in two television pilots, *Public Enemy* and *Turnpike*, neither of which found a buyer. Along the way, under Wynn Handman in New York City and Jeff Corey in Hollywood, Gifford took acting classes, which gave him, as he put it in his autobiography, "a little more personal confidence" and enabled him "for the first time . . . to perform before an audience without being self-conscious or inhibited."

In the early 1950s professional football had not yet become the immensely popular and lucrative national attraction that network television would make it. Even aside from taking heavy physical punishment for little glory and minimal pay, Gifford was very unhappy during his first seasons in the National Football League. As he recounted in his autobiography, he "ran into definite resentment" from some of his teammates, "crusty old veterans" who perceived him as "a media-made glamour boy, all glitz and no substance." "During practices, I'd get a thumb in the eye here or an elbow in the ribs there . . . ," he recalled in *The Whole Ten Yards*. "They also had their little cliques, and I didn't belong to any of them." At the same time, he was at odds with Steve Owen, the head coach, who consigned him chiefly to defense and would not even let him concentrate on that. In 1952, his first season with the Giants, he played in the shadow of the running back Kyle Rote. "Aside from a few fill-ins for Kyle when his knee acted up," he wrote in his book, "I played cornerback and handled kickoffs, and . . . quietly seethed. . . . I wanted to run the football, and I knew that I could."

In 1953, when the Giants won only three games, Gifford, who was making $8,000 a year (a figure that would quadruple before the end of his playing career), "almost packed it in" as a football player, as he related in his autobiography. "My problem was the exact opposite of the year before. I had started the season as a defensive back, but when Kyle Rote went down with an injury, I wound up going both ways. . . . I played halfback, cornerback, kicked off, and ran back kickoffs and punts. And when you do that with a bad team, it's hard to describe the physical beating you take. Somehow I survived it, but as exhausted as I was, I don't know how I got out of that year without getting hurt."

The situation changed radically for the better in 1954, after Jim Lee Howell succeeded Steve Owen as head coach of the Giants, and Vince Lombardi was brought in as offensive cordinator. "Just as Homer in high school and Jess in college rescued me from the defense and built their offense around me, so did Vince in the pros," Gifford has recounted. "Lombardi believed that the left halfback position—now my permanent home—was the key to a successful offense, the point of attack. That attack would basically hinge on three plays: the 49 and 28 power sweeps, in which I took a handoff from [quarterback] Charlie Conerly and followed two pulling guards around end; and the halfback option, the same play except that I either passed the ball or ran it. . . . What really turned me on . . . was passing the ball in Vince's option play. Ever since Bakersfield High, I'd been a frustrated quarterback."

In the first eight games of the 1954 season, Gifford averaged 5.6 yards per rush on the ground (the best in the conference) and a touchdown every four attempts in passing. The Giants were ahead of the Cleveland Browns, the previous year's winner, in the forefront of the race for the conference title when, in the ninth game of the season, Gifford and Kyle Rote were both injured when they collided in a 47 power play. Suffering a concussion, Rote, the Giants' leading receiver at the time, missed the next two games. With a severely injured knee, Gifford, the team's leading rusher, was finished for the season. The Giants lost three of their last four games, and the Browns again took the conference title. During the following nine years Gifford never played a game without being conscious of, and favoring, his right knee. "There were certain things I couldn't do anymore, like plant the knee a certain way," he wrote in *The Whole Ten Yards.* "I just knew that sucker was about to blow out."

In 1955 the Giants lost their first three games but were unbeaten in their last five. In 1956, after clinching their division title with an 8-3-1 record, they defeated the Chicago Bears to take the NFL championship. That year the NFL players voted Gifford the most valuable player in the league, and three years later he was MVP in the Pro Bowl. In 1957 the Giants finished second in the Eastern Conference. Over the following six years, they won five division titles, three of them under the field leadership of Y. A. Tittle, who succeeded Charlie Conerly at quarterback in 1960. Gifford suffered his most severe football injury on November 20, 1960, when an extraordinarily violent blind-side tackle by Chuck Bednarik of the Philadelphia Eagles sent him to the hospital with what doctors diagnosed as a fractured vertebra and deep brain concussion.

Thinking his football career was over, Gifford announced his retirement, but after recuperating he returned to action as a flanker in 1962, when he won NFL comeback-of-the-year honors in a UPI poll. His most memorable feat took place in the final game of the 1963 season, against the Pittsburgh Steelers. The turning point in that game, which decided the division title, was Gifford's one-handed shoestring catch of a pass from Tittle. In 1964 the Catholic Youth Organization named Gifford sportsman of the year. When he retired definitively from professional football at the end of the 1964 season, he had made All Pro eight times, at three different positions, and set Giant records in touchdowns scored (seventy-eight), points (484), and yards gained receiving (5,484), and he was second only to Alex Webster in rushing yards (3,704).

During his playing days, in addition to his work in films, Gifford moonlighted as a commercial model and did product endorsements, often on television. He also wrote a twice-weekly column, a public journal of his life as a member of the New York Giants, for a Bakersfield newspaper. On the strength of the column, he came, in 1957, to host a sports show, consisting of game wrap-ups and interviews, on television station KERO-TV, in Bakersfield. Later, filling in for Phil Rizzuto, he did five-minute baseball spots on the CBS radio network, and he cohosted some pregame shows before CBS's NFL telecasts. In 1961, during his premature retirement, he became a sports reporter for WCBS, the network's flagship radio station in New York City, appearing every night as part of the station's half-hour newscast.

Early in 1962, at about the time that he was deciding to try a football comeback, he joined the WCBS-TV evening news staff, appearing as a sports reporter on both the station's six o'clock and eleven o'clock local newscasts. He did those two telecasts for the next nine years, with the exceptions of the 1962, 1963, and 1964 football seasons, when he did the early news but not the late news, so as not to break his curfew as a player. Concurrently, on the network level, beginning in 1965, he worked for CBS Sports, doing color commentary on NFL games, covering the Masters golf tournament and some college basketball games, and hosting many segments of *Sunday Sports Spectacular,* a CBS series imitative of ABC's *Wide World of Sports.*

Roone Arledge, then the president of ABC Sports, and Gifford met at the golf course at Winged Foot, a country club in Westchester County, New York, of which both were members. Arledge told Gifford that at the beginning of the 1970 NFL season he was going to introduce at ABC the weekly broadcast of a football game of special interest, to be selected by league representatives. The game would be played and broadcast live on Monday nights. (At the time, pro football games were normally played only on Sunday afternoons.) He told him that Howard Cosell, the grandiloquent lawyer turned sportscaster, would be one of a trio of broadcasters on the show, and he wanted Gifford to be another, after working out his contractual option at CBS. In the meantime, Arledge, acting on Gifford's recommendation, hired Don Meredith, the former Dallas Cowboys quarterback, a jock whose country-boy manner would complement Cosell's city-slicker persona. Keith Jackson rounded out Arledge's original *Monday Night Football* trio of broadcasters.

In 1971, after fulfilling his contract commitment at CBS, Gifford moved to ABC and, replacing Keith Jackson as designated play-by-play announcer, joined Cosell and Meredith on *Monday Night Football* (*MNF*). Over the years, he would be the constant component in a configuration that changed several times in personnel as well as number (from three to two and then back to three broadcasters). Among the associates who, in succession, worked with him in the *MNF* broadcasting booth were Fred Williamson, Alex Karras, Fran Tarkenton, O. J. Simpson, and Joe Namath. In 1977 Gifford received an Emmy Award as television's outstanding sports personality. When Al Michaels joined him in 1986, Gifford turned the play-by-play responsibility over to him and switched to analysis. Michaels and Gifford worked as a pair until the beginning of the following season, when Dan Dierdorf joined them, making the *MNF* broadcast team once again a trio.

"Gifford has taken his share of shots from critics, but he always ranks high on fan-opinion polls," Martie Zad wrote in the *Washington Post* (November 20, 1987). "Viewers like him because he comes across as the true-blue straight arrow that he is, honest, earnest, sincere, and amazingly good-looking for a fifty-seven-year-old grandfather." Zad noted that some observers had thought that Dierdorf, with his "Type A delivery," might "overwhelm the soft-spoken Gifford." "Instead, Gifford's even-keeled analysis seems sharper than ever, and his bursts of humor and insight in tandem with Dierdorf make the telecasts a treat. . . . Gifford is renowned for his loyalty to the NFL; his critics have said he doesn't criticize players. A fairer statement is that he doesn't take cheap shots when a player drops a ball or misses an assignment. . . . His love for the game comes through clearly. More than a few times, he has cut off aimless banter and clowning in the booth with, 'Hey, guys, there's a game going on down there.' Criticism doesn't seem to wound him, either." Zad quoted Gifford: "In this arena you're going to have critics, and you better get used to it."

In addition to his *Monday Night Football* assignment, Gifford has covered numerous Olympic games as host of ABC's *Wide World of Sports*. He received the Christopher Award for his coverage of the 1983 Special Olympics on *Wide World of Sports*. His association with the Special Olympics goes back to 1968, when Eunice Shriver asked him to help promote that cause. He has chaired the Special Olympics sportscasting committee since 1974 and has been a member of the Special Olympics board of directors since 1983. For his work in behalf of the Multiple Sclerosis Association and the Multiple Sclerosis Society of New York, the society in 1984 honored him with its Founders Award. With his wife, Kathie Lee Gifford, he has raised hundreds of thousands of dollars for various charities, including those concerned with children born with crack-cocaine addiction or the virus that causes AIDS. They do their charity work chiefly under the aegis of the Association to Benefit Children and of the Variety Club International's Childhood Charity. Their philanthropic concentration at present is chiefly on two Manhattan facilities for terminally ill children and their families: the Variety Cody Gifford House for Children with Special Needs and Cassidy's Place.

Frank Gifford and Kathie Lee Johnson, as his wife was then known, met in 1982 on the set of ABC's *Good Morning America*, while he was filling in for David Hartman, the host, and she was doing an entertainment segment. He and Kathie Lee, who is twenty-three years his junior, were married on October 18, 1986. They have two children, Cody Newton, born in 1990, and Cassidy Erin, born in 1993. The Giffords have a home in Connecticut, a pied-à-terre in Manhattan, and a vacation home in Colorado. Frank Gifford was previously married and divorced twice. By his first marriage, to Maxine Avis Ewart, he has three grown children, Jeffrey, Kyle, and Victoria (who is married to Michael Kennedy, a son of Ethel and Robert F. Kennedy), and several grandchildren. His second marriage was to Astrid Lindley.

Gifford is a temperamentally shy person who projects a persona that is, in the words of David Behrens, "comfortable but reserved, civilized and somewhat inaccessible, in control and cool in crisis." Others have described him as "unflappable," with a "modulated" voice. Chet Forte, after directing *Monday Night Football* for more than a decade, pointed out to Behrens how Gifford "plays off each" of his broadcast-booth mates, "plays it like it lays." "In all the years I've known him, I've never seen Frank argue, get mad, or sulk," Forte said. "It's hard to say when he's unhappy. He buries it." In addition to his autobiography, Gifford has written *Frank Gifford's Football Guide Book: Basic Plays and Playing Techniques for Boys* (1965), *Frank Gifford's NFL-AFL Football Guide* (1968), *Pro Football Guide for 1970* (1970), and *Gifford on Courage* (1976). The latter, written with Charles Mangel, consists of profiles of ten of the most courageous athletes Gifford has known. Gifford was inducted into the collegiate National Football Foundation Hall of Fame in 1975 and the Pro Football Hall of Fame in 1977.

Selected Biographical References: Chicago Tribune III p17 S 25 '94; Inside Sports p16+ N '94 por; N Y Newsday mag p22+ O 19 '80, mag p13+ Ap 5 '84; People 33:162+ My 21 '90 pors; Sat Eve Post 250:62+ O '78 pors; Washington Post C p1+ S 9 '80 por, TV Week p11+ N 20 '87; Contemporary Authors vol 109 (1983); Gifford, Kathie Lee. I Can't Believe I Said That (1992); Who's Who in America, 1995; Who's Who in Football, 1974

Godwin, Gail

June 18, 1937- Writer. Address: c/o Ballantine Books, 201 E. 50th St., New York, NY 10022

Gail Godwin, the author of two collections of short stories and nine novels, including *The Odd Woman* (1974), *A Mother and Two Daughters* (1982), *The Finishing School* (1985), and *The Good Husband* (1994), is ranked among the most distinguished fiction writers in the United States. Although she is not considered strictly a feminist writer, her characters have often been women of great inner strength who nonetheless have reached points of crisis in their lives and are trying to discover their true selves. Many of her works portray events, relationships, and locations—particularly those in the South—that have parallels in her own life. In addition to her fiction, which has brought her numerous literary prizes, Godwin has written the librettos for several operas.

Gail Kathleen Godwin was born on June 18, 1937 in Birmingham, Alabama, the only child of Kathleen May (Krahenbuhl) Godwin and Mose Winston Godwin. Her father deserted the family shortly after her birth, and she was reared by her

Jerry Bauer

Gail Godwin

mother and grandmother in Asheville, North Carolina. In the book *Family Portraits* (1991), edited by Carolyn Anthony, Godwin wrote about her mother: "Even in this Era of the Working Mother, she would have been considered something of a heroine." Indeed, Kathleen Godwin supported the family by simultaneously teaching English composition and beginning Spanish at the local junior college, working as a reporter for the *Asheville Citizen-Times*, and writing romance fiction for such publications as *Love Short Stories*; she sometimes used the pseudonym Charlotte Ashe (the family lived on Charlotte Street in Asheville) in order to place more than one story in an issue of a magazine.

Kathleen Godwin also wrote several novels that failed to find publishers—partly because they did not conform to any one genre but also, as Godwin has written, because her mother "put fire and spite and rebellion and fantasy into them and ruined their chances of posing as Uplifting Narratives." "Charlotte Ashe, quite a bit of her, found her way into Gail Godwin," the writer recalled in *Family Portraits*. "I have learned to recognize her . . . whenever, after thinking I have been writing about one thing, I discover behind it her covert designs."

In contrast to the adventurousness of Godwin's mother was the overprotectiveness of her grandmother. A childhood friend of Godwin's suggested to David Streitfeld of the *Washington Post* (March 7, 1991) that Godwin's girlhood shyness and fearfulness could be traced to her grandmother's influence: "Cold weather could hurt you, cars could run you over, bad people could talk to you on the street. Gail was brought up cautioned against danger and is very conscious of the fact that things can go wrong. It goes along with her melancholy." (Several members of Godwin's family appear to have suffered from that "melancholy": her father, who was chronically depressed, eventually committed suicide, as did her uncle and half-brother.) While Godwin was not physically daring as a child—she has recalled, for example, having "never been athletic"—she found vicarious adventure through reading and writing. She was fond of the Mary Poppins series of books, by P. L. Travers, and at the age of nine she composed her first story—"about a henpecked husband." She has been writing fiction ever since.

Godwin attended Peace Junior College, in Raleigh, North Carolina, from 1955 through 1957 before matriculating at the University of North Carolina at Chapel Hill, where she earned a B.A. degree in journalism. Following her graduation, in 1959, she took a job as a reporter for the *Miami Herald*. After about two years, her tendency to suffuse the bare facts of her stories with drama led to her being fired from the newspaper. "I wasn't consciously embellishing," Godwin told Hilary DeVries for the *Christian Science Monitor* (March 14, 1985), "just trying to make [the articles] more interesting." Soon after that incident she married Douglas Kennedy, a Florida photographer. She later described their union, which lasted only three months, in her first, unpublished novel, "Gull Key," the manuscript of which was lost after she sent the only copy to a London publisher.

Following the breakup of her marriage, Godwin went to Europe, where she would work and travel for the next six years. During an interview for *Contemporary Literary Criticism* published in 1992, she explained to Joyce Renwick her reasons for living abroad: "I knew that the longer I stayed away from the South the more I would lose of that lovely southern *mulch* that clung to [the] pages [of celebrated Southern writers]. I risked losing the little bit I had—my Southern heritage—which for many writers has given them a head start: that decorous, stately flow of language, the tendency to make myths out of the past, out of your family's past, and a sense of nostalgia, and that special, almost religious, sense of place. But I had to risk losing all that, because for me the alternative would have been to stay home and become trapped. A Southern writer who is not a genius is often overwhelmed by the great nostalgic myth of 'The South' that other writers have created."

Godwin eventually settled in London, where she took a job as a travel consultant for the United States Embassy. During that period she married Ian Marshall, a psychiatrist she had met in a creative-writing class. Although the class resulted, indirectly, in a second marriage that proved to be as ill-fated as her first (the couple split up in 1966), Godwin nonetheless found that seeking instruction in writing had been a beneficial move. One of her assignments at the London City Literary Institute was to write a short story that began, "'Run away,' he muttered to himself, sitting up and biting his nails." "When that must be your first sentence," Godwin has written, "it sort of excludes a story about a woman in her late twenties, adrift among the options of wifehood, career, vocation, a story that I had begun too many times already—both in fiction and reality—and could not resolve." The story that resulted from the assignment, "An Intermediate Stop," was among those later collected in *Dream Children* (1976). In the meantime, an earlier draft of the piece won her admittance to the exclusive graduate writing program at the University of Iowa, in Iowa City, which she entered in 1967, at the age of thirty.

"Thank God for the Iowa Writers' Workshop," Godwin told Joyce Renwick. "That's where it all began for me. I had been struggling to write fiction since age nine, but it wasn't until Iowa that the whole thing jelled." She studied there under, among others, the novelist Kurt Vonnegut, and one of her fellow students was John Irving, who would go on to write such highly regarded novels as *The World According to Garp*, *A Prayer for Owen Meany*, and *The Cider House Rules*. For Mary Vespa's profile of Godwin in *People* (March 8, 1988), Vonnegut recalled the young Godwin and compared her to Irving: "They started out with considerable stature. What remained was simply to put on a little weight, a little muscle, and gain some wisdom." Godwin received her M.A. degree in 1968 and her Ph.D. degree, in English, in 1971. Her thesis, the novel *The Perfectionists*, was published in 1970.

The Perfectionists, which was inspired by Godwin's relationship with her second husband, is told from the perspective of Dane Empson, a young American woman married to John Empson, a hyperanalytical British psychotherapist and self-styled spiritual guru. Over the course of a vacation in Spain with her husband, one of his patients, and her distressingly silent, three-year-old stepson, Dane comes to regret her theoretically perfect but unsatisfying marriage. Like *The Perfectionists*, Godwin's second novel, *Glass People* (1972), focuses on an unhappily married woman—the beautiful Francesca Bolt, who is little more than a trophy in the eyes of her husband and whose struggle for self-realization is the theme of the story. Both novels enjoyed generally positive reviews but modest sales.

Godwin garnered more attention with *The Odd Woman*. The protagonist of that novel is Jane Clifford, a thirty-two-year-old literature professor. Untenured and unattached but for her on-again, off-again romance with a married man, Jane feels rootless and directionless, and, in seeking a sense of order in her own life, she examines the lives of other women, both real and literary. During her interview with Joyce Renwick, Godwin recalled about the writing of the book, "I was in an academic setting. My mind was attuned to seeing life through the patterns of literature, and so my heroine saw destinies in terms of her favorite heroines in novels. It came out of her but out of me also." Evaluating the novel for the *New York Times Book Review* (October 20, 1974), Lore Dickstein wrote, "*The Odd Woman* is written with a light, witty touch. It is a cerebral, reflective novel—most of the action takes place in Jane's mind—and a pleasure to read. Godwin's prose is elegant, full of nuance and feeling, and sparkling with ironic humor." The work was nominated for a National Book Award.

Most of the stories in *Dream Children* (1976), Godwin's first book of short fiction, concern women seeking—through various external pursuits—an escape from the pain of broken relationships, unrealized aspirations, or other emotional setbacks. The collection was published to mixed reviews. "These new stories are not all well shaped—some read like sketches for longer works and so seem to gallop across their twenty pages breathlessly, loose ends flying," Katha Pollitt wrote in the *Saturday Review* (February 21, 1976), "but the best have the sharp humor and sharp eye that marked [Godwin's] earlier work."

Godwin drew the inspiration for her next novel, *Violet Clay* (1978), from the passage in Mozart's opera *The Magic Flute* in which the character Tamino asks, "When will my eyes see the light?" and the priests answer, "Soon, soon, Youth, or never." "It has been that image of that 'never' time that has spurred me on," the novelist told Joyce Renwick. "For a long time I used to imagine myself old, alone, poor, having failed to become a writer, and living in a rented room, maybe with a cat, maybe not even with that luxury. And that was somehow so unbearable, and I knew I was not the type to kill myself, that the negative image drove me on. The thing about the 'soon or never' moment is that you reach a point where the light is going to come soon or it's never going to come." The character that emerged from that theme, the eponymous protagonist of *Violet Clay*, is a painter who once aspired to be a genuine artist but has settled into the world of commercial illustration. A series of personal crises lead her to renew her commitment to producing serious works.

Godwin told Mary Vespa, "When I was writing *Violet Clay* and [John Irving] was writing *The World According to Garp*, we exchanged chapters as we wrote them. It was funny. In my first draft I started off with Violet's birth, and in his he began with Garp as a grown man, middle-aged and looking for something to do. He advised me to change mine, to start off when Violet is mature enough for the reader to be interested in her, and he was right. Then later he decided to start his novel with Garp's birth, and that decision made the book." Reviewers were divided over the merits of Godwin's novel. "The trouble with *Violet Clay* may be that it is too intelligent for its own good," John Leonard wrote in the *New York Times* (May 18, 1978). "It is overgrown with ideas. You can't see the feelings for the ideas." On the other hand, Judith McPheron, who critiqued the novel for *Library Journal* (May 15, 1978), felt that it reinforced Godwin's status as "one of our most intelligent, engaging makers of fiction." *Violet Clay* was nominated for a National Book Award, as was Godwin's next full-length work, *A Mother and Two Daughters*.

The latter novel became a best-seller (outselling her previous books combined) and greatly expanded Godwin's following. The title characters are Nell Strickland, a recently widowed sexagenarian, and her daughters—the rebellious Cate, a twice-divorced college professor, and the more staid Lydia, herself a mother of two, who has just left her husband. Through more than five hundred pages, the novel explores the main characters' relationships with one another, such issues as abortion, and the attitudes of the "new" South, in which the story is set. *A Mother and Two Daughters* was the first work in which Godwin told a story from the perspective of more than one character. "For a long time I was influenced by Henry James, with the idea that there could only be one center of consciousness," Godwin told a reporter for *Publishers Weekly* (January 15, 1982). "Suddenly I found I didn't care anymore. I found I could be anybody, could enter fully into them." In a representative assessment of the book, Edmund Fuller wrote in the *Wall Street Journal* (January 11, 1982): "Few women thirty-six and older will fail to recognize at least some aspects of their own experience, and that of others they know, among the women in *A Mother and Two Daughters*. The novel confirms . . . Godwin as the maturely gifted artist that she is."

Mr. Bedford and the Muses, a well-received collection of Godwin's shorter fiction, followed a year later. In 1985 the writer published her sixth novel, *The Finishing School*, which, together with *A Mother and Two Daughters*, solidified her reputation as a major American fiction writer. *The Finishing School* is narrated by Justin Stokes, a successful actress in her forties, who recalls the relationship she had as a fourteen-year-old with Ursula DeVane, the woman who inspired her attempt to live an extraordinary life—and whom she eventually betrayed. "Justin and Ursula are characters realized in full complexity," Frances Taliaferro declared in the *New York Times Book Review* (January 27, 1985). "Vivid, overwhelming Ursula might have presented a problem for the novelist—the temptation would be to make her an Auntie Mame, a stock eccentric. Miss Godwin avoids this trap, rendering both the enchantment and the flaws of her character. Justin is a classic adolescent, piecing together a world of her own from fragments of experience and surmise, but she is also Justin, a person of specific intelligence and ardor. Her characterization is one of the most trustworthy portraits of an adolescent in current literature. *The Finishing School* is a strikingly accurate examination of the affinity between adolescence and middle age."

The writer's next two novels were set in her native South and drew on the facts of her own life. The suicide of her half-brother, Tommy, provided the impetus for *A Southern Family* (1987), in which the brother of the novelist Clare Campion dies suddenly and violently while she is visiting her family in the fictional Mountain City, North Carolina (also the setting of *A Mother and Two Daughters*). The novel won the Janet Heidiger Kafka Award from the University of Rochester as well as the Thomas Wolfe Memorial Literary Award. Four years passed between the appearance of that book and the publication of *Father Melancholy's Daughter* (1991), Godwin's novel about the role-reversal that takes place between Margaret Gower and her father, Walter, a Virginia church rector, after Margaret's mother abandons the family. The depression suffered by Walter Gower had its factual counterpart in the angst that plagued Godwin's father. *Father Melancholy's Daughter* won the Alabama Library Association's Best Fiction Award.

Godwin returned to the theme of matrimony in her most recent novel, *The Good Husband*. Set in a college town, the story focuses on two couples in its exploration of what marriage can and cannot achieve. The first couple consists of Magda Danvers, a brilliant academic dying of cancer, and her husband, Francis Lake, who has made it his life's work to serve her. The second couple is the Henrys: Hugo, an egocentric southern novelist, and Alice, his wife, who benefits from the wisdom of the rapidly deteriorating Magda while suffering emotional crises of her own. The critical response to the novel was varied. "The real problem is that *The Good Husband* is overloaded with attempts to make it a larger-scale book than it is," Sara Maitland wrote in the *New York Times Book Review* (September 4, 1994). "The novel is overambitious, too full of unnecessarily 'meaningful' symbolism. . . . [*The Good Husband* is] a perceptive domestic novel heavy with pretension." On the positive side, a reviewer for *Publishers Weekly* (June 20, 1994) declared, "Godwin's nuanced portraits of the four principals display her usual gift for probing the complex wellsprings of human behavior, but here she has dared risk two major characters—Magda and Hugo—who are not intrinsically sympathetic: each is boastful, domineering, demanding—and fascinating. This is Godwin's best book to date, a landmark achievement."

With her companion, the composer Robert Starer, whom she met in 1972 at the Yaddo writers' colony, Godwin has collaborated on several operas—she writes the librettos, he, the music. The first of these, *The Last Lover*, was first produced in 1975; the couple's other collaborations include *Appollonia* (1979), *Anna Margarita's Will* (1981), and *Remembering Felix* (1987). Godwin wrote in a *New York Times Magazine* article (December 15, 1985) that part of the lure of this work is that it allows her to have "fun in the absorbed, unselfconscious way [she] used to have when [she] wrote stories or painted as a child," and she explained further that "many phrases that look overwrought or even embarrassing in the cold medium of print sound just right when sung with the proper musical setting and dramatic shaping."

Gail Godwin lives in Woodstock, New York, in a house that has a view of the mountains and an indoor swimming pool. Over the years she has taught English and creative writing at schools including the University of Iowa; Vassar College, in Poughkeepsie, New York; and Columbia University, in

New York City. She also edited, with Sharon Ravenel, *The Best American Short Stories of 1985*. Among the honors she has received are the John Simon Guggenheim Fellowship, National Endowment grants for both fiction and libretto writing, and the award in literature from the American Academy and Institute of Arts and Letters.

David Streitfeld portrayed Godwin in his *Washington Post* profile as someone given to gloom, quoting her as saying, "We all have these constellations, and one of my stars is the melancholy star." As a graduate student, she recalled, she took antidepressant drugs, which "just ruined [her] mind." She found that the medication, beyond alleviating her emotional state, also nullified a part of her personality that, perhaps, contributes to her success as a writer. "My favorite part of my thought processes is that they're so associative," she revealed to David Streitfeld. "I'll think one thing, and there'll be a whole cluster that goes with it."

Selected Biographical References: Christian Sci Mon B p1+ Jl 21 '83 pors; People 17:69+ Mr 8 '82 pors; Washington Post D p1+ Mr 7 '91 pors; Contemporary Literary Criticism vol 69 (1992)

Terry O'Neill

Goldman, William

Aug. 12, 1931– Writer. Address: Janklow & Nesbit Associates, 598 Madison Ave., New York, NY 10022

William Goldman is a prolific novelist and, with two Academy Awards and a number of critically acclaimed movies to his credit, one of the most successful screenwriters of all time. Praise for Goldman's work, which includes the smash hit film *Butch Cassidy and the Sundance Kid* and the novels *Marathon Man* and *The Princess Bride*, has focused on his gift for dialogue, his knack for rendering bleak events with humor, and his talent for creating swiftly moving plots without neglecting character development. In addition, Goldman has produced a body of nonfiction, much of it frontline reportage on the industries he has come to know well in his nearly forty-year career. The best-selling *Adventures in the Screen Trade*, for example, is a veteran's view of Hollywood, sketched with Goldman's characteristic biting wit.

William Goldman was born on August 12, 1931 in Chicago, the son of Maurice Clarence Goldman, a businessman, and Marion Weil Goldman. His brother, James, is also a writer; his credits include the Academy Award-winning screenplay for *The Lion in Winter*, adapted from his own play. The Goldman brothers grew up in suburban Highland Park, where William spent what he remembers as "countless hours" watching movies in the Alycon Theater—an activity that was to influence his career. As Ralph Tyler reported in his profile of the writer for the *New York Times* (November 12, 1978), Goldman has traced a memorable scene in *Butch Cassidy*—the one in which the characters played by Paul Newman and Robert Redford leap off a cliff into a raging river—to a similar sequence he remembered from the 1939 film *Gunga Din*. "I seem to be repaying the pleasure movies gave me when I was a kid," he told Tyler.

Goldman attended Oberlin College, in Oberlin, Ohio, where he pursued writing but received little encouragement. He has recalled submitting what he considered to be his best short story for publication sixty-nine times without success, and he could not get his work printed in the college literary magazine, which had a policy of anonymous submissions, even though he was its fiction editor. Upon receiving his B.A. degree from Oberlin in 1952, he fulfilled his military obligation by serving a two-year hitch in the United States Army, then continued his education at Columbia University, in New York City, which awarded him a master's degree in English in 1956.

Although he might have remained at Columbia to work toward a doctorate, Goldman was by that time "sick of school," as he himself put it. Instead, in the summer of 1956, he "sat down and . . . wrote in wild desperation [his] first novel—*The Temple of Gold*—in ten days." Within a short time of its completion, Alfred A. Knopf accepted the novel, about a young man's search for direction in life, for publication. "If [the manuscript] had not been taken, I would have gone into advertising . . . or something," Goldman told Ralph Tyler.

The Temple of Gold received good reviews overall, with Henry Greene observing in the *Chicago Tribune* (October 13, 1957), "William Goldman has chosen a difficult theme for his first book and has pulled it off with flying colors. . . . [He] should do well."

Your Turn to Curtsy, My Turn to Bow (1958), whose protagonist suffers from delusions that eventually bring about a mental breakdown, was followed by *Soldier in the Rain* (1960), which some rate the best of Goldman's early novels. Set in an army training camp in the southern United States after the Korean War, the novel is, according to Charles Poore of the *New York Times* (July 14, 1960), replete with both "wonderfully funny" and "touchingly tragic" scenes. During the early 1960s Goldman also became involved in Broadway theatre, collaborating with his brother, James, on *Blood, Sweat and Stanley Poole*, a comedy about army life, and the musical *A Family Affair*, which one critic dismissed as "hopelessly ordinary." Neither production fared well at the box office, and Goldman later advised, "If you ever have an urge to write for Broadway, be kind to yourself and write a long novel instead."

Heeding his own counsel, Goldman completed the 623-page *Boys and Girls Together* (1964), a novel he had begun several years earlier and then put aside to work on the two plays. The story of the complex relationships among a group of young artists in New York City, *Boys and Girls Together* received mixed reviews. The British critic David Galloway, writing in the *Spectator* (March 12, 1965), called it "a polymorphous book that spins together with unflagging vitality and inexhaustible inventiveness the multiple, frequently contradictory experiences and values which make up American life." William Whitworth, in an evaluation for the *New York Herald Tribune* (July 23, 1964), took exception to what he viewed as the book's "presumptuous size" and chastised Goldman for his "gimmicky, cutie-pie" style of writing. Still, *Boys and Girls Together* turned out to be Goldman's first commercial success, and it has proved to be a durable best-seller.

As Goldman has often recounted in various interviews over the years, his introduction to screenwriting came about as the result of a misunderstanding on the part of the actor Cliff Robertson. By chance, Robertson read an early draft of Goldman's novel *No Way to Treat a Lady* (published in 1964 under the pseudonym Harry Longbaugh) and mistook it for a film treatment. On that basis, he asked Goldman to write a screenplay from a Daniel Keyes short story, "Flowers for Algernon," which the actor had optioned. Goldman, who, by his own admission, knew nothing about writing for the movies, accepted the assignment, then rushed out to purchase a book on screenwriting to use as a guide. Although Robertson ultimately decided not to use Goldman's scenario, the actor was instrumental in getting Goldman hired to help write the script for *Masquerade* (1965), a British-made thriller in which Robertson was appearing. Goldman shared the writing credit on that film with Michael Relph.

In the mid-1960s Goldman suggested to the producer Elliot Kastner that they collaborate on a film based on a work by the mystery writer Ross Macdonald. When Kastner agreed, Goldman wrote a screen adaptation of the novel *The Moving Target*, and the resulting film—Jack Smight's stylish *Harper*, starring Paul Newman as a cynical private eye—was released in 1966. Goldman has identified *Harper* as the project on which he "first began to learn at least a little about the craft of screenwriting." His statement was borne out by the enthusiastic notices the movie received. Although he was beginning to make a name for himself in Hollywood, Goldman did not abandon fiction writing. In 1967 he published the novel *The Thing of It Is . . .* (1967), about the disintegration of a marriage, which was praised by the critic Warren French, among others, for the "economy and precision" of its writing. "Beside [Goldman] the affectations of acclaimed stylists like [the novelist John] Updike appear trivial," French declared.

In addition, Goldman indulged his longtime interest in theatre by embarking on a project for which he attended nearly every play produced on Broadway during the 1967–68 season. He also sat in on rehearsals, went to out-of-town previews, and interviewed scores of actors, producers, directors, and critics. His impressions of the state of mainstream theatre were published as *The Season: A Candid Look at Broadway* (1969), a controversial work in which he assailed everything from the performances of individual actors to the gullibility of patrons to the myopia and cruelty of drama critics. Many of those who reviewed *The Season* took Goldman to task for what they saw as a lack of objectivity but nonetheless found the book to be highly readable. A representative assessment was that of Haskel Frankel in the *National Observer* (November 17, 1969): "*The Season* is not an investigation; it's just a new approach to Broadway bitchery. Taken as that, it won't let you down."

The publication of *The Season* roughly coincided with the release of the film that is arguably Goldman's biggest screen success, *Butch Cassidy and the Sundance Kid*. The story of the Hole-in-the-Wall Gang (or the Wild Bunch, as the gang was sometimes called), a group of turn-of-the-century bandits headed by Butch Cassidy, had fascinated Goldman since the 1950s, and he spent the better part of the following decade researching the subject. His account of the relationship between Cassidy and the gunslinger Harry Longbaugh, who was known as the Sundance Kid, came to the screen in 1969. The humorous, wistful movie presented its title characters, played by Paul Newman and Robert Redford, respectively, as outlaws with a difference—affable men not too proud to turn and run when a posse sets out after them. For his work on George Roy Hill's enormously popular film, Goldman received $400,000, which was at the time the highest fee ever paid for a movie script. *Butch Cassidy and the Sundance Kid* garnered an Academy

Award for Goldman for best original screenplay, and, as Botham Stone remarked in an article about the writer for the *Dictionary of Literary Biography* in 1986, the film "continues to be one of the most influential works in Hollywood, still defining a standard for entertainment movies."

Despite the acclaim he received as the scenarist of *Butch Cassidy*, Goldman still saw himself as a novelist at heart, as he told Jerry Parker for a *New York Newsday* (October 10, 1969) profile: "I consider myself, hopefully, a novelist. But do you know how much a novelist makes? I don't mean Harold Robbins and Jacqueline Susann. I mean most novelists. I have a family to support, so I write movies." He offered a somewhat different description of his career in his interview with Ralph Tyler. "I have a theory that we gravitate toward affection," he explained. "Since . . . people seemed to want my screenplays, I gravitated toward that affection."

Whatever his motivation, in the early and mid-1970s Goldman provided the screenplays for a number of major releases. He adapted Donald Westlake's comic novel *The Hot Rock*, about incompetent jewel thieves, for the 1972 film of the same name, starring Robert Redford and directed by Peter Yates. Another novel he translated to the screen was Ira Levin's *The Stepford Wives*, in which women in a Connecticut town are murdered by their husbands and replaced by replicas. Goldman told John Brady, in an interview for Brady's book *The Craft of Screenwriting* (1982), that he was unhappy with the final version of that 1975 film because its director, Bryan Forbes, "rewrote *all* of *Stepford*, until the last twenty minutes of the film." "I'm not saying that it would have been better if it had been mine," he said, "but I'm saying it *isn't* mine, and I wanted my name off it, but they wouldn't take it off." *The Great Waldo Pepper* (1975), directed by George Roy Hill from Goldman's original screenplay and starring Robert Redford, concerned barnstorming pilots in the early days of aviation.

In the meantime, Goldman had continued to write books at a steady rate. *Father's Day* (1971) focuses on a divorced composer whose relationship with his young daughter is his sole link to reality. *The Princess Bride: S. Morgenstern's Classic Tale of True Love and High Adventure* (1973), which Goldman has singled out as his favorite among his novels, is built on an unusual premise. In the book's introduction, the narrator recalls having been spellbound as a boy when his father read to him from the classic *The Princess Bride* (an invention of Goldman's); when his own son found the book to be boring reading, the narrator perused it himself for the first time and discovered that his father had skipped the book's duller sections while reading it aloud. The narrator then presents Morgenstern's "adult fairy tale"—involving a virtuous young woman, an evil prince, and various fantastic beasts—in an "abridged" form, cutting or telescoping some parts and embellishing others to make them more exciting. Critics praised the novel as "daffy" and "delightful." Some years later, Goldman wrote the screenplay for Rob Reiner's popular film version of *The Princess Bride*, released in 1987.

The protagonist of *Marathon Man* (1974), Goldman's ninth novel, is Thomas ("Babe") Levy, an idealistic graduate student of history who dreams of being a great long-distance runner. Following the violent death of his older brother, whom he believed to be a businessman, Babe finds himself caught in a nightmare of international espionage complete with a double-talking government agent and a sadistic ex-Nazi named Szell, and he is forced to resort to violence in order to survive. Assessing the novel for *Library Journal* (September 15, 1974), Eric Moon wrote, "Goldman's brilliant construction holds the interest and helps build the excitement. This book gradually eases you to the edge of your chair, then keeps you there with that combination of terror and pleasure that only the superb thriller can achieve." John Schlesinger directed the popular and critically acclaimed 1976 movie version of the story, which starred Dustin Hoffman and featured Laurence Olivier in a terrifying performance as Szell. Although Goldman wrote the screenplay, he has disavowed the ending of the film, which is somewhat less disquieting than the book's conclusion.

Goldman won considerable praise as well as his second Academy Award for best screenplay for Alan Pakula's *All the President's Men* (1976). That film, based on the best-selling book of the same title by the *Washington Post* reporters Bob Woodward and Carl Bernstein, recounted the journalists' exposure of the Watergate break-in and subsequent cover-up—the political scandal that ended the presidency of Richard Nixon. As Botham Stone observed in the *Dictionary of Literary Biography*, Goldman perceived the story as being as much about the way Woodward (played by Robert Redford) and Bernstein (Dustin Hoffman) overcame their personal differences to work together as about their investigation itself. A less successful adaptation of a nonfiction work was Richard Attenborough's film *A Bridge Too Far* (1977), which Goldman took from Cornelius Ryan's account of the World War II Allied defeat at Arnheim. Despite an all-star cast that included James Caan, Elliot Gould, Robert Redford, and Maximilian Schell, the three-hour film—which one critic called "a movie much, much too long"—was both a critical and commercial failure.

Like *Marathon Man*, Goldman's novel *Magic* (1976), about a disturbed ventriloquist whose dummy becomes his jealous, murderous alter ego, was subsequently adapted for the screen by the author himself. The book received mixed reviews; the film, directed by Richard Attenborough and starring Anthony Hopkins, was almost universally panned upon its release in 1978. In the following year Goldman wrote the screenplay *Tom Horn*, based on the true story of a western scout, but his treatment turned out to be too long for a feature film. The script was eventually produced as a four-hour made-for-television movie. He wrapped up the decade with another novel, *Tinsel* (1979), an exposé of the crassness and decadence of Hollywood.

The 1980s found Goldman at work on a variety of projects. The novel *Control* (1982), which uses a large cast of disparate characters to explore the notion of controlling the future by altering the past, drew positive notices, with a reviewer for *Publishers Weekly*, for example, calling it a "work of dazzling entertainment." Three more novels followed: *The Color of Light* (1982), a breezy account of the tribulations of a writer; *Heat* (1985), a hard-boiled tale of revenge set in Las Vegas (Goldman also wrote the screenplay for the 1987 film version); and *Brothers* (1986), a sequel to *Marathon Man*. Meanwhile, Goldman provided a wealth of inside information about the film industry in *Adventures in the Screen Trade* (1983), an anecdotal account of his experiences in Hollywood that included advice for aspiring writers as well as scathing passages about actors, studio executives, directors, and the moviemaking process. In an article about Goldman for *Publishers Weekly* (March 18, 1983), Sybil S. Steinberg called it a "funny, irreverent, lusty-languaged look at the movie industry. . . . [written] in fast-paced Hollywood lingo, conveying the casual earthiness of typically inbred movieland conversation." Readers seemed to agree, for *Adventures* quickly became a best-seller. In 1988 Goldman collaborated with the sports columnist Mike Lupica on *Wait till Next Year* (1988), a survey of the previous year's football, baseball, and basketball seasons.

By all accounts, one of Goldman's most effective screen adaptations of recent years was the psychological thriller *Misery* (1990), directed by Rob Reiner from the popular Stephen King novel of the same name. In that film, James Caan portrayed a highly successful romance novelist who yearns to write more serious fiction. After a car accident in a remote area leaves him helpless, he is rescued and subsequently terrorized by a demented fan (Kathy Bates, in an award-winning performance) intent upon seeing him write another romance. Jay Scott, who evaluated the movie for the *Toronto Globe & Mail* (November 30, 1990), described it as "gut-grindingly intense," adding, "William Goldman's deft adaptation of *Misery* is a piece about pain . . . and about putting pain to use, both in terms of public profitability and personal growth." Perhaps because they came in the wake of the box-office smash *Misery*, which took in more than twenty million dollars in its first two weeks of release, Goldman's next two film credits—*Year of the Comet*, a comic caper directed by Peter Yates and referred to by one critic as a "black hole of a movie," and the Chevy Chase vehicle *Memoirs of an Invisible Man*—left most observers unimpressed.

Goldman's next project was *Hype and Glory* (1990), a wry account of his experiences as a judge at the 1988 Cannes Film Festival and, later in the same year, at the Miss America Pageant. "Because it deals essentially in trivia, *Hype and Glory* lacks the resonance of Goldman's best nonfiction," Clive Davis observed in *New Statesman & Society* (November 2, 1990). "Yet the truth is that he is capable of making any subject seem absorbing. . . . We are so used to thinking of him as a purveyor of screenplays that we forget that he is an extraordinarily vivid prose writer." For the past several years, Goldman has been a regular contributor to *New York* magazine, writing mainly about film and occasionally about sports. He is also the author of a children's book, *Wigger*, published in 1974. *William Goldman: Four Screenplays*, containing the movie scripts of *Butch Cassidy and the Sundance Kid*, *Marathon Man*, *The Princess Bride*, and *Misery*, each printed with an introductory essay, was published late in 1994.

William Goldman married Ilene Jones, a photographer, on April 15, 1961; he has two daughters, Jenny and Susanna, from that marriage, which ended in divorce in 1991. A longtime resident of Manhattan, Goldman has said that he prefers New York City to Hollywood because "it's too beautiful in Los Angeles." "I'd never get any work done," he told Suzy Kalter of *People* (August 20, 1979). "Out there actors can get famous and then divorce their old wives and marry new wives because they don't want to be reminded of who they were before. I think there's something very important about a writer remembering his childhood and who he was." Goldman writes in an office rather than in his home because it "gives validity" to what he does, as he put it, and while he is writing he listens to music appropriate to his subject. When she met Goldman in 1983, Sybil S. Steinberg of *Publishers Weekly* found him to be "earnest, circumspect, sensitive, a gentleman to his toes." In addition to his two Academy Awards, in 1983 Goldman received the Laurel Award for lifetime achievement in screenwriting.

Selected Biographical References: N Y Times II p23+ N 12 '78 por; Brady, John. The Craft of Screenwriting (1982); Contemporary Literary Criticism vol 48 (1988); Dictionary of Literary Biography vol 44 (1986); Goldman, William. Adventures in the Screen Trade (1983); Who's Who in America, 1995; World Authors 1970–1975 (1980)

Grafton, Sue

Apr. 24, 1940– Writer; screenwriter. Address: c/o Molly Friedrich, Aaron Priest Agency, 708 Third Ave., 23d fl., New York, NY 10017

"My goal in life is to write one perfect mystery," Sue Grafton, the creator of the fictional private investigator Kinsey Millhone, told an interviewer in 1992. With the twelve linked suspense novels that she has written to date in Kinsey's voice, Grafton

Steve Humphrey/Henry Holt and Co.

Sue Grafton

has staked out a prominent position in the province of American detective fiction, a domain dominated until recent years by male writers, and she has been recognized as "perhaps the best of the new breed of female mystery writers." She began her critically acclaimed, hugely popular series with *"A" Is for Alibi* in 1982. Eleven books and thirteen years later, the abecedarian series reached *"L" Is for Lawless*, and according to Grafton, it will end with *"Z" Is for Zero* by around the year 2008. "Intelligent, fast-paced, and filled with memorable characters," as Nancy S. Dye wrote in the *New York Times Book Review* (July 28, 1991), each of the mysteries is narrated by the brashly independent Kinsey Millhone, "a tough cookie with a soft center" who is "attractive, capable, caring, funny, and courageous as well as highly professional," "endearingly sardonic," and "armed with matchless powers of observation," as critics have described her, and who is also "flawed and inconsistent," in the words of her creator. "Kinsey is my alter ego—well, not even very alter," Grafton has said of her heroine, whose wry comments on people, situations, and the human condition enrich each story.

Grafton's career as a writer began in the late 1960s, with the publication of her novel *Keziah Dane*. She adapted her next book, *The Lolly-Madonna War*, for a feature film that premiered in 1973. For more than a decade beginning in the mid-1970s, she wrote or cowrote scripts for television series and films that were produced in Hollywood. Her suspense novels have won many prizes, including several Shamus Awards from the Private Eye Writers of America, and most of her mysteries have been best-sellers. "Even in a less than top-notch performance," the screenwriter Ed Weiner wrote in an assessment of *"F" Is for Fugitive* for the *New York Times Book Review* (May 21, 1989), "Ms. Grafton's work surpasses most of what limps along as detective fiction these days. And throughout her work, . . . she is consistent in accomplishing two extremely difficult tasks. First, she has successfully replaced the raw, masculine-fantasy brutality and gore of the [Robert B.] Parkers and [Jonathan] Valins and [Elmore] Leonards with heart-pounding, totally mesmerizing suspense. It's tough to do, and she's a master at it. Tougher yet, she has made Kinsey Millhone real, somebody we believe actually exists." "Despite the pace of production, there's nothing mechanical about Grafton's novels," Anita Manning wrote in *USA Today* (July 2, 1992). "With each one, she and her witty detective . . . grow more accomplished." "I want to be the king of American mysteries," Grafton declared to Deborah Starr Seibel during an interview for the *Chicago Tribune* (May 11, 1992). "Not the queen, please. I want to be the king."

A daughter of Cornelius Warren ("Chip") Grafton and Vivian Boisseau (Harnsberger) Grafton, Sue Grafton was born in Louisville, Kentucky on April 24, 1940. She has at least one sibling, an older sister. Her father, an attorney and writer, and her mother, a high school chemistry teacher, both suffered from alcoholism. In *USA Today*, Anita Manning reported that Grafton considered what she termed her "peculiar" childhood to be "a gift" despite the difficulties of her early years, in part because, as a result of her parents' "benign neglect," she was given an unusual amount of freedom. She has credited her troubled home environment in addition with fostering her creativity and motivating her to succeed. "When you grow up in a dysfunctional household," she explained to Manning, "you quickly tune in to what's going on under the surface. From age five or six, I was scanning, figuring out all the stuff not being discussed." She also said, "One of my theories is that no one with a happy childhood ever amounts to much in this world. They're so well-adjusted, they never are driven to achieve anything."

Grafton's parents encouraged her to read widely, and as an adolescent, while her friends were still engrossed, as she had been, in the popular girls' mystery series about the amateur detective Nancy Drew, Grafton began reading hard-boiled adult crime fiction by such celebrated practitioners of the genre as Mickey Spillane, Raymond Chandler, Dashiell Hammett, and Ross Macdonald. She had many conversations with her father about the craft of writing, she told Bruce Taylor during an interview for the *Armchair Detective* (Winter 1989). "He taught me to write with clarity and simplicity," she recalled. "He said it was never my job to revise the English language or to play games with punctuation, spelling, or capitalization." He also stressed the importance of transitions in holding the interest of the reader between the "big scenes" and of developing minor characters as carefully as major ones, and he "talked a lot about how to survive as a writer, how to deal with rejection." During the

1940s her father wrote one "straight" novel, as she has described it, and three mysteries, including *Beyond a Reasonable Doubt*, which is widely regarded as a classic courtroom drama. Sue Grafton told Bruce Taylor that she had read *Beyond a Reasonable Doubt* "about eight times" and that it had "astonished" her every time. "I'm sorry I never had a chance to ask [my father] how he put [that book] together, because I think it's so intricately constructed," she remarked. (Chip Grafton died in the early 1980s.)

Grafton majored in English at the University of Louisville. She married during her sophomore year and became the mother of a daughter the next year. Soon after her graduation, with a B.A. degree, in 1961, she divorced and then remarried. In 1962 she and her second husband moved to California, where within the next four years she gave birth to two more children. During the 1960s she held a series of jobs, including several in hospitals or doctors' offices and one as a secretary at Danny Thomas Productions, in Hollywood. At home, to maintain her mental equilibrium in "an otherwise chaotic existence," as a reporter for *Redbook* (April 1986) put it, she began to write fiction.

Grafton's first book, *Keziah Dane*, a Depression-era story about a strong, warm-hearted widow, was published in 1967. Although, by her own admission, Grafton "knew nothing about the Depression," she was—apparently despite her father's tutelage—"so innocent about the writing process that [she] did no research whatever" for the book. In *Publishers Weekly* (August 21, 1967), a reviewer described *Keziah Dane* as a "curious" and "folksy" tale whose appeal would be limited; nonetheless, the reviewer wrote, Grafton showed "storytelling promise." According to some critics, that promise was not evident in her second published book, *The Lolly-Madonna War* (1969), which centered on two feuding Appalachian families. "Sue Grafton's previous novel was worthwhile, if sentimental, but this one is unconsciously comic," Maurice Capitanchik wrote in the *Spectator* (September 27, 1969); in the *Listener* (October 2, 1969), Kenneth Graham reported that he had approached *The Lolly-Madonna War* "with some expectations," only to find what he labeled "antique preposterousness." Grafton herself is among the severest critics of her early works. "In those days I often wrote quite strange books," she told Bruce Taylor. "I don't know where these books came from, and I was very happy when they finally went away, because I don't think I was meant to be a mainstream writer."

The lack of critical acclaim for *The Lolly-Madonna War* notwithstanding, Metro-Goldwyn-Mayer bought the screen rights to it and hired Grafton and Rodney Carr-Smith to write the script. The film premiered in 1973, with a cast that included Rod Steiger, Robert Ryan, and Jeff Bridges. It was "a fine, fine cast, but [it was] not a good movie . . . ," Grafton said during her interview with Bruce Taylor. "When I saw a rough cut of the film, I thought, what kind of sicko put that together? And then I realized it was me." Sometime later, at the suggestion of an agent, she sent a script on spec to the producers of the popular television comedy series *Rhoda*. Although that script and the next one that she offered on spec were rejected, they were sufficiently impressive to land her an assignment. Her contracted script was produced as an episode of *Rhoda* in the spring of 1975. During the next few years she wrote scripts for various other television series and also adaptations of novels by other people for a number of telefilms, including *Walking through the Fire* (which won a Christopher Award in 1979), *Sex and the Single Parent* (1979), *Nurse* (1980), and *Mark, I Love You* (1980).

In the 1980s Grafton collaborated with her third husband, Steven F. Humphrey, whom she had married in 1978, on at least five scripts that were produced as television movies: *A Caribbean Mystery* (1983), which was adapted from an Agatha Christie novel; *A Killer in the Family* (1983, with Robert Aller as cowriter); *Sparkling Cyanide* (1983, with Robert Malcolm Young as cowriter), another adaptation of an Agatha Christie story; *Love on the Run* (1985), which was nominated for an Edgar Award by the Mystery Writers of America; and *Tonight's the Night* (1987). By her own account, the substantial financial rewards that she and her husband were getting as television writers were overshadowed by Grafton's increasing irritation with the attitude prevalent in Hollywood toward scriptwriters: they were considered "trash, but well paid," in her words. She was also feeling increasingly intolerant about rewrites of her scripts by committees ("They were always nice and polite, but they wrecked your work," she explained to Enid Nemy of the *New York Times* [August 4, 1994]) and critiques of her work by fledgling network executives who, in her estimation, knew nothing about writing. She and Humphrey eventually became so distressed, she told Nemy, that they began to spend a substantial part of their earnings on "extra presents to [themselves] to compensate" and on psychotherapy.

Grafton's unhappiness with her working conditions in the television industry was a major factor behind her decision to try her hand at writing a mystery novel. "I finally reached a point where I felt that if I wanted to redeem whatever minimal writing skills I had left, I'd better get back to solo work," she recalled to Bruce Taylor. Another impetus was the repeated criticism that while she was skilled at character development, her plots were weak. Writing a mystery, where plot is crucial, she reasoned, would be a good exercise for her. A further inspiration was the example that her father had set. "Since my father wrote [mysteries], I guess, in the back of my mind, I always thought I'd do a mystery one day," she told Bruce Taylor.

Grafton has traced the genesis of her first Kinsey Millhone story in addition to the bitter child-custody battles in which she was embroiled for a total of about six years with her second husband. "Like many women," Grafton told Deborah Starr Seibel, "I had not been taught how to fight. I found myself feeling frustrated and powerless, and, under those circumstances, often homicide seems like a quite reasonable solution to your problems. However, I am personally such a law-abiding little bun that I knew I would never actually act it out. And if I did, I would never get away with it. So the next best thing was to put it in a book and get paid for it." Every night as Grafton lay in bed, thinking "how much nicer it would be if [her second husband] were a dead person instead of a live one," as she recalled during an interview with Susan Goodman for *Modern Maturity* (July/August 1995), she could smell the fragrance from the blossoms of an oleander that grew outside her bedroom window, and she began fantasizing about murdering her husband by putting a powder made from the poisonous leaves of the shrub into his allergy capsules. Transforming her fantasy into art, she incorporated the idea as an element of the plot of what would become her first mystery novel.

During the five years that Grafton worked on that book, she spent a lot of time doing extensive research into such crime-fiction fundamentals as investigative techniques, insurance fraud, ballistics, and toxicology. At some point she learned how to handle a gun and pick a lock and took classes in self-defense and marksmanship. Through the years she has acquired many books on subjects related to crime and crime-fighting, and she maintains extensive files of newspaper and magazine articles. "[Kinsey] can only know what I know, so I have to keep learning things," she pointed out during an interview with Katrine Ames for *Savvy Woman* (June 1989).

Reluctant to complete her book without a guarantee that she would be paid for her efforts (she had become accustomed to such assurances as a Hollywood scriptwriter), Grafton wrote sixty-five pages and then sent the partial manuscript to prospective publishers. A half-dozen of them rejected her concept before Holt, Rinehart and Winston (now called Henry Holt and Company) bought it. The sequential titles of two of her father's books—*The Rat Began to Gnaw the Rope* and *The Rope Began to Hang the Butcher*, which are lines from a nursery rhyme—and alphabet-based series of illustrations by the artist Edward Gorey led her to envision her book as one in a linked series, in which the titles would be one of the links. It was thus that she selected the title *"A" Is for Alibi.*

Published in 1982, *"A" Is for Alibi* was offered as a main selection by the Mystery Guild, and it received favorable reviews. After identifying it as "the first in what promises to be an excellent series," a writer for *Publishers Weekly* (March 12, 1982) reported that "Grafton's characterizations are colorful and credible" and added that "she certainly knows how to tell a good story, one that keeps you guessing all the way." Similarly, in *Newsweek* (June 7, 1982), Katrine Ames praised both the plot, which she labeled "smart, well paced, and very funny," and the characterizations, not only of Kinsey Millhone—"a woman we feel we know," in Ames's words—but also of several minor characters, about whom she wrote, "One hopes [they] will be a regular supporting cast. " *"A" Is for Alibi* won the 1982–83 Mysterious Stranger Award from the Cloak and Clue Society.

Fearing that her second mystery might not live up to the expectations generated by the first, Grafton struggled with a severe case of writer's block after the publication of *"A" Is for Alibi*, and three years passed before the appearance of *"B" Is for Burglar*. A main selection of the Mystery Guild, in 1985 it won both the Shamus Award for best hardcover private-eye novel, from the Private Eye Writers of America, and the Anthony Award for best hardcover mystery, from the Mystery Writers of America. Grafton has produced a Kinsey Millhone mystery annually ever since. *"C" Is for Corpse* (1986), which was also a Mystery Guild main selection, was followed by *"D" Is for Deadbeat* (1987), *"E" Is for Evidence* (1988), *"F" Is for Fugitive* (1989), *"G" Is for Gumshoe* (1990), *"H" Is for Homicide* (1991), *"I" Is for Innocent* (1992), *"J" Is for Judgment* (1994), *"K" Is for Killer* (1994), and, most recently, *"L" Is for Lawless* (1995).

Many of Grafton's books have reached both the hardcover and paperback best-seller lists (*"L" Is for Lawless* leaped to the number-one spot for fiction on the *New York Times* hardcover best-seller list almost immediately after publication), and with each addition to the series, Grafton's readership has steadily grown. Nine hundred thousand copies of the paperback edition of *"H" Is for Homicide* were printed before the official publication date, and *"L" Is for Lawless* had a first printing of three-quarters of a million copies. Hardcover sales of *"A"* through *"K"* have reached one-and-a-half million copies, and paperback sales of the same titles currently total thirteen million. Grafton's books have pleased juries of her peers as well as lay readers: *"C" Is for Corpse* won an Anthony Award, *"E"* through *"I"* each won a Doubleday Mystery Guild Award, and *"F"*, *"G"*, and *"I"* also won other awards (both a Shamus and an Anthony award in the case of *"G"*). A three-book contract that Grafton signed with Henry Holt in 1991 amounted to several million dollars, according to an article in *McCall's* (August 1991).

"[*'E' Is for Evidence*] is the best detective fiction I have read in years," the writer Vincent Patrick declared in the *New York Times Book Review* (May 1, 1988), in one of the many laudatory reviews that have greeted the publication of Grafton's mysteries. The plot thickens "to precisely the right consistency . . . ," Patrick reported. "[It] does what a plot ought to in a good detective novel: it keeps us turning pages and serves as a vehicle for the *really* interesting stuff, an unveiling of the characters' foibles by the worldly-wise but uncorrupt private eye. And this is where Sue Grafton shines." The relatively few negative assessments of Grafton's books have been counterbalanced by positive ones. *"G" Is for Gumshoe*, for example, struck Alex Kozinski as "devoid of intellectual challenge and completely forgettable," as he wrote in the *New York Times Book Review* (May 27, 1990), but in *People* (April

23, 1990), Lorenzo Carcaterra hailed *"G"* as "the best" of Grafton's mysteries up to that date. Grafton, he declared, "works with a cinematic eye, possessing a keen visual sense of detail, color, and style. The pace is fast, the crime difficult to solve. The secondary characters . . . are strong enough to stand on their own."

Grafton has received universal praise for her deft characterization of Kinsey Millhone. Orphaned at the age of five and raised thereafter by an unmarried aunt, Kinsey is a twice-divorced former police officer who is in her thirties; she has gotten a year older every two-and-a-half books, and Grafton anticipates that the private eye will turn forty in *"Z" Is for Zero.* The resourceful, outspoken, tough-minded Kinsey lives by herself in a converted garage in Santa Teresa, a fictional town north of Los Angeles that bears a strong resemblance to Santa Barbara, California, where Grafton lives. Like the author, who has jogged six mornings a week for nearly a quarter of a century, Kinsey keeps in shape by means of a daily run before breakfast. She is conspicuously casual about both her appearance and her eating habits, as Enid Nemy noted in the *New York Times*: "She has been known to cut her hair with nail scissors, has one all-purpose dress, and often faces a cupboard barren of just about everything but peanut butter, uncooked lentils, and maple syrup." Other than her landlord, a retired baker in his early eighties, and the owner of a tavern where she sometimes eats, Kinsey appears to have no close friends, and, in the course of the series, she has had few romantic encounters.

In her assessment of *"H" Is for Homicide* for the *New York Times Book Review* (July 28, 1991), Nancy S. Dye described Kinsey as "wry and considerably less sentimental than many of her male counterparts," "remarkably equable about human nature," and, "best of all, . . . very funny." "Like most fictional characters—male and female—she sometimes walks a fine line between the mainstream and the margins of society," Dye observed. "There has always been something of the outlaw in Kinsey Millhone—what she herself calls 'the latent felon in me.' Fond of disguises, Kinsey also relishes lying, which she does frequently and without guilt. And like most detectives, she is comfortable with the anarchic side of herself." "Kinsey's the person I would have been if I had not married young and had children," Grafton told Andrea Chambers for *People* (July 10, 1989). "We have the same sensibilities, though we have different biographies." Grafton has cited her resemblance to Kinsey as one reason why she has resolved never to allow her mysteries to be adapted for film.

By her own admission, contrary to her expectations, Grafton has discovered that the difficulties of writing mysteries have increased rather than decreased with each of her books. During an interview with Charles Hix for *Publishers Weekly* (January 22, 1992), she said, "I run into the same problem every time, which is: Do I have anything left? I'm always working right out on the edge of my abilities, and it's very hair-raising for me." "I write in a state of hysteria," she told Katrine Ames for *Savvy Woman.* "I never relax." Each story emerges from a journal in which, in a process that she has likened to stream of consciousness, Grafton records her ideas about possible murders, victims and wrongdoers, motives, "challenges to each supposition," and information she has gained through research. Working from a very sketchy outline or without one, she writes two pages a day, a task that can take her from as little as twenty minutes to as much as sixteen hours. She spends a great deal of time revising what she has written, so that, as she told Bruce Taylor, her books require little editing.

"What I love about the mystery is that it is the one form in which the reader and the writer are pitted against each other . . . ," she told Charles Hix. "I am doing sleight of hand. And the readers' job, in part, . . . is to see if they can get me at what I'm up to." Although she has said that she does not think it is her duty "to convert anyone to anything"—"A writer's job is to entertain in the best sense of the word," she said to Bruce Taylor—she has consciously made Kinsey Millhone a medium for social commentary. "I think the private eye has always functioned literally as a private eye—as an observer and as someone who comments on society and on family relationships and on the state of justice," she told Rosemary Herbert, who interviewed her for *Publishers Weekly* (April 13, 1990).

Sue Grafton has been described as being outspoken and irreverent and as having a "don't-mess-with-me attitude." She has characterized herself as a feminist who has "no interest in being politically correct" and as "tough in a psychic sense." "I'm certainly tough in my persona *and* I am also mild, soft-spoken, timid, and genteel," she told Rosemary Herbert. "But I enjoy competition; I like to test myself in an arena such as hard-boiled private-eye fiction . . . , to get in there and knock elbows with those guys whom I greatly admire." She enjoys talking to readers during promotional book tours, and she answers every letter that she receives from people who have read her books, some of whom have advised her to find a husband for Kinsey or give her a pet cat—suggestions that, along with most if not all of the others that have been offered to her, she has rejected. Grafton and her husband, Steve Humphrey, who has a Ph.D. degree in philosophy and who teaches in colleges in California, own homes in both Santa Barbara and Louisville, Kentucky. They walk several miles together most afternoons and reportedly get to bed each night by 8 o'clock. "I live a very ordinary lifestyle," Grafton told Marlene Cimons for *Runner's World* (June 1992). She maintains a close relationship with her children: her daughter Leslie, who is the mother of Grafton's two granddaughters, her son, Jay, and her daughter Jamie.

Selected Biographical References: Armchair Detective 22:4+ Winter '89 por; Chicago Tribune V p1+ My 11 '92 por; Modern Maturity 38:74+

Jl/Ag '95 pors; N Y Times C p1+ Ag 4 '94 pors; People 32:81+ Jl 10 '89 pors; Runner's World 27:37+ Je '92 pors; USA Today D p4 Jl 2 '92 por; Contemporary Authors new rev vol 31 (1990); Who's Who in America, 1995

AP/Wide World Photos

Grant, Hugh

Sep. 9, 1960- British actor. Address: c/o Creative Artists Agency, 9830 Wilshire Blvd., Beverly Hills, CA 90212

Hugh Grant, the star of the immensely popular British romantic comedy *Four Weddings and a Funeral* (1994), has revived the long-lost art of endowing a romantic role with both intelligence and an endearingly bumbling comic presence. In many of his films he has played a repressed Englishman confronted with uninhibited sexuality, frequently in the form of people from former colonies, among them Australia and the United States. As John Petrakis suggested when he interviewed Grant for the *Chicago Tribune* (March 20, 1994), many of his characters have suffered from an "inherent Englishness." "Well, it's a bit of a cliché, isn't it?" Grant replied. "But I think we are sort of a little bit nervous or uncomfortable with our deepest, darkest instincts and emotions." "He is actually two people," Mike Newell, who directed Grant in *Four Weddings*, told Cyndi Stivers for an article in *Premiere* (May 1994). "There is at least as much of Hugh that is charismatic, intellectual, and whose tongue is maybe too clever for its good as there is of him that's gorgeous and kind of wooly and flubsy. . . . He has all the lineaments of a star, and at the same time he's a God-given character actor. He can do both." John Duigan, who directed the actor in *Sirens* (1994), agreed, as he told Stephen Farber of the *New York Times* (February 25, 1994): "Hugh has the capacity to be a terrific player of light comedy, in the tradition of Cary Grant and David Niven. He has the same ease and urbanity in the way he moves and talks."

Hugh Grant was born on September 9, 1960 in London, into what he has described as a "very ordinary, middle-class family." His father, James Grant, is a retired carpet salesman who paints in watercolor; his mother, Finvola Grant, is a teacher; and his older brother, Jamie, is a banker at J. P. Morgan in New York City. Both brothers attended the all-boys Upper Latymer School, in the Hammersmith section of West London. Referring to Grant's upper-class accent, Bruce Perkins, his language teacher and rugby coach, told a reporter for *People* (July 10, 1995), "That's partly natural, partly a put-on. He has always been putting on different personae, anything to make an effect on other people."

With characteristic self-deprecating humor, Grant informed Rita Kempley of the *Washington Post* (March 20, 1994) of the origins of his interest in acting: "I was extraordinarily moving as the White Rabbit in *Alice and Wonderland*. Well, you probably heard about it. It was a huge success. . . . And it just went on from there, just spiraled out of control after that, my career." In fact, Grant entered Oxford University in 1979 not with the intent of becoming an actor but to study English literature, on a scholarship. In an interview with Lucy Kaylin for *GQ* (December 1994), he described himself as "dull as dirt" at Oxford: "I went to the pub the first year and drank beer and was quite studious and occasionally had a game of darts." He did not become involved in theatrical projects until his senior year. "No one there took him very seriously as an actor," an acquaintance told David Gritten, who profiled Grant for *Cosmopolitan* (January 1995). "But I must say, a lot of girls were smitten with him." While at Oxford, he was interviewed for the unlikely role of Tarzan in the movie *Greystoke*. After some time had passed and he still had not heard from the casting director, he sent her some photos of himself slathered in baby oil, wearing only his shorts, with the note, "Just in case you're wondering about my body." "I think those pictures must go down as the most humiliating experience of my life," he admitted to Candace Bushnell years later, in an interview for *Vogue* (July 1995).

Before graduating with a degree in English from Oxford in 1982, he played Lord Adrian in the student film *Privileged* (1982), produced by the Oxford Film Foundation. Then known as Hughie Grant, he also appeared with the Oxford University Dramatic Society and, according to Kaylin, donned full drag attire for an exclusive party thrown by the Piers Gaveston Society (named for the male lover of Edward II). Following his graduation Grant wrote—and sometimes performed—ad copy for radio commercials for Red Stripe beer and

Brylcreem, work in which he appears to have taken much pride. "It was just sort of manly to have a deadline," he told Kaylin. "We were trying to sell a product, and it was good to see more cans of Red Stripe lager going out of the shop, rather than some review in an arty-farty newspaper. I think it's more rewarding."

In 1984 Grant began making regular trips to the London Library, where he attempted to write a novel—or at least the first page of one, over and over again, as he told Candace Bushnell. "I'm sort of a joke there, going with my folders with pages and pages of notes. I write a hysterically funny first paragraph and then I go have my lunch, and when I come back I gibber with embarrassment and put it in the bin and start again," he said. Acting, he added, "was just one thing that I thought I might have a crack at." He made his stage debut in 1985, at Nottingham Playhouse, but he soon grew tired of repertory work. "I was bored playing the tree that waved in the wind and the fourth angry peasant," he told Ginia Bellafante of *Time* (April 25, 1994). After cofounding the comedy troupe Jockeys of Norfolk, he wrote and directed the revues in which he performed.

In 1987 Grant landed his first film role since his student days, that of Clive Durham, a British homosexual aristocrat and Cambridge undergraduate who falls in love with a fellow student, in the meticulous James Ivory-Ismail Merchant production *Maurice*, based on a 1913 novel by E. M. Forster. "Funny enough," Grant recalled to John Petrakis, "I got *Maurice* directly through my comedy work. James Ivory kept saying, 'I've cast you because I want you to bring some humor to this role.' But I never saw any humor in it whatsoever, and brought none whatsoever to it." Nonetheless, most critics felt that Grant had acquitted himself admirably in a role that required him to shift from being the aggressor to being the reluctantly pursued lover who abandons his homosexuality for a secure married life in politics. Writing in his *Movie and Video Guide 1994*, Leonard Maltin declared *Maurice* to be "beautifully realized and extremely well-acted all around, but overlong." For his role in *Maurice*, which made him a minor gay icon in England, Grant won a best-actor award (shared with his costar James Wilby) at the Venice Film Festival and became an overnight sensation in Japan, where two books were published about him. "For a few years," he told Bellafante, "I was getting sacks full of origami and very sensitive letters which said I have sensitive eyes and a kind face. Little did they know I wanted their money, not their love."

For the next four years, Grant made a slew of mostly forgettable films, miniseries, and television movies. "I'm the first to admit that I'm the master of the stinker," he told Candace Bushnell. "I must have done a dozen in my life. 'Euro-puddings,' as they call them." In 1988 alone he appeared in five films, playing Harry in Robert Knights's *The Dawning*, a chronicle of political turbulence in southern Ireland in 1920, starring Anthony Hopkins; Allan in *La Nuit Bengali (The Bengal Night)*; Lord James D'Ampton, an archaeologist, in Ken Russell's horror farce *The Lair of the White Worm*, adapted from a novel by Bram Stoker; Lord Byron in *Remando al Viento (Rowing with the Wind)*; and Hugh Dickinson in Michael Radford's *White Mischief*, a steamy mystery that was derived from James Fox's book about a real-life murder that scandalized a British colony in Kenya during World War II. In 1990 Grant appeared with Liam Neeson and Joanne Whalley-Kilmer in David Lelan's *Crossing the Line*, a drama based on William McIlvanney's novel *The Big Man* (the title under which it was rereleased, in 1991).

In the meantime Grant was also finding steady work in television, both British and American. In 1985 he appeared as Peter Baines in the syndicated made-for-TV movie *Jenny's War* and played Apsley Cherry Garrard in the *Masterpiece Theatre* miniseries *The Last Place on Earth*. The following year he acted in two series, *The Demon Lover* and *Ladies in Charge*. In the 1987 PBS presentation *Lord Elgin and Some Stones of No Value*, he portrayed William Hamilton. The miniseries *'Til We Meet Again*, broadcast in 1989, featured Grant as Bruno de Lancel. In the same year he completed two more television movies: *The Lady and the Highwayman*, based on a Barbara Cartland romance novel, in which he played the male title character, Lord Lucius Vyne, and *Champagne Charlie*, in which he portrayed Charles Heidseick. Recalling the latter movie in his interview with Lucy Kaylin, he said, "Apart from my enormous fee, the whole thing was so abominable that it didn't matter that I played the entire role rolling drunk because they had champagne on the set all the time." He portrayed a gay man in *Our Sons* (1991), costarring Julie Andrews and Ann-Margret, and he was most recently seen on television in a production of the Jacobean tragedy *The Changeling* (1994). Grant also appeared in *The Detective, Handel, Dangerous Love, Honour, Profit and Pleasure*, and in episodes of *Shades of Darkness*.

In stage director James Lapine's sumptuous cinematic debut, *Impromptu* (1991), Grant portrayed the Polish composer and pianist Frederic Chopin, the object of the strong affections of the novelist George Sand (Judy Davis), whose controversial adoption of a masculine pseudonym, attire, and manners provided a stark contrast to Chopin's consumptive vulnerability and sensitivity. Sand, Chopin, the poet Alfred de Musset (Mandy Patinkin), the composer Franz Liszt (Julian Sands), Liszt's mistress Marie d'Agoult (Bernadette Peters), and the artist Eugène Delacroix (Ralph Brown) are guests at the country home of the ditzy Duchess d'Antan (Emma Thompson), who has invited the artists for a fortnight of entertainment. It is there that Sand first encounters Chopin, in whose music she hears a confluence of spiritual and artistic truth that captures her heart. Setting out to win his love, she ultimately seduces him despite several inauspicious early attempts. Most critics found the movie to be an amusing, intellectual romp. Kathleen Carroll of the New York *Daily News* (April 12,

1991) wrote, "Hugh Grant has a shy demeanor that makes him convincing as the priggish Pole," but Janet Maslin of the *New York Times* (April 12, 1991) suggested that Grant's robustness lent little credence to Chopin's frailty, and another critic found him to have been "at his most foppish."

Grant himself was not keen on playing such a humorless character and tried to make the crew laugh during rehearsals. "That's my way, my center," he explained to John Petrakis. "The comic element. It has to be there. I'm not really interested in dour, gloomy stuff." Although he succeeded in that endeavor on the set of *Impromptu*, the director was less amused, so Grant bowed to his wishes for the filming. In his next picture, Roman Polanski's *Bitter Moon* (adapted from a novel by Pascal Bruckner in 1992 but not released until 1994), Grant was left to decide for himself whether his part was meant to be funny. A tale of sexual obsession aboard a cruise ship, *Bitter Moon* revolves around an uptight Englishman named Nigel (Grant) and his sexually repressed wife, Fiona (Kristin Scott Thomas), who are seduced by the sadomasochistic games of a self-destructive couple (Peter Coyote and Emmanuelle Seigner). "I was sure there was comedy in my part," Grant told Stephen Farber, "in the English reaction to what is going on. What I never really felt I could discuss with Polanski was whether he was serious about the relationship between [Coyote and Seigner]. You hardly go up to your director, particularly Roman Polanski, and say, 'Are you joking?' Just in case the answer is no." Reviewers seemed to be unsure about the movie's intentions. Some rejected it as failed pornography or criticized its tone for veering incoherently between comedy and dark eroticism, while others felt it was hilarious. "It seems clear," Jami Bernard wrote in the New York *Daily News* (March 18, 1994), "that Polanski has cloaked true emotional torment in the bitterest of humor so that the audience can swallow it—but just barely."

After a small role as the journalist Cardinal, Lord Carrington's nephew, in the Merchant-Ivory film *The Remains of the Day* (1993), featuring Anthony Hopkins and Emma Thompson in a story of love foregone in pre-World War II England, Grant honed his "repressed Englishman" persona in two films released in 1994: *Sirens*, directed and written by his Australian friend John Duigan, and Mike Newell's sleeper hit *Four Weddings and a Funeral*. In *Sirens*, which is also set in the 1930s, only this time in Australia, Grant's Anglican vicar, Anthony Campion, tries to persuade a libertine artist, Norman Lindsay (Sam Neill), to abandon the erotic content of such paintings as his *Crucified Venus*. The minister and his innocent wife (Tara Fitzgerald) are ultimately drawn into the artist's circle of unconventional friends and habitually nude models. "*Sirens* I very much like," Grant told John Petrakis. "I'm very proud of it. I'm proud of the part," he said, because it was his idea to give the minister a humorous side. "I suddenly thought, 'Well, if he's the kind of minister that I used to know in my youth, who thinks he's very groovy, very avant-garde, and quite hip, then there was a lot of fun to be had with it.' And that's the way I played it." Critics were once again divided on the merits of the film, some dismissing it as trite and hypocritical and others deeming it a highly enjoyable sex comedy. In his review for the *Chicago Tribune* (March 11, 1994), Michael Wilmington singled out "Grant's Anthony, who considers himself immune to erotic danger," as "the film's great character. His is a comic performance so consummate and clever that he easily turns what could have been labored ribaldry into wry delight."

In the inveterate bachelor Charles in Mike Newell's *Four Weddings and a Funeral*, written by Richard Curtis, Grant found a character whose personality closely resembled his own, according to many friends and acquaintances. Attending the weddings of his friends, Charles remains cynical and unmoved, feeling only squeamishness in the presence of a number of heartbroken ex-girlfriends, until he encounters Carrie (Andie MacDowell), an irrepressible American who seduces him. "I do share some of [Charles's] fear of commitment, but he really isn't me," Grant told Stephen Farber. "I'm not nearly as nice or as diffident. I can be quite hard and nasty. So I do think some acting was required." When *Four Weddings* opened at the Sundance Film Festival in January 1994, according to Andrew Sarris, writing in the *New York Observer* (March 14, 1994), it "was immediately discounted by the snowswept cineastes in attendance for its anachronistic lack of violence, madness, malignancy, incest, kinky sex, and all-around grunginess. Instead, all it could offer was charm, grace, wit, humor, and the most delicate feelings—qualities singularly lacking in mainstream Hollywood entertainments."

Perhaps because of its uniqueness among American offerings, *Four Weddings* became a tremendous success with moviegoers and critics alike, and it was nominated for an Academy Award for best picture. Along with the writer and director, Grant, who won a Golden Globe Award for best actor for his performance, was credited by most critics with saving the film from the sentimentality and sappiness that mar many of the genre's other examples. Reviewing the movie for *Variety* (January 24–30, 1994), Todd McCarthy declared that the actor "emerges as a first-class romantic *farceur* who, in his ability to absorb innumerable comic arrows with grace, recalls [Cary Grant]. [Hugh] Grant's got just the combination of good looks, rueful self-disparagement, quickness, and bespectacled nerdiness to carry off refined, sophisticated screen comedy."

Riding into 1995 on the crest of his seemingly overnight success with *Four Weddings*, Grant was lionized by the American press, which discovered that he had a huge, overwhelmingly female, following. In short order he made another film for Mike Newell, *An Awfully Big Adventure*, which was released in late July 1995; teamed up with his *Sirens* costar Tara Fitzgerald in Christopher Monger's *The Englishman Who Went Up a Hill but*

Came Down a Mountain; turned in a cameo performance as a seventeenth-century portrait painter in Michael Hoffman's *Restoration*, starring Robert Downey Jr. and Meg Ryan; and wrapped up production of his first American big-budget movie, Chris Columbus's *Nine Months*, in Hollywood. Then suddenly the future of his skyrocketing career appeared to be in jeopardy when, on June 27, 1995, he was arrested for engaging in what police called a "lewd act" with Estelle Marie Thompson, a prostitute known to clients as Divine Brown, whom he had picked up on Sunset Boulevard. Sentenced to a two-year term of unsupervised probation, Grant was fined $1,180. (Brown, meanwhile, was paid $150,000 for her version of events by the British tabloid *News of the World*.) He immediately issued a statement of apology, saying, "Last night I did something completely insane. I have hurt people I love and embarrassed people I work with. For both things I am more sorry than I can ever possibly say."

Feeling he "owed" it to the producers of *Nine Months* to promote the film according to a prearranged schedule, Grant embarked on a round of talk-show appearances, earning high Nielsen ratings everywhere he went. Newspaper columnists and even op-ed writers weighed in on the topic, evidently finding it hard to resist speculating about the actor's motives. When asked publicly about the incident, Grant replied, "I did a bad thing," winning points with commentators for facing the situation bravely and "staying in character." His American fans, at least, seemed charmed by his polite contrition.

The incident generated considerable publicity for *Nine Months*, which was well attended despite mixed reviews. Released in early July, the movie showcased yet another of Grant's befuddled, determinedly misogamic Englishmen—in this instance Samuel, a child psychiatrist with no great love for children, who is forced to face up to his responsibilities when his girlfriend, Rebecca (Julianne Moore), becomes pregnant. Costarring Joan Cusack and Tom Arnold as another set of parents, Jeff Goldblum as a fast-lane friend, and Robin Williams as a Russian obstetrician, the film provided irresistible parallels to Grant's real-life travails, but most reviewers were pleased with the movie's broad, if predictable, comedy. Although some critics had wearied of Grant's stammering and blinking mannerisms, many gave him credit for more than holding his own with Arnold and the manically spontaneous Williams. Todd McCarthy of *Variety* (July 10, 1995) seemed to sum up the critical consensus: "Grant does lay on the mugging and facial contortions a bit thick at times, but his debonair manner and appealing personality do a lot to put the film over."

By some accounts Grant was more impressive as a cartographer in the awkwardly titled *The Englishman Who Went Up a Hill*, the story of the inhabitants of a Welsh town thrown into turmoil in 1917 by the threatened reclassification of their prized mountain as a hill. Perhaps too quirky to remain long in the theatres, the film—and Grant's performance—nonetheless garnered superlative-laden notices. Typical was Michael Wilmington's review for the *Chicago Tribune* (May 12, 1995), in which he praised Grant's "diffidence, wit, and razor-sharp timing" as well as his restraint. "By not trying to unbalance the picture," Wilmington wrote, "Grant takes effective control of it, ensuring its success." Grant's most recent project is a role in Ang Lee's *Sense and Sensibility* (1995), adapted from Jane Austen's novel by the actress Emma Thompson, who also stars in the film.

According to Candace Bushnell, "Grant is at once charming, deliciously nasty, silly, insecure, arrogant, and hysterically funny—in short, the best company you could hope for." He seems ambivalent about his new-found fame, reveling in its attendant first-class luxuries yet decrying the loss of privacy and leisure time. "There are some days," he admitted to Bushnell, "when I feel quite aggressive and driven, and other days I think, 'Why, it couldn't matter less. Bring me another chocolate-covered biscuit.'" He conceded in his interview with *Cosmopolitan*'s David Gritten, "My vanity is atrocious—I can hardly pass a shop window without stopping to check my reflection. I can never be recognized too often. I adore the attention." On the other hand, he told Bushnell that his social life has suffered because of his recent success. "Interestingly, people who were my friends are genuinely embarrassed," he said. "It's rather like walking into a room and everyone knowing you have cancer. It's acutely awkward. Your fame sits beside you like an incubus, and people are embarrassed and want to leave the room. It's very unhappy-making. And you've got to endlessly run yourself down, and even that becomes a boring joke." More than one interviewer has tried to probe behind his shield of ironic witticisms, and Bushnell seems to have found at least one plausible explanation for his reluctance to give a straight answer to even the most innocuous questions. "I don't believe in truth," he said. "I believe in *style*. I think the truth is a tremendous chimera. Or maybe I don't understand it. There's a kind of authenticity in good style which is far more interesting than something which is a scientific analysis. I quite like people to be charming, to be stylish. I don't really care if it *means* anything. It's enough in itself."

In 1994 Grant signed a two-year agreement with Castle Rock Entertainment, which is run by the actor/director Rob Reiner and four partners, to develop material in which he will star and/or produce. He manages Simian Films, in South Kensington, London, with his longtime girlfriend, the actress and Estee Lauder model Elizabeth Hurley, who is also Simian's development executive. The couple divide their time between a farmhouse in West Littleton and a two-bedroom apartment in the Earl's Court section of London. Named one of *People* magazine's best-dressed people in 1994 and one of that magazine's fifty most beautiful people in the world in the same year, Grant enjoys watching cricket on television, playing tennis, and swimming, but he stops short of working out in a gym. After telling Rita Kempley about the time his offer to do a nude scene for *Sirens* was refused once he had begun disrobing, he said, "I suppose I could go to a gym, but you have to make all those hideous faces and grunt like an ape. I really couldn't bear it."

Selected Biographical References: Chicago Tribune XIII p10+ Mr 20 '94 pors; Cosmopolitan 218:118+ Ja '95 pors; GQ 64:196+ D '94 pors; N Y Times II p 17 F 25 '94 pors; Premiere 7:78+ My '94 pors; Time 143:87 Ap 25 '94 pors; Vogue 185:142+ Jl '95 pors; Washington Post G p3 Mr 20 '94 pors; Contemporary Theatre, Film, and Television vol 8 (1990); Who's Who in America, 1995

Chicago Tribune

Greene, Bob

Mar. 10, 1947- Journalist; writer. Address: c/o Chicago Tribune, P.O. Box 25340, 435 N. Michigan Avenue, Chicago, IL 60625-0340

"Water covers two-thirds of the earth," a writer for *Playboy* once observed, "and Bob Greene covers the rest." Through his column in the *Chicago Tribune*, which is syndicated to more than two hundred newspapers nationwide, Greene has earned a reputation for exploring the human side of a dizzying array of subjects, from presidential politics to homelessness to the indecipherable and often-debated lyrics of the rock-'n'-roll classic "Louie Louie." His fourteen books include several collections of his columns as well as full-length works, such as *Good Morning, Merry Sunshine* (1984), a best-selling account of the first year in the life of his daughter; *Hang Time: Days and Dreams with Michael Jordan* (1992), a chronicle of two years spent off-court with the legendary athlete; and *Rebound: The Odyssey of Michael Jordan* (1995). "One thing that sets Greene apart from other well-known syndicated columnists," Daniel B. Wood wrote in the *Christian Science Monitor* (December 17, 1985), "is that his topics cut a swath across politics, sports, family life, education, and pop culture. In doing so they explore that gap behind the headlines and in front of the statistics and demographic shifts where the true humaneness, irony, and humor of America reside."

Robert Bernard Greene Jr. was born on March 10, 1947 in Columbus, Ohio, the son of Robert Bernard Greene, a business executive, and Phyllis Ann (Harmon) Greene. He has recalled having a happy childhood in which, early on, he demonstrated an interest in newspapers and other news media. One of his most treasured memories, he has written, is of working as a "staff boy" on local radio broadcasts of basketball games at the age of twelve. Beginning in the seventh grade, Greene wrote for the Bexley Junior High School *Beacon*. As he recounted in 1988 in an interview with Jean W. Ross for *Contemporary Authors*, he and a friend managed to get an interview with a star basketball player for Ohio State University whom professional journalists had been unable to reach. "Here two twelve-year-old kids had a national exclusive," Greene told Ross. When he was sixteen, he landed a job as a copyboy at a daily paper in Columbus. He received local attention during his senior year of high school when his essay on the first anniversary of the assassination of President John F. Kennedy appeared in a magazine for teenagers and then in the Columbus *Citizen-Journal*.

In 1965 Greene entered Northwestern University, in Evanston, Illinois, as a journalism major. During his college career he was an editor of the *Daily Northwestern*, the campus paper, and worked part-time as a stringer for the *Chicago Tribune*. That experience led to his being hired, immediately after he received his bachelor's degree, in 1969, by the *Sun-Times*, Chicago's morning tabloid. Assigned to the usual stories on a cub reporter's beat, Greene covered sports, city news, and politics. His editors soon noticed the distinctive style that he brought to even the most mundane news stories and also became aware of the attention that readers accorded Greene's byline. After two years, an unusually short apprenticeship by newspaper standards, the *Sun-Times* gave Greene his own column. "I didn't feel I was so young; it just seemed to me I was doing what I ought to be doing," Greene told Peter Benjaminson in a 1981 interview for *Contemporary Authors*. "I always wanted to be, and I basically consider myself to be, a storyteller. I always wanted to tell stories, whatever format they were in. So it was natural that when I was working for newspapers I should be writing a column." He also began contributing pieces to various magazines, including *Harper's* and *Rolling Stone*.

Greene's first book, *We Didn't Have None of Them Fat Funky Angels on the Wall of Heartbreak Hotel, and Other Reports from America* (1971), comprised fifteen of his daily columns as well as articles for the *Sun-Time*'s Sunday magazine, *Midwest*. The title piece was a sketch of the rock-'n'-roll legend Elvis Presley, in Las Vegas for his first personal appearance in thirteen years. The book also included accounts of the 1969 inauguration of President Richard Nixon, a revealing interview with the comedian Jack E. Leonard, and "I Don't Know How You'd Make a Horse Back Up," a deft portrait of the newscaster David Brinkley.

In 1972, acting on an idea that came to him while he was interviewing the rock star Rod Stewart, Greene signed on with the press corps covering that year's presidential campaign. "Stewart and I were talking about the world of a touring band," Greene has recalled. "I had always wanted to do a long, extended tour; not just five or six days, but a whole exhausting, killing thing to see what it does to a person, what it's like to live on a constant edge of fatigue for months on end while the country flashes past you, and you see more crowds, more adulation every day." Although he decided to trail politicians rather than musicians, Greene was less concerned with the candidates' political positions than with covering the campaign as "a massive unique road show."

Written in journal form, *Running: A Nixon-McGovern Campaign Journal* (1973) chronicled Greene's travels with the entourage of press and politicos that followed George McGovern as he made his doomed 1972 run for the presidency against the incumbent, Richard Nixon. Greene captured the disorder of McGovern's campaign, the posturing of Vice-President Spiro T. Agnew, and the atmosphere of the Nixon White House. *Running* won acclaim from such veteran journalists as Joe McGinnis, Pete Hamill, and David Broder and high marks from critics. "The detail is rich and the observations sharp, albeit without more than casual political insights," L. C. Lewin wrote in the *New York Times Book Review* (May 20, 1973). "As you follow even the most superficial moves of the players, you will not fail to get a solid sense, from their behavior and style in playing out the game, of their real political sensibilities and why they do what they do."

For his next book, *Billion Dollar Baby* (1975), Greene abandoned the stance of outside observer for that of participant when he took a leave of absence from the *Sun-Times* in 1973 to accompany the enormously popular and self-consciously outrageous Alice Cooper Band on the road. He told Peter Benjaminson, "It seemed to me that the American Dream for kids growing up in the 1940s and 1950s was to become a baseball star, to be Joe DiMaggio or Mickey Mantle. By the 1970s, the dream had turned into the rock'n'-roll dream, and the greatest fantasy a young male could have was to be a rock-'n'-roll star. . . . I'd been on rock tours before as a reporter, but I always thought it would be fascinating to step across the footlights and see what it would be like on the other side." He performed as a back-up singer on one of the group's albums and also appeared on stage, playing the part of Santa Claus and receiving a mock beating from the band at the end of each performance.

In *Billion Dollar Baby*, Greene not only recounted his experiences as a performer but showed the negative side of the "dream" as well—the boredom of the superstar's lifestyle, made evident as Alice Cooper (the stage name of Vincent Furnier) and company passed their days watching television in hotel rooms. "I've never seen so many desperately unhappy young millionaires," Greene said later. "The book was a story about the American Dream and what happens when you achieve it." *Billion Dollar Baby* received extensive praise in the press, with Maureen Orth in *Newsweek* (January 13, 1975) commending Greene for "stripping away the glamour surrounding the big-name rock band and exposing it for what it is—a carefully promoted . . . group of young millionaires of questionable talent whom he genuinely likes."

The title of the four-hundred-page collection of some of Greene's most memorable pieces, *Johnny Deadline, Reporter* (1976), came from the nickname given to him by his coworkers at the *Sun-Times*. In 1978 Greene left that newspaper, moving to the *Chicago Tribune*, which he felt had become one of the country's best dailies. At the *Tribune* he began his current practice of writing four weekday columns and dropped his Sunday piece, in the belief that his readers incorporated his column into their workaday routines. In addition, in 1980 Greene began writing a monthly feature, "American Beat," for *Esquire*, and he also broke into television when he became a correspondent for ABC's *Nightline* in 1981, covering as wide a variety of stories on the air as he did in print.

Another compilation of Greene's columns, *American Beat*, appeared in 1983. A particularly intriguing—and to some, disconcerting—piece in the collection was Greene's interview with the convicted mass murderer Richard Speck. Although Speck usually shunned the press, he agreed to meet with Greene, saying, "I read your column, man." "Reflections in a Wary Eye" was an account of Greene's interview with Richard Nixon after the latter had resigned the presidency. For the purpose of encouraging would-be authors, Greene also passed on the story of Chuck Ross, who had retyped Jerzy Kozinski's popular novel *Steps* and submitted the manuscript under his own name to some thirteen publishers and the same number of literary agents—all of whom rejected it as unpublishable or unworthy of representation.

For years, Greene's journalistic use of his own experiences was mainly restricted to brief asides in stories on other subjects. But after the birth of his daughter, Amanda, Greene started keeping a journal in which he chronicled in intimate detail the first year of her life and the effect of her presence on himself and his wife. The idea for the journal, which was excerpted in *Esquire* and *Redbook* and later published as *Good Morning, Merry Sunshine*, came to Greene when, as a father-to-be, he searched bookstores for literature that "could tell him what might lie ahead" but failed to find "anything that dealt on a human level with what happens when a man and a woman bring a new baby home—when a house that held two people suddenly holds three."

Good Morning, Merry Sunshine was generally well received, with Larry L. King saying in the *Chicago Tribune* (May 6, 1984) that Greene had written "an honest and valuable book, one dealing with new career conflicts, the changing relationships with Greene's own parents, the complex and painful evolutions between married lovers when a strong new force intervenes." Some reviewers were less enthusiastic, complaining that Greene had failed to examine his feelings about fatherhood in an engaging way. David Owen of the *New Republic* (October 1, 1984) called *Good Morning, Merry Sunshine* "a book about Susan Greene's second baby written by her first" and added, "The really annoying thing about the book is that both Greene and his publisher present it as a manifesto of sensitive fatherhood. . . . But Bob Greene's vision of manly child-rearing is quite reactionary. He ducks all the major chores and responsibilities in order to savor his daughter from afar." Nevertheless, with rave notices from the likes of the popular columnist Erma Bombeck and the talk-show host Phil Donahue, *Good Morning, Merry Sunshine* became Greene's most commercially successful book to date.

The high points of *Cheeseburgers: The Best of Bob Greene* (1985) include a humorous tour of the Playboy Mansion in Chicago, soon after it was permanently vacated by the publisher Hugh Hefner and donated to a local university, and a more in-depth account of Greene's meeting with Richard Nixon, during which the ex-president, "as the hours went by . . . loosened up . . . and began to talk freely, about his days in the White House, about his relations with the news media, about his views on television, about his new life in New York," among other topics. In the *Christian Science Monitor* (December 17, 1985), Daniel B. Wood complimented Greene's "uncanny way of writing about personal things—his mother, his diary, his father's baby-shoe-bronzing business—without exuding ego" and his ability to "touch the human element in a story without waxing sentimental . . . in ways that derive universal import from the particular incident."

By 1986 Bob Greene had written, by his own count, some three thousand columns, exclusive of magazine articles. The effect of such prolificacy on his personal world-view was substantial. "What has happened," as he put it in an article for *Esquire* (December, 1986), "is that I have become virtually incapable of experiencing things in life and then keeping them inside myself. My life runs in twenty-four-hour cycles: I go out and live the day, talking with people and noticing things, and then the next morning I am back in front of a word processor, turning those things into a column for public consumption. . . . I think I have lost the ability to live my life if it's not going to end up on paper." Greene had by that time reduced the number of his appearances on ABC's *Nightline* because "things were finally threatening to get out of hand." "I wasn't even able to sleep anymore," he has said.

It was perhaps in an effort to reclaim a time when he had put his thoughts on paper for purposes other than public consumption that Greene published *Be True to Your School: A Diary of 1964* (1987). That book was a partially rewritten version of the diary he kept during his junior and senior years of high school, when he was taught that the practice was a good one for an aspiring journalist. Writing about his everyday life, he had sketched a teenager's world that he felt was universal in many aspects since, as he has put it, "everyone falls in love and has his first beer and a best friend and cruises his town in a car and maybe gets into a fight." Greene took some flak for this effort at reconstituting the past, with the *Christian Science Monitor* (March 23, 1987) calling the book "slow and overlong" and "not quite journalistic Muzak, but close" and Joanne Kaufman, in the *New York Times Book Review* (June 7, 1987), finding Greene to be "not nearly as compelling here as he thinks he is." Still, the book found a wide readership, including a large number of teenagers, and it became a best-seller. Lou Orfanella, a teacher at Webutuck Junior/Senior High School in Amenia, New York, reviewed *Be True to Your School* for *English Journal* (November 1993) and revealed that he had assigned the book to his senior students to use as a model for their own journals.

The spiritual wounds left by the Vietnam War were the topic of Greene's next book, *Homecoming: When the Soldiers Returned from Vietnam* (1989). In his column Greene had requested veterans to write to him concerning the reception accorded them on their return from the Vietnam War. He received more than one thousand responses, mostly from men who had been literally spat upon by antiwar protestors or who had been "made to feel small and unwanted in so many other ways that it felt like being spat upon." Instead of interpreting the letters he received, Greene merely collected and edited the first-hand accounts. In the *New York Times Book Review* (January 22, 1989), Doug Anderson evaluated the book thusly: "Underneath the anger in *Homecoming* is a desire for what the veterans suffered to have meaning in the larger scheme of things. . . . If you have a taste for historical irony, you will like *Homecoming*."

He Was a Midwestern Boy on His Own (1991), Greene's fifth compilation of columns, took its title from a song by Bob Seger. The book featured an account of Greene's high-school class reunion; an interview with Sean Connery titled "So . . . We Meet At Last, Mr. Bond"; and the story of Elvis Presley's offer, made to President Nixon in 1970, to become a federal agent to help in the fight against, in Presley's words, "drug abuse and Communist brainwashing techniques." Regardless of its subject, each piece was undergirded by Greene's particular vision of the world. "I have gone out to see some things, but part of me is still on Main Street," he has explained. "It's as if the kid on Main Street is always waiting for me to come back and tell him what I have found."

Greene's book *Hang Time: Days and Dreams with Michael Jordan* came about as an indirect result of what he has described as a midlife crisis. The experience was made worse for Greene by his having recently covered a story of shocking child abuse that left him in despair over the prevalence of such inhumanity. It was during this period, in 1990, that Greene befriended the Chicago Bulls basketball superstar Michael Jordan. *Hang Time* is at once a portrait of the athlete, a recounting of two of the basketball seasons in which Jordan led the Bulls to the NBA championship, and a reflection on the solace that Greene drew from his friendship with Jordan.

"What makes *Hang Time* absorbing is not so much Jordan as Greene," Armen Keteyian declared in the *Chicago Tribune* (November 8, 1992). "When he is clear-eyed and committed, he remains one of the most penetrating and evocative voices in print. And here he is very good, offering a vivid, enlightening portrait of the world's ultimate sports star. . . . The book does have drawbacks. One is Greene's tendency to gloss over or quickly dismiss the self-absorbed side of Jordan. . . . Then, at times, there is the syrupy tenor of the storytelling. . . . Green also has a tendency to stretch his journalistic eye a bit far, trying to find deep meaning in the bounce of a basketball. . . . But it is Greene's ability to stretch and see beyond basketball that has allowed him and Jordan to connect. And because he does, we do too." Greene's second book about the basketball hero, *Rebound: The Odyssey of Michael Jordan*, was published in the fall of 1995.

In the meantime, in 1993 Bob Greene had published his first novel, the semiautobiographical *All Summer Long*, which tells the story of three middle-aged friends who briefly leave their families and careers behind and set out on a trip across the United States in an attempt to recover some of the glory of their youth. The novel impressed a writer for *People* (June 14, 1993), who described it as "a testament to the homespun values of family and friendship that endure no matter how far you roam from Small Town, U.S.A." The reviewer judged *All Summer Long*, "despite [its] tendency to be a bit too sweet," to be "as refreshing as a tall glass of iced tea on a July afternoon."

On February 13, 1971 Bob Greene married Susan Bonnet Koebel, a paralegal. Their daughter, Amanda, was born on June 11, 1983. Greene has won a number of awards and honors, including the National Headliner's Award for the best American newspaper column in 1977, and the Peter Lisagor Award in 1981. He has received numerous other honors as well, and he explained in an article for *Esquire* (December 1986) what he does with the "plaques, trophies, warm letters and reviews, photographs of himself with celebrities," and other "artifacts that come in on a fairly regular basis": He keeps them for a while, during which he treasures them, and then, lest they make him feel self-satisfied and lessen his desire to keep working, he throws them away.

Selected Biographical References: Esquire 106:54+ D '86 por; Pub W 225:60+ My 4 '84 por; Contemporary Authors vol 107 (1983); Contemporary Authors new rev ser vol 27 (1989); Who's Who in America, 1995

AP/Wide World Photos

Grodin, Charles

Apr. 21, 1935- Actor; director; producer; writer; television talk-show host. Address: CNBC, 2200 Fletcher Ave., Fort Lee, NJ 07024

The multitalented Charles Grodin, who has described himself as "low-key but . . . high strung," has been a droll and quirky presence in American theatre, television, and film for almost four decades. Grodin began his theatrical career in the late 1950s, made his Broadway debut in *Tchin Tchin* in 1962, and later starred on Broadway in *Same Time Next Year*. Among his scores of other theatrical credits are those as the author of *One of the All-Time Greats*, as the author and star of *The Price of Fame*, and as the producer and director of *Thieves*. He made his breakthrough to movie stardom as the caddish title character in *The Heartbreak Kid* (1972), one of the many roles in which he demonstrated his ability to lend charm and vulnerability to egocentric knaves and bumbling jerks. After surviving a series of setbacks, he reached the height of his career as a film actor with the improvisational chemistry that he, with Robert De Niro, brought to the action comedy *Midnight Run* (1988), his twenty-first motion picture.

On television, where most of his early credits were as an actor and director, Grodin became better known in recent years for the comic tension he created with his mock hurt feelings and hostility and tongue-in-cheek peevishness as a guest on the *Tonight Show* and other television talk formats. In January 1995 he became host of his own talk program, *Charles Grodin*, on the cable television network CNBC. In each presentation of the nightly show, he delivers a laid-back, apparently extemporaneous monologue and interviews celebrity guests from show business and other fields—ideal chores for an irrepressible raconteur who obviously delights in exercising his oblique and deadpan sense of humor. Despite his success on camera, Grodin is said to regard himself first and foremost as a writer. In addition to plays and screenplays, he has published several books, including an autobiography and two volumes of personal reflections on show business and life in general.

Charles Grodin, who is of Russian Orthodox Jewish heritage, was born to Theodore and Lena Grodin in Pittsburgh on April 21, 1935. His father, the proprietor of a wholesale store supplying dry goods to tailors, dressmakers, and cleaners, died when Charles was a teenager. Grodin has an older brother, Jack, a certified public accountant and lawyer. In talking about his ambivalence regarding his chosen profession, Grodin has often said that he sometimes wishes that he had followed in his brother's footsteps. "I'm serious," he insisted in an interview with Robert Wahls for the New York *Sunday News* (April 27, 1975). "I think the basis for acting is deeply neurotic, something to do with not getting recognition when I needed it. Now, when I'm getting the attention I once needed, I just don't need it that much anymore."

By his own account, Grodin was "a rough kid, always getting kicked out of class." Other sources suggest that he was not so much rough as compulsively argumentative and basically shy. His only strong extracurricular interest was in sports, especially basketball, and at age thirteen he made second string on the basketball team at the local Y. He was elected president of his class in each of his four years at Peabody High School in Pittsburgh, and he was valedictorian at his graduation in February 1953. At the time he had no firm career plans. That changed when he saw the film *A Place in the Sun* and was inspired by Montgomery Clift's performance in that movie to become an actor. (His other formative models in acting included Paul Muni and Sir Ralph Richardson.) "It was a very disturbed choice . . . ," he told Ellen Cohn in an interview for the New York *Sunday News* (June 3, 1973). "At that age you can't possibly be thinking of illuminating elements of life for people—which is a good reason to be an actor—or hoping to be an artist. You don't know what an artist is, if you ever know. I just wanted to be on stage and hear the laughter and applause."

Grodin studied acting at the University of Miami for six months and, on a scholarship, at the Pittsburgh Playhouse School of the Theater for a year and a half. In retrospect, he views his experience at the school as less than satisfactory. "They ridiculed the Method at the Playhouse," he wrote in his autobiography, *It Would Be So Nice If You Weren't Here: My Journey Through Show Business* (1989), "because they could neither do it nor understand it." Meanwhile, he appeared in summer stock at the Little Lake Theater in Washington, Pennsylvania in 1954 and 1955. At the end of the 1955 season, armed with two letters of recommendation addressed to film studio talent departments, he traveled to Hollywood. Summarily rejected there, he turned around and headed for New York City with the intention of studying at the renowned Actors Studio under Lee Strasberg, a leading interpreter of the so-called Method acting technique developed by Konstantin Stanislavsky.

In Manhattan, Grodin learned that the Actors Studio auditioned more than a thousand hopefuls a year. After failing his initial audition (without meeting Strasberg), he studied acting under Uta Hagen for three years. During that time, and for several years thereafter, he supported himself by working nights at such jobs as cab driver, postal clerk, and Pinkerton watchman. Through the actress Eleni Liamos, he eventually met Lee Strasberg, who accepted him as a student in 1959, and the director Joan Horvath, who cast him, without pay, in *Don't Destroy Me*, a play she was directing on a shoestring in the lower depths of Off Off Broadway. A one-line favorable notice in a trade paper about that performance led to Grodin's acquisition of an agent, who got him an audition for an *Armstrong Circle Theatre* network television production, a drama about the *Nautilus*, the first nuclear submarine to go under the North Pole. Precisely because he unintentionally came across as physically clumsy in that audition, he was chosen for the role of a young naval officer named Phelps, a total klutz.

Soon after appearing on *Armstrong Circle Theatre*, Grodin was cast in the leading role in the weekly *My True Story* television series, a villainous part in the teleplay *Black Monday* on public television, and small parts in various other dramatic programs, and he had regular work in such Sunday morning television shows as *Camera Three* and *Lamp unto My Feet*. In the following years his television credits included stints on the soap operas *Love of Life* and *The Young Marrieds*, regular appearances as the vicious hired gunslinger Bells Pickering in the television western series *The Guns of Will Sonnett*, performances as a heavy in other westerns, and some work, including directing, on *Candid Camera*.

Meanwhile, during the 1960 summer season at the Woodstock Theater in Woodstock, New York, Grodin had played roles, usually leads, in eight plays in eight weeks. He made his Broadway debut in 1962, drawing good notices for his support of Anthony Quinn and Margaret Leighton in *Tchin Tchin*. The three-character play ran for more than a year. In 1964 he was cast as a young business school graduate in the Broadway comedy *Absence of a Cello*. He cowrote and directed the 1966 Off-Broadway show *Hooray! It's a Glorious Day . . . and All That*, a send-up of big Broadway musicals. During the following two years, he helped Renee Taylor and her husband, Joe Bologna, hone twelve short pieces they had written about love and marriage into the play *Lovers and Other Strangers* and directed them in that production from highly successful tryouts in Detroit to Broadway. His next theatrical credit was as one of the succession of actors fired from the leading male role in the not-very-successful Off-Broadway production of Bruce Jay Friedman's play *Steambath*. That experience both gave him, as he recounted in his autobiography, "nightmares about not being wanted every night for weeks" and inspired him to write *One of the All-Time Greats*, a play about a stage director's "fear of being replaced." With Alan Arkin in the male lead, that play was given its premiere production in summer stock in 1972.

Grodin made his movie debut in the shelved, low-budget film *Sex and the College Girl* (1964). After passing up the chance to star in another low-budget film—the 1960s classic *The Graduate*—reportedly because the pay was too low, he appeared as the more sympathetic of the two gynecologists in the chiller *Rosemary's Baby* (1968). For the popular musical duo Simon and Garfunkel, in 1969 Grodin produced, cowrote, and directed a politically charged, highly controversial network television special that, in Grodin's words, "essentially said: 'Let's get out of Vietnam, let's stop persecuting blacks, let's show what's wrong with America and raise a banner for the more tolerant, compassionate side of the American character."

After making a total retreat into writing and directing, Grodin was persuaded by the director Mike Nichols to appear in the minor role of the United States Army Air Force navigator Aardvark in Nichols's intensely dark comic film *Catch-22* (1970), based on Joseph Heller's surreal and sarcastic World War II novel. During the filming of *Catch-22*, Grodin wrote a screenplay adapted from Jordan Crittenden's novel *Balloons Are Available*, but he was unable to find a producer for that property. He also wrote the original screen adaptation of Woody Allen's stage comedy *Play It Again, Sam*. (Ultimately, Allen wrote his own adaptation, after deciding that he himself would star in the movie.)

Grodin's breakthrough screen role was the title character in the tartly comic 1972 hit film *The Heartbreak Kid*, by the comedienne-turned-director Elaine May, who, along with Mike Nichols, was then promoting Grodin to anyone who would listen as "the best young actor in America." He played Leonard Alan Cantrow, a brash and selfish young Jewish sporting goods salesman from New York who ditches his Jewish bride of five days in the midst of their honeymoon in Miami Beach to pursue a man-teasing WASP (Cybill Shepherd) to her native Minnesota and to his ultimate rue. Grodin was aware of the danger of his being identified with the cad on the screen, and indeed, he reported that "after seeing the movie, a lot of people would approach me with the idea of punching me in the mouth." But, as Bob Salmaggi of the New York *Daily News* observed, he played Lenny "so artlessly and beguilingly that you may have actually liked the character a little while writing him off as [no good]." Others described the character portrayed by Grodin as "one of the suavest losers the twentieth century has yet produced," ranking "among the screen's greatest jerks—in a funny, infuriating, and thoroughly original way." The picture made numerous "Ten Best" lists, and Grodin was nominated for a Golden Globe award for best actor.

Much of the boost given Grodin's career by *The Heartbreak Kid* was negated by *11 Harrowhouse* (1974), a spoof of caper films in which Grodin was cast in the leading role of a diamond salesman who is drawn into a massive heist. That movie was panned by a number of influential critics and failed at the box office. On television, Grodin directed two specials written by Renee Taylor and Joseph Bologna. One was the Emmy Award-winning *Acts of Love and Other Comedies* (1973), starring Marlo Thomas as a character who comments on dating, romance, marriage, infidelity, and life in general as she progresses from adolescence to motherhood.

In 1974 Grodin directed Marlo Thomas in Herb Gardner's stage comedy *Thieves*, about a group of neurotic New Yorkers trying to recover their sanity and innocence in the midst of corrupting circumstances. With financing provided by Frank Yablans, the president of Paramount Pictures, Grodin became producer as well as director. The play, which had a moderately successful run in Boston, eventually came to Broadway, where it folded after receiving mixed reviews. Grodin was cast with Thomas in the film version of *Thieves* (1977), directed by John Berry.

Grodin starred opposite Ellen Burstyn in the hit Broadway comedy *Same Time Next Year*, about an adulterous tryst at a motel that is reenacted annually. The play opened in March 1975 and ran for 1,453 performances. Burstyn won the Tony Award for best actress of the year, and she and Grodin won the Outer Circle Critics awards for best actress and actor. Grodin's next stint on Broadway was in 1977, as the producer and director of Jordan Crittendon's comedy *Unexpected Guests*. Back on the screen, in Dino De Laurentiis's remake of *King Kong* (1976), Grodin brought some motivational credibility to the role of Fred Wilson, the greedy business executive who goes to Skull Island looking for oil deposits and instead brings back a show-business property in the form of an enormous ape that ultimately squashes him to death. In the film *Heaven Can Wait* (1978), director and actor Warren Beatty's imaginative remake of the 1941 tragicomic fantasy *Here Comes Mr. Jordan*, he was cast as the Beatty character's unscrupulous lawyer. For his contribution to *The Paul Simon Special*, televised on NBC on December 7, 1977, he shared an Emmy Award for writing with Lorne Michaels and others. In a production of *Charley's Aunt* for cable television, he played the leading role, a male college student who dresses up to impersonate the aunt.

On the screen, Grodin starred in *Sunburn* (1979) as an insurance investigator pretending to be a tourist while trailing a suspected murderer to Acapulco. He was truly in his element in Albert Brooks's *Real Life* (1979), a mock documentary in which Brooks, playing himself, heads a behavioral experiment dedicated to filming every detail of the day-to-day life of a "typical American family," the fictional Yeagers of Phoenix. As Warren Yeager, husband, father, and veterinarian, Grodin is, as reviewers of the movie noted, "wonderfully funny" as he "tries to feign nonchalance" while self-consciously playing to the camera. As the most platonic of the three leading characters in the triangular romantic comedy *It's My Turn* (1980), Grodin demonstrated, as one reviewer put it, "his verbal virtuosity—his gift for sparring with words." In the zany farce *Seems Like Old Times* (1980), he was cast as Ira, a district attorney with political ambitions whose career is jeopardized when the disreputable first husband (Chevy Chase) of his wife (Goldie Hawn) barges into their lives. In the ecology-minded cautionary comedy *The Incredible Shrinking Woman* (1981), he played an advertising man who promotes the very chemical-laden household products that have combined to cause the physical plight of his wife, the title character (Lily Tomlin). He was Steve Martin's partner in miserable bachelorhood in the comedy *The Lonely Guy* (1984), he had a minor role in *All of Me* (1984), also starring Martin, and he was one of the cronies of the Gene Wilder character in the broad farce *The Woman in Red* (1984).

In 1976 Grodin had begun writing a satiric scenario about a Hollywood studio that buys the famous title of a best-selling sex manual (*The Joy of Sex*, later changed to *Love in Sex*) and doesn't know what to do with it. After being rejected numerous times, the screenplay, with the title *Movers and Shakers*, was finally filmed with a star-studded cast that included Walter Matthau as the studio head and Grodin as the writer who is assigned the difficult project. It was released to poor reviews in 1985. Grodin's screen credits for the late 1980s also include a father not quite ready for the uninhibited hijinks he and his vacationing family encounter at a Club Med–type resort in *The Last Resort* (1986); a cynical CIA operative in *Ishtar* (1987); and a neurotic radio psychiatrist replaced by an imposter (Dan Ackroyd) in *The Couch Trip* (1988).

In *Midnight Run* (1988), Grodin was cast in the role of Jonathan Mardukas, a bail-jumping accountant who is being escorted from New York back to Los Angeles by the bounty hunter Jack Walsh (Robert De Niro), with the Mafia, from whom Mardukas embezzled fifteen million dollars, and the FBI in hot pursuit. As reviewers observed in glowing notices, the easy, humorous rapport between Grodin and De Niro raised the movie above formula. "De Niro is often said to be the best actor of his generation . . . ," Roger Ebert wrote. "In *Midnight Run* [Grodin] is every bit the master's equal, and in the crucial final scene, it is Grodin who finds the emotional truth that defines their relationship."

Grodin made his first New York stage appearance in fifteen years when his comedy *The Price of Fame* opened at the Roundabout Theatre (to mostly unenthusiastic reviews) in June 1990. He played the protagonist, Roger Carstairs, a movie star whose personal life suffers while he concentrates obsessively on the minutiae of his career. "In this play," Grodin explained to a reporter, "I was interested in presenting a man who's accused of being egocentric and self-involved and then having the audience walk out asking, 'Am I any better than that?'" Grodin's *One of the All-Time Greats*, which was originally a one-act play, was given its New York City debut in an expanded, two-act form under Tony Roberts's direction Off Broadway in 1992.

Grodin was among those who lent outstanding support to Kevin Klein in the Capra-like White House comic fantasy *Dave* (1993). His other screen credits during the early 1990s include a businessman whose lost Filofax enables a petty criminal (James Belushi) to assume his identity in *Taking Care of Business* (1990) and the migrating soul of a passenger killed in a bus crash in the lightweight comic fantasy *Heart and Souls* (1993). In the meantime, he concurrently was gaining wide public attention in movie roles in the "family entertainment" vein: a human rival to Kermit the Frog for the affections of the glamorous Muppet Miss Piggy in *The Great Muppet Caper* (1981); an uptight, harried father of four who becomes the reluctant owner of a huge Saint Bernard in *Beethoven* (1992) and *Beethoven's 2nd* (1993); and the adoptive father of the title character, a ten-year-old brat played by the adult comedian Martin Short, in *Clifford* (1994).

In his book *How to Get Through Life* (1992), Grodin offered entertaining commentary on eighty aspects of contemporary life, from family, social relationships, and sexual mores to restaurants and travel. With wisdom, insight, and his usual sense of humor, along with a rare hint of rancor, in *We're Ready for You, Mr. Grodin* (1994) he shared his behind-the-scenes experiences in show business. The title of that book is a reference to the combination of appreciation and nervousness with which he was greeted by Johnny Carson, David Letterman, and other television show hosts as they anticipated the tension he was likely to cause as a guest through feigned animosity and hurt feelings and verbal dueling. In addition to discussing the television programs on which he has appeared, including *Good Morning, America* and *Saturday Night*

Live, he provided glimpses of the myriad personalities with whom he has worked, including such kindred spirits as Albert Brooks, Andy Kaufman, and Louise Lasser. Reviewing *We're Ready for You, Mr. Grodin*, Jon Anderson of the *Chicago Tribune* (October 31, 1994) wrote, "For an actor, Grodin is a goodish writer, accurately catching the rhythms of his routines in print. He comes across as an intelligent, likeable fellow, unsullied by . . . fame."

In 1994 the King World Syndicate was testing talk-show formats for him, but he was unhappy with the kind of physical humor that had become standard spicing on late-night talk shows. "Today everybody says, 'Interesting talk makes compelling television—but let's also have a dog catch a Frisbee . . . ,'" he was quoted as saying in *Variety* (November 21, 1994). "They literally had me interviewing the world's most intelligent pig." Finally, for what he described as "way less money," he accepted from CNBC a talk-show offer with no "stupid pet tricks" attached. "It's a smaller audience," he has explained, "but it's on during prime time, and the CNBC audience is people I want to reach." In November 1994 he signed a two-year contract calling for him to tape 176 hours a year, and *Charles Grodin* premiered on January 9, 1995.

The shows, some live and some taped, are broadcast on weekday nights from the CNBC studios in Fort Lee, New Jersey, and repeats are televised on weekends. Each show begins with a monologue in which Grodin, in his charismatic, subdued, and off-the-cuff manner, talks to the television audience like a sensitive and funny friend dominating the conversation in their living room with a stream of stories from his life experience, pet peeves, and comments on current issues. During the rest of the hour, Grodin talks with guests (usually two) and invites questions from the television audience. A large number of the guests are drawn from Grodin's wide circle of friends and acquaintances in show business, interspersed with well-known figures from other fields. The program includes, and usually ends with, a tasteful acoustic performance by one of Grodin's favorite singers or musicians, typified by the likes of Art Garfunkel, Vic Damone, and the Manhattan Transfer. Early in the show's run, Ken Tucker observed in *Entertainment Weekly* that Grodin had expanded "his self-parodying loutishness in making the move from talk-show guest to host" and that "the results are yielding terrific television." In the *New York Times* (March 12, 1995), James Gavin wrote, "The show . . . has a very different kind of feeling from other talk shows. It is less predictable, less promotional, maybe even more truthful."

Charles Grodin, who is six feet, one inch tall and looks much topnger than the sexagenarian that he is, is prepossessing in appearance and has what has been described as a "complicated" and "ingenuous" grin. "Charles Grodin [is] an absolute peach," Larry Hackett reported in the New York *Daily News* (April 12, 1992). "But then this thing begins to creep over his face, this awkward half-smile just this far from a grimace." Grodin has described himself as "sentimental" and "vulnerable," and his colleagues have testified that he is "a dream to work with" and "very gentle and careful" in giving helpful criticism. By his first marriage, which ended in divorce in 1967, Grodin has an adult daughter, Marion. In 1985 he married Elissa Durwood, with whom he has a son, Nicky. The juvenile protagonist in Grodin's children's book *Freddie the Fly* (1993) is also named Nicky. Grodin also narrated an animated version of the popular children's story "Rotten Island," which is included in the video *Shelley Duvall's Bedtime Stories* (1993).

Selected Biographical References: After Dark 7:40+ D '74 pors; Christian Sci Mon p14 Mr 17 '73; Interview 20:78 Je '90; N Y Daily News mag p22+ Je 3 '73 pors, Leisure p8 Ap 27 '75 por, Leisure p9 F 27 '77 por; N Y Newsday II p3+ Je 12 '90 por; N Y Times II p5+ F 20 '77 por, II p19 O 19 '80 por, II p7+ Je 10 '90, II p35 Mr 12 '95 por; New York 21:34+ Jl 18 '88 pors; People 10:39+ S 25 '78; Playboy 21:174 Mr '74 por; Grodin, Charles. It Would Be So Nice If You Weren't Here (1989), How to Get Through Life (1992), We're Ready for You, Mr. Grodin (1994); Motion Picture Almanac, 1995; Who's Who in America, 1995

Hartley, Hal

Nov. 3, 1959– Filmmaker. Address: c/o True Fiction Pictures, 12 W. 27th St., New York, NY 10001

The filmmaker Hal Hartley, who has produced four features, numerous shorts, and one television movie since 1990, is among the most idiosyncratic voices to come on the American independent cinema scene in recent years. His work often elicits comparisons to that of Jim Jarmusch and Steven Soderbergh, for his films, like theirs, concern disaffected young people who are aware of, but not quite able to overcome, the absurdity and banality of contemporary life. Another distinguishing feature of Hartley's films is their highly stylized form: his characters' speech is terse and repetitive, and their movements and gestures are tightly choreographed. In this respect his films are reminiscent of the work of Jean-Luc Godard, the groundbreaking New Wave director to whom Hartley himself has acknowledged he owes a great debt. Because of the quirky subject matter and formalized style, his work is an acquired taste, though one that is becoming more widely shared. "I know I have a limited audience," Hartley told Martin Kihn in an interview for *GQ* (October 1992). "But people I thought would never go see my films not only see them but become obsessed by them. When you're hooked, you're hooked."

Robin Holland

Hal Hartley

The third of four children of an ironworker and his wife, Hal Hartley was born November 3, 1959 in Lindenhurst, New York, into a Catholic, working-class family. A defining event of his early life was the death of his mother, when he was eleven or twelve. In the following years he lived intermittently with his aunt, uncle, and cousins next door. "I became very introverted, very quiet," he told Ellen Pall, who profiled him for the *New York Times* (October 11, 1992). "I spent a lot of time doing art. I wasn't misanthropic, I was just happy to be left on my own." Besides painting, the activity he enjoyed most, Hartley spent a lot of time working on carpentry projects and playing the guitar, causing his father and two older brothers to worry about his apparent aimlessness. "It was clear I had a creative bent," he joked to Judith Weinraub in an interview for the *Washington Post* (August 4, 1990). "But it wasn't clear whether it was for carpentry or for telling elaborate lies."

Hartley's artistic interests led him to enroll in the Massachusetts College of Art, in Boston, in the late 1970s. During his one year there, he took a film course and was enthralled by the power of moving images. The experience helped him realize, he has said, that his "vague dissatisfaction" with his paintings derived from the fact that "they didn't move." "I remember the first emotions I had when I saw the images I had filmed," Hartley told Pall, "and some of them were very mundane, like water glasses in the window with light coming through them. I was just crushed with sadness—a good sadness, totally life-affirming."

In 1978 or 1979 Hartley left art school, and he spent the following year working part-time in a department store. During his free time he made a series of short films in Super-8, and on the basis of these he was admitted to the film program at the State University of New York (SUNY) at Purchase, where he studied under the film director and editor Aram Avakian. During a 1992 interview with John Fried for *Cineaste*, Hartley expressed his gratitude for the quality of the education he received at the university: "What really distinguishes Purchase, and makes it one of the most important film schools in the country, is its position as a working-class film school. It is one of the only places where blue-collar, lower-middle-class kids can go to study film." For his senior thesis film, Hartley made *Kid*, about a young man whose efforts to get out of Lindenhurst are constantly thwarted.

Following his graduation, with honors, from SUNY-Purchase in 1984, Hartley worked briefly as an ironworker alongside his father and brother. He then began scrounging for jobs as a freelance production assistant on other people's films. He found the film work exhausting—to such an extent that at the end of each day he had no energy left for his own film projects. "I decided if I was going to make films," he remarked to Martin Kihn, "the first thing I had to do was get out of the industry." Hartley did just that, when he accepted a job answering phones and running errands at Action Productions, a company in Manhattan that produced public service announcements. Taking that job turned out to be a serendipitous move, for the company's president, Jerome Brownstein, both recognized and nurtured Hartley's talent. "After a couple of weeks, I knew in my heart that this guy had a lot of potential, so, consciously, I took him under my wing," Brownstein told Martin Kihn. Brownstein even allowed Hartley to read and write when he had completed his office work. "That job made all the difference," Hartley told Kihn.

During his stint at Action, Hartley made two shorts, *Dogs* and *The Cartographer's Girlfriend*. While working on those projects, he also demonstrated that he had a talent for making quality films with extremely limited resources, for he used borrowed cameras and outdated film stock. "I made movies with whatever money I had," he told Helen Peterson in an interview for the New York *Daily News* (August 5, 1990). "If I had fifty dollars, I made a movie that cost fifty dollars. If I had three hundred dollars, I made a movie that cost three hundred dollars."

Through a combination of good fortune and his own resourcefulness, Hartley soon found himself with considerably more than three hundred dollars to work with. One day, while he was still on the payroll at Action, he saw a sign in a bank offering personal loans to buy home computers. He filled out an application and, to his surprise, the bank approved it. He then persuaded one of his brothers and a cousin to apply as well, and in this way accumulated twenty-three thousand dollars. Hartley had planned to use the money to make a feature film, *The Unbelievable Truth*, in sixteen millimeter (he had never intended to buy a computer), but those plans changed after Brownstein told him he would raise enough money for a thirty-five millimeter film if Hartley would first come up with a reasonable budget. Hartley submitted his budget, and Brownstein came through with an investment of more than fifty thousand dollars, giving Hartley a total of about seventy-five thousand dollars for the production of his film. Hartley believes that his demonstrated ability to make low-budget shorts inspired Brownstein's faith in him. "If you know what you're doing, you can usually manipulate less-than-perfect situations," he explained to Helen Peterson. "So the crucial thing was that I had developed skills in being able to work regardless of my means. And I think that's what really impressed the people who eventually put up the money for *The Unbelievable Truth.* They knew I could make a movie and finish it for very little."

To make the film Hartley recruited many of his friends from SUNY-Purchase to serve as cast and crew members. He also persuaded his father and several other relatives who lived in Lindenhurst to allow him to use their homes as locations during the eleven-and-a-half-day shoot. Once he completed the film, his next challenge was to find a distributor. "For nine months I dragged this thing all over the country trying to show it to people and nobody would look at it," Hartley told Peterson. The film's commercial prospects brightened considerably in 1989, when it became the surprise hit of the 1989 Toronto Film Festival. "The audiences just went wild. . . . We were inundated with offers," Hartley recalled to Peterson. Ironically, the ensuing bidding war involved many of the same companies that had initially turned down the film, among them Miramax, which eventually won the distribution rights.

The Unbelievable Truth, which was released commercially in 1990, is by any standard a decidedly eccentric movie. Set on Long Island, it concerns the relationship that develops between Audry, a high school senior who is convinced that a nuclear apocalypse is imminent, and Josh, a mechanic and ex-convict who had been imprisoned for killing the father and sister of one of Audry's friends. The two "are a perfect match, the weirdest but most sensible characters in Hal Hartley's droll, lucid black comedy," Caryn James observed in the *New York Times* (July 20, 1990). And they are sensible, the film suggests, because they think for themselves, whereas all the other characters conform without reflection to the conventions of suburban Long Island. In this respect, *The Unbelievable Truth* is reminiscent of Jim Jarmusch's film *Stranger Than Paradise* and Steven Soderbergh's *sex, lies, & videotape,* as Kevin Thomas pointed out in the *Los Angeles Times* (August 17, 1990): "Hartley brings to blue-collar types something of the oh-so-fashionable air of disaffection that Jarmusch brings to marginal people and Soderbergh to yuppies."

Like its predecessor, Hartley's second film, *Trust* (1991), is a dark comedy populated by eccentric Long Island suburbanites. It focuses on Maria, a selfish high school senior whose announcement that she is pregnant leads to her father's death from a heart attack, prompting her mother to kick her out of the house. Maria soon meets an electronics whiz who lives with his abusive father and whose barely submerged rage is epitomized by the hand grenade he carries with him at all times. During an interview with John Anderson for *New York Newsday* (July 25, 1991), Hartley talked about what inspired him to make the film: "I wasn't trying to portray Long Island. That's just the kind of family units I know. Not that I know anybody that was that wired. But young girls pregnant who wanted to get married, who considered that a real plus; getting married at seventeen, getting their own house. That's an aspect of middle America that I really wanted to get across."

According to Hartley, *Trust* also concerns "a human being's ability to transcend selfishness, and Maria does." Although at the beginning of the film Maria is immature and greedy, "she learns to get past herself, to become unselfish, to live for somebody else," Hartley has explained. Many critics agreed that the film, while on one level disturbing, also affirmed people's capacity for self-transformation. As Peter Travers observed in *Rolling Stone* (August 8, 1991), "Within its small, darkly funny range, *Trust* is an exceptional film that stays alert to the mysteries of love." The movie won the grand prize at the Houston International Film Festival and earned Hartley the screenwriting award at the Sundance Film Festival.

At the same time that he was making feature films, Hartley was also producing short movies for television. *Surviving Desire* (1989), an hour-long movie that he made for the *American Playhouse* series, centers on the relationship between a college professor and a student with whom he is infatuated. For PBS's *Alive from Off Center* series, he made two shorter pieces: *Theory of Achievement* (1991), which deals with a group of would-be artists in Brooklyn who contemplate philosophy and their underachieving lives while arguing about whether their neighborhood will be the new Left Bank, and *Ambition* (1991), which follows a young man on his way to work as he tries to remind himself he's good at his job while fending off attacks from a number of passersby. Some reviewers felt that the shorts lacked originality because they employed conventions used by Jean-Luc Godard. The critic Peter Hogue, however, was impressed by their "bold energy" and "brash originality." "Each is more an extension than an imitation of Godard," Hogue wrote in *Film Comment* (January 1993), "and Hartley seems to have found a distinctive film idiom of his own in passing through the territory mapped out between [Godard's films] *Breathless* and *Masculin Feminin.*"

The influence of Jean-Luc Godard was also apparent in Hartley's third feature, *Simple Men* (1992), according to some reviewers. Set in rural Long Island (but shot in Texas for financial reasons), the film focuses on the McCabe brothers: Bill, a robber, and Dennis, a college student. Together they search for their father, a one-time professional baseball player known as "the radical shortstop," who has been on the run for over twenty years for bombing the Pentagon. The film, which like its predecessors has a bizarre plot and quirky characters, is distinguished from them by the fact that it is much more stylized, with flat, deadpan dialogue and stiff, almost theatrical staging. For some critics, the result was gratifying. Writing in the *New York Times* (November 1, 1992), Caryn James described *Simple Men* as "the purest, funniest view yet of the Hartley world, a place where dialogue is everything though disaster is imminent, where characters speak with utter conviction but drop-dead cool. There isn't much space for naturalism as the actors dance on some imaginary line between the banal and the deep." Others, however, felt that in stepping further away from realism, and in relying too heavily on the work of Godard, Hartley was squandering his artistic vision. *Simple Men* "is mannered in the terrifically knowing way of someone who has looked too long at the movies of others, especially, in this case, at the movies and mannerisms of Jean-Luc Godard . . . ," Vincent Canby wrote in the *New York Times* (October 14, 1992). "[And it] is all technique, which is possibly a proper subject for a movie at a time when there are how-to videos for everything from self-analysis and childbirth to the building of a greenhouse. Technique of this rigorous kind is also a way of masking all thought, even all commitment to anything except the making of more movies."

"Since 1984, I've been a New York City dweller hanging out with writers, journalists, painters, and filmmakers," Hartley told Graham Fuller in an interview for the London *Observer* (December 19, 1993), "but it was frustrating to me that I could never afford to make a film here. I had to run away and make films in the suburbs, and I channeled my interests into story forms that could take place there. I was always anxious to get back to the city to talk about the world I know." With his fourth feature, *Amateur* (1994), Hartley was able to shift his focus from suburban Long Island to Manhattan. Yet, apart from the change in setting, the film is vintage Hartley, complete with oddball characters and an improbable story line. The film concerns an amnesiac with a lurid past who hooks up with an ex-nun who is trying to make a living writing pornography. The pair, along with the amnesiac's wife, a porn star, soon find themselves on the run from hit men working for a Dutch arms dealer.

The film's thriller framework notwithstanding, *Amateur* is not a genre picture, and the violence is as artificial and comic as might be expected in a film by Hartley. "I am not particularly interested in trying to show guns going off realistically or making gunshot wounds look real, because I find it boring," he told Graham Fuller, "but I am interested in maintaining the kind of storytelling voice where things that are fake-looking are affecting in a very real way." Terrence Rafferty, who reviewed the film for the *New Yorker* (April 17, 1995), agreed: "Hartley is obviously not interested in making a conventional thriller. The plot is pointedly silly, and Hartley puts ironic Godardian quotation marks around the violence. The antic suspense-movie motifs serve a purpose, though: they make Hartley's familiar obsessions look shinier and fresher."

Hartley works with a regular pool of actors, many of whom he met while he was a student at SUNY-Purchase. To elicit from them the highly stylized acting that marks his films, Hartley, unlike most filmmakers, puts his performers through extensive rehearsals, during which he determines precisely how each scene will be played. He even manipulates the actors like models, going so far as to adjust the angles of their heads and to tell them where they should look at any given moment. "I don't think there are many directors who are as specific as Hal," Elina Lowensohn, a frequent performer in his films, told Ellen Pall. "He doesn't want to see emotionality. He likes a certain remove. It's very much like choreography. It takes great concentration."

Hartley's scriptwriting style is similarly idiosyncratic. Often described as repetitive and emotionless, his screenplays are sometimes compared to those of David Mamet or Harold Pinter. During his interview with John Fried, Hartley talked about what he hoped to accomplish by writing highly formalized dialogue: "It's like Joyce's *Ulysses*. It's taking the form and having fun with it. . . . I like to think that I am getting through to the kind of audience that appreciates ongoing, creative formal exercises." Although Hartley's movies are unquestionably funny, they are also infused with great sadness, anger, and frustration. "When people ask me, 'Is this comedy or is this drama?' I don't have an easy time answering," Hartley told John Anderson. "Because I don't necessarily work that way. I don't consider myself a writer of comedies or a writer of dramas. Whatever works, works. Writing, I try to work out some sort of reconciliation of the incongruities I see in life. Sometimes they make me laugh, sometimes they make me laugh and cry. In any event, I think that's the stuff that's really rich—the stuff you can't figure out, the stuff you can't label, the stuff you can't categorize."

Hal Hartley, who stands six feet, three inches tall and is reed-thin, "looks like a stretched-out cross between Nicolas Cage and Ray Bolger," according to Judith Weinraub. He has been described as affable and talkative, and, in the opinion of Graham Fuller, he bears "an air of quiet conviction." He lives in a loft in Manhattan. *Flirt*, his next feature, will consist of three segments, one each set in New York, Berlin, and Japan, dealing with love and commitment.

Selected Biographical References: Atlantic 273:108+ Ap '92 por; GQ 63:166+ O '92 por; London Observer p6 D 19 '93 por; N Y Times II p11+ O 11 '92 por; Village Voice p56 Ap 25 '95 por; Washington Post G p7+ Ag 4 '90 por

Agence France Presse

Havel, Václav

(HAH-vel, VAHTS-lahf)

Oct. 5, 1936- President of the Czech Republic; playwright; essayist. Address: Kancelář prezidenta republiky, 119 08 Prague Hrad, Czech Republic

NOTE: This biography supersedes the article that appeared in *Current Biography* in 1985.

As his fellow playwright Arthur Miller has remarked, Václav Havel is "the world's first avant-garde president." The strength and influence that Havel brings to the presidency of the Czech Republic is based largely on the moral authority he gained as Czechoslovakia's foremost dissident and human rights champion during the two decades of hard-line Communist rule that preceded the so-called velvet revolution. During the short period of relative freedom that artists enjoyed in Czechoslovakia in the 1960s, Havel wrote several plays that were produced in Prague, including *The Garden Party* and *The Memorandum*, absurdist comedies satirizing the Communist bureaucracy and its distortion of language. The most important of his later, samizdat works are the three grimly ironic one-act plays *Interview*, *A Private View*, and *Protest*, all of which are about the rationalizations of conformists trying to reconcile with conscience their selfish collusion with an oppressive system, and the full-length plays *Largo Desolato*, his wrenching dramatization of the inner crisis of a man pitted against and persecuted by a totalitarian state, and *Temptation*, his version of the Faust legend.

A self-described political "agnostic" who is "shy" by temperament, Havel never "consciously decided to become a dissident," much less a politician. "We just happened to," he has explained. "We don't know how. And we started landing in jails—we also don't know how. We just did some things that seemed the decent things to do." With the collapse of the Communist regime in Czechoslovakia, in December 1989, eight months after his final prison term, Havel became president. In the new climate of freedom, old ethnic divisions arose, to Havel's dismay. He resigned the presidency in July 1992, when the Czechoslovak federation was clearly on the verge of splitting into Slovakia and the Czech Republic. In January 1993 the newly constituted parliament of the Czech Republic elected him to a five-year term as president. He is not known to have written any plays since *Tomorrow*, in 1988.

One of two sons of Václav M. and Božena (Vavrečková) Havel, Václav Havel was born into "grand-bourgeois" family, to use his description, prominent in what might be called free-lance civic planning, in Prague, Czechoslovakia on October 5, 1936. His paternal grandfather was an architect and contractor, and his father was a major commercial real-estate developer. By his own account, he grew up "surrounded by good books" in "the intellectual atmosphere of Masarykian humanism." Through his grandfather and father, who personally knew the authors, he had childhood access to the books, and in some instances the persons as well, of the philosophers Josef Safařik and J. L. Fischer, the journalist Ferdinand Peroutka, and such other writers as Eduard Bass and Emanuel Rádl. "When I was very young I was friends with Edvard Valenta, and at his place I first met Václav Cerný, Olga Scheinpflugová, and Pavel Eisner," Havel recalled in *Disturbing the Peace* (1990). That memoir, originally published in Czech in 1986, derived from a long-distance interview, conducted through letters and tape recordings, with his friend the Czech journalist Karel Hvížďala. Havel told Hvížďala that he had been writing both poems and prose "ever since they taught me the alphabet."

When the Stalinists took power in a Moscow-backed coup and nationalized business and industry in Czechoslovakia in 1948, Havel recounted in *Disturbing the Peace*, "they confiscated all our family's property and we became objects of the class struggle." In the new "people's republic," Václav (already teased by classmates for being overweight) and his brother, Ivan, being scions of capitalist privilege, were punitively denied automatic access to an education beyond elementary school. As a teenager Václav managed to complete his secondary education by attending night school while working for five years as a laboratory technician. After graduating from night school in 1954, he applied to various arts faculties to study art history and philosophy and to a university film school. Unsuccessful in all of those efforts, and otherwise facing military conscription, he settled for studying economics at the Czech University of Technology, beginning in 1955.

Meanwhile, as a teenager, Havel had embarked on his adventures in search of the "second culture," hidden below the official "socialist-realist" one. The search began on "the borderline between what was permitted and not permitted" before moving "beyond those borders." In the university library he devoured such books as the works of Jan Patočka, officially frowned on but not suppressed. Alone or with such friends as Jiři Kubena and Milos Forman, and often with his own early literary efforts, mostly poetic, in hand, he visited poets Jaroslav Seifert and Vladimir Holan and other well-known writers. A turning point came when he met the young poet Jan Zabrana, who introduced him to the underground literary world represented preeminently by Jiři Kolář and the members of Group 42. In 1952 or 1953 Havel and his closest literary companions and friends became regular guests at Kolář's famous table in Prague's Cafe Slavia. Eventually they collaborated in Kolář's projects, and with his blessing and encouragement they organized presentations at the Umělecká Beseda, or artists' club, and began to participate in the samizdat of the time. "It wasn't until . . . years later, in America and Western Europe, that I met many important personalities of prewar Czechoslovakia and of the period immediately after the Second World War," Havel wrote in *Disturbing the Peace.* "In 1968 I traveled a great deal and spent much of my time visiting exiles."

Havel studied at the Czech University of Technology until 1957, when he finally began his two-year term of military service. In the army, he cofounded a regimental theatre company. At the end of his army hitch, he applied for admission to the university drama school in Prague, which rejected him at the time but would virtually force an "external" diploma on him almost a decade later, after he had begun gaining fame and had lost interest in academic credentials. In 1959 he became a stagehand with Prague's old ABC Theatre, where he came to understand that theatre "must be . . . a living spiritual and intellectual focus, a place for social self-awareness . . . , an instrument of human liberation." In 1960 Havel published an article in defense of the "absurd" comedies being offered by the Theatre on the Balustrade and two other avant-garde Prague companies. Soon thereafter, at the invitation of its director, he moved to the Theatre on the Balustrade, which grew in influence with the political thaw that began modestly in 1962 and reached its nova in 1968. "Until 1968, when I left, I lived for that theatre, I helped to create its profile, and I identified with it entirely," he recounted in *Disturbing the Peace.* "I went through a number of jobs when I was there, from stagehand to lighting technician, secretary, reader, right up to dramaturge. . . . Often I held [the jobs] concurrently: in the morning I organized tours, in the evening I ran the lighting for the performance, and at night I rewrote plays."

Havel's first plays were the juvenilia *The Life Ahead* and *An Evening with the Family.* During his first two years with the Theatre on the Balustrade, he collaborated in the writing of the plays *Hitchhiking* and *Mrs. Hermannova's Best Years* and the cabaret revue *The Deranged Turtledove.* His first independent full-length play, *The Garden Party,* was set in 1963 (the year of its initial production), when the nascent, and ultimately aborted, transition from totalitarianism to relative liberalism was running into linguistic impasses and, thus, into vicious logical circles. In the play, efforts of government employees to dismantle a bureaucratic agency are hampered by the very language in which they are trapped, the soul-sapping bureaucratic clichés under whose force they succeed only in building a yet more monstrous agency. The British critic Kenneth Tynan described the surreal satire of *The Garden Party* as "absurdism with deep roots in contemporary anxiety."

In *The Memorandum,* Havel extended the theme of *The Garden Party* beyond the dehumanizing power of piecemeal words and phrases to a view of language as a total ideological web. He began writing that play, intended as a political/social metaphor not only about socialism or Communism but, in his words, "about all systems that destroy human personality," in 1960. After many revisions, it was finally produced at the Theatre on the Balustrade in 1965, and an Off-Broadway production received the Obie Award for best foreign play of the 1967–68 season. *The Memorandum* relates the vicissitudes in the life and career of Josef Gross, the managing director of a vast and anonymous office, as he attempts to comply with a directive, written in a new, synthetic official gibberish called Ptydepe, ordering the imposition of an artificial "scientific" language designed to make communication more objective and "precise" by making words as dissimilar as possible, although the complex analysis involved makes the language unlearnable and communication impossible.

The Czech-born English playwright Tom Stoppard, who discovered Havel's work in 1967 and became a good friend of his, as well as a translator of his work, wrote in his introduction to the Grove Press edition of *The Memorandum* (1980) that he regarded that play as "the one that best shows off the hallmarks of [Havel's] gift: the fascination with language; the invention of an absurd society raised only a notch or two above the normal world of state bureaucracy . . . ; and, not least, the playfulness . . . , the almost gentle refusal to indulge a sense of grievance, the utter lack of righteousness or petulance or bile." "Here," Stoppard concluded, "one revels in the joyous freedom of Havel's imagination." In her essay "Living in Lies: Václav Havel's Drama" in *Cross Currents* (Summer 1992), Phyllis Carey wrote: "In the tradition of Kafka, Camus, and Beckett, probably his most significant mentors, Havel explores in *The Garden Party* and *The Memorandum* the paradox of human rationality pushed to its absurd logical extreme."

In Havel's sardonic bedroom farce *The Increased Difficulty of Concentration,* first produced at the Theatre on the Balustrade in April 1968, the theme of fragmented consciousness is underscored by the cubist structure of the plot, which spirals repetitively, playing events back, like a film rewinding, and ending where it began. The protagonist of the play is Edouard Huml, a social scientist whose professorial statements on human values are counterpointed by the emotional and moral chaos of his personal life, in which he seeks escape from a dehumanized society by indulging in romantic excess. A computer programmed to analyze Huml as a "random sample" and measure his identity comes up with a zero, underscoring the play's message that the human heart is uncomputable. An Off-Broadway production of *The Increased Difficulty of Concentration* received the Obie Award for best foreign play of 1969–70.

During the 1960s, when the Communist regime's credibility was weakened by a progressively deteriorating economy, it grudgingly acceded to a limited relaxation of its stranglehold on life in Czechoslovakia, the beginning of what would become known as the "Prague Spring" in 1968. The change in the Czechoslovakian Communist Party occurred under the leadership of two members of the Slovakian national minority, Alexander Dubček and Gustáv Husák. Dubček, the staunchly liberal one of the two, led the opposition to the regime of Antonín Novotný and succeeded him as party first secretary and prime minister of Czechoslovakia in January 1968. During his brief term, Dubček initiated an accelerated program in the direction of democratization domestically and independence of the Soviet Union internationally. Havel, whose passport had been confiscated, had it restored to him, and he was able to travel to other European countries and to the United States. In New York City in the spring of 1968, he rejected his friend Joseph Papp's offer of a position with Papp's Public Theatre, which would have made possible his staying in the United States. He was, however, profoundly and enduringly affected by the American counterculture of that time, including its musical elements.

Dubček's effort at "socialism with a human face" was abruptly crushed by an invasion of Soviet and other Warsaw Pact troops in August 1968. He was replaced by the more pliable (in the Soviet view) Husak, who resolidified Czechoslovakia's ties with the Soviet Union and reimposed hard-line Communist Party control over the country's political and economic life. Havel's plays and writings were banned, and because of his conspicuous leadership in the resistance to the repression and his human rights advocacy, he was during the 1970s repeatedly arrested, jailed twice, and forced to earn his livelihood by doing menial work, stacking barrels in a brewery. His lifestyle, once almost dandyish, was drastically downgraded.

In his condition of persecution, Havel went through a crisis of creativity. In the early 1970s he wrote two cerebral plays with purgatorial, Sisyphean structures that brought to the fore his fundamental and abiding concern with existential schizophrenia and the disintegration of human identity. One was *The Conspirators*, in which he portrayed the history of the Communist revolution in Czechoslovakia, personified in four power-struggling public officials, as static, or tethered, always returning to its original state. The other was *The Mountain Hotel*, set in a windowless resort in which vacationers take turns remembering and forgetting the same sets of words, gestures, and occurrences.

In the mid-to-late 1970s, Havel wrote three semiautobiographical one-act plays that he and his associates presented clandestinely: *Audience* (1975), also known as *Interview*; *A Private View* (1975), also called *The Varnishing Day*; and *Protest* (1978). The protagonist in all three is Ferdinand Vanek, a dissident and persecuted writer who, like a Biblical prophet, confronts conformists who are in moral denial, rationalizing their accommodation to a repressive regime. While all of the Vanek plays involve judgment of moral irresponsibility, or the shirking thereof, in none of them does the hero—or, perhaps more properly, antihero—come across as holier-than-thou. "Rather, he comes off as a self-ironic, timid soul . . . , his humility and self-effacement pointing beyond the human to a standard of truth that enables the other characters to glimpse their own duplicity and that gives his own character both its quiet dignity and its self-parody," as Phyllis Carey pointed out.

In 1975 Havel was briefly arrested after writing an open letter to President Husak in which he described Czechoslovak society as an "order without real life." The turning point in the political radicalization of Havel, a rock-'n'-roll aficionado, came with the arrest and trial of the Plastic People of the Universe, a Czechoslovak rock band that had taken its name from a song by the American musician Frank Zappa. In January 1977 hundreds of Czechoslovak artists and intellectuals signed Charter 77, a manifesto protesting the failure of the Czechoslovak Socialist Republic to abide by the Helsinki Covenant on Civil and Political Rights, to which it was a signatory, and the human rights clauses in its own constitution.

There ensued a wave of arrests, accompanied by government warnings that "freedom of expression" had to be "consistent with the interests of the working people." As one of Charter 77's three principal elected spokesmen, Havel was arrested for the fifth time and jailed for four months, until May 1977. The following October he was brought to trial on a new charge, "subversion of the republic," for sending banned writings out of the country for publication or production abroad, and given a four-month suspended sentence. In 1978 some dozen Chartists, including Havel, founded an offshoot of the Charter 77 movement known as the Committee for the Defense of the Unjustly Persecuted. The membership of the committee was arrested piecemeal during 1979, and in October of that year the Prague people's court convicted six of the dissidents, including Havel, on charges of "subversion." Havel was sentenced to four-and-a-half years at hard labor. During his incarceration he fell seriously ill with pneumonia, complicated by a lung abscess. Following pressure from the international intellectual community, his sentence was suspended in February 1983, a few months short of its completion.

In commemoration and criticism of Havel's near-fatal imprisonment, Samuel Beckett wrote the short play *Catastrophe*. Havel responded with the short play *Mistake* (1983), which dramatizes the tendency of human beings not only to adapt to repressive systems imposed from above but to replicate them on their own level. It also implicitly chides liberals in the West for what Havel viewed as their preoccupation with "rights" that are trivial alongside the rights to identity and survival that are threatened in some places in the world. In *Mistake*, a group of prison inmates who have formed their own totalitarian society sentence a new inmate to death after their efforts to indoctrinate him fail.

Following his arrest in 1977, Havel, hoping to win release, had written to the public prosecutor a letter formulated in a way that he considered at the time to be, in his words, "tactical and cunning," containing nothing that he "did not believe or that wasn't true." Later, however, the authorities recast his words to make it appear that he had given in to pressure and betrayed the Charter 77 movement. In one of his prison letters to his wife, Olga, he wrote: "No one knows what I went through in that darkest period of my life. . . . There were weeks, months, years in fact, of silent desperation, self-castigation, shame, inner humiliation, reproach, and uncomprehending questioning."

An agony of conscience and crisis of identity comparable to Havel's own are suffered by the existentialist philosopher and dissident professor Leopold Nettles, the protagonist of Havel's play *Largo Desolato* (1984). (*Largo Desolato* won an Obie Award in 1986.) Havel went on to explore in depth how truth may be convoluted perversely in the full-length play *Temptation* (1985). In that play, Fistula, the Mephistopheles character, points out that "the truth isn't merely what we believe, after all, but also why and to whom and under what circumstances we say it." That statement is a paraphrase of a remark Havel made in one of the letters written to his wife from prison and contained in *Letters to Olga: June 1979-September 1982* (1983; English translation, 1989).

Reviewing that book in the *New York Review of Books* (June 14, 1990), Janet Malcolm observed: "What one marvels at when one marvels at the phenomenon of Havel is not that a writer has become president of Czechoslovakia but that a man who is not afraid of his own ambivalence has succeeded in public life." In *Vanity Fair* (August 1991), Stephen Schiff wrote: "Reading *Letters to Olga* is like witnessing the genesis of a secular saint—one who smokes and drinks and womanizes, one who irritably upbraids poor Olga . . . , one who spends page upon exasperating page misinterpreting Heidegger's phenomenology (by way of Havel's mentor Jan Patočka) and manages nevertheless to create a stirring and coherent political philosophy."

For inciting antigovernment demonstrations in January 1989, Havel served his final term in prison, from February to May 1989. During the following months, with President Mikhail Gorbachev opening the door to reform in the Soviet Union, a wave of democratization swept through eastern Europe. In November 1989 Havel participated in the founding of the Civic Forum, the first legal opposition group in Czechoslovakia in forty-one years. Against the backdrop of mass demonstrations mounted by the Civic Forum and its Slovak counterpart, Public Against Violence, officials of those groups held talks on political reform and power-sharing with the Communist prime minister. Following the resignation of President Husák, on December 10, an interim coalition cabinet was formed, a multiparty political system was written into law, and free elections were scheduled.

Reluctantly, Havel agreed to become a candidate for president, and the interim cabinet unanimously elected him on December 29, 1989. In retrospect, he would see himself as a man who was "simply 'pulled forward by Being'" to become what he called "an instrument of the time." "With no embarrassment, no stage fright, no hesitation, I did everything I had to do," he recalled in *Summer Meditations* (1992), a book of reflections on the nature and practice of politics, the original version of which was written in the summer of 1991. "I was capable of speaking extempore (I who had never before spoken in public!) to several packed public squares a day, of negotiating confidently with the heads of great powers, of addressing foreign parliaments, and so on . . . not because historical opportunity suddenly uncovered in me some special aptitude for the office, but because . . . that special time caught me up in its wild vortex and—in the absence of leisure to reflect on the matter—compelled me to what had to be done."

What had to be done was, in his words, "to help this country move from totalitarianism to democracy, from satellitehood to independence, from a centrally directed economy to market economics." In an address televised on New Year's Day 1990, Havel described Communism as "a monstrous, ramshackle, stinking machine" whose worst bequest to Czechoslovakia was not the country's economy but "a spoiled moral environment." "We have become morally ill because we are used to saying one thing and thinking another," he pointed out. "We have learned not to believe in anything, not to care about each other. . . . Love, friendship, mercy, humility, or forgiveness have lost their depths and dimension. . . . They represent some sort of psychological curiosity, or they appear as long-lost wanderers from faraway times."

Characteristic of Havel's unusual style as president was his bringing into an official position in the Ministry of Culture Frank Zappa, whose band the Mothers of Invention had been one of his favorites since the 1960s. In February 1990 Havel visited Washington, D.C., to discuss with President George Bush not financial aid but such matters as initiatives and technical assistance that would enable

Czechoslovakia to compete more effectively in the international marketplace. In an address before a joint session of Congress, he said that the best way for the United States to help Czechoslovakia and the rest of eastern Europe was to help the Soviet Union find its way to democracy. Meeting in Moscow several days later, Havel and Mikhail Gorbachev agreed on a fast-paced timetable for the withdrawal of the seventy thousand Soviet troops that had been stationed in Czechoslovakia since 1968 and on an end to cooperation in espionage directed against the United States, among other matters. Not long afterward, in Prague, Havel addressed a conference of approximately fifty representatives of pro-democracy movements from around the world, including the Soviet republics. Havel's first term as president ended on June 5, 1990. A new Czechoslovak parliament, seated after non-Communist parties swept the free elections held later that month, reelected Havel president by a vote of 234 to 50 on July 5, 1990.

With democratization, the dormant separatist sentiment among the Slovak population of Czechoslovakia was awakened, and that sentiment was abetted by the growing difference of opinion between Czechs and the poorer Slovaks regarding the privatization of state-run industries, which was scheduled to proceed at too-rapid a pace in the view of most Slovaks. When Havel traveled to Bratislava to open a Slovak branch of his presidential office there in October 1991, he was turned away with jeers by demonstrating Slovak separatists. In an interview with Adam Michnick for a Polish periodical, later published in translation in *World Press Review* (March 1992), Havel said: "I wrote some time ago . . . that Communism, in a certain manner, immobilized history. . . . Metaphorically, Communism was a kind of narcotic, and now some nations are waking up to their previous state of mind and problems. Judging by what is beginning to appear in Czechoslovakia, the most menacing demons are anti-Semitism, ethnic intolerance, and xenophobia, which all can be observed in Slovakia and, in somewhat different forms, in Czech regions."

The results of the legislative elections of June 1992 gave the left-wing nationalist Vladimir Mečiar's Movement for a Democratic Slovakia just short of an absolute majority in the Slovak parliament and the second-biggest representation in the federal parliament, while the right-wing federalist Václav Klaus and his Civic Democratic Party scored strongest in the Czech regions. With the Slovak nationalists blocking his reelection, and the dissolution of Czechoslovakia being clearly imminent, Havel resigned the presidency on July 20, 1992, three months before the formal end of his term. He exited Prague Castle in a symbolic manner, wearing a T-shirt and carrying a backpack.

During his presidency of Czechoslovakia, Havel had drawn the ire of a large segment of the population by phasing out the country's arms industry and its overseas weapons sales. In his general approach to building a market economy, he was accused by right-wingers of being a "crypto-socialist," because he believed that government had to be involved in "planning" and in contributing to "an industrial strategy," while left-wingers thought he was pushing for too swift a pace of privatization. "The most virulent attacks focused on Havel's opposition to the 'lustration' law that stripped former Communist office-holders of their civil rights regardless of whether they had themselves engaged in human rights violations . . . ," Erwin Knoll wrote in the *Progressive* (March/April 1993). "This suggested to me that Havel was a decent, thoughtful, generous, and compassionate human being . . . and . . . that the Czechs were in the extraordinary, almost unique position of having a leader better than they wanted or deserved."

On August 26, 1992 the Czech and Slovak political leaders announced their intention to dissolve the Czechoslovak federation. The dissolution became effective on January 1, 1993, when the Czech Republic and Slovakia became independent of each other. When invited to run for the presidency of the Czech Republic, Havel at first demanded that the constitutional power base of the office—the power to veto legislation and to dissolve parliament—be expanded. He finally accepted the invitation without winning that concession. On January 26, 1993 the Czech parliament elected Havel to a five-year term as president of the Czech Republic. He was chosen over the Left Bloc (the reincarnation of the old Communist Party) and right-wing Republican Party candidates. While Havel is internationally better known and more influential, Prime Minister Václav Klaus is the more powerful figure in Czech national politics.

Václav Havel, or Living in Truth (1986), edited by Jan Vladislav and translated by Paul Wilson, contains six essays by Havel and sixteen essays appreciative of him by Samuel Beckett and Heinrich Böll, among others. *Open Letters* (1991) comprises selected speeches, newspaper articles, and other prose pieces written by Havel between 1965 and 1990, along with several interviews from that period, edited and in some instances translated by Paul Wilson. In his *Vanity Fair* (August 1991) profile of Havel, Stephen Schiff wrote of his oeuvre: "The plays have a chilly technical perfection [as] thumbnail sketches of totalitarian bureaucracies whittling down their minions like so many pencils. . . . Havel's essays . . . are richer. Their forthrightness and generosity of spirit can be moving, and there's something exhilarating about the dogged way Havel sniffs and digs at his ideas until every bony chip has been unearthed. Here too [as in his plays] the strongest meditations are about language, and also about the insidious nature of official lying—about the way every unquestioned falsehood drops the temperature another degree, until in the end freedom itself is frozen in its tracks. But Havel the stylist can be clunky and overemphatic, and he doesn't cover much ground that the great antitotalitarian thinkers—George Orwell, Arthur Koestler, Hannah Arendt—haven't already excavated. . . . And yet something draws us to Havel anyway. That paradoxical combination of heartfelt humility and brick-wall moral conviction is as plain in his written voice as in the public man, and it's enormously appealing."

Shortly after Havel joined the Theatre on the Balustrade as a stagehand, Olga Splíchalová quit her job as an office clerk to be near him there, working as an usher. They have been married since July 9, 1964. The Havels' civilian residence is their own small villa near Prague Castle, the official presidential residence; they also have a farm cottage in Bohemia. Václav Havel is short, with graying hair, a moderate walrus-style mustache, and what have been described as "attentive blue eyes," a "slumped posture," a "warm handshake," and an "almost offhand delivery." He is generally viewed as a nonreligious humanist, but he has said that while he is "not a practicing Catholic," his "whole view of the world arises from a Christian background, from a certain Christian experience of being." "Some say I'm a naïve dreamer trying to combine the incompatible: politics and morality . . . ," he wrote in *Summer Meditations*. "My experience and observations confirm that politics as the practice of morality is possible [although] not always easy. . . . What I would like to accentuate . . . in my practice of politics is culture. . . . I am convinced that we will never build a democratic state based on law if we do not at the same time build a state that is . . . humane, moral, intellectual and spiritual, and cultural."

Selected Biographical References: Christian Sci Mon p14 D 14 '89 por; Deutschland p14+ F '95 pors; Esquire 119:84+ F '93 pors; Guardian p23 S 15 '90 por, p23 S 25 '92 por; Humanist 52:19+ Ja/F '92 por; London Observer p13 Je 16 '91; Mirabella p92+ Je '90 pors; N Y Times C p17+ F 8 '90 por, A p3 S 30 '92; People 33:44+ Ja 22 '90 pors, 34:141+ S 10 '90 pors; Time 135:62+ Ja 8 '90 por; Vanity Fair 59:124+ Ag '91 por; Village Voice p31+ Ja 16 '90; Washington Post A p3 Jl 26 '92 por; Kriseova, Eda. Václav Havel: The Authorized Biography (1993); International Who's Who, 1994–95

AP/Wide World Photos

Hill, Anita

July 30, 1956- Lawyer; professor; writer; lecturer. Address: University of Oklahoma, College of Law, 300 Timberdell Rd., Norman, OK 73109

When, in October 1991, University of Oklahoma law professor Anita Hill accused President George Bush's Supreme Court nominee Clarence Thomas of having sexually harassed her when she worked for him in the early 1980s, first at the Department of Education and later at the Equal Employment Opportunity Commission, her riveting testimony to the Senate Judiciary Committee during Thomas's confirmation hearings polarized television audiences throughout the United States. Deified by feminists for single-handedly revitalizing the women's movement by forcing the issue of sexual harassment to the forefront of public debate, Hill was also castigated by supporters of Thomas's conservative political views and by African-Americans who were angry with her for attempting to undermine the advancement of one of their own. Although Hill lost a battle when Thomas won Senate confirmation, by a 52–48 vote, allowing him to fill the seat vacated by the retired liberal justice Thurgood Marshall, the first and only other African-American to have served on the Supreme Court, her testimony irrevocably altered the political landscape. Membership in feminist organizations increased dramatically, and the record number of congressional seats won by women in the elections of November 1992 has been attributed to the galvanizing effect—on female voters and female candidates alike—of watching the treatment Hill received at the hands of the all-male, all-white Judiciary Committee. To rid the committee of its uniform appearance, chairman Joseph R. Biden Jr., a Democrat from Delaware, actively recruited two women elected to the Senate in 1992: Dianne Feinstein, a white Democrat from California, who remains the panel's sole female member, and Carol Moseley-Braun, an African-American Democrat from Illinois, who relinquished her seat two years later for a slot on the more-powerful Finance Committee.

In addition to drawing attention to the consequences for women and minorities of being poorly represented in government, Hill has been credited with improving the lot of women in the workplace, where the issue of sexual harassment was treated by some employers with a renewed sense of commitment in the wake of the hearings. Sexual harassment claims filed with the EEOC rose about 60 percent during the first half of 1992. When asked if she would still testify if she had it to do over again, Hill has always answered in the affirmative, despite the character defamation she has endured on television and in print. "Testifying has helped me understand that one individual's behavior and actions make a difference," she told Jill Nelson in an interview for *Essence* (March 1992). "That my actions are important to people other than myself. . . . Had I not come forward, I would have a real problem living with my own conscience." The poet June Jordan, a professor of African-American studies and women's studies at the University of California at Berkeley, published an article in the *Progressive* (December 1991) in which she declared her intention to write to Anita Hill, thanking her for speaking out and reassuring her of "her rights, her sanity, and the African beauty of her earnest commitment to do right and to be a good woman: a good black woman in this America . . . who is somebody and something beautiful and precious and exquisitely compelling."

Anita Faye Hill was born on July 30, 1956 in Lone Tree, Oklahoma, just outside the town of Morris. She is the youngest of the thirteen children of Albert and Erma Hill, devout Baptists and Roosevelt Democrats of African-American and Creek Indian descent. Growing up without indoor plumbing in a clapboard house on a 250-acre farm, Anita Hill, who is known to her family and friends by her middle name, picked peanuts and chopped cotton during her round of daily chores. "My childhood was one of a lot of hard work and not much money," she told the Senate Judiciary Committee during the Thomas hearings, "but it was one of solid family affection." After attending segregated public schools through the ninth grade, she became one of about ten black students in her class of sixty at Morris High School, where she was a member of the student council, the National Honor Society, the Future Homemakers of America, and the pep club. A straight-A student, she was valedictorian of her class of 1973. Classmates later described her as "a sweet" person who eschewed drugs and alcohol and had ample opportunity but little time for dating. "It was like even back then, you could sense she was going places," her high school peer Billy Reager told Jane Mayer and Jill Abramson in an interview for their book *Strange Justice: The Selling of Clarence Thomas* (1994). "If there was a perfect person, it was Faye," he added. "Everyone just loved her."

A National Merit Scholar and a Regents Scholar, Hill graduated in 1977 with a B.S. degree in psychology from Oklahoma State University in Stillwater. Her longtime interest in civil rights led her to complete a summer internship with a judge and to apply to law school. Accepted at Harvard and Yale law schools, she enrolled at Yale University Law School, in New Haven, Connecticut, which she attended on an Earl Warren scholarship from the Legal Defense Fund of the National Association for the Advancement of Colored People. During the summer before her final year at Yale, Hill worked in Washington, D.C., as a law clerk for the prestigious firm of Wald, Harkrader & Ross, which she joined as an associate in August 1980 after earning her J.D. degree earlier that summer. The circumstances surrounding her departure from the firm, after only eleven months, were considered suspicious by Thomas's supporters, who produced as evidence an affidavit from John L. Burke Jr., a partner with the firm during Hill's employment who claimed that Hill's work had been unacceptable and that she had been asked to leave. Refuting Burke's claim were three other Wald partners, one of whom stated that Hill had been "well-regarded" and had left of her own volition in good standing. Further light was shed on the circumstances of Hill's departure by Mayer and Abramson, who reported in their book that the firm's records indicated that Hill had not worked directly with Burke, who, the authors suggested, may have confused Hill with another black female associate, who experienced difficulties at the firm and who left shortly after Hill did.

On the recommendation of Wald partner Gil Hardy, Clarence Thomas hired Hill as his special counsel in July 1981, when he was appointed head of the Office of Civil Rights in the Department of Education. During the Thomas confirmation hearings, Hill alleged that within three to five months of her assuming the job Thomas had begun sexually harassing her, repeatedly telling her she "ought to" go out with him and persistently addressing her in a lewd manner, describing pornographic movies to her, and bragging about his sexual prowess. According to Hill, she clearly and repeatedly told Thomas that she was not interested in going out nor in these conversations. Hill said the harassment stopped after several months, around the time Thomas became involved in a relationship with another woman, and had not yet resumed when he became chairman of the EEOC, in May 1982, bringing Hill with him as his assistant, to be in charge of reviewing EEOC policy. In the fall, however, according to Hill, Thomas again began harassing her.

At the EEOC, Hill recalled in her interview with Jill Nelson, she had, in her words, "consistently pursued an approach consistent with the longstanding policy of the commission, which was often antagonistic to the position of the Reagan administration." In an interview with Lynne Duke and Sharon LaFraniere of the *Washington Post* (October 9, 1991), Michael A. Middleton, a former colleague of Hill's at the Department of Education and the EEOC who later became a law professor at the University of Missouri, described Hill as "your typical brainy, dedicated egg-head type" and

Thomas as a "hard-working, no-nonsense kind of guy," adding, "I can't believe that she is inventing this, but I can't believe that Clarence Thomas took inappropriate liberties." Another former EEOC colleague, J. C. Alvarez, a Thomas supporter, told the Senate Judiciary Committee that she remembered Hill as "a relentless debater, . . . the kind of woman who always made you feel that she was not going to be messed with."

In January 1983 Hill began looking for another job. In July of the same year, five months after she was hospitalized with an undiagnosed stomach ailment that she has attributed to "stress at work," Hill left the EEOC to begin teaching at the O. W. Coburn School of Law at Oral Roberts University, in Tulsa, Oklahoma, an ultraconservative, almost all-white, and strictly religious institution. She arrived with a recommendation from Thomas to Charles Kothe, the dean of the law school, who worked concurrently as Thomas's special assistant at the EEOC beginning in 1984. Hill experienced difficulty gaining the respect of her unruly students, many of whom were her own age and could not see beyond her status as a quota-filling "double minority"—a woman and an African-American. Even Kothe perceived her this way, as he was quoted by Mayer and Abramson as saying: "Here we had a chance to hire the first black woman Yale Law graduate in the Southwest—it was a coup whether she could teach or not." When the Coburn school closed in 1986, Kothe, who was still friendly with Thomas, recommended Hill for a teaching position in commercial law at the University of Oklahoma's College of Law in Norman.

Thus it is not difficult to understand, Hill's supporters have argued, why she remained on cordial terms with Thomas in the years after she left the EEOC, a fact that damaged her credibility during the hearings in the view of those who wondered why she did not charge Thomas with harassment after she left the EEOC, thereby burning the most important bridge of her professional life to that date. (Thomas was among the Reagan administration's most powerful black men in the civil rights arena, in which Hill had always wanted to make her mark.) Moreover, sexual harassment law was in its infancy in the early 1980s, and in her job as an assistant to the man responsible for enforcing such laws, Hill had witnessed firsthand the limits of the law as a remedy for victims. Those few who did complain of being harassed were often branded as whistle blowers or liars, and their careers were sometimes permanently derailed as a result. Furthermore, Hill found it unlikely that she would be believed, given Thomas's position—especially after she confided in a friend who found her story incredulous and said so.

In terms of her career, Hill's reticence paid off handsomely. At the University of Oklahoma she was involved with minority student organizations and law school committees, and she served on the boards of a transportation service for the handicapped and of a shelter for battered women. In the summer of 1987, she conducted a research project at American University's Washington College of Law. In 1990, four years after her arrival in Norman, Hill was awarded tenure. Later she was elected by her colleagues to a select committee overseeing hiring, tenure, and salaries.

Hill was therefore at the height of her career when, on July 1, 1991, the White House announced that Clarence Thomas, then a judge on the federal appeals court, had been nominated by President Bush to the Supreme Court. "I had no plan in my mind to come forward [with allegations of sexual harassment]," she told Mayer and Abramson, recalling her reaction to the news, "not one single thought about it." After all, she had never been asked about her relationship with Thomas during any of his confirmation hearings for previous positions. But this time she was not only approached but forced to speak out publicly after her accusations were leaked to the press despite a promise of confidentiality. Researching the source of the breach, Mayer and Abramson discovered that in late July Hill had told an old law school friend, Gary Phillips, of Thomas's behavior and had asked his advice on whether to become involved. Phillips, who worked for the Federal Communications Commission in Washington, D.C., told some friends of the scandal without naming Hill, and one of those friends circulated the story at a dinner party. One of the party guests then told Nan Aron, a liberal lobbyist for the Alliance for Justice. Aron, suspecting that Hill was the only person whose career path went from Yale to the EEOC to Oklahoma, tipped off the staff of Judiciary Committee member Howard Metzenbaum, a Democrat from Ohio.

For weeks, according to Mayer and Abramson, the crucial information lay undisturbed—until one of Metzenbaum's aides scrutinized Thomas's travel records and noticed a number of trips to Oklahoma (which turned out to be visits to Kothe). Hill's name once again made its way into investigators' discussions, and in early September she received—and returned—several phone calls regarding Thomas from aides to Metzenbaum and Senator Edward M. Kennedy of Massachusetts, another Democratic member of the Judiciary Committee. Both Metzenbaum and Kennedy were also members of the Labor Committee, for which the aides who called Hill worked. On September 10, 1991, Hill, under the impression that her comments would be confidential unless other women were also willing to speak out, and believing also that other sexual harassment complaints against Thomas were being investigated, agreed to detail her allegations in a conversation with Metzenbaum's Labor Committee aide James Brudney, whose notes of the interview, according to Mayer and Abramson, match Hill's testimony very closely.

Brudney informed Metzenbaum of Hill's allegations later on the same day. Metzenbaum's immediate reaction, as quoted by Mayer and Abramson, who cited *Time* magazine's Capitol Hill reporter Hays Gorey as their source, was to tell Gorey, "If that's sexual harassment, half the senators on Capitol Hill could be accused." Metzenbaum, who thought it might look unseemly for his Labor Committee staff to handle the investigation further, passed the information to the staff of Joseph Biden, the chairman of the Judiciary Committee. His staff indicated that Hill would have to initiate contact with them if she wanted to be heard. On September 12, two days into Thomas's confirmation hearings, Hill called Harriet Grant, chief counsel to Biden's nominations unit, who informed her that if she wanted to pursue the allegations, her name would have to be used in a confrontation with Thomas. Grant thought she sounded discouraged, and when she informed Biden of her talk with Hill, she gave him the impression that Hill did not want her name to be used (an assumption that Hill later disputed, according to Mayer and Abramson), so Biden dismissed the charges for the time being.

Meanwhile, as the circle of congressional aides and others who knew about Hill widened, a few of them understood that the Judiciary Committee could appear to have failed in its task of weighing Thomas's nomination if Hill's charges ever became public, and these few finally persuaded Biden, who ordered an FBI investigation, to take her accusations more seriously. The two-day inquiry ended inconclusively on September 25. Two days later, after reviewing the FBI report, the fourteen-member Judiciary Committee dismissed the charges without making them public, and split evenly on whether to recommend Thomas's confirmation in a first round of voting. A second round of voting the same day accumulated thirteen votes in favor of sending the nomination to the full Senate, but without a recommendation. A floor vote of all one hundred senators was scheduled for October 8.

Not wanting the FBI to misconstrue her charges, Hill had written a four-page statement of her allegations on September 23, which she faxed to Biden's staff, who then passed it on to an aide to Senator Strom Thurmond, Republican of South Carolina, whose staff failed to inform his Republican colleagues on the committee of Hill's existence, flaunting a Judiciary Committee rule that all members should be notified of any FBI investigation within twenty-four hours. Thus the September 27 vote had taken place with most of the Republican senators in the dark about the FBI report and Hill's typewritten statement. The Democrats on the committee, most of whom were expected to approve the nomination, did not see her statement until the very morning of the vote. Convinced that there was a story to be broken, Nina Totenberg of National Public Radio and Timothy Phelps of *New York Newsday* separately traced their hunches to Anita Hill, having been leaked various parts of the story by several sources simultaneously. Totenberg's interview with Hill, in which the law professor said Thomas had used his power in an "ugly and intimidating way," was broadcast on NPR on October 6, the same day on which Phelps's story was published in *Newsday*.

The media blitz that resulted shocked Hill. "I had no idea there would be television cameras camped out in my neighbor's yard," she later recalled in her interview with Jill Nelson. "Did they want me to give my testimony to them, prior to the hearings? Had I not been a lawyer, perhaps that would have happened." At a news conference the following day, Hill chided Biden for the delay in distributing her statement to his colleagues—criticism that was echoed by many of the women in Congress, lawyers, and feminist lobbying groups throughout the Capitol, all of whom converged on the Senate to insist on a postponement of the vote in order to give Hill's remarks full consideration.

On October 7, a day before the Senate vote was scheduled, Senator Paul Simon, a Democrat from Illinois, called for a one-week delay. The Senate postponed the vote and subpoenaed Hill for testimony during the hearings, which resumed on October 11. Believing that she could approach the hearings objectively and professionally, Hill planned to face the Judiciary Committee without outside legal representation. When her friend and fellow law professor Emma Coleman Jordan learned this, she was "stunned" and hurriedly recruited a volunteer team of advisers composed of law professors and a public relations consultant. Hill gave seven hours of testimony during the televised confirmation hearings, which lasted through October 14. Several of her friends and coworkers testified that she had told them of Thomas's alleged harassment years earlier. In the middle of the proceedings, to counter the assertion of Senator Arlen Specter, a Republican from Pennsylvania, that Hill was a perjurer, she successfully underwent a lie-detector test and made the results public. In his testimony Thomas, who refused to submit to a polygraph exam, categorically denied her charges, memorably characterizing the hearings as a "high-tech lynching for uppity blacks." On October 15 the Senate confirmed Thomas's nomination by a vote of fifty-two to forty-eight, the second narrowest approval margin for any nominee to the Supreme Court in history. A *New York Times*/CBS News poll conducted on October 13 found 45 percent of Americans in favor of Thomas's confirmation and 20 percent opposed, with 58 percent saying they believed Thomas and 24 percent backing Hill.

During and after the hearings, at which expert testimony on sexual harassment was prohibited, Republican senators postulated that Hill was a "scorned woman" willing to perjure herself to get revenge. Her attackers also attempted to portray her by turns as a politically motivated puppet of liberal interest groups or as a conservative who opposed affirmative action, insinuating that she was a pawn of those who opposed Thomas's nomination because of, respectively, his conservative views or his race—theories she described as "absolutely absurd" in her interview with Jill Nelson. "The whole process," she said, "was trying to paint me as an arch-conservative, someone who was duped by somebody else, the scorned woman, someone who was deluded, a fantasizer. All those were really attempts to avoid dealing with the issue, to avoid dealing with me as a person. . . . Most Senate members probably have not dealt with an African-American woman as a peer or someone who has come before the committee. They couldn't deal with me, Anita Hill, as an individual and with the issue before them other than in a political way."

The hearings caused many observers to fault the entire process by which Congress confirms presidential appointees. The eminent trial lawyer F. Lee Bailey, writing in the *ABA Journal* (January 1992), decried the "offensive, even downright mean-spirited" manner in which Hill was questioned during the hearings, and stated that the inquiry should have been conducted under the procedural safeguards of a legal trial and with the assistance of experienced trial attorneys trained to root out facts. In Bailey's opinion, many of the senators' questions were merely "polemic, self-serving babble designed only to capture votes." In an article for *Social Work* (January 1992), Ann Hartman wrote that the hearings had revealed "how men will join together to defend each other when one of their own is called to account." In his analysis of the hearings for *Harper's* (December 1991), Lewis H. Lapham declared, "The Republicans carried out the White House brief to do whatever was necessary to discredit the woman's statement. They did so with a mean-spirited singleness of purpose that was as effective as it was dishonorable." Rather than deploring the hearings, however, Lapham felt they "cast a clear and welcome light on the character and conduct of some of the disreputable politicians who govern the state. . . . They made a show of their venality and cowardice that was marvelous to behold."

Asked how she managed to remain poised throughout the ordeal of the hearings, Hill told Nelson, "I stayed focused on the reason I was in Washington, D.C.—to bring the information before the committee. Spiritually, I drew on resources I had developed during my childhood. I kept in touch with my family by telephone, and I saw them on the day of the hearing." In December 1991 Hill predicted that within a year she would have returned to being just "a cog in the machine." Although she insisted that she was not interested in seeking public office, the reaction to the Thomas hearings had forced Hill to reexamine her aversion to public life. As she told Nelson, "I will not be satisfied anymore with living my life simply for myself. Other issues are much broader than my own little world." Motivated to learn more about sexual harassment by the letters she received from women detailing their own experiences, some of which harked back fifty years, Hill researched the topic and began revealing her findings in lectures, beginning in November 1991. When members of her audiences would ask for the correct pronunciation of the word "harassment," Hill would say, "Once and for all, let's pronounce it dead."

Besides speaking out about sexism, Hill also felt compelled to address the political split among African-Americans that was thrown into stark relief by the Thomas hearings. "As African-American women," Hill explained to Nelson, "we are always trained to value our community even at the expense of ourselves, and so we attempt to protect the African-American community. We don't want to say things that will reflect negatively on it." Addressing the charge that she had "betrayed" a black man, she told Nelson, "It doesn't do us any good as black people to hide what we believe is wrong because it may be perceived as a betrayal. . . . It's interesting that people haven't seen the harassment of black women as a betrayal."

Although Hill had chosen to break the unwritten rule that blacks should not air their differences in public, especially to an all-white audience (such as the Judiciary Committee), she was troubled by the fact that her actions were lauded by some women for being purely feminist, without any racial context. Hill addressed that topic a year after the hearings, at a conference at Georgetown University Law School entitled "Race, Gender, and Power in America." "Not only did the Senate fail to understand or to recognize me because of my lack of attachment to certain institutions, like marriage and patronage," Hill explained, "they failed to relate to my race, my gender, my race and gender combined, and in combination with my education, my career choice, and my demeanor."

While polls taken during the confirmation hearings had shown popular support for Thomas, surveys conducted in 1992 and in 1993 showed that the proportion of those who believed Hill had risen dramatically. Much of the evidence that might have convinced the Senate and the public that Hill was telling the truth did not emerge until three years after the hearings, when *Wall Street Journal* reporters Jane Mayer and Jill Abramson published *Strange Justice: The Selling of Clarence Thomas*, in which they reported that four women had been prepared to corroborate Hill's allegations, but Biden had refused to allow them to testify. The Thomas hearings provided grist for several other books (in addition to the transcripts of the hearings), among them *Capitol Games* (1992), by Timothy M. Phelps and Helen Winternitz, and *The Real Anita Hill* (1993), a best-seller by David Brock that sought to discredit Hill. Abramson, who, along with Jane Mayer, wrote an unfavorable review of Brock's book for the *New Yorker* magazine, told Barbara Brotman of the *Chicago Tribune* (December 18, 1994) that they had interviewed many of Brock's sources in the course of writing *Strange Justice*: "We found that people said their words had been twisted to form a false thesis." In his memoir *Resurrection: The Confirmation of Clarence Thomas* (1994), Senator John Danforth, a Republican from Missouri, admitted that he had pledged his support to Thomas "whether or not [Hill's] charge was true."

Other books on the subject include *Race-ing Justice, En-gendering Power: Essays on Anita Hill, Clarence Thomas, and the Construction of Social Reality* (1992), edited and with an introduction by

Toni Morrison, and *African-American Women Speak Out on Anita Hill-Clarence Thomas* (1995), a collection of essays edited by Geneva Smitherman. A seventy-six-minute video documentary, *Sex and Justice: The Highlights of the Anita Hill/Clarence Thomas Hearings*, with commentary by Gloria Steinem, was released in 1993. There has even been a theatrical version of the event: Mame Hunt's *Unquestioned Integrity*, which was produced by Studio Secondstage, Washington, D.C., in the summer of 1994.

Named Woman of the Year in 1991 by the editors of *Glamour* magazine, Anita Hill was honored in 1992 by the American Bar Association's Commission on Women in the Profession, which bestowed upon her the Margaret Brent Women Lawyers of Achievement Award. In April 1993 a private group raised $120,000 towards endowing a chair at the University of Oklahoma in Hill's name, for research on women's rights issues. This set off a new wave of controversy in her home state, where conservative enmity towards her had never really subsided. In December 1993 Hill signed a million-dollar agreement with Doubleday to write her autobiography and a historical account of sexual harassment. In order to write the books, she took a one-year unpaid leave of absence from her teaching position in August 1994 and moved to the more tranquil environs of Laguna Beach, California. In July 1995, a month before she was scheduled to resume her professorial duties at the University of Oklahoma College of Law, it was reported that Hill hoped to raise $150,000 for the college education of six children who survived the April 19, 1995 bombing of the Alfred P. Murrah Federal Building, which housed their day-care center, in Oklahoma City. Anita Hill enjoys taking long walks and listening to the music of Mozart.

Selected Biographical References: Essence 22:54+ Mr '92 pors; N Y Times A p1+ O 11 '91, A p1+ O 12 '91 pors; People 36:40+ O 28 '91 pors; Who's Who Among Black Americans, 1994–95; Who's Who of American Women, 1995–96

Thinking Machines Corporation

Hillis, W. Daniel

Sept. 25, 1956- Computer scientist. Address: Thinking Machines Corporation, 245 First St., Cambridge, MA 02142.

After building a ticktacktoe-playing computer out of Tinkertoys as an undergraduate at the Massachusetts Institute of Technology, W. Daniel Hillis, commonly known as Danny, began putting his mind to work designing more practical computers. The result of that work was the blueprint for an innovative computer, the Connection Machine, that uses thousands of microprocessors instead of just one, which had been the number routinely used by even the most powerful computers. To produce and market the Connection Machine, in 1983 Hillis founded the Thinking Machines Corporation, with the ultimate aim of developing a computer that lived up to the company's name. Although that lofty goal has yet to be realized, the Connection Machine revolutionized the supercomputer industry. Ignoring those who said that computers with multiple processors—known as massively parallel computers—were impractical, Thinking Machines, with Hillis as chief scientist, developed the Connection Machine into the fastest computer in the world, with as many as sixty-five thousand microprocessors (each equivalent to a desktop computer) working together.

Thinking Machines quickly became dominant in the nascent market for parallel computers, but the high price of supercomputers limited their sales to research institutions, very large corporations, and the government (particularly the military). Although its technology had become the industry standard, the company, hurt by increased competition and defense cutbacks, filed for bankruptcy protection in 1994. Undaunted by those problems, Hillis, whose research has often dealt with artificial intelligence, foresees a future where robots perform household chores and massively parallel computers, such as the Connection Machine, serve as public utilities, to which all homes and business are networked. As he sees it, the only limits on the Connection Machine's power are those imposed by a lack of creative vision for new ways to use the young technology.

Born in Baltimore on September 25, 1956, William Daniel Hillis Jr. is one of the three children of William Daniel Hillis and Argye Idell (Briggs) Hillis. While he was growing up, Danny lived in many different places, for his father was a doctor who traveled around the world studying epidemics. As a youngster, Danny was an avid reader of science fiction, which inspired him to build such things as rockets and robots, forging each creation out of paint cans, light bulbs, and a motor. His interest in science fiction, particularly Robert Heinlein's *Have Spaceship Will Travel*, led him to attend the Massachusetts Institute of Technology (MIT), where he hoped to gain an understanding of human thought processes by studying neurophysiology. An adviser, however, convinced him that he could learn more about the mechanism of thought in the artificial intelligence (AI) lab. Hillis accepted the advice, and in the AI lab he studied such problems as how a baby learned to recognize its mother's face. While an undergraduate at MIT, Hillis demonstrated his ingenuity in computer design by constructing a hand-cranked computer, made of fishing line and ten thousand Tinkertoys, that was unbeatable at ticktacktoe. (The large creation is now housed at the Boston Computer Museum.) His ingenuity also landed him a summer job creating electronic toys for Milton Bradley. Hillis earned a B.S. degree in mathematics, an M.S. in electrical engineering, and, in 1988, a Ph.D. in electrical engineering, all from MIT. For his doctoral dissertation, he designed a revolutionary supercomputer, which he called the Connection Machine.

At the time he developed the Connection Machine, the accepted technology in computing was sequential architecture, in which one microprocessor—some supercomputers had up to four—is used to process all information, even in the most powerful computers. Regardless of their power, microprocessors can process only one piece of information at a time, which means that the speed of the computer is determined entirely by the speed of the microprocessor. Hillis's interest in the human thought process convinced him that sequential architecture was inefficient. While it easily handled simple problems, as a sequential computer was given more information it became slower, or, in effect, dumber—unlike humans, who become smarter with more information.

Although computer chips are thousands of times faster than neurons, the brain is much better and faster at processing certain types of complicated information, such as recognizing words or images. Hillis reasoned that the difference in speed must be due to the difference in structure. "If you try to make the computer smarter by giving it more information, it takes longer to process the answer, so it gets more stupid," Hillis explained to a reporter for *Fortune* (October 13, 1986). "It can take hours to recognize a face. I had this intense feeling that we ought to do better than that. One of the few things we know about the brain is that it has slower components than a computer, but there are more of them. So it must be somehow using them in parallel. That led to the idea of looking at a problem from the beginning as if it were broken into millions of small pieces." Hillis's vision was a parallel architecture, in which, theoretically, millions of microprocessors concurrently process small parts of a problem, much like the brain does. Although so-called massively parallel computers were not a new idea, the conventional wisdom was that such a system was impractical, mainly because of communication and programming difficulties inherent in coordinating all of the chips.

In 1983, with the help of Sheryl Handler, who had earned a Ph.D. in urban studies from MIT, Hillis formed the Thinking Machines Corporation (TMC) to build and market the Connection Machine, with Handler as president and Hillis himself as chief scientist. The name of the company reflects his ultimate goal. "My dream is to make a thinking machine," Hillis has often informed interviewers, "a machine that could be proud of me." "We have deliberately chosen a goal that's hard enough to keep pulling us forward for years to come," he told Gino Del Guercio for an article in *World Monitor* (July 1989). To start the company, Handler gathered a team of experts in artificial intelligence, circuit design, computation, and other disciplines and secured $16 million in backing from venture capitalists. Thinking Machines' first home was a mansion in Waltham, Massachusetts, the ballroom of which was filled with nine powerful computers. In late 1984 it moved to a more conventional office building in Cambridge, Massachusetts.

The toughest hurdle Hillis faced in making the Connection Machine was to build a sort of telephone network through which the thousands of processors could communicate with one another. Eventually, the TMC scientific staff designed a communication system that had more switching capacity that a telephone company. Completed in May 1986, the first Connection Machine contained 65,536 small processors, each with its own small memory. The processors chosen could handle only words of one bit at a time—the industry standard was a processor that could handle thirty-two-bit words—but the Connection Machine was still more than twice as fast and more flexible than other supercomputers. The small processors held the cost down, and the Connection Machine sold for $3 million, compared to $10 million for other mainframes. A computer maker from Connecticut told a reporter for the *Economist* (May 10, 1986) that the Connection Machine was "the most significant single major advance in large-scale computing in several decades." Designed by the architect Maya Lin, the exterior of the exotic-looking computer's five-foot cube was black, with red blinking lights. "[The red lights] have some diagnostic use," Hillis told Doug Stewart during an interview for *Omni* (October 1992), "but basically, who wants to spend his life working on something that looks like a refrigerator?"

Although it was a major breakthrough in computer technology, the first Connection Machine disappointed some industry observers, who pointed to programming difficulties and the fact that each processor lacked sufficient memory to work with optimum efficiency. Because it was a new technology, and because the software that ran on sequential machines did not run on the Connection Machine, users were forced to develop their own software for the new computers. Although writing programs for parallel machines is not inherently more difficult than writing them for sequential machines, programmers were all trained in using the latter, so the development of efficient programs for the Connection Machine was a slow process. Exacerbating the problem was the fact that the Connection Machine did not use Fortran, which was the programming language favored by most scientists and engineers, who are the main users of large computers. (Fortran was soon updated for use with the Connection Machine.) Within a year Connection Machine 2, which uses processors with sixteen times more memory than the original, was unveiled. Although it was an improvement on the first Connection Machine, Connection Machine 2 still failed to generate enthusiasm among some would-be users. Again the major source of disenchantment was the lack of existing programs. While the criticism was not without merit, part of the problem may have been jealousy in the computer world, especially over the amount of publicity and government support given to TMC.

One of the major benefactors of TMC was the Pentagon's Advanced Research Projects Agency (ARPA), which funded parallel computer research in the belief that better computers meant better national security. In addition to awarding millions of dollars ($12 million in 1989 alone) directly to TMC, ARPA also helped researchers test prototypes and buy finished Connection Machines so that they could conduct research on new software. While they were not the only companies to receive ARPA funding, TMC and the Intel Corp. did get the lion's share, with the result that by 1993 the two companies dominated the rapidly growing field. Acting on complaints from other computer makers, the congressional General Accounting Office concluded that while funding the development of the computers themselves was appropriate, "ARPA [did] not appear to be justified in restricting the [subsequent software research] program to only those machines it helped develop." ARPA responded by changing its policies to open the door to more companies.

One of Hillis's objectives for TMC was to advance the science of artificial intelligence, but the advancements in AI that he had hoped to achieve have been slow in coming. Although computers are infinitely more efficient than humans at such tasks as solving complex mathematical problems, tasks that come naturally to humans (such as those involving the senses) are very complicated (sight, for example, requires one-third of the brain's power) and prove difficult for computers. Nevertheless, vision is one area of AI in which substantial progress has been made at the Vision Laboratory at MIT, one of the first purchasers of a Connection Machine. Although the goal of designing a computer that sees as well as humans do has not been achieved, by 1989 a Connection Machine attached to cameras was able to recognize objects, though not as efficiently as humans. It takes humans one-thirtieth of a second to recognize an object, whereas it takes the Connection Machine several minutes. (It would take hours with a sequential computer.) "That's been one of my disappointments," Hillis admitted to Gino Del Guercio for the *World Monitor* article. "It's not made the progress I'd hoped it would, except in some specific areas like vision. But in terms of knowledge or common-sense reasoning, I've been surprised at how little progress there's been. In retrospect, I think I was personally naïve about how difficult common-sense reasoning was. I still have long-term optimism about it, but no time in the next few years will I expect there to be great things in this area." "Right now the science of intelligence resembles astronomy before Galileo invented his telescope," Hillis told the reporter for *Fortune*. "It wasn't a science really. I am like a telescope builder."

The criticisms and disappointments notwithstanding, the Connection Machine irrevocably altered the future of supercomputers, and by May 1989 thirty-five of the machines had been sold at a cost of $2 million to $10 million each. Most of them were bought by research institutions for purely scientific purposes, such as studying earthquakes; by such large companies as Boeing, to design airplanes, and Dow Jones, to analyze the financial markets; and by the Pentagon. The cost of the Connection Machine, while lower than that of other supercomputers, still limited its market. With that in mind, in May 1989 TMC released a scaled-down version, CM-2a, which cost less than $1 million and could use anywhere between four thousand and nine thousand microprocessors.

Over the next several years, the Connection Machine continued to evolve, and in 1991 TMC increased its flexibility by using a much larger microprocessor in the CM-5, which was fitted with thirty-two microprocessors but could be expanded to use sixty-four thousand. Able to process 60 billion operations per second, CM-5 was the fastest commercially available computer in the world. The high-profile buyers of the computer, which cost between $1.5 million and $30 million, depending on the number of chips, included the Sandia and Los Alamos National Laboratories, the Army High Performance Computing Research Center at the University of Minnesota, the University of California at Berkeley, the University of Wisconsin, the oil-services company Schlumberger (which intended to use the machine to interpret seismic data in searching for oil deposits), and American Express (which purchased two to analyze customer buying habits).

By 1991 the computer industry was beginning to accept the fact that parallel technology was the wave of the future and that TMC was leading the pack. "Everybody laughed at first," Hillis told Andrew E. Serwer for *Fortune* (Autumn 1993). "Now competitors are copying us." Thinking Machines realized $65 million in sales in 1991, and in a major concession that TMC was indeed the industry leader, IBM, which had been working on its own parallel technology for years, formed a joint venture with TMC to incorporate parallel technology into IBM computers. In an effort to attract a wider range of users, TMC introduced CM-5 Scale 3 in late 1992. Containing up to thirty-two processors, the Scale 3 was attractive to a new level of users not only because of its relatively low price of $750,000 but also because its simpler design ran better on existing software.

Although Thinking Machines was the country's second-largest supercomputer maker, the company lost $17 million in 1992. The loss can be attributed to federal budget constraints and increased competition. By 1993 TMC had grown to more than five hundred employees, had sales of $90 million, and, with Intel, controlled 50 percent of the parallel computer market, but the company was still struggling and was troubled by inner turmoil. Late in the year, amid reported tension between Hillis and Handler, Harvey L. Weiss, after only seven months on the job, was replaced as CEO, reportedly at Hillis's command, by Richard P. Fishman. There were rumors that Hillis was planning to limit his work with TMC in order to concentrate on different basic research, but he assured Fishman that he would not leave. Handler resigned from the company in April 1994.

Hurt not only by changes in management and setbacks in their development schedule but also by federal cutbacks, competition from companies offering low-end machines for less than $500,000, and a shrinking demand for supercomputers, in August 1994 Thinking Machines announced that it would lay off one-third of its employees and seek bankruptcy protection in the courts. Assessing the situation, most analysts agreed that it was a lack of business acumen, not a lack of technical vision, that caused TMC's problems. Indeed, the technology the company developed has become the industry standard. "The nation set a goal that was clear and specific, and now they've changed the goal, and we're left having made the investment . . . ," Hillis explained to John Markoff of the *New York Times* (August 7, 1994). "We may die, but we didn't fail." Hillis has predicted that the company will adjust to the ever-changing realities of the supercomputer industry by marketing its technology instead of its computers.

Hillis got his start in the AI lab at MIT, and artificial intelligence research has remained a major part of Thinking Machines. His current research is centered on computer evolution—a process by which computers will be able to learn and solve problems on their own, without the aid of programs written by humans. Each computer would essentially write its own programs by learning from its mistakes; bugs, which are inherent in programs written by humans, would thus be eliminated. Learning through its mistakes, the computer would evolve like organisms do, but thousands of generations of computer evolution would take only a few minutes. "The dream," Hillis told Steve Ditlea for *Omni* (December 1990), "is to evolve programs that solve problems we don't know how to solve but merely know how to state."

Thinking Machines' financial problems notwithstanding, Hillis sees a bright future for parallel computing. He is convinced that once people more fully realize the possibilities presented by Connection Machines, the computers will become an integral part of everyone's life. "The limits [of parallel computers] are much more in how we take advantage of this increase in power to do things in a completely different way [than in how fast the computers can be]," he explained to Doug Stewart. "When television first came out, networks televised radio shows with singers standing in front of microphones. Over time, people began to realize they could do things with TV they couldn't with radio; there was a whole new dimension to exploit. Today, many people just use parallel computers to do faster versions of what they did with sequential computers. This will change. . . . I think parallel computers will evolve over the long run into a public utility. Like electricity, your demand for computation fluctuates wildly. A network will tie your desktop computer into a shared Connection Machine somewhere. If you ask your computer a hard question, it will tap into this bigger machine to get the answer quickly." Another advancement envisioned by Hillis is the home robot, which will be able to do housecleaning and other tasks. While the technology for such a machine is within reach, it would be impractical for any one person to have a computer powerful enough to coordinate the tasks required of a robot (including, among other things, vision, motor control, and recognition of objects). If each household tapped into a municipal Connection Machine, however, the cost would become manageable.

Danny Hillis, who is widely known in Cambridge for driving around town in an old fire engine, often wears shorts, T-shirts, and sneakers to his office, which is filled with toys. He and his wife, Pati, adopted newborn identical twins in the early 1990s. In addition to serving as an editor for several scientific journals, Hillis is a member of the science board of the Santa Fe Institute, the advisory board of the *OS Journal of Computing*, and the external advisory board of the Institute for Biospheric Studies. He holds thirty-six United States patents and has been honored with the Association for Computing Machinery's Grace Murray Hopper Award, the Spirit of American Creativity Award, and the Ramanujan Award.

Selected Biographical References: Fortune 114:56 O 13 '86 por; *Newsweek (Access)* 103:52 Fall '84 por; *Omni* 15:101+ O '92 pors; *USA*

Today B p2 Ag 17 '94 por; World Monitor 2:38+ Jl '89 por

Donna Dietrich

Hooks, Bell

Sept. 25, 1952– Writer; poet; educator. Address: 291 West 12th St., New York, NY 10014

The African-American feminist writer Bell Hooks has been referred to on separate occasions as "one of America's most indispensable and independent thinkers" and as "one of the foremost black intellectuals in America today." The author of a dozen books and more than thirty essays, Hooks has focused attention on the myriad forms of racism, from subtle to blatant, in the United States. She has also criticized the way in which the plight of black women has been either ignored or worsened not only by what she has termed the "white supremacist capitalist patriarchy" but, in many instances, by the mainstream feminist movement and the black-liberation struggle. In recent months Hooks has also participated in discussions of those subjects on television and radio programs, in order to ensure that her opinions are heard outside the world of academia. "We are looking at a culture where millions of people don't read or write," she has said. "If I want to get the message out there, I have to use some other format." Far from merely making use of the mass media, she has frequently cited the roles played by television, film, and advertising in perpetuating racism and sexism. Hooks is on the faculty of the English Department at the City College of New York.

Bell Hooks was born Gloria Jean Watkins on September 25, 1952 in Hopkinsville, Kentucky, the daughter of Veodis Watkins, a custodian employed by the postal service, and Rosa Bell Watkins, a homemaker. She has a brother, Kenneth, and five sisters: Sarah, Theresa, Valeria, Gwenda, and Angela. While she was growing up, one interest that her family shared was poetry. Hooks has recalled that when storms caused power outages in her neighborhood, her family would sit in their candlelit living room and stage impromptu talent shows, and during those events Hooks recited the works of such poets as William Wordsworth, Langston Hughes, Elizabeth Barrett Browning, and Gwendolyn Brooks. Her family's love of poetry inspired her to write verses of her own, some of which were published in a local Sunday school's magazine.

Hooks was exposed early on to the racism and sexism that she would make it her life's work to oppose. The southern community in which she grew up was segregated, and she has written that her father held rigid, traditional ideas regarding sex roles. Those influences were offset, however, by the actions of other people with whom she had regular contact. "Though I admired my father," Hooks wrote in *Black Looks: Race and Representation* (1992), "I was more fascinated and charmed by black men who were not obsessed with being patriarchs." Such figures included Felix, "a hobo who jumped trains, never worked a regular job, and had a missing thumb," and her maternal grandfather, Daddy Gus, who "spoke in hushed tones, sharing his sense of spiritual mysticism." As she wrote in *Sisters of the Yam: Black Women and Self-Recovery* (1993), it was Daddy Gus who taught her that "everything in life was a dwelling place for spirits, that one only had to listen to hear their voices."

Hooks's environment was also replete with strong female role models. She wrote in *Sisters of the Yam* that life in her community involved "an ever-present and deep engagement with the mystical dimensions of Christian faith" and that, "despite the sexism of that segregated black world, the world of spirituality . . . was one where black women teachers, preachers, and healers worked with as much skill, power, and second sight as their black male comrades." The accomplishments of those women gave Hooks faith in her own capabilities, and she decided as a young girl that she would be a writer.

After graduating from Crispus Attucks High School, in Hopkinsville, Hooks enrolled at Stanford University, in Stanford, California, from which she obtained a B.A. degree in English in 1973. Three years later she earned her master's degree in the same subject at the University of Wisconsin in Madison. She then embarked on her teaching career, serving as an English instructor and as a senior lecturer in ethnic studies at the University of Southern California, in Los Angeles, where she remained until 1979. In the early 1980s she taught courses in creative writing, African-

American literature, composition, and other subjects at various institutions, including the University of California at Santa Cruz and San Francisco State University. Concurrently, she worked toward her doctorate, which she received from the University of California at Santa Cruz in 1983, having written her dissertation on the works of the African-American novelist Toni Morrison.

In the meantime, Hooks had published a chapbook of poems, *And There We Wept* (1978), and her first full-length work, *Ain't I a Woman: Black Women and Feminism* (1981), a book she had begun writing when she was nineteen years old. For those projects the author had adopted the pseudonym Bell Hooks. She explained to Rebecca Carroll for *Elle* (December 1994) that one of her great-grandmothers, a Native American, was named Bell Hooks and that her own use of the name is "about celebrating female legacies." The lower-case spelling Hooks prefers, she said, is "about ego: What's in a name? It is the substance in my books, not who is writing them, that is important."

Ain't I a Woman took its title from the refrain in a speech delivered in the nineteenth century by the black feminist Sojourner Truth. In her book, Hooks challenged certain ideas regarding the place of black women in the feminist and black-liberation movements. With respect to the latter, Hooks castigated the unabashedly sexist treatment of women on the part of male black leaders, but she also described such behavior as being indicative of the internalization, begun during the years of slavery, of American patriarchal values. "Clearly," she wrote, "black men need to employ a feminist analysis that will address the issue of how to construct a life-sustaining black masculinity that does not have its roots in patriarchal phallocentrism." In addition, she found fault with the theory, put forth in studies by Daniel Patrick Moynihan and others, that black men have been psychologically castrated by a lack of economic opportunity, a situation that has in turn led to the predominance of matriarchs in the black community. That theory is unsound, Hooks claimed, because the word "matriarch" suggests power that most black women—whether or not they are heads of their households—do not possess and because black males have never viewed their masculinity as being determined solely by their ability to act as breadwinners.

Hooks documented the way in which white advocates of women's rights in the late nineteenth and early twentieth centuries not only excluded black women from their platforms but also convinced white supremacists that suffrage for white women would help strengthen institutionalized racism. She cited the contributions to freedom that were made, in spite of such exclusion, by black feminists, among them Truth, Mary Church Terrell, and Frances Ellen Watkins. She also attacked what she felt to be the arrogance of present-day white feminists, who have invited black women to join "their" struggle and thereby revealed their belief that "the word woman is synonymous with white woman, for women of other races are always perceived as Others, as dehumanized beings who do not fall under the heading woman." At the conclusion of *Ain't I a Woman*, Hooks declared, "I have . . . heard black women express a belief in feminism and eloquently critique the women's movement, explaining their refusal to participate. . . . Only a few black women have rekindled the spirit of feminist struggle that stirred the hearts and minds of our nineteenth-century sisters. We, black women who advocate feminist ideology, are pioneers. We are clearing a path for ourselves and our sisters. We hope that as they see us reach our goal—no longer victimized, no longer unrecognized, no longer afraid—they will take courage and follow."

The critical response to *Ain't I a Woman* was largely positive. "This exciting book reveals [Hooks] to be a lucid, persuasive writer and an extraordinary penetrating and original thinker," Mary Biggs wrote in *Library Journal* (December 1, 1981). "Her wide-ranging analysis of sexist and racist oppression of black women in America . . . leaves no group uncriticized, no assumption unchallenged, no doctrine unravaged, no sacred cow ungored. . . . Her book should be widely read, thoughtfully considered, discussed, and finally acclaimed for the real enlightenment it offers for social change." A writer for *Choice* (April 1982), while holding that Hooks's "simplified assertion that nineteenth-century black women were more feminist than their twentieth-century counterparts is never carefully demonstrated," nonetheless found *Ain't I a Woman* to be "a provocative, readable, and worthwhile study."

Hooks expanded on many of the arguments put forth in *Ain't I a Woman* in her next book, *Feminist Theory: From Margin to Center* (1984). That work called for a new direction for the women's movement, toward a recognition of the diversity of women's backgrounds and experiences. Such recognition would be achieved, according to Hooks, by an acknowledgement that race and class play as big a role as gender in the subordination of poor and nonwhite women. In *Ms.* (October 1985), Paula Giddings took exception to one of the conclusions in *Feminist Theory*: "[Hooks] writes, 'Revolutionary ideology can be created only if the experiences of people on the margin who suffer sexist oppression . . . are understood, addressed, and incorporated.' Understood, addressed, incorporated by whom? By her terms of address, Hooks, perhaps unwittingly, has assigned proprietary rights to the same 'privileged' women she criticizes for their narrow perspective. . . . Hooks fails to make an important distinction: women on the margin of this society are not necessarily on the margin of feminist aspirations or activism." That criticism aside, Giddings found the premise of *Feminist Theory* to be "especially provocative."

In *Talking Back: Thinking Feminist, Thinking Black* (1989), Hooks recounted some of her personal experiences as examples of ways that readers might overcome the psychological injuries inflicted by a racist and sexist culture and apply to their daily lives informed thinking about race, sex, and sexual orientation. *Yearning: Race, Gender, and Cultural Politics* (1990) comprised essays in which Hooks analyzed, from a black and feminist perspective, films, rap songs, and advertisements. Evaluating *Yearning* for the *Women's Review of Books* (September 1991), P. Gabrielle Foreman noted the wide range of subjects covered as well as the unpredictable nature of the author's opinions. "Inevitably," Foreman wrote, "a reader will cheer through one essay and scowl through another." Writing in *New Statesman* (November 30, 1990), Barbara Burford pronounced *Yearning* to be "a formidable step forward on the way to creating a black cultural criticism."

Breaking Bread: Insurgent Black Intellectual Life (1991) is a collaboration between Hooks and the African-American writer, educator, and activist Cornel West. *Breaking Bread* consists of five chapters penned alternately by Hooks and West, two sections in which one writer interviews the other, and two "dialogues" between the authors. The book outlines the forces motivating and the challenges facing black intellectuals and addresses the connection between scholarship and social activism. "*Breaking Bread*'s fundamental contribution," Patricia Hill Collins wrote in *Signs: Journal of Women in Culture and Society* (Autumn 1994), is that "it not only theorizes about how a transformed intellectual power might fuse deep moral concern and political engagement—it actually does it."

The title of Hooks's seventh book, *Black Looks: Race and Representation*, refers both to the way African-Americans are depicted in film, television, advertisements, and literature and to what Hooks feels is the need for blacks and others to "see" the continuing hold of racism on the American imagination and thereby allow their minds to be "decolonized," to use her term. She was especially critical of what she called the "commodification" of blacks—the profit-driven use of black images to generate and satisfy a public hunger for "different" cultural experiences, a practice she saw as a modern version of colonization and a reflection of a desire simply to consume other cultures. In Hooks's opinion, the appropriation of such images should be, but rarely is, accompanied by an openness toward the values—and not merely the symbols—of the peoples being represented. For example, she faulted Jennie Livingston's film *Paris Is Burning*, the videos of the pop-music icon Madonna, and the ads of the clothing manufacturer Benetton for reducing African-American culture to spectacle.

Black Looks met with qualified praise from most reviewers. "The twelve essays are uneven in their analytical complexity and originality of thought," D. Soyini Madison wrote in the *New York Times Book Review* (February 28, 1993), adding that many of the book's passages nevertheless "provide insight into race, representation, and dominance." Itibari M. Zulu observed in the *Multicultural Review* (March 1993), "At times Bell Hooks's essays are a bit preachy (or overly politically correct), but she redeems herself by revealing a witty personal experience related to the sermon that flows through [most of] her narrative." Evaluating the book for *Library Journal* (July 1992), Beverly Miller offered a favorable opinion: "Hooks continues to produce some of the most challenging, insightful, and provocative writing on race and gender in the United States today."

Sisters of the Yam: Black Women and Self-Recovery was the culmination of several projects undertaken by Hooks. In the 1980s she had established a support group for black women after realizing that many of her female African-American students, regardless of their economic backgrounds, were suffering psychologically as a result of either physical abuse or "fear of being unmasked as the inferiors of their white peers." She had also begun writing a monthly column, addressed to black women, in *Zeta* magazine. Both the column and the support group were called Sisters of the Yam, after a passage in Toni Cade Bambara's novel *The Salt Eaters*. Hooks considered the yam to be "a life-sustaining symbol of black kinship and community," for "everywhere black women live in the world, [they] eat yam. It is a symbol of [their] diasporic connections. Yams provide nourishment for the body as food, yet they are also used medicinally—to heal the body."

The theme of healing runs through *Sisters of the Yam*. One crucial step in the healing process, Hooks wrote, is to do away with "the myth of the 'strong' black woman," according to which every African-American female is "somehow an earthy mother goddess who has built-in capacities to deal with all manner of hardship without breaking down, physically or mentally." Adherence to that myth, she claimed, obscures and contributes to the fact that black women have often turned to drugs and alcohol rather than acknowledge their need for viable support systems. Hooks called for communication and bonding among black women, for the good of individuals but also for the political and social gains of the group as a whole. "When wounded individuals come together in groups to make change, our collective struggle is often undermined by all that has not been dealt with emotionally," she wrote. Finally, *Sisters of the Yam* was intended as a celebration of the bonding that had already taken place among black women.

Reviewing *Sisters of the Yam* for *Library Journal* (July 1993), Kathleen E. Bethel noted, "Readers trying to unlearn racism and sexism will respect Hooks for politicizing the self-recovery movement. Highly recommended." In the *Women's Review of Books* (October 1993), Vanessa Northington Gamble granted that black women "know how to survive" and "how to struggle" but added, "Bell Hooks reminds us . . . that we must break out of 'struggle mode.' We have to develop habits of caring, loving, and flourishing. Thank you, Bell, for starting us on that journey."

The year 1994 saw the publication of two works by Hooks, *Teaching to Transgress: Education as the Practice of Freedom* and *Outlaw Culture: Re-*

sisting *Representations*. In *Teaching to Transgress*, Hooks sought to apply to American society the philosophy of the progressive Brazilian educator Paulo Freire, who has advanced the idea that students must develop "critical consciousness" by becoming participants in, and not mere receivers of, their own educations. Like *Yearning* and *Black Looks*, *Outlaw Culture* is comprised of essays on a wide array of subjects, including the writings of Camille Paglia and Kate Roiphe, contemporary films, rap music, and perceptions of beauty. In his review of *Teaching to Transgress* and *Outlaw Culture* for the *New York Times Book Review* (December 18, 1994), Jerome Karabel expressed the opinion that the first-named book was "often marred by a disconcerting reliance on pop psychology." He noted, however, the "jarring character of [the book's] insights" and declared that both works force readers "to confront the political undercurrents of life in America."

The writer's rapid rate of publication continued in the following year. *Art on My Mind: Visual Politics* comprises essays on contemporary art, focusing on the discord between the traditional Western aesthetic and the aims of black artists. *Killing Rage: Ending Racism* is also a collection of articles, which, while not setting forth "a comprehensive plan for achieving the subtitle's promise," display Hooks's "sensitivity to the intersection of race, class, and gender," in the opinion of a reviewer for *Publishers Weekly* (July 17, 1995). In 1996 the publishing company Henry Holt will release *Black Is a Woman's Color*, the first of a two-volume set of Hooks's memoirs. The second book will be titled *Cat Island Woman*.

In addition to her books, Hooks has contributed dozens of essays to such publications as *Callaloo*, *Emerge*, *Essence*, the *Utne Reader*, and *Catalyst*. She also founded a literary magazine, *Hambone*, with the poet Nathaniel Mackey, whom she met while she was an undergraduate at Stanford and with whom she lived for more than ten years. Her second poetry collection, *The Woman's Mourning Song*, was published in 1993. In 1985 Hooks taught African and Afro-American studies and English at Yale University, in New Haven, Connecticut. In 1988 she was an associate professor of women's studies and American literature at Oberlin College, in Oberlin, Ohio, and in 1994 she accepted the post of distinguished professor of English at the City College of New York, where she currently teaches. Later in the same year, she received the Writer's Award, which brought with it a cash prize of $105,000, from the Lila Wallace-Reader's Digest Fund.

Bell Hooks stands five feet, three inches tall and has short black hair and brown eyes. She divides her time between an apartment in the Greenwich Village section of New York City and a house in Oberlin. She loves the color red, deep shades of which can be found in the furniture and art in her two homes. She has described herself as being "into" Buddhism and "the spiritual experience." In her interview with Rebecca Carroll for *Elle*, Hooks said, "My idea of a delicious time is to read a book that is wonderful. And then I have the usual passions: romance, fashion—I am totally into shoes. People are constantly calling me Imelda Marcos 2d. . . . I'm a big fashion girl. And I'm really into art and deeply into culture. I am passionate about leading my life with a certain quality of elegance and grace. But the ruling passion of my life is being a seeker after truth and the divine. That tempers everything else."

Selected Biographical References: Elle p78+ D '94 por; Contemporary Authors vol 143 (1994); Hooks, Bell. Talking Back: Thinking Feminist, Thinking Black (1989)

Imagine

Howard, Ron

Mar. 1, 1954- Actor; filmmaker. Address: Imagine Entertainment, Inc., 1925 Century Park East, Los Angeles, CA 90067

NOTE: This biography supersedes the article that appeared in *Current Biography* in 1979.

"What I like most are entertaining movies with a fairly wide appeal," the filmmaker Ron Howard said in 1985. "A lot of directors start out making wonderful, interesting, and also very entertaining and accessible movies. Then they become a little more ambitious or more uneasy, and as their pictures become real personal, they also become less entertaining and crowd-pleasing. I want to guard against that happening to me." Howard has so far avoided such a fate, as demonstrated by the popularity of many of his character-driven movies, among them *Splash* (1984), *Cocoon* (1985), *Parenthood* (1989), and, most recently, *Apollo 13* (1995).

Prior to his career as a film director, Howard had been imbedded in the public consciousness as the embodiment of boyhood innocence, thanks to his roles in two immensely popular television sitcoms: in the 1960s, beginning when he was only six years old, he portrayed Opie Taylor on *The Andy Griffith Show*, and in the following decade he played the teenage Richie Cunningham on *Happy Days*. While those shows live on in syndication, Howard has managed to carve a new reputation for himself as a director of movies and also as an executive producer, of such films as *Clean and Sober* (1988). In addition, he is the cochair, with Brian Grazer, of Imagine Entertainment, which since 1986 has produced films by Howard and others.

Ronald William Howard was born on March 1, 1954 in Duncan, Oklahoma, the older of the two sons of Rance Howard, an actor, director, and writer, and Jean Howard, an actress. His brother, Clint, is also an actor. The family's theatrical connections led to Howard's first acting credits. When he was eighteen months old, he appeared in his first movie, *Frontier Woman* (1956), and at the age of two he was seen on stage in a summer-stock production of *The Seven Year Itch*, directed by his father at the Hilltop Theatre in Baltimore. On television, the medium with which he would be primarily associated for many years, he turned up in an episode of *Kraft Television Theatre* and on an installment of *The Red Skelton Show*, both in 1956. Howard has recalled that acting was never "pressed" on him but was, rather, a pastime he fell into naturally when he was a toddler: during the time that Rance Howard directed a production of *Mister Roberts*, Ronny (as he was then known) memorized some of the dialogue and, as a game, played Ensign Pulver to his father's Mister Roberts. "When I started [acting] with other people," Howard told Edwin Miller for *Seventeen* (March 1975), "it was just a matter of playing the game with them, something I did for fun." In 1959 he was cast in the CBS teleplays *Black December*, on *Playhouse 90*, and *Barnaby and Mr. O'Malley*, on *General Electric Theatre*, and in the feature film *The Journey*, a drama starring Yul Brynner and Deborah Kerr and set during the 1956 Hungarian revolt.

After Howard's family moved to California, he was hired as a regular on *Playhouse 90*. "In those days TV was still live," Rance Howard explained to Dwight Whitney for *TV Guide* (December 9, 1978). "The town was so awed by a five-year-old who could be depended upon not to fall apart in mid-scene that he did twenty-five shows in a row." Howard's later television credits included appearances on *The Danny Kaye Show* and roles in episodes of *The Many Loves of Dobie Gillis*, *The Danny Thomas Show*, *Dennis the Menace*, *Dr. Kildare*, *The Fugitive*, *Gomer Pyle*, *The FBI*, *The Big Valley*, and *I Spy*. Among his film credits in the 1960s were roles in *Five Minutes to Live* (1961; rereleased in 1966 as *Door-to-Door Maniac*), *The Music Man* (1962), *The Courtship of Eddie's Father* (1963), and *Village of the Giants* (1965).

Meanwhile, the television producer Sheldon Leonard, who had seen Howard's performance in *Barnaby and Mr. O'Malley*, had cast the young actor in *The Andy Griffith Show*, which began its eight-year run on CBS on October 3, 1960. The gentle comedy was set in the sleepy town of Mayberry, North Carolina, and centered on the daily lives of the widowed sheriff Andy Taylor (Griffith), his young son, Opie (Howard), Aunt Bee (Frances Bavier), who served as Andy's live-in housekeeper and Opie's surrogate mother, and Barney Fife (Don Knotts), Andy's inept deputy. The sensitively drawn scenes between Andy and Opie were inspired in part by Howard's relationship with his father, who helped to write some of Opie's lines. On the set, Rance Howard became a mediator of sorts between his son and the other actors, keeping the adults from teasing the boy too much and also instilling in Ronny the idea that acting was a thing to be taken seriously.

Howard's parents intervened in other ways to ensure that his being a child star did not have a negative effect on other aspects of his life. They saw to it that his contracts included clauses exempting him from promotional tours, and when he was not working, they enrolled him in public schools, so that he would be able to interact with other children his age. "In school I was always a novelty at first," Howard told Edwin Miller. "People got very jazzed up about the idea of having a kid actor in class. That would blow over in a couple of weeks, and then I was able to blend right in." At Burroughs High School in Burbank, Howard made the basketball team, and he turned down acting assignments so that he would not miss games. "I didn't work for nine months," he has recalled, "and that's when I learned I missed acting."

Following the termination of *The Andy Griffith Show*, in 1968, Howard landed parts in episodes of several network series, including *Judd for the Defense*, *Gunsmoke*, and *Lassie*. His second continuing role was as the son of a police detective, played by Henry Fonda, in the drama *The Smith Family*, which aired from January 1971 to mid-1972. On the big screen, Howard was featured (along with his brother) as a member of a pioneering Western family in *The Wild Country* (1971), and he shared credits with Patricia Neal and Cloris Leachman in the horror film *Happy Mother's Day, Love George* (1973).

The latter film was released in the same year as Howard's first major movie hit: *American Graffiti*, the director George Lucas's low-budget depiction of life in a small northern California city in 1962. The action, set during one night in late summer, focuses on four recent high-school graduates, two of whom (Howard and Richard Dreyfuss) struggle with decisions that will affect the rest of their lives. A critical as well as commercial success, *American Graffiti* received five Academy Award nominations, including one for best picture. It also helped to usher in a period in film and television that was characterized by nostalgia for the supposedly uncomplicated era of the late 1950s and early 1960s.

Howard contributed further to that trend with his role on the long-running ABC sitcom *Happy Days*. The pilot for that series was "Love and the Happy Day" (also starring Howard), a 1972 installment of the weekly comedy anthology *Love, American Style*. First telecast in January 1974, *Happy Days* was set in Milwaukee during the 1950s and focused initially on the misadventures of the clean-cut teenager Richie Cunningham (Howard). Most episodes showed Richie at home with his family or plotting escapades with his high-school pals at the local hamburger shop, where a jukebox played rock-'n'-roll songs of the period. Although the show struggled in the ratings for a time, Laurence Laurent, writing in the *Washington Post* (February 24, 1974), predicted that it would eventually thrive, not due to its "hokey format," but rather because of "the skill of the oldest young professional performer in television, Ron Howard." Instead, the show's popularity increased along with its concentration on one of the supporting characters, the auto mechanic and high-school dropout Arthur Fonzarelli (Henry Winkler), better known as Fonzie or the Fonz. A leather-jacketed tough guy and consummate ladies' man, the Fonz served as Richie's mentor and as the personification of "cool." By the start of the 1975–76 season, Winkler had become the star of *Happy Days* in everything but name, and his character had grown into perhaps the biggest popular-culture icon of the 1970s.

While Howard admitted to feeling "awkward" at first over the show's change of focus, he came to regard the situation philosophically, telling Judy Klemesrud of the *New York Times* (June 22, 1977), "Maybe if Henry Winkler and I hadn't liked each other, and if we were two different people, there would have been problems. But we're all on the series to make it as successful as possible, and it benefits us all that Fonzie is tremendously popular." Winkler, in turn, paid tribute to Howard, as quoted by Dwight Whitney in the *TV Guide* article: "Ron has been acting for twenty years, and what he doesn't know about his craft is hardly worth knowing. . . . Creatively, the man's a volcano."

Indeed, Howard took on a number of projects during the run of *Happy Days*. He starred in a variety of challenging television film dramas, including *The Migrants* (1974), in which he won praise for his portrayal of a fruit picker struggling against poverty, and *Locusts* (1974), which found him playing a young man who returns from Navy flight school to his home in Montana after his friend is killed in a training accident. On the big screen, he took the part of an impressionable Texas farm boy in *The Spikes Gang* (1974), also starring Lee Marvin; appeared in the elegiac western *The Shootist* (1976), John Wayne's last film; and starred in the grade-B car-chase film *Eat My Dust* (1976).

The last-named film was significant for Howard not because of its large profits, its critical reception (which was dismal), or even his enjoyment of his role (he has claimed that he "hated" the film), but because it provided him with the opportunity to establish himself as a filmmaker. At the age of about fifteen, he had become "obsessed," to use his word, with making films, and he had begun shooting movies with a Super-8 camera. He pored over the copy of *The Cinematographer's Manual* given to him by Henry Fonda, and, following his graduation from high school, in 1972, he enrolled in the film program at the University of Southern California, which he left after a couple of years on the theory that he could learn about directing films "on the job." He began to question the directors with whom he worked, including George Lucas, about their techniques, and he eventually met the producer and director Roger Corman, who had given Francis Ford Coppola, Martin Scorsese, and others their first directing opportunities. Initially, Corman was interested in Howard only as an actor, seeing in him "a [1970s] Jimmy Stewart," as he told Dwight Whitney. After viewing a sixteen millimeter film Howard had shot, however, he agreed to help the aspiring filmmaker direct his own feature, stipulating that Howard first star in the Corman-produced *Eat My Dust* and that Howard's own film also be a car-chase comedy.

As a result, Howard's first project as a director, based on a screenplay he cowrote with his father, was *Grand Theft Auto* (1977), in which he also played the lead. The movie received respectable reviews, with a writer for *Variety* (June 15, 1977) declaring that Howard had "directed with a broad but amiable and well-disciplined touch." "It clearly would not have been what I would have chosen as my first film," Howard said in an interview with Todd McCarthy for *Film Comment* (May/June 1984). "As an actor, I felt that my strength would be scenes, character, and trying to help people evolve performances, and *Grand Theft Auto* was hardly a performance picture. But it turned out to be a great experience for me." The movie proved to be worthwhile in other ways as well. Shot in twenty-two days for $602,000, it grossed some fifteen million dollars and as a consequence opened the door for Howard to direct three television movies: *Cotton Candy* (1978); *Through the Magic Pyramid* (1981); and *Skyward* (1981), which featured Bette Davis.

Howard's last major acting credit to date was the sequel to *American Graffiti*, B. W. L. Norton's *More American Graffiti* (1979), which, in contrast to the unanimous praise accorded its predecessor, received disparate critical responses. Janet Maslin of the *New York Times* (August 17, 1979) described it as so "grotesquely misconceived . . . that it nearly eradicates fond memories of the original," but Charles Champlin of the *Los Angeles Times* (July 29, 1979) characterized the effort as "an uncommonly evocative trip back to our common past. . . . On the must-see list." Critics were similarly split regarding Howard's next directing venture, the comedy *Night Shift* (1982), about two men (Henry Winkler and Michael Keaton) who manage a ring of prostitutes out of a New York City morgue.

Gary Arnold of the *Washington Post* (July 30, 1982) called Howard's directing "delightfully ingenious and astute," and David Denby of *New York* (September 13, 1982) agreed, citing Howard's "excellent comic timing" and crediting him with the "sense to give his actors some room to breathe in." Kathleen Carroll, however, panned the picture in the New York *Daily News* (July 30, 1982), concluding dourly that "Howard's directing career may go to the dogs if he continues to choose such shoddy projects as *Night Shift.*"

It was with the fantasy/romantic comedy *Splash*, starring Daryl Hannah, Tom Hanks, and John Candy, that Howard established his reputation as a director to be reckoned with. In that film, Hanks played a New York City greengrocer who falls in love with a mermaid (Hannah). "The mermaid story has always been a negative thing, the love you can never have," Howard told Jim Jerome for *People* (April 9, 1984). "We flipped that, and it came out fresh." Most critics agreed with that assessment. David Ansen wrote in *Newsweek* (March 12, 1984) that Howard had "fashioned . . . a romantic comedy that is truly romantic and truly comic, a deft blend of hip satire and fairy-tale charm," and Rita Kempley of the *Washington Post* (March 9, 1984) called the movie "a triumph."

Howard's next film was *Cocoon*, a fantasy about members of a Florida retirement community who are magically rejuvenated after swimming in a pool inhabited by beings from another world. Although he had reservations about taking on a project similar in some respects to *Splash* and to other films featuring benign aliens (among them *Close Encounters of the Third Kind* and *ET*), Howard was so intrigued by the characterizations of the senior citizens that he agreed to work on the film and proceeded to embellish the scripted roles of the retirees. Working with a cast of veterans that included Jessica Tandy, Maureen Stapleton, Hume Cronyn, Wilford Brimley, Don Ameche, and Jack Gilford, Howard gave his actors freedom to improvise.

The result was, in the opinion of Kathleen Carroll of the New York *Daily News* (June 21, 1985), a "poignant, wonderfully buoyant film." "The concept is fraught with perils," David Ansen noted in *Newsweek* (June 24, 1985). "Mawkishness and cutesy condescension loom around every corner. . . . but Howard has the rare quality of tact. . . . He has the grace and good sense not to force pathos out of scenes already brimming with emotional content. *Cocoon* is crowded, not with high-tech space battles and cliff-hanging plot twists, but with humanity." There were those, such as Stanley Kauffmann in the *New Republic* (July 15–22, 1985), who dismissed the film as "silly," but Lawrence O'Toole of *Maclean's* (July 1, 1985) was in the majority in his belief that *Cocoon* was "tenderhearted and beautifully structured." For Howard, O'Toole wrote, "youth is merely a capacity of the imagination—the ability to dream. In *Cocoon* he uses that ability extraordinarily well, making the audience feel ageless."

Perhaps surprisingly, given the wide praise accorded his two previous projects, Howard's social comedy *Gung Ho* (1986), about a Japanese auto company's opening a factory in a small Pennsylvania town, drew little attention. By contrast, his fifty million-dollar mythical fairy tale *Willow* (1988) attracted considerable interest, although probably not of the kind he had sought. Virtually all of the notices for *Willow* lambasted its plot as a mishmash of elements "patched together from tatters of the Brothers Grimm, Saturday morning cartoons, and the New Testament," as one critic phrased it. That reviewer went on to deride the movie as "anemic."

Howard bounced back, in the opinion of many, with his next film, *Parenthood*. Wanting, as he put it, to immerse himself in a project that would be "smarter, tougher, a little more painful in places" than his earlier efforts, he worked with the writers Lowell Ganz and Babaloo Mandel and the producer Brian Grazer to develop a film about the trials and joys of family life. The four men, who among them had fifteen children, based their script largely on their own experiences. "The four of us would sit there talking about how we felt as kids, as parents, how our kids perceive us," Howard told Kim Masters for an article in *Premiere* (August 1989). "It was kind of therapeutic. It was cleansing. But we were always looking for a comedy nugget." At the same time, he added, they wanted the movie to convey the message that having a family is a worthwhile experience. "It is fraught with little traps, the potential for hurt feelings, and even disastrous predicaments," Howard said. "But it's what human beings do, and it feels good."

David Ansen of *Newsweek* (August 7, 1989) described the resulting film as a comedy "[whose] laughs are rooted in pain, disappointment, and exasperation." With a large cast that included Steve Martin, Mary Steenburgen, Dianne Wiest, Keanu Reeves, and Jason Robards, *Parenthood* touched on issues ranging from teen sex to the extent to which parents are responsible for the actions of their grown children. "Howard's touch hasn't been this sure since *Splash*," Ansen declared. While a reviewer for the London *Observer* (January 14, 1990) concluded that "the film poses serious questions about the responsibilities of parents and then proceeds to provide glib, evasive, and dishonest answers," a writer for *Rolling Stone* (August 24, 1989) expressed "surprise" that "a comedy directed by Ron (Opie) Howard and loaded to bursting with gurgling infants, bratty kids, horny teens, and parents who can't cope" was both "heartfelt and howlingly comic" and "spiced with risk and mischief."

The next three movies directed by Howard received mixed reviews. For *Backdraft* (1991), a story about firefighters, Howard had his actors, among them Kurt Russell, William Baldwin, and Donald Sutherland, undergo training in the field. The film won praise for its fire-fighting scenes and performed well at the box office, but critics were reserved in their overall assessment. "*Backdraft* has some of the raw filmmaking excitement that has been missing from Howard's recent work," Owen Gleiberman wrote in *Entertainment Weekly* (May 31, 1991). "Yet," he continued, echoing the thoughts of other critics, "this movie, too, is conventional."

As he revealed to Meredith Berkman of *Entertainment Weekly* (April 1, 1994), Howard intended his 1992 epic romance *Far and Away*, about a young Irish couple (Tom Cruise and Nicole Kidman) who immigrate to America in the nineteenth century, to be "almost fairy-tale-ish, a family fable." While critics agreed that he had produced just such a story, they were divided on its value. Julie Salamon of the *Wall Street Journal* (May 21, 1992) thought *Far and Away* offered an "enjoyably old-fashioned vision of American history," but Manohla Dargis of the *Village Voice* (June 9, 1992) called it a "staggeringly retro" film in which the cast "reenact[ed] the great fiction that everyone in the promised land volunteered for service." Unlike the majority of Howard's other films, *Far and Away* was a box-office failure, earning slightly less than the sixty million dollars it cost to shoot.

Preparatory to filming *The Paper* (1994), a comedy-drama about tabloid journalism starring Michael Keaton, Robert Duvall, Glenn Close, and Marisa Tomei, Howard spent a considerable amount of time at the offices of the *New York Post* and the New York *Daily News*. Jack Mathews of *New York Newsday* (March 18, 1994), while conceding that the film "got a lot of the newsroom nuts and nuances right," concluded that *The Paper* was "about the newspaper business in the same way the Road Runner cartoons are about wildlife in the American Southwest." On the other hand, Jami Bernard, in the *Daily News* (March 18, 1994), praised the picture for "perfectly captur[ing] the exciting claustrophobia of New York City tabloid journalism."

Whereas reviewers had disagreed on the merits of *Backdraft*, *Far and Away*, and *The Paper*, they were unanimous in their praise for Howard's *Apollo 13*, a drama about the jeopardized 1970 American space mission. "*Apollo 13* unfolds with perfect immediacy, drawing viewers into the nail-biting suspense of a spellbinding true story," Janet Maslin wrote in the *New York Times* (June 30, 1995). "Better even than Mr. Howard's sure hand with this fascinating material is his film's unexpected restraint. *Apollo 13* understands the difference between movie bravado and real courage, and it celebrates the latter in inspiring ways that have almost gone out of style." Maslin went on to declare that the film—which starred Tom Hanks, Kevin Bacon, and Bill Paxton and featured the filmmaker's mother and brother—was "far and away the best thing Mr. Howard has done."

Among the directors Howard has credited with influencing him most is George Lucas, who was, in Howard's words, "important in [his] understanding the difference between shooting television and shooting features," in part because Lucas was "so much more interested in detail than the television directors [he] had worked for." The actor Brian Dennehy, whom Howard directed in *Cocoon*, praised the filmmaker to Stephen Farber of the *New York Times* (June 16, 1985): "Ron prepares as well as any director I've ever seen, but he doesn't take himself that seriously. He's very easygoing on the set, and yet he can be ruthless in the editing. With many directors it's the opposite, and that's when you're in trouble." Howard "has seen absolutely everything that can possibly happen on a set, because the man started doing it three months before he was born or something like that," Tom Hanks told Jim Jerome for the *People* article. "Ron's the king."

While Howard is no longer identified solely with his characters on *The Andy Griffith Show* and *Happy Days*, he has retained one vestige of his former roles: the image of the quintessential "nice guy," a perception reinforced by Dennehy and others with whom he has worked. "I went through a period where I thought I should rebel," Howard confessed to Peter Gethers of *Esquire* (December 1986). "When I gave an interview, I'd act tough, and I'd be sure to swear." That stance, he admitted, lasted "about a week. It really wasn't me." By his own account "a little shy," Howard has said that his acting experience gave him "a certain amount of self-confidence." The blue-eyed, red-haired Ron Howard married Cheryl Alley, his high school sweetheart, on June 7, 1975. The couple live quietly in Cos Cob, Connecticut, with their four children: daughters Bryce, Jocelyn, and Paige and son Reed.

Selected Biographical References: Entertainment W 216: 22+ Ap 1 '94 pors; Esquire 106: 256+ D '86 pors; Film Comment 20:40+ My/Je '84; Newsweek 114:56+ Ag 28 '89 pors; N Y Times p21+ Je 16 '85 por; TV Guide 26:12+ D 9 '78 por; Aylesworth, Thomas G. Hollywood Kids (1987); International Motion Picture Almanac, 1995; International Television and Video Almanac, 1994; Who's Who in America, 1995

Huizenga, H. Wayne
(HY-zeng-uh)

Dec. 29, 1939- Corporation executive; entrepreneur. Address: c/o Huizenga Holdings, 200 S. Andrews Ave., Fort Lauderdale, FL 33301

"I enjoy building something good and having a successful product and making money," the entrepreneur H. Wayne Huizenga has said. The hero of a real-life Horatio Alger story, in his early twenties Huizenga worked as a garbage-truck driver. Striking out on his own, he started a one-man trash-collection operation that, within a decade, had grown into a highly profitable enterprise providing employment for several dozen people. In 1968, combining his business with three other companies, he created Waste Management, Inc., which,

Blockbuster Entertainment Corp.

H. Wayne Huizenga

when he resigned as president and chief operating officer in 1984, having decided to retire, ranked as the largest trash haulage and disposal business in the world. Bored with inactivity, he began buying properties in Fort Lauderdale, Florida, his adopted hometown, and soon became a major player in the city's economy.

In 1987 Huizenga and two partners acquired a nineteen-store chain called Blockbuster Video. As chairman of the board and chief executive officer of Blockbuster Entertainment Corp., he used his skills as a master dealmaker to help transform the business into the world's largest video-rental chain and, in the words of one reporter, into "the company that is to videos what McDonald's is to hamburgers." With revenues of more than $2 billion in 1993, its share of the market has reached 20 percent, and it has reportedly grown larger than the next 550 video-rental chains combined. After Blockbuster's merger with the media giant Viacom, in 1994, Huizenga was named vice-chairman of Viacom and chairman of a new entity called the Blockbuster Entertainment Group. In 1995 he left Blockbuster to become the chairman and chief executive officer of Republic Waste Industries, a relatively small solid-waste collection business. As the owner of the Miami Dolphins football team, the Florida Marlins baseball team, and the Florida Panthers hockey team, Huizenga is the only person in the United States whose holdings include three professional sports clubs.

The first child of Jean (Riddering) Huizenga and G. Harry Huizenga, a cabinetmaker turned builder, Harry Wayne Huizenga was born on December 29, 1939 in the Chicago suburb of Evergreen Park, Illinois. Pat Jordan, who interviewed him for the *Sporting News* (February 14, 1994), described Huizenga's upbringing as "strict and disciplined, with old-fashioned, workingman's values." On Sundays the Huizenga family, which belonged to the doctrinally rigorous Dutch Christian Reformed Church, spent many hours in church; at home, reading the comic pages of the newspaper was forbidden. Even on weekdays, as a youth Harry Wayne Huizenga had to sneak out of the house to attend movies or dances. In early 1953 Huizenga and his family moved to Fort Lauderdale, Florida, where his father hoped to take advantage of a real-estate boom. Shortly thereafter, his parents divorced, and Jean Huizenga was awarded custody of Harry and his eleven-year-old sister, Bonnie. (The Huizengas remarried in 1978.)

Around the time that Harry Wayne Huizenga graduated from the Pine Crest School, a private high school, where he had played center on the football team, he began to identify himself as Wayne. After working as a bulldozer driver, spending three semesters as a student at Calvin College, in Grand Rapids, Michigan, in 1957-58, and serving briefly in the United States Army, he returned to Florida, where one of his father's friends hired him to drive a garbage truck in Pompano Beach. In 1962, heeding the advice of his father, that "you can't make any real money working for someone else," and following in the footsteps of his paternal grandfather, a Dutch immigrant who had owned a garbage collection business in Chicago called Huizenga & Sons, he started his own company, with a single truck and five hundred dollars' worth of accounts acquired from a Broward County, Florida garbage collector. He collected trash from 2:00 A.M. until noon and then canvassed the neighborhood door-to-door to solicit new business. "I didn't know anything about the business," he told Pat Jordan during the interview for the *Sporting News*. "I just worked hard and gave good service. If I was late picking up the garbage, the customer would call me at home to complain about the driver. *I* was the driver."

Huizenga had launched his business at a time of rapid population growth in southern Florida, and his industry and aggressiveness soon began to pay off. Aided also by Florida's right-to-work laws and spared the hassling that many trash-collection operations in the Northeast suffered at the hands of organized-crime syndicates, he steadily extended his reach. By the late 1960s the Southern Sanitation Service, as he had named his business, was operating twenty garbage trucks, with drivers covering routes along Florida's east coast as far south as Key West, and Huizenga had become a millionaire. In 1968 he merged his company with three Chicago firms to establish Waste Management. Two of the three, Richard Sandomir reported in a profile of Huizenga for the *New York Times Magazine* (June 9, 1991), were "successors" to Huizenga & Sons, and one of those two was headed by one of Huizenga's cousins by marriage, Dean L. Buntrock.

Buntrock entered their partnership with the idea of creating a nationwide sanitation company, and Huizenga took on the task of making the deals that would translate that vision into a reality. Their plan, Huizenga told Richard Sandomir, entailed "selective acquisitions" of small businesses familiar to them. In 1972, a year after Waste Management made a public offering of its stock, Huizenga bought ninety competing trash-collecting companies in just nine months, an accomplishment that sometimes required his presence in three cities on a single day. "It was during this frenzied time that he developed some of the key strategies and skills that he would later use to run his other companies," Richard Sandomir noted. Waste Management grew by other means as well, by positioning itself, for example, to fill the need—generated by the plethora of new government regulations aimed at maintaining specified standards of environmental quality—for technologies capable of handling toxic waste. By the early 1980s it had become the biggest company of its kind in the world, with contracts to collect garbage in such far-flung places as Saudi Arabia and Argentina and with annual revenues in excess of $1 billion.

During the years that Huizenga served as the vice-chairman, president, or chief operating officer of Waste Management, the company paid millions of dollars in fines or settlements for such infractions as bribery, harassment of competitors, intimidation of customers, and illegal dumping and storage of waste materials. In 1976 the Securities and Exchange Commission named Huizenga in a charge stating that the company had made improper political contributions. The charge was dropped after Huizenga, while neither admitting nor denying guilt, signed a consent decree according to which he agreed to stop making such payments. Years later, Gail DeGeorge reported in the January 22, 1990 issue of *Business Week* that Huizenga had come to regret signing the decree.

Weary of commuting each week between Waste Management's headquarters in Oak Brook, Illinois and his home in Fort Lauderdale and bored with a job in which he had become more or less bound to his desk, Huizenga retired in 1984. He remains a major stockholder in the company, which is now known as WMX Technologies. (According to an article by Anita Sharpe for the *Wall Street Journal* [September 30, 1994], as of mid-1994 he owned 4 million shares, valued at $100 million.) Becoming restless after just a few weeks of retirement, Huizenga began to acquire hotels, office buildings, and small businesses, especially those associated with such unorganized and unglamorous service industries as pest control, lawn care, insurance, bottled water, auto-parts cleaning, and dry cleaning. His relentless pursuit of additional holdings prompted one of his associates to describe him as a "deal junkie." He has said of his modus operandi, as quoted in David Whitford's book *Playing Hardball* (1993), "Keep putting the pressure on the competitor. Hopefully someday he'll go out of business and we'll get all of his business. That's really what we're after." By the end of 1986, Huizenga had bought more than one hundred businesses, which together generated $100 million in annual revenues. Before long Huizenga Holdings, as he called his parent company, "so dominated Fort Lauderdale that a typical resident could pass an entire day using nothing but his services," in the words of Pat Jordan, in his *New York Times Magazine* (December 5, 1993) profile of Huizenga. Currently, Huizenga's properties in Florida include warehouses, office buildings, shopping centers, airplane hangars, resorts, a helicopter delivery service, and a company that conducts drug tests at the behest of employers.

By his own admission, Huizenga had never owned a VCR, rarely patronized movie theatres, and had no interest in the video-rental business when, in early 1987, John J. Melk, then an executive at Waste Management, persuaded him to check out a Dallas, Texas-based chain of eight video-rental stores and eleven franchised establishments known as Blockbuster Video. His visit showed Huizenga that he had been mistaken in believing that video-rental stores were nothing more than dingy outlets for pornography. The Blockbuster stores were large, clean, well run, well stocked, and brightly lit establishments staffed by neatly dressed, personable clerks. Having made a great deal of money by renting out such things as Dumpsters and portable toilets ("If I rent something, basically I'm selling the same thing over and over," he has explained), Huizenga immediately recognized Blockbuster's built-in profitability and its potential for growth. Within a week he, Melk, and Donald F. Flynn, another Waste Management executive, bought a nearly 35 percent interest in Blockbuster for $18 million. When David P. Cook, Blockbuster's founder, left the company a few months later, Huizenga took on the title of chairman. Inspired by the marketing model presented by the McDonald's chain, he and his partners began to acquire additional video-rental stores. As he has done throughout his career, Huizenga, who eschews the accumulation of debt, opted to finance his purchases by issuing stock or using cash generated by operations.

In expanding Blockbuster Video, Huizenga maintained the qualities that he had admired in the company's original stores. Unlike the typical neighborhood video-rental outlet, a cramped facility that seldom offered more than a thousand titles, each conveniently located Blockbuster store covered between six thousand and eight thousand square feet and stocked at least eight thousand different titles, including instructional, exercise, and sports videos, video games, and many movie classics as well as recent releases—but no films rated X or NC-17. Advertising itself as "America's Family Video Store," Blockbuster even removed crude language and depictions of violence and sex from the trailers shown in its stores.

Although the company retained ownership of many of its stores, Blockbuster's expansion received big boosts from the entrance of such franchisees as United Cable Television Corp., which opened one hundred stores in 1988 and 1989. By the end of 1991, Blockbuster had more than two thousand outlets in the United States and overseas, and its income had surpassed that of its closest ninety-nine competitors combined. In 1993 revenues reached $2.2 billion, according to an article by Don L. Boroughs in *U.S. News & World Report* (May 16, 1994). In the United States alone, Huizenga reported in 1993, 50 million people held Blockbuster video-rental cards worldwide, and 10 million videos were rented from Blockbuster every week. By the latter half of 1994 Huizenga had built what had become Blockbuster Entertainment Corp. into an empire of more than thirty-nine hundred video stores in the United States, Canada, Puerto Rico, Mexico, Chile, Venezuela, the United Kingdom, Italy, Austria, Spain, Guam, Australia, and Japan, with a new store opening every twenty-four hours. The company also signed development agreements with franchises in Argentina, Brazil, and Israel.

Huizenga has consistently dismissed predictions that as technology improves—and, in particular, as fiber-optic cable replaces coaxial cable in homes, thus permitting residents to get movies on demand—the video-rental business will wither. In *Billboard* (May 25, 1991), Paula Parisi quoted him as saying that "pay-per-view is available now, and the customer does not watch it." "I don't think they're going to watch it when they have ten more channels or twenty more channels," he maintained. In a conversation with David Whitford in 1992, he said, "The pie is big enough that you can share it. The industry's still growing at a billion dollars a year, and they still sell 10 million VCRs a year. . . . I'm convinced that five years from now, we'll have more customers in our stores than we do now."

Nevertheless, in the early 1990s Huizenga began to diversify Blockbuster, by such means as selling (as well as renting) movie videos, acquiring the music-store chains Sound Warehouse and Music Plus, forming a partnership with Philips Electronics to sell compact discs, and selling music videos and tapes in a worldwide chain of stores owned jointly with the Virgin Retail Group of London. Blockbuster properties currently include more than 570 music stores. In 1993 Huizenga paid $140 million for a 54 percent stake in Spelling Entertainment Group, which holds the rights to such television shows as *Dynasty* and such films as *Rambo* and its sequels. Later that year Blockbuster gained a 78 percent ownership of the entity formed through Spelling's acquisition of Republic Pictures Corp. It also secured a 49.9 percent stake in a chain of indoor playgrounds known as Discovery Zone and, most recently, joined with Sony and Pace Entertainment in plans to build and operate concert amphitheaters in the United States and Europe. In collaboration with IBM, Blockbuster technicians have devised a machine to produce compact discs on demand in the Blockbuster stores (a project that initially aroused vehement opposition in the record industry) as well as a mechanism to produce copies of video games for customers who want titles that have been checked out by other people. In an article for *Time* (October 11, 1993), Cathy Booth and Jeffrey Ressner reported that Huizenga planned to transform Blockbuster outlets by the year 2000 into "one-stop family centers" that would house virtual-reality parlors and children's playgrounds as well as offer film and music videos, tapes, and compact discs. "We're going to be your neighborhood entertainment experience, your neighborhood Disney," they quoted Huizenga as saying.

Beginning in 1990, Huizenga extended his grasp in the sphere of entertainment to the arena of professional sports, by purchasing, through Huizenga Holdings, a 15 percent share in the National Football League's Miami Dolphins and a 50 percent share in Joe Robbie Stadium, in Dade County, Florida. (He later gained total ownership of the team and the stadium.) The stadium then served as the site of only occasional concerts and the Dolphins' home games. With the goal of increasing patronage by filling the stadium eighty-one additional days a year with baseball fans, Huizenga spent $10 million to improve the field and to create such amenities as an adjoining picnic area. Then, representing Miami and armed with, among other funds, $25 million that he had raised by selling 10 percent of his Blockbuster stock, he competed against ten other cities and in 1991 made what proved to be the successful bid—$95 million in cash—for one of two new National League franchises. The Florida Marlins played their first season in 1993.

At the time of his triumph in establishing Florida's first professional baseball team, spectator sports, with the possible exception of football, had never held much interest for Huizenga. Vying for the franchise was simply the logical next step after investing in Joe Robbie Stadium. "The way to think about this is as a real-estate play . . . ," he told Joseph Nocera during an interview for *GQ* (June 1992). "I'm competitive, but I want to win on the bottom line as well as on the field." "I'm a virgin in baseball," he admitted to Pat Jordan for the *New York Times Magazine* article, "but I don't see it as different than any other business. I won't lose money on the Marlins. Money is how you keep score." In 1992, inspired by the realization that "South Florida is home to millions of transplanted northeasterners and Canadians," in his words, Huizenga sought and won (at a price of $50 million) a franchise for one of two new National Hockey League expansion teams and thus became the owner of the Florida Panthers.

After purchasing Joe Robbie Stadium, Huizenga spent more than $40 million to buy hundreds of acres between Miami and Fort Lauderdale, as the first stage in launching a project that was christened Blockbuster Park by Huizenga but became familiarly known in southern Florida as "Wayne's World." A planned sports and entertainment complex that was described by Larry Rohter in the *New York Times* (April 4, 1994) as potentially "the biggest new tourist attraction to arise in Florida since Disney World," it aroused a great deal of controversy, with Florida environmentalists and homeowners in nearby communities bitterly opposing the project and various public officials and other local residents supporting it.

Plans for Blockbuster Park were scrapped in 1994, after Blockbuster Entertainment Corp. was purchased for $7.6 billion by Viacom, the media giant that had grown even larger three months before through its acquisition of Paramount Communications Inc. "These are very tough times for me," Huizenga told Blockbuster shareholders at the meeting at which they approved the sale, as quoted by Diane Mermigas in *Advertising Age* (October 3, 1994). "I personally do not want to sell the company or merge the company. I'd like nothing better than to continue doing what I've been doing." "But this is in the best interest of our stockholders," he added, according to a Blockbuster spokesman, and he reportedly had to fight back tears as he recalled his seven years with Blockbuster. According to Diane Mermigas, Huizenga held a 3 percent interest (worth about $500 million) in Viacom, where he was given the title of vice-chairman; he was also named chairman of the Blockbuster Entertainment Group, which was created after the merger.

Huizenga told reporters that he intended to leave Viacom within a year. "I can't work for someone else," Diane Mermigas quoted him as saying. "I am not an employee; I'm an entrepreneur." He suggested that he would probably acquire companies (by his own account, the nature of their products or services was immaterial to him) with sales between $300 million and $500 millon and then try to double their revenues. "I'd rather build a company than manage one," he commented. In May 1995, in a partial fulfillment of his prophecy, Huizenga gave up his positions at Blockbuster to assume those as chairman and chief executive officer at Republic Waste Industries, Inc., which, at that time, owned nine landfills in six states and had annual revenues of $50 million. He invested $27 million of his own money in Republic and moved its main office from Atlanta to Fort Lauderdale. According to an article by Anita Sharpe for the *Wall Street Journal* (May 23, 1995), Huizenga has "bold plans" for the company.

During an interview with Steve Berkowitz for the *Washington Post* (April 30, 1991), Charles Lewis, a managing director at Merrill Lynch and Huizenga's investment banker, described Huizenga as having "an unquenchable thirst for challenges and learning." "When he starts to learn about a business, he's very much like a young student who comes across an area of study and becomes consumed by the passion of learning about it," Lewis said. "He immerses himself so totally that within a year or two, he's competing with people who have been doing it for years." Berkowitz quoted Elliott Barnett, a Fort Lauderdale lawyer, as saying that "the more complex the situation, the more [Huizenga] gets going. It isn't the money that drives him. . . . It's the challenge of dealing with problems." Dean Buntrock told Richard Sandomir that during internal company discussions, Huizenga "always liked to take the adversary position on an issue. He'd take both sides and argue them well. That forces you to think through a decision." Noted for his seemingly limitless energy, Huizenga routinely works twelve to fourteen hours a day and, when traveling for business reasons, flies (in one of his three planes) at night, to avoid wasting time. His personal worth has been reported as $700 million or $800 million.

H. Wayne Huizenga's most distinctive physical feature may be his ice-blue eyes, which, because of the sometimes high intensity of his gaze, some of his employees have referred to as "Wayne's lasers." He has a reputation for "shrewdness, toughness, and smarts, for being a real businessman's businessman," in the words of David Whitford, and also for being "gracious, confident, and brutally honest," as Mark Vancil wrote in the *Sporting News* (April 19, 1993). With Huizenga, Vancil added, "there are no hidden agendas, no measured words." As a host in his Joe Robbie Stadium box, Pat Jordan reported in his *Sporting News* profile, Huizenga is "almost deferential" to all his guests, including reporters from local newspapers, and behaves "as if their comfort superseded his own."

Among Huizenga's many honors are the entrepreneur of the year award from the Wharton School of the University of Pennsylvania, in 1989; the Silver Medallion Brotherhood Award from the Broward Region National Conference of Christians and Jews, in 1990; the CEO of the year bronze award from *Financial World* magazine, in 1991 and 1993; and a Horatio Alger Award, in 1992; also in 1992 Yale University selected him as a Gordon Grand Fellow. The many civic groups of which he has been an active member include the Florida Chamber of Commerce, the Broward County Economic Development Board, and the board of governors of the Friedt School of Business and Entrepreneurship at Nova University, in Fort Lauderdale. His community activities also include service on the board of advisers of the Salvation Army, as the chairman of the Florida Council on Economic Education, and as the vice-president and director of the Boys Club of Broward County.

From his first marriage, which ended in divorce during the 1960s, Huizenga has two adult sons; from his second marriage, on April 17, 1972, to the former Martha ("Marti") Jean Pike, a onetime secretary, he has a stepson and a stepdaughter. He and his wife were named outstanding philanthropists for 1990 by the Greater Broward/Fort Lauderdale chapter of the National Society of Fund Raising Executives. The couple live in Fort Lauderdale in a Spanish-style house on spacious grounds bordered by canals on two sides and by the New River on another. The walls of their billiard room are decorated with photographs of Huizenga with five United States presidents and Generals Colin Powell and H. Norman Schwarzkopf and framed magazine covers featuring Huizenga's portrait. Huizenga and his wife also own a vacation home in North Carolina. H. Wayne Huizenga's avocations are playing golf and collecting vintage automobiles. "It's a business investment," he told Pat Jordan, while speaking of his 1931 Dusenberg, 1937 Rolls Royce, and other cars during an interview for the *New York Times Magazine*. "They should appreciate in value. I couldn't have fun if I wasn't making a profit."

Selected Biographical References: Bsns W p47+ Ja 22 '90 por; Chicago Tribune VII p1+ Ag 27 '95 por; NY Times Mag p22+ Je 9 '91 pors, p54+ D 5 '93 pors; Sporting N 217:13+ F 14 '94 pors; Wall St J B p1+ S 30 '94; Whitford, David. Playing Hardball: The High-Stakes Battle for Baseball's New Franchises (1993); Who's Who in America, 1995

ERGO

Humphry, Derek

Apr. 29, 1930– Organization official; social activist; writer; journalist. Address: c/o ERGO, 24829 Norris Ln., Junction City, OR 97448-9559

The "ultimate civil liberty," according to Derek Humphry, arguably the leading spokesperson in the United States for voluntary euthanasia for the terminally ill, is "the freedom to select one's own manner of dying without interference from others, but with help if we choose." Since 1980, when he founded the Hemlock Society, the British-born Humphry has campaigned nationwide for the passage of legislation that would permit physicians, in compliance with strict guidelines, to help incurably ill patients end their lives. In becoming a full-time crusader for what has been termed legalized aid-in-dying or self-deliverance, he abandoned a career in journalism that spanned some thirty-five years, including about fifteen years as a reporter for the London *Sunday Times*. In 1993, a year after resigning from the Hemlock Society, which he had served for twelve years as executive director, he founded the Euthanasia Research and Guidance Organization. Known as ERGO, its goal is to ensure that, once physician- assisted suicide becomes legal, the laws are properly administered.

Humphry is the author or editor of ten books, five of which—among them the prizewinning *Because They're Black*—address racial issues. He attracted widespread attention in the late 1970s with the publication of *Jean's Way*, his account of the carefully considered suicide of his first wife and his role in that event. *Final Exit* (1991), his best-selling, detailed instruction manual on voluntary euthanasia, triggered impassioned debate nationally about the ethics of his position. Nearly a million copies have been sold worldwide. Writing in *Harper's Magazine* (April 1994), Anne Fadiman, who has reported extensively on the right-to-die movement, credited *Final Exit* as the primary force behind the "monumental shift in popular thinking about suicide—about what is taboo and what is not"—that has occurred in the last few years in the United States. "I enjoy being part of social progress, combating the forces of darkness," Humphry has said.

Derek Humphry was born on April 29, 1930 in Bath, in the county of Somerset, England, to Royston Martin Humphry and Bettine (Duggan) Humphry. When he was very young, his parents separated. His mother, a sometime model, settled in Australia, and his father, a traveling salesman, got custody of Derek and his older brother, Garth. Soon afterward the boys were placed in a series of foster homes. Humphry did not see his mother again until 1953, when, during a brief visit to England, she awakened in him the idea that they would become close. After she returned to her adopted country, however, he never heard from her, and his attempts to track her down ended in failure. "I didn't think I would lose her again," he told Erica Goode during an interview for *U.S. News & World Report* (September 30, 1991), adding, "I'm someone who likes to tie up loose ends." (In 1992 he traced her to a remote part of Australia, only to find that she had died six months earlier.)

In 1939, after the outbreak of World War II, Humphry became one of the thousands of British children who, to protect them from bombings, were evacuated from urban areas. He was sent to live with a couple who farmed in the Mendip Hills, near Bath. By his own account, the extensive reading that he did on his own and the BBC news broadcasts to which he listened avidly each day during the war years constituted an important part of his education. After the war ended, the fifteen-year-old Humphry quit school and got a job in London, as an editorial messenger for the *Yorkshire Post*. At sixteen, after reading *The Origin of Species by Natural Selection*, in which the British naturalist Charles Darwin introduced his revolutionary views on evolution, Humphry's already-weakening belief in the existence of God vanished altogether, and he turned his back on all religions, including Anglicanism, the denomination in which he had been raised.

In 1946 Humphry got a job in southwestern England as a cub reporter with the *Bristol Evening World*. His five-year association with that newspaper was interrupted by his service in the British army, from 1948 to 1950. Between 1951 and 1955 he worked as a junior reporter with the *Manchester Evening News*. Continuing to advance in his career in journalism, he became a reporter for the *Daily Mail* in London (1955–61), deputy editor of the *Luton News* (1961–63), and editor of the *Havering Recorder* (1963–67). As home affairs correspondent of the London *Sunday Times* (1967–78), he specialized in issues and events involving immigration, race relations, civil liberties, and the fighting in Northern Ireland.

During his stint at the *Sunday Times*, Humphry produced six books, the first five of which were published in the United Kingdom but not in the United States. *Because They're Black* (1971), which he wrote with Gus John, won the Martin Luther King Memorial Prize in 1972 for its contribution to racial harmony. *Police Power and Black People* (1972), which Humphry has described as "an outright attack on the London police for failing to combat racism in their own ranks" and which was adopted as a textbook at some universities, was followed by *Passports and Politics* (1974), cowritten by Michael Ward. *The Cricket Conspiracy* (1976), a short book that Humphry wrote for the National Council for Civil Liberties, is an account of the trial of Peter Hain, an antiapartheid demonstrator who had been charged with conspiracy. *False Messiah* (1977) is about Michael de Freitas, also known as Michael X, a Black Power leader in Great Britain during the 1960s.

Jean's Way, Humphry's sixth book, which he wrote at the suggestion of and with Ann Wickett, his second wife, was published in England in 1978. The book describes the events that followed the discovery in late 1972 by his first wife, the former Jean Edna Crane, of a lump in one of her breasts, and her subsequent mastectomy. Less than a year later, the Humphrys learned that the cancer had spread to her bones. Despite aggressive treatment, Jean's condition deteriorated, and at times she experienced severe pain. Having witnessed the agony that her mother had endured before dying of lung cancer, she "resolved with a vengeance that such a fate would never befall her," Humphry reported in *Jean's Way*. One day she said to him, "Derek, I simply don't want to go on living like this. . . . I want you to do something for me so that if I decide I want to die, I can do it on my own terms and exactly when I choose. . . . I want you to promise me that when I ask you if this is the right time to kill myself, you will give me an honest answer one way or another, and we must understand . . . that I'll do it right at that very moment. You won't question my right and you will give me the means to do it." Humphry responded that if their positions were reversed, he knew he would make the same request. "I rebelled at the thought of Jean's ever dying," he recalled, "and a part of me strongly resisted being an accomplice; however, when the request for help in dying meant relief from relentless suffering and pain, and I had seen the extent of this agony, the option simply could not be denied. . . . And certainly Jean deserved the dignity of selecting her own ending." Humphry promised his wife that he would honor her wish.

By early March of 1975, Jean's bones had become so weakened by cancer that one of her ribs cracked when she bent over one morning. Her doctors told Humphry that she would not survive much longer. Upon awakening on March 29, Jean found that she could no longer move her neck. "Is this the day?" she asked Humphry. "I panicked . . . ," he reported in *Jean's Way*. "It was the most awful moment of my life. However, I had to answer, 'Yes, my darling, it is.'" The Humphrys spent the next few hours reminiscing about their twenty-two-year marriage. In the afternoon, at an hour of her own choosing, Jean drank a cup of coffee that Humphry had laced with a powerful mixture of two prescription drugs that he had carefully stored for months after obtaining them from a physician friend of his. She soon lost consciousness, and fifty minutes later she died. (Years later Humphry assisted in the suicide of Ann Wickett's ninety-two-year-old father, who was suffering from congestive heart failure. He has also participated in an act of what is known as passive euthanasia: his brother's death, in 1986, followed the disconnection, at Humphry's request, of the mechanical support systems that had kept him alive after he suffered irreversible brain damage during surgery.)

During the week in 1978 that *Jean's Way* reached bookstores in Great Britain, a documentary about Jean Humphry's life and death aired on London Weekend Television. For days afterward, London newspapers presented front-page articles about the manner of her death, and an Associated Press account appeared in hundreds of newspapers worldwide. In the following weeks Humphry was interviewed on many British radio and television programs. "I was amazed at the response to my book," Humphry told E. Robert Sinnett, Rodney K. Goodyear, and Valarie Hannemann during an interview for the *Journal of Counseling and Development* (June 1989). "I was staggered . . . that this dear little book which was a love story, a memoir, created a national furor."

Meanwhile, because, according to English law, helping anyone to commit suicide is a crime punishable by up to fourteen years in prison, the office of the London public prosecutor began an investigation into Jean's death and pressed Humphry to reveal the name of the physician who had given him the drugs. Although he unhesitatingly gave the police a statement describing his role in his wife's suicide, he refused to identify the doctor. The prosecutor eventually decided that there was insufficient evidence to charge Humphry with a crime. By that time—mid-summer of 1978—Humphry and Ann Wickett, an American whom he had married in 1976, had settled in California, where Humphry had gotten work as a features writer with the *Los Angeles Times*. In 1979 he became the London *Sunday Times*'s roving correspondent in North America, a job he held until 1981.

As had happened in England, the publication of *Jean's Way* in the United States in early 1979 generated a great deal of interest and public debate. Humphry appeared as a guest on such television programs as *Good Morning America*, the *Mike Douglas Show*, and *Donahue*, and he was deluged, as he had been in England, with letters from people who had witnessed the suffering of a terminally ill loved one (or were currently ministering to such an individual), including a few letters from people who had helped a relative or friend commit suicide. Many of the writers wanted to know what drugs Jean had taken and how they could obtain them, and they asked questions about the law, religion, insurance, and other matters as they related to suicide.

During an interview that was recorded in 1979 for the television program *60 Minutes*, the broadcast journalist Mike Wallace asked Humphry what action he might take if *A Guide to Self-Deliverance*, a booklet published in England a few months before by a group called EXIT, were not also published in the United States. Humphry blurted out that he might form an organization that would address issues surrounding assisted suicide. He had actually been nursing that idea for a while, and the possibility that many *60 Minutes* viewers might interpret his response as a statement of intent spurred him to proceed. At a news conference held at the Los Angeles Press Club in 1980, Humphry announced the establishment of the Hemlock Society, which takes its name from the poison that the Greek philosopher Socrates used to kill himself in 399 B.C. Cofounders with Humphry were Ann Wickett, Robert S. Scott, a lawyer and physician, and Gerald A. Larue, a professor of biblical history at the University of Southern California who has also taught courses on death and dying. The society was funded initially by Humphry's royalties from *Jean's Way*, and for some time it operated out of the garage of Humphry and Wickett's house in Santa Monica, California.

In addition to publishing newsletters and books, the Hemlock Society's principal activities have been producing educational videos, conducting research, and organizing conferences, "all with the intention of raising consciousness about the right of terminally ill persons to choose to die in a manner of their choice," in Humphry's words. The society maintains computerized records of every reported mercy killing in the United States since 1920. Advice-giving about lethal drugs has been confined to recommendations of reading material.

In its infancy the Hemlock Society attracted primarily elderly women. With the advent of the AIDS epidemic, it drew increasing numbers of young men. At the end of 1985, the society had thirteen thousand members, only about 5 percent of whom, according to a study conducted around that time by demographers at the University of California at Los Angeles, had terminal illnesses. By 1992 membership had grown to fifty-seven thousand, and eighty-six autonomous chapters had been established in the United States. "The thing just took off," Gerald Larue told Mark O'Keefe for the *Oregonian* (November 1, 1994). "Of course, it was because of Derek and his tremendous energy." Humphry, according to Larue, "became the best-informed person in North America, and maybe the world, . . . [on the issue of] the right to die with dignity and the morals involved with it."

One product of Humphry's exhaustive research on euthanasia is *The Right to Die: Understanding Euthanasia* (1986), a wide-ranging examination of the subject that he wrote with Ann Wickett. According to their preface, *The Right to Die* constitutes "an attempt to explain the complexities of the most controversial issue of the decade against the historical, cultural, and legal background." In the *New York Times Book Review* (September 14, 1986), Earl E. Shelp judged the book "interesting to read but not intellectually convincing." "On the whole . . . ," he complained, citing a shortcoming also noted by other reviewers, "the authors do not provide the promised critical analysis of the moral and legal questions surrounding euthanasia." The strength of the book, he wrote, lay in "the numerous accounts of the conditions and circumstances of terminally ill people who elected to avoid some of the suffering of dying. These stories are sensitively told, eliciting in the reader an identification with the actors and a sympathy for their travail."

Humphry had compiled similar accounts earlier, in *Let Me Die Before I Wake* (1981). Moreover, in the course of describing various suicides in that book, he had offered explicit information about the dosages of the prescription drugs used. (Revised twice, *Let Me Die* has sold 130,000 copies.) His presentation of such material had aroused heated discussion in the media. But in both duration and intensity, those disputes were to pale in comparison with the controversy that followed soon after the publication by the Hemlock Society in 1991 of *Final Exit: The Practicalities of Self-Deliverance and Assisted Suicide for the Dying*.

Humphry wrote *Final Exit* because he decided that the time had come for him to take "a less philosophical, more pragmatic stance" toward euthanasia in his articles and books. "This is the scenario," the text begins: "you are terminally ill, all medical treatments acceptable to you have been exhausted, and the suffering in its different forms is unbearable. Because the illness is so serious, you recognize that your life is drawing to a close. Euthanasia comes to mind as a way of release." A few paragraphs later Humphry advised, "If you consider God the master of your fate, then read no further. Seek the best pain management available and arrange hospice care."

In subsequent chapters, Humphry discussed ways of finding a doctor who supports euthanasia, the legal implications of helping someone to die, the importance of telling close friends or relatives about one's plans, and matters regarding life insurance policies. He pointed out the drawbacks of most means of suicide and the benefits of relying on an overdose of certain drugs. He also explained ways of obtaining effective drugs and the proper way to store them, listed lethal dosages of common prescription drugs, and spelled out precisely how to administer them.

Final Exit attracted little notice until, several months after its publication, an article about it appeared in the *Wall Street Journal*. Features that aired soon after on television news programs brought it to the notice of people nationwide, and the first printing of forty-one thousand copies quickly sold out. On August 18, 1991 *Final Exit* topped the *New York Times Book Review*'s hardcover "Advice, How-to, and Miscellaneous" list, and it remained on the list for several months. To date, more than five hundred thousand hardcover copies have been purchased in the United States and Canada, and the book has been translated into eleven languages.

In a favorable essay about *Final Exit* for *Nature* (August 15, 1991), an anonymous writer observed that "as the average age of the population increases, the abstract debates of ethicists about informed consent and of physicians about the duty to heal will come face to face with realities and indignities of incapacitating illness that in an earlier age would have claimed its victims swiftly. The 'ethic' of using technology to prolong life when life is ebbing should give way to the ethic of individual choice, including the right of physicians to choose to assist in dying." In the *New York Times* (August 14, 1991), the columnist Anna Quindlen offered a similar view: "Advances in medical technology have left some of us more afraid of dying than of death. . . . Sometime in the future, faced with terminal illness, I may feel so bereft of strength, purpose, stamina, and the will to live that I may want to know what constitutes a lethal dose of Seconal. And if that day comes, whose business is it, really, but my own and that of those I love? . . . Instead of worrying about [the contents of *Final Exit*], we should look for ways to insure that dignified death is available in places other than the chain bookstore at the mall."

"Let's face it," Mary R. Mallison, a registered nurse who edits the *American Journal of Nursing*, declared in that publication (September 1991): "The popularity of *Final Exit* is largely a response to inadequate resources. Those who know what's clinically possible believe that very few people would choose voluntary euthanasia if they had access to appropriate care. . . . Too many dying people . . . will never experience the proper relief of symptoms or the passionate advocacy of hospice nurses." She suggested that it was not only a fear of suffering or of "clinicians who believe they must not only resuscitate, but resurrect" that arouses in people the desire to control their manner of dying, but also depression and the fear that "the cost of one's final illness will impoverish or otherwise burden the survivors."

Among the deeply religious, *Final Exit* was denounced for implying that the individual, rather than a higher creator, is supreme. In the *Human Life Review* (Summer 1992), Maria McFadden labeled Humphry a "demagogue of death" who "offer[s] 'solutions' that trivialize dying." "His work allows no discussion of the human areas touched on when dealing with death: emotions, psychology, religion and metaphysics, the fallibility of human nature, and the importance of the law for protection of humans, even from themselves," she wrote. Many critics of *Final Exit* predicted that the information it provided would propel depressed people—particularly teenagers and the elderly—to kill themselves. "Even if only one teenager is now helped to suicide, Derek Humphry will have a lot to answer for," the physician and bioethicist Leon R. Kass wrote in *Commentary* (December 1991), in an article in which he condemned *Final Exit* as "evil" and as "an exquisite model of modern rationalism gone wrong." Raising what is known as the slippery-slope argument, Kass maintained that sanctioning assisted suicide will inevitably lead to society's acceptance of involuntary euthanasia and ultimately to the sorts of atrocities that were perpetrated by the Nazis. "The partisans of 'right to die' and the partisans of 'cut the costs' . . . are incubating a deadly outcome for the vulnerable, the elderly, and the powerless," he warned.

Humphry has countered that such abuses would not be possible in a democratic nation. "If the electors ever vote into power a Nazi-like government, then the consequences would be disastrous for the healthy and the sick alike," he wrote in the *Humanist* (March/April 1988). He has also pointed out that depressed people already have at their disposal many means of suicide and that information about lethal doses of prescription medication has appeared for decades in books readily available in stores and libraries. "Suicide as such should be prevented whenever possible," he told Timothy Appleby during an interview for the *Toronto Globe and Mail* (December 7, 1994). "I would campaign against suicide for the elderly, or the disabled, or mentally ill. That's . . . morally wrong."

In addition, Humphry has rejected the contention that legalizing doctor-assisted suicide would irreparably compromise the relationship of trust that exists between physicians and their patients. "It would inspire greater confidence, because the physician would be seen as capable of this final act of compassion," he has said. Moreover, as he has learned from many doctors and nurses, euthanasia in various forms is already practiced in hospitals and elsewhere, although few medical professionals have acknowledged that fact publicly. Legislation, he has asserted, would simply codify and regulate such deeds. (Initiatives to legalize doctor-assisted suicide were defeated by voters in Washington State in 1991 and in California in 1992. A similar measure was passed by a bare majority of voters in Oregon in 1994, but a court ruling has blocked its implementation.) Humphry has criticized the pathologist Jack Kevorkian, who has assisted nearly a score of people to end their lives by means of his "suicide machine," for not only failing to support organized legal-reform efforts but also for ridiculing such campaigns and thus provoking backlashes in some states.

"Having the idea to start Hemlock, laying out the blueprint for the organization, and drawing together a multitude of kindred spirits over twelve years has been the crowning achievement of my life," Humphry wrote in the *Hemlock Quarterly* (April 1992), in announcing that he would be retiring from the position of executive director of the Hemlock Society in August 1992. His resignation followed a period of dissension among the society's board members, which was precipitated by Humphry's acrimonious separation from Ann Wickett in 1989 and their divorce in 1990, events that unfolded in the glare of the public spotlight. (Wickett committed suicide in 1991.)

Derek Humphry has served as secretary and treasurer (1983–84), president (1988–90), and director (1992–94) of the World Federation of Societies for the Right to Die, and he has edited the federation's newsletter (1979–84 and 1992–94). The author most recently of *Dying with Dignity: What You Need to Know About Euthanasia* (1992) and *Lawful Exit: The Limits of Freedom for Help in Dying* (1993), he is currently writing a history of the euthanasia movement and an autobiography that he has entitled *Seesaw*. Humphry, who has retained his British citizenship, works in a small office next to his house, which rests on a hill near Junction City, in western Oregon, a short distance from Eugene. His property overlooks a reservoir, where he enjoys sailing his twenty-one-foot boat. His other main avocational interest is gardening. Humphry married the former Gretchen Crocker in 1991. From his first marriage, he has three sons, Clive, Edgar, and Stephen, the last of whom was adopted and is of mixed-race parentage.

Selected Biographical References: N Y Times Mag p46+ D 8 '91 por; Oregonian A p1+ N 1 '94; People 33:76+ Mr 12 '90 por; Toronto Globe and Mail A p10 D 7 '94 por; U S News 111:88+ S 30 '91 por; Contemporary Authors new rev vol 41 (1994); Humphry, Derek. Jean's Way (1979)

Ice Cube

1970– Rap artist; actor. Address: c/o Priority Records, 6430 Sunset Blvd., Hollywood, CA 90028

Priority Records

Voicing the rage of the underclass with searing conviction and rhetorical flair while also articulating a militant political agenda, Ice Cube has become one of the best-selling musical artists of the 1990s. He is the quintessential angry young man of rap, the musical component of hip-hop culture that was first heard on the streets of the South Bronx, New York, in the late 1970s, having originated in a game called "the dozens," in which players hurl an escalatory litany of insults and boasts at one another. A progenitor of the West Coast subgenre known idiomatically as "gangsta rap," Ice Cube emerged in 1989 as the chief lyricist for the popular hard-core group Niggas with Attitude (N.W.A.) before launching a solo career a year later and subsequently giving a memorable performance in the highly acclaimed film *Boyz N the Hood* (1991), John Singleton's realistic depiction of street life in the gang-infested war zones of South Central Los Angeles, where Ice Cube grew up.

After joining the Reverend Louis Farrakhan's radical Nation of Islam sect, Ice Cube began to interject strident political commentaries into his feral, yet musically engaging and thematically compelling, raps. He has been pilloried in the press and neglected by radio not only because of his sexist, homophobic, and racially divisive language but also for the views such epithet-laden hate speech implies. The rock critics who have been able to hear the deeper message of Ice Cube's confrontational lyrics have emphasized the potential value that would accrue to all races who heed his wake-up call. It is Ice Cube's hope that black teenagers who listen to his music will avoid the dead-end life of crime he chronicles and that whites will come away with a better understanding of the sources of black rage. "I'm pro-black," he explained to Amy Linden of *People* (January 11, 1993). "The only thing I'm anti is poor. I'm talking to the brothers out there who are killing their own kind, and I ain't with that. . . . There's a bigger enemy than another black man in the same situation you're in."

Born O'Shea Jackson in Los Angeles, California in 1970, and named after O. J. Simpson, his mother's favorite football player, Ice Cube is the second son and the youngest by eight years of Doris Jackson and Hosea Jackson's four children; a half-sister died when he was about fourteen. His mother, who hailed from South Carolina, and his father, who had moved to California from Louisiana, were hard-working homeowners in the South Central section of Los Angeles. Doris Jackson was a clerk at a University of California at Los Angeles (UCLA) hospital, and Hosea Jackson worked as a groundskeeper at UCLA. Ice Cube attended Hawthorne Christian School but transferred to another school after the third grade because he disliked the uniform he was required to wear. A B-student who played football and basketball, he was "a very nice young man," as his mother told Mike Sager of *Rolling Stone* (October 4, 1990). "Every time someone would take him on a field trip or something, they always had something good to say about him." Although he vandalized some cars and got into a few fights, he never joined N-Hood, the gang that ruled his neighborhood's streets. "My father always instilled in me that it's more important to be a man than a superhero or a sports player," Ice Cube recalled in an interview with Greg Kot of the *Chicago Tribune* (July 14, 1991). "Instead of looking up to Superman, Batman, [or pro football star] Marcus Allen, I looked up to my father. He was my idol. I was more afraid of him getting on my case than I was the neighborhood gang. Peer pressure wasn't a factor, my father was a factor."

In a discussion with the black poet Abiodun Oyewole that was moderated by Sheila Rule for the *New York Times Magazine* (April 3, 1994), Ice Cube said that he had been a rap fan since the age of ten. "I was just out of nursery rhymes," he recalled. "So I tried it and fell in love. I said, 'I'm going to do records my homeboys down the street like.' That was my main concern, you know, just recognition in the neighborhood. What I wanted to do was be witty." After composing his first rhyme when he was in the ninth grade, Ice Cube started rapping at clubs and parties, and he was a finalist in a radio-station rap contest at the Hollywood Palladium. In 1986 he met the Ruthless Records label founder Eazy-E, a former drug dealer from Compton, California. At Eazy-E's request, Ice Cube collaborated with the rapper Dr. Dre on a song for HBO, a rap group from New York City that had just signed with Ruthless. Containing harshly realistic, profanity-laced raps, which were intended to lend a trademark style to the fledgling label, the resulting song,"Boyz-n-the-Hood," was an unflinching depiction of life on the streets of Compton. When HBO rejected the rap because it described a locale in California, Eazy-E recorded "Boyz" as a solo track on *N.W.A. and the Posse* (1987), the debut album by N.W.A., which Eazy-E had formed with Dr. Dre, Ice Cube, M.C. Ren, and Yella.

With Ice Cube rapping, writing songs, and fostering his image as the group's scowling, streetwise intellectual, N.W.A. was on the verge of a commercial breakthrough when Doris Jackson heard an unexpurgated version of Ice Cube's rap "Dope Man." When she asked her son, who had not been allowed to curse at home, why he spewed profanities on his raps, Ice Cube replied, as quoted by Mike Seger, "This is what the kids want to listen to." Urged by his parents to continue his education before becoming a professional rapper, he completed a one-year course in drafting at the Phoenix Institute of Technology in September 1988. He then wrote almost half of the raps that appeared on N.W.A.'s *Straight Outta Compton*, which was released in February 1989. Although the collection received scant radio airplay, *Straight Outta Compton* commanded glowing critical notices, and by the time N.W.A. embarked on a fifty-city tour, the album's hit track, an incendiary anticop number, had become a gangster-rap anthem.

Midway through N.W.A.'s 1989–90 tour, Ice Cube left the group because of a financial dispute with its manager, the industry veteran Jerry Heller, who had tried to give each member of N.W.A. seventy-five thousand dollars for signing a contract with him. Spurning Heller's offer, Ice Cube hired an attorney and an accountant, who discovered that the rapper had earned only thirty-two thousand dollars from N.W.A.'s first two albums, which had sold more than three million copies by the fall of 1989, and that Ice Cube's earnings from the group's tour were paltry in comparison to the fees Heller had paid himself. Heller eventually compensated Ice Cube for his contributions to N.W.A., but he claimed that the young rapper's motivation for striking out on his own was jealousy of Eazy-E. "How can I be jealous of [someone] with no talent," Ice Cube responded when he spoke to Mike Sager. "He got money. I'm gonna have talent *and* money." Without their chief lyricist, N.W.A. quickly degenerated "into a pandering self-parody," according to Jon Pareles, writing in the *New York Times* (November 10, 1991).

In his solo debut, *AmeriKKKa's Most Wanted* (1990), which sold half a million copies within ten days of its release and achieved platinum status in just three months, Ice Cube embraced a radical and sometimes shocking political vision with his "searing tales of street life and crime that blurred the line between reality and fantasy," as Greg Kot put it in his article for the *Chicago Tribune*. In his review of the album for *Rolling Stone* (July 12, 1990), Alan Light called the collaboration between Ice Cube and Public Enemy's Bomb Squad production team "a disappointment": "The potential for this bicoastal all-star session was tremendous: N.W.A.'s furious gang-scapes given direction and sophistication by Public Enemy's ambitious street politics and whirling, dizzying funk. . . . But the relentless profanity grows wearisome, the Bomb

Squad beats lose steam, and Cube's attitudes toward women are simply despicable. . . . Ice Cube ultimately sounds like the Andrew Dice Clay of rap."

Responding to the accusation that he depicts all women as rapacious, money-hungry harlots, Ice Cube, who brought in his cousin Yo Yo, a feminist rapper, to present a woman's point of view on the track "It's a Man's World," explained to Greg Kot of the *Chicago Tribune* (December 15, 1991), "The women I'm referring to look at a man strictly in economic terms. If that's the sole reason they pick one man over another, that brings down the community as a whole. What you end up with is kids who don't have money looking to get money to impress these women, and that generates crime." Ice Cube followed *AmeriKKKa's Most Wanted* with *Kill at Will* (1990), an EP containing "Dead Homiez," an elegiac lament for victims of black-on-black homicide in which he backed away from his glorification of urban street gangs. In 1991 he produced Yo Yo's solo album *Make Way for the Motherlode*.

Drawing upon his background as a streetwise product of the inner city, Ice Cube was convincing in the role of a troubled teenager seeking revenge for his brother's murder in writer-director John Singleton's impressive debut film *Boyz N the Hood*, a harrowing coming-of-age tale of three friends seeking to avoid the dangers that can ensnare young blacks in South Central Los Angeles—Tre Styles (Cuba Gooding, Jr.), whose virtuous father (Laurence Fishburne) is steering him toward college, and two brothers, Ricky (Morris Chestnut), a gifted athlete who dreams of playing pro football someday, and Doughboy (Ice Cube), a tough, embittered homeboy who has survived a seven-year stretch in prison. Ice Cube found that he fell naturally into the role of Doughboy, telling interviewers that the only scene that required special preparation was the one in which his character, anticipating his imminent death, cries, something Ice Cube himself hadn't done in years. "Doughboy learns a lesson that the killing has got to stop," he explained in one of his interviews with Greg Kot of the *Chicago Tribune* (July 14, 1991), "but he already knows it's too late for him. He wants to start over, but knows he can't. He's already dead. It was a tough scene for me, because I'm a person who hides my emotions, who covers them up."

Considering himself to be primarily a rapper rather than an aspiring actor, Ice Cube did the movie at least partly because he believed in its message, as he told David Hinckley of the New York *Daily News* (July 11, 1991): "What's good about this movie is that even though [Doughboy] does these [bad] things, it's not like you want to toss him in jail and throw away the key. You understand him. . . . White people who see this movie will better understand why black Americans behave like they do." Noting in the same interview that "Doughboy wouldn't end up where he was if he had a father figure," Ice Cube had singled out the aspect of the film that most disturbed Terri Apter of the *Guardian* (November 5, 1991), who wrote, "What is most unsatisfactory about the film is the way in which it locates a son's failures in the mother's weakness and his successes in the father's strength. Neither mother nor father have full power over a child's development."

Ice Cube had met John Singleton at a rally for the Reverend Louis Farrakhan, the controversial minister whose militant Nation of Islam, a Muslim religious sect that advocates black self-reliance (and which has been accused by some of espousing racial demagoguery). By the time he released his second solo recording, *Death Certificate* (1991), Ice Cube had joined the sect. *Death Certificate* is divided into two sections—"The Death Side," which opens with a funeral and a sermon by the Nation of Islam's Dr. Khallid Muhammad, and "The Life Side," which begins with the simulated sounds of a woman giving birth. The two sides, Ice Cube has explained, comprised "a mirrored image of where we are today" and "a vision of where we need to go."

In his review of *Death Certificate* for *Entertainment Weekly* (November 15, 1991), James Bernard applauded Ice Cube for expressing "young black anger" and trying "to redirect it in a productive direction beyond blaming the white man." Discussing Ice Cube's music, Bernard noted that "many critics treat rap solely as an academic text, forgetting the magic of simply experiencing a rapper as skilled as Ice Cube. His mid-tempo delivery punches rather than jabs, stomping with urgency, grabbing you by the throat rather than dazzling you with tricks. The same is true for the beats, which, however, can be a little too seamless." Jon Pareles, writing in the *New York Times* (November 10, 1991), admired Ice Cube's "gift for storytelling and rhetoric," but he added that on *Death Certificate*, "it's hard to tell which is more obtuse, Ice Cube's gangster raps or his political statements." "Ice Cube seems to think that if he's not 'hard'—bloodthirsty, angry, foul-mouthed and woman-hating—he will lose credibility (and album sales) with rap's core audience," Pareles observed. "He may be right."

Although *Death Certificate* held the number-two position on *Billboard's* pop album charts, Ice Cube's inflammatory diatribes triggered a flurry of condemnations and calls for the withdrawal of the recording. In "No Vaseline," he called on N.W.A. to "put a bullet" in Jerry Heller's temple because "you can't be the nigga-for-life crew with a white Jew telling you what to do." "Black Korea" threatened Asian-American store owners who, Ice Cube charged, make black customers feel unwelcome in inner-city markets: "Pay respect to the black fist or we'll burn your store right down." He ranted against miscegenation in "Horny Lil' Devil," and many of *Death Certificate*'s raps contained homophobic messages.

Denouncing the album as "a cultural Molotov cocktail," Rabbi Abraham Cooper of the Simon Wiesenthal Center urged national record-store chains to suspend sales of *Death Certificate*, and in an unprecedented editorial in *Billboard* (November 23, 1991), Ice Cube's lyrics were described as an expression of "the rankest sort of racism and hatemongering." Although the influential trade journal rejected the Wiesenthal Center's call for a ban on the recording, the editorial stated, "Each of us must decide whether or not Ice Cube's record is fit to sell or purchase." And when the Korean-American Grocers Association protested "Black Korea" by launching a boycott against St. Ides, a malt liquor for which Ice Cube served as a celebrity promoter, the beer's parent company suspended the advertising campaign featuring the controversial rapper.

Writing in the *New York Times* (December 8, 1991), Jon Pareles hypothesized that *Death Certificate*'s commercial success owed more to record buyers' wanting to savor the "action-movie thrills of Ice Cube's dirty words, his machismo, his gift for violent imagery, and his general anger" than to widespread support for his racially divisive views. Although white listeners make up a substantial portion of Ice Cube's audience, his raps are addressed exclusively to the black community, and he has explained that his use of street vernacular, including such loaded epithets as "bitch" and "nigga," enable him to communicate with his core audience. "I can't go to the Japanese talking Chinese," he remarked to Abiodun Oyewole, who had explained that when he had used those words in a previous era, he had used them only to refer to specific individuals. Oyewole advised the rapper to adopt more "positive" expressions, "so that the beauty of your folks will emerge." But Ice Cube insisted that kids wouldn't listen to him unless he spoke in the same terms with which they were familiar: "I have to speak the language of the street to get their ear." And while he lashed out at whites, Jews, Koreans, gays, women, and the police on *Death Certificate*, his harshest criticisms were directed at the black community. In "True to the Game," he castigated middle-class blacks for abandoning the inner city, and in "Us" he declared: "We mess up and blame the white man. . . . Us will always sing the blues 'cause all we care about is hairstyles and gym shoes."

The Predator (1992) became the first album to simultaneously occupy the number-one spot on both the pop and rhythm-and-blues *Billboard* lists since Stevie Wonder's *Songs in the Key of Life* dominated the charts in 1976. Although Ice Cube continued to scapegoat women and gays on some tracks, as Amy Linden noted in her *People* (January 11, 1993) review of *The Predator*, his themes were more complex and his anger more focused than on previous albums, in part because he examined the rage that galvanized African-Americans in the wake of the Rodney King verdict in the spring of 1992. (Riots erupted in Los Angeles when an all-white jury returned a not-guilty verdict in the trial of white police officers who had been videotaped brutally beating King.) Ice Cube expressed ambivalence over the riots on one track while on another he combined an antigang message with revulsion for the white "devils" who "got nothing but a slap on the wrist" for beating King. "*The Predator* is a difficult, intense, and perversely engaging disc," Linden wrote. "But as long as Cube insists on bashing other minorities and disenfranchised people and lets hate cloud his vision, he diminishes his power to expose the real problems."

In Walter Hill's fast-paced action-adventure film *Trespass* (1992), Ice Cube again demonstrated his screen charisma, playing a gun-toting gangster opposite the rap artist Ice-T, who was cast as a drug-dealing crime boss. The two characters end up in a standoff with two white firemen who are holed up in an East St. Louis warehouse that contains hidden gold treasure. Originally called *The Looters* and scheduled to open in the summer of 1992, the film saw its release date postponed until that December, so that it would not follow hard on the heels of the Los Angeles riots. In a dismissive review of the more innocuously titled *Trespass* for the *Washington Post* (December 25, 1992), Hal Hinson called the film "mindlessly violent, profane, and insultingly racist; . . . a stale and routinely numbing exercise in swat-team cinema—men, guns, gold, blood, and death." Other critics found it highly entertaining, notwithstanding what all agreed was a thin plot, and singled out the performances of Ice Cube and Ice-T for praise. The two rappers also cowrote and performed the film soundtrack's title number.

By the time Ice Cube released his fourth solo album, *Lethal Injection* (1994), of which he was also the executive producer, a backlash had set in against radical rap artists. Because audiences sometimes mistake rap's "dramatic musical theatre" for "a call to violence," as a writer for *Time* (January 11, 1993) noted, rap concerts have occasionally been marred by armed confrontations, such as the one that resulted in several injuries after a 1992 performance in Seattle by Ice Cube. Moreover, several leading rappers, including a member of Ice Cube's backing group, the Lench Mob, have been indicted on felony charges ranging from sexual assault to murder. Ice Cube, however, has declared that attempts to muzzle hard-core rappers are misguided. "If I'm more of an influence to your son as a rapper than you are as a father, . . . you got to look at yourself as a parent," he said, as quoted by Mike Sager. In the same interview, he asserted, "White people don't like us having something of our own. Rap is ours! The whites are saying, 'Oh, wait a minute now, You can't talk among each other. You supposed to focus everything on hatin' us.' 'Cause if we keep hating them, that keeps them superior."

In accordance with that line of thinking, on *Lethal Injection* Ice Cube preaches the self-reliance and self-love that he has learned from the teachings of the Nation of Islam as well as from his own experience. "We need to love and respect ourselves before we can love anyone else," he said in a recent publicity release. "That's the key. Love does what a gun cannot. Love makes you run into a burning building to save a baby. It's a lack of love for the next man that keeps the world poor and raggedy." His most recent recording is *Bootlegs & B-Sides*, which contains B-sides, remixes, and two new tracks. The director of several music videos, Ice Cube was behind the camera for his own "Check Yo Self," Color Me Badd's "Time and Chance," and the singer formerly known as Prince's "Love Sign," among others. In 1995 three films starring Ice Cube were released: F. Gray Gray's comedy *Friday*, coscripted by Ice Cube, who also contributed to the soundtrack, and DJ Pooh; the independent writer-director Charles Burnett's *The Glass Shield*, a look at corruption in the Los Angeles Police Department; and John Singleton's *Higher Learning*.

Despite Ice Cube's considerable success—he has sold six million albums to date—he has not been content to rest on his laurels. In 1990 he announced his intention to retire from rapping within five years, after which he said he hoped to invest in shopping malls and apartment complexes. Instead, he is busier pursuing his artistic endeavors than ever before. In between recording raps, directing music videos, writing film scripts, and acting, he manages his South Los Angeles-based record company, Street Knowledge Productions, founded in 1990. He has one child who is about four years old. In a conversation with Dimitri Ehrlich that appeared in *Interview* (December 1991), Ice Cube declared his commitment to living in his hometown: "The white community doesn't need my money—they have enough money. The black community needs my money. They need for me to shop in black neighborhoods, stay where I'm needed, stay put. That's where I grew up, so why should I run as soon as I get some money? Just think: if all the athletes and entertainers stayed in the communities they grew up in, things wouldn't be as bad as they are now."

Selected Biographical References: Chicago Tribune XIII p6+ Jl 14 '91 pors; N Y Times Mag p40+ Ap 3 '94 pors; People 39:21 Ja 11 '93 por; Rolling Stone p80+ O 4 '90 pors; Who's Who in America, 1995

Michael Thompson

Iman

(ee-MAHN)

July 25, 1955- Model; actress; political activist; entrepreneur. Address: c/o Keeble, Cavaco & Duka, 853 Seventh Ave., Suite 10A, New York, NY 10019

"My whole nation is graceful," the Somali-born American model Iman has said. "Nobody has to tell us how to walk or how to stand. We have an air, a dignity: whatever happens, you keep your head up. It comes off as secure, but it isn't. It's like a duck gliding on water. Under the surface, where nobody can see, its feet are churning." Iman's arrival in the United States twenty years ago was heralded by rumors that she had been discovered herding sheep and goats in Africa; in fact, she had been studying political science and working as a translator. The advance publicity generated by tales of her exotic background gave her a running start in the highly competitive modeling business, in which she earned as much as two million dollars a year. Although she retired from runway modeling in 1989, she is still signing lucrative contracts for print advertisements, such as the milk-mustache campaign of 1995, a series of ads touting the health benefits of milk, sponsored by the National Fluid Milk Processor Promotion Board. An actress as well as a model, Iman has acted in a number of movies, and the television shows on which she has appeared include a BBC documentary about her 1992 visit to Somalia, which was riven by clan warfare that brought about widespread homelessness, famine, and disease. In 1994 Iman launched the Iman Cosmetics and Skincare Collection for all women of color, including African-Americans, Asians, Hispanics, and Native Americans.

Iman, whose name means "magnet," was born Iman Abdulmajid on July 25, 1955 in Mogadishu, the capital of Somalia, the daughter of a nurse and a teacher. "My parents started from nothing . . . ," the model told Charles Gandee in an interview for *Vogue* (June 1994). "They married very young, and they worked their way up. I would say I was raised middle class, upper middle class." Her father gave up teaching for diplomacy, eventually serving as the Somali ambassador to Saudi Arabia and Egypt, among other countries; her mother continued her medical training and became a gynecologist.

After graduating from high school (some sources say in Egypt, others, in Mogadishu), Iman, who speaks Somali, English, French, Italian, and Arabic, enrolled at the University of Nairobi, in Kenya, where she majored in political science. (Iman's two brothers and two sisters are also college-educated, courtesy of Iman's modeling earnings and sound financial management.) At some point, possibly between high school and college, she served for two years in the military in Somalia. "The hardest part was jumping from a plane in a parachute," she recalled in an interview with Earl Wilson for the *New York Post* (February 8, 1980).

It was while Iman was walking to class at the University of Nairobi that she was "discovered" by the American photographer Peter Beard. (According to Sheryl Fitzgerald, who interviewed Iman for *New York Newsday* (March 12, 1987), she was introduced to Beard by Mirella Riccardi, the author of *Vanishing Africa*.) At the time, Iman was also working at Kenya's Ministry of Tourism and Wildlife, in Nairobi, translating brochures into Italian. She agreed to allow Beard to photograph her in exchange for college tuition, and her portrait wound up on the announcement card for an exhibit of his work in New York City, where it was noticed by Wilhelmina, the owner of the modeling agency of the same name. Wilhelmina tried to persuade Iman to come to New York City with promises of instant stardom, but the young student had difficulty believing Wilhelmina was serious. She has claimed, on more than one occasion, that she was not considered attractive as a teenager and that her brother and father had paid a young man to escort her to her high school prom at a school in which the ratio of boys to girls was nine to one. Moreover, she did not aspire to be perceived as feminine. "My role models were men like Egyptian leader Gamal Abdel Nasser . . . ," she told Jamie Diamond, who interviewed her for *Harper's Bazaar* (June 1992). "I thought femininity was weak and frivolous."

Finally, after months of being courted by the Wilhelmina agency and being reassured repeatedly by Beard, Iman quit school and left Kenya without telling her parents, who had fled to Tanzania in 1972, fearing political persecution under the new Somali regime headed by Siad Barre. "They wouldn't have let me go," she explained to Carla Hall of the *Washington Post* (June 6, 1987). She did not mind giving up her education, as she told Jamie Diamond. "I realized that I didn't want to follow in my father's footsteps and become a diplomat. As a youngster, I thought I could make a difference. But I became disappointed. In my country, women were considered second-class citizens; most were not even sent to school."

Shortly after arriving in New York City, on October 15, 1975, Iman was beset by a flock of reporters whom Beard had fed wildly erroneous versions of her discovery. Expecting to meet a shepherdess or a princess who did not speak English, they directed all their questions to Beard, who was then supposed to translate for her. Even though Iman cut the fantasy short by revealing the truth about her background, the exotic tales proliferated, adding to her allure. Within days of her arrival, Iman was being photographed by Francesco Scavullo; within a year, she had become the first black model to sign a contract with a major American cosmetics company when she was chosen for Revlon's "most unforgettable women in the world" campaign. "I didn't believe the flattery," she told Jamie Diamond. "I thought the world had gone insane. I still believe I pulled the biggest con." In 1979 she agreed to represent Polished Ambers, a Revlon cosmetics line that was discontinued in the mid-1980s. In the late 1980s she introduced her own line of brightly colored body wraps, called *kikois*, which were marketed through the Echo Design Group.

Although she earned thousands of dollars a day, Iman was pulling in less than her white peers. "I could have made much more money if I weren't black," she asserted in her interview with Charles Gandee. One of only fourteen African-Americans out of the two hundred women represented by the Elite agency, to which she had switched from Wilhelmina, she was never selected to pose for the cover of *Vogue*, one of the most prestigious assignments in the modeling world. (Among the few black models to have been so honored as of 1987 were Shari Belafonte-Harper, Beverly Johnson, and Peggy Dillard.) Iman's outspokenness on such issues, combined with her innate reluctance to tolerate condescension in any form, has earned her a reputation for being difficult to work with, a state of affairs with which she has professed to be quite pleased. "I've been called everything from 'diva' to 'queen,' 'princess' to 'a bitch,'" she informed Carla Hall. "You know when someone is called all those, you know there's something special about them. Otherwise, if they don't think anything, you're just another one."

Iman withstood the first of three threats to her modeling career when she gave birth to her daughter, Zulekha, in 1979, at the age of twenty-three, when she was at the top of her profession. "Everyone said I couldn't come back," she told Mikki Garth-Taylor of *Essence* (January 1988). "And I did. I picked up right where I left off." Later, when she returned to New York City after two years in Los Angeles, where she had moved to be with her first husband (the former basketball star Spencer Haywood, to whom she was married from 1978 to 1986), she again resumed her career in Manhattan without missing a beat, contrary to the conventional wisdom. "It's not about confidence," she explained to Garth-Taylor. "It's about being exact. You have to know what you can do and what you can't."

The third and most serious challenge to Iman's modeling career came in 1983 in New York City, when a taxi in which she was a passenger was broadsided by a car driven by a drunk driver. The cab was pushed into a building and overturned. "Some fool just ran the red light and hit us," Iman recalled to Brooks Peters for *Vanity Fair* (October 1985). "Broke half my face, my ribs, my collarbone, everything." "It was a time to realize the frailty of physical beauty," she explained to Marion Collins for the New York *Daily News* (January 13, 1985). "If I wasn't repairable, if I couldn't model, so what? I was considered ugly all of my young life, then thought beautiful, and someone took it all away from me. It was a confusing time." After only two months of recuperation from five hours of reconstructive surgery on the left side of her face, Iman was back at work. Numerous photographs attest to the testimony of reporters that she bears no visible scars.

In 1989 Iman quit modeling and moved with her daughter to the Chateau Marmont on Sunset Boulevard in Hollywood. "The idea was film," Iman said, in explaining her move to Charles Gandee. "Unlike New York, where there's always something going on, here there's always nothing going on." Iman devoted much of her newly found free time to peronal development, enrolling in acting classes and entering psychotherapy. She had planned the transition carefully. "Before I left Manhattan, I made sure that I could comfortably take care of myself and my child for five years if I didn't work a day," Iman told Charles Gandee. "I was smart; I saved my money, I invested." Following a five-year hiatus after having made a "disastrous" debut in *The Human Factor*, in 1980, Iman began accepting small roles in other films, among them *Out of Africa* (1985), *No Way Out* (1987), *Surrender* (1987), *L.A. Story* (1991), *House Party II* (1991), *Star Trek VI: The Undiscovered Country* (1991), and *Exit to Eden* (1994). On television, she has been seen in *Miami Vice*, *The Cosby Show*, *In the Heat of the Night*, *Heart of Darkness*, and *Lies of the Twins*. She also appeared in two music videos: Michael Jackson's "Remember the Time" and Jermaine Jackson's "Do What You Do."

In June 1992, alarmed by the famine and violence that had recently descended upon her homeland, Iman decided to do her part to publicize the crisis. "I approached the BBC and told them I wanted to do a documentary about my return and let the Somali people speak for themselves," she explained to a reporter for *People* (November 9, 1992). "People get numbed when they see picture after picture, year in and year out, of people starving. I wanted to show that they are not a nation of beggars—that culture, religion, music, and hope are still there." Iman and her British film crew spent ten days in the troubled country in September and October of 1992 under the auspices of the International Committee of the Red Cross. The trip, which Iman described in detail in an article she wrote for *Vogue* (December 1992), was emotionally harrowing and physically dangerous. Visiting the house she grew up in for the first time in twenty years, she found four refugee families living within its bullet-riddled walls. She consoled the grief-stricken young parents of starving babies, witnessed the nightly collection of truckloads of small body bags containing mostly children's corpses, and survived being caught in the cross fire between two gangs of boys while driving on the outskirts of Mogadishu.

Although her body remained unscathed, her memory was seared by her overwhelming experiences, and Iman resolved to make helping Somalia a lifelong project. Two months after the BBC documentary of her journey aired in Britain, Iman appeared at a press conference to urge the warring clans to agree to a peace conference. "Military intervention alone is not enough," she said. From November 1991 to September 1992 fourteen thousand Somalis had been killed and twenty-seven thousand had been wounded in Mogadishu alone. By the time a United Nations peacekeeping force arrived in December 1992, the death toll in the country had climbed to a quarter of a million. During the peacekeepers' two-year stay, the international humanitarian effort managed to stave off a potentially more devastating famine but failed to reconcile the warring factions, who resumed fighting even as the last of the UN troops were withdrawing in February 1995.

Before traveling to Somalia, Iman had begun laying the groundwork for her own business. "I didn't want to always be the product," she explained to Gandee. "I wanted to be the owner of the product for once." In July 1994 the Iman Cosmetics and Skincare Collection debuted at two hundred J. C. Penney outlets. As she told Gandee, Iman chose that department-store chain because its merchandise was affordable and its policies were socially progressive. "They are very involved in ethnic communities, very diverse in their sponsorships," she said of the Penney's management team. The 132 items in the Iman line were specially formulated to suit the needs of all women of color, who constitute 30 percent of cosmetics buyers in the United States. A portion of the profits are channeled into the treasury of the Children's Defense Fund, one of Iman's favorite charities.

Standing five feet, eight-and-a-half inches tall and weighing around 115 pounds, Iman exercises regularly to maintain her slender figure. She once complained that if her waist weren't so small (twenty-three inches), she wouldn't have to work so hard to tone her thirty-five-inch hips. She does not fear the development of facial wrinkles, which, she believes, lend character to one's appearance, but she has blamed the fashion industry's emphasis on extreme youthfulness for the perception that all models are empty-headed. "The average model starts working at fifteen," she explained to Sheryl Fitzgerald, "and fifteen-year-olds are airheads. I was, you were, we were all airheads at that age. What else can you expect?"

Now an American citizen, Iman divides her time between a 640-acre estate in the hills of County Wicklow, near Dublin, Ireland, and homes in Lausanne, Switzerland and New York City, among other places. She lives with her husband, the rock star and actor David Bowie, whom she married on April 24, 1992 in a civil ceremony in Lausanne and again on June 6, 1992 in a church ceremony in Florence, Italy. "It's an unfortunate combination, though—the model and the rock star," Iman commented in her interview with Jamie Diamond.

"People think there's something *less* than meets the eye. They think I'm in it for the ride. They never ask why *he's* with me. . . . While it's the best thing that's happened in my life, in a way it's the worst thing for my career." Their homes are filled with her needlepointed cushions and tapestries and Bowie's portraits of his wife. The couple spends Christmas and Easter on Mustique, an island in the Caribbean. Iman's daughter, Zulekha, has lived with her father in Detroit since 1992.

Selected Biographical References: Chicago Tribune V p3 Ap 19 '87 pors; GQ 58:258+ Ap '88 por; Harper's Bazaar p82+ Je '92 pors; Interview 24:162+ O '94 por; N Y Newsday II p4+ Mr 12 '87 pors; Washington Post G p1+ Je 6 '87 pors; International Who's Who of Women, 1992; Who's Who in America, 1995

Agence France-Presse

Jiang Zemin

(jee-AHNG dzuh-MEEN)

Aug. 17, 1926– President of China; general secretary of the Communist Party. Address: Office of the President, Beijing, People's Republic of China

Jiang Zemin is the titular head of the People's Republic of China and the heir apparent to his political patron, the country's paramount leader, Deng Xiaoping. Formerly the mayor of Shanghai, Jiang was appointed general secretary of the Communist Party in mid-1989, following the so-called Tiananmen Square Massacre, in which several thousand student demonstrators lost their lives, and he has since assumed the positions of president and head of the military. His imposing titles notwithstanding, Jiang's real power is a subject of considerable debate among China-watchers, and his survival at the top after the death, which many believe to be imminent, of the aged and physically frail Deng, is by no means assured. Jiang shares with Deng a commitment to effecting economic reforms while remaining socially conservative, and he has continued to rein in dissent while promoting what he calls "market socialism."

Thought by his detractors to be more style than substance, Jiang was characterized by Lincoln Kaye of the *Far Eastern Economic Review* as being "finely tuned to the vicissitudes of palace politics," a description that echoes the views of others and explains one of his nicknames—"Weather Vane"—as well as his impressive rise within the Chinese governmental hierarchy. Having initially been without a power base beyond Deng's patronage, Jiang has moved in recent months, apparently with some degree of success, to consolidate his leadership.

Jiang Zemin was born on August 17, 1926 in Yangzhou City, Jiangsu Province, in eastern China. In an interview with the editors of *U.S. News & World Report* (March 12, 1990), Jiang explained that his family was made up of intellectuals, that his grandfather was "a doctor of Chinese medicine" and "also a very famous painter," and that his father, Jiang Shangqing, and his uncle were "also men of letters." "So from childhood," he revealed, "I read many, many poems and verses and listened to many, many proverbs." Jiang's father was a Communist and may have been killed by the Kuomintang, the Chinese Nationalists who fought a civil war with the Communists for the better part of two decades, beginning in the 1920s. After attending an American missionary school, where he learned English, Jiang enrolled at the prestigious Jiaotong University, in Shanghai, where he studied electrical engineering and from which he graduated in 1947. During much of his youth, from 1937 until 1945, Shanghai was under Japanese occupation, and as a student Jiang participated in the anti-Japanese movement before joining the Communist Party in 1946. According to one anecdote, he once managed to elude Communist-hunting Nationalist soldiers by hiding in the trunk of the car belonging to the principal of his school.

The triumph of Communist forces over the Kuomintang, which in 1949 brought Mao Zedong to power, shaped the direction of Jiang's early career, although there is little agreement on its details through the 1950s and 1960s. According to some sources, he was put in charge of a large foodstuffs factory in Shanghai in about 1949. The *Biographical Dictionary and Analysis of China's Party Leadership 1922–1988* (1990) states that in 1950 he served as director of the military engineering department of the Northeast Military Region and that from 1950 to 1955 he was a commercial counselor at the Chinese embassy in the Soviet Union. Most sources indicate that Jiang worked for a year during the mid-1950s in the Stalin automobile plant in Moscow; *Automotive News* (July 3, 1989), however, reported that he remained there for six years, returning in 1960 to China, where he was employed as a mechanical engineer in an automobile factory in Changchun. By other accounts, Jiang served in the Ministry of Machine-Building from 1956 until 1959 and then, as a brief summation in the *Beijing Review* has it, worked in industry as, successively, "factory director, research institute director, section chief, and finally department director."

Little information has been published in the Western press about Jiang's activities between 1966 and 1976, the period of the Great Proletarian Cultural Revolution in China, during which Mao carried out a sometimes violent campaign against those he accused of contributing to "a bourgeois dictatorship." In all probability Jiang's career, like those of almost all the Communist Party apparatchiks, did not advance. By 1978, however, two years after Mao's death and soon after Deng Xiaoping assumed power, Jiang was named adviser to the First Ministry of Machine-Building. From 1980 to 1982 he served as vice-minister of the State Administrative Commission for Import and Export Affairs, and beginning in 1981 he concurrently held the position of vice-minister of the State Foreign Investment Commission. In 1982 he was named vice-minister in charge of the electronics industry, and he was promoted to the minister's post the following year, a position he held until 1985. Beginning in 1984 Jiang also functioned as deputy head of the State Leading Group for the electronics industry, and during that period he traveled extensively in Europe, visiting Romania, Bulgaria, East and West Germany, and Poland. Meanwhile, he rose within the Communist Party hierarchy. In 1982 he served on the Central Committee of the Communist Party at its Twelfth National Congress, and five years later, at the Thirteenth National Congress, he was selected for the Politburo, the main decision-making body of the Communist Party.

In 1985 Jiang's career took a dramatic upswing when he was appointed mayor of Shanghai. One of the world's most densely populated cities, inhabited by more than twelve million people, Shanghai is a virtual province unto itself, and it is administered by the central government. As mayor, Jiang was credited by some China scholars as well as by Western businessmen with mounting a full-scale attempt to attract foreign investment, a key objective of the broad, capitalist-style economic reforms initiated by Deng Xiaoping. According to Richard Evans in his biography *Deng Xiaoping* (1993), Jiang "impressed Deng by drawing up and launching a program to modernize Shanghai, a city which had slipped from being one of the most modern in the world to one of the most backward." His tenure as mayor saw the opening of a Sheraton Hotel and the Shanghai Hilton, and he worked with Prescott Bush, the brother of former President George Bush, on the development of a modern golf course. Daniel Southerland of the *Washington Post* (December 14, 1986) described Jiang as "representative of the new type of educated, technically competent leader whom the country's top leadership [was] trying to promote over the heads of bureaucrats who are notorious for resisting the kind of changes Deng and the mayor are trying to introduce."

Other observers of Jiang's three-year term as Shanghai's mayor have described him as ineffectual and as largely disliked by the citizenry—mainly because, in spite of his business initiatives, the city's economy remained stagnant. Jiang was nonetheless able to use the position to get for himself a great deal of exposure in China and in the Western media, often for activities beyond the scope of his mayoral duties. The *Washington Post* (July 15, 1989) reported, for example, that in Shanghai, before an audience of some twenty thousand at the National Day celebration in 1987, he conducted a lively version of the Communist anthem, the "Internationale," amid "flashing red and green lights and clouds of vapor." On a tour of the Melbourne (Australia) Opera House in 1987, he is said to have spontaneously broken into song. Jiang's tendency toward exhibitionism earned him the sobriquet "Flower Pot," used in China to describe one who has a pleasing appearance but does nothing. He resigned the mayoralty in April 1988, the same year he was elevated to the position of secretary of Shanghai's Communist Party.

In the meantime, the first signs of student unrest had appeared at China's major universities in 1985, when young protestors in Shanghai demanded democratic reforms in government, freedom of the press, and recognition of the right to protest with a guarantee of personal safety. In December 1985 Jiang took the unusual step of meeting with students at his alma mater, Jiaotong University. During their discussions, he agreed to view the demonstrations as being within the law and pledged not to punish the leaders. He refused, however, to consider the possibility of greater press freedom or more rapid democratic reform.

Motivated in part by popular uprisings against the Communist governments in Eastern Europe, Chinese students intensified their demands for reform during the late 1980s. In the spring of 1989, following the death of the democratic reformer Hu Yaobang, the ostracized former general secretary of the Communist Party, memorial demonstrations staged by students and others turned into confrontations with the government, in which protesters called for the resignations of Deng and other government officials. Jiang reportedly spoke with student leaders in an attempt to calm tensions. After the Chinese government expressed its strong disapproval of the students' activities, however, Jiang changed his attitude, taking a firmer stand. When the *World Economic Herald*, a newspaper which for several years had served as a soapbox for outspoken intellectuals, published an issue partially devoted to a tribute to Hu Yaobang, Jiang intervened to censor the paper and suspend its editor.

On June 3, 1989, in Beijing, a massive occupation of ancient Tiananmen Square led the government to declare martial law and to launch a brutal attack on student protesters. The military's assault on the demonstrators, which resulted in the deaths of approximately five thousand people and was followed by the execution or imprisonment of many student leaders, attracted the attention and condemnation of the Western world. What came to be known as the Tiananmen Square Massacre effectively changed the course of Chinese politics and also determined the subsequent career of Jiang Zemin. Zhao Ziyang, then the general secretary of the Communist Party, had angered Deng and others by urging a conciliatory approach to the students, and Deng sought to replace him. While Deng was conservative politically and socially, which was made evident when he ordered the army to suppress the rebellion, his reformist stance with regard to China's economy prevented him from elevating Prime Minister Li Peng, a hard-line Communist, to Zhao's position. Deng therefore turned to Jiang Zemin, who had won praise from conservative Communists for his willingness to suppress publication of the *World Economic Herald*. Jiang was appointed general secretary in June 1989.

Many Western observers saw the choice of Jiang as an attempt to place in the ostensibly powerful position someone who would not challenge his superiors. Others conjectured that Jiang, who speaks several languages and is said to be able, for example, to quote passages from the American Declaration of Independence, was picked to lend an appearance of sophistication to, and improve the image of, China's forty-six million-member Communist Party. In attempting to explain why Jiang accepted the position, which some felt he would be unable to maintain after Deng's death, the *Washington Post* (July 15, 1989) quoted an Asian diplomat as saying that Jiang is "such an egomaniac" that "he couldn't say no."

Following Jiang's appointment, the Chinese government continued to take an uncompromising stand against the Tiananmen Square protesters, deciding, in the new general secretary's words, to "mete out severe punishments to the plotters, organizers, and behind-the-scene commanders who staged the turmoil and rebellion" and to offer "no iota of forgiveness." To members of the international press corps, Jiang said, "We do not believe there was any tragedy in Tiananmen Square," and he compared media reports of the cruel handling of prisoners to "fairy tales from the *Arabian Nights*." Jiang is widely believed to have overseen the extensive television campaign to provide the Chinese people with the government's version of the events in Tiananmen Square.

While strictly limiting political freedoms in China, Jiang took steps to continue Deng's policies of economic restructuring. In a September 1989 speech, he condemned "bourgeois liberalization," or Western-style capitalism, but promoted free-market reforms. Criticizing his predecessor's advocacy of the importation of capitalism, Jiang declared that Deng's "four modernizations"—the development of agriculture, industry, science, and technology—would lead to a state of perfect socialism. To that aim, by the end of 1989 the government had instituted price controls and put in abeyance programs of stock ownership, and plans had been made to limit income disparities. Jiang went on to describe those who spoke out against his economic strategy as pawns of foreign enemies who "foster blind worship of the Western world and propagate the political patterns, sense of values, decadent traits, and lifestyle of the Western capitalist world."

In November 1989 Jiang was elected chairman of the Central Military Commission, replacing Deng Xiaoping, who stepped aside in his favor. By that time Deng had named Jiang his successor as paramount leader, calling him the "core" of the third generation of Chinese Communist leaders, in the tradition of Mao and Deng himself. Although in principle that turn of events augmented Jiang's power, the extent of his political muscle remained a subject of considerable speculation. He was often compared to Hua Guofeng, who had been expressly chosen to succeed Mao Zedong only to lose all power soon after Mao's death. It was noted, in addition, that each of Deng's two previous hand-picked heirs to the throne had been forced to cede authority. As David Bachman pointed out in *Current History* (September 1990), "Aside from his formal positions," Jiang enjoyed "few other advantages," one of those being that "other Chinese leaders know that the failure of yet another erstwhile successor to become the successor will destroy the credibility of any succession arrangement and will further erode China's already diminished image in international affairs."

Although political repression was not new in China, the country's efforts to become a player on the world economic stage brought it unaccustomed political responsibilities, and the pattern of human rights abuses that continued in the wake of the Tiananmen Square Massacre drew persistent international criticism. In an exclusive interview with the editors of *U.S. News & World Report* (March 12, 1990), Jiang offered his explanation of China's position regarding political repression. Pointing to other world trouble spots, such as Panama and Azerbaijan, he suggested that China was being judged by a double standard. "Democracy and freedom are specific, concrete concepts which have to be linked to the economy, the culture, and the system of the country concerned," he maintained. Reiterating his view that human rights were an internal affair, he added, "We do not regret, or criticize ourselves for the way we handled, the Tiananmen event, because if we had not sent in the troops I would not be able to sit here today." In May 1990 Jiang told Barbara Walters, in an interview for the ABC television program *20/20*, "I don't have any regret about the way in which we dealt with the events which took place last year in Beijing. I don't think any government in the world will permit the occurrence of such an incident as happened in Beijing."

Jiang presided over the Fourteenth Congress of the Chinese Communist Party in October 1992, and in a long speech he reemphasized the government's commitment to economic reform, calling for what he termed a "socialist market economy." "Reform is also a revolution . . . whose goal is to liberate the productive forces," he said. "It is the only way to modernize China. . . . Poverty is not socialism." At the same time, he strongly restated the government's insistence on political order and made it clear that in this way China's "socialist democracy" would not resemble a Western parliamentary model. Underscoring that assertion was the example of Wu Shishen, the editor of the New China News Agency, who, as punishment for leaking the contents of Jiang Zemin's speech at the Fourteenth Congress to the Hong Kong media, was sentenced to life imprisonment.

On March 27, 1993 Jiang assumed the presidency of China, succeeding an aged Yang Shangkun. As more than one observer pointed out, Jiang could function more comfortably in an international environment as president than as general secretary of the Communist Party or head of the military commission. Indeed, a meeting between him and President Bill Clinton was arranged as part of the November 1993 summit of Pacific Rim leaders, in Seattle. At that meeting President Clinton insisted that economic ties between the United States and China depended on China's progress in human rights, and he also expressed concern about its escalating weapons sales—both subjects of continuing discussion between American and Chinese officials. In May 1995 new tensions arose between the two countries when President Lee Teng-hui of Taiwan received permission to make a private visit to the United States. The government in Beijing has never acknowledged the sovereignty of Taiwan, an island off the southeastern coast of China that declared its independence from the mainland in 1949, and by allowing Lee's visit, the United States reversed the sixteen-year-old policy that favored Beijing. In order to attempt to settle those and other matters, Jiang and Clinton met for discussions in October 1995.

Meanwhile, at home, during 1994 Jiang was apparently able to solidify his leadership by appointing an ally, Shanghai mayor Huang Ju, to the central committee of the Politburo as well as by finding a place in the party's secretariat for Wu Bangguo, another supporter from Shanghai. The men's new assignments signified Jiang's effort to expand his base of support. Jiang was also said to be moving toward better relations with the military leadership. In a show of power in the spring of 1995, Jiang spearheaded an anticorruption campaign that resulted in the arrests of dozens of local Beijing Communist Party officials, a move that received the backing of China's National People's Congress and seemed to indicate at least some support for Jiang in the government's upper echelon.

Jiang Zemin is married to Wang Yeping, his childhood sweetheart, who was formerly head of a Shanghai engineering research institute. The couple have two sons, who have studied in the United States. The portly Jiang sports western-style business suits and large, square-rimmed glasses. Some journalists have described him as being aloof, caustic, and arrogant while others have characterized his demeanor in favorable terms, on at least one occasion going so far as to compare it to the celebrated social grace of the American president John F. Kennedy. Jiang reportedly speaks Russian, Rumanian, and English (he is said to be very proud of having conversed in English with Queen Elizabeth II of Great Britain at their meeting in 1986) and is able to read French and Japanese. He particularly enjoys reciting poetry and proverbs in English and singing American songs from the 1940s.

Selected Biographical References: N Y Times I p10 Je 25 '89; U S News 108:50+ Mr 12 '90 pors; International Who's Who, 1994–95; Schell, Orville. Mandate of Heaven (1994)

Peter Nash/MCA

Jones, George

Sept. 12, 1931– Singer; songwriter. Address: c/o MCA Records, 60 Music Sq. E., Nashville, TN 37203; c/o Evelyn Shriver Public Relations, 1313 16th Ave. S., Nashville, TN 37212

A vocalist who has fused dazzling technique with intense emotionality, George Jones is widely regarded as "the finest, most riveting singer in country music," in the words of the *New York Times* music critic John Rockwell. Since launching his singing career in the mid-1950s, the Grammy

Award-winning Jones has made well over 150 albums and recorded dozens of hit singles, among them such quintessential country-music classics as "The Window Up Above" and "He Stopped Loving Her Today," demonstrating throughout his work a voice that has been described as "country music's best mixture of syrup and redneck fire." "Few other singers . . . can so effectively leave listeners hanging on their every word," the drummer and journalist Ben Sandmel has written. With the exception of a brief foray into rockabilly, Jones has ignored musical trends and steadfastly adhered to his traditional country style. Although his repertoire includes many high-spirited, up-tempo numbers, he favors heart-wrenching ballads, many of which focus on the kinds of sorrows and tribulations with which he has been intimately familiar in his much-publicized private life. Indeed, as John Morthland observed in *New York Newsday* (September 21, 1980), he has "lived those songs so fully that his life and his art have become inseparable." George Jones was elected to the Country Music Hall of Fame in 1992.

The second son and youngest of the eight children of George Washington Jones and Clara (Patterson) Jones, George Glenn Jones was born on September 12, 1931 in Saratoga, a small town in southeastern Texas. During Jones's early years his father drove a lumber truck, earning barely enough to keep his family out of poverty. In 1942, joining thousands of other rural Texans in the wartime exodus to cities where defense work was available, the Joneses moved to a public housing project in Beaumont, and George Washington Jones began working in a shipyard as a pipe fitter. In his book *Country Music, U.S.A.* (1968; second edition, 1985), the music historian Bill C. Malone observed that despite those changes in residence and in the father's occupation, the Jones family remained "typically southern and rural in its outlook."

The younger George Jones hated his father for his frequent bouts of drunkenness, during which the elder George sometimes terrorized his family. Jones has recalled getting beatings if he dared to balk at his father's demand, which he made during the night after rousing the boy from sleep, that he sing for him. Those events notwithstanding, from an early age Jones loved to sing. In a *Texas Monthly* (June 1982) profile of him, Pepi Plowman reported that some of his relatives remembered the four-year-old George "walking barefoot down a dusty road, banging on a pot and singing as loudly as he could." "I knew for a fact when I was a kid, when I was first learning to sing, I knew I'd do it 'til the day I died," Jones told John Morthland. He sang regularly at the family's church, a Pentecostal tabernacle where his mother played the piano. At the age of eleven or twelve, he began singing on Beaumont streets or "anywhere that a crowd was willing to listen," in the words of Bill C. Malone. Often, instead of going to school, he would spend the day outdoors, playing the "little old Gene Autry guitar," as he has called it, that his father had given him. "My Sunday-school teacher taught me the chords on it," he told Nick Tosches, who interviewed him for *Texas Monthly* (July 1994). "I just fell in love with it." According to most sources, he quit school after failing the seventh grade.

Jones got his first paying job as a musician at sixteen, when he joined Eddie and Pearl, a husband-and-wife team who had a weekday radio show. On weekends they performed in the eastern Texas and Louisiana taverns and dance halls known as honky-tonks, for their tawdry atmosphere and boisterous clientele as well as for the type of music they had spawned (much of which, as Nick Tosches wrote in *High Fidelity* [May 1977], consisted of "loud, driving, rough songs of whiskey and sex, stuff of drastic fatalism"). Eddie, who played guitar and blues harmonica, and Pearl, who played bull fiddle (double bass), became surrogate parents to Jones and provided his room and board in addition to his $17.50 weekly salary. In recalling his experiences with them on the honky-tonk circuit, Jones told James Hunter, who profiled him for the *New York Times Magazine* (March 15, 1992), "It was a lot of fun, except for the chicken wire we'd have to put up in front of us around the bandstands some places when [customers] got to fighting or throwing beer bottles."

Jones had become thoroughly steeped long before in what has been labeled hillbilly, country, or mountain music by listening every Saturday night to the Grand Ole Opry radio show, which was broadcast live from Nashville, Tennessee. "I lived and breathed [the legendary country singer] Hank Williams [Sr.] when I was growing up," he said to the British singer/songwriter Elvis Costello during a conversation for *Interview* (November 1992). Later, in addition, he listened to some of the hundreds of country-music radio programs that had come into being during World War II.

In 1951, faced with the prospect of being jailed for failure to send his ex-wife child-support payments (their short-lived marriage had ended before the birth of their daughter, earlier in the same year), Jones enlisted in the United States Marine Corps. During his two years of service, he was stationed at Camp Pendleton, in California, and whenever possible he would perform at base-side nightspots. After his discharge he returned to Beaumont and began working as a housepainter. In 1953 or 1954 he signed a contract with Starday Records, a Beaumont-based concern founded by Jack Starnes and Harold W. ("Pappy") Daily, the latter of whom was to serve as his producer and manager for the next fifteen years. Jones cut his first single in Daily's living room, which had been wallpapered with egg cartons in an attempt to create the proper acoustics.

As Jones recalled to James Hunter, he began that first recording session by "just messing around." "Finally," he continued, "Pappy Daily came in and said: 'George, for the last few hours you've sung like [the country singers] Roy Acuff, Lefty Frizzell, Hank Williams, and Bill Monroe. Can you sing like George Jones?' So we just grabbed onto another song . . . and sang it in more of a straight voice of my own, although I still used their phrasing. You can't get that out. I learned, though, that I had to sing like George Jones. Somehow, it developed until . . . I had my own sound, my own voice." In the first edition of *Country Music, U.S.A.*, Bill C. Malone noted that "Jones's voice sometimes takes on the wailing quality of Roy Acuff or the plaintive tone of Hank Williams, and he occasionally lets his voice slide and bend around notes in a manner reminiscent of Lefty Frizzell or Floyd Tillman. But despite the numerous influences that have worked upon his style, Jones has a manner of presentation that is original, and it has come to be copied as much as that of earlier singers."

In 1955 Starday released "Why, Baby, Why," the first Jones single to reach the Top Ten on the country-music charts. Cowritten by Jones and Darrell Edwards, the song is "an indignant plaint that . . . epitomizes [Jones's] heartbroken barroom eloquence," as the music critic Mark Coleman wrote in *The Rolling Stone Album Guide* (1992). "Why, Baby, Why" brought Jones to the attention of country-music audiences nationwide. On the strength of its success, he obtained regular guest appearances on the Shreveport show *Louisiana Hayride*, the most prominent of radio's regional "barn dances." In mid-1956 he won a spot on the far more influential Grand Ole Opry program. That same year his first album, *George Jones Sings*, was released, and three of his songs appeared among the country-music charts' Top Ten hits. Jones's outstanding talents were quickly recognized: *Country & Western Jamboree Magazine* and disk jockeys polled by *Billboard* selected him as, respectively, one of the best new country singers of 1956 and one of the year's most promising new vocalists.

Beginning in 1957, Jones's discs were released on the Mercury label, in a deal Starday arranged as a means of expanding the marketing and distribution of its recordings. Despite that tactic and the release in 1957 of what became two more Top Ten Jones hits—"Don't Stop the Music" and "Uh Uh No"—the singer's finances remained precarious, because "he commanded less than top dollar on the road and had yet to see his first record royalty check," as Bob Allen explained in the *Journal of the American Academy for the Preservation of Old-Time Country Music* (February 1994), in an article adapted from his book *George Jones: The Saga of an American Singer* (1984). Part of the blame for those problems may be traced to the advent of rock-'n'-roll, which is commonly dated to 1954 and which within two years had led to the phenomenal success of Elvis Presley. In an attempt to gain a toehold on the rock-'n'-roll bandwagon, Pappy Daily persuaded Jones to make some recordings in the hybrid style known as rockabilly. By his own account, those discs displeased the singer, who used the pseudonym Thumper Jones on their labels. "I never could get the hard-feelin' country out of my soul," he explained to James Hunter. "It was in there too deep. I did some rock, and I had fun with it. But it didn't touch my heart. I was always looking forward to . . . get[ting] back to a ballad."

Between 1957 and 1962 Jones had eighteen country hits. Among the best known is "White Lightning" (1959), written by Jones and J. P. Richardson (known to rock enthusiasts as the Big Bopper), an exuberant song about the pleasures of distilling and drinking moonshine whiskey. His first number-one single, it remained at the top of the country-music charts for five weeks and entered the national pop charts as well. "The Window Up Above" (1960), which reached number two on the *Billboard* country-music chart, is one of the small number of songs that Jones has written without a collaborator. Widely regarded as one of his finest creations, it is the first-person narrative of a man who discovers his beloved in the arms of another man. Bob Allen expressed the view that "its images of violence, rage, desire, betrayal, and voyeurism [offer] a fleeting glimpse into Jones's own complex, sometimes troubled psyche" and that, singing in a "taut, almost offhanded manner" that "barely hinted at emotions seething beneath the surface," Jones had produced "one of the most powerful, haunting, and unusual" performances of his career. Other notable hits that followed soon after included "Tender Years," a pensive ballad that remained at the number-one spot on the country-music charts for seven weeks in 1961, "Aching Breaking Heart" (1962), and "She Still Thinks I Care," one of Jones's first singles after leaving Mercury for United Artists Records. The last-named song was nominated for a Grammy Award in 1962 as best country-and-western recording. "The Race Is On," an up-tempo Jones composition, became a crossover hit in 1964–65.

The early 1960s marked Jones's emergence as the dominant figure in what Bill C. Malone described as "a honky-tonk resurgence" that stretched from Texas to California. In both 1962 and 1963, the Country Music Association (CMA) named Jones the year's best male vocalist, thereby acknowledging both his technical virtuosity—which includes the ability to sing through clenched teeth—and his genius at conveying with authenticity a gamut of powerful emotions, ranging from ecstasy and elation to guilt, fury, grief, and hopelessness. "His voice is a wondrous instrument," according to John Morthland, "a tormented tenor that seems to be somehow pinched out of the back of his throat, stretching one-syllable words out over whole lines or snapping them off abruptly, swooping up and down the scales, twisting over and around the melody. . . . He puts his ideas and feelings across with such precision that even when he's working with second-rate material, it sounds like something very special."

"Unlike most country singers, there is no cheap melodrama in [Jones's] singing," Nick Tosches observed in *High Fidelity*. In a conversation with James Hunter, Kyle Lehning, who produced *And Along Came Jones* (1991), the singer's first album for MCA Records (his current label), pointed to the "classic sonority and dark, varied colors" of Jones's voice, and in the liner notes for the CD *The Best of George Jones* (1991), Ben Sandmel noted its "rich mournful tone." Jones "moves effortlessly from backwoods whoops and hollers to a warm, mellow tone," Sandmel continued. "He toys with rhythm like the best jazz phrasers, rushing or sustaining here, pausing suspensefully there. He hits unexpected falsettos and deep, throaty growls and dramatically contrasts the two." "Perhaps no singer since Billie Holiday, Robert Johnson, or Hank Williams has so chillingly conveyed the lower depths of pain and desperation," he added.

In the *New York Times* (February 27, 1981), the music critic John Rockwell offered his analysis of Jones's achievements and popularity: "Distinction as a country singer . . . is attained less through virtuosity than subtlety and the projection of personality. Mr. Jones has a confiding baritone, which he can crank up for the obligatory, rousing rockabilly tune. But he prefers soulful ballads. In that kind of song, his seemingly intuitive gifts of phrasing can shine through unimpeded. Mr. Jones has a way of accenting a key word or note in a melody that can enliven an entire song. But technical description seems to mean less in country music than in more complex forms, and it is unadorned simplicity of expression that country fans find so appealing. The simplicity seems to allow the intensity of a strong personality, and the pain of misused lives (a motif that informs the lyrics of many country songs), to come through clearly. And nobody seems to have had more of a country-song life than George Jones."

Interest among country-music aficionados in Jones's private as well as public life increased exponentially in 1969, when, a year after the termination of his fourteen-year second marriage, he wed the singer Tammy Wynette. Commonly referred to during their marriage as "the president and first lady of country music," the couple performed together before enthusiastic audiences at sites as different as Philharmonic Hall, in New York City, and Possum Holler, a club that Jones had established in Nashville. Jones and Wynette made ten albums together, and more than a dozen of their singles—some of which date from after their divorce, in 1974 (1975 according to some sources)—became hits. In *USA Today* (March 15, 1994), David Zimmerman characterized such successful Jones-Wynette duets as "We Go Together" (1971), "The Ceremony" (1972), "We're Gonna Hold On" (1973), and "We Loved It Away" (1974) as "state-of-the-union messages to fans" during their stormy marriage. Three of their collaborative efforts—"Take Me," "Golden Ring," and "Near You"—were nominated for Grammy Awards in 1972, 1976, and 1977, respectively, as best country vocal performance by a duo or group.

"Two-Story House," another duet recorded by Jones and Wynette, was released in 1980, a year after the publication of *Stand By Your Man*, Wynette's autobiography. Dwelling at length on the Jones-Wynette marriage, the book describes "in excruciating detail," as John Morthland put it, Jones's frequent alcoholic binges and unexplained disappearances and the couple's many brawls. Jones has said that he has neither read the book nor watched the television movie, first aired in 1981, based on it. "I heard a lot about it," he told John Morthland. "I don't mind anything in the world that's true. Country-music fans will forgive you, 'cause they love you, they love what you're experiencing, as long as you aren't a phony, as long as you can walk out on that stage and say I am what I am." "All country music thrives on sentiment, but few idols have gone so far on such fragile feet of clay," Ben Sandmel observed about Jones.

Earlier, in 1965, Jones had left United Artists to record for Musicor. In 1971 he signed on with Epic Records, where, for the next twenty years, he worked with Billy Sherrill, the company's house producer. Sherrill had originated a style known as countrypolitan (also referred to as "the Nashville sound"), which made use of lush string accompaniments, large complements of background singers, and "rhythms rendered with more technological punch," in the words of James Hunter. But "no matter how full and engulfing these accoutrements might be," as Bill C. Malone wrote, "they could not blunt or hide [Jones's] distinctiveness." In 1977 Jones was named country artist of the year by *Rolling Stone*. By that date, according to Nick Tosches, his discography would have shown "well over a hundred" albums but for the fact that apparently neither Jones nor anyone else had maintained a complete list. In the *Washington Post* (May 25, 1981), Richard Harrington estimated that as of mid-1981 Jones's albums numbered 150.

Sometimes referred to as "a singer's singer," Jones has won the highest admiration of top vocalists in various genres, among them Elvis Costello, Bob Dylan, Merle Haggard, Emmylou Harris, James Taylor, Randy Travis, and Waylon Jennings, the last of whom declared, in the 1970s song "It's Alright," "If we could all sing like we wanted to / We'd all sing like George Jones." Several of those admirers, along with Linda Ronstadt, Johnny Paycheck, Willie Nelson, and others, joined Jones in duets and trios to make *My Very Special Guests* (1979). By his own admission, Jones felt very unhappy about his performance on that album. "I let 'em all down," he told John Rockwell, referring to his fellow singers.

Scores of times in the years preceding that release, Jones had disappointed concertgoers, often in sold-out halls, by failing to show up for performances. (He thereby earned the nickname "No Show Jones," which became, in 1982, the title of a hit Jones-Haggard single.) While, to all appearances, the loyalty of his fans had remained unshaken, angry promoters had filed a slew of lawsuits against him. His troubles did not end there, however. Recklessly extravagant with his earnings, he had amassed such cripplingly large debts that he had been forced to declare bankruptcy, and he had run up a huge bill for delinquent taxes. He had fallen afoul of the law in other ways as well, by driving while intoxicated and firing a gun at one of his friends. At the end of 1979, his weight having dropped by a third, to little more than a hundred pounds, and with perhaps just two months to live, as one physician warned him, he was hospitalized for severe alcoholism and addiction to cocaine.

Jones has traced his alcoholism to his constant exposure to heavy drinkers as a teenage performer and also to the pressures of his enormous success; others have pointed to his nearly paralyzing stage-fright, which for years he apparently could surmount only with the aid of alcohol, and his deep-seated insecurity and lack of confidence in his abilities. Although his problems with alcohol lingered until about 1984 and led to at least one more hospitalization, Jones has said that his realization in 1979 that he had hit bottom marked a turning point for him. He has attributed his now decade-long sobriety and other aspects of his current stability to the financial and emotional help of friends, a $1 million loan from a fan, and the unwavering support of Nancy Sepulvado (or Sepulveda), whom he married in 1983 and who became his manager in 1986. At her suggestion, in the early 1980s he gave many concerts gratis to appease the promoters who had sued him.

Among the most popular of Jones's offerings at those concerts was "He Stopped Loving Her Today" (written by Bobby Braddock and Curly Putnam), one of country music's all-time greatest hits, a song about a man whose anguish from unrequited love ends only with his death. Jones won a Grammy in 1980 for best country vocal performance by a male artist for "He Stopped Loving Her Today." The CMA named the song the single of the year in 1980 and Jones the male vocalist of the year in both 1980 and 1981. The year 1980 also marked the release of *I Am What I Am*, the first Jones LP to sell more than half a million copies. In 1986 Jones won the CMA's video of the year award for "Who's Gonna Fill Their Shoes," and in 1993 he won the CMA's vocal event of the year award for "I Don't Need Your Rockin' Chair."

Although his diminished lung capacity, a consequence of his decades-long chain-smoking habit, has forced Jones when concertizing to include instrumental numbers after every few songs, in recent years he has maintained a performance schedule of about one hundred dates annually. In a review of a concert that he gave in 1992 at Tramps, a New York City club—where, according to Jon Pareles of the *New York Times* (November 14, 1992), he received "an adoring welcome from the packed crowd"—Doug Simmons of the *Village Voice* (November 24, 1992) declared that Jones "was in glorious voice, wringing more emotion out of a syllable or two . . . than most interpreters get from an entire song." "As an unexpected bonus, this notoriously shy man glowed with confidence and humor," Simmons added. In his assessment of the concert for *Rolling Stone* (January 7, 1993), Ron Tannenbaum reported, "Jones mixed the intimacy of a porch sing-along with the drama of a Las Vegas floor show."

Jones's most recent albums include *High Tech Redneck* (1993) and *Bradley Barn Sessions* (1994). The latter featured duets with, among others, Mark Chesnutt, Trisha Yearwood, Emmylou Harris, Travis Tritt, Dolly Parton, and—in their first joint recording in nearly fifteen years—Tammy Wynette, with whom he sang "Golden Ring." Jones and Wynette teamed up again in 1995, to produce the album *One*. Their performance of songs from the album at the annual Fan Fair celebration in Nashville in mid-1995 launched a joint forty-engagement tour in the United States and Europe. At one of their recent concerts, at the Star Plaza Theatre, in Merrillville, Indiana, their rendition of the title track of *One* "was so compelling in its depiction of spiritual union that the singers' current spouses felt obliged to wander onstage to playfully 'defend their turf,'" as Kevin McKeough reported in the *Chicago Tribune* (September 6, 1995). "Wynette wrapped her warm and lovely twang around Jones's soft drawl," McKeough continued, "and their drawn-out harmonies were glories to behold on a fine 'Hold On,' stunning 'Near You,' and the spine-tingling conclusion, 'Golden Ring.'"

The five-foot seven-inch George Jones was described by Jack Hurst in the *Chicago Tribune* (October 26, 1980) as "a man of mercurial temper and swiftly changing moods" and by Jim Jerome in *People* (November 23, 1992) as "endearingly humble." "Talking about himself, he will use 'we' when the subject gets too personal to say 'I,'" John Rockwell noted. Jones underwent triple-bypass cardiac surgery in 1994, and he recently quit smoking. He and his wife, Nancy, a former telephone company employee, with whom he established and managed the Jones Country Music Park, in Colmesneil, Texas, in the early 1980s, live in Franklin, Tennessee. A short distance away is Jones's farm, where he spends much of his leisure time tending his herd of cattle. The singer's other main recreational interests are watching television and—every morning when he is not on tour—mowing his vast lawn. He gets his hair trimmed daily in his professionally equipped home salon. For the past couple of years, he has been working on his autobiography. From his first marriage, to the former Dorothy Bonvillion, Jones has a daughter, Susan; from his second, to the former Shirley Ann Corley, he has two sons, Brian and Jeffrey. He has one daughter, Tamala Georgette, from his marriage to Tammy Wynette, whose three older daughters he adopted, two step-daughters from his current marriage, and several grandchildren.

Selected Biographical References: Chicago Tribune mag p12+ Mr 22 '81 pors; Country Music p28+ Jl/Ag '95 pors; NY Times C p1+ Je 15 '95 por; N Y Times Mag p50+ Mr 15 '92 pors; People 38:109+ N 23 '92 pors, 44:54+ O 2 '95 pors; Texas Mo 10:144+ Je '82 pors, 22:64+ Jl '94 pors; Malone, Bill C. Country Music, U.S.A. (1968, 1985); Who's Who in America, 1995

Demmie Todd/PMK

Jones, Tommy Lee

Sept. 15, 1946- Actor. Address: c/o International Creative Management, 8899 Beverly Blvd., Los Angeles, CA 90048

For all the praise that greeted his work in such television movies as *The Amazing Howard Hughes* (1977) and *The Executioner's Song* (1982) and such feature films as *Coal Miner's Daughter* (1980), Tommy Lee Jones was for years chiefly relegated to parts in little-noticed pictures. Seemingly overnight, however, he became known as an "A"-list Hollywood talent, in large part due to his award-winning performance as a rough-edged federal lawman in the 1993 film *The Fugitive*. Since then he has been a ubiquitous screen presence, turning up, for example, in the 1994 films *Cobb, The Client,* and *Natural Born Killers* and as the director and star of *The Good Old Boys*, broadcast on TNT in the spring of 1995. Several of his recent, more prominent roles have been those of men whose tough exteriors belie their vulnerability—a pattern that has led to comparisons with a movie star of an earlier era, Humphrey Bogart.

An eighth-generation Texan, Tommy Lee Jones was born on September 15, 1946 in the small town of San Saba, the only child of Clyde Jones, an oil-field worker, and Lucille Marie (Scott) Jones, who worked variously as a police officer, schoolteacher, and owner of a beauty parlor. By all accounts, Clyde Jones was an abusive man whose relationship with his wife was stormy, and as a result Tommy Lee Jones's childhood was, as he described it to a reporter for *People* (June 15, 1981), "psychically horrifying." Because his father was continually in search of new oil fields, the family often relocated, "from one small West Texas town to another," as Jones has recalled. By the time of his early adolescence, Jones had developed a passion for football, which afforded him an escape from his tumultuous home life. "Football was a reason for living," he explained to Mimi Swartz, who profiled the actor for *Texas Monthly* (October 1993). "I'd lie awake at night dreaming of the day I could play." Weighing only ninety-eight pounds in the seventh grade, when he took up the sport, he competed against boys who were much larger than himself. "That made me faster, meaner," he told Swartz.

The course of Jones's life changed when his father decided to work in the oil fields in Libya. Wanting to continue playing football, Jones resisted a move overseas. He received an opportunity to stay in the United States when he earned a scholarship to St. Mark's, an elite preparatory school in Dallas. Although the school provided a refuge for Jones, he had difficulty adapting to the new setting, and his first-quarter report card described him as "sullen, morose, and belligerent." "As I look back, here was a kid who was completely alone in a big city, in a very challenging academic environment, living with people who occupied a social world that I'd never even heard of or thought of," Jones recalled in an interview with Lucy Kaylin for *GQ* (March 1994). "There were just enormous adjustments to make. There would have been enormous adjustments to make even if I'd been living at home with both parents."

Jones eventually thrived at St. Mark's, playing football, developing a passion for literature, and gaining his first exposure to the theatre. One day, he happened upon a rehearsal for a student production of *Mister Roberts* and was instantly captivated. He was soon performing in school plays, making his debut in *The Caine Mutiny Court-Martial*. The discovery of acting was a thrilling one for Jones. "I was very happy, elated, with this wonderful feeling of security, joy, and honor," he recalled, as quoted in the *New Yorker* (April 4, 1994).

Thanks in large measure to his prowess on the football field, Jones won a scholarship to Harvard University, in Cambridge, Massachusetts, where he roomed with future vice-president Al Gore. (The two have remained good friends.) As a guard on the football team, Jones made the All-Ivy and All-East squads and received an honorable mention on the Associated Press All-America list. He also played in the legendary 1968 Harvard-Yale contest, known since as "The Tie," in which Harvard scored sixteen points in the final forty-two seconds of the game to even the score at twenty-nine points. Another Harvard alumnus, the character actor John Lithgow, recalled to Lucy Kaylin, "I remember Jones describing in great detail what it was like after a football game . . . the serenity of it. He had an artistic appreciation of what it was like to be an athlete." Jones brought the same studied intensity to acting, performing in works by Euripides, Shakespeare, Bertolt Brecht, and Harold Pinter, among others, in college and in repertory theatres around Boston. He graduated cum laude in 1969 with a B.A. degree in English.

Lacking the girth necessary to become a professional football player, Jones concentrated on acting after leaving Harvard. Just ten days after he moved to New York City to pursue theatre work, he was cast in a Broadway production of John Osborne's *A Patriot for Me*, in which he had five different bit parts. In 1970 he made his first film appearance, as one of Ryan O'Neal's Harvard friends in the celebrated tearjerker *Love Story*. For the next several years, Jones supported himself by performing during the day as Dr. Mark Toland on the soap opera *One Life to Live*. During this period he also appeared in a number of stage productions. He had small parts in *Four on a Garden*, the collective title of four comic pieces starring Carol Channing and Sid Caesar. In the opinion of Richard Watts of the *New York Post* (November 30, 1972), Jones "seemed the best actor of the evening" in *Blue Boys*, a Civil War drama by Allan Knee. In *Ulysses in Nighttown*, an adaptation of James Joyce's *Ulysses*, he played Stephen Dedalus to Zero Mostel's Leopold Bloom. Although most reviewers found Jones's portrayal of Stephen to be bland, Jones was nonetheless thrilled by the opportunity to work with Mostel, for whom he had a high regard. "It was great to watch Mostel's energy, where he succeeded, where he failed," Jones told Bernard Weinraub for an article that appeared in the *New York Times* (August 1, 1993). "Every day was a brave new world for me. It was an important period in my life."

That experience notwithstanding, by about 1975 Jones had grown frustrated with the New York theatrical scene, having frequently lost coveted assignments to actors with less experience but greater name recognition. "I was bumping against a ceiling in the theatre," he explained to Weinraub. "I was told two or three times a year that, yes, I was the right actor for a role, but I wasn't famous enough. I saw roles that I should have had go to people whose qualifications as a theatre actor seem to have derived from sitcoms, from the fact that they were more famous." To remedy the situation, Jones moved to Los Angeles, where he again easily found work, including a featured part in the pilot for the television series *Charlie's Angels*.

Jones's first starring role was as the title character in the 1977 made-for-television movie *The Amazing Howard Hughes*, a portrait of the eccentric billionaire. Five years after that success, he again triumphed on the small screen, with his portrayal of Gary Gilmore, the convicted murderer who requested his own execution, in *The Executioner's Song*, based on the book by Norman Mailer. It was commonly agreed that Jones managed to elicit from the viewing audience a measure of sympathy for the killer. Yet his performance was also chilling, according to Cathy Horyn of the *Washington Post* (March 30, 1992), who found that Jones "inflamed Gary Gilmore with a quality of interior violence that made watching the television movie a nervous and exhausting experience." For his work in *The Executioner's Song*, Jones earned an Emmy Award.

Meanwhile, in feature films, Jones had appeared as violent or disturbed characters in a series of mostly forgettable projects. Among the first of these was *Jackson County Jail* (1976), in which he and Yvette Mimieux were cast as escapees from an Arizona jail. In *Rolling Thunder* (1977), he took the part of an ex-POW whose experiences have left him devoid of emotion, and he was a venal race-car driver turned automotive designer in the 1978 adaptation of Harold Robbins's steamy novel *The Betsy*. Later in the same year, in *The Eyes of Laura Mars*, which starred Faye Dunaway as a fashion photographer who has psychic visions of actual murders, Jones played a police lieutenant with a split personality. He had hesitated to accept that role because he thought the storyline was "preposterous," but in the end, he decided to attempt an authentic portrait of a psychopathic criminal, even consulting a therapist for advice. Jones was singled out by various critics as being an "inspired" casting choice and as "charming and believable," although many reviewers shared the actor's initial opinion of the story as a whole. In *Back Roads* (1981), another film that failed to impress reviewers, Jones's character was a petty criminal who supplements his income by taking dives in boxing matches and who teams up for adventure and romance with a prostitute (Sally Field).

The exception in that string of unremarkable films was the well-received *Coal Miner's Daughter*, in which Jones costarred as Mooney Lynn, the husband and manager of the country-music star Loretta Lynn (Sissy Spacek). As portrayed by Jones, Mooney is by turns supportive of his wife and resentful of living in the famous singer's shadow. In his review of *Coal Miner's Daughter* for *New York* (March 17, 1980), David Denby wrote, "The revelation here is Tommy Lee Jones. In some of his earlier pictures . . . , Jones, shy of acting, ducked his head away from the camera and ran through his lines skittishly, but now he has stopped fighting what he's doing. . . . He shows us the animal grace and the shrewdness inside the hick. His sudden, nervous grin, shading off into slyness, says to us, 'I'm not as dumb as I look.' . . . Jones gives Mooney a sweet, sodden dignity that's immensely touching."

Despite that winning performance and the accolades for his television work, the fame that was predicted for Jones continued to elude him, and throughout much of the 1980s he embodied assorted heavies and clever rogues in performances generally judged to be better than the movies themselves. On the big screen he played a swashbuckling pirate in *Nate and Hayes* (1983), a thief-for-hire in *Black Moon Rising* (1986), and a gambling boss in *The Big Town* (1987). His television work during those years included a turn as a strict father during the Revolutionary War in the 1988 entry *April Morning* and, in the same year, a portrayal of a Vietnam veteran fighting to prevent his ranch from being turned into a missile base in *Stranger on My Land*. Discussing Jones's portrayal of an evil entrepreneur in the film noir *Stormy*

Monday, Mike McGrady wrote in *New York Newsday* (April 22, 1988), "Some day, off in the future, when Tommy Lee Jones finally finds his way into a first-rate movie, people will wonder where he's been all these years. Where he's been, mostly, is adding sinew to movies such as *Stormy Monday*, tough-minded flicks that are better than just so-so but less than memorable."

His appearance as the taciturn cowboy Woodrow Call in the 1989 television miniseries *Lonesome Dove* brought Jones renewed attention as a serious actor. Based on the highly praised novel by Larry McMurtry, *Lonesome Dove* is the tale of a late nineteenth-century cattle drive from South Texas to Montana, led by Call and his irrepressible cohort Gus McCrae (Robert Duvall). Harry F. Waters spoke for many when he observed in *Newsweek* (February 6, 1989) that Jones and Duvall "clearly relished playing off each other, and their mutual affection for their irascible characters shines through brilliantly."

Because the physical and emotional landscapes of *Lonesome Dove* were very familiar to Jones, he was particularly enticed by the opportunity to play Call. He explained to Gavin Smith for *Film Comment* (January 1994), "It's the story of my country and my people in a very real way, so I found that important. It was a good testing ground for any thinking that I might have done on the abstract level about acting and having a creative life—if it's not gonna work there, it's not gonna work." Jones was touched by the exceptional viewer response to the program, telling Horyn, "People who saw *Lonesome Dove* wrote me letters about their experiences in Texas, about their grandfathers and their families. People who had done nothing for five generations except run cattle, who had been watching movies all their lives and had entirely given up hope of ever recognizing themselves in a Western. Letters that would break your heart."

In a departure from his previous, rough-and-tumble characters, Jones appeared as the flamboyant homosexual businessman Clay Shaw, one of those accused of conspiring to kill President John F. Kennedy, in Oliver Stone's *JFK* (1991). Many reviewers were fascinated by Jones's interpretation of his character, agreeing with David Ansen of *Newsweek* (December 23, 1991), who called Jones "a powerful, if too overtly sinister, presence," and with Jack Mathews of *New York Newsday* (December 20, 1991), who pronounced the actor to be "truly unnerving" as Shaw. Jones also earned praise for his performance from the writer Norman Mailer, who had met the actor during the filming of his book *The Executioner's Song*, and who, after seeing *JFK*, asked an acquaintance the name of the "marvelous actor" who had been cast as Clay Shaw.

In his interview with Gavin Smith, Jones referred to Shaw as "a dedicated sadomasochist," and he explained that he had wanted to portray fully that side of the character. The film drew protests from some gay groups because its three villains were homosexual; in his interview with Gavin Smith, Jones himself conceded that the actors had walked "a fine line, because you don't want to make it all about being gay, you don't want to *insult* anybody's sexuality, you don't want to make a blanket statement about any group of people. People don't exist as groups in my mind, and they shouldn't in an actor's mind. People exist as individuals." Jones was nominated for an Academy Award as best supporting actor for his performance.

The actor again teamed up with Stone for *Heaven and Earth* (1993), a tale of the Vietnam War seen from the point of view of the Vietnamese. He portrayed Steve Butler, a caring but volatile American soldier who marries a South Vietnamese woman (Hiep Thi Le) and moves with her back to the United States, where emotional crises begin to get the better of him. Jones's acting in the film drew responses ranging from "riveting" and "haunting" to Anthony Lane's comment in the *New Yorker* (January 17, 1994) that the highly emotional role was "a perfect demonstration of how not to use" Tommy Lee Jones, who had theretofore earned a reputation for portraying men whose feelings were held in check.

Jones has appeared in several films made by the thriller specialist Andrew Davis, among them *The Package* (1989), in which he played a psychopathic prisoner, and the Steven Seagal vehicle *Under Siege* (1992), in which he was a demented but charming killer. His most significant collaboration with Davis to date has been *The Fugitive* (1993), the film based on the long-running television series that starred David Janssen. Jones played the deputy United States marshal Sam Gerard, who doggedly pursues escaped prisoner Richard Kimble (Harrison Ford), a doctor wrongly convicted of killing his wife. "Jones swaggers lovably, leaking compassion around the edges, and his performance—charged with a particularly American mythos—steals the show," Joe Levy observed in the *Village Voice* (August 17, 1993). "To watch Jones's U.S. marshal in *The Fugitive* is to witness the exhilarating spectacle of a movie propelled inevitably forward by sheer personality. It looks like a lot of fun being around this guy, he can do what the hell he likes—and he's *cool*," Gavin Smith observed. For his contribution to *The Fugitive*, Jones won an Academy Award for best supporting actor as well as a Los Angeles Film Critics Award and a Golden Globe Award.

The success of *The Fugitive* catapulted Jones into leading-man status and precipitated an avalanche of offers. In 1994 alone he won kudos for his film portrayals of a prosecutor in *The Client*, directed by Joel Schumacher and based on the John Grisham novel; a prison warden in Oliver Stone's violent satire *Natural Born Killers*; an army engineer caring for his manic-depressive wife (Jessica Lange) in *Blue Sky*, the director Tony Richardson's last movie; and the belligerent baseball legend Ty Cobb in Ron Shelton's *Cobb*. (An exception was his portrayal of a mad bomber, opposite Jeff Bridges, in the critically reviled *Blown Away*.) Reviewing

Cobb, Janet Maslin of the *New York Times* (December 2, 1994) wrote that watching Jones perform was "a frankly captivating experience. He's an actor whom audiences would follow anywhere, one whose other work released this year . . . shows off a snappish, gritty presence that lends any film a little extra fury. . . . He easily inhabits this big, colorful role. He gives this film the entertaining demon it needs." In March 1995 Jones received generally good notices for *The Good Old Boys*, the made-for-television movie, taken from the Elmer Kelton novel, that marked Jones's debut as a director and screenwriter. Set in Texas in the first years of the twentieth century, the movie also starred Jones, as an aging cowboy in an era of rapid change. Later in the year, Jones gave an over-the-top performance as the villain Two-Face in Joel Schumacher's *Batman Forever*.

In his interview with Bernard Weinraub of the *New York Times*, Jones explained his attraction to acting: "The simple answer is, it seemed like fun. The complicated answer is, it has to do with an enjoyment of and necessity for a vital imagination. But I'm not that analytical. I'll stick with the simple answer. It's fun." Jones sees nothing amiss in making films that are intended as pure entertainment. "It's no mean calling," he told Richard Corliss for *Time* (September 6, 1993), "to bring fun into the afternoons of large numbers of people. That too is part of my job, and I'm happy to serve when called on." While Jones ascribes to no particular acting method, he believes acting requires detachment and astute observation. "Other people's experience is important. That's one of the best things about being an actor. I have a real interest in people—for entirely *selfish* reasons," he explained to Gavin Smith. "I don't forget anything. You try to be *thoughtful* about the experience of other people. And I don't take life all that personally."

Texas remains vital to Jones's sense of self. "Natives of my region are heirs to a society whose language, manners, cuisine, habits of dress, transportation, and ways of socializing with one another are not so removed from location as others are," he remarked to Richard Corliss for the *Time* profile. "We're still tied to a place. We happen to think it's important to be from some place." Jones married Kimberlea Cloughley, whom he had met when she was working as an extra on *Back Roads*, on May 30, 1981. They subsequently moved back to San Antonio, where they lived together until they were separated in 1995. From that marriage Jones has two children, Austin and Victoria. (His first marriage, to Kate Lardner, the granddaughter of the writer Ring Lardner, ended in divorce in the late 1970s.) Jones owns a cattle ranch that reportedly encompasses four thousand acres, a space that also enables him to indulge his passion for polo, which he described to Kaylin as "the finest thing a man and a horse can do together." Every fall, he invites the Harvard polo team to practice on his property.

Jones has on occasion come across as taciturn during interviews, inspiring frequent comparisons to those of his characters who are gruff but sensitive and vulnerable below the surface. With his coarse features and pock-marked face, he is not classically handsome, yet many seem drawn to other aspects of the actor. Sissy Spacek, his costar in *Coal Miner's Daughter* and *The Good Old Boys*, probably spoke for others when she explained her affinity for Jones: "I've always been attracted to men who have a strong inner life, who are smart and not quite perfect and who tend to be misunderstood a lot." Speaking to Richard Corliss, Andrew Davis compared Jones to the screen legend Humphrey Bogart. "He's not the most attractive, smooth-faced guy in the world, yet he has this sexuality. He really is the southwestern Bogart."

Selected Biographical References: Film Comment 30:30+ Ja '94 pors; GQ 64:210+ Mr '94 pors; N Y Times II p11+ Ag 1 '93 pors; New Yorker 70:57+ Ap 4 '94; People 40:83+ S 6 '93 pors; Texas Monthly 21:106+ O '93 pors; Time 142:65 S 6 '93 por; Washington Post B p1+ Mr 30 '92 pors; Who's Who in America, 1995

AP/Wide World Photos

Karadžić, Radovan

(KAH-rah-jeetch, RAH-doh-van)

1945(?)- Bosnian political leader; psychiatrist. Address: c/o 71000 Sarajevo, trg Dure Pucara bb, Bosnia and Herzegovina

The death in 1980 of the Yugoslav dictator Josip Broz Tito, combined with the disintegration of the Soviet bloc a decade later, set the stage for the June 1991 breakup of Yugoslavia, an ethnically diverse country comprising six constituent republics born in the aftermath of World War II. In 1992 one of those republics, Bosnia and Herzegovina, under a Muslim-controlled government, gained formal recognition as an independent state. Following that development, Radovan Karadžić, the elected representative of the Bosnian Serbs, carried on a campaign of savagery against Bosnian Muslims. From Slobodan Milošević, the president of neighboring Serbia, Karadžić received strong moral and military support for the war against the Muslims, who greatly outnumbered Serbs in Bosnia but were poorly armed. The atrocities on the part of Karadžić's troops were committed in the name of "ethnic cleansing."

Karadžić, a psychiatrist by training, by turns rationalized and denied the violence, and until recently he took advantage of the international community's reluctance to combat his army. He inspired the war against civilians through jingoistic appeals to Serbian patriotism and by creating fear, unwarranted in the view of most observers, that the Muslim government would transform Bosnia into a Muslim fundamentalist state. Karadžić stated that the Serbs, most of whom belong to the Serbian Orthodox church, had "been betrayed for centuries" and could not "live with other nations." Between 1992 and 1995 the Serbs killed as many as two hundred thousand of their former countrymen and uprooted at least one million, in an apparent drive to claim Bosnia as part of a Greater Serbia. In April 1995 Radovan Karadžić was formally named as a suspected war criminal by an international tribunal established by the United Nations. Four months later, following yet another massacre of civilians at the hands of Bosnian Serbs, NATO launched a two-week-long series of air strikes that curbed the aggression of Karadžić's troops and forced him to engage in peace negotiations.

Radovan Karadžić was born in about 1945 in Montenegro, a constituent of Yugoslavia. Although the details of his background are sketchy, it is known that at the age of fifteen he moved to an area just outside Sarajevo, the capital of Bosnia, as part of a larger migration of peasants to urban areas. During an interview with Maggie O'Kane for the *Guardian* (August 10, 1992), one observer explained that Karadžić arrived in the city "with all the complexes of a barefooted peasant boy," and that he felt excluded from the more cosmopolitan Sarajevan society. It has been surmised that any resentment he may have developed toward the residents of Sarajevo during his boyhood may have found expression in his future military campaign against the city. Karadžić eventually studied medicine and specialized in psychiatry, spending the 1974–75 academic year at Columbia University, in New York City. After returning to Yugoslavia, Karadžić held a variety of positions as a physician and psychiatrist and is said to have specialized in the treatment of paranoiacs. He worked for, among other concerns, the state hospital system, the large Yugoslavian company Unis, and the Sarajevo rugby team.

In about 1985 Karadžić was imprisoned for eleven months, charged with having misused funds marked for house loans; he has claimed that his incarceration was the result of his anti-Communist stance. He began his political activities shortly after that episode. Beginning in the mid-1980s, Serbian nationalists stepped up their activities, evoking past conflicts among Serbs, Croats, and Muslims, calling for a unified ethnic state, and declaring, for example, that "not even a hundred thousand dead will be too many" if the result were the establishment of a Greater Serbia. In the summer of 1990, Karadžić helped to found, and assumed the presidency of, the Serbian Democratic Party of Bosnia and Herzegovina. Soon thereafter the party disseminated propaganda calling on Serbs to participate in the "historic ethnic struggle" and fabricated the notion that the Bosnian Muslims were preparing a *jihad*, or holy war, against non-Muslims. "It was manifest rubbish, as any Serb who had lived with Bosnia's Muslims knew only too well," Ed Vulliamy wrote in his book *Seasons in Hell* (1994). Nonetheless, Karadžić successfully used stories of Muslim-perpetrated violence—exaggerated or simply invented—to stir up anti-Muslim sentiment among Bosnian Serbs.

Karadžić's propaganda campaign took place against the background of the Yugoslav federation's spectacular disintegration into component states. Following conflicts between Croats and Serbs in Croatia, in 1991 both Croatia and Slovenia seceded from the federation and established themselves as separate nations, with Bosnia and Herzegovina soon following suit. In the latter case, however, after Bosnian Croats and Muslims voted in favor of a new government, Bosnian Serbs, who had largely boycotted the elections, declared the establishment of a Serbian Republic, of which Karadžić would be president and which would remain part of Yugoslavia. In April 1992, shortly after President Alija Izetbegović took the reins of the newly independent republic of Bosnia and Herzegovina in Sarajevo, Bosnian Serb troops closed the roads to the city, set up blockades and sniper posts, and began a long and bloody siege. "We are not going to accept an independent Bosnia [and] Herzegovina," Karadžić stated on March 2, 1992, warning that the civil war to come would make the conflict in Northern Ireland seem by comparison like "a seaside holiday."

Indeed, in the months that followed, Serbian troops set about to destroy the city of Sarajevo while Bosnian villages in Serb-held territory were "cleansed" of Muslims as well as other non-Serbs. Forced relocations to concentration camps, sometimes in railroad boxcars, recalled Nazi deportations of Jews and were accompanied by robbery, arson, and massacres. Widespread reports of torture and rape by Serbs were countered, though not convincingly, by Karadžić with stories of Muslim atrocities. Although he eventually moved his headquarters to an underground bunker, Karadžić made himself available to the press. In an interview with John F. Burns in the *New York Times*

(May 17, 1992), he stated his belief that it would be "impossible for Serbs to live together with other peoples in a unitary state."

The initial response of the international community to the strife in Bosnia went little further than the UN Security Council's institution of a "no-fly" zone over Bosnia and Herzegovina in October 1992. Meanwhile, in the summer of the same year, Karadžić journeyed to London to take part in an internationally sponsored peace conference. In an interview with Nathan Gardels that appeared in *New Perspectives Quarterly* (Fall 1992), Karadžić said that he did not consider the talks a success because they were "too one-sided against the Serbs, as if we were to blame for everything. There are eleven million Serbs. We are about to stand up and say to the rest of the world, 'That is enough. Get your hands out. We want to make our own state, and we don't need you since you are not interested in our survival.'"

In January 1993, in Geneva, Switzerland, a new round of talks began. Cyrus R. Vance, a United Nations representative and former United States secretary of state, and David Owen, a former British foreign secretary, presided over negotiations among Karadžić; Alija Izetbegović; the Bosnian Croat leader Mate Boban; Franjo Tudjman, the president of Croatia; and Dobrica Cosić, the leader of what remained of Yugoslavia. The proposed Vance-Owen peace plan advocated the division of Bosnia into ten provinces—three populated chiefly by Muslims, one peopled mainly by Serbs, five in which power would be divided between Muslims and Croats or Muslims and Serbs, and one that would encompass Sarajevo, which would be an open city.

Within days of the commencement of the talks, the Muslim and Croatian factions had agreed to the terms of the plan, leaving as the only holdout Karadžić, who called for the recognition of an independent Serbian state in Bosnia. Under pressure from the West, however, Karadžić agreed to the plan—but then announced that it had to be ratified by the eighty-one-member, self-declared Bosnian Serb parliament. The group voted to approve the plan, although some felt they had done so only to assuage the West and to buy time to work toward the creation of a separate Bosnian Serb state. There also remained the question of where to draw the borders of the proposed provinces, and new rounds of talks began. In the meantime, violence on the part of the Bosnian Serbs continued; while Izetbegović called for the West to initiate air strikes to end the fighting, Karadžić threatened "another Vietnam" if the UN or the United States sent ground troops to Bosnia.

In early May 1993, after the peace plan had been amended to allow for a corridor that would connect Serbs in eastern Bosnia with those in the western part of the country, Karadžić signed the agreement. The plan was subsequently defeated by the Bosnian Serb parliament. By the end of July, Lord Owen and Cyrus Vance's successor, Thorvald Stoltenberg, had devised a new proposal, which called for the conversion of Bosnia into a union of three independent states created along ethnic lines. That plan was killed by a 65-0 vote in Bosnia and Herzegovina's Muslim-controlled parliament, whose members felt that to cede a third of Bosnia to the Serbs would be to validate Bosnian Serb aggression.

Despite having threatened prolonged violence in the event of the Muslims' rejection of the peace plan, Karadžić was conciliatory in the fall of 1993. His army's guns fell more or less silent, and the siege of Sarajevo was discontinued. Karadžić gave assurances that the Bosnian Serbs did not "intend to resume the war" and that, "for us, the war is finished." He said further that he regretted "every single lost life, no matter whose lost life," that his troops would allow UN trucks to bring wood for fuel into Sarajevo, and that one day Serbs would help Muslims rebuild the city. Karadžić's sudden change of approach, as John F. Burns put it in the *New York Times* (October 10, 1993), seemed to be inspired less by a love of peace than by a desire to "[encourage] reservations in Washington about the part of a peace plan that would involve sending a fifty thousand-member NATO force . . . to put the accord into effect."

Indeed, the proclaimed peace did not hold: in November 1993, just before talks were to begin on yet another peace plan—this one calling for Bosnian Serbs to yield to Muslims more land than they had agreed to surrender under the previous accord—Serb shelling killed five people in Sarajevo. "This is our territory," Karadžić was quoted as saying in the *New York Times* (November 29, 1993). "This land is Serbian land." In January 1994 Karadžić refused UN requests to open the airport in the city of Tuzla to enable the Muslim community, still under Serbian attack, to receive humanitarian aid. Karadžić also rejected the notion, proposed by the United Nations, of a loose confederation of separate Croat, Serb, and Muslim states within Bosnia. Karadžić seemed more committed to warfare than ever, perhaps because of new military losses suffered by his troops at the hands of the Bosnian military, and he was blustery in the face of renewed threats by NATO to conduct air strikes in the event of a continued siege of Sarajevo: "I accuse the international community. . . . They are responsible for initiating the war, and they are responsible for continuing the war. Everyone can realize that the Muslims are encouraged to fight."

Although Karadžić denied that his troops had launched a mortar that killed sixty-eight civilians in Sarajevo on February 5, 1994, the UN nonetheless began to threaten air strikes on Serbian weapons emplacements around the city. On February 28, 1994 NATO forces shot down a quartet of Serbian bombers that were in violation of the "no-fly" zone. A month later the undeterred Bosnian Serbs launched a battle to gain control of Goražde, designated as a "safe" area (one protected by UN troops). This led to further air strikes on April 10 and 11 to counter the growing Serb offensive. The following day Karadžić declined to meet with UN officials and instead visited his troops near Goražde. On April 17 Serbs downed a British jet fighter that had attempted to immobilize the Serb tanks firing on the area, and within days Goražde fell to the Bosnian Serbs.

That bloody victory created new impetus in the international community for another diplomatic initiative, and a "Contact Group" of representatives from the United States, Russia, Britain, France, and Germany was soon formed. In July the group developed a peace proposal that was comparatively tough on Serbian aggression: it would have required, among other things, that the Bosnian Serbs return about one-third of the territory they had gained (they had seized approximately 70 percent of the country) and would not have recognized an independent Bosnian Serb state. Not surprisingly, Karadžić and the Bosnian Serb leadership rejected the plan. Shortly thereafter, Slobodan Milošević, pressured by the UN's newly aggressive economic sanctions, shut the borders between Serbia and the Bosnian Serbs and hinted at the discontinuation of military aid. In response, Karadžić voiced defiance and urged self-reliance among his troops. "We are prepared to be hungry, naked, and barefoot, but we must fight for our freedom," he stated on Bosnian Serb television.

Although the autumn of 1994 brought battlefield losses and tougher economic sanctions to the Bosnian Serbs, by late November they were once again on the offensive. They undertook a siege on Bihać, a Muslim enclave in northwestern Bosnia, which had previously been declared a "safe" area. On November 30 Karadžić refused an invitation to meet with the UN secretary general, Boutros Boutros-Ghali, and his troops kidnapped seven UN peacekeepers. Former United States president Jimmy Carter offered his services as a peacemaker to Karadžić in the following month, in an effort to bring about a cease-fire. The mission's accomplishments, like those of all previous initiatives in the conflict, were short-lived.

On April 23, 1995 the International Criminal Tribunal for the former Yugoslavia named both Karadžić and General Ratko Mladić, the commander of the Bosnian Serb army, suspected war criminals. The tribunal, established by the UN security council in 1993, cited Karadžić for "genocide, murder, rape, mistreatment of civilians," and other offenses. Karadžić had periodically denied any involvement in the killing of civilian Muslims, although he acknowledged possible violence on the part of Serbs acting on their own initiative. Since 1992 there had been speculation on the part of some that Karadžić had lost control of the siege he had begun. During the peace talks, Karadžić's willingness to accede to some of the terms of the various proposals had seemed to put him at odds with members of the Bosnian Serb parliament, who were more hard-line than their leader. On the other hand, some observers have viewed Karadžić's reversals of direction, his frequent self-contradiction, and his alternating between the roles of negotiator and warlord as ways of sowing confusion and buying time while his troops continue their landgrab.

In 1995, for the first time since hostilities commenced, the Bosnian government army began to make significant gains. Partly breaking the Serbian grip on Sarajevo in the early summer of 1995, Muslim troops mounted an effort to control Serbian supply routes to Pale, where Karadžić had been headquartered since the war began. But Karadžić's Bosnian Serbs, meanwhile, had taken UN peacekeepers as hostages, either detaining or surrounding some 350 soldiers altogether, at least in part to discourage air strikes. The last of these hostages were eventually released on June 18, 1995, after the UN and NATO gave up their joint effort to protect Sarajevo from Bosnian Serb bombardment and to collect some of the heavy artillery surrounding the city. NATO also agreed, in effect, not to undertake any of its planned air strikes or to use any other method involving force.

At the same time that the hostages were released, and shortly after he had written President Bill Clinton to propose a "Camp David–style conference" to resolve the conflict, Radovan Karadžić declared to his countrymen a "state of war" and called for all Bosnian Serbs over the age of eighteen to report for military service. On July 11 Bosnian Serbs entered Srebrenica, another "safe" area, and took more UN hostages. Ten days later NATO renewed its threats of air strikes in a move designed to defend the remaining "safe" regions. Within a week Croatia sent thousands of its troops into Bosnia to fight the Serbs.

In August 1995 Karadžić faced new threats, internal as well as external. Following his attempt to relieve Ratko Mladić of command, a move supported by the Bosnian Serb parliament, Mladić's troops declared their loyalty to the general, stating that they would follow Mladić's orders rather than Karadžić's—and leading observers to speculate about a possible coup. On August 29, the day after Bosnian Serb shelling killed thirty-seven residents of Sarajevo and wounded more that eighty others, NATO undertook its most forceful retaliatory measures since the start of the Bosnian conflict, initiating a prolonged series of air strikes against Bosnian Serb targets. Karadžić remained defiant in the face of the bombardment, promising that his troops would continue to fight. Eventually, however, he pleaded with NATO to stop the bombing. In mid-September, after the Bosnian Serbs agreed to place their weapons at a safe distance from Sarajevo, NATO ended the air strikes, and a monthe later all sides declared a cease-fire in the region. In the face of the West's new stance with regard to the conflicts in the former Yugoslavia, Karadžić submitted to Milosevic's plans to participate in United States-sponsored peace talks that began in November 1995.

Radovan Karadžić has been described with varying degrees of hostility by Western journalists and others who have met him. A "pathological liar and a psychopath" and "the butcher of Bosnia" are among the phrases that have been used to characterize him. "The portly Dr. Karadžić buttons up his jacket as he waddles towards you as a gesture of feigned respect," Ed Vulliamy wrote in *Seasons in Hell*. "He greets you with his troubled frown, . . . runs his fingers through a dash of grey hair and invites you into his lair, a converted hotel in Pale, for coffee, French cognac and cheese." His wife, Liljana Karadžić, is a psychiatrist who specializes in group analysis. The couple has two children, one of whom, Sonja, has served in an increasingly important capacity as an aide to her father. An admirer of the American poet Walt Whitman, Karadžić has himself written three books of verse.

Selected Biographical References: Guardian p19 Ag 10 '92 por; N Y Times IV p7 My 17 '92 por; International Who's Who, 1995-96; Gutman, Roy. A Witness to Genocide (1993); Vulliamy, Ed. Seasons in Hell (1994)

Clein & White Inc.

Katzenberg, Jeffrey

1950- Film industry executive. Address: DreamWorks, 100 Universal Plaza, Bungalow 477, Universal City, CA 91608

"I love my job because I entertain people. I bring joy and happiness to them and make them laugh and cry," Jeffrey Katzenberg told a British journalist in 1989, at the midpoint of his decade as chairman of the Walt Disney Studios, whose preeminence in animated films had been established with such perennial children's favorites as *Snow White and the Seven Dwarfs* (1937) and *Cinderella* (1950). After the death of founder Walt Disney in 1966, the company seemed to lose its focus; it had recently been the target of fierce takeover battles when Katzenberg arrived, in 1984, with Michael D. Eisner, who had been named chairman and chief executive officer of the Walt Disney Company in the same year. Credited with reviving Paramount Pictures, where Katzenberg had gotten his start working for Eisner in the mid-1970s, the Eisner-Katzenberg team set out to rescue the foundering Disney company by applying what they had learned at Paramount, the crux of which was to keep costs down while making concept-driven movies based on good scripts rather than on the box-office appeal of a hot celebrity or on the prestige of a demanding auteur.

By all accounts Katzenberg and Eisner succeeded beyond their wildest dreams in resuscitating the moribund corporation. Although attendance at theme parks, including Disneyland in Anaheim, California and Disney World in Orlando, Florida, has been down in recent years, the Walt Disney Studios' reputation for producing first-class animated features has been indisputably restored with such hits as *The Little Mermaid*, *Beauty and the Beast*, *Aladdin*, and *The Lion King*. Katzenberg has also triumphed in the live-action arena with the popularity of *Pretty Woman*, *Good Morning, Vietnam*, and *Three Men and a Baby*, among other films. Widely acknowledged to be one of the hardest-working executives in Hollywood history, he took the studio from $1.4 billion to $8.5 billion in revenues in a decade.

According to colleagues and competitors alike, Katzenberg owed his success not only to his cost-conscious strategies and hardball negotiating tactics but also, in no small measure, to his confidence and legendary perseverance. Often compared to the legendary MGM studio chief Irving Thalberg, Katzenberg has "that kind of vision," as Sam Goldwyn Jr. told Frank Rose for an article in *Premiere* (November 1990). "He's got an instinct for what he wants, and he trusts that instinct. . . . He's a picture maker, as opposed to most of the guys running studios, who are deal makers." Considered for years to be primarily a creative talent by many in the film industry, Katzenberg has since shown that he is also a master of the art of the deal, as he demonstrated with his most recent career move. Stunning the Hollywood community, he resigned as chairman of the Walt Disney Studios in September 1994, after Eisner failed to promote him to succeed company president and chief operating officer Frank G. Wells, who had died in a helicopter crash in April of that year. A free agent for the first time in his professional life, Katzenberg had his pick of jobs with existing corporations, according to industry observers, but he decided instead to form a new studio with two longtime friends, the hugely successful filmmaker Steven Spielberg and the billionaire recording impresario David Geffen. In October 1994 DreamWorks joined the ranks of Hollywood's studios in what a *New York Times* reporter hailed as "the biggest merger of talent since Charlie Chaplin, Mary Pickford, Douglas Fairbanks, and D. W. Griffith founded the United Artists movie empire in 1919."

Jeffrey Katzenberg was born in 1950 and grew up on Park Avenue in the New York City borough of Manhattan. His father is a stockbroker; his mother is a talented craftswoman who wove tapestries and made beadwork. Nicknamed "Squirt," Katzenberg attended the Fieldston School in Riverdale, New York, one of the city's three Ethical Culture Schools that were founded by the philosopher Felix Adler. He spent his summers at the fiercely competitive Camp Kennebac in Maine. "There is nothing in my background to suggest my future career," Katzenberg told Adrian Turner in an interview for the *Guardian* (December 14, 1989). "I was not a movie-smitten child, I am not a movie buff, I'm not a student of film, I'm not a historian. In fact you would probably be surprised by how little I actually know about film."

There's plenty in his background, however, that presaged his ambitious rise to the top in a cut-throat industry. At the age of fourteen, after he had purposely gotten himself ejected from summer camp by playing poker for candy, he volunteered to work for John V. Lindsay's New York City mayoral campaign of 1964. "I had no idea what Lindsay's politics were," Katzenberg recalled in an interview with Aljean Harmetz for the *New York Times Magazine* (February 7, 1988). "But it was a better camp than the one I got thrown out of." For the following seven years, he worked for the mayor, performing every task from sweeping the floors to organizing campaign stopovers. During Lindsay's 1972 campaign for the Democratic presidential nomination, Katzenberg served as controller. "I was out there being an adult," he observed in an interview with Elaine Dutka for *American Film* (June 1990). "I never had a normal high school or college environment. I never took drugs. I hate the taste of alcohol, wine, [and] beer. Give me a piece of rum cake and I gag."

In 1972 Katzenberg, who had dropped out of New York University, in Manhattan, in his sophomore year, held a series of odd jobs before landing at Paramount sometime between 1972 and 1975 (sources vary). After Lindsay lost the Democratic nomination to George S. McGovern of South Dakota, three of the candidate's most enterprising young aides, including Katzenberg, started a restaurant called Jimmy's, a project from which he disengaged himself shortly thereafter. Before beginning his career at Paramount, Katzenberg worked as a talent agent and developed material for Lindsay's friend David Picker, an independent producer who introduced him to Barry Diller, the chairman and chief executive officer of Paramount Pictures in New York City from 1975 to 1977. Plucked from the studio's mailroom to be Diller's assistant for those two years, Katzenberg was promoted in 1977 to executive director of marketing.

A few months later, Michael Eisner, the president of Paramount, sent Katzenberg to California to be vice-president of programming at Paramount television for a year. Although his attempt to create a fourth commercial television network failed, his career progressed rapidly from then on, especially as his ability to search out bright ideas before anyone else could claim credit for them earned him a reputation for being Eisner's most astute "Golden Retriever." Vice-president of feature productions at Paramount from 1978 to 1980, Katzenberg then became senior vice-president of production at the motion picture division, a position he held from 1980 to 1982, when he was named president of production for motion pictures and television.

Katzenberg's rise at Paramount was marked by a string of spectacular successes, the first of which was *Star Trek—The Motion Picture* (1979), for which he was a production executive. In addition to two *Star Trek* sequels (more would follow Katzenberg's 1984 departure), such hits as *Airplane!*, *Beverly Hills Cop*, *Flashdance*, *Raiders of the Lost Ark*, *An Officer and a Gentleman*, and *Footloose* also pulled in more than their share of profits for the financially strained studio. While at Paramount, Katzenberg developed an enviable roster of contacts through his relentless networking, which eventually included making over a hundred ninety-second phone calls a day. In that manner he would stroke actors' egos to cajole them into working for him or prod agents to give him a better deal. "If Jeffrey were any more aggressive, he'd be in jail," the producer Dan Melnick quipped to Aljean Harmetz. "Jeffrey's always had this extraordinary ability to keep in touch with a lot of people . . . ," Dawn Steel, a former Paramount colleague, told Peter J. Boyer for an article in *Vanity Fair* (November 1991). "No matter whether they're mad at him or not, it's 'Hello, Jeffrey!' and they feel connected to him."

Few industry analysts were surprised when Eisner brought Katzenberg with him to Disney in 1984, because the two men worked so well together as a team. As company chairman and CEO of Disney, Eisner devoted most of his working hours to developing corporate policy and improving the theme parks, while Katzenberg, as chairman of Walt Disney Studios, concentrated on beefing up Disney's filmmaking capacity. "At Paramount, Jeff brought home the bacon," Eisner told Aljean Harmetz. "Now he knows how to cook it." In 1984 Disney ranked last among the nine major Hollywood distributors. Katzenberg's arrival yielded immediate results when he approved Paul Mazursky's *Down and Out in Beverly Hills* (1986), which became the studio's first R-rated picture, and decided to distribute the television sitcom *The Golden Girls*, the only new hit of the 1985–86 season. In 1985 Katzenberg formed a television syndication division to sell material to independent television stations, which would then have thirty years' worth of movies and television programs from the Disney library to choose from, excluding the company's animated feature films. By 1988 the studio had climbed to first place, and four of the year's ten top-grossing films carried the Disney name.

One of the ways in which Katzenberg achieved such phenomenal growth was by increasing output, which he accomplished by creating, in 1988, Hollywood Pictures, a new studio division, to complement the existing Walt Disney Pictures, which created primarily animation and family fare, and the more adult-oriented Touchstone Pictures, which was responsible not only for *Down and Out in Beverly Hills* but also for the hits *Tin Men*, *Three Men and a Baby*, *The Color of Money*, *Ruthless People*, *Good Morning, Vietnam*, and *Dead Poets Society*. All three divisions' films are distributed by Buena Vista. Because of flops like *An Innocent Man*, *Gross Anatomy*, and *Blaze*, Disney wound up in third place in 1989, behind Warner Bros. and Universal. Although Disney rallied in 1990 with *Pretty Woman*, the Julia Roberts–Richard Gere vehicle that grossed $178.1 million, the company nonetheless ran into trouble in the same year with Warren Beatty's *Dick Tracy*, whose $104 million in box-office receipts barely covered its $46.5 million in production costs and $54.7 million in distribution expenses.

Nonetheless, an impressive 70 percent of the forty-four films produced under Katzenberg's auspices by 1990 turned a profit, and the studio head began looking for ways to broaden Disney's reach without assuming the risk. In the same year, Katzenberg sealed a five-year distribution and marketing deal with Cinergi Productions, headed by Andy Vajna, and in 1992 he brought aboard Joe Roth, the former film-studio head of Rupert Murdoch's Twentieth-Century Fox, and Roger Birnbaum as founders of Caravan Pictures, whose movies are distributed by Buena Vista under the aegis of one of Disney's three studio divisions.

In the following year Katzenberg concluded an agreement with the producer Ismail Merchant and the director James Ivory to cofinance and distribute the output of Merchant Ivory Productions, the company responsible for *A Room with a View* and *Howards End*, among other highly acclaimed fare. Later in 1993 Katzenberg persuaded Eisner to acquire Bob and Harvey Weinstein's New York City-based "art-house" studio, Miramax. In 1994 the Walt Disney Studios—encompassing Hollywood Pictures, Touchstone Pictures, and Walt Disney Pictures—released twenty-nine films. As an autonomous division of Buena Vista, Miramax, which still distributes its own films, released a string of major and minor hits in 1994, including *The Crow*, *Clerks*, *Bullets over Broadway*, *Ready to Wear*, and *Pulp Fiction*.

Whereas Disney's overall live-action scorecard was decidedly mixed, its animated-features record was an unqualified success during Katzenberg's tenure, a circumstance the executive, in an interview with John Culhane for the *Chicago Tribune* (November 24, 1991), attributed to his "creative listening" skills: "When you are in a business which is primarily dependent on originality and creativity at its purest for your future growth and success, when creativity is at the essence of what you do, you must by definition be an exceptional listener. . . . You must have your antenna up." The first two animated movies that Katzenberg "put into production" were *The Great Mouse Detective* (1986) and *Oliver and Company* (1988), the latter being a retelling of the Oliver Twist story with an orphaned kitten as the main character. *The Little Mermaid* (1989), Disney's first feature to be based on a classic fairy tale (by Hans Christian Andersen) since *Sleeping Beauty* (1959), grossed more than $80 million in box-office receipts. Based on a French fairy tale, *Beauty and the Beast* (1991), which featured the voice of Robby Benson as the Beast and that of Paige O'Hara as Belle, took in $106.4 million and was the first animated film to be nominated for an Academy Award for best picture. *Aladdin* (1992), an Arabian Nights tale utilizing the voice of Robin Williams as the Genie, won two Academy Awards and earned $240 million at the box office and an additional $465 million in worldwide video rentals.

The first of Disney's thirty-two animated features to be made from an original script rather than adapted from a fairy tale, children's story, or historical legend, *The Lion King* is the tale of a cub, Simba, who goes up against his malevolent uncle, Scar, to claim the throne left vacant by the death of Simba's father, King Mufasa. With voices provided by James Earl Jones, Matthew Broderick, Jeremy Irons, and Whoopi Goldberg, among others, *The Lion King* yielded a number-one soundtrack scored by Elton John. By March 1995 the film, which had cost only $40 million to make, had taken in $312.5 million at the box office, making it the fourth-highest-grossing film in Hollywood history and Disney's most successful movie ever. (The 1995 release *Pocahontas* was less successful.)

In addition to having restored Disney's lustrous reputation for producing top-notch animated features, in 1991 Katzenberg also brought aboard the top-rated television show *Home Improvement*, based on the comedy of Tim Allen and produced by Disney's Touchstone Television division for ABC. All in all, the studio's revenues leaped from $1.4 billion to $8.5 billion in a decade. During the same period, pretax profits jumped from $2 million in 1984 to $800 million in 1994, making it the most profitable studio in the world.

Given the role Katzenberg played in Disney's phenomenal success, many in the industry were shocked when he was snubbed by Eisner, who in 1994 denied him a promotion, thus precipitating his resignation. The seeds of strain between Eisner and his protégé could be traced to Katzenberg's infamous cost-cutting memo of January 11, 1991, in which he warned of impending doom despite Disney's continuing profitability. The memo, which was leaked to the press and which was soon followed by a witty, anonymously authored parody, reportedly infuriated Eisner, even though Eisner had written a similar memo, at Paramount in 1981.

Derided by some as a bland potpourri of common sense and lauded by others as a prescient document that had industrywide impact, Katzenberg's memo singled out *Dick Tracy* as an example of the kind of film project to avoid in the future. "As profitable as it was," Katzenberg wrote, "*Dick Tracy* made demands on our time, talent, and treasury that, upon reflection, may not have been worth it." He also castigated agents for jacking up the cost of moviemaking by putting together expensive "package" deals in which a producer, director, screenwriter, and actors are shopped around to the studios with the idea that the package would work based on the box-office appeal of the stars no matter what type of movie was made. Katzenberg worked in the opposite manner, first finding what he hoped would be a solid script, then hiring low-fee actors (like Bette Midler and Tom Selleck) whose careers were languishing or who had worked only in television, and signing them to multipicture deals. Thus Disney was able to come out on top by restricting costs rather than simply by beating the competition at the box office.

One year later Hollywood players were still discussing the Katzenberg memo, but by that time his stridency had been somewhat vindicated. In the eighteen months following the release of the memo, Katzenberg reduced the average cost of his movies from twenty-four million dollars to sixteen million, at a time when the industry average was thirty million. "The fact that Jeffrey placed his thoughts on paper—whether every sentence is appropriate or not—forced him to come to grips with the problem," Eisner told Bernard Weinraub of the *New York Times* (February 11, 1992). "Then he did something about it. I loved that. Whether I would have changed a sentence here or there, yes. But the memo he wrote was a kind of map. . . . He's done a spectacular job."

Although Katzenberg's talents and achievements were undeniable, he was reportedly not deemed to have the skills necessary to succeed company president Frank G. Wells, who died in a helicopter accident on April 3, 1994 while on a ski trip in Nevada. Although he was given responsibility for Hollywood Records and for interactive games and telecommunications, Katzenberg was not promoted to Wells's position, possibly because, as many observers speculated, his strengths were too similar to Eisner's and far different from those of Wells, who was a financial strategist and a behind-the-scenes deal maker who had never sought the limelight. There were also rumors that Eisner, who had undergone quadruple coronary-bypass surgery that summer, didn't want a strong second-in-command in any event, and that he preferred to disperse power among several deputies. Some analysts reported that the company's diversification and acquisitions lent credence to that theory.

"It's about a father not being able to accept a son," Katzenberg said of his longtime mentor and friend's refusal to promote him, when asked by Richard Corliss of *Time* (September 5, 1994) to come up with an allegorical interpretation of the dissolution of their partnership. "I still don't understand it, and it's hard to reconcile." Terminating a nineteen-year partnership that has been lauded as one of the most successful in the industry's history, Katzenberg announced on August 24, 1994 that he would resign on September 30, 1994, upon the expiration of his contract. After his departure, Katzenberg's duties at Disney were shared by Joe Roth, who was put in charge of live-action films; Richard Frank, formerly president of Disney studios, who took over television and telecommunications duties; and the team of Roy Disney, Walt's nephew, and Peter Schneider, who were given responsibility for animation.

No sooner had Katzenberg announced his resignation than his future began to take shape. His friend Steven Spielberg, the most successful filmmaker of all time, called from Jamaica to wish him well, and the two began talking about starting their own studio. "We were teasing, I guess," Katzenberg recalled in an interview with Bernard Weinraub for the *New York Times* (October 16, 1994). "But there was a moment it went from a playful and fanciful idea to a great idea." On October 12, 1994 Katzenberg, Spielberg, and another close friend, the recording-industry executive David Geffen, announced the first formation of a major new studio since Disney itself was founded over sixty years ago. "This has got to be a 'dream team.'" Katzenberg said, adding, "Certainly it's my dream. . . . There's opportunity for us here to have a revolution." The three partners made equal financial investments totalling $250 million to launch DreamWorks, which would produce live-action films (overseen by Spielberg), animated features (supervised by Katzenberg), record albums (produced by Geffen), and multimedia (interactive software) products. Under the terms of a separate agreement announced in November 1994, Spielberg, Katzenberg, and Geffen would produce television shows in an unprecedented revenue-sharing joint venture with Capital Cities/ABC Inc., a seven-year deal that was made possible by the impending demise of the financial interest and syndication rules that have prevented ABC, CBS, and NBC from owning the prime-time series that they broadcast. (The television-studio deal was completed when, on July 31, 1995, the Walt Disney Company acquired Capital Cities/ABC Inc. for nineteen billion dollars.)

DreamWorks negotiated a number of partnership arrangements in 1995 as well. In March the cable television company HBO signed a ten-year agreement to buy an estimated ninety to a hundred future films from DreamWorks, and the computer software company Microsoft announced the formation of a thirty million-dollar joint venture with DreamWorks, tentatively called DreamWorks Interactive, which will produce interactive software for adventure games and stories for cartridge, CD-ROM, online networks, and interactive television. The first titles, which will run on Windows-based personal computers, are scheduled for release at the end of 1996. On May 31 Dreamworks inked a fifty million-dollar deal with Silicon Graphics Inc. to develop a new computer animation system. (Spielberg had collaborated with Silicon Graphics on the enormously successful dinosaur movie *Jurassic Park.*) A week later DreamWorks signed an agreement with IBM Corp. to acquire a computerized storage system that will enable the new studio to store its original film, video, and audio recordings on digital servers. On June 13 MCA/Universal became DreamWorks' chief distributor; on August 16 the studio signed Hasbro to create a line of toys; and on September 21 Scholastic agreed to produce CD-ROM versions of *Goosebumps* children's books.

Standing five feet, seven-and-a-half inches tall, the diminutive Jeffrey Katzenberg often applies his seemingly boundless energy to several tasks at once, such as reading the newspaper in between sets at the gym or making some of his legendary hundred-plus daily phone calls while driving. "Compared to Jeffrey," Geffen told Elaine Dutka in an interview for her *American Film* profile of his friend and colleague, "everyone else in this town is on vacation." Katzenberg lives in Los Angeles with his wife of twenty years, Marilyn (Siegel) Katzenberg, a former schoolteacher, and their twelve-year-old twins, Laura and David. He regularly squeezes in three movies a weekend, and he attends baseball games and rock concerts. For several years he has driven a black Mustang convertible. "A Jaguar or a BMW would make me feel too adult," he has said, as quoted by Dutka. He and Spielberg recently teamed up with restaurateurs Mark and Larry Levy to open Dive, a submarine-sandwich eatery in Century City, California. Katzenberg is reportedly as generous with his friends as he is tough at the negotiating table. "Jeffrey's relationships are both genuine and strategic," the producer Mark Johnson maintained in a conversation with Dutka. "It's not as calculating as it sounds. Jeffrey just chooses his friends from a limited universe. The people he tends to socialize with are those who have the most to offer."

Selected Biographical References: Am Film 15:40+ Je '90 por; N Y Times Mag p29+ F 7 '88 pors; New York 24:33+ O 7 '91 pors; Premiere 4:102+ N '90 por; Vanity Fair 54:140+ N '91 pors; Grover, Ronald. The Disney Touch: How a Daring Management Team Revived an Entertainment Empire (1991); International Motion Picture Almanac, 1995; Who's Who in America, 1995

Keen, Sam

Nov. 23, 1931- Writer; philosopher; lecturer; group leader. Address: 16331 Norrbom Rd., Sonoma, CA 95476

Jerry Bauer/Bantam Books

In 1991 Sam Keen's best-selling book *Fire in the Belly: On Being a Man* joined the poet Robert Bly's *Iron John: A Book About Men* (1990) at the top of the reading list for the so-called men's movement, which had been steadily but quietly evolving since the 1970s, when significant numbers of men began to believe that the patriarchal system so deplored by feminists was as harmful to themselves as to women. Sometimes misinterpreted as a backlash against women's striving to transcend gender-based expectations, the men's movement, as envisioned by Keen, shares the feminist premise that masculine and feminine stereotyping is detrimental to members of both sexes in denying each the right to possess and express the full spectrum of human emotions, desires, and characteristics. In redefining masculinity as the result of an inner journey toward "sexual-spiritual maturation," Keen drew on a wealth of experience as a professor of philosophy and, subsequently, a leader of men's groups. In much of his writing about personal growth and in many of his workshops, Keen has emphasized the roles played by the persistence of ancient myths and by autobiographical storytelling in one's becoming a healthy, whole, fully individuated being. His most recent book is *Hymns to an Unknown God: Awakening the Spirit in Everyday Life* (1994).

Of Scottish descent, Sam Keen was born on November 23, 1931 in Scranton, Pennsylvania, the son of J. Alvin Keen and Ruth (McMurray) Keen, both of whom were musicians. Sam and his two younger sisters, Ruth Ann and Edith, and his older brother, Lawrence, grew up in a series of small towns in Alabama, Tennessee, and Delaware. "My family moved every year or two, so my brother and I were always outsiders," Keen wrote in one of his books. "We were the strange ones, the ready-made enemies of the established gangs, and we spent much of our time playing alone in the woods. Consequently, membership has always been difficult for me, while the virtues and vices of individualism come easily."

After graduating from P. S. duPont High School in Wilmington, Delaware, Keen earned a bachelor of arts degree in 1953 from Ursinus College, in Collegeville, Pennsylvania. He then enrolled at Harvard Divinity School, in Cambridge, Massachusetts, where he earned a bachelor of the science of theology degree in 1956 and a master's degree in theology in 1958. Two years later he earned a master's degree in the philosophy of religion from Princeton University, in Princeton, New Jersey, where in 1962 he completed a doctorate in the same subject (his thesis explored the concept of mystery). For the following six years, he was a professor of the philosophy of religion at the Louisville Presbyterian Theological Seminary, in Louisville, Kentucky. Before he left the seminary, he had published his first book, *Gabriel Marcel* (1967), an introduction to the philosophy of the French existentialist.

In 1968 Keen moved to California and, in the following year, began a twenty-year association with the popular monthly magazine *Psychology Today* as a contributing editor. Nine of his interviews for that magazine, including conversations with the philosophers Norman O. Brown and Herbert Marcuse and the mythologist Joseph Campbell, were collected in the book *Voices and Visions* (1974). From 1969 to 1970 he did postdoctoral work at the Western Behavioral Sciences Institute, in La Jolla, California, on a fellowship from the National Institute of Mental Health. In 1970 he held an appointment as a professor of the philosophy of the person at Prescott College, in Prescott, Arizona, and in 1972 he was a professor at the Humanistic Psychology Institute, in San Francisco. With the exception of serving as a visiting professor of medical ethics at the University of Florida Medical School in 1983, Keen has held no formal academic appointments since 1972, when he embarked on a full-time freelance career as a writer, lecturer, group leader, and consultant for more than two hundred colleges, universities, clinics, institutes, and corporations.

From 1968 to 1970 Keen conducted workshops in personal mythology (an amalgam of storytelling, introspection, and autobiography) at the Esalen and Kairos Institutes in California. The move from a seminary professorship to the vanguard of the human-potential movement reflected Keen's disillusionment with the ability of churches to help modern humanity find answers to spiritual crises. Religion, according to Keen, projected too much negativity to promote spiritual growth. "That's not the business I'm in," he told John Dart of the *Los Angeles Times* for an article that was reprinted in the *Washington Post* (June 20, 1970). "The place where my work connects with religion is on the question of how you make human life sacred and keep it that way. In the old sense those were religious questions."

In his workshops Keen sought, among other things, to help participants discover a more meaningful existence that is full of grace, which Keen defined in his conversation with Dart as "the natural mark of a fully human life." "It does not need," he continued, "to be conferred by Jesus Christ nor confirmed by the church. . . . The spiritual questions are being asked with more integrity and more earnestness outside the church on such crying issues as war, ecology, community, survival of the person, and returning sacredness to these things." But Keen had lost confidence in the rhetoric-driven human-potential movement as well, in part because it overemphasized personal problems at the expense of drawing connections to societal and political causes and solutions. "I think we have to laugh at all these communities of salvation that take themselves too seriously," he explained to Dart, adding that "as much growth [as occurs in human-potential centers] can take place over teacups or with friends or just getting a good night's sleep. Taking a walk in the Grand Canyon—that will blow your mind."

Keen had advocated a recapturing of the capacity for remaining in awe of ordinary phenomena as well as of the Seven Wonders of the World in his second book, *Apology for Wonder* (1969). Claiming that the imperatives of modern technological society have replaced the childlike wonder of what he calls *Homo admirans* with the alienation and indifference of *Homo faber*, Keen called for a balancing of the two extremes in an ideal *Homo tempestivus*, who would be "timely, seasonable, or opportune" in expressing gratitude for the joys of human existence while remaining aware of the horrors and injustices of life. Maryellen Muckenhirn of *Commonweal* (September 5, 1969) called *Apology for Wonder* "a delightful and profoundly stimulating book. It is not really about theology, but rather about the kind of men and women who might live and experience and reflect and do some vital philosophy and theology today."

In *To a Dancing God* (1970), Keen demonstrated his personal approach to affirming sacredness in his own life. Although some reviewers took exception to Keen's literary devices, including dialogue and a journal form, the book did have its supporters. In his review of the book for *Commonweal* (November 6, 1970), Bernard Cooke wrote, "*To a Dancing God* is marked by a brightness of style and enthusiasm for life." Cooke also lauded the author's "gift of probing in clear and strikingly imaginative form the most basic and critical questions of our contemporary world."

The late 1960s and early 1970s were a transformative period for Keen, who during that time left behind what he has called his "discarnate years as a professor," divorced his wife after seventeen years of marriage, turned forty, and made a final attempt (through love affairs) to avoid confronting the existential despair that is often referred to by the term "midlife crisis." Keen emerged intact from those simultaneous transitions, apparently by practicing what he was preaching in his books and seminars. Chief among his methods of "becoming himself" was his effort to create a personal mythology, the dire need for which he realized upon the death of his father in 1964, an event that shattered his sense of security. Nine years later, after having grappled with the question of his identity in workshops, through continual study, and via his interviews with other philosophers and psychologists for *Psychology Today*, Keen coauthored, with Anne Valley-Fox, *Telling Your Story: A Guide to Who You Are and Who You Can Be* (1973); an updated edition was published in 1989 as *Your Mythic Journey: Finding Meaning in Your Life Through Writing and Storytelling.*

"We tell stories—myths—about who we are, where we come from, where we are going, and how we should live," he wrote in an article for *Psychology Today* (December 1988). "And the myths we tell become who we are and what we believe—as individuals, families, whole cultures. . . . Personal myths become constricting and boring unless they're examined and revised from time to time," Keen explained. "We need to reinvent ourselves continually, weaving new themes into our life narratives, remembering our past, revising our future, reauthorizing the myth by which we live." Keen also contributed to *Sacred Stories: A Celebration of the Power of Stories to Transform and Heal* (1993), edited by Charles and Anne Simpkinson.

In 1975 Keen published *Beginnings without End*, a compendium of three years' worth of diary entries and his own commentary on them, poems, fantasies, and family stories. Writing in the *Library Journal* (January 15, 1976), B. Y. Beach found the book to be "a moving, lucid, and penetrating account of 'the places where [Keen] found an oasis, a helping spirit, a devouring demon, a rushing river, or a tree with magical apples.'" Along similar lines, Keen cowrote, with Jim Fowler, *Life-Maps: Conversations on the Journey of Faith* (1978), edited by Jerome Berryman. Keen explored the role of boredom in personal growth, revealing its positive, healing qualities, in *What to Do When You're Bored and Blue* (1980); a revised edition was published in 1992 as *Inward Bound: Exploring the Geography of Your Emotions.*

Drawing again on his own experiences, Keen chronicled the pursuit of ideal love in *The Passionate Life: Stages of Loving* (1983), a step-by-step approach to enhancing intimacy. The stages of love Keen describes start with the mother-child bond, which later breaks down into adolescent rebellion. In young adulthood sexuality passes into a more cohesive stage until that is disrupted by a second rebellion, in midlife. One can then arrive at the fifth and fully evolved stage of love, which, in Keen's eyes, is built on kindness, forgiveness, friendship, justice, and respect for nature. Assessing *The Passionate Life* for the *Christian Century* (August 31–September 7, 1983), James Allen Sparks wrote, "Keen's occasional flights into obscure imagery and clever idiom can leave us breathless and groping for his meaning. Nevertheless, *The Passionate Life* is a probing book that goes beyond analysis, guiding without preaching, and pointing toward love's potential without being simplistic." Reviewing the book for *Library Journal* (May 15, 1983), Elise C. Dennis deemed it "an eclectic mix of Kundalini yoga, Norman O. Brown, and those aspects of Christianity with which Keen identifies [that] integrates insights on sex, spirituality, and social criticism in a genuinely provocative way."

While exploring the obstacles that impede sexual maturity, Keen was prompted to examine what keeps people from becoming truly compassionate beings—in other words, how people have been conditioned to hate and to fear. His research led him to an exhaustive study of wartime propaganda in *Faces of the Enemy: Reflections of the Hostile Imagination* (1986), which examined the ways in which visual propaganda is used to incite and reinforce hatred of wartime enemies. With 322 illustrated examples, the book shows how enemies are depicted in posters and cartoons as barbarians, rapists, criminals, imperialists, and as the personification of death itself.

That the imagery seems to possess certain similar characteristics from country to country and from conflict to conflict, Keen decided, demonstrates a human psychological need to find enemies on which to affix these common images. In Keen's view, propaganda allows individuals to project the traits they most dislike about themselves onto the enemy. This process dehumanizes one's enemies, making them easier to kill. Rather than merely despairing at that conclusion, Keen has discovered within it a measure of hope for the future of humankind. "We demean our enemies not because we are instinctively sadistic, but because it is difficult for us to kill others whom we recognize as fully human beings," he wrote. "Our natural empathy, our instinct for compassion, is strong: society does what it must to attempt to overcome the moral imperative that forbids us from killing. . . . If it is difficult to mold men into killers, we may still hope to transform our efforts from fighting an outward enemy to doing battle with our own paranoia. Our true war is our struggle against the antagonistic mind."

Calling *Faces of the Enemy* "extraordinary" in his evaluation for the *Christian Century* (June 3–10, 1987), James J. Farrell added that "some of Keen's conjectures are simply not believable. But others are so provocative, so suggestive that even the paranoid turns eagerly to his prescriptions for a change from paranoia to metanoia (literally, 'change of mind')." In his review of the book for the *Journal of the American Medical Association* (August 7, 1987), Neil J. Elgee wrote, "Vivid and jolting, this book is a major new contribution to the literature of the psychology of war and hence to the prevention of the final epidemic. . . . While Keen writes with a disarmingly calm grace, both the pictures and his verbal images arrest us so that we are forced to explore more deeply the ugliest of human attributes." In 1987 *Faces of the Enemy* was made into a public-television documentary that was nominated for an Emmy Award.

With the publication in 1991 of *Fire in the Belly: On Being a Man,* which spent more than twenty-five weeks on the *Publishers Weekly* best-seller list, Keen became one of the leading flag-bearers of the men's movement, which urged men to reclaim their masculinity in a way that allowed for the expression of aggressive energy as long as it was not inexorably bound up with hostility. In order to develop their own, positive definition of masculinity, according to Keen, men must first recognize the ways in which WOMAN—Keen uses capital letters to denote not real women but that collection of various threatening archetypes men carry around in the deepest recesses of their minds—has power over them. Keen has labeled those archetypes "goddess and creatrix," "mother and matrix," and the "erotic-spiritual power."

"Before a man struggles to become conscious of the nature and limits of his virility," he wrote, "the essence of the threat he feels from WOMAN lies in its vagueness. She is the soft darkness at the core of his psyche, part of him, not a stranger." Keen philosophizes that men become uncomfortably bound to WOMAN through their mothers during childhood. "A large part of the reason that WOMAN looms so large in a man's life from early childhood on is because we created a society in which men were absent from the home," he said in an interview with Donna Jackson for *New Woman* (June 1993). "As boys, we men got most of our feedback from females." With mothers, female neighbors, and female teachers constantly telling them how to behave, men have learned to see women as the ones who define appropriate behavior, Keen said, even if their advice conflicted with what he considers to be men's true natures.

Because the father is often absent from the home, whether he abandons his family or just goes off to work each day, the boy wins the Oedipal conflict, becoming something of a "mama's boy" for whom, as an adult, no actual woman is good enough, according to one of the many scenarios that, in Keen's view, result from this early "perversion" of relations between the sexes. Men can come into their own, according to Keen, only by separating from the world of women and allowing themselves to feel and experience all their emotions and instincts. "We must make use of the warrior's fierceness, courage, and aggression," Keen wrote, "to break through the rigidities of old structures of manhood and explore the dark and taboo 'negative' emotions that make up the shadow of modern manhood."

In 1978 Keen had formed his first men's group when several of his friends who were having trouble with their relationships with women began to hold weekly consciousness-raising sessions to confront their hostility, denied emotions, and repressed selves. Sometimes called SPERM, which stands for the Society for the Protection and Encouragement of Righteous Manhood, the men's group and others like it have inspired suspicion among women, who fear that "there might be a lot of woman-bashing going on in these all-male groups," as Donna Jackson put it in her interview with Keen. He responded that the men in his group not only avoided criticizing women but that they "didn't let each other get away with a lot of negative, unfocused hostility toward women. [They] called each other on [their] hostility and destructive patterns in love." Consequently, their relationships with women improved, according to Keen.

"*Fire in the Belly* is that rare thing: a literate and lyrical self-help book," Richard Stengel wrote in his review for *Time* (July 8, 1991). "Like Bly, who uses a Grimm brothers' myth as his framework, Keen takes up the ancient theme that each man is on a spiritual journey, a quest for the grail of manhood." Guiding men through that journey, Keen advises "the spiritual traveler how to avoid the dead ends of combative machismo and the blind alleys of romantic obsession . . . ," Stengel continued. "*Fire in the Belly* is as much about being human as being a man." Evaluating the book for the *Library Journal* (February 15, 1991), John Moryl called it "challenging, well written, recommended, and definitely not for men only."

Hymns to an Unknown God (1994) is Keen's most recent book about the inner journey that must be undertaken by anyone, male or female, to achieve spiritual maturity. According to a summary of the book by a writer for *Publishers Weekly* (July 11, 1994), Keen defined the "unknown" god as "'some missing value, some absent purpose, some new meaning, some presence of the sacred.'" "A soulful life," Keen suggested, "is more about getting rhythm and tuning into the music of the spheres than it is about getting the words correct." In *Hymns to an Unknown God,* according to *Publishers Weekly,* Keen provided readers with "rituals for consecrating sex and work, family and other relationships, local communities, and the global environment."

For relaxation and rejuvenation, Keen "practices the flying trapeze," as he told *Current Biography;* he also enjoys riding horses, cooking, and tending the gardens and orchards of his sixty-acre ranch in Sonoma, California. Keen has two grown children—a daughter, Lael, and a son, Gifford—from his first marriage; he and his second wife, Jananne Lovett-Keen, have a teenage daughter, Jessamyn.

Selected Biographical References: Contemporary Authors vol 137 (1992); Keen, Sam. To a Dancing God (1970), Beginnings without End (1975)

Dennis Turner/Turner Management Group

Kenny G

1957(?)- Saxophonist; composer. Address: c/o Turner Management Group, 3500 W. Olive Ave., Ste. 770, Burbank, CA 91505

The saxophonist Kenny G, who was reported by the trade-magazine *Billboard* to be the world's best-selling jazz artist of 1994 and the top instrumentalist of the past decade, with sales of twenty-seven million albums worldwide, composes and plays sweet, melodic tunes that he has described as "contemporary jazz." Every album he has released since his 1986 *Duotones* has gone multiplatinum—that is, sold several million copies—and his 1992 album *Breathless* has sold over seven million. "Kenny G is of a new generation of players whose accessible style comes across in his songs—strong melodies with a good groove plus a touch of soul and jazz," Stephanie Stein observed in a profile of him for *Down Beat* (January 1988). His music can be heard not only on both jazz and Top Forty radio stations but also in supermarkets, elevators, airplanes, and, according to one source, the waiting room of the royal palace in Monaco. Among his legion of fans is President Bill Clinton, who invited Kenny G to play at his inauguration in 1993.

Despite his popularity, or perhaps because of it, jazz critics have tended either to overlook or scorn Kenny G's work. Among those given to the latter tendency is Peter Watrous, who after writing in the *New York Times* (March 21, 1993) that "rarely has anybody sold so many records and been so firmly ignored by critics," observed, "Kenny G either can't play jazz or won't, and his music is spectacularly lacking in any of the characteristics that define jazz as a genre." Maintaining a gracious attitude toward his critics, Kenny G told Bob Cannon of *Entertainment Weekly* (April 2, 1993), "It's the intellectuals who write the reviews. . . . Maybe I'm a dreamer, but I think the ordinary guy has just as much right to say 'This is a good song' as somebody who is in the music business."

Born Kenneth Gorelick in Seattle in about 1957, Kenny G is the middle child of Moe Gorelick, who owned a plumbing-supply business, and Evelyn Gorelick. The family lived in an African-American neighborhood, and Kenny G attended racially mixed schools, where he was influenced by the rhythm and blues music preferred by most of his fellow students. At the age of ten, he was "completely enthralled," as he put it, when he heard a saxophonist featured in a big band on a television program. He began taking saxophone lessons, and later, in high school, he studied the clarinet and flute. "I can't really say I learned anything at the lessons," he recalled to Stephanie Stein. "You learn a few technical things, but nobody can teach you how to solo. That's just whatever you have in you."

After his first application to play in the Franklin High School jazz band was rejected, Kenny G redoubled his efforts to master the saxophone. In his junior year he became the band's lead saxophonist, and he later played with the group during a European tour in 1974. Afterward, one of the Franklin High band directors arranged for Kenny G to play with Barry White and his Love Unlimited Orchestra during a Seattle appearance. "They needed a sax player who could [sight] read and solo in a soulful style, and I really was the only person in Seattle that could do both," Kenny G told Stein. "It was really funny, because I hadn't played professionally before. . . . When I showed up, the band could not believe it—here was this tiny little kid. But I did a great job—I even got a standing ovation because I had such a long solo."

Although he aspired to becoming a professional musician, Kenny G enrolled in an accounting program at the University of Washington in Seattle to be sure he would always have a way to support himself, and he eventually graduated magna cum laude. He didn't take music classes while in college, because, he was quoted as saying in the *Chicago Tribune* (November 6, 1994), "I didn't like the analysis of music. I liked the beauty of it." He did, however, play in the college band, and its director, Roy Cummings, booked him to perform with celebrities who came to Seattle, among them Liberace, Johnny Mathis, Diahann Carroll, and the Spinners. He also played and recorded with a local funk band called Cold, Bold and Together.

In 1979 Kenny G was invited by Jeff Lorber, one of the pioneers of "fusion" jazz—a musical style that blends bebop, funk, and rhythm and blues—to audition for his band. For the next four years, Kenny G played with Jeff Lorber Fusion, acquiring knowledge about musical style and innovation that he would later incorporate in his own work. He recorded two albums with Lorber's ensemble: *Wizard Island* (1979) and *Step by Step* (1984); the latter includes several songs that he cowrote with Lorber.

"When I first joined Jeff, I was just a kid from Seattle," Kenny G told Stein. "Four years later I was a pretty experienced musician."

Lorber's manager arranged for Kenny G to record his own album for Arista Records. Produced by Lorber, *Kenny G* was released in 1982. It received little notice at the time; in a retrospective review of the album for *Rolling Stone Album Guide* (1992), J.D. Considine described Kenny G's sound as "light jazz in a Grover Washington vein." Frustrated that his premiere album sounded more like Lorber's music than his own, the saxophonist resolved to work harder to create a signature style. Toward that end, he listened to records and then spent several hours daily reworking certain passages to his own liking.

For his second album, *G Force* (1983), Kenny G worked with the rhythm-and-blues producer Kashif. The album sold about two hundred thousand copies, but when he and Kashif collaborated on another record, *Gravity* (1985), the result was less successful. J. D. Considine, in the *Rolling Stone Album Guide*, dismissed both *G Force* and *Gravity* as "feckless, funkless attempts at an R&B identity." Kenny G believes his second album failed because his musical vision was out of sync with Kashif's. "He's more of a vocal producer, and he was hearing hit vocal songs, and I was hearing instrumentals," he told Stein. "We had a lot of vocal tunes on the record, and I felt like we weren't going in the right direction."

Arista executives decided to give Kenny G—the only instrumental artist on their label—one last chance to come up with a successful formula. With Narada Michael Walden as his executive producer, Kenny G shared the production work of *Duotones* (1986) with Preston Glass. Although he included some vocal tracks, Kenny G made sure that they fit into an integrated album sound. *Duotones* was a smash hit, selling two million copies in its debut year and another million since. "It blew me away," he told Pat Cole in an interview for *Down Beat* (November 1992). "I never expected it to happen." Invited to appear on the *Tonight Show with Johnny Carson* soon after the album's release, Kenny G mesmerized the audience with a *Duotones* selection, "Songbird," an instrumental ballad he had written for his girlfriend (and future wife), Lyndie G. Benson. After its release as a single, "Songbird" became a Top Ten hit.

Asked during his 1988 *Down Beat* interview how he accounted for his success, Kenny G replied that he was "in the right place at the right time with the right song." "I also think part of it is the whole yuppie thing—meaning people who are working really hard in this business-oriented upper demographic period of time," he added. "People are looking for ways they can relax. . . . If people are using my music for that purpose, I think I'm providing a valuable service. I don't consider myself as 'going commercial.' It's just the fact that music like mine has *become* commercial." Kenny G's success brought him requests to record with such vocalists as Smokey Robinson, Dionne Warwick, and Aretha Franklin. In the early fall of 1987, he went on tour as the opening act for the singer Whitney Houston. That November he followed up with a tour as a headliner, bringing along a band made up of his musician friends from Seattle.

Kenny G's next album, *Silhouette* (1988), proved to be as hugely popular as *Duotones* had been. Even reviewers who had ignored him in the past felt compelled to give the work a backhanded compliment or two. "It's not a bad album, really," J. D. Considine acknowledged, "particularly when [Kenny] G gets to play off Smokey Robinson's silken phrasing in 'We've Saved the Best for Last.'" David Hiltbrand, writing in *People* (December 5, 1988), noted that on *Silhouette*, Kenny G's technical prowess on the saxophone was "nimble and fluid"; the music, however, was, in his view, "excruciatingly pretty." The release of *Kenny G Live* (1989), a recording of an outdoor concert in San Diego, was greeted enthusiastically by fans and sold about 2.5 million copies. J. D. Considine, in the *Rolling Stone Album Guide*, panned both *Kenny G Live* and the musician's next release, *Dying Young* (1991), a soundtrack album for the movie of the same name: "*Live* barely shows a pulse and *Dying Young* turns out to be dead on arrival."

Although Arista executives wanted Kenny G to finish another studio album quickly, he preferred to proceed more slowly and act as his own producer. Working in the forty-eight-track digital recording studio he had installed in his Seattle home, Kenny G took nearly two years to create his album *Breathless* (1992). "I wish I could have done it in a year," he told Craig Rosen in an interview for *Billboard* (February 27, 1993). "But you're talking about a creative process I take very seriously. It's not just a piece of product to me. . . . It just took me that long to compose and record the songs that I was satisfied with." Within six months of its release, *Breathless* had sold three million copies, and "Forever in Love," a single from the album, had become a Top Forty hit. Geoffrey Himes, who reviewed *Breathless* for the *Washington Post* (February 7, 1993), noted that the album is "built on Kenny G's most obvious strengths: his knack for writing hummable pop 'hooks' and his ability to play those radio-friendly melodies in a breathy, fluid style that invites the listener to lie back and relax. . . . Yet there's so little tension on *Breathless*, so little resistance to the sax's meandering melodies, that the music's prettiness seems like a small victory indeed."

Kenny G has worked diligently to make sure his music is aired on a wide range of radio formats—jazz, new age, adult contemporary, pop, and rhythm and blues. When *Breathless* was released, he met with radio-programming executives across the country to promote it, as he had for his previous albums. "If the radio people know you as a person, the chances of them supporting you is a lot better," he explained to Pat Cole. His promotional efforts have extended overseas, where he released slightly different versions of *Breathless* to appeal to local markets. For example, he included a rendition of the traditional Chinese song "Jasmine Flower" on albums released in the Far East.

A popular live performer, Kenny G has given concerts all over the world. He has made a habit of leaving the stage during performances to walk through the aisles while he plays a solo. "Going out in the audience is the ultimate in breaking down any walls between the performer and the audience," he said to Joe Brown in an interview for the *Washington Post* (June 4, 1993). "People touch me, grab my hands, slap me on the back. That's the best. I like to make the people that are sitting far back finally have a front-row seat." A fellow saxophone player, Eric Marienthal, who saw the enthusiasm Kenny G generated at a concert, has called him a "master" at communication. "He was able to get that real connection that a lot of musicians aren't as successful at doing," Marienthal told Pat Cole. Another audience pleaser is Kenny G's ability to hold a note for minutes at a time by employing a technique called circular breathing, in which he stores air in his mouth and draws on it while playing.

As Kenny G's popularity has grown, so, too, has the refusal of critics to consider his music to be authentic jazz. "His work is improvisationally empty and doesn't swing, there's no blues sensibility, and he hasn't figured out the difference between emotionalism and sentimentality," Peter Watrous wrote in the *New York Times* after the release of *Breathless*. "No wonder people who have spent their whole lives trying to master the art form [of jazz], to little recognition, get resentful [of Kenny G]." Watrous further observed that "a simple change in nomenclature" would help. In his view, Kenny G's music should be called "instrumental pop music." While acknowledging that he is not a purist, Kenny G has declined to give up the association with jazz altogether. The "purist critics," he told Stephanie Stein, "don't know anything about the style of contemporary jazz we play. I live that, I'm one of the creators of it. So is Lorber—we're the young players who have created something new and different that's still called jazz."

In 1994 Kenny G received a Grammy Award for the single "Forever in Love," an award that, in his view, "has to kind of legitimize the music." At the end of that year, he released *Miracles: The Holiday Album*, a collection of Christmas classics and two original songs: "Miracles," written for his son, and "The Hanukkah Song," written in recognition of his Jewish heritage. The album was the first holiday record to top the Billboard Top Two Hundred since 1962.

Slightly built and energetic, Kenny G has shoulder-length curly brown hair. He shares two homes, one in Seattle and the other in Los Angeles, with his wife, Lyndie, whom he married in 1992, and their son, Max, who was born in 1993. A flying enthusiast, he has a pilot's license and owns a Glassair III prop plane, which he uses for touring; he also enjoys skiing and bike riding. Kenny G appreciates his success and has tried to savor it, because, as he told Pat Cole, "I remember the time when I didn't have a gig. It's a dream. I'm waiting for the dream to end, and I hope it doesn't."

Selected Biographical References: Chicago Tribune XIII p38 N 6 '94 por; Down Beat 55:16+ Ja '88 pors, 59:22+ N '92 pors; Entertainment W 164:24+ Ap 2 '93 pors; Contemporary Musicians vol 14 (1995); Guinness Encyclopedia of Popular Music vol 2 (1992)

Agence France-Presse

Kieślowski, Krzysztof
(kyesh-LOF-skee, KSHISH-tof)

June 27, 1941– Polish filmmaker. Address: c/o Ministry of Culture and Arts, Cinematography Authority, Krakowskie Przedmiecie 21/23, 00071 Warsaw, Poland

With the release of his biblically inspired *Decalogue* in 1988, the Polish filmmaker Krzysztof Kieślowski earned a place among the most acclaimed contemporary European filmmakers. He came to the attention of American audiences several years after that, following the release of his poetic, resonant *The Double Life of Véronique* and his *Three Colors* trilogy, the third installment of which is his much-praised *Red*, which in 1994 was nominated for an Academy Award. Kieślowski began his career as a documentarian, hoping to use his work to draw attention to the social ills that afflicted Poland after it fell under the domination of the Soviet Union. He also made several overtly political feature films, but by the late 1970s he had concluded that it was fruitless to continue to try to depict his country's flaws and that it was more important for the artist to probe "the interior of the human being." Much of his work from the latter half of his career thus attempts to explore the emotional landscape of human relations. "The interior of a human being is full of mystery," he told David Sterritt in an interview for the *Christian Science Monitor* (December 6, 1994), "full of things that are not expressed or said, full of intuitions, and full of fear."

Krzysztof Kieślowski was born on June 27, 1941 in Warsaw, Poland. His father, a civil engineer who suffered from tuberculosis, spent most of his adult life in various hospitals. As a result, the family moved often, to be near whatever hospital Kieślowski's father was in at the time. Since the father was often unable to work, the family had to subsist on the meager income of Kieślowski's mother, an office clerk. Krzysztof, who as a child was also sickly, was occasionally admitted to sanatoriums for children, which were free of charge. When he was living at home, he spent many of his bedridden hours reading books—everything from Dostoyevsky to cowboy stories, he has recalled.

Because the family moved so frequently, it was not unusual for Kieślowski to attend two or three different schools in a year. He was a good student, though he did not particularly enjoy studying, and when he completed high school he decided against going to college. "I thought I knew everything I needed to know, like most teenagers," he explained to Danusia Stok in an interview for *Kieślowski on Kieślowski* (1993), a book consisting mainly of interviews Stok conducted with the filmmaker. Realizing that he had to find a way to make a living, he took his father's advice and entered a training program to become a firefighter. "My father knew perfectly well that when I got back from that fireman's training college I'd want to study," he told Stok. "He was right, of course. In three months I came back, wanted to study—at any cost."

Kieślowski has said that he might have ended up pursuing a different vocation if his parents had not persuaded a distant relative who happened to be the director of the Państwowe Liceum Techniki Teatralnej, a school for theatre technicians, in Warsaw, to help their son gain admission to the school, for it was during his years there that he first encountered serious theatre, cinema, and literature. "Once I saw that such a world existed, I realized that I could live like that, too," he told Stok. "I hadn't known this before." Kieślowski subsequently resolved to become a theatre director. To achieve that goal, he decided to enroll at a film school. "I thought, 'Why not study at film school to become a film director, as a way to becoming a theatre director?'" he has recalled. "They're both directors."

Kieślowski's first two attempts, made in successive years, to secure admission to the School of Cinema and Theatre, in Łódź, the prestigious training ground of virtually every postwar Polish director, were unsuccessful. He ended up working as a clerk and writing poetry at the Department of Culture and, in the evenings, serving as a dresser in a theatre. Later, to avoid being drafted into the army, he entered college, where he studied to be an art teacher. Then, in the early 1960s, the political climate in Poland became more repressive. Partly as a result, the theatre was no longer as vibrant as it had once been, and Kieślowski's interest in becoming a director—in either film or theatre—began to wane. It was thus "only through sheer ambition," as he has put it, that he made a third attempt to attend film school. This time he succeeded.

In 1969, the year he graduated from the Łódź film school, Kieślowski's graduation film was released, becoming his first professional screen credit. Entitled *Z Miasta Łodzi* (From the City of ódź), the film is a short documentary about the city in which he had been living. Throughout the 1970s he released one documentary after another, for a total of more than twenty. His ambition in those days, as he put it to Stok, was "to describe the world"—not as the Communist regime saw it but as he saw it. "The Communist world had described how it should be and not how it really was . . . ," he continued. "It was fascinating to describe something which hadn't been described yet. It's a feeling of bringing something to life, because it is a bit like that. If something hasn't been described, then it doesn't officially exist." His documentaries included *Byzem Żolnierzem* (I was a Soldier; 1970); *Robotnicy 71 nic o nas bez nas* (Workers '71; 1972), and *Z punktu widzenia nocneo porteria* (From a Night Porter's Point of View; 1977). After Kieślowski completed *Dworzec* (Station), in 1981, the police confiscated some of his footage. Realizing that his documentary work could be used to assist the state in its surveillance of ordinary citizens, he decided not to make any more documentaries.

The transition to feature filmmaking was not too difficult, for Kieślowski had been making feature films for several years. His first, *Podziamne Przajście* (Pedestrian Subway), a short television film, was completed in 1973. His first feature for the cinema was *Blizna* (The Scar; 1976), which he dismissed in *Kieślowski on Kieślowski* as "badly made." One of his more important early features was the television film *Spokój* (Stillness; 1976), about a man just released from prison who finds work on a building site. "It's a film about our country, about our system where you can't get what you want, even if all you want is a television and a wife," the director told Stok. "And he didn't want anything else." *Spokój* was not broadcast for six or seven years because it depicted a labor strike, an event that had never before been shown on Polish television.

The first of Kieślowski's features to attract international attention was *Amator* (*The Camera Buff*; 1979). Indeed, it is considered by some to be one of the best examples of Poland's "cinema of moral anxiety," a movement that examined the moral and ethical challenges encountered by those living in Soviet-dominated Eastern Europe. The film tells the story of a young man who, after buying an eight-millimeter camera to record his newborn's first days, becomes obsessed with using film to document the moral decay pervading Polish society. Trouble ensues when the ideas expressed in his films are viewed as being at odds with the official version of reality. *The Camera Buff* won the top awards at the Moscow and Chicago film festivals.

At the end of the 1970s, Kieślowski decided to stop making films with political themes, having concluded, in his words, that "there was no point in describing this world any further." *Przypadek* (*The Accident*), which was shot in 1981 but banned until 1987, thus became his first film to take as its subject an individual's inner life. *The Accident* is "no longer a description of the outside world but rather of the inner world," he has explained. "It's a description of the powers which meddle with our fate, which push us one way or another." *The Accident* explores the different directions the life of the protagonist, a young medical student, could take, each of which depends on whether or not he catches his train. In one scenario, he becomes a Communist Party official, while in another he joins the opposition. A third possibility is that he becomes a happily married, apolitical doctor. "Every day we're always faced with a choice which could end our entire life, yet of which we're completely unaware," he explained to Stok, elaborating on the theme of the film. "We don't ever really know where our fate lies. We don't know what chance holds in store for us."

Kieślowski completed *The Accident* just before martial law was imposed in Poland, in late 1981. The changing political situation in his homeland sent both his personal life and his career into limbo. Feeling compelled to help Poland get back on the right track, Kieślowski, who was then a member of the independent trade union Solidarity, began signing petitions and letters in opposition to martial law. His activism unnerved his wife, who felt he was ignoring his responsibilities to her and their young child. "That's precisely an example of a situation where you can't make the right choice," he reflected in one of his conversations with Stok. "If you make the right choice from the social point of view, you make the wrong one from the point of view of the family. You always have to look for the lesser evil. The lesser evil consisted of my going to bed and sleeping, like a bear." Kieślowski has said that he slept for about five months.

When he emerged from his slumber, Kieślowski decided to make a movie about the Polish legal system. He intended to film people being sentenced to extended jail terms for such activities as possessing underground newspapers or breaking the curfew, and he eventually received permission to shoot footage in court. The presence of his cameras apparently had an effect on the judges: whenever cameras were present, they would not impose prison sentences. The film was never completed. Kieślowski's experience with the Polish legal system and martial law in general left him dispirited, and he eventually resolved to try to convey on film the sense of despair that he and many others of his generation felt. To help him write a script, he enlisted Krzysztof Piesiewicz, a young lawyer who had defended many people accused of crimes under martial law. Their collaboration marked the beginning of a professional relationship that continues to this day. The result of their initial joint effort was *Bez Końca* (*No End*; 1984), in which a lawyer who is to defend a strike organizer dies. His widow, who struggles to rediscover meaning in her life, ends up committing suicide.

Upon its release, which was delayed for over a year, *No End* was castigated not only by the government but also by the Roman Catholic church, which deplored the film's handling of the suicide, and the political opposition, which objected to its pessimism. The public's response, on the other hand, was overwhelmingly positive. "Never in my life have I received as many letters or phone calls about a film from people I didn't know as I did after *No End*," Kieślowski told Stok. "All of them, in fact—I didn't get a single bad letter or call—said that I'd spoken the truth about martial law. That's the way they experienced it, that's what it was like. . . . It was a film about the state of our minds and the state of our hopes rather than about the fact that it was cold outside and that we were being interned or shot at."

Kieślowski's next project grew out of Piesiewicz's suggestion that he make a film that would take the Ten Commandments as its inspiration. "My interest in the Commandments comes from an obvious contradiction," the director said of his motivation in making the film, as quoted in *Variety* (February 28, 1990). "These rules have existed for thousands of years, and everyone more or less agrees that they are right. But in practice, we all violate them every day." *Dekalog* (*Decalogue: The Ten Commandments*; 1988), as the film was entitled, gradually evolved into a gargantuan project: the completed film was actually a series of ten hour-long segments for Polish television that took one year to write and another to film. Because of the rushed production schedule, Kieślowski often shot scenes from several episodes on the same day. "That kept me from getting bored," he joked to Annette Insdorf in an interview for the *New York Times* (October 28, 1990).

Each episode in *Decalogue* is a self-contained entity, though it is linked to the others, for they all take place in the same Warsaw apartment complex and the lead characters in one story sometimes turn up as incidental characters in another. The episodes are also similar in that none promotes a particular religious or moral point of view, despite the biblical connection. Rather, "the series covers a dazzlingly wide range of human experience and human emotion," as Dave Kehr observed in the *Chicago Tribune* (October 8, 1989), "moving between the poles of comedy and tragedy as it probes the ethical underpinnings of everyday life." Echoing the comments of reviewers on both sides of the Atlantic, Kehr described *Decalogue* as "one of the major artistic accomplishments of this decade."

Two episodes from *Decalogue*, *Krótki film o miłości* (*A Short Film about Love*; 1988) and *Krótki film o zabi janiu* (*A Short Film about Killing*; 1988), were expanded into feature-length films and released theatrically. The latter, which depicts a brutal, motiveless murder and the even more gruesome details of the murderer's execution by hanging, elicited a wide range of reactions from reviewers, the Polish government, and film festival judges. Suzanne Moore, writing in *New Statesman and Society* (November 24, 1988), described it as "filmmaking of immense concentration and gut-clenching clarity. . . . The film grabs you by the throat from the very start." Caryn James, on the other hand, writing in the *New York Times* (September 23, 1989), felt that it "forces the audience to confront the most vile aspects of life, without offering enough intellectual substance to justify sitting through such brutality." *A Short Film about Killing* also led to the enactment of a five-year moratorium on executions in Poland. The winner of the Jury prize at the 1988 Cannes Film Festival, it was named best picture at the first European Film Awards.

Somewhat curiously, *Decalogue* was not enthusiastically embraced by the Polish public, a response Kieślowski attributed to his having lost his feel for the concerns of his countrymen. Partly because of the Poles' lukewarm reception of the film, but also because the Polish government had reduced subsidies for motion pictures, Kieślowski began to toy with the idea of collaborating with Western studios on future projects. He ended up doing just that: his next film, *The Double Life of Véronique* (1991), was a Polish-French coproduction set in both countries. The film concerns two young women (both played by Irène Jacob) who lead parallel lives, in that both are musically talented, have heart conditions, were born on the same day in 1966, and were raised by their widowed fathers. What distinguishes their lives is that Weronika is molded by the repressive atmosphere of the post-1968 Communist Poland in which she grew up, while Véronique is the product of the anything-goes sensibility that dominated post-1968 France. Although the two never meet, the death of the more energetic and determined Weronika is somehow communicated to the more diffident Véronique, whose grief over the ineffable loss enables her to learn intuitively from the experiences of her Polish counterpart.

The unorthodox narrative of *The Double Life of Véronique* was baffling to some—Polish reviewers in particular were puzzled by the film—but most, especially Western European and American critics, thought it was brilliant. The latter group included Dave Kehr, who observed in the *Chicago Tribune* (January 5, 1992) that the film "not only respects the intelligence of its audience but actively solicits it, demanding imaginative leaps to bridge the gaps in the narration and interpretive flights to align and analyze the dense patterns of imagery and metaphor." For her dual role, Irène Jacob won the best-actress award at the Cannes Film Festival.

Kieślowski's *Three Colors* trilogy, comprising the films *Blue*, *White*, and *Red*, grew out of Piesiewicz's idea for a film based on the colors of the French flag and the ideals—liberty, equality, and fraternity—they symbolize. "Why not try to make a film where the commanding dictums of the *Decalogue* are understood in a wider context?" Kieślowski asked Danusia Stok, in explaining his interest in taking on the project. "The West has implemented these three concepts on a political or social plane, but it's an entirely different matter on the personal plane."

In *Blue* (1993), the first installment of the trilogy, the freedom that Kieślowski explores is not the type granted by governments, such as freedom of speech, but the less-concrete idea of individual freedom. As Geoffrey Macnab observed in *Sight & Sound* (November 1993), Piesiewicz and Kieślowski's "almost Proustian project is to consider how far individuals are able to detach themselves from family, memory, and material objects, the very things which give most lives a definition." To explore this subject, Kieślowski focused on the life of Julie, a Frenchwoman (Juliette Binoche) who, after ostensibly becoming "free" following the deaths of her beloved husband and daughter, tries to erase all remnants of her previous life. At the 1993 Venice Film Festival, *Blue* won the top prize, and Binoche was named best actress.

For the next installment of the trilogy, Kieślowski adopted a completely different tone: *White* is a black comedy about Karol Karol (Zbigniew Zamachowski), a Polish hairdresser who, divorced and humiliated by his French wife (Julie Delpy), returns to Poland to earn his fortune and plot his revenge. Discussing the theme with Tony Rayns in an interview for *Sight & Sound* (June 1994), Kieślowski said, "The conclusion we came to about equality is that nobody really wants it. Karol in *White* doesn't want equality, he wants to be better than others." The film earned Kieślowski the best director award at the Berlin Film Festival.

In *Red*, Kieślowski revisited one of his favorite themes: the extent to which fate determines the course that an individual's life takes. The film tells the story of a Swiss model (Irène Jacob) whose life becomes intertwined with that of an embittered retired judge (Jean-Louis Trintignant), whose own life, in turn, is strangely mirrored by that of a young law student (Jean-Pierre Lorit). "It seems all but impossible to account for the emotional impact of the last two reels of *Red*, an impact that reaches far beyond the narrative events depicted," Dave Kehr wrote in *Film Comment* (November/December 1994). In his 1994 article for *Sight & Sound*, Tony Rayns considered the three films as a whole and concluded that *Three Colors* "is finally a trilogy about love in the '90s. . . . All three films quicken in pace as they move towards climaxes in which the characters discover in themselves an unsuspected capacity for reciprocating intense emotions. In all three cases, this involves putting behind them earlier relationships they believed at the time to be happy and fulfilling." For *Red*, Kieślowski received an Academy Award nomination for best director, and he and Piesiewicz received a nomination for best original screenplay, an unusual accomplishment for a non-English-language film.

Kieślowski, a self-confessed "professional pessimist," was described by Dave Kehr in his 1989 *Chicago Tribune* article as "an intense, graying man who hides a cynical regard behind a huge pair of glasses." After completing the *Three Colors* trilogy, Kieślowski announced his retirement from filmmaking. When asked by a *New York Times* (November 20, 1994) reporter what he planned to do with his time, Kieślowski offered a characteristically sardonic response: "Just sit in a room and smoke." He and his wife, Marysia, have one daughter, Marta.

Selected Bibliographical References: Film Comment 30:10+ N/D '94 pors; Guardian p6+ O 15 '93 por; N Y Times II p29 N 20 '94 por; Sight & Sound 59:162+ Summer '90 por, 4:8+ Je '94; International Dictionary of Films and Filmmakers vol 2: Directors (1991); Kieślowski, Krzysztof. Kieślowski on Kieślowski (1993)

Agence France-Presse

Kim Young Sam

Dec. 20, 1927- President of South Korea. Address: Office of the President, Chong Wa Dae, 1 Sejong-no, Chongno-ku, Seoul, Republic of Korea

More than thirty years of military rule in South Korea, formally known as the Republic of Korea, ended in February 1993 with the inauguration of Kim Young Sam as president. For decades prior to his election, Kim had been a leader among those calling for democratic reforms in his country, and he suffered political ostracism and repeated arrests for his outspokenness. In 1990 he appeared to many to have given up his struggle for freedom in favor of personal ambition when he merged his opposition party with the ruling party in the National Assembly, South Korea's parliament. Kim, however, maintained that he had taken the action in order to reshape his country's government from within, and he silenced his critics when, after assuming the presidency, he instituted many of the changes he had long advocated, creating what the *Financial Times* (February 23, 1994) termed "one of the most politically free societies in Asia" and "the most democratic government in Korean history." The challenges Kim has faced since becoming president have included reversing his nation's economic downturn and determining the proper course to take to improve relations with North Korea in the face of that country's reported development of nuclear weapons.

The only son of Kim Hong-Jo, a prosperous fishing and shipping merchant, and Park Bu-ryon, Kim Young Sam was born on December 20, 1927 in Koje-gun, in the province of South Kyongsang, Korea. Although one source reports that Kim was not an exceptional student in elementary school, his family moved to Pusan, South Kyongsang's capital, so that he could attend the prestigious Kyongnam High School. What he lacked in studiousness he seems to have made up for in ambition, for he once put up a banner in his classroom that read, "Future President Kim Young Sam." He continued his studies at Seoul National University, South Korea's leading academic institution.

Kim's education was interrupted in 1950 when the army of Communist North Korea marched across the thirty-eighth parallel and into South Korea. (Korea had been occupied, from the end of World War II, by American troops in the south and Soviet troops in the north. In May 1948 the American-occupied zone was declared the Republic of Korea. In September of that year, the Communist-administered zone was proclaimed the Democratic People's Republic of Korea, commonly known as North Korea.) During the resulting war, in which the United States-supported South Korean military fought the Chinese-backed invading troops to a stalemate, Kim Young Sam served as a propagandist for the Seoul government. He nonetheless managed to complete his studies in 1951, two years before the Korean War ended with the cease-fire of July 1953.

Following his graduation from Seoul National University, Kim obtained a post in the administration of President Syngman Rhee. In 1954 he ran for the National Assembly, winning a seat as the representative of a district in Pusan and thus becoming, at the age of twenty-seven, the youngest member of the governing body. It was not long before he established a reputation as a rebel. After Rhee attempted to change South Korea's constitution so that he could extend his presidential term, Kim broke away from the government's ruling party and in 1955 formed the Democratic Party, the first of several opposition groups with which he would be affiliated. Five years later Rhee again tried to prolong his hold on the presidency—this time by election tampering—but his unethical behavior sparked student demonstrations that forced him to resign. Following the brief, unstable rule of the United States-supported John M. Chang, a bloodless coup on May 16, 1961 resulted in the installation of General Park Chung Hee as South Korea's president, and Kim joined those who protested the undemocratic nature of Park's ascendancy.

Kim's rise to prominence came in the 1960s, with his emergence as floor leader of the New Democratic Party (NDP), the chief rival of Park's ruling Democratic Republican Party. In that capacity, he leveled charges of corruption against Park's administration, which, although nominally civilian, was controlled by the generals who had engineered the 1961 coup. He criticized in particular the government's continuous monitoring of opposition parties and the media, a practice that Park insisted was necessary to maintain national security and guard against military aggression from North Korea. By extension, Kim complained about the pervasiveness of South Korea's Central Intelligence Agency, claiming to be "90 percent sure" that the organization was behind the July 1970 incident in which a bottle of acid was hurled into the car he was driving. (He was not seriously hurt.) At the time of the attack, Kim was in the midst of a campaign—an unsuccessful one, as it turned out—to stop the National Assembly's passage of a bill allowing Park to run for a third term as president.

In 1971 Kim himself sought his party's nomination for the presidency, but he lost out to his fellow assemblyman and opposition leader Kim Dae Jung, who in turn fell to Park in the general election. Park's apparent popularity among the people was due to his having improved South Korea's economy while also strengthening its military. Although the opposition NDP enjoyed the support of intellectuals and residents of large cities such as Seoul, it failed to inspire enthusiasm among South Korea's large rural population, which backed Park's Democratic Republican Party.

Park put that backing to the test on October 17, 1972, when he declared martial law, stating that he was doing so in part to prevent any "social unrest" that might develop as a result of the changes he planned to make in government. Those changes included a new constitution, adopted in November, that effectively gave Park unlimited authority. Among other things, the constitution severely limited freedom of speech, allowed Park to appoint one-third of the members of the National Assembly, and set no term limits, making it possible for a president to rule for life.

Kim assumed the leadership of the New Democratic Party in August 1974. He used the post as a platform from which to call for Park's resignation and for a new constitution, one that would provide for direct presidential elections to replace the electoral college system, which gave an advantage to ruling party candidates. He demanded the release of the two hundred students, clergymen, and others who had been arrested as political dissidents; charged that the government's blatant disregard for human rights had tarnished South Korea's standing in the international community; and expressed skepticism that Park's actions had been taken in order to maintain the appearance of national unity before North Korea. Emergency Decree Number Nine, which outlawed criticism of Park's administration in the presence of foreigner, went into effect on March 26, 1975. Thereafter, Kim—who had thrice been held for questioning by the authorities during Park's presidency—risked further punishment by continuing to air his grievances for the benefit of the international media.

While the members of the NDP were united in their desire to change the constitution, there were divisions among their ranks over other issues. Some in the party accused Kim himself of dictatorial behavior, and others, sobered by the fall of South Vietnam to Communist forces in April 1975 and fearing a similar fate for their own country, embraced a less radical antigovernment stance. A violent confrontation took place on May 25, 1976, when NDP members opposed to Kim's having a second term as party leader barred him from the party's convention. Kim and his supporters repaired to NDP headquarters, where he won election to a new term; meanwhile, however, the rival faction had formed a group leadership for the party. The two sides took their differences to the nine-member Central Election Management Committee, which ruled that neither election had been valid. On June 11, 1976 Kim resigned as president of the NDP, maintaining that government instigators had caused the split in his party and adding defiantly, "I may be politically dead, but they can't obliterate the party."

Indeed, in the 1978 National Assembly elections, the NDP for the first time received more popular votes than did the ruling party. While Park's Democratic Republican Party still held a majority of seats, due to his being able to appoint one-third of the representatives, the election results appeared to pose a threat to the president's rule. Perhaps motivated by that realization, and by the fact that in May 1979 the outspoken Kim had again won the leadership of the NDP, on August 11, 1979 the government dispatched an estimated one thousand riot police in a raid on NDP headquarters in Seoul. (The action was carried out on the pretext of having to remove 170 recently fired female textile workers who were staging a sit-in on the premises.) During the course of the operation, the police brutally assaulted NDP leaders, provoking condemnation from the United States government and from Kim, who called the raid "Park's gravest act" up to that time. Kim also suspected the government of being behind the lawsuit, brought against him by several NDP members two days after the raid, charging that his election as party president had been conducted improperly.

Kim appealed to the United States to help restore the observance of human rights in his country. "You have got American boys here," he said, as reported by the *New York Times* (August 20, 1979), referring to the thirty thousand American troops then stationed in South Korea. "If we ever had another war with North Korea, the United States government and public opinion would want to know whether they are fighting for democracy or for a dictatorship, which is what we have here in fact." A few weeks later the *New York Times* (September 16, 1979) quoted him as saying, "Whenever I tell American officials that only by direct pressure on Park can the United States bring him under control, they say that they cannot interfere in the domestic politics of South Korea. . . . Doesn't the United States have thirty thousand ground troops here to protect us? What is that if not interference in domestic affairs?"

After Kim called Park's administration a "minority dictatorial regime," on October 4, 1979 the ruling party expelled him from the National Assembly. All seventy opposition representatives, including those NDP members who had opposed Kim's leadership, resigned their posts in response to the action, bringing parliamentary functions to a halt. In the southern cities of Pusan, Masan, and Changwan, demonstrations protesting the expulsion devolved into riots. The violent clashes with police, which Kim said were indicative of the "widespread discontent" throughout the country, resulted in the declaration of martial law in Pusan and garrison command law in the other two cities.

On October 26, 1979 President Park was assassinated by Kim Jae Kyu, the director of the South Korean CIA, apparently as the result of a confrontation between the two men over the walkout by opposition members. Following Park's death, Kim Young Sam and Kim Jong Pil, the new president of the Democratic Republican Party, agreed to form an ad-hoc National Assembly committee to amend the constitution, implement democratic rule, and establish guidelines for direct presidential elections, to be held the following year. In the meantime, Kim bickered with Kim Dae Jung, the NDP's 1971 presidential candidate, over which of them should seek their party's nomination. The issue soon became moot, however, for in May 1980 the acting president, Choi Kyu Hah, responded to the many antigovernment demonstrations staged by students and others by instituting martial law throughout South Korea and ordering the arrests of hundreds of people labeled as dissidents—among them Kim Young Sam, Kim Dae Jung, and Kim Jong Pil. Electoral college balloting held in August installed the recently retired general Chun Doo Hwan, the only candidate, as president.

Having assumed leadership of the South Korean CIA in April 1980, Chun had taken effective control of the country even before his election as president, and in the process he had banned more than five hundred people, including Kim, from political activity. After winning the nation's top post, he took measures that rivaled Park's in severity. Under Chun's orders, the government confiscated the building that housed the NDP's headquarters, and it prevented the party from nominating candidates for the 1981 National Assembly elections. Consequently, the elections were swept by the Democratic Justice Party, which had been founded by Chun. Meanwhile, Kim, emerging from more than a year of house arrest, attempted to rebuild the NDP. His hopes of doing so were dashed, however, when he was again placed under house arrest, in June 1982, and was forbidden to participate in politics until 1988.

Still in custody in May 1983, Kim went on a hunger strike, demanding the release of all political prisoners, the implementation of democratic rule and direct elections, and the restoration of free speech. The government set him free at the end of May, at which time he checked into a hospital but continued his hunger strike and refused medical treatment. Reportedly near death, he ended his fast after twenty-three days, saying that he wanted to live in order to continue his struggle for democracy in South Korea. Kim's actions appeared to have a galvanizing effect on the theretofore dispirited members of the fractured opposition movement; many joined the Council for the Promotion of Democracy, a new umbrella group cochaired by Kim Young Sam and Kim Dae Jung ("the two Kims," as they came to be called). That organization contributed to the founding, in December 1984, of the New Korean Democratic Party (NKDP), whose membership consisted of former opposition leaders who had recently been released from the political ban.

In the meantime, President Chun had pledged to work toward a more democratic political system. While repressiveness continued to be a defining characteristic of his rule (for example, he placed strict limits on freedom of the press, and on six occasions in January 1985 alone the police prevented Kim from attending political meetings), Chun did restore free legislative elections. As a result of that, in February 1985 the NKDP emerged as the largest opposition party in the 276-seat National Assembly, winning nearly 30 percent of the vote. The political ban on Kim Young Sam, Kim Dae Jung, and others was lifted in March.

The two Kims continued to call for direct presidential elections. Electoral reform became an even more frequent subject of debate with the approach of the end of Chun's seven-year term, for he had promised to step down and make way for a democratic presidential election. By 1987, with prodemocracy demonstrations continuing to take place in many cities, both the NKDP and the majority Democratic Justice Party had expressed the desire to change the electoral system, but the two sides disagreed on the form the new system should take: the ruling party favored British-style parliamentary elections, while the NKDP advocated a system based on that used in the United States. In the spring the two Kims, who felt that NKDP president Lee Min Woo was being too heavily influenced by the majority party, led seventy-three other NKDP members in a walkout, rendering the party—with only sixteen members remaining in the National Assembly—ineffectual. After the government put Kim Dae Jung under house arrest, Kim Young Sam formed, and assumed the leadership of, a new opposition group, the Reunification Democratic Party (RDP).

In the summer of 1987, following talks with Kim and still more student-led demonstrations, Chun gave the National Assembly permission to draw up a new constitution. The RDP and the ruling party each composed a draft, then met to compare the two documents and determine the points of agreement. A single draft was finally submitted to the National Assembly, which in October voted overwhelmingly in favor of the proposed constitution. Under the new system, the president would have less power and would be elected directly by the people to a single, five-year term. The military would play no part in government.

Also in October 1987, Kim Young Sam declared his candidacy for the presidential election to be held two months later. Shortly thereafter, Kim Dae Jung, the head of the new Peace and Democracy Party, did the same. Many opposition members and ordinary citizens feared that with both men in the race, the opposition vote would be split, thus granting a plurality of votes to the Democratic Justice Party candidate, Roh Tae Woo. As it turned out, those fears were realized in December, when Roh received 36 percent of the ballots to defeat the two Kims, who together had drawn 55 percent of the votes. Both Kim Young Sam and Kim Dae Jung were roundly criticized for putting personal ambition ahead of the good of their cause.

Legislative elections in February 1989 made Roh the first president in South Korea's history to lose control of the National Assembly. Kim Young Sam's Reunification Democratic Party and Kim Dae Jung's Peace and Democracy Party, winning fifty-nine seats and seventy seats, respectively, together outnumbered the Democratic Justice Party, which claimed 124 spots. But in 1990 Roh, to the astonishment and disappointment of many, persuaded Kim Young Sam to merge the RDP—by then the largest opposition bloc—with the Democratic Justice Party to form the Democratic Liberals, which instantly commanded a substantial majority of seats in the National Assembly. Some speculated that Kim had allowed Roh to command the majority party in exchange for Roh's promise to support him in the next presidential election.

Given that theory, it was perhaps not surprising that Kim declared himself a candidate for the presidency in 1992. His opponents were the longshot Chung Ju Yung, the founder of the Hyundai corporation, and, once again, Kim Dae Jung. As Andrew Pollace pointed out in the *New York Times* (November 22, 1992), the platforms of the three candidates were strikingly similar: each man advocated stimulating South Korea's stagnating economy by supporting small business, and all three favored reunification with North Korea. As a result, the race was largely a contest of personal styles, with the fiery Kim Dae Jung offering a contrast to the staid Kim Young Sam. In the end, many voters appeared to prefer the latter's more pragmatic, cautious approach to governing, for Kim won the election on December 18, 1992 with 42 percent of the ballots.

Soon after taking office, Kim demonstrated that he had not abandoned the causes of freedom and reform. Breaking with the tradition of the previous three decades, he appointed to his cabinet people from business, academia, and politics rather than the military. In March 1993 he granted amnesty to forty-one thousand political prisoners, dissidents, and criminals. John Burton of the *Financial Times*, evaluating Kim's success one year after the beginning of his presidency, credited the South Korean leader with having "purged the remnants of the military elite," "curbed the powers of the once feared intelligence agency," and contributed to an "improving" economy in which exports had risen by 9.6 percent. Kim has also launched a campaign against governmental corruption and expressed a willingness to increase further South Korea's participation in international trade. He continues to face the challenge of maintaining diplomatic relations with North Korea, with which he has predicted his country will reunite by the year 2000.

Kim Young Sam has been described as handsome and as a "small, lively" man. Since 1951 he has been married to Sohn Myoung-Soon, with whom he has three daughters and two sons. *International Who's Who* lists mountain climbing, swimming, jogging, and calligraphy as being among his interests. He is a Presbyterian. Towson State University, in Baltimore, awarded him an honorary doctorate in 1974. Kim is the author of four books: *There is No Hill We Can Depend On*, *Politics is Long and Political Power is Short*, *Standard-Bearer in His Forties*, and *My Truth and My Country's Truth*.

Selected Biographical References: Christian Sci Mon p1+ F 8 '85 por, p6 D 21 '92 por; N Y Times p1+ D 19 '92 pors, p3 D 20 '92 por; Washington Post A p17+ N 2 '87; International Who's Who, 1994–95

King, Mary-Claire

Feb. 27, 1946- Geneticist; epidemiologist; educator. Address: Department of Molecular and Cell Biology and School of Public Health, University of California, Berkeley, CA 94720

"One of the most fascinating paradoxes of the human condition is that we are all different, yet we are all the same," the geneticist and epidemiologist Mary-Claire King has said. As a graduate student in the early 1970s, King made the startling discovery that more than 99 percent of the DNA of human beings is identical to that of chimpanzees. Since

Jane Scherr/courtesy U.C.-Berkeley

Mary-Claire King

then, in focusing on the much smaller differences in genetic inheritance among people, she has become a leading figure in the revolution that is unlocking secrets of the human genome. In 1990 she and her research team at the University of California at Berkeley mapped a gene responsible for early-onset breast cancer, and the next year she and other researchers announced that they had pinpointed the chromosomal location of a gene that causes a form of inherited deafness. King's discoveries also include genetic clues to why some men infected with HIV-1 develop AIDS faster than others.

"Nearly everything [King] has ever chosen to work on has had, at its core, a deep sense of humanity," the science reporter Natalie Angier has noted. Combining her expertise in DNA sequencing with her passion for justice, King has helped the Argentine human-rights organization Grandmothers of the Plaza de Mayo to establish the identities of some of the hundreds of children kidnapped during the so-called dirty war conducted by the military in Argentina between 1976 and 1983. Thanks to her efforts, more than fifty of those children have been reunited with their relatives. King has also used DNA sequencing to identify the remains of villagers murdered by Salvadoran death squads in 1981. "I've never believed our way of thinking about science is separate from thinking about life," she remarked to David Noonan, who profiled her for *Discover* (October 1990). "Whether we realize it or not, we are all political animals." For the past two decades, King has taught at the University of California at Berkeley, where since 1994 she has held the title American Cancer Society professor of genetics and epidemiology.

Mary-Claire King was born on February 27, 1946 in Wilmette, Illinois, a suburb of Chicago, to Harvey W. King, who was in charge of personnel at Standard Oil of Indiana, and Clarice King. She has a brother, Paul King, a mathematician who owns an aluminum smelter and a consulting firm that specializes in long-term business planning, a half-brother, and a half-sister. In 1966, after just three years as an undergraduate, she earned a B.A. degree, cum laude, in mathematics from Carleton College, in Northfield, Minnesota, where she was also elected to Phi Beta Kappa.

Motivated by the idea of applying her mathematical talents to problems in medicine, King began working toward a doctorate in biostatistics at the University of California at Berkeley. On a whim, she enrolled in a course taught by the renowned geneticist Curt Stern. Each time the class met, Stern would pose a baffling question about heredity. Then, Fran Smith reported in a profile of King for the *San Jose* (California) *Mercury News* (May 19, 1991), he would proceed through "calculation, clues, missteps, and leaps of thinking to arrive at the answer that seemed utterly inevitable—*after* he gave it away." The operation fascinated King, who, since childhood, has loved puzzles, conundrums, and mysteries. "It was like reading mystery novels and solving crossword puzzles and all those kinds of things rolled into one," she explained to Smith. "And furthermore, it had the possibility of actually being good for something. Good for people." Having lost much of her enthusiasm for the purely abstract aspects of mathematics, she changed her area of concentration to genetics. Between 1968 and 1972, she held a National Science Foundation graduate fellowship.

The University of California at Berkeley had attracted King because of its reputation for political activism as well as its academic merits, and as a graduate student she spent many of her extracurricular hours organizing and participating in protests against the Vietnam War. In 1969, disheartened after campus antiwar disturbances prompted Ronald Reagan, then the governor of California, to call in the National Guard, she took a leave from graduate school to work for the consumer activist and lawyer Ralph Nader. As a research fellow at Nader's Center for the Study of Responsive Law, in Washington, D.C., she assisted in a project to determine the effects of pesticides on farm workers, among other assignments.

In graduate school, King had come up with ideas for several innovative research projects, but the lack of sufficiently sophisticated techniques and instrumentation had prevented her from "get[ting] any experiments to work," as she recalled to David Noonan. While trying to decide whether to abandon her academic pursuits and accept an offer from Nader of a permanent job, she sought the advice of Allan C. Wilson, a professor of biochemistry and molecular biology at the University of California at Berkeley whose research focus was evolution. In response to King's description of herself as "a complete disaster in the lab," Wilson observed that "if everyone whose experiments failed stopped doing science, there wouldn't be any science." At Wilson's invitation, she began conducting research toward her doctorate in his laboratory.

As a means of possibly bolstering his theory that humans and apes had evolved from lineages that diverged five million years ago, rather than, as many paleontologists had postulated from fossil evidence, at least fifteen million years ago, Wilson suggested that King investigate the genetic differences between humans and chimpanzees. "I couldn't seem to find any differences," King told Thomas Bass, who profiled her for *Omni* (July 1993). "I'd do tests involving migration rates of proteins, and I'd see a difference in one out of a hundred tests. I was in despair, but Allan kept saying, 'This is great; it shows how similar we really are to chimps.'" King eventually demonstrated that the genomes of human beings differ from those of chimpanzees by less than one percent. Her research became the subject of her doctoral dissertation and also of a paper, cowritten with Wilson, that was published as the much-discussed cover article of *Science* in April 1975.

After earning her Ph.D. degree in genetics from the University of California at Berkeley in 1973, King went to Santiago, Chile, where, as a visiting assistant professor, she taught science for a year at the Universidad de Chile in an exchange program funded by the Ford Foundation. She also participated in medical research programs funded by the Chilean government, which was then headed by Salvador Allende Gossens. On September 11, 1973 Allende was assassinated during the military coup that toppled his Socialist government. In the suppression of suspected leftists that followed, friends and students of King's were murdered, and others were forced to go into hiding or flee the country. "It was hell," King told David Noonan, in recalling the events of that period.

In 1974–75 King did postdoctoral work in epidemiology at the San Francisco branch of the University of California. The next year she secured a job as assistant professor of epidemiology at the School of Public Health at the University of California at Berkeley, where she was promoted in 1980 to the rank of associate professor and in 1984 to that of professor. Since 1989 she has held, concurrently, the title of professor of genetics in the university's Department of Molecular and Cell Biology. An instructor of both graduate and undergraduate students, she regards teaching "not as drudgery but [as] a pleasure," Natalie Angier reported in the *New York Times* (April 27, 1993), noting that such an attitude is "rare for a research professor."

In 1975 King began to search for the causative factor in what appeared to be hereditary cases of breast cancer. Several years later, after exhaustively analyzing the medical histories of the families of more than fifteen hundred women who had breast cancer, she concluded that in at least 5 percent of the victims (and possibly as many as 10 percent), many of whom became ill in their twenties, thirties, or early forties, the disease could be traced to a dominant gene that each woman had inherited from either her father or her mother. "It's important to understand that breast cancer is *always* genetic," King explained years later, during an interview with Natalie Angier for *Glamour* (December 1993). "It's the result of mutations, or alterations, in our genes. But women who develop hereditary breast cancer were born with these mutations, while others develop genetic alterations at some point in their lives. . . . For women born with the genetic mutation, the risk of developing breast cancer is over 80 percent." (The chance of developing ovarian cancer is also significantly higher than average for those women.) King has also explained that "if all the genes causing breast cancer can be mapped [and] identified and their functions understood, the disease could be detected and treated very early in its development."

Pinpointing the location of the breast-cancer gene on the twenty-three pairs of chromosomes that reside in every human cell (except the gametes, which contain a haploid set of chromosomes) proved to be a far tougher problem than building the case for its existence. King has likened the difficulty she faced in the early years of her research to that of trying to locate, while driving at night, an address in a unfamiliar town in which streetlights have been installed only on every tenth block. She made little headway until the early 1980s, when breakthroughs in molecular biology led to the mapping of many more genetic markers—the streetlights in King's analogy. Her research received an additional boost in 1985, with the advent of the polymerase chain reaction technique and the identification of a new type of DNA marker. During the next few years, King and her staff systematically ruled out one likely location after another. The turning point came when Beth Newman, then a postdoctoral researcher in her lab, suggested mathematically plotting their test results according to the date of onset of breast cancer in the 146 stricken members of the twenty-three extended families in this phase of their study. "So we lined them up," King told Fran Smith. "And there it was!" In 1990 King announced that early-onset familial breast cancer was linked to 17q21, meaning that the gene responsible for hereditary breast cancer was located midway down the lower arm of chromosome 17.

Having narrowed their search for BRCA1, as the gene was dubbed, to a well-defined neighborhood of "no more than a few million nucleotides," King and her coworkers now focused their energies on locating the gene's precise address. At the same time, guided by King's discovery and proceeding in an atmosphere of intense scientific competition, researchers in a dozen other laboratories struggled to reach the same goal. "We're obsessed with finding the gene," King, speaking for the twenty or so members of her laboratory team, admitted to Natalie Angier in April 1993. "I want it to happen in our lab." That hope was dashed when, in September 1994, a group of scientists led by Mark H. Skolnick of the University of Utah Medical Center, in Salt Lake City, succeeded in identifying BRCA1. After acknowledging her disappointment and praising the work of the Skolnick team, King alluded to her next, immediately adopted cancer-research objective by remarking to Natalie Angier during an interview for the *New York Times* (September 15, 1994), "It's going to take a lot of work from everybody in the field to figure out how this gene works." The accuracy of King's prediction, which she made with the knowledge that BRCA1 is ten times larger than the average gene, sharpened with the finding that BRCA1 is unusually prone to mutation (by November 1994 King's team and two others had discovered a total of about thirty distinct mutations).

Propelled by what Angier characterized as a "pronounced bedside bent," King has continually addressed the concerns of women with an inherited susceptibility to breast and ovarian cancer. In a paper for the *Journal of the American Medical Association* (April 21, 1993), for example, that was written with the oncologist Susan M. Love and the epidemiologist Sarah Rowell, she described the medical, pharmacological, and surgical strategies (among them constant surveillance, use of the experimental drug tamoxifen, and preventive mastectomy or ovariectomy) available to those women. "We do not have a good option, or even a good combination of options, for women with inherited risk," she admitted. Such women, she continued, "need to be told honestly what we know and what we do not know, so they can decide what to do. . . . [A woman's] decision, with its enormous consequences, should never be rushed, and all providers need to respect both the process and her conclusion."

King has approached the genetic analysis of breast and ovarian cancer not only as a researcher but also as the sister or sister-in-law of two women who were diagnosed with breast cancer and, in addition, as a potential breast-cancer victim herself and as the daughter and mother of other potential victims. (Current statistics indicate that one out of eight American women will eventually get the disease.) Similarly, when she was enlisted to help the Grandmothers of the Plaza de Mayo and Argentina's National Commission on the Disappearance of Persons, she brought to her task not only scientific expertise but strong feelings of empathy for the victimized families and a sense of outrage regarding the "dirty war" conducted by the Argentine generals who overthrew the government of Isabel Perón in 1976. Before its ouster in 1983, the military junta had trampled the civil and human rights of most Argentineans and murdered an estimated twelve thousand to twenty thousand people in an attempt to rid the country of "all the subversives, . . . their collaborators, . . . their sympathizers, . . . those who remain different, and . . . the timid," in the words of the Argentine general Iberico Saint Jean, whom King quoted in an account for *Grand Street* in 1992.

The victims included women who had been pregnant when seized by the military or the police and who were killed shortly after giving birth. Their infants, as well as the infants of other parents (who were murdered along with their older children), had been, in effect, kidnapped—given to, or taken by, military officers or prison employees or sold on the black market. Although, with few exceptions, the new "parents" pretended the infants were their own biological offspring, word of what had actually happened began to spread, and in 1977 some of the grandmothers of the kidnapped babies, defying the government's ban on public gatherings, began marching every Thursday morning in the Plaza de Mayo, in Buenos Aires, as a means of attracting attention and thereby gaining clues to the whereabouts of the "disappeared," as the children and their parents (and others who had been killed) came to be called. In the next six years, the Grandmothers of the Plaza de Mayo filled hundreds of black binders with the information they had uncovered.

Within a day of her arrival in Buenos Aires in mid-1984, King had learned of the existence of 145 missing children. "And those were cases where the Grandmothers actually had a *lot* [of information]," she told Fran Smith. To determine whether a particular child was related to a particular grandmother, King decided to compare their HLA (human leucocyte antigen) genes. Those genes, which "code for the histocompatibility antigens that must match for tissue transplants," as she wrote in her *Grand Street* article, were at that time "the most varied human genes known" and thus were particularly useful for resolving questions of identity. King engaged a local laboratory to carry out the typing of HLA genes in both the child's blood (which she obtained with a court order) and the blood of the grandmother and, if possible, other relatives. The "imposter" parents invariably refused to be tested.

The first case that King tackled was that of Paula, an eight-year-old girl who had disappeared in 1978 and had been traced to the home of a former police chief. "We proved with 99.9 percent certainty, on the basis of HLA testing and blood groups, that Paula was a descendent of the three living grandparents who claimed her," King told Thomas Bass. "When she went back to her grandparents' house, which she hadn't seen since she was two, she walked straight to the room where she'd slept as a baby and asked for her doll." In 1988, after the introduction of the polymerase chain reaction, King abandoned HLA matching in favor of the much more reliable technique of comparing mitochondrial DNA, which is inherited only through the maternal line and thus, for purposes of comparison, permits the substitution of any maternal relative in cases in which the grandmothers are no longer alive or reachable. As of 1994, King had helped to reunite more than fifty children with their blood relations. In another twelve cases, in which King proved that the "imposter" parents were not related to the children in question, the natural parents have yet to be identified. "I think the fundamental parts of everybody's life are love and work, and it's very nice when they can touch," King observed to David Noonan, in reflecting upon her efforts in Argentina.

In the past few years, King has used her skills in genetic sleuthing not only in Argentina but also at the United States Army Central Identification Laboratory, in Hawaii, to identify the recently recovered remains of soldiers who had been listed as missing in action during the Vietnam War. She has also assisted in attempts to identify the remains of the five hundred villagers killed during a massacre by Salvadoran armed forces in El Mozote, El Salvador, in 1981. In cases where no dental or bone X rays of the victims exist, she has proceeded by extracting and sequencing tiny amounts of mitochondrial DNA from teeth, a technique she perfected in 1992 in collaboration with the Berkeley research geneticist Charles Ginther and Laurie Issel-Tarver, then a graduate student. Their method may prove valuable to law-enforcement agencies, as she and Ginther showed in the same year, when they used it to identify the skeletal remains of a teenage boy who had been missing for ten months in upstate New York. Stretches of DNA from the boy's teeth exactly matched DNA from a blood sample obtained from the woman that police had suspected was his mother.

Sequencing of mitochondrial DNA also lies at the heart of the Human Genome Diversity Project, an undertaking in which King has been working closely with Luigi Luca Cavalli-Sforza, a professor of genetics at the Stanford University Medical School, in California, and a coauthor of *The History and Geography of Human Genes* (1994). King has lobbied energetically for governmental support of the project, the goal of which is, in her words, "to understand who we are as a species and how we came to be." The project calls for the linkage of molecular analysis of the human genome with population genetics, epidemiology, anthropology, archaeology, linguistics, and other disciplines. Studying human genome diversity will enable scientists to address questions ranging from how humans migrated out of Africa to how, given the same exposure to viruses or bacteria, some people become ill while others do not. King and other participants in the Human Genome Diversity Project have developed a plan for obtaining both DNA samples and anthropological information from twenty-five individuals in each of four hundred populations, with an emphasis on those (such as some groups of Pygmies, in Africa, and the Basques, in Europe) that have long been relatively isolated from other peoples. At a hearing held before the United States Senate Committee on Governmental Affairs on April 26, 1993, King and Cavalli-Sforza expressed the hope that the findings that may emerge from the project will "undercut conventional notions of race and underscore the common bonds between all humans," as Louise Levathes quoted them as saying in the *New York Times* (July 27, 1993).

In other research that King has conducted since the late 1980s, she and other scientists at Berkeley have demonstrated that differences in the rapidity at which homosexual men infected with the HIV-1 virus develop AIDS or AIDS-related complex correlate with differences in the men's HLA genes. Another of King's research projects, which she has carried out in collaboration with scientists at both Berkeley and the Universidad de Costa Rica, concerns an inherited form of deafness that leads to total loss of hearing by age thirty. Through genetic studies of a large, extended Costa Rican family, many of whose members inherited that form of deafness, King and her coworkers determined the exact location, on chromosome 5q, of the gene responsible. King's current research projects include the genetic analyses of systemic lupus erythematosus, rheumatoid arthritis, and migraine and the genetic epidemiology of perinatal transmission of HIV.

King has served on the Special Commission on Breast Cancer of the President's Cancer Panel; the Board of Scientific Counselors of the Division of Cancer Prevention and Control of the National Cancer Institute as well as various institute task forces; committees of the National Academy of Sciences/National Institute of Medicine; and the advisory board of the National Institutes of Health Office of Research on Women's Health. Her professional activities also include service as a consultant to the UN's Forensic Anthropology Team. She has written or cowritten more than 120 journal articles and book chapters. In the *New York Times* (April 27, 1993), Natalie Angier reported that King passed up an opportunity to be considered for the directorship of the NIH in 1991. "I'm not interested in a job with that level of administrative responsibility," King told Angier. "It would be too far removed from what I love to do, which is science."

"Of course I feel overwhelmed!" King acknowledged in answer to a question put to her by Natalie Angier regarding the many demands on her time. But she refuses to let that feeling hinder her, and, according to Angier, "in spite of [all her responsibilities], she manages to look young for her age." Angier also reported that King "walks and talks so swiftly that by comparison one feels trapped in resin" and that "she speaks her mind, goes after what she wants, and will never cede her ground." Eric Lander, a molecular biologist and friend of King's, has described her as "insightful, irreverent, energetic, a wonderful antidote to the notion people have of scientists as lifeless, bloodless drones."

In 1973 King married Robert Colwell, an ecologist; the couple were divorced about seven years later. Emily King Colwell, their daughter, who was born in 1975, plans to specialize in constitutional law. Among other honors, King has received the Alumni Achievement Award and an honorary doctor of science degree from Carleton College, in 1982 and 1992, respectively; the Susan G. Komen Foundation Award for Distinguished Achievement in Breast Cancer Research, in 1992; and the Clowes Award for Basic Research from the American Association for Cancer Research, in 1994. In 1993 the

American Association for the Advancement of Science elected her a fellow, and *Glamour* magazine selected her as a woman of the year. In 1994 the American Cancer Society named her the first recipient of the Walt Disney Research Professorship for Breast Cancer, the most prestigious of the society's cancer-research awards.

Selected Biographical References: Discover 11:46+ O '90 por; NY Times C p1+ Ap 27 '93 por; Omni 15:68+ Jl '93 por; Who's Who of American Women, 1993

George Bennett/CNN

Kinsley, Michael

Mar. 9, 1951– Political commentator; writer; editor; television host; lawyer. Address: CNN, 820 1st St. NE, Washington, D.C. 20002

As the cohost representing the political left on the Cable News Network's daily debate program *Crossfire*, the extraordinarily articulate and quick-witted Michael Kinsley is a formidable participant in fast-paced repartee, countering the verbal punches of his right-of-center opponent with stinging bons mots, usually delivered with an insouciant smile. While able to adapt to the polarized format of *Crossfire*, which recruited him in 1989, Kinsley is a more complex intellectual than the television show makes him appear. Outside of television, as a writer and editor, he has for most of his career been associated with the *New Republic*, the once-leftist weekly journal of opinion that began moving to the center after Martin Peretz became its publisher two decades ago. "I don't think we're centrist by any motivation to be moderate," Kinsley once wrote of the *New Republic*'s position. "In fact, what we are is sort of schizophrenically extremist. Sort of all over the place rather than right down the middle."

Kinsley joined the *New Republic* as managing editor in 1976, when he was completing his law studies. He became editor and writer of the magazine's "TRB from Washington" column of political commentary in 1979 and remained in those positions on and off through the 1980s. On leave from the *New Republic*, he edited *Harper's Magazine* for one and a half years and was a guest American editor with the *Economist* in London for six months. Earlier in his career, he had been managing editor of the *Washington Monthly*. While editing the *New Republic*, he was seen on television regularly on William F. Buckley's PBS political discussion show *Firing Line* and occasionally on such Washington-oriented programs as the weekly public events and issues roundtable *The McLaughlin Group*, also on PBS.

Since becoming cohost of *Crossfire* in 1989, Kinsley has remained associated with the *New Republic*, with the title of senior editor. While no longer writing the TRB column, he contributes occasionally to the magazine, about an article a month. He also contributes ten essays a year to *Time*, the weekly news magazine. A collection of his TRB columns and other published articles was issued under the title *Curse of the Giant Muffins and Other Washington Maladies* in 1987. Among the salient characteristics of the pieces are a clever style, a distinctive sense of humor, and an unconventional neoliberal approach to ideas and issues. In his column in *New York*, the media critic Edwin Diamond once described Kinsley as "perhaps the best current practitioner of analytical journalism, of Washington political writing as hip essay."

Michael E. Kinsley, the grandson of Jewish immigrants from Eastern Europe and the son of George and Lillian (Margolis) Kinsley, was born in Detroit, Michigan on March 9, 1951, and he grew up in the city's suburbs. After graduating from the Cranbrook School in Bloomfield Hills, Michigan, he matriculated at Harvard College, in Cambridge, Massachusetts. As an undergraduate at Harvard, he had, according to Jerry Adler in *Esquire* (May 1990), a reputation as "a gifted iconoclast" with "contrarian instincts." While opposed to the American military intervention in Vietnam, he did not join in the student demonstrations supporting Ho Chi Minh, and he was similarly nonconformist in his wardrobe. "He eschewed the small but commonplace hypocrisy of dressing for class at Harvard Yard as if on his way to the hills to fight by the side of Che Guevara," Adler wrote. "He wore button-down Oxford shirts and permanent-press chinos, a uniform that in that place and time was as attention-getting as a velvet opera cloak."

After taking his B.A. degree at Harvard in 1972, Kinsley spent the next two years in England on a Rhodes scholarship at Magdalen College, Oxford University. In 1974 he returned to the United

States and entered Harvard University Law School. While studying for his law degree, he worked for Ralph Nader, the crusading consumer advocate, as one of "Nader's Raiders"; more important, at the end of his first year in law school, he joined the staff of the *Washington Monthly*, and he eventually became managing editor of that small but influential publication. In his *Esquire* profile, Jerry Adler, after placing Kinsley "at the center of a loose network of writers [including James Fallows and Nicholas Lehman] who have disassembled the conventional wisdom of Washington, finding the rot of self-interest and the rust of sentimentality and wishful thinking that underpin the great gray monolith of opinion," went on to observe that "Kinsley and most of his cohorts began their careers at the *Monthly*, learning to pillage reputations under the Fagin of young liberal skeptics, editor Charlie Peters. Kinsley was one of the most radiant of Peters's protégés."

Kinsley also put in a stint as a summer associate with the Los Angeles law firm of Gibson, Dunn & Crutcher, but by the fall of 1976, when he was beginning his third year in law school, he had decided to try to pursue a career as a journalist rather than as an attorney. "I applied all over the place," he recounted to Lynn Hirschberg in an interview for *Rolling Stone* (May 1988). "Fortunately for me, the managing editor of the *New Republic* had just quit. And Martin Peretz [the editor in chief and owner of that publication] was desperate for a managing editor. . . . He said, 'You can have this job of managing editor if you take it right away.' So I went to Harvard Law School, and after endless negotiations they said I could finish up at night at the George Washington University Law Center, which is what I did." Studying law nights while working at the *New Republic* days, he took his doctorate in jurisprudence in 1977.

Kinsley was managing editor of the *New Republic* from 1976 until 1979, when he became editor. "[The *New Republic*], which just celebrated its seventy-fifth anniversary, was a high-minded journal of tired liberal thought that had fallen on hard times when Peretz bought it in 1974," Jerry Adler wrote in his 1990 *Esquire* piece. "Kinsley was the right person to inject fresh ideas. . . . He brought the same contrarian instincts [he had exhibited at Harvard] to the *New Republic*, both as editor and author of the 'TRB from Washington' column." In surveying the Washington scene, Adler observed, Kinsley sometimes created a sensation by daring to attack by name some prominent "pompous twit" whom others were dismissing only privately. "Disdaining most Washington social life," Adler explained, "Kinsley was impervious to the sanction of being excluded from it. In a small coterie of fellow journalists, acquaintances from England, and people he'd gone to law school with, Kinsley hid from the social-climbing, name-dropping, leak-mongering whirl that most people in Washington have instead of friends." Even in his intimate circle, he was known for his "irascible sensibility," his "unblinking frankness," and his "impatience with activities that failed to meet his high standards." "He would bring dinner parties to an early close," Adler wrote, "[and] walk out on movies in the first five minutes if they threatened to bore him." One writer who had worked under Kinsley told Adler, "As an editor, he could be brutal. Where someone else might say, 'Oh, I think *this* is what you're trying to say,' Kinsley would write, 'This is crap. Cut it.'"

Kinsley resigned as editor of the *New Republic* for a brief period during 1979, after Martin Peretz spiked an article by Suzannah Lessard titled "Kennedy's Woman Problem, Women's Kennedy Problem," which Peretz judged to be in violation of responsible standards of taste and ethics. Upon returning to his editorial post, Kinsley wrote regarding the contretemps: "The article was a feminist argument that a certain matter should be of serious political concern to women. The particular example was the presidential candidacy of Senator [Edward M.] Kennedy. [Peretz], as I understood his position, did not necessarily disagree with the author's argument. The problem arose from her forthright definition of the matter she was concerned about." Lessard's article was later published in the *Washington Monthly*.

Accepting the position of editor of *Harper's Magazine* in 1981, Kinsley left the *New Republic*, where Hendrik Hertzberg succeeded him as editor. During Kinsley's nineteen months as editor of *Harper's*, that publication received a National Magazine Award for general excellence. Among the several articles he wrote for *Harper's*, the one that attracted the most attention was "Nuclear Holocaust in Perspective" (May 1982), a review of Jonathan Schell's book *The Fate of the Earth*, a jeremiad that had been published originally in the *New Yorker*. "Perhaps it is lese majesty to call a major three-part series in the *New Yorker* 'pretentious,'" he wrote, "but *The Fate of the Earth* is one of the most pretentious things I've ever read." Beyond being amused by "the pompous generalities that come attached to *New Yorker*-style cautionary notes" and "a lot of wacky judiciousness," Kinsley took issue with what he perceived to be Schell's belief that "the nuclear peril outweighs all other considerations" and his apparent willingness to trade away individual liberty and national sovereignty for an international order conducive to the emergence of a postnuclear world that would be, in Kinsley's words, "a delightful lion-and-lamb affair, no nation-states, no war, free hors d'oeuvres at the Algonquin bar . . . ."

In retrospect, Kinsley would write three years later: "Now that the fever of nuclear monomania has passed, it's hard to remember the thrall in which this silly book [*The Fate of the Earth*] held the American intelligentsia. The praise was so ecstatic, and so unanimous, that when I and one other reviewer (John Leonard of the *New York Times*) dissented, this affront was considered worthy of an article in *Time* magazine. The piece was the beginning of the end for me as editor of *Harper's*. The chairman of the board, a pompous investment banker, stormed into the office waving the magazine and thundering, 'I have grandchildren!' . . . Despite the ever-present peril of imminent doom, my former boss has found the courage to complete his new house in the Hamptons . . . , and if he has given two seconds' thought a week to nuclear destruction recently, I'd be very surprised. There's been an amusing role reversal on nuclear matters during the past few years. . . . The right has decided that the very existence of nuclear weapons is intolerable and has taken up all the childish rhetoric about wiping them off the face of the earth. Meanwhile the left has gone all sophisticated and pragmatic and rediscovered the strategic magic of nuclear deterrence."

The friction between Kinsley and some of his superiors at *Harper's* was exacerbated by a disagreement over his propensity for junketing. The breaking point came when he refused to apologize for accepting an invitation to visit Israel and Lebanon at the expense of the Israeli government. Resigning his position at *Harper's* in 1983, he returned to the *New Republic*, where he resumed writing the TRB columns while Hendrik Hertzberg continued as editor. Kinsley's columns in 1983 included "Decisions, Decisions," about a South Carolina judge's sentencing of three convicted rapists to their choice of thirty years in prison or castration; "Welcome to the Power House," about Alejandro Orfila's resigning as secretary general of the Organization of American States to join the lobbying firm of Gray & Company ("yet another watershed in the astonishing evolution of Washington's influence-peddling industry"); and "Away with a Manger," about the United States Supreme Court's hearing of oral arguments about a nativity scene in Pawtucket, Rhode Island ("It's getting to be that time of year again, and Christmas just wouldn't be Christmas without the American Civil Liberties Union's annual campaign to rid the nation of religious displays on government property").

The July 16, 1984 issue of the *New Republic* carried a diatribe against the *New Yorker* by Kinsley titled "William Shawn and the Temple of Facts." He began that article by citing "a dyspeptic friend, who earnestly dislikes the *New Yorker* for its smug insularity, its tiny dada conceits passing as wit, its whimsy presented as serious politics, and its deadpan narratives masquerading as serious journalism." He went on to say that he had had his suspicions about the *New Yorker*'s vaunted fact-checking department ever since a dinner party at which he heard a *New Yorker* fact checker regale the gathering "with tales of chartering airplanes to measure the distance between obscure Asian capitals, sending battalions of Sarah Lawrence girls to count the grains of sand on a particular beach referred to in an Ann Beattie story, and suchlike tales of heroic valor in the pursuit of perfect accuracy."

Among the other subjects Kinsley addressed in the *New Republic* in 1984 were the advertising or promotion of products and causes by direct, or "junk" mail ("For cynical manipulation, deception, and sheer malarkey, political mailings make even the wildest TV commercials look like models of Socratic dialogue"); press exploitation of the casual remarks of politicians ("A Gaffe Is When a Politician Tells the Truth"); the Democratic Party platform ("No human sorrow is alien to the Democratic Party. First we need to 'know more.' Knowing more will lead to a Government program, and soon the problem will be solved"); the investment banker Felix Rohatyn ("Rohatyn's progress from Felix the Fixer to Felix the Philosopher is one of the great public relations ascents of our time"); the American Jewish electorate ("Jews live like Wasps, the saying goes, and vote like Puerto Ricans. . . . Like other late-arriving ethnics, American Jews got their Democratic politics early on, in the slums and sweatshops. But unlike other ethnics, Jews rarely change their politics with their economic status. That's because (and I generalize grossly—but I'm entitled) Jews are slower to forget. . . . Also . . . although it annoys Jewish hard-liners and anti-Semites alike, mainstream American Jews traditionally have felt they can't behave like any other selfish interest group. They must be like Caesar's wife.")

In 1985 Hendrik Hertzberg, moving to contributing editor, relinquished the editorship of the *New Republic* to Kinsley, who continued to write the TRB column. In "Abortion Time Bomb" (February 25, 1985), Kinsley discussed what he saw as the unfortunate boomerang legacy of *Roe v. Wade*, the 1973 Supreme Court case in which the majority of the court voted in favor of declaring abortion to be a constitutional right. "One of the worst things that ever happened to American liberalism was *Roe v. Wade*," he wrote. "Almost overnight, it politicized millions of people and helped create a mass movement of social-issue conservatives that has grown into one of the most potent forces in our democracy. . . . The reasoning in *Roe* was, in a word, a mess. There was almost no effort to explain where this 'right' to an abortion came from. Previous 'privacy' rulings had involved . . . matters that feature prominently in the Bill of Rights. Abortion doesn't. . . . There is a time bomb ticking away inside *Roe v. Wade*. Scientific developments of the past decade, allowing us to peer into the womb, have affected the emotional climate and a lot of people's thinking about abortion. . . . Less widely noted outside legal circles is how other medical developments have started to undermine abortion's legal basis. . . . What this saga of judicial folly makes clear is that abortion just doesn't belong in the Constitution. . . . The greatest danger is a future Supreme Court ruling that not only is not required by the Constitution, but actually is forbidden as a denial of due process to the fetal 'person'. . . . Abortion is another area of the law where conservatives are discovering the joys of 'judicial activism,' and liberals may soon discover the virtues of 'judicial restraint.'"

Analyzing public-opinion polls under the title "Vox Pop Crock" in the September 10, 1985 issue of the *New Republic*, Kinsley dissented from the common complaint that such polls lead to democratic excess. "Polls undermine democracy . . .

because polls don't measure public opinion," he wrote. "They create it, often with building blocks of ignorance, prejudice, and simple muddle. Worse, they reinforce the impression . . . that untethered opinion is what democracy is about. . . . No poll allows you to express reasoned views. . . . Even the granddaddy poll question is essentially unanswerable. The classic formulation is, 'Do you approve or disapprove of the way President Reagan is handling his job?' I think Reagan has done brilliantly at 'handling his job.' I just disagree with him about nearly everything. What am I supposed to say? At their sleaziest, polls take a subject on which the vast majority of people are completely ignorant, implant a prejudice, call it an opinion, and serve it up as a basis for policy."

In the article "Dohrn Again," in the October 14, 1985 issue of the *New Republic*, Kinsley wrote of the reemergence of the 1960s New Left revolutionary Bernadine Dohrn as a Long Island yuppie housewife and member of a prestigious New York law firm: "It's hard to know which is more appalling, Bernadine Dohrn embracing the establishment, or the establishment embracing Bernadine Dohrn." In "Saint Ralph" (December 9, 1985), Kinsley attested that while his former employer Ralph Nader was "actually quite warm and funny in person," Nader the social reformer reminded him of Miss Birdseye in Henry James's 1886 novel *The Bostonians*, a character who, in James's words, "always dressed in the same way" and "was in love . . . only with causes." Regarding the long-held cynical expectancy that Nader would, like "the normal person," sell out for financial or political gain, Kinsley wrote, "But Ralph Nader is not a normal person. Operating on the mental fringe where self-abnegation blurs into self-obsession, Ralph is living proof that there isn't much difference between a fanatic and a saint."

The sharpest disagreement between Peretz and Kinsley at the *New Republic* came in 1986, when an editorial, approved by Peretz, favoring aid to the Nicaraguan *contras* was rebutted in a column by Kinsley in the same issue. Other subjects addressed by Kinsley in the *New Republic* in 1986 included Armand Hammer ("an extreme example of the sort of capitalist whose only measure of a government is whether it is willing to 'do business'—the sort that his friend Lenin observed would sell the Soviets the rope they needed to hang him with") and Democratic Party policy ("Much of what the Democratic Party currently stands for domestically is nothing more than an expression of [New York governor Mario] Cuomo's ideological sleight of hand: peddling selfishness as progressivism"). Among his writings published outside the *New Republic* was a piece in the *Washington Monthly* (April 1984) about the controversy over the disclosure that the political columnist Alexander Cockburn ("rhymes with 'slow burn'"), an unabashed hard leftist and critic of Israel, had received a ten-thousand-dollar grant from the Institute of Arab Studies. Kinsley noted that Cockburn had been described, "accurately enough," as both "irresistibly readable" and "a talented, despicable writer who enjoys vicious teasing as a kind of journalistic blood sport."

Kinsley was among thirteen journalists whose names appeared in a list of "150 Who Make a Difference in American Politics," published in the *National Journal* in the summer of 1986. In *New York* (August 4, 1986), Edwin Diamond noted that Kinsley had no interest in investigative journalism. He quoted Kinsley as saying that he doesn't "spend time with news sources because [he doesn't] *have* any news sources." "On paper," Diamond wrote, "the Kinsley journalistic operation seems unworkable. In Washington, the ultimate insiders' town . . . , Kinsley is an outsider. [His] paradoxical successes—as the outsider in the insiders' game, the dove working for hawk Peretz—are a tribute to a sharp intelligence."

Forty-eight of Kinsley's *New Republic* articles, along with thirteen others, including the Cockburn piece and articles that had originally appeared in *Harper's*, the *Wall Street Journal* (where his writing often appeared on the Op Ed page), and *Fortune*, were brought together in *Curse of the Giant Muffins and Other Washington Maladies*. (In the title essay Kinsley quotes a statement about the financial sacrifice involved in public service made by a former solicitor general of the United States, who hadn't realized what scrimping was until he found himself in a Giant supermarket considering buying the cheaper store brand instead of his preferred brand of English muffins.) Reviewing the collection of articles in the *Washington Post* (September 6, 1989), John Kenneth Galbraith wrote, "They are admirably written, topical, and informative, especially on Washington people, scene, and culture." With tongue at least partly in cheek, Galbraith went on: "However, the interest comes not just from the good writing, the clear, effective, resourceful prose, but also from the superb consistency of the author's views. . . . [Kinsley] concerns himself . . . with people or tendencies that are morally defective, intellectually perverse, financially depraved, or, by way of variation, 'egregious,' 'odious,' and 'piteous.' The list of those so usefully characterized is very impressive. Ronald Reagan . . . , Ed Meese . . . , Howard Baker . . . , James Buchanan, the last Nobel economics laureate . . . , Armand Hammer, Mary Cunningham, Tish Baldridge, Felix Rohatyn . . . , Lloyd Cutler, Michael Deaver . . . , a wide assortment of Washington lobbyists . . . , [and] an especially large number of other journalists."

In *Vanity Fair* (September 1989), Christopher Hitchens observed that Kinsley "deftly avoids" conventional political partisanship in *Curse of the Giant Muffins*. "He thinks that the Reagan era has been a fraud on the public, but he also thinks that the liberals kind of asked for it," Hitchens wrote. "This is the strength and weakness of a book that simply delights the reader. [The book] is funny, sometimes extremely funny, and it is also mordant and clever. Unlucky is the fraud or windbag who catches Kinsley's eye." In *Rolling Stone*, Lynn

Hirschberg described the writing in the collection as "clever and amusing, insightful and prescient." She elaborated: "Kinsley has a remarkable ability to sort out differing points of view and make his opinion seem like the only opinion worth having. He has a gift for spotting phonies and scams and ridiculous trends, and, more impressively, he has a way of attacking his targets with humor and precision. . . . He's the grand antagonist of the tax shelter, the country-club write-off, the bullshit speech writer, and the overpaid 'consultant.'"

Although the *New Republic* editorially endorsed the candidacy of Al Gore for the Democratic presidential nomination in 1988, Kinsley's personal first choice was Michael Dukakis. In his 1988 interview with Lynn Hirschberg for *Rolling Stone*, he explained: "On most of the issues we editorialize about, we come to some kind of consensus. Or [if] it's a subject on which most people don't feel strongly, . . . the one who does writes the editorial. Like, nobody else around here could care less about taxes and tax reform, but it happens to be an issue I'm very interested in, and I wrote, or at least heavily edited, most of the stuff about that. And on foreign policy, I probably disagree with most of what we say, but it's not my specialty, so I let it go by. And in the end . . . Marty Peretz has the last word."

On leave from the *New Republic* beginning in 1988, Kinsley spent six months in London as guest editor of the "American Survey" department of the *Economist*. Meanwhile, on American television he had over the years been a regular participant in William F. Buckley's weekly PBS political and social debate forum *Firing Line*, and more recently he had also been seen on *The McLaughlin Group* and other such television shows. Shortly after his return from London, in the summer of 1989, he was approached by the producers of CNN's half-hour program *Crossfire*, a furiously paced debate on a hot political issue televised weekday afternoons from CNN's Washington, D.C., studios. Accepting their invitation, he succeeded Tom Braden in the liberal chair on the show, opposite conservative Pat Buchanan. Since then, when Buchanan has taken leave, to seek the Republican presidential nomination and for other reasons, Kinsley has been faced on the right by others, most often by Robert Novak or John Sununu. In addition to the two hosts, the program includes two similarly polarized guests, chosen with regard for the issue being debated on the given day.

With his slim physique, neat grooming, clear-rimmed glasses, and general buttoned-down appearance, Michael Kinsley still projects, in his mid-forties, an air of what Jerry Adler in *Esquire* called "schoolboyish insouciance." Kinsley lives in Chevy Chase, Maryland, in a house that he bought in 1987 after living in a condominium in the District of Columbia for many years. According to Jerry Adler in *Esquire*, the house is appointed with "spare white furniture from Ikea." At about the same time Kinsley bought the furniture, he also bought an automobile. After interviewing him in his book-lined *New Republic* office in Washington, D.C., for *Rolling Stone* in 1988, Lynn Hirschberg wrote, "Kinsley, who is unmarried, seems to be fairly consumed with his work. During this conversation . . . Kinsley was charming and engaging, but rarely self-reflective. It's as if he simply doesn't concern himself with the more mundane aspects of life—like what socks to wear or who said what to whom in the elevator. . . . Kinsley is busy. There's work to be done."

Selected Biographical References: Esquire 113:100+ My '90 pors; New York 19:23+ Ag 4 '86 por; Rolling Stone p187+ My 19 '88 por; Vanity Fair 50:39+ S '87; Who's Who in America, 1995

Paul Cox/Warner Bros.

Knopfler, Mark

(NOF-ler)

Aug. 12, 1949- Rock musician; songwriter; composer. Address: c/o Warner Bros. Records Inc. 3300 Warner Blvd., Burbank, CA 91505

"Dire Straits albums sounded as though [Mark] Knopfler had examined life's great truths under a microscope and wanted to project what he found onto the very heavens above," Karen Schoemer declared in the *New York Times* (September 22, 1991). As songwriter, singer, and lead guitarist for Dire Straits, Knopfler, who was described in *Rolling Stone Album Guide* (1992) as an "acerbic tunesmith and virtuoso guitarist," has made his band one of the most distinctive and, in the mid-1980s, one of the most popular in rock music. Heavily influenced by authentic blues, early rock-'n'-

roll, and country, he incorporated elements of those genres into Dire Straits' unmistakably unique form of pop music. Bursting onto the scene in 1978 with its first single, the bluesy hit "Sultans of Swing," Dire Straits was a musical anachronism in the waning days of the punk and disco era, and the band managed to stay out of the limelight until the release of its fifth album, *Brothers in Arms*, in 1985. The most popular album ever issued in England to that date, it sold over fifteen million copies worldwide, and the opening line of the number-one hit single "Money for Nothing" ("I want my MTV") virtually came to define that era of pop music.

In addition to his work with Dire Straits, Knopfler has scored several films, including *Local Hero* and *Last Exit to Brooklyn*, worked regularly as producer or sideman for such artists as Eric Clapton and Bob Dylan, formed a band called the Notting Hillbillies to cover old country, blues, and traditional songs with a few rustic sounding originals thrown in, and teamed with the country guitar legend Chet Atkins on several Grammy-winning guitar duets. He concentrated on those alternate careers when he fled the spotlight after the tremendous success of *Brothers in Arms*, and Dire Straits did not reform until the 1991 offering, *On Every Street*. Praised as a "new kind of guitar hero—a tasteful, tuneful craftsman rather than a star-tripper," by Liam Lacey of the Toronto *Globe and Mail* (July 26, 1985), the unassuming Knopfler, who plays without a pick, is reluctant to accept the honor of "guitar hero." "It's nonsense. I don't want it, and I don't think it's fair—to anyone," he told Lacey. "I don't feel as if I know *anything* about guitar. I can't see how anyone could elect a picker and strummer to that position, anyway. As you learn more, you discover how much you don't know. You set yourself a goal—sometimes just a textural thing—and you work on that. It's a matter of exploring different channels that are interesting—to keep myself awake, to make sure the music doesn't become soporific. I don't mean I'm on any quest for perfection—I'm just playing."

Mark Knopfler was born on August 12, 1949 in Glasgow, Scotland. His father was an architect from Hungary, and his mother was a school teacher. He moved with his family, which struggled financially and was unable to afford a television or a car, to Newcastle, England during his boyhood. As a teenager in Newcastle, Knopfler, who was inspired by the music of the Everly Brothers, Lonnie Johnson, and B. B. King, among others, longed to play the guitar. "I remember standing outside music stores with my nose pressed up against the glass, just staring at those electric guitars," he recalled in an interview with Jonathan Cooper for *People* (September 2, 1985). "I used to smell Fender catalogs, I wanted one so bad." His father finally bought him a Fender guitar but innocently neglected to purchase an amplifier for the instrument, and Knopfler was unable to muster the courage to tell him that a vital element was missing. To overcome that shortcoming, he tried to amplify the guitar through the family radio, which he thus destroyed.

At the age of seventeen, Knopfler left home to attend journalism school. After obtaining his journalism degree, he landed a job as a reporter and music critic for the *Yorkshire Evening Post*. After two years he left the paper to enter Leeds University, from which he earned a degree in English, but instead of utilizing his academic credentials, Knopfler, aching for a career in music, went to London and joined a band. Struggling to survive, he lived in a room without heat and slept on an ambulance stretcher, barely able to make enough money to buy food. "It was really horrible," he told Liz Derringer of the New York *Daily News* (September 25, 1985). "I think of it now, hitchhiking around with guitars, getting on buses with two guitars to go to an audition for a band. Now it's like, 'How did I do all that?' You do it because you're so totally into it. You're really in love with it, and that's it. Everything else is just staying alive."

Finally reaching his limit, Knopfler took a part-time job teaching English at Loughton College, near London, but continued to play in pub bands. After teaching for three years, Knopfler's musical aspirations came to the fore in 1977, when he met John Illsley, a bass player who was working in a lumber yard. Returning to music full time, Knopfler formed Dire Straits (the name reflects the band members' financial situation) with Illsley, Pick Withers on drums, and Mark's younger brother David on rhythm guitar. As lead guitarist, singer, and songwriter, Mark Knopfler was clearly the band's driving force. They pooled together $320 to record a five-song demo and persuaded Charlie Gillett, a local disc jockey, to play the song "Sultans of Swing," which brought a strong response and gained the attention of several record executives.

After signing a record contract, Dire Straits landed a gig opening for the Talking Heads on a tour of the United Kingdom in January 1978, followed by three weeks in the studio to record their eponymous first album. The June release of *Dire Straits* was preceded, in May, by the group's first single, "Sultans of Swing." Amid the era of disco, punk, and new wave, *Dire Straits* stood out for its integration of blues, country, and old fashioned rock-'n'-roll into a distinctive style that sounded old and new at the same time. Both the single and album made the top ten in Great Britain and in the United States, and *Dire Straits* reached the top of the charts in France, Germany, the Netherlands, Australia, and New Zealand. Ken Emerson of the *New York Times* (March 5, 1979) described Knopfler's highly individual guitar playing in his review of the band's New York City debut: "Knopfler . . . plays nimble lead guitar with a light-fingered touch like no one else's. . . . The elegant restraint of Mr. Knopfler's guitar style is not without precedents, . . . but today, Mr. Knopfler's terse, tart runs and delicate shivers of vibrato are all his own."

"Dire Straits is a success, I think, because they have a warm, relaxed, understated, very melodic, and danceable sound that is a virtual catalog of the most popular and enduring styles of rock and roll,"

William Carlton wrote in the New York *Daily News* (March 2, 1979). "This is background or foreground music. They fill the gap for those repelled by punk, disillusioned with disco, and bored with the Stones." Despite their immediate success, the members of Dire Straits refused to go out of their way to gain attention, preferring to let the music make their point for them. As Knopfler told Cutler Durkee for *People* (March 26, 1979), "We don't want a lot of attention diverted to things like wearing pink plastic trousers, which we're not."

Dire Straits followed its acclaimed debut recording with *Communiqué* in 1979 and, after the departure of David Knopfler, *Making Movies* in 1980, both of which, according to most reviewers, fell slightly short of the high standards set by the first outing. With *Love Over Gold* (1982), most critics agreed, the band not only regained but surpassed the level of *Dire Straits*. Moving to a five-person lineup on *Love Over Gold*, Dire Straits was better able to sustain and explore extended musical ideas, such as on the fourteen-minute epic "Telegraph Road." Despite the departure of Pick Withers, who left the band in late 1982, leaving Mark Knopfler and David Illsley as the only remaining original members, Dire Straits was named best British group at the second annual BRIT awards in early 1983. Over the next two years, the only Dire Straits offerings were the EP *Dancing by the Pool* (1983) and the live album *Alchemy* (1984), but when the band members finally returned to the studio they produced what would become the best-selling album of all time in England.

Having gained a reputation for high production values with the early albums, Dire Straits was a natural for the nascent compact-disc format, which would make Knopfler's often soft and subtle guitar wizardry even more noticeable. Released at the dawn of the CD age, in 1985, *Brothers in Arms* debuted at the top of the British charts, held on to the top spot in the United States for nine weeks, and became the best-selling recording on the CD format up to that time, eventually selling over fifteen million copies. Among the many critical plaudits was Liam Lacey's comment in the Toronto *Globe and Mail* that, with *Brothers in Arms*, Knopfler "emerged more strongly than ever as [a] songwriter of steely clarity." "Perhaps the LP's most telling instrument is Knopfler's voice, a rock-hard diamond in the gruff cut by years of pub singing and a penchant for Dunhills," Jonathan Cooper wrote for *People* (September 2, 1985). "At thirty-six, the singer sounds like a cross between Bob Dylan and Leonard Cohen."

The single "Money for Nothing"—the lyrics of which Knopfler took verbatim from a conversation that he overheard between two employees in an appliance store, who were discussing the unfairness of musicians earning millions of dollars for the "easy" work of making videos for MTV—topped the American charts for three weeks. Although "Money for Nothing" can be read as a swipe at MTV, its opening words, "I want my MTV," sung by Sting, became an advertising slogan for the music video station. Responding to some criticism of the song, particularly over the use of the word "faggot," that was made under the misconception that the song represented his own point of view, Knopfler told Stephen Holden of the *New York Times* (March 28, 1990), "Anybody who didn't get that song is just an ignoramus."

In addition to winning another best-British-group honor at the 1986 BRIT awards, Knopfler and Dire Straits dominated the 1986 Grammy Awards, garnering a total of eight nominations. The band earned kudos for best rock performance by a duo or group with vocal, for "Money for Nothing," and best engineered recording (non-classical), for *Brothers in Arms*, while Knopfler and one of his heros, Chet Atkins, won honors for best country instrumental performance, for their guitar duet "Cosmic Square Dance." Dire Straits gained more accolades at the MTV awards, where "Money for Nothing" won best-video and best-group-video honors. Although *Brothers in Arms* was released in 1985, it was still winning awards for the band in 1987, when it took best British album at the 1987 BRIT awards. The video *Dire Straits Brothers in Arms* captured the prize for best music video, long form at the 1987 Grammy ceremony. In June 1988, 162 weeks after debuting on the charts, *Brothers in Arms* climbed back into the top twenty after Dire Straits (with Eric Clapton sitting in on guitar) headlined the "Nelson Mandela's Seventieth Birthday Party" concert at Wembley Stadium, near London, which was televised worldwide. In addition to Dire Straits' success, Knopfler's song "Private Dancer" became a hit single for Tina Turner in 1985.

After supporting *Brothers in Arms* with a grueling year-long world tour that included shows in twenty-five countries, Dire Straits did not release another album until 1991, but Knopfler was not idle. Since the band's inception, he had often lent his skills as a guitarist or producer to other artists. As a performer, he played with Bob Dylan on the album *Slow Train Coming* (1979) and with Steely Dan on *Gaucho* (1980), and as a producer, he worked on Dylan's *Infidels* (1983) and Aztec Camera's *Knife* (1984). He also began a thriving second career writing and performing soundtracks with his score for Bill Forsyth's film *Local Hero* (1983), which won a British Academy of Film and Television Award.

"Initially I had no idea how to score a film," Knopfler recalled in his interview with Liam Lacey of the *Globe and Mail*. "I did it all wrong. For *Local Hero*, I wrote the music first, then I discovered it doesn't work that way. Mostly, I stumble from crisis to crisis. Film is very good for you, though, because you don't have any words, which sounds ridiculously simple, but it's the most important thing. The music helps determine the meaning of the pictures. . . . So you learn that you have to be quite precise about the sounds you use—and not to overstate your case." The single "Going Home," from the soundtrack album, made the British charts and took top honors as best film theme or song at the 1984 Ivor Novello awards; the album climbed to number fourteen on the British charts. Knopfler also wrote and performed the music for the film *Cal* (1984) and teamed up again with Bill Forsyth by writing the score for *Comfort and Joy* (1984).

Making the most of his sabbatical from Dire Straits, Knopfler composed the film scores for *The Color of Money* (1986), *The Princess Bride* (1987), and *Last Exit to Brooklyn* (1990). Selections from Knopfler's four soundtrack albums (*Local Hero, Cal, The Princess Bride,* and *Last Exit to Brooklyn*) were released in 1993 on the collection *Screenplaying*. Among other projects, he produced Randy Newman's album *Land of Dreams*; played guitar on Joan Armatrading's *Shouting Stage*, Sting's *Nothing Like the Sun*, and the Judds' cover of the Dire Straits song "Water of Love"; took up the role of rhythm guitarist on an Eric Clapton tour; and recorded *Neck and Neck* (1990), an album of duets with Chet Atkins. Knopfler welcomed being off center stage for a change. "Singer-songwriters are, by and large, a pretty egocentric bunch of people," he admitted to Rob Tannenbaum for *Rolling Stone* (April 5, 1990). "It's good to get away from that and do the best you can for somebody else. There's something decent in it. Singing your little songs around the world and ordering people in the road crew about can be a pretty narrow way of life." Although out of the spotlight, he was still getting plenty of critical acclaim, for the collaboration with Atkins earned the two guitarists the 1991 Grammy Awards for best country vocal collaboration, for "Poor Boy Blues," and best country instrumental performance, for "So Soft, Your Goodbye."

In 1990 Knopfler joined his longtime friends Steve Phillips, who had played in a duo with Knopfler in the late 1960s and who makes some of Knopfler's acoustic guitars, Brendan Croker, and Guy Fletcher, who had played keyboards on the *Brothers in Arms* tour, to record an album of old country, blues, and traditional songs, with a few roots-flavored originals thrown in. Recorded over eighteen months in Knopfler's home studio in the Notting Hill section of London, the collection was called *Missing . . . Presumed Having a Good Time* by the Notting Hillbillies. In his interview with Stephen Holden, Knopfler discussed the reasoning behind this phase of his somewhat atypical career as a rock star: "I don't think about career stuff, and I'm not a long-term planner. I have no strategy. I just get seduced by things as they come up. The Notting Hillbillies became a band by accident. . . . Initially I was just going to produce an album for Steve and Brendan, but because I'm obnoxious and pushy, I started to come up with ideas for songs and insisted on playing the guitar."

Although, in 1988, Knopfler had announced the end of Dire Straits, he and Illsley returned to the studio with a new lineup to record *On Every Street* (1991). Knopfler explained the long hiatus from Dire Straits after *Brothers in Arms* to Rob Tannenbaum: "A lot of press reports were saying we were the biggest band in the world. There's not an accent then on the music, there's an accent on popularity." Heavily influenced by the considerable time Knopfler had spent in Nashville, Tennessee over the preceding few years, *On Every Street*, which featured the renowned Nashville session musician Paul Franklin playing pedal steel guitar on most songs, has more of a country flavor than any previous Dire Straits effort. *On Every Street* drew mixed reviews and was a commercial disappointment following the huge success of *Brothers in Arms*. Complaining that the lyrics "retread a surprising amount from past albums," Karen Schoemer of the *New York Times* called it "Dire Straits' least ambitious album." "Knopfler's past achievements lay in his ability to stretch the rock idiom, expand it—to use rock's limitations as his starting point," Schoemer wrote. "Here he seems content to work within boundaries." Conversely, the reviewer for *Rolling Stone Album Guide* found it to be top-notch Dire Straits: "Although the album has its lighter moments, such as the dead-Presley 'Calling Elvis' or the consumerist sarcasm of 'Heavy Fuel,' the bulk of its songs find Dire Straits doing what they do best, stretching dry, reflective words and tunes over moody, effortlessly maintained grooves." After a tour supporting the album, Knopfler again took a respite from Dire Straits to devote time to the other aspects of his career.

"He's so unpretentious musically and personally," Chet Atkins told Stephen Williams of *New York Newsday* (August 23, 1987), "but he's so good." Indeed, Mark Knopfler, who enjoys watching sports in his spare time, prefers quiet nights at home to the stereotypical pursuits of rock musicians. In keeping with his growing fascination with country music, he took up the pedal steel guitar in the early 1990s. He maintains two residences, one in the Notting Hill section of London and one in Greenwich Village in New York City, and lives with his second wife, Lourdes Salamone, and their children. His first marriage ended in divorce during his difficult pub-band days. In an interview with Andy Widder-Ellis for *Guitar Player* (June 1992), Knopfler offered advice on making good music: "Be concerned with the soul quotient of your music, the sheer joy of being in the heart of something. And don't be concerned about the marketplace. The music business is something that's *completely* and utterly separate from music. Don't think about singles. Just do what the hell you really want to do. Learn to hear music, so whatever is going on, you find a way to help it. Finding parts is a *musical* musician's speciality: parts are what make great records—not producers. It's not a question of what you know. It all comes down to this: What are you prepared to give of yourself?"

Selected Biographical References: Guitar Player 26:30+ Jn '92 pors; N Y Newsday II p9 D 29 '85 por, II 3+ Ag 23 '87 por; People 11:79+ Mr 26 '79 pors, 23:55+ S 2 '85 pors; Rolling Stone p26 Ap 5 '90 por; Toronto Globe and Mail p12+ Jl 26 '85 por; Washington Post N 12 F 21 '92 por

The Brokaw Co.

Kotto, Yaphet

(KOH-toh, yah-FET)

Nov. 15, 1944(?)–Actor. Address: c/o Metropolitan Talent Agency, 4526 Wilshire Blvd., Los Angeles, CA 90010

With his continuing role as the police lieutenant Al Giardello on the television drama *Homicide: Life on the Street*, Yaphet Kotto has added another subtle characterization to his long list of acting credits. The physically imposing actor first made a name for himself on Broadway in the late 1960s with his portrayal of the tormented boxing champion Jack Jefferson in the long-running play *The Great White Hope*, and he has since been seen in numerous feature films, television series, and made-for-TV movies. In many of his more prominent roles, whether in such serious films as *Brubaker*, or in lighter fare, such as *Midnight Run*, Kotto has projected an image of controlled anger. The filmmaker Barry Levinson, who is the executive producer of *Homicide*, has said of Kotto: "Yaphet has great credibility, a simple strength, a quiet passion."

Yaphet Fredrick Kotto was born on November 15, 1944 in Harlem, in the New York City borough of Manhattan, the son of Gladys Maria Kotto, a Panamanian nurse, and Yaphet Kotto (one source gives his name as Abraham Kotto), a construction worker and former merchant marine from what was then the Cameroons, in western Africa. (Some sources give 1937 as the actor's year of birth.) Kotto has at least one sibling, a sister, Deborra. While he was growing up, Kotto was exposed to an eclectic mix of cultures. In an interview with Desson Howe of the *Washington Post* (July 21, 1985), he revealed that his father's friends were from "all over Africa," that his father, who descended from a long line of Jews, "spoke about nine or ten languages, [as did] all of his friends," and that during his own formative years there were "thousands of languages going on and all different colors of people" around. Kotto was initially reared as a Jew and was bar mitzvahed, but following his parents' divorce (after which he was brought up by his maternal grandparents), he was baptized a Catholic. He has recalled being, in his word, "confused" regarding religion. "For years, I had a Torah in one hand and the Bible in the other," he told Desson Howe. He said in another interview that it "definitely wasn't too cool being black and Jewish," for he was sometimes beaten in Harlem for wearing his yarmulke, and, on some occasions when he left Harlem, he was attacked by bigoted whites.

During his adolescent years Kotto belonged to street gangs. As he explained to Peter Bailey for a *New York Times* (October 26, 1969) profile, his family "had to get [him] out of Harlem to save [his] life," and they eventually moved to the Bronx. At the age of sixteen, he dropped out of school. Kotto has admitted to telling his family that he was out looking for a job when he was actually spending his days in movie houses. "One day . . . I walked into this theatre showing *On the Waterfront*, and I saw Marlon Brando for the first time," he recalled to Barry Koltnow for the *Chicago Tribune* (January 23, 1994). "I couldn't speak. It was like somebody had punched me in the stomach. It was like someone had crashed cymbals in both ears. I was blasted out of the theatre. I knew from that moment that I wanted to be an actor."

Kotto found odd jobs, as a dishwasher, a dock worker, a shoeshine boy, and even a numbers runner, to make ends meet while he went about training himself for an acting career. Part of that training involved improving his diction. "When I came out of Harlem, I couldn't speak," he confessed to a reporter for *New York Newsday* (September 3, 1969). "I had a street voice, with a high nasal pitch, and I punctuated everything with 'Hey, man.'" To correct the problem, he recorded the voice of the radio and television personality John Cameron Swayze and studied his way of speaking. He also consulted books on dance, in order to learn how "to walk and move," and took lessons from his aunt, who ran a dance studio. The other impediment to his development as an actor was his growing realization that a black person would have a difficult time making it onto the stage or screen. "Then I went to see *The Defiant Ones*," Kotto explained to Barry Koltnow, "and standing right there on the screen was this tall black man [Sidney Poitier], and I said to myself, 'I could be like him.'"

The young actor was eventually able to receive formal instruction at the newly founded American Conservatory Theatre, which was then based in Pittsburgh. After cutting his teeth in summer stock in Massachusetts, appearing, for example, as the title character in *Othello* when he was just nineteen, Kotto landed roles in several Off-Broadway plays, including Athol Fugard's *The Blood Knot* and Reginald Rose's *Black Monday in White America*. When he was about twenty, he decided to try his luck on the West Coast. There, he won parts in regional theatre productions and also broke into television, with guest spots on numerous dramatic series, among them such popular shows as *Bonanza, Daniel Boone, The Big Valley*, and *Gunsmoke*. He made his film debut as a supporting player in Michael Roemer's *Nothing But a Man* (1964), a study of racial attitudes in a town in Alabama. (Although it took two awards at the Venice Film Festival, Roemer's movie was nonetheless rejected by the major film distributors and faded into obscurity. Nearly thirty years after its completion, it emerged on the art-house circuit and drew the attention of Desson Howe, who noted the performance by the "engagingly youthful" Kotto.) Later in the decade Kotto appeared in supporting parts in the films *Five Card Stud* (1968) and *The Thomas Crown Affair* (1968).

Kotto's first assignment on Broadway was in the musical comedy *The Zulu and the Zayda*, which premiered at the Cort Theatre on November 10, 1965. The play told the story of a family of Jews living in South Africa who hire a young Zulu, played by Louis Gossett Jr., to look after their *zayda*, or grandfather. Kotto's big break, however, came in 1969, when he succeeded James Earl Jones as the lead in Howard Sackler's phenomenally successful Broadway play *The Great White Hope*, based on the life of Jack Johnson, the first black heavyweight boxing champion. Kotto appeared to be undaunted by the prospect of taking over the role that had made Jones a star. His self-assurance seems to have been warranted, for his portrayal of the boxer, who was ultimately a victim of the prejudiced attitudes of his day, drew overwhelmingly positive notices. "Mr. Kotto gives a more physical, a more angry performance than did Mr. Jones . . ." Clive Barnes observed in the *New York Times* (September 27, 1969). "With Kotto the prizefighter is more of a man and less of a hero." Admitting that he had never heard of Kotto before the actor was cast in *The Great White Hope*, Barnes predicted, "Mr. Kotto will never be unheard of again."

In 1970 Kotto was among the cast of William Wyler's film *The Liberation of L. B. Jones*, about a black Tennessee undertaker (Roscoe Lee Browne) who is killed after threatening to expose his wife's affair with a white, racist policeman (Anthony Zerbe). The movie was widely panned for its overwrought and outdated treatment of race relations; Kotto, however, in the role of the young man who avenges the undertaker's murder, came in for considerable praise, with a reviewer for *Cue* (March 28, 1970) writing, "Yaphet Kotto . . . quickly establishes himself as a forceful new film actor. He is strong in face, voice, and the ability to convey the intensity and depth of frustration." In his interview with Peter Bailey, Kotto reflected on his characters in *The Great White Hope* and *L. B. Jones*, calling them "real" men as opposed to the "overgrown boys" often portrayed by black film and stage actors. His character in *L. B. Jones*, for example, "does the things that a man has to do to survive, including killing when necessary," Kotto explained. "He is a beautiful cat." He added, "I am not a militant myself, so the best way I can express my feelings is to play these parts."

Kotto's other film credits from the early 1970s include *Man and Boy, Across 110th Street*, and *Bone*, and he had a part in the 1970 made-for-television movie *Night Chase*, starring David Janssen. *The Limit* (1972), in which Kotto starred, also marked his debut as a film director, producer, and scenarist. His role was that of a Los Angeles policeman who takes on a motorcycle gang. In a representative review of the movie, William Wolf of *Cue* (November 25, 1972) declared, "A certain honesty keeps poking through what is basically a jumbled, heavy-handed film. It is still a loser, but one leaves with admiration for actor Yaphet Kotto and anticipation that maybe, in another try at film directing, he'll come up with something more worthwhile." Less-qualified praise came Kotto's way the following year, for his work in *Live and Let Die*, the eighth in the series of films featuring the fictional master spy James Bond. Playing the villain, a Harlem drug smuggler, Kotto gave "high-class support" to the film's star, Roger Moore, in the opinion of Judith Crist of *New York* (July 9, 1973). Two decades after that movie's release, Barry Koltnow looked back on Kotto's performance as a breakthrough of sorts: "After he appeared in *Live and Let Die* . . . it no longer seemed unusual to have a black villain worthy of James Bond."

While Kotto's film career was taking off, his personal life was in turmoil. His marriage to Rita Dittman, a Danish woman he had wed when he was about twenty-one, was failing, and his career success was having an adverse effect on his friendships. He has mentioned in particular "antagonism from fellow black actors." "I didn't go around calling myself a star, but suddenly all my buddies were gone," he told Lois Armstrong, who interviewed him for *People* (July 21, 1980). "To have any friends I had to throw a party." Kotto found relief from his unhappiness—as well as an end to any lingering confusion about religion—when he became a member of the Self-Realization Fellowship, a religious sect whose tenets are drawn from the Bhagavad-Gita as well as from the New Testament. The actor Dennis Weaver, another convert to the fellowship, "helped [him] tremendously," Kotto has recalled. "Here was an actor with the same kind of experience I'd had." In observance of the sect's guidelines, which also forbid the consumption of meat and alcohol, Kotto began to meditate three times daily. He also left behind the glitz and glamour of California to pursue a simpler domestic life in Washington State.

Meanwhile, Kotto's acting career was proceeding apace. In the mid-1970s he turned up in a half-dozen feature films, including *Truck Turner, Report to the Commissioner, Sharks' Treasure*, and *Drum*, and he took on the part of the Ugandan dictator Idi Amin in the acclaimed made-for-television movie *Raid on Entebbe* (1976), for which he earned an Emmy nomination for best actor. Paul Schrader's *Blue Collar*, one of the films that Kotto has cited as being especially important to his professional development, was released in 1978. Costarring with Richard Pryor and Harvey Keitel, he played an ex-convict, one of a trio of friends working on an automobile assembly line in Detroit. Struggling to survive financially, and exploited by their labor union as well as by their employers, the three decide to rob the safe in the union office, with disastrous consequences.

Critics hailed the performances of *Blue Collar*'s three leading actors. In the *Saturday Review* (April 15, 1978), Arthur Schlesinger Jr. wrote that Kotto "play[ed] the ex-con with great force and charm," and Robert Martin, assessing the film for the Toronto *Globe and Mail* (April 10, 1978), declared that of the three performers, "Kotto [came] across best despite the fact that his motives [were] left unexplored." At least one reviewer noted the similarities between *Blue Collar*—one of Kotto's favorites among the films in which he has been featured—and *On the Waterfront*, which impelled Kotto's decision to become an actor and which, like *Blue Collar*, examines union corruption.

The following year found Kotto in a supporting role as an astronaut in the space-adventure film *Alien*, one of the biggest hits of 1979. In Stuart Rosenberg's *Brubaker* (1980), starring Robert Redford as a prison warden who tries to reform the corrupt system at an Ohio penitentiary, Kotto played Dickie Coombes, an armed trusty in the prison, who eventually comes to admire the new warden. During a conversation with Richard Christiansen for the *Chicago Tribune* (August 24, 1980), Kotto discussed the techniques he used to demonstrate his character's personality, including his decision to dress in a tattered poncho that hid most of his body: "The purpose of that was to show that this guy wants to keep every part of himself concealed, so that no one can guess what's inside him." His approach proved to be effective, for while some critics dismissed *Brubaker* as sanctimonious, many complimented Kotto's characterization of the tough trusty. More than one reviewer described his portrayal as "powerful," and the notoriously hard-to-please Pauline Kael of the *New Yorker* (July 7, 1980), in her evaluation of the movie, called Kotto a "solid, great actor."

After his appearance in *Brubaker*, Hollywood producers considered Kotto to be a "bankable" actor, as Diane Duston of *New York Newsday*, among others, pointed out. Indeed, in the early and mid-1980s, he was a nearly ubiquitous figure in film and television. On the small screen he lent his talents to such movies as *Rage*, *Women of San Quentin*, *Playing with Fire*, and *Badge of the Assassin*, and he delivered an effective performance on the dramatic series *Hill Street Blues* as a community activist whose frustration with "the system" leads him afoul of the law. Among Kotto's feature-film credits from that period are *Fighting Back* (1982), *The Star Chamber* (1983), *Warning Sign* (1985), and *Eye of the Tiger* (1986). Later in the decade he showed up in, among other movies, Martin Brest's action-comedy *Midnight Run* (1988). That film starred Robert De Niro as a bounty hunter who takes a fugitive accountant (Charles Grodin) from New York to Los Angeles, half a step ahead of pursuers on both sides of the law. Kotto turned in a hilarious portrayal of an unamused FBI agent thwarted at every turn by De Niro's character.

The actor's projects in the early 1990s included the films *Tripwire*, *We're Back*, and *Freddy's Dead: The Final Nightmare*, an installment of the Nightmare on Elm Street series of horror movies. Among his television credits for the same period were the films *After the Shock*, about the hours immediately following the 1989 San Francisco earthquake; *Chrome Soldiers*, whose main character (Gary Busey), an air force colonel, enlists the aid of friends to avenge his brother's death; and *The American Clock*, a multicharacter portrait of the Depression, adapted by Frank Galati from Arthur Miller's 1980 play.

January 1993 saw the debut of *Homicide: Life on the Street*, an NBC television crime drama based on David Simon's book about Baltimore police officers and produced by the esteemed feature-film director Barry Levinson. *Homicide* broke stylistic ground with its use of overlapping—and sometimes improvised—dialogue and its complete reliance on hand-held cameras. It also features a collection of quirky characters—detectives under the supervision of the no-nonsense Lieutenant Al Giardello, played by Kotto. Like the actor who portrays him, Giardello is a product of different cultures: he is half black and half Italian. The critically acclaimed series, after starting out with a solid viewership, fell victim to scheduling difficulties and was temporarily pulled from the air after losing its ratings battle with the enormously popular ABC sitcom *Home Improvement*. Since it was revived during the 1993–94 television season, however, the show has held its own, both critically and commercially.

Although Kotto was offered two movie projects at about the same time that the opportunity to join the cast of *Homicide* arose, he accepted the television role without hesitation. As he explained to Barry Koltnow, "The whole idea of acting is to work with the best people, so why not go back to television to work with the director [Levinson] who made *Rain Man*?" He apparently has not regretted his decision. "The script [for the first episode] was so good and the camera work so different than what I was used to that I forgot my lines," he confessed to Koltnow. "I was really embarrassed. That had never happened to me before. But the other actors came over to me and told me the same thing had happened to them. Then Barry gave me a few words of advice, and I was back in acting school again, and this man was giving me acting lessons. It proves you're never too old to learn."

"When I was a kid," Kotto told Desson Howe in 1985, "I could see these films of black people . . . scratching their head and taking [abuse], and I swore when I was nineteen I would never do that on the screen. I would always stand up tall and straight. I was not going to leave an image of people to feel ashamed of. . . . I've upheld that in every single film I've done." That resolution seems to have sprung from a simple sense of dignity rather than from any bitterness connected with race, for during his childhood he never heard "stories about slavery and the horrors that black Americans went through." "None of my family came from the South, none of them were slaves," he explained to Fred Brack for *Dial* (February 1982). "Because of that, I think I was endowed with a certain lack of hostility, so my consciousness does not have the rage that many of my brothers have." He mentioned another consequence of his lineage: "I guess I'm one of the few black people born in this country who have their own name. I have not been anglicized with a surname that comes from an Anglo-Saxon background. . . . I can't tell you the number of letters I get from black kids who think I am a cultural hero for that. They say, man . . . you're the real thing! Your father is actually from Africa, and you were born in the United States! You're a legitimate Afro-American!"

Yaphet Kotto stands six feet, three inches tall and weighs well over two hundred pounds. Richard Christiansen of the *Chicago Tribune* described him as having "hooded eyes in a large head atop a bull neck." The actor currently divides his time between homes in Los Angeles and a suburb of Toronto. From his marriage to Rita Dittman, he has three children: Natasha, who is a lawyer, Frederick, a stockbroker, and Robert, a medical student. He also has three children—Sarada, Mirabai, and Salina—from his marriage to Antoinette Pettyjohn, whom he met at a Self-Realization Fellowship workshop in the mid-1970s and from whom he is now separated. As of 1994 Kotto was engaged to be married for the third time.

Selected Biographical References: Chicago Tribune XIII p16 Ja 23 '94 por; Dial 3:44+ F '82 por; N Y Newsday II p30 Jl 1 '80 por; N Y Times II p3 O 26 '69 por; People 14:106+ Jl 21 '80 pors, p67+ Ja 31 '94 pors; Washington Post G p3 Jl 21 '85 por; Who's Who Among Black Americans, 1994–95

Kruger, Barbara

(KROO-ger)

Jan. 26, 1945– Artist; writer; media critic. Address: c/o Mary Boone Gallery, 417 W. Broadway, New York, NY 10012

Timothy Greenfield Sanders

Barbara Kruger's red-framed, black-and-white photomontages constitute, in the artist's description, "a series of attempts to ruin certain representations and to welcome the female spectator into the audience of men," as she told Carol Squiers in an interview for *ARTnews* (February 1987). Typically appropriated from magazines, how-to manuals, or advertisements of the 1920s through the 1960s, the photographs she selects are closely cropped, sometimes revealing only a hand or a face, and collaged with concise textual phrases that subvert the messages conveyed by the images, which are often seductive and/or menacing. Deliberately ambiguous, her slogans usually employ personal pronouns whose meaning changes according to the identity (and, often, gender) of the viewer. Among her better-known works are those that proclaim "We don't need another hero," "Your manias become science," "I can't look at you and breathe at the same time," "Your life is a perpetual insomnia," "Buy me I'll change your life," and "When I hear the word culture I take out my checkbook."

"I'm interested in coupling the ingratiation of wishful thinking with the criticality of knowing better," Kruger declared in an interview with Jeanne Siegel for *Arts* (Summer 1987). Frequently censorious of the inequities produced by sexual stereotypes; of militarism, prejudice, and uncritical thinking; and of the power of advertising to channel desire into consumption, Kruger's work has changed little over the past fifteen years, but it has extended its reach well beyond galleries and museums. Her images have appeared on billboards, bus shelters, shopping bags, T-shirts, refrigerator magnets, postcards, book and magazine covers, and posters announcing political marches and artists' conferences. She has recently mounted installations that cover the floor, ceiling, and walls of a gallery space and are accompanied by a soundtrack. A former photo editor and graphic designer for women's magazines, Kruger has also taught art at the university level, curated shows, written poetry, and worked as a film and television critic.

Barbara Kruger was born on January 26, 1945 in Newark, New Jersey. An only child, she grew up in that city's South Ward. Her father was a chemical technician for Shell Oil; her mother, a legal secretary. After graduating from Weequahic High School in 1964, Kruger enrolled at Syracuse University, in upstate New York, whose students hailed mainly from a socioeconomic background that seemed alien to her. "I felt like a Martian," she told Carol Squiers. "I was the only woman on my dorm floor who hadn't had facial surgery and who knew words other than Pappagallo and Evan Picone." Following the death of her father, a year after her arrival at Syracuse, Kruger transferred to Parsons School of Design, in New York City, where she studied under the photographer Diane Arbus, whom she has referred to as her first female role model, and the graphic designer Marvin Israel, who had recently made his mark as an art director of *Harper's Bazaar.* "He was power hungry and manipulative," Kruger told Squiers. "But he was the first person who ever told me that I was special and that I could do *anything.*"

Israel advised Kruger to prepare a graphic arts portfolio. Copying the style of *Nova,* a trendy British magazine, she made up some page designs and presented them to the head of the art department at Condé Nast Publications, who hired her in 1967 to illustrate women's shoes and accessories for *Seventeen* and to make up ads for the back pages of *Mademoiselle.* Within a year she was promoted, at the age of twenty-two, to chief designer of *Mademoiselle,* a position she held for the following four years. For the ensuing decade Kruger supported her artistic production by freelancing for Condé Nast as a photo editor, by teaching, and by designing book jackets, mostly for political texts.

Making the transition to less-commercial artistic pursuits was not easy for Kruger, who has said that she felt intimidated by the art world. In the 1960s she had begun frequenting the nightspot Max's Kansas City, where, as she told Squiers, "charming grotesqueries destroyed themselves for the benefit of famous silver-haired voyeurs, and a bunch of horrible painters and minimalists would hold court, harassing the waitresses and reading Marx out loud. It was just a *zoo* of retching and male hysteria." Max's was so hostile to women that unaccompanied females were often prohibited from entering "on the grounds that they might be 'procuring,'" as Squiers reported. Perhaps because of the unwelcoming atmosphere, Kruger's first artworks, produced in 1969, were what she has called "woman's work"—woven-and-stitched-together fiber hangings inspired by a show of the work of Magdalena Abakanowicz that she had seen at the Museum of Modern Art in New York City. "I was allowed that," Kruger noted in her interview with Squiers. "And I didn't have to deal with all those horrible men who were in the art world." In her conversation with Jeanne Siegel, however, Kruger emphasized that she did not "subscribe to the uncritical celebration of this work, which might suggest that women have a genetic proclivity toward the decorative arts."

Kruger proceeded to turn out a series of round wall pieces that were amalgams of brightly colored cloth, sequins, and feathers—"very decorative, very gorgeous, very sexualized," in the artist's description. In the early 1970s her circular format was, in Squiers's words, "exploded outward, broken by curvilinear projections that gushed out like waves or flames." After viewing some such pieces at Kruger's studio/loft in lower Manhattan, Marcia Tucker, then a curator at the Whitney Museum of American Art, in New York City, decided to include some samples of Kruger's work in the prestigious Whitney Biennial in 1973. Solo exhibitions followed in 1974, at Artist's Space, and in 1975, at the Fischbach Gallery, both in New York City.

After producing abstract paintings—thick black and white stripes to which she would add a single third color—for a year in the mid-1970s, Kruger came to view her work as a "literal baroque potpourri of decorative exercises . . . ," as she told Kate Linker in an interview for *FlashArt* (March 1985). "I felt I was giving my mind Demerol. I had started writing at the time, and . . . I couldn't help but compare the exhilaration, liveliness, and generativeness of the writing activity with this manual labor, this busywork." In 1974 Kruger began giving readings of her poetry, which was influenced, she told Squiers, by the "transgressive female presence" of the poet and rock singer Patti Smith. In the mid-1970s she began associating with a group of young artists who had recently arrived in New York City from the California Institute of the Arts in Valencia, among them David Salle, Ross Bleckner, Eric Fischl, Ericka Beckman, and Barbara Bloom. Kruger had finally found "a generation of men who were not *cowboys* and among whom women could be *artists,*" as she told Squiers. In contrast, she discovered that women took a back seat at the gatherings of Artists Meeting for Cultural Change, a left-leaning organization whose meetings she attended in the summer of 1976. Kruger was nonetheless intrigued by the group's unofficial syllabus, which included works on cultural theory by Walter Benjamin, Roland Barthes, Max Horkheimer, and Theodor W. Adorno.

Kruger stopped painting in 1976, and for the next few years she spent most of her time reading, watching movies, and teaching, beginning with a stint as a visiting artist at the University of California at Berkeley in the fall semester of 1976 and including sojourns at the California Institute of the Arts and the Art Institute of Chicago. She resumed her art making in 1977, with the help of a Creative Artists Service Program grant. It was then that she turned to photography, which had recently enjoyed greater acceptance as an art form, partly as a result of the progressive dissolution of the boundaries between fine art and commercial art. In an exercise that recalled an assignment Arbus had given her, Kruger took photographs of residential buildings, then paired her images with fictional descriptions of the "furnishings" and "inhabitants" of the buildings. A typical example of such work, which was collected in Kruger's self-published book *Picture/Readings* (1979), is a photograph of the upper story of a house and, on the facing page, its accompanying text, which reads, in part, "Gloria is still in bed. . . . She is aware of Harold's stillness, somewhere in the next room."

Kruger's next two series of text-and-photography works, shown in 1979 at the Franklin Furnace Archive in New York City, were about "daily life," as the artist explained to Squiers: "Rather than abstracting or repressing daily life into busywork, I became a reporter. Because I felt that daily life and the social relations around it are what is repressed in art." Those series were followed by the four-paneled "Hospital Series," in which she used appropriated images for the first time. The first panel contained one of her own photographs; the second, such nonnarrative texts as "The honing of the functional gesture" and "The blaming of the victim"; the third, a previously published photo of two or more people interacting; and the fourth, such condensed messages as "Please," "No," or "Not that."

In 1979 Kruger began to superimpose the words on the pictures. One piece shows an image of a woman surrounded by fashion magazines. To that appropriated photograph, she added lines, colorful geometric shapes, and, slanting across the top of the frame, the word "deluded." For *Untitled (Dual)* (1979), Kruger used a photograph of a woman sitting on the floor, her face buried in her arms, which rest on the seat of a chair; its superimposed text recalled the color mark-ups of art direction: "Black=opaque assumptions," "Pink=emotive transparency." Although this work, like her later creations, is reminiscent of the early-twentieth-century collage and poster art of John Heartfield, among others, Kruger has rejected such categorization, pointing out that it applied only to the formal elements of her work and not to its content. "When people start talking about my similarities with Heartfield," she said in an interview with Suzanne Moore for the *Guardian* (January 22, 1994), "I say, excuse me, but I didn't know that he did any work on gender. The similarity is just that we both worked on magazines."

Although the feminist implications of a work like *Untitled (Deluded)* may be evident, Kruger has said that the art she produced beginning in 1980 was even more explicitly direct and aggressive. Exhibited along with the work of Jenny Holzer, Mike Glier, and Keith Haring at the Annina Nosei Gallery in New York City, in a 1981 group show called "Public Address," Kruger's pieces were prime examples of what has since come to be understood as her mature work: red frames surrounding black-and-white photographs, upon which blocks of bold-faced type have been laid. In 1980 she accompanied a photo of a stone sculpture of a woman's head, in profile, with the words, "Your gaze hits the side of my face." A 1981 photograph of a man's face obscured by the shadow cast by his hat, his finger raised to his lips, is captioned, "Your comfort is my silence." *Untitled (We have received orders not to move)* (1982) shows a profile of a seated woman, bent slightly forward, with what appear to be needles or pushpins stuck in the outline of her spine and the backs of her legs. "The image," according to Kate Linker, writing in *Love for Sale: The Words and Pictures of Barbara Kruger* (1993), "is at once an invocation of social stasis and a feminist retort to the controlling structures of patriarchy, which perform the function . . . of getting woman into place." A selection of Kruger's images from this period was published in 1982 as *No Progress in Pleasure*.

When Kruger is asked to explicate her creations, she invariably declines. "When I show my work, people ask questions," she told Squiers. "When ever they ask what a work means, I say that the construction of meaning shifts. And it shifts according to each spectator." Although each image may be open to a multiplicity of meanings, each viewer is encouraged to take a stance, a manipulative effect achieved largely through Kruger's use of personal pronouns. Referring to a 1985 poster of a boxer whose nose is being smashed by an opponent, with accompanying text that reads, "We get exploded because they've got money and God in their pockets," Kruger told Squiers, "We're *all* exploded. The 'they' could be women, too." She went on to say that her interest is not to indict any viewer but to expose a power structure. "With the question of You I say that there is no You; that it shifts according to the viewer; that I'm interested in making an active spectator who can decline that You or accept it or say, 'It's not me, but I know who it is.'"

If the interpretation of a given work depends upon the viewer, some critics have wondered, how much responsibility does the artist bear when her message is lost altogether, its irony swallowed up by the very forces that are being criticized? For instance, Kruger has been disparaged for transforming her art into a commodity while purportedly attacking the power of the marketplace. This issue was brought to the fore when a 1987 work of a hand holding a white-on-red, credit-card-shaped sign emblazoned with the words "I shop therefore I am" was printed on canvas shopping bags, whose owners may or may not have perceived the self-deprecation inherent in the message, which may be read as a straight admission of one's obsession or as an indictment of a society that validates individual identity through a person's acquisitiveness, among other possible interpretations. Another example is the acquisition by the Museum of Modern Art of her montage of the Sistine Chapel ceiling, cropped to reveal only the hands of God and Adam, and overlaid with the words "You invest in the divinity of the masterpiece."

Kruger spoke to Anders Stephanson for *FlashArt* (October 1987) about her need "to comment on the financial proclivities which enveloped her: to be in and about consumption at the same time." "These were objects," she told Squiers. "I wasn't going to stick them on the walls with pushpins. I wanted them to enter the marketplace because I began to understand that outside the market there is nothing—not a piece of lint, not a cardigan, a coffee table, a human being. That's what the frames were about: how to commodify them. It was the most effective packaging device: signed, sealed, and delivered."

Knowing that pedestrians in New York City's Times Square were surrounded by signs and ads and X-rated marquees all clamoring for their attention, Kruger immediately set out to disarm them in her text-only piece for the area's Spectacolor light board in December 1983. "I'm not trying to sell you anything," it began, after which it exhorted spectators to think about the TV news. The work went on to explain that "wars happen" because world leaders are "worried about the size of their weapons; worried about their manhood" and concluded, "So I guess the TV news is really the hottest sex show going." The smaller lettering on the final screen—which read: "And a lot cheaper than paying out five bucks a shot at the movie around the corner"—functioned as a sly parenthetical device. "The city took it off after two weeks," Kruger told Jeff Giles for *Mother Jones* (May 1989). "They said it had no Christmas spirit."

By 1986 Kruger was sometimes using color photographs, color silk-screen prints, photolithography, and lenticular pictures—ribbed plastic screens whose images change when the viewer shifts position. One of her more sumptuous works in color is a tray of glazed pastel petits fours, framed in pink, with fuchsia script lettering demanding, "Give me all you've got." Another is a close-up of flowers that says, "Jam life into death." One lenticular work shows, from one angle, a circular saw blade overlaid with the words "You make the world safe for democracy"; from another perspective, the viewer reads, in white lettering against a solid lavender background, "I've seen this movie before."

The visual power of moving images, particularly television, is a recurring theme in Kruger's conversation and in her written work. In 1984 she edited *TV Guides*, a collection of essays on broadcast media. *Artforum* magazine's film critic since 1982 and its television critic since 1987, she published a collection of her essays that had previously appeared in that and other magazines under the title *Remote Control: Power, Cultures, and the World of Appearances* (1993). In 1988 Kruger participated in the Whitney's Artists & Writers project, a collaborative venture that had her designing a limited edition of a forty-page chapbook, with a story by the horror novelist Stephen King, entitled *My Pretty Pony*.

Until the mid-1980s Kruger's work had been seen mainly in traveling group and solo shows throughout the United States and Europe, including the prestigious Venice Biennale, in Italy, and the Documenta VII, in what was then West Germany. Since that time Kruger has been involved in a multitude of public projects, including billboards that proclaim, "Surveillance is your busywork," bus-stop posters, and visual editorials for the *New York Times*. In 1989 she created a widely distributed poster for a pro-choice rally that presented a 1950s-era woman's face, split down the middle between its photographic negative and positive exposures. Superimposed on the image were the words "Your body is a battleground." A music video for Vanessa Williams and an AIDS poster (her second) followed in 1992, then billboard, radio, and video work to combat domestic violence. "I'm always suspicious when people say being marginal is liberating," she told Jeff Giles. "Well, I say, 'Try it, buddy.'"

In 1992 Kruger entered the mainstream with a series of magazine covers. In January *Ms.* ran a Kruger cover that included the words "Women+Rage=Power." This was succeeded in May by an *Esquire* cover featuring a photo of the controversial radio talk-show host Howard Stern, overlaid by the words "I love myself and you hate me for it." The artist wrote an accompanying essay in which she championed Stern for his sense of humor and for his "unrelenting penchant for 'truth' telling, his dumbly extemporaneous brand of performance art." In June she illustrated a *Newsweek* cover story on family values with the phrase "Whose values?" In the same month the *New Republic* ran a cover parody of Kruger's work, confident that its readers would be familiar with her art, for a story on "the idiot culture." When Charles Hagen of the *New York Times* (June 14, 1992) asked Kruger if she minded such plundering of her signature style, she replied, "What are you going to do? I don't have a copyright on Futura Bold Italic." An editorial feature by Kruger was included in the February 1994 issue of *Harper's Bazaar*, a fashion magazine.

The ubiquity of Kruger's work led Peter Schjeldahl to admit in the *Village Voice* (March 29, 1994) that while he himself has resisted being manipulated by her images, she "is an artist of tremendous achievement and really vast influence, . . . among the most consequential graphic inventors since El Lissitzky, the stylistic codifier of Russian Constructivism." For the past few years, Kruger, who has been a recipient of a National Endowment for the Arts grant, has been mounting installations that combine text and imagery to affront, confront, accuse, and amuse the viewer. Reviewing a 1991 project that was exhibited at the Mary Boone Gallery, in New York City, Ken Johnson wrote in *Art in America* (March 1991) that it was "sensational—an explosive wedding of hyperactive form and vehement polemic, a spectacular theatre of dissent." While he found the experience of moving through the installation "fun" and "rousing," he nonetheless felt that it lacked Kruger's usual "poetic ambiguity" and "incisive aphoristic wit." A 1994 exhibit, also at the Mary Boone Gallery, was savaged by Roberta Smith in the *New York Times* (March 18, 1994) as an "installation-cum-harangue" that seemed outdated. Addressing that type of criticism in her interview with Anders Stephanson, Kruger said, "I disagree with the post-modern philosopher Jean Baudrillard in his pronouncement that power and the masculine no longer exist. . . . Nothing crawls as profoundly between laughter and tragedy as power's cutely disingenuous attempts at selfeffacement." (Baudrillard is nonetheless one of Kruger's favorite writers.)

Barbara Kruger's expressive face is framed by long corkscrew-curled hair. When asked by the editors of *FlashArt* (November/December 1988) to submit a photo and a statement about her work, she wrote that her portrait was "an approximation of how she chooses to be seen." "It joins with other received information about 'Barbara Kruger,'" she continued, "and works to biographize my body, siphoning out the palpability of incremental moments, laughs, and touches, leaving an outline, a figure which has a life of its own." For the past twenty-five years, Kruger has lived in a loft in the TriBeCa section of lower Manhattan, where she derives inspiration for her art making and her writing from multifarious sources: comments overheard on the street or in a restaurant, television programs, movies, political campaigns, radio shows, and the "art world" itself. "I think the division between notions of public and private, work and spare time, is spurious," the artist told Squiers. When Suzanne Moore asked her how she had fun, Kruger replied, "I would rather use the word pleasure. I like walking down the street. I like the sun on my face. I live in the present as much as possible. I am not nostalgic about the past."

Selected Biographical References: ARTnews 86:76+ F '87 pors; Arts 61:17+ Summer '87; FlashArt p36+ Mr '85; Guardian p27 Ja 22 '94 por; N Y Times II p25 Je 14 '94; Linker, Kate. Love for Sale: The Words and Pictures of Barbara Kruger (1990); Who's Who in American Art, 1991–92; World Artists 1980–1990 (1991)

Michael Slobodian/The National Ballet of Canada

Kudelka, James

(koo-DELL-kah)

Sept. 10, 1955– Canadian choreographer. Address: c/o The National Ballet of Canada, 157 King St. E., Toronto, Ontario M5C 1G9, Canada

According to the Canadian choreographer James Kudelka, dance is "a language to talk about something—not just steps," a conviction reflected in the wide-ranging ideas and themes he has explored through his deeply expressive, highly original works. Passion, sexual repression, homosexuality, and death are among the subjects Kudelka has addressed during the course of his choreographic career, which began when he was a teenager studying ballet in Toronto. As a dancer, he stood out for his innate musicality, but he remains best known internationally for the works he has created for the National Ballet of Canada, where he is currently artist in residence, for Les Grands Ballets Canadiens, and for a number of American companies, including the Joffrey Ballet, the San Francisco Ballet, American Ballet Theatre, and the Martha Graham Dance Company.

Although he earned a reputation early in his choreographic career for his imaginative settings of such literary works as Henrik Ibsen's *Hedda Gabler*, Henry James's *Washington Square*, and Bram Stoker's *Dracula*, Kudelka gradually moved away from traditional narrative forms and developed a more allusive and ambiguous style. To date, his ouevre consists of about fifty works, in radically different styles, but critics have noted several commonalities, including a commitment to emotional expression and a dedication to the classical idiom of dance. Recognized as one of the most important choreographers in North America, Kudelka has received enthusiastic praise from dance critics, among them the highly respected Anna Kisselgoff of the *New York Times*, who has called him "the most interesting choreographic voice to come out of ballet in the last decade."

The fifth of six children, James Kudelka was born on September 10, 1955 in Newmarket, Ontario, about thirty miles north of Toronto, where his father, a Hungarian immigrant, and his mother, a native Ontarian, had a farm. He began dancing at the age of seven, following his sister Jan to ballet classes in Newmarket. Recognizing his innate musicality and his natural aptitude for dance, Kudelka's teachers soon arranged for him to receive instruction in Toronto. When he was ten, he was accepted into the National Ballet School, the Toronto-based educational institution associated with the National Ballet of Canada. One of only seven boys in his grade five class, the precocious youngster quickly earned a reputation as a prodigy. Meticulous and scrupulously hard-working, the young dancer demonstrated extraordinarily clean technique and an exceptional ability to portray character through dance. He appeared in the National Ballet's production of *The Nutcracker* during his first year at the school, impressing his older colleagues by learning not only his own role but most of the others in the ballet as well. "I'd see him in the studio showing the other children every step of the whole ballet," the veteran ballerina Nadia Potts recalled to Penelope Doob in an interview for *Dancemagazine* (March 1977). "He knew the pas de deux, the girl's step, the boy's step, every bit of every dance." "I always watched rehearsals as much as I could," Kudelka explained to Doob. "I wasn't even aware of trying to learn the steps. I just picked them up. I was fascinated."

Kudelka began experimenting with choreography of his own during his first year at the school. His teachers were amazed by the complexity of one work he created for a parents' night performance in the late 1950s; the piece was based on George Balanchine's *Concerto Barocco*, which he had seen only three times. The promising pupil often tried their patience in other ways, however, by asking unusually difficult questions during classes. "You had to find a convincing reason for everything," Betty Oliphant, who was then the director and principal of the school, told Penelope Doob. "He had to understand something before he could accept it and that impressed me very much." Self-assured and confident of his own talent, the young dancer frequently recognized other students' technical flaws, and he wasn't averse to pointing them out. One dancer remembered Kudelka, at the age of twelve or thirteen, intently watching a professional soloist and then advising her, correctly, that she was off time. His comment was a reflection of his inherent sensitivity to music, which became even more evident when, at fourteen, he created his first pas de deux, *Encounter*, set to the music of Johann Sebastian Bach.

Although Kudelka was an excellent student and exhibited a wide range of artistic interests, which his parents actively encouraged by taking him to art galleries, concerts, and plays, he chose not to complete his academic course of study, opting instead to enter the National Ballet company, at Oliphant's suggestion, in 1972. He was just sixteen years old. Among his early assignments as a member of the corps de ballet was his first solo role, the challenging part of the Peasant Boy in Erik Bruhn's production of *La Sylphide*, which he danced during the company's debut season in London, in 1972. Later in the same year, Veronica Tennant, one of the troupe's principal dancers, asked him to create a work for her. The result was *Sonata*, a brief pas de deux, set to the first movement of César Franck's Sonata in A Major for violin and piano, that was given its world premiere at the company's annual workshop in 1973.

It was *Sonata* that brought Kudelka to the attention of Canadian dance critics, among them John Fraser of the Toronto *Globe and Mail*. After seeing a subsequent performance of the piece, Fraser expressed ambivalence toward its "loose, almost treacly form of movement," but he praised Kudelka's musicality. "Kudelka showed an impressively secure knowledge of what to do with difficult music," Fraser wrote in his review of November 29, 1974. "There were so many bits of lyrical bliss strewn about in this ballet which seemed to be taking the music to a new direction, that watching James Kudelka is going to be an important and rewarding task in the days ahead." *Sonata* won for Kudelka the Jean A. Chalmers Award for Choreography. He used part of his prize money to finance a trip to Hamburg, Germany to observe the work of John Neumeier, an internationally acclaimed choreographer whose dance-dramas he especially admired.

Meanwhile, Kudelka's career as a dancer was proving to be as promising as his choreography. In 1975 he was promoted to second soloist and a year later, to first soloist. His repertoire was unusually broad, ranging from the great nineteenth-century classics to abstract modern works. Kudelka's clean elegant line and sparkling technique stood him in good stead in such virtuoso showcases as the Neapolitan Dance in *Swan Lake* and the Diamond Pas de Deux in *The Sleeping Beauty* and his flair for comedy enlivened his portrayals of such parts as Franz in *Coppélia* and the Mouse King in *The Nutcracker*, but he was, by all accounts, most effective in contemporary narrative ballets. Because of his rare ability to suggest character through movement alone, Kudelka was an uncommonly affecting interpreter of the tortured adolescent Boy in Rudi van Dantzig's *Monument for a Dead Boy* and of Paris and Benvolio in John Cranko's version of *Romeo and Juliet*.

As more than one reviewer noted, Kudelka's attention to character details was particularly apparent in his interpretation of Romeo's friend Benvolio. "Benvolio is very minor in the ballet," Kudelka explained in his interview with Penelope Doob, "but since Benvolio and Mercutio so often do the same steps, Benvolio could easily become a mirror image of Mercutio if you hadn't studied the play. So I try very hard to be unlike Mercutio." His success in that effort was borne out by the overwhelmingly favorable notices he received. "Kudelka's Benvolio becomes a focal point for the development of dramatic tension," Penelope Doob observed. "He's the one character who clearly sees the tragedy to come and yet is powerless to prevent it. Cranko's ballet gains immensely in power when Kudelka dances Benvolio."

While the critics applauded Kudelka's intensity and theatricality as a performer in others' ballets, they reserved their most enthusiastic praise for his own choreographic endeavors, which he began to create in increasing numbers during the late 1970s. *A Party* (1976), his first major work for the National Ballet of Canada, demonstrated the fledgling choreographer's talent for etching character through movement and gesture. Set to *Variations on a Theme of Frank Bridge*, by Benjamin Britten, the thirty-minute, one-act work featured ten clearly defined characters, led by the worldly Hostess, a role devised for Veronica Tennant. Other characters in the cast include a boisterous Bachelor, a shy Single Girl, a Chic Couple who crash the party, and the hostess's Former Lover, performed at the premiere by Kudelka himself. "The party in question is one we've all been to, with its standard complement of small talk, awkward moments, and secure and insecure people," wrote William Littler in an assessment for the *Toronto Star* (February 18, 1977). "What gives it vitality as a ballet is Kudelka's cleverness in bending classical movement vocabulary to yield psychological undertones."

Anna Kisselgoff of the *New York Times* was equally impressed when she first saw *A Party* during the National Ballet's engagement in New York City in 1978. "While no one expected a workshop product from a relative beginner to be a masterpiece, the fact is that Mr. Kudelka showed off a real talent," Kisselgoff wrote in her review of July 30, 1978, in which she commended the young choreographer for his "interesting ideas" and "firm grasp of dramatic structure" and likened him to the British playwright Harold Pinter. "Mr. Kudelka has the same interest in dramatic undercurrents, and on the surface, his characters too imply situations without telling us very much overtly."

Kudelka further explored the dynamics of human relationships in his next major project for the National Ballet: *Washington Square* (1979), a work that reflected his early interest in ballet as a narrative form. Based on the Henry James novella of the same name, about a sheltered heiress named Catherine Sloper who falls in love with a young man whom her father suspects (rightly, as it turns out) is interested only in her money, *Washington Square* was set to an original score by Michael Conway Baker. After several viewings of the ambitious hour-long work, Stephen Godfrey concluded in the Toronto *Globe and Mail* (February 19, 1979) that while it succeeded as musical theatre, it fell short as a ballet, because the choreography failed to reveal character. "What seemed on Friday night to be choreography hampered solely by the strictures of the story now seems choreography that is thin, no matter what its context," Godfrey said, singling out in particular the limited classical vocabulary that comprised Catherine's steps—"endless pique turns, arabesques, and petit battements"—and the flamboyantly virtuosic, yet psychologically unrevealing, solos assigned to the young suitor.

In September 1979 Kudelka began a six-month sabbatical from the National Ballet, motivated at least in part by frustration over what he saw as a lack of artistic opportunity. (Although he was allowed to choreograph, he felt increasingly limited under the artistic directorship of Alexander Grant, who Kudelka felt didn't give enough priority to new works.) With the assistance of a grant from the Canada Council, he traveled to Europe, where he visited London, Paris, Hamburg, Stuttgart, Salzburg, and Copenhagen, and spent as much time as possible absorbing dance, art, and music. Upon his return to Canada in the spring of 1980, he embarked on a serious exploration of contemporary dance at the second Canadian National Choreographic Seminar, a three-week summer course in Banff, Alberta that brought together modern dancers, choreographers, and avant-garde musicians from across Canada. "It was an extraordinary experience," Kudelka recalled to John Gruen, who interviewed him for the *New York Times* (April 10, 1985). "I worked with dancers who moved in a completely different way—it was a new vision of dance, and it was an intense collaborative process, with new scores, new ideas, new ways of moving. All that just seeped into my brain."

Reinvigorated by his experience at the Banff workshop, Kudelka abandoned many of the conventions that had previously restricted him. The change was readily apparent in the first new work he created upon his return to the National Ballet of Canada in 1980, as its resident choreographer. The abstract *Playhouse* (1980), set to some piano pieces by Dmitri Shostakovich, combines elements of vaudeville with images intended to suggest children's playhouses, fun houses, and madhouses. One of the most unconventional aspects of the work is its central character, an impresario/lunatic designed to be performed alternately by male and female soloists. In his review of November 30, 1980, the *Globe and Mail*'s dance critic Stephen Godfrey described *Playhouse* as "light and breezy," especially in comparison to *Washington Square*, an indication, in his view, that Kudelka's artistic range was expanding. Although he felt that the piece was marred somewhat by an abrupt change of tone at the end, Godfrey noted several delightful examples of "dance 'play,' which seemed to indicate the growth of that light touch one associates with really fluent choreography."

His appointment as choreographer in residence notwithstanding, under the National Ballet of Canada's new artistic director, Erik Bruhn, Kudelka still devoted more of his time to dancing than choreography; consequently, when his contract expired, he declined to renew it. Instead, he accepted an offer from the Montreal-based Les Grands Ballets Canadiens, which invited him to join the company as principal dancer in 1981, with the understanding that he would create new ballets on a regular basis. (He was officially named the company's resident choreographer three years later.) The change of venue sparked a wave of creativity in Kudelka, who devised some three dozen new works over the next decade, most of them—beginning with the aptly titled *Genesis* (1982), to a jazzy suite by Igor Stravinsky—for his new company.

Kudelka made his international breakthrough with *In Paradisum* (1983), an off-pointe work, to an original modular score by Michael J. Baker, that has since been recognized as a landmark in the choreographer's oeuvre, because of its abstract nature and total reliance on modern-dance vocabulary. The hauntingly beautiful, visually stunning work represented Kudelka's attempt to come to terms with the impending death of his mother, Kay, who was terminally ill with cancer. In an early program note, Kudelka acknowledged his debt to the writings of Elisabeth Kübler-Ross, who identified the various psychological stages an individual passes through before accepting death. *In Paradisum* presents those stages—from denial to anger to acceptance—in a gripping series of snapshots, separated by brief blackouts. Kudelka designed the two leading roles in the ballet so that they could be danced by either men or women, and during the work's premiere run, male and female pairs alternated performances without changing the steps.

The critical response to *In Paradisum* was enthusiastic and overwhelmingly positive. In a typical review, for the Toronto *Globe and Mail* (October 26, 1983), Stephen Godfrey hailed the work's rich and assured movement, in both ensembles and solos. "It is [Kudelka's] best dance to date and shows astonishing growth," Godfrey wrote. "Works like *Washington Square* and *Playhouse* seem light years away." *In Paradisum* earned him national attention and provoked a flurry of commissions from Canada's top ballet and contemporary dance companies. It was also well received in the United States, where Jack Anderson of the *New York Times* led the applause, calling it a compelling work of "enormous urgency and drive."

Kudelka's reputation in the United States was further enhanced in the mid-1980s by the positive notices accorded several other works, including *Passage* (1981), *Hedda* (1983), and *The Heart of the Matter* (1986), all of which were commissioned by companies other than Les Grands Ballets Canadiens. Presented by American Ballet Theatre II, the plotless *Passage*, to Thomas Tallis's motet *Spem in Alium*, revolves around a Christ-like figure who appears to offer salvation to those around him. In a review for the *New York Times* (January 15, 1983), Anna Kisselgoff pronounced the "disturbing" but strangely haunting piece the hit of the evening program. Taking note of the ways he managed to extend the classical idiom of ballet "with body-language gestures and compositional patterns that set up clearly defined emotional relationships," she called Kudelka a "special talent" and compared him favorably to Antony Tudor, an acknowledged master of dance-drama. Kisselgoff's impression was reinforced when she went to Toronto to see the National Ballet of Canada dance the world premiere of *Hedda*, Kudelka's distillation of Henrik Ibsen's play *Hedda Gabler*. Despite some minor reservations about the work, she contended in her review of February 26, 1983 that the Canadian was "one of the few new ballet choreographers in North America worth following at all."

Commissioned by the Joffrey Ballet and set to the Second Piano Concerto of Sergei Prokofiev, *The Heart of the Matter* was the first of Kudelka's pieces to be showcased by a major American dance company. The ballet's opening performance was met with cheers by the audience at the New York State Theater and by rave reviews in the press, including one from his longtime champion, Anna Kisselgoff. Writing in the *New York Times* (April 5, 1986), she acclaimed Kudelka's exploration of male-female relations through the work's intricately choreographed, and vaguely menacing, central pas de deux. "A ballet different enough from anybody else's to be termed truly original, inventive in its treatment of movement to the point of strangeness, fluent in its choreographic structure, highly dramatic and yet completely plotless—if you combine these elements with a wonderfully danced performance by the Joffrey, you have a ballet that marks Mr. Kudelka's arrival as a choreographer to reckon with on the international scene."

Kudelka's credits for Les Grands Ballets Canadiens during the mid- and late 1980s include, among others, *Alliances* (Brahms, 1984), *Diversions* (Britten, 1985), *Le Sacre du Printemps* (Stravinsky, 1987), *La Salle des pas perdues* (Brahms, 1988), *Signatures* (Beethoven, 1988), *Ouverture Russe* (Glinka, 1989), and *Schéhérazade* (Rimsky-Korsakov, 1989). Perhaps the most notable of these works is *Le Sacre du Printemps* (The Rite of Spring). Although a number of high-profile choreographers had already set the Stravinsky score, Kudelka left his artistic mark upon the piece through several changes he made in the traditional scenario. In his version, the role of The Chosen One, a sacrificial figure central to the work, is divided between two characters, a pregnant woman and her husband. Kudelka also shifted the focus of the story to birth, rather than ritualistic death. Transplanted to an unidentified, middle-European country, Kudelka's revamped narrative revolves around the anticipated birth of a boy who will ensure the continuity and mythology of the people's native culture. When the pregnant woman does not produce the desired firstborn son, the townspeople turn hostile. In a review syndicated by the Southam News wire service on March 31, 1987, Jamie Portman applauded the work as "an absolute knockout": "Mounting psychological horror is a hallmark of this work. Kudelka brings it off by taking Stravinsky's pulsating score and assigning to it a dance language which is an audacious and highly personalized fusion of the classical and modern."

After nearly a decade with Les Grands Ballets Canadiens, Kudelka decided to strike out on his own. "The party was over in Montreal," he explained in an interview for *Dancemagazine* (February 1994). "There was a new artistic director who wanted to do his own thing, and my history got wiped out. I had been very influential in that company, and suddenly I was put on contract work. A series of painful setbacks made me realize that Les Grands wasn't home anymore." As a freelance choreographer, he created a dozen new works in the early 1990s, many of which were remarkable for their distinctly sensual character (both *Désir* and *Fifteen Heterosexual Duets*, for example, feature fervid pas de deux), but the choreographer felt increasingly distanced from the passion that had illuminated his work for years. "It was all vicarious, physically and emotionally," he told Robert Everett-Green of the Toronto *Globe and Mail* (July 18, 1992). "I decided I actually wanted to stop doing these pieces and start living it." He went so far as to begin assigning exit titles to his ballets, such as *Fare Well* (Mozart, 1991), a piece he made for the National Ballet of Canada, and *The End* (Brahms, 1992), created for the San Francisco Ballet.

In 1992 Kudelka accepted an appointment as artist in residence with the National Ballet of Canada. The move back to Toronto was a difficult one for him, given the anxiety he had experienced there previously, but discussions with the National Ballet's new artistic director, Reid Anderson, convinced him that his works would receive more active support. Anderson had been trying to entice Kudelka to return to the company ever since the premiere of *Pastorale*, which the choreographer had created for the National Ballet in 1990. Set to Beethoven's Sixth Symphony, *Pastorale*, which depicts a visit to the country by a group of aristocrats but is, as Anna Kisselgoff noted in the *New York Times* (May 15, 1990), "sexual, anguished, elegant . . . ; anything but the lighthearted frolic its title suggests," was a huge hit with critics and audiences alike. "I know great choreography when I see it," Anderson, a veteran dancer, told Paula Citron. "I'm enthralled by the way his steps are appliquéd onto the music—not only reflecting the music but taking it beyond what the composer tells you alone. James is not just a person making steps; he's a total artist."

Since rejoining the National Ballet of Canada, Kudelka has choreographed a half-dozen new ballets, for his own company and other troupes. Some of those works have revealed facets of his personality that had previously been unexpressed—his sense of humor, for example, and his homosexuality. *Making Ballet*, a work he designed for Ballet British Columbia, satirizes classical ballet traditions. Danced in silence, the piece features swan queens, in sylph wings and tutus, partnered by princes discarding handfuls of feathers, but the centerstage spoof is set against a troubling backdrop: a pair of men in shirts, ties, and undershorts dragging each other in a circle around the dancers, raising the specter of AIDS and ultimately questioning the relevance of art to life. Other notable recent works include *Cruel World* (Tchaikovsky), "a near-perfect ballet," to borrow Anna Kisselgoff's description, that earned a roaring ovation at its world premiere in May 1994, and *States of Grace* (Hindemith, 1995), both for American Ballet Theatre, and, for the National Ballet, a nightmarish new version of the *Miraculous Mandarin* (Bartók, 1993) and *The Actress* (Chopin, 1994), a showpiece for the company's reigning prima ballerina, Karen Kain. Although recurrent back injuries caused him to curtail his dancing some years ago, Kudelka recently returned to the stage himself, in the character role of the dollmaker Dr. Coppelius in the National's production of *Coppélia*.

James Kudelka has a reputation for being remote and moody, but interviewers have invariably found him to be articulate and at times amusing, even when discussing the years of therapy he has undergone to deal with the physical and emotional stresses that have accompanied his career. "I get used and abused quite easily," he admitted to the Toronto *Globe and Mail*'s Robert Everett-Green, who nonetheless noted that a boyish smile frequently cracked "the Dostoevskyan severity of Kudelka's face—solemn, searching, with a stubble of black beard." Kudelka is the recipient of several awards for his choreography, including the Isadora Duncan Award and the Dora Mavor Moore Award. Besides commissions from major dance companies, he has created works for individuals and for smaller ensembles, including Montreal Danse, Dancemakers of Toronto, and Hubbard Street Dance Chicago, and he choreographed pieces for Expo 1986 (*Collisions*) and the 1988 Winter Olympics Arts Festival (*Concerto Grosso*). By Kudelka's own admission, much of his work reflects his life. "My entire creative career has been autobiographical," he confessed to Paula Citron. "And the choreography has been most successful when it has come from a deep place."

Selected Biographical References: Dance 51:69+ Mr '77 pors, 68:94+ F '94 pors; Macleans p 62+ F 21 '94 por; N Y Times II p25+ Ap 10 '88, II p1+ Ap 17 '94 pors; Toronto Globe and Mail p79 N 23 '94 por; International Dictionary of Ballet, 1993

Lamb, Brian

Oct. 9, 1941– Cable television executive; interviewer. Address: c/o C-SPAN, 400 N. Capitol St. NW, Washington, DC 20001

With the monkish air of tranquility, detachment, and meticulous fairness that he brings to his television appearances, Brian Lamb sets the tone of the Cable-Satellite Public Affairs Network, better known by the acronym C-SPAN, the nonprofit, nonsense, no-frills "anti-network," to use James Lardner's term, of which he is the founder, chairman, and chief executive officer as well as a program host. C-SPAN regards itself as "America's electronic town hall," keeping cable television viewers abreast of public events and issues and providing them with an interactive link to their elected officials in Washington and other federal government officials. Others have described it as

C-SPAN

Brian Lamb

"video vérité" and "television for the postmodern age" and hailed it as the most important breakthrough in broadcasting since cable itself. "This is not television," Lamb himself has said of his creation, meaning that it represents the antithesis of the other networks, with their slick packaging, sound-biting of news and public affairs, and commercial interruptions. As conceived by Lamb, C-SPAN is dedicated in large measure to chronicling America's public life through an unblinking and unfiltered camera eye, preferably live, as open-endedly as possible, and without a hint of editing, spin, or biased commentary (on C-SPAN's part). Funded entirely by the cable television industry, C-SPAN began televising the proceedings of the United States House of Representatives live and gavel to gavel in 1979. Since 1986, when it expanded to include a second channel, it has been covering the Senate as well, on C-SPAN 2.

In addition to the floor proceedings, C-SPAN regularly covers selected congressional committee hearings. Outside of Congress, it offers detailed coverage of the workings of the federal government's executive and judicial branches, of other areas of American public life, and of some international events. The network takes its cameras to such events as White House press briefings, other governmental news conferences, and speeches and symposia on public issues in such venues as the National Press Club, political think tanks, and university forums. It provides marathon coverage of political campaigns and the national political conventions, does in-depth profiles of political figures, and takes its viewers behind the scenes in media, including radio talk shows, which it occasionally simulcasts. The programming, set in its Capitol Hill studios, includes journalistic roundtables, call-in shows (including the three-hour *Washington Journal*, each morning), and interviews with writers and others. C-SPAN transmits twenty-four hours a day with a staff and budget that are shoestring in comparison with the Cable News Network and even with National Public Radio: approximately 200 employees and an annual budget of about $24 million. Carried by more than 90 percent of America's cable systems, it serves some 60 million households with some 140 million potential viewers.

Brian P. Lamb, the son of a tavern owner turned wholesale beer distributor, was born in Lafayette, Indiana on October 9, 1941. James Warren, the media critic of the *Chicago Tribune* (March 15, 1992), considered it "a bit ironic" that Lamb would be "the one to illuminate the political system for so many," considering "the political lesson of [his] dad's career." "Because of Indiana's [liquor] licensing system, the father, and many others, were beholden to the political establishment," Warren wrote. "Every time a new governor was elected, Democrat or Republican, the father had to 'keep on the guy's good side,' the son says, and contribute financially." "It made me sick," Lamb said, as quoted by Warren.

At Jefferson High School in Lafayette, Lamb was junior-class president, the basketball team's water boy, and founder and president of the Bronco Broadcasters, a club for aspiring radio and television broadcasters. Bill Fraser, the club's adviser, later recalled how Lamb, "fascinated with broadcasting," would come to the local radio station where Fraser worked to observe the proceedings there. After graduating from high school, Lamb majored in speech and communications at nearby Purdue University, where he was president of his senior class. According to Henry Rosenthal, the owner and manager of radio station WASK-AM, in Lafayette, where Lamb had been a part-time disk jockey during his student days, Lamb "had no other interest but media and politics." During the summer between his junior and senior years at Purdue, Lamb created and hosted *Dance Date*, a daily show patterned after *American Bandstand*, at a local television station.

Upon his graduation from Purdue, Lamb enrolled in the law school at Indiana University at Bloomington, but he soon dropped out and enlisted in the United States Navy, in 1964. Following two years at sea, he was assigned, with the rank of lieutenant junior grade, to the Pentagon's public affairs office, where his chief task was fielding telephone calls from reporters. Observing the media coverage of events in Washington, D.C., to which he himself was a witness, such as demonstrations against the war in Vietnam, he realized that what television audiences were seeing was "only a portion of what was really going on," and he dreamed of the possibility of focusing a raw and dispassionate eye on public affairs.

Following his discharge from the navy in 1967, Lamb worked briefly as an assistant manager of a television station in Indiana. Returning to Washington in 1968, he worked there over the following three years as, successively, a radio reporter for United Press International and press secretary to Senator Peter H. Dominick, Republican of Colorado. He began to see the feasibility of his idea of a public-affairs television forum when, beginning in 1971, he was working in President Richard Nixon's White House as an assistant to the director of the Office of Telecommunications Policy, which was charged with deregulating the telecommunications industry and leaving it free to utilize the emerging satellite and cable-television technology—including duplexing, multiplexing, parabolic dishes, and transponders. "You could begin to see how you could put something together that didn't require megabucks," Lamb told Thomas J. Meyer, who interviewed him for the *New York Times Magazine* (March 15, 1992). "When I finally understood the economics of it, I knew it would work." By the time he left the Office of Telecommunications Policy, in May 1974, he had conceived what his friend Henry Goldberg, the communications lawyer, has described as a plan for "a network that relied on the alternative media of cable and satellite to bring Washington into people's homes."

After leaving the Office of Telecommunications Policy, Lamb became the editor of the newsletter *Media Reports* and the Washington bureau chief for the trade magazine *Cablevision*. At the same time, he began seeking support for his envisioned network from cable-system operators, pointing out that they would thus distinguish themselves in the eyes of the public by providing a service not rendered by the traditional television industry. He was encouraged in that effort by Robert Titsch Sr., his superior at *Cablevision*. "Brian was driven by the dream," Titsch told James Lardner for a profile of Lamb in the *New Yorker* (March 14, 1994). "He felt that the American public was getting screwed by television. He felt that the government—the most powerful government in the world—was hidden from its constituents and that people should see it."

"There was a tremendous amount of rejection," Lardner quoted Lamb as saying with regard to the early response to his efforts. "People would pat you on the head, and say, 'Nice little boy, keep it up, Brian.'" The cable industry, then barely a decade old, was still composed largely of its original operators, a group not noticeably disposed to looking beyond profit and loss to public service. Amos B. Hostetter Jr., the chairman and chief executive officer of Continental Cablevision and a member of C-SPAN's board of directors, told Lardner: "These people were not Time Warner or Cox Broadcasting. They were small-town appliance dealers who put an antenna up on a hill and brought a wire down from there to hook your television set up, so they could sell you the television set."

The idea of introducing television cameras into the House of Representatives had been circulating for years, with the assumption that the television industry would be in control, selecting bits of footage for inclusion in news broadcasts. When Thomas P. ("Tip") O'Neill Jr. became Speaker of the House in 1977, he made it known that he would favor the installation of television cameras in the chamber, but with the proviso that they be under the control of the House, an arrangement unacceptable to both the commercial networks and the Public Broadcasting Service. In October 1977 Lamb, a pragmatist who was willing to accept O'Neill's terms as a trade-off for the opportunity to initiate C-SPAN, informed Representative Lionel Van Deerlin, the chairman of the House Communications Subcommittee, that House sessions might be carried in full through a cable linkup. At the urging of Van Deerlin, and over the objections of the networks, the House voted to approve O'Neill's plan for installing television cameras during the Ninety-fifth Congress.

In the meantime, Lamb had been winning support for his venture from some progressive cable executives, including Robert Rosencrans, the founder of Columbia International Cable, which developed into United Artists Cable. Following the House vote, Lamb, seeded with twenty-five thousand dollars from Rosencrans, collected from within the cable industry the financial backing necessary for the launching of his nonprofit corporation, the projected annual budget of which at that time was in the magnitude of four hundred thousand dollars, minuscule by television industry standards. Through the intermediacy of Bob Schmidt, the president of Communications Technology Management, and Gary Hymel, an aide to Representative O'Neill, he met with the House speaker and came away with a verbal accord. In the following months Lamb formed the corporation called C-SPAN with the help of Robert Rosencrans and others. Rosencrans, who had joined forces with Madison Square Garden, the sports and entertainment center in New York City, to form the MSG Network, made it possible for C-SPAN initially to use that evening-oriented network's satellite channel during the day at a reduced rate. Rosencrans became first chairman of the board of C-SPAN.

C-SPAN, with a staff of four and one telephone line, was originally headquartered in a five-hundred-square-foot office in an apartment building in the Washington, D.C., suburb of Arlington, Virginia. It began transmitting to as many as 3.5 million households on a trial basis on March 19, 1979, and the system was officially approved by the House two weeks later. Its first annual budget was $480,000, and during the network's first five years of operation its total cumulated budget was comparable to the current annual salary of the ABC television broadcast journalist Diane Sawyer, according to James Lardner. During those years the television cameras in the House of Representatives were trained exclusively on the representatives who were speaking. That situation changed in the spring of 1984, when a small group of conservative Republicans began to take political advantage of "special orders," a time slot in which speeches can be made on the House floor following the end of the day's normal legislative proceedings. House Speaker O'Neill viewed the tactic as "the lowest thing" he had seen during his career in the House. Lest the lack of response to the partisan speech-making give the wrong impression to the television audience, in May of that year he ordered that the cameras occasionally pan the virtually empty chamber. The contretemps brought C-SPAN into the national front-page news for the first time.

Outside the House, C-SPAN began practicing a different form of political coverage during the Democratic presidential primaries of 1980, when it had a staff of seven network-wide. At a rally for Massachusetts senator Edward M. Kennedy in Philadelphia, it trained its cameras not on Kennedy and others on the podium but on the crowd, occasionally focusing on an individual. C-SPAN staffers later chatted with campaign workers at independent candidate John Anderson's headquarters in Philadelphia, and still later they talked with political reporters at a Philadelphia newspaper office. "We wanted to go out and do no editing, no embellishments," Lamb explained to James Warren of the *Chicago Tribune*. "It's the same now. We try to give people the sense of what you'd see if you were actually in the room."

The most popular of the extracongressional offerings introduced on C-SPAN in the early 1980s was a morning call-in program devoted to discussing how the news of the day was variously presented in newspapers across the country. "It's pure television, with all the hokum taken out," the Washington-based journalist Charles McDowell commented, as quoted in the *Chicago Tribune* (June 18, 1985). "A man holds up a newspaper in front of a camera. What a remarkable notion! A throwback to some linear age." By the mid-1980s, C-SPAN had ninety employees and an annual budget of $5.9 million (roughly the cost of two evenings of prime-time programming on a mainstream network), and it was being carried by two thousand cable affiliates with a potential audience of twenty-one million households. In 1984, in addition to fourteen hundred hours of House floor debate and committee hearings, C-SPAN produced 865 hours of live call-in programming in which more than twelve thousand callers in more than two thousand cities participated. While the mainstream networks limited their coverage of the Democratic and Republican conventions to the prime-time hours that year, C-SPAN covered both conventions in their entirety and provided the Public Broadcasting Service with its convention footage.

On May 4, 1987 the *Miami Herald* broke the story of aspiring Democratic presidential nominee Gary Hart's alleged adulterous fling with Donna Rice. The following day, when the press in general was zeroing in on the scandal, C-SPAN, typically, was alone among the electronic media in broadcasting Hart's entire foreign-policy speech. In the presidential primaries of 1988, C-SPAN followed candidates out on the stump, televising "extraordinary wireless mike sessions," as Douglas Davis observed in the *New York Times* (July 10, 1988). "The channel's cameras are allowing the much-abused medium of television to reveal its basic strengths," Davis wrote. "Where the commercial networks strive at great expense to distill and therefore distort the world, C-SPAN can only afford to turn it on. C-SPAN gives us the visual world as a spontaneous, unrehearsed feast, in which the viewer is the guest of honor." Davis confessed to being part of a national addiction to C-SPAN, a habit he touted as "a singular sign of growing political sanity, of a lust for unmediated access to public affairs."

In 1991, a year before Arkansas governor Bill Clinton declared his candidacy for the Democratic nomination for president of the United States, Clinton's media strategists saw that his ability to talk about issues extemporaneously could be shown to advantage before C-SPAN's running cameras. Accordingly, they arranged for him to speak, to saturation effect, at Democratic Party events that C-SPAN was covering. Thus did C-SPAN inadvertently contribute to the emergence of Clinton as the front-runner in the Democratic primaries of 1992. During the 1992 Democratic National Convention, at which Clinton was nominated, C-SPAN was widely praised for letting the television audience directly witness the proceedings on the podium, without the often obtrusive commentary on other networks. Similarly, while the other networks presented bowdlerized footage of the "march on Washington" by gay activists in 1993, C-SPAN televised the event intact, including every obscenity and every instance of foul language caught by its cameras and microphones. "We think that people should have a chance to see the whole thing and make up their own mind," Lamb explained. When the Persian Gulf war was taking shape, C-SPAN displayed its characteristic thoroughness by documenting in almost tedious detail, in footage lasting eight hours, a National Guard unit's odyssey from North Carolina to Saudi Arabia. That project was child's play in comparison with the network's presentation, day in and day out, of World War II footage and live coverage on the occasion of the fiftieth anniversary of the D-Day invasion, in June 1994. Also during 1994 C-SPAN televised reenactments of the Lincoln-Douglas debates from the cities and towns in Illinois where they had originally taken place.

Since the mid-1980s C-SPAN has been headquartered in a suite of offices in view of the Capitol in Washington, D.C. Among the programs broadcast from there are viewer call-in shows, filling some three hours every day, which give viewers the opportunity to speak directly to their legislators, other policymakers, and journalists; a Sunday morning retrospective of the issues raised by the previous week's events; and *Booknotes*, an interview with an author conducted by Lamb on Sunday evenings. C-SPAN camera crews go out into the field, to the White House Rose Garden and other locations, for such programs as *Event of the Day*. The weekly program *Road to the White House* looks at potential presidential candidates. In Congress, where the cameras are still in the hands of the House and Senate, C-SPAN is actively seeking to install and control its own cameras. Another goal is to add to its programming schedule the televising of arguments before the Supreme Court, where cameras have thus far been forbidden. From overseas, C-SPAN brings to its viewers the daily *Evening News from Moscow*, the British prime minister's "question time" in the House of Commons, other public-affairs programming from Britain, and periodic coverage of legislative activity in other countries. Since November 1993 C-SPAN's "School Bus," a motorized exhibit, has been traveling all over the United States, demonstrating to local communities the usefulness of the network in educating citizens in public affairs and bringing them in closer touch with their government.

By policy, C-SPAN has no on-air stars. Those who appear on-camera as moderators or interviewers (including Susan Swain, a senior vice-president, and Bruce Collins, the network's legal counsel) do so not only secondarily to their full-time off-camera duties but also as self-effacingly as possible—almost anonymously. None adheres to this rule more strictly than Lamb, who is the network's most conspicuous face but has never uttered his name or revealed a personal bias on camera. "I am not a Ted Turner, who first built the [CNN] network on personality," he explained to Sharon Geltner for her profile of him in the *Saturday Evening Post* (December 1985). "In order for C-SPAN to work, it has to be cooperative. This can't be an ego trip or be seen as empire-building." At every opportunity he lavishes praise on his staff, who are kept aware of his favorite motto: "You can accomplish anything as long as you don't mind who gets the credit."

Brian Lamb is a little below average in height, has bright blue eyes set deep in a round, usually serene face, and dresses impeccably, in dark, classically cut suits, pressed white shirts, and conservative ties. On-camera, his strongest reaction is expressed in a benign, controlled smile. Off-camera, he remains generally mild-mannered but is more animated and less laconic, and he can be emotional (such as on the occasions when he rails against the "television tyranny" of the New York-based networks) without losing his self-assurance. Both on- and off-camera, he is unassuming.

Self-described as "your ultimate news and information junkie," Lamb reads or scans about nine newspapers a day, many of which he picks up on his arrival at C-SPAN's offices on Capitol Hill each morning between six and eight o'clock, the exact time depending on his schedule for the particular day. According to Rayne Pollack, C-SPAN's former publicist, Lamb "has no hobbies, other than reading books for *Booknotes*." His one conspicuous private extravagance is his Acura Legend automobile. He works long days, seldom takes a vacation, and, eschewing the celebrity network of dinners and parties, is not in the Washington "game." "Money doesn't move him," according to someone who knows him well. "Nothing moves him, except putting out a good product." Lamb himself has said of his relationship to C-SPAN: "This is my fun. . . . This is my dedication."

Selected Biographical References: Chicago Tribune II p4 Je 18 '85 por, Tempo p1+ Mr 15 '92 por; N Y Times II p31 Jl 10 '88 por, B p8 Mr 28 '89 por; N Y Times Mag p46+ Mr 15 '92 por; New Yorker 70:48+ Mr 14 '94 por; Sat Eve Post 257:70+ D 85 pors, 258:46+ Ja/F '86 pors; Time 140:29 Ag 24 '92 por

---

R. R. Jones

Lanting, Frans

July 13, 1951– Photographer. Address: 1985 Smith Grade, Santa Cruz, CA 95060

By immersing himself intellectually, emotionally, and physically in the lives of wild animals ranging from elephants and lions to albatrosses and penguins, the internationally renowned Dutch-born photographer Frans Lanting has captured on film arresting images that illuminate seldom-seen aspects of the natural world and "excit[e] a sense of shared discovery for the viewer, a feeling of seeing a well-known creature as if for the first time," as Steven Werner wrote in *Outdoor Photographer* (May 1993). Lanting's photo-essays "bring to life remote geographic areas . . . and often even create the public image of these landscapes and animals for a worldwide audience," Uta Henschel observed in the German edition of *Geo* (February 1992). His pictures have also been credited with focusing attention on environmental problems and, in some cases, spurring governments and nongovernmental groups to act upon them. "I may be part of the last generation of photographers able to show wildlife in all its glory," Lanting told Michael McRae during an interview for *Outside* (October 1992). "The next generation may have better technology, but what wildlife will be left? Wherever I go I see whole ecosystems unraveling. The long-term pattern is the demise of wilderness as we know it. I'd rather go at a more leisurely pace, but I'm in a very privileged position, being the eyes of the world."

One of the most widely published photographers in his field, Lanting has contributed thousands of pictures to *Natural History*, *Audubon*, *Life*, the Italian nature magazine *Airone*, the German magazine *Stern*, and many other prestigious periodicals. On commissions from *National Geographic*, he has tackled difficult assignments in Antarctica, Madagascar, Botswana, and the rainforests of Borneo, Belize, Peru, and the Congo Basin, producing work of such outstanding quality that Wilbur Garrett, who served as the editor of *National Geographic* during the 1980s, came to regard him as "the finest nature photographer working today." "[His] aesthetic vision and knowledge of the subject matter are unlike those of any other natural history photographer [*National Geographic*] has used," according to Thomas R. Kennedy, the magazine's director of photography. "He's able to understand and anticipate animal behavior with the same kind of alacrity that a photojournalist would who is making pictures of people. The animals are unconscious of his presence, and as a result he can get closer." Lanting's photos illustrate ten books, four of which—*Madagascar: A World Out of Time* (1990), *Peace on Earth* (1993), *Okavango: Africa's Last Eden* (1993), and *Forgotten Edens: Exploring the World's Wild Places* (1993)—he wrote or cowrote. Many of the seventy-five thousand images in his collection of color transparencies have appeared in other books as well, and also in advertisements, filmstrips, greeting cards, posters, and annual reports, among other vehicles. Lanting was named BBC Photographer of the Year in 1991.

Frans Lanting was born on July 13, 1951 in Rotterdam, the Netherlands. As a child he identified closely with the hero of two children's books by the Swedish writer Selma Lagerlöf, a boy named Nils Holgersson, who, after being shrunk by a magician to less than half his original size, joins a flock of wild geese and becomes an accepted member of the animal world. At one point the leader of the geese tells him, "If you have learned anything from this journey, Nils, you might no longer be of the opinion that man alone should rule the world. See, you people have so much land just for yourselves, so perhaps you could leave some marshy lakes and swamps and sea cliffs and distant forests to us. That way, we animals can live in peace. All my life I have been persecuted and hunted. It would be a good thing if creatures like us could find a refuge somewhere." In 1994 Lanting told an interviewer that Lagerlöf's story "really set the stage for a lot of what [he is] doing now." He believes that, like Nils Holgersson, he plays the role of a "mediator" between humans and other species. "I stay with wild animals, and then I come back to my own people to tell them about life in nature," he has said.

At the age of twenty-one, Lanting spent a school holiday hiking and taking pictures in national parks in the United States. His photographs disappointed him, so, thinking that the fault lay with the camera, which he had borrowed from his mother, he bought himself a better one and began educating himself in its use in a Rotterdam city park and in the Dutch countryside. He also developed his skills by studying the work of established photographers and reading how-to articles. By his own account, he has been strongly influenced by "native ways of looking at animals," and through the years his imagination has been fired by cave paintings, Chinese landscape paintings, and other artworks.

Lanting earned a master's degree in environmental economics from Erasmus University, in Rotterdam, in 1977. In 1978 he enrolled in a postgraduate program in environmental planning at the University of California at Santa Cruz. He left the program about two years later to devote himself full-time to photography, thereby reportedly dashing his family's hopes that he would someday take over his father's business. "I've always been interested in the natural world, and I love photography, so it seemed a good idea to combine the two," he told Cathy Joseph during an interview for *Amateur Photographer* (September 11, 1993). He also felt, as he explained to Antus M. Theurmer Jr. for *Jackson Hole* (Winter 1994–95), that "a bad day in the field is better than a good day in the office." In 1980 a collection of Lanting's photographs of the Dutch landscape was published in the Netherlands, with the title *Holland: The Magic of Reality*.

After abandoning his academic career, Lanting continued to live on the California coast, where he found limitless inspiration and a wealth of wild subjects to photograph. "The vitality of this coast amazes me, despite the obvious urbanization and commercialization . . . ," he told Uta Henschel. "It is just as fantastic as if bisons were still running through the suburbs of Chicago." The sanderlings (a type of sandpiper) that foraged along the seashore fascinated Lanting, and he set about learning as much as he could about them. In line with what he has described as his "tendency . . . just to look for a neighborhood and make a commitment to a group of animals or a small patch of land," he observed them for weeks on end and even followed them for some distance when they migrated. In time he became intimately familiar not only with their behavior as a species but also with the idiosyncracies of individual birds. As they got used to his presence, he was able to come increasingly close to them, and the birds eventually seemed to accept him as simply another feature of their environment.

Lanting "discovered his photographic style" during his work with the sanderlings, Uta Henschel reported, and by his own account, that long-term project provided the foundation for his later success in photography. "Right from the start Frans had a deep, abiding love for the natural world," the photographer David Cavagnaro, with whom Lanting collaborated to produce the book *Feathers* (1982), told David M. Roth for *Departures* (September/October 1994). "That was apparent in his earliest work; and as a photographer I know the kind of hardship it takes to do the work he was doing. He would dog something endlessly until he got it, and he had the patience to sit quietly. Those are gifts few photographers really have."

"Animals communicate a lot with body language and thus are very sensitive to what others are demonstrating with their bodies," Lanting has observed. Lanting's highly developed ability to unobtrusively enter the worlds of animals—to live "eye to eye" with them and "com[e] to know their most intimate, desperate, and ordinary moments," in his words—has aided him not only when he photographs species that are skittish or shy, when his greatest risk is scaring his subjects away, but also when the objects of his attention are potentially dangerous: elephant seals, for example, which, in another of his major undertakings on the California coast, he began photographing in the early 1980s. Any action interpreted by the elephant seals as threatening, or as interfering with their searches for or defense of harems of females, might have resulted in his being killed by one or more of the adult males, which when fully grown may weigh more than three tons. In another instance, in Botswana Lanting photographed elephants while positioned within a stone's throw of them. While working in Africa, he also followed a pride of lions for a month, "liv[ing] with them as an auxiliary lion, so to speak," as he told Victor Goodpasture for *Confetti* (May/June 1992). One night the lions killed a giraffe, and, again from a distance of just a few feet, he spent hours photographing them as they devoured every part of the animal but the bones.

In what amounted to a veritable coup for a fledgling wildlife photographer whose career had not yet reached the three-year mark, Lanting's photo-essay "Elephants on the Beach" was published in January 1982 by the National Audubon Society's wildlife and conservation magazine *Audubon*. Later that year a photo-essay by him about the wildlife of California's Channel Islands was published in *National Parks* (July/August 1982); another story, illustrated with his photos of snow geese, appeared in the German edition of *Geo* (September 1982) and drew "international attention," according to Cathy Joseph. "Despite the routine nature of his early subjects," Steven Werner noted, "Lanting had a talent that made them appear novel and exotic. Through his lens, even a common beach scavenger like a seagull seemed remarkable."

"I try to control situations only to a point and then leave the door open to chance by allowing the animals choices or leeway, which then forces me to improvise and react," Lanting told Werner, in describing his working methods. "It becomes more of an interaction than a one-way street where an animal can do only one thing or stay in only one position. . . . My photographic approach has long been to show the context within which wildlife lives or has to live. . . . I try not to show only the totem animals, but include little critters that are often overlooked to show that they're all expressions of vital ecosystems. Beyond that, I go to great lengths to illustrate relevant connections between people and animals, be they positive or negative."

In 1985 Lanting's career got another big boost, when *National Geographic* commissioned him to record on film the environmental crisis on Madagascar. "Madagascar had not been explored in a modern sense," Lanting recalled during an interview with Tim Gallagher for *Living Bird* (Summer 1993). "It was very exciting to be in the vanguard, providing the first documentation of species that had never before been photographed. . . . I actually photographed a species of lemur that hadn't even been named yet. It doesn't get any more exciting than that, sitting face to face with an unknown primate, alongside the scientist who discovered it."

Acting in accordance with his conviction that the formula for success for someone in his realm of photography is "part science, part expedition skills, and part human-relations skills," in his words, Lanting initiated many conversations with farmers, subsistence hunters, government officials, scientists, and other Malagasy during the year that he worked on Madagascar, and he thereby became intimately familiar with the country's economic and social problems as well as its environmental troubles. His thorough research, which also included extensive reading, "enabled him to make photos that were more moving than anything previously done on Madagascar," David M. Roth wrote. According to Roth, even if Lanting "had never snapped another frame [after leaving Madagascar], he would have been assured a place in photo history because of a single iconic image—that of a Malagasy tribesman clutching an enormous egg [that of an elephant bird, an extinct species] and spear."

Lanting's pictures of the land, people, and wildlife of Madagascar, which accompanied the article "Madagascar: A World Apart," in the February 1987 issue of *National Geographic*, and which subsequently appeared in many other periodicals, awakened a great deal of interest in Madagascar's multiple problems, and since the late 1980s scores of foreign scientists and conservationists, in collaboration with their Malagasy counterparts, have launched projects on the island with the linked goals of halting the destruction of the environment and combating the country's economic and social ills. With financial aid from the United States Agency for International Development and various conservation organizations, the Malagasy government has increased its annual support for parks and reserves from less than one thousand dollars to millions of dollars, and a growing tourism industry has bolstered the economy.

After the publication in *National Geographic* (December 1990) of Lanting's photographs of the wildlife of the eighty-five-hundred-square-mile Okavango Delta, in Botswana, scores of Americans contacted the Botswana embassy in Washington for information about tours or the possibilities of starting businesses there. The publicity that that *National Geographic* issue generated also reportedly led the Botswana government to alter its policies regarding a portion of the delta so as to ensure its conservation. Lanting's impressions, in words as well as pictures, of the region appear in his book *Okavango: Africa's Last Eden*. In a review of the book for *Photo District News* (April 1994), in which she commented that "Lanting's commitment to wildlife photography is justly legendary," Nancy Madlin observed, "It's hard to believe that, after we've seen so much, any book on African wildlife can still impress us to marveling. But that's exactly what this one does." In the *Boston Globe*, Mark Wilson, who called Lanting "perhaps the most versatile wilderness photographer working today," wrote, "The photographer wanting to learn from [his] pictures needn't go far into the book. Patterns, symmetry, eye shine, action, expressions, perspective, and color swirl about the viewer in a concert of the finest kind." "In documenting the cycles of the Okavango, Lanting's photographic skills are seemingly boundless," Ray Olson wrote in *Booklist* (November 15, 1993). "His viewpoints, lighting, backgrounds, and composition are unparalleled. From vast aerial shots to closeups of lionesses lapping water, each extraordinary photo conveys life and power and feeling."

In another enthusiastic assessment of *Okavango*, for the *New York Times Book Review* (January 9, 1994), the renowned zoologist George B. Schaller wrote, "[Lanting] celebrates the land and its wildlife with spare, evocative prose and with photographs that are extraordinary in capturing motion, form, and color. . . . [He] possesses not only the clear vision and technical virtuosity of the world's best outdoor photographers, he also has the unusual ability to create mood and mystery. . . . Lanting's photographs take creatures that have become ordinary and familiar and transform them into haunting new visions. . . . Admire this book for its beauty. But remember also that it bears witness to our moral obligation to protect a unique environment; it demands compassion, concern, action, and global commitment to help 'Africa's last Eden' endure."

Lanting's photos also illustrate *The Total Penguin* (1990), by James Gorman, and two books for younger readers by Sylvia A. Johnson—*Elephant Seals* (1989) and *Albatrosses of Midway Island* (1990). The pictures in *Peace on Earth* (1993) appeared first in fifty-two consecutive weekly Lanting portfolios in the Japanese magazine *Asahi Graph*, in 1992. Dozens of articles illustrated solely with his photos appear in other periodicals each year. Among other subjects, Lanting has created feature stories on the life cycle and migration of the monarch butterfly, penguins of the Falkland Islands and South Georgia Island, and the bonobo (also known as the pygmy chimpanzee), which lives in the Congo Basin. He spent one summer on the west coast of Canada, photographing Kwakiutl Indian artists who carve masks inspired by the natural world, and he took pictures of giant tortoises inside a volcano in the Galápagos Islands. In a remote region of the upper Amazon Basin, he focused on wild macaws while perched eighty feet above the forest floor on a tower that he had constructed to get treetop views. He has expressed the hope that his pictures of orangutans and other creatures on Borneo will help attract attention to the destruction of Borneo's tropical forests, which are disappearing even faster than the rainforests of Amazonia.

According to David M. Roth, Frans Lanting "looks more like a tweedy college professor than a camera-toting Crocodile Dundee. He's soft-spoken, mild-mannered, and unprepossessing. . . . His large doleful eyes are his most striking feature; in an instant they can switch from an unfathomable melancholy to a gleaming smile: a polarity of expression that reflects his having witnessed the extremes of earthly paradises (and their development-driven destruction)." Wilbur Garrett has observed that Lanting is "more meticulous than most people. And that goes for everything—from cutting his toenails to maintaining his cameras."

Lanting lives near Monterey Bay, a few miles from Santa Cruz, with the writer Christine K. Eckstrom, who edited his book *Okavango* and cowrote *Forgotten Edens*. Bobcats and coyotes sometimes wander into the meadow that surrounds their house, which, David M. Roth wrote, is "filled with African artifacts . . . all precisely placed." Lanting is a founding director of the North American Nature Photography Association, a columnist for *Outdoor Photographer*, and a roving editor for the National Wildlife Federation, and he serves on the board of the National Council of the World Wildlife Fund. In addition to the 1991 BBC Wildlife Photographer of the Year award, which he received for his work in Botswana, Lanting's awards include top honors in the 1988 and 1989 World Press Photo competitions, for his images of Madagascar and Antarctica, respectively; a PATA (Pacific Asia Travel Association) Gold Award, for his photo-essay on the Hawaiian island of Kauai, which appeared in the magazine *Island*; and, for his photos of Okavango, the 1993 Kodak Fotobuch Preis and the 1995 Kodak Fotokalener Preis.

Selected Biographical References: Departures p124+ S/O '94 por; [KLM] HollandHerald p24+ S '93 por; Outdoor Photographer 9:34+ My '93 por; Wildlife Conservation 97:56+ My/Je '94 por

AP/Wide World Photos

Leakey, Richard

Dec. 19, 1944- Paleoanthropologist; conservationist; writer. Address: P.O. Box 24926, Nairobi, Kenya

NOTE: This biography supersedes the article that appeared in *Current Biography* in 1976.

As recently as a century ago (one hundred years is but a moment in geologic terms), anyone interested in investigating the human family's origins had to be part adventurer and part naturalist. All of them lacked formal training, because no training was to be had. Since then, paleoanthropology has become as rigorous as any other scientific discipline, and to gain credibility among colleagues one generally has to have the proper credentials. But the grand old tradition of the unschooled fossil-hunter lives on in Richard Leakey, the son of the famous husband-and-wife fossil-hunting team Louis and Mary Leakey, who, despite his lack of an academic degree, went on to become a highly respected paleoanthropologist in his own right. Indeed, Leakey has been credited with organizing some of the most successful paleoanthropological expeditions of this century, in the Lake Turkana region of northern Kenya. "Without a doubt," Ian Tattersall, an anthropologist and curator at the American Museum of Natural History, in New York City, told Elizabeth Schick, who profiled Leakey for *The World & I* (August 1994), "Richard's contribution lies in his locating the site at Turkana and organizing the logistics" of the expeditions, which led to the discovery of "an incredibly rich trove of fossils."

Two decades after he began prospecting for fossils at Lake Turkana, Leakey remains perhaps the best-known living paleoanthropologist. His name alone is enough to attract large crowds of natural-history buffs to lecture halls to hear him speak, and his books invariably sell well. Given his reputation, it is somewhat ironic that Leakey has not done much fossil hunting in recent years. From 1989 until 1994 he served as director of the Kenya Wildlife Service, which manages the country's animal life, a precious resource for the cash-strapped African nation, and in early 1995 he helped to found a political party in Kenya. Leakey possessed no formal training for those jobs, either. But he has never described himself as a wildlife manager or politician and even seems reluctant to characterize himself as a scientist. "I'm not a biologist. I'm not an evolutionist. I'm a naturalist," he told *Current Biography*. "I think I'm somewhat old-fashioned in being fairly competent in a lot of different areas but probably not a master of any. I'm a generalist. A very inquisitive generalist."

Richard Erskine Frere Leakey was born in Nairobi, Kenya on December 19, 1944, the son of Louis Leakey and Mary (Nicol) Leakey. He has an older brother, Jonathan, a herpetologist, and a younger brother, Philip, who is the only white member of Kenya's parliament. Although Leakey's parents eventually became world famous for their discoveries of hominid fossils at Olduvai Gorge, in Tanzania, and elsewhere in East Africa, during his youth their work did not generate much interest within the paleontological community. This was partly because, despite years of searching, they had not found anything to confirm Louis Leakey's belief that Africa was the birthplace of mankind. (In those days most scientists were convinced that humans first appeared in Asia.) It was not until 1959 that they made their first important find: the Nutcracker Man, which was the most ancient human ancestor then known.

While Louis Leakey, who died in 1972, remains perhaps the better known of the pair, Mary Leakey made most of the important discoveries, including that of the Nutcracker Man; Louis, a relentless self-promoter, was simply better at publicizing the couple's work. According to Gilbert M. Grosvenor, the president of the National Geographic Society, Richard Leakey inherited the best of each of his parents' talents. "From his mother, I think he earned the Ph.D. in paleontology," he said at an award ceremony during which Leakey was presented with the Gardiner Greene Hubbard medal, the society's highest honor, in early 1994. "From his father, a Ph.D. in communications, public awareness, debating, and above all an incredible nose for finding fossil-rich cliffs and riverbeds."

Leakey was not always interested in human prehistory. In fact, as a youth he wanted to have nothing to do with his parents' line of work, and he did not even particularly enjoy accompanying them on their fossil-hunting expeditions. To make those excursions tolerable, he spent his time wandering around in the African bush and tracking wild animals. His affinity for the ways of the wild led him, while still a teenager, to become a supplier of animals to research institutions. He preferred this work to attending school, and at seventeen he left high school without graduating to establish a photographic safari company, which soon became a thriving enterprise.

His professed disinterest in human evolution notwithstanding, Leakey soon found himself drawn to the same questions about human prehistory that so preoccupied his parents. This fascination led him, while he was in his late teens, to join the fossil-hunter Kamoya Kimeu, who had worked with his parents, in prospecting for fossils at Lake Natron, on the Kenya-Tanzania border. The turning point for Leakey came in 1967, when he joined an international paleontological expedition in the Lower Omo Valley, in Ethiopia, as a team leader for the Kenyan contingent, for it was during that expedition that Leakey took his now-legendary flight from the Omo camp for a brief visit to Nairobi, during which he peered out of the window and saw what he thought might be fossil-bearing sedimentary rock. His preliminary survey of the area, in the Lake Turkana region, seemed to confirm his hunch, so he asked the National Geographic Society to fund an exploratory expedition, with him as the team leader. It was an audacious proposition, given the fact that he had not even completed high school. Nevertheless, the society was sufficiently persuaded by his confidence and hands-on experience to provide him with twenty-five thousand dollars to fund an exploration of the area.

By this time Leakey, having decided to pursue a career in paleoanthropology, had realized that he needed to establish his credibility among his university-trained colleagues. At the time, the National Museums of Kenya was in the midst of a search for a replacement for the departing British director. Leakey saw a great advantage in becoming affiliated with an institution where he could carry out his research, and so he applied for the post. In his favor was the fact that he had opted to become a citizen of Kenya, rather than retain British citizenship, when the country achieved independence in 1963. His cause was also helped by his considerable skills of persuasion. "Nobody in their right mind should give a twenty-three-year-old with no education and no experience a job of being director of a museum," he joked to *Current Biography*. "But because I was a Kenyan and capitalized on the nationalism of the day, the unpopularity of having the British people run things, I was able to influence decisions and get in the back door. You couldn't do it in the contemporary situation. And I'm not sure I should have been able to get away with it then."

Thus equipped with funds and a job at a research institution, in 1968 Leakey organized an expedition to excavate the eastern shore of Lake Turkana. As he had predicted, the site proved to be rich in ancient hominid fossils, the oldest being between two and a half million and one million years old. "I think I knew enough about geology and certain geological formations that when I flew over Lake Turkana in 1967, a casual observation told me . . . volumes," he said of his success in discovering such an important site in his interview with Schick. "Nobody with that sort of preset knowledge had flown where I had flown at that particular moment."

In the nearly three decades since he initiated the excavation of the Turkana basin, Leakey's team of scientists has unearthed more than two hundred hominid fossils—a large number compared with other sites. The Leakey fossils are also of an unusually high quality, for among them are perhaps a dozen skulls, a number of fairly complete jaws, and some partial skeletons. The collection's greatest treasure is Turkana Boy, a remarkably complete *Homo erectus* skeleton that is estimated to be 1.6 million years old. "I had no professional degrees or training, but I wound up with something even more important: ancient bones of my own," Leakey was quoted as saying in the *Chicago Tribune* (November 20, 1992). "The total number of fossils of early man that have been recovered is exquisitely small. So I could trade access to my set of fossils for being allowed to study other paleontologists' collections, and I thus gained back-door entrance to the profession." As might be expected, some paleoanthropologists at first dismissed Leakey's efforts, not only because he lacked a university education but also because he was not always directly involved in the actual discovery, analysis, and interpretation of the fossil material collected by his team. Nevertheless, most have since come to acknowledge that he has made a significant contribution to the profession.

In terms of modern science's understanding of human evolution, what was particularly exciting about the Turkana specimens was that they indicated that between two and a half million and one million years ago, the region was home to at least three different kinds of early humans. There was *Australopithecus boisei*, a small-brained creature equipped with huge jaws and molars, which it used for consuming large amounts of plant material. There was also an as-yet-unnamed, small-brained animal with a more delicate dental apparatus that presumably enjoyed an omnivorous diet. And finally, there was a creature with small teeth and jaws and—its hallmark—a comparatively large brain; this was *Homo habilis*, the earliest known species belonging to the genus *Homo*, which includes modern humans.

The discovery that several hominid species lived at Turkana contemporaneously forced scientists to reformulate their ideas about human evolution, for until Leakey and his team of scientists began excavating at Turkana, the prevailing wisdom had been that *Australopithecus africanus*, an early hominid species that lived in southern Africa some three million years ago, evolved into two distinct lines. According to this view, one line gave rise to other australopithecine species, all of which eventually became extinct, and the other to the human lineage, the only surviving member of which is *Homo sapiens*. With the addition of the Turkana specimens, however, it became clear that human evolution did not fit into this simple Y-shaped pattern and that it was considerably more complicated than had previously been supposed.

It was revealed to be more complicated still in 1985, when Leakey's longtime colleague Alan Walker discovered on the western shore of Lake Turkana what became known as the Black Skull. An analysis of its anatomy, combined with its great age—it was dated to be two and a half million years old—suggested to Leakey that it represented yet another branch on the human family tree. "Our family tree was getting bushier and bushier," he wrote in *Origins Reconsidered* (1992), "and the west Turkana expeditions had played a major role in its growth." As for what paleoanthropological research will yield in the future, Leakey remains confident that his long-held belief in the antiquity of the genus *Homo*—the notion that members of the genus did not evolve from australopithecines but, rather, originated deep within prehistory—will eventually be proved correct. For the time being, though, most scientists maintain that the *Homo* lineage evolved from the australopithecines, the earliest known species of which appeared around four million years ago. The dispute will remain unresolved in the absence of additional fossil evidence.

In addition to providing him with the means to achieve his own professional goals, Leakey's directorship of the National Museums of Kenya benefited his country. When he took the job in 1968, the museum consisted of a few underfunded departments employing a handful of people. By the time he left, in 1989, it had mushroomed into a complex of nine regional institutions that, collectively, make up one of the few museums in Africa to claim international stature. His other achievements included establishing an education department at the museum and expanding its research programs, which have come to encompass not only paleontology and archaeology but also zoology as well as the study of Kenyan culture and traditional medicine, to name just a few subjects. In addition, Leakey, a fervent nationalist, helped to formulate Kenya's antiquities laws, ensured that Kenyan citizens were hired to fill key positions, and worked hard to persuade Western philanthropic organizations to provide the institution with financial support. For his efforts he won the admiration and respect of his Kenyan colleagues. "He's very hard-working, and he's a kind person, always encouraging people to explore further in their field," James Maikweki, the curator of the Nairobi Museum, told Schick. "That's why people like him."

Leakey's career at the museum, as well as his active involvement in the field work at Turkana, came to an end in 1989, when the Kenyan president, Daniel arap Moi, named him the director of the Kenya Wildlife Service (KWS). The appointment came as a surprise to many wildlife conservationists, for Leakey's mandate was challenging: he was to bring an end to the rampant elephant poaching that had decimated the country's elephant populations and that, as a result, had devastated the tourist trade, a vital part of the national economy. (The elephants were being poached for their tusks, the source of ivory, which has been used to make everything from billiard balls to jewelry to piano keys.) What made Leakey an attractive candidate for the job were his management experience, his fund-raising skills, and his international stature, all of which would be needed to turn Kenya's precarious wildlife situation around.

Leakey accepted the appointment, both out of his desire to further Kenya's development and because he has long been an avid conservationist, a fact that has been overshadowed by his paleoanthropological work. During the award ceremony at which Leakey received the Hubbard medal, Gil Grosvenor told a story that illustrates Leakey's empathy for wild creatures. The two men had been driving toward Nairobi when Leakey stopped in an area that he described as being prime puff adder habitat. "I thought it was rather strange that Richard would stop in a puff adder habitat," Grosvenor said, "until Richard went around to the back of the Land Rover, opened the door, and pulled out these two gunnysacks that he'd been carrying back there, very carefully untied the ends of them, shooed me back in the Land Rover, and out slithered a couple of puff adders. I said, 'Richard, why didn't you tell me they were back here?' He said, 'They won't bother you. . . . They're a nuisance around camp, and I wanted to bring them to a place I thought they'd like.'"

In his effort to preserve Kenya's elephants, Leakey, in one of his first acts as head of KWS, took a public stand in favor of a proposal, then being considered by over one hundred nations, to list the African elephant as an endangered species. (Kenya's elephant problem was actually part of a broader crisis involving all of Africa's elephants, whose numbers had been reduced by more than 50 percent—from 1.3 million to 600,000—from 1979 to 1989.) His efforts, combined with those of many others, paid off in October 1989, when a majority of those countries endorsed the proposal, which made all international trade in elephant products illegal. As Leakey and many other conservationists had predicted, the ban, which went into effect in early 1990, led to a precipitous decline in the price of ivory, which in turn made poaching an unattractive enterprise throughout Africa and helped eliminate the problem in Kenya.

Leakey's other accomplishments at KWS include raising some $150 million from Western governments and donor organizations to support wildlife conservation in Kenya; increasing park entrance fees; and setting aside some of the agency's funds for community development projects. (He carried on with those efforts even after he lost the lower half of both legs in a 1993 plane crash.) The community development initiative was aimed at easing the competition between people and wild animals over access to land. If monies earned from tourism could be shared with the locals, Leakey and other conservationists reasoned, they would have more of an incentive to help protect Kenya's wildlife. "We've reckoned that only 30 percent of our wildlife is inside the national parks. Seventy percent is outside," he told Schick in January 1994, shortly before he resigned from the agency. "This land is under private ownership, and there's lots of animals all over it. . . . And in fact the animals are destroying their crops, killing their cattle, killing their people, and the people are getting nothing back. . . . That's why we're experimenting with all sorts of landowner rights over wildlife and community projects and sharing revenue, building schools, and so on."

Several powerful members of Kenya's parliament disagreed with Leakey's handling of the issue; instead, they wanted the KWS to allocate funds directly to the county councils, which would then distribute the resources themselves. Leakey would not hear of it, on the grounds that the money would end up paying government salaries and not benefiting the community. Although he retained the support of many Western conservationists and prominent Kenyan political leaders, he became the object of increasingly bitter attacks by his opponents. In response, he submitted his resignation in January 1994. President Moi refused to accept it, but in March, amid increasingly heated criticism of his leadership, Leakey resigned from KWS for good.

Based on what he learned during his years at KWS, Leakey has a message for Westerners, especially those who believe humans have a responsibility to preserve Earth's wild creatures. In his view, the West cannot expect Third World governments, many of which are so poor they can scarcely provide their citizens with adequate health care, education, and other basic services, to commit large amounts of money to wildlife conservation. "The one thing that's clear is that the Third World doesn't have any money . . . ," he said during a lecture at the American Museum of Natural History in May 1994. "It's no good saying that they've got to do the job themselves since they're the ultimate beneficiaries. They can't." The solution, he suggests, is that concerned citizens of the wealthier countries of the industrialized world must take an active role in the preservation of wild creatures.

Leakey has drawn much the same conclusion from what he has learned about the history of life, as revealed by the fossil record. "Five times in the distant past," he was quoted as saying in the *Chicago Tribune* article, "life on Earth went through what paleontologists call the 'great extinctions,' when, because of climatic changes, volcanic eruptions or other natural disasters, great numbers of species died out. Now we're in the midst of a sixth extinction, when the number of living species may be reduced by as much as 50 percent. This time it's happening simply because human populations are expanding so rapidly that the natural habitat of other species is being destroyed." Although Leakey believes that Earth will survive modern man's negligence, he does not believe that humans are therefore absolved of responsibility for preserving its flora and fauna. "Our greater intellect may confer on us an enhanced ability to exploit the natural resources of the world," he wrote in *Origins Reconsidered*. "But—and I feel this very strongly—it also lays on us an enhanced responsibility to husband those resources carefully, to be sensitive to the knowledge that a species, once extinct, is destroyed forever. By impoverishing the environment, we impoverish our own lives, in this short-term tenancy we have on planet Earth."

Soon after leaving KWS, Leakey said he hoped to relax a bit and to do more writing for popular audiences, and he vowed not to take on another administrative post. Yet in May 1995 he took on a new challenge that is unlikely to provide him with much opportunity for relaxation: he and several prominent members of Kenya's political opposition established a new political party, Safina, with the aim of "cleaning up" Kenya's corrupt, and increasingly repressive, political establishment. Shortly after the creation of the party, about one hundred armed Masai tribesmen arrived at Leakey's home outside Nairobi, which was unoccupied at the time, and demanded that he leave the country.

Richard Leakey has been married since 1971 to the former Meave Epps, a zoologist who completed her doctorate with Louis Leakey and went on to become a key member of Richard's team of scientists at Lake Turkana. (His first marriage, to Margaret Cropper, who had been Mary Leakey's assistant at Olduvai, ended in divorce.) They have three daughters, Anna, Louise, and Samira.

Selected Biographical References: Chicago Tribune V p1+ N 20 '92 pors; N Y Times Mag p28+ Ja 7 '90 pors; Time 110:64+ N 7 '77 pors, 142:51 Jl 19 '93 por; U S News & World Report 107:58+ O 2 '89 pors; World & I 9:206+ Ag '94 pors; Who's Who, 1995

Lee Kuan Yew

(lee kwahn yoo)

Sept. 16, 1923– Senior minister of Singapore; lawyer. Address: Istana Annexe, Istana, Singapore 0923

NOTE: This biography supersedes the article that appeared in *Current Biography* in 1959.

"Singapore today is the house that Lee built," the foreign correspondent Lewis M. Simons wrote in the *Atlantic* in 1991. Simons was referring to Lee Kuan Yew, the chief architect of the remarkable transformation of Singapore, a small island with virtually no natural resources, from an impoverished British colony plagued by racial friction and unemployment into a thriving, politically and socially stable city-state that boasts a strong industrial base, the world's second-busiest harbor, nearly full employment, and the third-highest per capita income in Asia. Lee served as Singapore's prime

Tommy Cheng/Agence France Presse

Lee Kuan Yew

minister for thirty-one years, from 1959 until his voluntary resignation, in 1990. He then became the senior minister, a position in which he has continued to wield substantial power. Considered to be one of the world's most adept politicians and reputed to be completely incorruptible, he headed the People's Action Party (PAP), Singapore's ruling political party for thirty-eight years, from its founding, in 1954, until 1992. "I make no apologies that the PAP is the government and the government is the PAP," he was quoted as saying in *Singapore: The Legacy of Lee Kuan Yew* (1990), by R. S. Milne and Diane K. Mauzy. Invoking the names of towering British statesmen, the former American president Richard Nixon once expressed the view that in a different era, Lee might have "attained the stature of a [Winston] Churchill, a [Benjamin] Disraeli, or a [William Ewart] Gladstone."

A highly controversial figure, Lee Kuan Yew began his political career as a Socialist and anticolonialist. Even after adopting a conservative political outlook, he remained enamored of aggressive social engineering. In creating "an oasis of ordered cleanliness," as a writer for the *Economist* (November 22, 1986) called Singapore—a place where slums, begging, vandalism, littering, and disorderly conduct have all but disappeared and where governmental services are performed with breathtaking efficiency—he also established a society that many Western observers have described as excessively regimented and totalitarian in atmosphere. Determined to silence dissent, as prime minister he suppressed his political opponents, reined in the press, hobbled the trade-union movement, and abolished the jury system, among other actions. He has steadfastly rejected many arguments for individualism and democracy and insisted on the necessity of maintaining traditional values and strict order in Singapore's multiethnic society. "I say without the slightest remorse," he told Singaporeans during a televised speech in 1986, "that we . . . would not have made the economic progress if we had not intervened on very personal matters—who your neighbor is, how you live, the noise you make, how you spit (or where you spit), or what language you use. . . . It was fundamental social and cultural changes that brought us here." In a *New Yorker* (January 1, 1992) profile of him, Stan Sesser declared, "Lee has put his stamp on Singapore to an extent that few political leaders anywhere in the world have ever matched."

Lee Kuan Yew (his name sometimes appears as Lee Kwan Yew) was born in Singapore on September 16, 1923. Longstanding residents of the city, the Lee family were of Chinese origin. Lee's father, Lee Chin Koon, worked as a depot superintendent for the Shell Oil Company, and his mother, Chua Jim Neo, was a well-known cooking teacher. After completing his primary-school education, in classes conducted in English, Lee enrolled at Raffles Institution, a preparatory school, from which he graduated in 1939. With the outbreak of World War II, he abandoned his plans to continue his studies in England and instead attended Raffles College (which was later renamed the University of Singapore), where he studied economics as well as mathematics and English literature.

The Japanese invasion of Singapore, in 1942, provoked in Lee, as in many of his fellow countrymen, a nationalist response. Although he became proficient in Japanese and worked as a translator for the official news agency, he was later quoted as saying, "We decided that from then on our lives should be ours to decide, that we should not be the pawns and playthings of foreign powers." In about 1946 Lee became a law student at Fitzwilliam College, Cambridge University, in England, where he earned a "double first" and led the honors list. In a speech that he gave in 1956, Lee said that his education at Cambridge had been designed to make him "an educated man—the equal of any Englishman—the model of perfection!" But by the time he graduated, he felt that "the whole set of values was wrong, fundamentally and radically wrong."

In 1950, after being admitted to the British bar, Lee returned to Singapore. With his wife, whom he had met at Cambridge, he set up the law firm of Lee and Lee. Nominally a Socialist but by no means a Communist, he became associated with Singapore's labor-union movement, as a lawyer representing more than one hundred trade unions. In 1952 he helped the postal workers' union win an important strike, and he subsequently defended *Fajar*, a student newspaper that had been prosecuted under sedition laws, in a celebrated trial in which he passionately argued for the right of freedom of expression. By the mid-1950s he had become a well-known left-wing, nationalist figure and had secured for himself a position in the vanguard of the anticolonialist movement.

In 1954 Great Britain, which had reoccupied Singapore in 1945, granted the colony a constitution and offered plans by which the partially enfranchised citizenry would elect a head of government. Later that year Lee helped to found the People's Action Party, which was initially a left-wing, populist organization, and he was named the PAP's secretary general. In 1955 he won election to the legislative assembly as the candidate from Tanjong Pagar, a district with a large population of poor people, after campaigning in English (he had begun studying Mandarin but was not yet fluent; he later also learned to speak Malay) on a platform that called for Singaporean self-rule. By adopting during the campaign a strategy that projected the PAP as a revolutionary party, he had solidified his support with students and trade unionists. To reach the goal of self-rule, after his election Lee collaborated with Singapore's Communists.

During the next several years, Lee consolidated his position as leader of the PAP and gained control of the party's central executive committee. According to an article by Claudia Rosett in the *Wall Street Journal* (November 7, 1990), within a short time he succeeded in purging the PAP of Communist members, by resorting to Communist tactics: he instituted a "Leninist cell system," whereby the executive committee would be chosen not by regular party members but by "a select, secret group of 'cadre' members," who "would be appointed by the central committee. No longer could the PAP rank and file call its leaders directly to account." "Essentially the same vehicle" existed three decades later, Rosett wrote: "In other words, Mr. Lee appoints the cadres, and they elect Mr. Lee." Stan Sesser quoted Chan Heng Chee, a leading Singaporean political scientist who has served as Singapore's ambassador to the UN, as saying that "Singapore is the world's only example of forming a united front with the Communists and defeating them."

In 1959 Great Britain ended its occupation of Singapore, while retaining control of its defense and foreign affairs. Campaigning that year in the now self-governing country's general elections, Lee and other PAP candidates continued to use left-wing, anticolonialist rhetoric, and the PAP won forty-three of the fifty-one seats that then constituted the assembly. The British governor Sir William Goode asked Lee to form a government, and on June 5, 1959 he was sworn into office as prime minister. He immediately chose his cabinet (which, with its company of intellectuals, became known as the cabinet of dons) and then announced a five-year plan that called for, among other measures, "the development of industry, . . . a reorganization of city administration, increased liberal and technical education, and the emancipation of women." He also proclaimed the launching of a broad-ranging cleanup campaign in which jukeboxes, pinball machines, and all forms of pornography were banned. In an interview with Nathan Gardels for *New Perspectives Quarterly* (Winter 1992), Lee recalled, "As prime minister of Singapore, my first task was to lift my country out of the degradation that poverty, ignorance, and disease had wrought. Since it was dire poverty that made for such a low priority given to human life, all other things became secondary."

In 1961 Abdul Rahman, called "the Tunku" ("prince"), the leader of Malaya, formally proposed that Singapore join Malaya, North Borneo (now called Sabah), and Sarawak to create the Federation of Malaysia. Lee wholeheartedly supported the plan. In his book *The Battle for Merger* (1961) and in a series of radio talks and in other arenas, he argued that the union would help bring about greater economic prosperity and political stability. (According to Stan Sesser, some Singaporeans suspected that his enthusiasm for the federation stemmed from the idea that he "might someday preside over the Malaysian federation himself.") A referendum was held in 1962, and Singapore joined the Federation of Malaysia in September 1963. As stipulated by the terms of the merger, Lee remained prime minister of the State of Singapore, but final authority over Singapore rested with Abdul Rahman.

Much ambiguity about the nature of the alliance remained after the federation was established. Long negotiations concerning economic, social, and cultural matters degenerated into a feud between Singapore and her partners about such matters as a proposed common market and Singapore's financial contributions to the federation. The conflict intensified when Indonesia severed trade relations with Malaysia, an event that had especially harsh consequences for Singapore; it worsened with the outbreak of race riots between Malays and Chinese in Singapore and came to a head when ten members of the PAP sought seats in the Malaysian parliament in elections held in 1964. "By contesting those seats, we alarmed [Malay politicians]," Lee told Stan Sesser, "because they could see that we could organize and rally not only Chinese but also Indians and Malays in the towns." On August 9, 1965, under pressure from Rahman, Singapore withdrew from the federation. In an emotional televised speech, Lee declared that all his life he had "believed in merger and unity of these two territories . . . its people connected by geography, economics, and ties of kinship," and then, breaking into tears, he requested that the television cameras be turned off.

After the rupture Singapore faced formidable economic problems. "Most factories have cut production drastically," a *Time* (January 7, 1966) article reported. "They are plagued by strike-prone unions [and] face increasingly stiff competition from aggressive and more experienced manufacturers in Hong Kong, Japan, and Formosa [now Taiwan]. Singapore may face insurmountable odds." Those odds worsened after Great Britain announced in 1968 that in the following few years, it intended to withdraw all British defense forces from Singapore and, in the process, close a huge naval base and other facilities that, in total, accounted for what various sources have reported as one-tenth or as much as one-fifth of the island's income.

Undaunted, Lee instituted an aggressive policy designed to entice business from abroad. Having recognized "very early on," according to an article in *Forbes* (June 11, 1990) by former United States secretary of defense Caspar W. Weinberger, that "socialist economics do not work, and that a free-market economy will work if encouraged by a government that knows it can attract capital only if capital knows it will be rewarded," he introduced free-trade policies and industry-friendly legislation, including laws aimed at holding labor unrest in check. He also oversaw major improvements in the nation's infrastructure. In addition, proceeding in the conviction that "a country succeeds" by "pick[ing] winners"—"You concentrate on those items, on those skills, on those products, which will sweep the market," he was quoted as saying in the *Economist* (November 22, 1986)—he promoted industries such as shipping, ship-repairing, shipbuilding, oil-rig construction, printing, and electronics, all of which indeed proved to be winners for Singapore, while avoiding industries that were "vulnerable to regional competition and Western protectionism." (Years later, in 1979, the government put into place a "restructuring program" that was designed to discourage labor-intensive industries while keeping wages high.) By abolishing "many traditional impediments to the movement of capital," as John Quirt noted in the *New York Times* (July 28, 1974), Singapore also became an important center for international finance, and skyscrapers housing the offices of dozens of foreign banks came to replace the city's quaint money-changing stalls.

By 1978 the per capita income in Singapore had grown to about $3,000 per year, a fivefold increase since 1960. According to the 1986 *Economist* article, the gross domestic product (GDP) in Singapore rose in real terms by an average of 9.4 percent annually between 1969 and 1979 and 8.5 percent between 1980 and 1984 despite global recessions and two energy crises. In 1985, in the midst of a recession that gripped nations on the rim of Asia and elsewhere, Singapore experienced an economic downturn after nearly two decades of uninterrupted growth. More than forty thousand jobs were lost before the economy began to recover in mid-1986. By 1989 the GDP per person (the population—currently 2.7 million—of the 210-square-mile main island is about 76 percent Chinese, 15 percent Malay, and 6 percent Indian, with Eurasians constituting most of the remainder) had reached $10,500, a figure topped in Asia only by Japan and the oil-rich kingdom of Brunei.

Meanwhile, early on in his regime, Lee spearheaded a variety of urban reforms. Singapore's vast slums, in which thousands of people had lived in conditions of extreme squalor, were systematically bulldozed and replaced by blocks of uniform apartments equipped with such modern amenities as refrigerators. In 1974 Sydney H. Schanberg reported in the *New York Times* (June 7, 1974) that Singaporeans were "well dressed and well fed" and that most of them "seem[ed] satisfied with their lives." In the early 1980s the United States Department of State estimated, as reported in its publication *Background Notes: Singapore* (May 1990), that the construction industry was responsible for "as much as 30 percent" of the country's total economic growth, through the construction of housing complexes, airports, roads, and port facilities. According to Lewis M. Simons in the *Atlantic* (July 1991), "80 percent of the population are homeowners, thanks to mandatory participation in a superbly invested government fund." Lee also introduced a program of universal health care.

On the political front, the withdrawal of the Socialist opposition from Parliament in 1966 left the PAP as the sole remaining party with legislative representation, and its power increased commensurately. In the 1968 elections the PAP won all fifty-eight seats in Parliament, with fifty-one of their candidates running unopposed. Repeats of that performance, in 1972, 1976, and 1980, while indicative to some extent of the popularity of Lee and the PAP in a period of remarkable growth, serve also as evidence of the government's willingness to curb political dissent. Political prisoners were detained indefinitely, and in 1971 the government shut down two newspapers that voiced opposition to Lee's policies.

At the same time, observers noted that life in Singapore was becoming more and more regimented. "Whichever way Singaporeans turn there is a uniformed organization waiting for them," T. J. S. George reported in his book *Lee Kuan Yew's Singapore* (1973). Citing an array of police units, people's defense corps, vigilante groups, and other patriotic associations, all of which helped to enforce bans on such things as long hair for men and the sale of *Playboy* magazine, George stated, "Together these organizations and activities reinforce the impression of a militant people dedicated to upholding high moralistic and nationalist values." Through the years the government has imposed fines for such infractions as failing to flush public toilets, littering, and smoking in restaurants, government offices, or public conveyances.

In 1982, in another move to ensure that Singapore would remain strong and independent, Lee—who has continually urged his constituency to work hard and eschew moral laxity and excessive materialism—announced plans to revive the study of Confucianism, the ancient Chinese philosophical system of ethical precepts, in the nation's schools. According to an article by Colin Campbell in the *New York Times* (May 20, 1982), Lee's plans had grown out of his belief in the advantages of the tradition of the extended family, in which several generations live under the same roof, and his conviction that the trend toward the nuclear family must be reversed, because with the latter arrangement, in Lee's words, "the survival chain is weakened and a civilized way of life is coarsened." Within a few years Lee also set about improving Singapore's "genetic outlook," by taking steps to discourage poorly educated, low-income mothers from having more than one or two children and by other measures—such as the formation of the Social Development Unit, a government body that in effect runs a dating service—to encourage college-educated women to marry and produce several children.

During the early 1980s signs of social discontent, although mild, began to appear. The PAP won every seat in the legislature in the 1980 elections, but its share of the popular vote declined from a 1968 high of 84.4 percent to 75.5 percent. In a 1981 by-election, the PAP lost a seat in Parliament to the Workers' Party candidate Joshua Benjamin Jeyaretnam, and three years later it lost two seats in Parliament. In 1986 Jeyaretnam was jailed; later, based on a series of technicalities, he was banned from Parliament. Among other actions designed to stifle opposition, Lee's government revoked the right to habeas corpus, forbade political activism by organizations that had not received express government approval, and restricted or banned certain publications, including the widely respected *Far Eastern Economic Review*. In 1987 twenty-two Singaporeans were arrested and charged with being party to a Marxist plot to overthrow the government, accusations widely considered to be as absurd as the detainees' televised confessions. "Long regarded as an authoritarian state," a 1989 report by the human rights organization Asia Watch declared, as quoted by Claudia Rosett, "Singapore has moved in the direction of totalitarianism as it succeeds in dismantling its civil society and the rule of law." All the while, Lee dismissed criticisms of his actions. In a speech that he gave in April 1988 during a visit to the United States, for example, he said, "The American concept of the marketplace of ideas, instead of producing harmonious enlightenment, has, from time to time, led to riots and bloodshed."

In August 1990 Lee Kuan Yew resigned from the position of prime minister of Singapore. He was succeeded by Goh Chok Tong, a longtime cabinet member. Lee became the cabinet's senior minister, a change in title that in fact represented a lateral career move and not a diminution of power. Since then, in addition to his continued immersion in the affairs of Singapore, Lee has taken upon himself the role of international social critic. His sometimes scathing opinions of the United States were the focus of an interview with Fareed Zakaria for what turned into a much-discussed article in *Foreign Affairs* (March/April 1994). After expressing admiration for, in his words, "the free, easy, and open relations between people [in the United States] regardless of social status, ethnicity, or religion" and "a certain openness in argument about what is good or bad for society; the accountability of public officials; none of the secrecy and terror that's part and parcel of Communist government," he said, "As a total system, I find parts of it totally unacceptable: guns, drugs, violent crime, vagrancy, unbecoming behavior in public—in sum the breakdown of civil society."

"The liberal, intellectual tradition that developed after World War II claimed that human beings had arrived at this perfect state where everybody would be better off if they were allowed to do their own thing and flourish," Lee explained to Zakaria. "It has not worked out, and I doubt if it will." In the same interview, he questioned the wisdom of the philosophy of one man, one vote. "I'm convinced . . . that [Singapore] would have a better system if we gave every man over the age of forty who has a family two votes because he's likely to be more careful, voting also for his children. . . . At sixty they should go back to one vote," he added, "but that will be difficult to arrange."

In 1994 the clash between Eastern and Western values was epitomized in the case of Michael Fay, an American teenager living in Singapore, who was sentenced to be caned after confessing to various acts of vandalism, including spray-painting automobiles. Caning is intensely painful, and the imposition of the sentence provoked a storm of protest in the United States. Strong objections from the administration of President Bill Clinton led the Singaporean government to reduce the number of lashes Fay received from six to four. Lee Kuan Yew stoutly defended the use of corporal punishment. "I am an old-style Singaporean who believes that to govern you must have a certain moral authority," he said during an interview for *Time* (May 9, 1994). "If we do not cane [Michael Fay] because he is an American, I believe we'll lose our moral authority and our right to govern."

In another incident that aroused the indignation of many Westerners, Singapore police interrogated Christopher Lingle, an American who had been teaching at the National University of Singapore, about an op-ed article that he wrote for the *International Herald Tribune*, which is owned jointly by the *New York Times* and the *Washington Post*. The article, which appeared in the *Tribune*'s October 7, 1994 issue, criticized what Lingle identified as "Asian states" as being "intolerant regimes" that suppress free speech, censor the media, and rely on "compliant judiciar[ies] to bankrupt opposition politicians." Although the article did not mention Singapore (or any other country) specifically, the police warned Lingle that he might face criminal charges, and he left the country. Despite protests by the Clinton administration, in January 1995 a Singapore judge found Lingle, the *Tribune*, its publisher and editor, and its Singapore printer guilty of contempt of court and ordered them to pay thousands of dollars in fines and court costs. Although the *International Herald Tribune* published two apologies to Lee Kuan Yew, who claimed that he had been defamed by Lingle's assertions, Lee filed libel suits against both Lingle and the newspaper.

When Lewis M. Simons interviewed Lee in 1991, he was "struck by how little he'd aged since [Simons] had first interviewed him, some twenty years earlier." "His hair had turned white, and the pockmarked skin of his craggy face had smoothed out somewhat," Simons wrote. "But his body was as trim and lithe as ever, dominated by a large head and a heavy, overhanging brow. Certainly his verbal combativeness has not diminished." Fareed Zakaria described Lee as being unlike any politician he had ever met—"there were no smiles, no jokes, no bonhomie"—and reported that he has "an inexpressive face but an intense gaze." "The quickness and acuity of Lee's mind are impressive to witness . . . ," Stan Sesser wrote; "several times, as I started to ask [him] a long question, he interrupted after only a few words, and he never failed to deduce just what I was going to say." According to the 1986 *Economist* article, Lee's "many strengths" include "a formidable self-discipline and the ability always to obey his head and not his heart." Notwithstanding his lifelong respiratory allergies, Lee is an avid golfer, jogger, and swimmer. He has received many honorary degrees and awards, among them the Order of Sikatuna, from the Philippines, in 1974, and Most Honorable Order of Crown of Johore (First Class), from Malaysia, in 1984, and he was named an Honorary Freeman, City of London, in 1982.

Lee lives in Singapore, in a house that has been described as modest, with his wife, Kwa Geok Choo, whom he married in 1950. As of 1991 Kwa Geok Choo headed the law firm of Lee and Lee along with Lee Kuan Yew's brother, Dennis. The Lees are the parents of two sons and one daughter and have several grandchildren. Many observers have speculated that their older son, Lee Hsien Loong, a former brigadier general in the Singaporean army who has served as the minister for trade and industry in the nation's cabinet and is currently the deputy prime minister, will someday follow in his father's footsteps and become the prime minister of Singapore.

Selected Biographical References: Atlantic 268:26+ Jl '91 por; Economist 317:19+ O 27 '90; Foreign Affairs 73:109+ Mr/Ap '94; N Y Times p6 Ag 10 '65 por; NY Times Mag p66+ O 31 '65 pors; New Yorker 67:37+ Ja 13 '92; International Who's Who, 1994-95

Claudel Huot/Union des Artistes

Lepage, Robert
(le-PAHZH)

1957- Canadian actor; director; playwright. Address: c/o l'Union des Artistes, 1290 rue St-Denis, Montreal, Quebec, H2X 3J7, Canada

"A sorcerer of the stage," in the opinion of one admiring critic, Robert Lepage has created a theatrical style that transcends the spoken word. His plays and solo performances often feature dialogue in several languages, yet remain accessible to audiences worldwide through the richness of his visual imagery. Acclaimed by reviewers for his fluid staging and stunning use of theatrical metaphor, the Canadian director, who also cowrites, designs, and acts in many of his productions, has become one of the most sought-after artists in theatre. Since making his debut as a director in 1985, he has mounted productions at major international venues, including the Royal National Theatre, in London, where he staged a controversial and highly unorthodox version of Shakespeare's *A Midsummer Night's Dream*, the Edinburgh Festival, and the International Theatre Festival of Chicago.

Known for using an unconventional creative method that relies heavily on input from the actors involved, Lepage develops his productions through a collaborative process that includes days of discussions and improvisational sessions. He explained that process to Karen Fricker in an interview for the *Financial Times* (August 13–14, 1994): "Before we even start to write or explore a show, it exists. It has a subconscious of its own. The actors, in their improvisations, are digging in the piece, and they uncover things—objects, relationships, coincidences, facts. Then we have discussions to figure out how we can connect these things we have discovered with the things we already know. . . . There is no recipe, no series of rules, no theory behind what we do. You cannot put a Shakespeare play and a Tennessee Williams play in the same microwave oven and expect them to be 'done.' How is the meal going to be cooked? We'll have to discover that as we go along."

Robert Lepage was born into a working-class family in Quebec City, in the Canadian province of Quebec, in 1957. His father was a taxi driver; his mother, a homemaker. The four Lepage children exemplify Canada's policy of official bilingualism: Robert and his biological sister are francophones, while an adopted brother and sister count English as their first language. During his childhood, Lepage developed alopecia, a disease that caused him to lose all his hair, including his eyelashes and eyebrows. At least partly because of his illness, he was a painfully shy youngster and suffered periodic bouts of depression. Instead of playing with his schoolmates, he spent most of his free time in solitude, watching soap operas and situation comedies on the television in his parents' bedroom. His interest in visual imagery began when, at the age of twelve, he first saw the multimedia performance artist Laurie Anderson and the musical group Genesis, whose innately theatrical presentations captivated him. Required to take an arts course in order to graduate from his school, Lepage initially chose visual arts, but he soon tired of that subject and switched to music. Finding that he lacked a musician's ear, he changed again, this time to theatre.

After years of sharing his life with fictional television characters, Lepage found companionship in the theatrical community. "What I found was a hiding place much larger and infinitely more exciting than my parents' bedroom," he told Alberto Manguel for *Saturday Night* (January 1989) magazine. "Keeping yourself hidden until the moment you chose to be someone else was ordinary stuff for them. My depression disappeared." Bolstered by his newfound confidence, the fledgling actor won his first role, a bit part in a school production, and made a fortunate discovery: onstage, he never had to feel shy. As he explained to Alberto Manguel, "I realized that . . . if speaking made me uncomfortable, I could use my gestures, if both were not enough I could move, use the space around me, the lights, the props." This revelation prompted Lepage to study drama at the Conservatoire d'Art Dramatique de Québec. Upon graduating from that institution in 1978, he continued his training in Paris, where he studied under the Swiss director Alain Knapp, whose instruction left an indelible mark on the Canadian. Knapp stressed what Lepage has described as a "global" approach to theatre, teaching his students to write and direct as well as act, and encouraging them to rely on intuition and gut instinct rather than intellect.

In 1980 Lepage returned to Quebec City, where he distinguished himself as a player in the Ligue Nationale d'Improvisation, a French-language improvisational league in which teams of actors play off one another. He became one of the league's top performers, winning its most-popular-player trophy. Then, in 1982, he joined an experimental company called Le Théâtre Repère. The young actor was drawn to the troupe because it was using a new creative method called RSVP Cycles, based on research done by Anna and Lawrence Halprin of the San Francisco Dancers' Workshop. Consisting of four steps, known as **r**esources, **s**core, e**v**aluation, and **p**resentation (RSVP), the method is unique in its emphasis on drawing creative inspiration from concrete objects rather than from ideas or themes. Dialogue, sets, costumes, and plots are developed organically through the exploration of a central object or image—the "resource." (In French, the RSVP method translates as *REPÈRE*, which literally translated means landmark, reference, or point of view but which also serves as an acronym for the four steps: *ressources, partition, évaluation*, and *représentation*.) The resource that serves as the genesis for a dramatic work may be something as mundane as a fried egg. "It doesn't matter where you begin," Lepage told Alberto Manguel. "As long as it's not with a theme but with a sign, a resource. . . . Once you find that first resource, that first image, everything falls into place." After participating in the process as an actor, Lepage made his debut as a director, using the *REPÈRE* model to develop a work called *Circulations*.

Embarking on the creative process with a map of the northeastern United States as their principal resource, Lepage and three Théâtre Repère colleagues collectively shaped a work that used the map as a metaphor for two journeys: the actual trip the lead character, Louise, takes from Quebec City to New York and an inner odyssey that involves her coming to terms with an unhappy past. The play's dialogue, which alternates between French and English and is sometimes deliberately distorted by a "vocoder," underlines Louise's increasing sense of isolation and alienation. The work's expressionistic lighting, haunting electronic score, and striking visual effects impressed Canadian critics, among them Matthew Fraser of the Toronto *Globe and Mail*. In his review of March 1, 1985, Fraser commended Lepage for treating audiences to "visual and aural poetry," singling out for special praise a scene in which Lepage and his fellow actor François Beausoleil created an artful trompe l'oeil by showing an episode set in a motel room from two different perspectives. The effect was achieved by turning the lights down for a split-second set change; when the lights came back up, the audience saw what appeared to be the same room, but this time from above, for the actors were "sitting" on chairs laid on their sides on the floor. "The creators of *Circulations* are exceptionally talented artists who are stretching and twisting the language of theatre into bizarre and fascinating shapes," Fraser wrote. Following its run in Toronto, *Circulations* toured Canada, and it was named best Canadian production at the 1984 Quinzaine theatre festival, in Quebec City.

Lepage's next project, *The Dragon's Trilogy*, featured an equally wide array of visual effects and showcased the director's talent for imbuing everyday objects with emotional significance. A parking lot in Quebec City that lies over the razed remains of the city's former Chinese quarter served as the resource for the work, which depicts life in three Canadian Chinatowns—in Toronto, Vancouver, and Quebec City—over a span of approximately seventy years. Lepage had been interested in Quebec's Chinatown for years, having heard numerous stories about it from his mother, who once lived there. With the work's central resource in place, he encouraged the members of his cast to explore virtually any idea they felt might serve as a starting point for the play. Explaining the results to Alberto Manguel, Lepage recounted the experience of one of the actresses, who turned to the I Ching and discovered an image of a water well, which led to associations with digging, both physically and psychologically, that were eventually incorporated into the work.

The Dragon's Trilogy premiered in Quebec City in 1985 as a ninety-minute work, with Lepage and five other actors credited as cowriters. The play, whose dialogue is in English, French, and Chinese, was designed to be performed on a deceptively simple set consisting of a rectangle of sand, a lamppost, and a parking-lot attendant's booth, which under Lepage's direction was magically transformed into a dragon's lair, a stairway, and the cave of the rising sun, among other things.

Buoyed by virtually unanimous praise from the critics, Lepage expanded *The Dragon's Trilogy* to three hours for a highly successful international tour that began at Toronto's World Stage Festival in 1986. In a representative review of that production, Ray Conlogue of the *Globe and Mail* remarked that although the narrative was occasionally weak and slightly contrived, Lepage demonstrated a remarkable ability to turn ordinary objects into evocative theatrical metaphors. In one scene, for example, clerks in a shoe store—suggested by several shoe boxes and a couple of chairs—are unpacking pairs of children's shoes. Suddenly, a soldier on ice skates bursts in and viciously tramples the shoes while the helpless onlookers scream in terror. What had been an unremarkable domestic scene has become a horrific vision of war marked by a level of violence that Conlogue called "overwhelming." "On one level, there is something simpleminded and kitschlike about Lepage's ideas in themselves . . . ," Conlogue wrote. "But then, unexpectedly, the scenes lapse into a lyrical and symbolic mode where they become painfully true and captivating."

In 1986 Lepage also premiered a one-man performance piece, *Vinci*, at the Théâtre de Quat'Sous, in Montreal. The play revolves around a young photographer named Philippe, who sets off on a therapeutic trip to Europe after learning that a close friend has committed suicide. His travels eventually take him to the birthplace of Leonardo da Vinci, where he reflects on the nature of art and the transience of human existence. Like many of Lepage's works, *Vinci* contains narrative elements that stem from his own experience: one of Lepage's friends, a painter, had recently attempted suicide in order to avoid succumbing to what Lepage called "the greed of the commercial world." Matthew Fraser, writing in the Toronto *Globe and Mail* (March 11, 1986), spoke for most of his counterparts when he hailed Lepage's "astonishing" accomplishments. Noting the director's tendency to use a host of gadgets and special effects, including a toy train that circles the stage, Fraser contended that although the work seemed at times to be overly ambitious, Lepage deserved credit for aiming high: "*Vinci* is a fascinating work that is sure to reinforce Lepage's reputation as a theatrical innovator whose work is changing the very language of the stage." A huge hit in Canada, *Vinci*, which Lepage has performed in both English- and French-language versions, was equally popular in France, where it won the 1987 Coup de Pouce prize.

During the late 1980s, Lepage assumed the directorship of the Théâtre Repère, a position that expanded his influence on the Canadian theatrical scene. Internationally, his name was becoming increasingly familiar as a result of various productions of *The Dragon's Trilogy*, which was well-received at the London International Festival of Theatre, the Festival des Francophonies de Limoges, in France, and the 1988 Adelaide Arts Festival, in Australia. An expanded, six-hour version that was performed at the Festival de Théâtre des Ameriques in Montreal in 1987 was awarded the Grand Prix and the Quebec Theatre Critics Association award for best production of the year.

The year 1988 saw Lepage dividing his time among a variety of projects, including playing the role of Pontius Pilate in the critically acclaimed Canadian movie *Jesus of Montreal*, directing a French-language version of Shakespeare's *A Midsummer Night's Dream* at the Théâtre du Nouveau Monde in Montreal, and unveiling two original productions: *Le Polygraphe* (The Lie Detector) and *Tectonic Plates*. The latter, which starred Lepage and other members of Théâtre Repère, was given its world premiere at the World Stage Festival in Toronto. On one level, *Tectonic Plates* is simply a series of interwoven stories about Quebecers traveling around Europe and the United States, but the work also uses shifting geological plates as a metaphor to explore the themes of separation and reconciliation between opposing forces, such as the old world and the new, English and French, love and hate, life and death.

As Lepage related to Nigel Hunt in an interview for the summer 1989 issue of *Drama Review*, the piece was developed from three related resources: tectonic plates, dinner plates ("you could break a plate so it suddenly looks like the continents, fractured like a big puzzle"), and boats ("a continent is a very big boat, a society that floats away"). The production's inventive set, created by the Canadian stage designer Michael Levine, features a stage divided by a swimming pool and, suspended from the ceiling, a sky-blue baby grand piano (one of the stories is about a pianist) and enough chairs and music stands for a small orchestra. During the course of the play, two baby grands on opposite sides of the stage glide silently toward each other and fit seamlessly together, serving as an apt symbol of the cultural links between Europe and North America.

Tectonic Plates opened in Toronto as a work in progress. At the end of a rehearsal the day before the premiere, Lepage still hadn't arrived at a suitable ending for the play. Unperturbed, he told Alberto Manguel, "The show will grow, evolve, progress. It isn't over. It hasn't found its ultimate shape. But that's the point. Theatre is change. . . . This show still has a lot to teach us. And we have a lot to learn." Despite its unfinished state, Canadian critics were enthusiastic about the work. In a typical assessment, Rick Groen of the Toronto *Globe and Mail* (June 7, 1988) commended Lepage's evocative use of symbols and imagery. "[*Tectonic Plates*] is at once intensely thoughtful and brightly playful, provocative and puzzling and paradoxical too. For what seems to be an essentially modern play, a nonlinear piece shy of narrative and short on naturalism, is actually a brave return to drama's deepest roots, an attempt to convey ideas and emotions through theatrical metaphor, through the 'word made tangible.'" *Tectonic Plates* was subsequently performed to great acclaim at the Royal National Theatre's studio space and at a number of other venues. A filmed version was seen on British television in 1992.

Lepage's second premiere in 1988 was the French-language *Le Polygraphe*, which he and his cowriter, the actress Marie Brassard, billed as a "metaphysical detective story." The ninety-minute work, which opened at the Théâtre Quat'Sous in Montreal in November of that year, revolves around three characters—a waiter, a criminologist, and a movie actress—whose lives are mysteriously connected by a murder. Although the events of the play are fictional, they are based on personal experience. In the fall of 1980, after a friend of his was murdered, Lepage was for a short time a suspect in the subsequent criminal investigation, and police detectives subjected him to intense interrogation, positing a series of possible events that could have culminated in Lepage's committing the murder.

Le Polygraphe is Lepage's depiction of the events leading to a crime. Comprised of twenty-five separate sequences, each introduced by a supertitle, the play assumes the form and texture of a film, making use of the theatrical equivalents of a variety of cinematic techniques, such as dissolves and slow-motion sequences. Lepage's role in the work was typically multidimensional: besides collaborating on the writing of the play, he served as its director and set designer and also appeared as a cast member.

Given the enormous popularity of Lepage's earlier efforts, critics and audiences alike had high expectations for *Le Polygraphe*. As Pat Donnelly pointed out in the *Montreal Gazette* (November 18, 1988), "The Quebec City wunderkind director . . . was not only expected to come up with another hit this time around—he was supposed to walk on water." With *Le Polygraphe*, however, Lepage seemed to fall short of achieving miracles. Donnelly's review of the work suggested that the play was marred by technical glitches and imagery that was "worked to death." Nevertheless, Donnelly wrote that the work provided some "ingenious moments in mime and dance heightened by superb lighting effects." When a revised, English-language version of the piece was staged at the Brooklyn Academy of Music, in New York, two years later, Stephen Holden found it to be reminiscent of Michelangelo Antonioni's 1966 mystery film *Blow Up*. "If Lepage is hardly the first director to attempt a synthesis of the vocabulary of film and theatre, his particular blend shows an exceptional visual flair, rhythmic energy, and deftness in the manipulation of symbols . . . ," Holden observed in his *New York Times* review of October 27, 1990. "He also has a special talent for finding symbols that at first seem arbitrary but that through intensive reworking assume an epic richness and significance."

In a departure from his usual practice, Lepage based his next work, *Echo*, on a prose poem: *A Nun's Diary*, by the Canadian writer Ann Diamond. Adapted and directed by Lepage as the first production of Theatre 1774, a repertory company dedicated to bridging the gap between French and English theatre in Quebec, *Echo* revealed the risk inherent in Lepage's creative method, for despite the official opening in Montreal, *Echo* was clearly a work in progress. "The occasional powerful moments seem the hasty work of a director who seems to have thrown several themes in the air, and still doesn't know where they are going to land . . . ," Stephen Godfrey complained in the *Globe and Mail* (November 10, 1989). "*Echo* displays Lepage's talents clearly; too bad it puts so few of them to use."

Returning to his successful one-man show format, Lepage next created a new solo production called *Needles and Opium*. Written, performed, and designed by Lepage, the work explores surrealism, existentialism, jazz, and other cultural developments of the twentieth century through a narrative inspired by the connections he saw between two pathbreaking artists: the French writer and filmmaker Jean Cocteau and the American jazz trumpeter Miles Davis. In researching their lives, Lepage discovered that the two men had much in common beyond their addictions to drugs—Cocteau to opium and Davis to heroin. "This European and this American, one old and the other young, one black and the other white, one who is of the ear and the other of the eye—they represent a way of showing what went on in the century artistically," he explained to Michael Church of the London *Observer* (April 19, 1992). "They *complete* each other on a lot of levels." To broaden the play's appeal, he added a third character, Robert—"a Mr. Everybody," in his words—who is at least partly based on himself. In the show, Lepage played Cocteau and Robert. (Davis was represented by the plangent sound of his trumpet and projected photographs of him and the French singer Juliette Greco, who was his lover at the time the play is set.) Lepage performed most of the work in midair, in a harness suspended from the flies, both to symbolize an airborne Cocteau, en route home to France aboard a transatlantic flight after a sojourn in New York, and to explore the idea of being suspended between two worlds. The harness also facilitated spectacular effects, such as the illusion of freefalling, which was achieved by projecting images of skyscrapers on a screen at the rear of the stage.

Needles and Opium opened in Ottawa in 1991, then traveled to New York City in 1992 as part of the Next Wave Festival at the Brooklyn Academy of Music, where it was cheered by critics. In the *Village Voice* (December 22, 1992), Michael Feingold reserved his highest praise for the show's panoply of effects: "Cleverly juxtaposing slides, film clips, opaque projections, silhouettes, and onstage imagery, [Lepage] builds a world of shadows, suggestions, joyously unnerving dislocations of scale, into which text—his own or quotes from Cocteau's *Lettre aux Américains*—poke like thorns of emotional or intellectual substance. . . . Intelligent art executed this stylishly deserves to be cherished for its sublime playfulness." When Lepage performed the piece at the Royal National Theatre in London, however, Deborah Levy expressed reservations, echoing the concerns of some reviewers that Lepage tends to emphasize form at the expense of content. "He conjures up compelling atmospheres and situations," Levy wrote in *New Statesman and Society* (May 8, 1992), "but they leave us suspended, like his central image, because the controlling idea feels incomplete."

Lepage is perhaps best known for another work he staged at the Royal National Theatre: his controversial 1992 production of Shakespeare's *A Midsummer Night's Dream*. In keeping with his group-oriented creative method, he began rehearsals with a four-day workshop, during which he asked his actors to draw the images that the play inspired in their minds on a large map on the floor. The process yielded an earthy, unusually sensual interpretation mounted in a boldly unconventional setting: a circular pool of mud. (Audience members in the first three rows were handed raincoats to protect themselves against the wet spray that splattered the stage area during performances.)

Critical reaction to the production, which premiered on July 9, 1992, varied widely. Robert Hewison of the London *Sunday Times* raved, "Someone is bound to fulminate against Lepage's Canadian bespattering of our literary heritage. Nonsense. The visual poetry surpasses any music the rhetoric misses. Lepage understands that this is a play about night and dreams. This justifies the extreme conception." Many commentators, Hewison among them, compared the production favorably to Peter Brook's legendary circuslike version for the Royal Shakespeare Company, in 1971. Among those who took exception to Lepage's concept was Paul Taylor of the London *Independent*. Condemning the production's focus on visual effects, Taylor cited a scene in which the significance of a key speech by Theseus is undermined by the onstage antics of several characters who are using chairs as stepping stones to progress across the mud.

In the fall of 1992, Lepage announced he was stepping down as artistic director of French theatre at the National Arts Centre in Ottawa, a post he had held for two years (some sources say three years), to devote more time to his own projects, which at the time, included directing a double bill of one-act operas—Béla Bartók's *Bluebeard's Castle* and Arnold Schoenberg's *Erwartung*—for the Canadian Opera Company. After an initial run in Toronto, the productions moved to the Brooklyn Academy of Music, where they garnered mixed reviews. Edward Rothstein of the *New York Times* (February 12, 1993) found "something dutiful and submissive" in both presentations, noting that some visual effects, such as a slow-motion sequence in *Erwartung* in which a hand emerged from a wall to grab its victim, bordered on "cinematic cliché." Peter Goodman, writing in *New York Newsday* (February 12, 1993), gave the double bill a positive review, calling it "fresh, enlightening, and seductive" and crediting Lepage with connecting the two works in "ways that the composers themselves could never have intended, yet which make for a persuasive evening of music-theatre." Later in 1993 the operas were remounted at the Edinburgh Festival, where they won the Critics Award and the coveted Scotsman Hamada Festival Prize.

Other projects Lepage undertook in 1993 included designing a high-tech stage show for the rock musician Peter Gabriel and directing productions of Shakespeare's *Macbeth*, *The Tempest*, and *Coriolanus* in French translation. In the following year, he offered an abbreviated version of his most recent major work, *The Seven Streams of the River Ota*, at the Edinburgh Festival. Ultimately intended to run seven hours, the play, which Lepage has described as being an exploration of "sex and death," spans several decades and continents and makes reference to Nazi concentration camps, postwar Japan, 1960s Paris, and 1970s New York, among other things. Reviewers who attended the world premiere at the Edinburgh Festival were generally unimpressed, although a few, among them the critic for the *Guardian*, felt that it might yet develop into "something remarkable."

From the beginning of his career, Lepage has maintained strict control over his public image. He grants few interviews, and broadcasters have been bound by contract to erase the videotapes of conversations with him after they have been aired. "Lepage concedes that records of his work are rare, and he seems to like it that way," Christopher Winston observed in *Shift* (Summer 1994). "His generous and calm manner doesn't suggest that he is an obsessive egomaniac. Perhaps he simply prefers to have his work exist only on the stage."

Although he is reluctant to discuss his personal life, Lepage appears to enjoy talking about his work with interviewers. A serene, self-assured man with a pale complexion and brown eyes, he was described by Matt Wolf, who interviewed him for the *New York Times* (December 6, 1992), as "more boyish-looking than he appears onstage, his aspect softened by a noticeable absence of facial hair." He usually wears a wig in public. Future projects Lepage has mentioned to reporters include the completion and release of his first feature film, *Le Confessional*, which he shot on location in Quebec City and Montreal during the summer of 1994, a production for the 1996 Olympic Games, in Atlanta, and a theme park in Barcelona, Spain, on which he is collaborating with Peter Gabriel, Laurie Anderson, and the music producer Brian Eno. Among his many honors and distinctions is the 1994 Governor General's Performing Arts Award, Canada's most prestigious performance prize.

Selected Biographical References: London Observer p52 Ap 19 '92 por; Maclean's 101:53 My 23 '88 por; Saturday Night p33+ Ja '89 pors; Toronto Globe and Mail C p1 N 4 '89 por

---

Ingrid Von Kruse/HarperCollins

Lessing, Doris

Oct. 22, 1919- British writer. Address: c/o Jonathan Clowes Ltd., Iron Bridge House, Bridge Approach, London NW1 8BD, England

NOTE: This biography supersedes the article that appeared in *Current Biography* in 1976.

"Every novel is a story, but a life isn't one, more of a sprawl of incidents," the British writer Doris Lessing wrote in *Under My Skin: Volume One of My Autobiography, to 1949* (1994). Yet the incidents that have formed Lessing's life, which began in the Middle East just after World War I and continued in southern Africa, where she lived from 1924 to 1949 before moving to England, have been shaped by her into the carefully structured narratives of her short stories, the five Children of Violence novels featuring Martha Quest, her masterpiece *The Golden Notebook*, and her forays into "inner space fiction" and science fiction. Her themes have ranged from racial injustice, sexual oppression, and the nature of political power to the interior journey toward self-understanding that few dare to push to the spiritual limits. In an essay for *World Authors 1950-1970*, Lessing wrote, "Yeats said that a writer must work a way inwards, into self-knowledge. I am always surprised at what I find in myself, and this to me is the most rewarding part of being a writer."

Doris Lessing was born Doris May Tayler on October 22, 1919 in Kermanshah (now Bakhtaran), an ancient trading town in what was then known as Persia and is now called Iran. Her father was Alfred Cook Tayler, a former captain in the British army who had lost a leg during World War I, and her mother was Emily Maude (McVeagh) Tayler, a former nurse of Irish and Scottish descent whose "great love," a doctor, had drowned during the war, while she was nursing Captain Tayler back to health. Doris was not yet two years old when her brother, Harry, was born. A few months later the family moved to the capital city of Tehran, where Alfred Tayler worked as a manager for the Imperial Bank of Persia.

"I was a terribly damaged child, terribly neurotic, over-sensitive, over-suffering," Lessing said, in describing her early years in an interview with Michele Field for *Publishers Weekly* (September 19, 1994). "I could say that my mother loved my brother and she didn't love me—but that's very common, isn't it? I do think it had more to do with my father and his perpetual talk of the war." In her autobiography, Lessing recalled, "I used to feel there was something like a dark gray cloud, like poison gas, over my early childhood. Later I found people who had the same experience. Perhaps, it was from that war that I first felt the struggling panicky need to escape, with a nervous aversion to where I have just stood, as if something there might blow up or drag me down by the heel." One of Lessing's methods of coping with that feeling seems to have been her adoption of the temperament of the fictional character that gave her her nickname—Tigger, from A. A. Milne's Winnie-the-Pooh stories. As she recalled in *Under My Skin*, "This personality was expected to be brash, jokey, clumsy, and always ready to be a good sport, that is, to laugh at herself, apologize, clown, confess inability." She did not shed the serviceable yet ultimately disagreeable moniker, conferred when she was eight, until she was thirty.

In 1924, after two years in Tehran, the Taylers became, according to Lessing, the first foreign family to travel around the newly formed Soviet Union, where the ravages of the recent civil war following the revolution were everywhere in evidence. They eventually made their way to England, and it was during their stay there that Alfred Tayler, beguiled by the promises of the Empire Exhibition of 1924, decided to settle in the district of Lomagundi in the northeastern part of Southern Rhodesia (now Zimbabwe). His plan was to grow rich by farming maize and then tobacco and also by prospecting for gold, but prosperity perpetually eluded the Taylers, who lived in a mud-and-thatch house in which they slept under mosquito netting to keep out multifarious marauding insects. During her childhood, Lessing suffered from malaria, dysentery, and measles, among other diseases that could be life-threatening in the days before antibiotics. But all her senses were fully alive on the farm, where, in the surrounding bush, she found the solitude she needed for peace of mind, enjoying a freedom of movement and a feeling of safety that, she has noted, would be impossible today, in Africa or anywhere else. With the assiduous attention to detail of an archaeologist or a historian, Lessing attempted to recreate in her autobiography the lush sounds and sights of the irrevocably lost wilderness of her childhood.

Having received her early education at home from her mother, in 1927 Lessing was sent to board at the Roman Catholic Convent School in the capital city, Salisbury (now Harare). After four seemingly interminable years under the nuns' strict instruction, she was removed from the school but not before she had, at the age of ten, converted briefly but passionately to Roman Catholicism. Her faith was destroyed when her mother, a Protestant, told her of the crimes of the Inquisition. "I was listening, full of cold loathing for what I saw as illogic masquerading as virtue," she recalled in *Under My Skin*. "I lost religion in a breath; Heaven fled from me on the wings of Reason, when I said that everything she said was true of the Protestants, who had burned Catholics at the stake, just as Catholics had burned Protestants." Lessing has remained an atheist ever since, without necessarily relinquishing her respect for the potency of religion and mysticism to some individuals and among various groups of people.

After a year as a boarding student at the Girls' High School, Lessing dropped out at the age of fourteen, claiming that her vision had been impaired by pinkeye, even though a doctor had pronounced her recovery complete. In between visits home and short stays with friends of the family in Umtali, Johannesburg, and Salisbury, where she held various jobs—working in a dress shop, writing advertising jingles for a furniture store, and serving as a nursemaid—Lessing read classic literature voraciously, including works by Virginia Woolf, Olive Schreiner, Marcel Proust, Thomas Mann, D. H. Lawrence, Tolstoy, Dostoyevsky, Chekhov, and Turgenev. Meanwhile, she sold two short stories to a South African magazine, works she has since dismissed because they were "written to suit a market," as she put it in *Under My Skin*. Back on the family farm by 1937, she wrote, in her words, two "bad apprentice novels" that she tore up, but she continued writing short stories. Returning to Salisbury, she worked for a year as a telephone operator. "It suited me very well," she wrote in her autobiography, recalling the disapproval that usually greeted news of her having performed such putatively unsuitable work. "For one thing," she continued, "I understand absolutely why women, asked why they put up with boring and repetitive work, go on with it, saying, But it allows me to think my own thoughts."

When she was in her late teens, Lessing dreamed of going to London, but she did not have enough money for the journey. Leading an active social life in Salisbury, she often went drinking and dancing, and she came to know a wide variety of people. At around that time she was introduced to members of the Left Book Club. "Their unlikability postponed my involvement with the Left for four years," she recalled in her autobiography, citing in particular the way the women "demeaned and diminished their children, talking in front of them, as nuisances, as burdens—unwanted." On April 6, 1939 she married Frank Charles Wisdom, a thirty-year-old civil servant with whom she had a son, John, in 1942 and, about a year later, a daughter, Jean.

In 1942 Lessing ran into a former member of the Left Book Club who told her that some "revolutionaries" had been wanting to meet her. She began spending time with a group of Royal Air Force pilots and European refugees who had, as she explained in her autobiography, become Communists as a result of cynicism, idealism, an affinity for conspiracy theories, or intoxication with the potential for heroism or martyrdom, among other reasons. "In my case," Lessing explained, "it was because for the first time in my life I was meeting a group of people (not an isolated individual here and there) who read everything, and who did not think it remarkable to read, and among whom thoughts about the Native Problem I had scarcely dared to say aloud turned out to be mere commonplaces. I became a Communist because of the spirit of the times, because of the *Zeitgeist*." Having started out with the intention of infiltrating low-level governmental organizations, the cadres soon found themselves involved primarily in social work.

Frequently faced with incredulity when she has tried to explain to members of younger generations the attraction communism held for her, Lessing observed in *Under My Skin*, "Facts are easy. It is the atmospheres that made them possible that are elusive." Thus she believes that her novels are more useful than nonfiction or interviews in conveying the truth of the times. (A Communist from 1942 to 1944 in emotional or ideological terms, Lessing did not formally join the Communist Party until 1951; she drifted away within a few years, but it was not until the 1960s that she "ceased to feel residual tugs of loyalty," in her words.)

Lessing's newfound camaraderie with the Left necessarily excluded her civil servant husband, whom she divorced in 1943, leaving her two young children in their father's custody. Later in the same year, Lessing, who was then working as a typist in a law firm, married Gottfried Anton Nicolai Lessing, a German Communist who had joined the same firm. Although they were not in love, they were the only members of her left-wing group who were unattached, and they began to have an affair. "It was my revolutionary duty to marry him," Lessing has written, explaining that the exposure of her affair with an "enemy alien" during World War II would have landed him in an internment camp. Having married with the intention of getting an amicable divorce after the war, they had one son, Peter, in 1946, whom Lessing ended up having to raise alone, because her husband moved to East Germany. Years later, she discovered that Gottfried Lessing may have been a KGB agent; he was killed in 1979, during the overthrow of Idi Amin, while trying to flee Kampala, Uganda, where he had been serving as the East German ambassador.

When World War II ended, in 1945, there were so many people in Southern Rhodesia and South Africa who were trying to obtain passage to England that the colonial bureaucracy was clogged for years. Lessing herself had to wait until the end of 1948; she has since described that period as "certainly the worst time in [her] life." She sought solace in reading poetry, composing verses in her head, and writing (and selling) short stories. She also took lessons in Afrikaans. Finally, in 1949 she moved to England with her son Peter, regained her British citizenship (which she had lost upon her second marriage), obtained a divorce from Gottfried Lessing, and began immediately to earn her living as a professional writer.

Whereas many an aspiring writer would have been daunted by the difficulty of getting established in the literary world, especially while caring for a small child, Lessing was not. "If you're not thinking that a particular situation is an obstacle, then it isn't," she told Dana Micucci of the *Chicago Tribune* (January 3, 1993). "It depends on how you look at things. Suppose you don't expect anything to be easy? I never did. I had sticking power, which is just as important as literary talent. I just got on with the work. And I think there are such things as writing animals. I simply have to write." In an interview with Roy Newquist for the book *Counterpoint* (1964), she noted further that it was "easier to be a writer in England than in America because there is much less pressure." "We are not expected to be successful," she explained, "and it is no sin to be poor." Moreover, she has said that having to raise a child was a blessing, in that her responsibility prevented her from falling into a dissolute, bohemian lifestyle. She treated her early years in London with ironic humor in the nonfiction book *In Pursuit of the English* (1960), which was adapted for the stage in 1990.

Lessing had arrived in London armed with an almost fatalistic optimism and the manuscript that would become *The Grass Is Singing*. None of her friends in Africa had liked the story, a study of the nervous breakdown of the English-born wife of a white farmer in Southern Rhodesia and her obsessive sexual relationship with her African house servant (who eventually murders her), mainly because it "did not give a hopeful picture of race relations," as Lessing recalled in *Under My Skin*. A British literary agent bought the manuscript and sold it to the publisher Michael Joseph, which printed it in 1950. *The Grass Is Singing*, which was highly praised for its psychological depth and maturity, has since become one of Lessing's most enduring novels. It was adapted for the screen in 1981.

Like *The Grass Is Singing*, many of Lessing's stories, especially those set in Africa, have been perceived—erroneously, according to Lessing—by critics to be solely about racism. "Color prejudice is not our original fault, but only one aspect of the atrophy of the imagination that prevents us from seeing ourselves in every creature that breathes under the sun," she has explained, as quoted by Michael Thorpe in *British Writers Supplement I* (1987). Thorpe suggested that "where Lessing does write explicitly of the 'color problem,' what interests her most is not the crass exercise of white power, but the complex predicament of the 'good' white. . . . Together, *The Grass Is Singing* and *African Stories* [1964; reprinted in two volumes in 1973] provide a complex inner portrait of an anachronistic society, which has failed to adjust to the pace of change; they make us see and feel that it consists of people little different from ourselves, who demand understanding, even sympathy, as well as judgment."

During the ensuing decades Lessing interspersed the publication of novels, among them *Retreat to Innocence* (1956)—the only novel that Lessing has refused to allow to be reprinted, according to Claire Sprague's essay for the *Explicator* (Spring 1992)—with short-story collections, nonfiction monographs or essay collections, and the occasional play (*Play with a Tiger*, 1962) or volume of poetry (*Fourteen Poems*, 1959). Her short stories and novellas have been collected in *This Was the Old Chief's Country* (1951), *Five: Short Novels* (1953), *The Habit of Loving* (1957), *A Man and Two Women* (1963), *African Stories*, *The Temptation of Jack Orkney and Other Stories* (1972), and *Stories* (1978), among other volumes. Many of the stories appear in more than one collection. *The Doris Lessing Reader* (1989) contains stories, essays, and excerpts from novels selected by the author. Reviewing *The Real Thing: Stories and Sketches* (1992), a collection of eighteen fictional and nonfictional pieces about London, Carolyn See wrote in *New York Newsday* (June 9, 1992), "These new stories are written with age in mind—that time, as E. M. Forster said about his own *Howards End*, when the people we know (and love, and hate) become less important, somehow, than the places we inhabit, the landscape in which we abide, the feel of life itself."

While the significance of place has infused Lessing's fiction from the beginning of her career, the subject has also imbued her nonfiction with a poignancy more often found in other genres, as when she wrote in *Going Home* (1957), a description of her first visit, in 1956, to Southern Rhodesia since she settled in England: "The fact is, I don't live anywhere; I never have since I left that first home on the kopje." After she returned to England, she was banned by the white government of Southern Rhodesia as a "prohibited immigrant" because of her political views. Lessing was unable to revisit what had become Zimbabwe until the ban was lifted in 1980, after white-minority rule was ended following a ten-year civil war. In *African Laughter: Four Visits to Zimbabwe* (1992), she lamented the loss of wildlife and the devastation of the natural beauty that had so enriched her childhood and decried the insularity of the paranoid white community, whose members talked incessantly about "taking the gap," that is, fleeing to South Africa, then still ruled by the white minority under the system of apartheid. The bitterness Lessing perceived among the population during the first of her four visits to Zimbabwe, in 1982, had given way to exhilaration and hope when she returned to the country in 1988, but Zimbabweans' euphoria was short-lived, as she observed during her subsequent trips, in 1989 and 1992.

Reflecting on the lost Africa of her youth, whether in *Going Home*, *African Laughter*, or *Under My Skin*, Lessing was able, with the benefit of hindsight and an extraordinarily keen memory, to limn the lives of white settlers in Southern Rhodesia with an acuity shared by few other chroniclers of that society. But as a novelist in the realist tradition of George Eliot and Joseph Conrad, she proved capable of imparting an even greater sense of "being there," as she told *Publishers Weekly*'s Michele Field: "I think autobiographical *novels* are truer than autobiography, even if half the novel is untrue. *Martha Quest*, which is full of made-up characters and invented situations, in fact gives the flavor of that time much more than *Under My Skin*. I am too old now to put all that violent emotion in it."

The first volume of the Children of Violence quintet, *Martha Quest* (1952) takes the eponymous heroine, a white farmer's daughter born at the end of World War I in Africa, up to the time of her marriage, which is described in *A Proper Marriage* (1954). The third novel in the series, *A Ripple from the Storm* (1958), which took its title from the Soviet novelist Ilya Ehrenburg's epic about World War II, concerns Martha's involvement with communism. Dealing with the claustrophobic limitations of the provincial white society from which Martha yearns to escape, *Landlocked* (1965) explores telepathy, ESP, and Sufism as possible responses to the problems of the world. The apocalyptic final installation in the series, *The Four-Gated City* (1969), is one of Lessing's most ambitious novels. Set in London, the novel finds Martha embarking on a search for self-understanding while simultaneously trying to enlarge her awareness of her responsibilities to the collective. The book ends with the destruction of the earth. "Not since Virginia Woolf," Michael Thorpe observed, "has an English novelist explored so thoroughly the labyrinth of the strained sensitive mind or pleaded so strongly for a more enlightened science of the mind than a dogmatic psychiatry provides."

According to most critics, *The Golden Notebook* (1962) remains Lessing's major achievement. A complex novel of ideas about freedom and responsibility, breakdown and wholeness, the book was taken up as a battle cry for feminism, to the initial consternation of the author. In her preface to the 1972 edition, she explained that her central theme was the self-healing properties of what used to be called a nervous breakdown. Lessing at first thought that the book was a failure because readers inevitably became overemotional in ways she had not anticipated. A manifesto to feminists, *The Golden Notebook* was seen by others as a treatise on politics or mental illness. As she explained in her preface, Lessing ultimately concluded that such "misunderstandings" were productive: "The book is alive and potent and fructifying and able to promote thought and discussion *only* when its plan and shape and intention are not understood, because that moment of seeing the shape and plan and intention is also the moment when there isn't anything more to be got out of it."

Delving further into the realm of what she has called "inner space fiction," Lessing explored the implications of mental breakdown for self-understanding and for societal chaos in *Briefing for a Descent into Hell* (1971), in which she questioned the traditional meanings of "sanity" and "normality," building on or sharing the ideas of Carl Jung, Michel Foucault, and R. D. Laing, as Michael Thorpe pointed out. In *The Summer Before the Dark* (1973), Lessing placed the search for identity through painful "rebirth" in the context of the midlife crisis of a woman who had allowed herself to be defined solely by her roles as wife and mother. The plot of *The Memoirs of a Survivor* (1975), the manuscript for which was subtitled "An Attempt at an Autobiography," was described by Lessing in *Under My Skin* as "a middle-aged person—the sex does not matter—observ[ing] a young self grow up" in a world of disintegrating values.

From 1979 to 1983 Lessing disappointed some fans by abandoning realism for the "space fiction" of the Canopus in Argos: Archives series, the first installment of which was *Re: Colonized Planet 5-Shikasta* (1979), in which she set forth a thirty-thousand-year vision of the struggle between good and evil as played out among outer-space empires, planets, and civilizations, with strong parallels to modern world history. Less a sequel than a novel-sized digression, *The Marriages Between Zones Three, Four, and Five* (1980) explores the masculine/feminine dualism at the heart of many power struggles. The themes of the first two archives were further developed in *The Sirian Experiments* (1981), *The Making of the Representative for Planet Eight* (1982), which served as the basis for her libretto for Philip Glass's opera of the same name in 1988, and *Documents Relating to the Sentimental Agents in the Volyen Empire* (1983), a political satire.

In a somewhat mischievous yet successful attempt to expose the obstacles facing new writers, including the prejudice among critics against unknown authors, Lessing wrote *The Diary of a Good Neighbor* (1983) and *If the Old Could. . . .* (1984) under the pseudonym Jane Somers. The books were accepted by three European publishers but sold fewer than 3,000 copies each in United States, where they went largely unreviewed until the author's identity was revealed. "It was terribly entertaining," Lessing told Michele Field. "I thoroughly enjoyed every minute of it." The two books were subsequently published together, under Lessing's name, as *The Diaries of Jane Somers* (1984).

Although they generally welcomed Lessing's return to realism in the mid-1980s, many critics faulted *The Good Terrorist* (1985), about a seemingly ordinary woman involved with a group of would-be terrorists, for what they considered to be its lifeless prose and underdeveloped characters. In Lessing's most recent novel, *The Fifth Child* (1988), a happy family of six is destroyed by the birth of a veritable monster—more a preternaturally strong and ill-tempered troll than a baby—they can't control. "*The Fifth Child* confidently bends the conventions of realism in order to persuade us to cross over into domains beyond realism," Catharine R. Stimpson wrote in *Ms.* (March 1988); "to notice the 'not us' that we blindly wish were like us; to engage with the possibility of the presences of creatures different from us."

Among Lessing's nonfiction works are *Prisons We Choose to Live Inside* (1986), a collection of lectures; *The Wind Blows Away Our Words* (1987), an appeal for the cause of Afghan refugees, which was roundly criticized for numerous factual errors but praised for its courage and sense of outrage; and *Particularly Cats . . . and Rufus* (1991), a reissue of a 1966 volume. Lessing is the recipient of an Austrian State Prize for European Literature (1981), a Shakespeare Prize (1982), Italy's Grizane Cavour Award (1989), and an honorary doctor of letters from Princeton University (1989), among other honors.

Doris Lessing, who lives in London, is "still very robust," according to Michele Field. "Her voice is higher than expected, but her eyes are stronger and more steely." Lorna Sage reported in the London *Observer* (April 17, 1988) that "in person she's so still and steady of gaze, she makes one twitch and ponder one's neuroses." Lessing was motivated to write her highly praised autobiography when she heard that unauthorized biographies of her were being written by authors unknown to her. For her official biographer, she has chosen Michael Holroyd, the biographer of George Bernard Shaw and Lytton Strachey, among other subjects.

Selected Biographical References: Pub W 241:47+ S 19 '94 por; Contemporary Authors new rev vol 33 (1991); Contemporary Literary Criticism vol 40 (1986); Dictionary of Literary Biography vol 15 (1983); Dictionary of Literary Biography Yrbk: 1985 (1986); Lessing, Doris. A Small Personal Voice: Essays, Reviews, Interviews (1974), African Laughter: Four Visits to Zimbabwe (1992), Under My Skin: Volume One of My Autobiography, to 1949 (1994); Scott lvert, Ian, ed. British Writers Supplement I (1987); Who's Who, 1995; World Authors 1950–1970 (1975)

The Nature Company

Levy, David H.

(LEE-vee)

1948– Amateur astronomer; writer. Address: c/o Plenum Publishing Corp., 233 Spring St., New York, NY 10013

"There is very little in my life that is more personal and more important to me than comets," the amateur astronomer David H. Levy told Terence Dickinson in an interview for *Equinox* (May/June 1994). "Not just discovering them but watching them, learning about them, writing about them, understanding what they do. It makes observing the sky intensely personal. I feel when I find a new comet that a door has been opened and I have seen a slightly new aspect of nature. There is this object in the solar system that—for a few minutes or a few hours—only I know about. It is like trying to pry a secret out of nature. It is a very special feeling."

Ever since he was a child, David Levy has been enthralled by the night sky and the wonders it reveals to dedicated watchmen. He developed a special affection for comets before he reached his teens, though it was not until 1984—after nineteen years and more than nine hundred hours of combing the sky in search of them—that he discovered his first one, from a small observatory that he had built in his backyard. Since then, he has discovered or codiscovered twenty more, making him one of the world's premier comet hunters. His most celebrated find is periodic comet Shoemaker-Levy 9, which he made with the husband-and-wife comet-and-asteroid-hunting team Eugene and Carolyn Shoemaker. The comet's dramatic collision with Jupiter in July 1994, which constituted "the greatest planetary show in recorded history," to quote Malcolm W. Browne of the *New York Times* (July 26, 1994), captivated not only astronomy buffs but the general public as well. Although he is "only" an amateur astronomer—he earns his living by lecturing and writing books and magazine articles on astronomical topics and by working with Project Artist, a Tucson-based project devoted to introducing astronomy to elementary school children—he has won tremendous respect from his credentialed colleagues for his success in tracking down comets. "David Levy is one of those rare individuals blessed with the gift of discovery," David Hartsel, who serves on the board of directors of the Richland Astronomical Society, in Ohio, has said. "Even rarer is his ability to let others share in the excitement and wonder of those discoveries through his writing and lectures."

David H. Levy was born in 1948, in Montreal, Canada, and it was not too long after that that skywatching became his principal avocation. He was just five years old when he talked one of his brothers into showing him the Big Dipper, and a few years later he chose as his subject for a public-speaking project at school the process by which comets are born. His school buddies apparently recognized his interest in the outer reaches of the universe, for when David was about eight, they gave him a book entitled *The Big Book of Stars*. When he was twelve, his cousin presented him with *Our Sun and the Worlds Around It*; it was that book, Levy has recalled, that "convinced [him] that [he] wanted to be an astronomer—or else an author who writes astronomy books." Also at the age of twelve, Levy made his first visit to the Royal Astronomical Society of Canada's Montreal Centre, where he obtained a map of the moon detailing three hundred of its craters and twenty-six of its mountain ranges, among other features. With the map and a three-inch reflecting telescope that his uncle had given him in the same year, Levy practiced identifying the moon's various features—a first step in learning the art of skywatching.

Levy is awed by all of the many celestial objects revealed in the night sky, but none more than comets. This obsession with them began in October 1965, when he caught a glimpse of comet Ikeya-Seki 1965f, an unusually bright one that made a much-anticipated rendezvous with the sun that month. (Comets are named after their discoverer or discoverers—in this case Kaoru Ikeya and Tsutomu Seki—and the year in which they are found; the letters correspond to the order in which comets are discovered in a given year.) Levy recalled the thrill he experienced on sighting it in his book *The Quest for Comets* (1994): "When I awoke on Friday, October 29, the clear sky outside my window sent a chill through me. I dashed downstairs and hopped on my bike, racing toward Summit Park in time to beat the dawn. Completely out of breath, I reached the summit lookout and stopped. The view that morning was splendid. Beyond the expanse of the city lights, beyond the distant St. Lawrence River, a mighty searchlight beam rose out of the southeast like an exclamation mark." That experience prompted him to launch a comet-hunting program of his own.

In a 1970 issue of the *Royal Astronomical Society of Canada*, David Levy wrote: "Comet hunting has attracted the fancies of many, including William Brooks, who, in the late nineteenth century, hunted in his yard with a nine-inch refractor and picked up over twenty comets, Charles Messier, better known for his 'non-comets,' Leslie C. Peltier, who between 1925 and 1954 gathered twelve comets and an assortment of novae, and David H. Levy, who between 1965 and 1970 has found nothing—absolutely nothing." Levy's searches in the following decade similarly failed to bear fruit, though his lack of success was due at least partly to the fact that he was then devoting considerable time to his schoolwork (he attended Acadia University, in Wolfville, Nova Scotia, from 1968 until 1972, when he received his B.A. degree, and Queen's University at Kingston, Ontario, from 1977 until 1979, when he took an M.A. degree in English literature) and thus had less time to spare for observing the sky.

Another reason for Levy's failure to find a new comet was that the Canadian sky provided him with comparatively few clear nights. To improve his chances of success, in 1979 he made what turned out to be an important decision. Following a visit with his brother Gerry, who was then living in Tucson, Arizona, which has been dubbed the "astronomy-research capital of the world" because of its dry climate and clear skies, Levy decided to relocate there himself. He settled in a community outside the city and, in his backyard, built his own observatory in a garden shed. To pay the bills, Levy taught for a time, worked as a research assistant at several local observatories, and contributed articles to astronomical magazines. But whenever he could, he would search for comets from his private observatory.

On November 14, 1984, after having logged 917 hours "at the eyepiece," as he has put it, Levy finally discovered his first comet. He had been making a routine search of the sky from his backyard observatory when he caught a glimpse of "a faint fuzzy object" near a cluster of stars. He recalled the experience in *The Quest for Comets*: "My first reaction was, 'Why have I never seen such a thing? It should be pictured in all the astronomy books.' Another atlas check confirmed my growing suspicion: The cluster belonged there; the faint fuzzy spot did not. Within a few minutes, I was sure that the object was moving very slowly in the direction of the cluster. A comet! My heart rate soared."

But according to the rules of the sport of comet hunting, Levy had not yet crossed the finish line. After all, other astronomers, amateur or professional, could have observed the same comet. So Levy quickly collected himself and communicated the comet's coordinates, brightness, speed, and other descriptive data to the Central Bureau for Astronomical Telegrams (CBAT), the astronomical equivalent of a referee. As it turned out, another amateur astronomer, Michael Rudenko, independently observed the same comet the next night; as a result, the discovery was named comet Levy-Rudenko 1984t.

Meanwhile, in addition to comet hunting, Levy was devoting time to magazine and book writing about astronomical topics. Since one of his interests is educating children about the wonders of the night sky, he wrote *The Universe for Children: How Astronomy-Minded Adults Can Teach Children to Love the Sky* (1984). "I don't think an astronomer can do anything more significant than teach about the stars and the beauty of the night sky to the youngsters . . . ," he told Robert Reeves, who interviewed him for *Astronomy* (April 1994). "Take the kids out and say, 'See those points of light? They are going to be your friends.'" Levy's other books published during the 1980s are *The Joy of Gazing* (1982), *Observe: Comets* (1985; with S. J. Edberg), *Observe: Meteors* (1986; with S. J. Edberg), and *Observing Variable Stars: A Guide for the Beginner* (1989).

The last-named book received a glowing review from Wayne M. Lowder, who declared in *Astronomy* (April 1989), "As a simple introduction to variable stars and a guide for the novice observer, this volume has no rival. . . . The two outstanding virtues of this book are the quality of writing and the consistency of presentation. The beginner will have no problem understanding the points the author is making and is very likely to be responsive to his obvious enthusiasm." Expressing a sentiment that would be repeated in the years to come by many of Levy's readers, Lowder concluded, "If you weren't already looking at variable stars, you should start! Levy's enthusiasm is likely to lead you down the garden path to your telescope or to a dark-sky location where a pair of binoculars will expand your universe." Nigel Henbest, writing in *New Scientist* (August 31, 1991), was similarly moved on reading Levy's book *The Sky: A User's Guide* (1991): "In some quarters, an amateur astronomer means a dedicated devotee in an anorak, mouthing esoteric catchphrases. But not for Levy: he has a love affair with the sky, and he wants everyone to join in. This joyous enthusiasm sets this book delightfully apart from run-of-the-mill guides to the sky. Levy is comprehensive in the parts of the sky he takes you to: from using your eyes to spot meteors and the phases of the moon to what an affordable telescope will show. But each episode is also a moment of adventure and excitement, illustrated by personal stories."

During the 1980s Levy also began writing about astronomers. What launched his career as a biographer was a profile of Bart Bok that he wrote for a 1982 issue of *Astronomy*. Eleven years later Levy's book *The Man Who Sold the Milky Way: A Biography of Bart Bok*, was published. In 1985 he began work on *Clyde Tombaugh: Discoverer of Planet Pluto* (1991), which a reviewer for *Sky & Telescope* described as "a warm, often personal biography [that] conveys the joy and passion of discovering new worlds." "It took six years," Levy told Robert Reeves, "but I wanted to write about Clyde because his life is an inspiration to those of us who want to go into the same field."

Meanwhile, on the comet-hunting front Levy had scored success after success since making his first discovery. Between 1984 and the end of 1994, he either discovered or codiscovered twenty new comets, for a total of twenty-one, eight of them from his backyard observatory. The remainder were found in partnership with Eugene Shoemaker, a geologist who specializes in the impacts of comets on Earth and other worlds, and his wife, Carolyn, who had joined her husband in his asteroid-and-comet-trolling expeditions in 1982. Since 1989 Levy has spent one week out of every month perusing the sky with the Shoemakers at their base of operations, Palomar Observatory, on Mount Palomar, in California. He works with them on a volunteer basis, receiving as his only compensation reimbursement for expenses. "David has become an integral part of the Shoemakers' program, which has been extremely successful at discovering comets," Brian Marsden, an astronomer who heads CBAT, told Terence Dickinson.

Levy's work with the Shoemakers is somewhat different from the comet-hunting expeditions he carries out in his backyard. At home he searches for comets visually (or "in real time"), by looking through his eight-inch-diameter Schmidt telescope or sixteen-inch Miranda. At Palomar Observatory, on the other hand, Levy and the Shoemakers use an eighteen-inch photographic telescope, which takes pictures of large swaths of the sky. The photographs are then viewed through a stereomicroscope, which provides a three-dimensional view of the photographed objects. According to the routine they have worked out, Levy and Eugene Shoemaker share the duties of preparing the film and "guiding" the telescope, while Carolyn Shoemaker examines the photographs. "In this curious exercise called guiding," Levy wrote of his task in *The Quest for Comets*, "I must keep the star exactly centered on the crosshairs of the eyepiece. It is a challenge, for even though the telescope is electrically driven to follow the star, it often lurches forward or backward a bit. If I can't keep the star centered perfectly on the crosshairs of the guiding eyepiece, the resulting film will show jerks and wiggles instead of starry points of light. This is a battle between me and the telescope, with the distant star as referee. For eight minutes I freeze the sky on film and only imagine the wonders that may later be found there."

As might be imagined, it is much easier to locate comets and asteroids with a photographic telescope than with a visual one. "Discovering a comet in real time by looking at the sky is tremendously hard to do," Brian Marsden told Terence Dickinson. "Most comet hunters who do succeed at it find one or maybe two. To discover eight that way is a remarkable accomplishment." Whichever method he is using, though, the sky demands that Levy assume the role of a humble and infinitely patient observer. "When I start a session, I have only a vague idea of what I may find in the next hour or so as I move the telescope forward for a few minutes across a region of sky, then backward through the next sector," he wrote in *The Quest for Comets*. "Whether I find a star cluster or a galaxy, a red star, or a bright double star, is really up to the sky, not me. The sky is the master, my telescope the receiver, and I am the watchman."

By the late 1980s David Levy had developed a reputation among astronomy buffs as a premier comet hunter and respected author. Nevertheless, he sometimes found it difficult to make a living through his writing. His prospects brightened in 1993, when he received three new book contracts, and he now supports himself mainly through his writing. Those contracts resulted in *Skywatching*, a richly illustrated guide to astronomy, *The Quest for Comets: An Explosive Trail of Beauty and Danger*, and *An Observing Guide for Comets, Asteroids, Meteors, and Zodiacal Light*, on which he collaborated with S. J. Edberg. All three books were published in 1994.

Coincidentally, 1994 was also the year of an unprecedented astronomical event: in July periodic comet Shoemaker-Levy 9—Levy's nineteenth comet discovery—crashed into Jupiter, marking the first time in recorded history that a substantial celestial body was observed colliding with a planet. Not surprisingly, the prospect of the impact focused considerable media attention not only on astronomical phenomena but on Levy and his colleagues as well. He was interviewed by *Time* magazine, CNN, and National Public Radio and was commissioned to write an article about the event for *Smithsonian*.

The Levy-Shoemaker team discovered the comet on March 25, 1993. Ironically, their observing run of the previous week had not gone all that smoothly. One problem was that some of the film they had used had been exposed to light; worse still, the observing conditions that week had been less than ideal. But on March 25 Carolyn Shoemaker, while examining the photographs the team had taken several nights before, noticed an odd-looking object that she likened to "a squashed comet." The object was in fact a comet, but rather than being a round ball of light, this one was flat. Seeking to confirm that this weird-looking object was a comet, Levy called his friend Jim Scotti, an astronomer at the University of Arizona's Lunar and Planetary Laboratory. Later that night Scotti e-mailed his analysis to CBAT: "It is a unique object, different from any cometary form I have yet witnessed. In general, it has the appearance of a string of nuclear fragments spread out along the orbit with tails extending from the entire nuclear train, as well as what looks like a sheet of debris spread out in the orbit plane in both directions."

As it turned out, the "string of nuclear fragments" (which was later more poetically described as "a string of pearls") represented the remains of a single comet that in July 1992 had passed within twenty thousand miles of Jupiter—too close to withstand the planet's gravitational forces. "Its icy interior long since cloaked by an inert crust, in July 1992 a comet wandered so close to Jupiter that the planet's tidal forces tore it apart," Levy wrote in *The Quest for Comets*, describing the comet's recent history. "As the ancient body traveled away from Jupiter, its pieces moved slowly apart, and a string of new comets was born, their freshly exposed materials brightening rapidly." Even more dramatic news came in May 1993, when Brian Marsden announced that periodic comet Shoemaker-Levy 9 would crash into Jupiter in July 1994. During an interview with Terry Gross for National Public Radio's *Fresh Air* in 1994, Levy described the magnitude of the impending collision: "If you were to take all of Earth's nuclear weapons, everything that was owned by the former Soviet Union and the United States at the height of the Cold War, put them in a box, and light a match to it, and multiply the result by about ten thousand times—this is about the energy we're talking about that will be released in the explosions this summer."

The fragments collided into the solar system's largest planet over a weeklong period, beginning on July 16. Although the moments of impact themselves could not be directly observed by Earth-based telescopes, because the fragments struck Jupiter's far side, the energy released by the collisions was so enormous that observers peering through even small telescopes could catch glimpses of the fireworks display. (The spacecraft Galileo, which was on its way to Jupiter, was able to observe the impacts directly.) Also, as Jupiter rotated, the impact sites became visible to Earth about twenty minutes after each collision. Malcolm W. Browne, who was on hand to observe the show, recounted in the *New York Times* (July 17, 1994) that after fragment A, thought by some to be a kilometer wide, pierced the planet's atmosphere, it "exploded with a bright flash and hurled a white-hot plume of gas high above the giant planet, leaving a huge, circular wound in Jupiter's dense cloud cover."

According to Levy, who watched the results of the collisions from a large refractor telescope at the United States Naval Observatory in Washington, D.C., an analysis of the plumes of gas and other observational data is important because it will yield new insights into the nature of both Jupiter and comets as well as information about cometary collisions with planets. Over the eons, Earth itself has been hit by comets, probably once about every one thousand years. Comets may have been responsible for bringing Earth not only its supply of water but also its carbon, hydrogen, nitrogen, and oxygen—the elements necessary for life. And some scientists have speculated that the extinction of the dinosaurs 65 million years ago may have been caused by a cometary impact.

For his discoveries, David Levy has received many awards, including the Chant Medal, the Leslie C. Peltier Award, and the Bruce Blair Award. He has also had a celestial object—asteroid 3673 Levy—named in his honor. In the years to come, Levy hopes to write another biography. "I live and breathe the sky, so if I find an astronomer whose story needs to be told, and I feel I can tell it, I'll be interested in a third project," he told Robert Reeves. "My heart is drawn toward talking about the lives of inspiring people with important ideas." But it goes without saying that he will continue his comet-hunting expeditions. "In my dreams back in the mid-[1960s], I wanted to find just one comet," he told Robert Reeves. "Now, I have [twenty-one]. . . . The movie *Field of Dreams* is one of my favorites because it really examines that question of doing something in your life to make your dreams come true. But you really have to work at it. I love watching that movie and then going outside and watching my own field of dreams."

Selected Biographical References: Astronomy p13+ Ap '94; Equinox p64+ My/Je '94 por; The Sciences p31+ My/Je '94; Levy, David H. The Quest for Comets; An Explosive Trail of Beauty and Danger (1994)

Mary Bachmann

Link, O. Winston

Dec. 16, 1914- Photographer. Address: c/o Thomas H. Garver, P.O. Box 3493, Madison, WI 53704-0493

Early in 1955, driven by the knowledge that the era of steam locomotion in the United States was rapidly drawing to a close, the photographer O. Winston Link began recording on film the activities of the Norfolk and Western Railway. Every few months Link would take a break from his work as a successful New York City commercial photographer and travel south, to take pictures of the N&W's freight and passenger trains, all of which were then pulled by steam engines. "The train is as close to a human being as you can get," he once told a reporter. "It talks, it moves, it grunts and groans. And each engine has its own characteristics—its own sounds and smells and sights." Remarkable portraits of "the most aesthetic of man's mechanical creations," Link's photographs of steam trains evoke "a myriad of emotions associated with romance, mystery, adventure, loneliness, power, sorrow, and, somehow, comfort," as Tim Hensley wrote of the trains themselves in *Steam, Steel & Stars: America's Last Steam Railroad* (1987), a collection of Link's pictures. Focusing as well on employees of the railroad and people who lived along its right-of-way and whose lives often revolved around it, Link produced not only what Andy Grundberg of the *New York Times* (September 4, 1983) described as "delightful and frequently incredible depictions of the allure of steam" but also a chronicle of a vanishing way of life in rural and small-town America in the mid-twentieth century. "Perhaps, in retrospect," Carolyn Kinder Carr wrote in 1983, for an exhibition of his photos that she curated at the Akron Art Museum, in Ohio, "Link should be seen not merely as one who depicted the last years of steam train activity on the N&W Railway, but also as one who documented the waning years of America's age of innocence."

"The handling of scale, balance, lighting, and composition in Link's photographs makes it hard to believe that he never studied art in general or photography in particular," Anthony Korner observed in *Artforum* (May 1989), in an assessment of some of the approximately twenty-five hundred photos that Link took during his five- to six-year N&W project. A civil engineer by training, Link shot many pictures during the day and about two hundred photos in color, but most of his N&W pictures were taken with black-and-white film at night. Using his unique, complex system of flash photography to illuminate his subjects with the equivalent of as many as three hundred thousand sixty-watt bulbs, he produced stirringly dramatic images that display striking contrast and great depth of field. "Both lighting and/or unusual juxtapositions lend a surreal quality to these images . . . ," Carolyn Carr observed. "Whether staged . . . or a marvelous coincidence, . . . the photographs both conform to and confound our expectations. Whether primarily of trains or people, his photographs speak about both the uniqueness of the moment and the universality of the event." The Museum of Modern Art and the Metropolitan Museum of Art, in New York City, the Art Institute of Chicago, and the Victoria and Albert Museum, in London, among other institutions, hold photographs by O. Winston Link in their permanent collections.

Known nearly all his life as Winston, Ogle Winston Link was named for two of his maternal ancestors, both of whom served in the United States Congress in the nineteenth century. The second of four children (one of whom died in infancy), he was born on December 16, 1914 in the New York City borough of Brooklyn to Earnest Albert Link (called Al), an elementary-school carpentry teacher, and Ann Winston (Jones) Link, a homemaker. In a profile of O. Winston Link that appears in *The Last Steam Railroad in America*, a compilation of his photographs that was published in 1995, Thomas H. Garver, a one-time assistant of Link's and now his agent, reported that Link's father exerted a powerful influence on young Winston in matters ranging from human relations to the manual arts. In addition to woodworking, Link recalled to Garver, his father taught him, among other lessons, "the importance of accuracy, patience, consideration of others, and honesty" and, in Garver's words, "to despise greed . . . and slipshod work."

"My father introduced me to all kinds of things to see what might take hold," Link told Garver. One of those things was photography. On day trips with his father, he would take pictures at the New York harbor and other city sites. Sometimes he aimed his camera at trains, which had intrigued him since the age of four, when he saw a train set in a store window. As a teenager he liked to go with neighborhood friends to railroad hubs in New Jersey. He especially enjoyed seeing the "Blue Comet," a Jersey Central train with a royal blue engine that, in a conversation with David E. Outerbridge for *Connoisseur* (December 1989), he labeled "a masterpiece." He developed his film at home and printed his pictures with an enlarger that he built himself.

At Manual Training High School, a public school in Brooklyn that was renowned for its outstanding math curriculum, Link received a rigorous education in math, science, and other academic subjects. His extracurricular activities included playing on the ice-hockey team and taking pictures for the student yearbook. To earn spending money he did small carpentry jobs in his neighborhood. Having been "indoctrinated" by his father "with the idea that he was going to be an engineer," as he recalled to Thomas Garver, he enrolled at the Polytechnic Institute of Brooklyn (now called Polytechnic University), where he had won a scholarship to study civil engineering. During each of his four years at college, he was elected president of his class, and in his junior year he was selected for membership in Tau Beta Pi, the honorary engineering society. He served as both photo editor and photographer on the campus newspaper; outside of school he sometimes worked as a wedding photographer.

By his own account, at college Link indulged his fondness for buffoonery and mimicry. Making full use of his talents as a clown and a mimic, he entertained students and guests at a banquet held by the campus newspaper shortly before his graduation. His hilarious act prompted one guest, an executive with the public relations firm Carl Byoir and Associates, to offer him a position as Byoir's first photographer. Since it seemed potentially more interesting than the few civil engineering jobs then available, Link accepted the offer. He began working for Byoir in 1937, immediately after graduating from the Polytechnic Institute with a bachelor's degree in civil engineering.

Although Link had had no formal training in photography, his experience, technical skills, creativity, aesthetic judgment, knack for storytelling, wit, and sense of the ridiculous proved to be ideal for fulfilling his assignments at Byoir. One of his widely circulated photos, which he produced for an ad campaign for plate glass mirrors, showed a hippopotamus having its teeth examined by someone holding a gigantic dental mirror. To demonstrate the ability of a new type of glass to withstand extreme heat or cold, he photographed a bathing-suit-clad young woman primping atop huge blocks of ice that rested on a glass tabletop supported by additional blocks of ice; on the floor below the tabletop, a fire blazed. *Life* magazine later cited the photo as a "classic publicity picture."

In 1942, eager to contribute to the United States effort in World War II, Link left Byoir to take a job in Mineola, New York as an engineer and photographer for a war-related project at the Airborne Instruments Laboratory, a facility run by Columbia University's Office of Scientific Research and Development. (Link's nearly total deafness in one ear, a consequence of a case of mumps during his adolescence, made him ineligible for active military duty.) In addition to helping to develop a device for detecting enemy submarines from low-flying planes, Link documented the work of the laboratory in photographs that he took both indoors and outside. The nearness of the laboratory to tracks of the Long Island Rail Road gave him an opportunity to take pictures of steam locomotives (he ignored the wartime ban on railroad photography), and his interest in trains, which had been "largely dormant since high school," according to Thomas Garver, revived. With the idea of taking dramatic railroad photographs at night without having to string electrical wire to flashbulbs, for several years he worked with some of the engineers at the lab to create a system in which radio signals would activate the bulbs. "But the hardware had not been developed (and maybe still hasn't been) to make it possible," Link has explained, "because the huge steel mass of the trains blocked the radio signals from reaching some of the lights."

At the end of the war, the Airborne Instruments Laboratory was disbanded. Rather than accept Carl Byoir's offer to rehire him, Link went into business for himself as a professional photographer specializing in industrial subjects. In 1947, after about a year in which he worked out of his house in Hempstead, on Long Island, he moved back to Brooklyn, to live and work at his childhood address. (His parents' nineteenth-century townhouse remained his home until 1983.) In 1949 he moved his photographic operations to a rented space in Manhattan. By the early 1950s his clients included New York City's Triboro Bridge and Tunnel Authority, such giants of industry as Freeport Sulphur, the Ethyl Corporation, Alcoa Aluminum, B. F. Goodrich, and Texaco, and several top advertising agencies. He sometimes got assignments from the *New York Times* and other newspapers and from fashion houses as well. Link handled all his work with the help of only one or two part-time assistants. "I wanted to take pictures—not manage a lot of people," he told Thomas Garver. "I wasn't running a business; I was doing something that I liked, and I managed to get paid for it."

In January 1955, on an assignment for an ad agency, Link went to Staunton, Virginia to take pictures of air conditioners at a Westinghouse factory. One evening he drove to the nearby town of Waynesboro, to see a Norfolk & Western train that was scheduled to pass through. At the invitation of a railroad worker, Link wandered around the Waynesboro train yard, repair shop, and refueling facilities. "Inspecting the premises, he became aware of the traditional appurtenances of railroading that he knew had not endured elsewhere," Tim Hensley wrote in *Steam, Steel & Stars*: "a Seth Thomas clock on the wall . . . the sweet scent of kerosene . . . men in bib overalls, bright bandannas, and Kromer caps . . . the chatter of telegraphic communications . . . warmth from a pot-bellied stove . . . the ruby glow of a lantern." Later that night, with growing excitement, Link watched the passage of a freight train and all the platform activity precipitated by the arrival and departure of a passenger train. Both were pulled by steam engines; unlike nearly all other major American railroads, which by the mid-1950s were far along in the process of scrapping their steam locomotives and replacing them with diesels, the N&W still used only steam power.

Virtually overnight after visiting Waynesboro, Link developed an obsessive desire to record the twilight years of steam locomotion. He returned to the station the next evening and took several pictures of arriving trains. Back in New York, he mailed prints of a couple of the photos and examples of his commercial work to the N&W headquarters in Roanoke, Virginia, along with a proposal for a project. "Have you ever noticed the dearth of photographs of railroad scenes at night?" he wrote, as quoted by Tim Hensley. "I would like to make a series of well-planned night photographs of exceptional quality and interest showing the railroad at work as the passenger sleeps. For human interest, I would like to show an employee in every picture. On this proposed long-term project, all I could hope for from your railroad would be some sort of cooperation in picking locations and obtaining necessary permission to enter yards. Do you think your management would be favorable?"

Both Ben Bane Dulaney, the head of the N&W's public relations and advertising department, and Robert H. Smith, the president of the railroad, responded enthusiastically. "I never knew what word [Smith] passed down the line, but it seemed to me that he gave me 2,300 miles of track, 450 steam locomotives, and all the employees of the N&W to help me get the job done," Link has said. In the course of his project, he was given a key to the railroad's switchboxes, so that he could phone dispatchers to find out the precise time of arrival of a specific train at a particular location. Sometimes crews timed the passage of a train to accommodate him.

Link scheduled his commercial work so that, every few months or so, he would have one to three weeks free to spend in N&W country, some six hundred miles from New York City by car. During his early visits he concentrated on selecting sites to photograph. First, while riding in N&W passenger trains, he surveyed both sides of the main route and the branch lines (which extended from Virginia into West Virginia, North Carolina, Kentucky, Ohio, and Maryland). Then he scouted roundhouses and other railroad facilities and made forays by car into the towns and countryside along the tracks, noting such potential photographic subjects as bridges and places rich in natural beauty.

Next, by means of his remarkable "photographic vision"—"the ability to visualize photographs before they are created," in Thomas Garver's words—and with what David Outerbridge labeled "mind-boggling precision," Link planned every aspect of each picture that he had decided to take, ranging from the overall composition, including exactly what point he wanted the engine of a moving train to have reached, to the placement and activities of the human subjects and such details as the presence of a lighted window in a trackside private house. Thanks to Link's warmth and friendliness and his obviously genuine affection and respect for the railroad employees and other inhabitants of the region, people that he approached invariably agreed to pose for him or help him with whatever else he asked of them. "Link did not work like a street photographer, grabbing images from the unsuspecting, nor was he a Margaret Mead documenting the tribal habits of an exotic and alien culture," Carolyn Carr observed in *Ghost Trains*, a catalog published in 1983 by the Chrysler Museum, in Norfolk, Virginia, for the exhibition of Link's photographs that Carr had mounted earlier at the Akron Art Museum. "For Link these people are family and friends." The names of the people he had photographed were always included in the detailed notes that Link kept about each of his photos.

Link took many photos during the day, among them images of train-crossed landscapes and railroaders whose expressions reflected their pride in their work. The most celebrated of his daytime shots is "Maud Bows to the 'Virginia Creeper'" (Green Cove, Virginia, 1956), which he himself has described as "one of the most serene and beautiful pictures [he has] ever made." The photo shows the train known locally as the "Virginia Creeper" approaching the Green Cove station, where, harnessed to a dray, a horse named Maud stands facing the track, with her head lowered "as if acknowledging the superiority of the railroad," in Anthony Korner's words.

In part because "you can't control the sun," as Link told a reporter, he preferred to photograph at night. By working at night with flash, "you can control the light and accent what you want," he explained to David Machalaba for the January 13, 1986 issue of the *Wall Street Journal*. (In one of its rare deviations from tradition, the *Journal* printed one of Link's photos on the front page of all its domestic and international editions that day.) Darkness also added a significant element of drama and romance to the events that he photographed, and, as Anthony Korner pointed out, "white smoke, steam, fire, bright lights, oiled pistons, and the gleaming metal of locomotives show up to best effect for the camera" at night.

Link relied on a synchronized flash system of his own design in which up to sixty flashbulbs were mounted in brushed aluminum reflectors that had been manufactured to his specifications. A battery capacitor that he designed and built himself provided the power for both the flashbulbs and the solenoids that triggered the release of the shutters in his cameras (he used up to three 4X5 view cameras simultaneously). To properly highlight selected portions of the scene that he wanted to photograph, Link had to determine the correct placement of each of as many as fifteen flash reflectors (the largest of which could hold eighteen flashbulbs)—an exceedingly technical task for which his engineering background stood him in good stead. Depending on the complexity of the arrangement, he used as much as three-quarters of a mile of electrical wire to connect everything. Because the components of his system were joined in series, a single break anywhere in the connections would cause the whole setup to fail. According to Tim Hensley, "breaks in the line were frequently a problem, because the wires often stretched across streets, fields, or even rivers, as well as around or through buildings." Since flashbulbs could be used only once, Link tested the connections by means of a separate circuit that did not activate the bulbs.

The job of setting up all the necessary flash equipment and cameras was both arduous and time-consuming. The groundwork for his picture "104 on the Turntable" (Bristol, Virginia, 1957), for example, entailed hours of labor in a busy train yard, where Link contended with smoke, steam, and moving trains while running wires up and down walls and under "what seemed to be a thousand rails," as he wrote in his notes. For "Gooseneck Dam and No. 2" (near Natural Bridge, Virginia, 1956)—a photo in which "earth, air, fire, and water are united in a zigzag of illumination," in the words of Anthony Korner—Link and his assistants placed equipment on the rocky banks of the Maury River and even on rocks midstream. Lacking a boat or a bridge, they crossed the river on a two-cable span, the higher one for their hands and the lower one for their feet, and they built ladders in trees to reach their trolley cable. The preparations took six days to complete.

"Although Link's technical expertise commands admiration," Carolyn Carr observed, "ultimately his photographs compel attention because of the manner in which he repeatedly transforms the ordinary into the extraordinary." Link's most famous picture, "Hot Shot Eastbound" (Iaeger, West Virginia, 1956), shows a young couple seated in a convertible among other cars at a drive-in theatre; they face an image of an airplane on the movie screen, while on an embankment just beyond the parking area, a steam train rushes by. "Living Room on the Tracks" (Lithia, Virginia, 1955) is a scene at once cozily domestic and reminiscent of the surreal paintings of René Magritte: while a young mother sits apparently lost in thought in an upholstered chair and a cat and a dog sleep on a braided rug, the woman's little son looks out a picture window and waves at a steam engine that appears to be just a few feet from the house. In "Egg, Stove, and Bananas" (Vesuvius, Virginia, 1957), a locomotive is visible through the window of a well-stocked general store in which the proprietor weighs a bunch of bananas for a customer while other townspeople chat near a pot-bellied stove. In "Giant Oak" (Max Meadows, Virginia, 1957), a picture that Anthony Korner described as "haunting and poignant," the branches of an enormous oak tree cover a plume of white smoke stretching the length of the engine and cars of the "Birmingham Special." "On one level Link's photographs bring out the child in us," Anthony Korner reflected; "on another, we can marvel as adults at the serene mastery of a difficult technique harnessed to innate artistry and dedicated patience. . . . Patience and hard work rewarded Link with these effortless-looking images, . . . for which he had only the equipment for one shot in the dark."

Link continued to photograph N&W trains until May 1960, when the railroad retired its last steam engine. (In 1982 the N&W became a subsidiary of the Norfolk Southern Railroad.) For most of the previous year, however, he had concentrated on tape-recording the sounds of locomotives and other railroad-related sounds. After he returned to full-time commercial photography, he tried to market his N&W photos to book publishers. Failing to generate any interest in them, he stowed his negatives in a fireproof vault in the Empire State Building. Then he proceeded to market a series of long-playing records that he had produced from his tape-recordings. According to Thomas Garver, Link hopes to reissue one or two of the records in the near future.

Link spent twenty thousand dollars of his own funds in the course of his N&W project, and other than tiny payments for the rights to reproduce a few of his pictures (from railroading magazines and from the N&W, for its 1957 booklet "Night Trick"), he had received no financial compensation for his efforts. Then, in 1976, John Szarkowski, at that time the director of the Department of Photography at the Museum of Modern Art, purchased six Link photos for the museum's permanent collection. After seeing one or more of them, Alan Ripp wrote an article about Link's work for the magazine *American Photographer* (June 1982). Link has credited Ripp's article with sparking a sudden burst of interest in his work. In 1983 two solo exhibitions of his N&W photos were mounted. One of them opened at the Photographers' Gallery in London and then traveled to fourteen other sites in Great Britain. The other, which opened at the Akron Art Museum, in Ohio, was later shown at more than half a dozen other museums and galleries in the United States, with excerpts from Link's sound recordings piped into the exhibit rooms. Nearly three dozen solo exhibitions of his work have been held worldwide. Prints of his photographs, which thirty or forty years ago sold for a few dollars, now cost as much as three thousand dollars apiece.

In a widely quoted characterization, John Szarkowski, in a letter to Thomas Garver, described O. Winston Link as "one of nature's noble men, a legitimate American genius, and a nut." "The artist in O. Winston Link is well-hidden beneath a thick crust of avuncular, all-American down-to-earthness," Kathy Field Stephen reported in the *Christian Science Monitor* (September 19, 1983). According to Thomas Garver, one of Link's most noticeable mannerisms is his laugh—"half bark, half machine-gun fire, rising and falling, on and on." In a profile of him for *Norfolk Southern Focus* (March 1987), William F. Noall wrote that he "comes across as a wise, old, and lovable eccentric. He smiles often and finds a humorous or ironic twist in just about everything said. . . . He shoots out ideas like water gushing from a firehose. Yet his friendly expressions make him easy to listen to."

O. Winston Link and the former Marteal Oglesby were divorced in 1948 after six years of marriage. In 1993 Link's second, ten-year marriage also ended in divorce, after a court trial in which he testified that his second wife, Conchita Mendoza, had stolen some two thousand of his prints, cameras, and a substantial part of his earnings. Along with his nephew, who was a party to Link's civil suit, he was awarded five million dollars in damages, but as of mid-1995, when Mendoza was formally charged with grand larceny, it seemed unlikely that he would get any of the award. (The criminal action action against Mendoza may be dropped if she returns his prints and other property.) Since retiring from his business in 1983, Link has lived in Mount Kisco, New York, where he continues to make prints from his negatives. He has one son, Winston Conway Link, from his first marriage. *Trains That Passed in the Night* (1990), a documentary about Link that was filmed for British television by Paul Yule, has aired on cable and public television stations in the United States.

Selected Biographical References: Christian Sci Mon p20+ S 19 '83; Connoisseur 219:122+ D '89 por; N Y Times III p20 Ag 26 '83 por; Norfolk Southern Focus 3:8+ Mr '87 pors; Railfan and Railroad 1:26+ Fall '76 por; Roanoke [Virginia] Times & World News E p1+ N 6 '83 por; Hensley, Tim. Steam, Steel & Stars (1987); Link, O. Winston and Thomas H. Garver. The Last Steam Railroad in America (1995)

Loach, Ken

June 17, 1936- British filmmaker; television director. Address: c/o Judy Daish Associates, 83 Eastbourne Mews, London W26LQ, England

AP/Wide World Photos

"I want to make films which are real, which correspond faithfully to experience," the British film and television director Ken Loach has said. "To describe what is going on between people; to be authentic about the world." In a career spanning more than three decades, Loach has been doing just that, with particular emphasis on giving voice to the concerns of the working poor and the downtrodden. Loach conceived his distinctive approach to filmmaking during the 1960s, while he was working at BBC television. "For the first time, the viewer at home experienced the jolt of seeing real people in real situations that were not confined to the reassuring Home Counties, BBC-accented, middle-class milieus of heretofore," Gavin Smith observed of Loach's early work in *Film Comment* (March 1988). It was during this period that Loach made such socially conscious television programs as *Up the Junction*, about three women down on their luck, and *Cathy Come Home*, about homelessness. Both are considered to be among some of the best British television dramas produced in the 1960s. By the end of the decade, Loach had become one of the most widely imitated directors in British cinema and the recognized creator of the docudrama genre.

During Margaret Thatcher's tenure as prime minister, which began in the late 1970s and continued through the 1980s, Loach, who has long been a committed leftist, began to make films that were more overtly political and that frequently aroused controversy. He found it increasingly difficult to obtain financing for his movies in England, with the result that he made only two feature films during the 1980s. In contrast, he has long been revered in continental Europe (he has won four awards at Cannes—more than any other British filmmaker). In recent years, however, he has enjoyed a resurgence in his popularity, with films such as *Riff-Raff* and *Raining Stones* gaining attention in the United States. With more than a dozen feature films and almost thirty television dramas and documentaries to his credit, Loach remains uncompromising in his desire to re-create real life on film as authentically as possible. "All I hope, when people see my films, is that they say, 'Yes, that's how things are,'" he was quoted as saying in the *New York Times* (January 31, 1993). "And if that's how things are, then shouldn't we try to change it? If that means I'm a political filmmaker, then so be it."

Kenneth Loach was born on June 17, 1936 in Nuneaton, Warwickshire, in the Midlands of England, to John Loach, an electrician in a machine tools factory, and Vivien (Hamlin) Loach. He has described his childhood as perfectly ordinary, happy, and secure. The first in his family to attend a university, he won a scholarship to Oxford University, where he studied law. Rather than focus on his studies, he devoted much of his time to working in the theatre. Among other activities, he became president of the school's Experimental Theatre Club, for which he performed sketches with the future film star Dudley Moore. When Loach left Oxford, he dreamed of launching a regional theatre, but he instead ended up taking a job as an understudy in a comedy revue, doing stints as a teacher, and working with a repertory company that toured schools.

In the early 1960s Loach began working in television, a career move that he has described as "a desperate bid to earn money and pay the rent." After serving as a trainee director with ABC Television, one of England's independent commercial production companies, he moved to the government-run British Broadcasting Corporation. While there, he directed its highly popular police action series *Z-Cars*, in which the police officers were portrayed as being as flawed as anyone else.

Some observers have described British television dramas of the 1960s as being little more than filmed theatrical productions. Loach was uncomfortable with this artificial style, and so, while directing episodes of the series *Diary of a Young Man*, he came up with new techniques to make the program more cinematic. In addition to shooting on location, he used many experimental elements, such as voice-overs, title cards, and monologues spoken directly to the camera. During this period Loach also became determined to use television to portray the lives and predicaments of the working classes, with the aim of legitimizing their concerns and forcing people to recognize the political and economic structures that influence their condition.

Loach's aesthetic and political sentiments were shared by the television producer Tony Garnett, who recruited Loach to work as his director on *The Wednesday Play*, which many consider to be among the best British dramatic anthology series of the 1960s. To achieve his objectives, Loach decided to film each drama as if it were a documentary film: instead of using a thirty-five millimeter camera and a tripod, he took to the streets with a handheld sixteen millimeter camera. The idea that the plays were a reflection of real life was enhanced by the fact that each aired immediately following the nightly newscast. "We wanted to keep the feeling of the news, to stop it being like, 'Here's the real world, now here's the fiction,'" Loach told Gavin Smith in an interview for *Film Comment*'s March 1994 profile of the director. "We wanted to keep the same perception and critical attitude in the audience."

The first of *The Wednesday Play* programs to attract widespread attention was *Up the Junction* (1965), based on a book by Nell Dunn. In Loach's hands, the story, which he has described as "a little kaleidoscope of life in a working-class area of London," became a film depicting the lives of three young women as they dealt with such issues as love, sex, and abortion. It "had a sort of anarchic, rough edge, which got everybody worked up, so it was a sort of national issue for a short time," Loach has recalled. Notable for its earthy subject matter and milieu and its obscene language, *Up the Junction* was among the first programs Mary Whitehouse, self-appointed spokesperson for the public conscience, ever protested.

The following year another entry in *The Wednesday Play* series, *Cathy Come Home*, provoked an even stronger reaction. The play, which tells the story of a poor family forced into homelessness, culminates with the heroine's losing custody of her children to the government's social services agency because she is unable to provide for them. The program not only led to some changes in housing laws and the creation of a charity named Shelter, but it also influenced many who would go on to be among Britain's most acclaimed filmmakers, including Stephen Frears, Alan Parker, and Roland Joffe. Alan Parker, for instance, described *Cathy Come Home* as having been "the single most important reason why he wanted to become a film director." Roland Joffe seconded that opinion in an interview with Jonathan Hacker and David Price for their book *Take 10: Contemporary British Film Directors* (1991): "The first time that I saw *Cathy Come Home* I was ravished because these were 'people.' This is a man who allows people to be. I wanted to embrace everything that Ken stood for." For his part, Loach, who is almost as well known for his self-criticism as he is for his films, believes that as an activist film *Cathy Come Home* failed, because, instead of recognizing the need for significant political action, people responded emotionally to the individual case. "If the inference was that the difficulties of the homeless could be solved by forming a charity, it was a backward step," he was quoted as saying in the London *Observer* (March 22, 1987).

While *Cathy Come Home* and *Up the Junction* were two of the most talked-about films that Loach produced during this period, all of his works had a defining influence on others working in the industry. "When I started making films, he was making the best ones around," the director Stephen Frears told Simon Hattenstone in an interview for the *Guardian* (October 8, 1993). "He seemed to have a limitless spring of creativity. All of us at the BBC were dominated by him. His films had an authenticity and poetry which was inspiring and infuriating." According to Hattenstone, Loach "became a Pied Piper, idolized and imitated by just about every aspiring filmmaker." His style became the archetype for realist drama, and he is said to have created the docudrama genre.

Loach's first feature film, and, in the view of many, his most commercial one, was released in 1967. Entitled *Poor Cow*, it concerns a young woman who, after her husband is sent to jail, hooks up with another petty criminal who is subsequently imprisoned. In her book *5001 Nights at the Movies* (1991), the legendary film critic Pauline Kael called it "ambitious but flat." Loach himself is even more critical of the movie. "I made every mistake you could possibly make," he told Gavin Smith. "It was a very valuable film because I learned all the things not to do. . . . I hadn't really got to grips with what the core of the film was about, and it was terribly self-indulgent." *Poor Cow's* enormous commercial success in Europe has been attributed at least partly to its raw language and graphic depictions of casual sex.

By the end of the 1960s, the cinematic style pioneered by Loach was so widely imitated—even television commercials had adopted it—that he began to think about taking a new approach. Concluding that "the real excitement is in what's happening in front of the camera, not in making the camera wobble," he began to develop a much simpler style, one that would allow "people to reveal themselves as much as they could." Filming in such a manner would enable him "to put forward more sympathetic arguments, more observant; more thoughtful," he told Hacker and Price. Those who have worked with Loach admire his technique. "The thing about working with Ken is that you learn very, very quickly that he wants a very sensitive, quiet camera that isn't going to impose a style on the actors or the script," Chris Menges, a cinematographer who has collaborated with Loach on many of his films, has said. "It should quietly observe."

Loach first employed this new approach to filmmaking, which would dominate his work for the next twenty years, in his second feature, *Kes* (1969). But while the style was new, the content was vintage Loach. The film, which was adapted from a novel by Barry Hines, revolves around Billy, a lonely fourteen-year-old boy who lives in Yorkshire with his emotionally vacant mother and his tough half-brother. School provides no stimulation for the child, because it serves mainly as a holding pen for children until they are old enough to go to work in the local mines. The only meaning in Billy's life is derived from his relationship with a wild kestrel. When his half-brother pointlessly kills the bird, the flicker of hope that had come into Billy's life is extinguished. As Hacker and Price observed, "The film poignantly shows how the repressed working class turn their frustrations in on themselves, and how the vitality and energy of youth is so often snuffed out."

Kes was enthusiastically received at the 1969 London Film Festival. Nevertheless, it failed to arouse much interest among distributors, who had doubts about its commercial prospects because of the characters' thick accents, the story's somber mood, and their own uncertainties over how to market such an offbeat film. Only after British critics pressured distributors to release it did the film enjoy a commercial run. Contrary to the distributors' initial expectations, *Kes* went on to become one of the most commercially successful British films of the period and an acknowledged classic of British cinema. According to the film critic David Robinson, as quoted in *World Film Directors* (1988), it was "not only one of the best and most original British films in a long time but also one of the most directly appealing and entertaining—very funny and feeling and with vivid illumination of aspects of our society often forgotten."

The 1970s were not kind to Loach. His 1971 film, *Family Life*, "didn't pay for the usherettes," he said in the interview with Hattenstone. In the same year, he faced personal tragedy when his five-year-old son and his mother-in-law were killed and his wife seriously injured in an automobile accident. The grieving Loach stopped working for about a year. "I just tried to cope with things, I suppose," he told Hattenstone. Throughout the rest of the decade, as the British film industry declined, Loach was unable to obtain financing for his movies, with the result that he concentrated on directing television dramas. In time, as the BBC lost interest in broadcasting political dramas, even these opportunities dwindled.

In the few programs that he was asked to direct, Loach demonstrated that he had not lost his political edge. His most ambitious project was *Days of Hope* (1975), a four-part dramatic series for the BBC that was set in Britain between the end of World War I and the 1926 General Strike. In the program Loach drew parallels between what he deemed to be the Labour Party leadership's betrayal of ordinary people in both that period and in contemporary times. Although acclaimed, the miniseries drew fire from some historians for its alleged oversimplification of events.

It was not until 1979 that Loach made another feature film, *Black Jack*. As has often been the case in his career, he experienced considerable difficulty in raising money for the project. This time, though, he faced resistance because of his refusal to use professional actors. After being turned down by all the major studios in both Britain and the

United States, he managed to secure funding from the National Film Finance Corporation and from sources in France and Germany.

Adapted by Loach from a best-selling historical novel for children by Leon Garfield, *Black Jack* chronicles the adventures of an eighteenth-century draper's assistant and a bandit named Black Jack. "I found Garfield's book on one of my children's shelves," Loach explained to Derek Malcolm in an interview for the *Guardian* (March 2, 1980), "and I thought it was the perfect answer to all the sex and violence on the screen today." Loach also wanted to adapt the story because he had never before done a historical feature film. "The language I wanted was one which would evoke the past properly, colloquial without seeming quaint," he told Malcolm. "I also wanted to get on film the extraordinary quality of the pre-industrial revolution English landscape—that and the harshness of the lives of those who lived in it. . . . Above all, I wanted to get away from the usual clichés of historical film, to get somewhere near the truth of those lives." According to many viewers, Loach achieved his objective. "The location photography is often stunning," Malcolm was quoted as saying in the *World Film Directors* biography of Loach, "and the dialogue has that sense of reality Loach always manages to impart." *Black Jack* won the International Critics' Prize at the Cannes film festival.

During the 1980s Loach, who remained steadfast in his left-leaning political beliefs, found himself increasingly out of sync with the conservative political and social climate that prevailed in Britian. As a result, he found himself unable to line up financial backers, not only for his feature films but for television dramas as well. As a consequence, he had little choice but to make documentaries, which were frequently subjected to political opposition and censorship. For instance, he was forced to cut *A Question of Leadership* (1980), which dealt with the 1980 British steel strike, before it was broadcast. *Questions of Leadership* (1983), a four-part series about the failures of the trade union leadership, was banned outright and has yet to be televised. *Which Side Are You On?* (1984), which anthologized the songs and poems spawned by the 1984 miners' strike, was turned down for being too political and for allegedly lacking artistic merit. Channel 4 eventually aired the film, but only after it won a prize at a documentary festival in Florence, Italy. In 1987 *Perdition*, Jim Allen's play questioning the politics of Zionism that Loach was to direct at the Royal Court Theatre, London, also faced political opposition and was withdrawn the day before its scheduled opening. "The whole *Perdition* episode was the worst in my life," Loach told Richard Brooks in an interview for the London *Observer* (May 6, 1990). "All the newspapers lined up against the play. . . . It was a very organized campaign."

In the 1980s Loach made just two feature films, *Looks and Smiles* (1981) and *Fatherland* (1987), the latter of which was released in the United States as *Singing the Blues in Red*. He has since dismissed both as failures. Characteristically self-critical, he has blamed himself for his meager output during the 1980s. "What I regret most is that I didn't come up with the right ideas for five or six years," he explained to Hattenstone. "The right idea always comes with the writers, and I didn't look hard enough to find new writers. Instead we were battering our head against a brick wall doing documentaries." Eventually, even the documentary film assignments dried up, and the only work he could find was directing commercials. "I did it to survive," he admitted to Hattenstone. "They were for Tetleys Bitter and the *Guardian*. It could have been worse."

Loach's career prospects began to improve when the producer David Puttnam suggested that he make a film about John Stalker, an English police officer whose investigation into the Royal Ulster Constabulary's brutal tactics in Northern Ireland was thwarted by the authorities, forcing him to go public with his findings. The result was *Hidden Agenda* (1990), a drama in which Loach conflated the Stalker case and two similar cover-ups. As might be imagined, the film stirred considerable controversy among Britons. A Tory politician who had not even seen it condemned it as "an IRA film," and when it was screened at the 1990 Cannes International Film Festival, it was reviled by conservative British journalists attending the event.

The reaction of film critics to *Hidden Agenda* was mixed. Verina Glaessner, writing in the *Monthly Film Bulletin* (January 1991), was not alone in concluding that the film was a "mish-mash of televisual blandness and warmed-over conspiracy-theory plotting that fails to make much contribution to the debate of issues crucial to daily life in this country." Other reviewers, however, forgave Loach for his obvious partisanship and appreciated the film for its artistic merits. In his review for the *Los Angeles Times* (December 21, 1990), Peter Rainer observed, "The movie has a documentarylike atmosphere, but the confrontations are brilliantly staged and the dialogue is heightened for dramatic effect. . . . It may be studded with political theory, but it really *moves*." *Hidden Agenda* won the Special Jury Prize at the 1990 Cannes festival.

Reinvigorated, Loach next made *Riff-Raff* (1991), which concerns a motley group of undocumented construction workers and centers on Stevie, a young Scottish ex-con who is struggling to make a new life for himself. The film's humanism and empathy for people like Stevie recalled the early films upon which Loach had made his reputation. What distinguished *Riff-Raff* from his earlier efforts, however, was his attempt to show "what the effects of the early Eighties and Thatcherism had been, but to do it without a political lecture, with some warmth and humor," as he put it. According to many reviewers, Loach succeeded in imbuing the film with a sharp comic edge that had not been evident in his earlier work. "Opening his work to whimsy and foolishness hasn't compromised Loach's message; it's as lucid as ever," Georgia Brown observed in the *Village Voice* (February 9, 1993).

In the United States, *Riff-Raff* was among the few English-language films to be subtitled, in order to make the plethora of English, Scottish, and Irish accents comprehensible to American ears. Reflecting the deep admiration for Loach among continental Europeans, the film won both the International Critics' Prize at Cannes and the European Film Academy's best-film award. In England, however, Loach could not find a distributor for *Riff-Raff* until, following a week's run at the British Film Institute, it was loudly praised by reviewers. In spite of the critical acclaim, the film was never widely released in the United Kingdom.

In *Raining Stones* (1993), Loach provided viewers with one of his most moving portraits of real people struggling to retain their dignity and spirit under grim circumstances. The film tells the story of Bob, an unemployed Manchester man who devises a variety of schemes to earn enough money to buy his daughter a dress for her first communion. In the *New York Times* (October 2, 1993), Vincent Canby described *Raining Stones* as "brisk, richly characterized fiction that cuts as deeply and truly as any documentary. The movie slides effortlessly from farce to melodrama . . . and on into affecting domestic drama." The film received the Jury Prize at Cannes, making it Loach's third consecutive film to be honored there, and it was shown at the 1993 New York Film Festival. His most recent film, *Ladybird, Ladybird,* which premiered in Berlin in February 1994 and which was screened in the United States later in the same year as part of the New York Film Festival, focuses on a mother whose habit of getting involved in abusive relationships and whose own lack of control cause her to lose custody of six of her nine children.

Loach is known for both the easy rapport he maintains with actors and his ability to elicit extraordinary performances from nonprofessionals. Most of his actors, in fact, are ordinary people whose only qualification is that they come from the community in which the film is set. In the rare instances where he works with trained actors, Loach requires that they have relevant life experience to draw upon. To ensure that the performances are as authentic as possible, he shoots the scenes of his films in sequence and typically gives his actors their lines just before filming. "It takes amazing discipline and unerring instinct to use a style this free and bring it off," Michael Wilmington wrote in the *Chicago Tribune* (January 20, 1995). "Loach succeeds where dozens, or hundreds, of experimental dramatists and filmmakers routinely fail."

Although frequently referred to as a Marxist, Loach is uncomfortable with such political labeling. "I don't want to be pigeonholed as extreme left," he explained to Leonard Quart in an interview for *Cineaste* (Fall 1980), "and I lead a relatively comfortable, bourgeois existence, relegating my political activity to my films." By all accounts, Loach is quiet, affable, and extremely modest. He has been married to Lesley Ashton since 1962; they have two surviving sons and two daughters.

Selected Biographical References: Film Comment 24:38+ Mr '88 pors, 30:58+ Mr '94 por; Guardian p6+ O 8 '93 por; N Y Times X p20 Ja 31 '93 por; Village Voice p110 N 27 '90 por, p56+ F 9 '93 por; Hacker, Jonathan and David Price. Take 10: Contemporary British Film Directors (1991); Who's Who, 1995; World Film Directors, vol 2 (1988)

Anthony d'Offay Gallery, London

Long, Richard

June 2, 1945– British artist. Address: c/o Anthony d'Offay Gallery, 23 Dering St., London W1, England

"My work is about an emotional, one-on-one relationship with nature," the British artist Richard Long told an interviewer in 1986. "It's intensely physical, about a real engagement with the world. . . . It's an engagement with the possibilities of real time, real distance, real rocks." Described by one observer as "an artist who is at once traveler, nature-lover, and adventurer," Long has gained renown for creating so-called earth art during the course of planned walks that are themselves, according to Long, works of art. Nearly always unaccompanied, he walks in uninhabited and often remote locales, proceeding in a particular area for as little as an hour or as long as a month. In the course of his walks, when so inspired, he collects natural materials—most often stones—and then uses them, at a site along his route, to form a circle, line, cross, or other shape that, in his judgment, fits aesthetically into the landscape. "A walk is a line of footsteps, a sculpture is a line of stones,"

Long has said. "They're interchangeable and complementary."

To document his walks, which he has executed on every continent except Antarctica, and his outdoor sculptures, which few, if indeed any, other people are likely to see, Long takes photographs of his creations and of such things along his routes as geological formations and panoramic vistas. He also marks his itineraries on maps and keeps logs. His photos and maps and distinctively designed, typeset versions of his notes are an integral part of his art, and they have been displayed in more than 150 solo shows and some 200 group exhibits in museums and galleries throughout the world. In addition, for each exhibit of his work, Long constructs, on site at the museum or gallery, one or more sculptures that resemble what he creates during his walks. Also on site at exhibition spaces, using mud that he has scooped from the banks of the Avon River or other places, he often produces paintings by placing muddy handprints, footprints, or variously fashioned mud circles on a wall or floor or by flinging the mud at a wall.

"The classical simplicity of Long's work deftly sidesteps questions about its meaning," Roger Housden wrote in a highly favorable assessment of it for the *Guardian Guide* (June 1, 1991). "In fact, it sidesteps the intellect altogether and evokes a direct, visceral response from the senses. This, I suggest, is why it sometimes confounds critics, why it can raise the question as to whether it is art, and why it fills the Tate [Gallery, in London,] and elsewhere with the general public. . . . The sheer and mysterious pleasure of being alive in the natural world is what Richard Long's work communicates." Widely acclaimed as one of Great Britain's greatest contemporary artists, Richard Long represented Great Britain at the Venice Biennale in 1976. He received the Kunstpreis Aachen (known also as the Ludwig Prize) in 1988 and the Turner Prize, an award equivalent in prestige in the world of art to that of the Booker Prize in literary circles, in 1989.

Richard Long was born on June 2, 1945 in Bristol, a port city in southwestern England. In *Richard Long* (1986), which was published in conjunction with the artist's retrospective exhibition at the Guggenheim Museum, in New York City, R. H. Fuchs reported that starting in his early childhood, Long enjoyed doing things by himself and relying on his own resources. Also from a young age, he felt drawn to the outdoors. He spent countless hours exploring the bogs and moors near Bristol, and he was fascinated by the Avon River and its high, muddy banks. "One of the great influences of my childhood was seeing this enormous great river empty of water," he told Douglas C. McGill during an interview for the *New York Times* (October 26, 1986). "As a kid I made little plaster models of rivers in plaster of Paris that I filled up and emptied. I never made model airplanes or anything." His favorite activities also included walking with his grandparents in Dartmoor, a twenty-mile-long wild moorland plateau about a hundred miles from Bristol, hiking with his parents during their so-called "walking holidays" in the countryside, and going on backpacking expeditions with his father. Indoors, he especially liked to paint and draw.

Long studied traditional painting and sculpture at the West of England College of Art, in Bristol. He remained there from September 1962 until March 1965, when, for reasons that, by his own account, remain a mystery to him, school officials requested that he leave. Meanwhile, he recalled to Douglas McGill, he had "started to move out into the landscape." "I had a feeling it was the right thing to do," he explained. In an interview with Roger Housden for the *Guardian Guide*, he said, "Every artist makes a choice, and mine at that time was to place myself firmly in the tradition of . . . people who stand for pushing the edge, exploring the unknown, rather than looking over their shoulders at history. It's a question of faith, really, and making a commitment to your particular point of view." Sometime in 1965 Long made one of his first earth sculptures: lines, holes, and hollows in grass-covered soil that he had dug and in some of which he had poured plaster. He created *Turf Circle* (1966), another early work, by removing from the ground a circular slice of soil and the next thin layer of soil and then placing wedges cut from the first slice into the depression so that they formed a pattern similar to that of a spoked wheel. Although such relatively benign alterations of land are transient, Long has since abstained from cutting into or otherwise deforming the earth.

From 1966 to 1968 Long was enrolled at St. Martin's School, in London, which at that time was considered, along with the Royal College of Art, one of the two "most lively seedbeds for sculpture" in England, as Lynne Cook wrote in an essay that appears in Graham Beal's book *A Quiet Revolution: British Sculpture Since 1965* (1987). The staff at St. Martin's included Anthony Caro and Phillip King, catalysts in the movement that revolutionized British sculpture during the 1960s and two of the originators of the now-famous course of study that Long pursued. The student body included Barry Flanagan, Hamish Fulton, Gilbert Proesch, and George Passmore (the last two of whom work together as Gilbert & George), all of whom, like Long, have become highly successful sculptors.

The St. Martin's faculty gave Long free rein (and academic credits) to explore unorthodox approaches to sculpture. In one or more of his projects, he used sand and/or water to make "landscapes" on the roof of the school and photographed them to record the effects of changing daylight. He incorporated bicycling and walking as integral aspects of other projects. To create his seminal sculpture *A Line Made by Walking, England* (1967), he repeatedly walked back and forth along a straight line in a field of grass and then photographed the line of trodden grass. "The camera's viewpoint is Long's as he walked, and it takes no great effort for viewers to re-create the walk in their own imagination, vicariously sharing the effort and the achievement," Graham Beal wrote in *A Quiet Revolution*. "Thus is the artist's presence evoked, although he is no longer there. Long's act comes to symbolize all the paths that have been made by men throughout history, and his photograph of his sculpture becomes a metaphor for the transience of human life in the face of geological time—all this from a simple photograph of a simple activity."

For *England* (1968), Long removed the heads of hundreds of flowers in a field of daisies to form a pattern in the shape of a cross. His photo of the cross of stems appeared in his first solo exhibition, which was held in 1968 at the Konrad Fischer gallery in Düsseldorf, in what was then West Germany. The show featured a sculpture that Long made at the gallery with willow twigs, each cut to the length of a pencil, laid end to end in lines that covered much of the floor of a small, narrow room. Indiscernibly off-parallel, the lines converged very slightly as they neared the far end of the room. "The result was magical, a sustained illusion," a writer for *World Artists, 1980–1990* reported: "the real length of the room became impossible to measure; the physical was undermined and the metaphysical emphasized."

In 1969, in addition to the Konrad Fischer gallery, museums or galleries in New York, Paris, Milan, in Italy, and Krefeld, in West Germany, held one-person shows of Long's work. Every year since then Long has had at least three solo exhibitions, and sometimes as many as a dozen. In addition to the Guggenheim Museum, sites have included the Museum of Modern Art, in New York City (1972), the Scottish National Gallery of Modern Art, in Edinburgh (1974), the National Gallery of Victoria, in Melbourne, Australia (1977), the Fogg Art Museum of Harvard University, in Cambridge, Massachusetts (1980), the National Gallery of Canada, in Ottawa (1982), the Century Cultural Center, in Tokyo (1983), the Kunstsammlung Nordrhein-Westfalen, in Düsseldorf (1994), and the Palazzo Dell Esposizioni, in Rome (1994).

In 1976 the thirty-one-year-old Long received the coveted honor of representing Great Britain at the famous Venice Biennale. Using pieces of red limestone that he had collected from a quarry in Verona, Italy, he created a single, large sculpture—an "angular spiral," as Robert Hughes described it in *Time* (July 26, 1976), that snaked along the entire floor of the British pavilion. "It is an unexpectedly moving work, a metaphor of landscape done with elegant economy and, oddly enough in view of its material, as unaggressive as any English watercolor," Hughes wrote, after judging it to be "outstanding" among the works on view at all the national pavilions.

In his 1991 article for the *Guardian Guide*, which appeared two weeks before the opening of *Richard Long: Walking in Circles*, Long's survey exhibit at the Hayward Gallery, in London, Roger Housden suggested that despite its seeming incongruity, displaying earth art in an indoor setting offers rich rewards for the viewer. "It is startling . . . to walk into an art gallery and be confronted with concentric circles of muddy handprints, or a circle of rocks, or a long rectangle of random footprints," he observed. "A circle of rocks is very concrete, situated in the real world of present time and space. It returns us to our senses, and it is partly that which startles. Then there is the jolt of being in a sophisticated, sanitized gallery, and gazing at the rough and raw material of uncut rock and mud placed on the floor in clear and simple geometric shapes. It is as if the wilderness from which the rocks came has crept into our tamed and domesticated lives under the guise of art, and we jump in some flicker of recognition of our kinship with nature's rhythms, shapes, and materials. . . . If you can find meaning in rocks, you may say, you can find it in anything. Well that, I believe, is no bad thing: the soul of the world is alive in more ways than we know, but [it] is under threat from a culture which no longer hears its voice in the wind. Long manages to personify that voice in the most concrete of materials: his work breathes life and pleasure back into the senses; and that is not only art but art that our desensitized culture badly needs."

The American painter Peter Plagens judged the Long exhibition at the Hayward Gallery to be "generally fetching," as he wrote in a review for *Newsweek* (July 29, 1991). "*Cornwall Circle 1991* looks gorgeously paleolithic deployed in the middle of the Hayward's polite gallery floor," he wrote. "Framed typographical pieces like *Desert Flowers* (1987) somehow manage to evoke hot days, cold nights, and furtive wildlife. And [Long's] photographs of patches of the Sahara or Nepal are as deliciously textured as [Timothy H.] O'Sullivan's or [Carleton Emmons] Watkins's from the golden age of landscape photography in the nineteenth century." Plagens concluded, "The best thing that art can do is to give us some sense of what it means to be a human intrusion on this natural planet. In its poetry and economy, *Walking in Circles* gets straight to the point."

For nearly three decades, Long has spent on average a total of about six months a year walking in circles and otherwise producing art in conjunction with walking. His walks are often both temporally and spatially modest, as some of his titles indicate: *A Walk of Four Hours and Four Circles. England* (1972); *A 5 Mile Circular Walk on Dartmoor Passing Over 409 Rock Slabs & Boulders* (1980). Others, like *A 113 Mile Walk in 3 Days from Windmill Hill to Coalbrookdale Wiltshire to Shropshire England* (1979), are more ambitious. For *A Thousand Miles, a Thousand Hours* (1974), Long walked twenty-four miles a day to form a clockwise spiral in central England. Like those journeys, many of his other walks have taken place in what he has called the "very rich" landscapes of Great Britain. He has also created art during perambulations in Alaska and other parts of the United States and in Canada, Mexico, Iceland, Lapland, Switzerland, Bolivia, Peru, Australia, Japan, India, Zambia, and Tanzania, among other places.

With few exceptions—among them undertakings that are not recommended for the solitary hiker, such as climbing Mount Kilimanjaro, in

Tanzania, or trekking in Nepal—Long has carried out his walks unaccompanied. By his own account, he has never felt lonely out-of-doors and "think[s] about everything" while he walks. "Somehow having the rhythmic relaxation of walking many hours each day puts me into a state of mind which frees the imagination," he told Richard Cork for an interview that appears in *Richard Long: Walking in Circles* (1991), the catalog for his Hayward Gallery show. "Quite often I get ideas for new works by doing a walk." In addition to food, clothing, and a tent, if needed, he brings only a few tools and pieces of equipment: a string, which he uses to make circles, a pencil, a notebook, a camera, maps and a compass, and gloves for moving rocks.

Although Long researches all his trips in advance, the extent of his planning for them and the closeness with which they follow his itinerary and time frame vary considerably. Many of his walks have proceeded precisely according to plan; what he has described as an "instantaneous feeling" has suddenly ended others. Sometimes environmental or other circumstances have forced Long to alter his plans. During one of his trips to Africa, for example, his expectation that he would find loose stones on a mountain in Malawi failed to materialize, so that instead of forming the circle of stones that he had envisioned, he made a circle with pieces of lightning-burned cacti that he found scattered about. Deep snow has occasionally thwarted his plans, but in the main, inclement weather has seldom deterred him. At times, since he can hike only where water is readily available, rain has even benefited him. One year, shortly before he departed for a planned trip to the Sahara Desert, a series of unusual—and for Long, highly fortuitous—rainstorms left pools of water in a mountainous part of the desert. The location of the pools determined the path he took, and when, after six days, the water disappeared, having seeped into the ground or evaporated, he had to end his walk.

During his conversation with Richard Cork, Long declared that a circle "can be a vehicle for perhaps any idea under the sun." After noting that he could make circles of words, stones, and mud and could also walk in circles, he said that the circle is "a completely adaptable image and form and system." "The first time I used a circle I had no idea why I used it," he recalled to Cork. "It seemed like a good idea at the time, but having made it, it looked great and seemed a very strong and powerful image. . . . There are a lot of things theoretical and intellectual to say about lines and circles, but I think the very fact that they are images that don't belong to me and, in fact, are shared by everyone because they have existed throughout history, actually makes them more powerful than if I was inventing my own idiosyncratic, particular Richard Long-type images. I think it cuts out a lot of personal unwanted aesthetic paraphernalia. . . . [Circles and lines] allow me to home in on other things, so the circles stay the same in the different places I make them around the world, but the places change. It means that the viewer of my work is noticing that there are circles, but he is also seeing that the places are changing and the materials are changing." In a review of Long's retrospective at the Guggenheim for the *New York Times* (September 12, 1986), Michael Brenson wrote that the artist's constructed lines suggest "an eternal beginning," and his circles, "eternal return."

After completing a circular walk in Scotland in 1979, Long used his notes about the trip to produce one of his "wordwalkworks," as Clive Phillpot, then the director of the library of the Museum of Modern Art, in New York City, labeled them in the *Print Collector's Newsletter* (September/October 1987). *A 2½ Day Walk in the Scottish Highlands/Clockwise* (1979), as the work is called, measures 42.5 by 61 inches; it shows, arranged around an unmarked circle and mostly at regular intervals, twenty-eight words, phrases, or place names set in capital letters in sans-scrif type. When read clockwise, starting from the words "WHITE OWL," which lie approximately between what would be the 6 and 7 on a clock, the following appears: "DEER / RED STONES / AM MEADAR / ALLT A'CHAMA CHOIRE / FIRST NIGHT / UP BRUTHACH CHIULAM / IN THE CLOUDS / PEAT / BY A'MHARCONAICH / MAOL AN T-SEILICH / UNDER THE CLOUDS / DAM / SLOW GROUND [at the 12 o'clock position] / IN THE CLOUDS / BY MEALL AN UILLT CHREAGAICH / WHITE GRAVEL / HEADWIND/ SECOND NIGHT / SIDEWIND / WEATHER ROUNDED GRANITE / BEINN DEARG / HIGHEST PLACE / SLEET / WADING / LOWEST PLACE / BURNT HEATHER." As Jill Johnston pointed out in a discussion of Long's work for *Art in America* (April 1987), the typeset texts of his "word-pieces" often mirror the contours of the routes he has taken.

Long's work has sometimes been greeted with skepticism, and some critics and laypeople have questioned whether it can even be considered art. "Well, I am the artist, the person who is making it, and I am telling you it is art," Geordie Greig quoted Long as saying in the London *Sunday Times* (June 16, 1991). "I can't analyze why it is mysterious, why it is beautiful to walk across Dartmoor in a straight line all day, but it is. And because it is beautiful for me to do that, it is good enough for me to make it into art. If other people find it is insignificant, it is not for me to speak for them." Some critics have found shortcomings in particular aspects of Long's art. After noting, for example, that "behind Long's respect for surface is an almost pantheistic reverence," Michael Brenson observed, "If this respect for surface helps explain the work's strength, however, it also suggests its limits. Work that is not going to challenge the surface and that has Long's feeling for impermanence and lightness is going to be heavily conceptual—even when the inspiration is earth and stone. Although Long wanders and loves the texture of this planet, there is no sense that he loses himself in it. His works are thoughtful and analytical, but they are not searching."

Peter Plagens voiced another complaint: "Like vacation snapshots of the Grand Canyon, there's no smell, no wind, no traveler's fatigue in Long's re-creations, only the feeling that it must have been great for *him* to be there." And Clive Phillpot expressed reservations about the sculpture that Long constructed in museums and galleries: "Unlike his outdoor pieces, which clearly belong to the open countryside, the affinity of his indoor sculptures to their environment is more like that of stuffed animals to a natural history museum. The works look impressive, but dead and out of place."

Phillpot declared, nevertheless, that "Long has given us some of the most vivid visual inventions of the last twenty years." In the *Manchester Guardian Weekly* (June 23, 1985), Waldemar Januszczak described him as "the most revolutionary British landscape artist since [J. M. W.] Turner." Many other critics and connoisseurs of art also rank Long's work with that of the greatest contemporary British artists or even the most important artists of modern times. In 1991, for example, in developing a new national curriculum for the teaching of art, a twelve-member committee appointed by the British government, which was chaired by Lord Renfrew, the master of Jesus College, Cambridge University, and which included such prominent critics as Marina Vaizey, an art columnist for the London *Sunday Times*, selected Richard Long, along with such masters as Turner, John Constable, and Henri Matisse, as one of sixty artists, designers, and craftspeople whose works should be studied by British students.

Long has also achieved notable commercial success. In 1989, at the height of the art market, *Whitechapel Slate Circle*, which Long had created in 1981 with approximately four hundred stones, was sold for $190,000. *Avon Pacific Dark Mud Drawing* (1987), a work on paper in six parts, sold at an auction at Sotheby's in New York City for $27,500 in 1992. *Summer Slate Ring* (1985), which consists of forty-four pieces of slate assembled in a circle, sold for about $46,000 in 1993. According to a representative of Sotheby's in London, works made with stones, which necessarily must be dismantled for transport, are sold with detailed instructions, signed by the artist, that stipulate precisely how the stones should be reassembled.

Long's oeuvre includes more than two dozen so-called artist books (or booklets, as Clive Phillpot suggested they be called, because, as he pointed out, "few are hardbound"). Produced in very limited runs, they are also conspicuously limited in content. *Richard Long Sculptures England Germany Africa America 1966–1970*, for example, which was issued as a catalog for an exhibition held at the Stadtisches Museum in Monchengladbach, in what was then West Germany, in 1970, is a fifteen-page, five-by-seven-inch book that was printed in an edition of 330 copies. The book contains thirteen black-and-white photographs of Long's sculpture and comes in a box, on the inside of which a text of five short paragraphs is printed. Each of the one hundred copies of *Mud Hand Prints* (1984) contains a print of Long's left hand and, on the facing page, a print of his right hand. There are no other images and no text. Each of the thirty-five sets of *Rock Drawings* (1994), his most recent book, consists of a special case that contains a certificate and thirteen screen prints produced from photographs of rock rubbings that Long made during an eight-day walk in the Rimrock area of the Mojave Desert, in southern California.

In the London *Sunday Times* (October 14, 1990), Marina Vaizey described Richard Long as "tall, lean, [and] extremely fit." "Long has almost everything of the artist about him . . . ," Tom Lubbock wrote in the British newspaper the *Independent* (June 23, 1991). "He is serious, uncompromising, methodical, [and] obsessive." According to Geordie Greig, the "critical ambivalence" with which Long's work has been greeted has made him "defensive and brusque." Long once ended a television interview after just thirty seconds, Greig reported, and his responses to questions "can be caustic or sarcastically dismissive." Long rarely submits to interviews, and little information about his personal life has appeared in print. He lives in Bristol, and according to one source, he has two daughters.

Selected Biographical References: Art in America 75:161+ Ap '87; Guardian Guide p12 Je 1 '91 por; N Y Times II p31+ O 26 '86 por; Beal, Graham. A Quiet Revolution: British Sculpture Since 1965 (1987); Fuchs, R. H. Richard Long (1986); World Artists, 1980–1990 (1991)

Lopez, Barry

Jan. 6, 1945– Writer. Address: c/o Peter Matson, Sterling Lord Literistic Inc., 65 Bleeker St., New York, NY 10012

"Apart from the ceaseless task of working with the language in order to tell a good story well, the most important issue to me as a writer is how to be responsible to society," Barry Lopez has said. Self-described as "a writer who travels" and characterized by T. H. Watkins of the *Washington Post* (May 5, 1988) as "one of the most fully involved and supremely articulate chroniclers of the land," Lopez is the author of the prize-winning books *Of Wolves and Men* and *Arctic Dreams* and many other critically acclaimed works of nonfiction and fiction. Notable for the clarity, richness, eloquence, and power of its language, his work is informed by what the *New York Times* book reviewer Michiko Kakutani called his "deep, almost mystical reverence for nature" and a vision of humankind's place in the environment that, while firmly rooted in history, cultural anthropology, and biology, is deeply spiritual as well.

Lopez's writings, which have often been compared to those of Henry David Thoreau, Edward

Mike Mathers/Fairbanks Daily News-Miner

Barry Lopez

Abbey, and Edward Hoagland, among other masters of American literature, offer "an endless supply of fresh, often unsettling looks at creatures, landscapes, and human behavior," Michael Coffey reported in *Publishers Weekly* (July 27, 1990). "When you write about animals and landscape and wilderness, you write about what appears to be natural history," Lopez has explained. "But my principal interest is in human beings and how we arrive at our ideas. My lifelong commitment is to some kind of elucidation of these ideas—what is prejudice, what is tolerance, and what does it mean to lead a dignified life."

Barry Holstun Lopez was born on January 6, 1945 in Port Chester, New York, a few miles from Mamaroneck, the town on Long Island Sound where he lived until age three. His mother, then Mary Frances (Holstun) Brennan, whose ancestors included seventeenth-century Pennsylvania settlers, worked in advertising and as a newspaper columnist before her marriage to John Edward Brennan, whose field was also advertising. In 1948, the year that Lopez's brother, Dennis, a carpenter, was born, the family moved to Reseda, in a semirural area of California's San Fernando Valley. After her divorce from John Brennan, in 1950, Mary Brennan taught home economics in secondary schools and at a junior college. In 1955 she married Adrian Bernard Lopez, a businessman, who legally adopted her sons and whom Barry Lopez regards as his father. During a conversation with Alice Evans for *Poets & Writers Magazine* (March/April 1994), he said that he had not seen his biological father since early childhood.

Lopez has recalled "walking out into Long Island Sound as a three-year-old, up to [his] neck, and the longing to go farther." "The space out over the water, and the light out over the water, was an *attraction* to me," he explained to Douglas Marx, who interviewed him for *Publishers Weekly* (September 26, 1994). "I wanted to go out in the morning and *be* in that." As a youngster living in Southern California, he "formed the rudiments of a local geography—eucalyptus trees, February rains, Santa Ana winds," as he wrote in an essay that appeared in the anthology *Finding Home* (1992), and he visited such places as the Mojave Desert and the Grand Canyon. "That's where I got the feelings about landscape that have remained with me the longest," he told Nicholas O'Connell for *At the Field's End: Interviews with 20 Northwest Writers* (1987). He completed grades one through six at Our Lady of Grace, a Roman Catholic school in Encino, California.

In 1956 Lopez and his family moved to the New York City borough of Manhattan, where his mother got a job as a junior high school teacher and he enrolled at the Loyola School, a Jesuit-administered institution. "New York was such a shock . . . ," he recalled to Alice Evans. "It was a very different flavor from what I'd had growing up. My emotional and metaphorical frameworks were set in my involvement with animals and the desert when I was a kid in California, and then at the age of eleven I got this sort of overlay, of school and intellection and reading and a formal exposure to the arts." In high school his extracurricular activities included dramatics, public speaking, soccer, basketball, and track. As a senior he served as president of the student body. He spent the summer following his graduation, in 1962, in Europe, "to see the landscape, the architecture, and the art that had been so much a part of [his] prep-school education," in his words.

Halfway through his freshman year at the University of Notre Dame, in South Bend, Indiana, Lopez changed his major from aeronautical engineering to communication arts and embarked on a program that focused on writing, theatre, and literature. The syllabus also included classes in philosophy and theology—courses that he has described as "of lasting importance . . . not because you believed one way or the other, but because you realized from them that you had to be responsible in your life for what you did." As an undergraduate he played intercollegiate soccer, participated in theatrical productions as an actor or member of the technical crew, and, all four years, worked at the campus radio station as a newsman and announcer. Disregarding a college rule, Lopez kept a car off-campus, and on weekends and during intersessions, either alone or with a friend, he would drive "terrific" distances, often "just to see the country," in his words. "As a boy I felt a hunger to know the American landscape that was extreme," he has explained; "when I was finally able to travel on my own, I did so."

By the end of his senior year, Lopez had visited nearly every state. He and a friend repeatedly returned to the West Virginia farm of Odey Cassell, whom they had met on one of their weekend excursions and with whom they shared stories. "When we unraveled our stories," Lopez recalled in his essay "Grown Men," which is in his book *Crossing Open Ground* (1988), "Odey listened as keenly as we had to him, strengthening the flow of our narrative with a gentle question or two, helping us shape it." In the summers following his sophomore and junior years, Lopez worked on a Wyoming ranch as a horse wrangler and packer, gaining experiences that he has characterized as "crucial to the development of his work." He earned a B.A. degree cum laude from Notre Dame (where he had been on the dean's list for three years) in 1966.

By his own account, as a youngster who was raised in the Roman Catholic faith, Lopez had been "deeply affected" by "the tradition of the desert fathers, the Jesuits, and the monastic tradition." In his senior year in high school, he had considered entering a seminary, and as a college senior he contemplated becoming a monk. "I was thinking, 'How can I be of service, how can I be of service?' . . . ," he recalled to Alice Evans. "I thought, 'You can be of service by planting things in the ground and by being an instrument of grace.'" Attracted by the idea of devoting himself totally to hard work and prayer, after graduating from college he visited Gethsemane, a Trappist abbey in Kentucky. While there, he decided that the monastic life would be "too easy," he told Alice Evans, and subsequently, according to Evans, he "drifted away from the formal institution of the church." For about a year, beginning in 1966, he worked as a representative of the New American Library, a publishing company.

Lopez had begun writing short stories in high school, and several of his stories and book reviews were published while he was in college. "I had no clear idea that I was going to be a writer," he told Nicholas O'Connell. "I guess it was just what I was, and after a while I was aware of that." ("My place is working alone in front of a typewriter and exercising a sense of social responsibility that's been there since I was very young," he has said.) In 1967, proceeding on the belief that he would never be able to earn a living as a writer and that, as a teacher, he "would write, like everyone else did, on the side," as he told Jean W. Ross during an interview for *Contemporary Authors* published in 1987, he entered a graduate program in teaching and English at Notre Dame, with a full scholarship and a stipend for living expenses.

In 1968, after earning an M.A. degree in teaching, Lopez began working toward an M.F.A. degree in creative writing at the University of Oregon, in Eugene. He also took courses in folklore and journalism and, under the guidance of Barre Toelken, one of his teachers, began an intensive study of Native American culture. "Until then I had not known what to do with this correspondence I'd felt between the things I was trying to articulate and what I was feeling while reading about Native American people," Lopez has noted. A character, known as the trickster figure, common to many Native American cultures became the subject of his first book, *Giving Birth to Thunder, Sleeping with His Daughter: Coyote Builds North America.* A collection of his retellings of various trickster stories, it was published in 1978, a decade after he wrote it and two years after the appearance of *Desert Notes*, his first published book.

Beginning in the mid-1960s, Lopez had begun contributing articles to national magazines and newspapers and selling some of his photographs of landscapes. In 1969 he dropped out of the University of Oregon, partly because he had gained confidence in his earning potential as both a writer and a photographer and also because he had lost his eagerness to teach and had decided that the university's writing program had "too much of a sense of the writer and not nearly enough sense of the reader," as he told an interviewer. For a while in 1969 he handled publications assignments part-time at a community college in Oregon. Since then, except for a semester in 1985 during which he taught at Eastern Washington University and another, in 1989, at Notre Dame, and short stints as a "distinguished visiting writer" at three universities, he has devoted himself virtually full-time to writing and research. Other than book tours, he gives readings and lectures only two or three times a year. "While I think this schedule is right for me," he told *Current Biography*, "I'm ambivalent about not accepting more university invitations because I feel an increasing responsibility to younger people, to share whatever it is I know that is useful to them."

Lopez has not taken photographs since 1981, in part, he explained to *Current Biography*, because he became uneasy about "what making photographs was doing to his sense of perception." His interest in photography remains strong, however. In 1990, for example, he spoke at the opening of an exhibition of the work of the photographer Robert Adams that was held at the Amon Carter Museum, in Fort Worth, Texas. "I . . . feel, as a writer, an affinity for Robert Adams's work . . . ," he said during his talk. "He reminds me of my obligations and my ideals. . . . He speaks to me as a human being, to my dreams for grace and dignity, and I would say holiness in the world." In words that echo observations that have been made about his own work and reveal his preoccupations, Lopez said that Adams, through his photographs, "urges us to overcome anger and bitterness, he urges us to be present in the present. Not to be aloof, unseeing and uncaring. . . . And when this message comes . . . from someone you could imagine as a neighbor, not as a posturer or a pontificator, then you sense that it might be a message worth listening to. To speak of Adams's work is to speak of faith, of hope, of compassion, of that which is sacred. He has fused art and religion not by creating icons but by inquiring after the fate of what is holy." Lopez maintains close friendships with photographers, composers, painters, dancers, and other artists as well as writers, all of whom, he has said metaphorically, are "seated at the same table" and many of whom are "struggling with the same conceptual problems" as he is.

Among the literary works that have emerged from Lopez's struggle with those problems are dozens of short stories. "My interest in a story is to illuminate a set of circumstances that bring some understanding of human life, enough at least so that a reader can identify with it and draw some vague sense of hope or sustenance or deep feeling and in some way be revived . . . and can say 'I have been brought to a state of wonder by contact with something in a story,'" Lopez told Jim Aton for *Western American Literature* (May 1986). In his trilogy of short-story collections that began with *Desert Notes: Reflections in the Eye of a Raven* (1976), Lopez, combining an "unsentimental naturalist's knowledge" with a "profound love-of-land," as David Graber wrote in the *Detroit News* (November 4, 1979), drew a strikingly individualistic, illuminating picture of particular natural landscapes.

In *River Notes: The Dance of Herons* (1979), the second book in the series, Lopez created "a small world of relationships among people, herons, salmon, cottonwoods—and all creatures drawn to . . . the river," David Miller noted in the *Progressive* (May 1980). In his review, Miller described the book as "a thing of beauty in itself, as tantalizingly real and yet as otherworldly as your own reflection on a river's surface. . . . It is a rare achievement; perhaps . . . a work of genius." A writer for *Publishers Weekly* (September 25, 1994) listed "The Negro in the Kitchen," "Sonora," "Empira's Tapestry," and "Conversation," which appeared in *Field Notes: The Grace Note of the Canyon Wren* (1994), the last work in the trilogy, as stories that Lopez "has not surpassed." "All the stories contain moments of sheer magic," the *Publishers Weekly* writer added, "and all reflect Lopez's abiding passion for the beauty and mystery of the earth and its creatures."

In an assessment of *Winter Count* (1981), an earlier collection of Lopez's short stories, Elaine Kendall observed in the *Los Angeles Times* (May 9, 1981), "There's a boundary, no wider than a pinstripe, where fact and fiction barely touch. With so much room on either side and assorted areas where overlap is expected, few writers choose to confine themselves to that fine line where the two simply meet. Lopez makes that delicate border his entire territory. *Winter Count* is a small and perfectly crafted collection of just such encounters between imagination and reality." *Winter Count* received the Distinguished Recognition Award from Friends of American Writers in 1981.

Earlier, in 1976, on an assignment for *Smithsonian* magazine, Lopez had gone to Alaska to gather information for an article about wolves. "That research catalyzed a lot of thinking about human and animal relationships which had been going on in a vague way in my mind for several years," he said later. "I realized that if I focused on this one animal, I might be able to say something sharp and clear." *Of Wolves and Men* (1978) came out of that realization. Based not only on extensive fieldwork, during which he interviewed scientists, trappers, and native peoples, but also on considerable scholarly research, it is at once an extraordinarily comprehensive scientific account, a history of humankind's relationship with wolves (and Western societies' relentless destruction of them), a treasury of wolf lore gleaned from aboriginal societies, and a study of the wolf in literature, folk tales, and popular belief.

In a representative review of the book that appeared in the *Washington Post* (November 27, 1978), Whitley Streiber judged it to be "a very important book by a man who has thought much on his subject. Above all he has listened to many people who claim to know about wolves. In coming to terms with the difference between what we know and what we imagine about the wolf, Lopez has shed light on some painful truths about the human experience. By laying no blame while facing the tragedy for what it is, he has made what we have done to the wolf a source of new knowledge about man." *Of Wolves and Men* won the John Burroughs Medal, a Christopher Medal, and a Pacific Northwest Booksellers award in 1979, and it was nominated for an American Book Award in 1980.

In 1978, soon after *Of Wolves and Men* was published, Lopez returned to Alaska "to hang out and watch animals and play," in his words. He recalled to Alice Evans, "I [thought], 'Oh, I've missed something here. I've been looking at wolves so long I've missed these other things.' And so that's where *Arctic Dreams* started." During the next four years, in the course of investigating the Arctic's "other things," he traveled along the Arctic Circle, between the Bering and Davis straits, on his own and in the company of wildlife biologists, archeologists, artists, petroleum geologists, and Inuit hunters. He delved deeply into the natural and social history of the Arctic while, at the same time, examining his own experience of it. "I was obsessed with the incredible beauty of that landscape," Lopez told Trisha Todd during an interview for *Publishers Weekly* (October 11, 1985). "I was haunted. I had the same quickness of heart and very intense feelings that human beings have when, in an utterly uncalculated way, they fall in love. *Arctic Dreams* is about that experience—what happens between the heart and a piece of land, what happens between the mind and a piece of land."

Arctic Dreams: Imagination and Desire in a Northern Landscape (1986) "is a book about the Arctic North in the same way that *Moby Dick* is a novel about whales . . . ," Michiko Kakutani wrote in the *New York Times* (February 12, 1986), in a review in which she described the work as "dazzling." "It treats the distant snowy world of the Arctic as a place that exists not only in the mathematics of geography, but also in the terra incognita of our imaginations. For Mr. Lopez, it is a land where 'airplanes track icebergs the size of Cleveland and polar bears fly down out of the stars,' a land rich in imagery and metaphor. . . . He communicates to us a visceral sense of his own understanding and wonder, as well as an appreciation for this distant country that flickers insistently like a flashbulb afterimage in our minds long after we've finished reading. . . . Mr. Lopez takes his place among those . . . individuals who ventured to the northern limits of the earth and made of their journey a lasting record of its fierceness and its beauty." *Arctic Dreams* won a National Book Award, a Christopher Book Award, a Pacific Northwest Booksellers Award, and the 1987 Francis Fuller Victor Award in nonfiction from the Oregon Institute of Literary Arts, among other honors.

"When I was at work on *Arctic Dreams*, I was trying to understand the relationship between landscape and imagination," Lopez wrote in a proposal, which he sent to prospective publishers in 1989, for his next book-length work of nonfiction, a study of "the scale of human time in remote landscapes." "What I want to look at now is the relationship between landscape and emotion, particularly the emotion of hope. . . . I want to raise questions about who we are and where we are headed as a species. And I want to introduce something quite dark about human life, our capacity to murder, for example, for without this knowledge an inquiry into the worth of human life falls flat." In addition to extensive library research, Lopez's preparations for writing the book have included travels in northern Kenya, the Northern Territory in Australia, the Galápagos Islands, Antarctica, and the Arctic. "Offshore," an essay that he has described as "bearing heavily" on the book, appeared in the Winter 1994 issue of *Orion*.

Essays and journalistic pieces that Lopez has written during the past quarter century have appeared in such periodicals as *National Geographic*, *Harper's*, *Antaeus*, *Outside*, *Aperture*, and the *New York Times* as well as *Orion*. Many have been included in anthologies, among them *The Sophisticated Traveler: Enchanting Places and How to Find Them* (1986), *On Nature* (1987), *Wild Africa* (1993), *A Thousand Leagues of Blue* (1994), *Major Modern Essayists* (1994), which is a widely used college text, *American Nature Writing* (both the 1994 and 1995 collections), and *Best American Essays* (1995), which is a compilation from the *Best American Essays* annuals. A dozen of his essays, dating from 1979 to 1986, are collected in revised form in *Crossing Open Ground* (1988). Among his recent short stories are "The Interior of North Dakota" (*Paris Review*, Winter 1992), the Pushcart Prize-winner "Benjamin Claire, North Dakota Tradesman, Writes to the President of the United States" and "The Hitter" (*North American Review*, September/October 1992 and July/August 1993, respectively), and "Thomas Lowdermilk's Generosity" (*American Short Fiction*, Winter 1993). *The Rediscovery of North America*, a 1990 memorial lecture in which he considered the consequences of Christopher Columbus's voyage to the Western Hemisphere, was published as a book in 1991.

Lopez wrote *Crow and Weasel* (1990), which he has described as "a hero myth of sorts," "a coming-of-age story," and "an allegory of hope," for younger readers as well as adults. A sixty-four-page fable set in "myth time," *Crow and Weasel* is about two young men from the northern plains of North America, who, during a courageous journey to a land farther north than any of their people have ever gone, gain knowledge about the natural world, "awareness of the spiritual dimension of the landscape," and insights into the importance of community and friendship. Illustrated by Tom Pohrt, it won a Parents Choice Foundation Award. An adaptation of *Crow and Weasel* for the stage, which was commissioned by the Sundance Children's Theatre, premiered in Minneapolis, Minnesota in 1994, in a sixty-three-run performance at the Children's Theatre Company. The play was written by Jim Leonard Jr. with Lopez's assistance.

In 1985 Nicholas O'Connell described Lopez as "a sturdy, thick-chested man . . . who looked as if he'd be as much at home following a wolf biologist around the Brooks Range in Alaska as doing research in the Pierpont Morgan Library in New York." "Wonder and curiosity animate his brown eyes," Douglas Marx wrote in 1994. "He's trim and fit, . . . and his tan face is that of a young man, still open, wiser, sadder, perhaps, but with no trace of the stereotypical hardened explorer's creased ruddiness." Lopez and his wife, the former Sandra Jean Landers, a book artist, were married on June 10, 1967. For the past twenty-five years, they have lived in Oregon, in a house overlooking the McKenzie River, on the forested, western slope of the Cascade Mountains. Among other honors and prizes, Lopez received an award in literature for his body of work from the American Academy and Institute of Arts and Letters (1986), a Guggenheim Foundation fellowship (1987), the Governor's Award for Arts (1990), the Lannan Foundation Award (1990), and an honorary doctorate from the University of Portland (1994).

"I find myself in the middle of a community of writers trying especially to reach people who make decisions in our society, trying to create an atmosphere of hope for all of us who are reading," Lopez told Ray Gonzalez during an interview for the *Bloomsbury Review* (January/February 1990). When Douglas Marx asked him for a capsule description of his philosophy as a writer, Lopez said, "I like to use the word 'isumataq.' It's of eastern Arctic Eskimo dialect and refers to the storyteller, meaning 'the person who creates the atmosphere in which wisdom reveals itself.' I think that's the writer's job. It's not to be brilliant, or to be the person who always knows, but it's to be the one who recognizes the patterns that remind us of our obligations and our dreams." He added, "My themes will always be dignity of life, structures of prejudice, passion, generosity, kindness, and the possibility of the good life in dark circumstances."

Selected Biographical References: Poets & Writers Mag 22:62+ Mr/Ap '94 por; Pub W 241:41+ S 26 '94 por; Contemporary Authors new rev vol 23 (1988); O'Connell, Nicholas. At the Field's End (1987); Who's Who in America, 1995; World Authors, 1980–1985 (1991)

Douglas C. Pizac/AP/Wide World Photos

Louis-Dreyfus, Julia

(LOO-ee-DRY-fuss)

Jan. 13, 1961- Actress. Address: c/o Producers Entertainment Group, 9150 Wilshire Blvd., Suite 205, Beverly Hills, CA 90212

"It's probably the best job I'll ever have," Julia Louis-Dreyfus has said about her role on the NBC comedy megahit *Seinfeld*. "It's maybe the best job there is." Louis-Dreyfus, who served as a member of the cast of *Saturday Night Live* for three disappointing seasons during the early 1980s and, in 1988, as the star of a failed situation comedy, hit the jackpot in 1989, when she was cast as Elaine Benes, Jerry Seinfeld's ex-girlfriend, on the show about a group of friends who live in New York City. *Seinfeld*, which survived several shifts on NBC's prime-time schedule from 1990 to 1992, has been a top-rated show since 1993, when it replaced the long-running show *Cheers* on Thursday nights.

Elaine is considered unusual on television because she shares the spotlight equally with the show's other three main characters, all of whom are men. Louis-Dreyfus "could have been relegated, like many women in prime-time, to fourth-banana status," Elizabeth Gleick wrote in *People* (November 23, 1992), "but as Elaine, she actually steals scenes" from the men. Louis-Dreyfus, who was nominated for an Emmy award for best supporting actress in a comedy series for the years 1992 through 1995, brings an exuberance and comedic talent to Elaine that many people find amusing. "Julia can be so deft with tricky material, yet she's great at swinging-from-the-heels comedy," Seinfeld told Betsy Sharkey in an interview for *US* (May 1993). "It's really astounding to me the variety of things she does well—she's such a *broad* broad."

Julia Louis-Dreyfus was born on January 13, 1961 to William Louis-Dreyfus, an attorney, and his wife, Judith, a writer. When she was one year old, her parents divorced. She grew up in Washington, D.C., with her mother and her stepfather, L. Thompson Bowles, a doctor, and visited her father and stepmother, Phyllis, a teacher, at their home in northern Westchester County, New York, during vacations and summers. "I got a lot of those little flying-wing pins," Louis-Dreyfus told Pat H. Broeske during an interview for *Redbook* (January 1994). "Divorce is not a lot of fun, but as divorces go, it was amicable." She has four half-sisters, two from each parent. Growing up in a family where everybody was funny, including her great-grandmother, contributed to Louis-Dreyfus's sense of humor. She has said that her childhood heroes were the television stars Lucille Ball and Mary Tyler Moore and that she admired them because they didn't give up their femininity in order to be funny. Louis-Dreyfus attended a girls' private school, Holton-Arms, in Bethesda, Maryland, where many of the students were the children of Washington notables, among them Susan Ford, the daughter of President Gerald R. Ford. "I wish I hadn't gone there for ten years," Louis-Dreyfus told Broeske. "But I must say, I got a great deal out of it. It gives women an advantage in a lot of ways. Because there's no social pressure, you have an opportunity to excel that you wouldn't have in a coed situation. It gives you a stronger sense of self."

A standout in high-school plays, Louis-Dreyfus found her niche in improvisational comedy at Northwestern University, in Evanston, Illinois, which she attended from 1979 to 1981. She was the only female member of an improvisational troupe called the Practical Theatre Company, which was run by a fellow student, Brad Hall, whom she married in 1987. One of her favorite skits during that time was an impersonation of the evangelist Tammy Faye Bakker. After seeing Louis-Dreyfus and Hall perform in a Chicago comedy revue in 1981, the producers of the NBC program *Saturday Night Live* invited both to join the cast of the show. Leaving college before her senior year, Louis-Dreyfus went to New York to begin the 1982–83 television season. She has said that being discovered so young made her feel "like Cinderella."

As a regular on *Saturday Night Live*, Louis-Dreyfus worked with the actors Billy Crystal, Eddie Murphy, and Joe Piscopo, among others. "I came in and had a lot of enthusiasm, if that's style," she told Betsy Sharkey. "But it wasn't like I'd been working on an act and a bunch of characters for years that I could drop into the show, so that was a problem." She did develop several signature performances, including impersonations of Linda Ronstadt and Liza Minnelli. She was also the host of "The Julia Show," a skit in which she chatted endlessly about herself rather than interview "celebrity" guests. Working for *Saturday Night Live* was not a happy experience for Louis-Dreyfus. "It was a real induction, a very hard experience," she told Pat Broeske. "Everyone was vying for material every week. It was definitely *not* an ensemble." The lesson she learned from her three years with the show, she has said, was that "it's not worth it unless you're having a good time."

After leaving *Saturday Night Live* in 1985, Louis-Dreyfus got small parts in several movies, including *Troll* (1986), *Hannah and Her Sisters* (1986), and *National Lampoon's Christmas Vacation* (1989). In 1988 she was back on television, in her first situation comedy series, the short-lived *Day by Day*. She played an ornery, fast-track stockbroker named Eileen Swift who, despite her dislike for children, becomes involved in her friends' day-care operation. A ratings disaster, the show was off the air by 1989. The casting of Louis-Dreyfus as a baby-hater amused Brad Hall, who told a reporter for *People* (April 18, 1988) that his wife loved children so much that she "would walk across a fiery pit to goo-goo and ga-ga a baby."

In the summer of 1989, the pilot episode of a show called *The Seinfeld Chronicles* (later renamed *Seinfeld*), about the private life of a stand-up comedian and his cadre of offbeat friends, aired on NBC. Network executives were sufficiently impressed by the pilot to order four new episodes as a summer replacement series in 1990. The cocreators of the show, Jerry Seinfeld and Larry David, had not originally envisioned a regular female role in the show, but after the pilot was broadcast, Seinfeld, feeling the program "lacked estrogen," decided to add a woman to the cast. Approximately one hundred actresses read for the part of Elaine. "We had a very vague idea of Elaine," Seinfeld told Elizabeth Kolbert of the *New York Times* (June 3, 1993). "But once Julia walked in, we knew who Elaine was. We created her together." Seinfeld also said that the "chemistry" between himself and Louis-Dreyfus just felt right. "She had an intelligence and appeal that was exactly what we were looking for—the ex-girlfriend you can't seem to get past," he was quoted as saying in *People* (November 23, 1992).

Louis-Dreyfus was impressed by *Seinfeld* after reading an early script in 1989. "The writing was truly spectacular—no bull," she has said. The show is not plot-driven in the way traditional situation comedies are; instead, it takes as its inspiration the typical annoyances of urban life—such as waiting for what seems like forever for a table at a Chinese restaurant, or trying to remember where a car is parked in a multilevel garage. The predicaments the characters get into are often unusual and frequently hilarious. A 1992 episode, noted for its controversial humor, was reviewed by John J. O'Connor in the *New York Times* (May 30, 1993): "One of the best episodes of the past season managed to be all about masturbation without ever once mentioning the word. The code phrase, always a handy Seinfeld device, became 'master of my domain.'" Louis-Dreyfus told Betsy Sharkey that the "subject matter was racy and groundbreaking for television, and it was so superbly crafted writing-wise that it was fun to perform."

Besides Seinfeld and Elaine, the show's central characters include George (Jason Alexander), Seinfeld's neurotic best friend, who regularly gets himself into trouble, and Kramer (Michael Richards), a neighbor whose bizarre behavior often complicates the lives of his friends. In an article for *Glamour* (May 1993), Louis-Dreyfus described how delighted she was to be the only female member of "an all-boys club." "Treating me as one of the boys is, in part, what's good about the show," she wrote. "The situation in reality (me and three guys) is the same as on the show (me and three guys). But much to the dismay of those who analyze *Seinfeld* too deeply, I'm not there to represent the female point of view. I'm just another actor in the cast. I have no agenda except to be funny." Harry Stein declared in a column for *TV Guide* (October 17, 1992) that what he admires about the character of Elaine is that she actually likes men and does not simply write them all off as sexist bores, a perspective he called "a welcome relief" from what is often depicted on television. Elaine is "a real sport," in Louis-Dreyfus's words, ready to help her male friends deal with their peculiar life situations or to be a full participant in their adolescent games.

The four stars of *Seinfeld* all have very strong personalities, but they nonetheless get along very well, Louis-Dreyfus has said. "We have a shared sensibility about what's funny," she explained to Betsy Sharkey. "We make each other laugh, which is crucial. We enjoy each other's company, we really do." During the taping of the show, cast members often laugh so much that the scenes have to be reshot. "To tell you the truth, I think we find our show funnier than anybody else who watches," Louis-Dreyfus admitted to Elizabeth Kolbert. The show is taped on Tuesday nights, and afterwards, the actors go out to dinner together to unwind and analyze the episode. Those dinners are often punctuated by laughter, too. "We remind each other about the lines, howling, howling," she told Kolbert.

Louis-Dreyfus, who is often asked to compare herself to the character she plays, has said, "Elaine is very much like myself, times one hundred and fifty." The biggest difference between the two is their private lives: unlike Louis-Dreyfus, Elaine has gone through a string of unsuccessful relationships. The actress described her character in an interview with Diane Bailey of *TV Guide* (August 3, 1991) as "the neurotic woman of the nineties. She vacillates in her day-to-day desires." It is appropriate to have "Elaine bouncing off the walls emotionally," she told Bailey, because the conflict of awkward romantic liaisons is often the heart of *Seinfeld*'s humor.

During the hiatus after *Seinfeld*'s first full season, Louis-Dreyfus took a dramatic role in the film *Jack the Bear*, about a father (Danny DeVito) who must raise two sons alone after his wife is killed in a car crash. She played a coworker of the DeVito character. The film, which was released in 1993, was not well-received. Leah Rozen of *People* (April 5, 1993) called the plot "melodramatic" and "herky-jerky" and observed that Louis-Dreyfus was "given nothing more to do than smile benevolently or frown disapprovingly at DeVito's antics." In the following year Louis-Dreyfus landed her first major screen role, in *North*, which was directed by Rob Reiner. The movie is a comic fable about a boy named North who wanders the countryside in search of new parents because his preoccupied mother and father are too busy to spend time with him. Louis-Dreyfus played North's mother; the father was played by her *Seinfeld* costar Jason Alexander. The movie received mixed reviews and fared poorly at the box-office.

Louis-Dreyfus, who is five feet three inches tall, has long, naturally curly, voluminous hair that has become a trademark of sorts. In 1993 she signed an advertising contract with Clairol Inc., which makes hair-care products, and she has done several amusing television commercials for Nice 'n Easy hair coloring. After missing the first four episodes of *Seinfeld*'s 1992–93 season, following the birth of her first child, Henry Hall, Louis-Dreyfus returned to work with baby, nanny, and lactation pump in tow. She has said that if she had not been able to bring the baby to work, she probably would have dropped out of the series. "I'm not interested in having anyone else raise my kid," she told Pat Broeske. "It doesn't sit well with me to be apart from him for an extended period of time." Seinfeld joked to Broeske that motherhood hasn't really affected Louis-Dreyfus because "she hasn't become any less silly."

Julia Louis-Dreyfus lives with her husband and their son in a four-bedroom, country-style house in the hills above Westwood, California. Brad Hall, who is a television producer, told Broeske that the constant changes in the couple's lives have helped keep their relationship fresh. "We started out as students and then we were avant-garde theatre artists," he said. "Then we became *Saturday Night Live*-y people in New York. Then we became television people. Now we're parents. It's been a constant journey." As for her fame and the success of *Seinfeld*, Louis-Dreyfus told Lisa Liebman of *New Woman* (July 1993) that she is trying to keep things in perspective. "To tell you the truth, what's happening right now is a very surreal experience," she said. "I mean, I sort of stand back from it all. You know, it's a job—a fun job, there's no doubt about that—but it's not real. And I'm well aware of the fact that it can all be very fleeting, so you can't put too much emphasis on it in your life. The success of the show is wonderful, and I hope it continues. But one day it will be over, everyone will move on, and, you know, it's just *entertainment*."

Selected Biographical References: Glamour 91:208 My '93 por; N Y Times C p1+ Je 3 '93 por; New Woman 23:21 Jl '93 por; People 29:79+ Ap 18 '88 pors; 38:165+ N 23 '92 pors; Redbook 182:57+ Ja '94 pors; TV Guide 41:18+ D 18 '93 pors; US p63+ My '93 pors; Who's Who in America, 1995

Mike Maicher/Philadelphia 76ers

Lucas, John

Oct. 31, 1953– Basketball coach; business executive. Address: c/o Philadelphia 76ers, Veterans Stadium, Philadelphia, PA 19148

"I came back from the dead," John Lucas, the head coach, general manager, and vice-president of basketball operations of the Philadelphia 76ers, has said of his recovery from drug and alcohol abuse and subsequent return to professional basketball. Lucas began his career as the top college pick in the National Basketball Association's 1976 draft. Although he posted respectable numbers over his fourteen years as a southpaw point guard, he "squandered as much talent as any player in National Basketball Association history," Mark Starr wrote in *Newsweek* (March 1, 1993). As a result, Lucas bounced around the league, playing for six different teams, and he was suspended several times because of his drug use. He hit bottom in March 1986, when he blacked out after a night-long cocaine binge and woke up with no memory of where he had parked his car or why he was wearing five pairs of athletic socks and no shoes. "Something happened that night that said: 'I have had enough,'" Lucas told Douglas C. Lyons in an interview for *Ebony* (June 1993). Lucas, who had tried unsuccessfully to quit drugs several times before, entered a treatment center and recovered. He returned to the NBA, and by the time he retired as a player in 1990, he had begun a second career as the owner of a company whose mission is to help recovering athletes and other substance abusers maintain their sobriety.

In 1992 Red McCombs, the owner of the San Antonio Spurs, hired Lucas as head coach, making him perhaps the most prominent ex-drug addict to lead a major professional sports team. Lucas helped the Spurs rebound from a 9–11 start in the 1992–93 season to a second-place finish in their division. He often inspired players with the lessons of self-discipline and self-reliance that he had learned from his battle with drug abuse. The following year the team had one of its best regular seasons ever but lost in the first round of the play-offs. After the ownership of the Spurs changed hands in 1994, Lucas resigned from the team and accepted the head coaching position with the struggling Philadelphia 76ers. He has written a book with Joseph Moriarity about his life titled *Winning a Day at a Time* (1994). "It's taken a lot of work to find out who I am," Lucas told Ken Denlinger of the *Washington Post* (January 20, 1993). "And even now all I can tell people is that I am a grateful recovering addict and alcoholic. I'm grateful I didn't get what I deserved."

John Harding Lucas Jr. was born in Durham, North Carolina, on October 31, 1953, the younger of the two children of Blondola Lucas, who served as the principal of Durham's Shepard Junior High School, and John Harding Lucas, who was principal of the city's Hillside High School. In an interview with Hank Whittemore for *Parade* (May 16, 1993), Lucas recalled that he idolized his father: "He became God in my life, and I wanted to be just like him. He was so successful—one of the first desegregation leaders in the South—but the biggest thing was that he worked all the time. And it was like I got into competition with him. In sports, I applied the same habits that he used in his work."

Indeed, by the time he was ten years old, Lucas was playing in national tennis tournaments. He competed in the United States Open Junior Championships at the age of thirteen and made the Junior Davis Cup Team when he was seventeen. As a basketball player, he shattered "Pistol" Pete Maravich's North Carolina high-school scoring record. He graduated in 1971 from Hillside High School, where he was the valedictorian of his class, declaring in the yearbook his ambition to become the first black president of the United States. Yet as is sometimes the case with overachievers, Lucas was unable to fully enjoy his many accomplishments. "It sounds strange, but no matter what I achieved, I never knew when it was good enough," Lucas told Whittemore. "I think I was trying to be perfect—in my daily life *and* on the tennis or basketball court. It was just too much pressure." In an attempt to ease the pressure, when he was fifteen he began drinking alcohol, a habit that continued for over two decades.

Offered sports scholarships by 401 colleges, Lucas chose the University of Maryland, where he played basketball and tennis. He was named to All-America teams in both sports in 1975 and 1976. From his freshman year, he was a star on the Terrapins basketball team, and he finished his college career as the squad's all-time leader in points (2,015) and assists (514). In tennis, he won two Atlantic Coast Conference singles titles. A business administration major, he earned a B.A. degree in 1976; he later returned to the University of Maryland on a part-time basis and was awarded an M.A. degree in education in 1982.

After signing with the Houston Rockets as the nation's top draft pick in 1976, Lucas played point guard on a team that included some of the league's most talented scorers—shooting-guard Calvin Murphy, center Moses Malone, and forward Rudy Tomjanovich. Averaging 5.6 assists and 11.1 points per game during the 1976–77 season, he was named to the NBA's All-Rookie team, and he helped Houston advance to the Eastern Conference finals in the play-offs. Although he was the youngest starter on the veteran club, he quickly earned his teammates' respect with his crisp passes, court awareness, and unselfish play. During the 1977–78 season, Lucas handed out 9.4 assists a game, the second-highest average in the NBA, and increased his per-game scoring to 12.4, for which he was named to the league's All-Star team. When the injury-riddled Rockets failed to qualify for the play-offs in 1978, he used the time off to play World Team Tennis (WTT) for the New Orleans Nets. Lucas, who spent several more seasons on the WTT circuit, thus became the first athlete to play both basketball and tennis professionally.

In 1978 Lucas was sent to the Golden State Warriors as compensation for the Rockets' acquisition of Rick Barry, the Warriors' perennial All-Star. Lucas racked up 9.3 assists and 16.1 points per game in his first season with Golden State and recorded 7.5 assists and 12.6 points in the 1979–80 campaign. During his third season with the Warriors, Lucas's performance began to slip. He showed up late for team trips and missed practices, causing the Warriors to suspend him. And in the sixty-six games in which he played, he posted lower than usual numbers (an average of 7 assists and 8.4 points). As a result of his poor performance, he was released by the Warriors at the end of the season. The Washington Bullets, who had lost their star point guard to an injury, decided to take a chance on Lucas and signed him as a free agent in the fall of 1981.

During his years with the Warriors, Lucas's problems with both cocaine, which he had begun using in college, and alcohol had worsened. He told Hank Whittemore that he had turned to alcohol and drugs to relieve the boredom of "down time" during long road trips: "I knew I did drugs and drank too much, but I didn't know I had a *living* problem. I used drugs to *medicate* my emotions and fears, because I had no tools to go through those feelings and handle them." After arriving late for a meeting before the Bullets' home opener on November 3, 1981, Lucas shocked his coaches and teammates by telling them about his drug problem and asking for their help. Although it was well known that some NBA players used cocaine, no player had ever before publicly admitted using the drug. Lucas met with the NBA commissioner, Larry O'Brien, in January 1982, and after assuring O'Brien he was drug free, he agreed to enter a rehabilitation program sponsored by the league. Lucas was warned that if he was caught using drugs, he would be suspended. Meanwhile, Bullets coach Gene Shue decided to replace Lucas in the starting lineup with rookie guard Frank Johnson. For the 1981–82 season, Lucas averaged 6.9 assists and 8.4 points as Washington advanced to the semifinal round in the play-offs before losing to the Boston Celtics.

Lucas returned to the Bullets for the 1982–83 campaign, but he played sparingly in thirty-five games and averaged just 2.9 assists and 4.1 points per outing. Despite his assurances to the contrary, he continued to use drugs over the next few years and was suspended several times, then reinstated after undergoing treatment. He landed in San Antonio for the 1983–84 season and showed flashes of his old brilliance, scoring 10.9 points and chalking up a career-best 10.7 assists per game. In the following season, Lucas returned to Houston for a two-year stint with the Rockets, who were then emerging as a Western Conference power with their "twin-tower" center tandem of Hakeem Olajuwon and Ralph Sampson. Playing in forty-seven contests, Lucas averaged 6.8 assists and 11.4 points a game for the 1984–85 campaign.

In the first sixty-five games of the 1985–86 season, Lucas averaged an impressive 8.7 assists and 15.5 points. Then, in March 1986, he went on a cocaine binge, blacked out, and awoke on a downtown Houston street. After he failed a team-administered drug test, the disgusted Rockets head coach, Bill Fitch, threw him off the team with a finality that Lucas later said probably saved his life. When he checked himself into a hospital in Van Nuys, California, on March 14, Lucas feared that he might not get any more breaks and believed that his basketball career was over. He eventually recovered, and he now counts the date he entered the Van Nuys hospital as the "anniversary" of his sobriety.

Lucas was permitted to return to the NBA in the following winter. He spent two seasons with the Milwaukee Bucks, averaging 17.5 points and 6.7 assists in his first year and 9.2 points and 4.8 assists in the 1987–88 campaign. Playing a backup role in 1988–89, he averaged 4.2 points and 3.5 assists for the Seattle SuperSonics before closing out his playing career in 1990 back at Houston, with an average of 5.8 points and 4.8 assists. Over his fourteen-year career, Lucas averaged 10.7 points and 6.9 assists a game. He is ranked ninth on the list of NBA career-assists leaders, and he holds the record for assists in one quarter, having dispensed 14 in the second period of an April 15, 1984 game between the San Antonio Spurs and the Denver Nuggets.

Meanwhile, in 1986 Lucas had founded John H. Lucas Enterprises, a company that runs drug-treatment programs designed for professional athletes but open to others. The centerpiece of the program is a rehabilitation clinic called "The House." It is affiliated with a Houston hospital and provides substance abusers with both psychological counseling and a rigorous program of physical exercise. "I don't like [to use] medicine to get people off medicine," Lucas explained to Frank Lawlor of the *Philadelphia Inquirer* (June 21, 1994). "I substitute physical fitness. . . . When you are in recovery, if you don't look healthy, you're in trouble, because people can't see a healthy mind, but they can see a healthy body." Lucas's company has also set up aftercare centers in NBA and NFL franchise cities across the country.

In 1991 Lucas purchased the Miami Tropics of the United States Basketball League, a minor-league team, as a vehicle for recovering athletes to test themselves under the pressure of game conditions. Lucas appointed himself coach and also acted as a drug tester and therapeutic counselor to the six men on the ten-player team who were former substance abusers. "It was the closest team I've ever been on," Lucas told Jill Lieber, who profiled him for *Sports Illustrated* (January 11, 1993). Lucas led the Tropics to a 24–4 record, and the team won the league's 1992 championship. He also found the time to spread his antidrug message at schools and churches and made himself available to talk to addicts in crisis. "He would go anywhere to get someone, into crack houses and police stations," Kevin Mackey, a former college coach who was treated in Lucas's program, told Paul Attner of *Sporting News* (March 29, 1993). "I don't think there is a limit to his generosity."

When San Antonio Spurs owner Red McCombs, himself a recovering alcoholic, asked Lucas to succeed Jerry Tarkanian as head coach of the team, Lucas eagerly accepted. He took over twenty games into the 1992–93 season, inheriting a disappointing 9–11 record. "No one knew what to expect when he arrived," center David Robinson, the team's superstar, told Douglas Lyons for the *Ebony* profile. "It was a shock to us that he was chosen." Lucas ignited the Spurs' running game by promoting point guard Avery Johnson to the starting lineup and letting him run the offense. But the change Lucas brought to the team was more than strategic. He used some of the lessons he had learned in drug recovery to foster, in his words, "the kind of environment [he] would want to play in." He gave the team's leaders, especially Robinson, the opportunity to take more responsibility for the team's performance by allowing them, on occasion, to run team huddles during game timeouts and mete out fines and other disciplinary measures against players who arrived late for team meetings or trips. "I've been trying to build character," Lucas explained to Lyons. "I've attacked their basketball character, not them personally. If we can build quality character, we can build good men. If we build some good men with quality character, then we'll win games because they will want to win for themselves."

The Spurs responded to Lucas by turning their season around: they won twenty-four out of the next twenty-eight games, including a franchise-record ten in a row. The team finished second in the Midwest Division, with forty-nine wins and thirty-three losses, and beat the Portland Trail Blazers in the first round of play-offs before losing to the Phoenix Suns in the Western Conference semifinals. "Every single guy is playing better since he came," McCombs was quoted as saying in *Newsweek* (March 1, 1993). Robinson told Lyons that the good-humored, hard-driving Lucas had become "a friend and father-figure to all of us."

Compiling a record of fifty-five wins and twenty-seven losses during the 1993–94 season, San Antonio finished just behind Houston for the division title, but the team was upset by the Utah Jazz in the first round of the play-offs. Displeased by the team's post-season performance, the consortium of local entrepreneurs who had purchased the Spurs from McCombs considered firing Lucas but instead dismissed his principal supporters, general manager Bob Bass and president Bob Coleman. Facing an uncertain future in San Antonio, Lucas resigned in June 1994 to become the coach, general manager, and vice-president of basketball operations for the Philadelphia 76ers, who had lost fifty-seven games during the 1993–94 season.

The 76ers won only twenty-four games and lost fifty-eight during the 1994–95 season, Lucas's first with the team. Lucas has said he welcomes the challenge of building a new foundation for the team. "I love putting something back together that people around the league said couldn't be fixed," he told Pat O'Brien in an interview for *Inside Sports* (June 1995). "I know about hopeless situations; that's where I've come from. We're going to grow—not overnight, but it's going to happen."

As the 1995–96 preseason began, Lucas's team included three players with troubled pasts: point guard Vernon Maxwell, who was released by the Houston Rockets after months of erractic and disruptive behavior; forward Richard Dumas, who had had drug problems during his two seasons with the Phoenix Suns; and point guard Charles Smith, a former Georgetown University player who served twenty-eight months in prison for vehicular homicide. In an article about the 76ers, Clifton Brown of the *New York Times* (October 15, 1995) wondered: "Lucas is a man who believes in second chances. But is he taking a few chances too many [with the new players]?" In response, Lucas told Brown, "Believe me, I'm well aware that I have to win games. But I have to keep an open mind about everybody, because somebody kept an open mind about me. You think just anybody would give me a second chance? Here I am, a recovering addict-alcoholic who messed up what could have been a great career, and now I'm coaching in the NBA. Guys seek me out, because they feel I'll give them a fair look."

Soon after Lucas joined the 76ers, his book, *Winning a Day at a Time*, was published. Wes Lukowsky, who reviewed it for *Booklist* (September 1, 1994), wrote, "There's plenty of basketball here, but sports isn't really the subject. John Lucas lost control of his life. With help, he got back on track and now helps others. It's an inspirational story, and it's well told." Charismatic and intense, Lucas prowls the sidelines during games with an energy that seems boundless. He looks considerably older than he is, a fact he blames on his past use of cocaine, but he prides himself on being physically fit, and he likes to challenge basketball players half his age to hard-fought games of one-on-one.

Lucas tries to attend Alcoholics Anonymous meetings daily, no matter where he is, and after almost a decade of sobriety his worst dependency is on the low-calorie soft drinks he imbibes almost continually. He has been married since 1978 to his grade-school sweetheart, the former Debbie Fozard. The couple has a house in Houston, where they live with their daughter, Tarvia, and their sons, John Jr. and Jai. The years Lucas was abusing drugs and alcohol were hard on his wife and children, but the family stayed with him. "I knew John long before his drug problem," Debbie Lucas was quoted as saying in *People* (July 13, 1992). "I knew he was a good-hearted person."

Selected Biographical References: Ebony 48:94+ Je '93 pors; Newsweek 121:65+ Mr 1 '93 pors; Parade p14+ My 16 '93 pors; People 38:67+ Jl 13 '92 pors; Philadelphia Inquirer D p1+ Je 21 '94 pors; Sporting N p33+ Mr 29 '93 pors; Sports Illus 78:46+ Ja 11 '93 pors; Washington Post C p1+ Ja 20 '93 pors; Who's Who in America, 1995

White House

Magaziner, Ira C.

Nov. 8, 1947– Management consultant; adviser to the president of the United States. Address: c/o The White House, 1600 Pennsylvania Ave., Washington, DC 20500

"Like many in the new administration, including the president, Magaziner stands at the radical center of American politics," Steven Pearlstein wrote of Ira C. Magaziner, President Bill Clinton's senior adviser for policy development, in the *Washington Post Magazine* (April 18, 1993). "This is not the mushy center defined by a middle-of-the-road position on every issue, but a hard-edge center that draws its preference for free-market solutions from the right and a commitment to social and economic justice from the left." Magaziner's commitment to social and economic justice, though not his faith in free enterprise, dates from his youth, when he earned a reputation as something of a radical. He reaffirmed that reputation during his college years, at Brown University, where he tried to reform the school's graduation requirements and curriculum—a task that he accomplished and that has since made him a legendary figure among Brown students and alumni. His youthful idealism had its first brush with reality soon after he completed his college education, in the early 1970s, when he attempted and ultimately failed to reverse the downward economic spiral of the shoe-manufacturing town of Brockton, Massachusetts. As it turned out, his failure to improve economic conditions there precipitated his own transformation: he began to realize that economic growth could not be achieved without taking into account the principles of the free market.

During the 1970s and 1980s, thanks in large measure to the combination of his pragmatism and 1960s-style idealism, Magaziner became a successful—and highly paid—management consultant to such corporations as Corning Glass and Rubbermaid and to the governments of a number of foreign countries, including Sweden and Japan. Working first for the management consulting company BCG and later for his own firm, Telesis, Magaziner would typically conduct in-depth studies of the company or country that retained him, and then provide a framework for economic growth. (While his success is indisputable, several commentators have pointed out that it is difficult to gauge the extent to which his advice resulted in an increase in growth.) His approach to problem-solving made him an attractive candidate for the task of reforming the nation's unwieldy health-care industry, but in September 1994 the plan he and his staff conceived at the behest of the Clinton administration died in Congress.

Ira Charles Magaziner was born on November 8, 1947 in the New York City borough of Queens, the son of Sylvia Magaziner, a homemaker, and Louis Magaziner, a bookkeeper in a tomato-packing business who moonlighted at a bank. He attended public schools on Long Island and distinguished himself as an A-student in Hebrew school. Magaziner has credited his parents with instilling in him and his sister, Sheila, a respect for knowledge and the belief that obtaining a good education would, in his words, place him on "a path to a better life."

Magaziner grew up in a household in which liberal politics was a family tradition. His paternal grandfather, who lived in Czarist Russia, had backed the moderate but short-lived Kerensky government before it fell to the Bolsheviks. His parents' political icons were Franklin and Eleanor Roosevelt, New York Democratic governor Herbert H. Lehman, and Robert F. Wagner, a Democrat who represented New York State in the United States Senate from 1927 to 1949. They were also committed supporters of Adlai Stevenson, the Democratic candidate in the presidential campaigns of 1952 and 1956.

Ira Magaziner's somewhat quixotic belief in his ability to bring about social and political change dates from his adolescence, if not earlier. As a young man, he led a labor strike against unfair working conditions at a summer camp in the Adirondack Mountains at which he was working as a waiter. "I got fired and everyone else got more money," he said of the outcome of the strike in the interview with Steven Pearlstein. While attending high school, he was expelled from the National Association of Student Council Presidents for leading an antisegregation boycott. He also sold tickets to a Lena Horne concert to benefit the Congress for Racial Equality, marched on Washington in 1963 for civil rights, and picketed against exclusionary housing practices in the town of Hempstead, Long Island.

At Brown University, in Providence, Rhode Island, which he entered in 1965, Magaziner deepened his commitment to a life of political activism. He initiated his most memorable project during the summer of 1967, when, with a fellow student, Elliot Maxwell, he studied the university's educational system with a view to reforming it. After completing their research, the pair wrote a report some four hundred pages long entitled "Draft of a Working Paper for Education at Brown University," in which they concluded that the Brown curriculum suffered from "a lack of vitality and meaningfulness." To make the educational experience at Brown more rewarding, they recommended that distribution requirements be eliminated, that interdisciplinary programs of study be established, and that grades be replaced by written evaluations. The underlying theme of their analysis was that students are capable of designing their own courses of study and therefore ought to have the freedom to do so.

When, during his junior year, the faculty committee assigned to consider his report failed to act, Magaziner opened a round of intense politicking for acceptance of his principles. He dispatched three-student teams, armed with copies of the report and supporting arguments, to persuade faculty members to endorse his recommendations. What the university finally adopted in the spring of 1969 came "pretty close" to what the report advocated, as Magaziner told Jacob Weisberg, who interviewed him for the *New Republic* (January 24, 1994). Indeed, in addition to eliminating required courses, Brown decreased the number of credits required for graduation and liberalized the grading system, doing away with Ds and allowing Fs to be stricken from transcripts. Magaziner's recommendations, many of which are still in place, transformed Brown into "one of the hottest schools in the country," Magaziner's friend Derek Shearer told Jacob Weisberg. "A great deal of Brown's popularity flows from the 1969 curriculum," Elmer E. Cornwell Jr. told Robert Pear in an interview for the *New York Times* (February 26, 1993). "We were viewed as an avant-garde kind of place." On the other hand, critics have argued that Brown's curriculum offers students too much freedom, pointing out that it is possible to graduate from the school without having read Shakespeare or Plato or having learned the fundamental principles of modern scientific thought.

During his years at Brown, Magaziner was also active in student government, serving as class president in each of his four years there. He was also elected vice-president and president of the student government. He caused one last stir before leaving the school when, in his speech at the graduation ceremony (he was valedictorian of his class), he urged his fellow students to demonstrate their opposition to the war in Vietnam by rising and turning their backs on Secretary of State Henry Kissinger, who was to receive an honorary degree at the ceremony. Nearly all the graduating seniors complied.

Following his graduation from Brown, Magaziner entered Balliol College, at Oxford University, as a Rhodes scholar. During his two years there, Magaziner put into practice the ideas he had formulated at Brown by designing his own course of study in economics and history. His stay at Oxford also marked the beginning of his friendship with Bill Clinton, a fellow Rhodes scholar, who shared with Magaziner a desire both to work for social justice and to see the United States end its involvement in Vietnam.

On returning to the United States in 1971, Magaziner embarked on yet another experiment in social reform—undoubtedly his most challenging one up until that time. With a number of fellow idealists, he settled in Brockton, a moribund shoe-manufacturing town near Boston, Massachusetts. He had chosen the town as a kind of test site for ideas he had formulated on urban economic and political rejuvenation. Indeed, his self-appointed mission was to effect the sort of a change on a citywide scale that he had achieved at Brown University. "In Ira's mind, this [the Brockton experiment] could be a fundamental building block for the renewal of blue-collar communities around the country, a model," Joshua C. Posner, a participant in the project and former Brown student, told Steven Pearlstein.

Characteristically, Magaziner and his army of activists began the project with a six-month study of the city's politics, economy, and social history. Based on what they learned, they then started a food co-op, a weekly newspaper, a tenants' rights organization, and a nonprofit housing corporation. To earn their living, they took jobs in schools, banks, and other local businesses. They worked hard for about two years. Magaziner himself got out of bed at 4:00 A.M. every morning to buy food for the co-op and then spent his evenings working on the loading dock of a local trucker.

Within two years of his arrival in Brockton, it had become clear to Magaziner that his dreams of urban renewal were not going to materialize. With foreign competition precipitating the closure of two shoe factories and inflation wreaking havoc on the local economy, economic conditions in Brockton failed to improve, despite the assistance of the youthful intellects and energies. Magaziner, who was one of the first to leave Brockton, has since said of the experiment, "It was a naïve, ineffective attempt to do some things." But while he has since acknowledged that the venture was ill-conceived, Magaziner learned some important lessons. "We overreacted against big business," he told Peter Petre, who profiled him for *Fortune* (August 31, 1987). "The private corporation drives productivity and raises the living standard. I think that's good, I think that's right, and I don't think you want to centralize things."

Magaziner left Brockton in 1973, and, with the help of a glowing recommendation from a Brown University trustee, he landed a job with Boston Consulting Group (BCG), an innovative management consulting firm. He brought with him no formal business training—only his native intelligence and an ability to put in long hours of hard work. In consideration of his inexperience, his starting salary was fifteen thousand dollars—about half of what the firm's newly hired business and law school graduates earned—but it was not long before he began to close the gap. He established himself as a serious player at BCG when, based on his own research of the steelmaking industry worldwide, he defied conventional wisdom and predicted—correctly—that demand would be flat and advised his client, the expansion-minded parent company of a steel manufacturer, to conduct business accordingly.

BCG had acquired its reputation as a leading management consulting company by helping its clients achieve higher levels of profitability, which it accomplished by figuring out which of the client company's constituent parts should be invested in and which should be used to generate cash to fund investment. Magaziner soon came up with a variation on that strategy: BCG could do for entire countries what it was already doing for corporations. In 1977 he received an opportunity to test this ambitious idea, when he persuaded Volvo, a BCG client, to help fund a study of the Swedish economy. After scrutinizing the country's economy, company by company, for six months, Magaziner wrote up his findings in a document entitled "A Framework for Swedish Industrial Policy." His recommendations—that the Swedish government stop pouring large amounts of capital into the country's shipbuilding, forest products, and iron ore and steel industries, which he argued were unlikely to compete well in the world marketplace, and invest greater resources in the nascent high-tech industries—touched off a national debate in Sweden. They were "naturally not popular with recipients of the government largesse," Magaziner explained to *Current Biography*. Nevertheless, he added, "our predictions turned out to be true and our recommendations were followed."

In 1978 (or 1979, according to one source), Magaziner left BCG to organize his own consulting firm, Telesis (the word means "intelligently planned progress"), with the intention of conducting country studies similar to the Swedish project he had carrried out to do at BCG. Working out of offices in Providence, Rhode Island, where Magaziner had maintained ties since his student days at Brown, as well as in Paris and Melbourne, Telesis did just that, accepting commissions for studies of Ireland, Australia, and Israel, among other nations. It also did work for private corporations. In establishing the firm, Magaziner was joined by five of his colleagues from BCG, one of whom was his wife-to-be, Suzanne McTigue, a graduate of both the Harvard law and business schools whom he had met at work. ("Where else would you meet Ira?" she asked Steven Pearlstein.) Before long, Telesis gained a solid reputation within the industry, with Magaziner charging his clients six hundred dollars an hour and delivering speeches to the CEOs of blue-chip companies for ten thousand dollars an appearance.

Magaziner's most widely publicized project during this period was not a country study but his plan to reverse Rhode Island's declining economic fortunes. The result of his efforts was the Greenhouse Compact, a report some one thousand pages long recommending that the state offer local corporations incentives, in the form of tax breaks and research grants, to nurture new enterprises in such high-tech fields as robotics, photovoltaics, medical technology, and computers. The ultimate aim of the proposed plan was to change fundamentally the character of the state's economy by creating high-wage jobs in those emerging fields. Magaziner reportedly managed to convince the state's political, corporate, and union leaders, as well as church leaders and community groups, that his scheme would regenerate the state's ailing economy, and it has been suggested that the initiative might have been implemented if it had been left to legislative action alone. (The state legislature in fact endorsed the proposal.) But Magaziner felt strongly that it should be put before the people of Rhode Island. When the referendum was held, in April 1984, voters roundly defeated the plan, at least partly because of their opposition to the tax that was to finance it.

Many of the ideas developed by Magaziner during this period found expression in his three books. In the first, *Japanese Industrial Policy* (1979), Magaziner and his coauthor, Thomas Hout, described the steps taken by the Japanese government to build the country's auto, steel, telecommunications, and computer industries. In *Minding America's Business: The Decline and Rise of the American Economy* (1982), which he wrote with Robert B. Reich (a fellow Rhodes scholar at Oxford who had recently joined the faculty of Harvard's John F. Kennedy School of Government), the authors investigated the reasons behind America's loss of industrial leadership in the international marketplace and then recommended remedial measures, such as retraining workers, establishing government funds for research and development, providing loans for investment in high-risk ventures, and investing in high-tech enterprises. Their key recommendation was that the business community and government collaborate in cultivating new businesses that have the potential for high growth and in encouraging those that had outlived their usefulness and profitability to decline gracefully. Magaziner's third book, *The Silent War: Inside the Global Business Battles Shaping America's Future* (1989), which he wrote with the journalist Mark Patinkin, consists of nine case histories describing the relationships between governments and businesses worldwide. The theme of the book echoes that which Magaziner and Reich presented in *Minding America's Business*: the winners of the trade wars will be the nations in which businesses and governments cooperate.

By the mid-1980s Magaziner had become "bored" with his work at Telesis, Mark Patinkin told Jacob Weisberg. "What he really wanted to do was economic strategy on a national basis." With that goal in mind, in 1986 Magaziner sold Telesis to Towers Perrin, a large management consulting firm, for an estimated six million dollars, and in 1990 he organized another firm to serve as a personal policy study institute. He called the new company SJS, Inc., after the first initials of his three children: Seth, Jonathan, and Sarah. One of the projects that he carried out during this period was a report for the National Center on Education and the Economy, of which Hillary Rodham Clinton, a successful attorney and the wife of then-Arkansas governor Bill Clinton, was a board member.

In 1991 Magaziner was recruited by his old friend Bill Clinton, who was then running for the Democratic nomination for president of the United States, to help out with the upcoming campaign. Magaziner had the satisfaction of seeing a number of his ideas incorporated into Clinton's campaign manifesto, *Putting People First*, of which he was one of the main authors. After the 1992 elections, President-elect Clinton named Magaziner his senior White House policy adviser, with responsibility for working with Hillary Rodham Clinton on reforming the country's unwieldy $900 billion health-care industry. Magaziner promptly organized a five hundred-member staff of volunteers and government employees to assist him in this effort. While the first lady had the lead role in the reform effort, Magaziner was, in Steven Pearlstein's words, the "behind-the-scenes mastermind."

During the first few months of 1993, Magaziner held meetings with his staff to hammer out the details of a workable health-care plan. Sessions often lasted into the early hours of the morning. In an interview with Michael Duffy and Dick Thompson for *Time* (September 20, 1993), Linda Bergthold, a private consultant from San Francisco, described these conferences, during which task-force leaders presented progress reports and Magaziner asked questions, as "a cross between Ph.D. orals and the Spanish Inquisition." The plan, which was made public in September 1993 and was set forth in a 1,342-page report, turned out to be enormously complicated and controversial. And despite the intense lobbying efforts of the president, the first lady, cabinet secretaries, and White House aides, it failed to win the endorsement of Congress. In addition to continuing to advise President Clinton on health care, since 1993 Magaziner has been involved in projects aimed at evaluating the United States' international trade strategy and urban policy.

Magaziner, whom some members of Congress have found to be arrogant, inflexible, and difficult to work with, has himself confessed to being somewhat uncomfortable with the political bureaucracy in Washington. "Working in the federal government," he told Julie Kosterlitz, who interviewed him for the *National Journal* (January 15, 1994), "is everything I thought it would be and worse." He is also considered to be shy, though self-confident, and he prefers operating out of the public eye, behind the scenes. He is "the brains behind the brawn," as one Washingtonian told a reporter for *People* (October 11, 1993). His style, as described by Mark Patinkin, is "messianic. He does crusades, not studies." His disdain for appearance fits that picture. Patinkin told Robert Pear that Magaziner's wardrobe consisted of "one rumpled suit which he doesn't press." Like his disheveled appearance, Magaziner's addiction to junk food is legendary: pizza, pretzels, Mallomar cookies, and colas comprise the core of his daily diet. He stands six feet, two inches tall, weighs 190 pounds, and has an aquiline nose and salt-and-pepper hair.

A multimillionaire, thanks to his success as a management consultant, Magaziner gives generously to causes in which he believes. He and his wife live in a $1.25-million home in Washington with their three preteen children. His long hours at the office leave him little time to pursue hobbies, but he does manage to unwind by reading, particularly biographies of American presidents, or by watching *Star Trek* with his children. Professionally, Magaziner has a reputation for cool intellectuality, but "with his kids," his former colleague Francis Scricco told Steven Pearlstein, "you get a sense that his emotional jets are on."

Selected Biographical References: Fortune 116:69+ Ag 31 '87 pors; N Y Times A p14 F 26 '93 por; People 40:61+ O 11 '93 pors; Washington Mo p11+ My '93 por; Washington Post mag p12+ Ap 18 '93 por

---

Malone, John C.

Mar. 7, 1941- Telecommunications executive; engineer. Address: c/o Tele-Communications, Inc., P.O. Box 5630, Denver, CO 80217-9523

Widely known as the "king of cable television" and arguably the most powerful figure in the cable television industry, John C. Malone is the president and chief executive officer of Tele-Communications Incorporated (TCI), which, since he joined the company in 1973, has become the biggest operator of cable television systems in the United States. TCI has wired communities in forty-nine states for cable television and currently controls access to more than 20 percent of the homes that subscribe to cable service. In addition, it holds a significant stake in many of the major cable networks and exerts great influence over cable television programming. An electrical engineer, Malone is recognized for his technical expertise, business savvy, brilliance as a strategic thinker, and skills as a deal-maker. By means of hundreds of often staggeringly complex acquisitions, he transformed TCI from "a nearly bankrupt compendium of backwater cable systems," as Bill Powell described it in *Newsweek* (June 1, 1987), to an industry leader with an annual cash flow well in excess of a billion dollars.

Tele-Communications Inc.

Over the course of TCI's development, Malone established a reputation for using strong-arm tactics in his business transactions and became, as L.

J. Davis wrote in the *New York Times Magazine* (December 2, 1990), "indisputably, one of the most feared" men in the television industry. "Wall Street analysts don't call [TCI] 'The Empire' and Malone 'Darth Vader' for nothing," Bill Powell noted, in a reference to the evil dominion and sinister warlord featured in the *Star Wars* movie trilogy. Although Malone failed in his highly publicized attempt, in 1994, to merge TCI with the Bell Atlantic Corporation, one of the country's main regional telephone companies, he remains determined to play a commanding role in the creation of the information superhighway, in which the technologies of television, telecommunications, and computers are being united. "In a world where massive industries are converging with astounding speed, with consequences that less adroit competitors may grasp too late, Malone understands not only the technology but also the art of the deal," Andrew Kupfer observed in *Fortune* (June 28, 1993). "That makes him a rare double threat." Malone is also the chairman of Liberty Media Corporation, which was created and is owned by TCI.

The second of two children, John Charles Custer Malone was born on March 7, 1941 in Milford, Connecticut. He grew up in an eighteenth-century Colonial-style house in a working-class part of Milford, an affluent town about ten miles southwest of New Haven on Long Island Sound. His mother became a full-time homemaker after the birth of her first child, Malone's sister, and resumed her career as a schoolteacher many years later. In a profile of him for the *New Yorker* (February 7, 1994), Ken Auletta reported that Malone's mother was "a remote figure, who did not hug her daughter or her son." She apparently played a far less significant role in his childhood and youth than his father, whom he idolized. A strict Calvinist and "an intellectual with white socks," as Malone has described him, his father worked for General Electric as an engineer and inventor. (According to one source, he held the title of vice-president.) The elder Malone's personal creed included a firm belief in thrift, and he impressed upon his son the importance of hard work and of succeeding professionally. Malone also took to heart his father's often-expressed disapproval of the policies of President Franklin D. Roosevelt, whom his father regarded as "a socialist, or worse," as Ken Auletta wrote.

Since his early years Malone has wanted, in his words, "to be different . . . to be unique"—an aspiration prompted to some degree by the repugnance he felt when, as a child, he passed cemeteries, where, to his eyes, nothing distinguished one tombstone from any other, thus implying the sameness of the people whose graves they marked. As a youngster he earned money by selling, for seven dollars, surplus General Electric radios that he had bought for a dollar and then repaired. During his teens he enjoyed tinkering with cars and driving up and down Milford's main street with his friends. Indeed, by his own account, his social life closely resembled those of the teenagers depicted in George Lucas's 1973 coming-of-age film *American Graffiti.*

After Malone transferred, in 1957, from a local high school to the Hopkins Grammar School, a preparatory school in New Haven to which he had won a scholarship on the strength of his uncommon abilities in math and science, his comfortable relationships with his blue-collar, neighborhood friends deteriorated. Accused by them of turning into a preppie, he became the victim of their jeers and their fists. Malone, who viewed himself at that time as "neither a preppie nor a town kid," as he said to Ken Auletta, reacted by resolving that he would excel in sports at school. Through "raw drive, not skill," in his words, he earned letters in soccer, fencing, and track. Thanks in part to his almost photographic memory (according to Auletta, he could remember verbatim "entire passages from textbooks"), he compiled an outstanding academic record as well.

Following his graduation from the Hopkins Grammar School, Malone entered Yale University, in New Haven. Heeding the advice of his father, who had urged him to become an engineer, he majored in electrical engineering. "Instead of getting bogged down in fancy analysis, I learned to develop an educated feel or horse sense for things," he told Mark Ivey for *Business Week* (October 26, 1987), in recalling his undergraduate engineering studies. Engineering fascinated him. He especially liked the fact that answers to problems in engineering were either right or wrong. In his social-science classes, in contrast, where he presented his opinions as a self-described "individualist conservative," he apparently failed to convince his professors—whom he has labeled "socialistic"—of the correctness of his arguments, and he did not get good grades. He did very well in courses in economics, however, and graduated from Yale, in 1963, with a dual B.S. degree in electrical engineering and economics. He was elected to Phi Beta Kappa.

Malone's first job after completing his undergraduate education was at Bell Laboratories, a division of AT&T, where he worked as an economic planner and handled assignments in research and development. During the next four years, with financial assistance from Bell, he earned at least two advanced degrees: an M.S. in industrial management from Johns Hopkins University in 1964 and a Ph.D. in operations research (which has been defined as "the analysis, usually involving mathematical treatment, of a process, problem, or operation to determine its purpose and effectiveness and to gain maximum efficiency") from Johns Hopkins in 1967. According to several sources (but not Malone's official company bio), he also earned an M.S. degree in electrical engineering from New York University in 1965.

By the time he received his doctorate, Malone had reportedly become convinced that, if he remained at Bell Labs, eventually he would resemble many of his coworkers, who, he assumed, had begun their careers there as he had, with high hopes of making a significant contribution, but who had become what he regarded as mere ciphers in a stifling bureaucracy. In 1968 he left Bell Labs to take a job as a management consultant at McKinsey & Company, which is currently the biggest general management-consulting firm in the world. His clients included such corporate giants as IBM and General Electric, and his responsibilities entailed a great deal of traveling. Because of his wife's unhappiness with his prolonged absences from home, Malone quit that job in 1970 and was hired as a group vice-president at the General Instrument Corporation (GI). He was soon promoted to the presidency of Jerrold Electronics, a GI subsidiary, which manufactured equipment for cable television systems and, in the early 1970s, acquired a leading position in the nascent cable television industry.

At Jerrold, according to Mark Ivey, Malone "learned a lot about hardware but learned even more about how to deal with people . . . [and] managed to win the trust and loyalty of his cable operator customers." He also gained a familiarity with complex financial arrangements, as John Dempsey noted in *Variety* (April 26, 1993). His performance impressed, among others, such pioneers in cable television as Steven J. Ross, the chairman of Warner Communications Incorporated, and Bob John Magness, a part-time cattle rancher who, in the mid-1950s, had started a small cable company, which he later renamed Tele-Communications Incorporated, to serve small western communities and farms that received the major networks' signals poorly or not at all.

In 1972 Steve Ross offered Malone the top job at Warner Communications' cable division, which had headquarters in New York City. At about the same time, Bob Magness asked him to come to work at the much smaller, Denver-based TCI. Although Malone "liked [Ross] an awful lot," as he told Ken Auletta, he foresaw that at Warner, he would almost certainly have felt compelled to dismiss particular senior managers whom he considered to be his friends. He also knew that his wife did not want to remain in the East and that, having continued to devote far more than thirty-five hours a week to his job, he had not fully lived up to his promise that their family (which by that time included their first child) would "have a more normal life," in his words. He accepted Magness's offer even though doing so required him to agree to a 50 percent reduction in pay, to sixty thousand dollars a year. In 1973 he joined Magness as the president and chief executive officer of TCI.

According to L. J. Davis's *New York Times Magazine* profile of Malone, Bob Magness conducted his business in accordance with the maxim "Pay interest, not taxes"—in other words, as Davis explained, "the most effective way to accumulate assets is to borrow copiously while reporting very little profit." When Malone arrived at TCI, the company was nearly bankrupt: while its revenues totaled $19 million, its debt burden had reached $130 million. "We looked catastrophe in the face every day," Malone acknowledged to Ken Auletta. For the next five years, he spent most of his time negotiating with bankers in New York City and Boston. "The early years of me and TCI were really a workout," he told L. J. Davis. "TCI was struggling. It was overextended. But I liked the entrepreneurship. I liked the people. I wanted a career." Determined to cut costs wherever they could, Malone and Magness shared motel rooms when they traveled together, and they became very close personally as well as professionally. Malone has said that he regards Magness not only as his partner but as, in his words, a "mentor, a father figure, [and] a friend." In an interview with Christopher Knowlton for *Fortune* (July 31, 1989), Magness said that he and Malone always "talk very freely and quickly." "We seldom disagree, and when we do, we never get upset about it," he said.

Former Colorado senator Timothy E. Wirth, who is currently the United States undersecretary of state for global affairs, met Malone at a meeting concerning cable television that was held in Denver in 1973, when Wirth was an environmental consultant for a consulting firm. "I remember Malone's determination [to change cable regulations]," he told Ken Auletta. "You could see his crooked little smile. He looked at you with that smile and you could tell that behind it was a tank." The television executive Bill Daniels also met Malone soon after the latter started working at TCI. In a conversation with Jennet Conant, who profiled Malone for *Esquire* (June 1993), Daniels recalled, "He was extremely gifted with numbers. You could sit down and talk to him about a deal in detail, and he wouldn't take down a note. The next time you'd see him, he'd remember it all."

The media analyst Richard J. MacDonald, of the investment-banking firm MacDonald Grippo Riely, offered another view of Malone when he spoke with L. J. Davis. "Malone understood the nature of the [cable] business sooner, quicker, and more profoundly than any of the others did," he said. "He realized that large size meant lower costs. The bigger he was, the better the deals he could cut with his suppliers, which in turn boosted his cash flow. Everyone else in the industry stood around worrying about what Wall Street would think about their earnings. But Malone quickly realized that the debt market was awash with cheap money, and he went after it."

TCI's fortunes took a dramatic turn for the better in 1977 or 1978 (sources differ as to the year), when Malone obtained a line of credit totaling over seventy million dollars from seven insurance companies (including the Teachers Insurance and Annuity Association and the Equitable Life Assurance Society of the United States), thus enabling TCI to refinance its debt with long-term capital. The sum amounted to "the largest cable loan in history to that point," according to L. J. Davis, who noted that it "was made possible by the company's improved cash flow, by then $31.5 million and growing." In the early 1980s the company increased its revenues substantially by forging agreements with programming networks whereby, in exchange for access to TCI's cable systems, the networks paid TCI in advance of the airing of their shows. TCI thus obtained, "in effect," as Davis pointed out, "tens of millions of dollars in interest-free loans."

In the 1980s Malone began spending what by the end of 1987 added up to over three billion dollars to buy more than 150 smaller cable systems. TCI also became a partner in hundreds of additional systems. Its approach contrasted sharply with that of some of its major competitors, which incurred huge losses through prodigal operations in large urban centers. (In remarking on the differences between TCI and those companies, Malone told Bill Powell, "We weren't going to build libraries, give away free fire engines, and send the mayor's eighteen illegitimate kids to college.") In addition, TCI bought substantial stakes in at least three large cable operations, paying more than a billion dollars for shares in United Artists Communications and similar amounts for shares in Storer Communications and Heritage Communications. In a widely quoted summing-up, L. J. Davis reported that "by mid-1989, after sixteen years with TCI, Malone had done an incredible 482 deals, on average one every two weeks."

According to Paul Kagan Associates, an investment analyst and media research firm, between 1974 and mid-1989 the value of TCI stock increased by 55,000 percent. "It was a very clever game that was played all the way," Marc Riely, of MacDonald Grippo Riely, told Jennet Conant. "The company reported almost no earnings, but the stock just kept going up, almost magically, people thought. It was just stunning." Meanwhile, Malone's personal worth as well as that of many of the businesspeople with whom he had formed partnerships and that of long-time TCI shareholders had increased astronomically, too. "Even some TCI secretaries are worth a million dollars, compliments of the stock in the company's retirement plan," Christopher Knowlton wrote.

By mid-1987, according to Bill Powell, "one out of five cable viewers in the United States—7.7 million people—watch[ed] systems in which TCI [had] an interest." Powell quoted one media analyst as saying that TCI had become "a proxy for the [cable] industry." "They can't exactly control the industry," the analyst explained, "but they can dictate what will happen." By 1989 TCI owned a thousand local cable systems, and it had become nearly three times as large as its next-largest rival. It had a remarkable $1.3 billion-a-year operating cash flow—more than ABC, CBS, and NBC combined. In addition, having bought a controlling block of stock in United Artists Entertainment Company in 1987 and thus gained control of UA's movie-theatre-division—the country's largest theatre chain, with some twenty-five hundred screens—TCI had become a major force in the entertainment industry. (It later sold the theatres.)

Furthermore, in the 1980s TCI had entered the field of television programming, by acquiring a significant stake in BET (Black Entertainment Television), the Discovery Channel, CVN (Cable Value Network), and AMC (American Movie Classics). In 1987, in a highly publicized transaction in which more than a half-billion dollars changed hands, Malone teamed up with a group of other cable-industry players, including Time Incorporated, to rescue the Turner Broadcasting System from financial ruin. By acquiring a 21 percent stake in Turner Broadcasting—and thus interests in CNN, TBS, and TNT—for TCI, he significantly increased the clout of his company and his personal influence in the cable-television industry.

While steadily gaining power, Malone and TCI had also become known for business practices that, in the opinion of various observers, warranted such labels as arrogant and ruthless. In dealing with complaints about poor signals or about repairmen who failed to keep appointments, for example, the company "established a reputation for treating customers with utter disdain," L. J. Davis reported. When, in 1973, local regulators in Vail, Colorado refused to agree to rate increases that Malone had proposed, he blocked all regular television programming for an entire weekend and, instead, to convey the message that the mayor and the city manager were responsible for the blackout, aired nonstop their names and home telephone numbers. Following a deluge of phone calls from viewers, Vail acquiesced to TCI's demands. In 1981, in another frequently cited example of TCI's arm-twisting tactics, the company forced officials in Jefferson City, Missouri to renew its franchise by warning that it would cut off all cable service to city residents—a threat that was described as "nothing short of commercial blackmail" by the judge who presided over the antitrust suit subsequently brought against TCI by a competing cable company. The jury in that case awarded the competitor a total of $35.8 million in actual and punitive damages.

More recently, TCI coerced the music-video network MTV and the all-sports network ESPN to cancel proposed fee increases by threatening to drop their programs, and it effectively forced NBC to abandon its plan to create an all-news cable network by refusing to carry it. "We always had to back down [when negotiating with TCI]," a former program executive told Bill Powell. "It's a simple equation. Without TCI no program channel can survive. Period. They enjoy a feared position in the industry. They are bullies." According to Bill Powell, "Malone rejects any charge of unfairness and doesn't apologize for his actions." "Sure it's a threat," Malone said to Powell about his modus operandi, "but it's good business, too." "When you're driving plate tectonics, you're going to squeeze people's tails," he told Andrew Kupfer. Many media observers identified Malone as the key, albeit behind-the-scenes, player in QVC's ultimately unsuccessful hostile bid to take over Paramount Communications Incorporated in 1992–93. In June 1993 TCI, along with six other companies, settled an antitrust suit that the attorneys general of forty states had filed against them for restricting the access of smaller companies to programming that the larger companies owned.

Meanwhile, beginning in the 1980s, various members of Congress, most prominent among them Ohio senator Howard Metzenbaum, had been growing increasingly concerned about what they viewed as TCI's monopolistic practices. In 1990, partly as a way of placating Metzenbaum and other lawmakers who wanted to reestablish federal regulations on cable television (which had been more or less lifted in 1984), Malone spun off from TCI a new company, called Liberty Media, to handle most of TCI's programming interests. Malone, who, while holding the CEO position at TCI, served as the new corporation's CEO as well, transferred most of his investments in TCI to Liberty. After a series of transactions that included three stock splits, on October 8, 1993 TCI bought back Liberty, thus enriching Malone, as Carol J. Loomis explained in *Fortune* (November 15, 1993), by more than $600 million.

Five days later Malone and Raymond W. Smith, the chairman of Bell Atlantic, announced that TCI and Bell Atlantic planned to merge into a single giant entity that would provide "wire and wireless service, video-on-demand, and interactive media, all rolled into one" and would "make the electronic superhighway we've been talking about for a while a reality," in Smith's words. On February 23, 1994 the $33 billion deal fell through. TCI and Bell Atlantic blamed its demise on the FCC's adoption, the day before, of rules requiring that cable-television rates be cut by 7 percent, the implementation of which, company spokespersons contended, would significantly decrease the cable industry's cash flow for many years to come. Most media observers, however, attributed the scrapping of the deal to the decline in the value of Bell Atlantic stock in the previous four months. Bell Atlantic was to have used some of its stock to purchase TCI and Liberty Media.

In 1993 TCI embarked on a $2 billion development project to replace the copper wiring in its cable systems with high-capacity fiber-optic lines, as a means of greatly increasing the number of channels that could be carried. In 1995, among other actions that it has taken to ensure its place on the information superhighway, TCI invested $125 million for a 20 percent stake in the Microsoft Network, Microsoft Corporation's new online network, and joined with the venture capital firm Kleiner Perkins Caufield & Byers to form a new company that, sometime in 1996, will offer TCI's eleven million cable customers high-speed access to the Internet computer network.

In September 1995 Liberty Media gained control of fifty-seven million shares of Time Warner stock (worth $2.3 billion), and thus a 9 percent stake in Time Warner, as a result of the merger of Time Warner and the Turner Broadcasting System. TCI emerged from the weeks-long negotiations that had preceded Time's purchase of TBS with a number of preferential agreements, including a long-term agreement to carry TBS channels on TCI cable systems—deals that Malone secured by threatening to veto the merger. Since TCI held more than a fifth of TBS stock, TBS and Time could not join their operations without the approval of TCI.

With his sturdy build and rugged features, as Christopher Knowlton observed, John C. Malone "could pass for a Marine Corps sergeant." In *Business Week* (April 13, 1990), William C. Symonds wrote that Malone is "often propelled by impatience." Mark Ivey reported that he "frequently salts his conversation with profanity," and Ken Auletta noted that he is "an intense listener." In the *New York Times* (February 24, 1994), Joshua Mills observed that the TCI executive "can be abrupt with the press, piercing with his critics, [and] contemptuous of . . . legislators and regulators." Malone and the former Leslie Ann Evans, who have been married since 1963, have two grown children—a daughter, Tracy, and a son, Evan. Most weekdays Malone leaves his office to have lunch with his wife at their home, just outside Denver, and they often go to a health club together after he finishes work in mid-afternoon. They keep on their property a stable of riding horses and Malone's collection of antique cars. By his own account, Malone stays up later than he would like to so that he can listen to broadcasts by the radio and television commentator Rush Limbaugh. Twice a year he and his wife travel in their bus-sized recreational vehicle to Boothbay, Maine, to vacation at their two-hundred-acre hilltop farm. In Maine, Malone's primary leisure activities are gardening and piloting his fifty-nine-foot sailboat.

Malone has served the National Cable Television Association (NCTA), a politically powerful industry lobbying organization, as director (1974–77 and 1980–93) and treasurer (1977–78). His honors include the NCTA's Vanguard Award (1983), the *Wall Street Transcript*'s Gold Award for the cable industry's best chief executive officer (1982, 1985, 1986, and 1987), the award of merit for distinguished entrepreneurship from the Sol C. Snider Entrepreneurial Center of the University of Pennsylvania's Wharton School, and an honorary doctorate from the University of Denver (1992). He was named the CEO of the Year in 1993 by *Financial World.*

Selected Biographical References: Bsns W p88+ O 26 '87 por, p152 Ap 13 '90 por; Esquire 119:86+ Je '93 por; Fortune 120:97+ Jl 31 '89 por; New Yorker 69:52+ F 7 '94 por; NY Times Mag p16+ D 2 '90 por.

Mandela, Nelson

July 18, 1918- President of South Africa. Address: Private Bag X1000, Pretoria 0001, South Africa

NOTE: This biography supersedes the article that appeared in *Current Biography* in 1984.

John Parkin/AP/Wide World Photos

Nelson Mandela

In August 1962 Nelson Mandela, who not long before had emerged as a leading member of the African National Congress (ANC), South Africa's oldest civil rights organization, was arrested on charges of inciting workers to strike and leaving the country without valid travel documents. When he appeared in court for a formal remand, which was attended by a number of white attorneys who knew him personally, Mandela had a revelation of sorts. He sensed that on some level the spectators knew that he had committed no crime and that he was simply, in his words, "an ordinary man being punished for his beliefs." "In a way I had never quite comprehended before," Mandela wrote in his autobiography *Long Walk to Freedom* (1994), "I realized the role I could play in court and the possibilities before me as a defendant. I was the symbol of justice in the court of the oppressor, the representative of the great ideals of freedom, fairness, and democracy in a society that dishonored those virtues. I realized then and there that I could carry on the fight even within the fortress of the enemy."

Mandela went on to do just that, not only in the 1962 trial and in the famous Rivonia Trial of 1963–64, in which he was convicted of treason and sentenced to life in prison, but also throughout the twenty-seven years of his incarceration. Mandela has continued to fight for the creation of a truly democratic society in South Africa since his dramatic release from prison in 1990, first as the guiding force in the ANC's negotiations with the white-minority government to end apartheid and to replace it with a multiracial government of national unity and then, since 1994, as South Africa's first freely elected president. Yet as far as Mandela is concerned, the challenge of transforming South Africa into a nonracial society has only begun. "I have walked that long road to freedom . . . ," Mandela wrote in his autobiography. "But I can rest only for a moment, for with freedom comes responsibility, and I dare not linger, for my long walk is not yet ended." For his efforts, in 1993 Mandela won the Nobel Peace Prize, which he shared with his predecessor, F. W. de Klerk, the former president of South Africa.

Nelson Mandela was born Rolihlahla Dalibhunga Mandela on July 18, 1918 in the village of Mvezo, in the Transkei, a region on South Africa's southeastern coast. His father, Gadla Henry Mphakanyiswa, was the chief of Mvezo and a member of the royal house of the Thembu tribe, and his mother, Nosekeni Fanny Mandela, was one of his father's four wives. Following his father's death, when he was nine, Mandela came under the guardianship of Jongintaba Dalindyebo, the powerful regent of the Thembu people, who groomed him for tribal duties as counselor to the chief and whom he came to admire greatly. In fact, Mandela's mature ideas about leadership, especially his belief in the importance of leading by consensus, were inspired by the example set by the regent, as Mandela revealed in his autobiography: "I always remember the regent's axiom: A leader, he said, is like a shepherd. He stays behind the flock, letting the most nimble go out ahead, whereupon the others follow, not realizing that all along they are being directed from behind."

As a youth Mandela was also influenced by certain Western cultural values that prevailed at the Methodist primary and secondary schools he attended. The schools were modeled after British schools, and as a result Mandela and his classmates were taught to aspire to be "black Englishmen," he has recalled somewhat ruefully. Mandela's identification with British interests remained strong at the University College of Fort Hare, in Alice, which he entered at the age of twenty-one at the urging of his guardian. Indeed, when the South African government entered World War II on the side of the Allies to help liberate Europe from German domination, Mandela and his classmates heartily supported the move—"forgetting," he has written, "that we did not have that freedom here in our own land."

Mandela's exposure to Western culture also distanced him from Thembu traditions, to the extent that he could not bring himself to submit to his guardian's wish that he marry a woman of the guardian's choosing, in accordance with Thembu custom. To avoid marrying the woman, in 1941 Mandela fled to Johannesburg, where, with the help of Walter Sisulu, a prominent black businessman from the Transkei, he soon got a job as a law clerk in the office of a liberal Jewish law firm. Concurrently, he began a correspondence course from the University of South Africa, which awarded him a B.A. degree in 1942.

During his early years in Johannesburg, Mandela was surrounded by people of all political persuasions, but he did not allow himself to feel pressured to embrace any one particular philosophy. Instead, he carefully considered all points of view, including not only those of friends who belonged to the Communist Party and the African National Congress (many of whose members were students at the University of the Witwatersrand, which Mandela entered in 1943 with the aim of obtaining a bachelor of law degree) but also those of his white employers, who did their best to discourage him from pursuing a career in politics.

After much thought, Mandela found that he had the greatest affinity for ideas promoted by the ANC, whose principal goal was the liberation of black South Africans from the shackles of racism. "I had no epiphany, no singular revelation, no moment of truth, but a steady accumulation of a thousand slights, a thousand indignities, a thousand unremembered moments, produced in me an anger, a rebelliousness, a desire to fight the system that imprisoned my people," Mandela wrote in his memoir. "There was no particular day on which I said, From henceforth I will devote myself to the liberation of my people; instead, I simply found myself doing so, and could not do otherwise."

Mandela joined the ANC in 1944, and shortly after that he and others helped establish the ANC Youth League, which eventually came to dominate the ANC and whose aims were nothing less than "the overthrow of white supremacy and the establishment of a truly democratic form of government," as Mandela has described them. Those goals became more elusive than ever after the Afrikaner-dominated National Party came to power in 1948. In the following years the Nationalists passed a series of sweeping laws that transformed from custom into law the system of racial segregation known as apartheid. In addition to requiring each of South Africa's racial groups to live in separate, designated areas, the laws prohibited marriage between people of different races, mandated that all South Africans be registered according to their race, and outlawed the Communist Party in terms so broad that almost anyone could be considered a member.

In response to the new measures, the ANC leadership felt compelled to rethink its strategy to protest the oppression of black South Africans. That rethinking ultimately prompted the ANC to demand, in a letter to the prime minister in 1952, that the government repeal the discriminatory laws. When the demand was rebuffed, as expected, the ANC launched the Campaign for the Defiance of Unjust Laws, which Mandela helped organize. Those involved in the campaign committed such nonviolent—and, according to the new laws, illegal—acts as entering proscribed areas without permission, using "whites only" facilities, including toilets and railway station entrances, and taking part in strikes. Because of his role in the campaign, Mandela, along with many others, was found guilty of "statutory communism," despite the fact that he did not even belong to the party. As a punishment, he was "banned," which meant that he was prohibited from attending rallies or other gatherings (even nonpolitical ones) for several months. (In 1952 Mandela, having already qualified to practice law, established the first black-run law practice in South Africa, with his friend Oliver Tambo.) Mandela was later banned again, and as a result he did not return to the public eye until 1955.

On December 5, 1956 Mandela was among 156 resistance leaders charged with high treason—specifically, committing acts aimed at toppling the government and replacing it with a Communist regime—an offense punishable by death. The acts in question included the Defiance Campaign of 1952 and similar challenges to the government's legitimacy. In the trial, which did not begin until 1959 (Mandela was free on bail during the interim), the government was unable to show that Mandela or the ANC had plotted any sort of violent revolution, and on March 29, 1961 he and his comrades were acquitted. Mandela was pleased by the verdict, though he regarded it not "as a vindication of the legal system or evidence that a black man could get a fair trial in a white man's court," as he wrote in *Long Walk to Freedom*, but rather as "a result of a superior defense team and the fair-mindedness of the panel of these particular judges." His circumspection proved to be well founded, for not long after his acquittal a warrant for his arrest was issued, the ANC having been banned by the government in 1960. In the following months Mandela thus lived as a fugitive, posing variously as a chauffeur, cook, or gardener.

Throughout his years of involvement with the ANC, Mandela was committed to fighting to end apartheid through nonviolent means. By the early 1960s, however, he, along with other ANC leaders, began to question the effectiveness of this approach, for increasingly the government was responding to the ANC's actions with violence. One of the more infamous instances in which the government resorted to violence occurred in the town of Sharpville in 1960, when sixty-nine protesters were killed by police. Whether or not to launch an armed struggle subsequently became the subject of heated debate, especially at an ANC meeting in June 1961. For his part, Mandela, having become convinced that "it was wrong and immoral to subject [his] people to armed attacks by the state without offering them some kind of alternative," argued that the ANC had no choice but to take up an armed struggle against the state. Notwithstanding his lack of military experience, Mandela was given the task of organizing an armed wing of the ANC, Umkhonto we Sizwe (Spear of the Nation), whose mission was to organize acts of sabotage against the state with the aim of overthrowing the white-minority government. Mandela now had more reason than ever to be mindful of his movements around the country. His uncanny luck and success in evading capture earned him the nickname "the Black Pimpernel," after the Scarlet Pimpernel, the title character of a book by Emmuska Orczy who eludes capture during the French Revolution.

Mandela's underground existence came to an end on August 5, 1962, when he was arrested on charges of inciting workers to strike and leaving the country without valid travel documents. In the trial that followed, in which he conducted his own defense, he never denied the government's charges, for he had indeed organized workers to strike and left the country without proper papers. Instead, he argued that the state had no jurisdiction over his activities since its laws had been made by a government in which he had no representation, and that it was merely his natural desire to live as a free man in a state that denied him freedom that had put him on the wrong side of the law. "There comes a time," he declared to the court at the trial's conclusion, "as it came in my life, when a man is denied the right to live a normal life, when he can only live the life of an outlaw because the government has so decreed to use the law to impose a state of outlawry upon him." On November 7, 1962 he was sentenced to five years in prison with no chance of parole.

Eight months later South African authorities raided the ANC's headquarters at a farm in Rivonia and seized documents outlining the organization's plans to wage guerrilla warfare in South Africa. That discovery enabled the state to try Mandela, along with several other top ANC officials, on new and more serious charges. The Rivonia Trial, as it became known, ended with the defendants being convicted of treason. Although their crime was punishable by death—an outcome that Mandela fully expected—the court sentenced them to life in prison, with no chance of parole, on June 12, 1964. The trial was the subject of considerable media attention around the world, and appeals for clemency were received in South Africa from abroad. An editorial writer for the *New York Times* predicted that history would judge that "the ultimate guilty party is the government in power—and that is already the verdict of world opinion."

For the next eighteen years, Mandela was confined to the maximum-security prison on Robben Island, off South Africa's coast. His first cell there was seven feet square, with a single light bulb and a mat on the floor for sleeping. He had the right to receive only one brief letter and one visitor every six months. But in spite of the harsh conditions, Mandela was determined not to surrender to despair. Indeed, he has said he never seriously considered the possibility that he would not one day walk on South African soil as a free man.

Within a year or two, conditions at Robben Island improved somewhat, in part through the efforts of the International Red Cross. Mandela was permitted to take correspondence courses from the University of London, and he and the other prisoners were eventually provided with desks and, later, stools. Still, virtually all conversation among the prisoners was forbidden, and they were not allowed to read newspapers, which they nevertheless felt duty-bound to try to do (and which they succeeded in doing), so as to keep abreast of political developments in South Africa. Beginning in the 1970s, as conditions permitted, Mandela and his ANC comrade Walter Sisulu led political study groups. Mandela also drafted judicial appeals for other inmates, often piecing together the details of a case as information slowly came to him through the prison grapevine.

In 1980, at the urging of several top ANC officials, the *Johannesburg Sunday Post* launched a campaign to free Mandela by printing a petition that readers could sign to demand that he and other political prisoners be released. Although it met strong resistance from the government—newspapers had long been barred from printing Mandela's photograph or citing his words—the campaign established him more firmly as the embodiment of black South Africans' fight for freedom.

In 1982 Mandela was transferred to Pollsmoor Maximum Security Prison. By then the effort to end apartheid had taken on greater urgency among the younger generation of black South Africans and as a result was gaining attention and sympathy abroad. There were also signs that the South African government was not impervious to the mounting international criticism of its policies, and that, more important, it realized it might eventually have to accommodate at least some of the concerns of the country's increasingly militant black majority.

One such sign came in 1985, when President P. W. Botha offered to free Mandela and all other political prisoners if they agreed to "unconditionally" repudiate violence. Mandela refused, for the same reason that he had committed himself to the armed struggle against apartheid more than two decades before—namely, that the government, by resorting to violent means itself, had left the ANC with no other course of action. But he saw in Botha's offer a change in attitude and decided to take a chance. Later that year, on his own initiative, he began exploring the possibility of conducting secret talks with the government. Such an effort, not coincidentally, had only then become logistically feasible, because in that year Mandela was moved to a cell where he had little contact with his colleagues and could thus speak with government officials privately.

Mandela at first told no one about his plan. "There are times when a leader must move ahead of the flock, go off in a new direction, confident that he is leading his people the right way," he wrote in his memoir. He took some consolation in the fact that his "isolation furnished [his] organization with an excuse in case matters went awry: the old man was alone and completely cut off, and his actions were taken by him as an individual, not as a representative of the ANC."

By 1987 Mandela had had several secret discussions with the minister of justice, Kobie Coetsee, the upshot of which was that the government appeared to be interested in reaching some sort of compromise with the ANC. In late 1988 Mandela was transferred to Victor Verster Prison, also near Cape Town, where he was provided with a cottage with a swimming pool and allowed to keep his own schedule. There, the talks continued.

In 1989 Botha stepped down both as head of the National Party and as president; he was succeeded by F. W. de Klerk. At first Mandela, like most political observers both within and outside South Africa, viewed de Klerk as simply a party man, but he soon came to see the new president as "a man who saw change as necessary and inevitable." And as it turned out, change was not long in coming. Shortly after taking office, de Klerk overturned many of the laws that constituted petty apartheid (such as those segregating parks and restaurants and other public facilities), released a number of black leaders from prison, and met personally with Mandela. Then, in a speech before parliament on February 2, 1990, de Klerk lifted the ban on the ANC as well as on other opposition organizations, declaring, "The time for negotiations has arrived." The following week he told Mandela that his release was imminent.

Mandela's release from prison, on February 11, 1990, was one of the most dramatic news events of the year. A few months later Mandela embarked on a world tour, making stops in major cities throughout North America and Europe, where he was welcomed as a hero and a world leader. In Great Britain he met with Prime Minister Margaret Thatcher. In the United States he addressed a joint session of Congress and conferred with President George Bush. After his meeting with Bush, the two men held a press conference on the White House lawn.

The task of establishing a truly democratic, nonracial government in South Africa fell to the multiparty Convention for a Democratic South Africa, which began in December 1991. The negotiations that ensued, led by Mandela and de Klerk, were by no means without conflict and were broken off at various points. A major hurdle was crossed on September 26, 1992, when Mandela and de Klerk signed the Record of Understanding, which formalized their agreement that a single, freely elected constitutional assembly would both serve as the transitional legislature and draft a new constitution. Another milestone was reached on June 3, 1993, when it was agreed that the first elections open to all South African citizens would be held on April 27, 1994. For their efforts to bring South Africa to that point, Mandela and de Klerk were awarded the 1993 Nobel Peace Prize.

Few were surprised when Mandela became a candidate for president in those elections. As expected, the ANC won handily, capturing 62.6 percent of the popular vote. "The images of South Africans going to the polls that day are burned in my memory," he recalled in his autobiography. "Great lines of patient people snaking through the dirt roads and streets of towns and cities; old women who had waited half a century to cast their first vote saying that they felt like human beings for the first time in their lives; white men and women saying they were proud to live in a free country at last. The mood of the nation during those days of voting was buoyant. The violence and bombings ceased, and it was as if we were a nation reborn."

In the months that followed his inauguration, on May 12, 1994, Mandela and the government of national unity began to draft a program of reconstruction and development aimed at both satisfying the demands of long-disenfranchised blacks and attracting new investments from abroad. While it remains to be seen how successful the new government will be in achieving those goals, Mandela has already been credited with one major accomplishment: significantly advancing the cause of mutual understanding and tolerance among his country's diverse ethnic and political groups. He has done so by including in his cabinet not only members of the ANC but also members of the Inkatha Freedom Party, with which the ANC has long been in conflict, and of the National Party. He also led discussions with members of the right-wing Conservative Party, while one of his ministers held similar talks with the neo-fascist Afrikaner Resistance Movement. As a result, he has succeeded in gaining the confidence of the more conservative elements of South Africa's electorate. "Even if Mandela achieves little more before he retires, he will have won a special niche in South African history as the dignified, white-haired patriarch who won the respect of his political enemies," Patrick Laurence wrote in *Africa Report* (November/December 1994).

From his marriage to Evelyn Mase, a nurse, which lasted from 1944 until 1956, Nelson Mandela has three children (a fourth died in infancy). In 1958 he married Nomzamo Winnie Madikizela, then a young social worker. The couple had two daughters in the four years they lived together before Mandela's imprisonment. Winnie Mandela became her husband's principal supporter and spokesperson during his years in prison, and she ultimately developed a political power base of her own. Her reputation was later marred by charges of criminal behavior. Following Mandela's release, the couple became estranged, and they separated in April 1992.

In addition to the Nobel Prize, over the years Mandela has received numerous honors and awards. He won the Bruno Kreisky Prize for Human Rights in 1982, and he was named an Honorary Citizen of Rome in 1983. He received the Sakharov Prize in 1988 and the Gaddaff Human Rights Prize in 1989 and shared the Houphouet Prize in 1991. He has received a great number of honorary doctorates, including a joint honorary degree from thirty-eight traditionally black American universities, which he received in 1990 during a ceremony at Morehouse College, in Atlanta.

"The policy of apartheid created a deep and lasting wound in my country and my people," Nelson Mandela concluded in his autobiography. "All of us will spend many years, if not generations, recovering from that profound hurt." Mandela nevertheless remains full of hope that such a recovery will eventually take place. "My country is rich in the minerals and gems that lie beneath its soil, but I have always known that its greatest wealth is its people, finer and truer than the purest diamonds."

Selected Biographical References: Ebony p40+ Ag '94 por; Benson, Mary. Nelson Mandela: The Man and the Movement (1986); Mandela, Nelson. Long Walk to Freedom(1994); Meer, Fatima. Higher Than Hope (1990); International Who's Who, 1994–95

Ambrosio/Mortimer & Associates, Inc.

Mary Alice

Dec. 3, 1941- Actress. Address: c/o Ambrosio/Mortimer and Associates Inc., 9150 Wilshire Blvd., Suite 175, Beverly Hills, CA 90212

In 1987 the actress Mary Alice gained widespread acclaim, as well as a Tony Award, for her Broadway portrayal of Rose Maxson in August Wilson's Pulitzer Prize-winning play *Fences*. Since then she has earned kudos—and more honors—for her strong performances in projects ranging from the movie *To Sleep with Anger* (1990) to, most recently, the Broadway hit *Having Our Say*, based on the best-selling book of the same name by the centenarian Delany sisters. Before appearing in *Fences*, Mary Alice worked for many years in relative obscurity in a host of Off-Broadway plays and in a number of films. While the financial rewards for her efforts failed to match her devotion to her craft during that period, she concluded, and has continued to maintain, that satisfaction lies in the act of performing itself. "It's all about the work," she told Nancy Anita Williams for *Essence* (August 8, 1987). "Anything else can be taken away from you."

Mary Alice Smith was born on December 3, 1941 in Indianola, Mississippi, one of the five children of Sam and Ozelar (Jurnakin) Smith. Her family moved to Chicago when she was an infant. "We never lacked for anything," Mary Alice recalled about her working-class family, during a conversation with Robert Blau for the *Chicago Tribune* (February 27, 1986). "But my parents got up before the sun rose and worked all day. My father was tired. My mother had to cook." She suggested during another interview, with Eleanor Blau for the *New York Times* (September 1, 1990), that the family's circumstances led on occasion to strained relationships among its members: "I love my family, but I always wanted it to be a certain way, and it was never that." As a result, she spent time by herself, "imagining that [her] family was perfect"—a pastime that, she explained, foreshadowed her later interest in acting.

Mary Alice told Leslie Bennetts of the *New York Times* (March 30, 1987) that her mother had wanted to be a nurse but that family obligations had interfered with her plans. For her part, Mary Alice was determined to attend college. "I think I decided very early that I did not want—well, not so much that I did not want to get married, but that I did want to find out about the world," she said to Bennetts. "I did that through college, through learning, through books and travel." In 1965 she graduated from the teachers' college at Chicago State University, and for the next two years she taught the third and fourth grades at the Victor Herbert School in Chicago.

Meanwhile, Mary Alice had become active in community theatre. "Very frightened" of performing at the outset, she took on administrative duties at a small theatre company. Eventually, she joined the cast of an all-black production of the Tennessee Williams play *Cat on a Hot Tin Roof*, and she found the experience to be such a positive one that afterward she "took whatever [she] was cast in." One of her assignments was as a bit-part player—and laundress—for a Chicago production of Douglas Turner Ward's plays *Happy Ending* and *Day of Absence*, which were performed as a double bill.

After the shows closed, Ward persuaded Mary Alice to go to New York City, where he was in the process of founding the Negro Ensemble Company. She moved to New York in 1967 and auditioned for membership in the troupe, only to be turned down. Ward arranged, however, for her to receive theatrical instruction from Lloyd Richards, the first black director to mount a Broadway play (the 1959 production of Lorraine Hansberry's *A Raisin in the Sun*) and the future artistic director of the Yale Repertory Theatre as well as of the National Playwrights Conference of the Eugene O'Neill Theater Center. "I'm an actor today because of that," Mary Alice said of Richards's teaching, in an interview with Patricia O'Haire of the New York *Daily News* (August 15, 1990). Richards returned the compliment in a conversation with Gene Seymour of *New York Newsday* (August 27, 1990): "The thing I noticed right away was her energy, her imagination. The power she conveys on stage was always there. It was bursting out. All it took was honing it and controlling it. But she had all the talent going in."

By the time of her Off-Broadway debut, in a 1967 staging of the one-act plays *The Trials of Brother Jero* and *The Strong Breed*, by the Nigerian playwright Wole Soyinka, the actress had dropped her surname and was billed as Mary Alice ("to make her stage name catchier," as Eleanor Blau phrased it). The title character in *Brother Jero* is a combination preacher and lecherous con man; the more serious *Strong Breed* focuses on a teacher who is made the "carrier," or scapegoat for all sins, in his African town. Of her performance in the latter play, a reviewer for *Variety* (November 15, 1967) wrote, "The support is mostly good, notably Mary Alice as a young girl who tries to help the victimized teacher." At the Arena Stage, in Washington, D.C., Mary Alice took the part of Cordelia in a 1968 production of *King Lear*. In 1969 she made her first—and, for nearly two decades, only—Broadway appearance, in Charles Gordone's play *No Place to Be Somebody*. She was featured prominently in the same year in *A Rat's Mass*, Adrienne Kennedy's poetic, nonlinear, and densely written work about a black brother and sister shackled by their shared adoration of a white woman. "Mary Alice and Gilbert Price . . . gave fine, controlled performances of the brother and sister 'rats,'" Marilyn Stasio wrote in *Cue* (October 4, 1969).

Throughout the 1970s Mary Alice was active in Off-Broadway theatre, turning up in *The Duplex* (1972), *Miss Julie* (1973), *House Party* (1973), and *Black Sunlight* (1974). Her work in *Terraces*, Steve Carter's quartet of sketches about black residents of a "pseudo-posh" housing development in Harlem, was thought to be "particularly impressive" by Edith Oliver of the *New Yorker* (April 22, 1974). *Terraces* was presented by the Negro Ensemble Company, as were the 1974 stagings of *Heaven and Hell's Agreement* and *In the Deepest Part of Sleep*, in which Mary Alice also appeared. Critics were at odds over the actress's performance as Reba, a woman who longs for her husband to display more "manliness," in the 1977 run of *Cockfight*, Elaine Jackson's study of attitudes about marriage and sex roles. While Richard Eder of the *New York Times* (October 17, 1977) felt that Mary Alice's interpretation of her character was "all performance with nothing underlying it," John Beaufort wrote in the *Christian Science Monitor* (October 26, 1977), "Mary Alice is extraordinarily touching as the affectionate, wishfully trusting, but finally disillusioned Reba."

By contrast, there was little disagreement about the quality of Mary Alice's work in the 1978 revival of Athol Fugard's *Nongogo*, set in Johannesburg, South Africa. She played Queeny, the jaded proprietor of an illegal liquor joint and a former prostitute (or *nongogo*), who briefly embraces hope in the form of a naïve young salesman. Mary Alice "grasps all of [her character's] emotional drives in her gallant and touching portrait of Queeny," John Beaufort declared in the *Christian Science Monitor* (December 6, 1978). In the *Village Voice* (December 18, 1978), Terry Curtis Fox expressed a similar view: "The cast is quite wonderful, but Mary Alice . . . is exceptional. Her Queeny is a woman who plays a constant game of emotional hide-and-seek until, in a breakdown at the evening's end, her callous mask becomes wedded to emotion in a truly horrifying way. Mary Alice is so exact that she can turn her back on the audience and we will still know what her face is doing—hers is a tour-de-force performance totally at the service of the play." Although Richard Eder of the *New York Times* (January 26, 1979), reviewing a black and Hispanic production of *Julius Caesar* at the Public Theater, found Mary Alice's portrayal of Portia to be "both overwrought and emotionally obscure," Michael Feingold of the *Village Voice* (February 5, 1978) pronounced the actress to be "the best Portia [he had] ever seen." For her performance in that role, she won an Obie Award.

Among Mary Alice's Off-Broadway credits in the 1980s were Charles Fuller's *Zooman and the Sign* (1980) and *Glasshouse* (1981), by Fatima Dike. In the former, she played the mother of a young girl murdered by a street thug. It was the opinion of Edith Oliver of the *New Yorker* (December 22, 1980) that "as the mother, Mary Alice—a fine actress and a beautiful woman—[became] Hecuba, her face ravaged by sorrow; the performance [had] depth and validity." *Glasshouse* tells the story of two South African women, one black, one white, struggling to maintain their long friendship in the shadow of their country's system of racial apartheid. Douglas Watt, writing in the New York *Daily News* (March 23, 1981), found that Mary Alice—"she of the woeful but pretty countenance that can turn suddenly radiant with joy"—was "appealing" in her role.

"Creatively," Mary Alice has said, "I have found [acting on the stage] to be more rewarding than doing films simply because the final product is not in the actor's hand when you do film or television." Still, concurrent with her stage work in the 1970s and early 1980s, she had made appearances—mostly in small roles—in a handful of made-for-television movies and feature films. On the small screen, she turned up in *The Sty of the Blind Pig* (1974), *Just An Old Sweet Song* (1976), *This Man Stands Alone* (1979), *Concealed Enemies* (1984), and *The Killing Floor* (1985), and she was seen on the big screen in *The Education of Sonny Carson* (1974), based on the autobiographical book by the black activist; *Sparkle* (1976), about a successful female singing group (modeled loosely on the Supremes); *Beat Street* (1984); and *Teachers* (1984).

In spite of those projects and her considerable body of stage work, the mid-1980s found Mary Alice, after almost twenty years in New York City, unable to earn a comfortable living solely through acting. For a time she taught drama at the high-school level, and at one point she took work as a substitute teacher. ("The kids abused me," she told one reporter. "Maybe I'm not qualified anymore.") For the 1986 *Chicago Tribune* profile, she revealed to Robert Blau that she had briefly considered giving up acting—but that she had then had a personal revelation. "I really didn't feel I wanted to act anymore," she said. "I was sitting down. I got up, and I had . . . a feeling, a feeling with such clarity, and I had no doubt what it was. It was my God. The voice said to go home, that everything is going to be all right. As long as you do work, it said, don't worry about the money."

It was in 1983, at the National Playwrights Conference run by Lloyd Richards in Waterford, Connecticut, that Mary Alice created the character Rose Maxson in *Fences*. (At the annual conference, actors are invited to spend two weeks performing in works in progress.) *Fences* is set in Pittsburgh in 1957 and focuses on a lower-middle-class black family; Rose is the longtime, not-always-silently suffering wife of Troy, the bombastic, complex, difficult patriarch. "I knew these people," Alice told Robert Blau, referring to the characters in the play. "Troy is . . . like my grandfather. There were men like [Rose's stepson] in my neighborhood, men who had no jobs but who wanted to look good. And Rose is like my Aunt Mary, who was strong and loyal in her love and a good person. She raised eleven children by herself. A lot of Aunt Mary is in me."

With Mary Alice as Rose and James Earl Jones in the part of Troy, *Fences* debuted in 1985 at the Yale Repertory Theatre, in New Haven, Connecticut, and it was later staged in Chicago and in San Francisco. The play opened on Broadway in March 1987 and was an immediate popular and critical success. The press lavished praise on the entire cast, and Michael Feingold of the *Village Voice* (April 7, 1987) had this to say about Mary Alice's performance: "Possibly to contrast with Jones's extrovert assertiveness as Troy, she treats her showy, long speeches as bursts of half-audible internal monologue, often while sauntering upstage. That she can rivet an audience even in that position is all I need to say about the power of her presence, and the moments when she turns it on facing downstage center are jaw-droppers."

Mary Alice's character delivers one of the play's most consistently audience-rousing lines, after Troy brings home the child that he has fathered by another woman: "From right now," Rose tells her husband, "this child got a mother, but you a womanless man." In Mary Alice's view, Rose's appeal for theatregoers cuts across racial lines. "I think that black women sitting there know Rose immediately," she explained to Leslie Bennetts. "With white women, they learn by the end of the play that she is not that different from them; her circumstances might be different, but her needs and desires and dreams are not. It's the same experience." Mary Alice's performance in *Fences* won her a Tony Award and a Drama Desk Award.

The success of *Fences* brought the actress financial stability as well as offers of roles in a variety of media. For a year and a half, beginning in 1988, she played the dorm director on the popular NBC sitcom *A Different World*, about life at a black college. In 1989 she was seen in the television adaptation of Gloria Naylor's novel *The Women of Brewster Place*. Her credits in 1990 included the New York Shakespeare Festival's production of *Richard III*, in which she played Queen Margaret, opposite Denzel Washington in the title role; the screen version of Tom Wolfe's novel *The Bonfire of the Vanities*; and Charles Burnett's critically acclaimed movie *To Sleep with Anger*. In the latter film, Mary Alice earned praise for her portrayal of Suzie, the mother of a middle-class family whose lives are disrupted by the visit of an old friend (Danny Glover) who is not quite what he seems. She received an Emmy Award for outstanding supporting actress in a television drama series for her work on *I'll Fly Away*, on which she played an eccentric baby-sitter. In 1992 she appeared in Spike Lee's film *Malcolm X*, and in the following year she had roles in James Lapine's *Life With Mikey*, starring Michael J. Fox, and in Clint Eastwood's *A Perfect World*, starring Kevin Costner as an escaped convict with a kidnapped boy in tow.

Mary Alice won a Tony Award nomination—and aged nearly half a century—for her role as Annie Elizabeth ("Bessie") Delany in the Broadway hit *Having Our Say*. The play was based on the best-selling memoir of the same name by Bessie and Sarah ("Sadie") Delany, two accomplished, centenarian black sisters who recalled the myriad social and political changes that they had witnessed over the course of their lives. While Mary Alice felt that the sisters were "both wonderful people," she was drawn more to the part of Bessie, the more blunt-spoken of the two women. *Having Our Say*, directed by Emily Mann, opened at the McCarter Theatre, in Princeton, New Jersey, and moved to Broadway in March 1995.

Vincent Canby, the *New York Times* (April 7, 1995) drama critic, wrote that Gloria Foster (Sadie) and Mary Alice "performed . . . with a collaborative spirit and skill equaled this season only by the performances of Vanessa Redgrave and Eileen Atkins in *Vita and Virginia*." Canby perhaps paid a bigger compliment than he realized: Mary Alice had told Eleanor Blau in 1990, "When I grow up—as an actress—I want to be like Vanessa Redgrave." Her "favorite actor in the whole world," she has said, is Robert De Niro, with whom she worked in Penny Marshall's 1990 film *Awakenings*, about a man who awakens from a thirty-five-year catatonic state.

Among the people who Mary Alice feels contributed to her development as a performer are Ellen Stewart, the founder of La Mama Theatre, the scene of some of the actress's Off-Broadway work. It was Lloyd Richards, however, who taught her that "you must always have secrets on stage, because that's the resource you draw from every night," as she told Gene Seymour for the *New York Newsday* profile. "You can give as much from that character as you have in your life." As an example of what she meant, she recalled, "My father died in April of [1987], and I left [*Fences*], went to his funeral in Chicago, came back. And the first week after his funeral . . . , I just didn't know how I was going to do this performance. Emotionally, I was somewhere else. And I said, 'What I have to do is use this.' And what I did was say that the reason why Rose feels the way she feels is because she has just returned from burying her father. . . . And later on, I had to do the same thing with my mom. Because she died in November of the same year."

Mary Alice, who has been described more than once as reminiscent of a "favorite aunt," continues to make her home in New York City. She explained to one journalist that she has reached the point in her career where she accepts only those projects that truly interest her. Asked by Tony Vellela of the *Christian Science Monitor* (May 10, 1995) if she had any plans to write an autobiography, she responded with a laugh, "I'm so tired of these people writing about their lives. They're not worth the money—and besides, they're not telling everything!" She stated several years ago that she hoped to return to teaching some day "on the college or university level."

Selected Biographical References: Chicago Tribune V p7 F 27 '86 pors; N Y Daily News p3 My 31 '87 pors; N Y Newsday II p9 Ap 21 '87 por

---

Bruce Bennett Studios

Messier, Mark

(MES-ee-yay)

Jan. 18, 1961- Hockey player. Address: c/o The New York Rangers, Madison Square Garden, 4 Pennsylvania Plaza, New York, NY 10001

The best all-around player in hockey may be Mark Messier, a sturdy center with a baleful glare, rough-hewn features, and square jaw who won five Stanley Cups with his hometown Edmonton Oilers and led the long-suffering New York Rangers to their first National Hockey League championship in fifty-four years. A remarkable combination of speed and strength, Messier is a missile on skates—lethal on the power play and a dangerous penalty killer as well—but it is the intangibles that set him apart from other hockey superstars. Energetic and tough, he body checks with authority, projects an intimidating on-ice aura, and plays through injuries that would sideline less dedicated athletes. He is also an accomplished playmaker, and with his consuming will to win, he is an inspirational figure both on the ice, where he leads by example, and in the locker room, where he asserts himself through the force of his personality. The consummate team player, Messier has described himself as a blue-collar athlete who would "rather be remembered as being on a great team than as a great individual player." In an interview with Leigh Montville for *Sports Illustrated* (March 16, 1992), Adam Graves, who has played with Messier in Edmonton and in New York, said, "Just his presence in the locker room, the intangibles he brings, make us a better team. . . . I'd say he has to be the premier leader in professional sports right now. Any team. Any game. Who'd be better?"

Mark Messier comes by his hockey skills naturally: his maternal grandfather, Jack Dea, was a goaltender for the Edmonton Eskimos; his great-uncle, Murray Murdoch, captained the New York Rangers; and his father, Doug Messier, was a rugged defenseman in the Western Hockey Association. The third of Doug and Mary-Jean Messier's four children, he was born in Edmonton, in the Canadian province of Alberta, on January 18, 1961. He has an older brother, Paul, and two sisters, Jennifer and Mary-Kay. Messier spent his early years in Portland, Oregon, where his father played minor-league hockey for the Portland Buckaroos, and, during the off-season, in Edmonton, his parents' hometown. Introduced to hockey by their father, Mark and his brother started out shooting pucks in the carport of the family home in the Edmonton suburb of St. Albert. "I took to it naturally," Mark Messier recalled to Stan Fischler of *Inside Sports* (November 1987). "I got a lot of hockey knowledge watching my dad play, and being around hockey all my life helped. He knew what it took for me to play pro. Not that he pushed me. He more or less let me make my own decisions about playing hockey. When I made that decision, he helped me out tremendously."

After Doug Messier quit playing hockey, in 1970, he completed work on a master's degree in special education at Portland University, then moved with his family back to Edmonton. Embarking on a new career as a coach, he guided the Spruce Grove (Alberta) Mets to the Canadian Tier Two Junior Championship in 1975 and, one year later, coached both of his sons on a Tier Two junior team in St. Albert. Weighing only 155 pounds, Mark was the better skater, but his brother, a gifted puck handler and scorer, was the star of the team. "I still hadn't grown," Mark told John Feinstein of *Sports Illustrated* (February 21, 1983). "I wasn't sure I could make the team, so I worked like crazy all summer." Over the next two seasons of Tier Two junior hockey, he bulked up to 190 pounds and blossomed into a promising player with an enforcer's disposition and the physical strength to back it up.

In 1978, just two credits shy of obtaining his high school diploma, Messier made the leap from amateur to professional hockey, trying out for the Indianapolis Racers of the World Hockey Association (WHA). On the strength of his five-game trial with the Racers, he landed with the Cincinnati Stingers for the remainder of the 1978–79 season, but scored just one goal, a fluke shot from center ice, in forty-seven games. "Maybe I was in a little over my head, but I thought I could play well enough to get by," Messier recalled in a conversation with Jim Matheson of the *Sporting News* (December 17, 1984). Despite his limited scoring ability, Messier had impressed Glen Sather, the Edmonton Oilers coach and general manager, by dominating Oiler forward Dennis Sobchuk in a junior game, and when the WHA disbanded, in 1979, the Oilers took Messier as their second pick in the 1979 National Hockey League draft. "Coming off what he did in Cincinnati, he was no sure thing," Sather said to John Feinstein. "But I had seen him play as a junior, and he had been a real leader. We were gambling on young players anyway, so we drafted him. When he made the team it was by design, not accident. We wanted players we could teach the game to."

Following a brief holdout for more money, Messier arrived at the Oilers' training camp brimming with confidence. "I remember going into that camp I still felt a little ahead of some guys coming out of junior, maybe not in talent, but psychologically," he told Jim Matheson. His cocky attitude, combined with a few late arrivals at practice and a missed team flight, soon earned him a spot in Sather's doghouse and a four-game demotion to the minors. "He just wasn't dedicated to the game," Sather explained to Feinstein. "He had a man's body but a kid's maturity. He had a lot of learning to do." In his rookie season, Messier was a one-dimensional player who, in Stan Fischler's words, "skated hard and slapped the puck ferociously, but did little else to please the coach." "I suppose I was pretty wild," Messier admitted to Feinstein. "I don't exactly go home after every game and bake cookies now, but I know there's a limit to how much you can do before it affects your hockey."

After posting only twelve goals and twenty-one assists as a rookie and twenty-three goals in 1980–81, Messier, at Sather's suggestion, developed wrist and snap shots to go along with the slap shot he had already mastered. Sather's coaching began to pay dividends in the 1981–82 season, when Messier emerged as an offensive threat, scoring fifty goals and becoming a first-team All-Star. "I went straight from Tier Two hockey to the pros and it took a long time for me to adjust," Messier said, explaining his slow start to Fischler. "By 1981–82 I was feeling a lot more comfortable. I always thought I had the ability to play, it was just going to take time." Messier's contributions helped the Oilers clinch first place in the division and, with it, a trip to the 1982 play-offs, where they were upset in the first round by the Los Angeles Kings.

In the 1982–83 season, Messier scored forty-eight goals and, with fifty-eight assists, broke the one hundred-point plateau for the first time in his career. The Oilers advanced to the Stanley Cup finals, where they bowed to the powerful New York Islanders. During the following season Messier moved from the left forward spot to center, and his goal production dropped to thirty-seven—he served a six-game suspension for clubbing Vancouver's Thomas Gradin over the head with his stick—but his sixty-four assists pushed him over the one hundred-point mark for the second consecutive year. Performing brilliantly in the postseason, Messier gave Edmonton a hard-nosed presence in the pivot that effectively neutralized the Islanders' All-Star center, Brian Trottier, in the Stanley Cup finals. With Messier winning the Conn Smythe Trophy as the most valuable player in the play-offs, the Oilers won their first-ever NHL title by dethroning the league's four-time defending champs. Although he would have been a valuable commodity on the free-agent market, he eagerly re-signed with the Oilers, a young team with dynastic aspirations and a front line that paired Messier, the hometown hero, with hockey's acknowledged "Great One," Wayne Gretzky.

Playing in the shadow of Gretzky, the high-scoring, charismatic superstar who became a hockey icon during the 1980s, Messier steadily improved his game. By 1987, when Edmonton bested the Philadelphia Flyers in the Stanley Cup finals for the second time in three years, he was widely considered to be the best all-around player in the league. A less-prolific scorer than his legendary teammate, Messier notched 35 goals and 49 assists for a total of 84 points in the 1985–86 season and 37 goals and 70 assists (107 points) in 1986–87, while Gretzky scored 215 points and 183 points, respectively. But Messier outweighed the 170-pound Gretzky by almost 40 pounds, giving the Oilers' muscular center a superior checking ability and a distinct physical advantage in a sport in which fighting is prevalent and clutch-and-grab tactics are tolerated by referees.

Moreover, because of his combination of speed and strength, the explosive Messier "ranks with the most feared skaters in history," as Stan Fischler noted. Bob Johnson, a former coach for the Calgary Flames, agreed. "Messier is to hockey what Jimmy Brown once was to pro football," Johnson told Fischler. "He's a bull—with finesse. What gives Messier an advantage, is his ability to play *any* team, *any* style, over an eighty-game schedule. Put him up against a rough club like Philadelphia or Boston and he'll play as well as he would against the Rangers or North Stars. He can kill penalties or work the power play. He has the ability to be the best all-around player in the business." "They're both great, but the difference is between finesse and strength," the Philadelphia Flyers' goaltender Ron Hextall said of Gretzky and Messier when Stan Fischler interviewed him for the *Inside Sports* profile of Messier. "Gretzky is more of the finesse player and Messier has the strength *and* speed. He's fast enough to move around your defensemen and still get off his wrist shot, which is *really* good. Gretzky won't go around a bunch. He'll pop up and try to hit the late man. Choosing between them isn't easy."

Messier spent the 1987 off-season helping Team Canada win the Canada Cup international hockey tournament, which the Canadians eventually captured with a dramatic 6-5 victory over the Soviet national team. A few weeks later he rejoined the Oilers for the 1987-88 campaign. An astute decision maker on the ice throughout his career, Messier developed into one of the league's best playmakers during that season, registering a career-high seventy-four assists and scoring thirty-seven goals as the Oilers won their fourth NHL championship in five seasons. In August 1988, when the Oilers made Wayne Gretzky hockey's first million-dollar man by trading him to the Los Angeles Kings, Edmonton became Messier's team.

Playing in seventy-two games in his first season as the Oilers' acknowledged leader, Messier scored ninety-four points on thirty-three goals and sixty-one assists, but Edmonton came up short in the 1989 play-offs. "He was put in a difficult situation . . . ," Oilers defenseman Kevin Lowe told Jim Matheson of the *Sporting News* (December 11, 1989). "It all rested on his shoulders for the first time in his life. Mark will disagree with me, but I think he tried to do too much. Instead of being a power forward, he tried to be everything. At times he tried too much to be a playmaker." But as Wayne Gretzky observed to Austin Murphy of *Sports Illustrated* (May 9, 1988), "The measure of Mark's game is not in goals and assists. The statistic he cares about is Number of Stanley Cups Won."

Scoring a career-best 129 points on 45 goals and 84 assists in 1989-90, Messier was named the league's most valuable player by the Professional Hockey Writers' Association. By his own account, he was even prouder of winning the Lester B. Pearson Award, which is bestowed upon the year's outstanding athlete by his fellow players. Although Gretzky's departure seemed to signal the end of the Edmonton dynasty, Messier's will to win proved decisive in the 1990 play-offs. With his team trailing the Chicago Blackhawks two games to one, Messier dominated the series' pivotal fourth game, scoring two goals and assisting on two others as Edmonton posted a 4-2 victory. "I don't think I'd ever seen anybody take control of a game like that before," Steve Larmer, who played right wing for Chicago in that contest, told George Vecsey of the *New York Times* (May 27, 1994). "He's a big, strong person, and he plays a physical game, and when he gets that look in his eye, there's no stopping him." The Oilers swept the next two games with the Blackhawks and went on to take the Stanley Cup for the fifth time in seven years with a victory over the Boston Bruins.

The 1990-91 season proved to be a long one for Messier, who missed twenty-seven games because of injuries to his knee and thumb and totaled just sixty-four points and twelve goals, the fewest since his rookie year. In an effort to rebuild the team around Messier and lower-paid youngsters, the Oilers had been trading away expensive veterans for several years, and in the 1991 off-season Messier himself began to entertain thoughts of leaving Edmonton. At an annual salary of one million dollars, the nine-time All-Star, who had scored more than one thousand points in his twelve seasons with the team, was playing for considerably less than his market value. The Oilers nevertheless rebuffed him when he sought the security of a long-term contract. "I'd always thought I'd play in one place for all of my life," Messier explained to *Sports Illustrated*'s Leigh Montville. "But I looked at some of the people who'd left—Wayne Gretzky, Paul Coffey, Jari Kurri—and none of them had suffered. I started thinking it would be good for me, too. Maybe I'd done as much as I could in Edmonton. It was time for another team, another place. It would be good for me financially, and it would be sort of a rejuvenation."

After leading Team Canada to another Canada Cup, in October 1991 Messier, who had asked to be traded to a title contender, was dealt to the New York Rangers in exchange for the veteran Bernie Nicholls and two young prospects, Steven Rice and Louie DeBrusk. His contract, reportedly worth three-and-a-half million dollars in salary and bonuses, made him one of hockey's highest-paid players. "I was looking for that mind-set of a winner to bring into the locker room," Neil Smith, the Rangers' general manager, told Montville. "It's that repetitive mind-set that thinks only of winning, that knows how to win. I think that's very big in hockey, why you see so much repetition in the teams that do win. They *expect* to win. . . . I thought that Mark, no matter how long he played for us, would leave us with something we didn't have before. Maybe that would be how to win."

Two days after he signed on with the Rangers, Messier was named team captain. "Burdened by glorious ancient history and a dismal recent past," as Robert Lipsyte put it in the *New York Times* (January 19, 1992), the Rangers had last won a Stanley Cup in 1940, and in recent seasons New York had mounted Patrick (now Atlantic) Division title drives only to falter in the play-offs. "When I first put on the Rangers' sweater, I knew I also took on that history, that tradition—and 1940 . . . ," Messier told Larry Wigge of the *Sporting News* (June 27, 1994). "There were a lot of hurdles to overcome. In Edmonton, we were kids. We didn't have history or anything to fall back on. In New York, it was fifty-four years of frustration. The toughest challenge in professional sports is to come here and try to win a championship." Leading the Rangers to a league-best record of fifty wins, twenty-five losses, and five ties, Messier, who finished the 1991–92 season, including the play-offs, with thirty-five goals and seventy-two assists, was chosen by the *Sporting News* as player of the year for the second time since 1990. New York, however, failed to survive past the second round in the play-offs.

In the following season the talent-laden Rangers collapsed, finishing last in their division. Although Messier scored ninety-one points on twenty-five goals and sixty-six assists, he was hobbled by injuries and distracted by a feud with head coach Roger Neilson. Early in the campaign, while the Rangers were struggling, Messier singled himself out as, in his words, the "leader of the players" who must take it upon himself to "feel their tempo and pulses" and "address a situation inhibiting them from playing to their capabilities." "It was kind of a declaration of war against Neilson," Robert Lipsyte observed in his *New York Times* (June 10, 1994) column, "and it tore the team apart. Older players, such as the gifted Mike Gartner, were less than charmed by Messier's Captain Dad approach." When Neilson was fired midway through the season, a move that further divided the team, Messier, for the first time in his career, was accused of sowing locker-room discord.

"It was a disaster," Neil Smith said of the 1992–93 season in an interview with Austin Murphy of *Sports Illustrated* (February 21, 1994). "The team needed a coach who would come in and kick its butt." To deliver that kick, Smith hired Mike Keenan, an iron-willed disciplinarian who had coached Messier in the 1987 and 1991 Canada Cups and had twice lost to Messier's Oilers in the Stanley Cup finals when he was coaching the Philadelphia Flyers. Embracing Keenan's program of rigorous conditioning, Messier installed a gym in his off-season home in Hilton Head, South Carolina and, instead of spending his vacation waterskiing and playing golf, devoted himself to the team's conditioning regimen. Moreover, Messier and Keenan enjoyed a cordial relationship based on mutual respect that infused the Rangers with a winning attitude.

Led by Messier, who played through a serious midseason injury to his wrist, the forwards Esa Tikkanen and Adam Graves, who had played with Messier in Edmonton, defenseman Brian Leetch, and goaltender Mike Richter, the Rangers finished the 1993–94 season with the league's best won-lost record. In the play-offs, the Rangers were trailing the New Jersey Devils three games to two in the Eastern Conference finals when Messier brashly guaranteed a game-six victory and then made good on his prediction by scoring a game-winning hat trick in the third period. With Messier netting one goal and assisting on another, the Rangers ended their fifty-four-year title drought with a heart-stopping 3–2 victory over the Vancouver Canucks in the seventh game of the Stanley Cup finals.

Taking advantage of a clause in the five-year, thirteen million-dollar contract he had signed in December 1991 that allowed him to renegotiate if the Rangers won the Stanley Cup, in January 1995 Messier signed a two-year extension (the Rangers have an option to add a third year) worth an estimated six million dollars per season. He entered the 1994–95 season as the second-leading scorer in play-off history, with 259 points, and his 99 postseason goals are third-best on the all-time play-off list, behind Wayne Gretzky (110) and Jari Kurri (102). Playing under a new coach, Colin Campbell, the Rangers clung to first place in the Atlantic Division for most of the lockout-abbreviated season, which did not get underway until late January, but they faded in the stretch to finish the year in fourth place, with a record of twenty-two wins, twenty-three defeats, and three ties. Fatigued by a down-to-the-wire battle for a play-off berth, the defending Stanley Cup champions survived the first round only to be swept in the Eastern Conference semifinals by the Philadelphia Flyers. "We were physically beaten up before the series even started," Messier said after the fourth and final game against the Flyers, as quoted in the *New York Times* (May 27, 1995). "When we see someone else carrying the cup around it will be that much tougher. We gave it all we had, and it wasn't enough." Over the course of the regular season, Messier notched 14 goals and 39 assists for a team-high 53 points.

During the hockey season, Messier makes his home in a brownstone on Manhattan's Upper West Side, while his parents look after his large, ocean-front estate in Hilton Head. As Filip Bondy noted in the *New York Times* (January 19, 1992), Messier's life has always been "defined by family." His father serves as his agent and negotiates his contracts, and his brother, Paul, and younger sister, Mary-Kay, handle his business affairs through the auspices of Messier Management International Inc., which they formed when Mark moved from Edmonton to New York. His son, Lyon, who lives with his mother, is a frequent visitor to Messier's homes. "Everything I do revolves around being good on the ice," Messier told Robert Lipsyte in an interview for the *New York Times* (February 9, 1995). "You must be willing to be consumed by this game for nine months, twenty-four hours a day, to be totally free to think about it, help a teammate, work harder. It's tougher on the married players, the ones with children. It's the reason I haven't committed myself to long-term relationships yet. Or to many endorsement contracts. I can't be distracted."

Selected Biographical References: Inside Sports p68+ N '87 pors; MacLean's 105:37+ Mr 30 '92 por; N Y Times p27+ O 5 '91 pors, VIII p1+ Ja 19 '92 pors, B p11+ F 9 '95 pors; Sport p64 O '90; Sporting N p40 D 17 '84 por, p32 Ap 13 '87 por, p43 D 11 '89, p51+ My 16 '94 pors; Sports Illus 58:54+ F 21 '83 pors, 68:52+ My 9 '88 pors, 76:44+ Mr 16 '92 pors; Toronto Globe and Mail A p20 O 26 '91 pors; Who's Who in America, 1995

Michel Lipchitz/AP/Wide World Photos

Mikhalkov, Nikita

(mi-KAHL-kof, ni-KEE-tuh)

Oct. 21, 1945- Russian filmmaker; actor. Address: c/o Sony Pictures Classics, 550 Madison Ave., New York, NY 10022

Nikita Mikhalkov, besides being an accomplished actor who has appeared in more than twenty-five films, is the most prominent and successful film director working in Russia today. He first gained attention in the West with his film *A Slave of Love* (1976), a bittersweet comedy about a group of Russian aristocrats living in the early twentieth century, just before their way of life disappeared forever. He has returned to the theme of dying cultures and ways of life in several other films, among them *An Unfinished Piece for Player Piano* (1976) and *Close to Eden* (1992). Because of his obvious reverence for the past, especially that of his native Russia, many reviewers have drawn parallels between Mikhalkov's sensibility and that of Chekhov, and in fact two of his films, *An Unfinished Piece* and *Dark Eyes* (1978), were inspired by the work of the great Russian writer. Mikhalkov's most recent effort, *Burnt by the Sun* (1994), which he wrote, directed, and produced and in which he also starred, won him his first Oscar, in 1995, for best foreign-language film.

Nikita Mikhalkov was born on October 21, 1945 in Moscow into a distinguished Russian family. His maternal grandfather, Pyotr Konchalovsky, and great-grandfather, Vasily Surikov, rank among Russia's greatest painters. His mother, Natalia, was a poet, essayist, and translator, and his father, Sergei, in addition to being a well-known poet, dramatist, satirist, and writer of children's books, served for a time as the head of the Soviet Writers Union and wrote the lyrics of the Soviet national anthem. His older brother, Andrei Konchalovsky, who uses their mother's maiden name professionally, is a prominent film director who has spent most of his professional life working in the West.

When Mikhalkov was a child, his mother wanted him to be a musician. The acting profession, with which he became acquainted when his brother was in film school, proved to have a greater hold over him, and as a youngster he studied at the children's studio of the Stanislavsky Theatre. He also studied at the Chuksin School of the Vakhtangov Theatre and the VGIK, the state film school in Moscow, which his brother had attended. Mikhalkov's first short, *I'm Coming Home*, was produced in 1968. His graduation film, *A Quiet Day at the End of the War*, is notable because it was the first project he worked on with his classmate Alexander Adabashian, who later became Mikhalkov's art director and the coscenarist of several of his films.

By the time Mikhalkov graduated from film school in 1970, he had already established a reputation as an accomplished actor. Even after he became a successful director, he continued to appear in films, including several of his own and a number of his brother's. Very often he was cast as a charming rogue. Two of his best-known performances were in *Station for Two* (1983), in which he played a black marketeer, and in *Cruel Romance* (1984), in which he played a callous womanizer.

Mikhalkov made his professional directorial debut in 1974, with *Svoi sredi chuzhikh, chuzhoi sredi svoikh* (*At Home Among Strangers, A Stranger at Home*), which has been described as a kind of Soviet western. Set during the civil war that followed the Russian Revolution of 1917, it focuses on a gang of thieves who steal a shipment of gold that was to have been used to buy wheat to feed the hungry. Two years later he made *Raba lubvi* (*A Slave of Love*), which brought him international attention. Like its predecessor, it is a period film, taking place in the Crimea during the revolution. It is also a tragicomedy, for it concerns a group of filmmakers who are so intent on their work—they are filming a melodramatic silent picture—that they remain oblivious to the cataclysmic events occurring to the north, in Moscow.

Many critics were impressed by the originality of *A Slave of Love*, given the strict censorship rules that governed the Soviet film industry. As Robert Hatch observed in the *Nation* (September 30, 1978), "It does seem astonishing that a picture so deft, so insouciant, so willing to acknowledge that flowers and sunshine do not ward off bullets, should come to us from the Soviet Union." Others admired Mikhalkov's ability to convey his fondness for the characters' aristocratic, luxurious lifestyle even while mocking their shortsightedness. "He clearly sees the bourgeois filmmakers' self-absorption as petty, but his artist's eye is drawn to the sensuous beauty of the White Russian style of life," David Ansen observed in *Newsweek* (August

27, 1978). "His ambivalence imbues the film with a Chekhovian sense of rueful comedy about the pipe dreams of a class on the edge of extinction."

Chekhov had an even more direct influence on Mikhalkov's next film, *Neokonchennaya pyesa dlya mekhanicheskovo pianina* (*An Unfinished Piece for Player Piano*), which was adapted by Mikhalkov and his collaborator Alexander Adabashian from *Platonov*, one of the Chekhov's early works. According to some critics, Mikhalkov was remarkably successful in capturing the spirit of the life lived by Russia's aristocracy in the decades before it was consumed by the changes wrought by the Russian Revolution. In his review for *Newsweek* (April 26, 1982), David Ansen observed that the film, which is set on a bankrupt estate populated by a group of aristocrats, evokes an "ineffable Chekhovian atmosphere: the idle heartiness that masks anxiety, the cynical jokes uttered by broken idealists, the sentimental idealism of pampered fools." The main character of the film is Platonov, a schoolteacher and one-time aspiring poet who has lost his ambition. Married to an adoring young woman, he is carrying on with the hostess of the estate when he becomes reacquainted with another woman who was the love of his youth. "With a poet's eye and an uncanny gift for revealing character at a glance, Mikhalkov sends these touching, absurd party-goers on a collision course that can veer at any moment from the tragic to the comic," Ansen continued. "When this lovely midsummer night's dream is over, you may well feel you know these vanished Russians as well as your own family." The film earned the top prize at the 1977 San Sebastian film festival and was a big success in the Soviet Union.

Neskolko dnei iz zhizni I. I. Oblomova ("Several Days in the Life of I. I. Oblomov," 1979), is another of Mikhalkov's adaptations of a Russian literary classic. Based on Ivan Goncharov's 1859 novel *Oblomov* (also the name under which the film was released in the United States), it revolves around the pleasant but hopelessly lazy and passive title character, who falls in love with a delightful woman named Olga but is unable to sustain the romance. Oblomov's character is brought into sharp relief by the presence of his more active, ambitious friend, Stolz, whom Olga eventually marries.

Mikhalkov has said he made the film because he felt that his countrymen's understanding of both Oblomov's character and the themes explored in Goncharov's book did not run very deep. "In the schools, they don't so much read it as use it," he explained to R. W. Apple in an interview for the *New York Times* (March 8, 1981). "I took a copy out of a school library, and I found that a few pages were dog-eared from repeated reading—the parts showing Oblomov's character—and the rest were unsoiled. The teachers impart the stereotype, but they make no effort to penetrate the essence." For Mikhalkov, one of the underlying themes of the book is that, contrary to popular wisdom, there are positive aspects to Oblomov's character, just as there are negative aspects to Stolz's. (Oblomov, among the best-known literary creations among Russians, inspired the term *oblomovshchina*, a synonym for slothfulness.) "There are things that must be felt rather than touched," Mikhalkov explained to David Sterritt in an interview for the *Christian Science Monitor* (April 9, 1981). "That's the story of Oblomov: he felt more than he could 'figure out,' and he suffered for that. But his friend Stolz, the man of action, was even more unhappy—because he understood more, and felt less." At least one film critic, Robert Hatch, writing in the *Nation* (March 28, 1981), felt that Mikhalkov failed to capture the essence of the book. On the other hand, Alan Brien, in a review for the London *Sunday Times* (September 13, 1981), found *Oblomov* to be "one of the most assured recreations of a great work of fiction to reach the screen."

During a break in the filming of *Oblomov*, Mikhalkov made *Pyat Vecherov* (*Five Evenings*, 1978), the first of three movies in which he dealt with more contemporary subjects and settings. *Five Evenings* is an existential love story set in 1956 in which a couple who had become separated as a result of World War II learn again how to communicate. *Rodnya* (*Kinfolk*, 1981) is a comedy about the trials of a dysfunctional family. Much darker is *Bez svidetelei* (*A Private Conversation Without Witnesses*, 1983), a two-character psychological drama about a man's coercive attempt to reunite with his ex-wife.

Mikhalkov returned to more familiar territory with *Otchi Tchornyia* (*Dark Eyes*), his first film to be produced outside of Russia. The film, an Italian production that is set in both Italy and Russia, began not with a script, story line, or even an idea for a story but with the mutual desire of Mikhalkov and the Italian actor Marcello Mastroianni to work together. Only after they agreed to collaborate did they settle on the idea of making a film adapted from four stories written by Chekhov. "We all understood it was ridiculous for Marcello to play a Russian character, and for me also to shoot an Italian film," Mikhalkov told Jerry Tallmer in an interview for the *New York Post* (November 9, 1987). "We tried to find someone we both love a lot, Marcello and I, and that was Chekhov." According to Mikhalkov, the film is less an adaptation of the four stories than it is an entirely new work inspired by them. "'The Lady With the Little Dog' was sort of a pretext for the film, not the subject," he was quoted as saying in the *New York Times* (September 29, 1987). "It's a movie that takes its motifs from Chekhov. I wanted to create a Chekhovian atmosphere."

Dark Eyes, which is set in the early twentieth century, focuses on Romano (played by Mastroianni), a charming Italian architect who, after marrying a woman from Italy's aristocracy, abandons his career plans, settles into a life of leisure, and devotes his energies to engaging in casual love affairs. His life seems to have little purpose until he meets a married Russian woman, Anna, with whom he becomes obsessed. The critical response to the film was mixed. Among those who enjoyed it was Wendy Weinstein, who in *Film Journal* (October 1987) called it "intoxicating." Pauline Kael of the *New Yorker* (October 5, 1987) spoke for those who found little to admire in the film: "It features obviousness and mugging—each in almost unprecedented amounts. Everything in it is overacted, is too slow and too close." Still others took the middle ground, among them David Ansen, who wrote in *Newsweek* (October 5, 1987), "The movie is like a cake with too much frosting. . . . [It] wears its heart too much on its sleeve. Still, it should be seen: the heart beats, and the sleeve is gorgeous." *Dark Eyes* received an Academy Award nomination for best foreign-language film, and Mastroianni earned the best-actor award at the 1987 Cannes film festival and an Academy Award nomination for best actor.

Five years passed before Mikhalkov produced his next movie, *Close to Eden* (1992). The film is unusual in that it had its genesis in little more than his desire to work in China's Inner Mongolia. "One day, I had thought of making a film in Inner Mongolia," Mikhalkov recalled, as quoted in the production notes. "The starting point was geographical. I'm still not sure why. Maybe I was following some ancestral trail. All I had to start with was a five-page script, a few key words, and a bunch of ideas." He knew it would be difficult to obtain financing for the film and was thus fortunate to have met Michel Seydoux, a French producer with a reputation for taking chances with unconventional films. Seydoux agreed to produce it on the basis of Mikhalkov's spare script, his only requirement being that Mikhalkov make it a narrative film rather than a documentary and that he shoot spectacular images using state-of-the-art technology.

Close to Eden is about the confrontation between Western civilization and the ancient, nomadic culture of the Mongol people. It tells the story of two men: Gombo, a shepherd who lives with his mother, wife, and three children in a yurt in the Mongolian wilderness, and Sergei, a Russian who is building a road to bring modernization to the region and who in the process becomes mesmerized by the Mongols' rich culture, the viability of which is threatened by the encroachment of Western civilization. In terms of the setting and the feel of the movie, *Close To Eden* is "worlds apart from the rest of [Mikhalkov's] work," as Geoff Andrew observed in *Time Out* (February 5, 1992). Yet on a deeper level it shares with his earlier works a sadness at the impending loss of traditional ways of life. The movie earned the top prize at the 1991 Venice Film Festival and garnered Mikhalkov his second Academy Award nomination for best foreign-language film.

Mikhalkov's most recent effort is *Burnt by the Sun* (1994). The movie chronicles the events of the day in the summer of 1936 on which an upper-class Russian family is destroyed by Stalinism. Mikhalkov plays the lead character, Sergei Kotov, a retired army officer and hero of the 1917 revolution. At the beginning of the film, Kotov is seen enjoying himself at the family's country home with his beautiful young wife, their six-year-old daughter (played by Mikhalkov's own daughter), and their relatives and servants. Following the arrival of Mitya, an old family friend, their idyll is gradually consumed by impending doom, as it becomes clear that Mitya has been sent by the Soviet secret police to arrest Kotov on trumped-up charges.

According to Anthony Lane, the film critic for the *New Yorker* (May 8, 1995), "what makes the tale more than charming, and gives it real heft, is Mikhalkov's willingness to show that same pleasure dying in front of your eyes—to watch the poison of a political system creeping into the characters' veins." With Mikhalkov writing, producing, directing, and starring in the picture, *Burnt by the Sun* is also, in the view of Jack Mathews of *New York Newsday* (April 21, 1995), a "staggering personal achievement." Mikhalkov's third consecutive film to be nominated for an Academy Award, *Burnt by the Sun* won him his first Oscar, for best foreign-language film. It also won the Grand Jury prize at the Cannes Film Festival.

Mikhalkov has often been asked why he, unlike many filmmakers working in the Soviet Union, was able to produce films without making major compromises. According to Alesandra Stanley, who profiled Mikhalkov for the *New York Times* (March 21, 1995), the artistic freedom he enjoyed can be attributed at least partly to the fact that his Chekhovian cinematic explorations generally provided him with safe and apolitical themes. Yet "talent, determination, and a famous, well-connected father," Stanley wrote, also "helped shield [him] from the censorship and persecution that forced other filmmakers to curb their careers."

Since the collapse of the Soviet Union, Mikhalkov has become less reticent about expressing his political views. He often criticizes the Russian president, Boris Yeltsin, sometimes on television, and he has openly expressed his belief that Russia ought to be governed by a constitutional monarchy. "In 1918 the Bolsheviks put to death the czar and his family, without a trial," he told Edward Ball in an interview for the *Village Voice* (November 3, 1992). "There was no transfer of power. Because of this, every subsequent Moscow government has been illegal. Therefore, I believe the Yeltsin government should find a descendant of the Romanov family and negotiate a formal state transfer of power. That would give us a legitimate new start." Mikhalkov is also an avowed Orthodox Christian and Russian nationalist. "I am not a counterrevolutionary," he told Stanley. "I consider myself an enlightened conservative, an evolutionist."

Mikhalkov appears to be very conscious of his elite background; both he and his brother, according to Vincent Canby of the *New York Times* (May 24, 1987), "have the manner of aristocrats who are totally sure of their places in the world." Canby also observed hanging on the director's office wall a genealogical chart tracing his roots back to Tolstoy and Catherine the Great. Other interviewers have been struck by Mikhalkov's close resemblance to the stereotypical Russian. "With a walrus mustache, booming voice, and taste for black humor," Edward Ball observed, "Mikhalkov presents himself as, and may actually be, the ethnographic Russian subject. The stout, six-foot-four former actor fills his conversation with parables, big laughs, and wry pessimism straight out of Gogol." The internationally acclaimed director could easily find work in the West if he wanted to, but he has no interest in doing so. "Russia is like my battery," he was quoted as saying in the *New York Times* (September 29, 1987). "If my work interests people, it's because my view of the world is a Russian view of the world." Mikhalkov lives in Moscow with his second wife, a model, and four children.

Selected Biographical References: Cineaste 16:34+ 1987–88 por; Film Q 34:14+ Summer '81; N Y Times II p11+ My 24 '87, C p15+ Mr 21 '95 por; Galichenko, Nicholas. Glasnost: Soviet Cinema Responds (1991); World Film Directors 1945–85 (1988)

Nicole Miller Inc.

Miller, Nicole

Mar. 20, 1951- Fashion designer. Address: c/o Nicole Miller Inc., 525 7th Ave., New York, NY 10018

Until a few years ago, Nicole Miller and Bud Konheim, both of whom are principals in the dress-and-sportswear manufacturer Nicole Miller Inc., were content to remain out of the limelight and hold to their strategy of producing stylish, well-made clothing at affordable prices. It was a strategy that made their company highly profitable, but, in an industry where hype is as important as talent, it did not win Miller recognition as an important designer. Nor did her wildly successful line of splashy men's ties, which she introduced in the mid-1980s. So in 1990 Miller, wanting to attract a more exclusive clientele—and thus compete with the likes of Calvin Klein and Donna Karan—held her debut runway show. It was a smashing success. Not only did the fashion media pronounce her "an up-and-coming designer" but some department stores subsequently created separate boutique areas to sell her clothing, just as they had done for the industry's top designers. Now that she has captured the fashion media's attention, it remains to be seen whether her reputation will continue to soar. "It's hard to give up what you were known for and try to convince people you've grown," an unidentified New York City fashion editor told Aimee Lee Ball in an interview for *New York* (March 8, 1993). "I think she has talent for a lot of things. In terms of being the next big name, I don't know yet. She loves the trendy and the sexy, and that sometimes gets in the way. We're all waiting to see what happens."

What sets Miller's designs apart from those of her competitors is their sometimes lighthearted, sometimes daringly sexy, and often "just-wanna-have-fun" attitude. Her core customers are urban women who frequent the trendiest clubs in town, but she also has a following among celebrities: the actresses Geena Davis, Meryl Streep, and Demi Moore and the writer and editor Martha Stewart, among others, have been spotted wearing her designs. Miller, who plays as hard as she works, has often said that her designs are inspired by her own lifestyle, an insight with which Kalman Ruttenstein, the fashion director at Bloomingdale's, agrees. "It seems to me that the designers who make the greatest impact are out and about," Ruttenstein told Aimee Lee Ball. "Nicole is one of the smartest designers we work with. She's on the town, she knows how sophisticated city women want to dress, and she knows how to produce these clothes at a price. A lot of customers are just discovering who she is. I think she will grow in her prestige and acceptability." In addition to dresses and ties, Nicole Miller Inc., whose sales in 1994 were reported to be about $48 million, produces outerwear, boxer shorts, shoes, socks, stationery, handbags, a women's fragrance, and a men's fragrance.

Nicole Jacqueline Miller was born in Fort Worth, Texas on March 20, 1951, the daughter of Grier Bovey Miller, an engineer who worked for General Electric, and his French-born wife, Jacqueline (Mahieu) Miller. She has a sister—Michele, a restaurateur—with whom she grew up in Lenox, Massachusetts. (According to one source, she has two siblings.) Miller, who has attributed her love of fashion to her mother, exhibited an original sense of style at an early age. "I come from this very conservative town where everybody wore heather-tweed skirts, penny loafers, and knee socks," she recalled to Joseph D. Younger, who profiled her for *Express* (November/December 1994). "I would go to New York and come back with these striped miniskirts and a Twiggy haircut and everybody would kinda go, 'Huh?'"

As a young girl Miller aspired to become a model, but that goal was never a realistic one because of her relatively short stature (she stands five feet four inches tall). When she reached high school, she was encouraged to study physics and math because of her aptitude for those subjects. She believes that the combination of her analytical mind and her flair for fashion is what enabled her to become a successful designer. "I have my father's mind," she told Aimee Lee Ball. "The way you figure out how to make something"—including clothing—"is engineering." After graduating from high school, Miller entered the Rhode Island School of Design, in Providence.

Although her mother took great pains to preserve her French identity and, presumably, to instill in her children a love of France (in addition to giving her daughters French names, she arranged for them to have dual citizenship and dressed them in French-style clothing), Miller never became particularly enamored of French fashion. She made her first trip to France during her sophomore year at design school, to study haute couture at the Chambre Syndicale de la Couture Parisienne. "I grew up thinking France was going to be the coolest place in the world," she told Aimee Lee Ball. "I went over there and said, 'Enough of this stuff—I'm American.' So I feel I'm one of the few designers who have no French complex." Nevertheless, she is grateful for what she learned about designing clothing while in France. "I got incredible training in the aesthetics of clothing that I never would have gotten anywhere else," she told Ball. "I think the cut of clothes is most important, and it's been instrumental in making my clothes sell. I'm so concerned about proportions and curves and necklines. It's a very subtle thing, and it goes beyond design. You put on a jacket that's magic, and you put on a jacket that's very similar and it's nothing."

After graduating from design school in the early 1970s, Miller invested in a boutique in Stockbridge, Massachusetts, using money that she had won in a design competition during her senior year. But her real goal was to see if she could make it in New York City's famed garment district. While in school she had gotten a taste of the intense competition that pervades New York City's fashion world, having arranged to intern at a company there that went out of business within two weeks of her arrival. That unpleasant experience failed to diminish the attraction that New York held for her, and after running the Stockbridge boutique for about a year, she set off for Manhattan, where she soon found a job designing raincoats for Rain Cheetahs.

Miller's big break came in 1975, when she responded to an advertisement for the position of head designer at P. J. Walsh, a dress-and-sportswear manufacturer. As part of the interview process, Bud Konheim, the president of the company, asked each of the applicants to choose a piece of fabric from the pile of samples on his desk and then come up with a design for it. "Most of them acted like I was asking them to undress," Konheim recalled to Aimee Lee Ball. "But Nicole knew exactly what she was doing." Konheim then asked the applicants "what would be their real measure of satisfaction, and most of them said something about their name on a label," he continued. "But Nicole said, 'I want to see everybody wearing my clothes.'" That sentiment—that a designer should aim to produce clothing that is not only aesthetically beautiful but sellable as well—matched Konheim's philosophy and thus gave Miller the necessary edge over the other 170 applicants for the job.

Over the next several years, Miller and Konheim developed a close working relationship. "It's like a marriage," she said in an interview with Cathy Horyn for the *Washington Post* (November 7, 1991). "We spent sixteen years working out the kinks." In 1982 Konheim bought out the owner of P. J. Walsh, made Miller a partner, and renamed the company Nicole Miller Inc. Their strategy was to produce moderately priced, couture-quality dresses (Konheim once referred to her style as "couture flea market"), and they did not have to wait long to achieve a measure of success. "Our first year in the business we made $1.4 million," Miller told Gretchen Morgenson, who interviewed her for *Forbes* (May 11, 1992). "The business is run very frugally. We didn't have any assistants; we had only two sewers. So we never had to go outside for financing." Miller and Konheim followed that formula for success for the next seven years. During that time Miller acquired a host of customers who appreciated her flattering designs. "The way I drape clothes tends to focus more on a woman's assets," she explained to Joseph Younger. "Some people are short-waisted, and some are long-waisted, and I take that into consideration in the way I fit the hips or the bust."

By the mid-1980s Konheim and Miller were ready to open their first boutique on Madison Avenue, in Manhattan, when competition from Nicole Miller knockoff manufacturers—firms producing less expensive versions of Miller's designs—began to affect the company's profitability. Miller, who is said to remain calm under pressure, tackled the problem head-on. She decided to revamp her collection by replacing the print fabrics she had been using with solid-colored fabrics. So as not to waste the discarded prints, she reprinted them on silk and turned them into women's scarves and, at Konheim's suggestion, men's ties. She and Konheim would have preferred to arrange for the ties to be sold at stores specializing in menswear, but "they would've laughed at us," Miller has said, so the two had little choice but to stock the ties at the Madison Avenue boutique.

What happened next was completely unanticipated. "Before we knew it, we ran out," Miller told Aimee Lee Ball. "We weren't trying to be in the tie business, but everybody was begging for more. The security guard at the door of our store moonlighted at the Met[ropolitan Opera], and he went to their gift shop one day wearing his theatre-ticket tie, and they were one of our first customers." Further spurring sales of Miller's ties was their popularity among such celebrities as the actors Charlton Heston and Chevy Chase.

Over the years, the tie line seems to have featured every conceivable theme. The "vice tie," for instance, sports images of cigarettes, dice, and martinis. Other ties feature basketballs, Absolut vodka bottles, Oreo cookies, Fritos corn chips, Elvis Presley, sushi, and poker chips. During her interview with Joseph Younger, Miller explained that her tie ideas are inspired by her personal experiences: "Like, I love conch chowder, so I made a tie that has conchs all over it and the word 'conch' in every language I could think of. That was my vacation-inspired tie." With each tie selling for around sixty dollars, the tie business eventually accounted for a significant percentage of the company's revenues. In 1994 the company raked in some $14.5 million—nearly a third of the company's total sales in that year—from tie sales alone.

The success of the tie line not only enhanced the visibility of Nicole Miller Inc.; it also changed Miller's understanding of how the industry works. "You can't really dictate much to the customer," she told Younger. "Customers see something they like and *they* create a fashion trend. We made these ties just for fun, and the customers found us." Following her success in designing ties, Miller launched her own lines of silk boxer shorts, robes, lingerie, bathing suits, and pajamas.

The challenges faced by Miller's company in 1988 were even more daunting than those posed by the competition from knockoff manufacturers. In that year Miller, thinking that hemlines were rising, designed shorter and sexier dresses for her next collection. Although short hemlines eventually came into vogue—in the early 1990s—at the time department-store buyers preferred a longer silhouette. As a result, the company had difficulty selling the dresses, to the extent that sales dropped 64 percent. Konheim had little choice but to lay off half his workers and scrap the pension plan. Thanks at least in part to its tie business, by 1990 the company had returned to fiscal health, with sales, according to one report, of about $35 million.

By the spring of 1990, Konheim and Miller had also decided it was time for the company to court a more exclusive clientele—and thus compete directly with such big-name designers as Calvin Klein, Ralph Lauren, and Donna Karan. To that end, they resolved to put on a fashion show to showcase Miller's talent. "I really wanted to do a show because I was thirty-nine and I thought, am I going to be the new kid on the block at fifty?" she explained to Aimee Lee Ball. "I just felt it was now or never. If I didn't do it, I'd never have any credibility as a designer." To handle the media, the company hired a public-relations firm, Keeble Cavaco & Duka. "A show was the next logical step for them," Paul Cavaco, then one of the principals of the firm, told Cathy Horyn. "Even if Nicole got a bad review, it wasn't going to hurt the business. Bud just felt that she should be recognized as a designer." As it turned out, the show, which featured 1960s-inspired clothing, was a huge success, and before long Miller's designs were appearing in many of the major fashion magazines. Miller since mounted several fashion shows.

Although since 1990 Miller has been trying to secure for herself a place alongside the world's top designers, she has no interest in catering to the tastes of the high-society set. "I would be happier to see Madonna in my clothes than a socialite," she told Aimee Lee Ball. And indeed, her signature style is marked not by sophistication but by a whimsical and an almost aggressively fun-loving spirit. She has a special affection for novelty prints; for instance, a 1991 collection featured sequined minidresses with racing-car designs. She also has more of an affinity for what is hip and sexy than for what is timeless and sensual. Her favorite items from her fall 1992 collection included a long, close-fitting, black-and-red-checked wool-and-Lycra stretch skirt and a leopard-print velveteen dress. Her spring 1994 collection was highlighted by "skimpy little nothings in matte jersey, georgette, embroidered stretch net, or beaded black net over shiny gold," Anne-Marie Schiro reported in the *New York Times* (November 3, 1993). "Nothing there for shrinking violets."

Notwithstanding the popularity of her designs among her core customers, Miller remains best known to the general public for her ties. "I know that the tie business detracts from the dress business because the ties make more noise and a bigger statement than the clothing," she told Aimee Lee Ball. "But I think my expertise is in cutting a dress." Apparently, her customers agree, for her skill in the craft helped make Nicole Miller Inc. worth about $48 million in 1994. Moreover, in 1992 Gretchen Morgenson conjectured that the company's operating profits in that year were around 20 percent—"double what the industry strives for."

Miller's clothes are inspired not by an idealized vision of femininity—a preoccupation of many designers—but by her own experiences, which include lots of parties and evenings out on the town, especially at some of New York City's trendiest nightclubs and restaurants. "I don't think designers are really creating fashion, a new look anymore," she told Aimee Lee Ball. "It's not the runway going to the streets—the streets are going to the runway." While she remembers wishing several years ago that her personal life also included marriage and a family, she is now more than content to be able to enjoy life on her own. "Five years ago, I was very jealous because a lot of my friends were getting married and having children," she was quoted as saying in *People* (April 19, 1991). "But life is always a trade-off. This is one of the better times in my life. . . . My last boyfriend used to always tell me, 'Grow up.' But I say, 'Why?'"

Selected Biographical References: Chicago Tribune VI p7 O 11 '92 por; Express p48+ N/D '94 pors; Los Angeles p14 My '93 por; New York 26:38+ Mr 8 '93 pors; People 35:128+ Ap 29 '91 pors; Washington Post C p1+ N 7 '91 por; Who's Who in America, 1995

W.W. Norton/*James L. Maris*

Millett, Kate

(MIL-it)

Sept. 14, 1934– Political activist; writer; feminist; artist; sculptor. Address: 295 Bowery, New York, NY 10003

NOTE: This biography supersedes the article that appeared in *Current Biography* in 1971.

Upon the publication in 1970 of her doctoral dissertation, *Sexual Politics*, Kate Millett, formerly an obscure sculptor and college teacher, was reluctantly crowned by the media as the "high priestess" of the second wave of the feminist movement. Delineating the degradation of women as reflected in the literature of D. H. Lawrence, Henry Miller, and Norman Mailer, among others, *Sexual Politics* stands as one of the earliest examples of feminist literary criticism, even though its author was concerned mainly with societal rather than textual analysis. Explaining gender as a function of social construction rather than biological difference, the book also provided one of the first feminist theories of the origins of patriarchy, filling the void between Simone de Beauvoir's *The Second Sex* (1949) and Betty Friedan's *The Feminine Mystique* (1963).

Abandoning the academic tone of her first book, Millett next produced two autobiographies in which she described—in a nonlinear, stream-of-consciousness style—her lesbian love affairs and her reactions to the sudden loss of privacy occasioned by the overnight success of *Sexual Politics*. Millett's subsequent works analyzed, often in excruciating detail, various forms of victimization, whether of women by men, children by adults, mental patients by the psychiatric profession, or political prisoners by the state. In addition to writing, Millett runs an artists' colony for women on a Christmas tree farm in upstate New York.

Katherine Murray Millett was born on September 14, 1934 in St. Paul, Minnesota to Helen (Feely) Millett, a farmer's daughter, and James Albert Millett, who was descended from a wealthy Irish-Catholic family. An engineer and contractor who worked for the state highway department, James Millett deserted the family when Kate was fourteen, her sister Sally, nineteen, and her sister Mary (who later changed her name to Mallory), nine. In the years immediately following World War II, the American labor force absorbed a huge influx of returning servicemen, many of whom displaced the female workers who had kept factories and corporations running during the war. Among the hundreds of thousands of women directly affected by the change in hiring policies was Helen Millett. Although she was a college graduate, she was offered only menial jobs before she finally landed a position selling insurance. Whereas her male colleagues were paid a weekly salary in addition to their commissions, she worked solely on commission. Kate Millett contributed to the family's income by working in a department store and by babysitting, and she also managed the household budget.

In 1952 Millett enrolled at her mother's alma mater, the University of Minnesota, from which she graduated with a bachelor's degree, magna cum laude and Phi Beta Kappa, in 1956. With the help of a wealthy aunt, Dorothy Millett Hill, who paid her tuition, she continued her education at St. Hilda's College at Oxford University in England, where she earned first-class honors in English literature in 1958. (Millett's most recent book, *A.D.* [1995], is a tribute to her aunt Dorothy, whom she had nicknamed Anno Domina.) After returning to the United States, Millett taught English at the University of North Carolina at Greensboro for half a semester, then abruptly resigned and moved to New York City. Settling into a loft in the Bowery, on the Lower East Side of Manhattan, she turned to painting and sculpting. She supported herself by working in a bank and, later, by teaching kindergarten in the Harlem district of the city. From 1961 to 1963 she studied sculpting in Tokyo, where she taught English at Waseda University and exhibited examples of her sculpture, which she constructed from metal objects that she had found, in a solo show at the Minami Gallery.

As an artist Millett has at various times produced pop furniture, such as chairs with legs resembling human limbs, wooden cages that imprison female forms, larger-than-life rag dolls, drawings, and silk-screen prints. Over the years, her art has been exhibited at numerous galleries, including the Judson Gallery and the Noho Gallery, in New York City; the Women's Building, in Los Angeles; the Andre Wanters Gallery, in Berlin; and the Courtland Jessup Gallery, in Provincetown, Massachusetts, which mounted an exhibition of her work as recently as 1994.

During her sojourn in Japan, Millett met the sculptor Fumio Yoshimura, with whom she returned to the United States in 1963 and whom she married in 1965, after immigration officials threatened him with deportation. From 1964 to 1970 Millett taught English at Barnard College, at the time the women's division of Columbia University, in New York City. (She has since taught at Bryn Mawr College, in Pennsylvania; Sacramento State College, in California; and the University of California at Berkeley.) In the meantime she had become involved in the burgeoning civil rights and feminist movements, having joined the Congress of Racial Equality and the newly formed National Organization for Women, which she served as founding chairperson of the education committee, from 1965 to 1968. She had also resumed her own studies. While she was teaching at Barnard, she completed work for a Ph.D. degree in English and comparative literature at Columbia University. After successfully defending her dissertation in March 1970, Millett was awarded a doctorate "with distinction." Six months later Doubleday published her doctoral thesis under the title *Sexual Politics.* Eighty thousand copies of the book were sold within its first year of publication.

Sexual Politics is divided into three sections. In the first, "Sexual Politics," Millett analyzed a passage from Henry Miller's *Sexus* and one from Norman Mailer's *An American Dream.* In each excerpt, a male hero is sexually brutalizing a passive, submissive female who is less a fully drawn character with her own thoughts and actions than a thoroughly objectified amalgam of body parts and animalistic reactions. Implying that the protagonists' behavior reflects the authors' attitudes toward women, Millett followed her discussion of Miller and Mailer with a short piece on the writings of Jean Genet, whom she praised for recognizing that "sexual caste supersedes all other forms of inegalitarianism: racial, political, or economic." Millett continued, "The political wisdom implicit in Genet's statement in his play *The Balcony* is that unless the ideology of real or fantasized virility is abandoned, unless the clinging to male supremacy as a birthright is finally foregone, all systems of oppression will continue to function simply by virtue of their logical and emotional mandate in the primary human situation."

In the second part of *Sexual Politics*, "Historical Background," Millett explained her theory of sexual difference as the result of patriarchal society's cultivation of "masculine" and "feminine" virtues in each gender, respectively, pointing out that if there are any (nongenital) biological differences between the sexes they could only be perceived after society has ceased to encourage traditionally masculine attributes, such as aggression, in boys and typically feminine ones, such as passivity, in girls. Contending that the first phase of the sexual revolution occurred from roughly 1830 to 1930, she argued that it was followed by a thirty-year counterrevolutionary period during which women's rights were rolled back by the policies of Nazi Germany and Soviet Russia and, in the United States, by the popularity of Freudian psychoanalysis. In the book's third part, "The Literary Reflection," she deconstructed the writings of D. H. Lawrence and returned to her discussion of Miller, Mailer, and Genet. In an interview with Marie-Claude Wrenn for *Life* (September 4, 1970), Millett commented on what she intended her book to accomplish: "I hope I pointed out to men how truly inhuman it is for them to think of women the way they do, to treat them that way, to act that way toward them. All I was trying to say was, 'Look brother, I'm human.'"

The numerous reviews of *Sexual Politics* ranged in tone from the outright hostile, replete with ridicule and ad hominem attacks on the author, to the reverential admiration expressed by Christopher Lehmann-Haupt in his two-part interview with Millett for the *New York Times* (August 5–6, 1970): "The book is supremely entertaining to read, brilliantly conceived, overwhelming in its arguments, breathtaking in its command of history and literature, filled with shards of wit and the dry ice of logic, and written with such fierce intensity that all vestiges of male chauvinism ought by rights to melt and drip away like so much fat in the flame of a blowtorch." Although some critics took issue with the desirability of her ultimate goal of sexual equality, fearing the eradication of sexual difference (on which male dominance is predicated, according to Millett), many reviewers found her arguments persuasive.

Millett soon found herself the subject of intense scrutiny by the media and by some feminists, who questioned her willingness to work with others in the women's movement. Having given generously of her time in speeches and interviews, she was appalled when an artist's rendering of her face, against her expressed wish, appeared on the cover of an August 1970 issue of *Time* magazine devoted to women's liberation. Unaware of Millett's suggestion that a crowd shot would more accurately represent the diversity of the women's movement, some feminists charged her with elitism and castigated her for presuming to speak for all women. In the autumn of 1970, one radical lesbian, falsely suspecting Millett of glossing over her sexual preference, asked her to admit her homosexuality at a women's conference held in a packed auditorium at Columbia University. Millett's public confirmation of her lesbianism was used by some members of the media to tar all feminists with the same brush. As a writer for *Time* (December 14, 1970) put it, "The disclosure [of her lesbianism, which in *Time* was termed bisexuality] is bound to discredit her as a spokeswoman for her cause, cast further doubt on her theories, and reinforce the views of those skeptics who routinely dismiss all liberationists as lesbians." Although many feminist leaders literally rallied to Millett's defense with a "Kate Is Great" press conference, the movement began to show signs of the coming split among lesbian separatists, heterosexual women who believed that lesbianism was a diversion from more pressing issues, and the (ultimately prevailing) feminists who believed that gay liberation should be an integral part of the fight for women's equality.

After writing and filming the documentary *Three Lives* (1971) and publishing transcripts of interviews with two prostitutes and a female Legal Aid worker in *The Prostitution Papers: A Candid Dialogue* (1973), Millett chronicled in minute detail her travels, her love affairs, and her state of mind in two autobiographical books, *Flying* (1974) and *Sita* (1977). *Flying*, which she has described as "symbolic of a turning point in women's literature," could hardly have been more different in form or content from her first book. Nonchronological and highly personal, it received many scathing critiques, a prime example of which was Rene Kuhn Bryant's in the *National Review* (August 30, 1974). Suggesting that "women's lib is the vehicle through which private psychosis is metamorphosed into public purpose," Bryant described *Flying* as "an endless outpouring of shallow, witless comment that is ungainly and graceless in its structure, gratingly obvious and banal in its observations, inchoate when it is not incoherent, blundering in its posture, and intolerable in its pretentiousness."

Contending that *Flying* would inevitably be misunderstood as long as it was held to the rigidly linear requirements of traditional (male) autobiography, more sympathetic reviewers countered that the circularity of *Flying*'s narrative, in which present-day events trigger memories that in turn spark a round of free associations, is truer to women's perceptions of their lives. In an article for *Contemporary Literature* (Autumn 1976), for example, Annette Kolodny pointed out that "any demand that women write the same kind of formal, distilled narrative we usually get from men implies a belief that women share the same kind of reality as men; clearly, this is not the case. . . . The narrative's refusal to obey normal rules of sequence and chronology reminds us how all past experience participates in the present."

Sita, a blow-by-blow account of the disintegration of Millett's three-year relationship with a university administrator, was subject to many of the same complaints that greeted *Flying*, but Nancy Manahan called it an "important book" in her review for *American Notes & Queries* (September 1977), "because it presents realistically a subject that has been neglected, sentimentalized, or deplored in most literature—lesbian relationships. . . . In addition, *Sita* explores in unprecedented depth the old themes of power and powerlessness and offers a model for emotional self-revelation of a kind traditionally found only under the cloak of fiction."

In her next book, *The Basement: Meditations on a Case of Human Sacrifice* (1979), Millett presented the horrific details of a true crime with which she had been obsessed ever since she first read about it fourteen years previously. *The Basement* is a study of the "philosophical implications" of the death on October 26, 1965 of sixteen-year-old Sylvia Likens, who had been kept in captivity in the basement of her foster family's home in Indianapolis. For months she had been starved, tortured, raped, beaten, and mutilated by her foster mother and foster siblings; at one time or another, a total of twenty-five other neighborhood children visited the scene of the crime as the torture was taking place. Identifying with the victim to a painful degree, Millett described the case as "a nightmare, my own nightmare, the nightmare of adolescence, or growing up a female child, of becoming a woman in a world set against us, a world we have lost and where we are everywhere reminded of our defeat."

Sometimes writing from the viewpoints of Sylvia and her foster mother in telling the story of what happened in the basement, Millett attempted to answer such questions as why the child (who was not tied up until the final two weeks of her ordeal) had not escaped, why the neighbors who heard her screams never called the police, why she was victimized at all, and what may have been the motives of her tormentors, some of whom were subsequently tried and convicted of her murder. Most critics agreed that *The Basement* was Millett's strongest work since *Sexual Politics*. Writing in the *New Republic* (July 7–14, 1979), the novelist Anne Tyler found Millett's prose to be "fully ripened, rich and dense, sometimes spilling out in torrents." Tyler concluded that the book was "an important study of the problems of cruelty and submission, intensely felt and movingly written."

In 1979 Millett traveled to Iran to speak at an International Women's Day rally on March 8 in support of women there who had recently lost many legal and civil rights in the aftermath of the Ayatollah Khomeini's Islamic revolution. Less than two weeks after their arrival, Millett and her companion, the photographer Sophie Keir, were deported for having made "provocations" against the new government. Their experiences there were recounted by Millett in *Going to Iran* (1982), which was described by Clifford D. May in the *New York Times Book Review* (May 16, 1982) as "a curious exercise that does not succeed as travel writing, political analysis, current history, or journalism." A reporter for *Ms.* magazine (May 1982), on the other hand, felt that "Millett and Keir capture the complexity of events often misrepresented by the press, as well as offering lessons for international feminist activity in years to come."

Between 1982 and 1985 Millett worked on her third autobiographical book, *The Loony-Bin Trip*, which was not published until 1990. Revisiting some of the territory mapped out in *Flying*, Millett revealed that she had had a nervous breakdown in the early 1970s and had been diagnosed as manic-depressive, a condition in which stages of enhanced creativity and hyperactivity alternate with periods of severe depression. After being institutionalized by her mother and sisters, she was released on the condition that she take lithium, a drug that moderates the mood swings of manic-depressive people but causes side effects that can be crippling for an artist (hand tremors) or a writer (slowed thought processes). After seven years on lithium, Millett stopped taking the drug in 1980. Later that year, while traveling in Ireland, she was incarcerated by authorities who had been told by her family that she was in need of psychiatric help. (She had been found by the police while she was taking a nap in an airport restroom, where she had washed her hair.) "Having committed no crime," Millett wrote, "one can . . . lose one's liberty for an indeterminate period, even for life." With the help of friends, Millett gained her release and returned to her farm in New York, where she tried to kill herself several times during her on-again, off-again course of lithium, from which she eventually withdrew, slowly and successfully, in 1989.

Arguing in *The Loony-Bin Trip* for a new perspective on those types of mental illness that may be diagnosed solely on the basis of observable behavior, Millett explained the difficulties in accepting a determination of insanity when the truth of the matter may lie in the mere unconventionality of the behavior deemed by others to be disturbing. Reviews of the book varied widely. "Not since Ken Kesey's *One Flew Over the Cuckoo's Nest* has the literature of madness emitted such a powerful anti-institutional cry," Marilyn Yalom wrote in the *Washington Post Book World* (May 13, 1990), adding, "Millett's prose is rich, her passion compelling." Joy Williams, who assessed the book for the *Chicago Tribune* (June 3, 1990), disagreed: "The tools Millett has as a writer are indignation, jargon, and an unfortunate reliance on tape recorders, old journals, and boxes of notes. The tools she lacks are lyricism, imagination, and a quest for meaning beyond cant."

Returning to a theme that she had first investigated in *The Basement*—the psychological effects of torture on the perpetrators, victims, and witnesses—Millett broadened her scope to encompass the entire world in *The Politics of Cruelty: An Essay on the Literature of Political Imprisonment* (1994), in which she examined state torture as practiced in Nazi Germany, the Soviet Union, South Africa under apartheid, and turn-of-the-century India, among many other places. The book also represents a return to the analysis of literature—in this case, *temoignage*, the literature of witness, which in Millett's study includes everything from documentary to memoirs to autobiography to fiction to film. Thus, in the first and third sections of her book, "The Mechanism" and "Recent Politics of Cruelty in Action," Millett analyzes excerpts from such works as Nien Cheng's autobiography *Life and Death in Shanghai*, Primo Levi's memoir *Survival at Auschwitz*, and Aleksandr Solzhenitsyn's novel *The First Circle*.

Although he praised the diversity of Millett's sources in his review for the *New Republic* (May 16, 1994), Michael Scammell, echoing a common complaint of the book's reviewers, stated that "each of these sources is treated as literally factual, with no distinction made between the sayings and doings of fictional characters and the historical actions of real people. . . . In the universe of Millett's book their experiences are endowed with equal ontological weight and validity." He added that whereas in *Sexual Politics* she had respected the autonomy of the novels and plays she analyzed, "here the works are plundered for circumstantial evidence, . . . used in an unsophisticated way as raw material for her purposes." Millett's purposes, as many critics noted, included an anti-Western, anticolonial agenda that was indicated in part by the relative amount of space she allotted to various regimes.

Millett was also taken to task by some reviewers for what they saw as the disturbingly titillating nature of the middle section of the book, "Imagination," in which she explored the eroticism of torture (a subject she had earlier touched upon when writing in the torturer's "voice" in sections of *The Basement*) in Georges Bataille's *The Tears of Eros*. In his evaluation of *The Politics of Cruelty* for the *New Republic*, Scammell compared Millett's method of repeatedly digressing (in her discussion of some photographs of a torture victim in Bataille's work) to the mechanism of deferred pleasure inherent in much pornography. Seeming to concur with such an assessment in her review for the *Village Voice* (March 22, 1994), Donna Minkowitz wrote: "Unfortunately, the very obsessive quality that often plagues the literature of torture imperils Millet's own work. Millett is so struck by torture, so aghast at what it can do, that she's unsure whether she wants to analyze torture imagery and its effects or merely tell her readers over and over how bad it is."

Notwithstanding such reproaches, a substantial number of reviewers were impressed by *The Politics of Cruelty*. In her appraisal of the work for *Booklist* (January 15, 1994), Mary Carroll declared that Millett's "powerful essay challenges the imperial circularity of the disease model of torture; she insists that both torture and resistance to torture are political acts with moral consequences and that individuals have the power, over time, to bring state terrorism to an end." In agreement with many who praised Millett for having had the courage to describe unspeakable acts in the hope that "more and more acts of description and definition like this" would eventually erode the protection that silence and secrecy have provided the torturers, Julie A. Mertus of *Ms.* (March/April 1994) called the book "a desperately needed wake-up call."

In her 1995 memoir, *A.D.*, Millett described her aunt Dorothy, who died in 1984, as "someone who made you think that life was a very big thing; really worth the trouble to live well and thoughtfully, whether it was lovely or hateful at a certain moment, season, or year. It was serious in the most beguiling way, whimsical in the most terrifying way, dull in the most fascinating way." Dorothy Millett Hill's influence on her niece was considerable; the elder's collection of rare books, her subscription to the local symphony orchestra's concert series, her pronouncements on art, her high standards, and her societal connections nurtured Millett's creativity, while Hill's snobbery and cold disapproval engendered fear and resentment. With a single act that was at once loving and cruel—Hill's exaction of a promise from Millett that she would abandon her female lover if Hill put her through Oxford—Hill set the stage for Millett's betrayal. Millett made the promise in order to receive an otherwise out-of-reach education, but she brought her lover with her to England. Hill discovered the deception and never forgave her niece, who wrote this achingly honest memoir in order to come to terms with her long-festering guilt. "Her healing book is a brave exorcism of anger and self-castigation," a writer for *Publishers Weekly* (June 19, 1995) declared. Although Elizabeth Gleick, in her review for the *New York Times Book Review* (August 13, 1995), described Millett's style as "flood-of-consciousness, with the combination of introspective candor and maudlin self-indulgence that implies," she commended Millett on "what must be her terrible honesty." "No thought here is left unexamined," Gleick continued, "including the ways in which her love for A.D. bordered on the incestuous, and no hazy filter of self-protection or vanity blurs the prose."

Kate Millett lives in New York City. Since 1980 she has spent summers at her Poughkeepsie, New York farm, which as of 1988 was a self-supporting community whose members cultivated thousands of Christmas trees during the mornings and devoted themselves to their artwork or writing in the afternoons. She has been divorced from Fumio Yoshimura since 1985 (one source indicates 1975).

Selected Biographical References: N Y Newsday mag p11+ My 8 '77 por; Cahill, Susan, ed. Writing Women's Lives: An Anthology of Autobiographical Narratives by Twentieth-Century American Women Writers (1994); Cohen, Marcia, ed. The Sisterhood: The Inside Story of the Women's Movement and the Leaders Who Made It Happen (1988); Contemporary Authors new rev vol 32 (1991); Contemporary Literary Criticism vol 67 (1992); Who's Who in America, 1995

Mirren, Helen

(MEER-in)

July 26, 1945(?)- British actress. Address: c/o Al Parker, 55 Park Lane, London W1, England

PBS

One of Britain's most celebrated classical actresses, whose stage credits include a wide range of Shakespearean heroines, including Cressida, Lady Macbeth, and a memorable Cleopatra, a role she has played twice—in 1965 and again in 1982–83—to considerable acclaim, Helen Mirren is nonetheless probably best known for her portrayal of Detective Chief Inspector Jane Tennison, the ambitious and uncompromising lead character in the award-winning British television series *Prime Suspect*. Since her debut with the vaunted Royal Shakespeare Company in 1967, Mirren has appeared in dozens of plays and numerous television productions, and she has made more than twenty-five films, the most recent being *The Madness of King George*; her touching portrayal of Queen Charlotte, the king's loving, protective wife, earned her an Oscar nomination as best supporting actress and the best-actress award at the Cannes International Film Festival, both in 1995. Fans of the actress in the guise of the obsessive, workaholic Tennison might not recognize her on the large screen, however, for her films, among them the art-house favorites *The Cook, the Thief, His Wife and Her Lover, The Comfort of Strangers*, and *Cal*, have typically highlighted her earthy sensuality.

Although Mirren's performances have invariably received glowing notices, few of her films have been box-office hits—a fact that is of little concern to her. A consummate professional who is totally dedicated to her craft, she is, by her own admission, "much happier with a good role in a small film than a bad role in a big film." She was consequently somewhat nonplussed by the enormous worldwide popularity of *Prime Suspect*, which has been broadcast in more than fifty countries since its British premiere, in 1991. Virtually without exception, critics have attributed the show's phenomenal success primarily to Mirren's nuanced, impassioned characterization of Tennison, which John J. O'Connor, the veteran television critic of the *New York Times*, described in his review of April 28, 1994 as "the kind of tour de force that leaves chronic television detractors stammering." James Wolcott, O'Connor's counterpart at the *New Yorker*, agreed, and went one step further. "Through Tennison, Mirren has created not only a pop-cult perennial . . . but a self-portrait of her fears, prides, and frustrations as a middle-aged actress trying to hold her own in a youth-and-beauty setup," Wolcott wrote in his column of January 25, 1993. "She confronts herself and comes out the other side reaffirmed."

Of Russian and British descent, Helen Mirren was born Ilynea Lydia Mironoff (or Mironov) on July 26, 1945 in London. (Some sources give 1946 as the year of her birth.) Her Russian émigré father, Vasily-Petrov Mironoff, who came from a prominent and once well-to-do Czarist military family that fled to England after the Russian Revolution, anglicized the family surname to Mirren in the mid-1950s. In an interview with Bernard Weinraub for the *New York Times* (April 23, 1995), Mirren described her background as "very working-class." During her childhood, her father, a former violist with the London Philharmonic Orchestra, worked variously as a freelance musician, a taxi driver, and a driving instructor. "It was a hand-to-mouth existence," Mirren told Weinraub. "You lived on what you earned that week." A solitary and somewhat secretive child, she settled on an acting career at an early age, because she, in her words, "wanted to be special." "In my sort of dreamworld as a little girl, I wanted to become a great actress," she said years later, as quoted in a publicity release for the film *2010*. "I didn't want to be particularly famous, but I wanted to be great in the old-fashioned and traditional sense. From the age of six, it was my absolute destiny, and I knew it."

While attending St. Bernard's convent school in Westcliff, near Southend-on-Sea, Mirren began to prepare herself for the stage by reading Shakespeare, and she played Caliban in a student production of *The Tempest*. Concerned about the precariousness of a life in the theatre, her parents strongly encouraged her to become a teacher—an occupation they considered to be more stable financially. In an effort to placate them, Mirren spent three years at a teachers' training college in north London, but her love of theatre eventually won out. "I knew [it] wasn't going to work when every history lesson turned into a theatrical event," she told Sally Ogle Davis in an interview for the *Chicago Tribune* (February 20, 1979). In the mid-1960s she joined the National Youth Theatre, an organization founded by the actor Michael Croft to give inexperienced young actors a solid foundation in Shakespearean performance. Shortly thereafter, in September 1965, she made her stage debut, in Croft's production of *Antony and Cleopatra* at the Old Vic in London. Among the host of critics who marveled at Mirren's surprisingly assured interpretation of the notoriously demanding part was the reviewer for the London *Times*, who found her "spectacularly glamorous" Cleopatra "continuously exciting both to watch and to hear. If majesty comes to her aid only at the close of the play, it does so after she has displayed all the other dangerous attractiveness that Shakespeare demands."

Mirren's performance in *Antony and Cleopatra* led to a stint at a regional repertory theatre in Manchester, in the north of England, where she took the parts of Nerissa in *The Merchant of Venice* and Kitty in the comedy *Charley's Aunt*, among other roles. In the spring of 1967, she fulfilled a dream when she joined the Royal Shakespeare Company (RSC). Over the next several years, she essayed many parts for the company, including the beleaguered Castiza in the rarely performed Jacobean drama *The Revenger's Tragedy*; Diana, the easygoing prostitute in *All's Well That Ends Well*, a character she played with "infectious merriment," according to the veteran British theatre critic Harold Hobson; the slandered Hero in *Much Ado About Nothing*; and Phoebe in *As You Like It*.

"She looked very nice and spoke well, but it began to seem possible that her Cleopatra had been one of those freakish amateur flashes in the pan . . . ," Ronald Bryden remarked, in looking back on Mirren's first few seasons with the RSC for the London *Observer* (July 11, 1971). Then, when she took the part of the heroine in John Barton's production of *Troilus and Cressida*, as Bryden went on to say, "the magic descended" once again: "Her special quality as an actress had declared itself. On the surface she looks like the ingenue next door . . . , but the moment she moves, something about her stride and carriage proclaims the temptress lurking inside: a line of White Devils, Lady Macbeths, and Cleopatras to come."

In the early 1970s Mirren's roles with the RSC ran the gamut from an endearingly childlike Ophelia in *Hamlet* to a strong-willed Harriet in George Etherege's *The Man of Mode* to the imperious and rapacious title character in August Strindberg's *Miss Julie*. Some critics rated her characterization of the mercurial Miss Julie as "an amorous boa constrictor," to use Milton Shulman's description, definitive. Mirren acquitted herself so well in the wide variety of parts assigned to her that the RSC named her an associate artist of the company in 1971.

Meanwhile, in 1969, Mirren had made her screen debut, as the sexually precocious beach girl Cora in Michael Powell's *The Age of Consent*. In 1972 she appeared as the free-spirited suffragette Gosh Smith-Boyde in *Savage Messiah*, Ken Russell's offbeat film portrait of the French sculptor Henri Gaudier, and in 1973 she was seen in Lindsay Anderson's picaresque satire *O Lucky Man!* In the same year, Mirren left the RSC to work with the International Center of Theatre Research, an experimental troupe headed by the iconoclastic director Peter Brook, whose stagecraft she had long admired. She toured Africa and the United States with Brook's company, then returned to the RSC in 1974 to play Lady Macbeth, opposite Nicol Williamson, in Trevor Nunn's staging of *Macbeth*, winning praise from Harold Hobson, among others, for the "civilized, controlled, intelligent, and irresistible sexuality" she brought to the part.

For the next ten years, Mirren worked steadily on the stage, though less frequently for the RSC, which she had come to see as "an elitist theatre . . . [with] no true commitment to finding new forms," as she put it in an interview for the London *Observer* magazine (November 30, 1975). Her credits for the company during that period include only Queen Margaret in *Henry VI*; the spunky, swaggering Moll Cutpurse, whom one reviewer described as "a kind of Lady Robin Hood," in the seldom staged Jacobean comedy *The Roaring Girl*; and, most notably, Cleopatra in Adrian Noble's acclaimed production of *Antony and Cleopatra*, which opened at the Other Place, the RSC's studio theatre in Stratford-upon-Avon, in October 1982. Christopher Hudson, the drama critic of the London *Evening Standard*, spoke for most of his colleagues when he rhapsodized, "[Mirren is] incontestably the finest Cleopatra I have seen on stage. . . . For once the legendary fascination Shakespeare gives to his Cleopatra is not betrayed by the reality. Mirren's wayward, cunning, passionately amorous serpent of the Nile dominates the action even when she is away from it; her changes of mood are electrifying in this small space . . . , and so sexually predatory is her nature that when near the end she declares with a half-smile, 'I have immortal longings in me,' one fears for the virtue of the gods."

During the late 1970s and early 1980s, in addition to her appearances with the RSC, Mirren performed with the adventurous English Stage Company at the Royal Court, as the boozy singer Maggie in *Teeth 'n' Smiles*, David Hare's play about the disintegration of a rock group—and an era—at the end of the 1960s, and as Grace, the long-suffering wife of the title character in Brian Friel's *Faith Healer*. Among her other assignments were the eponymous heroine in John Webster's *The Duchess of Malfi*, at the Royal Exchange in Manchester, and, in the West End—the London equivalent of Broadway—Nina in Anton Chekhov's *The Seagull* and Marjorie in *Extremities*, William Mastrosimone's play about one woman's revenge on a would-be rapist. Mirren was also seen frequently on television, where her roles included Rosalind in *As You Like It*, Titania in *A Midsummer Night's Dream*, and Imogen in *Cymbeline* for the BBC's esteemed series *The Shakespeare Plays*, which was broadcast in the United States by PBS.

In the late 1970s Mirren began to devote increasing amounts of time to film acting. She first came to international attention in 1980, when she appeared in *Caligula*, Bob Guccione's notoriously violent and sexually explicit film about the decadent Roman emperor. Described by the *New York Times* critic Vincent Canby as "the most expensive pornographic movie ever made," the seventeen million-dollar *Caligula* featured, in addition to Mirren, several other well-known British actors, including Peter O'Toole, John Gielgud, and Malcolm McDowell, whom reviewers credited with bringing moments of intelligence to an otherwise execrable film. Rex Reed, in his assessment for the New York *Daily News* (April 10, 1981), reviled *Caligula* as a "trough of rotten swill," but he had only admiration for Mirren, who played Caesonia, the emperor's wife, "as though she knows exactly what the film is about, even when nobody else does." (Mirren, who appeared fully clothed throughout the movie, has since dismissed it as "an unmitigated disaster.") In the following year, the actress won similar praise from Reed and others for giving the sorceress Morgana in *Excalibur*, John Boorman's version of the Arthurian legend, a diabolical intensity that Reed found "riveting." Her next film effort, John Mackenzie's *The Long Good Friday* (1982), in which she portrayed the classy and cool-headed mistress of a London gangland kingpin, fared better with the critics, winning virtually unanimous approval for its uncompromising look at organized crime and for the galvanic performances of Mirren and her costar, Bob Hoskins.

The year 1984 saw the release of the film that remains Mirren's favorite among all her screen credits—*Cal*, a bittersweet romance set against the bloody backdrop of violence in Northern Ireland. Sex, politics, and religion figure prominently in the relationship between Marcella (Mirren), the widow of a Protestant police officer murdered by an Irish Republican Army gunman, and Cal (John Lynch), a young Roman Catholic who, unbeknownst to Marcella, was involved in the shooting. In a review of the movie for the *New York Times* (August 24, 1984), Janet Maslin paid tribute to its two stars: "The love story, played in gentle, gradual stages . . . , brings out the best in both performers. Miss Mirren, through a reserve that disappears layer by layer, makes Marcella a woman of unexpected substance and generosity, one who is no more comfortable with the pain and paradoxes of Northern Ireland than Cal is himself." Patrick O'Connor's modest film was the official entry of the Republic of Ireland at the 1984 Cannes International Film Festival, where Mirren was awarded top honors as best actress.

Following the release of *Cal*, Mirren was seen in a series of films that further boosted her international profile. Her roles included the cosmonaut Tanya Kirbuk in Peter Hyams's *2010* (1984), the long-awaited sequel to Stanley Kubrick's classic *2001: A Space Odyssey*; the fading Russian ballerina Galina Ivanova in *White Nights* (1985), a romantic thriller that also starred the dancers Mikhail Baryshnikov and Gregory Hines; the loyal Mother in *The Mosquito Coast* (1986), a Harrison Ford vehicle based on Paul Theroux's novel of the same name; the bohemian painter Lydia Neuman in *Pascali's Island* (1988), a "psychological pas de trois," to quote one reviewer, in which she shared billing with Ben Kingsley and Charles Dance; and Georgina Spica, the bored wife of a crude and brutal gangster in *The Cook, the Thief, His Wife and Her Lover* (1989), Peter Greenaway's graphic postmodern fable about greed. The latter film eventually attracted a cult following among art-house audiences, although it provoked considerable dissension in the critical ranks. As for Mirren, by all accounts she once again seemed to triumph over her material. "Helen Mirren is all calm politeness and mute acceptance until her passion is aroused . . . ," the reviewer for *Variety* (September 13, 1989) wrote. "The actress is simply superb, as Georgina sheds her clothes and her inhibitions for a series of scorching lovemaking scenes." In an interview for *Harper's Bazaar* (February 1993), Mirren described the project as "great fun." "It was so off-the-wall, so wonderfully wild," she explained to Joe Morgenstern. "I have a propensity for that sort of thing. It's the more formal, mainstream things that make me uncomfortable."

Another erotically charged film, the quirky psychological thriller *The Comfort of Strangers* (1991), provided Mirren with her next major movie role. Directed by Paul Schrader, the broodingly atmospheric film revolves around a mysterious couple living in Venice—Caroline (Mirren) and her husband, Robert (Christopher Walken)—and a pair of British tourists they appear to meet by chance. A disturbing series of events unfolds as Caroline and Robert draw the British duo into a web of sexual manipulation and intimidation. Later in the same year, Mirren was seen in *Where Angels Fear to Tread*, Charles Sturridge's adaptation of E. M. Forster's novel of the same name. The film's story line is propelled by Mirren's character, Lilia, a headstrong widow who shocks her family by marrying a young Italian she meets during a holiday in Tuscany. Lilia's marriage and subsequent death in childbirth set off a chain of events that brings other members of her family to Italy, where their lives are irrevocably changed. The film drew strongly positive notices, many of which singled out Mirren for special commendation.

Her numerous film appearances notwithstanding, Mirren is best known in North America as Detective Chief Inspector Jane Tennison, the driven, hard-nosed, blunt-speaking, yet touchingly vulnerable veteran of the London police force who is the central figure in Granada Television's gritty police procedural *Prime Suspect*. In the initial installment of what was soon to become an eagerly anticipated series, Tennison, entrusted with her first homicide case, pursues a serial killer with unflagging tenacity while battling sexism among her male colleagues. A huge hit in Britain, where it was among the most popular programs in 1991, *Prime Suspect 1*, as it has since been retitled, was first shown in the United States in 1992 as part of the PBS *Mystery* series. The reviews were overwhelmingly favorable. Tom Shales of the *Washington Post*, who went so far as to venture that it was "better than *Masterpiece Theatre*," PBS's venerable dramatic showcase, cited Mirren as the "main reason" for the program's success. "Her portrayal of Tennison is ice-hard but not ice-cold, a brilliant parlay of backbone and heart," Shales observed in his evaluation of January 23, 1992. "Mirren doesn't take a breath or blink an eye that isn't in character. Everything contributes to a portrait of a cool, canny dynamo who knows she can't allow herself any signs of weakness or indecision. . . . [*Prime Suspect*] is sensational, and it's mostly Mirren's triumph."

Prime Suspect 2 and *Prime Suspect 3*, broadcast in the United States in 1993 and 1994, respectively, brought Mirren more critical bouquets and firmly established Tennison as one of the most popular female characters on television—"the PBS pinup woman of the decade," as David Ansen put it in *Newsweek* (May 16, 1994). In *Prime Suspect 2*, Tennison investigates a brutal murder that may have been racially motivated; she also demonstrates signs of having softened a little—enough to become romantically involved with one of her colleagues—but on the job she remains purposeful and tenacious. *Prime Suspect 3* found Tennison, recently transferred from the homicide division to the vice squad, looking into child prostitution as she tries to solve the murder of a young "rent boy." The fourth installment of the series, *Prime Suspect: The Lost Child*, in which Tennison, newly promoted to the rank of detective superintendent, wrestles with a puzzling case involving the abduction of a fourteen-month-old girl, was first broadcast in the United States in October 1995 as a two-hour segment of *Masterpiece Theatre*.

In reviewing the sequels, critics took note of Mirren's uncommon ability to take a fresh approach to her character, to present her in a new light. "She's a very different person a year on," Mirren said of Tennison when she spoke to William Grimes for the *New York Times* (February 2, 1993) shortly before PBS televised *Prime Suspect 2*. "She's met certain challenges and gained confidence from that. That's directly parallel to my personal journey playing the role. These are all my mates from the first series, so as an actress I had immensely more confidence. You think it's the character, but it's just as much the actress feeling self-confident. . . . The whole interest in doing something like this lies in watching a character who develops. You're almost watching her life as much as you are the intricacies of the police drama." The most highly rated series ever shown on PBS's *Mystery*, *Prime Suspect* has collected a basketful of honors, including an Emmy Award in 1993 for best miniseries, an Edgar Award for best television mystery, and for Mirren herself three consecutive best-actress awards from the British Academy of Film and Television Arts.

Although Mirren has concentrated on television and film in recent years, she has remained active in the London theatre, appearing in 1989 opposite Bob Peck in *Two-Way Mirror*, a double bill comprising Arthur Miller's two-character one-act plays *Some Kind of Love Story* and *Elegy for a Lady*, and in the short-lived farce *Sex Please, We're Italian* in 1991. Her portrayal of Natalya Petrovna, a bored and willful woman who becomes infatuated with her son's young tutor in Ivan Turgenev's *A Month in the Country*, enchanted London critics, who rewarded her with unanimous raves. Michael Billington of the *Guardian* (March 30, 1994) credited the actress with singlehandedly setting the tone for the sardonic social comedy: "Mirren, in one of her best-ever performances, plays Natalya as a woman constantly torn between headlong surrender to instinct and captious self-criticism. . . . The result is both devastatingly funny and not a little sad."

Billington and his colleagues were prepared to "lay down the red carpets the length of St. Martin's Lane to welcome [Mirren's] return" to the West End, as Jack Tinker put it in the London *Daily Mail* (March 30, 1994). When she reprised the role on Broadway for the Roundabout Theatre in 1995, their New York counterparts were, on the whole, similarly enchanted, although less given to hyperbole. To Vincent Canby of the *New York Times*, however, her characterization seemed underplayed and "small," perhaps because he was accustomed to seeing the actress in television close-ups. "The camera adores her," he explained in his review of April 26, 1995. "With a slight change of expression, she can look beautiful one minute and ravaged the next. Her fine, melancholy eyes reveal a succession of contradictory feelings." On stage, he said, she was "in a continuous long shot." Mirren's performance in *A Month in the Country* earned her a Tony nomination as best actress of the 1994–95 Broadway season.

Interviewers have invariably described Helen Mirren as self-possessed, soft-spoken, and amiable. Virtually all of them have taken note of the small tattoo of a South American Indian sign called a *lakesh*, signifying equality, between the thumb and forefinger of her left hand—a memento of her stint with Peter Brook's experimental theatre group. A self-professed socialist, Mirren is wary of celebrity treatment and generally shuns the public spotlight. She once asked that her name be withdrawn from the biographical directory *Who's Who*, because of its, in her view, elitist nature. "What's so special about me and not my mother and father?" she asked in an interview for the New York *Daily News* (May 12, 1982). "I can't stand it that some section of people decide who's who. I find it offensive." Since the mid-1980s Mirren has lived in Los Angeles with the filmmaker Taylor Hackford, who directed her in *White Nights*, although she has continued to spend a good part of each year in London, where she has an apartment overlooking Battersea Park.

Selected Biographical References: London Observer mag p16 Jl 11 '71 por; N Y Times II p5+ Ap 23 '95 pors; Newsweek 123:60+ My 16 '94 pors; Sunday Times mag p10+ Mr 19 '94; Toronto Globe and Mail C p1+ Ja 20 '93 por; Contemporary Theatre, Film, and Television vol 10 (1993); International Who's Who, 1994–95

New York Jets

Monk, Art

Dec. 5, 1957– Football player. Address: c/o New York Jets, 1000 Fulton Ave., Hempstead, NY 11550

"I don't consider myself a standout player," Art Monk, who caught more passes than any player in the history of the National Football League, said in one of his infrequent interviews, with Thomas Boswell for a *Washington Post Magazine* (September 2, 1990) profile. "I never thought I had the ability to play in the NFL. . . . Even now, when I see highlights of [San Francisco 49ers star] Jerry Rice, I say, 'Man! How does he do that?' But when I see myself, it doesn't look very special to me. . . . That's why I don't take anything for granted." Notwithstanding his self-effacing humility, Monk was perhaps the NFL's prototypical possession receiver throughout his fifteen-year professional career, which began when he joined the Washington Redskins in 1980. A running back and kick returner at Syracuse University, he was tall, strong, fast, and sure-handed, a virtual carbon copy of Redskin great Charley Taylor, a record-setting split end who had been one of Monk's childhood heroes and who, as the coach of the Redskins' receivers, helped Monk make the transition to wide receiver in the professional ranks.

Monk, however, doubted that he was good enough for the NFL. To overcome his anxieties, he adopted a grueling off-season conditioning regimen and simply worked harder year round than any other player on a team of blue-collar overachievers. In the process, he became the most prolific receiver in league history as well as a quiet, steady, respected leader on a team that won four National Football Conference championships and three Super Bowls in a span of ten years. "I remember playing against him when I was at Penn State and he was at Syracuse . . . ," the linebacker Matt Millen told Thomas George of the *New York Times* (October 23, 1991). "He is so tough and reliable. When the chips are down, you know where the ball is going, and he still comes up with it. The thing that impresses me most about Art is that he is always asked to do the things that other guys can't do, and that's block and catch the ball over the middle. Art excels at those tasks that other receivers hate."

James Arthur Monk, who has always been known as Art, was born in White Plains, New York on December 5, 1957, the second of the two children of Arthur Monk, a construction worker, and Lela Monk, who worked as a domestic in nearby Scarsdale, an affluent New York City suburb. He and his sister, Barbara, grew up in an apartment above the church the Monk family regularly attended, the Shiloh Gospel Chapel, in the racially integrated neighborhood known as Battle Hill. The Monks instilled in their children "the virtues of perseverance, patience, and hard work," as William Nack noted in his profile of the athlete for *Sports Illustrated* (September 7, 1992). "My parents always told us," Monk recalled, "'Nothing in life is free. Whatever it is you want, you have to knuckle down and work for it.' This wasn't just talk. They actually lived it. I *saw* that in them. . . . That was their way of life."

As a boy, Monk loved to play sports, especially football, but he suffered from a deep-seated inferiority complex. "When I was younger, I had very little self-esteem," he admitted in the interview with Thomas Boswell. "I didn't have confidence in myself. In a Pop Warner League tryout I didn't do very well. I didn't feel I was very good, so I didn't try hard. I didn't think I could do it, and people around me—with the exception of my family—didn't think I could either." During his childhood, he was, by all accounts, more successful as a musician—a talent he apparently came by naturally, for as he told Boswell, "music runs all through the family." (Thelonious Monk, the celebrated jazz pianist, was Arthur Monk's cousin.) By the time he was in junior high school, Monk had learned to play the tuba, bass guitar, drums, and trombone. According to William Nack, Monk's tuba teacher thought he might one day be accomplished enough to attend college on a music scholarship.

Monk's passion for football began to overshadow his interest in music while he was attending White Plains High School. A fan of All-Pro pass catchers like the rangy Charley Taylor and the fleet Paul Warfield, he dreamed of becoming a wide receiver, but he wound up playing on the junior varsity squad's offensive and defensive lines, because he was much taller and heavier than other boys his age. "Charley Taylor was one of my idols growing up," Monk recalled when he spoke to William C. Rhoden of the *New York Times* (January 22, 1992). "I always grew up wanting to be a wide receiver because I was big and playing in the sandlot with my friends. I caught the ball well. So I admired him and Otis Taylor because they were also big." To lose weight and improve his speed, Monk ran track in the spring of his sophomore year, and at the beginning of his junior year, he was named the football team's starting tight end. He was, however, largely overlooked in the team's passing game, which revolved around senior wide receiver Sam Bowers, a game-breaking high-school All-American. In his senior year, Monk, who had developed into a promising decathlete and a standout in the 330-yard intermediate hurdles, was moved to the running-back position by head coach Brant Wintersteen. After a slow start, he became a churning, between-the-tackles runner, and in the season's next-to-last game, against Newburgh High School, he scored four touchdowns and gained 105 yards on twenty-four carries. College football recruiters were especially impressed by the athleticism Monk displayed in track. As a senior he set state records in the intermediate hurdles (with a time of 37.1 seconds) and the 120-yard high hurdles (13.5 seconds), and he closed out his track career with a victory in the intermediate hurdles at a national meet in California.

Although Monk wanted to attend the University of Maryland, he bowed to his mother's wishes and enrolled instead at Syracuse University, in upstate New York, majoring in speech and communications. Head coach Frank Maloney played him at wingback, to take advantage of his running and pass-catching skills, but Monk's freshman season turned into a nightmare of dropped balls. "I couldn't catch a cold," he confessed to William Nack. "I don't know why. It was just a disaster. I remember practices where they'd throw the ball to me and it would hit my hands and I couldn't catch it. I *knew* I was better than that. I got really depressed and down on myself. And I just made up my mind that this wasn't going to happen again."

Driven to overcome his self-doubt and, at the same time, prove to the Syracuse coaching staff that he was "worthy of their scholarship," as he told Nack, Monk trained diligently in the off-season, and in his sophomore year he gathered in forty-one balls for 590 yards and racked up an additional 566 yards on the ground. By the end of his four-year career with the Orangemen, Monk had rushed for more than 1,100 yards, gained over 1,100 yards on kickoff and punt returns, and caught 102 balls for 1,644 yards, displaying the gift for making the tough catches in traffic that would become his signature in the NFL. "One of our most effective patterns was across the middle," Maloney recalled when he spoke to Nack. "Most of the receivers we had heard footsteps, always looking to see who was around. Not Arthur. He'd go for the football. He was a fearless guy with terrific hands, and a tremendous punt returner."

An elusive runner with 4.5 speed and classic "big receiver" size, the six-foot-three-inch, 209-pound Monk was nevertheless stunned when the Washington Redskins used their first-round draft pick to make him the eighteenth player selected in the 1980 NFL draft. In joining an organization that had shifted the Hall of Famers Bobby Mitchell and Charley Taylor from the running-back position to split end, Monk became the "third generation of a genre of wide receivers who helped expand and perhaps revolutionize the modern-day passing game," as William C. Rhoden observed in the *New York Times*. Like Mitchell and Taylor, Monk is tall and agile, combining a running back's power with a receiver's speed and grace, and his confidence began to grow with Taylor, the Redskins' receivers coach, serving as his mentor. "I was blessed," Taylor explained to Rhoden. "When I made the switch, I worked with Bobby Mitchell, who had done the same thing when he came over from Cleveland. I knew what Bobby and I did to get me where I had to be, so I just passed along to Art what I learned from Mitch. Art could move. He had my size, great skills. He had everything. The only thing that would hold him back were his feet, getting in and out of cuts." Making a successful transition from runner to receiver during his rookie year, Monk led the team in catches with fifty-eight (for an average of 13.7 yards per reception and three touchdowns), but the Redskins' disappointing record of six wins and ten losses cost head coach Jack Pardee his job.

Pardee's successor was Joe Gibbs, who had been an innovative offensive coordinator for the San Diego Chargers. In addition to overhauling the Washington passing game, Gibbs brought in the veteran halfback-receiver Terry Metcalf, a dedicated student of the game, who befriended Monk and served as his off-season conditioning guru. "Terry had a motor in him," Monk recalled to William Nack. "We'd go to a high school track at nine o'clock and run. We did a lot of agility work, running up and down stairs. Midafternoon we'd go and play eight games of racquetball. Then we'd play basketball at night. Or we'd go jogging. Or riding our bikes. One time we rode from Arlington to Redskin Park, twenty miles one way, and back."

Gaining quickness from his arduous workouts, Monk subsequently refined and adopted as his own the conditioning program he learned from Metcalf, who retired after the 1981 season. Moreover, he flourished in the H-back offense that Gibbs had devised in San Diego. In the H-back scheme, a physically imposing wide receiver or tight end—usually Monk in the Redskins offense—is constantly in motion near the line of scrimmage, to force on-the-spot defensive adjustments and give the receiver a clean, unimpeded release into the secondary. "I liked being in motion right away," Monk told Thomas Boswell. "I'm not a sitting target. I can get a release and also read the defense before the snap. If no one follows me, it's a zone. If someone does follow, I know he's my man. When I'm in motion, I can set up my defender by adjusting my speed. He wants to stay even with me, but as soon as I slow up, he's out of position."

Emerging as the Redskins' dependable possession receiver, Monk was especially adept at executing "the dodge," a perilous route that capitalized on his intelligence and fearlessness as well as his unique physical tools. The pattern required Monk to explode off the line of scrimmage, read the defensive coverage, cut quickly into an open area just five to seven yards downfield, and then catch the ball in traffic, leaving himself vulnerable to punishing blows by defenders. "We call [Monk] the Punjam of the Dodge," Charley Taylor said in his interview with Boswell. "He's awful quick for a guy so big. He's in a crowd, then he springs out of there free. That pattern brings out all the skills. Plus, you have to be a runner after you catch it, and you can't fumble." Joe Theismann, the Redskins' starting quarterback during Monk's first six years with the team, observed to Boswell, "The most important part of Art Monk to our teams was not his legs or his hands. It was his brain. In Joe Gibbs's system, with all the men-in-motion and the formation shifts, Monk was the key. He had to master four positions—both wide receivers, halfback, and tight end as well as all the inside slot routes. He had the whole week's game plan mastered in the first hour of practice. He was also the smartest receiver I ever had. When I was in trouble, I never had to look for Art. He was already coming back, finding me."

At least partly because of problems associated with adjusting to the new schemes that Gibbs was implementing, the Redskins opened the 1981 season with five losses, but the team rallied to win eight of the remaining eleven games. Monk's fifty-six catches for 894 yards (an average of 16 yards per reception) and six touchdowns were second best on the team, behind halfback Joe Washington, who hauled in seventy aerials. The Redskins' resurgence continued in the strike-shortened 1982 season, as the team captured the NFC East title with a record of eight wins and one loss. The team's leading receiver, with thirty-five catches for 447 yards and one touchdown, Monk broke his ankle in the regular-season finale against the St. Louis Cardinals and watched from the stands while Washington overwhelmed the Dallas Cowboys in the NFC championship game and bested the Miami Dolphins, 27–17, in Super Bowl XVII.

Monk had never before missed a game or even a practice due to injury, but the bad luck that sidelined him late in 1982 continued to plague him in the 1983 preseason, when he suffered a strained knee ligament that kept him out of action for the month of September. After his return to the lineup, Monk snared forty-seven balls for five touchdowns and a team-high average of 15.9 yards per catch, as Washington fielded one of the most potent offenses in NFL history, scoring a regular-season record 541 points en route to a league-best tally of fourteen wins and two losses. But after upending the San

Francisco 49ers in the NFC title game, the Redskins were stymied by the impenetrable defense of the Los Angeles Raiders in Super Bowl XVIII—Monk was held to just one catch for 26 yards—that paced the Raiders to an easy 38–9 victory.

Playing injury-free football in 1984, Monk shattered the NFL record for pass receptions in a season (101, set by the Houston Oilers' Charley Hennigan in 1964) with 106 catches for 1,372 yards (12.9 yards per grab) and seven touchdowns. The eleven-and-five Redskins captured the NFC East crown in that year but had their postseason hopes dashed in the play-offs by the Chicago Bears. Although Washington failed to qualify for postseason play in 1985, Monk was named to the Pro Bowl for the second consecutive year after reeling in ninety-one balls for 1,226 yards (13.5 yards per reception) and two touchdowns. With quarterback Jay Schroeder throwing for a club-record 4,109 yards in 1986, Monk was voted to his third Pro Bowl on the strength of a solid season that saw him catch seventy-three passes for 1,068 yards (14.6 yards) and four touchdowns; he was the second-leading receiver (behind Gary Clark) on a twelve-and-four team that advanced to the NFC title contest before losing to its divisional rival, the New York Giants.

Although he appeared in just nine games in the strike-abbreviated 1987 season, Monk caught thirty-eight passes for 483 yards (12.7) and six scores, and Washington won the NFC East title with a record of eleven and four. (Nonunion "replacement" players filled in for striking NFL veterans in three games, and Monk missed the final three games of the season as well as both conference play-off matches after tearing ligaments in his knee in a game against the Cardinals.) The injured Monk was limited to the role of third receiver in Super Bowl XXII, but his only reception, a forty-yarder from quarterback Doug Williams, helped the Redskins overcome a sluggish start to post a 42–10 blowout of the Denver Broncos.

Washington slipped to seven and nine in 1988, but a healthy Monk snared seventy-two passes for 946 yards (13.1) and five trips to the end zone. In 1989 the Redskins failed to make the play-offs for the second consecutive year, but they improved their record to ten and six, largely because Gary Clark, Ricky Sanders, and Monk—the team's brilliant trio of wide receivers, who dubbed themselves "the posse"—each racked up more than one thousand yards on pass receptions. The most prodigious receiver was Monk, who caught eighty-six aerials for 1,186 yards (13.8) and eight touchdowns and succeeded Charley Taylor as Washington's career receptions leader.

The humble, unselfish, and hard-working leader of a team on which "no one player tries to be an individual," as he described the Redskins in a conversation with William Gildea of the *Washington Post* (January 16, 1992), Monk, who feared that his struggling club was losing its status as a perennial Super Bowl contender, called a players-only meeting on the eve of the 1990 season's twelfth game. The usually taciturn wideout, who had never before publicly chastised his teammates, pledged to rededicate himself to a successful season, and challenged his fellow players to follow suit. The Redskins responded, finishing the season with a ten-and-six record and scoring a first-round play-off victory over the Philadelphia Eagles. Over the course of the season, Monk totaled sixty-eight catches for 770 yards (11.3) and five touchdowns. In 1991 he again topped the thousand-yard mark, hauling in seventy-one balls for an average of 14.8 yards per reception and eight scores, while the dominating, fourteen-and-two Redskins capped a banner season with a 37–24 thrashing of the Buffalo Bills in Super Bowl XXVI.

Monk moved past Steve Largent to become the NFL's career receptions leader when he registered his 820th catch early in the 1992 season. For the year, he snared forty-six balls for 644 yards (14.0) and three scores as the Redskins squeaked into the play-offs with a nine-and-seven record. Joe Gibbs retired after the 1992 season; his successor as head coach, Rich Petitbon, inherited an aging Redskins squad that dropped twelve of sixteen games to finish in the NFC East cellar in 1993, and although Monk had forty-one receptions for 398 yards and two touchdowns, his yards-per-catch average (9.7) dropped below ten for the first time in his career.

In a poll of Washington fans, Monk had been chosen as the greatest player in franchise history, but when he refused to accept a substantial pay cut, from $1.3 million to $600,000 for the 1994 season, the Redskins let him go. Two months later he signed a $500,000 contract to play for the New York Jets in 1994. Although a late-season collapse left the Jets with a sub-.500 record, Monk had another productive year, racking up forty-six catches for 581 yards and three touchdowns. He also became the league's first player to catch nine hundred passes in a career, and he broke Steve Largent's record for consecutive games with at least one reception when he extended his streak to 178 late in the season, in what turned out to be a losing effort against the Detroit Lions. He subsequently caught passes in the season's two remaining games to establish the record at 180. In February 1995 the Jets announced that the team would not try to sign Monk for another year.

Because he was basically a possession receiver, whose "designated role is to get hit by somebody," as Joe Theismann bluntly put it to Thomas Boswell, Monk absorbed tremendous physical punishment over the years. By all accounts, the thirty-seven-year-old receiver owed his longevity in the league to the off-season conditioning program that he scrupulously followed since 1981. During his tenure with the Redskins, Monk worked out with weights three days a week and ran sprints, distances, and a forty-five-degree, fifteen-yard hill every afternoon at George Mason University, in Fairfax, Virginia. After dinner, he donned a weight belt and jogged three miles before ending the day with a game of basketball or racquetball. "If there's even one guy who works as hard as Monk, I'd be surprised," Joe Theismann observed to Boswell. "I played with guys who had talent at Art's level but who didn't work hard, especially in the off-season. . . . Art shows what happens when you never miss a day." A computer enthusiast in his spare time, Monk is also a talented graphic designer, and he has indicated that he might someday pursue a career in commercial art. He and his wife, Desiree, who met when they were students at Syracuse, have three children—James Arthur Jr., Danielle, and Monica. "I do two important things in my life," Monk told William Nack. "I play football, and I spend time with my family. Most everything else is a distraction."

Selected Biographical References: N Y Times B p9 O 23 '91 por, B p7+ Ja 22 '92 pors, B p16 O 14 '92 por, B p7+ Jl 26 '94 por, B p19+ D 1 '94 por; Sporting N 208:22 Ja 1 '90 pors, 214:8+ S 7 '92 pors; Sports Illus 77:32+ S 7 '92 pors; Washington Post D p1+ Ja 18 '84, F p1+ S 22 '84 por, E p1+ N 27 '84, D p3 D 17 '84, F p1+ Ag 16 '88 pors, mag p14+ S 2 '90 pors, B p1+ My 28 '91 pors, D p1+ O 13 '91 pors, E p3 Ja 24 '92, M p6 Ag 30 '92 por, D p1+ S 6 '92 por, D p1+ Ap 7 '94 por, D p1+ Ap 10 '94 por

---

Paula Cooper Gallery

Murray, Elizabeth

1940- Artist. Address: c/o Paula Cooper, Inc., 155 Wooster St., New York, NY 10012

Known for her shaped and fractured canvases, her witty, cartoonish depictions of domestic objects and scenes, and her use of vibrant colors, the artist Elizabeth Murray is widely regarded as one of the enduring talents to have emerged from the commercial hype that suffused the art world in the 1980s. According to Deborah Solomon, who interviewed the artist for the *New York Times Magazine* (March 31, 1991), Murray's "work recapitulates great moments in twentieth-century art: cubism's splintered planes, fauvism's jazzy colors, surrealism's droopy biomorphic shapes, the heroic scale of abstract expressionism." Many of Murray's larger paintings are made of several canvases that overlap and curl around each other or appear to constitute a puzzle assembled from pieces that don't quite fit together. Her images, which blur the boundary between the abstract and the representational, are superimposed on the canvases, at once unifying the work and threatening to implode that unity. A painter of interiors, Murray uses contrasting colors to reflect emotional states as well as to render the inside of a kitchen or a bedroom. Multiple readings of her paintings emerge gradually or simultaneously or not at all, depending on the viewer.

"I want to make a possibility with a painting," Murray declared in an interview with Kay Larson for a profile in *New York* (February 10, 1986). "A painting is a still thing on a wall. I want this openness and indeterminacy, and yet the picture is very determined—once it's there you can't change it. My work is mute in a certain way. I think that's the beautiful thing about it—that it's so vulnerable. Something is exploded out of its ordinary context into a new state." In a Murray painting, such usually nonthreatening objects as spoons, tables, and cups can take on ominous connotations, appearing to be about to break apart, to thrust themselves into the viewer's psychological space, or to fly out of the painting altogether. "I want my paintings to be like wild things that just burst out of the zoo," Murray told Deborah Solomon. Writing in *Art in America* (April 1989), the artist Robert Storr described "the queasiness [Murray's paintings] sometimes occasion" as "that which accompanies a headlong leap into space, and Murray's has indeed been a very big leap forward. No one, to date, has gone as far as she in testing the tensile strength of the traditional structure of painting while managing to maintain a sense of the whole. A kind of pictorial yoga, Murray's work is an exercise in matter over mind—or, at any rate, in hands-on making over programmatic thinking—and as such, an object lesson in what can, rather than what 'should,' be done to a painting."

Elizabeth Murray was born in 1940 in Chicago, one of three children in an Irish Catholic family. When she was about eight years old, her father was compelled to give up his law practice after he fell victim to an obscure, physically and mentally degenerative ailment. In search of work that Murray's father could perform, the family moved to Three Rivers, Michigan and, about four years later, to Bloomington, Illinois, where they lived with one of Murray's grandmothers. Murray's father supported the family by working on an assembly line in a factory, while her mother, Dorothy, an aspiring commercial artist, painted porcelain miniatures at home. In her interview with Deborah Solomon, Murray described her parents as "unorthodox, goofball" people who allowed her to spend hours watching cartoons at the local movie theatre. "We lived on fantasy, not meat and potatoes," she said. It was not long before Murray decided she wanted to become a cartoonist. Her parents encouraged her to pursue her passion for drawing, as did her high school art teacher, Elizabeth Stein, who recalled that her former pupil "knew exactly what she wanted to do and was going to do it," as Stein told Kay Larson. "That kind of drive was unique among the students."

With the aid of a scholarship partially financed by Stein, Murray enrolled at the School of the Art Institute of Chicago in 1958. To get to her classes in commercial art, she had to walk through the institute's galleries. One day a Cezanne still life caught her eye. "It was like doors opening, to realize that paintings were the equivalent of books," Murray told Larson. "Just like Kafka could tell you about the mysteries of existence in words, Cezanne could tell you the same thing only in physical terms, using space."

Murray was soon following the prevailing dictum that fine art was superior to commercial art, as she explained in a 1982 interview with Kate Horsfield recorded for the Art Institute's Video Data Bank and published in *Profile* (Summer 1986): "At that age and in a school situation, you completely adopt the ideals of all the people around you: a fine artist was somebody who was really important, it was the *real* struggle, and it had intense meaning. Doing anything else was cheap in comparison. That whole hierarchy affected me a lot." By the end of her second year, she had dedicated herself to painting. Her initial experiences terrified her, because she had no idea how to work in the medium. "I had always thought of myself as gifted," she explained to Larson, "but it took a good year of struggle just to get the paint off the palette in a way that meant anything. . . . It's not that you learn how to paint—anybody can do that—but you learn how to be expressive with paint."

After graduating from the Art Institute with a bachelor of fine arts degree in 1962, Murray entered the graduate art program at Mills College, in Oakland, California, to which she had been awarded a scholarship. At Mills she befriended Jennifer Bartlett, who also became a well-known painter. "Elizabeth was the first woman I'd met who was as ambitious as any of the men I knew," Bartlett told Deborah Solomon. "She worked constantly, wouldn't go to meals and lived on Grape Nuts [cereal]. She was a real artist to me."

In her second year at Mills, from which she earned a master of fine arts degree in 1964, Murray married a sculptor, with whom she moved to Buffalo, New York, where she taught art at Rosary Hill College for two years. While she was living in Buffalo, Murray temporarily abandoned painting, instead creating large-scale sculptural pieces that were painted and had movable parts. Arriving in Manhattan in 1967, she began to write and to execute smaller sculptural works. It was not until 1971, two years after the birth of her son, Dakota Sunseri, that she returned to oil painting, motivated in part by the emotional openness that attended her experience of motherhood.

Purity of form had by then become the reigning motif under the sway of minimalism, whose leading exponents discouraged the creation of anything remotely representational except for the most basic cubes, grids, and the like. While art magazines were declaring that painting was dead, many artists began avoiding "easel art" and, eventually, two-dimensional imagery altogether, preferring to orchestrate "happenings" and performances. People who came to view Murray's work kept telling her that painting was a thing of the past. Although she persisted in following her instincts, she found the going more difficult than she had anticipated, as she recalled in her conversation with Deborah Solomon: "I thought that when I got to New York I would be happy just to be here working. Instead, I saw how out of it I was, and that was painful for me." Within a few years, however, her tenacity began to pay off as she hit her stride, working with colors of uncommon intensity while still adhering to abstract forms. "I was interested in minimalism and conceptualism," Murray told Kay Larson, "but I made a conscious decision to avoid them. Instead, I set about trying to make tough, clear, subjective painting. My heritage says that art is about more, not less. I felt painting was important and I wanted to bring it back into the world."

Despite the clarity of her goals, Murray was not fully confident until she was liberated from the psychological constraints of her first marriage, which ended in the early 1970s. "The breakup allowed me not to be afraid of being ambitious," she explained to Larson. "When [my husband] left, I decided I wanted to try to show my work." From 1972 to 1974, Murray, who was then unrepresented by a gallery, displayed her paintings in group shows at the Whitney Museum of American Art, in New York City, and at galleries in Paris, Cologne, and Washington, D.C.; a solo exhibition of her work was mounted in Toronto. In searching for an art dealer, she encountered considerable sexism from the male dealers who came to view her work until she met Paula Cooper, whose gallery was the first of many to open in Manhattan's SoHo district. The Paula Cooper Gallery exhibited Murray's work in four group shows between 1974 and 1976. When Cooper asked her to join the gallery, a signal of impending success, Murray accepted a teaching job in California instead, in order to detach herself from the pressures of living in New York City and to examine whether success was something she actually wanted.

In addition to the position Murray took in California, as a visiting instructor at the California Institute of the Arts, in Valencia, from 1975 to 1976, she was also a visiting instructor at Wayne State University, in Detroit, in 1975 and at the Art Institute of Chicago from 1975 to 1976. She was an instructor at Bard College, in Annandale-on-Hudson, New York, from 1974 to 1975 and from 1976 to 1977; at Princeton University, in New Jersey, in 1977; and at Yale University, in New Haven, Connecticut, from 1978 to 1979. In 1987 she was a lecturer at the New York Studio School of Drawing, Painting, and Sculpture.

It was in California that Murray began to make shaped canvases. Upon her return to New York in 1976, Murray joined the Paula Cooper Gallery, where she had her first one-woman show in the autumn of the same year. Describing one of Murray's paintings from that period, Kay Larson noted that "the fragmentation of her later canvases is predicted [in *Southern California*] solely through color." A flat, diamond-shaped plane features small blue, green, and purple comma shapes floating inside an immense orange-red parabola that nearly obscures the blue-black background. "The psychic pressure exerted against the edges of the picture is both euphoric and scary," Larson wrote, "as though the bursting bubble might shatter the tensile strength of the edge, destroying the universe within."

In 1979 and 1980 Murray began to break up her canvases into smaller pieces in such works as *Painter's Progress* (now owned by the Museum of Modern Art in New York City), in which nineteen conjoining shards of canvas are painted with the fractured image of a painter's palette and brushes. "At first I didn't tell people about the images," she told Kay Larson. "Nobody saw them, which interested me a lot. I realized that was how I felt about life. What I did is create this funny conflict—a painting in pieces—and inside that I painted an image that could come together as a whole." In the interview with Kate Horsfield, she said, "Taking something broken and then trying to make it conceptually whole is the fundamental drive behind all those paintings."

Murray's works became increasingly three dimensional in the mid- to late 1980s. Her paintings often incorporated objects of common experience in their texts—images of coffee cups, spoons, tables, windows, and chairs proliferated—and her deliberate use of the wall space between the puzzle-pieces of her canvases grew more sophisticated. Annual exhibitions of her work at the Paula Cooper Gallery were by that time events not to be missed in the art world, as she was increasingly recognized for expanding the limits of art. A touring ten-year retrospective of Murray's work, originating in 1987 at the Dallas Museum of Art and culminating in 1988 with an exhibition at the prestigious Whitney Museum, marked a new zenith in her career. Evaluating the show of twenty-eight paintings and twenty drawings, Theodore F. Wolff noted in the *Christian Science Monitor* (May 9, 1988) that "her large pastel drawings . . . project an aura of greater informality and warmth [than do her paintings]." In *Arts Magazine* (September 1987), Gregory Galligan wrote, "With a keen sense of art history, Murray integrates the past with pure, unbridled innovation—to such an extent, in fact, that her work rises above all descriptive categories. In a word, her painting has achieved a classical quality of expressive motion contained by a sure, conclusive framework."

While clearly building on her past body of work, Murray has continually set new standards of complexity and refinement without sacrificing her exploration of her inner life. Aiming to challenge rather than to pacify the viewer, she paints many birth images, complete with impossibly long umbilical cords winding out of holes. "My work has to do with the fact that I'm a woman; I've accepted it, loved it, and hated it," she told Elizabeth Hess in an interview for *Ms.* (June 1988). At the same time, she insisted that "good art rises above the issue of gender," as she commented in her conversation with Hess. "The fact that I'm a feminist is not always immediately clear in my work."

Some art critics have downplayed the value of Murray's art because of its "domestic" imagery of women's work and motherhood. In response to critics' implied derogation of her emotional engagement with everyday life, Murray has pointed out that Cezanne, who painted many domestic objects—apples, cups, saucers, and the like—was not dismissed on similar grounds. She has also wondered why some writers persist in labeling her cups "teacups." "It's as if the cups refer to a bunch of dainty ladies with nothing better to do than sit around and sip tea," she complained to Hess. On the contrary, her images of cups "are horrifying in some way," as she explained to Kate Horsfield. "They are large paintings on large shaped canvases that are split apart. And there are these big splashes that are coming out of the cup."

Other critics have championed this aspect of her art. Gregory Galligan wrote, "Like an autistic child who seems to commune with the most mundane kitchen utensils, Murray celebrates the domestic world with a spasmic, attractive sense of humor. Even more than her funky humor, it might be Murray's inherent sense of poetry that keeps one returning to her combustive images." In her catalog essay that accompanied the artist's 1988 retrospective, Roberta Smith proclaimed, "Murray has delineated the home front, the domestic situation, as the psychological war zone that it truly is."

At times, Murray has been surprised by the imagery that has come to her. "At times I think it's too psychological, it's too sexual," she told Horsfield. "It bowls people over, and I think, 'That's in me?' But that *is* in me. I made that image. To have that thrown back at you—what somebody else sees, likes, or is turned off by—is really amazing." Indeed, when people interpret her works differently from the way she had intended them to be read, she realizes "that it is the intention. . . . It doesn't seem to be consciously intended but I think it is."

Notwithstanding variations in interpretations of content, Murray's art lends itself to more than one way of seeing, as Amei Wallach pointed out in *New York Newsday* (May 1, 1988): "To Murray, the soap-opera details of day-old coffee, breakfast-table babble, and plumbing that doesn't work are grist for a systematic investigation into how we perceive and how you can depict that on canvas without lying about depth and perspective."

In recent years, Murray's work has become even more impressive, according to most critics. Writing in the *Village Voice* (April 21, 1992), Elizabeth Hess noted that Murray "revels in expanding painting's consciousness. The wild curvatures in her frames have transgressed all her previous boundaries. . . . There are endless quandaries and visual texts in these images, which slowly begin to gel." In an appraisal of a recent exhibition for the *New York Times* (April 10, 1992), Michael Kimmelman observed, "Murray's work manages to be funny in its cartoony imagery, yet wrenching and allusive. The process of deciphering her paintings is typically one of uncovering some sort of emotional predicament that is all the more affecting for being at first hidden. This kind of emotional complexity is a hallmark of her art." By 1994 her smaller canvases possessed "a compressed clarity of shape, color, and paint handling that her large, more looming efforts can sometimes lack," according to Roberta Smith of the *New York Times* (April 15, 1994).

Murray's first solo exhibition in seventeen years was mounted in 1995, at Feigen Inc., in Chicago. In it she displayed five large paintings, some of which were clearly representational, while others (*Unlocked* and *Calling*) were ambiguous. Writing in the *Chicago Tribune* (April 28, 1995), Alan G. Artner described Murray's most recent painting, *What Is Love* (1995), which depicts a four-poster bed adorned with a pillow and two cartoonlike hands on either side of a sheet that does not quite cover the bed: "Pillow and sheet have become a figure expressing exhaustion or boredom. And either condition surely has something to do with the detumescence suggested by drooping bedposts, especially in relation to the painting's title." Summarizing the show, Artner declared that it revealed an artist "breaking new ground less than reclaiming and extending earlier approaches. The constant is unflagging vitality expressed through the hum of Murray's color and the roar with which she applies it."

As the first woman involved in the Artist's Choice series at the Museum of Modern Art, in New York City, in which an artist selects pieces from the museum's collection for an exhibition, Murray chose over a hundred works by seventy women, representing the years 1910 through the 1970s. Mounted in the summer of 1995, the exhibition *Modern Women* began with works of the 1950s and 1960s by some of Murray's role models—among them Grace Hartigan, Joan Mitchell, Helen Frankenthaler, and Lee Bontecou—and continued with pieces by her peers Eva Hesse and Louise Fishman. Among the motifs Murray traced in this nonchronological show were the confluence of art and craft techniques and introspective abstraction. She included only one of her own paintings, *Mirror* (1963), which was described in Holland Cotter's review of the show for the *New York Times* (July 21, 1995): "Scruffily painted, with an off-kilter, hand-hammered frame, its central image is the newsprint image of a man's head torn in half and embedded in the paint, an idiosyncratic anti-masterpiece that makes sense within the exploratory, communal sensibility of the show." Cotter concluded that with *Modern Women* Murray had "done the right thing, done it well, and pushed art another step forward."

Developed through trial and error, the process Murray uses to create her paintings has remained unchanged in recent years. Before she begins painting, she draws a basic outline of the frame, makes a clay model of the whole piece, and shapes her canvases over curved armatures. When Murray paints, Hess wrote in *Ms.*, she "deliberately allows her unconscious to direct the end result." "If my work isn't spontaneous I feel like I'm cheating," Murray told Hess. The procedure can sometimes be slow, but she has never considered accelerating her production in order to increase her income (some of her paintings sell in the six-figure range). "I don't want my work to be a siphon, or used solely as a commodity," she informed Hess. "I want people to buy the work because they want it, not because they can sell it next week for a profit."

Murray received the Walter M. Campana Award from the Art Institute of Chicago in 1982, an award from the American Academy and Institute of Arts and Letters in 1984, the Skowhegan Medal for Painting in 1986, an honorary doctorate from the School of the Art Institute of Chicago in 1992, the Larry Aldrich Prize in Contemporary Art in 1993, and an honorary degree from the Rhode Island School of Design in 1993. Murray's *Terrifying Terrain*, (1990) which comprises several overlapping canvases and depicts, in shades of red and blue, a woman tied to unstable ground, was purchased by the Metropolitan Museum of Art, in New York City, in 1991, and her paintings have been exhibited throughout the United States, at, among other places, the Museum of Contemporary Art, in Los Angeles, the National Gallery of Art, in Washington, D.C., the Walker Art Center, in Minneapolis, the Museum of Modern Art and the Whitney Museum of American Art, both in New York City, and the Art Institute of Chicago.

Soft-spoken without being demure, Elizabeth Murray laughs frequently, and her modest, down-to-earth demeanor surprises visitors who expect to meet a formidable doyenne. She has frizzy gray hair and a girlish, makeup-free face that belies her years. She, her second husband, the poet Bob Holman, and their two young daughters, Daisy and Sophie, divide their time between their home in Manhattan and their farm in the Berkshires. Her son, Dakota, has graduated from college and lives on his own. Reflecting on what being an artist has meant to her, Murray told Kate Horsfield, "I think that my art has helped me to like myself a lot better. . . . It taught me—through my being able to make myself do it, continue it, and go deeper into myself and through it—that I am not so bad. That I can be honest, or if honesty doesn't matter, that I can be direct. That I can express what I am feeling from my heart and soul."

Selected Biographical References: Art in America 77:210+ Ap '89; Arts Mag 62:62+ S '87; Elle Decor p14+ Je/Jl '92 pors; Ms 16:34+ Je '88 pors; New York 19:40+ F 10 '86 pors, 21:78+ My 9 '88; N Y Times C pl+ O 21 '94 pors; N Y Times Mag p20+ Mr 31 91 por; Profile 5:2+ S '86 por; Village Voice p93 Ap 21 '92; Who's Who in America, 1995; World Artists 1980–1990 (1991)

Agence France-Presse

Mwinyi, Ali Hassan
(MWIN-yee, AH-lee HAH-sahn)

May 8, 1925– President of Tanzania. Address: c/o Office of the President, Dar es Salaam, Tanzania.

Although Africa has to a large extent retained its image in the West as a continent plagued by nepotism, ethnic strife, and chronic economic disarray, the reality is, according to many observers, in some ways more benign, for in recent years an increasing number of African politicians have committed themselves to reforming their countries not only economically but politically as well. The challenge confronting Africa's present-day leaders, many of whom belong to the so-called second generation of African politicians, is that of transforming their countries' state-run economies into free-market ones and of relaxing the restrictions on political freedom imposed by their socialist-minded predecessors. "There are few tasks more difficult, and more important, than those that face the second generation of African leaders," John Storm Roberts, a former editor of the newsmagazine *Africa Report*, told *Current Biography*.

One of these politicians is Ali Hassan Mwinyi, who became the president of Tanzania in 1985. He succeeded Julius Nyerere, who remains a respected figure in Tanzania because of his role in the country's struggle for independence but whose fidelity to his own distinctive brand of socialism contributed to its economic decline. In addition to improving his country's rickety economy, Mwinyi has permitted a free press, denationalized the country's formerly state-run businesses, and improved civil liberties. His staying power, as well as his success in instituting various reforms, has come as something of a surprise, for although he assumed the presidency through legitimate means, he was at the time of his election widely seen as a transitional figure, and he lacked a strong power base of his own.

Ali Hassan Mwinyi was born on May 8, 1925 in Kivure, in the then-British trusteeship territory of Tanganyika. His parents, who were Muslims, moved to the almost entirely Islamic island-group of Zanzibar and Pemba, just off Tanganyika's coast, when he was very young. Mwinyi trained as a teacher, completing his studies in England, at the University of Durham, in the last year of World War II. On his return to Zanzibar, he joined the staff of the Zanzibar Teacher Training College, of which he eventually became director.

Zanzibar, a British protectorate then ruled by a hereditary sultan, was and remains the heartland of the Afro-Arab Swahili culture. The inhabitants identified themselves as either Arabic or Afro-Shirazi (African), and the latter resented the politically and economically dominant Arab group. As a Muslim African whose mainland roots distanced him somewhat from the tangled ethnic/political conflicts of the time, Ali Hassan Mwinyi was politically valuable, and he was appointed permanent secretary to the minister of education when Zanzibar achieved independence from Great Britain in late 1963.

In January 1964 the Zanzibari government was overthrown. President Julius Nyerere of neighboring Tanganyika, also newly independent from Great Britain, sent security forces to the island nation to restore order, and soon after that the two countries joined to form the United Republic of Tanzania. Mwinyi spent the next six years as assistant general manager of the government-run Zanzibari State Trading Company. In 1970 he was appointed minister of state in the Tanzanian President's Office. He later became Tanzania's ambassador to Egypt, and in the early 1980s he served as minister of health and home affairs and minister of natural resources and tourism. During these years he gained a reputation as a moderate who was respected by both ideological socialists and those who were eager to reform the economy along free-market lines. Then, in 1984, Mwinyi was unexpectedly thrust into the most powerful political post in Zanzibar.

Mwinyi's emergence as a key player in Tanzanian politics was precipitated in part by the increasingly fragile relationship between the country's mainland and island constituents. The union had in fact been strained since its establishment two decades before, though official intolerance of dissent masked the tension in the early days. One source of discord was the lack of a common history and culture: while Zanzibar's history and Swahili culture were closely linked with that of the Tanganyikan coast, they were quite alien to those of the "upcountry," or inland, regions, from which many of Tanzania's politicians had come. Another was that while Zanzibaris were permitted to hold union government jobs, mainlanders were barred from working for the Zanzibari government. Zanzibar's semiautonomous status extended to the fact that mainland travelers to the island portion of the ostensibly united nation had to pass through customs, though the same was not true for islanders visiting the mainland.

Zanzibaris, too, were dissatisfied with the union. The defining document of Tanzanian socialism, the 1967 Arusha Declaration, had mandated the establishment of collective farms. The system, known as *ujamaa*, was said to reflect the traditional African extended family system, which was foreign to Zanzibaris. Particularly irksome to the Zanzibaris was the fact that the collectivization program had proved disastrous for the island's (as well as the union's) economy. By January 1984—ironically, the twentieth anniversary of the Zanzibari revolution and creation of the union—unrest on the island had become so serious that President Nyerere felt compelled to send troops to maintain order there.

In this tense climate, Mwinyi was elected president of Zanzibar and chairman of the Zanzibar Revolutionary Council. Later in 1984, as a result of a change in the constitution that made the Zanzibari president a vice-president of the union, he assumed the latter post as well. Mwinyi's position was further strengthened in August, when he won the vice-chairmanship of the country's sole political party, Chama Cha Mapinduzi (CCM, which in English means the Revolutionary Party), with 96 percent of the vote. Immediately after his election as president, Mwinyi tried to ease Zanzibari discontent by introducing economic reforms that gave private enterprise and free-market forces more of a role than the party traditionally permitted.

Mwinyi's rise to power came at a crucial period not only in Zanzibar's political history but Tanzania's as well, for Nyerere, the country's first and only leader, was then preparing to step down from the presidency. Partly as a result of the impending change in leadership, the positions of president and CCM chairman—both of which had been held by Nyerere—were separated, and that of the prime minister was strengthened. As Roger Yeager observed in *Tanzania: An African Experiment* (1989), those changes "made the national executive more potent without the CCM's ultimate control over public policy being sacrificed." They also allowed Nyerere to resign as president while retaining his overriding influence as party chairman, a position he said he planned to hold until 1987 but did not relinquish until 1990.

Mwinyi was a principal beneficiary of these events. On August 15, 1985, following a power struggle within the CCM between economic liberals and centrists, the delegates to a special convention of the CCM elected Mwinyi the sole candidate to succeed Nyerere as president of Tanzania. In October of that year, 92 percent of the Tanzanian electorate confirmed the party's choice, and on November 5 Mwinyi was sworn in as Tanzania's second president for a five-year term.

Because of his relative obscurity and his lack of a strong power base, Mwinyi was expected to be a transitional figure. And as might be imagined, given Nyerere's domination of Tanzanian politics for the previous two decades, most Tanzanians expected Mwinyi to defer to Nyerere, who would remain Tanzania's ultimate arbiter of power. This view was expressed by a businessman during an interview with Edward Girardet for the *Christian Science Monitor* (March 21, 1985) a few months after the election: "In this country, the party is the real government. Nyerere may have stepped down as president, but the landlord has not changed." Samuel M. Wangwe, a professor and dean of arts and sciences at the University of Dar es Salaam, agreed, telling Edward A. Gargan in an interview for the *New York Times* (November 3, 1985), "The party is the main policy-making organ. Mwinyi will not, cannot, make any major changes in the next two years. His principal problem is how to improve the performance of the economy, how to make people accountable for their performance."

Improving the economy ranked as the most daunting challenge any Tanzanian politician could have faced. As a Reuters reporter observed, as quoted in the *Guardian* (November 6, 1985), Mwinyi "inherited appalling economic problems, including sagging agricultural output partly due to poor government planning and excessive state intervention," which were compounded by an ambitious but unaffordable social agenda. An *Economist* (August 23, 1986) writer's assessment of the country's circumstances was even grimmer: "Tanzania is in a mess even by black Africa's gloomy standards." The economic crisis in which Tanzania found itself was generally attributed to "the failed system of *ujamaa*," as the *Economist* writer put it, which had been instituted and perpetuated by Nyerere. Under that system, some thirteen million peasants who had previously worked their own land had by 1976 been resettled, many of them forcibly, into eight thousand cooperative villages. Their crops were bought and distributed by the government, and the country's major industries were nationalized and operated by state-run companies. But because Tanzania lacked experienced civil servants, the nationalized economy had little chance of being managed efficiently. The net result was that following independence Tanzanians became progressively poorer, economic growth slowed, and the country became increasingly dependent on foreign aid. The nation even had difficulty feeding itself; between 1970 and 1984 agricultural output dropped dramatically—by 25 percent.

One of Mwinyi's first important moves as president—which also turned out to be one of his first successes—was to conclude an agreement with the International Monetary Fund according to which Tanzania would begin to introduce free-market reforms in return for new loans from the bank. As part of the reform effort, Tanzania's troubled state marketing organization, the Agricultural Products Export Corporation, was dissolved; the notoriously low prices that the government paid farmers for their crops were raised; some state-run businesses were privatized, and others were closed down; interest rates were raised; price controls on many consumer items were lifted; government spending was cut; and the country's overpriced currency was devalued. For its part, in 1986 the International Monetary Fund agreed to extend to Tanzania a standby loan of seventy-eight million dollars. The IMF agreement, the first such accord in six years, was welcomed by the international lending community, and in 1986 the World Bank, which had suspended assistance to Tanzania because the country was so far behind in its payments on previous loans, agreed to lend one hundred million dollars.

By 1987 ordinary Tanzanians were beginning to feel optimistic about their future. As Sheila Rule observed in the *New York Times* (April 15, 1987), Mwinyi "has gained popularity in this impoverished country as his government moved ahead with initiatives that moderated Mr. Nyerere's socialist principles and slowly eased economic decline. . . . Tanzanians credit Mr. Mwinyi's economic recovery program with much of what they are experiencing today, including higher crop prices, a greater role for private enterprise and more goods in the market. Even though prices remain out of reach of the ordinary Tanzanian, the people say they like to see more goods in the shops. There is a psychological benefit in this, they say."

Predictably, the reform effort was opposed by some members of the ruling party's socialist old guard. In 1987 these hardliners retaliated by excluding Cleopa Msuya, Tanzania's chief negotiator with the IMF, from the CCM National Executive Committee. They also launched a campaign among village party chairmen to persuade them to oppose grassroots reform. Popular support for Mwinyi's economic recovery program, too, dissipated somewhat, as Tanzanians began to realize that their circumstances were unlikely to improve significantly in the near term. (Indeed, in some respects their conditions worsened.) Despite these difficulties, Mwinyi's liberalization policies prevailed, to the extent that Tanzania's intellectuals and policy leaders became more accepting of them. As Yeager put it, "Even the former radical Abdulrahman Babu has extolled 'the dynamic practices of capitalism.'"

Another challenge confronting Mwinyi was the resurgence of hostility between Zanzibaris and mainlanders. Tensions flared in 1988, when, at a conference on women and development, Sophie Kawawa, the wife of the CCM secretary-general, said that Muslim law would be modified wherever it discriminated against women, particularly in regard to polygamy and inheritance. In Zanzibar, Muslim, conservative, and anti-mainland sentiment converged, culminating in a protest march to the State House by four thousand demonstrators. In the ensuing melee, two people were killed and dozens were wounded. Mwinyi flew to Zanzibar and promised that any changes in the nation's laws would be subject to constitutionally established procedures; he warned, though, that "any further threats to the union's peace and internal security would be vigorously prosecuted."

The year 1990 marked another watershed in Tanzanian political history, for in that year Nyerere relinquished the chairmanship of the CCM. Some political observers suggested that Nyerere's declining influence would provide Mwinyi, who succeeded Nyerere as party chairman, with an opportunity to take bolder steps in reforming the economy. As a writer for the *Economist* (June 2, 1990) observed, Mwinyi's "fragile economic improvements of recent years, including real growth of 4 percent a year since 1986, were achieved in the face of persistent meddling by his predecessor." By the time Mwinyi was reelected to a second term as president later in 1990, some observers were beginning to feel that Mwinyi's approach to Tanzania's problems had become less cautious. He took an important step in October 1993, when he opened a branch of the Meridien Biao bank, thus ending the government monopoly of the banking system.

In the 1990s Mwinyi began to liberalize Tanzania's political system. In 1991 he appointed a special commission on political reform, and in the following year the CCM leadership adopted the commission's recommendation that the government permit the formation of opposition parties. Another of the commission's recommendations—that a Tanganyikan government parallel to the Zanzibari government be established to ease the mainlanders' persistent resentment of the Zanzibaris—was ignored, however, and the mounting tension between the two sides in turn laid the groundwork for the worst crisis of Mwinyi's tenure as president.

The imbroglio was precipitated by the revelation that Zanzibar had secretly joined the Organization of the Islamic Conference (OIC) in clear violation of the union's secular constitution. Mwinyi at first tried to condone the move; he even went so far as to suggest that the union government might also join the OIC. But the fact that Mwinyi, a Muslim with strong ties to Zanzibar, appeared to be taking a partisan stand infuriated mainlander politicians, who in 1993 revived the proposal that a Tanganyikan government be established. When Nyerere was consulted for his views, he was openly critical of the government, and by implication, of Mwinyi. "Many observers were predicting the fall of Mwinyi and his top leadership within days," Louisa Taylor observed in *Africa Report* (May/June 1994). The crisis passed after the CCM leadership agreed to solicit the views of party members on the matter of forming a Tanganyikan government.

The debate over the relationship between the union's constituent parts is likely to feature prominently in the campaign leading up to the first multiparty presidential elections, scheduled for 1995. Louisa Taylor has said that "for all sides the elections have become the deadline for reform." The elections may also prove to be a turning point in Mwinyi's political career. As one Zanzibari official predicted in an interview with Taylor, "If the present structure is not changed, the union will break as soon as Mwinyi steps down. The pressure is coming from the mainland. They want him out; some people just can't stand the thought of Zanzibaris in State House."

Ali Hassan Mwinyi, who has a stocky build, is of medium height and has a predilection for conservative dark suits. A devout Muslim, he is said to be a modest, incorruptible man with a reputation for honesty and flexibility. Since 1960 he has been married to Siti A. Mwinyi, with whom he has five sons and four daughters.

Selected Biographical References: Guardian p9 O 18 '85 por; N Y Times A p4 Ap 15 '87 por; Toronto Globe and Mail p4 Ag 16 '85 por; Washington Post A p29 N 6 '85; Contemporary Black Biography vol 1 (1992); International Who's Who, 1994–95

David Cooper/The Shaw Festival

Newton, Christopher

June 11, 1936– Canadian theatrical director; actor. Address: c/o The Shaw Festival, Box 774, Niagara-on-the-Lake, Ontario L0S 1J0, Canada

One of Canada's most highly regarded actors and directors, Christopher Newton is internationally renowned for bringing a fresh artistic vision and commercial success to the Shaw Festival, a major Canadian theatrical institution that showcases the works of the playwright George Bernard Shaw and his contemporaries. As artistic director of the festival, which is located in Niagara-on-the-Lake, in southern Ontario, Newton has demonstrated shrewd management and programming skills, but perhaps his most remarkable accomplishment is his emergence as a preeminent director of Shavian drama. Theatre reviewers have frequently noted with irony that when Newton joined the festival, in 1980, he considered Shaw to be a tediously didactic playwright whose works were of limited dramatic interest. Newton's ambivalence toward Shaw was reflected in his initial productions, which were critical failures, but he gradually acquired an assured directorial style that has become a hallmark of the festival.

Visually imaginative and intensely theatrical, Newton's approach is typically distinguished by his bold explorations of the emotional and sexual themes underlying many of Shaw's plays. Reviewers have applauded his innovative interpretations, crediting him for imbuing works of intellect and ideas with an uncommon passion; actors have praised him for his active development of Canadian talent and his willingness to take theatrical risks. The explicit nature of some of his productions—one of the most notorious of which is his 1981 staging of Shaw's *Saint Joan*, which featured a brief glimpse of male nudity—has shocked a number of critics and audience members, some of whom have canceled their subscriptions. But the controversial director, whose early career included stints as the artistic director at Theatre Calgary and the Vancouver Playhouse, has staunchly defended his unconventional choices. "In a curious way, my imagination—my being—is not terribly interested in working out what people want and giving them that . . . ," he has said, as quoted in the summer 1979 issue of the journal *Performing Arts*. "My philosophy is not *non*populist. I want a lot of people to see my work. But the basic interest is in saying *this* is really exciting."

The oldest of the three children of Albert Edward Newton, who owned and operated a gas station, and Gwladys Maude (Emes) Newton, a kindergarten teacher, Christopher Newton was born on June 11, 1936 in Deal, a small town on the southeastern coast of England. He has two sisters, Josephine and Marguerite. Encouraged by his mother, whom he has described as "poetically inclined," early in his life Newton showed an interest in the arts, especially music. As a boy he learned to play the piano, cello, clarinet, and flute, and he dreamed of becoming a composer. But at Sir Roger Manwood's school, which he attended between the ages of eight and eighteen, his musical talents went largely unrecognized. He described his education at that venerable institution, which has catered to the English middle class for hundreds of years, to Keith Garebian for Garebian's book *George Bernard Shaw and Christopher Newton: Explorations of Shavian Theatre* (1993): "I was ultimately trained to be a district officer in the old empire. That's what this school trained for, without specifying this in any way. . . . It wasn't interested in any boys who were interested in anything that was out of the ordinary. In fact, my interest in music was regarded as weird."

As he grew older, Newton had little time for music in any case, for he was obliged by his family's straitened financial circumstances to help out after school at his father's service station, where he manned the gas pumps—a job he hated so intensely that he cannot tolerate the smell of gasoline to this day. He abandoned all plans for a musical career after he broke his left arm while playing cricket (he has never regained full use of it). By that time theatre had become another interest of Newton's—he had acted in several student productions at Manwood's school—but its precarious nature made it an unpromising career option, so he decided to study English literature in college. A strong writer and an exceptional student, he had received consistently high marks at Manwood's and was thus eligible to attend virtually any university, but instead of choosing a prestigious institution such as Oxford or Cambridge, Newton chose the University of Leeds, in Yorkshire, because of its more egalitarian environment. While at Leeds, Newton appeared in a variety of student productions, among them a memorable *Othello*, with the noted Shakespearean scholar G. Wilson Knight in the title role, and whenever he could spare the time, he traveled to London to see plays, especially Tyrone Guthrie's groundbreaking stagings of Shakespeare at the Old Vic.

Newton thrived in the intensely stimulating academic environment, so much so that he decided to continue his education at the graduate level. To that end, he sought a graduate assistantship at several American universities; the only one to offer him a position, as a teaching assistant in English literature, was Purdue University, in West Lafayette, Indiana. Arriving on campus in the fall of 1957, Newton took courses toward his master's degree and taught some undergraduate English classes, a task he found "incredibly boring." He eventually transferred to the University of Illinois in Urbana, where he completed work on his master's degree in English literature. While he was there, his interest in music was rekindled by his association with some of the avant-garde composers on campus, including John Cage and Lejaren Hiller, with whom he collaborated on an electronic score for a staging of the play *Cuthbert Bound*.

It was also during his two years at the University of Illinois that Newton became seriously involved in acting. After receiving his master's degree, in 1960, he spent the summer interning at the Oregon Shakespeare Festival, in Ashland, then began a year's appointment as the acting head of the drama department at Bucknell University, in Lewisburg, Pennsylvania. Although the department was small (there were only ten students in the acting program), the job was daunting for Newton, who had no formal academic or professional training in theatre. But the challenge appealed to him, and as the year progressed, he decided to pursue a theatrical career. "Running that little theatre, I thought, 'This is it! I want to be an actor!'" he told Gina Mallet in an interview for *Chatelaine* (August 1984). Following his second summer at the Oregon Shakespeare Festival, he tried out for the Stratford Festival, a classical repertory company based in Stratford, Ontario, but was turned down because the director assumed he was an American. Undeterred, Newton decided to move to Toronto, a major center for Canadian theatre.

Newton served his theatrical apprenticeship with the Canadian Players, a small touring troupe with whom he traveled around the country performing such parts as Cassius in *Julius Caesar* and Brother Martin in Shaw's *Saint Joan*, often for audiences with little or no knowledge of the theatre. "It was up to us to excite them, *reveal*, do all those things," he told Keith Garebian. "That's what I found wonderful. . . . And that was a learning experience. How to do that. How to hold the attention of an audience of native people in Lynn Lake." Newton subsequently played small roles on various Canadian radio and television programs, among them the journalist Robin Craven on the popular CBC serial *The Other Man*, and in plays produced at the Manitoba Theatre Centre, the Shaw Festival, and the Vancouver International Festival. At Vancouver, his assignments included the part of Algernon in Mike Nichols's staging of Oscar Wilde's *The Importance of Being Earnest*. Impressed by Newton's performance, in May 1965 Nichols tapped the young actor to succeed Brian Bedford in the leading role of Tom in the Broadway production of Ann Jellicoe's comedy *The Knack*.

As a result of his Broadway appearance, Newton was recruited by the Stratford Festival, the company that had previously spurned him. He eagerly accepted the festival's offer, and for the next several years he appeared regularly with the company, earning a name for himself as a talented and highly versatile actor. Among his more noteworthy characterizations were a self-adoring Orsino in *Twelfth Night* and the schoolmaster in Gogol's *The Government Inspector*. Gradually, however, Newton's enthusiasm for the Stratford Festival began to wane. Feeling that he was being typecast in "pretty parts," and discouraged by the lack of support he was receiving as a younger member of the company, he left Stratford in 1968 to become the founding artistic director of Theatre Calgary, a professional nonprofit troupe in Alberta. "There was never a real sense of company [in Stratford]," he explained to Keith Garebian. "That's what I missed. That's what I always wanted. And I think it was from that and from the idea that they turned down some of our suggestions to make it a company that I got turned off."

Strongly motivated by a desire to create a supportive environment for actors, Newton resolved to cultivate the talent of a resident group of performers at Theatre Calgary rather than import big-name celebrities for each production—a philosophy that he has espoused and resolutely followed throughout his career. Working with a small company of mostly young actors, he oversaw the staging of an unusually wide variety of works, ranging from a revival of *Dracula* to the Canadian premiere of Joe Orton's *Loot* to a campy, updated version of Ben Jonson's *The Alchemist* and including two original musicals—the space fantasy *Trip* and *You Stay Here, The Rest Come With Me*, a history of Calgary—that Newton himself cowrote. The response, from the city's relatively unsophisticated theatregoers and critics alike, was overwhelmingly positive. Jamie Portman, the Calgary *Herald*'s drama critic at the time, went so far as to rank Newton's "Chekhovian" reading of Noel Coward's *Private Lives* as "one of the best [he'd] ever seen." Newton also won praise for offering a series of lunch-hour shows, organizing an "actors to the schools" program, which established links between the theatrical community and local schools, and scheduling workshops on improvisation and basic acting techniques.

By 1971 Newton, having achieved most of his goals at Theatre Calgary, was keen to move on. Handing in his resignation at the end of the 1970–71 season, he took some much-needed time off before returning to work, as the artistic director of the Vancouver Playhouse, in British Columbia. One of his first acts upon assuming his new post, in 1973, was to ask the company's board of directors to cut his salary by three thousand dollars and use the money to help pay actors. He then assembled a small company of actors and began planning a series of productions that would shake up the conservative Vancouver arts community. Over the course of his career, Newton has demonstrated a proclivity for risk taking—an inclination that he clearly indulged during his years in Vancouver by mounting boldly unconventional productions, such as Derek Goldby's highly controversial version of Bertolt Brecht's *A Respectable Wedding*, about an ill-fated suburban wedding party. Goldby's radical reinterpretation, which ended with the groom's attempt to rape his bride with a wine bottle, shocked Vancouver audiences. Newton's own productions, which included a sexually charged translation of *Camille* by the Scottish playwright Robert David MacDonald and a "Fellini-esque," to use Newton's word, *Julius Caesar*, were equally provocative.

Dismayed by the notoriety that the new artistic director brought to the previously staid Vancouver Playhouse, Newton's detractors complained that his programming showed a lack of respect for his audience, but as several critics noted, more people walked into the theatre than walked out. Among the many box-office successes during Newton's tenure were critically acclaimed productions of such classics as *Oedipus*, *Macbeth*, *King Lear*, *Tartuffe*, and *Twelfth Night*, in which Newton himself took the part of Malvolio. He also appeared as Henry Higgins in Shaw's *Pygmalion*, the psychiatrist Martin Dysart in Peter Shaffer's *Equus*, and Henry Carr in Tom Stoppard's *Travesties*, earning virtually unanimous approval for the "dazzling, histrionic virtuosity" of his performance.

Newton's 1978 production of *Hamlet*, staged during his final season at the Vancouver Playhouse, was singled out by critics as one of the highlights of his term as artistic director. In a representative review for the syndicated Southam News Service, Jamie Portman praised Newton's decision to transpose the play's setting to the nineteenth century. By depicting Denmark as "a second-rate monarchy with a second-rate king on the throne," surrounded by legions of small-minded, puffed-up bureaucrats, Newton heightened the play's emotional impact, Portman wrote, by juxtaposing the mundane with the extraordinary. The result was a "stunning" and intimate exploration of human emotions. "Vancouver's production may end up on the traditionally violent level of revenge and retribution with bodies strewn about the stage," he concluded, "but the underlying emphasis is on the death of innocence." As Portman pointed out in his assessment of *Hamlet*, Newton, who had by that time accepted the directorship of the Shaw Festival, was "leaving behind a splendid legacy." In addition to his numerous production credits, his achievements at the Vancouver Playhouse include the establishment of the Playhouse Acting School and the creation within the resident company of two smaller troupes, one devoted to theatre in education programs and the other, made up mainly of young actors, to the presentation of new works.

When the Shaw Festival's board of directors first approached him, in 1978, the position of artistic director of the festival held little appeal for Newton, who made no secret of his lack of enthusiasm for the playwright. (He had, on several occasions, publicly dismissed Shaw as "boring.") But after five years at the Vancouver Playhouse, he was ready to take his artistic vision elsewhere. "I really like starting things up, changing things," he explained to Bryan Johnson in an interview for the

Toronto *Globe and Mail* (June 22, 1978). "That's what I'm best at. I don't like continuing."

In keeping with his team-oriented approach to leadership, Newton arrived in Niagara-on-the-Lake in January 1980 with many of his Vancouver actors and staffers in tow. He assumed responsibility for the Shaw Festival during one of the most difficult periods in its eighteen-year history. Without an artistic director since Paxton Whitehead's departure, in 1977, the festival had seen its reputation sink to an unprecedented low. Productions were generally so lackluster (the casts often included local amateurs in minor roles) that disgruntled subscribers had taken to calling it the "Shoddy Festival." With an accumulated debt of approximately $635,000, the festival was also in acute financial trouble. Intent on revitalizing the festival, Newton set out to eliminate the debt by presenting a first season that would make an immediate impact on the Shaw Festival audience. To that end, he hired an administrator, a controller, a production director, and an operations director. He then increased the number of productions from seven to eleven and made a major change in terms of programming: only two works scheduled for the 1980 season—*Misalliance* and *The Philanderer*—were by George Bernard Shaw. The other selections were by a wide variety of artists who lived during Shaw's lifetime, ranging from Anton Chekhov to the popular composer Irving Berlin. The expanded scope marked a significant departure for the festival, which had focused almost exclusively on Shaw under previous directors.

With the opening of the 1980 season, Newton once again found himself in the line of fire. Critics questioned the festival's eclectic program, and residents of Niagara-on-the-Lake expressed outrage over the inclusion of Derek Goldby's staging of *A Respectable Wedding*, which Newton had decided to revive at the Shaw. The production deeply offended some members of the community, a number of whom walked out in disgust during a preview performance. Scores of longtime Shaw subscribers canceled their subscriptions because of the play, and some members of the board suggested that Newton's appointment had been a mistake. Critical response to the production did little to marshal support for the beleaguered artistic director. The *Toronto Star*'s Gina Mallet denounced *A Respectable Wedding* as "unabashedly gross" and unfocused. While conceding that the production offered some "moments of wonderful mayhem," the *Globe and Mail*'s Ray Conlogue issued a warning to theatregoers who had grown accustomed to the festival's previous conservatism: "If *Respectable Wedding* is any indication of things to come under Christopher Newton, the staid old place is going to become Raunch City."

Reviews of the remainder of the season further undermined Newton's standing, both as head of the festival and as a director in his own right. His production of *Canuck*, a relatively unknown Canadian comedy from the 1920s, was generally dismissed as embarrassingly nationalistic, and *Misalliance* was faulted for what Frank Rich called "distressingly sloppy stage behavior" and several unfortunate casting choices. "Sad to say," Rich wrote in a review for the *New York Times* (May 31, 1981), "something has gone terribly wrong at Niagara-on-the-Lake." Derek Goldby's production of the French farce *A Flea in Her Ear* was one of the few successes during Newton's turbulent first season, which ended with the festival $120,000 deeper in debt.

The behind-the-scenes tension increased the following year, when Newton presented a daringly modernist production of Shaw's *Saint Joan* that downplayed the central character's saintliness, featured frontal nudity, and, in Newton's original conception, omitted the play's epilogue, which he felt was superfluous. (He restored the epilogue after the playwright's literary executor, appalled by the planned cut, denied the festival permission to stage the play.) Newton's controversial *Saint Joan* was lambasted by the critics, some of whom began to call publicly for the director's dismissal. Gina Mallet of the *Toronto Star* was among those who disputed Newton's suitability as the festival's artistic administrator. "After two seasons, and particularly after this season's egregious *Saint Joan*, in which the maid was projected as a kind of medieval freedom fighter, it is clear that Newton does not have the capacity to be a worthy interpreter of Shaw's plays," she wrote, as quoted by Keith Garebian. Garebian also quoted an ostensibly disinterested outside observer—Julius Novick, who assessed the festival's season for the *Village Voice*. Novick agreed with his Canadian counterpart, suggesting that the festival's board "either fire [Newton] or . . . , ideally, hire a codirector who likes and understands Shaw and leave Mr. Newton free to do what he does well." What he did well, in the view of Novick and his fellow reviewers, were plays like Robert David MacDonald's *Camille*, which Gina Mallet hailed as "a flamboyantly camp production directed by Newton with a confidence and style never seen in his efforts with GBS."

Advised by several members of the festival board that his chances for a reappointment after the completion of his three-year term were slim, Newton considered handing in his resignation at the end of the 1981 season, but he decided to stay on, motivated by a desire to prove himself and by a growing appreciation of Shaw's plays, which he was beginning to view as works full of passion and paradox. He explained his change of heart in his evaluation of the first installment of Michael Holroyd's three-volume biography of Shaw, which was published in 1988. "If you take the plays seriously and see them as profound plays, then they are profound plays," he wrote, as quoted in Keith Garebian's book. "Before I started directing Shaw, I always thought he was what I'd always seen him presented as—as some kind of drawing-room comedian who didn't work anymore. No! *Misalliance* is about a forest in which lovers move and get lost. *Heartbreak House* is a magical strange house. In *You Never Can Tell*, they're at the seaside, and the seaside is full of delight—sunbathing and sunshine let into rooms and craziness, delight, happiness."

With one year remaining in his contract, in 1982 Newton determined to turn the festival around financially without compromising his vision of the Shaw as a venue for innovative theatre. He managed to do so at least in part by choosing not to direct any plays by Shaw during the 1982 season, thus deflecting further criticism of his Shavian vision. Instead, he responded to audience demand for a musical by scheduling and directing Sigmund Romberg's operetta *The Desert Song*; he also revived his production of *Camille*. But the season's biggest crowd-pleaser was Derek Goldby's sumptuous production of Edmond Rostand's *Cyrano de Bergerac*, starring Heath Lamberts. A huge critical and box-office hit, the story of the romantic swashbuckler played to full houses throughout the season, helping the festival take in a surplus after expenses, which, when combined with a one-time government grant, reduced the deficit to about three hundred thousand dollars.

Impressed by Newton's successful third season, the festival board reappointed him to a second term. During the years that followed, he and his staff instituted a series of cost-control measures that virtually eliminated the festival's accumulated debt by 1985. As the company's finances continued to improve, Newton concentrated on expanding the festival's scope by founding the Academy of the Shaw Festival, which, according to a 1994 press release, the company sees as its "research and development arm." Among other things, the academy coordinates professional acting classes, exchange programs, and an annual Shaw Seminar. Newton also endeavored to extend the festival's season—and expand his actors' work opportunities—by coproducing several productions every winter in Toronto, a two-hour drive away.

Having proven his skill as an administrator, Newton gradually established himself as a Shavian director of originality and depth during the late 1980s and early 1990s. His most memorable stagings of the playwright's works include a hauntingly surrealistic treatment of *Heartbreak House*, set near the end of World War I. Visually, the 1985 production transfixed audiences, eliciting gasps of amazement with an opening scene that revealed a vast, empty Edwardian drawing room that grew visibly larger as the play began. The illusive beauty of the set created a striking backdrop for the unsettling behavior of a seemingly civilized English family. Newton's stunningly original interpretation was so widely admired that the Arena Stage, in Washington, D.C., asked him to serve as a consultant on its production of the play.

Newton's Shavian credits also include noteworthy stagings of *Major Barbara, You Never Can Tell, Pygmalion, Arms and the Man*, and *Man and Superman*, for which he won virtually unanimous critical acclaim. A spare, minimalist set conceived by Eduard Kochergin lent a fresh perspective to the last-named production, enabling Newton to strip the work to what the Shavian scholar Dan H. Laurence called its "passionate essentials"—namely, the tension between the superficial conventions of English society and the deep-rooted sexual repression that underlies them. "Freed of its usual realistic Victorian or Edwardian settings, the Shavian vision seems much more up-to-date and exciting," John Bemrose observed in a review for *Maclean's* (June 5, 1989). "Newton's production of the 1902 play has a great deal to say to the late twentieth century, and it says it with power and style."

In planning each season at the Shaw Festival, Newton has always been careful to balance such intellectually demanding works as *Man and Superman* with lighter pieces from the same period. In 1989, for example, in addition to *Man and Superman* and Ibsen's *Peer Gynt*, he programmed the Moss Hart–George S. Kaufman comedy *Once in a Lifetime*, J. B. Priestley's psychological thriller *An Inspector Calls*, *Berkeley Square*, John L. Balderston's adaptation of Henry James's unfinished novel, and the 1927 musical *Good News*. "These works help recreate the context of an entire era," he explained to John Bemrose for *Maclean's*. "To fully understand Shaw, for example, you must also understand the popular theatre of his time. After all, he drew on the techniques of popular theatre, even as he transcended them."

Newton has continued to act whenever his administrative and directorial responsibilities allow. Among the numerous roles he has undertaken to considerable acclaim at the Shaw Festival are the Noel Coward sophisticates Garry Essendine and Elyot in, respectively, *Present Laughter* and *Private Lives*, Captain Hook in J. M. Barrie's *Peter Pan*, Nikolai in the Canadian premiere of Stephen Poliakoff's *Breaking the Silence*, and the poker-faced Brasset in *Charley's Aunt*. He has also written several plays, including *Slow Train to St. Ives* and *The Sound of Distant Thunder*, that have been staged by such Canadian regional theatres as the Manitoba Theatre Centre, the National Arts Centre, and the Vancouver Playhouse.

In recent years Newton has found himself increasingly drawn to opera, which he first began to direct in the mid-1980s. "I like these old things, not just because they are old, but because they help reveal the present," he told Liam Lacey of the Toronto *Globe and Mail* (January 30, 1991). "I'm beginning to understand masterpieces and what their role in our life is. . . . I'm obsessed with showing the past to the present, or more properly, I suppose, with showing the present through the past." Numbered among his opera credits are *The Barber of Seville* for the Vancouver Opera, *Madame Butterfly* and *Die Fledermaus* for the Canadian Opera Company, and *Carmen* for Pacific Opera.

Tall and athletic with gray hair that contrasts with his otherwise youthful appearance, Christopher Newton was described by one interviewer as sounding and looking "like an English country gentleman." He is said to be poised and amiable with reporters but relatively restrained when discussing his personal life, particularly his sexuality; he is gay and has supported several gay causes, although he prefers not to "make a big issue of it," as he has put it. He makes his home in Niagara-on-the-Lake, in a nineteenth-century cottage filled with photos, prints, drawings, and paintings, many with theatrical subjects. In his leisure, he spends, by his own account, "a lot of time" reading and listening to music. His honors include the Queen's Silver Jubilee Medal, in 1977, and the Dora Manor Moore Award for best direction of a musical, for the Shaw Festival's staging of *The Desert Song*, in 1986. He is an honorary fellow of the Royal Conservatory of Music in Toronto, and he has been awarded honorary doctorates by Brock University and the University of Guelph. After more than a dozen seasons with the Shaw Festival, Newton remains committed to playing the role of *enfant terrible* on the Canadian theatre scene. "I keep writing notes to myself: 'Don't stop being daring,'" he told Keith Garebian. "When one stops being daring, that's when one fails in the theatre."

Selected Biographical References: Chatelaine p40+ Ag '84 pors; Maclean's 102:54+ Je 5 '89 por; Toronto Globe and Mail C p1+ My 30 '92 por; Garebian, Keith. George Bernard Shaw and Christopher Newton: Explorations of Shavian Theatre (1993); International Who's Who, 1994–95; Oxford Companion to Canadian Theatre (1989)

AP/Wide World Photos

Nicholson, Jack

Apr. 22, 1937– Actor; filmmaker. Address: 12850 Mulholland Dr., Beverly Hills, CA 90210

NOTE: This biography supersedes the article that appeared in *Current Biography* in 1974.

The screen legend Jack Nicholson, who gained fame in the 1970s for embodying the roguery and rebelliousness in ordinary men, has, in several of his more recent films, including *Batman* and *The Witches of Eastwick*, accomplished the opposite—lending human form, even charm, to absolute evil. Among his generation of film actors, which boasts the heavyweights Dustin Hoffman, Al Pacino, and Robert De Niro, Nicholson is unique, in that his individual characterizations have contributed to a distinctive persona, as was true of such earlier idols as Humphrey Bogart and Clark Gable. That fact has led to his being called America's "most charismatic movie actor" and "the greatest American film actor of his generation."

The aura that surrounds Nicholson derives in part from his notorious off-camera activities, and yet, while only a blurry line separates the lustfulness of some of his characters from the widely reported decadence of his own life, Nicholson does not merely "play himself," as evidenced by the wide range of movies that have featured his acclaimed work: dramas such as *One Flew Over the Cuckoo's Nest*, for which he won an Oscar for best actor; the horror pictures *The Shining* and *Wolf*; and comedies, among them *Prizzi's Honor*.

The actor was born John Joseph Nicholson on April 22, 1937 and was reared in Neptune City, New Jersey by Ethel May Nicholson, a beautician, and her daughters, June and Lorraine. (Some published sources indicate that he was born in New York City; others give the Jersey Shore Medical Center, in Neptune Township, as his place of birth.) Nicholson was thirty-seven years old when he discovered that the woman he believed to be his mother was actually his grandmother and that June Nicholson, whom he had thought to be his sister, had at the age of eighteen given birth to him out of wedlock. His namesake was Ethel May's husband, John J. Nicholson, who had a drinking problem and drifted away from the family when Jack was an infant. The identity of Nicholson's biological father is uncertain. "I'm not overly curious," he explained in an interview with Nancy Collins for *Vanity Fair* (April 1992). "I've always said I had the most fortunate rearing. No one would've had the courage to design it that way, but it was ideal. No repression from a male father figure, no Oedipal competition."

In about 1945 Nicholson moved with his family from working-class Neptune to a middle-class section of Asbury Park, a bustling resort town on the Jersey shore. While he was growing up, Nicholson loved to play sports, read comic books, and attend matinee showings at the local movie theatre. At about the time that he was ready for high school, the family moved again, to the prosperous seaside town of Spring Lake, where Nicholson attended one of the area's best schools, Manasquan High School. He wrote about sports for the student newspaper and was for a time active in sports himself, but as Paul Attanasio reported in the *Washington Post* (June 14, 1985), he was eventually barred from athletic activities after "trashing" the gymnasium of a rival team, whose members had abused one of his friends. Following that incident he began appearing in student theatrical productions because, as he put it in a conversation with Rita Kempley of the *Washington Post* (August 15, 1990), "all the chicks that I liked were doing plays." As a teenager Nicholson was outgoing and adept at cultivating friendships with his school's most popular students. His own popularity was apparent when, in his senior year at Manasquan, he was voted vice-president of his class as well as "co-class clown" and best actor.

His status as class clown notwithstanding, Nicholson earned good grades and was offered a scholarship to study chemical engineering at the University of Delaware. As Patrick McGilligan reported in the biography *Jack's Life* (1994), however, Nicholson took the advice of Lorraine Nicholson, who urged him to "live life a little" before going to college, and in 1954 he made what was initially intended as a visit to Los Angeles, where June Nicholson had moved. Before long he had made the West Coast his home. In May 1955 he was hired as a mail clerk at MGM, where he eventually became a gofer for the film company's prestigious animation studio. A year later he joined the Players Ring, a small repertory theatre company that served as a training ground for young actors. While continuing to work at MGM during the day, Nicholson apprenticed at the Players Ring in the evenings, working as an assistant on various productions and appearing as a walk-on in Robert Anderson's *Tea and Sympathy*. Nicholson's command of his craft deepened when he began to study acting in 1957 with the innovative Method teacher Jeff Corey. "Acting is life study," Nicholson told an interviewer for *Film Comment* (June 1985), "and Corey's classes got me into looking at life as . . . an artist."

Through Corey, Nicholson met the producer and director Roger Corman, whose low-budget but profitable B movies introduced some of the American cinema's most celebrated artists. Nicholson made his screen debut as the title character in Corman's *The Cry Baby Killer* (1958), about a young man who thinks he has committed a murder, and in 1960 he turned in an amusing portrayal of a masochistic dental patient in Corman's horror-comedy *Little Shop of Horrors*. Soon the young actor was making a living acting in B pictures. He played Buddy in *Too Soon to Love* (1960), which dealt with teenage sex, and had his first starring role in *The Wild Ride* (1960), a Corman-produced movie about a juvenile delinquent named Johnny Varron. In a change of pace from teen-oriented fare, Nicholson appeared next as Weary Reilly in director Irving Lerner's screen version of the James T. Farrell novel *Studs Lonigan* (1960), and in *The Broken Land* (1962), his first western, he was cast as Will Broicous, a gunfighter's law-abiding son.

Nicholson's other films of the early and mid-1960s were, with the exception of the unsuccessful *Ensign Pulver* (1964), low-budget affairs that offered little hope of making a star of the actor. Perhaps as a result, Nicholson, while continuing to act, tried his hand at other areas of filmmaking as well. His first screenwriting credit was a collaboration with Don Devlin on the script of *Thunder Island* (1963), a thriller about a plot to kill the former dictator of a Latin American country. Nicholson wrote and starred in *Flight to Fury* (1966), the story of a group of diamond hunters, and he scripted and co-produced *Ride in the Whirlwind* (1966), an unconventional western. Directed by Corman and written by Nicholson, *The Trip* (1967) dealt with a director of television commercials (Peter Fonda) who experiments with LSD and becomes a refugee from corporate America.

In spite of his varied functions in those films, acting remained Nicholson's chief interest. He made television appearances on *Divorce Court* and *The Andy Griffith Show*, and in the late 1960s he lent his talents to a number of films that exploited themes from the emerging hippie counterculture. In Richard Rush's box-office hit *Hell's Angels on Wheels* (1967), he played Poet, a sensitive gas-station attendant who tags along with the infamous biker gang, and he appeared opposite Bruce Dern and Diane Ladd as a sadistic motorcyclist in *Rebel Rousers* (1967). *Psych-Out* (1968) found Nicholson playing the pony-tailed leader of a Haight-Ashbury rock band, and *Head* (1968), directed by Bob Rafelson from a script he wrote with Nicholson, was a psychedelic film with avant-garde flourishes that attempted to do for the teenybopper band the Monkees what *A Hard Day's Night* had done for the Beatles.

In a part originally intended for Rip Torn, Nicholson at last rose to prominence as George Hanson, a good-natured, dipsomaniacal southern lawyer disappointed in himself and his country, in the quintessential counterculture film *Easy Rider* (1969). When the film's two main characters (played by Dennis Hopper, the film's director, and Peter Fonda, its producer) set off on an ill-fated cross-country motorcycle trip with the fortune they have made by selling drugs, Hanson joins them on their odyssey. For his work in *Easy Rider*, Nicholson won awards for best supporting actor from the New York Film Critics Circle as well as the National Society of Film Critics, and he was nominated for an Academy Award.

While Nicholson had gained recognition with *Easy Rider*, he began to build his reputation as an actor with two films made in the early 1970s, *Five Easy Pieces* (1970) and *Carnal Knowledge* (1971). The former, directed by Bob Rafelson, starred Nicholson as the lost soul Bobby Dupea, who has abandoned his privileged background for the blue-collar life of a Southern California oil rigger. Bobby defies everyone's ideas of what he should be, and the film's existentialist conclusion finds him running even from the new life he has built. *Five Easy Pieces* earned Nicholson his first Oscar nomination for best actor. *Carnal Knowledge*, which was directed by Mike Nichols from Jules Feiffer's screenplay, traces the lives of two friends, played by Nicholson and Art Garfunkel, from their college years to early middle age. Nicholson portrayed the more worldly of the two, the womanizer Jonathan, who fails to find a higher purpose than his own pleasure. Writing in *Cue* (July 3, 1971), William Wolf declared that Nicholson, in the part of Jonathan, was "more brilliant than he [had] ever been." The actor's other movie credits from that period included a brief appearance in *On a Clear Day You Can See Forever* (1970).

Adapted by Nicholson and Jeremy Larner from the latter's novel, *Drive, He Said* (1971) marked Nicholson's debut as a director. Although critics disliked the film's jumbled structure, Nicholson won praise for drawing stellar performances from a cast that included Bruce Dern, as a gung-ho college basketball coach, Robert Towne, as a professor, and Karen Black, as Towne's unfaithful wife. In the same year, Nicholson played the enigmatic lover of a young woman (Tuesday Weld) who travels erratically back and forth through time in the writer-director Henry Jaglom's *A Safe Place*. Bob Rafelson's drama *The King of Marvin Gardens* (1972) found Nicholson in the part of a morose intellectual, a radio disc jockey who fails to discourage his starry-eyed brother (Bruce Dern) from pursuing pipe dreams. Garnering his second Oscar nomination for best actor, Nicholson portrayed signalman first class Billy Buddusky, a raucous navy lifer assigned to escort an eighteen-year-old serviceman (Randy Quaid) to prison, in Hal Ashby's well-received comedy-drama *The Last Detail* (1973).

The cinematic tour de force *Chinatown* (1974), set in Los Angeles in the 1930s, featured Roman Polanski's moody, atmospheric direction, a witty, Academy Award–winning screenplay by Robert Towne, and one of Nicholson's most celebrated performances. The actor played J. J. ("Jake") Gittes, a cynical but principled private detective specializing in adultery cases. After he makes the acquaintance of a mysterious woman (Faye Dunaway) and her wealthy, sinister father (John Huston), Gittes finds himself ever more deeply embroiled in a situation in which, to paraphrase the Huston character, he thinks he knows what is going on—but doesn't. Nicholson's work in *Chinatown* earned him yet another Academy Award nomination for best actor.

The year 1975 was one of the busiest of Nicholson's career. He gave a low-key interpretation of the character David Locke, an alienated American journalist in revolutionary Africa, in Michelangelo Antonioni's *The Passenger*. In Ken Russell's film version of *Tommy*, the rock opera by the influential British band the Who, Nicholson made a brief appearance as a doctor. Directed by Mike Nichols, *The Fortune* was an unsuccessful screwball comedy about two inept lowlifes (Nicholson and Warren Beatty) scheming to part an heiress (Stockard Channing) from her money. In her book *5001 Nights at the Movies* (1991), Pauline Kael called *The Fortune* "a charmless slapstick farce" but praised Nicholson, who she felt "[came] through the best" and "at moments . . . lift[ed] himself single-handed into slapstick like a demented Laurel and Hardy in one."

Also released in 1975 was Milos Forman's screen adaptation of Ken Kesey's best-selling novel *One Flew Over the Cuckoo's Nest*. Nicholson starred as Randle Patrick McMurphy, who is admitted to a mental institution after pretending to be insane. The charismatic McMurphy inspires his withdrawn fellow patients to stand up to the domineering head nurse, played by Louise Fletcher. In 1976, *One Flew Over the Cuckoo's Nest* became the first movie since the 1934 comedy *It Happened One Night* to sweep the top five categories at the Academy Awards ceremonies, winning Oscars for, among other things, best picture and best actor (Nicholson).

The feisty but doomed McMurphy epitomized the rebellious antiheroes Nicholson specialized in playing in the 1970s—volatile characters who refused to conform to institutionalized codes of behavior. Writing in *Esquire* (September 1990), Steve Erickson observed that Nicholson alone among his box-office peers in the 1970s achieved the status of "counterculture movie star." According to Erickson, "[Nicholson's] stardom had more of a mythic dimension than any American actor's since [Marlon] Brando or perhaps Bogart, with both of whom he shared an outlaw's attitude and a contempt for anyone trying to sell him a bill of goods. 'Give me some more advice on the good life,' Nicholson sneers angrily to his oil-rigging partner in *Five Easy Pieces*, 'because it makes me want to puke.' It's a line not dissimilar in tone and cynicism to Bogart's 'I stick my neck out for no one,' or Brando's famous answer, when asked exactly what he's rebelling against, 'What have you got?' In tune with his times, Nicholson created his stardom by cross-circuiting old-fashioned movie chemistry with a rock 'n' roll sensibility."

Despite the ballyhooed pairing of Marlon Brando, cast as a bounty hunter, and Nicholson, playing a horse rustler, director Arthur Penn's *The Missouri Breaks* (1976) was burdened by a murky plot and eccentric acting on the part of Brando. "Only Jack Nicholson comes out of this mess well-nigh unscathed, almost succeeding in turning the nullity handed him by the filmmakers into a living character—a not-unremarkable feat," John Simon wrote in *New York* (May 31, 1976). Nicholson played a left-wing union organizer in *The Last Tycoon* (1976), directed by Elia Kazan from Harold Pinter's adaptation of the F. Scott Fitzgerald novel. He tried his hand at directing again with *Goin' South* (1978), a western comedy that marked the screen debuts of Mary Steenburgen and John Belushi. Although

Leonard Maltin, in his *Movie and Video Guide* (1992), credited Nicholson with having contrived an "amusing" film, Pauline Kael, writing in the *New Yorker* (December 11, 1978), complained that his "fatuous leering performance dominates the movie." "An actor-director who prances about the screen maniacally can easily fool himself into thinking that his film is jumping," Kael wrote; "Nicholson jumps, all right, but the movie is inert."

Based on Stephen King's best-selling horror thriller of the same name, *The Shining* (1980) allowed Nicholson to work with the celebrated director Stanley Kubrick. The actor portrayed Jack Torrance, a frustrated writer who serves as the off-season caretaker of a resort hotel with his wife (Shelley Duvall) and son (Danny Lloyd), who has terrifying psychic visions related to past incidents at the isolated, haunted resort. Torrance eventually loses his mind and goes on a violent rampage in the film, which received mixed reviews but enjoyed enormous success at the box office.

According to Nicholson, it was the eroticism that "tends to underlie everything that is in the story" that drew him to a remake of *The Postman Always Rings Twice*, the 1946 film-noir classic. Nicholson took the part of a drifter who conspires with a young woman (Jessica Lange) to kill her unsuspecting husband. Despite Bob Rafelson's direction and a screenplay by David Mamet that was faithful to James M. Cain's novel, the 1981 remake proved to be a critical and commercial failure. As a favor to his friend Warren Beatty, the film's director and lead actor, Nicholson agreed to play the writer Eugene O'Neill in *Reds* (1981), a sprawling romantic epic set against the backdrop of the Russian Revolution. His performance in the film brought him his second Oscar nomination for best supporting actor.

Nicholson once again played a hero bucking a corrupt system in director Tony Richardson's well-regarded *The Border* (1982), which dealt with the inequities of immigration control on the Texas-Mexico border. "Nicholson has played disaffected, cynical characters before," David Ansen wrote in *Newsweek* (February 1, 1982), "but as Charlie Smith, a border-patrol guard in El Paso, Texas, he hits new notes, creating a character whose complexities may in fact be greater than the script intended." A tearjerker with comic flourishes, *Terms of Endearment* (1983), which James L. Brooks directed from his own adaptation of Larry McMurtry's novel, dealt with the relationship between an overbearing mother (Shirley MacLaine) and her headstrong daughter (Debra Winger) over a period of three decades. Nicholson proved to be a scene-stealer as Garrett Breedlove, a lascivious, middle-aged former astronaut who woos the staid Aurora Greenway (MacLaine). A resounding commercial and critical success, *Terms of Endearment* cleaned up at the 1984 Academy Awards ceremonies, and Nicholson received the Oscar for best supporting actor.

John Huston's black comedy *Prizzi's Honor* (1985) starred Nicholson as Charley Partanna, an effective if slow-witted hit man for the Prizzi crime family who falls in love with a professional assassin (Kathleen Turner). His impersonation of Partanna brought Nicholson another best-actor nomination while his longtime real-life romantic partner Angelica Huston, the daughter of John Huston, won the Oscar for best supporting actress, for her portrayal of Maerose, a conniving Prizzi family member with romantic designs on Charley. Critics were less kind to *Heartburn* (1986), directed by Mike Nichols from the Nora Ephron novel about a writer (Meryl Streep) forced to confront the fact that her husband, a Washington political columnist (Nicholson), is a philanderer. A box-office disappointment, *Heartburn* suffered from a weak story "about two people who are only marginally interesting," as Roger Ebert noted in his *Video Companion* (1993). "Here is the story of two people with no chemistry played by two actors with great chemistry," Ebert declared. "The only way they can get into character is to play against the very things we like them for."

Nicholson received his first opportunity since *The Shining* to embody pure evil when he joined the cast of George Miller's *The Witches of Eastwick* (1987), loosely based on the John Updike novel. He tackled the role of Daryl Van Horne—the devil—who is conjured up by three women (Cher, Susan Sarandon, and Michelle Pfeiffer) yearning for the ideal man in a placid New England village. "As 'your average horny little devil,' [Nicholson] is so repulsive he's funny," Pauline Kael wrote in the *New Yorker* (June 29, 1987), "and he has invented some furiously demented slapstick; he's an inspired buffoon." Appearing in an unbilled cameo, Nicholson played a network news anchor in *Broadcast News* (1987), James L. Brooks's romantic comedy about the television news industry. Hector Babenco's *Ironweed* (1987), which William Kennedy adapted from his own Pulitzer Prize–winning novel about Depression-era hoboes in Albany, New York, starred Nicholson as the guilt-ridden Francis Phelan, a boozy street person haunted by his past, and Meryl Streep as Helen, his alcoholic companion. Although critics faulted Babenco's film for its somberness and overly deliberate pace, Leonard Maltin, in his *Movie and Video Guide*, praised Nicholson and Streep for delivering "rich performances" that "are a privilege to watch."

The actor turned in yet another seriocomic exploration of undiluted wickedness in *Batman* (1989), Tim Burton's dark, expressionistic screen version of the adventures of the "caped crusader." Nicholson stole the show as the Joker, the disturbed nemesis of the eponymous comic-book hero (Michael Keaton). With its extravagant special effects and stylish set designs, *Batman* became one of the cinema's top moneymakers of all time, with Nicholson earning an estimated sixty million dollars from his percentage of the gross and merchandise licensing fees alone (his fee for appearing in the film was six million dollars). Most critics agreed with Hal Hinson, who wrote in the *Washington Post* (June 23, 1989) that "Nicholson's maniacal Joker is the movie's engine." The Joker "takes riotous pleasure in his evil-doing," Hinson said, and "Nicholson, too, seems to be having a blast," bringing "a sense of dangerous hilarity to the character."

As Brian D. Johnson noted in *MacLean's* (August 20, 1990), Nicholson's *The Two Jakes* (1990) was "the most belated sequel in the history of Hollywood." He might have added that it was one of the most troubled. With Robert Towne directing from his own script, the long-awaited follow-up to *Chinatown* had gone before the cameras in 1985 with Nicholson and Robert Evans, who had produced *Chinatown*, cast in the title roles. The production closed down, however, when Towne fired Evans. Longstanding friendships were strained, and the film languished until 1989, when Nicholson took over as director. *The Two Jakes* was set in Los Angeles in 1948, eleven years after the events in *Chinatown*. Prosperous but emotionally scarred by the past, Jake Gittes (Nicholson) is drawn into an investigation of shady real-estate developer Jake Berman (Harvey Keitel) and Berman's unfaithful wife (Meg Tilly). A disappointment at the box office, Nicholson's film was thought by most critics to be ponderous, and it was hampered by a plot that proved to be nearly impossible to follow.

Even less successful was *Man Trouble* (1992), in which Nicholson was cast as a low-brow, womanizing dog trainer trying to seduce an opera singer (Ellen Barkin). That movie reunited the actor with the creative team behind *Five Easy Pieces*, the director Bob Rafelson and the screenwriter Carole Eastman, but their attempt to make a contemporary screwball comedy misfired. A reviewer for *Time* (July 27, 1992) pronounced *Man Trouble* "an enervated, despondent entertainment," and Leah Rozen, writing in *People* (August 3, 1992), called it a "dismal black comedy" that is "painful to sit through."

Nicholson rebounded with his work in Rob Reiner's courtroom drama *A Few Good Men* (1992), earning a best-supporting-actor Oscar nomination for his portrayal of Colonel Nathan Jessep, the snarling commander of a military base who tangles with a navy attorney (Tom Cruise). Directed by Danny DeVito from a David Mamet screenplay, *Hoffa* (1992) chronicled the rise of Jimmy Hoffa, the legendary Teamster boss (Nicholson). DeVito's film was criticized for its adulatory depiction of Hoffa, and while some reviewers hailed Nicholson's work in the film, others thought that he had failed to dig below the character's surface. David Sterritt of the *Christian Science Monitor* (December 28, 1992) wrote, "This is one of [Nicholson's] more imitative performances, . . . growing less from his own fertile imagination than from a desire to mimic Hoffa's actual appearance, manner, and voice." Expressing a different view, Vincent Canby declared in the *New York Times* (December 11, 1992) that Nicholson had delivered "a gigantic powerhouse of a performance" and applauded him for relying on his "crafty intelligence and conviction," rather than on the artifice of make-up and vocal tricks, to evoke Hoffa. In his most recent film, Mike Nichols's *Wolf* (1994), Nicholson appeared as a mild-mannered New York book editor who is a werewolf by night. While the film as a whole received mixed reviews, the actor gave what Janet Maslin of the *New York Times* (June 17, 1994) called "one of his subtlest performances in recent years."

Subtlety, or a lack of apparent effort, is Nicholson's goal in a performance. "I've always thought that the best work you can do as an actor is when the audience looks out and says, 'Oh, I could do that,'" Nicholson explained in 1985, during his conversation with Paul Attanasio for the *Washington Post*. On the subject of growing older in his profession, he said, "An actor's only got his life to offer. I cannot play an eighteen-year-old person now. I'm very different than I was at eighteen, and that's what I have to offer as a kind of ongoing dynamic: What do I see now? What do I feel now?"

Jack Nicholson stands approximately five feet, nine inches tall. Over the years a great many column inches in newspapers and magazines have been devoted to descriptions of his facial features, particularly his "killer" smile and his eyebrows, which Paul Attanasio termed Nicholson's "weapons . . . , marvelous protean creatures, sometimes bullwhips cracking from the bridge of his nose, sometimes the horizontal slits of sinister withdrawal." In 1991 Nicholson coproduced the as-yet-unreleased film *Blue Champagne*, whose cast includes Rebecca Broussard, the mother of Nicholson's children Lorraine and Raymond, and Jennifer Nicholson, the actor's daughter from his marriage to Sandra Knight, which ended in divorce in 1968. While his hedonistic escapades have provided fodder for the tabloids, Nicholson is regarded by by his friends as loyal and dependable. The actor maintains two homes near Aspen, Colorado as well as a primary hilltop residence in Beverly Hills, California, which houses his large collection of modern art. In 1994 he received the Am Film Institute's prestigious Life Achievement Award. An avid sports fan, Nicholson is a fixture at Los Angeles Lakers basketball games, where he cheers noisily from courtside.

Selected Biographical References: Am Film 15:20+ F '90 pors; Chicago Tribune XIII p9+ Je 16 '85 pors, XIII p4+ Ag 12 '90 pors; Esquire 44:164+ S '90 pors; GQ 60:128+ Ja '90 pors; Guardian Weekend p6+ D 19 '92 pors; MacLean's 103:36+ Ag 20 '90 pors; N Y Newsday p4+ O '74 pors; N Y Times Mag p28+ S 10 '89 pors; People 24:51+ Jl 8 '85 pors; Premiere 4:58+ S '90 pors; TV Guide 33:20+ Ag 11 '90 pors; Vanity Fair 49:60+ Ag '86 pors, 55:161+ Ap '92 pors; Washington Post C p1+ Je 14 '85 pors, C p1+ Ag 15 '90 pors; McGilligan, Patrick. Jack's Life: A Biography of Jack Nicholson (1994)

W.W. Norton/*Rex Features*

O'Brian, Patrick

1914– Irish writer. Address: c/o W. W. Norton & Co., 500 Fifth Ave., New York, NY 10110

In January 1991 Richard Snow, the editor of *American Heritage* magazine, declared in a front-page essay in the *New York Times Book Review* (January 6, 1991) that an obscure series of books set during the Napoleonic Wars comprised "the best historical novels ever written." Patrick O'Brian, the Irish-born author of the Aubrey/Maturin novels, as the series is called, had been publishing books in England since 1950, but his work had never found a secure foothold in the United States. In the fall of 1990, however, the publishing house W. W. Norton brought out number twelve in the series, *The Letter of Marque*, and began reissuing the previous volumes in paperback, starting with the first, *Master and Commander*. Other favorable reviews and word-of-mouth acclaim followed Snow's encomium, and by the spring of 1993, Norton had sold four hundred thousand copies of O'Brian's books.

Master and Commander introduced readers to Captain Jack Aubrey of Lord Nelson's navy, England's representative in its battles with France and Napoleon. Aubrey is ungraceful, uncultured, and always in debt, but his skill in commanding warships and the men who sail and fight on them has made him feared among the French. His friend and alter ego, Stephen Maturin, serves as the ship's surgeon, but he is also a linguist, a naturalist, and an occasional intelligence agent—three professions he has in common with his creator. The portrait of Aubrey and Maturin's relationship provides a window onto early nineteenth-century life that has led more than one critic to compare O'Brian with another acute observer of that period, Jane Austen. (In fact he is an admirer of Austen and supplied the introduction to a new edition of her 1814 novel, *Mansfield Park*.) John Bayley analyzed O'Brian's technique in a retrospective evaluation of the series for the *New York Review of Books* (November 7, 1991): "His most time-honored ploy is the two-man partnership, the accidental coming together of a dissimilar pair—Don Quixote and Sancho Panza, Holmes and Watson . . . who from then on are indissolubly wedded in terms of the reader's expectations and the novels' success." O'Brian's two protagonists have very different talents, styles, and goals, and the differences between them are explored to entertaining, but always believable, results.

Patrick O'Brian was born in 1914 in Ireland. His mother died when he was very young, and shortly after the end of World War I, he was sent to live with relatives in the west of Ireland and then with family friends in England. Prevented from attending school by a persistent lung illness, he was privately tutored, a circumstance that contributed to, as he has put it, "a very lonely childhood." His illness did, however, bring him two lasting companions: books and the sea. Enforced rest turned him into an avid reader of all kinds of literature. During periods when he was stronger, his physicians recommended sea air for his health, and O'Brian learned to "hand, reef, and steer" on an old merchantman belonging to a friend's cousin. He instinctively turned to writing, he said in an autobiographical essay, adding, "It had never occurred to me to do anything else."

A recurrence of his illness kept O'Brian out of active service during World War II. According to Mark Horowitz's profile of the writer in the *New York Times Magazine* (May 16, 1993), he instead drove ambulances in London during the Blitz and served in an intelligence unit with ties to the French Resistance. After the war he turned down an embassy post and moved to Wales, where he produced his first volume of short stories, *The Last Pool and Other Stories* (1950). Looking for a warmer climate, he then moved again, to what he has termed a "largely medieval" fishing village in the south of France, and with the money he earned from the book of short stories and an anthology he had edited (*A Book of Voyages*), he was able to install running water and electricity in his house. Money was scarce during this period of his life, but O'Brian has recalled being "upon the whole extraordinarily happy."

O'Brian's first published novel, *Three Bear Witness*, appeared in 1952. A love story with a dark ending, the novel, which is set in the Welsh mountains where he had lived, was critically acclaimed, particularly in the United States (the American edition was entitled *Testimonies*). Among its more enthusiastic admirers was Delmore Schwartz, who praised its "lyric eloquence." His second novel, *The Catalans* (1953), received mixed reviews. American critics were especially unimpressed. For example, writing in the *New Yorker* (October 24, 1953), Brendan Gill described the book as "a short novel in which everything is always just slightly out of whack" and declared, "O'Brian is clever by fits and starts and appears easily winded. We keep feeling that we could accommodate ourselves to his gait if he would only settle down to one, but he never does." O'Brian's next two books, *The Road to Samarcand* (1954) and *The Walker and Other Stories* (1955; subsequently published as *Lying in the Sun and Other Stories*), met with a similar fate.

The first of O'Brian's works to reflect his familiarity with the sea was his novel *The Golden Ocean* (1956), the story, based on naval history, of a young, inexperienced midshipman. This book, which was intended more for children than for adults, did not attract much attention, but O'Brian has claimed that he penned it largely for fun. "I wrote the tale in little more than a month, laughing most of the time," he has said. Two other novels, *The Unknown Shore* and *Richard Temple*, published in 1959 and 1962, respectively, also went virtually unnoticed.

In the late 1960s an editor at the American publishing firm Lippincott suggested to O'Brian that he write an adult book about the sea. The result was *Master and Commander* (1969), the first novel in what would be (to date) a seventeen-book series featuring Jack Aubrey and Stephen Maturin. The story is set in April 1800, when England is at war with France. Aubrey, newly made a captain, persuades his acquaintance Maturin to be the doctor on board his sloop, the *Sophie*. Stephen knows nothing of naval matters, which allows O'Brian to supply the reader with nautical information through explanations given to the doctor by various members of the *Sophie*'s crew. Aubrey's men win an unlikely victory against the crew of a battleship twice the size of the *Sophie*, but they are later forced to surrender when a squadron takes them by surprise.

Reviewing *Master and Commander*, Martin Levin reported in the *New York Times Book Review* (December 14, 1969) that O'Brian had "recreated with delightful subtlety the flavor of life aboard a midget British man-of-war plying the western Mediterranean in the year 1800. . . . Even for a reader not especially interested in matters nautical, the author's easy command of the philosophical, political, sensual, and social temper of the times flavors a rich entertainment." Many critics compared O'Brian, favorably and unfavorably, with C. S. Forester, the author of the popular series of novels chronicling the adventures of the fictional naval hero Horatio Hornblower, which are also set in the early nineteenth century. "Dashing, well-timbered, pickled in the period, and with strong human tensions and cross-currents, this is probably the best of many good novels about Nelson's navy since the loss of C. S. Forester," Benedict Nightingale maintained in the London *Observer* (January 18, 1970). "Certainly Aubrey, with his hangovers and impulses the extrovert antithesis of Hornblower, is a hero one hopes to hear more of."

American sales of *Master and Commander* were sluggish, but Collins, O'Brian's British publisher, had more success. The series continued in 1972 with the release of *Post Captain*, in which Aubrey and Maturin not only take part in naval battles that correspond to the historical record but also engage in skirmishes with creditors and eligible women back on land. The critical response in the United States was cool. The book was "overwritten for so little plot, which consists mainly of adventures at sea and the friends' feuding over their rather tedious women," a writer for *Publishers Weekly* (July 17, 1972) complained. A comparable reception greeted *H. M. S. Surprise* (1973). O'Brian spent the next three years researching and writing a biography of the artist Pablo Picasso, whom he claimed in his autobiographical essay to have known "moderately well." John Raymond assessed *Pablo Ruiz Picasso* for the London *Sunday Times* (September 19, 1976): "In a positive, original, diverting, and highly effective manner, O'Brian succeeds by the apparently simple formula of evoking the man in all his manifest vitality and contradiction and physically describing the paintings."

After two more Aubrey/Maturin novels, *The Mauritius Command* (1977) and *Desolation Island* (1978), the series was dropped by its American publisher. In England, however, O'Brian was beginning to receive more recognition than is usually afforded a writer of naval adventures. Such noted novelists as Iris Murdoch and A. S. Byatt praised the Aubrey/Maturin series, and T. J. Binyon, in a glowing article for the *Times Literary Supplement* (June 24, 1977), declared, "Taken together, the novels are a brilliant achievement. They display staggering erudition on almost all aspects of early nineteenth-century life, with impeccable period detail ranging from the correct material to grind a telescope lens . . . to the subtle points of a frigate's rigging . . . and at the same time work superlatively well as novels." Aubrey and Maturin fight in the War of 1812 at sea and on land in *Fortune of War* (1979), which was followed by *The Surgeon's Mate* (1980), *The Ionian Mission* (1981), *Treason's Harbor* (1983), and *The Far Side of the World* (1984).

The Reverse of the Medal (1986) was not markedly different from its predecessors, except that it was read in 1989 by Starling Lawrence, an American editor at W. W. Norton, partly at the urging of a cousin. Despite O'Brian's dismal sales history in the United States, Lawrence urged Norton to take a risk and release its own editions of the author's works. ("One of the nice things about working at a place like Norton," the editor told Mark Horowitz, "is that you get enough rope to hang yourself with.") Norton published *The Letter of Marque* in 1990 and made plans to reissue the previous eleven volumes in the series in new paperback editions.

Still, the Aubrey/Maturin novels seemed to be headed for obscurity for the second time until their rescue by Richard Snow's article "An Author I'd Walk the Plank For." According to Snow, "Patrick O'Brian presents the lost arcana of that hard-pressed, cruel, courageous world with an immediacy that makes its workings both comprehensible and fascinating. All the marine hardware is in place and functioning; the battles are stirring without being romanticized (this author *never* romanticizes); the portrayal of life aboard a sailing ship is vivid and authoritative. . . . On every page Mr. O'Brian reminds us with subtle artistry of the most important of all historical lessons: that times change but people don't, that the griefs and follies and victories of the men and women who were here before us are in fact the maps of our own lives." John Bayley's overview in the *New York Review of Books* pointed to one characteristic that distinguishes the Aubrey/Maturin novels from those of the "naval-romantic genre": O'Brian's detailed description of the sea as an ecosystem as seen through the eyes of Stephen Maturin, a fervent naturalist. Bayley stated flatly that "no other writer, not even Herman Melville, has described the whale or the wandering albatross with O'Brian's studious and yet lyrical accuracy."

More books and rave reviews followed. Of *The Thirteen-Gun Salute* (1991), Thomas Flanagan, himself a historical novelist of considerable distinction, wrote in the *New York Times Book Review* (August 4, 1991): "The plot . . . concerns a mission by Aubrey and Maturin to the South China Seas to thwart Bonaparte's agents. But Mr. O'Brian is in no particular hurry to get them there. . . . These eccentric, improbable novels seem to have been written by Patrick O'Brian to please himself in the first instance, and thereafter to please those readers who may share his delight in precision of language, odd lands and colors, a humane respect for such old-fashioned sentiments as friendship and honor." *The Nutmeg of Consolation*, also published in 1991, was followed by *The Truelove* (1992), which prompted Anthony Bailey to claim in the *New York Times Book Review* (May 31, 1992) that O'Brian is "one of the best storytellers afloat, whose chosen period is the great age of fighting sail but whose works have none of ye olde creaks and groans of period fiction."

Deluged by letters from delighted readers, Starling Lawrence told Maria Simson of *Publishers Weekly* (October 26, 1992), "I've never received mail such as we've had on O'Brian." In November 1993 Patrick O'Brian visited the United States for the first time in twenty years, on a publicity tour for the sixteenth Aubrey/Maturin book, *The Wine-Dark Sea* (1993). By that time W. W. Norton had produced a shelfful of uniformly designed paperbacks. Soon *People* (November 8, 1993) was referring to the series as a "cult hit." The publisher was quick to recognize the special nature of O'Brian's readership: once hooked, his fans wanted not just more books but more information about Aubrey and Maturin's world. It was thus that the *Patrick O'Brian Newsletter*, which provides, among other things, definitions of nautical terms and illustrations of frigates as well as information on upcoming titles, was launched.

In *The Wine-Dark Sea*, as in the previous works chronicling the adventures of Aubrey and Maturin, O'Brian used humorous dialogue to illustrate the contrast between the two men's world views. For example, when Maturin expresses a naturalist's desire to see the ice south of Cape Horn, O'Brian wrote the following exchange, beginning with Aubrey's response to his friend's request: "'With all due respect, Stephen, I must tell you that I utterly decline to go anywhere near any ice whatsoever, however thin, however deeply laden with seals, great auks, or other wonders of the deep. I hate and despise ice.' 'My dear,' said Stephen, pouring him another glass of wine, 'how well a graceful timidity does become you.'" *The Wine-Dark Sea* received many positive notices, although the place of the series in literature was questioned by some reviewers of the book. In the *Chicago Tribune* (December 19, 1993), Patricia Reardon maintained that "all [the novels] are at the same very high, but not quite highest, level of literary quality." Elliott Abrams expressed a somewhat less favorable opinion in the *National Review* (January 24, 1994), saying, "How anyone can think these stories to be fiction of the very first rank remains inexplicable." He nonetheless conceded that "taken on their own terms, O'Brian's books are marvelous novels."

In 1993 David R. Godine published the American edition of O'Brian's *Joseph Banks: A Life*, a biography of the eighteenth-century English naturalist who collected thousands of specimens of exotic plants and animals on his voyages to Tahiti, New Zealand, Australia and New Guinea. Linda Colley observed in the *New York Times Book Review* (March 28, 1993), "O'Brian documents these solid achievements sympathetically. But out of his own nautical element, his expertise sometimes wavers. Nor does the biographer succeed in fully explaining Banks as an individual." In *Natural History* (May 1993), Ghillean T. Prance was more approving, calling the work a "most readable biography" and "a rich portrait." A collection of O'Brian's short stories, many of them previously published, was released by Norton in 1994 under the title *The Rendezvous and Other Stories*. A reviewer for *Publishers Weekly* (July 11, 1994) judged, "These twenty-seven tales, many of which date back to the 1950s and the dawn of O'Brian's career, often lack narrative drive and any semblance of character development. . . . On the plus side, O'Brian's prose is often beautiful and always impeccably crafted, and his eye for detail in the wild gives a number of the stories considerable power and rural charm."

The seventeenth—and most recent—Aubrey/Maturin novel, *The Commodore*, was published in April 1995. The beginning of that novel finds the protagonists at home in England after having unsuccessfully supported a revolution in Peru. Before long, however, they are back at sea, one of their missions being to intercept ships engaged in the slave trade. Evaluating the novel for the *New York Times Book Review* (April 30, 1995),

Joel White declared, "There is a great deal to be said for reading Mr. O'Brian's novels in proper order, but if you cannot face the thought of a seventeen-novel excursion, read *The Commodore* as a freestanding event. You will soon find yourself at the local library asking for No. 1, *Master and Commander*, then *Post Captain* and *H.M.S. Surprise*. They're worth the trip."

Besides having produced biographies, short stories, and "a single five-thousand-page book," as Patricia Reardon described the Aubrey/Maturin series, O'Brian has found time to write poetry, book reviews, and, in 1974, a nonfiction book on Nelson's navy entitled *Men-of-War*. For that book, as well as for his historical fiction, O'Brian researched original sources, including ships' logs, public records, memoirs, correspondence of officers and sailors, and contemporary descriptions of battles. Aided by his fluency in French, Catalan, Spanish, and Italian, he has translated thirty-one books into English, including several works by the French feminist writer Simone de Beauvoir. Talking to Mark Horowitz about his writing, O'Brian said, "When you're taking a fence on a horse, you don't think much; your body does all the thinking, and you're over or you're not over. It's much the same when you are doing a tricky thing with a pen. There are times when I'm writing very, very fast. It's very like taking a hedge, or doing some rather dangerous thing that has to be done just so or not at all. It's not something you can dwell upon." His first drafts are written in longhand and are seen only by Mary O'Brian, his wife of more than fifty years. She types the final versions, and almost every book O'Brian has written is dedicated to her.

Patrick O'Brian, who was described by Malcolm Jones Jr. in *Newsweek* (November 15, 1993) as having a "lean, lined face framing a boy's keen eyes," lives quietly with his wife in the south of France in a small house with a view of the sea. He is very protective of his privacy and has often objected to interviewers' routine questions on the grounds that they are too personal. His preferred authors are Austen and Samuel Richardson, and he has numbered Marcel Proust among the few modern writers he has enjoyed reading.

Selected Biographical References: N Y Times Bk R p1+ Ja 6 '91; New York Times Mag B p31+ My 16 '93 pors; Cunningham, A. E., ed. Patrick O'Brian: Critical Essays and a Bibliography (1994)

O'Brien, Tim

Oct. 1, 1946–Writer; journalist. Address: c/o Houghton Mifflin, 215 Park Ave. South, 10th Floor, New York, NY 10003

"I find most writers came to writing because they wanted to write," the award-winning novelist and short-story writer Tim O'Brien told Wayne Warga of the *Los Angeles Times* (November 25, 1979). "I had never seriously considered writing as an occupation—but then I found I had different reasons for doing it. I came to it not to be a writer but because I had something substantive to say, I had strong feelings." For O'Brien, a Vietnam veteran, the war and its enduring personal legacy have provided enough material to fill six books, among which are *Going After Cacciato*, *The Things They Carried*, and *In the Lake of the Woods*.

Known for his spare, Hemingwayesque prose and his innovative literary forms, which range from straight reporting to dreamlike imaginings and stories within stories, O'Brien is widely considered to be one of the best American writers of his generation. "My life is storytelling," he admitted in an interview with D. J. R. Bruckner of the *New York Times* (April 3, 1990). "I believe in stories, in their incredible power to keep people alive, to keep the living alive, and the dead. And if I have started now to play with the stories, inside the stories themselves, well, that's what people do all the time. Storytelling is the essential human activity. The harder the situation, the more essential it is. In Vietnam men were constantly telling one another

Jerry Bauer

stories about the war. Our unit lost a lot of guys around My Lai, but the stories they told stay around after them. I would be mad not to tell the stories I know."

William Timothy O'Brien was born on October 1, 1946 in Austin, Minnesota, the son of William Timothy O'Brien, an insurance salesman, and Ava

Eleanor (Schultz) O'Brien, a schoolteacher. Both parents had served in the United States Navy during World War II. Tim O'Brien lived in Austin until the age of nine, when he moved with his family to Worthington, Minnesota, three hundred miles away. As a student at Macalester College, in St. Paul, Minnesota, he developed a reputation as an activist for social justice and improved education. He campaigned for the establishment of dorm libraries, the reform of the grading system, and, for twenty-one-year-olds, the privilege of bringing alcoholic beverages into the dorms; on behalf of female students, he advocated abolishing curfews and granting the privacy of closed doors when male guests visited during "open-house hours." Partly as a result of these efforts, he was elected student-body president in his senior year.

In 1968, a month after graduating summa cum laude from Macalester with a B.A. degree in political science, O'Brien, who had been offered a full scholarship to pursue a graduate degree at Harvard University, received his draft notice to fight in a war he had protested. He recalled his reaction to being drafted in his conversation with D. J. R. Bruckner: "I went to my room in the basement and started pounding the typewriter. I did it all summer. It was the most terrible summer of my life, worse than being in the war. My conscience kept telling me not to go, but my whole upbringing told me I had to. That horrible summer made me a writer." O'Brien had initially intended to seek refuge in Canada, but he changed his mind, as he explained in an interview with Jon Elsen for the *New York Times Book Review* (October 9, 1994): "I went to the war purely to be loved, not to be rejected by my hometown and family and friends, not to be thought of as a coward and a sissy." Ironically, he came to believe that his decision not to dodge the draft was the result of a lack of another kind of courage. "I was a coward. I went to Vietnam," he concluded in a highly introspective article he wrote for the *New York Times Magazine* (October 2, 1994).

In February 1969 O'Brien arrived in Quang Ngai Province as a private first class with Alpha Company, in the Fifth Battalion of the Forty-sixth Infantry, 198th Infantry Brigade. His unit's area of patrol included the village of My Lai, in the larger village of Son My. O'Brien has recalled wondering, at first, why the villagers were so hostile to the Americans. In a few months he, along with the rest of the world, learned of the massacre that had taken place in My Lai on the morning of March 16, 1968. Hundreds of women, children, infants, old men, and other civilians, in addition to virtually all the animals within firing range, were gunned down by the approximately 115 American soldiers of Charlie Company, commanded by First Lieutenant William L. Calley. The incident was successfully hidden from the American public for over a year, and it was not until the autumn of 1969 that the army was forced to investigate after a series of letters from a former soldier were sent to government officials. The death toll was officially estimated by the army to have reached nearly 350; a memorial in Son My commemorates over five hundred fatalities—virtually the entire hamlet of My Lai. The few villagers who survived the slaughter did so only because they were the first victims to be shoved into an irrigation ditch, where much of the killing took place, and the bodies subsequently piled on top of them served as a shield against the hail of bullets. The only punishment doled out to any of the handful of men who were court-martialed by the United States Army was four and a half months in prison for Calley, whose original sentence, life at hard labor, was repeatedly appealed and reduced.

O'Brien, who witnessed the death or maiming of friends in battle, has said that he did not to his knowledge kill anyone, allowing for the possibility that enemy soldiers may have died from one of his bullets fired blindly into the trees. ("In a war without aim, you tend not to aim," he has written.) He nevertheless has suffered from an ineradicable sense of guilt and responsibility. In his *New York Times Magazine* piece, he revealed that he was familiar with the feelings of anger harbored by the participants in the My Lai massacre. "This is not to justify what occurred here," he emphasized. "Justifications are empty and outrageous. Rather, it's to say that I more or less understand . . . how it happened, the wickedness that soaks into your blood and heats up and starts to sizzle. I know the boil that precedes butchery. At the same time, however, the men in Alpha Company did not commit murder. We did not turn our machine guns on civilians; we did not cross that conspicuous line between rage and homicide." Unlike many of his comrades, O'Brien regarded antiwar protesters back home as potential saviors rather than traitors. "I was glad for them," he told John Blades, who interviewed him for the *Chicago Tribune* (April 27, 1990), "because I didn't see much hope of winning the damn war. I was rooting for [Jane Fonda] or [Eugene] McCarthy or somebody to get the war over with and get me home." In March 1970 O'Brien was discharged from the army with the rank of sergeant. During his tour of duty in Vietnam, he had been awarded a Purple Heart for action in which he had sustained a superficial shrapnel wound.

Until recently, O'Brien consistently told interviewers that he had suffered no lasting psychological damage and had had no difficulty readjusting to civilian life upon his return to the United States. "It was land in Seattle—they process you out of the army in about two hours—say the pledge of allegiance, take off your uniform in a toilet, and fly to Minnesota," he recalled in an interview with Michael Coffey for *Publishers Weekly* (February 16, 1990). "It was fast and effortless, just like gliding out of a nightmare." In the fall of 1970, O'Brien enrolled at Harvard as a graduate student in government. "I think I thought I might become the next Henry Kissinger," he told Bruckner. After two summer internships at the *Washington Post*, he took a leave of absence from Harvard during the 1973–74 academic year to report on national affairs for that newspaper. Returning to Harvard in 1974, he continued working on his dissertation, "Case Studies in American Military Interventions," which he never finished. At night he wrote essays about his war experiences, having already published his first piece, in *Playboy*, while he was still stationed in Vietnam. (A novel he had written as an undergraduate during a summer vacation in Czechoslovakia remains unpublished.)

"There came a point when I had to decide where I was going to devote my time, and I decided that I wanted to be a writer and not a scholar," O'Brien told Michael Coffey, adding, "I'm glad I didn't pursue it." He dropped out of Harvard in 1976, after publishing two books, in order to write full-time. He explained his decision to abandon his academic career in an interview with Maria Lenhart of the *Christian Science Monitor* (August 13, 1979), in which he said, "I didn't have the answers to write definitive essays about the war. I'm not a polemicist, and I found the issues very complex and complicated. Also, I don't think the hellishness of war can be communicated through universal statements and abstractions." Another reason may have been his unsatisfying journalistic experience. As he told Wayne Warga, "I didn't like covering politics. You're forced to report platitudes, or what I call 'cover your ass statements.' I figured I can do better dialogue than that."

O'Brien's first book, a war memoir published in 1973, was a collection of essays, some of which had previously appeared in newspapers and magazines. Praised for its realism and honesty, *If I Die in a Combat Zone, Box Me Up and Ship Me Home* covered the author's basic training, combat duty, and last few months in Vietnam, which he spent as a typist behind a desk. "In a style which is lucid, relaxed, razor-sharp, and consciously dispassionate, the wasteland of Vietnam unreels before us," Chris Waters wrote in the *New Statesman* (January 4, 1974). "Without fuss or rhetoric [O'Brien] registers the arbitrary deaths and futile suffering of soldiers and citizens alike, and his descriptions are more powerful because of their reserve." Its respectable notices notwithstanding, the author has since dismissed *If I Die* as "trash," even after he excised what he has called its "purple prose" for the revised edition published in 1979.

Several critics thought that O'Brien's second book, the novel *Northern Lights* (1975), was reminiscent of Ernest Hemingway's *The Sun Also Rises*. A story of two brothers who lose their way in a blizzard while skiing, the narrative presents a classic role reversal as the skills of the purportedly courageous Vietnam veteran turn out to be less useful for surviving in the wilderness than those of his ostensibly cowardly brother who stayed home during the war. Evaluating the novel for the *New York Review of Books* (November 13, 1975), Roger Sale wrote, "The terms of potential combat dissipate into fleeting attempts to know what it means to be brothers facing annihilation. Freed from having to write much dialogue, O'Brien is free of Hemingway for more than a hundred pages, and the result is splendid clarity that is never nature writing, never heroics, never conscious understatement." Writing in the *New Republic* (February 7, 1976), Rosellen Brown noted that "in the end, [the brothers] survive moments of terror and of radiant transcendence (rendered by O'Brien with a kind of open-heartedness, pitched higher than Hemingway's but respectful of the same integrities of nature, in an amplitude of style that refuses to be self-consciously ironic or self-denigrating)."

The novel *Going After Cacciato* (1978), for which O'Brien received a National Book Award (which had been widely expected to go to his good friend John Irving, for *The World According to Garp*, or to John Cheever, for the collection *The Stories of John Cheever*), was considered by most critics to be a prime example of the South American literary form known as magical realism. Based partly on the author's own remembered daydreams of desertion, the novel follows the nocturnal reveries of Paul Berlin, a soldier on guard duty in Vietnam, who fantasizes that he and his squad follow Cacciato (Italian for the hunted, the pursued), a deserter, all the way to Paris, where they decide to capture him and return with him to Vietnam.

Many reviewers of *Going After Cacciato* compared O'Brien to Joseph Heller and, again, to Hemingway. "I read [Heller's] *Catch-22* in high school, but it didn't make any great literary impression on me," the author told Lenhart. "The comparison to Hemingway is more accurate—and terribly flattering—but I think overemphasized. All writers learn from other writers, but then learn to be themselves. Even Hemingway was once accused of imitating [Daniel] Defoe—I felt better when I learned that." After the novel was published, O'Brien was deluged with emotional letters and telephone calls from other Vietnam veterans. "It has been a bittersweet experience," he told Lenhart. "The letters mean a lot because I had wanted to touch on something that was common to us all. But I found myself involved in so many hour-long phone calls from shattered guys that it was like reliving the war all over again."

In an attempt to distance himself from the Vietnam era, O'Brien focused on the transformation of a 1960s peace activist into a 1990s uranium speculator (the story opens in 1995) in his next novel, *The Nuclear Age* (1985). "I know in my own experience," he told Maria Lenhart, "that I'm a total drop-out compared to how I was ten years ago when there were issues we all cared so much about—peace, poverty, civil rights. This book is confronting my own apathy." Generally deemed less successful than his previous books, *The Nuclear Age* was faulted by Michiko Kakutani of the *New York Times* (September 28, 1985) for presenting "a didactic pastiche of R. D. Laing and Jonathan Schell, bereft of originality or persuasive passion." Although Kakutani found the jokes to be "lame" and the characters to be little more than "pasteboard caricatures," other critics judged the novel to be entertaining, and Edith Milton of the *Boston Review* (November 1985) called it "mournfully persuasive, graceful, funny, and sane."

Returning to the literary landscape of his previous works, O'Brien produced one of his most highly acclaimed books in 1990. Taking its title from a short story that garnered O'Brien a National Magazine Award when it appeared in *Esquire* in 1987, *The Things They Carried* earned its author nominations for the Pulitzer Prize and the National Book Critics Circle Award and won him the *Chicago Tribune* Heartland Prize, the Melcher Book Award, and France's prestigious Prix du Meilleur Livre Etranger. Narrated by a character named Tim O'Brien, *The Things They Carried*, a compilation of interrelated vignettes (some previously published as short stories), is primarily about soldiers' emotional reactions to the Vietnam conflict: "grief, terror, love, longing, . . . shameful memories" and "the common secret of cowardice." "Men killed, and died, because they were embarrassed not to," O'Brien wrote in one chapter. (In another, "Sweetheart of the Song Tra Bong," he suggested that women would behave similarly in an identical situation.)

In *The Things They Carried*, O'Brien was more aware than ever of the nature of telling stories and getting at the truth through such fictional devices as putting faces on emotions. In "How to Tell a True War Story," he wrote, "A true war story is never moral. It does not instruct, nor encourage virtue, nor suggest models of proper human behavior, nor restrain men from doing the things men have always done. If a story seems moral, do not believe it. If at the end of a war story you feel uplifted, or if you feel that some small bit of rectitude has been salvaged from the larger waste, then you have been made the victim of a very old and terrible lie. There is no rectitude whatsoever. There is no virtue. As a first rule of thumb, therefore, you can tell a true war story by its absolute and uncompromising allegiance to obscenity and evil."

By his own definition, O'Brien's next and most recent novel, *In the Lake of the Woods* (1994), is a true war story. It is also a love story, a meditation on the nature of loss, and a mystery whose "solution" is given away in the beginning, insofar as the author/narrator reveals that there will not be any solution. Senatorial candidate John Wade's wife, Kathy, is declared missing—possibly lost or drowned or dumped in deep water after being hideously murdered—in the Lake of the Woods in northern Minnesota, to which the couple had retreated after John Wade lost a primary election because of the public revelation by his political opponents of his participation in the My Lai massacre. Through John Wade's flashbacks and through frequently appearing chapters called "Evidence," in which secondary characters reflect on what they know of the protagonists, or "Hypothesis," in which the author provides various accounts of the days leading up to Kathy Wade's disappearance, O'Brien reveals a marriage scarred by deceit on both sides. Most horrifying of all, perhaps, is the author's convincing illumination of the inner destruction wrought by self-deception: the more elaborately the edifice of false consciousness is constructed, he seems to suggest, the more tenuous is one's grip on sanity once the edifice crumbles. "The deceits I write about in the book are magnified versions of the secrecy and deceit I practice in my own life, and we all do," O'Brien said in his interview with Jon Elsen. "We're all embarrassed and ashamed of our evil deeds and try to keep them inside, and when they come out, the consequences are devastating." In writing *In the Lake of the Woods*, O'Brien intended to "write a book where craving for love can make us do really horrid things that require lifelong acts of atonement," he told Elsen. "That's why I write about Vietnam. It was given to me, and I'm giving it back."

Critics were divided over the merits of *In the Lake of the Woods*, for which O'Brien was awarded the Society of American Historians' James Fenimore Cooper Prize for best historical novel. Some saw it as a profound philosophical inquiry; others were irritated by the frequent interruptions in the narrative caused by the interpolated "Evidence" sections, in which excerpts from politicians' biographies are juxtaposed with testimony from the courts-martial in the My Lai investigation, quotations from such sources as a magician's handbook, and a recovery book for veterans' wives, and historical accounts of the battles at Lexington and Concord during the American Revolution and of federal troops' savagery in the eradication of Native Americans. William O'Rourke seemed to speak for many critics when he declared in the *Chicago Tribune* "Books" section (October 16, 1994) that O'Brien had "written a risky, ambitious, perceptive, engaging and troubling novel, full of unresolved and unresolvable energies and powerful prose, a major attempt to come to grips with the causes and consequences of the late twentieth century's unquenchable appetite for violence, both domestic and foreign."

O'Brien's short stories have been anthologized in *Prize Stories: The O. Henry Awards* (1976, 1978, 1982), *Great Esquire Fiction*, *The Best American Short Stories* (1977, 1987), *The Pushcart Prize* (vols. 2 and 10), and many collections and textbooks. Occasionally supplementing his income with part-time teaching jobs, he has received awards from the Guggenheim Foundation, the National Endowment for the Arts, the Massachusetts Arts and Humanities Foundation, the Bread Loaf Writers' Conference, the Vietnam Veterans of America, and the American Academy of Arts and Letters.

Tim O'Brien has lived in the Boston area since the mid-1970s. His 1973 marriage to Ann Elizabeth Weller, a magazine production manager, ended in divorce after around seventeen years. He usually writes about ten hours a day; he spends his evenings reading historical and philosophical works. He loves to watch film musicals, especially those of Gene Kelly and Frank Sinatra, and he enjoys working out, skiing, and playing golf and basketball.

Selected Biographical References: Chicago Tribune V p1+ Ap 27 '90 por; Christian Sci Mon B p3 Ag 13 '79 por; N Y Times C p15+ Ap 3 '90 por; N Y Times Bk R p1+ O 9 '94 por; N Y Times Mag p48+ O 2 '94 pors; Pub W 237:60+ F 16 '90 por; Contemporary Authors vol 128 (1990); Contemporary Literary Criticism vol 40 (1986); Dictionary of Literary Biography Documentary Series vol 9 (1991); Dictionary of Literary Biography Yearbook, 1980; Who's Who in America, 1992-93; World Authors 1980-1985 (1991)

AP/Wide World Photos

O'Donnell, Rosie

1962- Actress; comedian. Address: c/o ICM, 8942 Wilshire Blvd., Beverly Hills, CA 90211

Known to many filmgoers as the quintessential "b-est friend" for her wisecracking sidekick roles in *A League of Their Own*, *Sleepless in Seattle*, and *The Flintstones*, the versatile comedian and actress Rosie O'Donnell had been performing as a stand-up comic for fourteen years before breaking into Hollywood movies. She now has to her credit eight films, two television sitcoms, the Broadway musical *Grease!*, several television comedy specials, and a stint as a veejay on the music-video cable television channel VH-1. Throughout her career she has maintained a philosophical attitude toward her growing fame. "You could go crazy with all this attention," she acknowledged in an interview with Nancy Mills for the *Chicago Tribune* (August 22, 1993), "but I think I was really fortunate to do my first film with probably the most famous woman in the world [Madonna]. I've tried really hard to maintain my essence, which is what got me here in the first place." Whereas her essence encompasses an uncommon honesty and directness, her image is that of an irreverent, tough-talking New Yorker whose sense of humor combines gentle self-deprecation with an "everywoman" approach that appeals to broad sectors of the population.

Roseanne O'Donnell was born in 1962, in Commack (some sources say Huntington), Long Island, New York, the third of five children. Her father was a camera designer for spy satellites, and her mother, for whom she was named, was a homemaker who died of pancreatic and liver cancer when O'Donnell was ten years old. Under the influence of her mother, whom O'Donnell remembers as a gifted amateur comedian, she developed an appreciation for musical theatre, tap dancing, ballet, and other arts. Her idols were Barbra Streisand, Lucille Ball, Carol Burnett, and Bette Midler. "I lived all my emotional reality through theatre, movies, and books," O'Donnell recalled in her interview with Nancy Mills. "I come from an Irish Catholic family where emotions weren't dealt with on any kind of real level. . . . My father is very distant and emotionally unavailable, and I rarely speak to him. After my mother died, the five children fused together and became one functioning parent/children unit. We took turns being those roles for each other." O'Donnell's brothers are a lawyer, an accountant, and an advertising executive: her younger sister, Maureen, a former banker, is her business manager.

From the age of ten, O'Donnell was determined to become a movie star. She would gain entree, she eventually decided, through comedy. When she delivered a dead-on mimicry of Gilda Radner's character Roseanne Rosannadanna (which sounded so much like "Roseanne O'Donnell" when filtered through a microphone that an emcee christened her Rosie to avoid the confusion) in a high school skit, a member of the audience suggested she audition at his comedy club. Since she had already performed a few times at the local Ground Round restaurant, as she told Trish Deitch Rohrer for *Mirabella* (June 1993), she decided to give it a shot. After watching Jerry Seinfeld on the Merv Griffin or Mike Douglas show (the anecdote varies, even as she tells it), O'Donnell went on stage the following evening and performed his act. "I killed," she told Todd S. Purdum of the *New York Times* (May 8, 1994). "Everybody was screaming, 'That girl is so funny!' Then I walked off the stage, and all the comics descended upon me: 'You can't do that! Where'd you get those jokes?'" "'Well, forget it!'" O'Donnell responded, as she recalled in an interview with Robert Hofler for *Buzz* (August 1994). "'I'm not doing this. When you're an actress, they don't ask you to write the movie.' I was so mad. I was sixteen and I thought they were ridiculous."

By observing the acts of other comics, O'Donnell eventually mastered the art of being herself onstage. After graduating from Commack South High

School, where she had been elected prom queen, homecoming queen, most school-spirited student, and class president, O'Donnell went on tour at the age of seventeen, honing her act in forty-nine states over a five-year period. "I always did it with the hopes that someone would see it and put me in a sitcom, a movie, or a Broadway show," she admitted to Hofler. "I never did it with aspirations of being a monologist." Her colleagues, most of them men, were much older. "Everybody was doing drugs and drinking, and I was just this little girl on the road, scared in her room," she told Hofler. She refused to allow herself to be discouraged, despite the often-vocalized misgivings of family and friends. "Time and time again, people told me to quit, that I was too tough, I was too New York, I was too heavy," she said in the interview with Nancy Mills. "But I didn't listen to them. I thought, 'You're all idiots!'" Along the way, O'Donnell encouraged others. "Some women comics when I started were jealous of other women," she told Mills in an interview for the New York *Daily News* (July 25, 1993). "They thought, 'If she gets the *Tonight Show*, I can't.' My philosophy always was, 'If she did, we can too.' . . . . Success breeds success."

In the meantime, O'Donnell studied briefly at Dickinson College, in Carlisle, Pennsylvania, and at Boston University. In 1984 she used her winnings as a five-time comedy champion on the television show *Star Search* to move to Los Angeles. At Igby's comedy club in West Los Angeles, Brandon Tartikoff, then the head of NBC's entertainment division, caught her act and subsequently cast her in the supporting role of Maggie O'Brien in the final season of the popular NBC sitcom *Gimme a Break*, which ended its run in 1986. Shortly thereafter, O'Donnell was hired as a veejay on VH-1. When the music video channel discontinued its use of veejays a year later, she persuaded the station to let her host and produce *Stand-Up Spotlight*, a showcase for comedians, which subsequently became VH-1's highest-rated program. O'Donnell, who remains the show's executive producer, hosted the program for four years, until 1992.

By that time O'Donnell's credits included three Showtime television specials—*Showtime Comedy Club All-Stars* (1988), *A Pair of Jokers: Bill Engwall and Rosie O'Donnell* (1990), and *Hurricane Relief* (1992)—a costarring role with Melissa Gilbert-Brinkman in the short-lived Fox sitcom *Stand by Your Man* in 1992, and a guest spot on *Women Aloud*, also in 1992. In 1990 she had played a small part in the bumbling-cop movie *Car 54, Where Are You*, starring David Johansen, John C. McGinley, and Daniel Baldwin. Based on the television show of the same name, the film was not released until 1994, when it was panned by Ralph Novak of *People* (February 14, 1994) as a "pathetic sub-comedy."

O'Donnell's film career was launched in 1992, when the director Penny Marshall cast her as Doris Murphy, a dance-hall bouncer-turned-third baseman, in *A League of Their Own*, a humorous look at the All-American Girls Professional Baseball League, which was founded in 1943 to fill the gap in major-league baseball left by the male players who had joined the armed services during World War II. (The league disbanded in 1954.) Featuring an all-star cast that included Tom Hanks, Geena Davis, Jon Lovitz, and Madonna, with whom O'Donnell struck up a much-publicized off-screen friendship, the film was widely lauded for its broadly funny sequences but often lambasted for its alleged hypocrisy in stereotyping most of the roles and in trivializing its own ostensibly feminist premise. O'Donnell's performance was deemed "excellent" by Vincent Canby of the *New York Times* (July 1, 1992).

In the following year O'Donnell's acting résumé was enhanced considerably when she portrayed Becky, the best friend of Annie (Meg Ryan), in Nora Ephron's romantic comedy *Sleepless in Seattle*, which was based loosely upon the thwarted-love premise of the 1950s tearjerker *An Affair to Remember*, starring Cary Grant and Deborah Kerr. Although their characters were supposed to have been deeply moved while watching *Affair*, O'Donnell and Ryan found themselves thoroughly amused by the outdated lines and improbable plot. "We would be hysterical laughing at the film," O'Donnell told Mark Morrison in an interview for *Us* (July 1993). "It was ridiculous." Another aspect of *Sleepless in Seattle*'s script that O'Donnell thought was less than faithful to reality was the quick recovery of Sam's (Tom Hanks's) son from the death of his mother. The boy calls a local radio station and places an ad for a mate for his lonely father, which Annie answers; after the requisite complications and mixups à la *Affair*, including a planned meeting at the top of the Empire State Building, the couple live happily ever after. A big hit at the box office, the film received mixed reviews, but O'Donnell was well liked by most critics. "Rosie O'Donnell . . . has the bulk of the best one-liners, and her performance is a joy," Jack Matthews noted in his review for *New York Newsday* (June 25, 1993).

Later that year O'Donnell played Gina Garrett, an assistant district attorney, in John Badham's amiable farce *Another Stakeout* (also known as *Stakeout II* and *House of Cops*), starring Richard Dreyfuss and Emilio Estevez. She had been chosen for the part immediately after her name was mentioned at a Disney planning session by Jeffrey Katzenberg, then the chairman of the Walt Disney Studios. In the autumn of 1993, O'Donnell's cameo appearance in Carl Reiner's little-publicized *Fatal Instinct* (a spoof of *Fatal Attraction* and *Basic Instinct*, among other films) was followed by a small role in James L. Brooks's *I'll Do Anything*.

As Betty Rubble in Brian Levant's film version of the cartoon classic *The Flintstones* (1994), O'Donnell worked with Rick Moranis (Barney Rubble), John Goodman (Fred Flintstone), Elizabeth Perkins (Wilma Flintstone), and Elizabeth Taylor (Wilma's mother). Once again, O'Donnell's performance was received much more favorably than the film itself. "Before chiseling at what's wrong with *The Flintstones,*" wrote George Lange of *USA Today* (May 27, 1994), "let's toss a few pebbles of praise: Rosie O'Donnell's right-on Betty giggle." In an interview for a *Chicago Tribune* (May 29, 1994) profile of the actress, Brian Levant told Hilary de Vries, "Rosie is a very funny, talented performer. But," he added, "she is also extremely focused on her career. Her ambitions have served her well."

O'Donnell's first starring role was as an undercover cop-cum-leather-clad dominatrix in Garry Marshall's *Exit to Eden* (1994), which also featured Dana Delaney and Dan Aykroyd. The comically sexy role, which broke the "best friend" mold that had been O'Donnell's mainstay up to that point, had originally been offered to Sharon Stone, who turned it down. In any event, Marshall decided that O'Donnell was more adept at "mixing the comic with the erotic," as he explained to Patrick Pacheco for an article in *Cosmopolitan* (June 1994). "We were trying something very new, and we needed someone with whom the audience could identify to ease them into this slightly kinky, slightly threatening world. Rosie's innocent, but hers is a hip innocence. It helps take the edge off the sex in the movie. Yet she's still sexy and, for the first time in her career, she even has a romantic thing going. She's also very brave. . . . She doesn't worry about how she looks all the time. That can be very refreshing in Hollywood." Based loosely on Anne Rice's best-selling novel of the same title, *Exit to Eden* received mostly negative reviews. "With O'Donnell providing a voice-over that sounds suspiciously like a stand-up act," Richard Harrington wrote in the *Washington Post* (October 14, 1994), "*Exit to Eden* bumbles and falls, turning into an unintentional parody of HBO's *Real Sex*. It's 'Laverne and Shirley do S&M.'"

In May 1994 O'Donnell's childhood dream of starring in a musical materialized when she made her Broadway debut as the tough-talking Rizzo in Tommy Tune's revival of *Grease!* Inaugurating a nostalgic revival of 1950s music and television shows, *Grease!* first became a hit in 1972, six years before the popular movie of the same name was released. Tommy Tune's production, directed and choreographed by Jeff Calhoun, received lukewarm praise, as did O'Donnell's performance. Some critics found her "fine" and appropriately cast, but Ben Brantley of the *New York Times* disagreed. "The show's nominal star, Rosie O'Donnell, a winning film actress, may also be a winning stage actress," he conceded in his evaluation of May 19, 1994, "[but] . . . you can't tell it from this. As the salty-mouthed, promiscuous Betty Rizzo, she affects a stiff, Alfred Hitchcock walk and a droll, deadpan delivery that conveys the character's tough defensiveness with none of her exuberant carnality."

O'Donnell had accepted the role against the advice of her agent, who felt the Broadway run would not provide as much exposure as another film assignment. "[It's] the reason I went into entertainment to begin with," she told William Norwich for *Vogue* (June 1994). Her enthusiasm was tempered somewhat by her distaste for certain aspects of the musical, as she explained to Robert Hofler in her interview for *Buzz*: "In *Grease*, there are a lot of offensive lines. It's quite sexist, very homophobic, very racist. I don't even like the message of the play: If you're a nice, normal girl, change yourself into a trampy, slutty girl to be accepted by the cool boy. So when I see little girls, I want to say at the end of the show, 'Don't believe it!'" She added, however, that *Grease!* "is also a lighthearted romp through the fifties, and you can't dissect everything you do or you'll never have any art." Most recently, O'Donnell was featured in Lesli Linka Glatter's movie about female friendship, *Now and Then*, which was released in October 1995. In the same month she appeared on an episode of the television sitcom *Bless This House*, as the sister of its star character, Bert, played by Andrew Clay.

O'Donnell has been thrice nominated for an American Comedy Award, for her roles in *Stand-Up Spotlight*, *Another Stakeout*, and *Sleepless in Seattle*. Her hosting of *Stand-Up Spotlight* also earned her a Cable ACE Award nomination. When Nancy Mills asked her for the *Chicago Tribune* interview how she prepared for her film roles, O'Donnell admitted, "I don't really prepare. I read the script and think who the character is to me. . . . My movies have been funny and light and little pops, with well-written and well-defined characters. I haven't had to delve into who I think the person really is." Although O'Donnell used comedy as a steppingstone to acting, she may also have been acting in order to move on to directing, something to which she has aspired for some time. "To be a director I think is the most creative and all-encompassing part of the film industry," she told Allan Johnson of the *Chicago Tribune* (February 17, 1995), who reported that she already had several projects lined up. "When you're an actor, you're the paint, and when you're the director, you're the painter. I'd much rather be the painter." She has also written several screenplays. Yet no matter what she does, O'Donnell enjoys the work for its own sake, according to all accounts. Indeed, she returned to performing stand-up in February 1995, after a two-year hiatus, in order to prepare for the taping of her first HBO comedy special.

Standing five feet seven inches tall, Rosie O'Donnell usually weighs between 140 and 170 pounds. She spoke to Chantal Westerman for *Elle* (October 1994) about the anxiety she experiences at the prospect of being thin: "I think it's because I feel safest when I'm in control. If I'm interested in someone and want to have a romantic relationship with them, I feel like I can entice them with my wit or my intellect or . . . my essence. . . . Also, my mother got very thin before she died. . . . I associated getting thin with getting sick and going away. So it also makes me frightened of my own mortality." Despite her fame, O'Donnell has retained her down-to-earth attitude toward her personal appearance, her friends, and her work. "As much as I've achieved some sort of success in the film industry, I don't feel any different," she told Allan Johnson. "And I think people have this illusion, including myself before it happened to me, that everything was going to change once you sort of made it." After living in Los Angeles for a decade, O'Donnell returned to New York City, whose inhabitants, she feels, manifest a matter-of-fact attitude toward celebrities that is more in keeping with her antipathy to hype. "I find that living in L.A., your whole life is centered around show business, and the more successful you become in it, the harder it is to get away from it . . . ," she told Robert Hofler. "In New York, they could care less. People see me and go, 'Hey Rosie, how ya doing?' I go, 'Hi!' and it's over."

Selected Biographical References: Career World 23:14 O '94 por; Chicago Tribune XIII p7+ My 29 '94 pors; Mademoiselle 99:160+ Ag '93 pors; N Y Times II p8 My 8 '94 por; Newsweek 122:60 Ag 16 '93 por; People 38:65+ Jl 20 '92 pors; Premiere 6:60+ Jl '93 pors; TV Guide 39:10+ Ag 3-9 '91 pors; USA Today D p1+ Je 25 '93 pors; Contemporary Theatre, Film, and Television vol 12 (1994); Who's Who in America, 1995

AFP/EPA/Beril Willner/MPC

Otter, Anne Sofie von

May 9, 1955-Swedish mezzo-soprano. Address: c/o IMG, Media House, 3 Burlington Lane, Chiswick, London, W4 2TH, England

With her full-bodied voice, handsome, androgynous features, and tall and slender physique, Anne Sofie von Otter is a natural for the trouser roles (male characters written for female singers) in opera. Two of the most famous trouser roles have become her specialties: Octavian in Richard Strauss's *Der Rosenkavalier* and Cherubino in Mozart's *The Marriage of Figaro*, both of which she has recorded—with the Dresden Staatskapelle under Bernard Haitink and the Metropolitan Opera under James Levine, respectively. She has sung the roles frequently in many of the world's greatest opera houses, and it was as Octavian that she made her debut with the Metropolitan Opera, in New York City in 1988.

Von Otter, who made her first professional appearance as a member of the Basel Opera in 1982, would seem to be ideally suited to the part of the Cavalier of the Rose, because of her exceptional vocal flexibility and musical refinement, her dramatic flair, combining swagger with intensity, and her own natural personality. "Indirectly it has something to do with the way I am in private," she explained to Andrew Clark of *Opera* (June 1991). "I don't particularly like the flouncy, feminine women's parts." She has nonetheless performed, invariably to considerable critical acclaim, several "flouncy, feminine" characters, perhaps most notably Dorabella in Mozart's *Cosi fan tutte*. Her credits also include the Composer in Richard Strauss's *Ariadne auf Naxos*, Ramiro in Mozart's *La finta giardiniera*, Romeo in Bellini's *I Capuletti ed i Montecchi*, Angelina in Rossini's *La cenerentola*, and the title role in Rossini's *Tancredi*. By tackling such a wide range of operatic roles, as well as the vast concert and song literature, von Otter has established herself as one of the most versatile and exciting young mezzo-sopranos in the world.

Anne Sofie von Otter was born in Stockholm on May 9, 1955. Her childhood was spent variously in Stockholm, Bonn, and London, as her father, a Swedish diplomat, moved from one post to another. Although she grew up in what one writer described as "a reasonably musical household," she did not consider singing professionally until her mid-teens. "I wanted to be a ballet dancer," she told Richard Fawkes in an interview for the British periodical *Opera Now* (September 1992). "I had ideas about being a doctor or a farmer, definitely not a classical singer." By her own admission, she was an unusually slow starter in the world of music. She began singing when she was in high school, first as a member of a church choir and later as a soloist. Recognizing her innate musicality, her choirmaster encouraged her to pursue a career in music, but he advised her against trying to become a professional soloist. "At that point I thought of myself as a high soprano," von Otter admitted to Andrew Clark, for the *Opera* profile. "No wonder he didn't think I would make a good singer—my voice was obviously very strained at that time."

Upon completing her secondary education, von Otter enrolled at the Stockholm College of Music, with the intention of becoming a music teacher, and it was there, at the age of nineteen, that she had her first formal singing lesson. Six years later she entered the Guildhall School of Music and Drama, in London, where she first performed operatic roles, and where she met her principal teacher, Vera Rosza, an internationally respected vocal coach. She has continued her training with Rozsa over the years, and she has also studied song interpretation with two renowned accompanists, Erik Werba, a professor of song and oratorio at the Vienna Academy of Music, and Geoffrey Parsons, who has accompanied such legendary singers as Nicolai Gedda, Elisabeth Schwarzkopf, and Dame Janet Baker.

Vera Rosza described the development of von Otter's artistry to Antony Peattie for an article about the singer in BBC *Music Magazine* (February 1995): "I've had a lot of Swedish pupils. There's something in the culture which inhibits competition. They tend to be very careful not to succeed, yet when they catch fire they are marvelous. . . . When Anne Sofie first sang, she already had a beautiful voice, was an innate musician and extremely intelligent, but she looked and acted like a girl from the choir. Sweden has an outstanding choral tradition, and that's where her voice was first trained. Since then, she has learned a lot, not just about singing." Von Otter's Scandinavian education is also evident in her fluency in several languages, a great advantage for an opera singer.

Von Otter did not find her true voice as a mezzo-soprano, and with it her place in the operatic repertoire, for some time. "When I started to study singing, I wanted to sound like Julie Andrews," she confessed to John von Rhein of the *Chicago Tribune* (October 1, 1989). "I really thought I was destined to be a coloratura soprano; that shows you what I knew about singing! . . . Back then I didn't know a single opera, except maybe *Carmen*, which I sang, even though it didn't really suit me temperamentally, because it was low enough for my voice. When I began studying with Vera Rosza, . . . she made me sing all sorts of things I never dared to touch before, like the Rossini repertory, and Mozart's Cherubino and Sesto [in *La Clemenza di Tito*]." She told von Rhein that she first began to like opera when she saw Jean-Pierre Ponnelle's film version of Puccini's *Madame Butterfly*, with Mirella Freni and Placido Domingo under the conductor Herbert von Karajan. It would not be many years before von Otter would be performing alongside such luminaries, both on stage and on such recordings as James Levine's Deutsche Grammophon release of Tchaikovsky's *Eugene Onegin*, for which she and Freni sang the roles of the sisters Olga and Tatyana.

Von Otter came to public attention in 1982, when she won both the Tunbridge Wells International Young Concert Artists competition and the Benson and Hedges Gold Award at the end of her year at the Guildhall School. Her first professional engagement was a two-year contract with the Basel Opera Company, in Switzerland, beginning in 1982. She made her debut with the company in the role of Alcina, in Haydn's *Orlando Paladino*, winning a warm reception. That assignment was followed by the roles of Cherubino, Sesto, Hansel (in Engelbert Humperdinck's *Hansel and Gretel*), which she has since recorded with Jeffrey Tate for the EMI label, Clairon (in Richard Strauss's one-act opera *Capriccio*), and Hermia (in Benjamin Britten's *A Midsummer Night's Dream*).

Von Otter's success in the Basel ensemble led quickly to an active freelance career. She has not since attached herself to any one opera house. The turning point in her career came during the Christmas holidays in 1985, when she sang Cherubino at the Royal Opera House, in Covent Garden, in London, under the baton of Colin Davis. Other conductors took note, and opera company managers and record companies also began to show an interest in the young singer. Over the next three years, she made successful opera or concert debuts in Geneva, Berlin, Chicago, Philadelphia, Milan, Munich, Stockholm, Brussels, and New York City. Colin Davis played an especially important part in the early development of von Otter's career, having introduced her to audiences in New York City, Vienna, Paris, and Munich.

From the beginning of her career, Von Otter has taken pains to sing only with the best conductors, and she has steadfastly refused to perform Baroque or Classical music with conductors who do not share her taste for the authentic style in early music. Von Otter has had a unusually fruitful relationship with the conductor John Eliot Gardiner, who first engaged her to sing Marguerite on his Philips recording of Berlioz's *The Damnation of Faust*. With Gardiner, she has since recorded the roles of Sesto in *La Clemenza di Tito*, for Archiv, and Clytemnestre in Gluck's *Iphigenie en Aulide*, for Erato, as well as the mezzo-soprano part in Verdi's *Requiem*, for the Philips label. In interviews, she has numbered among her other favorite maestros Carlos Kleiber, Riccardo Muti, and Georg Solti, but she also enjoys working with such up-and-coming young conductors as Daniele Gatti and Carlo Rizzi, both of whom have conducted her in productions at the Royal Opera House in London.

In preparing an operatic role for the stage, von Otter first masters the music, then works with the director or producer to bring her character to life. "I'm very intuitive in the way I approach a character," she explained to Andrew Clark, "and that holds me back a bit. I try to listen to what the composer has said about the role—the only characterization I get is from the music. I'm not one of these people who sit and read about the backgrounds of different figures and make myself a picture in that way. What the composer has to say about the role is all I have to use, until the producer gives me something else to think about. . . . I'm delighted when a conductor or a stage director sees things in me that I don't." By her own account, she is more concerned with creating something entirely her own on the stage than with having a big effect. "I'd rather be known as a cool performer than an emoter," she told Clark.

Unlike many mezzo-sopranos, von Otter is not interested in pushing her voice up into a higher range, to make her eligible for the more lucrative soprano assignments. Indeed, she has indicated that if she makes any move at all it will more likely be down the vocal scale, toward the lower mezzo and contralto parts in opera. Some of the roles she has her eye on are the Philistine temptress Delilah in Saint-Saëns's *Samson and Delilah*, the Princess Eboli in Verdi's *Don Carlo*, Dido in Berlioz's *Dido and Aeneas*, and Charlotte in Massanet's *Werther*. Carmen is a role for which she is vocally ideal, and she has said that she may record the opera, although she has no intention of playing the part on the stage, unless, as she told Richard Fawkes, "the right director comes along who says he's looking for a tall, blonde Swedish mezzo to do it. If they want to put a curly black wig on me—no. . . . Some roles are very clichéd, and Carmen is the most clichéd of them all. People have a very clear picture in their minds of what Carmen should look like and that's not me. I'd look like a parody of Carmen, and I don't think I should do it like that." Rosina, in Rossini's *The Barber of Seville*, is another role she has said she is "very cautious about."

For the time being von Otter's repertoire of operatic roles remains rather small. Her Octavian is still her calling card. In 1990 she performed the role at the Metropolitan Opera, with Felicity Lott as the Marschallin and Barbara Bonney as Sophie, under the baton of Carlos Kleiber. Donal Henahan, who reviewed that production of *Der Rosenkavalier* for the *New York Times* (September 27, 1990), found her "utterly convincing, visually," and he felt that she "gained in charm and authority as the night went on." Von Otter was "particularly effective," he wrote, "masquerading as the tipsy Mariandel in the tavern scene."

When the same cast and conductor were reunited for *Der Rosenkavalier* in Vienna, Deutsche Grammophon recorded the performance for release on video and laser disc. Commenting on the Vienna *Rosenkavalier*, Nicholas Payne, the director of the Royal Opera in London, told Antony Peattie, "Octavian suits Anne Sofie von Otter—she sings the notes, for a start, which isn't true of all Octavians, since much of it is really a soprano role. She remains unfazed. And she looks wonderful. Perhaps her natural Swedish reserve helps—she has an innate aristocracy in her bearing. It can be embarrassing if an Octavian tries to 'act aristocratic.'" Von Otter herself told Peattie, "Octavian's bearing is not something I have to work at, but it must be more than a question of looking royal; he must be a real person. I try to make things true to myself and to those who listen. I don't like falseness." Since recording *Der Rosenkavalier* in 1990, she has made subtle changes in her interpretation of Octavian that, according to Antony Peattie, make the character "sexier, more engaged, more touching."

Now at the peak of her career, von Otter is in the enviable position of being able to turn down more offers than she accepts, both to preserve her voice and to maintain a serene family life. As she explained to Andrew Clark, "Being busy doesn't make you a better singer, it doesn't necessarily help your career either. I now really work quite hard to have a lot of free time between engagements, so that I can always go home, and so that my children know it's in Stockholm that we live, not in some hotel somewhere. I don't have a limit on the number of performances I do, but when I see my diary starting to turn black, I just put a stop to anything new that comes in. This annoys some people, and there are conductors who have decided they don't want to work with me again."

Von Otter's extensive work in recording has given her not only the flexibility of schedule she wants but also the opportunity to explore music beyond the limitations of the standard opera house repertoire. Her discography includes a wide range of music, from the seventeenth century to the twentieth, from Henry Purcell to Kurt Weill. Her longstanding interest in early music, which dates back to her days in the local choir, is reflected in her recordings of Handel's Marian Cantatas and Arias, with Reinhard Goebel and the Musica Antiqua Köln, and of Purcell's *Dido and Aeneas*, with Trevor Pinnock and the English Concert, both on the Archiv label. Assessing her performance as Dido on the Purcell disc for the *Guardian* (August 11, 1989), Edward Greenfield wrote, "Von Otter, both fresh and mature, sings her two big solos with a combination of weight, gravity, and expressive warmth, which is yet completely in scale. The final lament is faster than in traditional performances but conveys full tragic intensity apt for an epic story."

The French and German songs of the nineteenth century are central to von Otter's recital repertoire. For the Deutsche Grammophon label, she has recorded Berlioz's orchestral song cycle *Les Nuits d'été*, with James Levine and the Berlin Philharmonic, and a selection of his other songs, with the pianist Cord Garben; a group of Brahms's lieder, accompanied by the pianist Bengt Forsberg; and lieder by Hugo Wolf and Gustav Mahler, with the pianist Ralf Gothoni. In his review of the Wolf and Mahler album for *Musical America* (July 1990), Terry Teachout wrote that the disc, one of von Otter's earliest recordings, proved her to be "a fully formed artist of the highest order. . . . Her voice is wonderfully solid without a trace of plumminess, her diction is clear and engaging, and her interpretations are restrained but intensely involved. She does a masterly job of illuminating Wolf's emotionally complex Mignon songs, but just when you think you have her pegged as a 'serious' singer, she dances through 'Die Spröde' with delicious, lightfooted wit."

Von Otter's devotion to Scandinavian music extends to her recording for the Swedish label Musica Sveciae of the songs of Wilhelm Stenhammar, on which she collaborated with her compatriot

Håkan Hågegard. "[Von Otter] has a glowing high-mezzo sound that binds phrases and expands to climaxes, along with a well-schooled technique . . . ," Will Crutchfield observed in an evaluation of the album for the *New York Times* (September 2, 1990). "Both singers' basic fineness of tone and soundness of method make it a pleasure to hear the disk through even though a certain sameness creeps into the songs."

Perhaps von Otter's most successful recital disc to date is her recording with Bengt Forsberg of a selection of songs by the Norwegian Edvard Grieg, which was released by Deutsche Grammophon in 1993 as part of the record label's commemoration of the 150th anniversary of the composer's birth. The recording won the prestigious *Gramophone* award that year in the solo vocal category. Reviewing the recording in *Gramophone* (June 1993), Alan Blyth wrote, "Here we have a singer at the peak of her career glorying in what she can accomplish with her voice and deploying it in repertory she knows well and obviously loves. With performances of this kind of conviction, Grieg in this celebratory year emerges as a first-rank composer in the genre. For every mood, for every nuance of meaning, von Otter finds the right expression and has the wherewithal to fulfill her ambitious intentions." John Rockwell, writing in the *New York Times* (March 20, 1994), agreed: "Even in songs seemingly intended for an impetuous young man, . . . Ms. von Otter's experience in trouser roles . . . helps her create a convincing poetic illusion. And her wonderfully confidential singing, with a technique that allows her to project a full timbre in even the softest phrase, sounds like folk song transformed. Only the greatest lieder singers master the blend of refinement and innocence that recreates in performance terms precisely the folk inspiration and artful naïveté embodied in Grieg's music."

Earlier in her career von Otter felt that if the need arose she could easily turn her back on her singing career. "I used to think that if I lost my voice I would just do something else," she said in the interview for *Opera Now*. "Now I know I'd be miserable, and I'd make life for my family miserable. I live for appearing on the concert platform and on the stage. I delight in singing. It gives me such a kick. I just hope I can carry on for a long time." For the time being von Otter seems to be content just to maintain the current momentum in her career, with a schedule that combines opera performances, concert and recital appearances, and recordings. "I'll never be a star," she conceded to Andrew Clark in 1991, "because I don't want to be—I'll never be a publicity person. I hope my development continues, that my voice stays healthy, and that I can explore different sides of my acting. My ambition is not to have a huge repertoire—I want to find my way into the bel canto repertoire, see how I like it, and continue doing my Octavians and hopefully lots of concerts." By all accounts, von Otter appears to be a singer with real staying power. As her teacher Vera Rosza put it to Antony Peattie, "Today we have a new great singer every second day. And every third day they disappear. Not her. She's going to be around for a long time. She's someone who can always surprise you, give you a little bit more than you were expecting."

Offstage, Anne Sophie von Otter is unassuming and down-to-earth, not at all the stereotypical prima donna, as more than one interviewer has pointed out. Her short, almost punkish haircut and the faded blue jeans she favors are a sharp contrast to the powdered wigs and satin knee britches she dons to sing roles like Cherubino and Octavian. Married since 1987 to the Swedish actor Benny Frederikson, she lives with her husband and their two sons in an apartment in Stockholm that is decorated with posters featuring the work of such contemporary artists as Paul Klee and Edward Hopper as well as several eighteenth-century portraits of von Otter's ancestors. Marks on the wall near the piano record her sons' changing heights. "When I was single, I worked more, hopping from engagement to engagement, country to country," she said when she spoke with John von Rhein. "Now I try to turn off singing every so often, to make sure that I have enough free time to spend at home. Unlike a lot of performers who say they maintain an apartment somewhere, but who never actually live there."

Selected Biographical References: BBC Music Mag p32+ F '95 pors; Chicago Tribune XIII p10+ O 1 '89 pors; Opera p627+ Je '90 pors; Opera Now p21+ S '92 por; International Who's Who, 1995-96; International Who's Who of Women (1992); Slonimsky, Nicolas. Baker's Biographical Dictionary of Musicians (1992)

Ovitz, Michael S.

(OH-vits)

Dec. 14, 1946- Entertainment industry executive; talent agent; entrepreneur. Address: c/o Walt Disney Co., 500 S. Buena Vista, Burbank, CA 91521

Michael S. Ovitz, a cofounder of the Creative Artists Agency (CAA) and its chairman until October 1995, when he became president of the Walt Disney Company, is widely recognized as not only one of the most powerful people in Hollywood but also as "one of the most imposing entrepreneurs on the national scene," as Ronald Grover wrote in *Business Week* (August 9, 1993). Ovitz began his career at the William Morris agency, where in a remarkably short time, he advanced from a position at the very bottom of the corporate ladder to become one of the firm's most effective agents. Within a decade of its creation, in 1975, CAA became the leading talent vendor in Hollywood, thanks largely to Ovitz's skill at maintaining a huge network of valuable connections; his ability to attract the most

Donna Daley/Bettmann Archive

Michael S. Ovitz

sought-after actors, writers, directors, musicians, and other specialists to CAA's stable of clients; his brilliance at matching his clients with good projects; his precedent-setting application of the tried-and-true show-business formula known as the package deal; and his success in building a highly motivated, extremely disciplined staff, who work in an atmosphere of uncommon cooperation. In 1990 a film studio executive told a reporter, "The balance of power [in Hollywood] has shifted from the studios to the agencies in the last decade, and more than any other single factor, Michael Ovitz and CAA are responsible for that." According to Ronald Grover, Ovitz turned CAA into what may be "the world's preeminent authority on harnessing star power to commercial ends." "There hasn't been a phenomenon such as CAA since 1947, when Lew Wasserman and MCA [Music Corporation of America] dominated Hollywood," the legendary talent agent Irving ("Swifty") Lazar was quoted as saying in *Time* (February 13, 1989). "Comparing CAA to its strongest competition is like comparing Tiffany's to the A&P."

Starting in the late 1980s, Ovitz extended his professional activities far beyond those of a "superagent," as he was often labeled. Assuming the role of an international corporate and financial consultant, he assisted in the Sony Corporation's acquisition of Columbia Pictures Entertainment in 1989 and brokered the purchase of MCA by the Matsushita company for $6.7 billion in 1990, which was then the largest buyout ever of an American firm by a Japanese concern. In 1993 he was retained by the French banking giant Credit Lyonnais to help manage its financially shaky $3 billion portfolio of loans in entertainment businesses and the media and to suggest possibilities for future investments. Through deals with such corporations as Coca-Cola and Nike and three regional Bell telephone companies, Ovitz also entered such fields as advertising, communications technology, and televised sports. "As different as these deals appear, they all have something in common: they came about because of Mike Ovitz and his determination to push, push, push to the boundaries of what's possible," Johnnie L. Roberts observed in a profile of Ovitz for *Newsweek* (June 12, 1995), in which he labeled Ovitz "Hollywood's ultimate deal-maker." "I think we all tend to feel that we can only take on so much in our lives," Richard Koshalek, the director of the Museum of Contemporary Art in Los Angeles and a friend of Ovitz's, told Connie Bruck, who profiled Ovitz for the *New Yorker* (September 9, 1991). "Michael Ovitz is one of the few people I have ever met who feel they have no limits. Really, none."

Michael S. Ovitz was born in Chicago on December 14, 1946. His father was a wholesale liquor salesman. When Ovitz was six, his family, which by then included his younger brother, moved to a tract house in a working-class neighborhood in Encino, a suburb of Los Angeles, in California's San Fernando Valley. As a youngster he liked to ride his bicycle to the RKO Studio lot, where, after sneaking in, he would watch filmmakers at work. "It was amazing how they could make something magical out of such chaos," he recalled to Ronald Grover. At Birmingham High School, in the nearby town of Van Nuys, he was elected president of the student body. He was "someone the kids looked up to, a leader and a doer," as one of his former teachers told Sandra L. Kirsch for *Fortune* (January 2, 1989).

Urged by his parents to become a physician, in 1964 Ovitz enrolled at the University of California at Los Angeles (UCLA) as a premed student. He covered at least part of his tuition and other expenses by working as a tour guide at Universal Studios and then at the studios of Twentieth Century Fox. His social life revolved around his fraternity, Zeta Beta Tau. In the *New York Times Magazine* (July 9, 1989), L. J. Davis quoted Bruce Hensel, one of Ovitz's fraternity brothers, as saying that when Ovitz announced that he was running for the presidency of the fraternity, "he wasn't expected to win," because "he was too quiet and reserved." "But he worked at it, he won going away, and he was one of the best presidents we ever had," Hensel said. According to Hensel, it was also through hard work that Ovitz overcame the limitations imposed by his small physique and lack of natural athleticism to become one of the most valuable players on the fraternity football team. Ovitz struck Lenny LeVine, another of his fraternity brothers, as "always bright, quick, aggressive . . . very organized [and] ambitious," as LeVine recalled to Malcolm MacPherson of *Premiere* (May 1992). In UCLA's 1968 southern campus yearbook, he was referred to as "King Ovitz."

Instead of going to medical school in 1968 after his graduation from college, Ovitz got a job with the William Morris talent brokerage firm, in Beverly

Hills. "I realized that there were a lot of areas in the entertainment business that I was interested in, and the career that would offer me the widest exposure to the entertainment business was the agency business," he told L. J. Davis, after noting that as a studio tour guide, he had had contact with many agency-affiliated people. "Agents can allow creative people to achieve their visions, and that's why I did it." William Morris assigned Ovitz to a job in the mailroom, where the agency traditionally placed entry-level employees, and he enrolled in the firm's rigorous training program, which weeded out as many as 60 percent of the trainees. L. J. Davis reported that after "months of servitude" in the mailroom, Ovitz became a secretary to Howard West, an agent whose clients were connected with television variety shows. According to another version of his rise in the agency, Ovitz was still working in the mailroom when, having stayed very late one night, he so impressed the president of the agency with his diligence that he was promoted to agent; according to a third account, he substituted for the president's secretary, who was on sick leave, before advancing to the position of agent.

In any event, Ovitz left William Morris after about a year and entered law school. He dropped out a short time later and returned to work at William Morris. Although the agency almost never rehired employees who had quit, an exception was made for Ovitz because of the potential that he had displayed. "By Morris standards, Ovitz's subsequent rise was little short of meteoric," L. J. Davis wrote. Elliott Kozak, a department head with whom Ovitz worked, described him to Davis as "just incredible" and as "the best agent [he had] ever seen." Ovitz's clients included the talk-show host Merv Griffin, the producer Chuck Barris, and the game-show host Bob Barker.

During the early 1970s Ovitz became increasingly dissatisfied with his low wages and the lack of opportunity for advancement at William Morris. (Many older staff members who held high positions gave no indication that they planned to retire in the foreseeable future.) One day at the end of 1974 or the beginning of 1975, Ovitz and four similarly disgruntled William Morris employees—Ron Meyer, Michael Rosenfeld, William Haber, and Rowland Perkins—met over dinner to discuss forming their own agency. "We came as a duo and a trio, to play our music," Ron Meyer told L. J. Davis, "and by the time we left, we were the Mormon Tabernacle Choir. We all sang the same tune, and we came out of that dinner with a clear understanding of how we were going to do it." Within days, the William Morris management learned about their plan through a New York accountant whom Ovitz and his coworkers had apparently consulted about financing their venture, and all five men were fired.

The partners thereupon secured a twenty-one thousand-dollar bank loan, established a one hundred thousand-dollar line of credit, and opened the Creative Artists Agency for business in a borrowed office. They furnished the quarters they subsequently rented with card tables and folding chairs that they brought from their homes. "Of course I was scared," Ovitz was quoted as saying in *Time* (February 13, 1989). "I was barely twenty-seven at the time. We didn't take a paycheck for almost two years. Our wives took turns serving as secretaries. In the early years, I couldn't get a good table at a restaurant. I felt like an extra on a set." (By the late 1980s the five original partners had been reduced to three—Ron Meyer, William Haber, and Ovitz; Ovitz's departure for Disney leaves Haber as the sole remaining founding partner.)

In CAA's infancy, nearly all of the people on its small list of clients were associated with television. One of them was the impressionist Rich Little, who at that time had his own television show. CAA also drew income from an ABC game show called *Rhyme and Reason* and a program featuring the Jackson Five (the singer Michael Jackson and four of his brothers). To acquire additional clients, Connie Bruck reported, Ovitz embarked on "a series of assiduous courtships" of television executives and fledgling business managers and entertainment lawyers, who later recommended the services of CAA to actors and others who were disenchanted with their current agents. "[Ovitz] has developed a spiderweb of connections, though I don't mean that in a sinister sense," Alfred Checchi, a cochairman of NWA, the parent company of Northwest Airlines, and a close friend of Ovitz's, told Bruck. "He realizes that his assets are relationships. He is always meshing—his agents, his clients, the studios, the networks, the small production companies. He has a capacity to relate to whole bunches of people in that web—and he realizes that a twang over here has repercussions over there. So much of Mike's life is about sizing people up, seeing where the weaknesses are. He makes fewer mistakes in the area of people than anyone I know."

Among the most important figures in Ovitz's network was the literary agent Morton Janklow, who has represented such popular writers as Judith Krantz, Jackie Collins, and Sidney Sheldon. According to Connie Bruck, Ovitz and Janklow forged such a close business relationship that, after the mid- to late-1970s, "they function[ed], albeit informally, as partners." At the beginning of their first meeting, in Janklow's New York City office, Ovitz placed his watch on Janklow's desk and announced that he would present his ideas within a half hour. "He made this driven, dramatic pitch, with tremendous intensity and, I thought, incredible intelligence," Janklow told Connie Bruck, "and after thirty minutes, exactly, he put his watch back on and left." Every Thursday morning for weeks thereafter, at precisely 10:30, Ovitz would telephone Janklow, to try to persuade him to allow Ovitz to read galleys of forthcoming novels, which, if Ovitz deemed them promising, would become the basis for package deals that Ovitz would create for the television networks. "He kept up a constant level of communication," Janklow recalled to Bruck. "He was undaunted." Janklow eventually offered Ovitz a widely rejected literary property that Ovitz soon succeeded in selling as part of a package.

In a package deal, the services of a writer, director, composer, actors, and other creative talent necessary for a project are sold all together to a production company. As CAA's client list grew, its package deals became more expensive, and some of them have called for record-high salaries for actors or others slated to work on a film. Various sources have reported that because of Ovitz's power, studio heads have tended to accept CAA's terms. Moreover, Larry Rohter reported in the *New York Times* (October 5, 1990), "according to studio executives and movie producers miffed by having to pay what they regard as inflated salaries and fees," CAA "can heavily influence scripts, casting, and the choice of directors for film projects."

By 1979 or 1980 CAA's gross annual bookings had climbed to $90.2 million, and the agency had become the third-largest in Hollywood, after William Morris and International Creative Management. By the mid-1980s the agency had catapulted to the top of its field, and in late 1986 a front-page story about Ovitz appeared in the *Wall Street Journal.* Until then little had been known about him or about whom CAA represented or what television shows and films the agency had been involved with. In refraining from discussing CAA's affairs with members of the media and forbidding his staff from doing so, Ovitz had followed the example set by his hero Lew Wasserman, who led MCA for several decades and who was well known for his marked aversion to the limelight. According to Connie Bruck, Wasserman is "an almost iconographic figure" to Ovitz—"a man whom he observed, analyzed, and sought to emulate."

Moreover, according to Sidney Sheinberg, who was named chairman of MCA when Wasserman stepped down from that position in mid-1995, Ovitz "likes to do things with an aura of mystery," as Connie Bruck quoted him as saying. "Even in a profession where the time-honored rule says that an agent does not publicize himself at the expense of his client, Ovitz's preoccupation with secrecy is unusual," L. J. Davis observed. "He works diligently to suppress all information about his agency. . . . Directors and actors, who will talk up a storm about almost anything Hollywood, fall silent when asked about [him]." Many sources have reported that Ovitz inspired much fear among members of the entertainment community. According to L. J. Davis, "In today's Hollywood, if you want your career to thrive, you do not cross Michael Ovitz."

Among the approximately one thousand people who have chosen CAA to represent them are the actors Warren Beatty, Cher, Sean Connery, Kevin Costner, Tom Cruise, Robert DeNiro, Whoopi Goldberg, Gene Hackman, Tom Hanks, Dustin Hoffman, Jessica Lange, Demi Moore, Bill Murray, Paul Newman, Al Pacino, Brad Pitt, Robert Redford, Sylvester Stallone, Meryl Streep, Barbra Streisand, and Robin Williams; the directors Sir Richard Attenborough, John Hughes, Barry Levinson, Sidney Lumet, Mike Nichols, Alan Parker, Sydney Pollack, Martin Scorsese, Steven Spielberg, and Oliver Stone; the writers Chris Columbus, Stephen King, Nicholas Pileggi, Anne Rice, and Gore Vidal; the musicians and/or composers Eric Clapton, Neil Diamond, Philip Glass, Michael Jackson, Madonna, Prince, Tina Turner, and Stevie Wonder; and producers and other specialists of comparable caliber. The films with which CAA is closely associated—among them some of the biggest money-makers in Hollywood history—include *Tootsie* (1982), *Ghostbusters* (1984) and *Ghostbusters II* (1989), *Fatal Attraction* (1987), *Rain Man* (1988), *Mississippi Burning* (1988), *Dances with Wolves* (1990), *Goodfellas* (1990), *Sleepless in Seattle* (1993), and *Jurassic Park* (1993).

Ovitz demanded that the sixty to one hundred agents on the payroll of CAA share information and otherwise collaborate closely with one another, and he emphasized the importance of loyalty both among agents and to the firm. "I've tried to create an environment here where everyone's on the same team," he told L. J. Davis, thus contrasting CAA with many other talent agencies, where staff members compete fiercely among themselves. In formulating his management style, he explained to Davis, he drew upon, among other things, his study of Eastern philosophies and what he identified as "the Western sports concept." Ovitz commissioned the architect I. M. Pei to design the building in which CAA has maintained its headquarters since 1990. The fifty-seven-foot atrium-cum-lobby of the building features bridges that were designed to facilitate communication among the staff. It is also the setting for a huge painting by Roy Lichtenstein and works by other major artists.

In the late 1980s Ovitz began seeking ways to extend the reach of CAA into the world of international finance. When, in 1988, Sony sought his advice, along with that of a number of other people, on a deal to buy Columbia Pictures, Ovitz's corporate contacts proved invaluable. Soon after the conclusion of that $3.4 billion transaction, in 1989, executives from the Matsushita Electric Industrial Company, one of the world's largest manufacturers of consumer electronics products, hired Ovitz to orchestrate Matsushita's acquisition of an American "software" company, which it wanted to "complement its consumer electronic 'hardware' products," as Connie Bruck put it. Ovitz recommended the purchase of MCA, a conglomerate with interests in publishing, film, television, movie theatres, a record company, and theme parks. Among many other steps that he took to prepare for the negotiations, which he correctly anticipated would be extremely delicate because of American and Japanese cultural differences, he read *The Japanese Today* (1988), by the scholar and diplomat Edwin O. Reischauer, and several books by Konosuke Matsushita, the founder of the Matsushita company. As Matsushita's point man, Ovitz selected the bankers, lawyers, and public relations experts who represented Matsushita during the negotiations. Ovitz, who was reportedly paid

$10 million for his work in connection with the Sony-Columbia Pictures transaction, is said by various sources to have received between $8 million and $17 million or as much as $40 million for his contribution to the $6.7 billion Matsushita-MCA deal.

In 1991, in a move that shocked and alarmed many people in the advertising world, Coca-Cola engaged the services of CAA to create and produce a substantial portion of its global advertising, a highly lucrative job that for forty years had been handled by the advertising agency McCann Erickson. "Instead of creating a story that is TV- or feature-film length, we shifted to stories that are thirty seconds or sixty seconds long," Janice Castro quoted Ovitz as saying in *Time* (February 22, 1993). Castro described the Coca-Cola ads as "wry, hip, and charming"; a reporter for the *Economist* (April 24, 1993) judged them to be "good: fresher than anything McCann [Erickson] has done for Coke in years." In 1993 CAA announced that it would be collaborating with Nike to develop sports-related television programs for an international market, and that same year it gained control of Movie Tunes, a company that sells theatre advertising to record companies. In late 1994 Ovitz and three regional Bell telephone companies—Bell Atlantic, the Nynex Corporation, and the Pacific Telesis Group—completed plans to launch a video entertainment network that would deliver movies and other programs over home telephone lines.

Ovitz sometimes claimed that despite his increasingly varied professional activities, he still devoted 85 percent of each day to what he considered his primary responsibility—working for individual clients—and that his involvement in the development of new technologies related directly to that obligation. Pointing to his right during his interview with Janice Castro for *Time* (April 19, 1993), he said, "Imagine all of the most talented artists here." "Over there," he continued, gesturing toward a television set, "is a primitive version of a machine that will offer nearly unlimited possibilities for entertainment within about ten years. What I have to do is get these talented people through a period of relatively low demand the best way I can. Because once these new technologies are in place, there will be the most incredible shortage of product!" "It's our job to be ahead of the curve," he told Ronald Grover. "In the near future, someone with a book or a movie project won't have to be content with just putting it on television or film. And we'd better be able to tell our clients where they can find markets for their work."

In early 1995 Ovitz contemplated leaving CAA to become the head of MCA, which had been bought by the Seagram Company in April of that year. In June of that year, after several months of negotiations with Seagram, he announced that he would remain at the helm of CAA. "I can't predict the future, but the only thing that is for sure is that I love my life at CAA," Ovitz told reporters. Only two months later he surprised people in the entertainment business by accepting the position of president at the Walt Disney Company. In that job, which he began on October 1, 1995, he oversees the company's operations divisions: Capital Cities/ABC, which Disney acquired for $19.2 billion at the end of July 1995, and Disney's theme parks, consumer products, and entertainment segments. "It was time to do something different," he said on August 14, 1995, when his decision to join the Disney company was made public. "It was right for me. This opportunity was extraordinary." Ovitz reports to Michael D. Eisner, the chairman of Disney, who has been a close friend of his for many years. Ovitz has dismissed industry speculation that occupying a subordinate position, and particularly one in which his supervisor is a personal friend, will prove unsatisfactory for him. "I am working for Michael and the shareholders," he told Geraldine Fabrikant of the *New York Times* (August 15, 1995). "That is not different from working for my clients."

Michael Ovitz is about five feet nine inches tall and has a gap-toothed smile and a slight stoop. "He has an almost Rasputin-like ability to focus his eyes on you," one of his colleagues told Connie Bruck. "He uses his voice in a soothing, harmonic way—it does something to your brain waves. And he speaks a few decibels lower, to make you strain to hear. Because of that, you're constantly paying attention, leaning toward him. He has an aura." In *Premiere* (May 1992) Ovitz was described as tenacious and methodical and as having "a surprising sense of humor." According to Bernard Weinraub of the *New York Times* (April 13, 1994), he is "extraordinarily disciplined and far smarter and more complex than most of the people" he represented and also "one of the most enigmatic" people in the entertainment industry. He is well known for his short temper. Every day for half an hour after arising at around dawn, he reads six newspapers while pedaling on his exercise cycle. He spends the next hour in his home gymnasium practicing the Japanese martial art of aikido with a private instructor. A self-described "avid team-sports fan," he regularly attends Los Angeles Lakers basketball games. (The former Laker guard Earvin ["Magic"] Johnson is a CAA client.) Each summer he devotes a few days to planning his life in one-, three-, and five-year blocks.

Ovitz and his wife, the former Judy Reich, to whom he has been married since 1969, live with their three children in Brentwood, a fashionable section of Los Angeles. He also maintains an apartment in New York City. His collection of art, which includes Old Master drawings, African antiquities, and works by Pablo Picasso, Joan Miró, Jasper Johns, and Roy Lichtenstein, among other major artists, is considered by many experts to be one of the finest private collections in the United States. When he developed an interest in African art, Arnold Glimcher, the owner of the Pace art gallery, in New York City, and one of Ovitz's close associates, gave him a number of books on that subject. "About a month later, he started asking me the most ethnographically eccentric questions," Glimcher recalled to a reporter. "I swear he had memorized those books. People say, 'What is Michael Ovitz about?' Michael Ovitz is about self-improvement. He has the most amazing appetite."

Selected Biographical References: Bsns W 125:50+ Ag 9 '93 pors; N Y Times D p1+ Ap 13 '94 por; N Y Times Mag p24+ Jl 9 '89 pors; New Yorker 67:38+ S 9 '91; Newsweek 125:44+ Je 12 '95 pors; Time 133:58+ F 13 '89 por, 141:54+ Ap 19 '93 pors

---

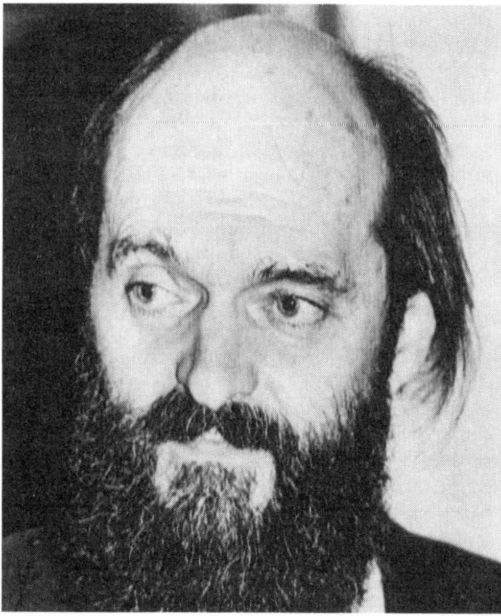

Lembit Michelson/Agence France-Presse

Pärt, Arvo
(payrt)

Sept. 11, 1935- Estonian composer. Address: c/o Universal Edition (London) Ltd., Warwick House, 9 Warwick St., London W1R 5RA, England

"I have discovered that it is enough when a single note is beautifully played," the Estonian composer Arvo Pärt has said. "This one note, or a silent beat, or a moment of silence comforts me." Since bursting onto the international music scene in the early 1980s through a series of enormously successful recordings on the ECM label, Pärt has captivated audiences and critics alike with his musically austere yet hauntingly beautiful, hypnotic compositions. His "tintinnabuli" compositional style, a term he derived from tintinnabulation, the ringing of bells, relies on a restricted musical vocabulary and frequent repetition, prompting some critics to label him a minimalist. But while his works contain some minimalist elements, his compositions, many of which are settings of sacred texts, are imbued with an emotional resonance and devotional quality that are heightened by his use of Renaissance and medieval techniques.

Pärt's distinctive compositional style emerged during the late 1970s, after he had produced a series of twelve-tone pieces that had established him as a radical musical innovator in what was then the Soviet Union. The majority of those works remain virtually unknown in the West, where his fame is based mainly on the popularity of his later, tintinnabuli works such as *Tabula Rasa* and *Passio*, an ethereal setting of the Passion according to St. John that has received considerable attention and earned him a reputation as a musical mystic. In a representative assessment of the composer's oeuvre, K. Robert Schwarz described his music as a balance between "serene mysticism and spiritual fire." Pärt himself rarely discusses his work and generally shuns personal appearances and interviews. "I cannot say in a thousand sentences what I can say in a few notes," he has explained, as quoted in *Fanfare* (April 1988).

Born on September 11, 1935 in Paide, Estonia, Arvo Pärt became interested in music after his family moved into a house with an old grand piano in it. Although the instrument was defective, particularly in the middle register, it enabled Pärt to begin experimenting with music. He began his formal training with piano lessons, at the age of seven or eight. "I thought I was playing Mozart," he said, recalling his early practice sessions for Richard Kostelanetz, who interviewed him for *Connoisseur* (April 1990). "It sounded like John Cage," he added, referring to the highly inventive and ultramodern American composer who is perhaps best known for his aleatoric, or chance, compositions. Pärt's first memory of classical orchestral music dates from his teen years, when he heard a new and unusual-sounding piece being transmitted over an outdoor loudspeaker in the town square. The experience reinforced his interest in music, although he wasn't able to commence serious study of the subject until after he had completed his compulsory service in the military, where he played snare drum in an army band.

Upon his discharge from the army, in 1958, Pärt enrolled at the conservatory in Tallinn, the capital of Estonia. Among his teachers there was the composer Heino Eller, a prominent Estonian musician who had trained at the St. Petersburg Conservatory under Alexander Glazunov. While at school, Pärt worked part-time as a recording engineer in the music division of Estonian Radio, a job he detested because of the low quality, in his opinion, of the music programmed for broadcast.

Pärt's own compositions during that period were favorably received by both the Soviet cultural authorities and audiences. One of his most popular early works was *Meie aed* (Our Garden, 1959), an exuberant cantata for children's choir and orchestra. Like many of his youthful efforts, most of which were written under Eller's guidance, *Meie aed* is a tonal composition. Energetic, melodious, and deeply rooted in Estonian choral tradition, the piece brought Pärt's name to prominence throughout the Soviet Union. Performances of his works were given in major Soviet cultural centers, such as Tallinn and Moscow, and at the 1960 Zagreb Festival, in what was then Yugoslavia.

During the 1960s Pärt began to explore new compositional techniques that were popular among composers in Western Europe at the time. The dodecaphonic, or twelve-note, system—a method of composition in which the twelve notes of the chromatic scale, arranged in a particular order called a tone row, provide the basis for both melodies and chords—especially interested him, since it represented, in his view, not only a mental discipline but a step toward greater expression in his music. His first large orchestral piece, *Nekrolog* (1960), was the first Estonian work composed according to the twelve-note system. Although Pärt didn't adhere strictly to all the rules of twelve-tone music, *Nekrolog*, which he dedicated to the victims of the Holocaust, showed enough of a Western influence to cause a stir among Soviet cultural officials and touch off a spirited debate about the relationship between artistic methods and the value of a work of art. The controversy did not prevent Pärt from receiving the top prize in the 1962 All-Union Young Composers' Competition, although he won it for two less contentious works: *Meie aed* and the oratorio *Maailma samm* (1961), which has been translated variously as The Pace of the World or The World's Stride.

Pärt graduated from the Tallinn Conservatory in 1963, the year he wrote *Perpetuum mobile*, another twelve-tone piece that consolidated the composer's reputation as a musical innovator. Rising as if from nothing to an explosion of rhythm and timbre, then ebbing away into silence once again, the deceptively simple work belies its meticulously crafted structure. "The formal simplicity and directness of expression evokes a definitely new, never-before-experienced musical feeling," Harry Olt observed in his 1972 book *Modern Estonian Composers*. "One might almost conceive of it as a gigantic deep breath."

With his symphonies nos. 1 (*Polyphonic*) and 2, written in 1964 and 1966, respectively, Pärt further explored twelve-tone composition. Symphony no. 2 is one of several works in which he employed a collage technique, incorporating snippets of other composers' music into his own. The Second Symphony, for example, which features melodic motives played against a background of aleatoric music and a chorus of children's squeak toys, ends, after a series of dramatic crescendos, with a serene quotation from Tchaikovsky's "Douce Reverie" (Sweet Dream), one of the twenty-four piano pieces that make up his *Album pour Enfants* (Album for the Young). Characterized by dissonance and abrupt changes of mood and texture, the symphony also contains "sudden bursts of tonality," to borrow the conductor Paul Hillier's phrase, offering listeners a foretaste of the style Pärt would later embrace.

Citations from the works of other composers are also apparent in *Credo*, a 1968 piece for piano, mixed chorus, and orchestra that placed Pärt at the center of controversy once again, because of its overtly religious nature. Based on a sacred text that included the line "I believe in Jesus Christ," the work was banned by Soviet officials. Musically, *Credo* is an unsettling juxtaposition of Bach's serene Prelude in C Major, from Book One of the *Well-Tempered Clavier*, and a slightly menacing orchestral part. The work ends on a C major chord, an indication that Pärt had abandoned atonality and concluded his foray into twelve-tone composition, in the opinion of the musicologist Susan Bradshaw. "The argument between two irreconcilable harmonic styles [i.e. twelve-tone and the conventionally harmonic] is finally resolved as the serial element is literally blacked out . . . for a triumphant consolidation of the work's underlying tonality," Bradshaw has explained, as quoted in *Connoisseur*. "In this respect the piece is not only a setting of the words of the Credo but also a personal affirmation."

After writing *Credo*, Pärt entered a phase that has often been referred to in the press as his "years of silence," a period of relatively low artistic output that lasted approximately eight years. During this time, Pärt left his job with the state radio network and devoted himself to intensive musical study, focusing on Gregorian chant, Notre Dame organum, the music of the fifteenth century, especially the works of Josquin Des Prez and Johannes Ockeghem, and Eastern Orthodox liturgical music. To support himself and his family during his self-education, he wrote dozens of film scores, an endeavor he disliked because, after editing, his music was, in his words, "no longer recognizable." Commenting on this period in his life in a rare interview with Paul Griffiths of the London *Times*, Pärt described it as a search for a new musical focus: "One day I realized that I possessed a great many things in my music, but I did not possess the most important thing. And so I set about eliminating everything that was extraneous."

Pärt's Symphony no. 3 (1971), one of only two major compositions he wrote between 1968 and 1976, showed signs of the new musical direction in which the composer was heading. Dedicated to a fellow Estonian, the conductor Neeme Järvi, one of his earliest champions, the twenty-minute piece is the first of Pärt's works to draw explicitly on medieval music. The symphony's medieval roots are apparent from its opening bars, in which an unaccompanied oboe suggests a Gregorian chant, receiving a modal "amen" response from the strings and a more forceful answer in the form of a fanfare from the brass and timpani. Critics also heard in the work, whose three movements share themes and are intended to be played without a break, the influence of Dmitri Shostakovich and, even more strongly, Jean Sibelius. As David Wright observed in his program notes for the New York Philharmonic's performances of Pärt's Third Symphony in November 1994, the "trans-Baltic connection to Sibelius" is especially evident in the composer's "lean yet vivid scoring, his seemingly glacial composure lit from within by a fire of passion." For Pärt, the work was, as he put it, "a joyous piece of music" but not yet "the end of [his] despair and [his] search." A year after writing the Third Symphony, he composed the symphonic cantata *Laul armastatule* (Song for the Beloved), then once again retreated into silence and contemplation.

The years of study and reflection resulted in a new compositional style that Pärt introduced through a string of compositions completed during the late 1970s. Characterized by an austerity derived from the works of the early masters he had studied, his new compositions were often created around the most basic musical elements, such as a triad, an arpeggio, or a scale. Using the three notes of the triad as a model to explain his new style, Pärt likened their sound to the pealing of bells and called his new approach "tintinnabuli style." Like the chiming of bells, the music written in Pärt's new style is in a state of constant flux, resonating with overtones and undertones, although the overall impression is one of stasis. To listeners, the music is characterized by a disarming simplicity, rhythmic calm, and shimmering triadic harmonies.

The work that appeared to mark the emergence of this new style was a quietly beautiful piano piece called *Für Alina* (For Alina, 1976), a simple composition constructed of notes at the extreme ends of the high and low registers, open intervals, and pedal points. "That was the first piece that was on a new plateau," Pärt is quoted as having said in the liner notes for the ECM recording *Tabula Rasa*. "It was here that I discovered the triad series, which I made my simple, little guiding rule." But it was the works that followed *Für Alina* that brought Pärt's unique style to the attention of Western audiences, after his emigration from the Soviet Union. At least partly because of his wife's Jewish heritage, he and his family were granted permission to leave Estonia for Israel in 1980, but they decided instead to remain in Vienna and become Austrian citizens. A year later, they moved to Germany and settled in a suburb of what was then West Berlin.

Pärt's international breakthrough came in 1984, with the release of his first recording on the ECM label. The disc was a collection of three works that remain among his best-known compositions: *Tabula Rasa* (1977), *Fratres* (1977), and *Cantus in Memory of Benjamin Britten* (1977). Entitled *Tabula Rasa*, the disc attracted considerable attention for what John Rockwell of the *New York Times* called its "quiet, compelling authority" as well as for its impressive roster of top-flight performers, including the conductor Dennis Russell Davies, the pianist Keith Jarrett, the violinist Gidon Kremer, and the composer Alfred Schnittke, who played the prepared piano on *Tabula Rasa*.

Tabula Rasa's title piece, a double concerto for two violins, prepared piano, and string orchestra, is typical of Pärt's later style, in that it relies on a restricted musical vocabulary, deriving virtually all of its musical material from one triad and its related minor scale. About thirty minutes long, *Tabula Rasa* makes use of one of Pärt's favorite Renaissance compositional techniques—namely, the mensuration canon, which bases its construction upon a central theme overlaid with rhythmic multiples of it in each voice. A haunting mysticism is evoked during the work's second section, entitled "Silentium," through a phrase played by prepared piano that calls to mind the distant ringing of church bells. A mensuration canon also serves as the foundation for *Cantus in Memory of Benjamin Britten*, a five-minute piece, scored for string orchestra and glockenspiel, that builds in intensity to reach an overwhelming climax through a series of repeatedly descending minor scales. *Fratres* achieves a surprising variety of sounds through the repetition and transposition of a simple six-measure theme. As he has done for a number of his compositions, Pärt has created several performing versions of *Fratres*, for violin and piano, for twelve cellos, and for baroque ensemble, the first two of which are included on the disc *Tabula Rasa*.

In a review of *Tabula Rasa* for *American Record Guide* (May/June 1987), Arved Ashby described Pärt's music as sounding like "a cooperative effort between the twentieth and fifteenth centuries that has chosen to ignore everything that came in between." "The listener finds himself toying with paradoxes in attempting to come to grips with this synthesis, and perhaps this quality is what makes each work beg for an immediate rehearing," Ashby continued. "It is music that is both greatly comforting and profoundly disturbing, both drained and full of deeply buried emotion. . . . One conclusion is inescapable: This music is profoundly original, and surely represents one of the most salient stylistic developments of the late twentieth century."

Pärt gained widespread recognition in North America during the mid-1980s through the release of two more ECM recordings and a number of performances of his works, including a retrospective program presented at Alice Tully Hall in New York City by the ensemble Continuum in 1984—an evening that K. Robert Schwarz described as a "transcendent mystical experience." "Pärt's emotional intensity, his quiet strength and simplicity, his meditative rapture, had brought a fleeting moment of repose to our hectic lives," Schwarz wrote in his review for *High Fidelity* (September 1984). "May he return to this country again soon." Pärt, who is customarily reticent in public, agreed to address the New York audience. In his brief statement, which he delivered in English, he described the mixed feelings of joy and helplessness he experiences when he first hears a new work in performance; he also expressed concern about whether the work was pleasing to God—a comment he has reiterated in his rare interviews.

Arbos, Pärt's second disc on the ECM label, collected a variety of works from the late 1970s to the mid-1980s that reaffirmed the composer's abiding interest in early music. Singling out for special praise a devotional work for four voices and organ called *An den Wassern zu Babel* (By the Waters of Babylon, 1976–84), Allan Kozinn described Pärt's music as a marriage of "antiquity and novelty." "Pärt indulges his antiquarian tastes fully, writing in long melismatic vocal lines (delivered without vibrato) and in harmonies that could pass for medieval organum," Kozinn wrote in the *New York Times* (March 26, 1989). "The work's structure and dynamic shape give away its contemporary provenance, but at its start, a listener might assume it was music from a distant age." The most substantial composition on the recording, *Stabat Mater*, a twenty-five-minute setting of the thirteenth-century Latin liturgical poem, advances stepwise through gradually descending melodic lines, emulating Mary's tears at the cross of Jesus, that bring to mind the composer's lament for Benjamin Britten.

Passio Domini nostri Jesu Christi secundum Joannem (1981–82), which is more commonly known simply as *Passio*, is the sole work on Pärt's third ECM recording. One of his most ambitious compositions to date, the seventy-one-minute, single-movement setting in Latin of the Passion according to St. John is scored for choir and soloists, accompanied by an instrumental ensemble of violin, oboe, cello, bassoon, and organ. In his version of St. John's narrative account of the arrest, trial, and crucifixion of Jesus of Nazareth, Pärt preserved the time-honored tradition of assigning the words of Jesus to a bass and those of Pontius Pilate to a tenor, but where other composers have usually written the role of St. John the Evangelist for a tenor, he chose to divide the Evangelist's narration among a quartet of singers—soprano, countertenor, tenor, and baritone—to emphasize various expressive points.

The ECM recording of *Passio*, which features vocal performances by the Hilliard Ensemble, a British group frequently associated with Pärt's work, received the highest praise from critics. In his assessment for *Musical America* (May 1989), K. Robert Schwarz saluted the composer's remarkable talent for creating unforgettable music through "deceptively simple" means, pointing out that most of *Passio* revolves around variations on a single minor tonic triad. "It creates a sense of ritual by means of repetition—not the kinetic repetition of [Steve] Reich or [Philip] Glass, but the slow-moving, circular repetition of a triad, a melodic fragment, or an ensemble refrain," Schwarz explained. "The result is a work that is deliberately undramatic, shunning all pictorialism, but spiritually intense; a work that overwhelms with quiet dignity and a sense of unspoken rapture." Kenneth LaFave of *Ovation* (September 1989) was similarly impressed. The "translucently beautiful" *Passio* was, in his view, "a masterpiece and one of the few indispensable works of the twentieth century." LaFave was especially taken by Pärt's "subtle, sober" tone-painting. He cited in particular one of the work's most poignant scenes, Peter's rejection of Christ: "Peter's triple denial gnaws at the listener—who could have known beforehand that four notes on the oboe would contain such loneliness?"

When asked to comment on the religious elements in his music, Pärt has been characteristically circumspect, telling John Rockwell of the *New York Times* (July 4, 1993), for instance, "For Bach, every piece that he wrote was praise of God, but I'm not worthy to say that." Of his most recent compositions, however, the vast majority, including such instrumental pieces as *Festina Lente*, an adagio for strings in the form of a mensuration canon, have had religious themes. Among them are the liturgical works *Miserere* (1989), for five solo voices, chorus, and orchestra; *Magnificat* (1989), for unaccompanied chorus; and *Litany: Prayers of St. John Chrysostom for each hour of the day and night*, which was given its world premiere at the Oregon Bach Festival, in Eugene, on June 26, 1994. Scored for chorus, orchestra, and the four vocalists of the Hilliard Ensemble, *Litany*, which takes as its text a group of fourth-century prayers, is sung in English. "The work has an unusually wide dynamic range for Pärt, and orchestra, chorus, and soloists eventually filled the hall with their fortissimo pleas . . . ," Chris Mohr, who was among the first-night listeners, recalled in a profile of the composer for *On the Air Magazine* (October 1994). "The music breathed new life into these ancient texts, giving a modern audience the chance to reexamine their meaning. It seemed perhaps that his purifying music was itself the answer to the prayers."

Standing almost six feet tall, Arvo Pärt has blue eyes and a dark, full beard that gives him the appearance of an Old Testament prophet, as more than one interviewer has noted. His public image is that of an intensely serious and meditative man, but friends and colleagues have described him as cheerful, witty, and high-spirited. His sense of humor is reflected in his 1976 work *Wenn Bach Bienen gezüchtet hätte* (If Bach Had Been a Beekeeper), in which minimalist buzzings are gradually transformed into a Bachian cadence. Pärt divides his time between two homes, one in London and another in Lichtenrade, on the outskirts of Berlin, where he and his wife, Nora, whom he married in 1972, live in a simple house with few signs of modern luxury. They have two sons. The awards and distinctions Pärt has received include the 1978 Estonian Music Prize, for *Tabula Rasa*, and two awards for the *Passio* recording: the Edison Award and an award from the Record Prize Academy, in Tokyo. He is a member of the Swedish Royal Music Academy and Ehrendoktor of the Tallinn Conservatory. Despite his accomplishments, Pärt is notoriously reluctant to discuss his music, explaining to Richard Kostelanetz for the *Connoisseur* profile, "Franz Schubert explained nothing; it is not necessary. He wrote songs. They are the best explaining."

Selected Biographical References: Connoisseur p66+ Ap '90 por; Chicago Tribune XIII p8+ Ap 3 '94 por; Musical Times p34+ Mr '89; On the Air 5:5+ O '94 pors; Contemporary Composers (1992);

International Who's Who in Music, 1993-94; Slonimsky, Nicolas. Baker's Biographical Dictionary of Musicians (1992)

Robert Sullivan/Agence France-Presse

Patterson, P. J.

Apr. 10, 1935- Prime Minister of Jamaica; lawyer. Address: Office of Prime Minister, 1 Devon Road, P.O. Box 272, Kingston 6, Jamaica

When, on March 30, 1992, P. J. Patterson was named by the People's National Party of Jamaica as the successor to Prime Minister Michael Manley, who was stepping down because of ill health, he was faced with the daunting task of repairing an economy hobbled by unemployment and an inflation rate that had soared to over 70 percent. A lawyer and longtime force in his party, Patterson had been the minister of finance and planning in Manley's cabinet until he was forced to relinquish that post in late 1991 amid a scandal involving tax breaks that he had granted and that allegedly benefited a high-ranking party official. The controversy, however, did little to diminish the respect Patterson had earned over the previous two decades of service to the People's National Party (PNP); just three months after he resigned from the cabinet, he was chosen to lead the party.

The PNP had traditionally supported a program of democratic socialism; as financial minister in Manley's administration, however, Patterson had implemented free-market reforms in an effort to revitalize the country's ailing economy. By continuing that policy as prime minister, he managed to rein in inflation somewhat in his first year in office. Although he is a low-key technocrat on an island governed since its independence, in 1962, mainly by charismatic figures such as Manley, Patterson has proved to be popular with both the masses and with business owners, many of whom are beginning to thrive under the new policies. Overcoming any lingering effects of the scandal and doubts about the still-fragile economy, Patterson retained the prime ministership with a landslide victory in the March 1993 general elections. Since the election he has stepped up his efforts to make Jamaica's monetary policy more creditworthy, and he has worked to attract foreign investment to achieve fuller integration into the world economy. "With creativity, discipline, determination, and hard work," he said, as quoted in *Black Enterprise* (December 1992), "we will enter the twenty-first century as a strong nation."

Born on April 10, 1935 in St. Andrew, Jamaica, Percival Noel James Patterson is the son of Henry Patterson, a farmer, and Ina James, a primary-school teacher. After attending Somerton Primary School in the province of St. James, he won a scholarship to Calabar High School, where he was a member of the table tennis and debating teams and edited the school magazine. Upon graduating from high school in 1953, he taught at Cornwall College for a short time and then, in 1954, enrolled at the University of the West Indies at Mona, where he was a founder and president of the Political Club. Patterson gave his first political speech in 1955, in support of a candidate in an election in the province of Western Hanover. After earning his B.A. degree in English with honors, in 1958, he became a party organizer for the PNP, a post he retained until 1960. During that period he also taught at Munro College and Jamaica College.

Patterson left Jamaica in 1960 to study law at the London School of Economics and Political Science. While there, he won the Sir Hughes Parry prize for excellence in the law of contracts. Following his graduation, in 1963, he passed the bar in England and Jamaica. Upon his return to Jamaica, Patterson resumed his work for the PNP, serving as a member of the party's Constituency Executive, National Executive Council, and Party Executive from 1964 through 1969. In 1967 he was appointed to the Senate, where he was leader of opposition business in 1969 and 1970. He was elected to the Jamaican House of Representatives in 1970, from the district of South-East Westmoreland, and he held that seat until 1980.

Named party vice-president in 1969, Patterson remained in that capacity until 1982. Among the other positions he held during that time were PNP campaign director in the 1972 and 1976 general elections, both of which the PNP won, minister of industry and tourism (1972–77), and deputy prime minister and minister of foreign affairs and foreign trade (1978–80). His legal training and nonconfrontational manner stood him in good stead as he played a major role in international negotiations. He represented Jamaica at meetings of the non-aligned countries, at Commonwealth Summit Conferences, in the negotiations of the Canada-West Indies Trade Agreement that was concluded in 1977, at meetings of the United Nations Conference on Trade and Development, and at other gatherings. Not only did Patterson lead the Jamaican delegations in international negotiations, but he also represented other nations in his region and developing countries in Africa and in the Pacific region in talks worldwide. He was an adviser to the government of Belize in the final negotiations that led to its independence, in 1982, and he subsequently assisted in drafting that country's constitution. When the PNP was voted out of office in 1980, and Patterson lost his seat in Parliament, he returned to the practice of law. His skills as an attorney led to his being called to the Inner Bar as a Queen's Counsel in 1984. In his spare time, he helped reorganize the party, serving as its chairman from 1983 to 1992.

Under Patterson's leadership as party campaign director, the PNP returned to power in 1989, and Patterson, who also regained his parliamentary seat that year, was appointed minister of development, planning, and production in the cabinet of Prime Minister Michael Manley. In the following year he was named minister of finance and planning, and as Manley began a shift away from the socialism of the PNP governments he had led in the 1970s and embraced free-market reforms, Patterson became a major architect of the transition. As finance minister, he was in charge of implementing Manley's program of privatization, trade liberalization, and deregulation of foreign exchange. Among Patterson's achievements were the drafting of a new banking act, replacement of a production tax with a general consumption tax, reduction of taxes on imports of raw materials and capital goods, removal of wage guidelines, increased revenue collection, and removal of income tax on approved productivity schemes. The abrupt transition threw the Jamaican economy into a turmoil as inflation skyrocketed.

Patterson was forced to resign as finance minister in December 1991, not as the result of the shaky economy but over accusations of conflict of interest stemming from his decision to waive import duties on gasoline for the Shell Oil Company, to the apparent benefit of a senior PNP official. He nevertheless retained strong backing in Parliament, and when Manley stepped down in 1992, the leading candidates to succeed him were Patterson and Portia Simpson, who was the minister for welfare, labor, and sports.

On March 28, 1992 thirty-two hundred PNP delegates assembled in Kingston to choose between Patterson and Simpson, a self-educated populist and champion of women's rights who had risen from a poor background and who, in contrast to the low-key Patterson, was "a sharp, exciting speaker," according to a reporter for the *Economist* (March 21, 1992). Speaking with Howard W. French for an article in the *New York Times* (March 29, 1992), one campaign worker expressed the emotional support typical of Simpson's backers: "If she loses it is only because they robbed her, because she is the people's choice. P. J. has never known hunger. It is only the big-belly guys who are behind him." Patterson and his supporters, on the other hand, emphasized Simpson's relative lack of experience. According to the correspondent for the *Economist*, Patterson's years in politics made him "a master of the island's system of patronage, trusted by its rich white and brown businessmen and supported by the rising black entrepreneurs who have long seen him as their man." Patterson argued that, with all its economic difficulties, Jamaica could not afford "the luxury of a learning curve." "P. J. has experience in every area of government," Terry Gillette, the minister of construction, told French. "The other candidate does not have the experience or ability to handle the situation hanging over us. She is a good horse running in the wrong race." After winning the delegates' endorsement by a margin of three votes to one, Patterson vowed to "reunite the party" in the wake of the sometimes bitter contest with Simpson.

Despite the Shell scandal, rising inflation, and dissention in the PNP, the rival Jamaican Labor Party (JLP), which was also plagued by infighting, got "curiously little mileage out of the government's difficulties," as the reporter for the *Economist* observed. "Some suggest it has no wish to be in power during such a difficult economic transition," the reporter added. Although Patterson was criticized by the JLP for failing to attract the new investments he had said his free-market policies would garner, he appeared to bring some stabilization to the economy during his first ten months in office, reducing inflation for the first nine months of the 1993 fiscal year to 17.9 percent, from 73.1 percent the year before.

Seeking to secure a direct mandate and to take advantage of the stabilizing economy, Patterson set an election date for March 30, 1993, a year earlier than required, and made his appeal to the Jamaican masses by adopting the slogan "black man's time has come," a reference to the fact that Patterson is only the second dark-skinned prime minister—none had ever won a general election—in the history of the predominantly black country. At the end of an election campaign marred by politically motivated violence that resulted in the deaths of more than ten people, the PNP won a two-thirds majority of the votes cast, and Patterson secured a five-year term as prime minister. "I have obtained from the people and for the people a mandate—live and direct," Patterson declared. Although he conceded that Patterson was clearly the winner, the JLP leader, Edward Seaga, referring to ballot-box theft and other polling irregularities, described the election as "the most disgraceful in the history of Jamaica." The JLP, however, was itself reportedly implicated in some of the election improprieties. Acknowledging such dissatisfaction and the violence surrounding the election, Patterson said, "We have to get rid of the bitterness, of any feelings of intolerance, of all forms of political prejudice . . . which have served in the past to divide our society."

Outlining his policy goals at a press conference on the day after the election, Patterson announced his determination to build a "broad consensus" among business, government, and labor and to institute programs for the education and training of workers in technical and service-industry jobs. In a speech he delivered on August 6, 1993, on the occasion of the thirty-first anniversary of Jamaica's independence, Patterson declared: "We must concentrate seriously on the development of our greatest asset—our human resources. We must widen our knowledge base and intensify skill training if we are to meet the challenges of the time." He added that Jamaica must reduce its crime rate in order, among other things, to maintain its thriving tourism industry, the country's biggest generator of foreign income. Calling on Jamaicans living abroad to contribute to the effort to revitalize the economy by investing in their home country, he implemented a plan to make doing so easier. As part of a scheme to integrate Jamaica more fully into the world economy, in 1994 Patterson's government oversaw the opening of the first Jamaican Life Insurance Agency in the United States. The financial services the agency provided, Patterson said, represented a new Jamaican export.

As part of a general campaign of divestiture of state-owned enterprises, Patterson privatized several state-run sugar factories and Jamaica's national airline, Air Jamaica, all of which had been losing money but were vital to the economy. "The decision to privatize . . . these entities was informed by the realization that the taxpayer should not be exposed to bearing the burden of further losses in the years to come," Patterson explained at an August 15, 1994 press conference. "Further major injections of equity capital were necessary in both cases to turn around two areas of strategic importance to the national economy, which were not available from public funds."

Edward Seaga contended that Patterson had done a poor job of implementing the free-market policies and, noting his own party's longtime advocacy of such policies, accused Patterson of "leading from behind." Charles Ross, the executive director of the Private Sector Organization of Jamaica, however, said that the economy had shown marked improvement under the new prime minister's leadership. "It's clear," Ross told Stephen Fidler of the *Financial Times* (February 28, 1994), "that barring a big collapse of the bauxite business or the tourism industry, the economy is much closer to self-sufficiency than it has been in any time in the last twenty years." According to a reporter for the *Economist* (March 27, 1993), entrepreneurs and small investors are especially pleased with Patterson and the "booming stock market" his policies have helped foster. "For those above the poverty line, life is in many ways more congenial than it was," the reporter wrote. "Telephones work. Cars can be imported without bribing anybody. It no longer takes all morning to get money from the bank."

P. J. Patterson has been described in the *Economist* (March 21, 1992) as "a reticent man in a loudmouth country." He enjoys listening to jazz and Jamaican music, and he is a fan of boxing, cricket, track and field, and tennis. A widower, he has a son, Richard, and a daughter, Sharon. In his thirty-first-anniversary message to Jamaica, he ended with a subject that he said was "especially close to [his] heart." "It concerns the values which we are teaching our children," he said. "Many of you are very conscious of the need to ensure that you instill in them the morals and discipline and give them the love that they need to develop their true potential. You understand the need to teach them to be proud of their heritage. As parents and close friends, you need to serve as good role models. . . . If our country is to grow and prosper, we need not only economic empowerment; we need men and women who appreciate giving of our best at the workplace; men and women with a feeling of self worth; and with a commitment to this great little island Jamaica, which we all love."

Selected Biographical References: Current World Leaders 21:9+ Jl '78; Economist 322:48 Mr 21 '92; Guardian p16 Mr 28 '92 por, p11 Ap 1 '93 por; Columbia Dictionary of Political Biography (1990); International Who's Who, 1994-95; Who's Who in the World, 1993-94

Payne, Roger S.

Jan. 29, 1935- Biologist; conservationist. Address: c/o Whale Conservation Institute, 191 Weston Rd., Lincoln, MA 01773

In the mid-1960s Roger S. Payne, who is widely regarded as the world's foremost cetacean biologist—and, in the words of the biologist Thomas Eisner, "possibly one of the two or three most interesting scientists alive today"—committed himself to doing whatever he could to preserve the world's remaining whale populations, and he has been honoring that commitment ever since. He began by investigating and publicizing the now-famous musical talents of humpback whales. Payne's efforts to educate the public about the animals' eerily captivating songs, through lectures and magazine articles, helped raise awareness of the plight of all species of whales, whose populations had been devastated by more than a century of commercial hunting for their oil, baleen, and other products and which are now being threatened by the effects of the toxins polluting their oceanic homes. "Roger gets people to care about all wildlife, about the sanctity of nature, and to see the importance of keeping it around," Eisner told Natalie Angier, who profiled Payne for *Discover* (April 1983).

Payne's other major research and conservation effort involves a population of right whales off the coast of Argentina, a group he has been studying

The Discovery Channel

Roger S. Payne

continuously since 1970. As the longest-running study of any whale species based on recognized individuals, the project is comparable to the work of such celebrated ethologists as Cynthia Moss, Biruté Galdikas, and Jane Goodall, who have been conducting similar studies of, respectively, the African elephant, orangutan, and chimpanzee. The right-whale study is carried out under the auspices of the Whale Conservation Institute, which Payne founded in 1971 and which, like Payne himself, is "dedicated to the conservation of whales through education and research." For his work Payne has received many awards, including a John D. and Catherine T. MacArthur Foundation "genius grant" in 1984. Payne has written about his research on and life among the world's largest living mammals in *Among Whales* (1995), his first book for a popular audience. In an advance review of the book, the writer Peter Matthiessen described it as "a thoughtful and beautifully written account of an eminent field biologist's passionate life among great whales."

The son of Edward Payne, an electrical engineer at Bell Telephone Laboratories, and Elizabeth Payne, a violinist and violist who taught at the Mannes School of Music before her marriage, Roger S. Payne was born on January 29, 1935 in the New York City borough of Manhattan, where he lived until he was nine. He has traced his fascination with wild animals and places to his childhood, even though Manhattan afforded him limited opportunities to observe the natural world. "I was always looking up at the sky," he recalled to Natalie Angier. "That was the only place you could find something that wasn't manmade." Neither of Roger's parents shared his passion for wildlife, which only intensified after the family moved to New Jersey. "It was a wildish place, and that's where I realized what I'd been missing," he told Angier. "I became fanatical about nature."

Payne's affinity for the natural world notwithstanding, his earliest career ambition was to follow in his father's footsteps and become an engineer. When he finally made the decision that steered him in the direction of a career in biology, he did so on something of a whim. It was at the beginning of his sophomore year at Harvard University, while he was standing in line to register for a course of study, that he elected biology as his major subject. "It was the first thing that came to mind," he explained to *Current Biography*. "Yet most important decisions—like marriage and career—one makes are based on the most meager evidence and thought. They're usually irrational decisions based purely on feeling."

At Harvard, Payne became interested in the acoustical abilities of various animal species, and, with D. R. Griffin, he did research on the directional sensitivity of bats' ears. After taking his A.B. degree in 1957, he entered Cornell University, in Ithaca, New York. There he studied animal behavior and neurophysiology, wrote his doctoral dissertation on how owls use sound to locate prey in the dark, and, with Thomas Eisner, did research on the defensive secretions of arthropods. From Cornell he moved on to Tufts University, in Medford, Massachusetts, both to teach and to do postdoctoral research on noctuid moths—"yet another creature for which sound is extremely important," he has noted. Payne has attributed his fascination with the ways animals use sound partly to his own interest in music (as a youth he had learned to play the cello). His dual interests in music and science were shared by Katy Boynton, whom he met at Cornell and married in 1960.

"Everybody has some such experience that affects him for life, probably several," Payne told Faith McNulty in an interview for the *New Yorker* (August 6, 1973). For Payne, one such experience occurred one night in the mid-1960s, while he was at Tufts. Upon hearing a report on the radio about a dead porpoise that had been found on a nearby beach, he decided to see the animal for himself. "It was a small whale—a porpoise about eight feet long, with lovely, subtle curves glistening in the cold rain," he later wrote of that night, as quoted by Faith McNulty. "It had been mutilated. Someone had hacked off its flukes for a souvenir, and two other people had carved their initials deeply into its side. Someone else had stuck a cigar butt into its blowhole. I removed the cigar, and I stood there for a long time with feelings I can't describe. . . . At some point the flashlight went out, but as the tide came in I could periodically see the graceful outline of the whale against the white foam cast up by the waves. Although it is more typical than not of what happens to whales when they encounter man, that experience was somehow the last straw, and I decided to use the first possible opportunity to learn enough about whales so I might have some effect on their future."

As it turned out, such an opportunity was not long in coming. In about 1967 Payne and his wife received an invitation to visit Bermuda and see their first live whales. While there they met Frank Watlington, an engineer with the Lamont Geophysical Field Station whose work entailed testing hydrophone arrays that the United States Navy used to listen to enemy submarines. Watlington invited the Paynes to listen to a tape of some unusual sounds that he had recorded in the course of his work—sounds that had been made by humpback whales, which migrated to the area each year to spend the winter. Except for a few biologists, Watlington had told no one about the sounds because he feared that the information might be useful to whalers.

The Paynes did not hesitate to take Watlington up on his offer. "Out of his tinny speaker came incredible sounds," Payne recalled, in describing the first time he heard the cries of humpback whales. "I had never heard anything like them. They riveted my attention as nothing ever had." He was so captivated by the haunting sounds, in fact, that he borrowed part of the tape, and, in the course of listening to it over and over, he ended up committing the songs to memory. When, in the following year, Payne returned to Bermuda to listen to the whales' songs again, he knew them well enough to recognize that the animals were emitting sequences of sounds that were similar to those he had heard on the tape. "This blew my mind," Payne told Faith McNulty. "It was confirmation that not only do individual humpbacks repeat their songs but other humpbacks may sing the same song at a different time and place."

By this time, in about 1968, Payne had joined both the New York Zoological Society's (NYZS) Institute for Research in Animal Behavior, as a research zoologist, and Rockefeller University, in New York City, as an assistant professor of biology, and he was actively pursuing his newfound desire to learn about whales. During his first few years at Rockefeller and the NYZS, he focused his research efforts on recording and then analyzing the humpbacks' sounds, with the hope of figuring out what purpose they served in the animals' lives. One of the first things that Payne and a colleague, Scott McVay, discovered was that what they were hearing was not a disorganized jumble of sounds but "songs" that obeyed rules of composition not unlike those employed by humans. They also learned that each song contains between two and nine phrases that are strung together without pause; that themes are reprised in the same order in successive songs; and that the animal "composers" make use of such musical conventions as rhythm, sometimes combining percussive sounds with tonal ones in proportions uncannily similar to those used by their human counterparts. The net result, according to Payne, is "an exuberant, uninterrupted river of sound that can flow on for twenty-four hours or longer."

Yet another tantalizing discovery, made by Katy Payne, is that humpbacks modify their songs from year to year. "In other words, the whales don't just sing monotonously throughout their lives," Roger Payne told *Current Biography*. "Rather, they compose as they go along, incorporating new elements into their old songs," he wrote in *National Geographic* (January 1979). "We are aware of no other animal besides man in which this strange and complicated behavior occurs, and we have no idea of the reason behind it." This observation is particularly astonishing in light of the fact that humpback whales are not closely related to humans (the evolutionary history of whales began more than fifty million years ago, while the earliest humans appeared a scant four to seven million years ago), and therefore developed this highly sophisticated ability independently.

It is tempting to conclude that the songs of the humpback whales, which are apparently produced only by the males, might be a kind of language, and some researchers have indeed suggested that the animals sing to share their experiences with one another. Payne, however, doubts that this is the case, for routine observations or events would probably be described by similar songs, and, as he has pointed out, the songs do not stay the same but evolve over time. Payne favors the idea that the songs are the means by which males attract females during courtship. "I think songs are sung by a male . . . in hopes of being more attractive than other males," he told Jonathan White, who interviewed him for *Talking on the Water; Conversations About Nature* (1994). "And I suspect that the form of the song is shaped and selected by females; in other words, males learn to sing what attracts females. That's my guess. There are all kinds of things the song could be. A good song might give a male a momentary advantage over other males, giving him more opportunities to mate with the female." Another possibility, suggested by others, is that the songs demonstrate how long a male can hold its breath and thus provide a female with a sense of the reproductive fitness of the male suitor.

In addition to studying the songs of humpback whales, Payne has concurrently pursued another line of research that is less widely known but arguably of even greater significance: since 1970 he has been studying a population of right whales, one of the more than seventy living species of whales and dolphins. The effort has been carried out under the auspices of the Whale Conservation Institute (formerly the Long-Term Research Institute and the Whale and Dolphin Conservation Society), which he established the year he began the project and which is headquartered in an old barn behind a farmhouse that Payne owns in Lincoln, Massachusetts.

In deciding to begin a long-term study of right whales, Payne joined the ranks of a group of pioneering ethologists that then included George Schaller, Jane Goodall, and Iain Douglas-Hamilton, who had already made important insights into the behavior of societies of gorillas, chimpanzees, and elephants, respectively. What distinguished Payne's ambition from those of his fellow researchers was the relative inaccessibility of his intended subjects. While it was difficult enough to trudge through the African bush in search of wild animals that might be inclined to charge an approaching human, observing the behavior of whales, which spend on average only 5 percent of their time near the surface of the water and most of whose migration routes were then unknown, seemed to most biologists to be considerably more daunting. In fact, one of the reasons so little was known about whales was that few scientists thought a field study was feasible. "When I started, three people told me that I couldn't study whales in the wild, that it was too difficult," Payne recalled to *Current Biography*. "But I knew that when statements are made with such inexperienced conviction, they're often wrong."

Many of the seemingly insurmountable problems associated with observing whales in their natural habitat vanished in 1970, when Payne, after hearing a definite report that large numbers of right whales had been sighted in the coastal waters off Peninsula Valdes, in southern Argentina, traveled with Katy Payne to the site to investigate. "They were concentrated in the southeast corner of a small bay about thirty miles long—an area flanked by tall cliffs that stretched along the coast to the north and west . . . ," Payne recalled to *Current Biography*. He wrote of his first visit to the site in an excerpt from *Among Whales* that appeared in *Natural History* (January 1994): "As the peace and stillness seeped into me, a whale started breaching far out in the bay, followed in the next few minutes by two others closer to shore. In all I counted thirty-two right whales." The group later proved to be one of the largest remaining populations of right whales in the world. The existence of such a throng of right whales came as something of a surprise, for they are the most endangered of all the whale species, their numbers having declined from a pre-exploitation high of between two hundred thousand and three hundred thousand to their current level of about three thousand. (The name derives from their reputation as commercially valuable, slow-swimming mammals that float when dead—according to whalers, they were the "right" whales to kill.)

The existence of this population meant not only that Payne could count on observing the same whales over the course of their lives, and thus learn about their mating behavior, feeding habits, and social organization, among other things, but that he could observe the animals relatively easily. The high cliffs above the bays afforded him an ideal spot from which to view the animals, which spent much of their time close to the shore. Payne and his colleagues eventually began to observe the animals by making aerial surveys, by sailing among them, and even by swimming among them. The problem of tracking individual animals was solved when Payne discovered that each right whale could be distinguished by distinctive patches of thickened skin, known as callosities, on its head. With a sizable population of whales at hand, the means to recognize which whale was doing what, and financial support from the NYZS, Payne had all that he needed to begin his project. "You don't even have to touch whales to study them," he told Natalie Angier.

In the twenty-five years since Payne launched the study of the Peninsula Valdes right whales, he and his colleagues have photographed and named more than twelve hundred individual whales and have gathered a wealth of information about their behavior and social organization. Among other things, they have learned that the mother and her calf, together with older siblings, form the basic unit of the right-whale social structure, with the young males leaving the group at a certain age and the females remaining until they themselves give birth; that groups of males cooperate when pursuing females for the purpose of mating; and that the whales sleep late in the mornings, when they can be seen "scattered throughout the bay like drifting logs, with the sounds of their snores filling the air," as Payne has written. The researchers have also found that the whales arrive in the waters off the Argentine coast in June, after having spent the austral summer feeding in the colder polar waters to the south, where there is an abundant supply of zooplankton, their main food source. During their four-to-six-month-long stay in the warmer Argentine waters and before returning to their feeding grounds some fourteen hundred miles to the south, the whales fast, living off the thick layer of blubber that they acquired during the feeding season.

Early on in his study, Payne encountered some difficulty in interpreting certain aspects of the whales' behavior, such as their playfulness. Because humans tend to associate playing with quick movements, he sometimes did not realize until the end of a day of observation that the long, slow movements he had described in his notes added up to nothing more than play. "Right whales spend hours and hours just fooling around, but it all happens in slow motion," he explained to Natalie Angier. "A calf slides off its mother's tail, and the mother rolls on her back and takes the calf in her arms and pats it. They stick their tails up in the air and use them as sails." "In order to observe whales, you must be willing to set your metronome on adagio," he has observed. "Then, to understand what you have seen, you must fast-forward through your observations by setting your metronome on allegro."

In spite of the fact that Payne and other researchers have collected a vast store of information on right and humpback whales and, to a lesser extent, on other whale species, much about the animals' lives remains shrouded in mystery—especially the question of what they use their highly sophisticated brains for. "There are reasons to suspect that the brains of whales—and I'm including dolphins—are of equal complexity to, or even greater complexity than, the brains of human beings . . . ," he told Diane Ackerman in an interview for the *New Yorker* (February 26, 1990). "During the first few weeks of life of a human being, whose brain-to-body ratio is not unlike that of a newborn dolphin, the brain requires about a third of the metabolism of the whole body just to run it. It's a very costly thing to have. So you don't just kind of end up having a fancy brain; you have a fancy brain because there's a compelling reason you need a fancy brain. It is selected for, and as soon as the advantage conferred by having it is gone you'd lose it, and lose it fast. What this means is that there must be something that dolphins and whales are doing with their brains that's fundamental to their lives and probably completely different from anything you and I use most of the computing power of our brains for. . . . It must deeply affect their reproductive fitness. It must be crucial to their survival. We just don't know what it is."

While Payne is considered to be a scientist of the first rank, he has never become so engrossed in the scientific aspects of his work that he has lost sight of what prompted him to devote his career to the study of whales in the first place: a desire to preserve their populations. He astutely realized early on that "if you want to have a lasting effect on anything, you can't do it by strictly pushing for legislation," as he told Roberta Brandes Gratz in an interview for the *New York Post* (November 27, 1970). "You must get whatever you want to protect to be part of people's emotional fabric so they can't be easily destroyed." Payne realized that the songs of the humpback whales, which deeply affected many of those who had heard them, could be used promote whale conservation. In addition to releasing recordings of the whales' songs, Payne has collaborated with several composers who wanted to incorporate the haunting sounds into their works. Perhaps chief among those collaborators was Alan Hovhaness, who integrated the taped voices of humpback whales into his orchestral piece *And God Created Great Whales*, which was given its world premiere in June 1970 by the New York Philharmonic, as part of its Promenade series. More recently, in the mid-1980s, Payne joined forces with the avant-garde composer Paul Winter on a similar project.

Payne has also hosted several documentaries describing the plight of whales and of marine life in general, including the Emmy-nominated Discovery Channel film *In the Company of Whales* (1990–92) and the Discovery Channel series *Ocean Planet* (1994–95). His message to viewers has been that pollution has supplanted commercial hunting as the principal threat to the whales' continued survival. Indeed, whales are now falling victim to the high concentrations of toxins currently found in the oceans, with the consequent damage inflicted upon their immune systems rendering them vulnerable to disease. As Payne told *Current Biography*, "We seem to have given the seas something that destroys the immune system of its inhabitants—not with a virus the way the AIDS virus destroys our immune systems, but with a lethal cocktail of carelessly discarded chemical wastes." The Whale Conservation Institute's ECOTOX Project was established to study the effects of such toxins on the whales and their aquatic environment.

In addition to the MacArthur "genius grant," Roger Payne has received many honors, both for his conservation efforts and his contribution to knowledge about whales. Among them are the Lyndhurst Prize, from the Lyndhurst Foundation (1994); the Joseph Wood Krutch Medal in Conservation, from the Humane Society of the United States (1989); and the Albert Schweitzer Medal, from the Animal Welfare Institute, which he shared with Katy Payne (1980). A member of the United Nations Environmental Program's "Global 500 Roll of Honor," he was named a Member of Honour by the World Wildlife Fund in 1980, and, in the same year, he was made a knight, and later an officer, of the Order of the Golden Ark by Prince Bernhard of the Netherlands.

In interviews and in his writings, Roger Payne has revealed himself to be a scientist who derives not only professional satisfaction but also pure pleasure from his work. Occasionally, he has expressed a reverence for the animals that is almost spiritual. During his interview with Jonathan White, Payne described one of his most memorable experiences: "One night just before leaving Argentina, my thirteen-year-old son and I took a long walk on the beach. As we did, we passed close to the water's edge where there was a mother whale and her calf. As she rolled, causing a great slow disturbance in the water, she raised her flipper into the air so it towered over us. It had the sense of a benediction. I mean, no pope could have waved in such a way as to give me a more complete sense of blessing. And what were we being blessed by? By life, I suppose. The feeling it gave me was unforgettable." From his marriage to Katy Payne, which ended in divorce in 1985, Roger Payne has four children: John, Holly, Laura, and Sam. He lives in London with his second wife, Lisa Harrow, an actress from New Zealand.

Selected Biographical References: Christian Sci Mon p1+ Mr 2 '87 por; Discover p40+ Ap '83 pors; National Geographic 155:18+ Ja '79 por; Natural History 103:40+ Ja '94; N Y Post p53 N 27 '70 por; N Y Times p1+ My 26 '70 por; Payne, Roger. Among Whales (1995); White, Jonathan. Talking on the Water; Conversations About Nature (1994)

Peres, Shimon

(PER-ez, SHEE-mohn)

Aug. 16, 1923– Israeli politician. Address: Ministry of Foreign Affairs, Hakirya, Romema, 91950 Jerusalem, Israel

NOTE: This biography supersedes the article that appeared in *Current Biography* in 1976.

Euro/Retna Ltd.

Shimon Peres

Shimon Peres, who has been a dominant figure in Israeli politics for the past two decades, has dedicated his life both to maintaining his country's national security and to upholding the ideals of its democratic socialist founders. An activist even as a youth, during the 1950s Peres served as minister of defense under Israel's first prime minister, David Ben-Gurion, a position in which he distinguished himself by developing Israel's weapons and defense industries. By the early 1970s he, along with Yitzhak Rabin, Menachem Begin, Yitzhak Shamir, and other members of the younger generation of Israeli statesmen, was at the forefront of politics, and in 1977 he was named chairman of the Labor Party, a position that made him the party's candidate for prime minister. Although he failed to lead Labor to a clear-cut victory in any of the elections held during his fifteen-year-long tenure as party leader, in 1984 Labor and Likud entered into a power-sharing arrangement according to which Peres served as prime minister from 1984 until 1986. In 1992, after Peres lost the party chairmanship to his long-time rival Yitzhak Rabin, Labor recaptured a majority of seats in the Knesset, the Israeli parliament, and Peres was named foreign minister.

Although at one time he was considered hawkish on defense issues, Peres has long been committed to a peaceful, negotiated settlement of Israel's long-standing conflict with its Arab neighbors and Palestinian population, and during the late 1980s he formulated a plan for implementing Israeli withdrawal from the West Bank and the Gaza Strip, territories occupied by Israel since the Six-Day War, in 1967 and for granting limited self-rule to the Palestinians. Most significant, he played a key role in the negotiations that led to the historic peace accord endorsed by Israel and the PLO in September 1993. For his efforts to forge a lasting peace in the Middle East, Peres, together with the PLO chairman, Yasir Arafat, and the Israeli prime minister, Yitzhak Rabin, was awarded the 1994 Nobel Prize for Peace.

Shimon Peres was born on August 16, 1923, in a small village in what was then Poland and is now Belarus. His parents, Yitzhak and Sarah Persky, were nonreligious Jews who embraced Zionist ideals, and according to one source Shimon was involved in the Zionist youth movement in Poland. In 1931 his father immigrated to Palestine, and two years later the rest of his family joined him. On settling in Palestine, Peres attended the Balfour primary school in Tel Aviv, where he was a good student. As he grew older he flourished in his studies, becoming an accomplished writer, rhetorician, and speaker. He also continued his involvement in Zionist youth organizations, including Hano'ar Ha'oved (Working Youth). He received a scholarship to the Ben Shemen Agricultural School, where he was sent by the Hano'ar Ha'oved to continue his education and to acquire the agricultural skills so highly valued by Palestine's Jewish settlers. Peres also found time to read poetry and study the works of Karl Marx.

While at Ben Shemen, Peres came under the influence of Berl Katznelson, an intellectual in the Jewish labor movement. In his book *From These Men: Seven Founders of the State of Israel* (1979), Peres described his relationship with his mentor and discussed his ideological development: "[Katznelson] was the cornerstone of the Labor movement; he showed the way and he was the fountain from which flowed the original and constructive spirit of the Labor movement in our country." Katznelson's lectures, Peres wrote, "left an indelible impression on many of us. They implanted in us a negative attitude toward the Communist revolution and Marxist dialectic, an attitude more interested in the values of the human race than in the study of Soviet Russian statistics." Also during high school, Peres joined the Haganah, the underground Jewish self-defense organization, which would later play a crucial role in Israel's winning the Arab-Israeli War of 1948 (also known as the Israeli War of Independence).

After leaving Ben Shemen in 1941, Peres continued his training at Kibbutz Geva and then went on to found Kibbutz Alumot, in the Jordan Valley, of which he was elected secretary. He devoted most of his energy, though, to his work with Hano'ar Ha'oved. "I traveled around the organization's farms, persuading the young people to lend their support to the unity of the movement," he recounted in *From These Men.* During this period he also joined the Mapai, the Israel Worker's Party, then the dominant political party in Palestine. According to Matti Golan, the author of *The Road to Peace: A Biography of Shimon Peres* (1989), "He was seen as a pusher in those early days, both in the field of action and in the realm of ideas. . . . He loved public affairs, felt driven to achievement, and sought positions which enabled him to implement his ideas."

In 1946 Peres attended the twenty-second World Zionist Congress in Switzerland, at which he proved himself to be a firm supporter of David Ben-Gurion, who was already a legendary figure in the Zionist movement and who was to become the first prime minister of Israel. In 1947, at the bequest of another key Israeli politician, Levi Eshkol, Peres became the director of manpower in the Haganah, in the Tel Aviv offices of the General Staff. Peres's duties included weapons procurement, which soon became his area of specialization. Not long after Ben-Gurion declared Israel a sovereign state, on May 15, 1948, Peres, along with the other members of the Haganah, was sworn in as a member of the Israel Defense Forces. During the War of Independence that followed, Peres served as the head of the defense ministry's naval department. Once the war had ended, in 1949, Prime Minister Ben-Gurion asked Peres to go to the United States as the head of a mission to continue to acquire arms for Israel. Because of the United States embargo on arms sales at that time, this task was an especially difficult one. Nevertheless, Peres accomplished his assignment. During this period he also attended the New School for Social Research and New York University, both in New York City, and Harvard University, in Cambridge, Massachusetts.

In early 1952, after returning to Israel, Peres was appointed deputy director-general of the ministry of defense, and several months later he was promoted to director-general. During his seven years in that position, Peres was responsible for developing Israel's government-owned weapons industry. He devoted special attention to nuclear research and weapons procurement, and, in the process, he became known for both his formidable negotiating skills and his conviction that Israel's survival depended on its technological development. One of his most notable accomplishments in that post was his success in forging a relationship between Israel and France at a time when Israel had few dependable allies. Israel's friendship with France, which supplied the newly independent country with much-needed weapons, was crucial to its success in capturing the Sinai Peninsula from Egypt in 1956. France remained Israel's principal supplier of arms for the next two decades. Equally significant, Peres conducted secret negotiations with West Germany on Israel's behalf in 1957, despite the fact that at that time diplomatic relations between the two countries did not exist. According to the Toronto *Globe & Mail* (September 13, 1986), the German-Israeli relationship proved to be important to Israel during the Six-Day War, by which time France had greatly reduced its commitment to Israel's defense. As a result of these achievements, Peres was regarded as a member of the "Young Mapai," a group that consisted of influential members of the younger generation of Israeli politicians.

Peres entered a new phase of his career in 1959, when he ran for and was elected to a seat in the Knesset, as a member of the Mapai Party. The party itself continued its domination of Israeli politics, with the result that Ben-Gurion remained prime minister. Ben-Gurion chose as his deputy minister of defense Peres, who held the position until 1965. One of the more notable events of his tenure was his visit to the United States in 1962, when Peres helped persuade the Kennedy administration to sell Israel its Hawk antiaircraft missile system. The purchase marked the beginning of a new phase in Israel's relationship with the United States, which after 1967 became Israel's main supplier of arms.

By the mid-1960s a rift had developed between David Ben-Gurion and several other key Israeli politicians, including Levi Eshkol, who became prime minister following Ben-Gurion's resignation from that post in 1963. Two years later the conflict between Ben-Gurion and Eshkol came to a head, with Eshkol declaring that Ben-Gurion's supporters had no place in the government. As a result, Ben-Gurion resigned from the Mapai Party and formed one of his own—Rafi, or the Worker's List Party. He was joined by a number of his supporters, including Shimon Peres, who became the newly formed party's secretary general. Within a few years, though, it became clear that Rafi was unlikely to win widespread popular support, and in 1968 it merged with other pro-labor groups (including the Mapai Party) to form the Israel Labor Party, of which Peres became deputy secretary general. In 1969 Peres was appointed to the cabinet of the new prime minister, Golda Meir. Over the following four years, he held a variety of cabinet portfolios, including immigration absorption (1969), transport and communications (1970–74), and information (1974); he also served as minister without portfolio with responsibility for economic development in the occupied territories.

Labor's fortunes—as well as those of Peres—changed dramatically after the Yom Kippur War of 1973. Israel proved to be profoundly ill-prepared to defend itself against its hostile Arab neighbors, and the Israeli public placed the blame squarely on the Labor-led government. Israelis' dissatisfaction with the government was compounded by rising inflation and generally poor economic conditions. Finally, in April 1974, continued public criticism of the government prompted Golda Meir to resign from the prime ministership, a move that required new elections to be held. Peres, who was then involved in a power struggle with Yitzhak Rabin—a military hero who, although he only recently entered into domestic politics, was extremely popular among the electorate—lost the party chairmanship to Rabin, who was elected the new Israeli prime minister in the 1974 elections. In a gesture of conciliation, Rabin appointed Peres minister of defense. During his three years in that position, Peres concentrated his efforts on reinvigorating the Israeli defense forces.

The rivalry between Peres and Rabin developed into a much-publicized feud for a period during the 1970s. According to the historian Howard Sachar, writing in his book *A History of Israel*, their inability to work together harmoniously "led to a near paralysis of executive responsibility. . . . The animus between [then–Prime Minister Rabin] and Peres became all but uncontrollable, intruding in ministerial discussions, even undermining the line of command in the defense establishment." Despite their difficulty in getting along, the two men put aside their differences and worked together on the dramatic rescue of the hijacked airline passengers in Entebbe, Uganda, in 1976. Peres was also involved in the negotiations that resulted in the 1975 disengagement agreement between Israel and Egypt.

In January 1977 Peres challenged Yitzhak Rabin for the chairmanship of the Labor Party, and for a second time he lost his bid to defeat his rival. Rabin went on to lead Labor to victory in the general elections, but several months later, following revelations that his wife had maintained a foreign bank account, a violation of Israeli law, he was forced to resign as both prime minister and party chairman. Rabin's indiscretion in turn cleared the way for Peres's election as Labor Party chairman in June 1977. If Labor had triumphed in the elections later that year, Peres would have become prime minister. But voters, frustrated by the continued high rate of inflation and lacking confidence in Labor's ability to defend the country against its enemies, gave the right-wing Likud Party, headed by Menachem Begin, the right to lead the country. Likud went on to dominate Israeli politics for the next seven years, a period during which Peres served as leader of the opposition.

Although he lacked a portfolio, Peres remained active on the foreign-policy front during the late 1970s, and in the process he succeeded in cultivating an image as a statesman. Traveling frequently outside Israel, he met with Egyptian president Anwar Sadat and leaders of both communist and noncommunist nations. In 1978 he supported the Camp David agreement, which Begin worked out with Sadat. Whereas Peres had long been regarded as a hawk on defense issues, when compared to members of the Likud he was decidedly dovish, for he was markedly more open to the idea of reaching a negotiated settlement with Israel's Arab neighbors and its Palestinian population. Peres also worked hard to breathe new life into the party so as to increase its appeal among the Israeli electorate.

The resignation of Menachem Begin in 1983 provided Labor with an opportunity to recapture its control of the government, and in fact Peres succeeded in leading Labor to a narrow victory over Likud, with Labor winning forty-four seats in the Knesset and Likud taking forty-one. Nevertheless, Peres was unable to form a government, with the result that the two parties came up with a novel power-sharing arrangement: they agreed to form a National Unity government, in which cabinet posts would be evenly divided between them and the leader of each would serve half a term as prime minister. Under this arrangement, Peres served as prime minister of Israel from 1984 until 1986.

According to many political observers, Peres was an unusually effective prime minister. His greatest achievement was his deft handling of the economic crisis in which Israel was mired. "We have to turn first of all to ourselves, control our standard of living, reduce our expenses, and make Israel self-reliant from an economic point of view," he declared soon after taking office, as quoted in *Time* (October 1, 1984). In addition to devaluing the shekel, he cut government spending, persuaded Israel's dominant labor federation to cut real wages, and convinced employers to freeze prices. The net result of these initiatives was that inflation dropped from an annual rate of about 445 percent (some sources give a much higher rate) in 1984 to 25 percent two years later. "Israel's success in halting inflation, with virtually no increase in unemployment, is almost unprecedented," Stanley Fischer, an economics professor at the Massachusetts Institute of Technology, told Thomas L. Friedman of the *New York Times* (October 13, 1986). "Argentina and Brazil both tried to do it at the same time as Israel, with nowhere near the same results."

Another of Peres's achievements as prime minister was his success in coordinating Israel's withdrawal from Lebanon, which the country had invaded in 1982. Its continued presence there was unpopular not only within the international community but also among Israelis. Peres also developed important diplomatic relationships. For instance, he made an official visit to Morocco, where he met with King Hassan II, an event that made him the first Israeli prime minister to be invited to an Arab country other than Egypt. He also met with President Hosni Mubarak of Egypt.

The principal disappointment of Peres's term as prime minister, according to many observers, was his failure to make any significant progress in the effort to resolve the Arab-Israeli conflict. A major stumbling block to any resolution of the conflict, though, was that Labor and Likud were fundamentally divided on how to negotiate a peace settlement. While Peres and other members of the Labor Party were willing to consider the possibility of turning over to Jordan the administration of the occupied territories in return for guarantees of Israel's security, Likud was adamantly opposed to relinquishing territory.

Despite the near impossibility of the two parties' seeing eye to eye on the issue, Peres received the most criticism for the government's failure to advance the peace process. "When it comes to changing the reality, Peres did nothing—for that you need courage," a left-wing member of parliament complained to Thomas Friedman. "I told him many times: 'With the present language of politics—the language of Golda Meir and Menachem Begin—you did the best you could. But you added nothing of your own—like recognizing the Palestinians' right to self-determination.' Peres did nothing to moderate the basic Israeli attitudes toward the West Bank or the Palestinian problems." Notwithstanding this failure, when Peres turned over the prime ministership to Yitzhak Shamir in October 1986 according to the previously agreed upon power-sharing arrangement, he ended what Abraham Rabinovich, writing in the Toronto *Globe & Mail* (September 13, 1986), called "one of the most successful terms of office ever served by an Israeli prime minster." Also according to the two parties' agreement, Peres at the same time became vice-premier and foreign minister.

In the campaign that preceded the 1988 elections, Peres and the Labor Party adopted a strategy that many observers considered to be risky: the party promised to resolve the conflict with the Palestinians—which had worsened considerably since late 1987, when the *intifada*, or uprising, erupted in the occupied territories—by trading land for peace. While the Israeli electorate was anxious to conclude a negotiated settlement with the Palestinians, in the end it was persuaded by Likud's argument that a dovish Labor-led government could not be trusted to protect Israel's security interests, and Likud scored a razor-thin victory over Labor, winning forty Knesset seats to Labor's thirty-nine. The outcome of the election left the two parties with little choice but to form another coalition government, though unlike the arrangement devised in 1984, Yitzhak Shamir was to serve as prime minister for the full four-year term. Peres, in addition to remaining leader of the opposition, served as vice-premier and finance minister.

By the early 1990s Israeli public opinion in regard to the Palestinian problem had changed dramatically. With the *intifada* continuing unabated, Israelis were growing increasingly dissatisfied with Likud's apparent unwillingness to advance the peace process. Moreover, the 1991 Persian Gulf war changed the geopolitics of the region in such a way that the United States had begun to exert considerable pressure on Israel to make peace with its Arab neighbors and the Palestinians. "We had reached one of those rare critical junctures," Peres wrote in *The New Middle East* (1993), "that enable discerning statesmen to make a quantum leap in their thinking—and perhaps turn the tide of history." Although officially out of power, during this period Peres directed a series of high-level meetings with PLO officials, meetings that were conducted in secrecy because all contact between Israelis and members of the PLO was prohibited by Israeli law.

Meanwhile, in 1992, the Labor Party elected Yitzhak Rabin as its new chairman, marking the end of Peres's fifteen-year-long leadership of the party. Rabin had emerged as a more attractive candidate for prime minister than Peres at least partly because of his reputation as a military hero: under his leadership, it was widely thought, Israel's national security would not be jeopardized. Following Rabin's election as prime minister in June of that year, Peres was named foreign minister.

According to an article in the *National Review* (March 7, 1994) that chronicled the secret PLO-Israeli negotiations that were conducted in the early 1990s, Peres spent the months following the 1992 election leading high-level discussions with the PLO. Then, in Oslo in the summer of 1993, an agreement between the two parties was reached, though it was not made public at that time. According to Mark Perry, writing in *A Fire in Zion* (1994), in August 1993 Peres secretly held an eight-hour telephone conversation with Yasir Arafat, and he later met with PLO officials to initial the "Declaration of Principles on Interim Self-Government Arrangements." This agreement was formally endorsed by both Israel and the PLO on September 13, 1993, on an occasion of state in Washington, D.C. Peres has provided his own vision of a land in which Arabs and Jews peacefully coexist in his book *The New Middle East* (1993), which he wrote with the Israeli political scientist Arye Naor and which one critic described as a "textbook lesson in how a small nation negotiates in the changed world after the Cold War, when even larger nations have given up some of their sovereignty."

On October 14, 1994 Shimon Peres, Yitzhak Rabin, and Yasir Arafat were jointly awarded the Nobel Prize for Peace. The announcement of the award was to some extent overshadowed by continuing violence in Israel, and when it was presented to the recipients, on December 10, 1994, the peace process was at a standstill. Nevertheless, each of the recipients of the prize remained committed to implementing the hard-won agreements. "There was a time," Shimon Peres declared on accepting the prize, "when war was fought for lack of choice; today it is peace that is the 'no choice' for all of us." A little less than a year later, the tortuous negotiations between the Israeli government and the PLO, led by Peres and Arafat respectively, had resulted in an important new agreement. Initialed by the two men on September 24, 1995, the accord outlined, in a step-by-step fashion, the transfer of power to the Palestinians in the West Bank. (The two sides had earlier reached an agreement on Palestinian self-rule in Gaza and the town of Jericho.)

Shimon Peres has been married to the former Sonia Gelman since May 1, 1945. They have a daughter, Zvia, two sons, Jonathan and Nechemia, and numerous grandchildren. In addition to the Nobel Prize, Peres has received a number of awards, including the French Legion of Honor. A poised, handsome man with a receding hairline and a cleft chin, Peres is not considered to be a charismatic politician. "Deep in my heart," he has said, "I'm convinced that I'm incorrigibly shy, but I must reconcile myself to the fact that many claim that I'm also a man who tried to leap forward—almost an arrogant man."

Selected Biographical References: N Y Times A p2 O 13 '86 por, A p12 S 19 '93; Nat R p28+ Mr 7 '94; Toronto Globe & Mail D p3 S 13 '86 por; Golan, Matti. The Road to Peace: A Biography of Shimon Peres (1989); Political Leaders of the Contemporary Middle East and North Africa (1990); International Who's Who 1994–95

Mark Cardwell/Bettmann

Perez, Rosie

1964(?)- Actress; choreographer. Address: c/o Creative Artists Agency, 9830 Wilshire Blvd., Beverly Hills, CA 90212

The multitalented actress and choreographer Rosie Perez is one of the few Hispanic performers to have carved a niche for themselves in Hollywood. She began her career in the late 1980s, as a dancer on the syndicated television program *Soul Train*, and, through a combination of talent, hard work, and luck, she soon found herself cast in the independent filmmaker Spike Lee's controversial 1989 movie *Do the Right Thing*. Since then, Perez has appeared in several more feature films, including the box-office hit *White Men Can't Jump*, and television programs. She has also choreographed many rap and rhythm-and-blues artists' stage shows and videos and has served as the resident choreographer for the television program *In Living Color*, through which she brought authentic urban hip-hop dancing to the masses. In her film work she has tried to prevent herself from being pigeonholed, by holding out for what she has often referred to as "Jessica Lange roles." Her most celebrated role to date, in the 1993 release *Fearless*, earned her an Academy Award nomination for best supporting actress.

Rosie Perez was born in Brooklyn, New York, the daughter of Ismael Serrano, a member of the merchant marine, and Lydia Perez, who had been a singer in Puerto Rico before moving to Brooklyn. According to one source, she was born in about 1964; other sources suggest that she may have been born several years later. One of eleven children (some sources say ten), Perez spent her early childhood in the Bushwick section of Brooklyn. She has spoken of having a troubled childhood, but the details are vague. She has said, for instance, that she once threatened a woman with a knife, while under the influence of drugs, and that she lived in several group homes, a claim her mother has denied. In any event, she apparently did live in an orphanage for a time. Happier memories are associated with an aunt, Anna Otero, with whom Perez lived while she was in high school, and her father, who doted on her and would write her long letters while he was out at sea. "If I've got an attitude," she told Veronica Chambers in an interview for *Premiere* (November 1993), "it's because my dad souped up my head when I was a little girl."

Both of her parents danced salsa, which sparked Perez's own interest in dance at a young age. "I always had a secret passion to be a dancer, so when they had a program for inner-city kids, I couldn't wait to go," she recalled to Gail Buchalter in an interview for *Parade* (September 19, 1993). "I was short and stocky—not like the other girls, who were white and willowy. I think that was the premise behind the lady's telling me I had no rhythm. I cursed her out, and she told me never to return." Thus prevented from taking dance classes, Perez thrust herself into the New York City club scene. By the time she was in her early teens, she was frequenting various venues with her older siblings, wearing heavy eye makeup to make herself look older.

Perez also had a special interest in the sciences, and after graduating from high school she moved to Los Angeles to study marine biology and biochemistry at Los Angeles City College and West Los Angeles College. She never lost her love for dancing, though, and in the evenings she would don her club attire to indulge her passion. One night the dance coordinator for the television program *Soul Train* saw her dancing at a local Latino club and asked her to appear on the show. During her stint with *Soul Train*, she received considerable camera time. Her work also attracted the attention of an executive at MCA Records, who asked her to choreograph a video and stage show for the singer Bobby Brown, a relative unknown at the time. Having never worked as a choreographer before, Perez was reluctant to accept the offer. "At first I told him I couldn't do it—I didn't know how," she told Gail Buchalter. "He told me I could. He presented the challenge, and I just had to take it." As it turned out, Bobby Brown's show was a smash hit. Its success translated into more work for Perez, whose choreographic credits soon included videos and/or shows for such performers as Diana Ross, The Boys, Heavy D, and LL Cool J, for whom she also served as tour manager.

Perez's big break came one day while she was dancing at a Los Angeles club called the Funky Reggae, where she was spotted by the filmmaker Spike Lee, who was celebrating his birthday there. After introducing himself, he gave her his business card and asked her to call him, though he did not say why. When she finally got around to contacting him, about a month after their initial meeting, she learned that he had her in mind for a part in the film he was then working on, *Do the Right Thing*, an explosive portrait of life on a Brooklyn block on the hottest day of the summer.

On hearing Perez read for the part, Lee's casting director, Robi Reed, instantly agreed that she was the ideal choice. "Rosie is a natural," Reed told Susan Howard in an interview for *New York Newsday* (November 28, 1990). "She has no formal acting training, but when she read for me she was so real that I cried. I called Spike and said, 'She's Tina.'" Lee, who had initially envisioned a black actress in the role, offered the part to Perez despite her utter lack of acting experience. For her part, Perez had mixed feelings about taking on the challenge. "I was so scared," she admitted to Renee Michael, who interviewed her for the *New York Times* (March 29, 1992). "But at the same time I wasn't going to say, 'Well, no, Spike. I'd rather not do this film.'"

Perez had little sympathy for the character of Tina, an emotionally demanding young woman who feels neglected by her boyfriend, Mookie (played by Spike Lee), with whom she has a child. "That character was so far removed from me," she explained to Buchalter. "I have a bad temper when there's something to be angry over, but Tina was angry because she had no one to blame. She was mad at her mother because she wouldn't baby-sit. Well, why should she? She was angry at her man because he was garbage, and she was angry because she had a kid. Those were *her* choices. I was disgusted with her." Perez's performance, like those of most of her fellow actors, was for the most part overshadowed by the furor generated by the film itself, which raised difficult questions about the nature of racism but pointedly did not offer any solutions. One of the film's most memorable scenes came during the film's opening credits, when Perez is dancing to the Public Enemy song "Fight the Power."

Perez's appearance in *Do the Right Thing* led to assignments on such television programs as CBS's *WIOU* and Fox's *21 Jump Street*. She also landed the role of Denise, a crack addict whose face is viciously slashed while she is being robbed, in the HBO made-for-television movie *Criminal Justice* (1990). Then, in 1992, she made a triumphant return to the big screen, in *White Men Can't Jump*, a comedy about two athletic con men, played by Wesley Snipes and Woody Harrelson, who support themselves by hustling basketball games at an outdoor court in Los Angeles.

As had been the case with *Do the Right Thing*, Perez was not an obvious choice for any of the characters in the film. She was too young to play the wife of Snipes's character, and Gloria, the girlfriend of Harrelson's character, was originally conceived as a privileged white woman who rebels by running away with a basketball player. Perez nonetheless auditioned for the role of Gloria, competing against such well-known actresses as Rosanna Arquette and Holly Hunter. "She gave a very surprising, honest reading," Ron Shelton, the film's writer and director, recalled to Renee Michael. "She was very focused, extremely prepared. I started to rethink the part." Indeed, with Perez in mind he changed Gloria from a Barnard graduate to an ex-disco queen, though he did not water down the character to conform to preconceived ideas about Hispanic women. (In both versions Gloria spends her days imbibing vodka and studying the *World Almanac* to prepare herself for her life's dream of appearing on *Jeopardy!*) "What was great about it, she was still well-versed," Perez told Douglas J. Rowe in an interview for the *Newark Star-Ledger* (May 17, 1992). "She was very intelligent. And she followed all of the characteristics that the original Gloria had. The dialogue never changed, and the storyline never changed." In fact, Perez found Gloria to be an unusually well-written female role. "I was funny, sexy. . . . I got to be neurotic," she told Rowe. "I got to just go off on these, like, tangents. It was just a very well-written role for a woman."

In their reviews of *White Men Can't Jump*, critics invariably singled out Perez's portrayal of Gloria as one of the main reasons to see the film. "The best thing about [Shelton's] engaging comedy . . . ," Georgia Brown wrote in the *Village Voice* (April 7, 1992), "is the commanding presence of the shrill, pint-sized motor-mouth Rosie Perez." That view was seconded by Kenneth Turan, who observed in the *Los Angeles Times* (March 27, 1992), "It is safe to say that Perez plays it like no one else on the planet. . . . To hear Gloria giving Billy a hilarious what-women-want lecture . . . is to feel in the presence of a true screen original."

Perez was next tapped for supporting roles in two offbeat films. In Jim Jarmusch's idiosyncratic *A Night on Earth*, about five taxicab encounters, she played a fiery Brooklynite named Angela who becomes involved in a screaming match with her brother-in-law (Giancarlo Esposito) over whether she should return home with him. Peter Rainer, who reviewed the film for the *Los Angeles Times* (May 8, 1992), was among those who were taken with Perez's performance: "She's the spirit of the streets, and she can belt out obscene epithets with a comic force that leaves you dazed—except that you're laughing so hard." The actress also won praise for her performance in the romance *Untamed Heart* (1993), in which she took the part of Cindy, a feisty waitress whose best friend and coworker, Caroline (Marisa Tomei), becomes involved with a dishwasher (Christian Slater). "It's Tomei and Perez who give *Untamed Heart* its buoyant wit," Peter Travers wrote in *Rolling Stone* (March 4, 1993). "Their friendship could have sustained an entire movie. It's certainly the best part of this one."

By the time she completed *Untamed Heart*, Perez was eager to expand her repertoire beyond Latina roles, which, in her view, all too often perpetuated the erroneous notion that Hispanic women are loud, boisterous, and volatile. She wanted, she has said, a part in which she would not be required to "[scream] at the top of [her] lungs." "I can be Hispanic and play a Jessica Lange role," she told Renee Michael. "All I need is the opportunity to go for it." Perez's "Jessica Lange role"—and her first starring part—came in *Fearless* (1993), a drama by the Australian director Peter Weir about the survivors of an airplane crash. She portrayed Carla, a young Puerto Rican mother grieving for the child she lost in the crash that she herself survived. The character was originally written as an Italian-American, but once again the role was rewritten with Perez in mind. "This was her part," Weir told Veronica Chambers for *Premiere*. "She had something to give. She was looking for a change of direction, and *Fearless* was it."

Playing Carla, a guilt-ridden, dazed, deeply religious woman, required a greater intensity and a wider range of emotions than any of Perez's previous roles—a fact that caused her considerable apprehension. "I would have these nights of anxiety before filming, and I called [Weir] up one night, crying hysterically, and I said, 'I'm so scared—I don't know if I can do this right,'" she recalled to Marisa Tomei in a conversation for *Interview* (March 1993). "And he's like, 'Oh, I'm so glad you came to me.' . . . He's an actor's director, totally. It was great to walk out there and know that someone is not gonna let you mess up. I was challenged in a lot of ways I've never been before, artistically, on this film. I needed a month to recover from it because I felt completely drained, but now that I look back on it, I feel *high* from it. Before, I used to make fun of actors being so deep. Now I know what . . . everybody was talking about." According to many reviewers, in *Fearless* Perez proved she can not only perform but act as well. As Michael Wilmington observed in the *Chicago Tribune* (October 15, 1993), Perez has always been "a whiz at hysterical fits and temper tantrums," but she "gets more shading here, more tenderness, than she's shown before." In rising to the challenge of serious drama, Perez earned an Academy Award nomination in the best-supporting-actress category.

Perez's most recent screen credit is Andrew Bergman's romantic comedy *It Could Happen to You* (1994), in which she played a part reminiscent of some of her earlier characterizations. Muriel is the screeching, greedy wife who becomes outraged when her husband (Nicolas Cage) gives half of his four million-dollar lottery winnings to a waitress as a tip. Terrence Rafferty, who reviewed the film for the *New Yorker* (August 1, 1994), was delighted by Perez's performance, calling Muriel "a hilarious caricature of a beady-eyed financial predator."

At the same time that Perez was pursuing her acting career, she was also accepting assignments as a choreographer. Shortly after making her screen debut, she had become the choreographer for the Fox network's comedy hit *In Living Color*. The show's creator, Keenen Ivory Wayans, had been searching for someone who would bring an edge to the series by arranging hip-hop dancing to accompany the show's rap soundtrack. "I wanted a choreographer who was unconventional, and Rosie is definitely that," he told Susan Howard. Perez has since been credited with imbuing the Fly Girls, *Living Color*'s dancers, with the street-smart air they had previously lacked. As Wayans observed, "She has taken something raw from the streets and given it a real sense of class and style without losing the essence."

Perez draws inspiration for her choreography from the club scene, and she prides herself on being able to capture the vitality of urban hip-hop in her television work. "Here's my dancer's arrogance," she told Gerri Hirshey, who profiled her for *GQ* (August 1992). "I haven't seen anybody who can articulate hip-hop the way I do, in such a clean, crisp way, and still be authentic. There are a lot who try and do it, and it comes off very corny. I still got the flavor." Perez has attributed the success of her choreography at least in part to the honesty of her friends who frequent the clubs and tell her immediately if her material is reductive or inauthentic. "There are times," she told Howard, "when they have called me and have said: 'Rosie, what . . . were you doing in that dance number? You better get back in the clubs, girl.'" Perez herself chose not to dance with the Fly Girls, mainly because she prefers to work behind the scenes. She gave Susan Howard another reason to stay offstage: "I dance like a guy. I would have thrown off the whole groove." "When I dance, it's for me and nobody else," she told Hirshey. "The best moves I come up with are if I'm in a club and nobody's looking at me. I come up with the fly things." Perez earned an Emmy nomination for her *Living Color* choreography.

Perez has also found time to involve herself in the business side of the entertainment industry. For instance, she served as executive producer for a three-part HBO series called *Rosie Perez Presents Society's Ride* (1993), which featured live performances by rap, rhythm-and-blues, and reggae acts. She also manages an all-female rhythm-and-blues band called 5 A.M., and she has directed a music video. According to many observers, she possesses uncommon business savvy. "I've never seen a more entrepreneurial actress," one of her colleagues told Charles Leerhsen for a profile of Perez in *Newsweek* (May 4, 1992). Perez herself has said she approaches her work in a businesslike fashion, something she learned to do early in her career. During her interview with Leerhsen, she recalled that while she was heavily involved in the Los Angeles club scene, four recording companies offered her contracts, despite her complete lack of singing talent. "All they knew was, she's got the packaging, she's got the look, and that was enough for them," she told Leerhsen. "I saw that, and I said to myself, 'Approach this like a business.'"

According to Mim Udovich, writing in *Vibe* (December 1993), Rosie Perez has "major-league dimples, the face of a demonic infant, the body of a petite but nonetheless solidly built brick house, and a vocal range that starts at Betty Boop and ends somewhere around car alarm." Despite the difficulties she has faced as a Hispanic actress in Hollywood, Perez remains determined to be a success. "The racism, the sexism, I never let it be my problem," she was quoted as saying in *Entertainment Weekly* (November 5, 1993). "It's *their* problem. If I see a door comin' my way, I'm knockin' it down. And if I can't knock down the door, I'm sliding through the window. I'll never let it stop me from what I wanna do."

Selected Biographical References: Chicago Tribune VII pJ F 19 '93 por; GQ 62:49+ Ag '92 pors; Interview 23:123+ Mr '93 pors; N Y Times II p28 Mr 29 '92 por; Newsweek 119:64+ My 4 '92 pors; Parade p12+ S 19 '93 pors; Premiere 7:86+ N '93 por; USA Today D p1 Ap 2 '92 por; Notable Hispanic American Women (1993)

Scott Davis/U.S. Army Visual Information Center

Perry, William J.

Oct. 11, 1927- United States Secretary of Defense. Address: The Pentagon, Washington, DC 20301

On February 3, 1994 William J. Perry was sworn in as President Bill Clinton's secretary of defense, after being unanimously confirmed by the United States Senate on the same day. For the eleven months preceding his confirmation, he had served as deputy secretary of defense under Les Aspin, who had incurred disfavor with the military for his managerial style, which some described as lax, and for what critics perceived as his blatant disregard for the opinions of top military commanders. The selection of Perry to succeed Aspin was widely praised by the Senate Armed Services Committee, military leaders, and major defense contractors, all of whom cited his decisiveness, his entrepreneurial background, and his academic credentials. "Aspin is concerned more about broad defense and foreign issues," Philip A. Odeen, a former Defense Department and National Security Council official acquainted with both men, told Eric Schmitt of the *New York Times* (January 26, 1994). "Perry is going to be focused on a combination of working the inside, budget and program issues, as well as on reforms in the acquisition area."

That Perry's mandate has so often been described in terms of managerial style represents the emerging priorities of the foreign policy establishment in the post-Cold War era, which are shifting from ideologically motivated geopolitical concerns to more pragmatic issues such as the cost-effectiveness of deploying troops overseas and the preservation of key weapons systems and industries in the face of shrinking defense budgets. The lack of a ready-made anti-Communist rationale for going to war has made it more difficult to explain distant military commitments to the American public, and the collapse of the Soviet Union has left the world with only one superpower, the United States, whose leaders have been faced with providing military protection for humanitarian relief operations without assuming the role of the world's policeman. During Perry's first year at the helm of the Pentagon, major national debates have erupted over the role of the American military in Somalia, where President George Bush committed several thousand American troops; the former Yugoslavia, where a civil war has continued despite UN and NATO actions; North Korea, where there have been persistent rumors of a covert nuclear weapons program; and Haiti, where a military coup ousted the impoverished nation's first democratically elected government. After a mildly controversial start, Perry has contributed a sense of policy continuity to these areas. Writing in the *Washington Post* (April 7, 1994), John Lancaster noted, "Perry benefits by comparison with [Secretary of State Warren] Christopher, who has been criticized for lack of leadership and clarity, and national security adviser Anthony Lake, who has largely avoided the limelight."

William James Perry was born on October 11, 1927 in Vandergrift, Pennsylvania, a small town thirty miles north of Pittsburgh. He grew up in the nearby town of Butler, where his father, Edward Martin Perry, worked as a grocer; his mother was Mabelle Estelle (Dunlap) Perry. As a student at Butler High School, Perry became interested in mathematics and music, and for a time he played piano in a swing jazz band called the 2 O'Clock Club. After graduating from high school in 1945, he enlisted the following year in the United States Army, serving as a noncommissioned officer with the occupational force in Japan, where he worked with the Army Corps of Engineers as a surveyor. In 1948 Perry joined the Reserve Officers' Training Corps, and in 1950 he was commissioned as a second lieutenant in the army reserves. While serving in an artillery unit, he suffered a slight, permanent hearing loss. In the meantime, he had studied mathematics at Stanford University, in Stanford, California, receiving a bachelor's degree in 1949 and a master's degree in 1950. In 1957 he earned a doctorate, also in mathematics, from Pennsylvania State University, in University Park, Pennsylvania, where he had served as a math instructor from 1951 to 1954. From 1952 to 1954 he had also been a senior mathematician at the HRB–Singer Company in the town of State College, Pennsylvania.

In 1954 Perry had begun what would become a long association with the private defense industry when he became director of defense laboratories with GTE Sylvania Company in Mountain View, California, a position he held until 1964. He resigned from GTE Sylvania in that year to cofound a military electronics company called ESL, Inc., in Sunnyvale, California, which provided the National Security Agency with sophisticated electronic surveillance devices. By the time he left the company in 1977 to become President Jimmy Carter's undersecretary of defense for research and engineering, Perry, who had also consulted for the Defense Department from 1967 to 1977, had taken ESL from "zero to $60 million a year," according to Carter's defense secretary, Harold Brown, as quoted by John Lancaster in the *Washington Post* (January 25, 1994). Prior to joining the Carter administration, Perry had become a millionaire upon the sale of his holdings in ESL.

As undersecretary of defense for research and engineering, Perry was responsible for weapons-systems procurement and research and development, and he advised the secretary of defense on technology development, communications, intelligence, and atomic energy. He soon developed a reputation as an avid supporter of high-technology weapons systems, and he was at the forefront in the creation of what became known as "stealth" (radar-avoiding) planes and laser-guided cruise missiles. In an interview with a reporter for *U.S. News & World Report* (September 8, 1980), Perry discussed his vision of the future of weaponry. "Electronics and microelectronics . . . will influence our weapons in two very important ways. First of all, they will allow us to have a revolutionary improvement in battlefield intelligence. Second, there will be a revolutionary change in the nature of firepower, brought about through the introduction of new and much more effective precision-guided munitions."

This "offset strategy," implemented by Perry and Secretary of Defense Harold Brown as well as by the Republican administrations that followed, was meant to compensate for the Warsaw Pact's numerical superiority in military personnel and armored equipment in Europe, which at the time was estimated at three-to-one over NATO forces. The goal was not simply to produce better weaponry with high technology but, as Perry explained in an article for *Foreign Affairs* (Fall 1991), to use the most advanced electronic and computer technology to enhance the performance of the available weapons and personnel: "The offset strategy was based . . . on the premise that it was necessary to give these weapons a significant competitive advantage over their opposing counterparts by supporting them on the battlefield with newly developed equipment that multiplied their combat effectiveness." Perry went on to describe how the pursuit of this strategy influenced allied successes in the Persian Gulf war, citing three key areas: command, control, communications, and intelligence, known as C^3I; defense suppression, or "the complex of systems designed to destroy or render ineffective the opposing air-defense system before it can function"; and precision-guided weapons, including laser-guided bombs, laser-guided missiles, and infrared-guided missiles, which cause fewer civilian casualties than the practice of carpet-bombing.

Perry's enthusiasm for such expensive technology has drawn criticism from some quarters. The B-2 Stealth bomber, for example, whose development was initiated in the late 1970s at a projected cost of $200 million per plane, ended up costing $2.2 billion per aircraft by 1994, when the air force finally began acquiring the planes. "Several defense analysts [suggested] that if Perry has a weakness," John Lancaster wrote, "it is that he places too much emphasis on technological solutions to military problems." One often-cited example of his high-tech bias is his development of the Strategic Computing Initiative, which would link battlefield weapons to high-powered, central computers meant to assist in some aspects of military decision making. As John Markoff reported in the *New York Times* (February 5, 1994), "Such a program could lead to weapons that can fire themselves." The murky ethics of automated weapons have not elicited much support among the industry leaders of Silicon Valley.

After leaving government service in 1981, Perry returned to the private sector, serving as executive vice-president of Hambrecht & Quist, a San Francisco-based investment banking firm that specializes in high-technology companies. Perry was responsible for the research department, as William Hambrecht recalled in an interview with John Markoff. "He was operating at a different level than a stock buyer," Hambrecht said of Perry. "He was interested in the substance of technology and less interested in third-quarter earnings." In 1985 Perry founded Technology Strategies and Alliances, a technologically oriented investment and consulting firm in Menlo Park, California, where he assisted large defense firms in acquiring smaller, innovative companies that were in the vanguard of current technology. Such acquisitions helped the larger companies save research and development dollars by enabling them to use the smaller companies' expertise; otherwise, the large corporations would have to develop their own in-house teams, an expensive prospect because of the overhead costs that must be factored into the budget. Among the high-profile acquisitions that were arranged by Technology Strategies and Alliances were Lockheed's $1 billion purchase of Sanders Associates in 1991, Chrysler's $367 million purchase of Electrospace Systems, and Boeing's purchase of Argo Systems for $275 million. With the end of the Cold War and the downsizing of the military, Technology Strategies and Alliances began working with contractors in diversifying their production to include products with civilian applications.

Clinton's nomination of Perry for the top job in the Defense Department was generally seen as a wise decision, politically safe and noncontroversial. Perry was already well known in the defense industry; as deputy secretary in 1993 he had been instrumental in managing the expenditure cutbacks so important to the fiscal policy of the Democratic administration. The Pentagon's much-criticized system of procurement, which requires contractors to produce goods to specifications unique to the Pentagon, has often been cited by Perry as the cause of vast overspending. "We cannot ignore how much it's costing us to do business any longer," Perry told Bruce B. Auster of *U.S. News & World Report* (September 13, 1993), "or we're going to have nothing left but overhead. . . . We have the two different segments of the national industry out there, virtually side by side," Perry continued. "If you cannot effect integration in the jet engine business [where there is a virtually identical civilian need] you probably can't effect it anywhere."

At the press conference announcing his nomination, Perry spoke about his plans to curtail spending by modifying procurement practices. "We have what I would call a window of opportunity to make a major reform to the defense acquisition system so that we can buy modern equipment for our military forces at affordable prices." Another early priority of Perry's in the area of management was to streamline the administration of the department. Aspin, who had sought to expand the department's influence into areas normally covered by the State Department, had created two new assistant secretary posts—one overseeing plans and policy and the other in charge of democracy and human rights—but the arrangement only contributed to the administrative traffic jams that so plagued Aspin's tenure. Within weeks of his confirmation, Perry abolished the two posts and reorganized the department, making it essentially the same as it had been during the Bush administration.

While it was widely acknowledged that Perry was more than capable of handling the administration of the Defense Department, many observers questioned his ability to lend a forceful voice to the complex military and foreign policy of the United States. At his confirmation hearing in February 1994, concerns were expressed about the administration's policy toward North Korea, which was then taking a defiant stance against allowing inspectors from the International Atomic Energy Agency (IAEA) to visit nuclear power plants where it was suspected that scientists were engaged in nuclear arms production. Perry told the Senate Armed Services Committee that a North Korean nuclear program would have a destabilizing effect on the rest of the area, possibly igniting an arms race among Japan, the Koreas, and Taiwan. He told the committee, "We see a very dangerous proliferation ahead of us," and outlined a series of measures he would follow to avert such a scenario. He also gave the senators a list of six priorities that would mark his tenure. First on the list was "reviewing and assessing war plans and deployment orders." Appearing last on the list—perhaps reflecting an effort to show that he was more than an astute manager—was the implementation of "innovative management techniques."

Another international priority for the new defense secretary was establishing a solid basis for relations with the four nuclear powers of the former Soviet Union: Russia, Kazakhstan, Ukraine, and Belarus. Since the breakup of the Soviet Union, the United States had sought to "denuclearize" the three smaller republics in the interest of international stability. On a tour of the republics in March 1994, Perry offered a financial assistance package, including $15 million to Kazakhstan and $100 million to Ukraine, in return for a commitment by the republics to surrender their nuclear stockpiles to Russia. In addition to helping to offset the cost of demilitarization, the financial aid was meant to help the republics convert their defense industries to commercial and civilian uses.

Perry has cited the instability in the former Soviet Union as part of the rationale behind the $264 billion defense budget sought by the Pentagon for fiscal 1995. Aspin had been chastised by conservatives for his insistence that Russia no longer posed a threat to the United States. Perry, on the other hand, took a harder line, saying that the internal instability so obvious in Russia justified sustaining high levels of investment in nuclear weapons systems. Although Perry acknowledged, in a speech delivered at George Washington University in March 1994, that the threats to international stability confronting the United States at the time did not, in themselves, warrant the entire amount of money requested by the Pentagon, he argued that certain defense industries must nevertheless be maintained in a state of readiness to protect the United States from future, possibly unforeseen, threats, such as a new arms race with Russia. Detractors have contended that such government intervention in the marketplace is contrary to the American belief in free markets. "This is not a bailout," Perry explained in 1993, as quoted by John Mintz of the *Washington Post* (January 26, 1994). "I explicitly reject the idea of sustaining a defense company just to keep it in business. We're not doing it to save jobs or help shareholders. We expect defense companies to go out of business. We will stand by and let that happen."

In April 1994 Perry was beset by his first controversy when, during questioning on the NBC News television program *Meet the Press* about the civil war in the former Yugoslavia, he stated that the

United States would not intervene to stop a Serbian assault on the predominantly Muslim town of Gorazde, in eastern Bosnia. That remark came one month after NATO had successfully brought a semblance of peace to Sarajevo, which had endured over two years of indiscriminate shelling, with threats of air strikes against the Serbian heavy weapons surrounding the city. The alliance had been widely praised for finally taking a firm stance, and Perry's flat rejection of such measures to save Gorazde was seen as implicitly granting the Serbs permission to continue their assault. Perry also said that he did not foresee the United States using nuclear weapons to protect its thirty-seven thousand troops in South Korea from aggression from the North.

Perry's candor was widely criticized by commentators who pointed to his remarks as evidence of continued disorganization within the Clinton administration's foreign policy team. In reference to Perry's comments on Gorazde, Clinton's national security adviser, Anthony Lake, was forced to make a speech later in the week saying that all options were under consideration and that nothing, including air strikes, had been ruled out. And in reference to Perry's comments about Korea, Brent Scowcroft, President Bush's national security adviser, was quoted in the *New York Times* (April 4, 1994) as saying, "Psychologically, it was the wrong direction to go. As long as they think the worst outcome for us is hostilities, then that is the direction they will try to push us to get us to back down."

Among the wars and conflicts around the world, Perry sees many, including the civil wars in the former Yugoslavia, Rwanda, and Somalia and the political instability in Haiti, as involving only limited American interests. More important to the national security of the United States, according to Perry, are maintaining relations with the republics of the former Soviet Union and containing the nuclear arms program of North Korea. With regard to cooperation with Russia, in October 1995 Perry was instructed by President Clinton, who had just met with Russian President Boris Yeltsin, to discuss with Russian defense minister Pavel Grachev the prospect of Russian troops' participation in a peacekeeping force in Bosnia, where prospects for a peace agreement were enhanced by the signing of an accord among the warring parties in September.

With his oversize eyeglasses and bookish manner, William J. Perry has a professorial air. (He is on leave from two posts at Stanford University: professor of engineering and codirector of the Center for International Security and Arms Control.) His long association with defense and computer industries has led many to label him a computer nerd, a description with which he has readily agreed. Since December 29, 1947 he has been married to Leonilla Mary Green, a certified public accountant, with whom he has five children: David Carter, William Wick, Rebecca Lynn, Robin Lee, and Mark Lloyd. The couple have eight grandchildren. Among the numerous awards that have been bestowed on Perry are the army's Outstanding Service Medal, in 1977; the Department of Defense's Distinguished Public Service Medal, in 1980 and 1981; a Medal of Achievement from the American Electronics Association, in 1980; NASA's Distinguished Service Medal, in 1981; the Federal Republic of Germany's Knight Commander's Cross, in 1981; France's Grand Officer de l'Ordre National du Mérite, in 1982; and the James Forrestal Memorial Award, in 1983 and again in 1993. He was honored with a Henry Stimson Foundation Award in September in 1994.

Selected Biographical References: N Y Times D p21 Ja 25 '94 por, A p9 F 5 '94; Washington Post A p12 Ja 25 '94; Who's Who in America, 1995

Chris Cuffaro/Virgin Records

Pop, Iggy

Apr. 21, 1947- Rock singer; songwriter. Address: c/o Virgin Records, 1790 Broadway, 20th Floor, New York, NY 10019; c/o Floyd Peluce, 449 Beverly Dr., No. 102, Beverly Hills, CA 90212-4428

Iggy Pop, who began recording in Detroit in 1969 with his band the Stooges, is widely acknowledged as the godfather of punk rock, in which attitude (usually hostile or angry) and energy (always raw and aggressive) rather than technical virtuosity or mainstream accessibility are the key factors. Blurring the edges between heavy metal and avant-garde performance art, the genre—multiple exceptions notwithstanding—is characterized by short, loud songs with a fast beat that rely on guitar-laden rhythm and percussion more heavily than on vocals, which often (and purposefully) approximate screaming more closely than singing.

The content of such songs, in Pop's view, should be truthful and sincere, as he explained in an interview with Anita Sarko for *Ray Gun* (August 1993): "One thing I really hate in music, particularly American music today, is these [rock stars] not telling what they feel in a song. They won't come out and say anything. They won't say, 'I'm hot, I'm cold, I'm hard, I'm soft, I'm tired, I'm happy, I'm thrilled, I'm disgusted.' [Instead,] it's all this . . . convoluted 'Well, if I was pink, you would be a fish swimming in the infinite collegiate miasma of crap.'" Referring in the same interview to his most recent album, *American Caesar* (1993), he said, "I wanted to come out and say things about how I felt, and I wanted to be specific in the songs. I didn't want to have any song where you couldn't tell who this guy was, where he is in the song, what he is doing exactly, who else is there with him, and what the surroundings are." A solo act since 1975 with more than a dozen albums to his credit, Pop has often collaborated with other rock artists, notably David Bowie.

Iggy Pop was born James Newell Osterberg on April 21, 1947 in Muskegon, Michigan, the only child of James Newell Osterberg, a high school English teacher, and Louella Kristine (Christensen) Osterberg, an executive secretary. Pop grew up in the Coachville Garden Mobile Home Court in Ypsilanti, Michigan. His father chose to live in a trailer park as an alternative to the suburban lifestyle he apparently abhorred, as Pop explained in an interview with Peter Gilstrap for the *Washington Post* (October 3, 1993): "My dad was a visionary, and he wanted to save money. He just didn't want to live in a house and be rooted and be part of the neighborhood barbecue association and the Little League and the PTA and all that." Pop's early life seems to have provided the basis for the outsider's perspective that informs much of his music, as he told Anita Sarko: "There was a big social stigma when I was in school, which really helped. It exerted a pressure that helped me later in my music, a kind of anger and a pressure against kids who would tease me about livin' in a trailer. Very helpful."

Pop has traced his desire to sing to the age of eight, when for the first time he heard Frank Sinatra sing. When he was in the tenth grade, in the Ann Arbor public school system, he formed his first band, the Iguanas, in which he sang and played drums and from which he earned the nickname Iggy (he took the surname Pop from the name of a local junkie, Jim Popp). The Iguanas released their first and only single in 1965, a cover of Bo Diddley's "Mona," and began playing professionally at the Ponytail Club in northern Michigan. After graduating from high school in 1965, Pop enrolled at the University of Michigan and joined a blues band called the Prime Movers, which performed at nightclubs in Detroit and, occasionally, in Chicago. Around that time he became enamored of the music of Howlin' Wolf, Otis Rush, the Butterfield Blues Band, and Little Walter. After completing only one semester, Pop withdrew from the university in 1966. "I didn't drop out," he insisted to Dave Thompson in an interview for *Alternative Press* (September 1993). "I finished my semester with a C average, and I was invited back. But I told them I didn't want to go, that I'd put it on hold for a little while."

Inspired by a Doors performance, Pop formed his own group in Detroit in 1967, with former Prime Mover Ron Asheton on bass and Asheton's brother, Scott, playing drums. The Psychedelic Stooges made their debut, on Halloween in the same year, in Ann Arbor. A few weeks later, Dave Alexander joined the band on bass guitar, and Ron Asheton switched to guitar, freeing Pop for singing and for performance showmanship. Iggy Pop and the Stooges (the band had dropped the word "psychedelic" from its name shortly after its first performance) were, according to the *Rolling Stone Encyclopedia of Rock & Roll*, "an appropriately frightening onstage sight: Iggy contorting his shirtless torso, letting out primal screams and guttural wails, rubbing peanut butter and raw steaks over his body, gouging his skin with broken glass, diving out into the audience; all while the Stooges played a raw, abrasive basic rock." (A 1970 *Downbeat* poll named Pop among the best instrumentalists for the use of his body.) Pop's onstage antics preceded by several years the practice of "slam dancing"—or slamming into fellow dancers like a human billiard ball—by members of the audiences at punk-rock concerts, a tradition whose recent incarnations include "moshing" and "crowd-surfing," in which performers as well as audience members dive from the stage or are lifted aloft and passed over the heads of the crowd in the "mosh pit."

Signed to a recording contract with Elektra in 1969 by Danny Fields, who had come to Detroit to sign the MC5, the Stooges recorded two albums: *The Stooges* (1969), which was produced by John Cale of the Velvet Underground, and *Fun House* (1970). Though both records would later be hailed for yielding such enduring punk singles as "No Fun" and "I Wanna Be Your Dog," they were only moderately successful in terms of sales. A series of personnel changes presaged the Stooges' breakup, due to drug-related problems, in 1971, and for a few months Pop lived in Florida, where he mowed lawns for a living and played golf.

In 1972 Pop was introduced to the British singer/songwriter David Bowie, a longtime admirer, at Max's Kansas City, in New York City. Bowie's manager, Tony DeFries of MainMan, signed Pop and offered to produce his and the Stooges' (who had regrouped) next album in London. Released by Columbia Records in 1973, *Raw Power* gained the attention of English rock fans and rose to number 182 on the American music charts. "*Raw Power* could not have been made in America . . . ," Pop told Dave Thompson. "It was a punk record. I didn't know that at the time, but it was punk." In fact, cover versions of some of Pop's songs were to be made within a few years by such prototypical punk groups as the Dictators, who did "Search and Destroy," the Damned ("1970"), and the Sex Pistols ("No Fun"), and by Joan Jett ("I Wanna Be Your Dog"). More recently, the Red Hot Chili Peppers, EMF, Peter Murphy, R.E.M., and Grace Jones have performed numbers by Iggy Pop. Commenting in his interview with Dave Thompson on the burgeoning of the punk and new-wave rock scene in middle America in the late 1970s, which followed upon the mid-1970s explosion in Britain of such bands as the Sex Pistols and in New York City of Talking Heads, among other groups, Pop said, "I saw a superficial correlation between punk and what the Stooges had been doing, and I knew exactly what was happening; that accidentally, the superficial aspects of noise, energy, aggression, irresponsible negative preening, and emotional exhibitionism were finally being adopted by the mob and their various frustrated mentors who couldn't create anything themselves."

Touring the United States after the release of *Raw Power*, the Stooges played their final two gigs, both of which ended in violence, in Detroit in October 1973 before splitting up in 1974. A bootleg recording of one of the shows was released by Skydog under the title *Metallic K.O.* in 1975. After the breakup of the Stooges, Pop checked himself into the Neuropsychiatric Clinic in Westwood, California to rid himself of a drug addiction. On weekend leave he recorded the vocals for some tracks he had been working on with some former Stooges; those sessions resulted in two albums, *Skydog in France* and *Kill City*, which were released in 1978 on the Bomp label in the United States and on Radar in Britain. "Listen to 'Kill City' itself," Pop advised Dave Thompson, "then play an Ice-T track from fifteen, eighteen years later. I said it all, right there, right then, before anybody else saw it coming. It's a concept album about Los Angeles and the future of America. I saw it, and I wrote it down as it was, and now it's come to pass."

Pop's monthlong rehabilitation at the clinic in Westwood was spent in near-total isolation, except for occasional visits by Bowie, who encouraged Pop to accompany him on his 1976 "Station to Station" tour, during which Pop sang Bowie's "Sister Midnight." Pop was also featured on Bowie's *Low* album. The pair eventually ended up living together for about two years in Berlin, a welcome haven from the image-conscious milieu of Los Angeles that had brought both artists close to the edge of insanity. In Berlin, Bowie recorded Pop's first solo album, *The Idiot*, which was released by RCA in 1977. *The Idiot*, which rose to number seventy-two on the album chart in the United States and to number thirty in Britain, contains Pop's version of "China Girl," cowritten by Pop and Bowie, which was to become a huge hit for Bowie in 1983. Later in 1977 Bowie produced and RCA released another Pop album, *Lust for Life*, which also charted on both sides of the Atlantic. Beginning that year, *The Iguana Chronicles*, a compilation of Stooges' recordings from 1972 to 1975, began to appear on various labels, among them Skydog, Revenge, and Bomp; *The Iguana Chronicles* comprise a projected fifteen-compact-disc collection, according to Dave Thompson. *TV Eye—1977 Live*, one of Pop's least favorite albums, was released by RCA in 1978.

By the late 1970s, Iggy Pop had moved to New York City and signed with a new recording label, Arista, which issued *New Values* (1979), *Soldier* (1980), and *Party* (1981), all of which were dismissed as "rather average albums" by a writer for the *Guinness Encyclopedia of Popular Music*. Speaking of *Party* in his interview with Dave Thompson, Pop said, "Not only is it my least favorite album, it was probably my least favorite to make as well. I'd really tried to go for an American hit, but the record company imposed this guy from the Monkees [Tommy Boyce] on me for the last four tracks, and it was terrible." In 1982 Pop made *Zombie Birdhouse*, which failed to chart, and published a book of autobiographical anecdotes, *I Need More*, which D. Keith Mano described in the *National Review* (July 22, 1983) as "a sharp, ozone-splitting and instructive autobiographical riff. . . . The natural prose excitement of *I Need More*—overdubbed atop a rock-lyric repetitious, insistent diction line—is, you might say, half machine and half hallucination."

In his interview with Dave Thompson, Pop referred to the end of the 1970s and the early 1980s as one of his "darkest" periods. Describing the 1993 Skydog release *We Are Not Talking About Commercial Shit!*, a collection of live recordings made between 1979 and 1985, Pop told Thompson, "There is a lot of struggle in those tracks, and you hear things you wouldn't hear from the usual air-brushed artist." By the end of that period, Pop had managed to purge himself of his drug addictions and straighten out his priorities, taking up jogging, painting, and acting. Reflecting upon that time in an interview with Josef Woodard of the Santa Barbara (California) *News-Press* (October 26, 1986), Pop said, "I felt my work was becoming diffused, losing clarity, punch and focus, if not in the public eye at least in my own eyes. I didn't feel much in contact with people in everyday life. I didn't know the price of a loaf of bread. I'd never gone out, tracked down and rented my own apartment, hassled with the landlady, done the vacuuming, taken out the garbage and shared the shopping. I've been doing things like that and having a really good time doing it."

Having made his acting debut in 1967 in a Françoise De Monierre film that featured Nico of the Velvet Underground, Pop renewed his interest in acting in the mid-1980s, taking lessons and obtaining membership in the Screen Actors' Guild. Although he was frequently denied movie roles, he did manage to land small parts in Alex Cox's *Sid and Nancy* (1985), about the Sex Pistol Sid Vicious and his girlfriend, and Martin Scorsese's *The Color of Money* (1987), starring Paul Newman. He later starred in John Waters's *Cry Baby* (1990) and, with Tom Waits, in Jim Jarmusch's *Coffee and Cig-*

arettes, which won the short-subject Palme d'Or at the Cannes Film Festival in May 1993. Pop's television credits include appearances in *Tales from the Crypt* and *Miami Vice* and, in 1990, as a guest on the premiere of the NBC series *Shannon's Deal*. His acting experience gave him the confidence boost he needed to carry on with his music. "I just felt myself getting sharper and sharper," he told Woodard, "until I finally thought, 'OK, I'm ready to roll. It's time to go out and do it right.'"

Having accumulated a small but adequate horde of savings through royalties and a thrifty style of living, Pop decided to tackle his next recording project without the initial aid of a record-label contract. In search of a collaborator, he approached Ric Ocasek of the Cars and Steve Stevens, who had played guitar with Billy Idol, before deciding on Steve Jones, the former Sex Pistols guitarist with whom he had earlier recorded the theme song to Alex Cox's movie *Repo Man*. After recording several songs in Los Angeles, Pop returned to New York City, where he once again hooked up with Bowie, who served this time not only as the producer but also as an equal financial and creative partner. The album, *Blah Blah Blah* (1987), spawned the hit singles "Cry for Love," cowritten by Steve Jones, and "Real Wild Child," a cover of Australian Johnny O'Keefe's often reworked original of 1957 that reached number ten in Britain. "I realized it's very important that this record sound as polished, as competitive as possible," Pop told Dave Thompson. "I didn't want there to be any obvious reasons why it shouldn't get on the radio." A writer for *Stereo Review* (February 1987) found *Blah Blah Blah* to be "both polished and gut-slamming at the same time. . . . [Pop's] love songs are puzzling but ultimately engaging non sequiturs. It's as though rock's angry young man were confused by the experience of having things work out right."

Blah Blah Blah was followed by *Instinct* (1988), another slickly produced album that featured Steve Jones on guitar. *Instinct* received mostly favorable reviews, even though it did not yield a hit single. Next came *Brick by Brick* (1990), which was produced by Don Was, the leader of the rock group Was (Not Was), with whom Pop had collaborated earlier on a song for the soundtrack of Ridley Scott's movie *Black Rain*, and included guest appearances by the singer/songwriter John Hiatt, the guitarist Waddy Wachtel, and two members of Guns N' Roses. The singer's duet with Kate Pierson of the B-52s, "Candy," from *Brick by Brick*, reached number twenty-eight on the American music charts. Writing in *Rolling Stone* (August 9, 1990), Paul Evans described the songs on *Brick by Brick* as "resolutely generic white-boy crunch rock with cocky, in-your-face conviction. . . . By now an elder statesman of the wild," Evans continued, "Iggy's role as criminal-with-a-conscience is both mythic and essential." Also in 1990, Pop recorded "Well Did You Evah," a duet with Debbie Harry, formerly the lead singer of the group Blondie, that was included on *Red Hot + Blue*, an AIDS-education benefit album comprising an anthology of Cole Porter songs.

Pop's most recent album, *American Caesar* (1993), features his own version of the Kingsmen's mock rock anthem "Louie Louie" as well as a guest vocal appearance by the former Black Flag frontman Henry Rollins. One of the songs on that album, "Hate," is about the conflict Pop feels between his misanthropic impulses and his need for friendly human contact, both of which are occasionally thrown into stark relief by the pressures of trying to lead an ordinary existence while being, if not famous on the scale of Madonna, then certainly a cult figure, an icon to the fringes rather than the masses. "I realized how much time I spend *hating* people," he told Anita Sarko. "I hate 'cause I'm *afraid*, and that's a really creepy thing!"

"Iggy's build is a mass of large bones and muscles somehow inhabiting a lithe, narrow frame," Anita Sarko reported, after interviewing him in 1993. To keep fit, he prefers practicing tai chi to working out with weights, because going to a gym is a "hassle" for him. As he told Sarko, "I just do these weird breathing exercises called *chi kwong*. It's like natural steroids. All the bulk comes from oxygen." According to Fred Schruers, in his profile of the singer for the New York *Daily News Magazine* (November 16, 1986), Pop "had a brief and cataclysmically bad marriage early in the Stooges' career," but no reference to that union appears in any other source. Iggy Pop, who answers to the names James, Jim, Ig, and Iggy, lives in an apartment near Tompkins Square Park in Manhattan with his wife, Suchi, a fan whom he met in Japan and married in October 1984. He also owns a home in a fishing village near Los Cabos, Mexico, a place to which he escapes whenever he, in his words, "can't stand it anymore." "[I] love my garden, my wife, my dog and cat, a lot," Pop wrote in a recent autobiographical press release, "but also love noise, aggravation, girls, regular guys, music, as much. . . . Ambition is to make better music, live life in peace, and then die."

Selected Biographical References: Alternative Press p52+ S '93 pors; N Y Daily News mag p24+ N 16 '86 pors; Rolling Stone p97+ N 20 '86 pors; DeCurtis, Anthony and James Henke, eds. The Rolling Stone Album Guide (1992); Larkin, Colin, ed. Guinness Encyclopedia of Popular Music vol 2 (1992); Pareles, Jon and Patricia Romanowski, eds. Rolling Stone Encyclopedia of Rock & Roll (1983); Pop, Iggy. I Need More (1982); Rees, Dafydd and Luke Crampton, eds. Rock Movers & Shakers (1991); Stambler, Irwin, ed. Encyclopedia of Pop, Rock & Soul (1989); Who's Who in America, 1995

Jon Gilbert Fox

Proulx, E. Annie

(proo)

Aug. 22, 1935– Writer. Address: c/o Charles Scribner's Sons, 866 Third Ave., 7th Fl., New York, NY 10022

The writer E. Annie Proulx emerged from obscurity to win, between April 1993 and April 1994, four major literary awards—one for *Postcards* and the remaining three for *The Shipping News*. While the settings of the two novels are different, each is as concerned with its characters' relationships to the land on which they live as with such universal themes as death and failed love. The careful depiction of place is crucial in the opinion of Proulx, who has said that if the setting of a story is handled well, "the characters will step out of it, and they'll be in the right place. The story will come from the landscape." Critics have also taken special note of Proulx's economical, poetic prose and of her beautiful, haunting imagery.

Only a few years before she became the toast of the international literary community, Proulx was virtually unknown. She did not publish her first book of fiction, *Heart Songs and Other Stories*, until she was in her early fifties. Fiction writing is only the most recent full-time pursuit for Proulx, who has also been a freelance journalist and a postal worker, among other things. "I certainly don't regret [becoming a writer] later because I know a lot more about life than I did twenty years ago, ten years ago," she told Sara Rimer for the *New York Times* (June 23, 1994). "And I think that's important, to know how the water's gone over the dam before you start to describe it. It helps to have been over the dam yourself."

The daughter of George Napoleon Proulx, the vice-president of a textile company, and Lois Nelly (Gill) Proulx, a painter, Edna Annie Proulx was born on August 22, 1935 in Norwich, Connecticut. Her mother's family had lived in Connecticut for three hundred years, and most of her maternal ancestors had earned their livings as farmers or mill workers. While she was growing up, her family moved frequently, and she lived in various towns throughout New England and in North Carolina. Proulx has credited her mother with helping her to develop the powers of observation she would later put to use in her fiction. "From the time I was extremely small, I was told, 'Look at that'," she recalled to Sara Rimer for the *New York Times* profile. She was taught to see "everything—from the wale of the corduroy to the broken button to the loose thread to the disheveled mustache to the clouded eye." When she was ten years old, Proulx wrote her first story. (She cannot remember its plot.)

In the 1950s Proulx enrolled at Colby College, in Waterville, Maine, but she left without graduating. It was not until 1969 that she obtained a bachelor's degree in history, cum laude, from the University of Vermont. In the meantime, she had supported herself by working variously as a waitress and a postal employee, among other jobs. In 1973, while she was living in St. Albans, Vermont, Proulx received a master's degree in history from Sir George Williams University (now Concordia University), in nearby Montreal. At the same institution, she began working toward a Ph.D. degree in history, but after passing her oral examination in 1975, she abandoned work on her dissertation in favor of a career as a freelance journalist, which she pursued from an isolated shack in the insular town of Canaan, Vermont. There, she fished, hunted, and foraged for her food, a practice that apparently suited what she has called her "fondness for harshness." Moreover, such a lifestyle "makes you very alert and aware of everything around you, from tree branches and wild mushrooms to animal tracks," as she explained to John Skow for *Time* (November 29, 1993). "It's an excellent training for the eye. Most of us stagger around deaf and blind."

For the next dozen or so years, Proulx churned out "tedious nonfiction," to use her term, including such books as *Sweet and Hard Cider* and *The Complete Dairy Foods Cookbook* and magazine articles on topics ranging from architecture to horticulture. After moving to Vershire—one of the thirteen Vermont towns in which she has lived—she founded a newspaper, the *Vershire Behind the Times*. In her spare time, she wrote short stories. "I yearned to write fiction, but there wasn't any money in it," she said to David Streitfeld in an interview for the *Washington Post* (April 21, 1993). "I could only write one or two short stories a year. It was my pleasure, my indulgence, when I wanted to do something that wasn't fishing or canoeing." Although her output was small, she was able to sell most of her stories, to periodicals ranging from *Blair & Ketchums Country Journal* to *Esquire*.

The nine tales collected in Proulx's first book, *Heart Songs and Other Stories* (1988), are set in rural towns in New England and concern the lives of working-class, chiefly male protagonists. In "On the Antler," for example, the two main characters, a storekeeper and a quiet, book-loving hunter, hatch plots against each other that exceed the bounds of practical jokes, and in "Bedrock" the devious central figure arranges a marriage between his sister and a widower for the purpose of gaining control of the widower's farm. Evaluating *Heart Songs* for the *Chicago Tribune* (December 11, 1988), Kerry Luft applauded Proulx's "lyrical" and "vivid" style and pronounced the book to be "such a dazzling debut" that the reader was made to "wonder where [Proulx had] been hiding." Kenneth Rosen observed in the *New York Times Book Review* (January 29, 1989) that Proulx's stories were "most compelling when they're rooted in a coarse rural sexuality" and that, at such times, her "sometimes enigmatic, often lyrical images seem to complement New England's lavish but barren beauty."

The contract that Proulx had signed with her publisher, Charles Scribner's Sons, called for her to produce, in addition to *Heart Songs*, a novel. Having written only short fiction up to that time, she "had not a clue about writing a novel, or even the faintest desire," as she admitted to Sara Rimer. "I thought of myself as a short-story writer. Period, period, period." After *Heart Songs* was published, however, and she was forced to confront the prospect of writing the novel, Proulx found her attention drawn to some old postcards she had been given years earlier. Dating from the 1930s and 1940s, the postcards featured reproductions of mug shots of escaped convicts. She was especially intrigued by one photograph, of a "really handsome guy" with "incredibly wavy hair," and, as she recounted to Rimer, "within a half-hour" of her sitting down to write, "the whole of *Postcards* was in [her] head."

The "handsome guy" who had piqued Proulx's interest became Loyal Blood, the central character in *Postcards* (1992). Early in the story, having killed and buried his lover, Loyal flees westward, leaving his parents and siblings with the seemingly impossible task of operating their Vermont farm without him. As the story progresses from World War II to the 1970s, the chapters alternate between those chronicling Loyal's meanderings across America and those depicting the Blood family's struggle for survival. Each chapter begins with a facsimile of a postcard, complete with address and cancellation stamp, written by a character familiar or unknown to the reader. The postcards, ambiguous in terms of the information they present, evoke, through their language and the subjects they discuss, the flavor of different time periods and geographical regions and thus provide a context for the narrative action. The technique, Proulx explained to one interviewer, lets the reader use his or her imagination in "filling in the blanks" in the book. "The reader writes most of the story," she said.

In the eyes of a majority of critics, *Postcards* represented a successful attempt to capture the essence of a particular people, place, and time. Declaring in the *New York Times Book Review* (March 22, 1992) that Proulx had "come close" to "writing a Great American Novel," the novelist David Bradley concluded his highly favorable appraisal by saying, "Story makes this novel compelling; technique makes it beautiful." Frederick Busch, evaluating *Postcards* for the *Chicago Tribune* (January 12, 1992), concurred. "This powerful novel is about powerful matters. It is made with a language that demands to be lingered over—for the pungent bite of its effect and for the pleasure of learning how good, and even gorgeous, sentences are written. . . . What makes this rich, dark, and brilliant feast of a book is its furious action, its searing contemplations, its language born of the fury and the searching and the author's powerful sense of the gothic soul of New England."

In a conversation with Esther B. Fein for the *New York Times* (April 21, 1993), Proulx reflected on the experience of creating *Postcards*: "It was astonishing how easy writing a novel was compared to writing a short story. I was so used to cramping thoughts and situations and cutting, and suddenly I had room to expand. It was like getting into a warm bathtub . . . ." Not surprisingly, her next fiction project was another novel, *The Shipping News* (1993). She had first visited its setting, Newfoundland, during a fishing trip in about 1987. As she related to John Blades for the *Chicago Tribune* (March 29, 1993), she "just fell quite madly in love with" the island. She described Newfoundland's coast as "rugged" and "immensely interesting" and its people as the "warmest, kindest, most interesting anywhere."

The protagonist of *The Shipping News* is Quoyle, a third-rate, small-town newspaper reporter and innocent soul described by the novel's narrator as having "a great damp loaf of a body," a "head shaped like a Crenshaw, no neck, . . . features as bunched as kissed fingertips," and a "monstrous chin, a freakish shelf jutting from the lower face." Widowed when his aggressively unfaithful wife, Petal Bear, is killed in an auto accident, after having attempted to sell their two young daughters to a pornographer, Quoyle is left "swimming with grief and thwarted love" until his indomitable Aunt Agnis comes to stay with him and his daughters and helps them rebuild their lives. Taking his aunt's advice, Quoyle attempts to make a fresh start by moving his family from upstate New York to Newfoundland, the land of his ancestors. There, he gradually finds a sense of belonging among his eccentric neighbors and his coworkers at the local weekly newspaper, the lurid and gossipy *Gammy Bird*, whose reporters invariably end up covering stories that exploit their "private inner fears," as one of Quoyle's colleagues points out. Quoyle, for example, is asked to photograph car wrecks, "while the upholstery is still on fire and the blood still hot."

Ironic, and sometimes comic, in tone, and written in spare language (including incomplete sentences such as "Then, at a meeting, Petal Bear. Thin, moist, hot. Winked at him."), *The Shipping News* inspired wide and largely unreserved praise. "As a stylist, Proulx is earthy and intelligent, never overwrought, grounding her lyric flights in extraordinarily vivid description," Dan Cryer wrote in *New York Newsday* (March 22, 1993). "If I have any complaint, it is that at times she carries her own brand of poetic compression too far," Howard Norman declared in the *New York Times Book Review* (April 4, 1993). Still, he complimented the novelist for her "surreal humor and . . . zest for the strange foibles of humanity" as well as for her "inventive language."

Literary enthusiasts who were not already aware of Proulx's work were soon alerted to her talents by the number of major awards she received in seemingly rapid succession over the thirteen months immediately following the publication of *The Shipping News*. In April 1993 she was given the PEN/Faulkner Award for fiction, for *Postcards*, becoming the first woman to be so honored; *Postcards* was selected over 284 other works for the prize. Four months later the *Chicago Tribune* chose Proulx as the recipient of its Heartland Award for fiction, for *The Shipping News*. In the following month that novel won the *Irish Times* International Fiction Prize, and, in November, it took the National Book Award. Early in 1994 *The Shipping News* was nominated for a National Book Critics Circle Award, and, finally, in the spring of that year, the novel won the Pulitzer Prize. "I've run out of being stunned," Proulx told David Streitfeld for the *Washington Post* (April 13, 1994), after learning of the last-named award. "Except I am stunned. Each time this happens, I can't believe it."

While Proulx has said that writing novels is "easy" compared with crafting short fiction, several reporters have noted the extensive research that went into both *Postcards* and *The Shipping News*. For the former, she traveled across the United States, just as her character, Loyal Blood, does in the book; for *The Shipping News*, which Howard Norman described as "almost an encyclopedia of slang and lore," she not only made several trips to Newfoundland but also pored over the *Dictionary of Newfoundland English* in order to capture the dialect of that island's inhabitants. "I literally slept with that book for two years, in the bed," she told Sara Rimer. "I'd fall asleep while I was reading it. This is the point in work. You get it right, or you don't do it. Everything depends on your getting it right."

E. Annie Proulx has been married and divorced three times. From her last marriage, to James Hamilton Lang, she has three grown sons: Jonathan Edward Lang, Gillis Crowell Lang, and Morgan Hamilton Lang. She has hinted in interviews at the "reckless," to use her word, nature of her past. In a letter to David Streitfeld of the *Washington Post*, she provided a list of her adventures (and misadventures) to illustrate her self-described recklessness: "Leaping a barbed-wire fence and not making it; being grabbed on a lonely back lane by a strange older guy but biting and escaping; running away through the rain on the eve of a wedding and finding self three-quarters across wet ties over railroad bridge over river when the train appeared at the far end of the bridge; getting caught in a thunderstorm on third flying lesson; throwing a knife at (and thank God missing) someone I thought I hated; driving north in the south-bound lane; hanging out with a wide variety of rough dudes in a wide variety of situations; swimming across a lake when eight months pregnant; speeding and rolling a car late one night on the way north and coming to in a hospital considerably messed up; using old shotgun that misfired; doing a 360 on icy street in Montreal morning rush hour; falling off ladder; ladder falling on me; etc., etc."

Proulx counts fly-fishing, canoeing, and playing the fiddle among her hobbies. According to David Streitfeld, she is also active in the fight against illiteracy—a cause she took up after learning that her great-grandmother, who left behind no letters or diaries upon her death, could not read or write. Proulx's passion, however, is clearly writing fiction. "I'm desperate to write. I'm crazy to write. I want to write," she told Sara Rimer. "I have . . . three novels sitting in my head, waiting to get on paper, and I know exactly how each one is going to go. Each one is like a wrapped package." At the time Rimer interviewed her in 1994, the novelist was living in Vershire, Vermont in a house that was "tall, strong, and unadorned, like her" and "cozy and welcoming" on the inside, "full of books and rocks and colors."

Selected Biographical References: Chicago Tribune V p3 Mr 29 '93 por; Maclean's 107:57 Ap 25 '94 por; N Y Times C p1+ Je 23 '94 pors; N Y Times Bk R p7 Mr 22 '92 por; Time 142:83 N 29 '93 por; Washington Post B p1 Ap 21 '93 por, B p1+ N 16 '93 pors; Who's Who in America, 1995

Rabin, Yitzhak

(rah-BEAN, YITS-ahk)

Mar. 1, 1922– Prime minister of Israel. Address: Office of the Prime Minister, 3 Rehov Kaplan, Hakirya, Jerusalem 91007, Israel

NOTE: This biography supersedes the article that appeared in *Current Biography* in 1974.

BULLETIN: Yitzhak Rabin was assassinated on November 4, 1995, as he left a peace rally in Tel Aviv, by Yigal Amir, an Israeli right-wing extremist opposed to the Israeli government's self-rule agreement with the Palestine Liberation Organization. *Obituary: N Y Times* A p1+ N 5 '95

Sven Nackstrand/Agence France Presse

Yitzhak Rabin

"The sight you see before you at this moment was impossible, was unthinkable just two years ago," Yitzhak Rabin, the prime minister of Israel, declared at the signing of the peace accord between Israel and the Palestine Liberation Organization in September 1995. "Only poets dreamed of it, and to our great pain, soldiers and civilians went to their death to make this moment possible." The agreement—which expanded Palestinian self-rule in the Israel-occupied territories of the West Bank (land Israel had captured in the 1967 Six-Day War)—has been hailed as a significant milestone on the road to peace in the Middle East. For Rabin, the hard-won accord with the Palestinians and the peace treaty Israel signed with Jordan in October 1994 are the crowning achievements in his long career as a soldier, diplomat, politician, and international statesman. A veteran of the 1948 Israeli War of Independence, Rabin played a key role in building up Israel's military might during the 1950s and 1960s, a period that culminated in Israel's victory in the Six-Day War, while he was army chief of staff. He gave up his uniform to serve as his country's ambassador to the United States from 1968 until 1973, and in 1974, as leader of the Labor Party, he became prime minister. A political scandal forced him to resign in 1977; for the next several years, Rabin, although he remained a member of the Israeli parliament, was relegated to the back benches. During the 1980s, when the right-wing Likud Party dominated Israeli politics, he served as defense minister, developing a reputation as a hard-liner in his efforts to quell the violence that had begun to spread among the increasingly discontented Palestinian population in the West Bank and Gaza Strip.

A frustrated Israeli electorate, discouraged by the lack of progress toward peace, voted the Likud out of power in 1992 and reinstated the more liberal Labor Party, and Rabin once again became the country's prime minister. Israelis seemed willing to trust Rabin to be a peace broker, confident that the man who had spent so much of his career defending the country against its enemies would be a reliable protector of its security. By 1992 Rabin had become convinced that it was time for Israel to conclude a political settlement with both its Palestinian population and its Arab neighbors. Among the reasons for Rabin's change in perspective were the end of the Cold War, which transformed the geopolitics of the Middle East, and Israel's failure to quell the *intifada*, the sustained uprising that had been raging in Israel's occupied territories since 1987. For his efforts to create a lasting peace in the Middle East, Rabin, along with Yasir Arafat, the chairman of the PLO, and Shimon Peres, Israel's secretary, won the Nobel Prize for Peace, on October 14, 1994.

The older of the two children of Nehemiah Rabin and Rosa (Cohen) Rabin, Yitzhak Rabin was born on March 1, 1922 in Jerusalem, in what was then Palestine. (Four months later the League of Nations adopted the British mandate for Palestine, which affirmed Great Britain's commitment to supporting the establishment of a Jewish homeland in Palestine.) Rabin has a sister, Rahel. His father, who emigrated from his native Russia to the United States as a boy and who later settled in Palestine, was a worker, intellectual, and member of the Jewish Legion. His mother, also a Russia-born Jew who immigrated to Palestine, became well known in the Yishuv, the Jewish community in Palestine, because of her work as a leader in the labor movement and as a member of the high command of the Hagana, the Jewish underground army. Both parents were nonreligious, Socialist Jews. Rosa Cohen, as she preferred to be called even after she got married, was the dominant figure in the family. Rabin has described her as "a very austere, extreme person, who stuck to what she believed in; there were no compromises with her."

Rabin began his education at the age of six, when he entered the Bet Hinuch, in Tel Aviv, where the family had moved several years before. The school had been established by Jewish settlers with the aim not only of educating students but also of providing them with the practical skills needed to settle what was then a largely undeveloped land. At the age of thirteen, Rabin entered Givat Hashlosha, an intermediate school organized by Rosa Cohen and modeled after Bet Hinuch. His mother's death in 1937 affected Rabin deeply. Following a period of mourning, he returned to Kadoorie Agricultural High School, which he had just entered, "with the feeling that [he] had crossed over the threshold of manhood," as he wrote in *The Rabin Memoirs* (1979). "Part of my home no longer existed," he continued, "and I had to strike out on my own path." Although on entering Kadoorie he had had no interest in pursuing a military career—"My purpose in life was to serve my country, and I believed that the best way to do it was to prepare myself to be a farmer," Rabin has said—that prospect became increasingly more likely as his years there passed.

After graduating from Kadoorie, with honors, in 1940, Rabin applied to the University of California to study hydraulic engineering. The idea appealed to him because an expertise in that field would serve the Yishuv well in the coming years, water being a scarce resource in the region. But the exigencies of World War II soon compelled him to abandon those plans. (Rabin's academic education thus ended when he left Kadoorie.) He instead joined the Hagana, the underground military arm of the Jewish Agency, and was assigned to the Palmach, the Hagana's secret commando force, soon after it was formed in May 1941. As part of the Palmach's campaign to prevent the Nazis from taking over the Middle East, in June of that year Rabin participated in sabotage operations conducted against the Vichy French government in Lebanon and Syria. He also attended a special military training course offered by the British, with whom the Hagana were allied.

Later in the war Rabin worked part-time on a kibbutz; all the while he remained in the Palmach, of which he was named platoon commander in 1943 and deputy battalion commander in 1944. According to Robert Slater, the author of the biography *Rabin of Israel* (1993), Rabin "acquired a reputation as one of the leading thinkers of the strike force. Other commanders, even his seniors, often sought his advice or opinion. He was not only a willing and persevering soldier, he had a special understanding of the unique role of the Palmach." With the conclusion of World War II, Rabin considered reapplying to the University of California, but he decided to remain in Palestine to take part in the creation of a Jewish state.

Following World War II the already unstable alliance between Jewish settlers in Palestine and the British deteriorated further. (The settlers and the British had been united in their opposition to the Axis powers, but were deeply divided politically; in 1939 Great Britain greatly reduced its commitment to the establishment of a Jewish homeland, when the fate of European Jewry was at its most precarious.) A major point of contention was Britain's policy on Jewish immigration; Britain not only opposed the immigration of Holocaust survivors to Palestine but sought to return those immigrants who had entered Palestine "illegally." A confrontation occurred in the summer of 1945, when the Palmach, in an attempt to thwart Britain's plans to evict illegal Jewish immigrants who were being held at the Atlit detention camp, set out to rescue the detainees. Still with the Palmach, Rabin was a key participant in the daring raid on the camp. (The raid was fictionalized by Leon Uris in his novel *Exodus*; Rabin was said to be the basis for the character Ari Ben-Canaan.) As a result of that and similar exploits, Rabin became a wanted man, and in June 1946 he was among the many Jewish settlers who were arrested and imprisoned by the British.

Soon after Rabin's release from prison, in November 1946, the British decided to relinquish their responsibilities under the mandate. A year later the United Nations voted to partition Palestine into two states—one Palestinian, the other Jewish. Rabin joined in the general celebration in Tel Aviv, but, as he wrote in his memoirs, he "harbored few illusions." "The irony of it all was that the success of our political struggle left us more vulnerable than ever to destruction," he continued. "We would now have to protect our political gains by force of arms." Indeed, the partition plan was rejected by the neighboring Arab states, which invaded Israel as soon as it declared itself a sovereign state in May 1948.

During the Arab-Israeli War of 1948 (also known as the first Arab-Israeli War and the Israeli War of Independence), Rabin played an important role as commander of the Palmach's Harel Brigade. Early in the war he was given "the extremely difficult task," as Avishai Margalit described it in the *New York Review of Books* (June 11, 1992), of securing the route linking Jerusalem and Tel Aviv, but he was unable to do so. He was also placed in charge of carrying out Israeli prime minister David Ben-Gurion's controversial order to sink the *Altalena*, which was defying government orders by transporting arms to the Irgun, a militia whose politics were at odds with those of the government. In the final phase of the war, Rabin helped to push back Egyptian forces into the Negev desert, and he took part in the negotiations for the 1949 armistice.

In late 1948 David Ben-Gurion, feeling that the Palmach constituted a threat to his authority, had dissolved the organization and integrated it into the new Israel Defense Forces (IDF). Ben-Gurion was also distrustful of some of the former Palmach members and saw to it that they had no place in the IDF. Rabin's loyalty was thus divided between the Palmach veterans and the government, and when the ousted Palmach members held a gathering to demonstrate both their solidarity and their opposition to the government's action, Rabin attended it despite government orders not to do so. According to some observers, Ben-Gurion delayed promoting Rabin to a top leadership position because of the act of disloyalty. Some insiders have claimed that Rabin would have been promoted to chief of staff by 1953 but for that blemish on his record; as it turned out, he did not receive that promotion until 1964.

Following the war Rabin was named commander of the brigade that patrolled the Negev and was recruited to help in the overall organization of the Israeli military. Although he had grown comfortable with the methods employed by the Palmach, which has been likened to a guerrilla organization, he nevertheless successfully adapted his skills to the needs of the regular army. In 1954, after spending a year at the British Staff College in Camberley, England, which offered a nine-month course in military education, he was promoted to the rank of major general and was asked to head the training branch of the IDF.

Rabin was appointed commander in chief of the Northern Front, on Israel's border with Syria, in 1956; he thus played no direct part in the Sinai Campaign, waged that year. At one point he considered leaving the military to enter Harvard University's Graduate School of Business Administration, but he decided to remain with the service when changes in command made it clear that he could advance to a top leadership position. Rabin's most significant promotion—to chief of staff, in 1964—not only placed him in charge of the army but also brought him into a leadership role with respect to the government.

Following his promotion, Rabin flexed Israel's military muscle against the Syrians and ordered reprisals against terrorist operations encouraged by the formation of the Palestine Liberation Organization in the same year. According to some Israeli political leaders, including David Ben-Gurion, Rabin's aggressive stance contributed to the escalation of tensions between Israel and its Arab neighbors in the spring of 1967. Shaken by the view of Ben-Gurion and others that he was leading Israel to the brink of war, in May of that year Rabin experienced a nervous breakdown that rendered him unable to perform his duties for a twenty-four hour period. "There can be no doubt that I was suffering from a combination of tension, exhaustion, and the enormous amounts of cigarette smoke I had inhaled in recent days . . . ," he wrote, as quoted by Robert Slater. "But it was more than nicotine that brought me down. The heavy sense of guilt that had been dogging me of late became unbearably strong on 23 May . . . Perhaps I had failed in my duty as the prime minister's chief military adviser. Maybe that was why Israel now found itself in such difficult straits. Never before had even I come close to feeling so depressed."

The heightened tensions between Israel and its neighbors culminated in the outbreak of the Six-Day War, on June 5, 1967, with Israel launching preemptive strikes against Egypt, Jordan, Iraq, and Syria. Whatever his role in provoking Israel's neighbors, Rabin prosecuted the war with great efficiency, to the extent that Israel succeeded in taking control of the Sinai peninsula, the western bank of the Jordan River, the Gaza Strip, and the Golan Heights—and thus in growing to three and a half times its prewar size. While the international media, enamored of the charismatic Israeli defense minister Moshe Dayan, gave most of the credit for Israel's victory to Dayan, among Israelis Rabin was the hero of the war. "No event shaped the image of Yitzhak Rabin in the pubic's mind as much as the Six-Day War . . . ," Robert Slater wrote. "When people asked themselves in later years whether Yitzhak Rabin would make a worthy prime minister or defense minister, his intimate involvement in the 1967 war was all the credentials he required. The Six-Day War . . . became Yitzhak Rabin's calling card for political leadership."

Before the war Rabin had lobbied to be appointed ambassador to the United States, which was proving to be Israel's most dependable ally, and in early 1968 he was posted to Washington, D.C. His assignment was to strengthen the relationship between the two countries, obtain economic and military aid, and gain support for Israel both within and outside government circles. Although he lacked the usual credentials of a diplomat, he made a highly creditable showing, and he succeeded in persuading the Americans to continue to supply Israel with arms and other forms of aid.

On his return to Israel in 1973, Rabin decided to run for a seat in the Knesset, Israel's parliament, as a member of the Labor Party. (Until 1971, when he joined Labor, he had not belonged to a political party.) The elections had been scheduled for October 31, 1973, but they were put on hold after Israel was attacked by Egypt and Syria on October 6, marking the beginning of the Yom Kippur War. While Israeli forces ultimately succeeded in driving back the enemy, the war was costly both in human and economic terms, and the government was blamed for having been poorly prepared to defend the country against attack. In the elections, held in December, Labor won a plurality of the vote, an outcome that enabled Prime Minister Golda Meir to form a government, but in April 1974 she resigned her post as a result of mounting public criticism of her government's lack of defense preparedness.

Rabin, who had won a seat in the Knesset in the elections, was a political beneficiary of those events. Thanks to his popularity among Israelis and his lingering reputation as the hero of the Six-Day War—and despite his lack of a solid political base within the Labor Party itself—he emerged as a candidate for prime minister. (The Labor Party's central committee was to choose the new prime minister, who would then form a new government.) His rival in the ensuing battle for the leadership of the party was Shimon Peres, with whom Rabin had never been on the friendliest of terms. In winning the contest, Rabin became Israel's youngest prime minister and the first sabra, or native-born Israeli, to hold that post.

During his three years as prime minister, Rabin's challenges included contending with a new wave of immigration, reviving the economy, which was plagued by high inflation as a result of the 1973 war, and accommodating the heightened domestic concerns for security, also a result of the war. By most accounts, he had some success in the economic sphere, and he made rebuilding the IDF one of his top priorities. In 1976 Rabin won considerable praise for authorizing what turned out to be the successful military operation at Entebbe, Uganda, in which Israeli soldiers rescued 103 airline passengers who had been held hostage by the PLO. Another of his successes was the conclusion, through the mediation of United States secretary of state Henry Kissinger, of Sinai II, one of several Israeli-Egyptian disengagement agreements, in 1975.

In late 1976, hoping to receive a mandate to continue leading the country, Rabin resigned in favor of new elections. His reelection campaign was soon beset by a variety of problems, among them the revelation that his wife had an active bank account in Washington, D.C., which constituted a violation of Israel's unusually strict rules governing such matters. Although initially a minor issue, it eventually developed into a full-blown political scandal that, in May 1977, prompted Rabin to abandon the race for the prime ministership. His rival Shimon Peres took his place as the leader of the party. In the elections the right-wing Likud Party gained control of the Knesset, beginning what was to become its fifteen-year-long domination of Israeli politics.

For the first half of that period, Rabin, who remained a member of the Knesset, was relegated to the party's back benches. With the publication of his memoirs in 1979, Rabin's rivalry with Shimon Peres became a much-talked-about news item, for in it he accused Peres of "subversion" and of undermining Rabin's premiership. In spite of the criticism he received for airing his grievances, by 1980 Rabin's popularity among the electorate had rebounded, to the extent that he was again considered a leading candidate for prime minister. But as it turned out, Peres received the party's nomination, and the Likud was returned to power in the June 1981 vote.

The surprise resignation of Menachem Begin in 1984 was followed by a closely contested election in which Labor captured forty-four seats in the Knesset, just three more than Likud. Neither party, however, could muster enough support from Israel's minor parties to form a government, with the unprecedented result that the two agreed to form a National Unity Government in which Shimon Peres and then Yitzhak Shamir would each serve a two-year term as prime minister. Also as part of this arrangement, Rabin was to serve as defense minister during the government's entire four-year term. The appointment reflected not only his return to a position of leadership within Israeli politics but also the confidence that both the left and the right had in his ability to head Israel's military establishment.

One of Rabin's major initiatives as defense minister was to withdraw Israeli forces from Lebanon, which it had invaded in 1982. Rabin had apparently supported the invasion initially but had later come to oppose it on the grounds that Israel's war aims, which included removing Syrian troops from Lebanon and trying to arrange the installation of a government friendly to Israel, were unattainable. The withdrawal was completed in 1985. Rabin was confronted with an even more serious problem when, in December 1987, impoverished and oppressed Palestinians living in the Gaza Strip and the West Bank launched a spontaneous revolt, which came to be known as the *intifada*. The revolt, which was characterized by mass demonstrations and random acts of violence, took Rabin, along with most Israeli and Arab leaders, by surprise, and he at first downplayed its significance. Viewing it as the work of a few extremists, he took a hard line against the rioters. Indeed, he is said to have commanded his soldiers not to shoot the demonstrators but to break their limbs—an order that many in the West found to be appalling. A. M. Rosenthal of the *New York Times*, for example, went so far as to call for his resignation.

Within several months, however, the failure of his policy convinced Rabin that the Palestinians could not be ignored indefinitely. "I've learned something in the past two and a half months—among other things that you can't rule by force over 1.5 million Palestinians," he said in early 1988, as quoted in *Time* (January 3, 1994). An alternative, he concluded, was to devise a political solution to the conflict. While he still opposed the creation of a Palestinian state, he came to believe that such a solution might involve ceding Israel's authority over territory inhabited by Palestinians to Jordan. He also expressed a willingness to negotiate with PLO officials, provided they adhered to certain conditions, including a recognition of Israel's right to exist. Rabin thus set himself apart from Yitzhak Shamir, who remained staunchly opposed to compromise of any kind.

Following the 1988 elections Labor and Likud again agreed to form a National Unity Government. Rabin retained the post of defense minister until 1990, when Yitzhak Shamir formed a new, more conservative government. Although in his public utterances Shamir expressed an interest in working toward peace, he failed to advance the peace process substantively. As a result, he not only alienated Israel's closest ally, the United States, but also taxed the patience of both the Israeli public and Israeli political leaders—factors that contributed to the fall of the Likud-led government in January 1992.

Notwithstanding popular dissatisfaction with Shamir and Likud, a Labor victory was far from assured, for the Israeli electorate, while fed up with Shamir, could at least trust that he would not jeopardize Israel's security. Labor's electoral prospects were therefore enhanced after Rabin succeeded in wresting control of the party from Shimon Peres, in February, for while Rabin appeared to be more willing than Shamir to negotiate a peace settlement—he went so far as to say that he would be willing to trade land for peace—he was, unlike Peres, someone who could be trusted not to jeopardize the country's security. As predicted by the polls, Rabin led his party to victory in the June 23, 1992 elections.

Once in office, Rabin set out to make good on his promise to make significant progress in negotiating a peace settlement. A breakthrough occurred in August 1993, following secret talks between the Israeli government and the PLO in Norway, when the two parties concluded a preliminary accord on Palestinian self-rule in the occupied territories. In another dramatic development, in September Rabin wrote a sober note to Yasir Arafat that stated, "Israel has decided to recognize the PLO as the representative of the Palestinian people and commence negotiations with the PLO within the Middle East peace process." According to the agreement on Palestinian self-rule, an interim Palestinian government was to be established in the Gaza Strip, the West Bank town of Jericho, and, later on, in the rest of the West Bank. At the historic signing of the accord, on September 13, 1993, in Washington, D.C., Rabin shook hands, albeit somewhat tentatively, with his former enemy Yasir Arafat. The signing of the accord was followed by a torturous but ultimately fruitful series of negotiations with other of Israel's neighbors. A peace treaty between Israel and Jordan was signed on October 26, 1994; it was the second peace treaty Israel signed with an Arab country, coming fifteen years after its accord with Egypt. At the historic signing ceremony, held at Arava Crossing, a desert outpost on the Israeli-Jordanian border, Rabin said: "For nearly two generations, desolation pervaded the heart of our two peoples. The time has now come not merely to dream of a better future but to realize it." By early 1995 Israel and Jordan had established full diplomatic relations and had also committed themselves to cooperate in such areas as agriculture, water, tourism, economic development, and environmental protection.

Eleven months after signing Israel's peace treaty with Jordan, Rabin put his pen to another historic document that expanded Palestinian self-rule in the West Bank and authorized the withdrawal of Israeli troops from cities where nearly half the West Bank population lives. The treaty with the Palestinians did not settle the final borders between Israel and the West Bank entity, which is not as yet—and may or may not become—a state. The pact with the PLO has aroused considerable controversy in Israel, where it is opposed by many in the Likud and other right-wing parties who see the West Bank as land to which Israel has a historical right. It has also generated opposition among radical elements of the Palestinians, who views peace with Israel as capitulation. Recognizing the fragility of the Israel-PLO accord, Rabin said at the signing cermony, "If all the partners to the peace do not unite against the evil angels of death by terrorism, all that will remain of this ceremony are color snapshots, empty mementos."

Yitzhak Rabin has been married to Leah Schlossberg, a German-born teacher he met in Tel Aviv, since August 28, 1948. They have a son, Yuval, and a daughter, Dalia. Rabin is known as a poor public speaker and is said to be uncomfortable in social situations. In addition to the Nobel Prize, he has received many honors, including honorary doctorates from Jerusalem University, Brandeis University, and Yeshiva University, among other institutions. When he received the Nobel Prize, Rabin claimed it was "for the whole nation, for the citizens of the State of Israel, for the bereaved families and the disabled, for the hundreds of thousands who have fought in Israel's war." "Today," he said, "the Palestinians face the moment of truth. If they do not defeat the enemies of peace, the enemies of peace will defeat them."

Selected Biographical References: London Observer p25 Je 28 '92; N Y R of Bks p17+ Je 11 '92; Time 143:40+ Ja 3 '94 por; International Who's Who, 1994-95; Rabin, Yitzhak. The Rabin Memoirs (1979); Slater, Robert. Rabin of Israel (1993)

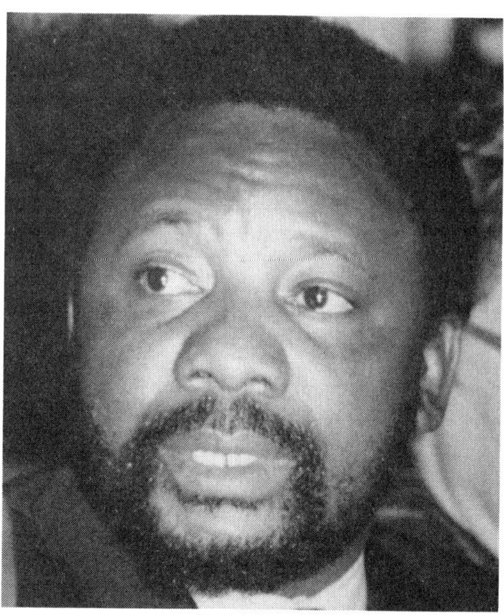

Dennis Farrell/AP/Wide World Photos

Ramaphosa, Cyril

(ram-uh-POHS-uh)

Nov. 17, 1952- South African labor leader; political leader. Address: African National Congress, P.O. Box 61884, Marshalltown 2107, South Africa

"Liberation—the struggle for national liberation against oppression and economic exploitation—that is the main thrust of our struggle," Cyril Ramaphosa, one of South Africa's most influential black leaders and its most powerful trade union leader, said in 1987. "The trade union work we are doing is part and parcel of the entire struggle. The struggle we are involved in on the mines is a training ground for our people for the ultimate goal, which is liberation." His words turned out to be prophetic, for in 1994 South Africa held its first-ever all-race elections, the results of which produced the country's first truly representative government. Ramaphosa's efforts to bring his country to that point began in earnest in 1982, when he was named head of the National Union of Mineworkers. By drawing on his pragmatism, negotiating skills, intelligence, and acute understanding of South African politics, he succeeded in strengthening the rights and improving the working conditions of black laborers, all the while earning the respect of his white opponents. "In ten years he has forged a trade union in the mining industry which has become a very powerful force," Adrian du Plessis, a mining industry official who represented white interests at the industry's wage negotiations, told John Battersby in an interview for the *Christian Science Monitor* (October 1, 1991). "It is a remarkable achievement and one which has taken decades in other countries."

The expertise Ramaphosa gained during that period made him an especially attractive candidate for the position of secretary-general of the African National Congress (ANC), to which he was elected in 1991. Over the next three years, he led the negotiations with members of the ruling National Party that resulted in the abandonment of the institution of apartheid and the inauguration of a new era of multiracial politics in his country. In addition to serving as secretary-general of the ANC, since 1994 he has chaired the new South African legislature, with responsibility for drafting a new constitution.

Matamela Cyril Ramaphosa was born on November 17, 1952 in Soweto, a collection of black townships located to the southwest of Johannesburg, South Africa. (Soweto is the acronym for Southwest Townships.) He is the son of Samuel Ramaphosa, a policeman, and Erdmuth Ramaphosa, and the grandson of a diamond-mine worker. Ramaphosa experienced the ugliness of South Africa's then-official policy of racial discrimination in 1960, in an encounter that affected him for years afterward. In that year, during the state of emergency that the government had imposed to quell unrest that erupted after police killed sixty-nine black demonstrators in the town of Sharpeville, white soldiers were stationed in the area where Ramaphosa's family lived. One day, as Ramaphosa was walking to school, a soldier kicked him into a ditch for no apparent reason. In response, Ramaphosa simply stared at the soldier, picked up his books, and continued on his way. The experience confused him, and the memory of it colored his thinking about white people. "I went to my mother and asked why," he recalled to Sheila Rule, who profiled him for the *New York Times* (September 2, 1985). "She told me that the government had decided to take over the township because black people and the African National Congress were putting pressure on the government. After being kicked like that, I felt bitter against white people, which took me a long time to overcome. But I began to realize that it was the reality of the South African situation."

Ramaphosa attended a boarding school in the town of Sibasa, in Vendaland. In 1972, according to *Time* (September 14, 1987), he enrolled at the University of the North at Turfloop, one of the ethnic colleges set up by the government, where he studied law and became actively involved in the emerging black consciousness movement. Unlike the leaders of the multiracial African National Congress resistance movement, black consciousness theorists maintained that white people should not be permitted to join the struggle of blacks to liberate themselves. Ramaphosa also served as head of the South African Students' Organization, which Sheila Rule described as a "militant group that gave birth to virtually all other student groups . . . working for change in the country."

In 1974 Ramaphosa's activism led him to organize a rally on the campus in support of Frelimo, the Mozambican resistance group dedicated to achieving Mozambique's independence from Portugal. For spearheading the demonstration, he was charged with violating South Africa's Terrorism Act and held in solitary confinement at the Pretoria Central Prison. During his eleven-month incarceration, he came to realize that the black consciousness movement, especially its insistence that blacks close ranks against even sympathetic whites, had, in his words, "come full circle and could take us no further." Following his release, he was denied readmission to the university, according to Sheila Rule. He was arrested again in 1976, this time for participating in the schoolchildren's uprising that year in Soweto. After his release six months later, he and his siblings insisted that their father resign from the police force, so that the family would have no connection with the government and its policies.

After Ramaphosa earned his law degree, by correspondence, from the University of South Africa, in 1980 or 1981, he decided against practicing law, because he realized that those who needed his services most would be unable to pay for them. A better way to further the cause of black liberation, he concluded, was to join the trade union movement, and so he took a job as a legal adviser for the Council of Unions of South Africa (CUSA). Before long he was asked to play a leading role in the establishment of a gold-miners' union. He agreed, and in 1982 the National Union of Mineworkers (NUM) was born. At its first conference Ramaphosa was elected its general secretary, a position that placed him in direct opposition to white South African interests. Just three years before, the government had legalized black labor unions, with the aim of pacifying blacks without ceding too much power. Ramaphosa's objective as the NUM's general secretary, on the other hand, was to increase the rights of black workers.

Among Ramaphosa's immediate goals was the recruitment of new members. (In the early days of the organization he was one of a staff of six administering to just six thousand fully paid members.) This task was complicated by the fact that mine owners had the right to prevent him from entering their property and to restrict his movements around the mines. He nevertheless managed to get around these obstacles, and in large measure through his efforts, the union's membership mushroomed. By 1984, according to NUM records, some 110,000 mineworkers belonged to the organization.

Ramaphosa's long-range aims included removing all restrictions on the professional and financial advancement of black miners. Although black workers performed tasks officially reserved for whites, he told one journalist, they did not receive pay increases or promotions for doing them. In seeking to abolish such practices, Ramaphosa wanted not only to improve the lot of black workers but to increase their political rights as well. "Our role is not just to look at the economic benefits our members can get," he told Alan Cowell in an interview for the *New York Times* (May 14, 1985). "It affects the right to live and sell your labor wherever you want to."

The union's goals became more overtly political in November 1984, when, under Ramaphosa's direction, it led the first legal strike by black workers in the history of South Africa, to protest the use of troops in the black townships, as Alan Cowell reported in the *New York Times Magazine* (June 15, 1986). With an estimated eight hundred thousand workers participating in the strike, the union proved itself to be a formidable force in South African politics. Within the next few months, Ramaphosa announced a series of new demands, including a 40 percent increase in pay (which he subsequently reduced), a shorter work week, and an end to the practice of reserving certain jobs for whites.

On August 4, 1985, after months of negotiations failed to secure a raise in pay for NUM members, Ramaphosa issued an ultimatum: another strike would begin on August 25 if NUM demands were not met. Among the union's other demands was an end to the state of emergency that had been imposed in July to put down the riots that had erupted in black townships when a new constitution failed to grant blacks political representation. The organization further called on the government to withdraw its threat to expel black workers who had come to South Africa from countries that had voted to impose sanctions against it. "The mine workers are like captive labor," Ramaphosa said, during his conversation with Sheila Rule, of his reasons for contemplating calling the strike. "Their situation is such that they can be manipulated completely by the mine owners. We've already said that if they use force, we are going to pull out our entire membership in the mines. But we don't foresee the workers holding out for too long, because they could be shipped out to the 'homelands,' and the law allows the owners to do just that. But taking strike action is the last weapon we have at this point."

Even before the strike officially began, the union's actions provoked an aggressive response from mine owners. According to Ramaphosa, the mine owners engaged in "activities similar to an army preparing for total warfare." In addition to threatening to dismiss anyone who participated in the strike, they erected fences around the single-sex hostels where almost all mine workers were required to live and instituted patrols of their properties by guards in armored trucks. The harsh tactics apparently had the desired effect. On September 1, 1985 a reported twenty-eight thousand miners—less than half the number NUM had anticipated—went on strike at five gold mines and two coal mines. (Mine owners claimed only fourteen thousand laborers took part in the strike.) Significantly fewer failed to show up at work the following day. "We underestimated management preparedness at the seven mines where we were supposed to go out," Ramaphosa was quoted as saying in the *New York Times* (September 3, 1985). "The intensity of the intimidation was a lot higher than we expected."

Union leaders asserted that many of their members had been forced to work at gunpoint and that "hundreds of workers" had been injured by rubber bullets, tear gas, and whips. An unidentified mining company spokesman declared the charges of intimidation to be "absolute nonsense." Meanwhile, the Anglo American Corporation, South Africa's largest mining company and the employer of a majority of NUM members, offered a wage increase close to what the union had demanded. As it turned out, the offer helped bring about an end to the strike, which Ramaphosa declared "suspended" on September 4, 1985.

Calling off the strike was a strategic move for Ramaphosa, for in so doing he reduced the risk that the mining companies would dismiss the strikers en masse. "Ramaphosa was not ready this year for a full-scale confrontation. He had too much to risk," an unidentified labor expert told Sheila Rule in an interview for the *New York Times* (September 6, 1985). "If he had gone into a full-blown strike with all his members and it had been unsuccessful, it would have led to disenchantment by all the workers and it would have seriously harmed his credibility as the man emerging as the single most important black trade union leader in the country." Equally important, in ending the strike Ramaphosa was able to maintain his relationship with the Anglo American Corporation, the labor expert told Sheila Rule.

By the time of the 1985 strike, the National Union of Mineworkers had become South Africa's largest and most powerful trade union, with some three hundred thousand members. Its strength increased considerably in November, when it left CUSA and joined thirty-two other trade unions to form the half-million-member Congress of South African Trade Unions (COSATU), which soon forged ties with the United Democratic Front, the largest nonparliamentary opposition group in South Africa, and the then-banned African National Congress. The "muscle of resistance in this country [is becoming] bigger and more organized," Ramaphosa, who was instrumental in the establishment of COSATU, told Alan Cowell in an interview for the *New York Times Magazine* article.

COSATU's strength was demonstrated in 1986, when it called on workers to stay away from their jobs on May 1 as part of its demand that the government make that day a paid holiday. An impressive one and a half million workers stayed home. Instead of experiencing the sort of intimidation that the mine workers had faced the year before, they "were allowed to take the day off, and to return safely to their jobs, without facing penalties,"

Cowell reported. What this indicated, Ramaphosa told Cowell, was that the trade union movement had become too powerful to be easily cowed. That assertion notwithstanding, the movement was far from invincible. Not long after the one-day labor action in May 1986, the South African government placed NUM's vice-president and a number of mine union leaders in detention, and Ramaphosa himself was forced to go into hiding for a time later that year.

In August 1987 Ramaphosa took his biggest gamble to that date, when he called what became both NUM's longest strike—twenty-one days—and one of the biggest in South African history. What prompted him to call the strike was the mine owners' failure to meet NUM demands for a 30 percent pay increase for all union members. At least 250,000 workers (out of the union's total membership of 350,000) at around fifty gold and coal mines participated in the strike. On August 26, the seventeenth day of the strike, the mine owners, who were losing between ten million and fifteen million dollars a day because of the strike, offered raises of up to 23 percent and increased fringe benefits. Although Ramaphosa and his negotiating partners had by then lowered their demand for an increase from 30 to 27 percent, they refused the owners' offer. "Union leaders did not need to make recommendations to our members because they found it was an offer that they could not even consider," Ramaphosa was quoted as saying in the *New York Times* (August 27, 1987), adding that the demands remained negotiable.

The mining companies, in turn, stepped up pressure on the miners, with Anglo American announcing that it would close some mine shafts and take "appropriate action" to resume operations at others. According to Ramaphosa, such action included intimidation of workers—a charge mining company spokesmen denied. In any event, clashes between strikers and company officials resulted in the deaths of nine mine workers and the injury of some five hundred, as David Beresford reported in the *Manchester Guardian Weekly* (May 3, 1992). When Anglo American began dismissing workers en masse—some forty-six thousand lost their jobs—Ramaphosa felt compelled to end the strike. He also concluded he had no choice but to accept the 15 to 23 percent pay raise first offered by the mining companies. The union suffered further losses following the strike, when 10 percent of its membership left the ranks. These setbacks notwithstanding, Ramaphosa also achieved a few victories. He won a battle in the courts, which forced Anglo American to reinstate some thirty thousand of the workers it had fired. More important, the strike "shifted the political balance between black and white and changed the face of industrial relations," in the words of John Battersby, writing in the *Christian Science Monitor*.

Ramaphosa's growing influence within the wider South African liberation struggle was underlined in 1988, when he served as the main negotiator during a rent boycott in Soweto, and in 1989, when he played a leading role in the Mass Democratic Movement's so-called Defiance Campaign against government repression. Ramaphosa by this time was also deeply involved in the activities of the African National Congress, of which he had become a member in 1986. Despite his nominal solidarity with the ANC, he may not have been entirely in sync with its politics, according to Tom Lodge, a political scientist at Witwatersrand University, in Johannesburg, who observed in the *World Policy Journal* (Fall 1993) that Ramaphosa's "statements during the 1980s were identifiably to the left of the official ANC policy." He also came from a background different from that of the ANC's patriarchs, many of whom had spent years in exile or prison. Nevertheless, Ramaphosa was selected to serve as the chief spokesman of the committee that was formed to oversee the celebrations surrounding the release from prison in 1990 of Nelson Mandela, who had come to be seen as a symbol of black South African resistance. Then, in the following year, in addition to being reelected head of the National Union of Mineworkers, Ramaphosa captured the post of secretary-general of the African National Congress, defeating his nearest rival by a margin of three to one. According to Tom Lodge, his victory was facilitated by the fact that the rapidly increasing membership of the ANC included a large number of trade union members.

The release from prison of Nelson Mandela was a historic event that marked the beginning of the end of the institution of apartheid in South Africa. The transition to black majority rule was accomplished through negotiations between the ANC, represented by Ramaphosa, among others, and the ruling National Party. The talks proved to be difficult and protracted. A major stumbling block was the white minority government's insistence on securing guarantees for the continuation of special rights for its constituency, including a veto for the white minority in the writing of a new constitution. In an attempt to force the government to be more flexible, on June 23, 1992 the ANC broke off talks. To further intensify the pressure, the ANC called on workers to engage in a two-day general strike, on August 3 and August 4, 1992.

In response, "at least four million" people stayed away from work, according to Ramaphosa, though business spokesmen placed the number of strikers at only two million. The ANC interpreted the strong showing of strikers as an endorsement of its decision to break off talks with the government. Tensions increased in early September 1992, when an ANC-organized march against the dictator of Ciskei, a South African puppet state, or "homeland," was broken up by homeland troops who fired on the marchers, killing twenty-four people. Ramaphosa was among those who had to dive to the ground to avoid being shot. "We are blaming [South African President F. W.] de Klerk for this," he told journalists. "The Ciskei is the creation of the apartheid regime, and they are responsible for the atrocities committed in its name."

Throughout the period during which negotiations were officially suspended, Ramaphosa worked behind the scenes to keep them alive. According to Tom Lodge, he remained "in almost nightly telephone contact with Roelf Meyer, the National Party's chief negotiator." Lodge attributed the eventual resumption of the talks to the mutual respect and professionalism of Ramaphosa and Meyer. (Their easy rapport was aided by the fact that their relationship predated the talks on the transition to majority rule.) By early 1993 Ramaphosa had finalized plans for national elections that were to result in a multiparty, multiracial "government of national unity." Partly in response to the criticisms of Winnie Mandela and others who alleged that the ANC had conceded too much to white South African interests, Ramaphosa stressed that "when the final agreement is reached and signed it will be an agreement that will finally lead to full majority rule that will deliver a full democracy and achieve nonracial society." In June 1993 the negotiators announced their choice of April 27, 1994 as the date for the first all-race elections in South African history.

His status as chief ANC negotiator left Ramaphosa at this point with only one serious rival—Thabo Mbeki, the ANC's foreign policy chief—as heir apparent to Nelson Mandela. In 1993, following an internal power struggle between the two men, Mbeki emerged victorious, for the time being at least, when he was appointed chairman of the ANC. The post established Mbeki as second in command after Mandela and his likely successor. Nevertheless, Ramaphosa finished second only to Nelson Mandela in an internal ANC election held in January 1994 to determine who was to run in the April election for South Africa's first all-race legislature.

Ramaphosa's less-than-secure standing among the more radical elements of the ANC, who felt that he had been too conciliatory in his dealings with the National Party, became evident in January 1994, when he and Joe Slovo, the chairman of the South African Communist Party, were the victims of an assassination attempt while they were touring a township that had been racked by factional violence. Violent incidents in the townships continued throughout the months leading up to the election, but the outcome of the April 27 voting was never seriously in doubt, with Mandela capturing the presidency and the ANC winning some 63 percent of the ballots and 252 of 400 seats in the new, transitional legislative assembly.

Many observers had predicted that, once elected, Mandela would select Ramaphosa as a deputy president in his government. Contrary to those expectations, Ramaphosa was not included in Mandela's cabinet, which was sworn in on May 11. The deputy president's post he had hoped for was given instead to Thabo Mbeki. According to a statement issued by the ANC, Ramaphosa himself had decided against taking a cabinet post, so that he could devote himself to strengthening the party. Casting doubt on the statement were reports that Ramaphosa made his decision after Mbeki was appointed deputy president. Ramaphosa, who had won a seat in the legislature, was later elected chairman of that body, in which capacity he began the task of drafting a new, permanent constitution for South Africa.

Cyril Ramaphosa, who stands five feet ten inches tall, is handsome and dapper. His devotion to his work is such that a writer for a South African newspaper observed that the labor leader, who is divorced, "now seems married to the union, and that is working out." When asked about the likelihood that the ANC would succeed in improving the lives of ordinary South Africans, Ramaphosa predicted that at the very least it would do a better job than the white-minority government had done. "They have been driven by racial and ideological considerations in virtually everything they have done in terms of running the country," he has said. "They were inherently undemocratic, and you cannot have progress, you cannot have full prosperity in an undemocratic dispensation." In October 1987 Ramaphosa was awarded the Olof Palme Prize by the government of Sweden, in recognition of his union's "courage and wisdom in its solitary struggle for human rights and dignity."

Selected Biographical References: Christian Sci Mon p4 O 1 '91; Financial Times p3 Je 11 '93 por; Manchester Guardian W p 21 My 3 '92; N Y Times A p6 S 2 '85 por, A p4 Ap 4 '92 por; N Y Times Mag p14+ Je 15 '86 pors; Time 30:42+ S 14 '87 por; World Policy J 65+ Fall '93; International Who's Who, 1995–96

Reeves, Keanu

(kee-AH-noo)

Sept. 2, 1964– Actor. Address: c/o Todd Smith, Creative Artists Agency, 9830 Wilshire Blvd., Beverly Hills, CA 90212

Since his impressive performance as an alienated teen in the 1987 film *River's Edge*, Keanu Reeves has been regarded by many as a talented young actor. On occasion he has also been described, less charitably, as one who "has a way of looking emptier than a sock drawer on laundry day," to quote one bemused critic. What some perceive to be "emptiness" may instead be a result of Reeves's singular approach to his craft. His willingness to "be filled" by his characters, as one movie reviewer phrased it, rather than animate them with aspects of his own personality is perhaps what has allowed him to be cast in such disparate roles, including that of a blissfully ignorant, time-traveling high-school student in *Bill and Ted's Excellent Adventure* and its sequel, *Bill and Ted's Bogus Journey*; a French nobleman in *Dangerous Liaisons*; the spiritual leader Siddhartha Gautama in *Little Buddha*; and a cop struggling to save a busload of passengers from death in the box-office smash *Speed*.

AP/Wide World Photos

Keanu Reeves

Keanu Reeves was born on September 2, 1964 in Beirut, Lebanon. His father, Samuel Nowlin Reeves, a geologist of Hawaiian and Chinese descent (the name "Keanu," shared by his paternal grandfather, means "cool breeze over the mountains" in Hawaiian), abandoned the family when Keanu was very young. He grew up primarily in Toronto, Canada, where he lived with his mother, Patricia, his younger sister, Kim, and his half-sister, Karina. A British-born costume designer, Reeves's mother married and divorced three men after divorcing Reeves's father. She provided her children with a life that was "long on love beads, incense, and visits from clients . . . such as [the rock star] Alice Cooper—but short on discipline," as Natasha Stoynoff put it in *People* (July 11, 1994).

That lack of discipline seems to have been reflected in Reeves's attitude toward school. Stoynoff quoted one of his teachers at Jesse Ketchum grade school as saying that Reeves was rarely, if ever, on time for his lessons but that when he did arrive, "he had a smile on his face." In high school Reeves was more concerned with his position as goalie on the hockey team (his prowess earned him the nickname "the Wall") than with his studies, as evidenced by the fact that he changed high schools four times before dropping out altogether in 1984, after unsuccessfully repeating his senior year. "I even flunked gym," he recalled in a conversation with Lynn Snowden for *Rolling Stone* (March 9, 1989).

While Reeves's upbringing did not incline him toward scholarship, it spurred his interest in the performing arts. He was impressed early on by the "exotic" people, to use his word, with whom his mother and stepfather associated. He has also recalled being captivated by such films as Stanley Kubrick's *A Clockwork Orange* (1971) and Peter Medak's *The Ruling Class* (1971), and he regularly attended screenings at Toronto University's Repertory Cinema, where he was exposed to a wide range of genres. At the age of fourteen, Reeves began landing bit parts in Canadian television series and American productions filmed in Canada. One of the secondary schools he attended was the High School for the Performing Arts in Toronto, and his first substantial theatrical outing came in a student production of Arthur Miller's *The Crucible*. A Coca-Cola commercial brought the budding actor his "first big paycheck," as Lynn Snowden put it. Reeves studied acting at the Hedgerow Theatre, in Moylan, Pennsylvania, during the summer that he was eighteen, and he later appeared on stage in Toronto in a production of Brad Fraser's play *Wolf Boy*. Deciding eventually that his dream of becoming a movie star could not be realized in Canada, in 1984 he moved to Los Angeles.

Among Reeves's earliest Hollywood credits was the feature film *Youngblood* (1986), a forgettable vehicle for Rob Lowe about a young hockey star. In the same year, he turned up in three made-for-television movies: *Act of Vengeance*, in which Reeves, as an assassin, became only the second person ever to kill a character played by the cinema tough guy Charles Bronson; *Under the Influence*, a drama about alcoholism; and the Christmas musical fantasy *Babes in Toyland*, a remake of the 1934 film. Evaluating *Babes in Toyland* for the *New York Times* (December 19, 1986), John J. O'Connor wrote, "Mr. Reeves, who in earlier television appearances this year was impressive as a young alcoholic . . . and a psychotic killer . . . looks understandably embarrassed each time he is required to join in another dreary song."

The actor's first attention-getting performance was in *River's Edge* (1987), Tim Hunter's disturbing tale, based on an actual incident, about a clique of affectless high-school students, one of whom, John, casually murders his girlfriend. Reeves's character, Matt, ultimately defies the leadership of Layne (Crispin Glover), who exhorts his friends to conceal the killing from the authorities. In the New York *Daily News* (September 14, 1988), Jim Farber pronounced Reeves to have been "so credible in his part" that "he seemed less an actor than some kid they ripped out of a Mötley Crüe concert."

On the strength of his work in *River's Edge*, in the following year Reeves appeared in several films. He essayed the supporting role of a young nobleman in eighteenth-century France in Stephen Frears's acclaimed *Dangerous Liaisons* (1988), which Christopher Hampton adapted from his own play based on *Les Liaisons Dangereuses*, Choderlos de Laclos's 1782 novel about games of sexual intrigue played by the aristocracy in pre-Revolution France. Reeves played the Chevalier Danceny, an earnest music teacher who falls in love with the young Cécile de Volanges (Uma Thurman), a convent-reared pawn in an erotic power struggle waged by the decadent Vicomte de

Valmont (John Malkovich) and the Marquise de Merteuil (Glenn Close).

In Thom Eberhardt's slight comedy *The Night Before* (1988), Reeves portrayed a nerdy teenager trying to remember what transpired at his high-school prom. More serious was Marisa Silver's 1988 release *Permanent Record*, in which the actor appeared as Chris, the best friend of a popular and gifted high-school student (Alan Boyce) who, without warning or apparent provocation, takes his own life. "Chris's gradual coming to grips with his sense of self gives the film its only point of interest, largely due to Keanu Reeves's performance, which opens up nicely as the drama progresses," a writer for *Variety* (April 20, 1988) declared. In *The Prince of Pennsylvania* (1988), a quirky comedy by Ron Nyswaner, Reeves took the part of a teenage free spirit trying to "find" himself while contending with his eccentric father (Fred Ward) and conducting a romance with an older woman (Amy Madigan).

The year 1989 was an equally busy one for the up-and-coming young actor. Directed by Stephen Herek, *Bill and Ted's Excellent Adventure* was an unpretentious comedy about two high-school boys (Reeves as Ted and Alex Winter as Bill) who are on the verge of flunking their history class when they discover a magical telephone booth that allows them to travel through time and meet such epochal figures as Socrates and Sigmund Freud. Although *Bill and Ted's Excellent Adventure* failed to impress the critics, it was a financial success, raking in more than forty million dollars. In *Parenthood* (1989), Ron Howard's gentle comedy about family and the complex ties between parents and children, Reeves was surrounded by an able cast that included Steve Martin, Mary Steenburgen, Dianne Wiest, and Jason Robards, and he turned in a strong, nuanced performance as a young husband. He also starred in *Life Under Water*, a made-for-television movie, based on the play by Richard Greenberg, about wealthy, cynical residents of Long Island.

Reeves demonstrated his ability to play a credible romantic lead in *Tune In Tomorrow. . . .* (1990), Jon Amiel's screen adaptation of the celebrated Mario Vargas Llosa novel *Aunt Julia and the Scriptwriter*. Set in New Orleans in the early 1950s, *Tune In Tomorrow. . . .* starred Reeves as an impressionable radio newswriter and aspiring novelist who falls in love with his sexy, older aunt by marriage (Barbara Hershey). Julie Salamon of the *Wall Street Journal* (October 26, 1990) felt that Reeves embodied his character "with just the right mix of innocence and smarts." Reeves and William Hurt were amusing as a pair of bumbling, drug-addled hit men in *I Love You to Death* (1990), Lawrence Kasdan's farce about a woman (Tracey Ullman) who puts out a contract on her philandering husband (Kevin Kline). A reviewer for *Variety* (April 4, 1990) pronounced Reeves to be "pleasantly dippy" in the movie. In director Kathryn Bigelow's offbeat action flick *Point Break* (1991), Reeves played Johnny Utah, a maverick FBI agent who goes undercover in a Southern California surfing community to investigate a series of bank robberies but falls under the spell of a charismatic gangster (Patrick Swayze). "A lot of the [film's] snap comes . . . from Mr. Reeves, who displays considerable discipline and range," Janet Maslin wrote in the *New York Times* (July 12, 1991). "He moves easily between the button-down demeanor that suits a police procedural story and the loose-jointed manner of his comic roles."

Bill and Ted's Bogus Journey (1991) found Reeves and Alex Winter returning as the sublimely vacant duo from Southern California, facing in this outing a villain (Joss Ackland) who attempts to alter history by having Bill and Ted killed, thus sending them on a journey through "a Dante-esque progression of Purgatory, Inferno, and Paradise, with side trips to several local mini-malls," as Dave Kehr summarized the plot in the *Chicago Tribune* (July 19, 1991). Roger Ebert, offering his opinion of the movie in the New York *Daily News* (July 19, 1991), praised Reeves for bringing "more artistry to this cretinous role than might at first meet the eye." He wrote in addition, "I have seen Keanu Reeves in vastly different roles (the FBI man in the current *Point Break*, for example) and am a little astonished by the range of these performances."

Reeves and River Phoenix starred in *My Own Private Idaho* (1991), the independent filmmaker Gus Van Sant's ambitious portrait of male street hustlers plying their trade in the American Northwest. Reeves was Scott, an upper-class vagrant slumming in the male-prostitute demimonde while waiting for the inheritance he will receive upon the death of his wealthy, powerful father, and Phoenix played the sweet-natured, narcoleptic Mike, who falls in love with Scott while searching for his long-lost mother. Van Sant layered *My Own Private Idaho* with conceits that, in the view of many critics, detracted from his lyrical and tender story of the two main characters, such as modeling Reeves's character after Prince Hal in *Henry IV* and burdening the actor with slang-ridden, modernized versions of Shakespearean speeches. Although David Ansen, writing in *Newsweek* (October 7, 1991), was impressed by Reeves and Phoenix, he noted that an "unmistakable self-consciousness comes over the movie in its boisterous Shakespearean passages, and you can feel Reeves, a good naturalistic actor, clenching whenever he shifts into Elizabethan rhythms." In the *New York Times* (September 27, 1991), on the other hand, Vincent Canby declared simply, "The performances, especially by the two young stars, are as surprising as they are sure."

Although Reeves was, by his own admission, not at his best in *Bram Stoker's Dracula* (1992), in which he took the part of Jonathan Harker, the young attorney whose fiancée (Winona Ryder) is the vampire's principal object of desire, director Francis Ford Coppola's erotic and visually striking film was well received at the box office and by many critics. Showing his versatility, Reeves followed his portrayal of the scheming Don John in

Kenneth Branagh's high-spirited Shakespearean romp *Much Ado About Nothing* (1993) with a turn as a South American freak-show performer in *Freaked* (1993), a comedy directed by Reeves's "Bill and Ted" costar, Alex Winter. Reeves played Julian Glitche, a love interest of Sissy Hankshaw (Uma Thurman), in *Even Cowgirls Get the Blues* (1994), Gus Van Sant's critically unsuccessful screen version of Tom Robbins's cult novel about a sexually liberated hitchhiker with oversize thumbs.

To prepare for the job of playing the young Siddhartha Gautama, who would go on to become the founder of Buddhism, in Bernardo Bertolucci's *Little Buddha* (1994), Reeves read extensively about Buddhism, learned the practice of meditation, and fasted while the film was being shot. "I knew people would find this an outrageous choice," Bertolucci said of his casting of Reeves when he spoke to Kristine McKenna for an article in *New York Newsday* (June 5, 1994). "How can Keanu, the idol of American teenagers, be Buddha? I tried to put such things out of my mind, and I'm enchanted with what he came up with—he seems as though he's not touching the ground when he walks in the film. Keanu has an innocence I felt was crucial to the role of Siddhartha—his innocence is on his face, and it goes to the core of his personality, and that's why I cast him."

The consensus of reviewers of *Little Buddha* was that the choice of Reeves was a good one. "Reeves's slightly blank aura is ingratiating here," Robert Horton wrote in *Film Comment* (July 1994). "He seems ready for anything, ready to be filled, ready to jump from his own private Idaho to the Himalayas—you can feel the happy energy of a young Hollywood actor asked to play one of the world's great spiritual leaders. So often in his movies Reeves gives you the feeling he hasn't quite found his own voice. . . . Here, he isn't required to say all that much, which helps, but even his uninflected voice is appropriate to his unformed character." That backhanded compliment was echoed by Janet Maslin of the *New York Times* (May 25, 1994): "Despite the fact that Mr. Reeves . . . retains traces of surfer-boy body language at the most unexpected moments, he more than commands interest during those sections of the film that depict Siddhartha's evolution. When a huge cobra magically appears to shield Siddhartha from rain, for instance, Mr. Reeves need only sit in meditation and look serene. That he can do."

After fasting to play the ascetic Siddhartha, Reeves pumped iron for the part of the police officer Jack Traven in Jan De Bont's popular thriller *Speed* (1994). Traven's nemesis is Howard Payne (Dennis Hopper), a bitter ex-cop who rigs a city bus with a bomb set to detonate once the vehicle's speed reaches, then drops below, fifty miles per hour. Traven tries to save the day as the bus hurtles wildly down the crowded streets and busy freeways of Los Angeles. Evaluating the film for the *Washington Post* (June 10, 1994), Hal Hinson wrote, "With his brush-cut [hair] and pumped-up physique, [Reeves] is barely recognizable as the loose, eager-puppy actor from his earlier films. As Jack, he reads every line as if he *really, really* cares, and though he's undeniably hunky and cute as a button, he's so earnest that he has no electricity, no life." In contrast, Jack Mathews of *New York Newsday* (June 10, 1994) felt that Reeves struck "a refreshingly different note" with his portrayal of Traven. "Using none of the pun-filled wit that has become the common denominator of the modern action hero, and with an intensity that may be a meditative hangover from *Little Buddha*, Reeves goes about his business with the concentration of someone actually trying to stop a killer."

After the success of *Speed*, Reeves's fee per film jumped to a reported seven million dollars, but instead of working for that price with the actors Al Pacino and Robert De Niro in a movie called *Heat*, he chose instead to play the title role in *Hamlet* at the Manitoba Theatre Centre in Winnipeg, Canada for the salary of two thousand dollars a week. "Shakespeare is physically thrilling," Reeves was quoted as saying in *Maclean's* (January 23, 1995). "It goes to my brain and into my heart." The twenty-four day run of Hamlet in early 1995 was sold out, as fans of the film star came from countries as far away as Argentina and Australia to see him on stage. Reviews of his performance were mixed: Brain D. Johnson, writing in *Maclean's* (January 23, 1995), carped: "He whipped through the soliloquies, the signature tunes of *Hamlet*, as if they were air-guitar solos. . . . He rode the play as if it were wired to blow up below a certain speed." The London *Sunday Times* critic, Roger Lewis, as quoted in *Vanity Fair* (March 1995), had a different impression: "He is one of the top three Hamlets I have seen. . . . He *is* Hamlet."

Two films in which Reeves starred were released in 1995: *Johnny Mnemonic*, a science-fiction thriller, and *A Walk in the Clouds*, a romantic drama set in the California wine country during World War II. Neither film was well-received by critics. "Keanu Reeves is not supposed to be a robot or an android or any other humanoid form in *Johnny Mnemonic*, but from his robotic delivery you'd never guess he's meant to be a flesh-and-blood man with a memory chip implanted in his brain," Caryn James wrote in the *New York Times* (May 26, 1995). In his review of *A Walk in the Clouds*, Michael Wilmington of the *Chicago Tribune* (August 11, 1995) dismissed the film as "silly," adding that Reeves's "performance actually fits right into the [movie's] aestheticized, swoony mood."

Carrie Rickey of the *Chicago Tribune* (June 26, 1994) described the dark-haired Keanu Reeves as a "reedy six-footer" whose "enigmatic face suggests a computer-generated composite of every known race and gender." Rickey went on to say, "His affect is pansexual and so is his appeal. At the trill of his name . . . fans female and male heave libidinal sighs." Although he has been perceived as inarticulate and vacuous, largely because of his tendency to lapse into the "valley" slang of his Ted character, Reeves has been said to read widely, and he is "very, very smart," in the opinion of Gus Van Sant, who was quoted by Chris Willman of *New York Newsday* (July 23, 1991). "He's the archetypal troubled young American," the actor John Malkovich, who appeared with Reeves in *Dangerous Liaisons*, told a reporter for *People* (July 11, 1994). "He's like your younger brother, someone you should be helping out in some way. He doesn't invite it. I don't think he would like it much. But if you're older, you feel you should protect him."

Reeves's screen work has been used as a focal point for a study of modern cinema in a course taught by the artist Stephen Prina at the Art Center College of Design in Pasadena, California. The actor currently lives at the Chateau Marmont hotel on Sunset Boulevard in Los Angeles. He relaxes by riding his motorcycle at high speeds (he bears numerous scars from crashes he has suffered) and by playing bass guitar with his "folk-thrash" band, Dog Star, at small clubs in Los Angeles.

Selected Biographical References: Am Film 16:32+ S '91 pors; Chicago Tribune XIII p16+ Je 26 '94 pors; Interview 20:132+ S '90 pors, 21:84+ N '91 pors; Maclean's 108:52+ Ja 23 '95 pors; N Y Daily News p35 S 14 '88 por, p31+ Jl 17 '91 pors; N Y Newsday p47+ Jl 23 '91 por, p8+ Je 5 '94 pors; People 42:49+ Jl 11 '94 pors, 43:70+ Je 6 '95 pors; Rolling Stone p31 Mr 9 '89 por; US 206:52+ Mr '95 pors; USA Today D p4 Ap 9 '90 por; International Television and Video Almanac, 1995

Ron Fricke

Reggio, Godfrey

1940– Filmmaker. Address: c/o Institute for Regional Education, P.O. Box 2404, Santa Fe, NM 87504

While Godfrey Reggio is usually described as a filmmaker, it might be more useful to characterize him as a creator of cinematic experiences, for his films, of which there are just three to date, employ none of the narrative conventions used by most filmmakers. Instead of telling a story in his films, Reggio provides viewers with his own distinctive metaphysical perspective on modern society, the natural world, and life itself, and he does so by joining a series of visually provocative images with a hypnotic musical score created by the avant-garde composer Philip Glass. "Language has lost its original charge," Reggio told Robert Epstein in an interview for the *Los Angeles Times* (December 12, 1991). "Here we fuse images and music. We use no language in the film because language has been stripped from us. We've lost how to use words." Only the titles of Reggio's films provide verbal clues to their content. Those of his first and second films, *Koyaanisqatsi* and *Powaqqatsi*, are words taken from the Hopi language, the former meaning "life out of balance" and the latter, "an entity, a way of life that consumes the life forces of other beings to further its own life." The title of his most recent film, *Anima Mundi*, is Latin for "soul world."

The progression of Reggio's career is almost as unusual as his approach to filmmaking. At the age of fourteen, already disillusioned with the modern world, he entered the monastic Roman Catholic order of the Christian Brothers. He spent the next fourteen years of his life fulfilling his monastic vows. Toward the end of that period, he began to work with street gangs and in behalf of various social causes. The disapproval his activism engendered among his fellow Christian Brothers contributed to his decision to leave the order. Once back in the secular world, Reggio cofounded the Institute for Regional Education (IRE), a not-for-profit organization based in Santa Fe, New Mexico that is devoted to community education and service. One of IRE's projects involved him in media advertising, which in turn led to his career in filmmaking, which he undertook even though he had no experience in the industry and had seen only a few films. While some viewers have been put off by Reggio's movies, finding them pretentious and self-indulgent, few would deny that they accomplish the director's intent, which is to tweak the viewer's subconscious. As he explained in an interview with Scott MacDonald for *A Critical Cinema 2* (1992), "I'm not interested . . . in creating an intellectual dialogue. I'm hoping that people can let go of themselves, forget about time, and have an experience."

Godfrey Reggio, who is of part-Cajun extraction, was born in 1940 in New Orleans. By the time he reached his early teens, he had already lived, in his words, "a pretty fast life," and had concluded that life in contemporary society lacked meaning for him. As a result of this realization, at the age of fourteen he joined the Christian Brothers, a Catholic teaching order. While his parents were not in favor of his becoming a monk, they did not try to prevent him from doing so.

Reggio was deeply moved by the example set by his fellow monks. "Those monks were very idealistic, they rejected the world, and, at the time, it made a lot of sense, it inspired me," Reggio told Kenneth Turan, who interviewed him for *GQ* (May 1988). "They became my idols. I also wanted to reject the world, to listen to another drum. I was inspired by Pope John XXIII; he was for me what Che Guevara was for some other person." In repudiating the world, Reggio adopted a lifestyle dominated by fasting, prayer, and silence. Indeed, during his first nine years with the order, he lived, in his words, "a very strict life of silence and manual labor and study," a way of life he has likened to that of the Middle Ages. "I had to have my head shaved. . . . I took it all very seriously," he recalled to Michael Dempsey for a *Film Quarterly* (Spring 1989) profile. "I wanted to be a saint, like you're supposed to want to be. . . . I collected holy cards, not baseball cards." Reggio took his preliminary vows at the age of eighteen and his final vows seven years later.

Meanwhile, by the age of twenty-three, Reggio had attended the Christian Brothers' College of Santa Fe, in New Mexico. He had also become active in the Santa Fe community, teaching in elementary and secondary schools and in college. It was as a result of the latter experience that he began to question the depth of his fellow monks' commitment to their vows. As he explained to MacDonald, he was troubled by what he saw as their failure to honor their pledge to "teach the poor gratuitously." "Almost all the children in the schools where I taught were middle-class kids, and yet I lived in *this* community where about 40 percent of the people had no access to primary medical care, and where the barrio was being eroded out from under the poor," he told MacDonald. "There was great social disintegration. . . . So there was a huge community of poverty, and I felt drawn to give some kind of assistance if I *could*."

For Reggio, serving his community meant working with its street gangs, which he did through Young Citizens for Action, an organization he was involved in founding, in 1963. He also helped to establish several medical clinics a few years later. Eventually, the Christian Brothers began to question Reggio's independent activities. "They felt that I was acting in a singular, rather than a communal way," Reggio told MacDonald. Despite his disagreements with the order, Reggio does not regret his years as a monk. "I feel my years with the Christian Brothers helped me a lot," he told Bob Strauss in an interview for the *Chicago Sun-Times* (May 8, 1988). "It detached me a bit from the objectives of the so-called world and the structure of the synthetic environment."

Reggio left the Christian Brothers in 1968. Four years later, in Santa Fe, he cofounded the Institute for Regional Education, which he has described as a "social, political collective." According to the production notes for *Koyaanisqatsi*, one of the institute's aims was to provide "information and research concerning social issues to the people of the American Southwest" through paid commercial advertising, including rush-hour radio spots, billboards, and prime-time television advertisements, rather than through public service announcements. Among IRE's earliest efforts was its 1974 campaign to raise public awareness of governmental invasion of privacy. The campaign featured a number of unconventional ads, including television commercials showing an eye that blinked to the sound of a camera shutter clicking. The television spots became so popular that viewers sometimes called the stations to find out when the next IRE ad would be aired.

The success of that campaign inspired Reggio to apply his talents to feature filmmaking—a rather audacious goal in view of the fact that he knew nothing about either the business or the art of filmmaking and in the course of his life had seen relatively few films. "As a child I'd seen Randolph Scott movies and stuff like that, and that was the extent of my viewing," he admitted to Scott MacDonald. "As a Brother, I saw a few religious films. I remember that *Monsieur Vincent* moved me greatly. But I had no real background." The film that most inspired Reggio was Luis Buñuel's classic *Los Olvidados* (The Young and the Damned; 1950), which he had used as a teaching tool while he was working with street gangs and which he eventually saw about two hundred times. "I felt that if I could be moved so thoroughly by this medium, then I could use it to express what I'm feeling," he said in an interview with Cressida Connolly for the British magazine the *Tatler* (June 1992). "It was clear that Buñuel's exercises were not merely entertainment, but a way of touching the human soul. That's what I want to emulate; that path to the source. I'm trying, principally, to speak to a person's heart." Thus, while Reggio lacked a firm idea of the kind of film he wanted to make, he knew the "feeling" he wanted it to convey. "And what I could feel, I could see," he told MacDonald.

By 1975 what had begun to take shape in Reggio's mind was a nonverbal film depicting, in his words, "ordinary daily living." With that seed of an idea, he and the cinematographer Ron Fricke began filming, in sixteen millimeter. Reggio was so thrilled by the results that he began showing his footage to potential investors in the hope of attracting enough money to film in thirty-five millimeter. But, as he recalled to a reporter for the Toronto *Globe and Mail* (January 20, 1984), persuading investors to commit themselves to the project was an uphill battle: "You can imagine what it was like. There was no dialogue. *There never would be any dialogue*. People would come out and be polite. My family thought I was insane." Reggio eventually succeeded in raising $2.5 million from seventy individuals, one of whom put up nearly $2 million.

Given the absence of dialogue, Reggio knew that the success of his film depended heavily on the musical accompaniment, which would provide coherence to the images. In 1979 he entered into a collaboration with the avant-garde composer Philip Glass, who would create the score. Glass was intimately involved in the editing of the film, to ensure that the images and music formed an integrated whole. "We wanted the images and the music to be coequal, so that you could actually hear the image and see the music," Reggio has said.

Reggio's principal aim in making his first film was to reveal the essence of both the natural world and modern society. "I was trying to look at buildings, masses of people, transportation, industrialization as *entities* in and of themselves, having an autonomous nature," he explained to Scott MacDonald. "Same thing with nature: rather than seeing nature as something dead, something inorganic like a stone, I wanted to see it as having its own life form, unanthropomorphized, unrelated to human beings, here for billions of years before human beings arrived on the planet." In keeping with those goals, *Koyaanisqatsi* (1983) begins with a progression of images of the landscape of Monument Valley—majestic cliffs, rolling clouds, and waves rippling over sand dunes. Eventually the images of nature give way to scenes, which flash across the screen with increasing speed, of vast transportation networks, assembly lines, skyscrapers, and other monuments of urban life.

Nonnarrative cinema is generally thought to have little or no commercial appeal. *Koyaanisqatsi* may therefore owe some of its box-office success to the filmmaker Francis Ford Coppola, who, after viewing the film, expressed his great admiration and offered to have his name listed in the credits as "presenter." The eighty-seven-minute film, which had taken seven years to produce, premiered at a special event at the 1982 New York Film Festival that was held at Radio City Music Hall. Following its screening at the festival, *Koyaanisqatsi* went on to become one of the few nonnarrative films ever to break into the mainstream movie market. Besides enjoying long runs in major American cities, it has been distributed in more than fifty foreign countries, and it was among the most frequently shown films on college campuses during the 1980s.

Koyaanisqatsi was also a hit with many film critics. While a handful of reviewers found the film preachy and naïve, most were intrigued by the film, and some even found it to be brilliant. One of its admirers was Alan Brien, who wrote in *New Statesman & Society* (September 2, 1983), "*Koyaanisqatsi* transmutes the realities of modern America into a succession of wonderful weird metaphors that positively invite anyone with a typewriter to match them with words." What particularly impressed some critics was the way in which Reggio manipulated his images. "Aerial photography makes fields of tulips seem like rows of bright knitting; the spines of mountains look like the gills of a fish, and vast whorls of sand in the desert resemble a finger print," Cressida Connolly observed. "Illuminated skyscrapers seem to be tiny microchips; endless rows of cars or tanks look like sweets and cockroaches, while a huge nuclear bomb is as shiny-brown and inviting as a little chocolate Easter egg." Reggio purposely accelerated the urban shots by employing time-lapse photography, an effect that gives the film a surreal air.

The techniques used in *Koyaanisqatsi* apparently made an impression on other filmmakers, for since the film's release many movies, music videos, and commercials have employed time-lapse photography in ways that bring to mind Reggio's work. Accelerated images of moving cars at night, which appear as streaks of light and which Reggio used in his film, for instance, have become commonplace. Even Francis Ford Coppola's *Rumble Fish*, which he shot just two months after seeing *Koyaanisqatsi*, appears to have been influenced by Reggio's scenes of swirling, rolling clouds.

Thanks to *Koyaanisqatsi*'s success, Reggio encountered considerably less reluctance among prospective investors when he set out to raise funds for his next project. He obtained more than half of the $4.2 million budget from Cannon Releasing Corporation and the remainder from the person who had been the majority participant in *Koyaanisqatsi*. And in addition to retaining the active support of Francis Ford Coppola, Reggio won another admirer in the director George Lucas, who shared the presentation credits of Reggio's second film, *Powaqqatsi*, with Coppola.

Like its predecessor, *Powaqqatsi* lacks dialogue and a conventional plot, is accompanied by a musical score composed by Philip Glass, and explores the impact of technological progress on society, though in the second film Reggio shifts his focus from the industrialized countries of the northern hemisphere to the developing world. During his interview with MacDonald, Reggio explained why he chose the Hopi word "powaqqatsi" to convey the impact that progress was having on traditional cultures: "The method of operation of a *powaqqa*, a black magician, is seduction and allurement. It's not an out-front aggression; it's subtle. I feel that's the way modernity operates: it doesn't say, 'This is going to be bad for you'; it creates desires that become 'necessities.'"

After developing the script, Reggio and his staff spent five months searching for locations, traveling to twenty countries in all. Then, working with two crews in twelve countries, including India, Egypt, and Brazil, he began what turned out to be a six-month shoot. In keeping with his conviction that people living in traditional societies are wrongfully being compelled to abandon their more slowly paced way of life by the encroaching industrialized world, Reggio decided to film the action in slow motion, to reveal the dignity of living life according to age-old customs. Individuals living in traditional societies "are what people in the Northern countries inaccurately refer to, out of cultural prejudice, as underdeveloped and lazy," he explained to Bob Strauss. "In fact, they're just moving more slowly with the rhythms of the natural order of life, rather than the synthetic order that *Koyaanisqatsi* tried to show."

Despite the similarities between the two films, *Powaqqatsi* was much less warmly received than its predecessor had been. Indeed, many American reviewers found it to be either boring (one likened viewing it to "being forced at gunpoint to flip through hundreds and hundreds of back issues of *National Geographic*") or offensive, because of what they took to be its implicit condemnation of Western culture. When he attended a screening at the Berlin Film Festival, Reggio was spat upon by people who felt he had "aestheticized poverty," as he put it. In the United States the film did not have an opportunity to develop an audience by word of mouth, as *Koyaanisqatsi* had, because soon after its release the distributor went bankrupt, abruptly ending its commercial run.

During his interview with Scott MacDonald, Reggio tried to account for the strong emotions generated by *Powaqqatsi*: "Some people felt, who am I to deny the opportunity of the Third World to make their lot better through industrialization. . . . But I feel there's a *fundamental* confusion between poverty and the norms of simple living. . . . Witness the collapse of repressive ideology in the East, and everyone opting for a market economy as the way to bring about some kind of sanity. Yet, the market economy only further removes them from sanity and leads toward bigger problems down the line. This is not a popular position to take, especially right now. East Berlin has this sinister, bureaucratic Stalinist architecture; you can feel the ghost of the Nazis. But the Disneyland of West Berlin is no answer: people are addicted to the materialization of all values through the market economy. We've created a need that we've become addicted to. My persuasions are also of the Left, but of a Left deeper than the ideological Left or the bureaucratized or the movement Left. Mine is more of an anarchist's Left." Reggio added that *Powaqqatsi* had been well received in the Third World, saying, "About 30 percent of the image is from India, and people from India felt that they were able to re-see the world they live in through someone else's eyes. I felt gratified by that." *Powaqqatsi* won the best film award at the São Paolo Film Festival, in Brazil.

Since completing *Powaqqatsi*, Reggio has been trying to drum up investor interest in *Naqoyqatsi*, which will be the final part of his "*qatsi*" trilogy. The subject of *Naqoyqatsi*, which he defines as "war as a way of life," will not be a military war but, as he explained to MacDonald, "the sanctioned aggression against the force of life, how we confuse human freedom with our pursuit of technological 'happiness' or material affluence."

In 1991 Reggio took a break from *Naqoyqatsi* to produce *Anima Mundi*, a film commissioned by Bulgari, the Italian jewelry company, for the World Wide Fund for Nature. The fund then used the film (according to a previously arranged agreement) as a promotional aid for its Biological Diversity Program, which was launched in the same year. Coincidentally, Reggio had thought of doing such a film before he was approached by Bulgari and the fund. "I wanted very much to get away from the idea that we sit on top of the pyramid as it were, we're the zenith of creation and the rest is inferior or below us," he said of his aims in making *Anima Mundi* during an interview with Alex Demyanenko for a 1992 issue of *Location Update*. "I felt that in putting a human presence in no more a quantitative presence than, say, the ostrich, kind of shows that we're part of a universe of creation that has a unity or a role that each must play in order to have it function in some sort of harmonious way."

Accompanied by the music of Philip Glass, the twenty-eight-minute *Anima Mundi* is a montage of intimate images of over seventy animal species, from a lemur to an aardvark to a grasshopper to a human embryo, that celebrates the magnificence and variety of the world's fauna. "Quiveringly alive and shown magnified in close-up," Stephen Holden wrote in his *New York Times* (May 7, 1993) review of the film, "the proud procession of life forms has an incandescence and mystery that neither still photographs nor museum exhibitions can begin to capture." The film was screened to great acclaim at the Venice, Telluride, São Paolo, and Oslo film festivals, and it subsequently enjoyed a limited commercial release.

After completing *Anima Mundi*, Reggio was asked by the sportswear executive Luciano Benetton and the photographer Oliviero Toscani to direct a new school of exploration and production in the arts, technology, and mass media. Called Fabrica Futuro Presente, it was scheduled to open in May 1995 in Treviso, Italy, just outside Venice. According to Reggio, the school's mission will be to bear witness to this world as it is transformed by technology. Thus, while the students' projects will be aimed at mass audiences and will be distributed world-wide, they will also explore with a critical eye the value of mass culture itself. "No one has clean hands by virtue of living in this world," Reggio told Virginio Briatore in an interview for *MODO* magazine. "We're all addicted to the current order of technological supremacy. We're trying to take that very addiction and make it the basis of the curriculum for Fabrica." In addition to directing the school, Reggio will continue his work on *Naqoyqatsi* at one of its studios.

Despite his slender frame, Godfrey Reggio, who stands six feet, six inches tall, has a commanding presence. "He comes across as a crusading prophet," Michael London wrote in the *Los Angeles Times* (June 18, 1983). "But his fanatical commitment to his work is tempered by an outsider's sense of humility, and of humor." Besides making films, Reggio frequently lectures on film, technology, and philosophy. He lives in Treviso, Italy.

Selected Biographical References: Chicago Sun-Times p11 My 8 '88 por; Film Q 42:2+ Spring '89; GQ 58:83+ My '88; Los Angeles Times V p5+ Je 18 '83 por; Toronto Globe and Mail p11 Ja 20 '84 por; MacDonald, Scott. A Critical Cinema 2 (1992)

Kate Kunz

Rose, Charlie

Jan. 5, 1942- Television talk-show host; broadcast journalist. Address: c/o Rose Communications, Inc., 499 Park Ave., New York, NY 10022

"I believe that there is a place in the spectrum of television for really good conversation, if it is informed, spirited, soulful," the television journalist and talk-show host Charlie Rose has said. "If it has passion, engagement, humor, surprise, spontaneity—if it has all that, there's a place for it. That has been my guiding vision." The widespread praise that he has received for his television interviews indicates that Rose has earned a niche for himself in that place. As the uncommonly knowledgeable, intensely interested, enthusiastic, effusive, and earnest host of the PBS show that bears his name, he has provided viewers with what the television critic Marvin Kitman has labeled "talk, as it was meant to be" and has created what the broadcast journalist Morley Safer has called "the last refuge of intelligent conversation on television." "He has tremendous intellectual vigor," former secretary of state George P. Shultz told James Barron for the *New York Times* (June 13, 1993). Writing in the *New Yorker* (June 14, 1993), the media critic James Wolcott declared that "compared with nearly everyone else on the dial, Rose has substance, standards, decorum." "You *always* come away from a Rose interview with the sense that you've learned something and were entertained in the process," Pete Schulberg wrote in the *Oregonian* (December 5, 1994). The hour-long *Charlie Rose*, which debuted in 1991 and went into national syndication in 1993, is broadcast five nights a week. Its guests have included heads of state and others who have won renown in the fields of politics, literature, the visual and performing arts, science, or sports, as well as lesser-known figures, each of whom, in Rose's opinion, has "a great story to tell." In addition to hosting the show, Rose has served as its executive editor and, for most of its existence, as its executive producer.

The Emmy Award-winning Charlie Rose entered television journalism full-time in 1974, when he became the managing editor of the PBS series *Bill Moyers' International Report.* He later worked with Moyers on two other series: *Bill Moyers' Journal* and *U.S.A.: People and Politics.* From 1984 to 1990 he anchored *Nightwatch*, the CBS television network's late-night interview series, and won for himself what some observers have described as a cult following for the in-depth conversations that have since earned him a reputation as "the best interviewer around today," in the words of Marvin Kitman. "[*Charlie Rose*] is the purest extension of my skills as an interviewer," Rose told Joyce Saenz Harris, who interviewed him for the *Dallas Morning News* (May 2, 1993). "Whatever craft there is, that's what it's about: stripping away all the barriers to good conversation. I'm looking for people to be at their best, their most real. If I can do that, it makes for telling television."

The only child of Charles Peete Rose Sr. and Margaret Rose, Charlie Rose was born Charles Peete Rose Jr. on January 5, 1942 in Henderson, North Carolina. He has been known as Charlie since his mid-teens. In choosing the name of his show, he recalled during an interview with James Brady for *Parade* (March 21, 1993), he decided against his given name because he thought it sounded "just too stiff and formal." Rose has characterized his mother as "a very strong person" who had a "tremendous influence" on him. In his conversation with Joyce Saenz Harris, he said that his father had uncommon intelligence and a prodigious memory and that he was, as Harris paraphrased his words, a "wise and wonderful storyteller."

The Rose family lived near the railroad tracks in Henderson, in rooms above the general store that Charles Rose Sr. owned and managed and where, starting at the age of seven, Charlie Rose helped out. At night, in the room that he shared with his maternal grandmother, he would read in bed by flashlight, his thoughts periodically transported elsewhere by the whistles of passing trains. Filled with curiosity about the world and always eager for knowledge, he enjoyed informational radio and television programs. As he grew older, he looked forward to reading *Time* each week, because, in his words, "it told you what was going on." Upon winning a contest sponsored by an area businessman, the teenage Rose was awarded a one-time chance to serve as a disc jockey on the local radio station. "I wanted just to be on the radio," he disclosed to Elise O'Shaughnessy, who profiled him in *Vanity Fair* (September 1993). "It sounded like a wonderful thing to me . . . to talk on the radio." "I didn't think of it as a career," he added, "because I didn't *know* any broadcasters." In the Raleigh, North Carolina *News & Observer* (October 19, 1993), Mary E. Miller reported that Rose knew from an early age that "he would be famous." "I have never in my life said, 'I can't do that,'" he has said. "Not about anything."

After graduating from high school, where he starred on the basketball team, Rose entered Duke University, in Durham, North Carolina, as a premed student. His extracurricular activities included working with children in a Head Start program. One summer, with the help of a family friend, he secured an internship in the office of North Carolina senator B. Everett Jordan. By his own account, his experiences as an intern turned him into a "political junkie," and upon returning to college, he changed his area of concentration to history. After receiving an A.B. degree, in 1964, he entered the Duke University School of Law, but sometime before or shortly after earning a J.D. degree, in 1968, he realized that the practice of law held little interest for him. As he explained to Scott Widener for the *Chicago Tribune* (January 7, 1993), "I was in some firm watching a lawyer advise a client one day, and it dawned on me that I was much more interested in the client than the lawyer. The client was the one trying to build something." Inspired by the idea of "building something" as an entrepreneur, he started taking classes at the New York University Graduate School of Business (he had moved to New York City in 1968) and accepted a job at Bankers Trust. But business, too, failed to engage his imagination fully. As he commented to Joyce Saenz Harris, "To know me is to know that [the business world] was not the right place for me."

Through his wife, who was doing research for the CBS television show *60 Minutes*, Rose became friendly with people employed in broadcasting, and he developed what soon became a passionate interest in the broadcast media. After his wife was hired by the BBC (in the United States), he handled some assignments for the British broadcasting service on a freelance basis. In 1972, while continuing to work at Bankers Trust, he landed a job as a weekend reporter for WPIX-TV, in New York City. But he found that occupation less than satisfying, primarily because it required him to limit his airtime reports or interviews to no more than a few minutes.

During his approximately one-year stint at WPIX, Rose tried several times without success to contact Bill Moyers for an interview. Then, in 1974, Moyers telephoned Rose, after Rose's wife spoke to Moyers about him at a social gathering. At their first meeting, Rose told Joyce Saenz Harris, he and Moyers felt an "instant chemistry," and within weeks he began working as the managing editor of the PBS series *Bill Moyers' International Report*. (Moyers has said that Rose served as his "alter ego" as well at that time.) In 1975 Moyers named him the executive producer of *Bill Moyers' Journal*, a PBS documentary and conversation series. Although, by his own account, Rose had "no great desire to be on camera," in the following year he became the correspondent for *U.S.A.: People and Politics*, Moyers's new weekly PBS political magazine series. "A Conversation with Jimmy Carter," one installment of that series, won a 1976 Peabody Award.

Later in 1976, after Moyers left public television to work for CBS, Rose accepted a Washington, D.C.-based job as a political correspondent for NBC News. In the belief that he lacked sufficient training to do a proper job and that he should "get the maximum amount of on-air experience," as he put it, he seized opportunities to host interview shows. He first appeared as a guest host on *Panorama*, on WTTG-TV, in Washington, D.C. In 1978, after leaving NBC, he served as a cohost on *AM/Chicago*, on WLS-TV. A year later Blake Byrne, the general manager of KXAS-TV, in Dallas-Fort Worth, hired him as program manager, and although, as Byrne has recalled, he "had no budget to pay [Rose] to do a talk show," he also offered him a time slot for what became *The Charlie Rose Show*. In carrying out his duties as program manager, Rose would sometimes work until 3:00 A.M., and he would be back at the studio to host his show by 9:00 A.M. "I don't know many people who could have done both jobs," Byrne told Joyce Saenz Harris. "But the guy's indefatigable." A daily, half-hour "Phil Donahue-style show," in the words of Jeanie Kasindorf, who profiled Rose for *New York* (June 22, 1992), *The Charlie Rose Show* featured prominent public figures, who submitted to questioning before a live audience. "It was where I sort of came of age as a broadcaster," Rose has said of his first eponymous show. "Because all the responsibility was on me. I was working alone; I wasn't cohosting. I produced the show, found the guests, researched the show. It was an extraordinary time for me." In 1981, with the goal (which he achieved) of securing national syndication, Rose moved *The Charlie Rose Show* to Washington, D.C., where, for the next two years or so, it was broadcast on the NBC-owned station WRC-TV. Concurrently, he hosted another, weekly interview show for WRC-TV.

At the end of 1983, Van Gordon Sauter, the president of CBS's news division, hired Rose to anchor *Nightwatch*, an interview program that was taped during the day and was broadcast five times a week between 2:00 A.M. and 6:00 A.M. Writing in the *New Yorker* (June 14, 1993), James Wolcott described *Nightwatch* as "a lonely orbit through the dark hours which won [Rose] a loyal core of news junkies and personal fans but scant prestige in the journalism biz. (It didn't help that CBS seemed to budget the show from loose change dug out of coin returns.)" The devotees of *Nightwatch* included the constitutional scholar Leonard W. Levy. "The only television I watch is Charlie Rose," Levy told Bill Moyers, as reported by Elise O'Shaughnessy. "He brings the world to me so enthusiastically that I can't help but listen."

Rose has recalled having "a wonderful time" during his six and a half years as the *Nightwatch* host. He told one reporter, "I would not be [in my current position] today without *Nightwatch*. [*Charlie Rose*] is a direct descendant of *Nightwatch*, because it's the same kind of guest list." Like that of *Charlie Rose*, the *Nightwatch* guest list was not confined to the world's movers and shakers. Among the other people whose activities or histories caught Rose's interest was the convicted murderer Charles Manson, with whom he talked for three hours. "At the beginning, Manson was really crazy . . . ," Jessica Matthews, a friend of Rose's, told Elise O'Shaughnessy. "But Charlie found a level on which to engage Manson and then finally brought him down to a more sane plane." The *Nightwatch* broadcast of Rose's interview with Manson won an Emmy Award in 1987.

In 1990 Rose left CBS to become the anchor of *Personalities*, a syndicated program produced by Twentieth-Century Fox Television. Chagrined to find himself associated with what proved to be a tabloid-type news show, he asked to be released from his contract after just six weeks (and, in doing so, turned his back on a salary said to have been set at more than one million dollars). "I felt my credibility, which I'd worked hard for, leaving me drip by drip and splashing on the floor," he explained to Lucy Kaylin for a *GQ* (December 1992) profile. He then retreated to the five-hundred-acre farm he had acquired in North Carolina the year before. About ten months later, acting on a friend's suggestion, he approached Bill Baker, the president and chief executive officer of the PBS-affiliated station Thirteen/WNET-TV, in New York City, with a proposal for a new interview show. "My vision was that talking heads done well can be engaging television and can attract an audience," he recalled to Scott Widener. "Bill Baker . . . saw merit in that vision, and I was on the air within a month after pitching the idea."

Charlie Rose premiered on Thirteen/WNET on September 30, 1991. During nine months in 1992, it also aired (a day later) on the Learning Channel, with ten minutes edited out to allow time for commercials. Syndicated nationally since January 1993, it currently airs on 215 PBS affiliate stations, and it is watched by an estimated 550,000–725,000 viewers (according to the Nielsen ratings, four-tenths of one percent of the 95.4 million American households that have televisions). The show is owned by Rose Communications, a corporation that Rose formed in 1991 with the aim of producing *Charlie Rose* and other programs. In 1994, faced with the probable loss of his studio, which was maintained by the then financially troubled WNET, he moved the show to a studio owned by Bloomberg Television News in a building on New York City's Park Avenue. (He also gained access to the fifty news bureaus maintained by Bloomberg worldwide and to Bloomberg television studios in Washington, Tokyo, and London, and he was able to interview guests via Bloomberg satellites.)

Telecast Monday through Friday from 11:00 P.M. to midnight (the show is picked up by some stations a half-hour later), Rose and his guest (or guests) sit across from one another at a round wooden table. "The key to the show is open space on the table's [near] perimeter," Phil Patton observed in *Esquire* (February 1993), "inviting the viewer to listen in. . . . Afloat in a black background, Charlie's table has become an island where savvy channel surfers put ashore each weeknight." With the exception of a series of introductory filmed images of some of his more easily recognizable past guests (including President Bill Clinton, Vice-President Al Gore, the tennis player Arthur Ashe, and Dan Rather, the veteran broadcast journalist), accompanied by an upbeat musical score, there are neither graphics nor music; nor is there a studio audience, an Ed McMahon-type sidekick, an opening monologue, or a skit.

"Night after night, Charlie Rose takes viewers on a thoughtful journey through politics and culture," an Op-Ed article in the New York *Daily News* (November 19, 1994) declared. Among the many notable guests whom Rose has interviewed are Nelson Mandela, the president of South Africa; Yitzhak Rabin, the prime minister of Israel; Jean-Bertrand Aristide, the president of Haiti; Mary Robinson, the president of Ireland; Boutros Boutros-Ghali, the secretary general of the UN; Congressman Newt Gingrich, the Speaker of the House of Representatives; the writer Maya Angelou; the dancer and choreographer Bill T. Jones; and the filmmakers Francis Ford Coppola and Martin Scorsese.

Unlike those of many other television talk shows, *Charlie Rose* guest lists have never included people selected solely because of their turbulent home lives or other personal problems. In "Rose On Rose: A Conversation with Charlie Rose," an interview for WNET, the talk-show host said that in choosing his partners in conversation, he tries to find people "who have unique experiences and accomplishments . . . who have spent a portion of their life working hard on a particular project . . . [and] who have a passion about their life and work and their ideas." To "tap into that passion," he explained, he first tries to establish rapport: "When [a guest] sit[s] down I make a quick, instinctive judgment about the person to decide how best to grab them and make that immediate connection." He then attempts to "energize the guest through [his] questions and curiosity." Observers have noted that Rose's intensely interested, unwavering gaze and sympathetic expression have served with uncommon effectiveness as triggers for thoughtful, forthright, revealing talk. "I forgot I was on TV," the fashion designer Donna Karan told Joyce

Saenz Harris, in speaking of her experience as a Rose guest. "I think he makes you feel so comfortable that you lose yourself in conversation."

"Watching Charlie's TV show is like being at a dinner party with Charlie as a host," Marvin Kitman wrote in *New York Newsday* (January 4, 1993). "There is all that relaxing, stimulating, nourishing talk, and the occasional madcap thing, like Bill Clinton suddenly breaking into an Elvis [Presley] tune." Commenting in the *New Yorker* (October 3, 1994) on interviews Rose conducted with the documentary filmmaker Ken Burns and with the sportscaster Bob Costas, Jesse Kornbluth wrote that "you felt you were watching smart people actually *think* in front of you." Rose has been cited for an "awed, almost breathless curiosity that might seem callow if not for his exhaustive preparedness," in the words of Lucy Kaylin, for what James Barron described as his "thoughtful, nonconfrontational, even courtly" interviewing style, and for what Walter Goodman, in a *New York Times* (January 13, 1993) article, called his "attitude of profound solicitousness." "Watch *Charlie Rose* on any given night and you're bound to hear the sincere refrain 'That's a good question' from one of his subjects—and that's because his questions invariably *are* good ones," Pete Schulberg wrote.

Some other observers have expressed the view that Rose avoids hard-hitting questions. In an interview with Barbara Kantrowitz for *Newsweek* (January 4, 1993), Rose countered such criticism. "Interviewing is about the craft of trying to have a guest justify an action, reveal themselves," he said. "It's not the posture of the interviewer that makes a difference. It's the intelligence of the question and the thoroughness of the follow-up that makes the difference." Rose is "a courtly North Carolinian," Arden Ostrander, a CBS producer who served briefly as executive producer for *Charlie Rose*, told Joyce Saenz Harris. "There's a certain civility involved in live TV. Charlie calls his interviews 'conversations,' and that implies some equality. . . . People who lacerate guests on live TV generally don't last too long." Neil Postman, the chairman of the Department of Culture and Communications at New York University, pointed out to James Barron that "Rose asks probing questions, but he surrounds the questions with so many prefaces and epilogues that you don't realize they're as good as they are."

Rose has also been criticized for repeatedly interrupting his guests. "I'm more conscious of [interrupting] now than I was in the past," he told Elise O'Shaughnessy. "But I don't think you should ever lose your spontaneity, you should never lose what it is that defines you. . . . Because all of a sudden you'll become homogeneous and bland and without distinction." Bill Moyers has attributed Rose's tendency to interrupt as arising from his "inner energy." "He engages almost physically in the conversation . . . ," Moyers explained to O'Shaughnessy. "In the South, to talk is to be. That's Charlie."

During his association with CBS News, Rose sometimes served as an anchor for such CBS programs as *Face the Nation*, *CBS Morning News*, *CBS This Morning*, and *Newsbreak*, and he occasionally also reported for *48 Hours*. In 1992 he hosted live, on-location broadcasts from the Republican National Convention, in Houston, Texas. He has moderated three national PBS specials: *Salmon Rushdie: A Conversation with Charlie Rose*; *America: The Fires Within*, during which, through a four-city remote hook-up, people talked about events sparked by the acquittal in 1992 of four white Los Angeles police officers accused of beating Rodney King, a black motorist; and *Public Television, Public Debate with Charlie Rose*, a face-to-face exchange between critics and supporters of federal funding of public television. *One on One with Roger Payne*, a Discovery Channel show in which Rose interviewed a leading American cetologist, won an Emmy Award in 1992.

"I'm just your very basic American. I love politics, I love sports. I love movies, I love books," Charlie Rose, a self-described "incurable romantic," told an interviewer. Lean and fit, the six-foot four-inch Rose is said to have "rugged good looks," "a genuinely easygoing, winning manner," "staccato energy," and "a bare wisp of a drawl." James Wolcott quoted a *Newsweek* reporter as writing that Rose "project[s] many of the same qualities" as President Clinton: "a manly sensitivity, an innate curiosity, a desire to please." "He's as kind to a security guard or a street person as he would be to Donna Karan," Arden Ostrander told Joyce Saenz Harris. "His rarely seen temper never lasts long," according to Joyce Saenz Harris, who also noted that when he is not working, Rose "favors rumpled khakis, pullover sweaters, and a well-worn navy blazer."

Charlie Rose's twelve-year marriage to the former Mary King ended in divorce in 1980. His ex-wife remains one of his closest friends, he has said. Rose rents a townhouse in Manhattan that, by his own admission, is filled with an "embarrassing amount" of electronic equipment. On weekends, when not enjoying the cultural life of New York City or preparing for his show, he travels to North Carolina or the upstate New York farm of a friend; during the long drives to his destinations, he listens to books on audiocassettes. Every weekday between 5:00 and 8:00 A.M., he spends what he has called his "favored hours" absorbing material written by or about his upcoming guests. At 10:00 A.M., after working out at a gym for about an hour, he meets with his staff to talk about the news and possible candidates for interviews. He also watches television news programs (he tunes in to CNN periodically throughout the day) and reads five newspapers daily and several books a week. Every afternoon at about 4:30, Rose, who has characterized himself as a "champion napper," naps for forty-five minutes or so.

A self-described workaholic who often devotes sixteen hours a day to his job, Rose "demands nothing of his ten-person staff that he does not demand of himself: only total commitment," Joyce Saenz Harris wrote. "It's hard to beat Charlie into the office," Nick Dolin, a *Charlie Rose* producer, told Peter Stevenson for the *New York Observer* (May 10, 1993). "It's hard to read anything before he's read it, see anything before he's seen it, and hear anything before he's heard it." According to the *Esquire* profile by Phil Patton, Rose's calendar is "so complex he keeps it on a Wizard pocket scheduler." His nightly routine includes, almost invariably, dinner in restaurants with, or at the homes of, prominent New Yorkers, a number of whom have appeared as guests on his show. "This is the most incredible, wonderful job in television," Rose has said. "No one, no one, *no one* has a job I would rather have than the one I do."

Selected Biographical References: Dallas Morning News E p1+ My 2 '93 pors; N Y Times II p30+ Je 13 '93; New York 25:32+ Je 22 '92 pors; Parade p14 Mr 21 '93 por; Vanity Fair 56:172+ S '93 pors; Who's Who in America, 1995

Atlanta Falcons

Sanders, Deion
(DEE-ahn)

Aug. 9, 1967- Baseball player; football player. Address: c/o Parker and Associates, 1080 Standard Federal Plaza, Ft. Wayne, IN 46802

Combining explosive speed, dazzling talent, and a flamboyant personality seemingly tailor-made for the spotlight, Deion Sanders is a force in both the National Football League and major-league baseball. Nicknamed "Prime Time" by a high school friend, for his play on the basketball court no less, he has lived up to the moniker in the NFL, not only as an All-Pro cornerback but also as a spectacular punt and kickoff returner and occasionally as a wide receiver. One of the few defenders who can dominate a game, he is viewed by many observers as the best defensive player in the sport. His development on the baseball diamond has been a little slower, but he has worked to make himself a dangerous leadoff hitter and one of the game's premier base stealers.

Even though he has excelled in both sports, Sanders's apparent inability to set his priorities during the three months when the baseball and football seasons overlap each year has made him the target of criticism, with some observers questioning his worth to any team in a sport not given his full attention. When he began his professional career, Sanders put football first, leaving baseball in early September, but after joining the Atlanta Braves, who were pennant contenders the three seasons he was on the team, he began to play both sports during baseball's division race and playoffs. In shuttling back and forth between the baseball diamond and the football field, Sanders, who had already become the only pro player ever to hit a major-league home run and score an NFL touchdown in the same week, became the first person to suit up for both professional sports in one day. After two chaotic years of trying to play both at the same time, he decided to stay with baseball for the duration of its season before turning to football. Perhaps even more impressive than Sander's playing two sports is his desire to play every down in football games. He has received limited play at wide receiver, but he wants to become as dominating on offense as he is on defense. "I've always been an offensive-type football player, even on defense," Sanders told Kevin Cook of *Playboy* (August 1994). "When I get the ball, people can see the offense in me—I'm taking it to the house, thinking about scoring every time I touch the ball."

Deion Luwynn Sanders was born August 9, 1967 in Fort Myers, Florida. His parents, Connie and Mims Sanders, divorced when Deion was two years old, and he was raised by his mother and her second husband, Willie Knight. "I grew up with my mother and stepfather, but my father was around," Sanders recalled in his interview with Kevin Cook. "We had our misunderstandings—he didn't do all the right things in life. He got caught up in drugs. Then he was finally getting his life together. We were becoming closer when he got sick and died of a brain tumor."

Growing up in a crime-ridden neighborhood, Sanders resisted the temptations to which his father had succumbed. "See, in my hometown, that was the community job," he explained to Curry Kirkpatrick of *Sports Illustrated* (November 13, 1989). "You graduated from high school to the streets and became a drug dealer." From a young age, Sanders excelled in athletics, which allowed him to appear cool in his friends' eyes without taking up dangerous habits to make an impression. "It would've been easy for me to sell drugs," he told Mike Lupica for an article in *Esquire* (June 1992). "But I had [sports] practice. My friends who didn't have practice, they went straight to the streets and never left." To this day, he eschews anything that will affect his athletic performance. "I have never tasted alcohol," he declared to Kevin Cook. "I have never smoked a cigarette. I have never tried drugs." At North Fort Myers High School, Sanders played quarterback and defensive back on the football team, and he was second-team All State in basketball. He was also good enough in baseball to be drafted by the Kansas City Royals, although he never signed a contract with the team. Instead, he accepted a football scholarship to Florida State University, in Tallahassee.

Quickly establishing himself as a key component of a strong Seminole defense, Sanders began what would become regular visits to the end zone when he returned an interception a school-record one hundred yards for a touchdown against the University of Tulsa. Against the rival University of Florida Gators later in the season, the defensive back, who was playing with a broken wrist, became the first Seminole in six years to return a punt for a touchdown. Switching to baseball after the football season ended, he batted .333 and stole eleven bases before an ankle injury limited his play. As a sophomore, he continued his excellent play on the gridiron, racking up four interceptions and eight deflected passes. Named Florida State's most valuable defensive player, he was also a finalist for the Jim Thorpe Award, given annually to the nation's top defensive back. As a baseball player, Sanders hit .221 and stole twenty-eight bases, and the school advanced to the College World Series, where it finished fifth. During his sophomore season, Sanders also began running track, but he competed only in relays. Once, between games of a doubleheader at the Metro Conference baseball tournament, Sanders, wearing his baseball uniform pants, helped Florida State win the 4x100 relay at a track meet. He then returned for the second game of the doubleheader and got the game-winning hit, "establishing himself as one of the most versatile college athletes of this or any other age," as Curry Kirkpatrick wrote.

Sanders entered his junior season at Florida State as a member of *Playboy* magazine's preseason All-America team and ended it as a consensus All American. In addition to setting a school punt-return record with 381 yards for the year, he intercepted four passes and shut down some of college football's top receivers. He was third in the Thorpe voting, and Florida State, whose only loss of the year was a one-point defeat early in the season at the hands of the eventual national champion, the University of Miami, finished the season with a Fiesta Bowl victory over Nebraska and a number-two ranking. Having decided against playing baseball that spring, Sanders had more time for track and began entering one-hundred- and two-hundred-meter events for the first time. Despite his inexperience, he captured the one-hundred- and two-hundred-meter Metro Conference titles in addition to running on the school's conference-best relay team. His times qualified him for the 1988 United States Olympic trials. "I don't believe in my experience in track and field, which spans twenty-three years, that I have ever been associated with, or witnessed, anyone that performed so well, so quickly," Florida State track coach Dick Roberts told Tom McEwen of the *Tampa Tribune* (May 29, 1988). "He was instantly good."

Although Sanders had skipped his junior baseball season, he was drafted by the New York Yankees in the thirtieth round of the June 1988 free-agent draft, and he spent the summer in the club's farm system. In twenty-eight games divided among three of the Yankees' minor-league teams (Sarasota, Fort Lauderdale, and Columbus), he batted .280 with fourteen stolen bases. Returning to Florida State for his senior year, he proceeded to improve his already outstanding football statistics. He broke his own school mark with 503 yards in punt returns, and his 15.2 yards-per-return average was the best in the nation. He also carried two of his five interceptions in for scores, topping off the season with a game-clinching pickoff in a 13–7 Sugar Bowl win over Auburn. The Seminoles, who were perfect after a season-opening defeat at the hands of Miami, finished the year ranked number three in the polls, and Sanders finally won the Jim Thorpe Award.

As a collegian, Sanders spent four years cultivating the "Prime Time" image, that of the flashy, super-skilled athlete loaded down with gold chains. (He was also dubbed "Neon Deion" while at Florida State, but he disdains that nickname.) Following his selection by the Atlanta Falcons as the fifth overall pick in the 1989 NFL draft, a swaggering, leather-and-gold-clad Sanders announced that he could also play in the NBA if he so desired and promised that his presence would bring new fans to fill the often empty seats of Atlanta-Fulton County Stadium, the Falcons' home field. Sanders's attention-getting paraphernalia and relentless boasting were not simply the result of an overactive ego but part of a carefully thought-out marketing strategy by a media-savvy young man, who knew that press coverage would bring endorsements. "I'm a businessman, and my product is Deion Sanders," he explained to Andy Friedlander of the *Sporting News* (June 12, 1989). "Prime Time is the way I market that product. I will do anything to promote that." His brash proclamations were proven to be more than hyperbole, for the Falcons saw a dramatic increase in attendance after he joined the team.

Belying his brash persona, one of Sanders's first big purchases was a new house for his mother. "I created the whole Prime Time image so I could get a big contract and build my mother her dream home," he told Kent Hannon for *Sports Illustrated for Kids* (August 1994). Indeed, many of those close to Sanders describe two contrasting personas, one the public Prime Time, the other the private Deion. "If he's around a crowd of writers, he'll show off," Florida State football coach Bobby Bowden said in an interview with Dave Scheiber of *Sports Illustrated* (July 3, 1989). "But by himself, he's very low-key and likable, and a very kind person." "It's like Michael Jackson," Sanders told Scheiber. "You think he wears that glove all the time? He puts it on for show, then takes it off. That's how I am."

Before joining the Falcons, Sanders spent the spring and summer of 1989 on the baseball diamond. He played thirty-three games of Double-A ball in Albany, New York before being called up to the Yankees on May 31, 1989. He got his first major-league hit and threw out a runner at third in his first game. Just four days later he hit his first home run. "[Playing in Yankee Stadium] was a dream come true," Sanders told Gary Pomerantz of *Inside Sports* (September 1991). "Everyone wants to experience the Yankees, but I think it's hard for a young player to experience the Yankees when they are losing. Every time you do something you are gonna get criticized for it."

On September 5, 1989 Sanders hit a homer for the Yankees in a game in Seattle. The next day, he signed a four-year, $4.4 million contract with the Falcons. In his first NFL appearance, on the following Sunday, September 10, he ran back a punt sixty-eight yards for a touchdown, to become the first person to hit a major-league home run and score an NFL touchdown in the same week. Sanders's batting average in his first year with the Yankees was .234. He was more impressive on the football field, finishing the season with five interceptions and averages of 11.0 yards per punt return and 20.7 yards per kickoff return. "In twenty-seven years in this league," Atlanta coach Marion Campbell told Curry Kirkpatrick, "I've never experienced the buzz that goes through a stadium when this guy gets near the football."

Sanders opened the 1990 baseball season with the Yankees, but after going zero-for-seven over eight games, he was shipped back to Columbus, the Yankees' Triple-A farm team. It was the first of several such trips he would make that year. When he left the Yankees to rejoin the Falcons, on July 30, Sanders was batting only .156 in fifty-seven major-league games. After a contract dispute with New York, he was given his unconditional release. His second season as a Falcon saw him gain a career-best 153 yards on three interceptions, two of which went for touchdowns. He also scored on another long punt return.

In January 1991 Sanders signed with the Atlanta Braves. He was the starting left fielder on opening day and stayed with the club until May, when he was sent to its Triple-A Richmond farm club. He was recalled in late June and spent a month with the Braves before leaving to play football. By late September, however, the Braves, whose top base-stealer, Otis Nixon, had been suspended, were in the thick of a pennant race and in desperate need of another fleet-footed base runner for the closing weeks of the season. Sanders persuaded the Falcons to release him from some practices so he could help the Braves chase the division title. "If Deion can help win just one game, either with his legs or his glove, then his salary would be a darned small price to pay," Braves manager Bobby Cox told Dave Nightingale of the *Sporting News* (October 7, 1991).

On September 25 Sanders, who had been named NFL player of the week for his outstanding performance against the Minnesota Vikings on the previous Sunday, began his double duty, as he practiced with the Falcons, then flew by helicopter to join the Braves. Serving as a pinch runner in both games of that day's doubleheader, Sanders stole a base. After spending the week with the Braves, he returned to football for the weekend, making two tackles, deflecting a pass, returning seven kicks, and playing three downs at wide receiver. The Falcons had a bye the next week, allowing Sanders to finish the regular season with the Braves. With Sanders's help the Braves overtook the Los Angeles Dodgers to capture the National League western division title. Although Sanders was not on their postseason roster, Atlanta advanced to the World Series, which they lost to the Minnesota Twins. Sanders ended the season with a .191 average and eleven stolen bases in fifty-four games with the Braves. Moonlighting as a baseball player apparently had no effect on his play for the Falcons, for he racked up six interceptions, including one for a score, and added his first kickoff-return touchdown for good measure. His All-Pro performance helped carry the Falcons to the playoffs for the first time since 1982.

Showing dramatic improvement in the 1992 baseball season, Sanders began the year with a fourteen-game hitting streak. In the ninety-seven games in which he appeared, he batted .304, stole twenty-six bases, and led the league in triples with fourteen, becoming the first player to top that category while playing fewer than one hundred games (except in strike-shortened seasons). Sanders's better numbers were the result of his increased dedication to the game. "Before, he would just grab his bat and helmet and go up there and hit," Clarence Jones, the Braves' hitting instructor, told Ed Hinton of *Sports Illustrated* (April 27, 1992). "Now he prepares himself before every game; who's pitching, what they're throwing, where they're throwing it, and how they're trying to get him out. Now he's using his head along with his ability."

Sanders's newfound hitting prowess was made doubly lethal by his tremendous speed on the base paths. Because of his base-stealing ability, a single by him was virtually the equivalent of a double. "He's one of a handful you can name that you definitely don't want to get on first base," a teammate, John Smoltz, said, in describing Sanders's prowess as a base stealer to Robert Markus of the *Chicago Tribune* (July 12, 1992). By this time the Braves were beginning to think of him as an integral part of their team, just as the Falcons did. "When he left last year, we missed him dearly, and part of the club went with him," fellow Brave Lonnie Smith told Markus. "Everyone here understands there are things he wants to do in his life outside of baseball, but he's a big key link to this club."

Sanders left the Braves early in September 1992 to return to the gridiron, but when the ball club made the National League playoffs, Sanders again pulled double duty. On Saturday, October 10, he played three innings against the Pirates in game four of the league championship series, then flew to Miami for the Falcons' Sunday meeting with the Dolphins. Returning to Pittsburgh immediately after the football game, he was back in his Braves uniform for game five of the championship series. Although he did not play for the Braves that night, he was nonetheless the first person ever to suit up for two different professional sporting events on the same day.

One of the low points of Sanders's career came following game seven of the National League Championship series, which Atlanta won to advance to the World Series. Upset after CBS sportscaster Tim McCarver declared that it was "flat-out wrong" for Sanders to divide his energies between two sports on the same day, especially since he had promised to be with the Braves full-time during the playoffs, Sanders dumped three buckets of ice water on the reporter during the Braves' postgame locker-room celebration. The incident generated considerable negative publicity for Sanders, but he refused to let the bad press affect his play in the World Series. Not only did he bat a stellar .533 in four games, but both he and his teammate Otis Nixon broke the all-time World Series mark for stolen bases in a six-game series, with five each. Their efforts were in a losing cause, however, as Atlanta fell to Toronto in six games. Following the World Series, Sanders returned to the Falcons for the remainder of the NFL season, during which he had three interceptions, returned two kickoffs for touchdowns, and made his first offensive score, on a thirty-seven-yard reception in a game against the Tampa Bay Buccaneers in December. Although the Falcons, with a 6–10 record, did not fulfill the promise of the previous season, Sanders was named second-team All Pro, and he played in the Pro Bowl.

Increasingly rancorous negotiations between Sanders and the Braves management marred the early weeks of the 1993 baseball season. Disappointed by his lack of playing time, which he felt was punishment for his not having signed a long-term contract, in late April, after his father's funeral, Sanders said that he would not return to the club, prompting the team to place him on the disqualified list, which meant he could not play for the Braves or for any other team until his name was removed from the list. He eventually signed a three-year, $10.75 million contract that committed him to play the entire baseball season and was taken off the disqualified list on May 21. Over the course of the season, Sanders played in ninety-five games, hitting .276, with six homers, twenty-eight RBIs, and nineteen stolen bases. In the late summer he had a team-best thirteen-game hitting streak, and he finished the season with a league-leading .429 average as a pinch hitter, going twelve for twenty-eight. In Atlanta's playoff series with the Philadelphia Phillies, which Philadelphia won in six games, he was hitless in his only three at-bats.

When Sanders joined the Atlanta Falcons for the sixth game of the 1993 football season, the team had yet to win a single game. With his return the Falcons were a changed club, winning five of the next six games, but it was not enough to overcome the slow start, and Atlanta was once again shut out of the playoffs. Sanders, who finished the season with seven interceptions and six receptions (one for a touchdown), joined the San Francisco 49ers wide receiver Jerry Rice as the only unanimous selections for the Pro Bowl that year, and he was again named to the All-Pro squad.

Following the departure of Otis Nixon prior to the 1994 baseball season, it appeared that Sanders would be the Braves' full-time center fielder for some time. Batting .288 with twenty-one RBIs, he was on his way to a fine year when, in late May, he was traded to the Cincinnati Reds for outfielder Roberto Kelly and minor-league pitcher Roger Etheridge. There were reports that the trade was made because Sanders was a disruptive presence in the clubhouse, but in speaking with Claire Smith of the *New York Times* (May 30, 1994), John Schuerholz, the Braves' general manager, cited a purely strategic reason for trading the left-hander: "We felt like we needed another right-handed hitter to balance our lineup." "I was surprised to be traded, but now I'm looking forward to the change," Sanders told Kevin Cook for the *Playboy* profile. "Actually, this is the best thing that could have happened. Everything has gotten comfortable for me. Now there's extra motivation. I'm going to go even harder to show everyone what I can do."

With the 1994 baseball season cut short in August by a players' strike, Sanders, who was a free agent in football, began to shop his talent around the NFL. Professing a desire to play for a contending team, he publicly stated that money was not his major concern. True to his word, he rejected lucrative offers from the New Orleans Saints, the Miami Dolphins, and the Falcons, who wanted to keep their popular star. After the second week of the season, he finally signed with the San Francisco 49ers, who were a preseason favorite to win a championship, for substantially less money than the other clubs had offered. Sanders's one-year, $1.1 million deal forced the 49ers to restructure the contracts of three other players to make room for him under the newly imposed salary cap. Sanders explained his decision to join the 49ers to Jarrett Bell of *USA Today* (September 16, 1994): "Winning was a factor, and I know we're going to win in San Francisco. They've won four Super Bowls. I'm here to make it five." True to his word, Sanders proved invaluable to the 49ers as they defeated the two-time defending champion Dallas Cowboys in the conference finals on their way to a record-setting fifth Super Bowl victory, over the San Diego Chargers. Despite his not having joined the team until the fourth game of the season, Sanders was chosen by Associated Press as the defensive player of the year.

When the major league baseball strike finally ended, in April 1995, Sanders returned to the Cincinnati Reds, only to be traded in July by the first-place Reds, who needed pitchers, to the struggling San Francisco Giants, who needed a box-office attraction. Sanders did not report immediately to the Giants, hinting that he might give up baseball, but after a couple of days of contemplation he reported to the team. In the waning days of the baseball season, while he was still playing for the Giants, Sanders was once again making headlines, for the bidding war over his gridiron services. Outbidding San Francisco and Denver, the Dallas Cowboys took a bold step toward regaining the Super Bowl title by signing him to a deal worth a reported thirty-five million dollars over seven years.

Deion Sanders, who stands six feet one inch tall and weighs 195 pounds, and his wife, Carolyn Chambers, have two children, Deiondra and Deion Jr. "I love fatherhood. It's changed me a lot . . . ," Sanders told Gary Pomerantz for *Inside Sports* after the birth of Deiondra. "Now, I have to do some things different in my life because that's the way I want my daughter to see me. . . . I don't want my daughter to see this guy who people think is so arrogant." Sanders lives with his family in Alpharetta, Georgia. In his few hours away from his life as a star athlete, he is an avid fisherman. He has also released a rap music album entitled *Prime Time*. As befitting his personal stance, Sanders works with antidrug programs and gives speeches to young people about the dangers of drugs and alcohol.

Selected Biographical References: Inside Sports 13:18+ S '91 pors; Playboy 41:51+ Ag '94 pors; Sporting N p47 Je 12 '89 por; Sports Illus 71:30+ Jl 3 '89 pors, 71:52+ N 13 '89 pors, 76:38+ Ap 27 '92 pors; Who's Who in America, 1995

Office of the Mayor

Schmoke, Kurt L.

(shmohk)

Dec. 1, 1949- Mayor of Baltimore. Address: Mayor of the City of Baltimore, 250 City Hall, 100 N. Holiday St., Baltimore, MD 21220

Throughout his two terms as mayor of Baltimore, Kurt L. Schmoke, who in 1987 became the first black elected to that office, has made improving the city's educational system, increasing the availability of affordable housing, and reducing its high rates of poverty, drug-related crime, and unemployment the key aims of his administration. He has thus distinguished himself from his predecessor, William Donald Schaefer, who centered his efforts on turning downtown Baltimore into a waterfront tourist attraction and bustling business district and who paid less attention to the city's underlying social and economic ills. While Baltimore continues to be plagued by a host of problems—for instance, a record-high 354 murders were committed in the city in 1993 and the illiteracy and teen-pregnancy rates remain among the highest in the country—Schmoke has won widespread respect for his commitment to improving the quality of life of city residents in troubled times. "Schaefer cleaned up the city and made us feel proud of our surroundings," Rick Sullivan, a former city policeman, was quoted as saying in *Business Week* (March 12, 1990). "Now, Schmoke is trying to make people feel proud of themselves."

Kurt L. Schmoke was born on December 1, 1949 in Baltimore, Maryland, the only child of Murray Schmoke, a civilian chemist at the United States Army's Edgewood Arsenal, and Irene Schmoke, a clerk-typist at the Social Security Administration. Both his parents (who divorced when their son was twelve) were college graduates, and they expected their son to go to college as well, preferably an all-black college like Morehouse University, his father's alma mater. Schmoke was a good, if unexceptional, student, and his most obvious talents lay in sports. While attending Baltimore City College, a public high school, he was a star quarterback.

Robert Hammerman, a white Baltimore judge who became Schmoke's mentor, saw in his young protégé yet another gift. "I felt immediately upon meeting him that here is a boy of tremendous leadership potential," Hammerman told Timothy Noah, who profiled Schmoke for the *Washington Post Magazine* (May 27, 1990). Schmoke may also have foreseen that his destiny did not lie in leading his team to victory on the football field, for at about the age of fourteen he vowed to become mayor of Baltimore. During his senior year in high school, Schmoke, at Hammerman's urging, entered the race to become school president. He won, and thus became the first black president of the predominantly white school. His status as school president, varsity quarterback, and the player principally responsible for leading the football team to victory in the state championship made Schmoke a minor celebrity in Baltimore.

Notwithstanding the attention he enjoyed as a result of his achievements at school, and the advances made for blacks by the civil rights movement (Baltimore's public schools were integrated not long before he entered City College), Schmoke also experienced first-hand the indignities of racism. He has recalled that his mother was not welcome to shop at some stores in Baltimore and that, at the age of thirteen, when he took a drive to South Carolina with his father, the two had considerable difficulty in finding a place to eat or a bathroom to use; his father ended up ordering dinner at the kitchen door at the back of a roadside diner.

After graduating from high school, Schmoke enrolled at Yale University, in New Haven, Connecticut; the news was reported on the front page of the *Baltimore Sun*'s sports section. As he had in high school, Schmoke excelled in sports and student leadership in college, serving as president of the black student association and, in his senior year, as class secretary. His leadership potential was clearly demonstrated in 1970, during a near-riot at Yale that had been triggered by the murder trial of Bobby Seale, a member of the black revolutionary group the Black Panthers. Schmoke, who was selected as a representative to voice the student demands to the faculty, issued a brief statement that impressed faculty and students alike. The writer John Hersey, a former Yale faculty member, wrote about Schmoke's speech in his book *Letter to the Alumni* (1970): "Kurt walked to the podium on the stage. What kind of abusive rhetoric would we hear? In a trembling voice, Kurt spoke only five or six brief sentences, to this effect: 'The students on this campus are confused, they're frightened. They don't know what to think. You are older than we are, and more experienced. We want guidance from you, moral leadership. On behalf of my fellow students, I beg you to give it to us.' Overcome by both the filial courtesy and the implacable challenge of these words, the entire faculty stood and applauded Kurt as he left."

Upon receiving his B.A. degree in history from Yale in 1971, Schmoke, as the recipient of a Rhodes scholarship, entered Oxford University, in England. On his return to the United States two years later, he enrolled at Harvard University's law school. He took his degree in 1976 and, after passing the bar, was hired as an associate at one of Baltimore's top law firms, Piper & Marbury. After spending just a year at the firm, he was recruited to serve as a member of the White House's domestic policy staff in the administration of President Jimmy Carter. Within about a year of beginning that job, Schmoke decided to return to Baltimore, because he wanted to become involved in local politics, and he accepted an offer to become a prosecutor for the United States attorney.

Schmoke's first opportunity to enter electoral politics came in 1982, when he decided to run for state's attorney for Baltimore, a position that in most cities is called district attorney. The challenge lay in persuading Baltimore's key voting factions—impoverished and prosperous blacks as well as liberal whites—that he was a better candidate than his opponent, the popular two-term incumbent, William A. Swisher. Rather than attack Swisher for what many considered to be his insensitivity to blacks, Schmoke focused on issues that were of grave concern to most Baltimore residents, particularly the need for more aggressive drug prosecutions. In the end, Schmoke won the election by some forty thousand votes.

As state's attorney, Schmoke implemented a number of reforms, which included an increase in the number of black and female attorneys; the creation of special narcotics, child abuse, and domestic-violence units; and the establishment of a community-liaison office to improve relations between the state's attorney's office and Baltimore's black and white communities. But while he was committed to improving the inner workings of the state's attorney's office, Schmoke's ultimate goal was much higher. He wanted to become mayor of Baltimore.

Since 1972 that office had been occupied by William Donald Schaefer, who in January 1987 stepped down to become governor of Maryland. Schaefer was automatically succeeded by Clarence H. ("Du") Burns, the city council president, who thus became Baltimore's first (unelected) black mayor. Despite Burns's close association with Schaefer, a beloved figure in Baltimore, Schmoke defeated Burns in a tight race for the Democratic nomination, in September 1987. On entering the general election campaign, in which he ran against Samuel A. Culotta, Schmoke was confident of victory. "General elections in Baltimore are usually an anticlimax," he told D. Michael Cheers in an interview for *Ebony* (February 1988). "There wasn't much doubt that I was going to beat this guy Culotta." As he had predicted, Schmoke won the election—by 74,111 votes, garnering about 65 percent of the white vote and 95 percent of the black vote.

After assuming office, Schmoke was frequently compared to Schaefer, who as mayor had won acclaim for giving Baltimore a new image to attract tourists and investors. While Schmoke never criticized Schaefer's efforts, he was convinced that the mayoralty should focus its attention on what he considered to be the more pressing problems of illiteracy, poverty, unemployment, crime, and drug addiction among city residents. He often remarked that Baltimore might be "prettier" as a result of Schaefer's efforts, but it was also "poorer." The remedy, according to Schmoke, was education; his goal, he often said, was to make Baltimore "the city that reads." "The hole in our development is in education," he told Paul W. Valentine in an interview for the *Washington Post* (December 20, 1988). "What we have is this terrible mismatch between a lot of jobs available and people lacking in the skills to take those jobs."

Comparisons between Schmoke and Schaefer did not end with the differences in their political agendas, for the two men also had dramatically different styles of leadership. Unlike Schaefer, a back-slapping politician who was perceived as a man of action, Schmoke preferred to study a problem at length before taking measures to address it. Schmoke was occasionally faulted for his cautious approach to problem solving. As Michael C. Middleton, the executive vice-president of MNC Financial Inc., told B. Drummond Ayres Jr. in an interview for the *New York Times* (March 12, 1990), "The mayor and everybody else knows by now what the city's problems are. So it's time the mayor sat down and stopped just studying things and scattering projects around. He needs to really lay out a game plan, make decisions, and get things moving. People are more than willing to work with him." In response to such criticisms, Schmoke told Margaret Garrard Warner in an interview for *Newsweek* (July 4, 1988) that he is "a firm believer in inching along" and that he does not "believe you ever win final victories in politics."

In keeping with his preference for studying a problem before taking action, early in his first term Schmoke hired a consultant to assess the quality of life in Baltimore. The result was "Baltimore 2000," a document that brought to light many alarming statistics about the city. For instance, the study found that 42 percent of the city's adult population under sixty-five was out of work; property taxes were astronomical because of a dwindling capital base; public school enrollment had dropped by nearly 50 percent since 1969; and 76 percent of all births in the black community were to unmarried women.

Among the programs that Schmoke implemented in an effort to reverse these social trends was the Baltimore Commonwealth, a partnership of the Baltimore City School Board, the Baltimore Office of Employment Development, and the Private Industry Council, among other public and private organizations. The commonwealth set up an endowment fund, which was to help college students pay for their tuition, among other services. "Getting the central players to the table was critical," Schmoke said of his efforts to establish the commonwealth, as quoted in *American City & County* (June 1988). "For the first time, they are buying into the same set of objectives as well as the strategies for achieving them. We are embarking on an ongoing partnership process that has the potential to reduce the dropout rate and make Baltimore a national model in providing opportunities and preparing youth for successful futures."

Other initiatives undertaken by Schmoke included the establishment of reading centers, whose aim was to help overcome the problem of adult illiteracy. Also on the literacy front, Schmoke organized a month-long Read-A-Thon, in which volunteers aged three to seventy-three read in the City Hall for twenty-four hours a day. To alleviate the severe housing shortage in Baltimore, Schmoke created the Community Development Financing Corporation, which provides low-interest loans for the rehabilitation of abandoned houses. The goal was to create one thousand new homeowners a year, by moving them out of public housing into low-income housing. In 1989 the program surpassed that goal, helping 1,473 Baltimoreans to buy their first homes.

Schmoke's accomplishments during his first term as mayor were offset by a few political missteps. For instance, at an early stage he was accused of alienating officials in both the mayor's and governor's offices. His critics complained that instead of seeking the advice of seasoned officials, he turned to a handful of aides who were as inexperienced in government as he was. An instance that was frequently cited as indicative of Schmoke's political naïveté was his controversial choice of Meldon S. Hollis Jr. as the school board president. Several months after Schmoke had selected him for the post—which he had done against the advice of some Baltimore officials—Hollis admitted to planting false stories with school board members as a way of determining who on the board was leaking information to the press. His actions left Schmoke with little recourse but to dismiss him as president.

Schmoke was also criticized by some black leaders for not speaking out enough on black issues. He has responded to such criticisms by remarking, as quoted in *Life* (Spring 1988), "Civil rights discrimination is still very important, but we no longer have to spend a lot of our time talking about it. I recognize that the black experience in America is different. The melting-pot effect does not apply to us. We are black this and black that. It is a great hurdle. So many other ethnic groups flourish, acquire economic power, and then become part of mainstream America. That's what I want." As it turned out, Schmoke's refusal to identify himself too closely with one segment of the city's population also won him the respect of many residents. As Walter Sondheim, a leading Baltimore businessman, told B. Drummond Ayres Jr. in an interview for the *New York Times* (April 14, 1988), "It's very reassuring. Kurt's already showing every indication of the kind of balance needed, reaching out to all elements. It's the kind of balance that people look suspiciously for in the first black mayor."

The biggest controversy of Schmoke's first term occurred in April 1988, when, without consulting his advisers, he delivered a speech at the National Conference of Mayors, in Washington, D.C., in which he called for a national debate on the legalization of drugs. Schmoke had planned to give a speech, prepared by his staff, on neighborhood "block watch" programs, but shortly before the conference he ripped it up and wrote the new one himself. "I know that even suggesting a possible decriminalization of narcotics is not popular," he declared at the conference, as quoted in *Jet* (May 23, 1988). "However, I also know that what we are doing now as a country not only is not working but also is hurting our communities." Schmoke also predicted that the United States would continue to fail in its war against drugs as long as drug abuse was treated as a crime rather than as a disease.

In an interview with Cynthia Cotts for the *Village Voice* (December 12, 1993), Schmoke recalled the hostility directed at him as a result of the speech: "You could have heard a pin drop. Then, when I got back to Baltimore, all hell broke loose. I got letters from elected officials, private citizens, people asking me to go lie down under the next train. The local TV station was running polls against me, and [Governor William Schaefer] just went ballistic." The controversy even touched his daughter, who came home from elementary school one day and asked him, "Are you really in favor of drugs?" The controversy might have been enough to ruin the career of a less popular politician, but Schmoke survived relatively unscathed. "Two things helped me weather the storm—the fact that I'd been a prosecutor and the fact that I'm black," he told Cynthia Cotts. "Proponents of legalization are often criticized by black leadership as being in favor of genocide, and a few made that suggestion to me. But it was just absurd on its face!"

Schmoke discussed his reasons for wanting to explore the idea of decriminalizing drugs during an interview with a reporter for *Ebony* (August 1989): "Drug trafficking is so profitable, and drug abuse such a serious disease, that no matter how many traffickers, pushers, and users we arrest, the illegal drug trade, with all of its attendant ills, especially in our urban communities, will continue. . . . We cannot prosecute our way out of drug abuse." While Schmoke remains convinced that the drug problem cannot be solved by locking up offenders, his ideas on the issue have evolved over the years. In the early 1990s he became a proponent of "harm reduction," an approach that advocates the implementation of needle-exchange and treatment programs as well as counseling for addicts. Supporters of harm reduction have argued that the cost of needle-exchange programs would be far less than that of treating addicts who become infected with the virus that causes AIDS, and that providing the offenders with managed doses of drugs will reduce the availability of illicit substances to the general public, because addicts will no longer be compelled to sell drugs to finance their habit. A needle-exchange program was scheduled to be launched in Baltimore in the summer of 1994.

Neither the uproar caused by his proposed solution to the drug problem nor the other controversies in which he was involved were enough to damage Schmoke's reputation among the public. In fact, he maintained such a consistently high approval rating that as his first term drew to a close many observers speculated that he would seek higher office. But Schmoke felt that there was more work to be done in Baltimore, and in June 1991 he announced his candidacy for reelection to the mayoralty, using the slogan that he would repeat throughout his campaign: "Stay on board with Schmoke."

Schmoke faced seven challengers for the Democratic nomination, including his former rivals Clarence Burns and William Swisher. Burns, who claimed that Schmoke had failed to achieve results in the battle against crime, drugs, and poor schools, expressed confidence in his ability to win the nomination. So, too, did Schmoke. "I feel good about this election," he told B. Drummond Ayres Jr. in an interview for the *New York Times* (September 11, 1991). "I think people understand that what I've been doing is laying a foundation for the city to move forward in the future. Some people may say I'm not very flashy and that this is a dull campaign. Well, protecting a city's bond rating may not be politically sexy, but it will pay off in the end." In the primary, Schmoke defeated Burns by a wide margin, receiving 61,681 votes to Burns's 31,748. Swisher came in third, with 10,482 votes. In the general election Schmoke faced Samuel Culotta, his Republican opponent, for the second time, and, as he had done four years earlier, he defeated him.

Two years later Schmoke appeared to be seriously considering making a bid for the governorship of Maryland, when he visited towns outside Baltimore and made what sounded to many like campaign speeches. While in Montgomery County, he was forced to answer some tough questions about how he would treat suburban districts if he were to win the 1993 election—questions that were prompted by a controversial move he had made early in his second term. In 1992 Schmoke had stated in a surprise announcement that he was joining the American Civil Liberties Union in a suit against Maryland for inequities in school funding among various districts. In so doing, he appeared to favor an increase in state funding to Baltimore at the expense of Montgomery County, a well-to-do suburb of Washington, D.C., where, according to one of his senior aides, more money was spent per student than in Baltimore. As might be expected, Schmoke's prospective candidacy for governor was greeted with skepticism by many Montgomery County residents. Later in 1993, he announced that he would not pursue the governorship but would run for a third term as mayor. "I have the fire in the belly, but it's for Baltimore," he told a reporter for *Jet* (October 18, 1993). In September 1995, in what had been expected to be a close race, Schmoke won the Democratic primary, by a margin of 59 to 39 precent. He won the mayorality for the third time when he easily defeated the Republican challenger, Victor Clarke, on November 7, 1995.

Kurt Schmoke, who has jokingly described himself as a "nerd," has been characterized by others as scholarly, congenial, self-effacing, and down-to-earth. He maintains a trim and athletic build, and he typically wears button-down shirts, pleated slacks, and wire-framed glasses. He and his wife, the former Patricia Locks, an ophthalmologist, have two children, Gregory and Katherine. While Schmoke has said that he is not yet ready to claim victory in his battle against the many social and economic ills that confront Baltimore, he has also refused to concede defeat. As he told the reporter for *Jet* (October 18, 1993), "While we're moving in the right direction, much more needs to be done. . . . One of the things that marks our programs is that these are works in progress."

Selected Biographical References: American City & County p62+ Je '88 pors; Ebony 43:180+ F '88 pors; N Y Times A p22 Ap 14 '88 por; Newsweek 62:18 Jl 4 '88 por; Washington Post mag p13+ My 27 '90 pors; Contemporary Black Biography vol 1 (1992); Who's Who in American Politics, 1993–94

University of California

Schopf, J. William
(shof)

Sept. 27, 1941- Geologist; paleobiologist; microbiologist; organic chemist; educator. Address: b. Center for the Study of Evolution and the Origin of Life, Institute of Geophysics and Planetary Physics, Department of Earth and Space Sciences, Molecular Biology Institute, University of California at Los Angeles, Los Angeles, CA 90024; h. 2581 S. Cotner Ave., Los Angeles, CA 90064

When did life appear on Earth? Was the appearance of life on Earth an inevitable event, or was it a highly improbable one? Does life exist elsewhere in the universe? Until the 1960s most scientists considered such questions to be firmly rooted in the realm of speculation, unanswerable by science. After all, paleontologists had been scouring fossil-rich sediments throughout the globe for nearly a century and had yet to turn up evidence of truly ancient living organisms. Nevertheless, as a young graduate student, J. William Schopf ambitiously took on the issue of the origin and earliest history of life as the subject of his doctoral thesis. "Scientists and family friends alike almost uniformly argued that I was not yet expert enough to take on such a basic question," Schopf, the director of the Center for the Study of Evolution and the Origin of Life, at the University of California at Los Angeles, told Anne C. Roark in an interview for the *Chronicle of Higher Education* (September 11, 1978). "Yet, the problem struck me as potentially solvable. It struck me as considerably interesting. And it struck me as certainly important. What didn't strike me is why I shouldn't do it."

Schopf's principal advantage in this endeavor was that, unlike many paleontologists, he did not expect to unearth fossil organisms that he could see and touch but instead suspected that his quarry was microscopic. That hunch proved to be correct. Not only did he go on to find relics of the earliest life forms known, but the discoveries that he and his colleagues have made over the past three decades, particularly those reported in a 1993 issue of *Science*, have shown that life is far more ancient than scientists had previously supposed. By 3.5 billion years ago—literally billions of years before the earliest humans or even the long-extinct dinosaurs appeared on Earth—the planet was home to thriving communities of biologically complex bacterium-like organisms, so complex that they may have performed photosynthesis. "By this time modern biochemistry was established, and it really has not changed much to modern times," Schopf told James Trefil in an interview for *Smithsonian* (February 1995). This and other findings have both given birth to an entire new scientific discipline, that of Precambrian paleobiology, and established Schopf as one of its founders. "Through his own dogged field work and his meticulous analysis in the laboratory," Wallace Ravven observed in a profile of Schopf for *Discover* (October 1990), "[Schopf] has done more than anyone else to bring the history of early life on Earth out of the dark."

James William Schopf was born on September 27, 1941 in Urbana, Illinois, to James Morton Schopf, a paleobotanist, and Esther (Nissen) Schopf, an information specialist. He first became interested in science as a child, when he and his brother would accompany their father to his university laboratory, where they would do odd jobs for him. It was not until his sophomore year at Oberlin College, in Ohio, though, that he became hooked on the study of the origin of life.

The pivotal moment came during a lecture in which his geology professor mentioned in passing that virtually nothing was known about the life forms that inhabited Earth during the first four-fifths of its history. A wide variety of organisms, mostly small, ocean-dwelling creatures, were known to have existed as far back as 550 million years ago; scientists knew that they must have evolved from simpler life forms, but without fossil evidence they could only speculate on what these organisms might have looked like. Intrigued, that night Schopf began reading Charles Darwin's *On the Origin of Species* and learned that the famed nineteenth-century naturalist himself had been perplexed by the lack of fossils from the Precambrian, the period during which the first life forms were thought to have evolved. "I thought, gee whiz, Darwin has got to be right, there has to be an earlier fossil record," he recalled in an interview with Neil A. Campbell for the *American Biology Teacher* (October 1989). "It seemed to me that there ought to be something out there to find."

Such evidence was not nonexistent, as Schopf discovered during one of his forays to Oberlin's library. On this occasion he read a little-noticed paper that had appeared in a 1954 issue of *Science*, on the discovery of fossil microorganisms in two-billion-year-old rock samples near Lake Superior. His interest heightened, Schopf visited Harvard University, in Cambridge, Massachusetts, to meet with one of the authors of that report, the paleobotanist Elso Barghoorn. He returned to Oberlin with chunks of the fossil-bearing sediment, his analysis of which formed the basis of his undergraduate thesis.

After taking his A.B. degree in geology, with high honors, from Oberlin in 1963, Schopf continued his study of ancient life at Harvard University. While working under Barghoorn, he discovered some fossil microorganisms on his own that were found to be 850 million years old. He made another important discovery in 1967. While analyzing 3.1-billion-year-old rocks from South Africa, he detected the presence of numerous amino acids, which living organisms use to manufacture protein. These constituted the oldest amino acids then known.

In the following year, after earning his A.M. and Ph.D. degrees, both in biology, from Harvard, Schopf joined the staff of the University of California at Los Angeles (UCLA) as an assistant professor of paleobiology. Within five years he had been promoted to professor and named a member of the Institute of Geophysics and Planetary Physics. During that period he also served as one of the principal investigators of lunar samples for the Apollo space program, with responsibility for analyzing moon rocks for evidence of life, either past or present. In addition, he took part in numerous fossil-collecting expeditions all over the world, including excursions to the Soviet Union, China, India, France, and Australia, as well as to various locales throughout Canada and the United States. He chose those destinations because they were known to possess some of the world's oldest rock, within which he hoped to find relics of primitive life.

Finding sediments of great antiquity was the key to Schopf's endeavor. As he has explained, over the eons heat, pressure, and volcanic activity have transformed beyond recognition much of the rock that formed in Earth's remote past. Such conditions not only make it difficult for geologists to date the rock; they also destroy any fossils contained within it. "If the rock is really heated up, as almost all the oldest rocks are, forget about finding a fossil," he told Wallace Ravven. "The minerals melt, and new minerals start to form. If you chip the rock, and if with a hand lens you can see the little bumps that form when the chert heated up and recrystallized, that's a sure sign that the rock has gotten fried. You'll have a hell of a time reconstructing what was once there." In fact, there are only a handful of rock formations left on Earth that date from the Archean era, the crucial period that stretches from 4.5 billion years ago, when Earth formed, to 2.5 billion years ago.

One place where Archean rocks can be found is Western Australia's North Pole region, which Schopf and some of his colleagues visited in 1982. "The Western Australia outcrops are among the best preserved Archean rocks on the planet," he told Ravven. "If you're going to find the fossils anywhere, that's where to find them." Specifically, what Schopf and his team of scientists were searching for in Western Australia were stromatolites, layered rock formations that resemble stacks of canned potato chips but that are actually produced by communities of microorganisms. Best of all were stromatolites composed of fine-grained cherts, for this type of rock, a variety of quartz, was likely to contain fossilized remnants of the microorganisms themselves. "If the cherts look black, that means there's organic matter inside—a sign of life . . . ," he told Ravven. "If you can manage to track down fine-grained black cherts associated with stromatolites, and if you're lucky, you might find a fossil. But the chances of finding a microfossil are infinitesimally small."

It was during the 1982 expedition to the region that Schopf and his colleagues discovered what they had long been searching for. Their analysis of the samples they collected revealed that the cherts contained simple cells resembling modern-day cyanobacteria, once known as blue-green algae, that were dated to be 3.5 billion years old. While earlier discoveries, by both Schopf and others, had lent support to the notion that life had originated in Earth's remote past, these fossils constituted the first solid evidence of the most ancient living organisms ever collected. "When we discovered we had some filament fragments and colonies of spherical cells, we knew we had the good stuff," he recalled to Wallace Ravven. "It was pretty neat. When you find filaments that have a series of cells in a row, they're complex enough that you can say that they can't be anything other than biological." Even more remarkable, these ancient microfossils appeared to have been capable of performing photosynthesis. "They divided by the same cell division as modern cyanobacteria, and they appear to have produced oxygen," Schopf was quoted as saying in a press release prepared by the UCLA communications department.

Despite what appeared to Schopf and others to be firm evidence that life had been biologically complex 3.5 billion years ago, some scientists have since expressed doubts about the accuracy of the ages derived for some of the fossils and even about their origin. The fossils may not have been produced by biological processes, they have suggested. These doubts were fueled by the fact that some of the fossil material might not have been as old as the rocks in which it was found. The reliability of other presumed fossil evidence was questioned when the site at which it had been collected could not be relocated by scientists.

Recent findings by Schopf seem to have put such doubts to rest. In a 1993 issue of *Science*, he reported on the discovery of more microfossils from Western Australia. They consist of eleven different species of tiny, filamentous cells containing fossil microorganisms that were found in sedimentary rock dated to be 3.465 billion years old. Unlike similar fossil material that had previously been questioned, these met all of the criteria necessary to state with confidence that they were made by bacterium-like organisms living at that time. Those criteria require that the fossils be found in reliably dated rock, that they are indigenous to the area and therefore not recent contaminants, and that they are biological in origin. "This is real firm," Schopf told John Horgan in an interview for *Scientific American* (August 1993). "It is the sort of thing that can get into the textbooks and stay there."

Based on these and other discoveries, Schopf has speculated that life spent the next 1.3 billion years simply reproducing and refining its chemistry. Then, around 2.2 billion years ago, an event of incomparable importance occurred: the sheer abundance of primitive life forms led to the production of an oxygen-rich atmosphere. In support of this claim, he cites the existence of 3.8-billion-year-old rust-bearing marine sediments. According to Schopf, the rust may have formed when iron in the oceans reacted with oxygen that had been produced by the earliest life forms. "Once oxygen levels got high enough to rust out the oceans," he explained to Wallace Ravven, "there would have been sufficient oxygen left over to support nonbacterial life." (The theory has been disputed by some researchers, who have pointed out that the rust could have been formed in other ways.) The creation of an oxygen-rich atmosphere in turn made possible the evolution of oxygen-dependent life forms.

While Schopf's discoveries have provided humans with an unprecedented glimpse into their own origin, he cannot answer definitively the question of when and where the very first cell, which actually may have resembled an oil droplet, appeared. He can, however, state with reasonable certainty that since life had already developed the ability to manufacture its own food by photosynthesis by 3.5 billion years ago, the very first living organisms must have evolved considerably earlier. An early origin would in turn lend support to the notion that life evolved quickly, for Earth itself formed 4.5 billion years ago, and, because of the intense meteoritic bombardment that it experienced during the first several hundred million years after its formation, it was probably incapable of supporting life until about 3.9 billion years ago, leaving just several hundred million years for life to achieve a relatively high degree of complexity.

In support of this view, which is disputed by some researchers on the grounds that inorganic molecules could not have organized themselves into biologically complex organisms in such a short period of time, Schopf has pointed to the rapid pace of evolution during the past 550 million years—the period during which the first vertebrates, a species of jawless fish, radiated into a vast array of backboned animals. "The problem with accepting this picture [of the rapid development of life] is psychological, not scientific," Schopf told James Trefil. "People think that life is so different from everything else, that there has to be a huge gap in time separating the living from the nonliving, but that's just not the way it is." A tantalizing corollary to this idea is that, as Schopf told Neil Campbell, life might have evolved "elsewhere relatively rapidly and there might be lots of life throughout the rest of the universe."

In addition to the tremendous amount of data he has collected on the origin of life, Schopf's research has given him a perspective on the earliest life forms and on the evolution of life itself. "The history of life is one of change, whether one examines humans, dinosaurs, or the saber-tooth cat," he was quoted as saying in the UCLA press release. "However, with cyanobacteria, the fossil record indicates that the same species that are alive today have been here for thousands of millions—that is, billions—of years. We cannot say that for any other species. The lifetime of typical mammals, such as ourselves, is about five million years. I can take fossils of cyanobacteria from two billion years ago and line them up side by side with modern species, and they look the same. This was absolutely unpredictable. . . . [They] can live virtually anywhere—in hot springs, in cold water, in the presence of oxygen, in the absence of oxygen; they can withstand submersion in liquid helium at 450 degrees Fahrenheit below zero and can even survive atomic bombs."

Besides conducting hands-on research on the earliest life forms, since 1984 Schopf has served as director of UCLA's Center for the Study of Evolution and Origin of Life, an interdisciplinary research center that he founded. Its multifaceted orientation reflects Schopf's conviction that scientists must be broadly educated if they are to contribute to man's understanding of the natural world. "Unlike our universities, nature is not compartmentalized," he told Neil Campbell. "The natural sciences have no real boundaries; if you want to question one aspect of science you really must be educated in ancillary disciplines. We come together once a week for dinner and discussion about a broad array of evolutionary problems—the evolution of the universe, the evolution of life, the origin of *Homo sapiens*, and musings about extraterrestrial life and future evolution."

The author of more than two hundred scholarly publications, Schopf has also served as editor of several books on the evolution of life, including *Earth's Earliest Biosphere* (1983), which discusses the major evolutionary events of the Archean era; *The Proterozoic Biosphere: A Multidisciplinary Study* (1992), which covers "almost everything that is known," in Schopf's words, about the history of life between 2.5 billion and 500 million years ago; and *Major Events in the History of Life* (1992), based on a symposium held at UCLA in 1991. He also finds time to teach undergraduate courses in paleontology, paleobotany, and the history of life, and graduate-level seminars.

For his efforts to extract from Earth's most ancient sediments their long-buried secrets about the origin of life, Bill Schopf has received many awards, including the 1986 Mary Clark Thompson Medal, from the National Academy of Sciences; the 1977 Alan T. Waterman Award, which the National Science Foundation presents to the country's "most outstanding young scientist"; the 1974 Charles Schuchert Award, from the Paleontological Society; the A. I. Oparin Medal of the International Society for the Study of the Origin of Life; and a Distinguished Teaching Award and the 1992 Gold Shield Faculty Prize for Academic Excellence, both from UCLA.

For all his hard work, Schopf has attributed his success in finding evidence of ancient life at least in part to luck, for when he started out he had no idea how abundant such evidence would be. "I could have been absolutely wrong and had no success at all," he told Campbell. "But I was young and I didn't know any better. It happened that I was fortunate and Darwin was right. There is an early fossil record, and I've had a lot of fun trying to find out about it." Since 1980 he has been married to Jane Shen Schopf, a professor of biology at UCLA. He has a son, James Christopher, from an earlier marriage.

Selected Biographical References: American Biology Teacher 51:396+ O '89 por; Chronicle of Higher Education p3+ S 11 '78 por; Discover 11:98+ O '90 por; Los Angeles Times D 27 '77 por; Sci Am 269:24 Ag '93; Science 260:640+ Ap 30 '93; Contemporary Authors vol 133 (1991)

Schultes, Richard Evans

(SHUL-tes)

Jan. 12, 1915- Ethnobotanist; conservationist; museum administrator; educator. Address: b. c/o Botanical Museum of Harvard University, 26 Oxford St., Cambridge, MA 02138; h. 78 Larchmont Rd., Melrose, MA 02176

For a dozen years beginning in the early 1940s, while researching rubber trees and conducting other scientific studies, the ethnobotanist Richard Evans Schultes dwelled nearly continuously among the native peoples of the Amazon Basin, mostly in Colombia, in some of the most remote places on Earth. In addition to collecting a remarkable total of some twenty-four thousand plant specimens, Schultes recorded information that the Indians shared with him from their trove of botanical lore. He thus learned about hundreds of plants that they use to cure specific infections or immobilize particular prey or for myriad other purposes. One of the few scientists at that time to recognize the importance of the Indians' encyclopedic knowledge of the flora in their environment to the welfare of people everywhere, Schultes returned to Amazonia almost annually for close to four decades after joining the staff of the Botanical Museum of Harvard University in 1953. He became a member of the university's faculty in 1970.

"The last of the great plant explorers in the Victorian tradition," as Wade Davis described him in his book *The Serpent and the Rainbow* (1985),

John Lupo/Harvard U. Biological Laboratories

Schultes is legendary among his colleagues for what Russell A. Mittermeier, the president of Conservation International, has called his "incredible field exploits." He has also gained international renown as "a true ethnobotanist, the incarnation and almost the inventor of this discipline," in the words of John Hemming, writing in the London *Times*

Literary Supplement (July 15, 1988), as an economic botanist of the first rank, and as a pioneer in tropical forest conservation. Since 1985 he has held the titles Edward C. Jeffrey professor of biology emeritus at Harvard University and director emeritus of the Harvard Botanical Museum.

The son of Otto Richard Schultes and Maude Beatrice (Bagley) Schultes, Richard Evans Schultes was born on January 12, 1915 in Boston. His father, a sanitary engineer, fashioned and installed plumbing in breweries until the 1920s, when, because of Prohibition, he turned to general plumbing and heating. His mother was an office worker before becoming a homemaker. "Something of a loner," according to E. J. Kahn Jr., in his *New Yorker* (June 1, 1992) profile of the scientist, Schultes grew up in East Boston, where his maternal great-grandparents landed when they immigrated to the United States from England, and he attended East Boston public schools. His interest in botany can be traced to the early years of his childhood. While visiting an uncle's farm as a young boy, for example, he would collect leaves and press them between the pages of the uncle's plant guide.

When Schultes was six or seven, a stomach ailment forced him to stay in bed for two months. Among the many books his parents read to him during that period, excerpts from Richard Spruce's *Notes of a Botanist on the Amazon and Andes* (published posthumously in 1908) made an especially powerful impression on the boy. By his own admission, as an adult Schultes modeled his career on that of Spruce, whom he has called "the greatest botanical explorer ever to have gone to South America, and one of the most careful and inquisitive botanical collectors of all times." A nineteenth-century British naturalist and teacher, Spruce explored Amazonia and the Andes of Ecuador for fourteen years, overcoming appalling difficulties to collect some ten thousand specimens of plants. Schultes's boundless admiration for his predecessor permeates his short biography *Richard Spruce Still Lives* (1953), in which he wrote—in words similar to those that others have used to describe Schultes's own achievements—"His researches and discoveries in the field of plant science have benefited mankind in all corners of the earth, and have helped to enrich governments and private enterprises in far-flung regions of the globe."

In 1933, after graduating from East Boston High School, Schultes enrolled at Harvard University, in Cambridge, Massachusetts, as a premed student, with a full scholarship for tuition. His extracurricular activities included membership in the university's botany club and a Unitarian association and working as a clerk in the library of the Harvard Botanical Museum. A course in economic botany so fired his imagination in his junior year that he decided to make botany rather than medicine his vocation. Known as Biology 104, "Plants and Human Affairs," the course was taught by Oakes Ames, an orchidologist and economic botanist of international repute and the director of the botanical museum, who became, according to E. J. Kahn Jr., "a kind of father figure" to Schultes. (Years later Schultes himself taught Biology 104, and he gained a degree of celebrity among Harvard students for his demonstration of the art of shooting a dart from a six-foot-long Amazonian blowgun.)

Having chosen the peyote cactus as the subject of his senior thesis, Schultes spent a month in Anadarko, Oklahoma, where he interviewed the local Kiowa Indians about their use of peyote as a cure for a variety of illnesses and as a mind-altering drug that enabled them to commune with their ancestors. He ingested the hallucinogen himself during all-night Indian ceremonies, albeit in smaller quantities than those favored by the Indians, and then recorded what he had experienced. In doing so, he inaugurated a practice that he was to follow repeatedly in his field studies in South America. In an article for the *Sciences* (March/April 1994), Schultes explained that South American Indians consider hallucinogenic plants sacred, and "it would have been an unpardonable rudeness to refuse them when the Indians were kind enough to offer them to [him] during a [religious] ceremony." Elsewhere, he has expressed the view that the minds as well as the bodies of humans need "curative and corrective agents" and that the full potential of hallucinogens as "aids to human needs" has yet to be fully recognized.

After earning an A.B. degree, cum laude, in 1937, Schultes entered Harvard's graduate program in biology. Intrigued by descriptions by sixteenth-century Spanish explorers in Mexico of *teonanacatl*, a hallucinogenic mushroom, and *ololiuqui*, a vine with psychoactive seeds, between 1938 and 1940 he made several research trips to the Mexican state of Oaxaca and, with the help of medicine men, collected specimens of both *teonanacatl* and *ololiuqui*. He later identified them as members of the genus *Panaeolus* and of the morning-glory family, respectively. Those and other of his findings appear in his doctoral dissertation, "Economic Aspects of the Flora of Northeastern Oaxaca." Schultes received an A.M. degree from Harvard in 1938 and a Ph.D. in 1941.

Immediately after receiving his doctorate, Schultes became a research associate of the Harvard Botanical Museum. He was also named a fellow of the National Research Council (NRC), which gave him a ten-month grant to find out which species of plants the Indians of Amazonia employed in making curare. Schultes's stint as an NRC plant explorer got off to an extraordinarily auspicious start. En route to the Colombian jungle, he had stopped in Bogotá, and on the very day of his arrival, while roaming the outskirts of the city, he came upon a new, half-inch-long species of orchid. (Oakes Ames later christened the species *Pachiphyllum schultesii*.)

Curare is a component of plants in the genera *Strychnos* and *Chondodendron*. A chemical compound in *Chondodendron* has been used since the 1930s as a muscle relaxant before surgical procedures and in treating certain neurologic disorders. In a far more concentrated form, it can cause rapid systemic paralysis and death, a property well known to the Indians of Amazonia, who for generations have included curare-tipped arrows in their arsenals of hunting weapons. Schultes eventually found out that "whereas some kinds of curare are made with only one plant species, other curares may call for as many as fifteen ingredients," in his words, and that the Indians prepare their different curares from more than three dozen species of plants. "His researches were the first steps toward identifying the more than seventy species of plants that can be used to make curare," E. J. Kahn Jr. reported.

Despite the remoteness of his study site, word of the Japanese attack on Pearl Harbor, on December 7, 1941, reached Schultes within a few weeks of the event. He eventually returned to Bogotá and went to the American Embassy to enlist in one of the armed services. But government officials decided that his botanical expertise would be far more valuable to the war effort than would military service. In particular, after the Japanese took control of the British and Dutch rubber plantations in Southeast Asia, the United States could no longer obtain the natural rubber necessary for the war effort, so getting the rubber from wild trees had become crucial. (Synthetic rubber did not provide an all-purpose substitute for natural rubber.) Accordingly, in early 1942 Schultes was hired as a field agent for a government entity known as the Rubber Development Corporation, which charged him with the tasks of finding rubber trees in Amazonia and teaching local Indians how to extract the latex. Later in the same year, he also received a Guggenheim Foundation fellowship for ethnobotanical research in the Amazon.

Over the next dozen years (for most of them, as an employee of the Bureau of Plant Industry, a branch of the United States Department of Agriculture), Schultes collected some thirty-five hundred specimens of *Hevea* (the genus in which the most important rubber-tree species are classified) and measured the latex yield of the trees the specimens came from. He also supervised the gathering of three tons of *Hevea* seeds suitable for cultivation. As E. J. Kahn Jr. reported, he was "well acquainted with all of the nine known species of *Hevea* and had collected material from seven. He had, furthermore, discovered a whole new variety, the members of which seldom exceeded ten feet in height and were thus less likely than their taller brethren to be toppled by monsoons." Beginning in 1947 Schultes extended his investigations of *Hevea* to Asia, most intensively in Ceylon and Malaysia, where, during the 1980s, he traveled annually. Since 1988 he has served as a consultant to the Rubber Research Institute and Development Board of Malaysia. In 1990 the board's chairman described Schultes's expertise in *Hevea* as "second to none."

Unlike Richard Spruce, in carrying out his work in South America, Richard Schultes was able to take advantage of the availability of antibiotics and, in the few urban or semiurban areas, motor vehicles, among other twentieth-century conveniences. But for the most part, his research in the forests entailed hardships similar to those that Spruce had faced, and it required a comparable degree of fortitude and determination. He suffered several attacks of malaria, for example, and bouts of beriberi as well, during one of which "he had to help paddle a canoe for forty days, his arms and legs growing increasingly numb, in order to reach a doctor better equipped than any shaman to treat him," as E. J. Kahn Jr. wrote.

Once, in 1947, while traveling on an Amazon tributary on a small, leaky barge with fourteen other people, pigs and other animals, and a cargo of odorous dried fish, Schultes fell ill with what he later learned was both malaria and beriberi. In her book *Green Medicine* (1964), Margaret B. Krieg quoted the entry that Schultes recorded that day in his field journal: "This afternoon I came down with a very high fever. Have rheumatic pains in every limb and back, continuous nausea. . . . Vomiting continuously, very weak, probably mostly from malnutrition—we have had no warm food, only a tin of sardines for supper last night." That night, the barge crashed into a tree that was leaning over the river. "With my flashlight, I saw that the tree was in young fruit, with a recently fertilized ovary, that is, so I broke off a few branches to put in the [plant] press later. When dawn came, I examined the plant—it was *Micandra minor*, which I am especially anxious to collect!"

Schultes's preferred means of conveyance on Amazonian rivers was an eighteen-foot, fifty-three-pound aluminum canoe, which he could paddle by himself, if necessary. More often he navigated with the help of local Indians whom he would recruit, sometimes with the help of missionaries, wherever he happened to be. In exchange for their labor, he would give them knives, scissors, pieces of bright-colored cloth, or aluminum pots. His pack contained little else: a change of clothing, a pith helmet, a notebook and pencils, a small medicine kit, a camera and film, a hypodermic and antivenin that he stored in his camera case, a hammock, a thin blanket, a machete, clippers and other plant-collecting and -preserving paraphernalia, and a few cans of food for emergencies. (According to Margaret Krieg, he and a guide once subsisted for four and a half days on a single can of condensed milk after they had lost all their provisions in some rapids.) Contrary to the belief of many Westerners, at times there is little fish, game, or even fruit available in the jungle. Schultes's diet consisted mainly of farina, made from ground tapioca, and *chicha*, a drink that the Indians brewed from fruit and that was often the only available liquid. "I do believe that [*chicha*] is nourishing, for I managed to live on it at times," he told Krieg.

Although Schultes has acknowledged proficiency in understanding only two Amazonian languages—those of the Witoto and the Makuna Indians—he apparently managed to communicate with little difficulty with tribal peoples who spoke other tongues. (In the *Boston Globe* [September 22, 1990], David Arnold reported that Schultes learned fifty tribal dialects.) He never carried firearms in the jungle, because he never felt threatened. "The Indians are extremely friendly and cooperative, at least until they acquire the sometimes unsavory veneer of Western culture . . . ," he wrote in his *Sciences* article. "The Indian leaders are gentlemen, and all that is required to bring out their gentlemanliness is reciprocal gentlemanliness." "The ethnobotanical researcher . . . must realize that, far from being a superior individual, he—the civilized man—is in many respects far inferior to the native in the native's own environment," he has been quoted as saying.

Schultes has also observed that "a sympathetic understanding and tolerance of his beliefs and ways and participation in his customs do more than anything else to win the Indian's respect and confidence." Those customs included the chewing of coca powder, which Schultes, in his words, "accepted as a fact of life," and which he himself often practiced during his years in the jungle. He has explained that, as used by the Indians, coca is nonaddictive and highly useful: "The stimulation and capacity for performance and endurance which coca affords the individual and its ability to suppress hunger pangs gives the drug the role of an indispensable vade mecum in the more or less itinerant life of deprivation which many Indians of the northwest Amazon must undergo."

In addition to their living quarters and food, the Indians shared with Schultes their vast knowledge of jungle animals and plants. Integral to the cultural heritage of many South American tribes, he discovered, is a wealth of explicit information about hundreds of useful plant species. Furthermore, he reported in the *Sciences*, "the forest peoples' acquaintance with plants is subtle as well as extensive. The Indians often distinguish 'kinds' of a plant that appear indistinguishable, even to the experienced taxonomic botanist. Moreover, they frequently identify such kinds from a considerable distance by sight alone." To date, only a small proportion of the plants used by the Indians (and a far smaller percentage of the world's estimated half-million higher plant species) have been chemically analyzed, but those analyses have almost invariably turned up biologically active substances. Determinations of the components of plants that the Indians rely on to cure conjunctivitis, ringworm, and various other infections, for example, have revealed the presence of antibacterial or fungicidal compounds. There is little doubt that untold numbers of substances valuable for medicine or industry await discovery by Western scientists in the forests of Amazonia, which support an estimated eighty thousand species.

In his preface to Schultes's book *Where the Gods Reign* (1987), the ethnobotanist and conservationist Mark J. Plotkin observed that Schultes "began writing about the importance of conserving ethnobotanical lore long before most biologists were aware of *any* conservation problems in tropical areas." In 1963, for example, Schultes warned, "Civilization is on the march in many, if not most, primitive regions. It has long been on the advance, but its pace is now accelerated as the result of world wars, extended commercial interests, increased missionary activity, widened tourism. . . . One of the first aspects of primitive culture to fall before the onslaught of civilization is knowledge and use of plants for medicines. The rapidity of this disintegration is frightening. Our challenge is to salvage some of the native medico-botanical lore before it becomes forever entombed with the cultures that gave it birth." He has repeated that message innumerable times since then. "Time is running out . . . ," he wrote in his *Sciences* article. "The Indians' botanical knowledge is disappearing even faster than the plants themselves."

Schultes took pictures as well as specimens of the medicinal, toxic, and narcotic plants to which he was introduced in Amazonia, along with photos and specimens of many other species. But of the approximately eight thousand images that he preserved on film, "as many seem to be of people as of plants," John Simon noted in an article for *World* (May/June 1992), the journal of the Unitarian Universalist Association. Some are portraits of the Indian boys who aided him in getting specimens; nimble climbers, they would use his machete to chop high branches (thus sparing the trees themselves). Under his guidance, a few of his helpers learned to operate his camera, and some of the pictures show Schultes himself. In one such photo, a small Indian boy is perched on his lap. "This little chap thought his mission in life was to come to my hammock and shake it at four or five o'clock in the morning," Schultes told John Simon. "He wanted me to have breakfast with him, breakfast being unleavened tapioca bread dipped in chili pepper." In a photo taken during a four-day ceremony in which Schultes took part while living with the Yukuna Indians, he stands barefoot and wears a long grass skirt and, draped over one shoulder, a strip of bark cloth decorated with an elaborate masklike face. The Yukunas, according to Simon, called him their brother, and when he left them, their medicine man gave him his brazilwood "wand of authority," which, Schultes noted, "must have taken months" to carve.

After about six years of work in the Amazon Basin, Schultes spent a short time in the United States. He then returned to Amazonia in the late 1940s for another half-dozen years. During those periods, Margaret Krieg wrote, he "became the first scientist to retrace most of Spruce's itinerary and to re-collect many of the plants [Spruce] discovered in the wilds of the Amazon a century earlier." Sometimes Schultes did not leave the forest at all for fourteen months at a time, because, as he told Margaret Krieg, "only through long and intimate association with a particular plant can [a botanist] really come to understand it." "A botanist literally must live with [plants] to be successful in his efforts," he explained. "He must study them throughout the year to obtain both flowers and fruit, watch changes in the leaves, and evaluate the effects of high and low water." To preserve his specimens, Schultes would saturate them in a mixture of formaldehyde and water and then press them between sheets of newspaper, placing the sandwich thus created in a rubber or plastic bag. On especially productive days he would collect as many as ninety specimens. "Somebody like Dick Schultes can go into a jungle and brush by zillions of things that he knows he knows, and then spot something that holds his eye," a colleague of Schultes's told E. J. Kahn Jr. Others have reported that Schultes has noticed unusual plants while seated in a fast-moving truck or in a plane during takeoff.

The vast amount of botanical and ethnobotanical knowledge that Schultes gained during his years in Amazonia provided the foundation for some of his nine books. Among them are *Plants and Human Affairs* (1960), written with A. F. Hill; *The Botany and Chemistry of Hallucinogens* (1968) and *Plants of the Gods* (1979), both of which he wrote with Albert Hofmann, the Swiss chemist who discovered and synthesized LSD; and, in collaboration with Robert F. Raffauf, a chemist who specializes in drugs of plant and animal origin, *The Healing Forest* (1990), which presents information on 1,516 plants used by the Indians of the Colombian Amazon, and *Vine of the Soul: Medicine Men of the Colombian Amazon—Their Plants and Rituals* (1992). Schultes's photos of Amazonia, which have been described as having "great beauty and tranquility" and as communicating "a deep understanding and great love of [Amazonian] peoples and plants," illustrate most of his books.

For some thirty-six years after he returned to Massachusetts in 1953, Schultes made almost annual field trips to Amazonian Colombia, as well as less frequent trips to many other places, until cardiac problems forced him to cut down on his traveling. But once he resettled in the United States, his theatres of operation shifted primarily to classrooms, meeting halls, and his office and laboratory at the Harvard Botanical Museum. From 1953 to 1958 he served at the museum as curator of the Orchid Herbarium of Oakes Ames. He then become the curator of economic botany, a job he held for the next seventeen years. From 1967 to 1970 he also held the position of executive director of the museum, and from 1970 to 1985, director. He has written and edited scores of articles published in the museum's scientific journal. To date, he has produced 455 scientific articles.

Concurrently, from 1957 until his retirement in 1985, Schultes taught Harvard undergraduate and graduate students and enrollees in the university's extension program. He was appointed Paul C. Mangelsdorf professor of natural sciences in 1973 and Edward C. Jeffrey professor of biology in 1980. "He inspired countless students (myself included) to pursue careers in the natural sciences," Mark J. Plotkin wrote in the preface to *Where the Gods Reign*. "His influence on young people has by no means been restricted to his students in Cambridge—he has traveled all over the world, giving lectures and serving on academic committees so that students who could not afford access to a Harvard education would have the benefit of his knowledge and experience."

Richard Schultes's numerous other professional activities have included service as a consultant to pharmaceutical and other companies and as a member and sometimes chairman of many scientific associations, commissions, panels, and advisory boards. He has participated in and occasionally organized dozens of scientific meetings. From 1962 to 1979 he edited the journal *Economic Botany*, and since the 1970s he has served as a member of the editorial boards of *Horticulture*, *Social Pharmacology*, the *Journal of Ethnopharmacology*, the *Journal of Latin American Folklore*, and other scientific periodicals. With Robert F. Raffauf, he has been editing *Psychoactive Plants of the World*, a series published by Yale University Press. In addition, he has appeared as an expert witness on narcotics in numerous trials in the United States, Canada, and England.

According to E. J. Kahn Jr., Richard Schultes "wears dark-wool three-piece suits and steel-rimmed spectacles, which, combined with a stately bearing and a fringe of white hair, give him the look of a sedentary Ivy League mentor." "Soon apparent to all who meet him is the Schultes brand of rugged individualism," Margaret Krieg reported. "A New Englander and proud of it, he says exactly what he thinks." Staunchly conservative in his political beliefs, as a protest he once wrote on a paper ballot the name of Queen Elizabeth II of England rather than vote for the Democratic or Republican candidate for president. He served for several years in the 1970s and 1980s as a vestryman at Kings Chapel in Boston, the Unitarian church where he has long been a member. Schultes's linguistic skills include proficiency in Latin, Spanish, and Portuguese and a working knowledge of French, German, and Scandinavian languages.

Schultes has been married since March 26, 1959 to the former Dorothy Crawford McNeil, an operatic soprano who sang professionally in Europe and the United States. In the couple's thirteen-room house in Melrose, Massachusetts, a suburb of Boston, he maintains an ethnobotanical library of three thousand volumes. The Schulteses are the parents of Richard Evans Schultes 2d (called Evans), a United Parcel Service manager, and the twins Neil Parker Schultes, a molecular geneticist at the Connecticut Agricultural Institute, and Alexandra Ames Schultes Wilson, a family physician who also teaches at the University of Massachusetts Medical School.

Richard Schultes's many honors include the Order of the Cross of Boyacá, Colombia's highest decoration (1983); the gold medal of the World Wildlife Fund (1984); the Tyler Prize for environmental achievement (1984); and the Lindbergh Award (1991). In 1986 the government of Colombia, in recognition of his contributions to conservation in that country, named a 2.2-million-acre protected tract

Sector Schultes. In 1992 Schultes received the Harvard Medal, for "extraordinary service to the university," and the gold medal of the Linnean Society of London, an award that has been called "botany's equivalent of a Nobel Prize." Three genera and more than 120 species of plants and a large species of Amazonian cockroach bear as part of their scientific appellations the name *Schultes.*

Selected Biographical References: New Yorker 68:35+ Je 1 '92; World 6:17+ My/Je '92 pors; Davis, Wade. The Serpent and the Rainbow (1985); Krieg, Margaret B. Green Medicine (1964); Who's Who in America, 1995

U.S House of Representatives

Schumer, Charles E.
(SHOO-mer)

Nov. 23, 1950- United States Representative from New York. Address: 2412 Rayburn House Office Bldg., Washington, DC 20515.

The publication *Politics in America* has referred to the "outsized" ego of the liberal Democratic congressman Charles E. Schumer, of Brooklyn, New York, and noted that his television talk-show appearances are so frequent that "it is sometimes hard to tell whether he is a guest or a host." Since he was first elected to the House of Representatives, in 1980, Schumer has put his self-confidence and his affinity for the limelight at the service of many causes—including gun control, affordable housing, and consumer advocacy—that touch the everyday lives of his fellow citizens, and he has addressed other issues as well. On the international front, for example, he has urged leniency toward economically depressed debtor nations for the sake of "putting the goal of growth above the goal of full repayment," and he has fought to force Japan to open its financial markets to American firms. In the wake of the April 1995 bombing of a federal office building in Oklahoma City, in which more than 160 people were killed, Schumer introduced President Bill Clinton's antiterrorism bill in the House. "If any member of the House—an immense and impossibly broad institution—can be called ubiquitous," a writer for *Politics in America, 1994* declared, "it is Schumer."

Charles Ellis Schumer was born on November 23, 1950 in Brooklyn, New York, the son of Abraham and Selma (Rosen) Schumer. He grew up in Brooklyn's Flatbush section, which he has represented for more than twenty years, first as a state assemblyman and then as a United States congressman. "My district has been my life," Schumer has said. He has occasionally poked fun at his background, once calling his manner of speaking "a colloquial form of English known as Brooklynese." Schumer's brilliance was evident when he was a young man: he earned an A.B. degree from Harvard University, in Cambridge, Massachusetts, in 1971, graduating magna cum laude, and he went on to receive a law degree, with honors, from Harvard in 1974. He was admitted to the New York Bar in the following year.

Schumer's work in politics began while he was still in law school. He served on the staff of United States senator Claiborne Pell, of Rhode Island, in 1973, and he also worked that year as a volunteer for Stephen J. Solarz, then a member of the New York State Assembly, during Solarz's unsuccessful bid for the Brooklyn borough presidency. When Solarz was first elected to the United States Congress, in 1974, Schumer, by then an associate at the law firm of Paul, Weiss, Ritking, Wharton and Garrison, campaigned successfully for Solarz's old seat in the assembly. Schumer was an assemblyman from 1975 to 1981, serving during that time as chairman of the Committee on Oversight and Investigation and chairman of the Subcommittee on City Management and Governance. During his tenure in the assembly, he developed a reputation for keeping in close touch with the needs of his constituency. In 1980, when Congresswoman Elizabeth Holtzman gave up her seat representing the Sixteenth Congressional District—comprising Flatbush and a few surrounding neighborhoods—to run what would turn out to be a losing race for the Senate, she endorsed Schumer as her successor.

Because the Sixteenth Congressional District had been a Democratic stronghold for more than fifty years, Schumer's real challenge was to win the Democratic primary. One of his opponents, Theodore Silverman, who later ran against Schumer as a Republican in the general election, favored the death penalty and thus attracted the support of the district's many Orthodox Jews. But Schumer, with the best political organization of the pack and with an important endorsement from Edward I. Koch, then the mayor of New York City, won the primary with nearly 60 percent of the vote and easily came out on top in the general election, which was held shortly before his thirtieth birthday.

Schumer arrived in Washington just after President Jimmy Carter had been defeated in his effort for reelection by the Republican Ronald Reagan and the GOP had wrested control of the Senate from the Democrats. That situation made Schumer only more determined to have an impact on congressional proceedings. "If I was a freshman Democrat during the [Democratic president Lyndon B. Johnson's] Great Society, there would have been very little need for Chuck Schumer," he told Steven V. Roberts of the *New York Times* (January 18, 1981). "But with a Republican president and a Republican Senate, there's a real need for my contribution." Schumer's voting record during his first term reflected his willingness to buck the Reagan administration. He opposed Reagan's programs more than 60 percent of the time, voting, for example, against the president's 1981 budget proposal, a balanced-budget amendment, and funding for the MX missile. His stances on those and other matters apparently met with approval in Brooklyn, as he was returned to Congress in 1982.

Indeed, despite that year's redistricting, which changed his jurisdiction from the sixteenth district to the tenth, and a subsequent redrawing of the map ten years later, which forced him to campaign in the new Ninth Congressional District, Schumer has consistently won reelection with more than 70 percent of the vote, and in the general election of 1986 he drew 93 percent of the ballots. He has also held true to his liberal principles over the years, as his votes on a host of issues attest. For example, he came out in support of both a nuclear freeze and the Equal Rights Amendment in 1983, and in the following year he opposed cuts in education spending. In 1986 he voted to block the manufacture of chemical weapons and to impose sanctions against South Africa, which then operated under a system of racial apartheid, over President Reagan's veto. He also voted to override Reagan's veto of the 1988 civil rights bill. He supported another civil rights bill in 1990; got behind the effort to shift funds from the defense budget to domestic programs in 1992; and voted in favor of the "motor voter" registration bill, which allows people to register to vote at motor-vehicle offices (as well as at military-recruitment offices and welfare offices), in 1993. In addition, he has been an unflagging supporter of abortion rights. As a member of the Foreign Affairs Committee, to which he was appointed during the 103d Congress, he has emerged as one of the House's most vocal defenders of Israel.

As a freshman representative, Schumer had decided to leave his family behind in Brooklyn while Congress was in session and commute home on weekends. He moved into a Capitol Hill townhouse, sharing it with three Democrats who were superior to him in rank. That living arrangement was one reason Schumer was able to gain the ear of the party's leadership. He obtained a position on the House Banking Committee and its Housing Subcommittee, where he quickly established himself as a leading spokesman for rent control, a vital issue to the many low- and middle-income families in his district. In the early 1980s, when President Reagan tried to eliminate federal subsidies for rental housing, Schumer fought hard against that policy, saying, "Rent control has become a bugaboo for people who want to blame the ills of the housing market on somebody." He also proposed a federal policy, passed into law in 1983, under which grants would be given to cities for construction and renovation in areas suffering housing shortages.

In 1983 Schumer devoted considerable attention to international finances, in the belief that, as he has put it, "unemployment in Pittsburgh and Detroit is related to debt in Nigeria and Brazil." In that spirit, he proposed an amendment to an appropriation bill for the International Monetary Fund that relieved developing nations of some of their debt by forcing banks to accept lower interest rates and longer payment schedules. The amendment also prevented the IMF from forcing countries, in return for funds, to adopt such potentially harmful and unpopular measures as cutting social programs and raising taxes. Schumer argued in an op-ed piece in the *New York Times* (October 24, 1983), one of many such pieces he has written for that newspaper over the course of his career, that easing repayment terms would "improve the chances banks will be repaid" and "promote political stability in Latin America." After Schumer's proposal failed on the House floor, the House Banking chairman, Democrat Fernand J. St. Germain of Rhode Island, drafted an ultimately successful compromise amendment that included many of Schumer's ideas.

During the mid-1980s Schumer focused on immigration, as a member of the House Subcommittee on Immigration, Refugees, and International Law. He tried to help rescue a bill intended to reform the nation's immigration laws, even though he had not been part of its creation. The bill died in a House conference in 1984, but Schumer became a key player in the efforts to get it passed in 1985 and 1986. "The Simpson-Mazzoli bill, first put forward in 1980, would institute a two-pronged immigration policy," he wrote in an op-ed piece for the *New York Times* (May 21, 1985). "To solve the problem of millions of foreigners who live here illegally and unprotected, it would gradually allow many of them to become full-fledged Americans. To alleviate the problems of the millions more who enter illegally every year—leaping ahead of those waiting for visas and taking jobs while millions of Americans can't find work—the bill outlined a system of penalties, targeted at employers, to deter new illegal immigrants." The two major objections to the resuscitated bill concerned the amount of money that would have to be spent on naturalizing immigrants and the possibility that sanctions against employers would bring about discrimination against legal aliens. By 1986 compromise provisions dealing with funding and anti-immigrant bias were worked out, but there remained a disagreement between farmers, who had historically relied on illegal aliens to harvest crops, and the farm workers' union, which represented the interests of the aliens in agricultural jobs.

A Brooklyn congressman may have seemed an unlikely choice to be the central player in farm-labor matters, but Schumer's objectivity on the agriculture issue led to his being accepted by all sides as an honest negotiator. In his view, the passage of an immigration bill was "a real institutional test for Congress in the twentieth century: can the general interest transcend the specific interest?" He hammered out a compromise that allowed foreign workers to pick perishable crops and linked it to a program designed to protect alien labor from exploitation. The landmark immigration bill passed during the Ninety-ninth Congress.

The mid-to-late 1980s also saw Schumer increase his involvement in financial affairs, following his appointment to the powerful Budget Committee. "Schumer was the personal favorite of those making the assignments," according to *Politics in America, 1988*. "They chose him, then settled down to haggling over the rest of the selections." One reason for his popularity among his colleagues was his pragmatism: despite his tendency to air his views strongly and publicly, he was willing to make compromises. "I've always had the feeling that if you want to stand on your white horse and just make speeches and not compromise, then don't be in Congress," he has said. "It's legitimate, but you really belong on the outside pushing Congress." Schumer took an active role in the battle to cap skyrocketing credit-card interest rates. That effort failed to get out of subcommittee, but he became so publicly tied to the issue that mail addressed to "Credit Cards, Washington, D.C." was delivered to his office. Through compromise, Schumer was able to pass a bill during the One Hundredth Congress that forces banks to disclose more fully the terms and provisions of credit-card agreements.

The issue that solidified Schumer's role as a congressional leader was the savings and loan crisis, which he had foreseen as early as 1985, after the failure of a small number of federally insured thrifts. "Revolutionary change began in the 1970s when the deregulation of money occurred and people could charge anything for interest," Schumer explained to Nathaniel C. Nash of the *New York Times* (May 12, 1985). "In an era I call 'go-go' banking, banks had to compete for deposits and find different places to put their money to make the spread they were accustomed to. So they put their money in riskier ventures. What does that mean? More banks are going to fail."

Indeed, two years later the nation's savings and loan associations suffered record losses. When a bill calling for a $132 billion bailout of savings and loan institutions came under consideration by Congress, Schumer led the call for stricter capital standards to be included as a condition of the rescue effort. He told Jill Dutt of *New York Newsday* (July 24, 1989) that he had never envisioned a key role for himself in the debate. "I was prepared on this bill to be the sort of voice in the wilderness, saying, 'It's not a good bill, I can't go along with it, how can we spend all this money and not toughen things up?' Instead, much to my delight, Congress came around to the view that I had." Schumer argued that a future crisis could be averted only by forcing thrifts to raise a substantial amount of new funds. After he helped to redraft the legislation, he described it to Dutt: "The theme of the bill is the thrift operator who has to have his or her own capital in the institution—his or her own money, up front. They can't just use the depositors' money for any godforsaken investment. That will make them, with the flick of a wand, much more careful."

The bailout bill made some strange political bedfellows, as Schumer found himself siding with the Republican president George Bush against many House Republicans. Still, he strongly opposed Bush's decision to keep the expense of the bailout separate from the federal budget. The bill, with Schumer's additions, passed in August 1989, but the congressman was still arguing over the funding aspect a year later: "When the cost of the bailout was placed off budget, the America people lost," Schumer wrote. "Interest payments on this money are going to cost taxpayers at least $300 billion over the next forty years. Almost more disheartening, putting the cleanup off budget whetted the ambition of many administration officials to sweep the thrift crisis under the rug. Some now want 'continuous authorization' of bailout funds—a fine-print way of guaranteeing that politicians will never again have to ask, publicly, for new money to cover mounting costs."

By the late 1980s Schumer had become a well-known public figure who was as effective at generating press coverage of his work as he was at crafting legislation, as evidenced by his withering questioning of James G. Watt, the former secretary of the interior under President Reagan. When Watt appeared in 1989 before the Banking Committee, which was investigating influence peddling at the Department of Housing and Urban Development, Schumer confronted him about the $420,000 consulting fee he had gotten from HUD soon after leaving office. "Was it moral what you did?" an outraged Schumer asked. "Were you lured by the crumbs of subsidies? Were you? Everyone in this room sees the hypocrisy of what you've done." A bill to reform HUD procedures, written largely by Schumer, was passed by Congress, and Schumer included in it housing provisions to create new rental property. In 1990 he was instrumental in the passage of a legal-immigration reform bill that changed the system by which visas were issued. Under the new law, individuals from countries that had been practically excluded under the old system were given opportunities to come to the United States.

Schumer saw his political capital take a temporary dip in 1991, after he voted against the use of force to oust Iraqi forces from Kuwait—a military campaign that received the overwhelming support of the American public. In an interview with the *New York Times* (April 7, 1991) Schumer insisted that his vote had not been a mistake. "I'm at peace with it," he said. "I wish, in a sense, I had the moral certitude of some of my friends who were very much opposed to the war and some of my friends who were very much for the war, but I agonized over it, and I think my district did too."

Schumer came into the national spotlight yet again in 1991, when he was selected by his fellow Democrats on the Judiciary Committee to lead the Crime and Criminal Justice Subcommittee. He wasted no time in working to change the public perception that Democrats were soft on crime. "The bottom line is that I think Democrats have a lot to say on the issue—with solutions," he said. Schumer spearheaded the effort to pass the so-called Brady Bill, named for the former White House press secretary James Brady, who had been severely wounded in the 1981 assassination attempt against President Reagan. The bill, which called for a waiting period before the purchase of a handgun so that authorities could check the buyer's background, was finally passed into law in 1994. In the meantime, Schumer had been the chief House sponsor of the Clinton administration's sweeping anticrime bill, which included an appropriation of more than twenty billion dollars for the rest of the decade to build new prisons, hire more police officers, expand federal law enforcement, and beef up crime prevention and treatment programs. In November 1993 the Senate passed a version of the bill that included a ban on semiautomatic assault weapons.

Schumer's actions made him an enemy of the powerful gun lobby headed by the National Rifle Association (NRA). In April 1994 the NRA took out a full-page ad in *USA Today* that featured a picture of Schumer with the headline "The Criminal's Best Friend in Congress." The ad accused Schumer of trying to "rob" the crime bill of eight billion dollars earmarked for prison construction and put it toward treatment and recreation programs that would "coddle" criminals. In addition to the newspaper campaign, the NRA purchased airtime on CNN for a commercial with a similar message. Schumer displayed a copy of the ad on the House floor and claimed the NRA attack was really about gun control. "But if they make that public, they can't win because they don't have the support," he said, as quoted by the *New York Times* (April 13, 1994). "So they've set up this subterfuge. They don't give a darn about the crime bill." The NRA campaign against Schumer provoked the condemnation of, among others, Attorney General Janet Reno, who wrote a letter to the *New York Times* (April 20, 1994) that said in part, "I can state unequivocally that I have never met a public official more dedicated to fighting crime than Mr. Schumer."

In the summer of 1994, after the crime bill, with the assault-weapons ban attached, had failed to pass the House, leaders of the House and Senate met to reconcile the differences between the bills. The House leadership told Schumer that he would have to give up the ban in order to ensure passage of the legislation. Schumer, however, refused to concede and pleaded for a few more days to try to get the eight additional votes needed to pass the bill with the ban intact. Targeting a group of moderate Republicans, he set his sights in particular on Mike Castle, a former governor of Delaware, whom he felt might be brought around to his point of view. Castle became the go-between through which the Democratic leadership communicated with Newt Gingrich, the Republican leader, whose seemingly endless list of counterdemands drove Schumer to a rare fit of frustration and despair. In the end, however, cooler heads in the Democratic Party prevailed, an agreement with the Republicans was reached, and the crime bill—with the assault-weapons ban included—passed.

After the national election in November 1994, in which the Democrats lost control of both the House and the Senate for the first time in four decades, Schumer did not mince words about the causes of his party's troubles: "Any Democrat who wants to revitalize the party has to start from the basic premise that while there were lots of other factors, the Democratic Party was ultimately to blame for the election fiasco. Yes, the Republicans were nasty. Yes, right-wing talk radio emphasized the negative. But those kinds of things can only succeed when there's a vacuum, and we created the vacuum." That mea culpa did not prevent Schumer from attacking the Republicans and their policies head-on. In January 1995, immediately after the new, Republican-controlled Congress convened for the first time, Schumer released a report, prepared by his staff, detailing what he claimed would be the enormous cost to his constituents of the legislation proposed in the Contract with America—the set of policy goals, including a balanced-budget amendment and a lower capital-gains-tax rate, on which the Republicans had campaigned. "To the surprise of no one who knows him," as Joyce Purnick phrased it in the *New York Times* (January 9, 1995), Schumer publicized the report at a news conference, which he had "timed . . . for maximum coverage."

In the wake of the terrorist bombing of the Alfred P. Murrah Federal Building in Oklahoma City, on April 19, 1995, Schumer introduced President Clinton's Omnibus Counterterrorism Act in the House. As he argued in a *New York Times* (April 28, 1995) op-ed piece, the proposed legislation would allow the federal government to combat terrorism effectively while preserving civil liberties. The act, he explained, would "allow the government to deport aliens who lay the groundwork for domestic terrorism" and would "surely be expanded to deal more fully with home-grown terrorism." He suggested that changes be made in existing guidelines so that the FBI would "know the extent of its investigative authority" and would not simply "investigate a group that did not 'smell right.'" Schumer wrote that the bill would "satisfy liberals and conservatives" and "produce the bipartisanship necessary for passage."

The anticipated bipartisan support failed to materialize, however, and initial attempts to win passage of the antiterrorism bill ended in defeat. Some political observers blamed the failure on conservative congressman, who opposed the bill because they felt that it gave federal agencies such as the FBI too much power. The conservatives' concerns took center stage during the summer of 1995, when the House Judiciary Committee held hearings on the federal siege of the Branch Davidian cult compound near Waco, Texas in 1993, in which about eighty cult members died. Contending that the hearings were a forum for hard-line Republicans to curry favor with constituents who oppose gun control by embarrassing the federal law-enforcement agencies that took part in the raid, Schumer accused the committee leadership of having forged an unethical alliance with the NRA, and he made public an instance in which an NRA consultant had posed as a Judiciary Committee staffer in order to interview a prospective witness.

Joyce Purnick referred to Charles Schumer, known to his friends as Chuck, as "an affable cross between the hard-working grind who makes the honor roll and the popular guy who becomes senior class president." Charles B. Rangel, a Democratic congressman from the New York City borough of Manhattan, expressed similar thoughts about his colleague's high profile: "We in Congress joke about Chuck. He's very ambitious. But he does his homework." For his part, Schumer considers his visibility to be an important aspect of his ability to do his job. He told Purnick, "I think that in this modern world, the media is not an end in itself. It's a means to getting things done. If I have an obsession, it's getting things done, and the power I have is the power of ideas and communication abilities. So I spend a good amount of time with the media. I don't apologize for it." Schumer continues to divide his time between his townhouse in Washington, D.C., and his home in Brooklyn, where his wife, Iris Weinshall—whom he married in 1980—and their two children reside.

Selected Biographical References: N Y Times I p30 Ap 7 '91 por; Politics in America, 1994; Who's Who in America, 1995

Shalikashvili, John

(shah-lee-kahsh-VEE-lee)

June 27, 1936- Chairman of the Joint Chiefs of Staff. Address: United States Department of Defense, Room 2E872, The Pentagon, Washington, DC 20318-9999

On October 25, 1993 John Shalikashvili, a native of Poland, was sworn in as the first foreign-born chairman of the Joint Chiefs of Staff, succeeding Colin L. Powell. A four-star general whose previous post was supreme allied commander of United States forces in Europe and of the North Atlantic Treaty Organization, Shalikashvili is the principal military adviser to the president of the United States, the secretary of defense, and the National Security Council, with responsibility for overseeing the United States Army, Navy, Air Force, and Marines. His Joint Staff includes fourteen hundred employees, most of whom are military analysts, distributed among eight directorates devoted to such areas as manpower, intelligence, operations, strategic planning, and communications.

When Shalikashvili assumed the post of chairman of the Joint Chiefs of Staff, the United States military forces faced unique challenges because of the shrinking budgets, base closures, and personnel reductions brought about by the end of the Cold War. As envisioned by Shalikashvili, the multiple purposes of the military are to deter war, to fight with resolve when deterrence fails, to participate in multinational peacekeeping arrangements, and to provide humanitarian relief to refugees. Ideally, he has said, military action of any kind should be undertaken only in cases that are characterized by clearly defined objectives, acceptable costs, widespread public support, a high likelihood of success, and the possibility of withdrawal without loss of credibility. "I firmly believe we have a strategy that requires us to be able to fight and win in two near-simultaneous major contingencies," he said in an interview with Tad Szulc for *Parade* magazine (May 1, 1994). "We have a force structure that is very lean but sufficient to accomplish its present and future missions. To be able to do that task, the readiness of the force has to be top-notch. Every last soldier and airman and marine and sailor has to be trained to the utmost. And all equipment must function perfectly."

John Malchase David Shalikashvili was born on June 27, 1936 in Warsaw, the second of the three children of Dmitri Shalikashvili, who hailed from the Soviet republic of Georgia, and Maria (Ruidiger) Shalikashvili, a Pole of half-German, half-Russian ancestry. Shalikashvili has forebears in the military on both sides of his family. His maternal grandfather served as a tsarist general, and his father fought with the monarchist White Army against the Red Army during the Russian Civil War, which lasted from 1918 to 1921. Soon after the war, Dmitri Shalikashvili became a training officer in the cavalry in Poland, where he met and married Maria Ruidiger, a refugee from St. Petersburg. Shalikashvili's maternal grandmother, then a flour-mill owner in Lublin, had at one time been a lady-in-waiting to the tsarina in St. Petersburg. "As I was growing up, my mother told me vivid stories about court life in St. Petersburg, about Rasputin, and about the family's flight from St. Petersburg after the Communists took over," John Shalikashvili recalled in an interview with Claudia Dreifus for the *New York Times Magazine* (May 21, 1995).

The Shalikashvilis were separated after Germany invaded Poland in September 1939. During the invasion Dmitri Shalikashvili defended his adopted land as a member of the cavalry, which surrendered to the Nazis after a few weeks. Briefly imprisoned, he was released with the help of his wife, who had relatives in Germany. In 1942, hoping to fight for Georgia's independence, he became a liaison officer for the German-organized Georgian Legion, which was instead sent to help repel the Allied invasion of Normandy in June 1944. Following the Allied liberation of France, he was transferred to a Georgian battalion in Italy under the command of the Waffen SS, Hitler's elite shock troops. John Shalikashvili did not learn about this part of his father's life until his confirmation hearings, nearly fifty years later.

Meanwhile, since 1942 the Shalikashvilis had been living in an elegant six-room apartment in Warsaw. In August 1944 the Polish Resistance waged a full-scale rebellion against the German occupiers, who crushed the sixty-three-day uprising with artillery shelling and bombing. With the Resistance forces fighting in the barricaded streets, Maria Shalikashvili moved her family into the basement. "All of us . . . were living on a shoestring," Othar Shalikashvili, John's older brother, now a retired United States Army colonel, recalled to John Lancaster of the *Washington Post* (September 21, 1993). "There was no water, no electricity, and essentially no food." In his interview with Claudia Dreifus, Shalikashvili himself said, "I remember moving through sewers because you couldn't get from one side of the street to the other. I remember being bombed in Warsaw and the building collapsing over us. I saw these things not with fear, but somewhat as an adventure. Children can be so resilient." With advancing Soviet forces poised on the outskirts of Warsaw, the victorious Germans evacuated residents from the city. Maria Shalikashvili and her children were transported by cattle car to a transit camp in eastern Germany. From there they traveled to Pappenheim, a Bavarian village, where they lived in a castle on the estate of wealthy relatives. The family was reunited when Dmitri Shalikashvili, who had been captured by the British in 1945, was released in 1946.

Sponsored by a branch of the Episcopal church and by relatives who were willing to conceal the Nazi connection, John Shalikashvili and his family immigrated to the United States in 1952 and settled in Peoria, Illinois. His father got a job in the accounting department of the local utilities company, and his mother went to work as a bank clerk. Enrolling as a junior at Peoria Central High School, Shalikashvili took a full course load, and after school he improved his English-language skills by watching John Wayne movies. It did not take him long to become assimilated. He joined the German and soccer clubs, played tennis, and competed in track, cross-country, and table tennis. A good student, he received a scholarship to Bradley University in Peoria, which he attended while living at home. He joined the Young Republicans and pledged a fraternity. He graduated with a B.S. degree in mechanical engineering in June 1958, a month after becoming a United States citizen and a month before he was drafted by the army. "An exciting three months for me," he remarked to Dreifus.

As a college freshman, Shalikashvili had enrolled in the Air Force ROTC, but his plans to become a pilot were thwarted because of his imperfect eyesight. "After that, I convinced myself that I really didn't want to be in the service," he told Dreifus. He nonetheless joined willingly when he received his draft notice in 1958. After serving the first six months of his hitch in Missouri and Arkansas as a private, Shalikashvili was selected for officer candidate school at Fort Sill, Oklahoma in 1959. Later that year he was commissioned a second lieutenant of artillery. His first field command, over a mortar platoon in Alaska from 1959 to 1960, proved to be so enjoyable that he decided to make the military his career. It was not until 1968, after stints in Fort Bliss, Texas and in West Germany, that he first experienced combat. By then he had attained the rank of major and had been assigned as a senior district adviser to South Vietnamese forces in Trieu Phong, an area rife with Viet Cong soldiers, just south of the North Vietnamese border. He earned a Bronze Star for leading an attack upon two enemy-held islands, but his responsibilities there went beyond fighting. He also helped supervise rice production, advised and trained the local militia, organized elections, and took part in various other political activities.

As he advanced in his career, Shalikashvili simultaneously furthered his education and broadened his experience to include personnel management, logistics, operations, and politico-military strategy. In 1970 he earned a master's degree in international affairs from George Washington University, in Washington, D.C. He has also completed courses of study at the Naval War College, in Newport, Rhode Island, and the United States Army War College, in Carlisle, Pennsylvania.

In 1971 Shalikashvili attained his first staff position, that of operations officer in South Korea. In 1975 he assumed command of an artillery battalion in Fort Lewis, Washington, and four years later he became a division artillery commander in Germany. In 1981 he began honing his diplomatic skills as chief of the Politico-Military Division, Office of the Deputy Chief of Staff for Operations and Plans at the Pentagon's Department of the Army. Promoted to brigadier general in 1983, he became deputy director of strategy, plans, and policy for the same organization, later advancing to director as a major general. Retired general Robert W. Riscassi, then his superior, recalled that Shalikashvili often took a moderate stance on reducing medium-range nuclear missiles in Europe. "There were camps that said we can't give up one iota of anything, and those who said maybe there are some things we can give up," Riscassi told Lancaster. "He just brought logic to the table. . . . His forte is knowledge." From 1987 to 1989 Shalikashvili served as Commander of the Ninth Infantry Division, in Fort Lewis. After receiving a promotion to lieutenant general, he returned to Germany, where he served as deputy commander in chief of the United States Army in Europe for two years.

Shalikashvili's next assignment marked a turning point both in his career and in the role of the United States military. In April 1991 he assumed command of Operation Provide Comfort, the largest humanitarian relief effort to that date. Involving a total of about twenty-three thousand troops from the United States, Britain, France, Italy, Spain, and the Netherlands, it provided food, clothing, and relocation services to about seven hundred thousand Kurdish refugees who had fled the troops of Iraqi leader Saddam Hussein in the wake of the war in the Persian Gulf. (After allied troops led by the United States had defeated the Iraqi army, Kurdish forces had taken over several cities in northern Iraq; the suppression of that uprising had created the refugee crisis.) Camped in the mountainous regions of the Iraqi-Turkish border, the refugees were dying at the rate of about a thousand a day. Compounding the difficulties Shalikashvili faced in saving them were diplomatic considerations, such as how to deal with the lack of full support for the effort from Turkey. The Turks feared becoming host to a permanent refugee population, especially one that had long sought to establish its own homeland, and as a result, the relief camps had to be set up in northern Iraq. (Dominated by foreigners since the fourth century B.C., in this century the Kurds had been fighting intermittently for an independent Kurdistan—comprising large areas of land now part of Turkey, Iraq, Iran, and Syria—since the 1920s.)

The implementation of Operation Provide Comfort was judged a remarkable achievement. "It was an incredibly successful thing to have returned half a million Kurds to their country, many to their homes, in a period of basically eight weeks," Morton I. Abramowitz, then the United States ambassador to Turkey, told Lancaster. "This required constant improvisation." One crucial decision Shalikashvili had made was to build the refugee camps in such a way that they would not survive the first winter. "If you make them permanent," he told Szulc, "they will be there—and we will have created another Gaza Strip. Today, there isn't a single camp anywhere. That, to me, is probably as satisfying as that we returned them to their own towns and villages." In December 1991 the United Nations Office of the High Commissioner for Refugees reported that about two hundred thousand Kurds had been driven back into the mountains by Iraqi shelling in the area around the cities of Erbil and Sulaymaniya.

Shalikashvili has credited Operation Provide Comfort with expanding his view of the role the military could play in the world. "That was the first time that I saw firsthand what an enormous capacity the armed forces have for doing good," he told Szulc. Since then, the scope of American military involvement in relief missions has increased dramatically. American peacekeeping forces stationed in famine-ravaged Somalia from December 1992 to March 1994 allowed food distribution to proceed securely. Just before the American troops withdrew from Somalia—and five months after he was appointed chairman of the Joint Chiefs of Staff—Shalikashvili flew there to tell them, "Your victory is counted by how many people are alive today." A few months later, American military personnel were dispatched to help alleviate the refugee crisis in Zaire that had been precipitated by the exodus of two million people from neighboring Rwanda, where a genocidal civil war had left half a million dead. "We have a capacity like almost no one else to help with tragedies of the magnitude we're witnessing now in Rwanda," Shalikashvili said, as quoted by Eric Schmitt of the *New York Times* (July 31, 1994). "But we also at the same time need to strengthen the United Nations so they can do more on their own without always having to call upon us, or that we don't have to play as large a part."

Another problem confronting the United States military during Shalikashvili's watch was a political crisis in Haiti, where people loyal to the country's first freely elected president, Jean-Bertrand Aristide, who had been exiled, frequently clashed with forces of Lieutenant General Raoul Cédras, who had come to power in a coup d'état. After Haitians began to flee the island en masse in mid-1994, the United States government devised a plan to invade the country to force Cédras to step down. As it turned out, Cédras agreed to relinquish power while United States invasion forces were en route to the nation. By the time they landed on Haitian soil, the mission of the American troops had thus been switched from "invade" to "stabilize"—though not to maintain law and order, as Shalikashvili explained at a White House briefing. "The task of keeping law and order in Haiti is the responsibility of the Haitian police force and the Haitian military," he said. "We are not in a business of doing day-to-day law and order, for that matter resolving or quelling any demonstrations, unless these demonstrations or this level of violence becomes so great that it threatens the overall stability and the security of our multinational forces, and then we will intercede." On October 15, 1994, after Cédras had resigned and accepted exile, Aristide was reinstated, and on March 31, 1995 responsibility for peacekeeping was transferred to UN forces.

The most intractable situation Shalikashvili has faced in recent years is the ethnic strife in the former Yugoslavia. When the current crisis in the Balkans began, with the June 1991 declarations of independence of Croatia and Slovenia from the Serb-dominated government of Yugoslavia, Shalikashvili had just completed Operation Provide Comfort. From August 1991 to June 1992 he served as assistant to Colin Powell, who was then the chairman of the Joint Chiefs of Staff. During that period fighting broke out between secessionist Croats and minority Serbs who resisted the secession. A UN-monitored cease-fire, which was violated frequently, was declared in early 1992 and coincided with the arrival in the area of UN peacekeeping forces, which eventually expanded to more than twelve thousand in Croatia and twenty-three thousand in Bosnia and Herzegovina, which had also erupted in violence. In spring 1992, after a Muslim-dominated government was elected in Bosnia and Herzegovina, the large Serbian minority rebelled and seized territory with help from Serbs in Serbia. By late 1992, when Serbian nationalists had gained control of roughly 72 percent of Bosnia and Herzegovina, the course of Shalikashvili's career had brought him much closer to the Balkan conflict. In June 1992 he had earned his fourth star as a general when he became supreme allied commander of United States forces in Europe and of NATO, a position he held until he assumed the chairmanship of the Joint Chiefs of Staff in October 1993.

There have been indications that Shalikashvili may have wanted NATO to act swiftly and decisively early in the conflict but that Powell had strongly opposed direct military intervention. The Bosnian crisis is "a lesson to all of us of the importance of America's leadership [and of] the price we pay when it isn't there," Shalikashvili said in June 1993, as quoted by Tim Weiner of the *New York Times* (August 12, 1993). "The United States did not lead in this operation from the very beginning, as it did in previous crises. America's leadership was not there." Shalikashvili declined to state explicitly what should have been done. He has said that air strikes would probably have been ineffective and that sending in sufficient numbers of NATO ground forces would have been politically unrealistic.

After three years of fighting that left two hundred thousand dead and a million homeless, NATO began launching air strikes against Bosnian Serb military targets in the summer of 1995. In September of that year, the warring parties in Bosnia signed an accord that was negotiated by Assistant Secretary of State Richard C. Holbrooke. The prospect that the accord may lead to a peace agreement, which would undoubtedly have to be enforced by the UN and/or NATO, prompted the Clinton administration to begin arguing for the sending of American troops to help NATO patrol new borders and protect humanitarian relief workers. Many Republican senators have questioned the need for American involvement, expressing frustration with the apparent inability of the Europeans to handle the Balkan crisis themselves. Testifying before the Senate Armed Services Committee in September 1995, Shalikashvili said, "We, as the leader of that alliance, cannot step away from the alliance when they are then asked to go and perform what I think will be a very challenging task. We cannot come in and out of the alliance and choose to lead when it's to our benefit and let them take the lead when we don't wish to. This is an alliance that has been built around the core of American leadership." According to a *USA Today*/CNN/Gallup Poll in October 1995, 67 percent of respondents favor sending American troops to Bosnia as long as none of them is killed, but only 21 percent would still approve of the deployment if the death toll were to rise to four hundred. Seeming to cover all bases, Shalikashvili has argued for strength in numbers, contending that the deployment must be large enough to take care of itself if threatened. The most serious threat to American national security, according to the general, lies neither in the Balkans nor elsewhere in the world. "The greatest demon," he told Dreifus, "is our own complacency, our sense that the world is safe and that we don't have to worry."

John Shalikashvili is regarded by his peers as "low-key, straightforward, self-effacing, and informal," John Lancaster wrote, "a four-star general who addresses his friends as 'turkeys' and answers his phone with a casual 'John Shali.'" Claudia Dreifus found the general to be "witty, thoughtful, [and] accessible. . . . He fudges rarely, and laughs often, sometimes at the ironies of his life story." Fluent in German, Polish, and Russian as well as English, Shalikashvili was asked by Dreifus whether he considers himself a man of the New World or the Old World. "The preponderance must be New World," he replied. "The proof of it is whenever I spend any time overseas, I am just delighted to come back to the United States. . . . I like more of what this country stands for." He lives in a three-story home in Fort Myer, Virginia with his wife, the former Joan E. Zimpelman, a full-time homemaker who volunteers her services on behalf of military families. Married since December 27, 1966, the Shalikashvilis have one grown son, Brant. Shalikashvili's first wife, Gunhild Bartsch, whom he had married in 1963, died in May 1965.

Selected Biographical References: Chicago Tribune I p1+ Ag 12 '93 por; N Y Times A p22 Ag 12 '93 por; N Y Times Mag p34+ My 21 '95 por; New Repub 209:13+ S 13 '93; Newsweek 122:14+ Ag 23 '93; Time 142:35 Ag 23 '93 por; U S News 113:69 N 9 '92 por; Vanity Fair 56: 150+ N '93 pors; Who's Who in America, 1995

AP/Wide World Photos, Inc.

Sharpton, Al, Jr.

Oct. 3, 1954- Baptist minister; political activist; politician. Address: 1133 Bedford Ave., Brooklyn, NY 11216

"Al Sharpton is an insurgent, an insurgent who will bring to the public's attention those conditions that ordinary poor black people have to live under," Andrew Cooper, the editor of the *City Sun*, a Brooklyn-based weekly newspaper, told Malcolm Gladwell of the *Washington Post* (June 2, 1994). "That's why people look to him and have no problem following his lead. He is the symbol of our attempt to get through the maze with the truth." Operating primarily in New York City, the Reverend Al Sharpton Jr. has promulgated his "No Justice, No Peace" stance by staging well-orchestrated protest marches to draw attention to what he considers racially motivated murders or other crimes against black people who otherwise might have died or suffered anonymously. From the mid-1980s through the early 1990s, he has been involved with one notorious case after another, including the alleged rape and abduction by white men of Tawana Brawley, a black teenager, whose claims were found by a grand jury to have constituted an elaborate hoax; killings in Howard Beach, Queens and Bensonhurst, Brooklyn; and riots in Crown Heights, Brooklyn.

Sharpton has been widely criticized—and also admired—for using his extensive knowledge of the media to promote his own agenda while ostensibly acting altruistically. "Most public relations people wish they were as good as he is," Dominick Carter, a reporter for the New York radio station WLIB, told Martin Gottlieb and Dean Baquet of the *New York Times* (December 19, 1991). "He knows how to manipulate the press. I mean that as a compliment." Sharpton does not pretend otherwise, acknowledging as much to Gottlieb and Baquet. Referring to his long, wavy hair, his trademark running suits, and his portly frame, he said, "I created Al Sharpton. I wore my hair like this. I dressed like this. I talked like this. I weighed this much. That was my persona. The media just covered it." By the late 1980s he had become so recognizable that he inspired a character in Tom Wolfe's novel of racial and class tensions in New York City, *The Bonfire of the Vanities* (1987).

By 1992, when Sharpton first ran in a Democratic primary for the United States Senate, his image had been overhauled to increase his appeal to mainstream voters. Although he lost that primary election, coming in third in a field of four, his showing was respectable enough to convince him to try again in 1994. His second attempt was also a failure, in that he lost to the Democratic incumbent, but he captured a larger percentage of the vote than he had two years earlier. The philosophy he had espoused in an interview with Mike Sager for *Esquire* (January 1991) perhaps explains why his electoral defeats have not discouraged him from running in future elections. "To a white mind, it's tangible wins and losses that count in the world," he told Sager, "so you can look at it like this: I got money in black banks, a seat on the MTA board, Howard Beach, Bensonhurst. Those, you could say, are wins. Brawley and them others might be losses. That's to a white mind. But to a black mind, I'm successful 'cause I'm still here."

Sharpton has been agitating for justice for African-Americans for as long as he can remember. "I yelled when I was hungry," he has said in speeches, describing his earliest protests in infancy. "I yelled when I was wet. I yelled when all those little black bourgeois babies stayed dignified and quiet. I learned before I got out of the maternity ward that you've got to holler like hell sometimes to get what you want." Alfred Charles Sharpton Jr. was born on October 3, 1954 in the Crown Heights section of the New York City borough of Brooklyn, the son of Al Sharpton Sr., a successful carpenter/contractor, and Ada Sharpton, a seamstress who had a son and a daughter from a previous marriage. A few years after Sharpton's birth, the family, which included his older sister, Cheryl, moved into a two-family home in the middle-class neighborhood of Hollis, in the borough of Queens.

From his earliest years, Sharpton's life was centered upon religion, particularly through the Washington Temple Church of God in Christ in Brooklyn, a Pentecostal church whose pastor, Bishop Frederick Douglas Washington, fascinated him. Baptized at the age of three, Sharpton preached his first sermon, titled "Let Not Your Heart Be Troubled," a year later, before he had learned to read or write. At the age of ten he was fully ordained as a Pentecostal minister. In the same year, his father deserted the family and withdrew all financial support, thrusting them into poverty. Ada Sharpton supported her children by working first as a domestic and later as a machinist. After living in a housing project for a year, they moved into what Sharpton has described as a "five-room ghetto apartment" in Brooklyn's Brownsville section.

The reduction in his standard of living did not escape the notice of the young minister, who acquired a keen awareness of social contrasts and inequalities. "I knew that the world was better than this," he told Catherine S. Manegold in an interview for the *New York Times Magazine* (January 24, 1993). "In the project, I thought: 'No, I don't have to accept this. I know there's a better life. I know there's good schools. I know that the garbage man picks up garbage in some neighborhoods, because I lived in them.' So that really gave me indignation." Sharpton became politically active at an early age. At various times throughout his educational career, he served as class orator, associate editor of the school newspaper, student council president, and leader of several student committees devoted to peace and civil rights. He also served as a student intern to Jule Sugarman, then New York City's human-resources administrator.

As a teenager, Sharpton was influenced by several other prominent African-Americans in addition to Bishop Washington, among them Congressman Adam Clayton Powell Jr., who was also a minister at the Abyssinian Baptist Church in Harlem, and Jesse Jackson, an up-and-coming leader in the national civil rights movement who had been an aide to the Reverend Martin Luther King Jr. In 1968 Sharpton served as the youth coordinator of the unsuccessful congressional campaign of James Farmer of the Bedford-Stuyvesant section of Brooklyn. In the following year Jackson chose Sharpton to be the youth director of the Greater New York chapter of Operation Breadbasket, a food-distribution program under the auspices of King's Southern Christian Leadership Conference.

When he was sixteen Sharpton founded his own political group, the National Youth Movement, whose aims included the eradication of drugs in black neighborhoods, the establishment of internships for teenagers with black entrepreneurs, and training programs for black health-care workers. In 1972, the year he graduated from Tilden High School in Brooklyn, Sharpton was chosen to be the youth director of Congresswoman Shirley Chisholm's presidential campaign. In the same year, Adam Clayton Powell died, but not before he had exhorted Sharpton to carry on for him, as Sharpton recalled in an interview with Peter Noel of the *Village Voice* (August 4, 1992): "Just before Adam died he told me, 'I want to tell you something. These yellow Uncle Toms are taking over the blacks in New York. Don't you stop fighting. If you wanna do something for Adam, get rid of these Uncle Toms.' I think what I am fighting is Adam's fight."

As he entered adulthood, Sharpton was temporarily sidetracked from the political activism of his youth. In 1973 he became closely associated with the soul singer James Brown, whose son, Teddy, had recently been killed in an auto accident. "James sort of adopted me as the son he lost," Sharpton told Joy Duckett Cain of *Essence* (August 1994), "and he became like the father I never had." During much of the 1970s, Sharpton arranged Brown's schedule, promoted his tours, and hired his musicians. He even adopted the singer's hairstyle, reportedly promising not to change it until after Brown's death. Brown introduced Sharpton to Don King, the flamboyant and influential boxing promoter, whose ability to successfully market million-dollar boxing matches was equaled by his affinity for self-promotion. "I did a lot of on-the-job training with people who are masters," Sharpton told Manegold. "To grow up under people like James Brown, Jesse Jackson, and a promoter like Don King, I would have to be totally incompetent not to learn something." The apex of Sharpton's career as a music promoter came in 1984, when he served as a community-relations adviser for the Jacksons' *Victory* tour.

Beginning in the mid-1980s, a series of racial incidents in New York City catapulted Sharpton into the limelight, and his role as an activist and protester increasingly became that of a recognized, albeit controversial, spokesperson for the African-American community. The first of those events was the death, on December 20, 1986, of Michael Griffith, a twenty-three-year-old black construction worker, who was fatally struck by a car after being chased onto a highway by white youths in the Howard Beach area of Queens, New York. His stepfather, Cedric Sandiford, was badly beaten in the attack. A third black man, Timothy Grimes, escaped unharmed. A day after the first anniversary of Griffith's death, Sharpton staged well-attended protests that snarled rush-hour traffic in Brooklyn and Manhattan for hours before the verdict in the first trial of the young white defendants was announced. Some of the protesters became enraged on hearing that no one was convicted of murder; three of the defendants were instead found guilty of manslaughter.

The case that garnered national attention for Sharpton was that of Tawana Brawley, an African-American teenager from Wappingers Falls in Duchess County, New York, who in November

1987 was found nude in a plastic garbage bag, her body covered with excrement and scrawled racial slurs. Brawley, who had been missing for four days, claimed that during that time she had been raped repeatedly by six white men, one of whom she thought was a police officer. After rejecting legal representation by the local chapter of the NAACP, Brawley's family chose Sharpton as their spokesperson and Alton H. Maddox Jr., who had represented Sandiford in the Howard Beach case, and C. Vernon Mason as their lawyers. On January 26, 1988 Governor Mario Cuomo of New York named as special prosecutor Attorney General Robert Abrams, who on February 29 empaneled a grand jury to investigate the case. In the same month, the actor and comedian Bill Cosby and *Essence* magazine publisher Edward Lewis put up a twenty-five thousand dollar reward for information leading to the arrest and prosecution of Brawley's alleged assailants, and the heavyweight boxing champion Mike Tyson contributed fifty thousand dollars to a foundation for young victims of violence; an equal amount was donated by Don King.

The story immediately became a media sensation, fed largely by unsubstantiated allegations originating from Sharpton-organized news conferences about the identities of Brawley's attackers, the "corrupt" American criminal system, a "massive cover-up" by the police, and even a connection to the Irish Republican Army. Sharpton, who advised the Brawleys not to cooperate with the grand jury investigation on the grounds that they could not expect justice from a racist system—a tactic that had produced results in the Howard Beach case—never provided any evidence to support his claims. The American public, which had at first seemed outraged by what allegedly happened to Brawley, soon became skeptical of the story, especially as it began to seem that Sharpton was using his influence to gain name recognition for himself. As his credibility began to suffer, so, too, did that of the silent Brawley, whose "statements" were made exclusively through Sharpton.

In the early months of the Brawley case, a reporter for *New York Newsday* (January 20, 1988) disclosed that Sharpton had been an FBI informant in investigations of organized-crime syndicates and of black civic leaders in the mid-1980s. Sharpton has acknowledged that he helped the FBI—but only in its drug investigations—to gain protection from threats by a certain unnamed mobster in the music industry. Seven months after Brawley's alleged abduction, Sharpton's image was further damaged when Perry McKinnon, a private investigator and former aide to Sharpton, denounced Brawley's trio of advisers, saying that they were fabricating accusations to gain political power for themselves. Having found no evidence of rape (hospital tests in the aftermath of the alleged attack turned up only a minor bruise on Brawley's scalp), the grand jury concluded in October 1988 that the whole affair had been a hoax. Abrams filed judicial complaints against Maddox (whose license was later suspended) and Mason for obstructing the investigation and making false statements about the case, and in 1989 Abrams convened a grand jury that investigated Sharpton on sixty-seven counts of tax evasion, larceny, and fraud. The felony counts were dropped after Sharpton pleaded guilty to the misdemeanor of failing to file a New York State personal-income-tax return for 1986.

The Brawley case generated a lot of publicity for Sharpton, but much of it was negative. A poll conducted in the spring of 1988 by the *New York Times* and a local television station found that although black respondents ranked Sharpton as the best-known African-American political figure in the city, they also gave him a rating that was more unfavorable than that given any other black leader. Writing in the *New Republic* (July 11, 1988), Stanley Crouch observed that the three self-appointed Brawley counselors had "successfully utilized an ethnic version of McCarthyism," in which the enemies are white racists and "rent-a-Toms" who collaborate with their oppressors. Sharpton's self-promotion also received a lot of negative press, but some observers of the Brawley case have credited him with possessing more than just media savvy. "Al Sharpton has gained prominence because he understands that there is in the inner city a constituency for a politics based on resentment, anger, and race hatred," according to Arch Puddington, writing in *Commentary* (January 1991).

In the early 1990s Sharpton, who, along with Maddox and Mason, was overseeing an organization called the United African Movement, again captured national attention by placing himself at the center of another violent crime with racial overtones. In the spring of 1990, a young, white Wall Street professional who was jogging in Central Park was attacked by a group of black and Hispanic teenagers, who raped and beat her nearly to death. Several of the defendants in the case made videotaped confessions to the police about their roles in the attack. As in the Brawley case, Sharpton leveled wild accusations, though this time not at the alleged attackers, but at the victim, charging variously, during protests outside the Manhattan Court House, that her boyfriend had committed the crime or that there had been no crime at all. "During the trial the testimony centered on constitutional rights and forensic evidence," Erika Munk reported in the *Nation* (October 8, 1990). "Meanwhile, the rhetoric outside the courthouse, though violently misogynous, was shouted as if it were a cry for racial justice. . . . Sharpton's demonstrators insisted they were talking race, not gender." Sharpton also helped to raise money for the defendants.

In August 1991 another racially charged crisis erupted in Crown Heights, Brooklyn, when a car driven by a Hasidic man jumped a curb, killing Gavin Cato, a seven-year-old black West Indian boy, and severely injuring his cousin, Angela Cato. Riots immediately broke out throughout Crown

Heights, where underlying tensions between blacks, on the one hand, and Hasidim, on the other, had long been smoldering. Sharpton, then the leader of an organization called the National Action Network, tried to organize some of the rioters to protest the failure of the New York Police Department to charge the driver with murder. In the course of three days of rioting, during which a visiting rabbinical student was killed and 67 civilians and 158 police officers were injured, Sharpton's role became that of negotiator. He met frequently with Mayor David N. Dinkins and other black leaders in order to bring the situation under control and to ensure that the black community's grievances received attention.

By the time he decided to enter the 1992 Democratic primary for the United States Senate seat held by the Republican Alfonse M. D'Amato, Sharpton had apparently realized that his image was sorely in need of renovation. (A 1990 poll by the New York *Daily News* had found that 90 percent of whites and 73 percent of blacks in the city felt Sharpton was worsening, not improving, race relations.) During the campaign he stopped making inflammatory remarks and accusations and began wearing business suits. He also broadened the range of issues he discussed and gathered endorsements from such prominent citizens as filmmaker Spike Lee and Betty Shabazz, Malcolm X's widow. It was not the first time Sharpton had tried to run for political office. In 1978 he had declared his candidacy for the New York State Senate from the Seventeenth District, which included the Ocean Hill-Brownsville area, but his name was removed from the ballot because he had used two different addresses when registering to vote.

Sharpton's luck was much better in 1992. Not only did he get his name on the Democratic ballot automatically, without having to submit nominating petitions, but he also won 15 percent of the vote in the primary election on September 15, including 21 percent of the vote in New York City and 67 percent of the black vote statewide—a surprisingly strong finish in the opinion of most observers. In that election Sharpton came in third in a field of four, trailing both Attorney General Robert Abrams, the victor, and former vice-presidential candidate Geraldine Ferraro, a member of Congress from Queens, and besting New York City comptroller Elizabeth Holtzman. Abrams was defeated by D'Amato in the general election in November by one percentage point, prompting Jim Sleeper to observe in the *New Republic* (September 19-26, 1994) that Sharpton's candidacy may have hurt the Democrats: "Black voters who had turned out heavily for Sharpton that year in his primary against Abrams sat on their hands in November."

Soon after the 1992 congressional elections, Sharpton once more found himself embroiled in controversy. In February 1993 the New York State Court of Appeals refused to hear his appeal of a 1990 criminal trespass and disorderly conduct conviction stemming from the marches he had organized to protest the murder of Michael Griffith. Sentenced to forty-five days in the Brooklyn House of Detention, Sharpton served twenty-five days before being released on March 30. During his imprisonment he fasted, preached to fellow inmates, and read about Martin Luther King Jr.

Meanwhile, Sharpton had never really stopped running for the United States Senate, having kept his campaign offices open as voter registration centers following his defeat in the 1992 primary. In the 1994 primary, he ran against Democratic incumbent Daniel Patrick Moynihan, garnering 26 percent of the vote to Moynihan's 74 percent. (Moynihan went on to triumph over the Republican candidate, Bernadette Castro, in the general election in November, capturing 55 percent of the vote.) In 1995 Sharpton returned to his role as an organizer. His most recent activities have included leading a march from New York City to Albany, the state capital, to protest proposed budget cuts by Republican governor George E. Pataki; traveling to Fairfax, Virginia, the home of Supreme Court Justice Clarence Thomas, to lead a protest against his conservative voting record; and speaking in Washington, D.C., to a huge crowd (estimates raged from four hundred thousand to a million and a half) of black men at the Million Man March rally, organized by Louis Farrakhan, the leader of the Nation of Islam, on October 16, 1995.

Al Sharpton, who in February 1994 was rebaptized into the Baptist faith, has returned in recent years to preaching, giving sermons to the congregations of three different churches in the Brooklyn area. He has recently trimmed nearly seventy pounds off his formerly three hundred-pound frame. Since 1980 he has been married to the former Kathy Lee Jordan, whom he met in 1977 while she was a backup singer for James Brown and who has served in the United States Army reserves since the 1970s. The Sharptons and their two young daughters, Dominique and Ashley, live in Englewood, New Jersey; Sharpton also maintains an apartment and an office in Brooklyn.

In 1993 Sharpton received the National Action Network's Dr. Martin Luther King Jr./Adam Clayton Powell Jr. Memorial Award for his "untiring efforts to keep the legacy of King and Powell alive." In his free time Sharpton enjoys reading history and biography and playing word games with his daughters. His decision to enter mainstream politics has been attributed to his brush with death in January 1991, when he was stabbed in the chest by one Michael Riccardi while leading one of thirty marches that he organized in the Bensonhurst section of Brooklyn to protest the verdicts in the racially motivated August 1989 slaying of Yusuf K. Hawkins, an African-American.

Selected Biographical References: Esquire 115:22+ Ja '91 pors; Essence 25:90+ Ag '94 pors; N Y Times A p1+ Ja 13 '91 por, B p1+ D 19 '91 por; N Y Times Mag p18+ Ja 24 '93 pors; New York 21:36+ Mr 28 '88 pors, 27:36+ Ap 4 '94 pors; New Yorker 68:55+ Ja 25 '93 por

Andrew Eccles/CNN

Shaw, Bernard

May 22, 1940- Broadcast journalist. Address: c/o CNN, 820 1st St. NE, Washington DC 20002-4205

Bernard Shaw, the principal Washington anchor for the Cable News Network, is one of America's most visible black newspeople and one of the country's most distinguished journalists by any standard. Best known for the sober, dispassionate baritone with which he delivers CNN's daily prime-time report, over the years Shaw has also gained recognition for his on-the-scene coverage, on CNN and other networks, of dramatic events around the globe, among them the Jonestown, Guyana mass suicide in 1978, the 1989 Chinese democracy movement, and, pivotally, the 1991 Persian Gulf war. During the last-named event, after every other news communication from Iraq to the world had been shut down, Shaw—together with his CNN colleagues Peter Arnett and John Holliman—reported live from the Al-Rashid Hotel, in Baghdad, as American bombs rained down. Following that journalistic coup, as before, Shaw resisted any attempts to portray him as part of the news story. His credo, which has won him the respect of his colleagues and the viewing public alike, remains one of strict professional integrity. He told Tony Chapelle for the *Black Collegian* (September 1989): "I'm not a personality or a star. Anchors are supposed to be bit players, not prime characters. The news is uppermost."

Bernard Shaw was born on May 22, 1940 in Chicago, Illinois, the son of Edgar Shaw, a housepainter and an employee of the New York Central Railroad, and Camilla (Murphy) Shaw, a housekeeper. Edgar Shaw, who had a passionate interest in current affairs, regularly brought home all four of Chicago's daily newspapers; by early adolescence, Bernard Shaw had inherited his father's appetite for news and his high regard for reporters and newsmakers, including those featured on what was then the fledgling medium of television, where the pioneer broadcast journalist Edward R. Murrow was making his mark. "I used to stand up my dates to watch Murrow specials," Shaw told Chapelle. "He was such a dominant force in television news when I was growing up. I said, 'I want to be like that man.'" Apparently, the absence of African-American television journalists in the 1950s did not cause Shaw to doubt his chances of realizing his goal. "I didn't see (Murrow) as white," Shaw revealed to Chapelle. "I saw him as a journalist."

On Sunday mornings, the teenage Shaw would walk to the Green Door bookstore, on the University of Chicago campus, to purchase the Sunday edition of the *New York Times*, often encountering the well-known Chicago journalist Clifton Utley, whom he would engage in conversation. He actively sought out both print and broadcast reporters, visiting newsrooms to question them about their profession. When he was only twelve years old, Shaw finagled his way into the Democratic National Convention, and he repeated the feat four years later, in 1956. "When I looked up at the anchor booths, I knew I was looking at the altar," he told Laurence Zuckerman of *Time* (February 22, 1988).

As a teenager, Shaw was also an avid baseball player, and he briefly flirted with the idea of trying to make the major leagues. "But I couldn't hit as well as I could pitch," he admitted to Norma Libman of the *Chicago Tribune* (February 9, 1992), and he decided unequivocally to pursue a journalistic career. While at Dunbar High School, Shaw produced morning radio programs over the school's public address system, served as the announcer at basketball games, competed on the debating team, and wrote for the school newspaper. "A sense of pride was deeply ingrained in him, that his family had standards to live up to and he didn't have time to waste on clowning or horseplay," Thelma Ford, one of his English teachers, recalled to Howard Kurtz of the *Washington Post* (January 22, 1991). "Bernie had within him this capacity for talking, for conveying ideas."

Shaw manifested such a high level of intelligence and ability in high school that both his teachers and his classmates expected him to attend a high-prestige university such as Harvard or Yale. The realization that his parents could not afford to send him to college initially devastated Shaw, but he then enlisted in the military as a path to a future college education. From 1959 to 1963 he served with the United States Marine Corps, the branch of the military he had singled out because of its emphasis on discipline.

During the years of his military service, Shaw maintained his focus on his career goal. In 1961, as a twenty-one-year-old corporal stationed in Oahu, Hawaii, he learned that one of his idols, Walter

Cronkite of CBS News, had come to town to film scenes for the show *The Twentieth Century*. Shaw traced Cronkite to the Waikiki Hotel and called his room "about thirty-four times," as he has recalled, in an effort to meet him. "He was the most persistent guy I've ever met in my life," Cronkite later told Howard Kurtz. "I was going to give him five begrudging minutes and ended up talking to him for a half-hour. He was just determined to be a journalist." "I told him, 'One of these days, you and I are going to be colleagues at the same network,'" Shaw recounted in an interview with Peter Benjaminson for *Contemporary Authors* (1987). "Ten years later I was hired by CBS . . . , and I had my first piece on CBS News. And there was this visible smile on Walter Cronkite's face when he said, 'And Bernard Shaw reporting,' as he was introducing the piece I did."

Upon his discharge from the marines, in 1963, Shaw enrolled at the University of Illinois, selecting history as his major. Following up on his earlier contact with disc jockeys and reporters at local radio stations, Shaw, while carrying a full college load, took an unpaid position in the wire room at a rhythm-and-blues station, WYNR. Within a few months, in 1964, the station renamed itself WNUS and switched to an all-news format. Later in the year, when Martin Luther King Jr. came to Chicago to stage a civil rights rally, Shaw talked the management of WNUS into hiring him for fifty dollars a day as the reporter on the scene. "I really hustled," Shaw told Benjaminson. "I worked very hard; I slept very little: a typical instance of a young novice getting an opportunity and going berserk in the process of doing the job. But I did so well they put me on staff."

In 1965 Shaw did his first television work, as a news writer for the Chicago station WFLD, before returning to radio in 1966 as a reporter for WIND, which was owned by the Westinghouse Broadcasting Company. Shaw was working for Westinghouse in Chicago in April 1968 when Martin Luther King Jr. was assassinated. Over two decades later, in a conversation with Lois Romano for *Redbook* (October 1991), Shaw recalled King's assassination as an event that had a lasting impact on his life. He was sent to Memphis, Tennessee to cover the story and was chosen by King's family as one of only two journalists who would join them on the flight to accompany King's body from Memphis to Atlanta. As it turned out, however, he could not make the journey, for he was summoned back to Chicago to cover the riots that had broken out there in the wake of King's murder. "I can still vividly recall standing next to the hearse on the tarmac, tears running down my face as they lifted the coffin onto the plane," Shaw told Romano. "It was one of the saddest days of my life. I felt I was saying goodbye to a man who held so much promise for this country's future."

Later that year, Westinghouse offered Shaw a prestigious promotion: a transfer to Washington, D.C., and an assignment to cover the White House. Shaw was plunged into a dilemma, because acceptance of the promotion would mean he would have to quit college, with one year remaining. In the end, the chance to work in Washington proved to be too tempting to pass up, and Shaw relocated to the nation's capital. There, in 1971, the dream he had had since his youthful idolization of Murrow and Cronkite was fulfilled, when CBS News offered him a job as a reporter. At that time, CBS News held unparalleled status in the profession of television journalism, and its Washington bureau included such luminaries as Dan Rather, Mike Wallace, Marvin and Bernard Kalb, Bob Schieffer, Eric Sevareid, and Roger Mudd. Shaw served as a CBS reporter from 1971 to 1974 and was then promoted to correspondent. During his years with CBS, Shaw covered the White House, the State Department, the Pentagon, and the Supreme Court, and he achieved an enviable feat when, during the time of the Watergate scandal, which led to President Richard Nixon's resignation, in August 1974, he obtained an exclusive interview with John Mitchell, who had resigned his post as attorney general to head Nixon's 1972 reelection campaign.

Although Shaw considered working at CBS to be "the primal experience" of his career, by 1977 he had grown eager to expand his journalistic horizons. Fluent in Spanish, and judging Latin America to be an "undercovered" part of the world, as he has phrased it, Shaw approached the management at CBS about the possibility of becoming a Latin American correspondent. When CBS rejected his proposal, he accepted an offer from ABC to become that network's Latin American bureau chief and correspondent. Based in Coral Gables, Florida, Shaw spent the majority of the next three years out of the country, covering everything from the renegotiation of the Panama Canal Treaty to economic problems in Chile; he also conducted an interview with Cuban president Fidel Castro.

In 1978 Shaw went to the jungles of Guyana to look into rumors of a tragedy there and thus became one of the first journalists to report from Jonestown, where more than nine hundred American followers of the religious cult leader Jim Jones lay dead as the result of a mass suicide. According to Howard Kurtz, Shaw obtained what turned out to be the only aerial photographs of the scene by ordering the pilot of his Lear jet to "fly low over the jungles of Guyana—so low that a stall would have meant certain death." The following year Shaw covered the Nicaraguan revolution, in which the country's dictator-president, General Anastasio Somoza, was ousted. At one point during the months of unfolding revolutionary events, Shaw left Nicaragua for an interview in Panama and was temporarily replaced by ABC News correspondent Bill Stewart. Stewart was killed while on the assignment, and Shaw was left badly shaken and guilt-ridden. "I concluded it would be safer for me back in Washington instead of running around in Latin America," Shaw told Tony Chapelle, citing the fact that he had two young children at the time. "ABC wasn't paying me enough to risk my life like that again."

Returning to Washington, Shaw became ABC's senior Capitol Hill correspondent; he was also chosen by the network to file special reports in late 1979 on the developing crisis in Iran, where radicals had occupied the American embassy in Tehran and taken the embassy staff hostage. Yet the fulfillment of Shaw's ultimate goal, to be a television news anchorman, remained in doubt—at least as far as ABC was concerned. Although Shaw felt he had acquired the requisite experience, having served "in the trenches," as he has put it, locally, nationally, and internationally, there was such a rich pool of talent at ABC that his promotion to anchorperson was far from assured.

Consequently, when ABC's former Washington bureau chief, George Watson, who had left ABC to help start a twenty-four-hour, all-news cable network, offered Shaw the position of chief anchor, Shaw accepted—although not without hesitation. Going to work for a cable news network, for which there was no prototype, seemed an enormous gamble, and Shaw's family responsibilities weighed heavily on his mind. "I walked the dining room floor for two weeks," he told Eleanor Blau of the *New York Times* (February 2, 1988). "The country was in a recession. Inflation was double-digit. ABC offered me a new contract. And I was thinking of going to work for a network that didn't exist." But as he recalled to Laurence Zuckerman for *Time* (February 22, 1988), he eventually decided that as a television reporter in the 1950s, Edward R. Murrow himself had been "on the threshold of the new age" and that CNN presented a similar opportunity for helping to revolutionize journalism. He also concluded, as he revealed in his interview for *Contemporary Authors*, that because "life is very brief," one must "move when the opportunity presents itself." Finally, Shaw's wife, Linda, persuaded him to take the job by telling him, "If you don't and CNN takes off, I won't be able to live with you."

CNN began broadcasting from Atlanta on June 1, 1980, with the staff manifesting a pioneering spirit befitting their work in what Shaw called "the last frontier in television." Gradually what had been dubbed the "Chicken Noodle Network" began to earn respect and to develop a significant viewership. Within its first decade, the company had capitalized on its initial investment of $40 million to reach an estimated value of more than $900 million, and it was operating twenty-one bureaus and broadcasting to more than eighty countries. The network's steady buildup of prestige culminated, in late 1987, in Shaw's joining the anchors Dan Rather of CBS, Peter Jennings of ABC, and Tom Brokaw of NBC in a nationally telecast interview with President Ronald Reagan days before Reagan's summit with Soviet president Mikhail Gorbachev. For those American households that did not receive cable, the interview served as an introduction to Shaw.

In October 1988 Shaw received nationwide, all-network exposure once again, when he acted as the moderator of the second presidential campaign debate between then-vice-president George Bush and the Democratic nominee, Michael S. Dukakis. Shaw later told Iva Sipal, who interviewed him for *Contemporary Black Biography* (1992), that, prior to the debate, he had spent over a day and a half preparing the opening question he would ask each candidate. Posing one of his hypothetical questions to the vice-president, Shaw asked whether or not Bush would be worried about the future of the country under the leadership of his controversial running mate, Dan Quayle, should Bush be elected and die before his inauguration. But it was the question Shaw put to Dukakis that was remembered long after the debate itself: would Dukakis still maintain his opposition to the death penalty, Shaw asked, if someone raped and murdered his wife, Kitty? Many commentators later pointed to Dukakis's reply, a passionless defense of his opposition to capital punishment, as the fatal blow to his candidacy.

In May 1989 Shaw and Dan Rather were the only American television network anchormen reporting live from Beijing, China on the summit visit by Mikhail Gorbachev. Taking advantage of the presence of the international media to publicize, on a grand scale, their demands for democracy, Chinese workers and students began mounting daily demonstrations in Beijing's Tiananmen Square. Those protests soon overshadowed Gorbachev's visit. When the Chinese government sent in the military in early June to crush the peaceful movement, Shaw was on hand to provide continuous live coverage of the massacre that ensued. For his reporting of those events, Shaw received the 1990 Award for Cable Excellence (ACE) for best news anchor and the 1989 National Association of Television Arts and Sciences' News and Documentary Emmy Award for outstanding coverage of a single breaking news story.

As dramatic as Shaw's experience in Beijing was, it was to pale in comparison with his landmark work during the Persian Gulf war. Shaw was in Baghdad in mid-January 1991 for a second interview with Iraqi president Saddam Hussein about his increasingly tense standoff with the United States over Iraq's invasion of Kuwait. Although Hussein abruptly canceled the interview, Shaw went on the air on January 15 and expressed, among other things, the view that a war could be avoided. The next evening, however—after the allied air attacks on Baghdad had begun, the transmissions of ABC, CBS, and NBC had been severed, and reporters from major Western newspapers had fled the country—Shaw found himself reporting from what he called "the center of hell," the ninth floor of the Al-Rashid Hotel. For sixteen-and-a-half hours, until Iraqi officials shut down the CNN phone line, Shaw and his CNN colleagues Peter Arnett and John Holliman offered to the world the only live coverage of the American bombing campaign, reporting via telephone after having lost their visual transmission. "By the time we stopped broadcasting to get some sleep, I was so tired I was making no sense whatsoever," Shaw recalled to

James Brady of *Parade* magazine (June 23, 1991). "I was no sooner in bed and asleep when the bombing started again, and I stumbled down the hall in my pajamas to the suite where we broadcast and went back to work."

The coverage by Shaw, Arnett, and Holliman inspired comparisons to the World War II London broadcasts of Edward R. Murrow, Shaw's boyhood idol. United States secretary of defense Richard Cheney and General Colin Powell, the chairman of the Joint Chiefs of Staff, both praised the CNN broadcasts, and Tom Brokaw acknowledged CNN's primacy by interviewing Shaw for the *NBC Nightly News*. In addition, as Matthew Cooper reported in *U.S. News & World Report* (January 28, 1991), "across the country, more than two hundred news directors at local affiliates often abandoned their own network's feed to get CNN material." Shaw's experience in Iraq would seem to fit what he described to a reporter for *Broadcasting* (April 24, 1989) as the most satisfying type of on-air journalism: "That is what I love about this business, when there are no scripts, when it is not a prepared newscast, and it's you against the world. It is . . . the consummate challenge." In recognition of his work in Baghdad, Shaw was honored with the George Foster Peabody Broadcasting Award as well as the ACE for best newscaster of the year.

In the wake of his success in covering the war, Shaw was not content to rest on his laurels. "So we did extremely well on that story — so what?" he asked Howard Kurtz rhetorically. "Next week we still have to be responsible and accurate and on top of the news. If you sit around fondling the clips, you're going to be in trouble." In the last few years, Shaw has provided coverage of other dramatic breaking stories. For example, in July 1993 he reported live from Tokyo, where President Bill Clinton's economic summit was in progress, and he was on hand to give the first national coverage of the January 1994 earthquake in Los Angeles, going on the air only eight minutes after the earthquake struck.

Shaw, who is one of the few African-Americans to become a network news anchor since Max Robinson broke the color barrier at ABC in the late 1970s, has downplayed the relationship of his race to his work, claiming that he is "just a reporter who also happens to be black." That comment has drawn criticism from some other black journalists, among them A. Peter Bailey, who told Tony Chapelle, "It's a defensive statement. It shows a sense of insecurity around white people, almost like saying, 'You don't have to be nervous about me.'" Shaw disagreed with that assessment, urging Chapelle to "ask Dukakis or Dan Quayle if [Shaw] can be trusted to be easy on them."

Throughout his career, Shaw has steadfastly maintained that the factor of race was never an impediment to his efforts. Following the civil unrest that erupted in Los Angeles in May 1992, after the jury acquittal of four white police officers who had been videotaped beating Rodney King, an African-American, however, he commented to Kenneth R. Clark of the *Chicago Tribune* (May 10, 1992), "Racism is America's society ozone; it permeates everything." Admitting to living with a "controlled rage," he added: "I can afford my controlled rage. People who have jobs, who are gainfully employed, and who get rewards for their efforts and contributions to society, can afford [controlled] rage. It would be insulting presumptuousness on my part to say that people in South Central Los Angeles or elsewhere who are rebelling against what they perceive as injustice should control theirs."

Once called "the Sergeant Joe Friday of anchoring"—a reference to the by-the-book police detective on the television series *Dragnet*—Shaw maintains a consistently dispassionate on-air demeanor, in keeping with what he regards as the seriousness of his work and the objectivity required. In a profile of the journalist for the *Chicago Tribune* (May 14, 1993), however, Allan Johnson reported that "Shaw's on-air persona" seemed "at odds with that of the easygoing, friendly man" Johnson interviewed. Shaw still abides by the advice Walter Cronkite gave him in 1961, to read omnivorously and to remain open and curious about all facets of human existence. He lives in a Maryland suburb of Washington, D.C., with his wife, Linda, his daughter, Anil, and his son, Amar. In his spare time, he tends his rose garden. Shaw has donated more than $130,000 to the Bernard Shaw Endowment Fund, which he established under the aegis of the University of Illinois Foundation in 1991. Among the many other awards and honors he has received are the Lowell Thomas Electronic Journalist Award, the 1991 David Brinkley Excellence in Communication Award from Barry University, in Miami, Florida, Arizona State University's 1994 Walter Cronkite Award for Excellence in Journalism and Telecommunication, and the University of Kansas's 1994 William Allen White Medallion for Distinguished Service.

Selected Biographical References: Black Collegian 20:50+ S '89 pors; Broadcasting 116:143 Ap 24 '89 por; Chicago Tribune X p6+ F 9 '92 por, V p1+ My 14 '93 pors; N Y Times C p18 F 2 '88 por; Washington Post B p1+ Ja 22 '91 por; Contemporary Authors vol 119 (1987); Contemporary Black Biography vol 2 (1992); Who's Who in America, 1995

Sin, Jaime L.

(HY-may)

Aug. 31, 1928- Roman Catholic prelate. Address: Office of the Archbishop, 121 Arzobispo St., Intramuros, P.O. Box 132, Manila, Philippines

"My role is to issue rulings on the morality of human activities," Jaime L. Cardinal Sin, the Roman Catholic archbishop of Manila, the capital of the Philippines, has said. "Politics, as a human activity,

Office of Cardinal Sin

Jaime L. Sin

has a morality. And I have to tell my flock how to make a moral choice." Acting in accordance with that conviction, on February 22, 1986 Cardinal Sin broadcast a radio appeal that spurred hundreds of thousands of people to rally on the streets of Manila in support of a surprise revolt against the administration of President Ferdinand Marcos, who had ruled the Philippines for more than twenty years. Sin thus became a key player in the bloodless "people power" revolution that led three days later to the fall of Marcos—a ruthless dictator who had trampled on the human rights of the Philippine people and drained the national treasury for his personal benefit, nearly destroying the country's economy in the process—and the accession of Corazon Aquino as president.

Renowned for his remarkable accessibility, diplomatic skills, joviality, and an earthy humor that sometimes borders on the risqué, Cardinal Sin is the effective head of the Roman Catholic Church in a nation where nearly 85 percent of the population, or some 55 million people, are Roman Catholic. After becoming the archbishop of Manila, in 1974, Sin criticized the Marcos regime with increasing frequency, but for a long time he nevertheless succeeded in maintaining what one reporter described as a "near-perfect balancing act" between supporters and opponents of Marcos. Moreover, according to an article by William Chapman for the *Washington Post* (September 25, 1983), during Marcos's reign some observers regarded Sin as "the strongest source of restraint on a government often given to extremes." During the administration of Corazon Aquino, he functioned as Aquino's de facto partner and adviser.

Since the election in 1992 of Fidel Ramos as president of the Philippines, the cardinal has resumed the role of outspoken critic of the government. In particular, he has fiercely condemned the Ramos administration's efforts to lower the country's birthrate of 2.5 percent a year by making artificial birth-control devices more widely available. "I criticize [Ramos] and the policies of the government because I want him to succeed," Cardinal Sin told reporters at the end of 1994, as quoted by William Branigin in the *Washington Post* (January 15, 1995). "How can he succeed if he will not be told what is wrong? . . . Had [Marcos] heeded our protests and listened to our criticisms, he would not have ended his presidency in shame." Sin was appointed to the College of Cardinals by Pope Paul VI in 1976.

The fourteenth of sixteen children, Jaime L. Sin was born on August 31, 1928 in New Washington, a small town on the Philippine island of Panay. He is called James by his family, and many of his friends still refer to him by his childhood nickname, Amé. The first seven of his siblings died in infancy, possibly, as Sin's brother Ramon, a physician, has suggested, because of an allergic reaction to their mother's milk. The next nine (four girls and five boys), all of whom were bottle-fed, survived, and all graduated from college and entered such fields as medicine, pharmacy, business, and education as well as, in the single case of Jaime Sin, religion.

Cardinal Sin's father was Chinese; after immigrating to the Philippines from Southern China, he changed his name from Sin Puat-co to Juan Sin. The cardinal's mother, Maxima ("Mimay") Reyes Lachia, was a Filipina of Spanish extraction. At her request, shortly before their marriage, her husband-to-be converted from Buddhism to Roman Catholicism, her faith. With savings that he accumulated as a junk dealer, Juan Sin opened a general store in New Washington; following his marriage, his wife helped to manage the store, and it became very prosperous. In his book *Cardinal Sin and the Miracle of Asia* (1987), the Philippine journalist Felix B. Bautista, who was the cardinal's personal assistant and speechwriter for many years and who edited two archdiocesan newspapers in Manila, wrote that when he died, in 1957, Juan Sin left an estate that included coconut groves, rice paddies, and oceanfront properties.

As a youngster Jaime Sin got average grades in school. He engaged in the same activities as the other boys in his neighborhood, but unlike most of them, he went to the parish church daily as well as on Sundays, when he served as an altar boy. Every morning, he has recalled, he would see his parents reciting the rosary at an altar in their bedroom, and he would be struck by their peaceful and happy expressions. Motivated by the conviction that "there must be something about religion that could make people look that way," in his words, he decided he would study for the priesthood. "You will become a priest because you are the ugliest [of all my children]," his mother, who reportedly selected the professions of all nine of them, told him at some point in his childhood, thus reinforcing (or perhaps inspiring) his career choice.

In mid-1941, upon graduating from the New Washington Elementary School, Jaime Sin entered the St. Vincent Ferrer Archdiocesan Seminary in Jaro, a district of Iloilo City. The seminary abruptly suspended operations in December 1941, when Japanese troops invaded the Philippines. For the next five and a half years, Sin lived at the church in Kalibo, a town near New Washington. In addition to serving as the altar boy, bell ringer, and housekeeper at the church, he ministered to the needs of the five retired priests who lived there. They, in turn, through their reminiscences, acquainted him with many facets of the priesthood. Despite an edict from the Japanese occupiers forbidding it, Sin listened to Voice of America broadcasts on a short-wave radio. After each broadcast, using equipment in the parish office, he would type and mimeograph a rough transcript of what he had heard and then distribute copies to various parishioners.

In June 1946 Sin returned to the seminary in Iloilo City. He distinguished himself neither scholastically nor athletically, but he was "a good friend to all [his fellow seminarians]," as one of them told Felix Bautista. "Above all, he was very prayerful," the priest recalled. "He would still be on his knees in the chapel long after the rest of us had gone to bed." Sin kept a special notebook in which he would write messages to the Virgin Mary, to ask her to help him pass an exam, for example. One day in 1953 he wrote a letter on seminary stationery in which he revealed to her his fear that, because of the frequent attacks of asthma that had plagued him since childhood, he would never be able to achieve his goal of becoming "the very best [priest] there is." "If by December 18 this year, the day before I am ordained a deacon, the attacks have not stopped," he wrote, "then I shall take it as a sign that I am not for the priesthood, that you have other plans for me." He placed the letter beneath a statue of the Virgin in the seminary chapel, and, by his own account, he never again had an asthma attack. His principal extracurricular activity at the seminary was performing in school theatrical productions. To improve his vocal projection, during the afternoon siesta he would stand at the far end of an athletic field and shout his lines. He spent summers in New Washington, teaching catechism to children. "We liked him because he had an endless stock of stories that made us laugh," a man who had attended his classes as a child told Felix Bautista.

Ordained a priest on April 3, 1954, Sin said Mass for the first time the next day, in New Washington. Overcoming the objections of his superior, Bishop Fondrosa, who wanted him to go to Rome to continue his studies, he began working as a missionary priest in the archdiocese of Capiz, in a mountainous part of Panay. On horseback or, more often, on foot, he would journey to villages that had no resident priest, to say Mass, hear confessions, preside at baptisms, marriages, and funerals, and prepare children for their first communions. At the request of Bishop Fondrosa, he gave up that mission after two years to become the first rector of the St. Pius X Seminary, in Roxas City. The seminary had not yet been built, however, so, as his first task, he had to procure money for its construction. He proved to be a talented fund-raiser, and it opened in June 1957, as a secondary school and seminary where all the students boarded.

In addition to handling all the duties of a principal—a role in which he donned the mantle of a strict disciplinarian who, at the same time, treated his charges with fairness and understanding—Sin taught classes in such secular subjects as history and Spanish. To fulfill the requirements set by Philippine law for teachers, he enrolled at the Immaculate Conception College in Roxas City and, in 1959, earned a B.S. degree in education. Among his other activities during his ten-year stint as rector, every Sunday afternoon he would broadcast catechism lessons and commentary in his own half-hour radio program. Also during that period, in 1960, the Holy See appointed him a domestic prelate of Pope John XXIII, thus conferring upon him the title "monsignor."

Sin left his position at the St. Pius X Seminary in 1967, to become the titular bishop of Obba and the auxiliary bishop of Jaro. His episcopal ordination was held on March 19 of that year. In taking up the rectorship of the cathedral in Jaro, he made good use of the administrative skills that he had honed at the Pius X seminary, where the day-to-day operations had had to meet the extremely high standards set by Bishop Fondrosa. As auxiliary bishop he oversaw the building of new schools and the establishment of new parishes. "Monsignor Sin was a go-getter," a Roman Catholic lay leader in Jaro told Felix Bautista, after noting that "the archdiocese had been pretty much in the doldrums when he came." "He involved himself actively in the various Catholic organizations, and he got things moving again."

In 1970 Sin was named an apostolic administrator in the archdiocese of Jaro. On March 19, 1972 he was named titular archbishop of Massa Lubrense and installed as the coadjutor archbishop of Jaro, with the right of succession. In October 1972, about half a year after the death of the incumbent archbishop, Sin became the metropolitan archbishop of Jaro. On March 19, 1974 he succeeded Rufino J. Cardinal Santos as the metropolitan archbishop of Manila. When, on May 26, 1976, Pope Paul VI named him a cardinal, he became the youngest member of the College of Cardinals to that date and one of the relatively small number from a developing nation.

Earlier, in 1969, President Ferdinand Marcos had been reelected to a second term amid circumstances marked by both violence and fraud. Even before his reelection, large segments of the Philippine citizenry had begun to feel increasingly unhappy with the Marcos administration, in which corruption was rampant. While most Filipinos were living under conditions of extreme poverty, Marcos, despite his modest salary, was amassing a fortune (as the extraordinary extravagances of his wife, Imelda, indicated), as were many of his cronies. The widespread discontent led to a series of civil disturbances, including, for example, an attempt by some two thousand demonstrators to storm the presidential palace in early 1970. On September 21, 1972, ostensibly in response to the threat of a takeover by Communist insurgents but in what was recognized as an action designed to enable him to stay on as president beyond the mandatory two-term limit, Marcos declared a state of martial law in all parts of the country and imposed tight government controls over the media. In an attempt to eliminate his political opponents, he ordered the detainment of many of his adversaries. Among the first to be imprisoned was Benigno Aquino, who was then serving in the national legislature.

The cardinal endorsed (or originated, as some sources have reported) the policy of "critical collaboration" with the Marcos government that the Catholic Bishops Conference of the Philippines adopted in 1973. In accordance with that policy, he maintained cordial relations with President Marcos and his wife. He regularly attended social events with the Marcoses, for example, and, if it were requested, he would say Mass at the presidential palace. He met with Marcos once a month, and on his desk he had a telephone with a direct connection to the palace. When questioned about his association with the Marcoses, Sin would offer such explanations as "If I don't attend to their spiritual needs, who will?" and "The Church takes care of both rightists and leftists."

Sin almost never criticized the Marcoses directly, but he sometimes twitted them. In the *New York Times* (December 12, 1982), Pamela G. Hollie reported that he enjoyed telling a joke about "the mining industry," in which a wealthy and powerful woman—presumably Imelda Marcos—points to everything in sight and declares, "That's mine! And that's mine!" By his own account, when Marcos said to him one day, "I admire the United States, because immediately after an election they can know the results," he replied, "You should admire the Filipino people—they know the election results before the election." Such barbs notwithstanding, Sin observed to Felix Bautista that until Marcos's downfall, he "was able to have rapport" with him. "He and I understood each other," he explained. And during an interview with Patty Edmonds for the *National Catholic Reporter* (September 16, 1983), he said, "I have told Marcos many times that we cannot see eye to eye, but we can work hand in hand."

By his own admission, the cardinal felt far less comfortable in his relations with Imelda Marcos, and sometimes he prevented her from realizing her ambitions. In one such instance, in 1982, he refused to affiliate himself with her plan to build the largest basilica in the world, where she intended to have the Pope officiate at a ceremony celebrating her twenty-fifth wedding anniversary. "The top priority today is for adequate housing for the poor and not luxurious housing for [the Christ Child]," Cardinal Sin admonished her. Since Sin's opposition to the basilica meant that no clergyman would ever say Mass there, she had to abandon the project.

According to Felix Bautista, for a long time Sin accepted Marcos's "constitutional authoritarianism" as a worthwhile experiment that might lead to a form of democracy suitable for the Philippine people; in the *New York Times* (October 18, 1974), Joseph Lelyveld quoted the cardinal as saying that martial law had produced "many good things" for the nation. Sin was nonetheless aware of the Marcos regime's increasing abuses of power, and, when he deemed it warranted, he publicly criticized actions of the government. One of the earliest such occasions occurred in September 1974, when Sin vigorously protested the administration's official account of a raid on a Catholic retreat house that the military had carried out while searching for a Communist party leader. After failing in his attempt to persuade the administration to admit that its story had falsely described Church officials as supporting and even assisting in the raid, Sin wrote a pastoral letter urging Catholics to pray "for those who are under detention and are suffering" and "that all of us may live under a reign of truth and justice, peace and freedom." Joseph Lelyveld described the letter, which was read in churches throughout the country, as "the most dramatic public challenge President Marcos [had] had to face" since he had assumed authoritarian power.

Sporadically during the next decade, at press conferences or during interviews with foreign journalists, at meetings with Catholic laypersons and clergy, and in pastoral letters, among other public venues, Cardinal Sin criticized the government for failing to address the needs of the Philippine people, for ignoring, and perhaps even condoning, the graft and corruption that pervaded all aspects of business and politics, and for rigging national elections in favor of Marcos and his cohorts. He expressed outrage about the climate of fear that had gripped the country and condemned the government for creating that climate by conducting searches without warrants, making illegal arrests, and subjecting prisoners to inhumane treatment and even torture. Among those imprisoned were nuns and priests who were accused of being Communist sympathizers.

On August 21, 1983 Benigno Aquino, who had been released from prison in 1980 to undergo surgery in the United States and had spent three years there in self-imposed exile, flew back to the Philippines to prepare for the parliamentary elections that had been scheduled to take place in 1984. As he stepped from the plane at Manila's international airport, he was fatally shot by an unknown number of assassins whom eyewitnesses asserted were members of the military and who, many Filipinos and foreign observers immediately suspected, had almost undoubtedly acted under orders from people at the top level of the government, if not Marcos himself. In the eulogy that Cardinal Sin gave at the funeral mass for Benigno Aquino, he challenged the government "to bring about reconciliation through the restoration of all those freedoms the people have lost" and "to restore the dignity of our people and to recognize their right to participate fully in the political process."

Within days of the funeral, fearing that the assassination of the popular and highly respected Aquino would precipitate violence throughout the Philippines, Sin urged Marcos to work toward "national reconciliation," as he called it, by holding free elections, restoring freedom of the press, creating an independent judiciary, and conducting a thorough and impartial public investigation of Aquino's murder. Marcos disregarded his recommendations. In September 1984, speaking from the pulpit of St. Patrick's Cathedral, in New York City, the cardinal reported that the people of the Philippines were still, as he put it, "enmeshed in an economic and political crisis of calamitous proportions."

In hopes of ending that crisis, Sin helped to persuade Corazon Aquino, Benigno Aquino's widow, to run against Marcos in the "snap" presidential election that Marcos announced would be held on February 7, 1986. (Marcos's surprising decision to hold an election had apparently come in response to increasing pressure from his opponents in the Philippines and from the United States, which had long been helping to prop up his regime with huge infusions of military and other aid.) On the day of the election, there were many reports of stolen ballot boxes, bribes, intimidation of voters, and even killings at the polls—events that prompted the Catholic Bishops Conference to issue a statement that described the fraud surrounding the election as "unparalleled" and endorsed nonviolent resistance to the anticipated claim of victory by Marcos. Although, as expected, Marcos declared himself the winner, rampant irregularities in the tallying process made the results of the election impossible to determine with certainty, and Aquino too announced that she had won.

The impasse dramatically ended during the last week of February. On February 22, Juan Ponce Enrile, Marcos's minister of defense, and Lieutenant General Fidel Ramos, the deputy chief of staff of the armed forces, announced their defection from the Marcos government and their support for Corazon Aquino. That day or the next, tanks and thousands of troops loyal to Marcos began to advance on the military camps where Enrile and Ramos and a couple of hundred other rebels had barricaded themselves. With their annihilation seemingly imminent, Enrile telephoned Cardinal Sin and pleaded with him for help. The cardinal immediately broadcast over Radio Veritas, the Church-owned radio station, a message that called upon Filipinos to protect Ramos and Enrile—"our idealistic friends," as he called them.

Hundreds of thousands of people, including many nuns, priests, and pastors, responded to the cardinal's appeal by forming a human barrier between the advancing forces and the defectors' redoubts, and the next day, in response to a second radio appeal by the cardinal, they and others—eventually about a million people were massed on the streets—brought food to the rebels. In a scene reminiscent of antiwar demonstrations in the United States during the 1960s, civilians gave flowers and candy to soldiers, and, except for the use of tear gas at one point, the massive rally proceeded peacefully. On February 25, under intense pressure from the administration of President Ronald Reagan, which promised him safe haven on American soil, Ferdinand Marcos fled to Guam, and Corazon Aquino was sworn in as president of the Philippines. At a huge open-air Mass that was held in Manila on March 2, hundreds of thousands of Filipinos cheered both Aquino and the cardinal.

A few days later Cardinal Sin went to Rome to meet with Pope John Paul II, who had expressed his uneasiness about what appeared to him to be the excessive involvement of the Philippine Church in the nation's politics. "I [told the Pope], 'This is not political. It is a moral dimension,'" Sin reported to E. J. Dionne Jr., who interviewed him for the *New York Times* (March 7, 1986). "And he smiled, because he understands. He came from Poland." During the last nine and a half years, Cardinal Sin has continued to maintain a high profile in the political life of the Philippines. During the parliamentary election campaign of 1987, for example, he advised Catholics to vote for candidates whose positions on matters of economic justice, land reform, and education could, as he wrote in a pastoral letter, "best serve the common good," and to vote against those who, contrary to Church teachings, supported abortion or divorce or adhered to a "godless ideology."

By publicizing, in a pastoral letter that he issued during the 1992 campaign, what he considered to be unacceptable traits or behavior in a candidate for president, Sin effectively rejected as unsuitable all the entrants in that contest except one—Ramon Mitra, whom he favored but who ultimately lost to Fidel Ramos, a Protestant, who had been Corazon Aquino's choice as her successor. During an interview with a reporter for the Associated Press in February 1995, the cardinal once again maintained that priests must speak out when the government of their country commits what they view as a wrongful act. "As a citizen of a country, whether you are a Catholic or not, you are duty-bound to participate and to share your views for the welfare of the people," he told the reporter, as quoted in the *Bangkok Post* (February 12, 1995).

Cardinal Sin lives in a suburb of Manila, in what used to be known as the archbishop's palace but which, since his residency there, has been called the archbishop's house. Every morning, the veteran Philippine journalist Amando Doronila reported in *Asiaweek* (January 6, 1995), people "humble and mighty" come there to speak with him. "Welcome to the House of Sin," the cardinal tells visitors, repeating one of the many quips by which he has poked fun at the incongruity of the name Sin for a man of the cloth. It is partly because of what he has called his "bad name" that the cardinal has consistently dismissed suggestions that he might be a serious—or even a long-shot—contender to succeed John Paul II as Pope. He offered a second reason to William Branigin: "[A prospective pope] should be highly intelligent [and] highly prudent, and I cannot find these qualities in me." Upon arising, well before dawn, and before retiring at night, the cardinal prays in the private chapel that adjoins his bedroom. The bedroom's sparse furnishings include a rowing machine and a stationary bicycle. Cardinal Sin's hundreds of honors include the Rajah Soliman Award for Distinguished Citizenry, presented to him in Manila in 1976; the Human Rights and Law Award from the Washington, D.C.-based International Human Rights Law Group and an award from the New York City-based International League of Human Rights, both in 1986; and more than two dozen honorary doctoral degrees, most of them from Church-affiliated colleges and universities, including more than a dozen institutions in the United States.

Selected Biographical References: Asian Survey 27:1240+ D '87; Asiaweek p26+ Ja 6, 1995 pors; National Catholic Reporter 16:7 Ja 18 '80 por, 19:1+ S 16 '83 por; NY Times IV p2 D 12 '82 por; Washington Post A p19 S 25 '83; Bautista, Felix B. Cardinal Sin and the Miracle of Asia (1987)

Buffalo Bills

Smith, Bruce

June 18, 1963- Football player. Address: c/o The Buffalo Bills, One Bills Drive, Orchard Park, NY 14127-2296

One of the fiercest pass rushers in National Football League history, Bruce Smith is the linchpin of the defense that helped carry the Buffalo Bills to an unprecedented four consecutive Super Bowl appearances in the early 1990s. After earning All-America honors as a defensive lineman at Virginia Tech, Smith was the first player selected in the 1985 NFL draft, joining a hapless team in one of the NFL's smallest media markets. Although he arrived in Buffalo overweight and overconfident, he quickly established himself as a force capable of singlehandedly disrupting offensive attacks. Smith was leaner by 1990, when the Bills emerged as the AFC's dominant team, and his explosive speed and overwhelming strength made him impossible to stop with one-on-one blocking schemes. His declared ambition was to become the most formidable defensive player of all time, but after undergoing knee surgery during training camp, he spent most of the 1991 season on the sidelines.

Despite his tremendous success, Smith's accomplishments have often been overshadowed by controversy. His cockiness and weight problem, elaborate dances after sacking quarterbacks, complaints that the Bills' defensive scheme limited him, and boastful declarations that he was the best defensive player in football drew more attention than his consistent Pro-Bowl caliber performances, but Smith apparently matured during his rehabilitation from the knee injury. Talking less but playing perhaps better than ever in 1992, he became less selfish in relation to his teammates on the defensive line and defended against the run as ferociously as he rushed the passer. Maintaining that level of performance through the 1994 season, Smith has become one of the top three sack leaders of all time. "I was an assistant coach years ago," Bills' coach Marv Levy told Frank Litsky for the *New York Times* (November 6, 1994), "when there were great defensive linemen with the Los Angeles Rams—Merlin Olsen, Deacon Jones—but I've never seen a better defensive lineman than Bruce."

Bruce Bernard Smith was born in Norfolk, Virginia on June 18, 1963, the youngest of George and Annie Smith's children. He grew up in a close-knit family that was cared for by hard-working parents. His father worked as a shipping clerk and a truck driver; his mother held a variety of jobs, and in her sixties she turned a deaf ear when her well-to-do youngest child begged her to quit her job as a bus driver for the city of Norfolk. Although his father had been a boxer and his mother played center on her high school basketball team, as a young boy Bruce shied away from sports while battening on the Southern-style foods prepared by his mother. "As a kid I'd eat at my mother's house, then go down the road to my girlfriend's and eat, and then sometimes go to my friend's house and eat again," Smith recalled in a conversation with Rick Telander of *Sports Illustrated* (September 2, 1991). "I could gain five pounds in a day."

Smith, who had ballooned to a weight of 270 pounds by the time he was a high-school sophomore, was teased by schoolmates and beaten up by neighborhood bullies because of his flabby physique. "Those were hard times growing up, dealing with my size and my situation," he said to Thomas George of the *New York Times* (December 9, 1990). "We didn't have a great deal of money though we were able to get necessities. You see your mother and father working two jobs apiece, and making the best out of everything, somehow, someway. I was too big, too slow and too fat for sports. Little success came easy for me in anything. . . . I lacked in confidence. It was a struggle."

That painful adolescence was ameliorated somewhat by the encouragement and companionship Smith received from his parents. They also dispensed advice in the form of homilies and truisms, telling him, "No one gets anything free"; "Whatever you do, do to the fullest"; and, "A diamond was once a piece of coal that did well under pressure." His family, Smith told Rick Telander, "did an excellent job of bringing [him] up with values," and in an interview with Thomas George for the *New York Times* (January 27, 1991), Smith credited his father with teaching him "the value of a dollar and of hard work." Indeed, he was especially close to his father, who took him fishing on the family's small boat and hunting on their tract of timberland in North Carolina. "I admired my father because he was a hard worker at the minimum wage," Smith explained to Edward Kiersh in an interview for *Inside Sports* (August 1991). "He worked ten to twelve hours a day, and yet he'd always find the time to watch me play sports. He was always there for me." At Booker T. Washington High School, Smith had developed into a dominating athlete, winning All-America honors as a lineman in football and, as a burly but high-scoring center, leading his team to a state basketball championship. When recruiters from the University of Virginia told Smith that he lacked sufficient speed and quickness to play for the Cavaliers, he enrolled at Virginia Tech, in Blacksburg.

In his four-year career at Tech, Smith made 180 tackles, including forty-six quarterback sacks and twenty-five stops behind the line of scrimmage. Twice named the team's most valuable player, as a senior he helped Virginia Tech earn a berth in the 1984 Independence Bowl, where Tech fell to the Air Force Academy, 23–7. Smith was chosen as the best collegiate football player in the state on two occasions, made the All-South Independent team for three consecutive years, and formed a friendly rivalry with Darryl Talley, a linebacker at West Virginia University who would become Smith's teammate and close friend in Buffalo. In his senior year, Smith, a consensus first-team All American, won the prestigious Outland Trophy, which is awarded to the best interior lineman in college football. The Buffalo Bills spent the first pick overall in the 1985 NFL draft on Smith, who was also chosen by the Baltimore Stars of the short-lived United States Football League. After a lively bidding war between Buffalo and Baltimore, Smith signed with the Bills, whose 1984 record of two wins and fourteen losses was the worst in the NFL.

The six-foot-four Smith, who had played at 285 pounds as a college senior, arrived at training camp cocky and out of shape, weighing in at a bloated 305 pounds. As Thomas George noted in 1990, Smith, who had boasted that he could eat fifty chicken wings before going home for dinner, "began his pro career continuing the eating habits he had developed in college: Wendy's, McDonald's, Burger King, and Popeye's Fried Chicken." Nevertheless, Smith, getting by on instinct and raw skill, started thirteen games and registered twenty-five quarterback pressures to go along with his team-leading 6.5 sacks. He also recovered four fumbles and lined up as a fullback from time to time in short-yardage situations. He was named the AFC's defensive rookie of the year, but, as Smith admitted to Rick Telander, he "didn't have [his] priorities in order." Having once again lost fourteen games in 1985, the Bills signed the gifted quarterback Jim Kelly from the USFL, which had just folded and, during the 1986 season, brought in a new head coach, Marv Levy. The Bills finished next to last in the AFC Eastern Division with a record of 4–12, but Smith's team-record fifteen sacks tied him for second place in that category in the AFC.

Although a players' strike kept veterans like Smith out of the lineup for three games and shortened the regular season by one game, the Bills' improving defense helped the team up its record to seven wins and eight losses in 1987. Smith led all AFC defensive linemen with twelve sacks in the abbreviated season. Among the numerous honors that Smith received after the year were the UPI defensive-player-of-the-year award, the Miller Lite/NFL award for defensive lineman of the year, and recognition as a first team All-Pro. Making an auspicious debut in the Pro Bowl, he earned the Dan McGuire Award as the game's most valuable player. Smith suffered a setback, however, when the league suspended him for the first four games of the 1988 season after he tested positive for the use of, according to Smith, a recreational drug. Despite missing those games, he led the team with eleven sacks. Buffalo finished in first place in the Eastern Division with a record of twelve wins and four losses, but Cincinnati bested the Bills in the AFC championship game in spite of two sacks by Smith. Again an All-Pro and a player in the Pro Bowl, he was also named AFC co-defensive player of the year by UPI.

In the off-season, the Denver Broncos tried to woo Smith with a five-year, $7.5 million contract, an offer the Bills matched, thereby retaining the services of the player Denver's head coach, Dan Reeves, called "the game's best defensive end." "I wasn't surprised when Buffalo matched the offer," Smith told Thomas George. "I think they knew the worst was behind me. I was losing my relationship with God and I kind of pushed it aside. My values had diminished. I had to regroup. I guess I was still maturing and I didn't handle success as well as I should have. In this business, I learned that you have to grow up in a hurry. You have to mature much quicker than you would in a normal life." When injuries retarded the defensive unit's effectiveness, Buffalo slipped from 12–4 to 9–7 in 1989, but that disappointing record was good enough to give the Bills their second consecutive Eastern Division crown. Although the AFC East champions were widely regarded as one of the league's most talent-laden squads, the Bills had not yet jelled as a team, as evidenced by internal dissension and public feuding that earned them the label "bickering Bills." Nevertheless, with his three-sack performance against the New York Jets in October of that year, Smith became the Bills all-time leader in sacks. For the season, he registered thirteen sacks, and he was selected as a Pro Bowl starter for the third straight year.

Smith approached the 1990 season determined to prove that he was the NFL's best defensive player. He had loose cartilage removed from his right knee in the off-season and undertook an ambitious workout program that involved Soviet-style weight lifting and strenuous daily aerobic sessions on a stair climber that were originally designed for marathoners. Smith also renounced fast foods in favor of a high-energy, low-fat diet of pasta and fish that helped him reduce his weight to 265 pounds, sculpt his body, and improve upon his already explosive quickness. "Now he's got the body fat of a wide receiver," Marv Levy told Thomas George. "Really, you look at him now and he looks like he's been carved out of wood. It has improved his endurance and his liking for the game. Our base defense is 3-4, but you name it and we've got it in our package, like most people. With a player like Bruce, you don't want too many schemes. You do enough where people don't zero in on him and you pick your spots to try and free him completely."

Relying on a smothering, Smith-led defense and a high-octane, no-huddle offense triggered by Jim Kelly, the versatile running back Thurman Thomas, and the sure-handed wide receiver Andre Reed, the Bills ran roughshod over the competition in 1990, posting a conference-best 13–3 record. Buffalo blasted the Los Angeles Raiders, 51–3, in the AFC title game to set up a showdown with the downstate New York Giants in the Bills' first-ever Super Bowl appearance. Although he was double- and triple-teamed all season long, Smith recorded a club-record nineteen sacks (one less than league leader Derrick Thomas), and his 101 tackles were second-best on the team. The consensus choice as NFL defensive player of the year, he made the All-Pro and Pro Bowl teams.

While preparing for a late-season road game against the Giants, Smith stirred up a media brouhaha in New York City when he boasted that he had replaced Giant linebacker Lawrence Taylor as the NFL's premier defensive player. In his postseason interview in *Inside Sports* with Edward Kiersh, Smith explained that he had spoken out because he wanted "more respect from the media." "If [the Buffalo Bills] were somewhere else—L.A., New York—then we would get the respect we deserve," Smith declared. "So many of our guys are underrated. Talley is the most overlooked player in the league. And [Thurman] Thomas, he should be compared to Barry Sanders. Let's face it: we're ignored. There are a lot of overrated guys in this league who get all of the coverage. We get none. We get no respect."

In the days preceding Super Bowl XXV, Smith angered the Giants when he expressed disappointment that the Bills were not playing the San Francisco 49ers, the previous year's champion and winner of four Super Bowls in the 1980s. "The 49ers are famous and everybody says they are this and that," Smith declared, as quoted by Thomas George in the *New York Times* (January 23, 1991). "It makes me sick. I wanted the 49ers." Although the Bills were favored to break the NFC's string of six consecutive Super Bowl victories, the Giants eked out a 20–19 win when Buffalo placekicker Scott Norwood missed on a game-ending forty-seven-yard field-goal attempt. Smith scored two points on an end-zone sack, but he was otherwise neutralized, and Buffalo's vaunted defense was worn down by the Giants' grind-it-out, ball-control attack.

After having arthroscopic surgery performed on his left knee during training camp, Smith missed eleven regular-season games in 1991. With Smith playing in a limited role on a knee that had not fully healed, the Buffalo defense was not the dominant force that it had been, but the team's explosive offense keyed a 13–3 campaign, and in the AFC title game the Bills edged past Denver by the score of 10–7. In Super Bowl XXVI, however, Buffalo's defensive shortcomings were exposed in a 37–24 loss to the Washington Redskins. The Bills had seemed to stumble even before the game's opening kickoff, reinforcing the perception that some of Buffalo's players were chronic, self-absorbed complainers. Smith began Super Bowl week by discussing racist hate mail he had received during the season, and he told reporters that he had asked the Bills' front office to trade him. Thurman Thomas, who, earlier in the week, had been named the league's most valuable player, complained that Jim Kelly was commanding too much attention from the media. Although Marv Levy chastised Smith for the poor timing of his remarks, Smith explained to Thomas George of the *New York Times* (July 6, 1992) that "the only way you can attack racism is to deal with it publicly and in a forum like [Super Bowl week] where everyone around the country will read about it and you can raise some eyebrows on the issue."

In the off-season, the twenty-nine-year-old Smith had bone chips removed from his troublesome left knee, but he exercised relentlessly to prove that neither age nor injury stood in the way of his quest to become "the best there ever was," as he put it. Although he played sparingly in the preseason, Smith reestablished himself as one of the league's most feared defenders in 1992, registering fourteen sacks and making the Pro Bowl for the fifth time. Although the Bills finished second in the AFC East with a record of 11-5 and demolished the division-champion Miami Dolphins, 29-10, in the AFC title game, the Buffalo defense watched helplessly in Super Bowl XXVII as the Dallas Cowboys seized nine turnovers en route to a 52-17 victory.

During the 1993 preseason, the Bills renegotiated Smith's contract, awarding him a four-year, $13.5 million deal that increased his annual salary by almost $2 million. Playing injury-free football for the first time in three years, Smith enjoyed what he has considered to be the best all-around season of his career, finishing second in the league in sacks with fourteen, recording a career-high 108 tackles, and leading the Bills in quarterback pressures with twenty-four. He was named the defensive player of the year by the *Pro Football Weekly*, won the George Halas Trophy as the Newspaper Enterprise Association's defensive player of the year, and made the Pro Bowl roster for the sixth time. (He skipped the Pro Bowl for the birth of his first child.)

Although the offense struggled somewhat in 1993, Buffalo relied on a stingy defense that paced the team to a 12-4 record as the Bills captured their fifth AFC East crown in six years. After routing the Kansas City Chiefs, 30-13, in the conference championship match, the Bills again came up short in the Super Bowl, squandering a 13-6 halftime advantage in a 30-13 loss to the Dallas Cowboys. The Bills' reign as AFC champions was unceremoniously ended in 1994, when they failed to make the playoffs with a record of seven wins and nine losses. Although bothered by a bruised tendon in his shoulder for much of the season, Smith finished the year with ten sacks and made the Pro Bowl for the seventh time.

"Bruce is the classic example of a guy that's matured over five, six, seven years," Marv Levy said to David Aldridge of the *Washington Post* (January 14, 1994). "He was somewhat self-indulgent when he came in, overweight. He had been able to totally dominate, I'm sure, all the way back to grade school. But somewhere when he got hurt, he began to realize the value of conditioning. Now, no one works out harder." Smith's maturity is evident in the way he refrains from the exuberant sack dances that he once performed over fallen quarterbacks. Having grown accustomed to the double- and triple-teaming that opponents routinely use to thwart him, he has accepted his role as the "marked man," as Rick Telander put it, in the Bills' 3-4 alignment even though he would probably register more sacks in a 4-3 defensive scheme. As Jennifer Frey reported in the *New York Times* (January 27, 1993), "Smith used to stomp to the sidelines and scream at his teammates and coaches, begging them to change the system so that he could get more sacks and more attention and more personal accolades. Now he won't even whisper a complaint." "He really has changed," the Bills' All-Pro center Kent Hull told Jennifer Frey. "At times you see him do things to help another defensive lineman that puts himself at risk. And I don't think you would have seen him doing things like that before."

Smith ranks third in the NFL in career sacks with 116, and he is the league's all-time playoff sack leader with twelve. Possessing extraordinary strength and speed, he can overpower blockers or use his quickness to blow past them. "You're talking about a guy who is stronger than a three-hundred-pounder and faster than a linebacker," the Buffalo center Kent Hull told Rick Telander. "His speed around the corner is unreal. And if you move out, he'll take one step upfield, spin inside and he's gone. I think he's double-jointed. He'll line up over me, and I'll try to hit him, and there's nothing there—he's going back and coming forward at the same time. I can't even explain it. There's no way a human being should do what he does."

Darryl Talley told Telander that Smith is "like a speed skater coming around the corner, he's so low to the ground, almost flat, with offensive linemen literally chasing him," and former Cincinnati Bengals offensive tackle Anthony Munoz said that Smith's "greatest asset is his ability to adjust, to use his momentum to his advantage." Smith plays football wearing the smallest pads he can find and no hip pads at all; he also eschews gloves in favor of small amounts of tape on his wrists and hands. "I'm a gladiator without any fear," he declared when he spoke to Edward Kiersh. Bruce Smith and his wife, Carmen, have one child, a son. They live in Norfolk, Virginia in a sprawling dockside house not far from the home that Smith built for his parents, in Virginia Beach.

Selected Biographical References: Chicago Tribune III p6 O 4 '92 por, IV p10 Ja 13 '94 por; Inside Sports p22+ Ag '91 pors; N Y Times VIII p1+ D 9 '90 pors, VIII p1+ Ja 27 '91 por, C p1+ Jl 6 '92 pors, B p8 Ja 27 '93 pors; Sports Illus 75:28+ S 2 '91 pors; Washington Post F p1+ D 22 '90 pors, C p5 Ja 14 '93 pors; Who's Who in America, 1995

Snowe, Olympia J.

Feb. 21, 1947- United States Senator from Maine. Address: 176 Russell Senate Office Bldg., Washington, DC 20510-1903

When asked in 1982 what she would like to accomplish as a member of Congress, Olympia J. Snowe of Maine, then a second-term Republican member of the United States House of Representatives, replied, "The thing that I would like to achieve most would be doing something for the women in the country. I think that my place in time in Congress gives me this opportunity and responsibility." In eight consecutive two-year terms as a representa-

U.S. Senate

Olympia J. Snowe

tive of Maine's Second Congressional District, Snowe established herself as a voice of moderation and independence as she sought to advance the role of women in Congress, in her own party, and at the grassroots level. In 1994 she became the first Greek-American woman elected to the United States Senate, succeeding the popular Democratic majority leader George J. Mitchell, who was retiring. Snowe is widely respected for her work on deficit reduction, fiscal issues, health care, women's issues, and foreign affairs.

Olympia Snowe was born Olympia Jean Bouchles on February 21, 1947 in Augusta, Maine, the daughter of George John Bouchles, a native of Mytilene, Greece, and Georgia (Goranites) Bouchles, whose parents had immigrated to the United States from Sparta. Snowe was orphaned at the age of nine when her father, a cook, died of heart disease, only a year after her mother had died of cancer. She was then raised in the factory town of Auburn, Maine by her uncle James Goranites, a barber, and her aunt Mary, a textile-mill worker, who had five children of their own. Her only sibling, a brother, was raised by another relative.

After graduating from St. Basil's Academy, a Greek boarding school in Garrison, New York in 1962, Snowe completed her secondary school education at Edward Little High School in Auburn. Shortly after her return to Maine, her uncle died, leaving her aunt, who worked the night shift, to rear six children alone. "Before we'd go to school, we'd pick her up [at the mill], and I thought how difficult it was," Snowe recalled in an interview with Susan Page for *Working Woman* (December 1983). "I guess that was when I began to realize the difficulties a woman faces, . . . the difficulties of raising a family on your own, as a single woman having lost her husband."

Following her graduation from high school, Snowe enrolled at the University of Maine at Orono, which awarded her a bachelor's degree in political science in 1969. By then she had already entered politics, having worked as a summer intern for Governor Kenneth M. Curtis, a Democrat. She switched parties sometime around 1969, when she married a Republican concrete-products business owner, Peter Trafton Snowe, who had become the youngest member of the state legislature when he took office in 1967. In 1970 Olympia Snowe worked as the Republican member on the Auburn Board of Voter Registration, and two years later she joined the staff of the district office of newly elected United States congressman William S. Cohen, a Republican.

In 1973 Snowe was elected to the Maine House of Representatives to fill the seat left vacant by the death of her husband, who had been killed in an automobile accident while returning from his office in Augusta during an April storm. "I certainly had not contemplated ever running for public office," Snowe told Susan Page, explaining, "I like behind-the-scenes work. I enjoyed what I was doing. The only reason why I decided I should probably do it was that I had such a strong passion for politics." Reelected to a full term in 1974, Snowe strengthened her position in Maine politics by serving as vice-chairman of the Auburn Republican City Committee, as a member of the Governor's Advisory Committee on the University of Maine, and as an alternate delegate to the 1976 Republican National Convention.

After she was elected to the Maine Senate in 1976, Snowe attracted the attention of not only the state's Republican Party but national party leaders as well. As a state senator, she chaired the Joint Standing Committee on Health and Institutional Services, where she gained particular recognition for her sponsorship of health-care legislation. When Congressman Cohen decided to seek a United States Senate seat in the 1978 elections, Republicans at the state and national level arranged for Snowe to run unopposed in their party's primary for the Second District House seat being vacated by Cohen. Her Democratic opponent in the general election was Maine's secretary of state, Markham L. Gartley, who had gained public notice for being the first prisoner of war released by North Vietnam. Gartley had run against Cohen in 1974 and had lost the election by a large margin.

During her 1978 congressional campaign, Snowe employed tactics she had learned while working under Cohen's tutelage, which included walking across her district—geographically the largest east of the Mississippi River—and attending town meetings and traditional bean suppers to discuss politics with voters. She also undertook efforts to "soften her 'Fifth Avenue' image," according to the 1990 edition of *Politics in America*, by "trad[ing] her designer clothes for a wool shirt and hiking boots." Her opposition to the construction of a large dam in her district and her support for the idea of national health insurance helped Snowe attract a sufficient number of crossover Democratic votes to win the election by a margin of ten percentage points, with 51 percent of the vote. Upon her victory, Snowe became, at the age of thirty-one, the youngest Republican woman, as well as the first Greek-American woman, to be elected to Congress.

Embodying the character traits that Maine natives are known for—rugged individualism and seeming indifference to national political trends—Snowe won her next five campaigns for reelection with at least two-thirds of the vote. "Independent and maverick candidates have often appealed to voters in Maine," Katharine Seelye noted in an article for the *New York Times* (March 8, 1994), "and more than a third of the state's voters are unaffiliated or attached to minor parties." Among the fifty states, Maine has the strongest record of favoring the loser in presidential elections, and has collectively tended to cast its votes for those perceived to be outside the political system. Both the Reverend Jesse Jackson and former California governor Edmund G. ("Jerry") Brown Jr., Seelye observed, have had strong showings in Maine during presidential primaries, and during the 1992 presidential elections Ross Perot garnered more votes there than did part-time Maine resident George Bush, the incumbent.

Snowe's constituency encompassed the entirety of Maine's northern half, a sprawling, sparsely populated territory filled with forests, which had supplied the state's wood and paper mills since the eighteenth century, and rural farmland dedicated to Maine's biggest cash crop—potatoes—as well as to apples, blueberries, corn, and poultry. While inhabitants of the district's rural areas tended to vote along Republican Party lines, residents of the factory cities of Lewiston, Auburn, and Bangor tended to favor the Democratic Party. Throughout the 1980s, the GOP held the advantage in the district, and this served Snowe well, even as she positioned herself as one of Congress's more moderate Republicans.

Taking a nonaligned stance on many issues, including health care and women's rights, Snowe proved to be an unbeatable candidate time and again. After achieving her first two reelection victories, against Harold Silverman in 1980 with 79 percent of the vote and James Dunleavy in 1982 with 67 percent, she went on to overwhelm Chipman C. Bull in 1984 by a margin of 76 percent to 23 percent. She topped that margin slightly in 1986, defeating Richard A. Charette with 77 percent of the vote. In 1988 she vanquished Kenneth P. Hayes by a margin of 66 percent to 34 percent.

During her first House term, Snowe worked to change federal aid formulas in an attempt to obtain for less-populous states, including her own, a larger portion of available subsidies. Toward this end, she was able to amend in 1980 a one billion-dollar antirecession aid bill to place a ceiling of 12.5 percent on the share of the total that any individual state, no matter what its size, could receive. She also began her association with the Congressional Caucus for Women's Issues, which she cochaired with Democratic congresswoman Patricia Schroeder of Colorado. As deputy whip in the House, Snowe was the only woman in the Republican congressional leadership.

When the Equal Rights Amendment was removed from the Republican platform in 1980, prior to Ronald Reagan's election, the women's caucus began developing the Economic Equity Act, a package of legislation that contained several of the ERA's key points, in somewhat modified form. "I think it's important for women in Congress to ensure equity for women," Snowe said in 1983, as quoted in the 1988 edition of *Politics in America*. "If we don't, who will?" Whereas the sweeping purview of the ERA, along with all of its implications and consequences, could be (and was) rejected in a single vote, the Economic Equity Act was divided into several different bills that addressed sex discrimination in insurance and pension laws and would have provided tax breaks for housewives and for parents who use day care. The probusiness Reagan administration, however, balked at many of the reforms, fearing that they would adversely affect the insurance industry.

Pointing out that the Republican party was gradually losing its attraction among many female voters because of its conservative stance on the ERA and reproductive rights, Snowe and Schroeder arranged a series of meetings between the caucus and the White House that would eventually lead to the administration's support of some components of the bill. "Olympia's insights have been invaluable to President Reagan and the administration," then-secretary of transportation Elizabeth Dole told Susan Page. "I don't expect to change [Reagan's] feelings or his way of looking at things," Snowe told Page. "The most important thing is to get him to sign on the dotted line."

Throughout the 1980s Snowe maintained her independence within the Republican Party. Voting for the administration's budget and tax cuts in 1981, she later modified her stance, calling for "a balanced and fair level of domestic spending," with protection for social programs and cuts in defense spending. She also changed her position on the nuclear-freeze resolution, first siding with the administration in opposition to the proposal and then voting for it after an alternative resolution failed to materialize. Nonetheless, she displayed characteristic courtesy to the party leadership in withholding a pro-freeze speech she had planned to deliver on the House floor. Meanwhile, she consistently opposed aid to the antigovernment rebels in Nicaragua until 1986, when she came around to the Reagan administration's point of view and voted to send the contras, as the guerrillas were known, $100 million in military and nonmilitary aid. In the 1987 and 1988 sessions of Congress, she supported President Reagan's positions on less than 40 percent of the House votes.

Snowe's differences with the Reagan administration regarding trade policy reflected her abiding concern for her constituency and contributed to the landslide election victories she experienced throughout the mid-1980s. Working with a group of northern, moderate Republicans referred to as Gypsy Moths, she won concessions from the administration on budget bills concerning increased aid to northern states. Among the programs for which she was able to gain increased funding were those promoting energy conservation and providing energy assistance to low-income households. Because of the effect of foreign competition on the textile, shoe, and timber industries of Maine's Second District, Snowe favored trade protection. In 1984, when the International Trade Commission recommended against import protection for footwear manufacturers, she introduced a bill limiting imports to 50 percent of the market. In August 1988 Snowe was one of only ten Republican House members to vote against the United States–Canada free-trade agreement because, she argued, it did not offset competition from Canada's government-subsidized businesses, particularly in that country's lumber and fishing industries.

Another area of frequent disagreement between Snowe and the Reagan administration was social issues. In the mid-1980s, for instance, much of her effort on the Foreign Affairs Committee dealt with maintaining the United States' commitment to United Nations–sponsored family-planning programs. In response to an effort by a Republican congressman to eliminate all American support of these programs, Snowe warned that "the antiabortion crusade has become an anti-family-planning crusade," as quoted in the 1988 edition of *Politics in America*. As a concession, she made a successful proposal to deny funding only to programs involving China, because its state-mandated one-child policy had resulted in serious human-rights violations, including forced abortions and female infanticide.

In 1988 Snowe sponsored a child-care proposal that sought to enhance the federal government's role in providing services through such measures as subsidies, employer tax credits, and various other strategies. In an effort to bridge the gap between the pro-choice and antiabortion camps, in 1989 Snowe and Schroeder introduced legislation authorizing more than seventy-seven million dollars for the establishment of five research centers that would study new methods of birth control and treatments for infertility under the auspices of the National Institute of Child Health and Human Development. A report issued on February 14, 1990 by the National Academy of Science's National Research Council and Institute of Medicine concluded that pharmaceutical research on contraceptives in the United States had virtually ceased due to the fear of product-liability lawsuits.

Such differences of opinion between Snowe and more conservative Republicans might have been expected to impair her effectiveness or damage her popularity, but her loyalty on key issues and willingness to compromise had earned her the respect and support of the party faithful at the highest levels of government. "She's a person you could work with," Congressman Trent Lott, Republican from Mississippi, told Susan Page. "Olympia usually tells you up front when she can't be there on a vote. She tries to have input that would make it possible for her to support the Republican Party position. And she usually does it without being cantankerous." Congresswoman Geraldine Ferraro, Democrat from New York, described Snowe in the same article as "very conscientious" and "a terrific legislator." Snowe also scored points for her initiative and ability to motivate others. Dissatisfied with her party's position in Congress as a "permanent minority," Snowe helped form the '92 Group, a collection of Republican moderates dedicated to gaining a House majority in the 1992 elections. She had supported George Bush's candidacy in the presidential race in 1988 (and would do so again in 1992), although she still criticized him for his positions on unemployment benefits and abortion rights, and in 1989 she had made the seconding speech to nominate Newt Gingrich (who was building his Conservative Opportunity Society) to the position of GOP whip.

Nonetheless, in 1990 Snowe faced a tough reelection campaign for the first time since her 1978 election victory. She was left vulnerable by the impact of the recession upon her district's industrial base, which lost forty thousand jobs during the late 1980s. Her support among voters was further eroded by with a series of budget cuts and tax increases imposed by Maine's Republican governor, John R. McKernan Jr., whom Snowe had married in 1989 after having dated him since the early 1980s, when they were colleagues in the United States House of Representatives. In the 1990 House elections, Snowe was challenged by Patrick K. McGowan, a member of the Maine House who accused her of spending too much time on foreign affairs at the expense of home-front issues. In November 1990 Snowe won the closest election of her career with 51 percent of the votes to McGowan's 49 percent, edging him out by a mere forty-nine hundred votes.

McGowan redoubled his efforts by immediately gearing up for the 1992 race, again attacking Snowe for her ties to the unpopular economic policies pursued by Bush and McKernan, as well as her much-publicized, and ultimately unsuccessful, effort to keep her district's Loring Air Force Base from being closed. Snowe counterattacked by linking her opponent to the state's House Democratic leadership, which was encountering increasing public dissatisfaction. The entry into the race of a third candidate, Jonathan K. Carter of the Green Party, also helped Snowe's efforts by luring voters away from McGowan. In the end, Snowe was reelected to her eighth term in the House by a margin of twenty-two thousand votes, or 49 percent to McGowan's 42 percent. From 1992 to 1994 Snowe concentrated on foreign-policy issues. She opposed deep cuts in foreign aid and criticized the bureaucratic red tape binding foreign spending procedures. As a member of the Budget Committee, she supported a constitutional amendment mandating a balanced federal budget, and as a member of the Select Committee on Aging, she backed more research into diseases affecting the elderly.

When Senate majority leader George J. Mitchell announced his retirement, after five terms, in March 1994, Snowe decided to enter the race to fill his seat. In the general election she faced Democratic congressman Thomas H. Andrews, Mitchell's handpicked choice for his successor; both candidates ran unopposed in their respective primaries. Because of her previous close calls in the races against McGowan, Snowe's campaign against Andrews was expected to be a close one. Falling in line with the Republican Party's well-organized and aggressive national strategy for 1994, Snowe portrayed her opponent as a tax-and-spend liberal and highlighted his support for the closing of the Loring Air Force Base and his unpopular votes for gun control. Snowe easily won the election; according to unofficial returns, she received 60 percent of the vote to Andrews's 37 percent.

Snowe's first year in the Senate has been marked by her efforts to balance the federal budget without sacrificing the interests of her constituents. In a speech to a Senate committee in January, 1995, she argued in favor of a constitutional amendment to balance the budget. "The people of Maine," she said, "have sent clear and unequivocal signals that we must have the courage and the will to balance the federal budget." At the same time, she has pushed for restoration of home-heating fuel subsidies, which were abolished by the House of Representatives in March 1995. Even while criticizing President Bill Clinton for his failure to sufficiently reduce the deficit, Snowe has pushed for the restoration of funding for a Job Corps center in Limestone, Maine, and she has tried to preserve the Portsmouth Naval Shipyard, in Kittery, Maine. Describing Snowe's seemingly conflicting stances in an article for the *New York Times* (May 20, 1995), Jane Fritsch observed that "she has demonstrated considerable aplomb in bouncing between budget slashing and budget loading." Snowe argued that her actions fell within the purview of what was expected of any senator. "We all fight for things we think are important," she said, as quoted by Fritsch.

In the 104th Congress, Olympia Snowe is a member of the Senate Committee on Commerce, Science, and Transportation, where she serves on the subcommittees dealing with fisheries and oceans, the merchant marine and other methods of surface transportation, consumerism, foreign commerce, and tourism. She also serves on the Senate Budget Committee; the Senate Committee on Small Business; and the Senate Committee on Foreign Relations, where she chairs the subcommittee on International Operations and serves on the subcommittees on European Affairs, Near Eastern and South Asian Affairs, and African Affairs. A member of the Holy Trinity Greek Orthodox Church of Lewiston-Auburn, Snowe is active in a number of civic and community organizations. She lives in Auburn with her husband, John R. McKernan Jr.

Selected Biographical References: N Y Times A p16 Mr 8 '94 por; Working Woman 8:96+ D '83 por; International Who's Who of Women, 1994; Politics in America, 1994; Who's Who in American Politics, 1993–94

White House

Stephanopoulos, George
(stef-ah-NOP-oh-luhs)

Feb. 10, 1961– Adviser to the President of the United States. Address: The White House, 1600 Pennsylvania Ave. NW, Washington, DC 20500

According to Robin Toner of the *New York Times*, George Stephanopoulos, a senior adviser to President Bill Clinton, is "one of those rare political staff members who move into the popular culture." Indeed, as director of communications for Clinton's presidential campaign, Stephanopoulos became a celebrity in his own right, primarily because of his intelligence, political savvy, and unflappable manner but also, in part, because of his telegenic looks and his youth (he was only thirty when he was entrusted with the important post). After Clinton's election victory, in November 1992, Stephanopoulos retained his position during the transition period and into the early days of the Clinton presidency.

It was not long, however, before Stephanopoulos, whose duties included briefing White House correspondents on a daily basis as well as advising the president, found himself at odds with the reporters. His difficult relationship with them and, by extension, with the press in general came to represent, in the eyes of some observers, the most troublesome aspects of an administration plagued by one controversy after another. When David Gergen was appointed communications director, in the spring of 1993, Stephanopoulos's reassignment was widely seen as a demotion. Washington insiders, however, pointed to his continued close working relationship with Clinton and his new title—senior adviser to the president for policy and strategy—as evidence that Stephanopoulos exerted as much influence in the White House as ever. The truth of that assertion has been borne out by the key role he has since played in Clinton's decision-making process.

Of Greek descent, George Robert Stephanopoulos was born on February 10, 1961 in Fall River, Massachusetts, the second of the four children of Robert Stephanopoulos, who is now the dean of the Holy Trinity Greek Orthodox Archdiocese Cathedral in the New York City borough of Manhattan, and Nikki Stephanopoulos. During his childhood, his family moved first to Rye, New York and then to Orange Village, Ohio, a suburb of Cleveland. Stephanopoulos is the grandson as well as the son of an Orthodox priest, and his older sister, Anastasia, is now a Greek Orthodox nun. Stephanopoulos himself once aspired to the clergy, and, as he told Joe Treen in an interview for *People* (October 26, 1992), "religion is still part of [his] whole life, [his] whole culture."

Although his family has been described as "nonpartisan," as a boy Stephanopoulos nonetheless received preparation for a life in politics. As Maura Sheehy reported in *Details* (March 1992), he "learned to craft a careful public persona for the spotlight" while assisting his father in church and accompanying him on pastoral visits in their neighborhood. In addition, Joe Treen quoted Nikki Stephanopoulos as saying that George "never played with toys" but, instead, read magazines and newspapers and was "always very involved in what was going on." At Orange High School, in Ohio, the trim Stephanopoulos took up wrestling, competing in the 105-pound weight class. Nikki Stephanopoulos told Joe Treen that the activity "disciplined and focused" her son.

Following his graduation from high school, Stephanopoulos enrolled at Columbia University, in New York City. His desire to be involved in politics surfaced during those years, although his party allegiance would later shift: in 1979, during George Bush's bid for the Republican presidential nomination, Stephanopoulos considered trying to become a delegate for Bush. As he explained to Maura Sheehy, Bush appealed to him at the time because he, Bush, was a moderate and because of his attacks on another Republican presidential candidate, Ronald Reagan. After Reagan had captured the White House, Stephanopoulos spent the summer between his junior and senior years working for Democratic representative Mary Rose Oakar of Cleveland, and, as he put it, he became "much more of a Democrat," because, in his view, President Reagan "didn't care about people."

Stephanopoulos graduated summa cum laude from Columbia in 1982 with a B.A. degree in political science. Delivering his class's salutatorian address, he condemned nuclear proliferation and praised the efforts of peace demonstrators in Europe. Following his graduation Stephanopoulos considered joining the Peace Corps, which had accepted his application, but instead became an intern at the Carnegie Endowment for International Peace, in Washington, D.C., which assigned him to the Arms Control Association. In 1983 and 1984, and again from 1986 to 1988, he served as an aide to Ohio congressman Edward Feighan, who later said of Stephanopoulos, "He is a one-man brain trust, and his advice is invaluable." Stephanopoulos was awarded a Rhodes Scholarship in 1984, and he spent the next two years at Balliol College, Oxford University, studying Christian political ethics and contemplating, as he phrased it to Maura Sheehy, "the whole question of whether you could even do politics and be a good person." Deciding in the affirmative, after he received his master's degree in theology from Oxford, he returned to the office of Congressman Feighan and attained the topmost rank, that of administrative assistant.

In 1988, during the presidential campaign, Stephanopoulos became deputy communications director for the Democratic nominee, Michael S. Dukakis. He had been eager to work for Dukakis, who was then the governor of Massachusetts, because of their shared Greek heritage and because Stephanopoulos felt confident of the candidate's chances for victory. It was while serving on Dukakis's campaign staff that he earned the nickname "Twins," for his ability to perform the tasks of two people. One of his duties was to help formulate responses to the accusations made against Dukakis by the Republican standard-bearer, then-vice-president George Bush. "We just weren't that good at it," Stephanopoulos admitted to Gwen Ifill of the *New York Times* (September 1, 1992). As quoted by Joe Treen, Stephanopoulos, musing on Dukakis's loss to Bush, stated that he and his colleagues had "underestimated the emotional power of Bush's attacks" on Dukakis's record with respect to crime and other issues. According to Fred Barnes, writing in the *New Republic* (September 6, 1993), however, Stephanopoulos and others in the Dukakis camp "worked up clever responses to attacks by Bush," but the candidate "wouldn't deliver" them.

Following Dukakis's defeat in the 1988 election, Stephanopoulos stayed away from politics for a short time, during which he held a high-ranking position with the New York City Public Library. In 1989, however, Tom O'Donnell, the chief of staff for the Democratic congressman Richard Gephardt, who was then the majority leader in the United States House of Representatives, recruited Stephanopoulos to serve as Gephardt's floor manager. In that post, which Joe Treen compared to "that of an air-traffic controller at a busy airport on a foggy night," Stephanopoulos was responsible for providing other representatives with details of the legislation Gephardt sought to pass. Stephanopoulos performed his job, which called for zealousness, tact, and a comprehensive knowledge of political issues and which kept him busy ten hours a day, seven days a week, well enough for Gephardt to tell Joe Treen, "There are lots of people up here who are good on the issues but sometimes lack diplomacy. George is good at both." Gephardt also recalled, "People liked [Stephanopoulos] instantly."

In 1991 Bob Kerry, the Democratic senator from Colorado, who was preparing to launch his presidential campaign, sought Stephanopoulos's services. Shortly after meeting with Bill Clinton, however, Stephanopoulos decided to cast his lot with the then-governor of Arkansas, whose dedication to providing economic opportunity while emphasizing personal responsibility he found appealing. As Clinton's deputy campaign manager and chief spokesman, Stephanopoulos set up office in the Clinton camp's modest, initially understaffed headquarters in Little Rock, Arkansas and took on tasks as numerous as they were varied. Among other things, he helped write Clinton's speeches, supervised polling, campaign ads, and contact with the press, advised the candidate on policy, and appeared on talk shows as his surrogate. Gwen Ifill reported that a "typical work day" for Stephanopoulos during the campaign lasted fourteen hours and found him "field[ing] one hundred telephone calls" and "mak[ing] half again that many himself."

Stephanopoulos also traveled extensively with Clinton as part of the candidate's efforts to meet a broad cross section of voters. He told Maura Sheehy that during a trip to New Hampshire, he "was in a dozen living rooms, seeing the people, hearing about their problems, seeing what moved them, what made them nod their heads." The conclusion he formed was that "the economy was slipping away from them, and Washington didn't seem to be paying attention." "For these people," he said, "I was part of the problem, even though we thought we'd been helping them." Discussing the application of that insight to his work for the Clinton campaign, Stephanopoulos told Sheehy, "We want to run the campaign that Bobby Kennedy started to run in [1968] and didn't get to finish," and he stressed the importance of "reaching out to every single part of the country, reaching their real needs and concerns, and actually touching them."

The nuts and bolts of "reaching" voters was an area in which Clinton's communications director showed particular brilliance. Maura Sheehy offered as one example of Stephanopoulos's method his skill in capitalizing on opponents' missteps. Learning that the Senate had voted on an amendment to a "compromise" unemployment bill (the original bill had been vetoed by President George Bush) and that the amendment sought to extend benefits in some economically depressed states, Stephanopoulos immediately set about learning whether Senators Kerry and Tom Harkin, another Democratic presidential aspirant, had voted. Upon receiving the news he had hoped for—that both Kerry and Harkin had missed the vote—Stephanopoulos contacted Clinton, who was scheduled to give a press conference later in the day, and, as Sheehy phrased it, began "giving the candidate stump lines: 'It's absurd. So the people who have been unemployed the longest get the least. This is Washington playing politics with people's lives, talking formulas while people can't put food on the table. In Washington, compromise means people get screwed. It's unfair, it's wrong, it's absurd. And it shows why we need people in Washington who understand as much about the workrooms of New Hampshire as the boardrooms of Wall Street and the back rooms of Washington.'" While Dukakis had been unwilling to make full use of Stephanopoulos's political cunning, Clinton was receptive to his aide's ingenious ploys as ways of distinguishing himself from his Democratic and Republican rivals. In that particular instance, Clinton scored politically by using Stephanopoulos's tip.

A significant part of Stephanopoulos's contribution to the Clinton campaign involved fending off attacks on his candidate's personal character. Responding to allegations that Clinton had engaged in a long-term extramarital affair and charges that he had unfairly avoided the draft during the Vietnam War, Stephanopoulos issued press releases denying any wrongdoing on Clinton's part and putting in perspective the importance of the accusations. In the midst of an unusually acrimonious campaign, however, Stephanopoulos did not lose sight of what he considered to be the single most important issue of all. "The difference between this and 1988," he told Joe Treen, "is that we are learning to stay focused and to stay on the economy." After Clinton defeated President Bush in the general election of November 1992, Stephanopoulos oversaw the communications process for the president-elect's transition team. When Clinton was sworn in, on January 20, 1993, Stephanopoulos, at the age of thirty-one, assumed the post of assistant to the president and director of the fifty-two-member White House communications department.

The friction between Stephanopoulos and White House reporters was evident at his first, half-hour press briefing, which, as Howard Kurtz of the *Washington Post* (January 22, 1993) put it, "wasn't pretty." Under persistent questioning regarding Clinton's ill-fated nomination of Zoë Baird for the position of United States attorney general, Stephanopoulos "lost his control early," in Kurtz's words, and gave vague answers "more appropriate to the transition period." Contributing to the strained relations between the communications director and the press corps were the new policy of barring journalists from the area behind the briefing room, where Stephanopoulos and White House press secretary Dee Dee Myers had their offices, and a general limiting of information given to reporters. That untenable situation, combined with a number of early public-relations gaffes made by the Clinton administration and the feeling that Stephanopoulos, as he himself later phrased it, was "doing too much" in his dual role as communications director and presidential adviser, led Clinton and his then-chief of staff, Thomas McLarty, to bring in David Gergen as the new White House spokesman in May 1993. Stephanopoulos was given the title of senior adviser to the president for policy and strategy.

While the shift of responsibilities generated considerable discussion in the print and broadcast media about his "fall," Stephanopoulos has continued to play a crucial advisory role on issues central to Clinton's presidency. He has also been instrumental in selling Clinton's position on those issues to legislators and others. For example, after Clinton's plan to lift the ban on gays in the military met with resistance from Pentagon officials, Stephanopoulos—once he was convinced that a compromise would still benefit gay people—worked with the Pentagon on the details of the "don't ask, don't tell" policy, under which homosexuals are not kept out of the armed services but are barred from revealing their sexual orientation. He also played an important part in getting the president's budget passed in the fall of 1993, securing three congressional votes by committing the president to making future spending cuts. (The budget passed by a margin of only five votes.)

Early in 1994 Stephanopoulos found himself at the center of a controversy that was part of a larger scandal surrounding the Whitewater real-estate development firm. In the autumn of the previous year, federal prosecutors had begun trying to determine whether President Clinton, during his tenure as governor of Arkansas, had received illegal political contributions from the Madison Guaranty Savings and Loan, whose owner, James B. McDougal, had also co-owned Whitewater with Clinton and his wife, Hillary Rodham Clinton. On February 25, 1994, after learning that Jay B. Stephens, a United States attorney who had previously criticized the Clinton administration, had been named as the Whitewater special prosecutor, Stephanopoulos telephoned his friend Joshua Steiner of the Treasury Department and reportedly asked whether that selection was final or if "anything could be done" about it. Stephanopoulos later said that he was told the appointment was final and that "that ended the matter, as far as [he] was concerned." When the conversation came to light, however, the White House and an independent counsel launched inquiries to determine whether Stephanopoulos's actions constituted obstruction of justice, and Stephanopoulos was called to testify before a grand jury. The independent counsel subsequently declined to bring charges against him. Michael Kinsley of the *New Republic* (April 18, 1994) may have put the matter in perspective when he wrote: "A White House official is told the rules and obeys them. Where is the scandal? Isn't that exactly what is supposed to happen?"

George Stephanopoulos, who has dark hair and brown eyes, stands about five feet, seven inches tall and weighs around 145 pounds. His boyish good looks and high profile have brought him fan mail from a legion of female admirers, and during the 1992 campaign, as Joe Treen reported, "his picture even grace[d] an admirer's wall at Bush-Quayle headquarters in Washington." Commenting on Stephanopoulos's highly regarded intellect, James Carville, Clinton's 1992 campaign strategist, told Gwen Ifill: "If George's IQ could be converted to Fahrenheit, that boy could boil water." Others have remarked upon his soft speaking voice (which one reporter called "a power whisper" that "makes people lean into him, like plants reaching toward the sun") and his willingness "to bury his own views for what he sees as a greater good." He has been described as "quiet, intense, internal," and, somewhat surprisingly, as a "born pessimist." Perhaps his defining trait, however, is the one noted by President Clinton: "No matter how hard George works, no matter how much pressure he is under, he is always cool under fire." In his free time, Stephanopoulos enjoys playing poker and listening to the music of Bruce Springsteen. In 1993 he received the John Jay Award for professional achievement from his alma mater, Columbia University.

Selected Biographical References: Details p98+ M '92 pors; N Y Times S 1 '92 por; New Repub 209:17+ S 6 '93; People 38:34+ O 26 '92 pors; Time 143:20+ Ap 4 '94 pors; U S News 113:34+ D 7 '92 pors; USA Today A p6 Je 25 '93 pors; Who's Who in America, 1995; Who's Who in American Politics, 1993-94

Stockton, John

Mar. 26, 1962– Basketball player. Address: c/o Utah Jazz, Delta Center, 301 W. South Temple, Salt Lake City, UT 84101-1404

Although he lacks Earvin "Magic" Johnson's dazzling showmanship, Anfernee Hardaway's soaring athleticism, and Isiah Thomas's flair for making sensational highlight-reel plays, John Stockton, the poker-faced point guard of the Utah Jazz, has quietly amassed more assists than any player in the history of the National Basketball Association. Drafted by the Jazz in 1984, he served a promising three-year apprenticeship behind the veteran point guard Rickey Green. But when Stockton became a full-time starter in 1987, he shattered Isiah Thomas's single-season assists record and teamed up with the All-NBA power forward Karl Malone to make the Utah Jazz a perennial play-off contender and Western Conference force. "You get the impression that he's not all that quick, or strong, and he's not really flashy," the Jazz forward David Benoit pointed out to Ira Berkow of the *New York*

Utah Jazz

John Stockton

Times (January 23, 1995). "I mean, his passes are usually straightforward, nothing behind the back or between the legs, and rarely a no-look. I know that a lot of other point guards in the league, especially black guys, have said, 'I can take that little white guy.' And then he makes dead meat out of them."

A member of the so-called Dream Team that captured the gold medal in men's basketball for the United States at the 1992 Olympic Games, Stockton has become the Bob Cousy of the 1990s—a heady court general who can knock down clutch three-point jumpers and apply relentless defensive pressure but primarily distributes the ball to open teammates for easy scores. "We had a saying in high school and college, 'Make your teammate an All-American,' and in this case, 'Make your teammate an All-Star,' and Stock is one of those guys," Karl Malone gushed when he spoke to Dan Diefenbach, who profiled Stockton for *Sport* (February 1995). "He always tries to go out and make his teammates All-Stars. People ask me what I would be without him, and I don't even want to think about it."

John Houston Stockton was born in Spokane, Washington on March 26, 1962, the younger son in Jack and Clementine Stockton's family of two boys and two girls. His father was the co-owner of Jack & Dan's Tavern, a popular Spokane watering hole near the campus of Gonzaga University. As a boy, Stockton spent virtually all his free time playing basketball. In all kinds of weather and at any hour of the day, he could invariably be found shooting baskets on the sloping driveway in front of his home. Mark Rypien, who quarterbacked the Washington Redskins to victory in Super Bowl XXVI, also grew up in Spokane, and, in an interview with Steve Rushin for *Sports Illustrated* (July 27, 1992), he recalled, "I remember driving by Stockton's house in high school. Ten, eleven o'clock at night, and he was out on the driveway, dribbling a basketball."

The constant practicing turned Stockton into a sure ball handler, but he was nonetheless bullied by his brother, Steve, in their no-holds-barred playground games of one-on-one. "Those were rough games and I'd get knocked around," Stockton admitted to Ira Berkow, "and I'd get knocked around when I played in other games in the neighborhood. And I remember when I was in the sixth or seventh grade, and I came home crying, my father said, 'Maybe you shouldn't play with those boys, maybe they're too rough.' He said it in a kindly way, but it made me take it as a challenge. Maybe I was stupid, but I went back out to show them I could play."

Unable to shoot over the taller boys, the wiry Stockton developed his passing game and became a relentless defender with an instinctive ability to swipe the ball from careless ball handlers. He also increased his speed and stamina by running track. According to Steve Rushin, as of 1992 Stockton still held the Spokane grade-school record for the mile run, which he set as an eighth-grader at St. Aloysius, a parochial elementary school. At Gonzaga Prep, he was a standout guard on the basketball team. In one memorable game, he torched Mark Rypien, who was then the point guard for rival Shadle Park High School, for forty-two points. Stockton's exploits on the basketball court earned him a place alongside Rypien and future baseball great Ryne Sandberg, then a three-sport star at Spokane's North Central High School, in the triumvirate of local sports folk heroes, but he was not considered to be a blue-chip schoolboy with NBA prospects. "The only person in the *world* who thought John would play in the NBA was John," Jack Stockton said to Steve Rushin.

Following his graduation from high school in 1980, John Stockton enrolled at his father's alma mater, Gonzaga University. He played sparingly for Gonzaga as a freshman, but the following year he posted an average of 11.2 points and averaged 5.0 assists per game. Although his field-goal percentage dropped somewhat in the 1982–83 season, from 58 to 52 percent, he averaged 13.9 points and 6.8 assists per outing. In his senior year his 20.9 points average (on 58 percent shooting) was the best in the West Coast Athletic Conference, and he also dished out 7.2 assists per game. Over the course of his 107-game career at Gonzaga, he tallied an average of 12.5 points and 5.2 assists while connecting on 56 percent of his field goals and shooting 72 percent from the free-throw line. In the first round of the talent-rich 1984 NBA draft, which included such potential hall-of-famers as Michael Jordan, Hakeem Olajuwon, and Charles Barkley, the Utah Jazz turned heads by gambling the sixteenth pick overall on Stockton, a scrappy but little-known playmaker from a small college who was, at six-foot-one and 175 pounds, short and slight by NBA standards.

Led by the high-scoring forward Adrian Dantley and the talented guard tandem of Darrell Griffith and Rickey Green, coach Frank Layden's Utah Jazz had won the Midwest Division title in 1984 before losing to the Phoenix Suns in the Western Conference semifinals. As a backup to Green, an NBA All-Star, at point guard, Stockton averaged 5.6 points and 5.1 assists in his rookie year while Utah struggled, losing half of its regular-season games. The team's one-rung-from-the-bottom finish in the Midwest Division enabled the Jazz to acquire the promising power forward Karl Malone in the 1985 draft, and in the 1985–86 season, Utah rebounded to a record of forty-two wins and forty losses. Stockton spent half of that season as the starting point guard, racking up 7.4 assists and 7.7 points per game while recording one of best assist-to-turnover ratios in the league.

Sharing the point guard duties with Green in 1986–87, Stockton handed out 8.2 assists and scored 7.9 points per game as the Jazz notched a 44–38 record that left the team eleven games out of first place in the Midwest Division. In the following season, his first as a full-time starter, Stockton emerged as one of the NBA's premier point guards, dispensing 1,128 assists to erase Isiah Thomas's single-season record and join Thomas and Kevin Porter as the only players in league history to exceed one thousand assists in a season. Stockton led the league in that category, surging past the perennial All-NBA point guard Magic Johnson with an average of 13.8 assists to Johnson's 11.9, and he finished third in steals, behind Michael Jordan and Alvin Robertson, with an average of just under three thefts per game. A deadly jump shooter with three-point range, Stockton averaged 14.7 points a game while draining 57 percent of his attempts from the floor. Powered by the high-scoring Karl Malone, the Jazz, the winner of forty-seven games during the season, proved to be a formidable opponent in the play-offs, extending the eventual NBA champion Los Angeles Lakers to the full seven games in the Western Conference finals.

Although he and Malone became the most potent guard-forward combination in the NBA, Stockton did not accumulate his impressive statistics simply by lobbing the ball to the burly Malone for easy buckets in the paint. As the point guard for the Jazz, he directed the offense and ran the fast break, distributing the ball to teammates with rifle passes that anticipated split-second openings in the flow of court traffic. "It wasn't all just feeding a post-up player," Frank Layden said to Lex Hemphill of the *Sporting News* (May 2, 1988). "It's been scattering the ball. The way we run our break, it could be confusing, because sometimes we have two and three men on one side of the floor. He seems to dish it off to the right guy." Stockton's skill in the open court notwithstanding, Jerry Sloan, who became Utah's head coach in 1988, told Hemphill that the playmaker's genius rested in his ability to "pick people out in a congested area." "John can let guys cross and go through and, all of a sudden, bang, something happens for him," Sloan explained. "From that standpoint, I'd say he's probably the best I've ever seen."

After claiming the Midwest Division title in the 1988–89 regular season with a record of fifty-one victories and thirty-one defeats, the Jazz were swept in the play-offs' opening round by the forty-three-and-thirty-nine Golden State Warriors. For the year, Stockton's 13.6 assists per game again topped the league, and he led the NBA in steals, with an average of 3.2. Moreover, he upped his scoring average to 17.1 points by connecting on 54 percent of his field goals and shooting 86 percent from the charity stripe. In 1989–90 Michael Jordan edged past him in thefts with an average of 2.8 steals to Stockton's 2.7, but the Jazz point guard posted a career-high average of 14.5 assists while contributing an average of 17.2 points per game. Utah won fifty-five regular-season contests during that campaign only to suffer a first-round elimination in the postseason for the second consecutive year.

The following season Stockton again scored 17.2 points per game and averaged 14.2 assists and 2.9 steals as Utah went fifty-four and twenty-eight and advanced to the Western Conference semifinals before losing in five games to the Phoenix Suns. In 1991–92 Utah's 55–27 record captured the Midwest Division title, and Stockton and Malone carried the squad to the conference finals, where the Jazz succumbed in six games to the Portland Trail Blazers. For the fifth season in a row, Stockton topped the one thousand mark in assists, averaging 13.7 per outing; he also stole the ball 2.4 times a game and nailed a career-best eighty-three three-point baskets. Although his increased number of attempts from the three-point arc, where he canned 41 percent of his shots, cut into his field-goal percentage, which fell slightly, to 48 percent, he still managed to average a respectable 15.8 points a game.

In late 1991 Stockton was the overwhelming choice of a thirteen-member selection committee to join Michael Jordan and Magic Johnson in the backcourt rotation for the men's basketball team that would represent the United States at the 1992 Olympic Games in Barcelona, Spain. (Guard Clyde Drexler was added to that collection of superstars in 1992.) Because Stockton played in a small-market city on a squad that had never reached the NBA finals, his selection to the Dream Team was perceived in some quarters as a slight to Detroit's high-profile playmaker Isiah Thomas, who had led the Indiana University Hoosiers to a national championship in college and spearheaded the Detroit Pistons' drive to capture back-to-back NBA titles in 1989 and 1990.

Although the Stockton-versus-Thomas controversy elicited some harsh comments about the Piston from Jazz president Frank Layden, the laconic Stockton, who has shunned the limelight throughout his career, refused to defend his selection or trumpet his qualifications. "I haven't been involved in any controversy," he told Jan Hubbard of the *Sporting News* (November 4, 1991). "It had nothing to do with me. The thing with Isiah was between him and the committee. I wasn't involved." The Jazz leader in consecutive games played, Stockton is widely considered to be an almost injury-proof iron horse, but a broken leg that he suffered during the Olympic qualifying round relegated him to spot duty in Barcelona, where the Dream Team overwhelmed their opponents.

Playing on the Jazz home court in Salt Lake City, Stockton and Malone combined to lead the Western Conference to a 135–132 overtime victory in the 1993 All-Star game. With Stockton delivering a game-high 15 assists and Malone outstripping all other scorers with 28 points, the Jazz stars shared the game's most-valuable-player award. Utah finished the 1992–93 regular season eight games out of first place in the Midwest Division, but Stockton topped the league in assists for the sixth straight year with an average of 12.0 per game, came in third in steals with a per-game average of 2.4, and scored 15.1 points, on 49 percent field-goal shooting. The stellar off-guard Jeff Hornacek, who was acquired in a trade with the Philadelphia 76ers, joined Stockton in the Jazz backcourt for the 1993–94 season, in which Utah won fifty-three regular-season games. In the play-offs, the Jazz made it all the way to the conference finals before falling in five games to the Houston Rockets, the eventual world champion. A first-team All-NBA selection for the first time in his career, Stockton put together an impressive list of statistics for the year, including averages of 12.6 assists, 2.4 steals, and 15.1 points, on 53 percent shooting from the floor.

Early in 1995, midway through his eighth season as a regular starter, Stockton became the NBA's all-time leader in assists, moving past Magic Johnson, who had handed out 9,823 assists in his twelve-year career with the Lakers. Stockton also tied the record of former Boston Celtic great Bob Cousy when he finished the year as the league's assist leader for the eighth consecutive season. Although the Jazz finished the 1995–96 season with the third-best record in the Western Conference, they were rewarded with the unenviable task of facing the defending champion Houston Rockets in the first round of the play-offs. Utah extended the series to the limit before Houston emerged victorious on their way to a second consecutive championship. Both Stockton and Malone were named to the All-NBA squad following the season.

Although he lacks the flamboyance of Isiah Thomas and Magic Johnson, Stockton executes the Jazz offense with almost flawless precision, and he possesses such an explosive first step that former Jazz swingman Kelly Tripucka was prompted to describe him to Lex Hemphill as "the fastest white guy" in the league. "He's a nuisance," Tripucka said, "and that's a compliment. He's like a fly that won't go out of the house." "When I first came into the league, I thought I could take him pretty easily," the veteran point guard Johnny Dawkins recalled to Ira Berkow. "But I learned that you can't relax for a second with him. He sees everything on the court, and he's aware of everything. You stand up for a moment and he's got that quick first step and he's got you on his hip, and he's either laying the ball in the hoop or dishing off to somebody for a basket. And then when you least expect it, when the game is on the line, he'll pull up for a three-pointer and hit one at the buzzer."

The unflappable Stockton is not known for histrionic outbursts or trash talking on the court, but in his will to win he is as determined and cold-hearted as a professional assassin. "There is a toughness in Stockton's game that one might expect from a tavern owner's son," Phil Taylor noted in *Sports Illustrated* (May 30, 1994). "Look closely at that stone-faced expression and it begins to resemble a scowl." "He's got a lot of street in him," Karl Malone told Taylor. Stockton himself has characterized his style of play as "irritating" rather than dirty. Among the opponents he has irritated is Dennis Rodman, the San Antonio Spur's bruising intimidator. During the 1994 play-offs, Rodman became so impatient with the impenetrable screens Stockton was setting that he flagrantly fouled the Jazz point guard. "Stockton's as mean as they come," Rodman said later, as quoted by Phil Taylor. "Everybody might think he's a choirboy, but he'll slip you an elbow when the refs aren't looking, or he'll talk some junk. I like that in a guy."

Stockton brings an elegant simplicity to the game that makes it easy for the stoic floor leader to be overlooked. "He's so good, you begin to take him for granted," Karl Malone observed to Berkow. "I've just come to always expect the perfect pass from him, and I get it. And I was thinking not long ago, even I don't appreciate him as much as I should." Stockton is a deft passer because, in addition to his vision and uncanny timing, he has enormous hands that allow him to palm the ball off the dribble. "Most other guys have to pick the ball up to grip it with two hands before they can pass," Jeff Hornacek explained in his interview with Berkow. "But I marvel at his anticipation. Like a quarterback. I'll come around off a pick and in the split second I'm open, the ball will just be sitting there waiting to be shot."

Unselfish and self-effacing, Stockton deflects attention from himself, declining requests for interviews so that lesser-known teammates can enjoy the media spotlight, and he is averse to making public appearances on behalf of the Jazz or Nike, the sporting-goods manufacturer whose sneaker he endorses. In the off-season, Stockton and his wife, the former Nada Stepovich, whom he married on August 16, 1986, live next door to the house in which John grew up, and they maintain a lakeside cottage in rural Washington State. They have three sons—Houston, Michael, and David—and a daughter, Lindsay. "He likes being home with us," Nada Stockton said of her husband when she spoke to Ira Berkow. "But even at home you can see how competitive John is. Like when he plays games with the kids, basketball or anything else." Stockton's college teammate Jeff Condill agreed, telling Steve Rushin, "He takes losing personally. Whatever he plays, Ping-Pong, golf, lawn darts. He holds the Jazz record on the treadmill, and he wants to defend that title every year."

Selected Biographical References: Chicago Tribune IV p1+ Ja 26 '94 pors; N Y Times C p1+ Ja 23 '95 pors; Sport 82:45+ D '91 pors, 85:41+ Jl '94 pors, 86:69+ F '95 pors; Sporting N p42 My 2 '88 por, p8 N 4 '91 por; Sports Illus p62+ Jl 27 '92 pors, 80:20+ My 30 '94 pors; Who's Who in America, 1995

F. Phipps/CBC

Suzuki, David T.

(soo-ZOO-kee)

Mar. 24, 1936- Canadian broadcast journalist; geneticist; writer; educator; environmentalist; civil rights activist. Address: c/o Sustainable Development Research Institute, University of British Columbia, Vancouver, British Columbia, Canada V6T 2A9

The Canadian broadcast journalist and writer David T. Suzuki, who has appeared on television for the past sixteen years as the eminently enthusiastic, engaging, and knowledgeable host of the celebrated CBC series *The Nature of Things*, has been recognized along with such figures as Jacques Cousteau and Carl Sagan as one of the world's most effective popularizers of science. A prize-winning geneticist and college teacher, Suzuki launched his first career, in zoological research, in the United States in 1961, after completing his undergraduate and graduate studies at American institutions. He returned to Canada a year later and, in 1963, set up a laboratory at the University of British Columbia, where he became a full professor at the age of thirty-three. His pathbreaking discoveries regarding temperature-sensitive genetic mutations in fruit flies earned him, in 1969 and the two following years, the E. W. R. Steacie award, which is given annually to the outstanding research scientist in Canada under the age of thirty-five.

In the 1970s Suzuki withdrew from active research to devote himself primarily to broadcast journalism. In the past quarter century, he has anchored dozens of popular and critically acclaimed radio or television series, miniseries, and specials. His credits include, on radio, *Quirks and Quarks* (1974–79), *Earthwatch* (1980), *Discovery with David Suzuki* (from 1983 on), and *It's a Matter of Survival* (1989), all of which he both originated and hosted, and on television, *Science Magazine* (1974–79), *A Planet for the Taking* (1985), and *The Secret of Life* (1993) as well as *The Nature of Things*, which currently airs in more than fifty countries. In addition to demystifying science for nonscientists, Suzuki, who is Canada's best-known environmental crusader and a dedicated civil rights activist, has frequently addressed in his broadcasts and other public forums such controversial issues as the social responsibilities of scientists, the social implications of gene therapy and other scientific innovations, the dangers posed by the economic and political pressures on scientists, deficiencies in science education, the consequences of underfunding basic research, and the unwitting or intentional misuses of scientific data and statistics.

Suzuki has also strived to alert people to the threats to the biosphere that have resulted from humankind's attempts to dominate the planet. "As a scientist, I know how ignorant we are of the biological and physical world," he wrote in *Metamorphosis* (1987), his autobiography, "yet we continue to cling to the lie that we *know* what we're doing. The truth is we have no idea." In the conviction that, in his words, "the ecological crisis that afflicts the world is, at its base, a result of the tremendous alienation that we feel from the natural world," he has also endeavored to foster, particularly in children, a "spiritual connection with nature," so that people will "consider the water and the air and the soil their home." In 1990 he and Dr. Tara E. Cullis, his wife, founded the David Suzuki Foundation, which, according to Suzuki, is dedicated to developing "a vision of sustainable communities living within the planets' carrying capacity, . . . a strategy for communities to work toward that vision, and a communications plan to help work through the strategy."

A third-generation Canadian of Japanese ancestry, David Takayoshi Suzuki was born on March 24, 1936 in Vancouver, British Columbia, to Kaoru Suzuki (called Carr) and Setsu (Nakamura) Suzuki (called Sue). His twin sister, Marcia, is a homemaker; his younger sisters, Aiko and Dawn, are a filmmaker and a dancer, respectively. For his first six years, Suzuki lived with his family in Marpole, a section of Vancouver, in the back of the dry-cleaning store that his mother and father owned and managed. Although they had both been born and educated in Canada and were upstanding members of their community, Suzuki's parents, like all other Japanese-Canadians, were not permitted to vote or to hold jobs in civil service, forestry, or various other professions. Military service was also closed to them. "We in British Columbia are firmly convinced that once a Jap, always a Jap," A. W. Neill, a representative in the Canadian parliament, said early in 1941, in a remark (quoted in *Metamorphosis*) that gave voice to the suspicions that many of his countrymen apparently harbored about the loyalty of Japanese-Canadians.

Shortly after the bombing of Pearl Harbor by Japan, on December 7, 1941, the Canadian government began relocating all Japanese-Canadians and confiscating their property. Men were sent to work camps, and women and children were incarcerated in remote ghost towns. Carr and Sue Suzuki lost nearly all their possessions, including their home, business, and insurance policies for their children's education. After working for about a year on the Trans-Canada Highway, Carr Suzuki joined his family in the single room allotted to them in a dilapidated building in Slocan City, an abandoned mining town in the Rocky Mountains. His earnings from a store job supplemented the small salary his wife received as a secretary.

It was not until 1943 that a school opened in Slocan City, with classes taught by young, untrained Japanese-Canadian women. Within a year David Suzuki progressed from the first grade to the fourth, in part because, unlike most of the other children, whose first language was Japanese, he spoke only English. His ignorance of Japanese, his outspokenness (a trait that Japanese people have traditionally frowned on but that his parents encouraged), and his identification with Canadians rather than the people of Japan alienated him from his schoolmates, and some of them regularly beat up on him.

At home, however, as the only son in a household where, as he wrote in *Metamorphosis*, the "cultural assumptions of male dominance" held sway, Suzuki was the "favored and most important child." Each day his father, whom he has described as his "greatest inspiration and role model," would ask him many questions about what he had learned in school. "He always listened carefully to my responses," Suzuki has recalled. "It gave me a sense that what I was reciting was important, and I loved dredging up all the details." "His vast faith in me gave me the nerve to try what my own inclinations often resisted," he has said. His father impressed upon him the belief that "for an Asian to do as well as a white, he had to be ten times as good," as William McCoy quoted Suzuki as saying in the *Dial* (July 1984), and repeatedly advised him, "Whatever you do, do it with everything you've got—whether it's scrubbing the floor, fishing for trout, or studying for exams." By his own account, thanks to such admonitions—and his wartime internment, an experience that "seared his soul," as he told Clyde H. Farnsworth for the international edition of the *New York Times* (December 28, 1994)—he developed a fierce desire to prove his worth.

A passionate outdoorsman and immensely knowledgeable avocational naturalist who had what Suzuki has described as an "enormous exuberance for life" and curiosity about everything, Suzuki's father powerfully influenced him additionally by vigorously encouraging his fascination with and love of nature. Carr Suzuki had begun taking his son fishing and camping and introducing him to the marvels of the natural world when the boy was little more than a toddler, and they often fished and hiked together during the war years. "Those activities shaped my interests for the rest of my life . . . ," David Suzuki has said, "and provided me with a base of intimate experience and knowledge on which my scientific career in biology would be built years later."

At the end of World War II, the government of British Columbia ruled that no person of Japanese ancestry could remain in the province. Faced with the choice of going to Japan—a foreign country for David's Canadian family—or moving east of the Rockies, the Suzukis settled in the province of Ontario. After living for a year in Olindo, where Carr Suzuki worked on a peach farm, they moved to Leamington, where he got a job at a dry-cleaning establishment. David Suzuki's bedroom in the family's Leamington home soon turned into an amateur naturalist's museum, with tanks of freshwater fish, collections of fossils and rocks, and displays of insects, skins of road-killed animals, and dried fish heads. As a ninth-grader at Leamington High School, he won a school-wide oratorical contest by presenting a speech on animal adaptations (which, with the meticulous coaching of his father, he had practiced for hours each day for weeks) and an extemporaneous speech in which, having been asked to imagine that he was three inches tall, he described being swallowed by a fish and surviving by entering the creature's air bladder. Within the next several years, he placed first in two Ontario-wide public-speaking competitions and third in another.

Following his family's move to London, Ontario, where Carr Suzuki worked as a carpenter and later as an insurance salesman, the fourteen-year-old Suzuki entered the London Central Collegiate High School, where he was one of only about a dozen nonwhite pupils. A good student with indifferent athletic and social skills in a school where academic excellence was downplayed, in his last year he nevertheless won election to the presidency of the student body, by campaigning on a platform that appealed to the many other members of Central Collegiate's out-group. Suzuki's sense of being an outsider, which had taken root during the war, had intensified during his adolescence and teens, and as a delayed consequence of the wartime propaganda that had associated Oriental facial features and skin color with perfidy, deceit, and fiendishness, he had also become acutely self-conscious about his appearance and consumed by self-hatred.

In 1954 Suzuki, with a full scholarship, entered Amherst College, in Massachusetts, where his obsessive desire to surgically enlarge his eyes, change his hair color, and anglicize his name gradually faded away. The camaraderie between faculty and students at Amherst and the college's small classes, intellectually rigorous curriculum, and emphasis on the process of acquiring knowledge rather than the absorption of facts all "brought out the best" in him and "extended [his] horizons in all directions," in his words. In addition to a class in embryology, Suzuki has identified as especially inspirational a course in genetics that William M. Hexter presented as if the subject were a detective story. "For the first time in my life, I sat in a class completely enthralled, my mouth hanging open in astonishment at the beauty of the insights and the elegance of mathematical precision absent from most other areas of biology," he has said of Hexter's class.

Guided by Hexter, Suzuki undertook a senior honors project in which, using as his experimental subjects insects of the genus *Drosophila* (commonly known as fruit flies), he investigated "the physical exchange of parts of similar chromosomes during the production of eggs," a phenomenon known in biology as "crossing over." The enthusiastic reception that greeted the lectures he presented to other students and faculty members on his research and the work of established scientists demonstrated to him that he had a knack for explaining highly technical concepts and contributed, along with his newly sprouted passion for genetics, to his decision to change his career objective from medical doctor to teacher and researcher. In 1958, after earning a B.A. degree in biology cum laude, he entered a graduate program in zoology at the University of Chicago, where he held a research assistantship and, in 1960–61, the John M. Prather Fellowship. For his doctoral project, he continued his investigations of chromosomal crossovers in fruit flies. Through meetings on fruit fly research that he helped to organize at Midwestern universities, Suzuki met many prominent scientists, among them the geneticist Dan L. Lindsley, of the Oak Ridge National Laboratory, in Tennessee.

In the summer of 1961, after receiving a Ph.D. degree (in the remarkably short time of less than three years), Suzuki did postdoctoral research as an National Institutes of Health fellow at the Rocky Mountain Biological Laboratory, in Colorado. That fall he began working as a research associate in Dan Lindsley's lab at Oak Ridge. Although the lab was racially integrated and the townspeople of Oak Ridge apparently treated Suzuki as if he were Caucasian, segregation was still entrenched in Tennessee, as it was throughout the South, and black people could neither live in Oak Ridge nor use such facilities as the launderette. As an undergraduate and graduate student, Suzuki had begun to identify with blacks and to see his "hangups about being Japanese in a white society as a mini-reflection of black problems," as he has said. In Tennessee, where he was the only nonblack member of the local chapter of the NAACP, his identification with blacks became so strong that "their resentments became [his]," as he recalled in *Metamorphosis.* "I began to feel a rage towards white people," he wrote. "A 'Whites Only' sign drove me into a frenzy of anger." "Eventually I became almost mentally unbalanced," he admitted to Blaik Kirby for the Toronto *Globe and Mail* (December 31, 1970). His bitterness and fury led him to reject excellent job offers from three top American universities, and, despite the abuses that the Japanese had suffered in Canada during the war and that the native peoples of Canada still endured, he returned to his homeland. "I felt there would be more opportunity for an individual to register an impact in Canada than in a huge country like the United States," he has explained. "To me, Canada still meant a civility that was missing in the States."

In 1962 Suzuki got a job as an assistant professor of genetics at the University of Alberta, in Edmonton. He left in 1963 to join, with the same academic rank, the Department of Zoology at the University of British Columbia, in Vancouver. His demanding course in genetics became so popular that he was forced to move the class from a small room to a lecture hall. "I tried to put myself in a beginner's place and to develop a sequence of lectures that would peel away the layers of mystery, just as Professor Hexter had done for me," he has said. In 1968 he was named runner-up for the university's first annual Master Teacher Award, and in 1969 he became a full professor.

When he was not teaching, Suzuki spent nearly all his daytime and nighttime hours in his lab, where, according to some sources, the atmosphere resembled that of a commune. In the course of his research, which focused on the behavior of chromosomes during cell division, he and his team discovered a genetic mutation in certain fruit flies that caused the insects to become paralyzed when their temperatures rose above a particular point. He and his assistants later identified many other genetic mutations in fruit flies that could be controlled by changes in temperature. In 1969, 1970, and 1971, in recognition of his discoveries, which advanced the understanding of genetics, neurology, and animal development and behavior, the National Sciences and Engineering Research Council of Canada awarded him the prestigious E. W. R. Steacie Memorial Fellowship.

Meanwhile, in 1962 Suzuki had entered the field of broadcasting, with eight lectures that he presented for an Edmonton community television program called *Your University Speaks.* "I found that performing in front of the unforgiving eye of the camera was not at all intimidating," he has said of that experience. During the next few years, he periodically gave interviews for television or radio and developed a reputation as an interesting and articulate interviewee. In 1969 or 1970, while making three television shows for the CBC in which he and another researcher shared their thoughts on a variety of scientific subjects, he realized, as he recalled in *Metamorphosis*, "what a powerful medium television could be." "I loved the *idea* of making science available to the layperson," he wrote.

The positive reaction of CBC executives to Suzuki's suggestion for a new science program resulted in the production of *Suzuki on Science*. Made with a minimal budget and devoted to a single topic in each half-hour segment, it began airing in January 1971. After observing Suzuki on the screen and also in the classroom, Alexander Ross reported in *Macleans* (March 1971) that he was "a natural performer whose passion for science comes across as well on TV as it does in the lecture room" and "a born teacher, one of those lucky people who is capable of communicating enthusiasm." (Suzuki himself has said, "If I have any ability, it is to be provocative and to stimulate people to think about things from a different perspective.") By talking with prominent scientists, including Nobel Prize winners, Suzuki gained familiarity with a broad range of subjects outside his own areas of expertise. He conscientiously honed his interviewing skills, with the goal of eliciting information from his guests with the deftness displayed by the prominent Canadian broadcast journalists Peter Gzowski and Patrick Watson, whom he admired because, as he put it, "they listen, they are not afraid to follow up on something unexpected, and they don't feel they have to impress the audience." His increasing dissatisfaction with the limitations of the talking-heads format of *Suzuki on Science* led him to turn down the CBC's offer of a third season, and he returned to full-time research.

Early in 1974 the CBC asked Jim Murray, the executive producer of *The Nature of Things*, which was then in its fifteenth season, to launch *Science Magazine*, a new series that would offer short reports on medicine, science, and technology in each half-hour segment. Some months later Murray invited Suzuki to come to Toronto to be interviewed for *Science Magazine* about his research. Unbeknownst to Suzuki, Murray was seeking a host for the program, and the interview provided him with a screen test that Suzuki passed with high marks. *Science Magazine* quickly attracted a large audience. The letters of protest that hundreds of listeners sent upon hearing, at the end of its first season, that it would be dropped persuaded the CBC to reinstate it, and Suzuki continued to host it until its cancellation, in 1979.

Meanwhile, the favorable impression Suzuki made on Diana Filer, another CBC executive producer, when he gave a speech for the University of British Columbia alumni association in 1974 led to his creation in 1975 of *Quirks and Quarks*, a weekly hour-long radio program on science, which he anchored for four years while he was also hosting *Science Magazine*. A mixture of such features as interviews with inventors, recorded statements by Sigmund Freud, Albert Einstein, and other famous scientists, and dramatizations of predictions that had been offered decades before in popular magazines, *Quirks & Quarks* became an immediate hit among scientists as well as laypeople. (In his 1991 book, *A Mirror to Nature: Reflections on Science, Scientists and Society*, Peter Knudtson reported that "its weekly excursions into the lives and laboratories of scientists still remain a virtual Canadian institution.")

Suzuki left *Quirks and Quarks* in 1979, when the CBC merged *The Nature of Things* with *Science Magazine* and invited him to host the product of that union—the one-hour weekly science show formally called *The Nature of Things with David Suzuki*. The program currently attracts about one-fifth of Canadian television viewers, and it is purchased by more stations outside of Canada than any other CBC offering. By his own account, Suzuki's involvement with it "ranges from writing and delivering a short introductory piece, to spending a considerable amount of time interviewing people and making on-camera commentaries on location." He also suggests ideas for the stories, which have been filmed all over the world and which have run the gamut from portraits of animal species to examinations of individual diseases, new synthetic fibers, and child sexual abuse.

After the airing of *A Planet for the Taking* in 1985, *The Nature of Things* and many of Suzuki's other broadcast and print media projects began to take what he has called "an overt environmental stand." In the face of such phenomena as the escalating destruction of wild lands, the steadily increasing consumption of nonrenewable resources, and, as the ecologist Edward O. Wilson and many other experts have predicted, the almost certain extinction within the near future of a significant number of the world's plant and animal species, Suzuki and his associates decided that they could "no longer afford the luxury of just doing pretty films," as he wrote in *Metamorphosis*. "We have to take a strong advocacy position and point out wherever we can the error in our assumptions," he maintained, among them that it is the right of humans "to exploit nature as we see fit, . . . to create more economic growth, to dump our wastes into the environment."

Acutely aware of the evil that has been wrought in the name of science—the misapplication of the principles of genetics, for example, contributed significantly to the institution of the United States' racial immigration quotas, the Nazis' wholesale murder of Jews, Gypsies, and others, and the internment of Japanese-Canadians and Japanese-Americans during World War II—Suzuki has also endeavored to alert people to the possibly unintended and undesirable ramifications of scientific and technological discoveries. "Science is a very powerful but limited way of knowing," he has said, as quoted in *David Suzuki* (1988), a biography by Ron Wideman for younger readers. "Science alone can never provide answers to important questions like what is right and wrong. If we are to control science, we must all learn how to think and to assess information for ourselves."

During the past quarter century, Suzuki has given more than five hundred lectures in Canada and other countries. In 1992 he and his daughter Severn, then twelve, both spoke at the Earth Summit Conference in Rio de Janeiro. He has written or co-written more than eighty major scientific articles and some seventy short pieces or abstracts for scientific journals and hundreds of articles for non-scientific magazines. His weekly columns have appeared in the *Toronto Star* (1985–86) and the Toronto *Globe and Mail* (1987–89), and since 1989 they have been distributed by the Southam Syndicate to thirty-one other Canadian newspapers. Suzuki has narrated science records, tape recordings, and films and written eight children's books and sixteen other books, including, with Peter Knudtson, *Genethics: The Ethics of Engineering Life* (1988) and *Wisdom of the Elders* (1992) and, with A. J. F. Griffiths, *An Introduction to Genetic Analysis* (1976; fifth edition, 1993), which is the most widely used genetics textbook in the United States and which has been translated into seven languages. In writing *Metamorphosis*, he has said, he tried "to show that scientists are people with foibles, idiosyncrasies, and passions." Since 1993 he has held the title of professor at the Sustainable Development Research Institute at the University of British Columbia.

In 1976 Suzuki was named an officer of the Order of Canada, that nation's highest civilian honor. Among his dozens of other awards and honors, which include a bevy of prizes for his work in broadcasting, are the Outstanding Japanese-Canadian of the Year Award (1972), gold medals from the Science Council of British Columbia (1981) and the Biological Council of Canada (1986), the UN Environment Program Medal (1985), UNESCO's Kalinga Award (1986), and a dozen honorary doctoral degrees. He was named Author of the Year by the Canadian Booksellers Association in 1990.

According to Clyde H. Farnsworth, Suzuki's "forest of graying tresses, laser-like gaze, and goatee" have become instantly recognizable throughout Canada. In a profile of him for *International Wildlife* (September/October 1988), Jerry Buckley wrote that Suzuki is "passionate, driven, irreverent, brilliant, charismatic, and controversial, usually all in the same sentence." From his seven-year marriage to the former Setsuko Joane Sunahara, which ended in divorce in 1965, Suzuki has two daughters, Tamiko and Laura, and a son, Troy. In 1972 he married Tara Elizabeth Cullis, who taught expository writing at Harvard University for five years and currently serves as president of the David Suzuki Foundation. He and his wife and their two daughters, Severn Cullis-Suzuki and Sarika Cullis-Suzuki, live in Vancouver. In addition to such sports as skiing, hiking, canoeing, and kayaking, Suzuki's main avocational interests are working for environmental causes and fighting for the human rights of Canada's aboriginal peoples.

Selected Biographical References: American Biology Teacher 55:31+ Ja '93 por; Amherst p16+ Summer '94 pors; Dial p25+ July '84 por; International Wildlife 18:34+ S/O '88 pors; Maclean's 84:36+ Mr '71 pors; Toronto Globe and Mail p17+ My 7 '77 pors; Suzuki, David. Metamorphosis (1987)

Bumble Ward & Associates

Tarantino, Quentin

1963- Filmmaker; screenwriter; actor. Address: c/o A Band Apart Productions, Capra Bldg. 112, 10202 W. Washington Blvd., Culver City, CA 90232

Quentin Tarantino, an aficionado of pop culture who never completed high school, is among the cinema's most controversial filmmakers. He made his debut as a director and screenwriter in 1992 with the audacious *Reservoir Dogs*, which earned him comparisons to Martin Scorsese and Sam Peckinpah because of his command of low-rent mise-en-scène and his staging of gut-wrenching scenes of gruesome yet poetic violence. In the following year, he saw the director Tony Scott score a hit with *True Romance*, for which Tarantino had written the script, and in 1994 his original story for *Natural Born Killers* was turned into a sensationally violent film by Oliver Stone. Tarantino shrugged off the sophomore jinx as a director with his critically acclaimed *Pulp Fiction*, which captured the Palme d'Or at the Cannes Film Festival in 1994 and was nominated for an Academy Award as best picture. His latest directorial effort, *Four Rooms*, a collaboration with three other directors, is scheduled for release in October 1995. His acting credits include supporting performances in *Reservoir Dogs* and *Pulp Fiction*, a starring role in Jack Baran's *Destiny Turns on the Radio* (1995), and appearances in two 1995 films by Robert Rodriguez: *Desperado* and *From Dusk till Dawn*. "Movies are so characterless these days that in the first ten minutes, the audience knows exactly what kind of movie it is going to be," Tarantino declared in an interview with Hilary de Vries of the *Washington Post* (September 9, 1993). "I try to work against those expectations. I don't want to just tell stories. My movies have to function on a number of different levels, so I like to work in the genre while subverting it from the inside."

Tarantino makes movies about movies—hybrid films that reflect a sensibility shaped by such diverse influences as blaxploitation flicks, Howard Hawks's studio masterpieces, and works by John Woo, the Hong Kong maestro of violence, and such avant-garde European masters as Jean-Luc Godard and Jean-Pierre Melville. "I think there are two ways you can go—the Hollywood-pack *Lethal Weapon* way or the art-house way—and both are dangerous and unrewarding," the filmmaker told Hilary de Vries. "And then there are directors like [Brian] De Palma and Scorsese who walk the middle. I don't want to be a hack. I want every single one of my movies to make money. . . . I'm trying to make a movie that I would want to go see. The kind of movies that aren't being made but that my friends and I would get a kick out of. This isn't some esoteric . . . kind of thing. Everyone else is invited."

Named for a Burt Reynolds television character (presumably Quint Asper, the blacksmith on *Gunsmoke*), Quentin Tarantino was born in 1963 in Knoxville, Tennessee, the only child of Tony Tarantino, an amateur musician, and Connie Tarantino, who was still a teenager when she divorced her husband and moved to California with her infant son. "I never met my father," Tarantino said in an interview with Peter Biskind for *Premiere* (November 1994). "My mom married him to get away from her family. Basically, they were bums. She ended up trading in one pair of bums for another bum." After settling in the South Bay, a heavily industrialized section of Los Angeles that borders on the sprawling, predominantly black neighborhood known as South Central, Connie Tarantino trained to become a nurse and ultimately landed a job as a corporate executive. Tarantino's stepfather, Curt Zastoupil, was a musician who "played at places like the lounge of the Ramada Inn," as Tarantino told De Vries. A rough-and-tumble area populated by Mexicans, African-Americans, and "white trash," to use Tarantino's phrase, South Bay included the middle-class neighborhood, Harbor City, in which Tarantino grew up and which lies between Torrance, a prosperous community, and Carson, a working-class town where Tarantino regularly attended kung-fu movies and low-budget flicks at the local Twin Cinema. "I grew up going to the grind houses and to the art houses and loving them both equally," he told David Wild of *Rolling Stone* (November 3, 1994). "That sort of defines my aesthetic. I mean, it's not like I'm some arty guy just getting off on myself."

A fan of comic books who taught himself to read at the age of three, Tarantino was a bright but hyperactive child whose mother resisted the efforts of school officials to regulate his behavior with the use of prescription drugs like Ritalin. In junior high school, he stood up to the bullies who picked on him, adopting a tough-guy pose that he maintained until he was in his early twenties. "I used to be concerned with not being pushed around," Tarantino told Clancy Sigal, who interviewed him for the *Guardian* (September 11, 1993). "I wanted to be the 'wrong guy.' You know, 'You picked the wrong guy to fool with, buddy.' So I created a personality that said, Don't mess with me or I'll take it all the way. I'd go wild, and it wouldn't be over until it was over. But life's too short, and that's kids' stuff." Although Tarantino scored above 150 on IQ tests, he hated school and had not advanced beyond the ninth grade by the age of sixteen, when he dropped out altogether.

Although he tuned out in the classroom, Tarantino was a keen student of the visual media culture that shaped his youth. "I'm thirty; [people my age] grew up through the seventies," he explained to Sigal. "The number-one thing we all shared wasn't music, that was a sixties thing. Our culture was television, and movies too. TV was what we all shared completely, passionately. It's a shared memory and language. The junk/trash culture made us. I like that stuff, I'm proud of it. A well-made hamburger is a great thing. We didn't have a Jim Morrison. Our Jim Morrison was Bruce Lee—our God." If movies and television occupied a larger space in Tarantino's adolescence than they might have during previous eras, he believes that that may have been a result of the void in values left in the wake of the sexual revolution and the political upheavals of the late 1960s and early 1970s. "The Vietnam War and Watergate were a one-two punch that basically destroyed Americans' faith in their own country," Tarantino asserted in his conversation with Biskind. "The attitude I grew up with was that everything you've heard is lies. The president is a monkey."

After dropping out of high school, Tarantino moved to Torrance and got a job as an usher at a theatre that showed pornographic movies. While studying acting, in Toluca Lake, he began writing scenes based on old films that he had seen. "Anything I couldn't remember, any holes, I'd fill in myself," he told Biskind. Eventually he began working on screenplays, some of which ran as long as thirty pages. "I saw different from the other kids in my class," Tarantino recalled in an interview with John Milward of the *Chicago Tribune* (October 25, 1992). "I saw movies in the big picture; all they cared about was their individual character." Before long he was dreaming of becoming a director rather than an actor. "My favorite actors were character actors, and I realized they still had to read for parts," Tarantino told Peter McAlevey, who interviewed him for the *New York Times*

Magazine (December 6, 1992). "I didn't want to be fifty years old and reading for parts. I wanted some control over my own destiny, and it seemed to me that directors [had control over theirs]."

By the time he was twenty-two, Tarantino had landed a minimum-wage job at Video Archives, a small rental store in Manhattan Beach that boasted one of the largest video selections in southern California. While working there Tarantino struck up a friendship with another aspiring director, Roger Avary, who told McAlevey that Video Archives "was less a video store than a film school. . . . We'd put a movie on . . . and we'd have these intense, eight-hour-long arguments about cinema," Avary recalled. "Customers would walk in and they'd get into it. It became this big clubhouse of filmmaking—and probably the best filmmaking experience anyone could ever get."

During the five years he worked at the video store, Tarantino would criticize himself unmercifully during his ritual, semiannual "Quentin Detest-fests," as he has called them. During his conversation with Biskind, he recalled that one day in 1990 he had told himself, "You have got to get . . . out of the South Bay. You are judging your progress rate by your friends at the video store. And they're not doing anything as far as a career is concerned. You need to move to Hollywood. If you run with the fast crowd, you will run fast, even if you run last." But he had no money with which to make the big move—until he received a thirteen hundred-dollar tax refund. "It showed up on the day that I decided to change my life . . . ," he told Biskind. "Things like that, when they happen, it just makes you think. It was almost as if God was waiting for me to . . . get my [act] together." Tarantino moved to Hollywood in 1990 and took a job with Imperial Entertainment as a telephone salesman for that company's line of low-budget videos.

Three years earlier Tarantino had completed his first script, *True Romance*, which he and Avary, who wanted to produce it, had been shopping around to potential financial backers ever since. Unable to find investors willing to let him direct *True Romance*, Tarantino turned the script over to Catalaine Knell of Cinetel Films, who hired him to doctor the script for Jan Eliasberg's *Past Midnight* (1992), a romantic thriller starring Natasha Richardson and Rutger Hauer. When Knell showed Tarantino's rewrite to her former boss, Tony Scott, the director of such box-office megahits as *Top Gun* and *Beverly Hills Cop II*, he was sufficiently intrigued to read *True Romance*, which he eventually purchased for fifty thousand dollars, according to Tarantino.

Using his fees from those two screenwriting jobs as seed money to film his script for *Reservoir Dogs*, Tarantino set about recruiting others for the project. While working at Imperial he had met Lawrence Bender, an actor and aspiring film producer, who initially failed to find investors willing to grant complete artistic control to a novice. As Tarantino recalled to Peter McAlevey, he and Bender finally decided to court "the one person we would want to have in this movie if we could"—Harvey Keitel, the respected method actor who was best known for his screen collaborations with Martin Scorsese and who had a penchant for accepting parts in avant-garde films. Through Bender's acting coach and his acquaintance with the cult filmmaker Monte Hellman, Bender submitted Tarantino's screenplay for *Reservoir Dogs* to Keitel, who told John Milward that he was "moved by the themes that Quentin was dealing with, like loyalty, betrayal, and redemption." Once Keitel had agreed to appear in the film— for substantially less than his usual fee—Live Entertainment, a division of Carolco Pictures, invested one and a half million dollars in the picture. It eventually grossed more than twenty million dollars in worldwide box-office receipts and video sales.

Echoing such disparate crime movies as Stanley Kubrick's *The Killing* (1956), Martin Scorsese's *Mean Streets* (1973), and Ringo Lam's Hong Kong shoot-'em-up *City on Fire* (1987), *Reservoir Dogs* is a high-testosterone talkfest with a ten-minute-long torture scene that left audiences gasping when it was shown at the 1992 Sundance Festival for independent American films. Tarantino's film centers on a group of gun-toting professionals who know each other only by their color-coded pseudonyms and who repair to an abandoned warehouse in the aftermath of a jewelry heist gone fatally awry. The robbery was planned by a savvy old crime boss (Lawrence Tierney), but the police had been tipped off, and the gangsters suspect that they have a traitor in their midst. The tension mounts as Mr. White (Keitel), the pivotal character, tries to keep up the spirits of Mr. Orange (Tim Roth), who lies slowly bleeding to death from a gunshot wound throughout most of the film. Meanwhile, Mr. White must restrain Mr. Pink (Steve Buscemi), who wants to grab the diamonds and run, and keep a wary eye on Mr. Blonde (Michael Madsen), a sadistic ex-con who has taken hostage a policeman whom he intends to torture. He finally does so, severing the officer's ear while dancing merrily to the strains of the Stealer's Wheel's 1973 bubblegum hit "Stuck in the Middle with You." One reason for the effectiveness of the mutilation scene is that "it's done in real time," as Tarantino told Lawrence Chua of the *Village Voice* (October 20, 1992). "Cinema isn't coming in with a lot of poppy cuts. I also like the fact that you get a chance to get into the beat of that song. I think it's almost impossible to watch Michael do his dance and not enjoy his performance and then, boom! You can't help but feel somewhat of a coconspirator for enjoying it."

A majority of critics hailed *Reservoir Dogs* as a flashy debut showcasing Tarantino's ability to create vivid characters out of dialogue that bristles with baroque profanities and clever allusions to such pop-culture touchstones as Madonna's song "Like a Virgin," which received an X-rated explication from Tarantino himself, who made an appearance in the film as Mr. Brown. Writing in *Premiere* (August 1992), J. Hoberman called *Reservoir Dogs* "a high-powered exercise in blood-soaked absurdism." In the *Village Voice* (October 27, 1992), Georgia Brown declared that, notwithstanding the movie's "nasty torture/mutilation scene," *Reservoir Dogs* was "a raucous black comedy . . . , a moving buddy picture, [and] an up-to-the-minute take on gangsters with their institutionalized codes of honor." Some critics, however, saw Tarantino's high-voltage first film as a stylish but glib exercise in cartoon nihilism. Terrence Rafferty, who reviewed the movie for the *New Yorker* (October 19, 1992), asserted that Tarantino mostly "tries to get by on film-school cleverness—a homemade pharmaceutical cocktail of allusions, pop music, and visual jolts," and Roger Ebert, in his *Video Companion* (1993), judged the film's screenplay to be its glaring weakness. "Having created the characters and fashioned the outline," Ebert observed, "Tarantino doesn't do much with his characters except to let them talk too much, especially when they should probably be unconscious from shock and loss of blood."

Like *Reservoir Dogs*, Tony Scott's *True Romance* (1993) contains a heavy dose of non sequitur speechifying and self-referential "movie-movie" qualities, to use the term Tarantino prefers to the more pretentious and overused "postmodern." The "knowingness" of the movie and its characters infused even their behavior. As Jessica Seigel noted in the *Chicago Tribune* (September 5, 1993) it was only after finishing the script that Tarantino noticed "how the screenplay's subtext grew out of his own movie-filled fantasies." "I realized," Tarantino said, "'Oh God, everything Clarence is doing he's seen in movies; he's never met any pimps. When he decides to do this, he's being a movie character.'"

Clarence (Christian Slater) is a comic-book salesman in Detroit who falls in love with a young prostitute named Alabama (Patricia Arquette) over a box of spilled popcorn at a triple-bill showing of kung-fu movies. Behaving like impulsively romantic B-movie characters, they get married, and Clarence, goaded by the imaginary Elvis (Val Kilmer), who serves as the voice of his conscience, guns down Alabama's drug-dealing pimp (Gary Oldman) and accidentally grabs a suitcase containing a fortune in uncut cocaine that belongs to a dapper mafioso (Christopher Walken). Sensing trouble, Alabama and Clarence set out in a fuchsia Cadillac for the land of their dreams—Hollywood. Although Tarantino preferred the bleak fate that befell Clarence in his original screenplay, he eventually endorsed the director's happy ending because, as Tarantino explained in an essay for *Projections 3: Filmmakers on Filmmaking* (1994), "[Scott] really liked these kids, and he wanted to see them get away." "What happened with that film was exactly what I wanted to happen in that I saw my world through Tony Scott's eyes," he wrote, adding that *True Romance* was his "most personal script." In his interview with Jessica Seigel, he recalled that when he wrote the script he was feeling very lonely. "I wanted to be loved, you know. I just was having a problem connecting with women. I never even had a girlfriend."

In her review of *True Romance* for the *New York Times* (September 10, 1993), Janet Maslin called it "a vibrant, grisly, gleefully amoral road movie . . . dominated by the machismo of Quentin Tarantino." In contrast, the next movie that was made from a script of Tarantino's was all but devoid of his unique point of view. Indeed, Oliver Stone's *Natural Born Killers* (1994), based on a story by Tarantino and rewritten by Stone, David Veloz, and Richard Rutowski, unmistakably bears the director's imprint and is so far removed from the original that Tarantino withdrew his name from the scriptwriting credits. A dark commentary on violence in America, Stone's somewhat heavy-handed film revolves around Mickey Knox (Woody Harrelson) and his young wife, Mallory, (Juliette Lewis), renegade mass murderers who become pop stars when they are glamorized by a cynical journalist (Robert Downey Jr.) on his tabloid TV show, *American Maniacs*. In her *New York Times* (August 26, 1994) review, Janet Maslin regretted that Tarantino's "distinctive voice is not heard" in *Natural Born Killers* and said that "as a satirist" Stone is "an elephant ballerina." Reviewing the movie for the *Washington Post* (August 26, 1994), Hal Hinson observed that Tarantino's story, as expanded by Stone and his collaborators, was "intended as a gonzo critique of the mass media and, by extension, of the bloodthirsty legions of couch potatoes whose prurient taste guarantees that the garbage rises to the top of the charts." But the film, Hinson wrote, "degenerates into the very thing it criticizes" because "the movie's jittery, psychedelic style is so obviously a kick for Stone to orchestrate."

Once again paying homage to the hard-boiled crime genre, in *Pulp Fiction* (1994) Tarantino knitted together three discrete vignettes, jumbling the chronology in a circular fashion so that the movie ends up a little while after it began, with an amateur holdup in a diner by a couple named Pumpkin (Tim Roth) and Honeybun (Amanda Plummer). In the first part, Vincent (John Travolta), a professional hitman, is charged with "taking care of" the wife (Uma Thurman) of his boss, Marsellus (Ving Rhames), who had her previous escort thrown off a balcony, allegedly for massaging her feet; the second story, written by Roger Avary, features a boxer, Dutch (Bruce Willis), who double-crosses Marsellus by not throwing a fight; and the final installment includes Tarantino in a cameo appearance and Harvey Keitel in a deus ex machina role, as a debonair sanitation expert who aids Jules (Samuel L. Jackson), a scripture-spouting hitman, in his quest for spiritual redemption.

The result was an ambitious film that was more complex than *Reservoir Dogs* but no less compelling or darkly humorous. According to Gavin Smith, writing in *Film Comment* (July 1994), "*Pulp Fiction* shares its predecessor's fetishes—violence as grammar; styling over pathology; plot as farcical, sadistic game; a hermetic, atemporal-yet-retro sense of the present—but is a far more adroit, nuanced work." In her review for the *New York*

Times (September 23, 1994), Janet Maslin declared that Tarantino had "come up with a work of such depth, wit, and blazing originality that it places him in the front ranks of American filmmakers." After winning the coveted Palme d'Or, the award for best picture, at the Cannes Film Festival, *Pulp Fiction* opened to critical acclaim at the New York Film Festival in the fall of 1994. Tarantino and Avary collected awards for best screenwriter from the New York Film Critics Circle and the National Society of Film Critics. Both groups also named Tarantino best director, and the latter organization voted *Pulp Fiction* best film. Garnering seven Academy Award nominations, including one for best picture, *Pulp Fiction* won in the category of best original screenplay.

In 1994 Tarantino served as executive producer of Roger Avary's directorial debut, *Killing Zoe*, and made a scene-stealing cameo appearance in Rory Kelly's *Sleep with Me*, as a film geek who delivers an impassioned exegesis of the homoerotic subtext of *Top Gun*. In Jack Baran's *Destiny Turns on the Radio* (1995), which also featured James LeGros, Dylan McDermott, and the comedian Bobcat Goldthwait, Tarantino starred as the ultrahip Johnny Destiny. "Filmed with iconographic admiration," Janet Maslin wrote in her review for the *New York Times* (April 28, 1995), "Mr. Tarantino glides through this smugly facetious film as a fount of cryptic wisdom, shedding the funny spontaneity that made him . . . a lively actor in films of his own. . . . His performance is a reminder that Mr. Tarantino, after all, established his reputation as a consummate hipster on the other side of the camera."

Most recently, Tarantino completed his segment of the anthology *Four Rooms*, which follows the rounds of a bellhop to four different hotel rooms, in each of which unfolds a story directed, separately, by Tarantino and his friends Allison Anders (whose previous films include *Gas Food Lodging* and *Mi Vida Loca*), Robert Rodriguez (*El Mariachi*), and Alexandre Rockwell (*In the Soup*). *Four Rooms*, whose cast includes Madonna, Bruce Willis, Tim Roth, Marisa Tomei, and Antonio Banderas, was scheduled to be released by Miramax late in 1995. Tarantino's latest acting credits are an appearance in Rodriguez's *Desperado*, starring Antonio Banderas, which premiered in August 1995, and a costarring role in Rodriguez's *From Dusk till Dawn*, tentatively scheduled for release in December 1995.

Despite his status as a much-in-demand Hollywood wunderkind, the tall, slender Tarantino remains unspoiled by success and lives in an unpretentious apartment near West Hollywood that once belonged to John Travolta. Decorated with movie posters and strewn with record albums, videocassettes, laser discs, books, and fan magazines, his modest dwelling looks like "a kitschy pop-culture Valhalla," as David Wild described it in *Rolling Stone*, and houses his treasured collection of board games based on hit television shows and movies. An animated, enthusiastic conversationalist with a staccato laugh that sounds like a cross between Woody Woodpecker and one or both of the MTV cartoon characters Beavis and Butt-head, according to interviewers, Tarantino dresses casually, shaves irregularly, and spends his spare time watching movies and television with friends, going to coffee shops, and working on screenplays.

Selected Biographical References: Chicago Tribune XIII p8+ O 25 '92 por, XIII p6+ S 5 '93 pors; Film Comment 30:32+ Jl '94 pors; Guardian Weekend p24+ S 11 '93 pors, p7 O 14 '93 por; N Y Times II p27+ pors, C p1+ S 23 '94 pors; N Y Times Mag p55+ D 6 '92 pors; Premiere 8:94+ N '94 pors; Rolling Stone p76+ N 3 '94 pors; Vanity Fair 57:94+ Jl '94 pors; Village Voice p60 O 20 '92 por, p29+ O 26 '94 por; Washington Post D p1+ S 9 '93 pors; Who's Who in America, 1995

Wendy's International Inc.

Thomas, R. David

July 2, 1932– Restaurateur. Address: Wendy's International Inc., PO Box 256, 4288 W. Dublin Granville Rd., Dublin OH 43017

Some of the most popular television ads of the last few years have been built around the deadpan, curmudgeonly persona of Dave Thomas, the founder, in 1969, of the Wendy's chain of fast-food restaurants. The image that he projects, of a bemused man with simple tastes, has helped to boost sales figures for the company, which experienced financial difficulties following its period of enormous prosperity in the late 1970s and early 1980s.

Wendy's currently boasts more than four thousand restaurants in countries around the world and sales of $3.8 billion. When he is not carrying out his duties as executive and spokesman for Wendy's, Thomas eagerly works to promote and facilitate the adoption of children, and to that end he established the Dave Thomas Foundation for Adoption in 1992. An adoptee himself, he is firm in his belief that "every child deserves a home and love. Period."

R. David Thomas was born on July 2, 1932 in Atlantic City, New Jersey and adopted soon afterward by Rex and Auleva Thomas, who lived in western Michigan. Auleva Thomas died of rheumatic fever when her son was five years old, and Rex Thomas, a construction worker whom Dave Thomas remembers as being an unaffectionate man, remarried three times, moving his family to numerous towns in the South and Midwest to take different jobs. By his own estimation, Dave Thomas had lived in a dozen places by the time he was fifteen, and as a result he "never felt [he] belonged," as he revealed to Marilyn Achiron for a profile in *People* (August 2, 1993). His feelings of alienation only increased when, at the age of thirteen, he learned from Auleva Thomas's mother, Minnie Sinclair, that he had been adopted. "It really hurt that nobody told me before," Thomas admitted to Marilyn Achiron. "It is a terrible feeling to know my natural mother didn't want me."

As Thomas wrote in his autobiography, *Dave's Way: A New Approach to Old-Fashioned Success* (1991), among the few constants in his early life were the summers he spent with Minnie Sinclair on her small farm in Michigan. He has described his adoptive grandmother as "strong and stern" and as "the most religious person" he knew but also as having "a good sense of humor." Thomas has credited her with giving him "a real sense of security" and with teaching him the value and pleasure of hard work. Perhaps as a result of her influence, Thomas, whose peripatetic lifestyle never allowed him to make many close friends, came to view work as a "constant companion."

To help make ends meet in his father's household, Thomas began working at the age of twelve, first delivering groceries and then manning a drug store soda fountain. He spent many of his off-hours eating in cheap restaurants with his father, an activity that seems to have influenced his career choice. He wrote in *Dave's Way*: "It was then that I decided I wanted to own my own restaurant because I liked to eat, and I just thought restaurants were really neat, exciting places." Marilyn Achiron quoted him as saying, "I thought if I owned a restaurant, I could eat all I wanted for *free*. What could be better than that?" When his family moved in 1947 to Fort Wayne, Indiana, Thomas found a job as a busboy in the local Hobby House restaurant. After finishing the tenth grade, he dropped out of school to work full-time at Hobby House, on the theory that he would then accelerate his education in his chosen field. Upon learning that his father was preparing to move yet again, he also decided the time had come for him to live on his own, and he took up residence at the local YMCA.

Shortly after the outbreak of the Korean War, Thomas enlisted in the United States Army, figuring that he would otherwise be drafted and that, by volunteering, he could exert more control over his assignment. He was stationed first at Fort Benning, in Georgia, where he attended the army's Cook and Baker's School, and then in Germany, where, as a cook and staff sergeant, he supervised three other men in the feeding of up to two thousand people per day. His experience in the army, Thomas wrote in his autobiography, gave him "some important skills about the big picture of feeding a lot of people," training that he "was glad to have later."

Upon his discharge from the service, in 1953, Thomas returned to Fort Wayne and to Hobby House, where he was hired as a short-order cook at a salary of thirty-five dollars a week. When Thomas's boss, Phil Clauss, opened a second restaurant called the Hobby Ranch House with Barbecue, he named Thomas assistant manager. In the mid-1950s Clauss met Harland Sanders, who would later become known to the public as Colonel Sanders, the founder of the phenomenally successful Kentucky Fried Chicken (KFC) restaurant chain. Sanders was then traveling around the country to sell his chicken recipe to restaurateurs in exchange for a commission on chicken sales, and when Clauss accepted the deal, Thomas began to learn about the preparation and marketing of chicken. Clauss later acquired four Kentucky Fried Chicken franchises in Columbus, Ohio, but he failed to make a profit on them. In an effort to save his new businesses, he went to Thomas with a proposition: if Thomas could take over the management of the outlets and make them solvent, Clauss would transfer to him 45 percent of the ownership of the restaurants. "The stores were practically bankrupt," Thomas has recalled. "I had four kids and a wife, and I was making $135 a week. But I made up my mind that I was going to be in business for myself."

In 1962 Thomas moved to Columbus to manage the outlets, which, under his stewardship, earned a tidy profit. His business acumen impressed Harland Sanders, who, like Phil Clauss, became a mentor for Thomas. While he learned a great deal about the fast-food business under Sanders's tutelage, Thomas also gave valuable advice to the older man. Marilyn Achiron reported that Thomas developed the idea for Kentucky Fried Chicken's now-famous revolving sign, and, according to Nancy Millman of the *Chicago Tribune* (March 2, 1993), he claims to have helped persuade Sanders to appear in television commercials for his restaurants, a move that increased the company's profits and made Sanders's face one of the best known in the United States. In 1968 Thomas sold his share of the franchises back to the Kentucky Fried Chicken Corporation for more than $1 million in KFC stock. Thomas then took a position at the parent company but left within a year, after a conflict with John Y. Brown Jr., who, with Jack Massey, had bought the business from Harland Sanders in the mid-1960s.

After leaving KFC, Thomas used part of the money from the sale of the franchises to build his own chain of restaurants, whose specialty would be hamburgers. His business would differ from other hamburger chains, he decided, by offering a variety of toppings, using fresh meat instead of frozen patties, and making the hamburgers to order rather than preparing them in advance and leaving them to sit under heating lamps. In picking a company logo, Thomas concluded that "a little girl's image is the greatest—wholesome and cute." By then the father of four girls and a boy, he had ready access to a model for his logo, and he settled on a likeness of his red-haired, freckled daughter Melinda Lou—nicknamed Wendy—who was eight years old when the first Wendy's Old Fashioned Hamburgers opened in Columbus on November 15, 1969.

The original menu at Wendy's consisted of chili, french fries, soft drinks, and the Frosty Dairy Dessert in addition to fresh hamburgers. With an eye toward creating a relaxed, homey atmosphere in his establishment, Thomas installed carpeting, Tiffany-style lamps, and bentwood chairs. Wendy's turned a profit within six weeks of opening its doors. In 1973 Thomas began to expand his business considerably, negotiating with entire cities and geographical regions rather than selling single franchises; as a result, during the next decade Wendy's became a ubiquitous presence in the United States.

Although he had built a successful enterprise, in the late 1970s Thomas began to reevaluate his own role in it. He had resisted the idea, offered by other senior officials in the company, of installing salad bars in the restaurants, because of his fear that Wendy's might lose its focus on hamburgers. After he begrudgingly approved the plan, and it proved to be immensely successful, Thomas thought that perhaps others were better qualified to run Wendy's. "Here's a company I didn't want to screw up," Thomas explained to Linda Killian for *Forbes* (August 5, 1991). "I see a lot of entrepreneurs start something they can't finish." In 1982 the restaurateur resigned as chief executive of Wendy's in favor of the more hands-off position of senior chairman.

At first the company continued to thrive. While Thomas began to spend time playing golf and investing in smaller businesses (pursuits that he, by his own account, "didn't find . . . very exciting"), Wendy's earned huge profits, particularly as a result of its popular "Where's the beef?" television ad campaign, which poked fun at the low meat content of some other restaurants' hamburgers. For a time during the early 1980s, the phrase "Where's the beef?" held such a firm grip on the public imagination that former vice-president Walter F. Mondale used it in a debate with other candidates for the 1984 Democratic presidential nomination. As Wendy's sharpened its marketing techniques, however, service at many of its outlets "began to get sloppy," as Linda Killian reported, paraphrasing Thomas. The restaurants started losing money as the decade progressed.

When, in 1989, Thomas asked James Near to become Wendy's chief executive, Near accepted the offer on the condition that Thomas return to his role as a guiding force in the company. Near felt that Wendy's, lacking Thomas's leadership, had lost touch with its founder's original vision. "I felt we needed [Thomas] as our focal point," Near told Linda Killian. Thomas, however, had little interest in overseeing the company's operations. The deal they worked out was that Thomas would have no management duties but would be, as Killian put it, Wendy's "spokesman, in-house cheerleader, and roaming quality-control man."

In one of his first acts in his new capacity, Thomas spoke to representatives of the New York City advertising agency Backer Spielvogel Bates, whose recent commercials for Wendy's he disliked. As Thomas recounted to Nancy Millman, he told Carl Spielvogel, "You don't know our business. And you better find out about it if you want to keep the account." That ultimatum resulted in a meeting between Thomas and other officials at the agency, during which the Wendy's founder explained the workings of, and philosophy behind, his restaurants. "I went to the agency and said, 'I want you to understand how we make a hamburger,'" Thomas recalled, as quoted in *Advertising Age* (August 6, 1990). "How we use only fresh ground beef. How we don't prepackage our hamburgers." Before long, one of the creative directors at the ad agency, Bob Lenz, came up with the idea of featuring Thomas himself in the commercials and having him explain to television audiences some of what he had told the employees of Backer Spielvogel Bates.

"Those first commercials, *oy gevalt!*" Jim McKennan, another official at the ad agency, exclaimed to Nancy Millman. The problem had to do with Thomas's way of speaking: more than one observer has commented on his scrambled syntax. As Millman wrote, despite Thomas's "immense fortune" he "still talks like the grillman he was when he got his start. He mixes up his verbs and comes up with words that can't be found in any dictionary." The agency's writers gave Thomas lines that he would never have spoken of his own accord and had trouble delivering before a camera. Eventually McKennan and others decided to turn the situation to their advantage by letting more of Thomas's real personality show through in the commercials.

The change proved to be for the better. Writing in *Advertising Age* (September 30, 1991), Bob Garfield, after calling Thomas's early ads "thoroughly pathetic in every respect," had only praise for his later efforts. In one "improved" commercial cited by Garfield, Thomas was shown in such glamorous locales as Paris and Osaka, Japan, waiting to be served in fancy restaurants more concerned with ambiance than with food; the spot ended with Thomas delivering the wistful line, "I sure could go for a Big Dave's Deluxe." Another ad, a spoof of the film *Field of Dreams*, featured a mysterious voice telling Thomas, "If you make a grilled chicken sandwich at Wendy's, they will come." "The new spots are hilarious, pointed, tactically sharp, and beautifully performed," Bob Garfield declared. "[Thomas is] still playing the part of a guileless bumpkin, but now . . . it's obvious he's playing a part."

Garfield was apparently not alone in responding positively to the new ads. Together with James Near's cost-cutting measures and Thomas's efforts at quality control (he regularly visits Wendy's restaurants around the country to boost employee morale and monitor operations), the commercials helped increase sales significantly. In early 1991, company officials reported that Wendy's had earned its highest profits in four years, with a sales increase of 3 percent per outlet. Explaining the appeal of his appearances in the television spots, Thomas observed in *Dave's Way*, "Food is a personal thing, and it's tied closely to family life. People want to know the values of the person ladling out the goods." In 1993, the company's fourth straight year with over 20 percent earnings growth, Wendy's opened 330 new outlets, for a total of 4,200 restaurants in more than thirty countries.

Meanwhile, Thomas had become active in the area of adoption. While he has acknowledged that his experience as an adoptee was not ideal, he has stated that it was "far better" than growing up in an orphanage would have been, and he believes that every child deserves the same chance that he had. Acting on that belief, he worked with the administration of President George Bush to focus attention on the adoption needs of older children and handicapped children. In 1990 he established the Wendy's corporate adoption program, through which the company helps pay medical and legal bills incurred by employees who adopt, and the Dave Thomas Foundation for Adoption began operations two years later. "People ask me, 'What about gay adoptions? Interracial? Single parent?'" Thomas told Marilyn Achiron. "I say, 'Hey, fine, as long as it works for the child and the family is responsible.'" Part of Thomas's aim is also to fight the negative connotations of what he views as an essential practice. "You'd be surprised the people who were adopted who don't want to talk about it," he has said.

Thomas interspersed throughout the narrative of his autobiography tips for business and personal success, such as: "*Keep checking to make sure the customer understands who you are.* Every month, we are out there asking five hundred people what they think Wendy's is and how they think we are doing. Most people think we're the best place for hamburgers, chicken sandwiches, and salads. When hamburger chains add things like pizza to their menu, I think that they have walked over the edge. People don't know what you are anymore." Another piece of advice offered in the book is: "*Don't just study people who succeed, study people who handle success well.* See how people who have succeeded financially live their lives, and learn from that. Some people can't handle money or success. It destroys them. They over-buy, drink, take drugs, become playboys or country-clubbers. Eventually they let their businesses slide, too, because they let their egos get in the way of their judgment. They forget about their families, their self-respect, and their fellow human beings." The book was published to positive reviews. With Ron Beyma, Thomas wrote *Well Done! Dave's Secret Recipe for Everyday Success* (1994), which, like *Dave's Way*, contains autobiographical information as well as advice for personal and professional well-being.

Dave Thomas and his wife, the former Lorraine Buskirk, whom he met in the Hobby House restaurant in Fort Wayne and married on May 21, 1954, are the parents of Pam, Ken, Molly, Wendy, and Lori. They have many grandchildren. Thomas sits on the boards of directors of Children's Hospital in Columbus and St. Jude Children's Research Hospital, in Memphis, Tennessee. He received the Horatio Alger Award in 1979. Thomas frequently addresses groups of teenagers, admonishing them to stay in school. Deciding to lead by example, in the early 1990s he earned his general equivalency diploma and graduated from Coconut Creek High School, in Florida. Thomas's classmates voted him "most likely to succeed."

Selected Biographical References: Chicago Tribune V p1+ Mr 2 '93 pors; Forbes 148:106+ Ag 5 '91 pors; People 40:86+ Ag 2 '93 pors; Thomas, R. David. Dave's Way: A New Approach to Old-Fashioned Success (1991)

Thompson, Emma

Apr. 15, 1959- British actress. Address: c/o Lorraine Hamilton Management, 19 Denmark St., London WC2H 8NA, England

"The key to everything that has happened to me," the British actress Emma Thompson told Russell Miller in an interview for the *New York Times Magazine* (March 28, 1993), "is people have approached me with wonderful opportunities. Whatever I've done has always seemed to be someone else's idea." According to Thompson and many of those who have worked with her, it is precisely her openness to serendipity, her natural attitude toward acting and toward being an actress, that have enabled her to invest her characters with emotional depth and credibility. Since the late 1970s, when she began performing in the Footlights revues at Cambridge University, Thompson has taken on an uncommonly diverse range of roles on stage, on television, and in films that have allowed her to demonstrate her comic bent, dramatic subtlety, and feminist commitment. Thompson's films include versions of Shakespeare's *Henry V* and *Much Ado About Nothing* directed by Kenneth Branagh, two Ismail Merchant-James Ivory collaborations, a *noir* thriller about reincarnation, a dra-

Jean Cummings/Retna Ltd.

Emma Thompson

matic interpretation of a notorious case of wrongful imprisonment, and, most recently, a comedy about male pregnancy. In the minds of many, her Oscar-winning performance as Margaret Schlegel in the 1992 Merchant-Ivory film adaptation of E. M. Forster's novel *Howards End* firmly established her as the heir apparent to such multifaceted British actresses as Vanessa Redgrave and Maggie Smith.

Emma Thompson was born on April 15, 1959 in London, England, the daughter of Eric Norman Thompson, an actor and director who created the popular children's television show *The Magic Roundabout*, and Phyllida Ann Law, a classically trained actress with a successful stage career who has appeared with her daughter in several recent films. Thompson's younger sister, Sophie, is also an actress. While she was growing up, Thompson was encouraged by her parents to pursue whatever interested her. "I had no rebellious state, because my parents gave me so much freedom that I didn't need to rebel," she recalled to Richard Corliss of *Time* (March 29, 1993). At the Camden School for Girls, in north London, Thompson was a serious and highly motivated student. Although at the time she had no interest in becoming an actress, intending instead to be a writer, she displayed an instinct for performing, reciting sketches from the popular offbeat television series *Monty Python's Flying Circus* into a tape recorder.

When Thompson entered Cambridge University's Newnham College, where she studied English literature, her interest in comedy blossomed. Finding the drama scene at Cambridge too staid, she became one of the few women to join Footlights, the celebrated Cambridge acting club that was the training ground for such *Monty Python* mainstays as John Cleese and Eric Idle, among others. After seeing her performance in one of the annual Footlights revues, a top London agent signed her up, even though she had two more years of school remaining. During her years at Cambridge, Thompson not only became the leading female performer in Footlights, she also cowrote, codirected, and coproduced *Woman's Hour*, the first all-female Cambridge revue, and played the part of Gwendolyn in a student production of Tom Stoppard's kaleidoscopic comedy *Travesties*.

Among Thompson's reasons for pursuing comedy was her desire to subvert traditional images of women. "I had tremendous resistance to the notion of women as a kind of romantic ideal, as something to be wondered at, as something beautiful," she explained to Russell Miller. "The thing I wanted to be was that kind of woman who could be strong and independent and jolly, but make people laugh, and break down all that 'I am a *wooo*-man. Don't touch me.'" In college she wore baggy clothing and wire-frame glasses, and at one point, she even shaved her head, because her boyfriend said it would make her look like Nefertiti. "I was doing what a lot of young women do, rebelling against looking remotely feminine . . . ," she told Georgina Howell, who interviewed her for *Vogue* (June 1993). "I went faintly radically feminist—which I still am! I was doing all the things you are supposed to do, discussing things, getting furious, thinking I was the only person ever to have thought things through. There's a point if you're female and growing up where you have to be quite rude and aggressive for a while in order to develop. Being compliant won't get you anywhere."

Thompson received her degree from Cambridge in 1982, after submitting a thesis in which she contended that George Eliot had failed to create in her novels a true female hero. After her graduation Thompson tried her hand as a stand-up comedian for a few months, but she found the experience to be somewhat frightening and thoroughly exhausting. In 1983 she joined her former Footlights colleagues Stephen Fry and Hugh Laurie in writing and performing in a Granada Television series called *Al Fresco*. Later in the same year, she appeared in her own television special, whose proposed title, "Sexually Transmitted," was deemed too suggestive by executives at Channel Four, who changed it to *Up for Grabs*. Two years later Fry recommended her for the female lead in the West End revival of Noel Gay's 1930s musical comedy *Me and My Girl*, whose book Fry had revised. For fifteen months, Thompson sang and danced in the long-running, award-winning musical, which starred Robert Lindsay, enchanting critics with her engagingly down-to-earth portrayal of a Cockney Cinderella.

In 1986 Thompson landed her first dramatic role, that of Harriet Pringle in the BBC miniseries *Fortunes of War*, based on Olivia Manning's Balkan Trilogy, which detailed the failing marriage of two young Britons (played by Thompson and Kenneth Branagh) living abroad during World War II. According to a writer for the London *Observer*

(August 6, 1988), the actress brought "star quality" to the role and appeared to be quintessentially "English, understated, receptive, [and] intense in repose." (*Fortunes of War* was subsequently broadcast in the United States on PBS.) On British television in 1987, Thompson portrayed a sharp-tongued Scot, Suzi Kettles, in John Byrne's comic miniseries *Tutti Frutti*, about an over-the-hill rock band. Recognizing her remarkable range, the British Academy of Film and Television Arts (BAFTA) honored her as best actress for both *Tutti Frutti* and *Fortunes of War*, and the Variety Club named her the year's most promising newcomer.

In 1988 Thompson created her own six-part television comedy series, *Thompson*, in which she costarred with her sister and mother. Largely because of her acting honors, the debut of *Thompson* was accompanied by considerable favorable publicity, but successive installments of the ribald revue, which included satirical sketches, monologues, and song-and-dance numbers, were increasingly faulted for being self-indulgent and poorly written, among other things. In an interview with Rachel Abramowitz for *Premiere* (April 1992), Thompson suggested that the unusually virulent criticism of her show was due in part to male reviewers' discomfort with female comedians: "They think I should just be attractive, do serious drama; they're threatened by a moderately good-looking woman who tries to be funny as well. . . . It confuses the signals. We are taught to take women only on a very few levels." Thompson found it especially ironic when, in returning to her comedic roots, she was "being accused of somehow cashing in on being a successful actress and trying to be a comedian," as she complained to Russell Miller. Although the hostile reception accorded *Thompson* was painful for her, she considered it to be a valuable learning experience, telling Georgina Howell: "My father told me, 'If you can't fail, you can't do anything.' . . . You learn much more from the experience of failing to please than you do from accepting an award."

In 1989, after a three-year courtship, Thompson married her *Fortunes of War* costar, Kenneth Branagh. "Through him, I lost my intimidation by the classics," she told Sid Smith of the *Chicago Tribune* (August 22, 1991). "He was full of the joy and enthusiasm for Shakespeare that I had for my work, and he didn't look down on what I was doing. It was a good marriage of ideas, because we agreed the important thing was to celebrate and tell these stories with as much joy and abandon as we could." She has often performed with Branagh's Renaissance Theatre Company, beginning in 1988 in Judi Dench's revival of John Osborne's explosive *Look Back in Anger*, a shattering study of a disintegrating marriage. According to Irving Wardle of the London *Times* (June 8, 1989), Thompson imbued the passive Alison Porter, the martyred wife of Branagh's furious Jimmy Porter, with strength, playing her "not as a defenseless drudge, but as a wife who knows how to defend herself with tactical silences."

Thompson subsequently appeared in two Shakespearean stage productions directed by Branagh, *A Midsummer Night's Dream*, in which she played Helena, and *King Lear*, in which she took the part of the Fool. Sid Smith described her unorthodox interpretation of the last-named role, which is almost always assigned to a man, in the *Chicago Tribune*: "Thompson took Shakespeare's most insightful court jester and turned him-her into an it, a 'swamp thing,' as she puts it, a deformed, tongue-tied ghoul that slashed Shakespeare's wit with razors and found extraordinary layers of pain and suffering in the character."

The first film in which Thompson and Branagh appeared together was *Henry V* (1989), for which Branagh received Academy Award nominations as best director and best actor. Cast in the relatively small part of the French princess, Thompson created "a delightfully droll Katherine, making you laugh out loud at her scenes, instead of smiling at them out of respect for the author," as Stuart Klawans observed in the *Nation* (December 11, 1989). Thompson's next two films allowed her to give her comic talents free rein. In *The Tall Guy* (1990), directed by another Footlights alumnus, Mel Smith, she portrayed Kate Lemon, a proper and acerbic nurse who falls in love with an American actor named Dexter (Jeff Goldblum) whom she met when she administered his allergy shots. Brian D. Johnson wrote in *Maclean's* (November 19, 1990) that Thompson "maintains a Julie Andrews sort of reserve—until she makes love with Dexter in a hilarious scene of sexual slapstick" in which they completely destroy an apartment. "She's got this fantastic clarity in her acting," Mel Smith told *Premiere*'s Rachel Abramowitz. "She's very uncluttered in what she does, because she's very intelligent in how she approaches the material. You really do feel an emotional appeal from her." Thompson also delivered a scene-stealing turn as the dizzy Duchess d'Antan in James Lapine's *Impromptu* (1991), a high-spirited period farce about the love affair between the novelist George Sand (Judy Davis) and the composer Frederic Chopin (Hugh Grant).

Thompson and Branagh teamed up for the second time on screen in his supernatural thriller *Dead Again* (1991), whose dual plot line harkened back to the melodramas of the 1940s. In black-and-white flashbacks to 1948, Thompson portrayed a concert pianist apparently murdered by her husband, an internationally renowned composer and conductor (Branagh). "I have a problem with violence against women in films," Thompson told Smith, "and ours is done in a very staged way. She also fights back, she has spunk." In the modern sequences, Branagh and Thompson play, respectively, a private detective and an amnesiac attempting to remember both her past and, possibly, her previous life as the 1948 murder victim. "Emma Thompson has a face that's magic in front of the camera," Owen Gleiberman wrote in an evaluation of *Dead Again* for *Entertainment Weekly* (August 30, 1991). "Her large, flat cheeks give her a masklike beauty, but with one quick curlicue of a smile, she becomes a radiant sprite, with hints of naughtiness. . . . [In the flashbacks, Thompson and Branagh] made me appreciate the *focus* of the great old stars, the way they could define, with intoxicating clarity, the emotions on which a scene spun."

It was Thompson's remarkable performance as Margaret Schlegel in *Howards End* (1992) that catapulted her into acting's upper echelons. Adapted by Ruth Prawer Jhabvala from the novel by E. M. Forster, the film explores the relationships between the intellectual, freethinking Schlegel family and the materialistic Wilcoxes in Edwardian England. Margaret strikes up a brief, yet profound friendship with the ethereal Ruth Wilcox (Vanessa Redgrave), who has an almost spiritual attachment to her country estate, Howards End. After Ruth's death, Margaret marries her widowed husband (Anthony Hopkins), much to the dismay of both families, and must then reconcile the families' conflicting values.

"[Margaret] was one of the best women's roles I'd ever read," Thompson told Lawrence Van Gelder of the *New York Times* (May 22, 1992). "She was morally very central to the piece. I get bored with women being marginalized. She was a complex, ambiguous, and fully rounded human being, and also somebody whose raison d'être is communication and the desire to connect people to each other." Thompson was so eager to play the part that she wrote to the film's director, James Ivory, requesting the assignment. Ivory, who had already offered it to her (their letters crossed in the mail), was happy to comply. "She is a bit like Margaret anyway," he explained to Rachel Abramowitz: "enormously rational, highly intelligent, and very assured. She has a great sense of society, and she played that to the hilt." True to type on the set as well as in the role, Thompson cheerfully but insistently argued with Ivory about how to approach her scenes. "I really enjoyed it," she told Abramowitz. "And I've never really done that before. I think that's to do with being over thirty and being married. You suddenly think, ' . . . I'll say what I think.'"

Thompson's attention to detail paid off handsomely, for *Howards End* was a favorite of most critics. "Thompson rises to the role's drama and fairly skates on its ironic wit," Richard Corliss wrote in *Time* (March 16, 1992). "She also displays the requisite magic of a period heroine: by her radiant example, she teaches the audience how a beautiful soul might behave." Terrence Rafferty of the *New Yorker* (May 4, 1992) saw Thompson's "thrilling and original" performance as a breakthrough for the actress, whose previous work had, in his view, "been marked chiefly by a wicked adeptness at caricature." In *Howards End*, however, "her acting is unmannered, daringly straightforward." For her performance Thompson earned an Oscar and a Golden Globe Award, and she was named best actress by the New York Film Critics Circle, the Los Angeles Film Critics Association, the National Board of Review, the British Academy of Film and Television Arts, and the London *Evening Standard*. The latter two British awards cited her for her work in both *Howards End* and in Branagh's well-liked ensemble vehicle *Peter's Friends* (1992), in which she played an "eternal-student type."

In her speech accepting the Academy Award for best actress, Thompson dedicated her Oscar "to the heroism and courage of women," adding, "I hope it inspires the creation of more true screen heroines to represent them." Thompson believes that a backlash against the advances women have made in society in recent years has resulted in a dearth of good parts for women. "I so rarely find roles that bear any relation to women I know," she told Caryn James of the *New York Times* (March 28, 1993). "Maybe I travel in the wrong circles, but I don't really know any bimbos." Because good parts are so hard to come by, Thompson has contended that actresses have a responsibility to try to generate them. "We need new writers to create roles where women are morally central to the story," she declared in an interview with Jack Kroll for *Newsweek* (January 4, 1993). "I grew up identifying with Marlon Brando. It's time we created new myths." Taking her own advice, Thompson worked off and on for several years on a screen adaptation of Jane Austen's novel *Sense and Sensibility*, which is to be released in December 1995. Directed by Ang Lee, the film will feature Thompson, Kate Winslet, and Hugh Grant.

Returning to comedy in 1993, Thompson took on the role of the witty and independent Beatrice in *Much Ado About Nothing* (1993). The acid-tongued Beatrice and the determinedly single Benedick (Branagh) spend much of the film verbally sparring, each enjoying the game but denying the slightest interest in the other until their friends trick them into revealing their true feelings. "It was great fun to create that relationship," Thompson said in an interview with Christopher Harris of the Toronto *Globe and Mail* (May 6, 1993). "They really like each other and they know each other. It's not really about romance, it's more about the recognition of your equal, your match, your pair." In approaching the role, she had wanted to ensure that her Beatrice was neither "girlish" nor "arch," as she explained to Harris: "I suppose I discovered how to play her as we went along, as happens with most films," she aid. "That's why filmmaking is such a mysterious and interesting process. You can prepare as much as you like, but until you get there you don't know what the hell you're going to do. You prepare beforehand and then you let it go."

Although critical reaction to the film itself was mixed, most reviewers agreed that, as Beatrice, Thompson again demonstrated her gift for comedy. Dave Kehr wrote in the *Chicago Tribune* (May 2, 1993) that she displayed a "flashing wit" and "an insolence that, like Lauren Bacall's, is tremendously sexy." An exception to the chorus of praise for Thompson was J. Hoberman's assessment in the *Village Voice* (May 11, 1993), in which he called her a "relentlessly mannered" actress and complained about her "overbright smile, ostentatiously furrowed brow, and extended display of eye-batting concern." For her performance in *Much Ado About Nothing* Thompson was nominated for best actress at the Independent Feature Projects/West's Spirit Awards.

To prepare for her role as Miss Kenton, the housekeeper whose love for a repressed butler (Anthony Hopkins) goes unnoticed in the Merchant-Ivory production *The Remains of the Day* (1993), based on Kazuo Ishiguro's 1989 novel of the same name, Thompson read William Shirer's *The Rise and Fall of the Third Reich*, in an attempt to get a feel for English society in between the two world wars. "She's got a good perspective," Anthony Hopkins told Georgina Howell. "A 'this is only a job' sort of attitude. . . . [She is] unique and a lot of fun. She comes well prepared, she's precise about the objective. She is one of the best actresses I have worked with." In 1994 Thompson was nominated for a BAFTA award as best actress for the highly acclaimed *The Remains of the Day* and for two Academy Awards, as best actress for *The Remains of the Day* and as best supporting actress for her role as a lawyer in Jim Sheridan's *In the Name of the Father* (1993), a dramatization of the case of the so-called Guildford Four, who were falsely accused by British authorities of an IRA pub bombing in the 1970s and imprisoned for fifteen years. Her most recent credits include the surreal *The Blue Boy* (1994), a BBC/Scotland-Masterpiece Theatre coproduction; Ivan Reitman's comedy *Junior* (1995), in which Thompson spoofed her own proper image with her portrayal of a madcap scientist who tends to a pregnant Arnold Schwarzenegger; Christopher Hampton's *Carrington* (1995), in which she stars as the painter Dora Carrington; and a forthcoming adaptation of Radclyffe Hall's 1928 lesbian novel *The Well of Loneliness*, to be adapted by the screenwriter Richard Friedenberg.

Thompson, who has had no formal professional training in her chosen career, has said that she instead relies on "blind instinct." In an interview with Lawrence Van Gelder of the *New York Times* (November 23, 1990), she likened discussions of role preparation to "asking a plumber to open his toolbox. One hopes the water will come out in a steady and convincing stream at the end of the job." Perhaps partly as a result of that commonsensical attitude, she is able to maintain a playfulness on the set. Stuart Oken, who produced *Impromptu*, told Rachel Abramowitz, "If it ever came down to a choice between her and another actress, I'd tell a producer to hire her, because you're just going to have a better time. She was happy to be there and worked to keep other people laughing even during difficult times." As Thompson herself explained to the television talk-show host Charlie Rose, in an interview rebroadcast on December 30, 1994, the joy of acting is in "losing yourself for a moment."

"I don't think I'd have any of this if I'd been looking for it in the first place . . . ," Thompson insisted in her interview with Charlie Rose. "I mean, it's everything . . . you could ever want. There's nothing more. . . . I think probably the art of life is to want what you've got, anyway." Despite her increasingly hectic schedule, Thompson manages to find the time to actively support such causes as Friends of the Earth, the Campaign for Nuclear Disarmament, and a political action committee dedicated to the election of female candidates. She has served on Central and South American action committees, protested the war in the Persian Gulf, and campaigned on television for the Labour Party. "Acting is the ultimate luxury," she told Richard Corliss. "This is one of the luckiest things you could possibly be doing. 'Hard' is going down a bloody coal mine or living in Somalia or in a war zone. That's hard."

Emma Thompson, who enjoys cooking and reading almost as much as acting, lives in an unprepossessing, Edwardian semidetached house in Cricklewood, in northwest London, across the street from her mother (her father died in 1982), and just down the road from her sister. Following their performance together in *Henry V*, Thompson and Branagh were enshrined in the media as England's golden acting couple and were frequently compared to Laurence Olivier, who had also directed himself in a screen version of *Henry V*, in 1944, and his second wife, the actress Vivien Leigh. "The Golden Couple myth was created by the press," Thompson has said, as quoted by Richard Corliss, "and then we were vilified by the press." One joke in circulation in 1994 went like this: "Branagh: 'I'm in the kitchen, darling!' Thompson: 'Ooh, can I be in it too?'" Thompson has reportedly turned down opportunities to work with Branagh when she deemed the role in question unsuitable. She nonetheless has thoroughly enjoyed working with him, as she told her colleague Robbie Coltrane for *Interview* (May 1993): "We tend to be happier when we're sharing the same routine, because you go home and have a bit of supper, chat about what's going on, and share all the same experiences. That seems to me to be the point of being married." She also has credited Branagh with having grounded her. "One of the most attractive male qualities is the capacity to earth a volatile woman," she told *Newsweek*'s Jack Kroll. "With Ken and me it's symbiosis. Together you're stronger, one and one make three." In October 1995 Thompson and Branagh issued a statement announcing their separation: "Our work has inevitably led to our spending long periods of time away from each other, and as a result, we have drifted apart."

Selected Biographical References: Chicago Tribune V p1+ Ag 22 '91 pors; Interview 13:119+ My '93; London Observer p13 Ag 6 '88 por; N Y Times Mag 6 p22+ Mr 28 '93 pors; People 36:61+ S 9 '91 pors, 39:51+ My 17 '93 pors; Premiere 5:109+ Ap '92 pors; Time 141:52+ Mr 29 '93 por; Vogue 183:188+ Je '93 pors; Shuttleworth, Ian. Ken and Em: A Biography of Kenneth Branagh and Emma Thompson (1995); Who's Who, 1995

Thompson, Tommy G.

Nov. 19, 1941- Governor of Wisconsin. Address: 115 E. State Capitol, Madison, WI 53702; 609 Academy St., Elroy, WI 53929

During his more than eight years as governor of Wisconsin, Tommy G. Thompson has received national attention for his role in shaping the debate on welfare reform. He has steered through the state legislature several radical proposals that, collectively, are aimed at weaning welfare recipients from their dependency on public assistance, providing incentives for them to become better educated and better trained, and requiring, rather than simply encouraging, them to become gainfully employed. According to his supporters, his "tough love" reforms are precisely what is needed to eradicate the entrenched bureaucracy of poverty in the United States. "Tommy is an example of an activist conservative," Newt Gingrich, the Speaker of the House and one of Thompson's longtime admirers, said of him in 1990. "He's open to conservative solutions, not just conservative opposition."

On the other hand, Thompson's critics fear that his programs will not only exacerbate public resentment of welfare recipients but will also fail to fundamentally improve their lives. "The governor's genius is in dramatically building a large number of welfare reforms and postponing the consequences," Michael Wiseman, the associate director of the La Follette Institute at the University of Wisconsin, told Norman Atkins in an interview for a *New York Times Magazine* (January 15, 1995) profile of Thompson. "If you look closely, you discover that many so-called reforms either haven't been implemented, are very small, or the evaluations are postponed for a very long period of time." For the time being, such expressions of skepticism seem unlikely to dampen the Wisconsin electorate's enthusiastic support for the governor, who was reelected to a third term in 1994, with 67 percent of the vote.

Thomas George Thompson, who was born on November 19, 1941 in Elroy, Wisconsin, stands out in the history of Wisconsin politics for his conservatism, for residents of the state have long prided themselves on their political progressivism. While Thompson's family is part of that liberal tradition—his maternal grandfather was a La Follette socialist (referring to Robert La Follette, the Wisconsin native and Progressive Party candidate who won 18 percent of the popular vote in the 1924 presidential election) who helped to organize a farm workers' union—his political orientation was shaped more by his father, Allan Thompson, a teacher and later a grocery store owner who taught his four children the value of hard work. According to a frequently recounted story, at the age of about four Thompson told his father that he wanted a tricycle. Instead of giving him one, his father provided him with the means to buy one himself: he offered to pay his son twenty-five cents an hour for doing odd chores. "I had to pay for everything myself," Thompson recalled to Norman Atkins. "But he always gave me the opportunity to work for what I needed."

In 1959, after graduating from Elroy High School, Thompson entered the University of Wisconsin at Madison. It was during his years there that he began to define himself politically. When he arrived on campus, he thought of himself as a Democrat, but early on he found that his commitment to the party did not run very deep. "At Madison, they were all so liberal that, bein' the rebellious sort, I sort of stood up and said, 'I'll take the contrary point of view," he told Rogers Worthington in an interview for the *Chicago Tribune Magazine* (April 10, 1994). "I did it more or less to be different from the majority of the campus." Later in college he served as a congressional intern in Washington, D.C., where he realized he had less of an affinity for the ideals of President John F. Kennedy than for those of Senator Barry Goldwater, especially those articulated in Goldwater's popular book *Conscience of A Conservative.*

On taking his bachelor's degree in political science from the University of Wisconsin at Madison in 1963, Thompson enrolled at the university's law school, from which he earned his J.D. degree in 1966. Later in the same year, he decided to enter the race for a seat in the state assembly. As might be imagined, few political observers thought the twenty-four-year-old Republican upstart had much of a chance of beating his opponent, a seven-term Democrat. His opponent, too, thought little of the competition—so little that he took a vacation during the campaign. "He thought I wasn't serious about running," Thompson told Worthington. But Thompson ran a vigorous campaign, promoting his candidacy at weddings, picnics, church gatherings, and even town bars. He not only won the election but went on to spend the next twenty years in the

Wisconsin assembly. For the last five of those years, he served as leader of the Republican minority. In that position he became known as a strident fiscal conservative, earning the nickname "Dr. No" for the consistency of his opposition to the Democratic agenda.

In 1986 Thompson decided to run for governor of Wisconsin. Because he was a conservative Republican running against a Democratic incumbent, Anthony Earl, in a traditionally Democratic state, the odds seemed to be overwhelmingly against him. In his campaign, Thompson pledged to improve economic conditions in Wisconsin by reducing state spending, creating new jobs, and overhauling the joint federal-state welfare system, officially called Aid to Families with Dependent Children (AFDC). Earl's strategy was to criticize Thompson's view of the welfare system and his opposition to abortion; he also called Thompson's integrity into question by reminding voters of the intensity with which he had tried to obstruct the Democrats' legislative efforts in the state assembly. "They tried to paint him as this Nixonian character, darkly complected and untrustworthy," Thompson's campaign manager, John MacIver, recalled to Norman Atkins. The strategy proved to be ineffectual, and to nearly everyone's surprise, Thompson was elected with 53 percent of the vote.

Once in office, Thompson wasted no time in launching an effort to reform Wisconsin's welfare system. In keeping with its reputation as one of the most progressive states in the union, Wisconsin had one of the nation's highest AFDC payment schedules. As a result, it had become, as Thompson repeatedly reminded his fellow Wisconsinites, a "welfare magnet," drawing poor people from neighboring states, such as Illinois, whose welfare payments were not as generous. In an attempt to transform the state's image, in one of his first moves Thompson sliced those benefits by six percent. They have remained at that level ever since.

Thompson then set about trying to reform the very nature of the welfare system itself. He began by instituting a program called Learnfare, in February 1988. This program authorizes the state to withhold welfare payments from a parent whose child has three or more unexcused absences from school in a given month. "The revolutionary theory here—that it is the responsibility of parents, not truant officers, to make sure children attend school—is still deemed scandalous in some parts of the state, like Madison," Daniel D. Polsby wrote in the *National Review* (May 16, 1994). "But the electorate seems to like it." One much-touted result of the program has been that the state saved an estimated $3.3 million in AFDC payments during the 1988–89 academic year.

Nevertheless, some political observers and advocates of the poor have questioned the success of the program. These critics have pointed out, as Alex Prud'homme reported in *Time* (August 19, 1991), that there was a substantial increase in the school dropout rate after Learnfare was implemented, from 10.5 percent in 1988 to 14.7 percent in the 1989–90 academic year. During that period approximately sixty-six hundred teens were cited for habitual truancy, yet in 1990 the Wisconsin legislature found that 84 percent of the truants who appealed their cases had them overturned because of errors in record-keeping. Partly as a result, Learnfare ran into legal trouble. In 1990 its constitutionality was questioned by United States District Court Judge Terence Evans, who temporarily suspended enforcement of the statute in Milwaukee. The city then upgraded its record-keeping methods, and in October 1990 the program was reinstituted.

Whether or not Learnfare fulfilled its promise, the program provided a political boost for the first-term governor. "Learnfare was such a no-brainer in most people's eyes," John Gard, a Republican assemblymen, told Norman Atkins. "How can you be against forcing kids to go to school? Tommy used the phrase 'tough love' and it sold. Two years after the governor took office, a lot of Democrats who fought it lost. So others became fearful of standing in the way of more welfare initiatives." The Learnfare program has since been expanded throughout the state.

Another of Thompson's early initiatives was aimed specifically at discouraging people from moving to the state simply because of its generous welfare payments. The Two-Tier Welfare Program, as it was called, was first proposed in 1989. Stipulating that recent migrants' welfare benefits remain at the level of those they received in their home state for six months after their arrival in Wisconsin, the measure won widespread support among both the electorate and state lawmakers. "We should not offer financial incentives for poor people to move here," State Senator Joseph Strohl, a Democrat, was quoted as saying in *Newsweek* (August 14, 1989). "If they're coming for other reasons, fine, but at least we won't be asking taxpayers to artificially stimulate that migration." Despite the widespread support for the proposal, as of 1994 it had yet to be signed into law, and, if passed, it is likely to face a constitutional challenge. (The Supreme Court ruled in a 1969 case that states did not have the right to impose residency requirements on welfare recipients.) Also during his first term, Thompson instituted Workfare, a program that requires welfare recipients either to work or to enroll in a vocational-training program. Those who fail to comply with the requirements are penalized with a reduction in their monthly welfare checks. Alex Prud'homme reported that by 1991 forty-five thousand of Wisconsin's eighty thousand welfare recipients were enrolled in job-training programs.

Following Thompson's reelection as governor in 1990, he remained as committed as ever to reforming the state's welfare system. Among the programs he undertook during his second term was the Parental and Family Responsibility Initiative, launched in February 1991. Under the rules that existed when Thompson announced his plan, two-parent families received less assistance from the state than single-parent ones—an arrangement that, according to Thompson, discouraged welfare recipients from marrying. To remove the disincentive to marriage, Thompson proposed to increase the amount of money paid to two-parent families; to compensate for the additional outlay, he suggested that the practice of automatically increasing payments to mothers who have more than one child be eliminated. To encourage recipients to find work, he proposed that the state increase to $14,500 the amount that could be earned without losing benefits.

The program, dubbed Bridefare by its critics, has proven to be highly controversial. Opponents of the plan have charged the governor with trying to impose his personal beliefs—that people ought to get married—on others through legislation. "To penalize people who don't get married in a society in which family ties are weakening in general seems like tough medicine," Professor Richard P. Nathan, the director of the Rockefeller Institute of Government at the State University of New York at Albany told Isabel Wilkerson in an interview for the *New York Times* (January 12, 1991). "This is not in the mainstream. This sounds like sledgehammer policy." Defending himself against such criticisms, Thompson told Wilkerson, "I certainly don't want to force anybody to get married, but don't think the welfare system should act as an impediment."

In 1993 Governor Thompson unveiled his most sweeping reform yet: a plan he called Work not Welfare, which not only requires welfare recipients to find work but also stipulates that cash payments are to be made for a maximum of two years, after which only food stamps and child care are to be provided (for one additional year). "This represents a genuine shift," Gerald Whitburn, the secretary of Wisconsin's Health and Social Services, told Edward Walsh in an interview for the *Washington Post* (December 5, 1993). "We are saying, 'No, this is not an entitlement. You will be getting twenty-four checks, not 260, not 2,600.' Recipients tell us they want to work, give us a chance. We're going to do that."

In May 1993 Thompson presented his plan to the state legislature, where it won bipartisan support. Over the next several months, it was expanded by Democratic lawmakers to include a provision requiring Wisconsin to withdraw from the federal welfare system by January 1, 1999—a provision that would make Wisconsin the only state to do so since the public-assistance program was instituted by President Franklin D. Roosevelt during the Great Depression. Many observers suggested that this provision was inserted into the bill by the Democrats to make it more difficult for the governor to sign. "Some members in our caucus wanted to embarrass him," Representative Antonio Riley, the bill's main Democratic sponsor in the assembly, told Jason DeParle in an interview for the *New York Times* (December 14, 1993). "They wanted a headline that said, 'Governor vetoes Democratic plan to end welfare.'" Thompson, however, was not to be intimidated, and in December 1993, he signed the bill into law. "We think the best thing to do is start over afresh, rather than tinker around the edges," he told DeParle.

Critics of the legislation have expressed anxiety over its central provision—the two-year limit on cash benefits—which went into effect on a trial basis in two counties on January 1, 1995. "My worst fear is that people will come in and sign the contract and still believe there is going to be a safety net somewhere for them, that they can't be cut off . . . and at the end of the two years, they'll not have the skills and experience to get a good job," Cyrina Kahut, a state county caseworker, told Rogers Worthington in an interview for the *Chicago Tribune* (April 2, 1995). Thompson has said he will give local employers financial incentives to hire former welfare recipients should they fail to find work. "If, in fact, we can't [find jobs for all of the recipients], there has to be some way to subsidize employers for that person to work in the private sector," he told Atkins. Yet another criticism of the plan is that it is being tested in two counties where the unemployment rate is very low. "This is not going to be an experiment that is going to provide useful information for national policy," Mark Greenberg, a senior staff attorney with the Center for Law and Social Policy, in Washington, D.C. told Edward Walsh. "The challenge isn't to implement welfare reform in perfect circumstances; it's to implement it in the real world." Notwithstanding these concerns, Wisconsinites have remained overwhelmingly supportive of the program. In 1994 Thompson was returned to the governorship for a third term, and in a 1995 poll some 75 percent of those questioned approved of his Work not Welfare program. In 1995 he considered running for the United States presidency, making several trips to Iowa and New Hampshire to gauge his prospects; in June he announced that he would not make a presidential bid but said that he would not rule out running for vice-president.

In addition to trying to reform the welfare system, during his tenure as governor Thompson has worked hard at improving the educational opportunities available to Wisconsinites. Many of his initiatives were thwarted by the Democratic state assembly, however. As Charles Sykes reported in the *National Review* (August 12, 1991), Thompson advocated "instituting statewide comprehensive examinations that would permit comparisons between schools; breaking up the city of Milwaukee's unwieldy school district into smaller units; offering special grants for effective schools; and permitting schools to contract privately with teachers for specialized programs." All these initiatives were defeated. "In the end," Sykes wrote, "Thompson won nationwide praise, but little in the way of actual legislation."

Thompson had more luck with his campaign to institutionalize school choice—the idea, advocated by many conservatives, that parents should be given the option of removing their children from the public school system and placing them in private schools, with the state partially subsidizing the tuition. In his first term he initiated the Milwaukee

Parental Choice Program, the country's first school-choice program, which provides parents who opt to send their children to private schools with a per-child tuition subsidy of $2,500. The program is limited to 1 percent of the system's students, and subsidies cannot be used for parochial schools. When the program was first proposed, some observers feared that it would prove to be beneficial only to children from middle-class families. But in his *National Review* article, Donald Polsby cited a study conducted by a professor at the University of Wisconsin indicating that such fears were unfounded. In February 1994 Polly Williams, the Democratic sponsor of the original bill in the assembly, and John Norquist, the mayor of Milwaukee, sought to expand the program and to remove the ban on religious schools.

Tommy Thompson has been married to the former Sue Ann Mashak, a schoolteacher, since 1968. The couple has three children: Kelli, Tommi, and Jason. An outgoing and gregarious politician who goes to great lengths to stay in touch with his constituency, Thompson typically peppers his speeches with references to Elroy, where he and his wife still live, and where they raised their children. He has received several awards, including *City and State* magazine's Most Valuable Public Official Award (1991), the American Legislative Exchange Council's Thomas Jefferson Freedom Award, and the Free Congress Foundation's "Governance" Award. Thompson is to assume the chairmanship of the National Governor's Association in August 1995.

Selected Biographical References: Chicago Tribune X p8+ Ap 10 '94 pors; N Y Times Mag p22+ Ja 15 '95 pors; Nat R 46:54+ My 16 '94; Almanac of American Politics, 1994; Politics in America, 1994; Who's Who in America, 1995

The Institute for Genomic Research

Venter, J. Craig

Oct. 14, 1946- Biochemist. Address: c/o The Institute for Genomic Research, 932 Clopper Rd., Gaithersburg, MD 20878

Working out of a former ceramics factory turned biotech research institute in Gaithersburg, Maryland, a group of some eighty scientists has been involved since 1992 in what the institute's president and founder, the biochemist J. Craig Venter, has called a "giant scientific, business, and social experiment." Their mission is to further scientists' understanding of both inherited diseases and human evolution, and they plan to accomplish those goals by employing a gene-hunting strategy that Venter has described as "the ultimate in simplicity." The strategy, developed by Venter, entails isolating the relatively small part of the human genome that consists of genes, partially sequencing them, and then, by relying on powerful computers to analyze the sequenced DNA fragments, deducing their functions. It is not the only gene-hunting method available to scientists—and, according to its critics, its usefulness has yet to be demonstrated—but it is the only one that yields sequenced gene fragments both quickly and inexpensively. "I don't see how this cannot revolutionize biology," Venter told Nicholas Wade in an interview for the *New York Times* (February 22, 1994). Described by one industry observer as "the most advanced gene-discovery laboratory in the world," Venter's brainchild, The Institute for Genomic Research, or TIGR (pronounced "tiger"), receives 80 percent of its funding from the for-profit enterprise Human Genome Sciences (HGS). According to some observers, the data that TIGR is bound by agreement to make available to its for-profit affiliate may help transform HGS into one of the leading pharmaceutical companies in the world.

Although Venter stands to earn a considerable amount of money from his institute's alliance with HGS (in 1994 the value of his stock in the company was $12 million), his motivation for entering into the venture was not financial gain, he has said, but rather a desire to achieve his research goals more quickly than he would have been able to at the National Institutes of Health, where he had worked since 1984. "I'm an impatient person," he admitted to Eliot Marshall in an interview for *Science* (October 14, 1994). Since TIGR was established, Venter and his colleagues have made considerable progress toward realizing their goals. By the end of

1994, they had discovered some thirty-five thousand unique human genes, and they expect to conclude their effort to sequence each of the estimated fifty thousand to one hundred thousand human genes within another two years.

J. Craig Venter was born in Salt Lake City, Utah on October 14, 1946. He spent part of his youth in San Francisco, where, as a high school student, he distinguished himself as a champion swimmer. He also enjoyed surfing, so much so that for a time he considered dropping out of school to devote himself to the sport. After his graduation from high school, he entered the United States Navy Medical Corps. During the last of his three years of service, he was stationed in Vietnam, where, among other duties, he provided medical care in an orphanage. On his desk in his office at TIGR, two photographs taken while he was in Vietnam serve as constant reminders of the suffering endured there. "Every year I've had since I have felt was a gift," he told Deborah Shapley in an interview for *Government Executive* (September 1994).

Venter's experiences as a medical corpsman in Vietnam contributed to his decision to pursue a career in medicine, and on his return to the United States he enrolled at the University of California at San Diego as a premedical student. He soon became more interested in research than in practicing medicine, however, and after graduating with honors and a B.A. degree in biochemistry in 1972, he entered the university's doctoral program in physiology and pharmacology. He received his Ph.D. in 1975, and in the next year he was hired as an assistant professor of pharmacology and therapeutics at the State University of New York (SUNY) at Buffalo. Venter remained affiliated with SUNY for eight years, rising to the rank of professor in the early 1980s. During part of that time, he worked concurrently at the Roswell Park Memorial Institute. The main focus of his research was on elucidating the structure and function of adrenergic and muscarinic cholinergic receptors. For his work he won the 1982 Boehringer Ingelheim Muscarinic Receptor Research Award, in 1984.

In the same year Venter became a section chief at the National Institute of Neurological Disorders and Stroke of the National Institutes of Health, in Bethesda, Maryland. During his eight years at the NIH, Venter centered his energies on understanding how signals are transmitted between nerve cells. To that end, he studied the genes that encode for the enzymes that help make neurotransmitters and receptors, molecules that are involved in neural communication. By using an automatic DNA sequencer produced by the California-based company Applied Biosystems to "sequence," or describe chemically, the genes in question, during the late 1980s Venter's lab succeeded in isolating several genes.

Despite his success, Venter was frustrated by the excruciatingly slow pace of gene discovery. Progress was slow—not just for Venter but for all gene hunters—because only about 3 percent of the human genome consists of genes, which carry the information needed to sustain life; the remaining 97 percent consists of "junk DNA," so called because it is made up of stretches of genetic material of no known function. Since these stretches of possibly meaningless DNA are interspersed not only between genes but within them as well, it is often difficult to figure out which parts of the gene are relevant and which are "junk."

Venter became especially frustrated by his and his colleagues' search for the genes located on chromosome 19. "We found that even when we had . . . sequences of human chromosomes, on the order of one hundred thousand base pairs of DNA, the sequence was, for all practical purposes, uninterpretable," he recalled to Gina Kolata in an interview for the *New York Times* (July 28, 1992). Venter was not alone in his frustration. In 1983 scientists had discovered that the gene that, when mutated, causes Huntington's disease (HD) resides on chromosome 4, but seven years later they had not yet found the gene. "We found it is not trivial to find the genes, even if you have the sequence," Venter told Leslie Roberts in an interview for *Science* (June 21, 1991). (The HD gene was finally isolated in 1993.)

In May 1990, while he was flying back to the United States from Japan, Venter was thinking about how to expedite the process of gene discovery, when he envisioned an alternative approach to gene hunting that exploits the fact that different genes are "expressed" in different types of cells. (Genes containing the information necessary to produce the protein hemoglobin are activated in red blood cells but not in other types of cells, for instance.) A gene is expressed after it translates itself into an intermediate, unstable molecule called messenger ribonucleic acid (mRNA). Thanks to a battery of molecular tools developed in recent decades, scientists are able to isolate a cell's mRNA and, using a special enzyme called reverse transcriptase, retranslate the mRNA back into DNA. The resulting molecule, known as complementary DNA, or cDNA, thus lacks the "junk" and contains only those parts of the original gene that encode for a protein that is being used by the cell.

According to the method developed by Venter, the cDNAs are partially sequenced, or "tagged," using an automated DNA-sequencing machine. The resulting sequences, called "expressed sequence tags," or ESTs, are about five hundred nucleotides in length—long enough to distinguish one from another. These fragments are then compared to known genes belonging to both humans and other organisms, including bacteria and yeast. Because many genes are not species-specific (for instance, more than 99 percent of human DNA is identical to that of chimpanzees, man's closest living relative), a close resemblance between one of Venter's ESTs and a known gene enables scientists to deduce the function of the gene from which the EST is derived. Using this method, Venter has said, he can infer the function of between 20 and 30 percent of the cDNAs he isolates.

On his return to the United States, Venter had considerable difficulty in persuading his researchers to test his idea. Part of the reason for its lack of appeal was that the idea had already been considered and rejected by some of the most eminent scientists in the world, on the grounds that the prevailing methods for isolating the cDNAs were unreliable. Finally, one of Venter's new recruits, Mark D. Adams, agreed to take on the challenge. "I couldn't convince anyone else in the laboratory to try this crazy idea," Venter told David L. Wheeler in an interview for the *Chronicle of Higher Education* (February 26, 1992).

As it turned out, Venter's EST method enabled him to accomplish just what he had hoped it would: he could thus sequence the information-carrying parts of the genome quickly. By July 1992 his lab had identified more than ten thousand genes, among them twenty-seven hundred that had previously been unknown. Traditional methods, on the other hand, had enabled scientists to discover just three thousand human genes over the course of a decade. Another distinguishing feature of the EST approach is that it is comparatively inexpensive. Venter told Gina Kolata that while it can cost as much as fifty thousand dollars to sequence a gene using traditional methods, his ESTs can be sequenced for just twenty dollars apiece.

The apparent advantages of Venter's approach to gene hunting failed to impress some of the most prominent members of the scientific community. According to critics, Venter's lab might be able to churn out the sequences of gene fragments rapidly, but how useful could this information be if the function of a majority of them remained unknown? It was more useful, even if more time-consuming, they argued, to focus on a particular biological phenomenon, such as an inherited disease, and work backwards to determine the gene or genes that caused it. Underlying much of the criticism was the notion that Venter's approach was a directionless and "unscientific" enterprise at least partly because it was heavily automated.

Many scientists' irritation with the EST approach was transformed into alarm during the summer of 1991, after the NIH applied for patents on 337 previously unknown human gene fragments that had been sequenced by Venter and his colleagues, and their alarm only intensified after the NIH submitted a second patent application on an additional 2,375 gene fragments in early 1992. "I think it's a terrible idea," Maynard Olson, a geneticist at Washington University, told Christopher Anderson in an interview for *Nature* (October 10, 1991). "If the law is interpreted to give intellectual property rights for naked DNA sequences, then the law should be changed. It's like trying to patent the periodic table. To put patent value on cream-skimming is sending entirely the wrong signal. Scientists who advocate such approaches are playing with fire."

A number of the scientists who objected to the patent application feared that if the patents were granted, other biotechnology firms would rush headlong into the business of sequencing gene fragments. Gene sequences could then become the property of private companies, an outcome that would inhibit collaboration among scientists. George Annas, a lawyer and medical ethicist at Boston University, for instance, told Gina Kolata that if the patent applications were approved, "we will have everyone trying to patent the entire human genome. This is not science. This is like the Gold Rush. That's why there are no scientists saying this is a wonderful thing." Especially biting were the criticisms expressed by James Watson, the legendary codiscoverer of the structure of DNA and the first head of the Human Genome Project, who, in addition to publicly voicing his opposition to the patent application, asserted that the automated sequencers used by Venter "could be run by monkeys." "It was a sad and frustrating situation for me," Venter recalled to Deborah Shapley, "to have the biggest star in the field, who had been a brief mentor, turn from my strong supporter into my biggest attacker."

For his part, Venter had become convinced of the need to file for patent protection on his gene fragments after discussing the matter with Reid Adler, an NIH lawyer. Adler explained that if Venter simply went ahead and published his data without having obtained patents on the fragments, biotechnology companies would be unlikely to use that information to develop gene-based products, the reason being that patents on products in the development stage are typically not granted if they are derived from data already in the public domain. "I thought it was just irresponsible to just dump all this stuff and make it so that the biotech industry and the pharmaceutical industry could not get patent protection," Venter explained to Gina Kolata.

While many in the biotech industry felt that the granting of patents would further complicate the conduct of business, most favored the NIH's application anyway, fearing that if the NIH did not file for the patents, other researchers would, a development that would undermine the United States' competitive edge in the biotech field. "If this becomes a race and if gene fragments become proprietary, then it is in the best interests of [the United States and its entities] to file for patents," Wallace H. Steinberg, the chairman of the board of HealthCare Investment Corp. and Venter's soon-to-be business partner, told Gina Kolata. Like many others, Steinberg also felt that the best possible outcome would be that the patent applications would be denied. (That is just what happened, in 1993; the NIH subsequently decided not to appeal the decision.)

Perhaps the principal reason the patent debate became so heated was the fact that Venter's patent application, and indeed his commitment to large-scale sequencing as a strategy for gene discovery, appeared to pose a threat to the goals of the Human Genome Project, an ambitious undertaking initiated by NIH and the Department of Energy in 1990. The key aims of the project, which was to cost $3 billion and take fifteen years to complete, were to be, first, to "map"—or find the approximate locations of each of—the estimated fifty thousand to one hundred thousand human genes and, second, to sequence all of the DNA—including the junk—in the human genome. Although Venter maintained that "the cDNA approach does not eliminate the need for the Human Genome Project," the fact that his method enabled scientists to sequence genes both more quickly and more cheaply than the approach advocated by the Human Genome Project appeared to undermine the legitimacy of the project. "There's an undercurrent of tension between those who advocate a cDNA approach and those who advocate the heavyweight sequence-to-the-end approach," one unidentified industry observer told Christopher Anderson. "Venter says he can do it cheaply. But the glory of it all gets dissipated to the wind once you've sequenced all the genes. It's a matter of who leads the project. The patent issue is just a lightning rod on the whole controversy." Venter's critics also feared that the government might devote precious dollars to large-scale sequencing efforts at the expense of the Human Genome Project. What would members of Congress think, they worried, when they heard that it was possible to sequence more genes for far less money than they had been led to believe?

The net result of the patent controversy was that Venter lost favor with many influential scientists working on the Human Genome Project. At the same time, however, the debate also brought him to the attention of the biotechnology industry. He was approached by a number of venture capitalists offering to fund his research, and he accepted one such offer from Wallace Steinberg. According to the deal worked out by the two men, Steinberg agreed to put up $10 million to launch Human Genome Sciences, Inc., which in turn would provide Venter with $85 million over the course of ten years to found and operate The Institute for Genomic Research. Venter, who was to serve as TIGR's president and director, would be free to pursue any research goals he desired, the only restriction being that he make his gene data available to HGS and wait twelve months before publishing any data the company might want to develop for commercial purposes.

Venter left the NIH in July 1992 to establish the institute. Joining him were his wife, Claire Fraser, who also worked at the NIH, Mark Adams, and a number of other researchers from his own lab. Since then, the pace of TIGR's sequencing effort has been so swift that by the end of 1994 more than thirty-five thousand human genes had been discovered. As might be imagined, those biologists who were dubious about large-scale sequencing when Venter first committed himself to it in 1991 were similarly unimpressed by the cDNA work done at TIGR. As David Botstein, a geneticist at Stanford University Medical Center, told Nicholas Wade, "No one ever doubted he could get one hundred thousand sequence runs. But it doesn't mean any more now than when he first proposed it." According to Mary Ann Liebert, the owner of a publishing company that specializes in scientific material, such criticisms may be rooted in part in jealousy. "There is envy that Craig Venter had gone and done this outside of NIH and created the possibility of becoming a wealthy individual in the process," she told Kathleen Day in an interview for the *Washington Post* (May 9, 1994). Liebert went on to say that Venter's "unabashed enthusiasm" for his work "is sometimes misinterpreted as overstatement."

Despite the widespread skepticism about Venter's sequencing initiative, TIGR can point to several indisputable successes. In 1993, for instance, the institute, in collaboration with researchers at the Centers for Disease Control and Prevention, in Atlanta, completed the sequence analysis of the variola genome, an achievement that makes the virus one of just a handful of organisms whose genomes have been sequenced. TIGR scored an even more important success in December of that year, after a team of scientists led by Bert Vogelstein and Kenneth Kinzler of Johns Hopkins University asked TIGR to assist them in their search for a gene that, when defective, causes hereditary nonpolyposis colon cancer, which is thought to be the most common inherited disease in humans. Previous research had led Vogelstein and his colleagues to suspect that their culprit was a mutant "mismatch-repair gene"—a kind of gene that, when healthy, is able to both identify errors that are introduced during replication and engineer the necessary repairs. If the gene becomes defective (as a result of exposure to environmental carcinogens, for instance), defects in other genes may remain uncorrected; if genes governing cell division are affected, a tumor may begin to grow, a process that can lead to cancer. Vogelstein's team, which had isolated a bacterial mismatch-repair gene, decided to turn to TIGR in the hope that a human gene with a sequence similar to that of their bacterial gene had been isolated by the institute's researchers and catalogued in its database. "Within a few minutes they told us that they had three such genes," Kinzler told Robert F. Service in an interview for *Science* (March 18, 1994). Subsequent research revealed that one of the three genes was responsible for 30 percent of hereditary nonpolyposis colon cancers; the other two are thought to play a role in an individual's predisposition to developing cancer.

In the eyes of some scientists, TIGR's role in helping to isolate the colon-cancer genes confirmed the merit of large-scale sequencing as a strategy for gene discovery. "[The Hopkins-TIGR-HGS] study provides a wake-up call to the future value of the databases that will hold cDNA sequences," Jefferey Trent, chief of the Laboratory for Cancer Genetics at the National Center for Human Genome Research, told Service. "The reason is very simple," Vogelstein added. "If TIGR or HGS has the gene already, it takes essentially five minutes to get this gene, whereas it could take months with the traditional approach." Venter won yet another convert in C. Thomas Caskey, a geneticist at Baylor College of Medicine, in Houston, who asked TIGR to do a database search in the autumn of 1994. "There's a gene I've been interested in for quite some time—a gene of no economic value but great biologic interest . . . ," Caskey told Eliot Marshall in an interview for *Science* (October 14, 1994). "In a minute and a half we got a strike . . . , and now we have the gene. It was beautiful to see how quickly it worked." As a result of his successes in large-scale DNA sequencing, Venter was recently awarded a three-year, $6.7 million grant from the Department of Energy for microbial genome sequencing.

Venter's current goals include developing computer programs that will facilitate the effort to deduce his gene fragments' functions. He also hopes his research will provide clues to how cancer develops. But he has said that his "real goal" is to use his data to understand the evolutionary development of humankind. "What we hope to do is follow evolution at the genome level," Venter told Nicholas Wade. "We will look for evolutionary events that lead to the development of new genes."

In addition to serving as director and president of TIGR, Venter serves on several editorial boards and is the editor in chief of the journal *Genome Science and Technology*, a member of several professional societies, including the Human Genome Organization, and cochairman of the Genome Sequencing and Analysis Conference. The author of more than 140 research articles, he has also edited a multivolume series of books on receptor biochemistry and methodology. His many awards include the Public Health Service Special Recognition Award, which he received for his isolation of some two thousand genes expressed in the human brain. Venter, "a soft-spoken biochemist who rarely dons a tie," according to Kathleen Day, lives with his wife in Potomac, Maryland. Venter has a son by a previous marriage.

Selected Biographical References: Chronicle of Higher Education A p6+ F 26 '92 por; Fortune 129:94+ My 30 '94 por; Government Executive p38+ S '94 por; N Y Times C p1+ Jl 28 '92 por, C p1+ F 22 '94 por; Science 252:1618+ Je 21 '91 por

---

Vermeij, Geerat J.

(ver-MAY, GEER-at)

Sept. 28, 1946- Evolutionary biologist; marine biologist; biogeographer; paleontologist; naturalist; educator. Address: c/o Dept. of Geology, University of California, Davis, CA 95616

Xiom Photo Design

"Few works of architecture can match the elegance and variety of the shells of mollusks," the Dutch-born scientist Geerat J. Vermeij has said. "Beauty is reason enough to appreciate and study shells for their own sake, but shells offer much more." Using his fingertips to examine their structures and surfaces, Vermeij, who has been blind since early childhood, can identify thousands of species and subspecies of present-day and fossil shells. His exquisitely sensitive, exceedingly detailed tactile explorations of shells have not only brought him endless aesthetic pleasure but in addition have yielded powerful clues to the histories of individual shells and the evolution of shell species and other organisms. Through his discoveries about the development of molluscan defenses and the weaponry of molluscan predators, he has demonstrated the importance of predation as a force in evolution.

Drawing upon those and other of his findings, an encyclopedic and probably unmatched knowledge of shells that he has gained through voluminous reading in the scientific literature as well as his own research, and his stores of information in such disciplines as zoology, botany, and geology, Vermeij has made significant contributions in biogeography, paleontology, paleoecology, and marine biology as well as evolutionary biology. Renowned as both "an acute thinker and an excellent observer," as the Harvard University paleontologist Stephen Jay Gould has described him, and as "a brilliant guy, an idea man, a synthesizer," in the words of David Jablonski of the University of Chicago, another leading paleontologist, in 1992 he received one of the prestigious fellowships, commonly known as "genius grants," awarded annually by the John D. and Catherine T. MacArthur Foundation. Vermeij taught at the University of

Maryland at College Park for seventeen years before joining the faculty of the University of California at Davis in 1989. He is the author of three books: *Biogeography and Adaptation: Patterns of Marine Life* (1978), *Evolution and Escalation: An Ecological History of Life* (1987), and *A Natural History of Shells* (1993).

"Without the support and encouragement of my parents and brother, and their fascination with plants and animals, I would not have chosen science or natural history as a career," Vermeij has said. The second of the two children of J. L. Vermeij and his wife, Geerat Jacobus Vermeij was born on September 28, 1946 in Sappemeer, in the province of Groningen, in the Netherlands. His brother is Arie P. Vermeij. When Geerat Vermeij was about two weeks old, he was diagnosed as having juvenile glaucoma, a condition so rare that it had never before been recorded in Groningen. As a baby and toddler, he spent much of his time in hospitals, where doctors administered various treatments in what proved to be a fruitless attempt to save his eyesight. Able at best to distinguish light and dark, colors, and hazy, distorted shapes, he became completely blind at the age of three. His last visual memory is of a blur of yellow.

According to an article by John Neary for *Life* (November 27, 1970), Vermeij lived for at least part of his childhood in Gouda, about twenty miles from the North Sea in northwestern Holland. He and his family often visited the seacoast, where he became familiar with "the chalky and rather sloppily ornamented clamshells that washed up in great profusion on the North Sea beaches," as he wrote in *A Natural History of Shells*. He received his earliest formal education at a residential school for the blind that he has described as "terrible." "The discipline was awful . . . ," he told Kenneth Brower, who profiled him for the *Atlantic Monthly* (November 1976). "I think if I stayed I would have gone nuts." His memories of his three years there are not totally negative, however, thanks in large measure to Miss Mooy, one of his teachers. The young Vermeij greatly enjoyed the class trips that she led in the woods surrounding the school, and he began collecting pinecones, beechnuts, and other things that Miss Mooy had showed to her pupils.

In 1955, having learned that public schools in several states offered blind children far more satisfactory educational programs than anything then available in Dutch institutions, Vermeij's parents immigrated to the United States with their sons. The family settled in Dover, a town in a rural part of northwestern New Jersey, where Geerat attended a local public school. Although the curriculum was significantly less demanding than that of his boarding school, "the social advantages outweighed the educational disadvantages," Vermeij said during an interview with Gerri Kobren for the *Baltimore Sun Magazine* (March 16, 1980).

At the age of ten, Vermeij had the "great fortune," as he has put it, to be placed in the fourth-grade class taught by Caroline Colberg. "The windowsills of her classroom held a display of the shells she had gathered on her travels to the west coast of Florida," he recalled in *A Natural History of Shells*. "My first glimpse of these shells is deeply etched in my memory. Here were elegantly shaped clam and snail shells, many adorned with neatly arranged ribs, knobs, and even spines. Not only were the shell interiors impossibly smooth to the touch, but the olive and cowrie shells were externally so polished that I was certain someone had varnished them. The contrast with the drab chalky shells from the Netherlands was remarkable. Why, I wondered, were warm-water shells so much prettier than the northern shells? When a classmate brought in some shells from the Philippines, which were even more spectacular in their fine sculpture and odd shapes, my curiosity was aroused even more. I resolved to begin collecting shells and to read as much as I could find about them."

In addition to what he learned through reading, Vermeij's knowledge of shells grew through the senses of touch, hearing, and smell. "When a shell falls into Geerat Vermeij's hand . . . , it is caught up in a kind of dance," Kenneth Brower wrote. "It revolves, flips, cants one way or another as his fingertips count whorls, gauge thicknesses, measure spires." "You're absorbing little details of the ribs, how many cusps there are in the spine," Vermeij explained to John Neary, in describing some of the things he looks for. "Are there little scales on this rib? Are there little sub-ribs?" When examining tiny shells, he uses his thumbnail rather than his fingertips. The faint sounds that he produces by gently rubbing the shell provide additional details about its structure. In addition to determining species and even subspecies, his inspections yield information about sediment content, the effects of wave action, damage from predator attacks and repairs to the damaged areas, and clues to the characteristics and identity of the predator. "He often has insights that are unencumbered by sight," Jerry Haresewich, a curator of mollusks at the Smithsonian Institution's National Museum of Natural History, in Washington, D.C., told Luther Young for the *Baltimore Sun* (December 12, 1988). "If a shell has a bright color pattern, sighted people might not pay attention to all the subtleties like he does."

In 1965, after graduating from a Dover public high school, Vermeij enrolled as a biology major at Princeton University, in Princeton, New Jersey, on a full scholarship. Overcoming the resistance of government officials who regarded his quest of a bachelor's degree in science as unrealistic, he obtained funds to hire people to read books and papers to him. In laboratory classes that required vision-dependent exercises, such as dissections or microscope work, he engaged in such alternative activities as studying plastic models.

Vermeij has described himself as a "life-long opponent of affirmative action." "I am a strong disbeliever in seeing things from the point of view of being handicapped, gender, race, and all the rest of it," he told Carol Kaesuk Yoon, who profiled him for the *New York Times* (February 7, 1995). "All my life I have fought hard to integrate into society, and I think that's the way any minority group should work," he explained. "If you give people preferential treatment, others will always say, 'Ah well, he got this because he's blind.' You can never live that down. The idea is to eliminate the barriers to the point that nobody will care." Vermeij believes just as strongly that "a policy of social integration does not absolve society from the responsibility to make science and other intellectual activities attractive and available to those who are socially handicapped," as he wrote in a letter to *Science* in 1978. "On the contrary, we should improve science education for the handicapped, stimulate the development of appropriate technology, and make the general public aware of the many opportunities that science can offer a handicapped person. In fulfilling this responsibility, we may bend some rigid rules to accommodate the handicapped, but we should not alter fundamentally the standards of performance."

During his second year at Princeton, Vermeij became friendly with the biologist Egbert G. Leigh Jr., one of his professors. A specialist in tropical rain forests, Leigh had many interests, among them evolution, animal shapes, and shells. Vermeij was surprised to discover that Leigh arranged his shell collection not in the usual way, by species and family, as Vermeij was grouping his, but rather according to their places of origin. "This arrangement made it possible to look beyond the particulars of individual species," Vermeij has noted. "The assemblage as a whole became the focus of attention. Leigh's appealing approach taught me that something as simple as the arrangement of a collection subtly directs one's thinking."

During the last of his three years at Princeton, Vermeij amassed specimens of mollusks from Curaçao, in the Netherlands Antilles, which he visited briefly while on a trip to Costa Rica with a class of graduate students. He earned an A.B. degree in biology from Princeton, summa cum laude and Phi Beta Kappa, in 1968. In the fall of that year, he began graduate studies in biology at Yale University, in New Haven, Connecticut, on a full scholarship. Before gaining acceptance to the university, he had been interviewed by a Yale professor who then harbored the widely held misconception that blindness precludes a career in science. "He asked me how I could possibly read the literature, how I could possibly do this, that, and the other thing," Vermeij told Carol Kaesuk Yoon. "He decided that the clincher would be for me to fail at the thing I was supposed to be the best at, shells." Vermeij's correct identification of shells that the professor pulled from a storage drawer at Yale's Peabody Museum of Natural History immediately dispelled his misgivings. "This incredibly skeptical man was transformed," Leslie Cole quoted Vermeij as saying in a profile for *UC Davis Magazine* (Winter 1992). "He just turned around and became an ardent supporter."

Vermeij received a master of philosophy degree from Yale in 1970. During the next year his interests, which until then had focused almost exclusively on mollusks, expanded to include all invertebrates and also biochemistry. Determined to complete his graduate work as quickly as he had his undergraduate studies so as not to be a "parasite," as he has put it, he earned a Ph.D. degree in biology and geology from Yale in 1971. By the end of that year, his name had appeared as the author or coauthor of eight papers published in scientific journals. The articles bore such titles as "Adaptive Versatility and Skeleton Construction," "The Geometry of Shell Sculpture," and "Gastropod Evolution and Morphological Diversity in Relation to Shell Geometry."

In mid-1971 the University of Maryland at College Park hired Vermeij as an instructor in the Department of Zoology. Once again, he had to prove that he was as capable as a sighted person, this time in order to progress from what the university designated as a trial position to a place on the tenure track. He was soon promoted to the rank of assistant professor (a title he held from 1972 to 1974) and later to associate professor (1974–80) and professor (1980–88). His receipt of the Award for Excellence in Research from the university's Division of Agriculture and Life Science, in 1983, further indicates his colleagues' recognition of his abilities. In 1976 and 1986 he served as a visiting associate professor and visiting professor, respectively, at the Friday Harbor Laboratories of the University of Washington, and in 1979, as a visiting associate professor at the University of Guam Marine Laboratory. Since 1989 he has held the title of professor in the Department of Geology at the University of California at Davis. He has taught courses in subjects ranging from general biology to evolution, ecology, paleontology, paleobiology, and the physics of organismal shapes. In addition, in the past two decades, he has served as the thesis adviser to fifteen students pursuing master's or doctoral degrees.

The genesis of Vermeij's research on shell form and the role that enemies of mollusks have played in molluscan evolution and distribution may be traced in part to two events that occurred when he was in his twenties. The first dates from the summer of 1968, when, as a participant in a National Science Foundation training program in molluscan biology, he gathered shells at Checker Reef, off the coast of Hawaii. Applying what he has described as the "valuable lesson" that he had gained from Egbert Leigh's unconventional arrangement of shells, he realized on one of his trips to the reef "how strikingly different the shells in Hawaii were from those at Curaçao," as he wrote in *A Natural History of Shells*. "The cones, drupe shells, and cowries of Hawaii had apertures so long and narrow and so restricted by barriers that there hardly seemed to be any room for the soft parts inside the massive shell." Moreover, the spines and other embellishments that covered the exteriors of the Hawaiian shells were far more highly developed than those adorning specimens from climatically similar, comparable Caribbean habitats.

The second significant event occurred during the summer of 1970, while Vermeij was doing fieldwork on the coast of Guam with the marine biologist Lucius G. Eldredge. One afternoon, while walking on a reef in Togcha Bay, Eldredge showed Vermeij a cowrie shell whose entire top was missing and then remarked that he had seen that type of damage in cowrie shells that had been broken by crabs. Vermeij had always attributed shell breakage to such phenomena as collisions with rocks and had always considered broken shells worthless. "The fact that many broken shells are found on sheltered shores, where the force of waves was minimal, had never occurred to me," he wrote in *A Natural History of Shells.* "Neither had the observation that many shells have repaired breaks, meaning that at least some shells sustain damage during the life of the builder. With the realization that predators might be responsible for shell destruction, I began to appreciate that broken shells contain information and should not simply be tossed away as ugly imperfections." Vermeij has described his experience on the Togcha Bay reef as one of the "defining moments" that "shaped his conception of how nature works."

In order to determine the significance of differences in shell forms and of the traces of successful and unsuccessful predation on shells, Vermeij set about collecting shells from climatically similar shallow-water habitats in tropical marine regions worldwide. The Organization of Tropical Studies, the National Science Foundation, and the National Geographic Society, among other organizations and agencies, supported his research. He had little difficulty obtaining grants, because, as he has pointed out, in the early 1970s funding agencies still looked with favor on what he has described as "thinly disguised fishing expeditions whose primary purpose was to uncover patterns and to make observations that might eventually serve as the basis for more directed research into underlying causes." "Nowadays," he observed in the early 1990s, "it is expected that every scientist, regardless of experience, have an unambiguous testable hypothesis before any money is risked on a project. The crucial first step of making observations or identifying a phenomenon or puzzle to be explained is either ignored or ridiculed as undirected and unscientific."

To discover how and why shell variations arose, Vermeij began to examine the fossil remains of mollusks and their predators. The nearness of College Park to Washington, D.C., enabled him to make frequent use of the National Museum of Natural History. As the repository of the world's largest collection of fossil and modern-day crustacean exoskeletons, the museum provided fertile ground for his investigations. Vermeij's research also required examination of shell breakage as well as observations of living creatures in marine environments in different parts of the world, to shed light on how crabs, sea stars, snails, and other predators killed or injured mollusks and which molluscan defenses were most effective. In collaboration with the molecular biologist Edith Zipser, his wife, Vermeij recorded what occurred when mollusks and their predators were brought together in laboratory settings. Between 1971 and 1978, when *Biogeography and Adaptation: Patterns of Marine Life*, his first book, was published, Vermeij and Zipser worked in nearly two-dozen far-flung places, among them Jamaica, Brazil, the Galápagos Islands, Madagascar, Ivory Coast, Israel, and the Philippines, and they subsequently did research in more than a dozen additional locations.

Kenneth Brower observed Vermeij in 1976 as he searched for mollusks along shores in the Palau Archipelago, in the Caroline Islands of Micronesia. Vermeij's fingers, Brower reported after watching them underwater through a face mask, "moved ceaselessly, meandering, then marching over the coral stones, pausing in crannies, moving on. They completed their scans so quickly that I found them hard to follow. When fingers met something animate, they retracted for a cautious instant, then returned, and in a flurry of touches they felt the thing out." Although he has been stung by such poison-bearing creatures as sea urchins, Portuguese men-of-war, and fireworms, Vermeij has avoided attack by the far more dangerous cone shells and sea snakes. "I've stuck my hands into more holes and under more rocks than I care to mention," he told Carol Kaesuk Yoon, "but my feeling is if you want to experience nature, you've got to be unconstrained." Warren Allmon, the director of the Paleontological Research Institution, in Ithaca, New York, once took Vermeij to a fossil bed in Florida that Allmon had investigated many times. "He stood there for maybe forty-five minutes feeling it," Allmon told Carol Kaesuk Yoon, "and then proceeded to tell me almost everything there was to know about it—the fighting conchs, the percent covered with barnacles, a layer of oysters. . . . He can do things with his hands that most of us can't do with our eyes."

Vermeij's research has revealed that compared with their fossil ancestors, modern-day mollusks are armed with thicker shells, narrower openings, tighter coils, and greater buttressing, and that the development of such defensive features—and, in a process known as escalation, of the devices with which predators try to overcome those defenses—is, on a geological time-scale, of relatively recent origin. "The arms races that mollusks have with their enemies have a lot to tell us about our own arms races," he has observed. He has also demonstrated that the shells of mollusks living in the Pacific Ocean bear, on average, more antipredatory defenses than those living in the Atlantic. If a proposed sea-level canal were to be constructed across the isthmus of Central America, allowing previously separated biotas to intermix, Pacific mollusk species might therefore have a distinct biological advantage over those of Atlantic origin. Vermeij's research has shown that many Pacific species invaded the Atlantic when, with the opening of the Bering Strait 3.5 million years ago, the Pacific and Arctic Oceans were connected, but "very little invasion in the opposite direction occurred." "The study of biotic interchange is important in view of the extensive biogeographical changes being brought about through human agency," he has pointed out. That study also has implications for the conservation of marine resources, a matter of deep concern to Vermeij.

In his interview with Leslie Cole, Vermeij noted that the findings of paleobiology are of relevance in human economics. "Most of the time, over geological time, mollusks and all other organisms have lived in a state of equilibrium or even decline," he said. "A state of growth is very much the exception to the rule. . . . Economists simply have to think about a world that isn't growing. And if they don't they're going to mislead us terribly with economic theories that simply won't work and with expectations that cannot be fulfilled." Vermeij has described his discoveries and theories in nearly ninety scientific papers in addition to his three books. He writes using either a Perkins Brailler—a typewriter that produces the raised dots of the Braille alphabet—or a standard typewriter.

According to Leslie Cole, "Vermeij fits the consummate image of a scholar, with his lean build, refined features, and short if slightly unruly brown beard and mustache." Carol Kaesuk Yoon noted his ability to "hold a visitor's attention with his quiet voice and a direct if unseeing gaze." Called Gary by his friends and associates, he is an accomplished punster. He and Edith Zipser, who also teaches at the Davis campus of the University of California, have one child. Zipser, who has been his constant companion and scientific collaborator since their marriage in 1972, "has plowed through innumerable papers with [him]," he wrote in *A Natural History of Shells*, "and helped in every imaginable research situation ranging from the sedate surroundings of the natural history library at the Smithsonian Institution to an encounter with spear-wielding islanders in the Aru Islands of Indonesia." Vermeij has also acknowledged as invaluable the assistance of Bettina Dudley, at the University of Maryland, and Janice Cooper, at the University of California, both of whom have read aloud to him thousands of papers and books, written not only in English but in any one of the six other languages he understands. He reportedly remembers the information contained in any given work after hearing it read aloud once.

Vermeij was awarded a Guggenheim fellowship in 1975–76. The five-year fellowship that the MacArthur Foundation awarded him in 1992 in recognition of his outstanding talents and creativity and "lasting discoveries" amounted to $280,000. He was named a fellow of the American Association for the Advancement of Science in 1981 and of the California Academy of Sciences in 1992. His interests include asymmetry in living organisms and the determinants of twining direction in vines. His favorite activities are collecting shells, traveling, and reading.

Vermeij has served as a consultant to the American Association for the Advancement of Science on scientific opportunities for the handicapped and has written several articles on teaching the blind. According to Leslie Cole, he has always considered his blindness "little more than an occasional inconvenience." He maintains that his problems do not differ fundamentally from those of other scientists. "I tend to see my career the way other biologists see theirs: good luck and bad luck and hard work," he said during a conversation with Luther Young. "Everyone in the world has to live with their own abilities and lack of abilities, and I do, too."

Selected Biographical References: Atlantic 238:94+ N '76; Baltimore Sun mag p15+ Mr 16 '80 pors, A p1+ D 12 '88 por; Life 69:R+ N 27 '70 pors; N Y Times C p1+ F 7 '95 por; UC Davis Mag p18+ Winter '92 pors; American Men & Women of Science, 1995–96

AP/Wide World Photos

Wayans, Keenen Ivory

June 8, 1958– Actor; screenwriter; filmmaker; television producer. Address: c/o PMK Public Relations, 955 S. Carrillo Dr., Suite 200, Los Angeles, CA 90048

"I'm not trying to change the world," the filmmaker and actor Keenen Ivory Wayans told Nick Charles of the New York *Daily News* (November 20, 1994). "It's not my job or my burden. I'm not naïve about what I do. People look at me for enjoyment, not education." The multitalented Wayans has provided plenty of entertainment for comedy lovers, moviegoers, and television viewers. A former stand-up comic who began his career by collaborating with the filmmaker and actor Robert Townsend and the comedian and actor Eddie Murphy, Wayans made his mark first in films, with *I'm Gonna Git You Sucka* in 1988, then in television, with the irreverent comedy/variety show *In Living Color*, which aired from 1990 until 1994. Few of his projects have escaped the charge that he is inadvertently perpetuating racial stereotypes by lampooning them, but Wayans has taken the criticism in stride with the knowledge that "you're damned if you do and damned if you don't," as he told Nick Charles, "so it's better to do."

Keenen Wayans was born on June 8, 1958 in Harlem in the New York City borough of Manhattan, the second son of Elvira Wayans, who earned a degree in social services after rearing her ten children, and Howell Wayans, a supermarket manager who later sold novelty items. (Early in his career Wayans acquired the middle name Ivory, in honor of one of his grandfathers.) Keenen's father, a Jehovah's Witness who imposed rigid discipline on his family, forbade his children to hang out with other kids in the neighborhood; consequently, the Wayans children provided their own entertainment. "Everything was a joke," Wayans told Tom Green in an interview for *Cosmopolitan* (November 1990). "If you got a whippin', when you got back to the table, you heard nine other people doing impressions of your screaming. Everything was funny to us."

When he was six years old, Wayans moved with his family to the Fulton housing project in the Chelsea district of Manhattan. It was around that time that he first saw Richard Pryor doing stand-up comedy on a television show. "He was doing routines about being poor, about looking for money, about being beaten up by the school bully," Wayans recalled to Dinitia Smith, who interviewed him for *New York* (October 8, 1990). "It was all happening to me at the time—and I'm laughin'!" Pryor became for him an idol to emulate and study, and from then on, Wayans has said, he knew what he wanted to do with his life.

At Seward Park High School, Wayans developed a reputation as a class clown. Resisting peer pressure to use drugs, he was satisfied with entertaining his friends with his wit when they were high. "They were the best audience in the world," he told Smith. At that time Wayans was putting in seventy hours a week as a manager at a McDonald's franchise to help support his family. Although the long hours took a toll on his academic performance, lowering his average from ninety-two to seventy-two, they did not prevent him from winning a scholarship to the Tuskegee Institute (now Tuskegee University) in Tuskegee, Alabama, where he studied engineering and did stand-up comedy for his new friends.

In the summer after his freshman year, Wayans auditioned at the Improv, a club on the West Side of Manhattan that has spawned many top comedians. He passed the audition on his second attempt. According to Dinitia Smith, no sooner did he resume his college education than he thought better of it, deciding instead to try his luck as a professional comic in New York City. (Other sources say he completed three years at Tuskegee.) "There was no need for me to be [in school] anymore," he realized, as he recalled to Smith. "It was a waste of time and money. If I got a degree and achieved a comfortable life, I would become complacent and not take risks. It would become something to fall back on. A college degree meant planning to fail." Within a few months of his return to New York City, he was regularly opening for jazz musicians at the Village Gate in Greenwich Village.

In 1980 Wayans moved to Los Angeles, where he made the round of comedy clubs and auditioned for television and film roles. A year later he won the part of Ray Brewster on the NBC pilot *Irene*, which failed to make the network's lineup, and appeared as a guest on the popular television series *A Different World*, *Benson*, *Cheers*, and *CHiPs*. Finally, in 1983, he was invited to appear on the *Tonight Show*, a breakthrough in terms of exposure for up-and-coming performers. In the same year he also appeared as a comic in the movie *Star 80*, Bob Fosse's harrowing dramatization of the murder of the *Playboy* centerfold model Dorothy Stratten (Mariel Hemingway) by her husband, Paul Snider (Eric Roberts). From 1983 to 1984 Wayans portrayed Duke Johnson, one of several peacetime army paratroopers in the NBC comedy/drama *For Love and Honor*, which starred Cliff Potts, Yaphet Kotto, Shelley Smith, and Rachel Ticotin, among others.

In a total of only fourteen days spread out over the next three years, Wayans collaborated on the movie *Hollywood Shuffle* (1987) with his friend Robert Townsend, whom he'd met while standing in line to audition at the Improv in the late 1970s. The film is a rough-edged satire about the racist casting practices that have led to a paucity of good movie roles for black actors, who have often been stereotyped in films as pimps, prostitutes, and thieves—a situation that has sometimes resulted in, among other things, black actors' being told that they are not "black" enough for roles. Townsend produced, directed, cowrote, and starred in the film, while Wayans cowrote the screenplay and portrayed two of the characters: Jerry Curl, who appears in a skit poking fun at black hair-care products, and Donald, a fast-food worker. Although most critics praised the film's creators for their caustic humor and original approach, some leavened their praise with the opinion that in focusing on black stereotyping as a subject, Townsend and Wayans were actually fostering racial categorization.

Hollywood Shuffle soon developed a cult following and led to a comedy special for the cable channel HBO, *Robert Townsend and His Partners in Crime* (1987), cowritten and coproduced by Wayans and Townsend, both of whom also appeared in the special. In the same year Wayans coproduced (with Robert D. Wachs) and cowrote (with Townsend, who also directed, and Eddie

Murphy) the opening sketch for *Eddie Murphy Raw*, a compilation of some of the stand-up routines of the eponymous actor, another friend from Wayans's Improv days. (Spoofing the "brat pack" label assigned to the crop of young white actors who arrived in Hollywood in the early 1980s, Eddie Murphy had labeled himself, Wayans, Townsend, and the future talk-show host Arsenio Hall members of the "black pack.")

Eager to emerge from what he considered Townsend's and Murphy's shadows, Wayans fought hard to maintain his independence by refusing to rely on his friends in any way when he directed, wrote, and starred in the genre-parodying *I'm Gonna Git You Sucka* (1988). "I've felt pigeonholed as Robert's partner, and I didn't want to take Eddie's money," Wayans explained to Jill Feldman of *Rolling Stone* (November 3, 1988). "It's like mom and dad. They're telling you you can always come home after you're finally setting out on your own. Coming home is your *worst* nightmare."

I'm Gonna Git You Sucka is an amiable sendup of such 1970s action movies as *Shaft* and *Superfly*, which belong to the genre commonly referred to as "blaxploitation" films, for their alleged exploitation of black experience. Wayans prefers not to use the term at all, as he explained in his interview with Nick Charles: "I think stereotype is attached to anything that we black filmmakers try to do. In the 1970s, they labeled those efforts 'blaxploitation,' and now they refer to them as stereotypes. [But] how can you call [*Shaft*], the first black film made for a major studio by a black director, blaxploitation? That film won an Oscar for [Isaac Hayes's] soundtrack," he added. Wayans believes that rather than exploiting blacks, those films provided black role models that were more positive than those that had been purveyed in previous Hollywood eras, as he explained to Alan Carter of the New York *Daily News* (January 12, 1989): "It was exciting to me to see something up on the screen that was so novel, so new, so exciting. To see a strong black male image was radically different from the image we were used to seeing. We saw diversity. I don't think the generation behind me saw that. They saw nothing but [blacks being portrayed as] gun-toting criminals." In establishing a strong black identity in his own film, in which blacks played the heroes and the villains, Wayans also strove to reach out to broader audiences. "We all experience the same things, and the trick in comedy is to find the proper language so that people can understand your experiences as their own," he told Sid Smith of the *Chicago Tribune* (December 18, 1988).

In *I'm Gonna Git You Sucka*, Jack Spade (Wayans) has returned home from ten years in the military, covered in medals for such skills as typing, shorthand, and surfing, only to find that his brother has died from wearing too many gold chains. Meanwhile, Spade's mother (Ja'net DuBois) uses martial arts—most memorably in a sequence in which DuBois's wig-wearing male stunt double has obviously replaced her—to fend off gold-chain-pushing gang members who want her to pay her dead son's debts. Among the movie's standout gags are an inner-city Olympics, featuring a race among street hoods carrying stolen television sets while being chased by Doberman pinschers, and a pimp-of-the-year contest whose winner is seen wearing Plexiglas platform shoes with enough room in the heels for live goldfish. In an inspired touch, Wayans enlisted the cooperation of many of the stars of the 1970s films, including Jim Brown (*Slaughter*), Bernie Casey (*Black Gunn*, *Hit Man*), Antonio Fargas (*Cleopatra Jones*), and Isaac Hayes (*Truck Turner*). (Richard Roundtree of *Shaft* and Ron O'Neal of *Superfly* were not cast.)

The movie's spoof of racial and sexual stereotypes as well as of bad filmmaking was praised by many critics. "*I'm Gonna Git You Sucka* is a lively but uncertain mixture of nostalgia, silliness, and genuinely unpredictable humor," Janet Maslin wrote in the *New York Times* (January 13, 1989), noting that the film "actually owes less to blaxploitation than to the anything-goes humor of the *Airplane!* school." But others, such as Desson Howe, who reviewed the film for the *Washington Post* (December 16, 1988), faulted Wayans for being what Howe called "slow on structure" and "too easily satisfied with predictable and sophomoric punch lines." Ultimately, critics seemed divided on the question of whether or not the movie was funny; their answers were influenced by individual taste, generational identification (that is, how they remembered the 1970s, with disgust, fondness, neutrality, or a mixture of all three), and whether they believed that parodying egregious stereotypes works to dispel or reinforce them. As a critic for the *Chicago Tribune* (December 14, 1988) put it, "Wayans probably will be accused, as was Philip Roth with *Portnoy's Complaint*, of somehow 'betraying' his people by holding ethnic foibles up to ridicule. But the wit and openness of *I'm Gonna Git You Sucka* has more to contribute to race relations than the smug piety of *Mississippi Burning*. As a positive image, a good, shared laugh is hard to beat."

Wayans had invited Fox Studio executives to a screening of *I'm Gonna Git You Sucka*, but representatives from Fox Broadcasting turned up instead. They were so impressed by the movie that they offered Wayans his own television show. "I really wasn't interested in television," he admitted to Charles E. Cohen and Vicki Sheff of *People* (June 11, 1990). "But they said the magic words, 'You can do anything you want.'" As the executive producer, Wayans, who also served as head writer and acted in some of the sketches, brought together a predominantly black cast, including his brother Damon, who in 1986 had been fired from the cast of *Saturday Night Live* for changing characters in mid-broadcast, and his sister Kim, who had been performing stand-up comedy in Los Angeles. Jim Carrey was one of the two white members of the team, which included an Asian and a Hispanic. Keenen's brother Shawn acted as the disc jockey for the Fly Girls, who between skits performed hip-hop/jazz dance sequences choreographed by Rosie Perez. Keenen's older brother, Dwayne, served as a production assistant.

Debuting in April 1990, the show was dubbed *In Living Color*, a title Wayans said was adapted from the old NBC-TV slogan, "The following program is brought to you in living color," which had also given rise, in 1985, to the name of the funk/metal black rock band Living Colour. Reprising one of the routines they had devised to amuse their family, Keenen and Damon portrayed employees of the Homeboy Shopping Network, who hawked stolen goods. Their childhood habit of reviewing films from an extremely effeminate perspective became the popular Men on Film routine, in which Damon Wayans and David Alan Grier played two outlandishly dressed, gay male reviewers whose criticism was never delivered without innuendo. Another favorite character was Damon Wayans's drunken homeless man, who gave *This Old House*–style tours of his cardboard-box home.

The nature of Keenen Wayans's material, which included a takeoff on the rap group 2 Live Crew, who are widely considered to be misogynistic, inevitably led to troubles with the network censors, whose scrutiny intensified when the show was scheduled for earlier in the evening in the fall of 1990. His exaggeration of ethnic stereotypes, such as a skit involving an overindustrious West Indian family, drew criticism from some quarters, as did the Men on Film bit, which was strenuously objected to by some members of the gay community (although others wrote to say how much they enjoyed it). More ironic was the concern, voiced primarily among white Fox executives, that Wayans's material would offend blacks. "I had to constantly remind them that I'm a black man with a very strong social conscience and a pretty decent education," Wayans told Marc Gunther for the *New York Times* (August 26, 1990). "I'm not a lunatic who's sitting around going, 'How can I totally degrade myself and my community?'" Wayans not only defended the innocuous nature of his work, he also contended that it can contribute to an improvement in race relations, as he explained to Gunther: "We take an exaggerated stereotype and really have fun with it. If I take something and ridicule it to such a degree that people could never look at it as anything real, then it really helps to destroy a preconceived notion."

Two months after the show's debut, it ranked among the Top Twenty programs in the Nielsen ratings. "Some of that success," noted the *Rolling Stone* writer Jeffrey Ressner (August 23, 1990), "can be traced to its blunt, unpretentious approach. Perhaps more important, however, is the funky, hip sensibility Wayans and his crew have injected into the tired 'skitcom' format. . . . *In Living Color* skewers ethnic and sexual stereotypes without coming across as mean-spirited or nasty." Indeed, Wayans scrupulously avoided jokes about AIDS, crack, Nazis, and the Ku Klux Klan. But occasionally his scathing humor cost Wayans a friendship, as in the case of Arsenio Hall, who was pilloried by Wayans's portrayal of him as a fawning interviewer with artificially enhanced buttocks. Many critics concluded, with Robert Goldberg of the *Wall Street Journal* (May 7, 1990), that the show "somehow manages to be simultaneously objectionable and funny."

After its first season, *In Living Color* earned Wayans an Emmy Award for outstanding variety, music, or comedy program in 1990; he was also nominated for an Emmy for outstanding writing in a variety or music program. In the following year he received another Emmy nomination for outstanding writing as well as a nomination for outstanding individual performance in a variety or music program. In 1990 and 1991 alone, Wayans appeared on no fewer than nine television specials: *Motown Thirty: What's Goin' On!*, *MTV's 1990 Video Music Awards*, the syndicated comedy special *A Laugh, a Tear*, the syndicated *Story of a People: The Black Road to Hollywood*, HBO's *Comic Relief V*, *A Comedy Salute to Michael Jordan*, *The Fifth Annual American Comedy Awards*, *The American Music Awards*, and *A Party for Richard Pryor*.

Throughout his helmsmanship of *In Living Color*, which ended when he terminated his contract with Fox in December 1992, reportedly because he was not consulted about scheduling changes, Wayans continued to pursue his film career. (At the time of his departure, *In Living Color* was rated Fox's third-most-popular television show.) In 1991 Wayans and Robert Townsend cowrote *The Five Heartbeats*, which Townsend also directed and starred in. The movie, about a Temptations-style musical group that struggles its way to the top through a corrupt and racist music business only to break up under the pressure of its success, received mixed reviews, with most of the criticism focusing on the mawkish tone of the film.

In 1994 Wayans signed a nonexclusive partnership contract with CBS-TV that would allow him to develop and produce network programs. The year also saw the release of his movie *A Low-Down Dirty Shame*, which he directed, wrote, and starred in with Jada Pinkett and Salli Richardson. As private detective Andre Shame, Wayans has to locate a Latin American gangster he thought he'd already killed. Featuring numerous explosions, shootouts, and fistfights, the movie was greeted with lukewarm praise. "Basically, *Shame* can't decide whether it wants to really be a thriller with a sense of humor, or a satire with a sense of adventure," John Anderson wrote in *New York Newsday* (November 23, 1994), adding that "it's definitely funny, if unevenly so."

Standing six feet, two inches tall, Keenen Ivory Wayans shaves his head and sports a fashionable goatee and mustache. He lives in Los Angeles. Although he has downplayed his engineering skills, telling Alan Carter of the New York *Daily News*, "I certainly wouldn't have gotten on any bridge *I* designed," he is reportedly a talented carpenter and renovator. He keeps physically fit by working out with weights and maintains his mental acuity by playing chess. Wayans is a member of the

Screen Actors Guild, the Directors Guild of America, and the Screen Writers Guild.

Selected Biographical References: Cosmopolitan 20:214 N '90 pors; N Y Daily News p42+ Ja 12 '89 por; N Y Times II p25+ Ag 26 '90 pors; New York 23:28+ O 8 '90 pors; People 33:75+ Je 11 '90 pors; Contemporary Theatre, Film, and Television vol 10 (1993); Who's Who Among Black Americans 1994–95; Who's Who in America, 1995

Max Hirshfeld

Wertheimer, Linda

(WORTH-hie-mer)

Mar. 19, 1943– Radio journalist. Address: c/o National Public Radio, 635 Massachusetts Ave. NW, Washington, DC 20001

Linda Wertheimer, a familiar voice to the nearly sixteen million listeners of National Public Radio, is one of the handful of women who broke through the gender barrier in broadcasting. "Twenty years ago Washington journalism was pretty much a male game, like football and foreign policy," Claudia Dreifus wrote in the *New York Times Magazine* (January 2, 1994). "But along came demure Linda, delicately crashing onto the presidential campaign press bus." Wertheimer began her career in 1967 as a researcher at WCBS Radio in New York, and in 1971 she joined the newly established NPR as the director of its weekday news program *All Things Considered*. Before long she was NPR's Congressional correspondent, a position that made her one of only a few female reporters to cover Capitol Hill in the early 1970s. Wertheimer thrived in the male-dominated political arena and developed a reputation for delivering dispassionate, objective reports. "I am by nature a watcher," she has said. "I never had any difficulty standing beside an event and divorcing myself from it."

In 1976 Wertheimer became a roving political correspondent for NPR, in which capacity she covered four presidential campaigns as a member of the press entourage that followed the candidates on grueling tours across the country. For nearly twenty years, she has also anchored NPR's election-night coverage. Her most recent promotion came in 1989, when she became a host of *All Things Considered*. Of the many young, female journalists who see her as a role model, Wertheimer has said, "I think they are wonderful. But of course it doesn't even dawn on them that anyone would have thought that they couldn't do this kind of work. That's the Dark Ages as far as they are concerned."

Linda Cozby Wertheimer was born on March 19, 1943 in Carlsbad, New Mexico, the first of the two daughters of June Gault Cozby and Miller Cozby, who owned and operated a local grocery store. "We were that immediate post-war generation, just before the baby boom, who grew up thoroughly cherished and absolutely well-educated in public schools and with all the optimism of that time poured into us," Wertheimer said of her childhood, in an interview with *Current Biography*. A favorite activity of her close-knit family was listening to the news on the radio and, beginning in the mid-1950s, watching it on television. On one such occasion, Wertheimer has recalled, she leapt out of a chair in excitement at the sight of a female reporter, Pauline Frederick of NBC, on the television screen. It was 1956, and Frederick was reporting on the Soviet Union's ultimately successful attempt to crush the popular uprising in Hungary that year. "I was thinking, 'I didn't know women could do that,'" Wertheimer recalled to Claudia Dreifus.

In 1961 Wertheimer graduated from Carlsbad High School and was awarded a scholarship to Wellesley College, in Massachusetts, where she struggled to do well. "I was always a sort of a serious, brainy child," she has said. "And I thought I was awfully smart, and I figured everything would always be very easy for me and Wellesley wasn't." She persevered and was awarded a B.A. degree in English literature in 1965. "I think going to a women's college made a big difference," Wertheimer told *Current Biography*. "It gave me the sense women could run things. . . . And I just never thought that it made sense to give that up."

After her graduation Wertheimer became an intern for the British Broadcasting Corporation in London, where she worked as a production secretary, a job that enabled her to learn the basics of radio writing and production. In 1967 she returned to the United States and applied for a reporting job at NBC in New York City, where her childhood heroine, Pauline Frederick, had worked. A male executive told her that women were not credible on the air and suggested that she aspire instead to a career as a researcher. After expressing her rage at him for his attitude, Wertheimer stomped out of his office. She ended up, however, accepting a research job at WCBS Radio in New York, for three reasons: the station had recently gone to an all-news format; a staff of talented journalists, among them Ed Bradley, had already been assembled; and she saw opportunities for advancement. Under the tutelage of Lou Adler, a prominent broadcaster at WCBS, Wertheimer improved her writing skills and was soon promoted to news writer and producer. "I was the only woman in the building who was not a secretary except for a vice-president of advertising," Wertheimer told *Current Biography*.

Following her marriage, on June 15, 1969, to Fred Wertheimer, a lawyer who later became president of the citizens' lobbying group Common Cause, she moved to Washington, D.C., where her husband was already living. For the next two years, Wertheimer stayed at home and enjoyed time off from her career. Then, in 1971, her husband told her about a new radio network, National Public Radio, that had come into existence as a byproduct of the Public Broadcasting Act, passed by Congress in 1967. She applied and was hired at NPR, as were several other women, including Nina Totenberg, who became a legal correspondent. NPR "was, and still is, a shop where a woman could get considerable visibility and responsibility," Totenberg told Claudia Dreifus. "NPR's wages were at least a third lower than elsewhere in the industry, and for what they paid, they couldn't find men."

On May 3, 1971 *All Things Considered*, a program that aired in-depth news reports and off-beat features, had its premiere broadcast, with Wertheimer sitting in the director's chair. "I have never forgotten the terror of directing the early programs," she has written. "I remember mistakes, dead air, missing tapes, and moments of panic as if they happened yesterday." Within weeks Wertheimer gave up directing to achieve her long-held dream of reporting, concentrating at first on consumer issues. By the end of 1971, she had become NPR's Congressional correspondent. "I have never been put off by politicians," she told *Current Biography*. "I know a lot of people don't like them, but I do. I just loved it [on Capitol Hill]." Working during a particularly turbulent time in American political history, she covered the House Judiciary Committee Hearings in 1974 on the impeachment of President Richard Nixon.

Keeping abreast of the myriad issues being considered by Congress was both challenging and "continually fascinating," Wertheimer has said. She had a knack for deciphering complex legislation, like tax reform, and for explaining it lucidly to listeners. And she had no hesitation about querying officials on controversial matters. "I never apologize for asking embarrassing questions," Wertheimer told Jamie Diamond, who profiled her for *Lear's* (February 1991). "After a while you stop seeing yourself as a solo performer and you see yourself as the tip of a spear. All of the people listening on the radio are back there somewhere, and I'm at the point. I ask the questions they would ask."

Wertheimer left her Congressional beat in 1976 to became a political correspondent for NPR. She was based in Washington most of the time but traveled around the country with the major candidates during four presidential campaigns, with 1988 being the last. While she enjoyed the challenge of covering national election campaigns, Wertheimer found the pace to be exhausting; she has recalled landing and taking off in an airplane six times in just one day. Despite the arduous schedule, Wertheimer filed in-depth and issue-oriented campaign reports at a time "when people were yelling and screaming" that most broadcast media reported only "sound bites," she has said. She also helped manage NPR's overall political coverage by staying in touch with other correspondents across the country. Her work ethic has been noted by her colleagues, among them Cokie Roberts, a reporter and commentator for NPR and ABC-TV, who told Dreifus that she envied Wertheimer's "incredible persistence." "I mean, when she goes to a live event, she can tell you every little detail down to the mortar in the cracks of the building she's about to sit in," Roberts said.

Wertheimer's memory has also served her well—and taken some of her interviewees by surprise. She angered Ross Perot, who ran as an independent candidate for president in 1992, by asking him during the campaign about a large tax break that he had received for his business in 1975. "Here's Linda's thoroughness again," Totenburg told Dreifus. "Linda had covered the tax bill, in which Perot had suceeded in getting himself a multimillion-dollar loophole of the kind that he was condemning all over the country. So she had him dead to rights because she'd been there when it happened. He went ballistic." Perot, who spoke to Wertheimer by telephone, accused her of arranging "a classic setup" and "doing a favor for someone" and then hung up.

In 1989, after working eighteen years as a reporter, Wertheimer became one of the three hosts of *All Things Considered*. "I had come off a campaign, I thought I had done a really great job, . . . and it just happened that the [host] job was open," Wertheimer said during her interview with *Current Biography*. "I thought, 'You know, I'd better jump now if I can talk them into letting me have it.' I think you should always change jobs when are not sure if you want to give up the one you have." As a host, Wertheimer is part of the collaborative team that decides what airs on the program, which expanded from one and a half to two hours in the spring of 1995. Her duties also include writing news copy, introducing correspondents' reports, and conducting interviews.

Wertheimer occasionally appears on television, most often as a guest questioner on CBS's *Face the Nation* and as a news analyst on CNN. But she is quite satisfied with her full-time radio position. "How can you beat this job I've got?" she asked *Current Biography*. "I can talk to anybody I want to, our program is respected, and we are nationally famous people but nobody knows what we look like. We don't make a lot of money, but then we work all the time, so how would we spend it anyway?" Her resonant voice is instantly recognizable to millions, and she is often complimented on her calm delivery. As she whimsically told Jamie Diamond, "Young women say to me, 'Your voice has so much depth and color. What sort of training did you have?' And I say, 'Turn forty. That helps.'"

To mark the quarter-century birthday of NPR, Wertheimer spent a year, with the assistance of researchers, reviewing tapes of the network's news programs. The resulting book, *Listening to America: Twenty-Five Years in the Life of a Nation as Heard on National Public Radio* (1995), is a chronological compilation of transcripts edited by Wertheimer, who also wrote short introductions to each piece. "You could have done this book ninety million ways," Wertheimer has said. "I chose to do it as a kind of informal history of the country over the last twenty-five years." A reviewer for *Publishers Weekly* (May 15, 1995) wrote, "Wertheimer has selected an eclectic set of stories, many covering the major events of the years (elections, disasters, world turmoil), others reporting on the culture (interviews with author Norman MacLean and Jack Kevorkian). NPR's strengths emerge clearly: it is literate and a forum for thoughtful callers and has a rich array of commentators."

A handsome woman, Wertheimer was described by Jamie Diamond as someone who "moves comfortably in her body and laughs freely. Nothing about her suggests the stereotype of the ballsy female reporter." She has won several reporting awards, including a special Alfred I. DuPont-Columbia University citation for anchoring the first live broadcast from the Senate chamber, the 1978 Panama Canal Treaty debates. She has also received an award from the Corporation for Public Broadcasting in 1988 for anchoring *The Iran-Contra Affair: A Special Report*, a series of forty-one half-hour programs, that summarized each day's congressional hearings. In 1992 she won an American Women in Radio/TV Award for her story "Illegal Abortion."

Linda Wertheimer lives in the Washington, D.C., area with her husband, Fred, who retired from his job as president of Common Cause in 1995. Her hobbies include gardening and cooking. As the daughter of a grocer, she grew up with a taste for overripe fruit and vegetables, and she learned from her mother how to make tasty, southwestern dishes.

Selected Biographical References: Lear's p48+ F '91 pors; N Y Times Mag p14+ Ja 2 '94 pors; Listening to America: Twenty-Five Years in the Life of a Nation as Heard on National Public Radio (1995); Who's Who of American Women, 1995–96

Green Bay Packers

White, Reggie

Dec. 19, 1961– Football player; minister. Address: c/o Green Bay Packers, 1265 Lombardi Ave., Green Bay, WI 54307-0628

Reggie White of the Green Bay Packers has tackled more quarterbacks behind the line of scrimmage than any other player in National Football League history. He achieved his record of 145 sacks through the 1994 season in spite of being routinely double- or triple-teamed by opponents. Using a combination of bullish strength and cannonball speed, White disrupts offensive blocking schemes and running patterns with fierce regularity. His eminence in the NFL became even more obvious in 1994, when he was selected to the Pro Bowl for the ninth consecutive year, making him the first defensive end in the league to be so honored. "Reggie White can change your whole defense," Mike Holmgren, the coach of the Green Bay Packers, has said. "He's the one guy other than a quarterback who can come in and change your whole program around." After eight years as the heart and soul of the Philadelphia Eagles' dominating defense, White, a free agent, was the object of an intense recruiting war until he signed a four-year deal with the Packers in 1993 that made him the highest-paid defender in the NFL at the time.

In addition to his career on the football field, White is an ordained minister. During his years in Philadelphia, he and his wife, Sara, spent many hours on street corners talking to inner-city youths about the dangers of drugs and alcohol and the importance of staying in school. He and Sara opened a residence on their Tennessee property in 1991 for unmarried pregnant women and new mothers. The home, called Hope Palace, is partially funded by the royalties from his book, *The Reggie White Touch Football Playbook: Winning Plays, Rules, and Safety Tips* (1991). White has pledged one million dollars toward another pet project, a community-development bank in Knoxville, Tennessee dedicated to helping inner-city borrowers. Asked by Vince Aversano of *Inside Sports* (August 1993) how he reconciled his Christian outreach work with the brutality of his football job, White replied, "One thing you've got to realize is that football is aggressive, not violent. Violence is what's happening on our streets, where our kids are dying. . . . I get a little fit when the game is labeled violent, because the game is not violent. We're not killing each other. I don't think too many guys go out with the intention to end anybody's career."

Reginald Howard White was born on December 19, 1961 in Chattanooga, Tennessee, to Charles White and Thelma Dodds Collier. "My dad and my mother were never married, but my dad was still a great man, and when my mother married my stepdad we got along real well as a family," White told Vince Aversano. His childhood hero was the white preacher of the all-black Baptist church he attended. As he recalled to Paul Zimmerman, who profiled the defensive end for *Sports Illustrated* (November 27, 1989), "Reverend Ferguson was the greatest man of God I ever saw. He had a way with kids and teaching. I always wanted to be a Christian, but I never knew how. He said that understanding was the first thing I had to know." White, who towered over his classmates, discovered around the time he was in seventh grade that he could use his size and strength successfully in football. Having announced to his mother at the age of twelve that he would be a football player and a minister when he grew up, he began preaching in churches when he was seventeen years old, while he was winning accolades as a high-school nose tackle and tight end. "I've always known that football was going to be a platform for me to help change people's lives for the sake of Jesus," he told Aversano.

At Howard High School in Chattanooga, White lettered three times in football, three times in basketball, and once in track, and he was named to the high school All-America team during his senior year. At the University of Tennessee, which he attended from 1980 until 1983, he was the defensive line stalwart on coach Johnny Majors's Volunteers team, and he was nicknamed "minister of defense" and "the big dawg." A consensus choice in 1983 for the All-America team as well as Southeastern Conference Player of the Year, White was also one of four finalists in the balloting for the Lombardi Award, given annually to the nation's outstanding college lineman. When the Volunteers celebrated their centennial football season, in 1991, White was named to their all-time team. According to some sources, White has a B.A. degree in human services, which he earned after he returned to the University of Tennessee in 1990.

Meanwhile, in January 1984, White had begun his professional career with the Memphis Showboats, a team in the short-lived United States Football League. On the strength of his 11 sacks over the course of the season, he made the league's all-rookie team. In 1985 he finished as the third-best sack artist with a 12.5 tally, and he was a first-squad selection for the All-USFL team. In his two years with the Showboats, White started in thirty-four games, registered 193 tackles (including 120 solo stops), 23.5 sacks, and 7 forced fumbles. The Philadelphia Eagles purchased his contract from the Showboats and added White to their roster after the third game of the 1985 NFL season. Making his debut against the New York Giants on September 29, White recorded 2.5 sacks and deflected a pass that one of his teammates intercepted and returned for the Eagles' lone touchdown in a 16–10 loss. The following week head coach Marion Campbell made White a starting defensive end. By the time the season was over, White had recorded 13 sacks, the fifth-highest total in the league, and he was named to the NFL's All-Rookie Team.

Campbell was fired before the last game in 1985 and was replaced in the offseason by Buddy Ryan, the defensive coordinator for the world-champion Chicago Bears. White flourished as a participant in Ryan's swarming, attack-oriented defensive schemes. The Eagles had a losing season in 1986, but White emerged as one of the league's premier pass rushers, posting a team-record 18 sacks. In his first trip to the Pro Bowl, he sacked the American Football Conference quarterbacks four times and was named the game's most valuable player. The 1987 season was shortened by a players' strike, but White posted a remarkable total of 21 sacks in only twelve games, missing the all-time league record for sacks in a single season by one. Named the National Football Conference Player of the Year by United Press International, White was unanimously selected to the All-NFL team.

Taking advantage of White's reputation as one of the most feared defensive players in the league, Buddy Ryan made a point of starting him at different positions. "That way," Ryan told Paul Zimmerman, "we can scare . . . a whole bunch of people instead of just one." During the 1988 season, the Eagles overtook their archrivals in the NFC East, the New York Giants, beating them twice. Double-teamed by the Giants' offensive line, White still posted 2.5 sacks in the first Eagles-Giants contest and knocked quarterback Phil Simms out of action in the second. "In high school and college you're taught to hit the ground on a double team," White told Zimmerman. "Here you're expected to take it on. I get double-teamed on every play, so I expect it. Sacks are great, and they get you elected to the Pro Bowl. But I've always felt that a great defensive lineman has to play the run and the pass equally well."

League rivals marveled at the speed and strength of the six-foot, five-inch White, who weighs close to 300 pounds. He was clocked by the Eagles as running 40 yards in 4.69 seconds, and in a weight-lifting test, he was able to bench-press 425 pounds. "He can kill you with his speed," San Francisco 49ers offensive tackle Harris Barton told Paul Zimmerman. "But if you overplay it and open up too wide, he'll bull-rush inside and you're finished. The first thing you have to worry about is his power. If he gets his hands into you, then he's like an offensive lineman—he'll drive you right into the backfield. You've got to be perfectly balanced, and you can't let him get those hands into you." In 1988 White posted a league-best tally of 18 sacks as well as 133 tackles, 96 of which were unassisted. The Eagles won their division with a 10-6 record, but the Bears eliminated them from the play-offs with a 20-12 victory. Voted the NFL Player of the Year by the Washington Touchdown Club, White finished second to Bears linebacker Mike Singletary in the Associated Press balloting for most valuable player.

In 1989 the Eagles defensive unit recorded a team record 62 sacks, with White posting 11 of them. Despite their second consecutive regular-season sweep of New York and an overall 11-5 record, the Eagles finished second in the division, behind the 12-4 Giants, and they were eliminated by the Los Angeles Rams in the first round of the play-offs. In a 1989 poll conducted by *Sports Illustrated*, NFL players were asked to choose the best defensive player in the league; 38 percent named White, who got three times as many votes as the closest runner-up. In 1990 White led the bullying Eagle defense with 14 sacks (the second-best total in the NFC, and the fourth-best in the league), and he made his second career interception on a deflected pass thrown by Washington Redskins quarterback Jeff Rutledge that he returned 33 yards. The Eagles finished the season in second place with a 10-6 record, then lost to the Redskins in the first round of the play-offs.

Ryan, who was fired after the 1990 season, was succeeded by rookie head coach Rich Kotite, who led the team to a 10-6 record in 1991. Although the Eagles failed to qualify for the play-offs, White's performance was not to blame—he spearheaded the defensive unit with 15 sacks and recorded 100 tackles, including 72 solos. In a CBS Sports poll conducted during the season, most NFL club general managers chose White when they were asked which player they would most like to build their defense around. Play-off success finally came to the Eagles in 1992, when the team beat the New Orleans Saints by a score of 36-20. They lost in the second round, however, to the Dallas Cowboys, in a game that featured 7 tackles and a sack by White. During the regular season, he posted 14 sacks—it was the eighth consecutive year he had recorded more than ten—and 81 tackles, 27 of them unassisted.

Off the field White made a big impact in another arena. He was the lead plaintiff in a class-action suit brought by the players against the NFL for antitrust law violation. The players sought a system of unrestricted free agency, which team owners contended would bankrupt the sport. After hearing legal arguments in the dispute, in late 1992 David Doty, the United States District Court Judge of Minneapolis, ordered both sides to resolve their differences or face a court-imposed labor settlement. An agreement was worked out in early 1993 between team owners and the players' union whereby free agency was instituted in exchange for a cap on players' salaries. A writer for the *Sporting News* (January 3, 1994) noted, "Twenty years from now White . . . will be remembered not only for his Hall of Fame skills, but also for his role as a free-agent pioneer who paved the way for non-quarterbacks to finally get their due."

After the institution of free-agency, a host of players went on the shopping block, none of whom was more sought after than White. In March 1993 he and his wife embarked on a thirty-seven-day tour of cities with NFL teams interested in his services. Vince Aversano described how White was treated during the tour: "He was greeted at airports by marching bands—even was introduced to the mayor in some cities—and was wined and dined by team presidents and general managers in the hopes that the best defensive lineman in pro football would sign his name on their dotted line. Press conferences were held just to announce that Reggie was in town *thinking* about playing for the local team."

Surprising many people who had expected him to choose a Super Bowl contender in a large media market, White elected to go to the Green Bay Packers, a mediocre team in a small city. He accepted a contract that offered him a large chunk of his seventeen million-dollar salary up front. Crediting divine intervention as the primary reason for his choice, White said he was also influenced by the fact that coach Mike Holmgren had hired two African-Americans as assistant coaches. In 1992, the year before White joined the team, the Packers' defensive unit ranked twenty-third in the NFL in yards allowed per game. With White stationed at left defensive end in 1993, the Packers' defense jumped to second in the league. He recorded 13 sacks and 98 tackles (including 31 solo stops) in a year that saw the 10-6 Packers lose in the first round of play-offs to the Dallas Cowboys.

Having suffered an elbow injury late in 1994, White finished the season with statistics that were, by his own account, below par—he made 8 sacks and recorded 59 tackles while the Packers finished with a 9-7 record. There were games during the year, however, when the veteran defensive lineman was overpowering. In a contest on October 20 against the Minnesota Vikings prior to his injury, White lifted Vikings wide receiver Cris Carter and dropped him on the ground before chasing quarterback Warren Moon fifteen yards for a sack. On another play, he grabbed offensive lineman Bernard Dafney with seeming ease and tossed him aside during a move upfield. White has a reputation for trying to spread the gospel among opposing tackles, and Vikings offensive lineman Chris Hinton told Don Pierson of the *Chicago Tribune* (October 30, 1994) that he got the message during the

October 20 game. "I was praying there was a tight end beside me," Hinton said.

Known for his work in the community as well as for his football achievements, White was given the Byron White Humanitarian Award in 1992 by the NFL Players Association. Dale D. Buss observed in an article about White for *Christianity Today* (October 24, 1994) that the defensive end's goal is "to tackle the roots of economic despair. He believes investing in people financially will help save them spiritually." Toward that end, White has been trying to encourage investors to help him set up more banks similar to the one he established, the Knoxville Community Development Bank, in Tennessee. The bank's mission is to rejuvenate Knoxville's inner city by providing business and personal loans to borrowers considered "at risk" by other banks. "I don't have enough money myself to do what I need to do," he told Dale Buss. "God has given me a powerful vision and a platform in this game to express it. I'm only on his agenda. I'm challenging the church to come and get with me in this."

A mimic of some repute, Reggie White enjoys doing impressions of such celebrities as Muhammad Ali, Elvis Presley, and Bill Cosby. His favorite hobby, he has said, is spending time with his family. He married the former Sara Copeland on January 5, 1985. They have two children: a son, Jeremy, born on May 12, 1986, and a daughter, Jecolia, born on May 24, 1988. The Whites live on a thirty-two-acre farm in Maryville, Tennessee.

Selected Biographical References: Chicago Tribune III p1+ O 30 '94 por; Christianity Today 38: 94 O 24 '94 pors; Inside Sports 15:26+ Ag '93 pors; Sports Illus 71:64+ N 27 '89 pors; 78:20+ Mr 15 '93 pors; Who's Who Among Black Americans, 1994–95

Todd Neil Michael

Whitman, Christine Todd

Sep. 26, 1946- Governor of New Jersey. Address: Office of the Governor, CN-001, Trenton, NJ 08625

Perhaps the most popular and widely imitated Republican politician of the post–Ronald Reagan era is Christine Todd Whitman, who was elected the fiftieth governor of New Jersey on November 2, 1993, becoming the first woman in the state's history to win its highest elective office. Invoking in her inaugural speech the philosophy of the Great Communicator himself, as President Reagan was known, Whitman declared, "Our principal problems are not the product of great global economic shifts or other vast, unseen forces. They are the creation of government."

A former county freeholder, a wealthy investor, and a sometime farmer, Whitman was virtually unknown until 1990, when she ran against the incumbent Democratic senator Bill Bradley. Coming within two percentage points of unseating him, she immediately set her sights on the job of Governor James J. Florio, whose approval rating had plummeted when he enacted a major tax increase shortly after taking office in 1990. Elected on a pledge to cut taxes by 30 percent over three years, Whitman has followed through on her promise in a mere two years, slashing taxes by 15 percent in her first year in office alone and simultaneously wiping out the two billion–dollar state budget deficit. As Republican candidates throughout the United States, running as self-described "Christie Whitman Republicans," lined up to benefit from her campaigning and fund-raising services in the elections of November 1994, they elevated her stature among party leaders to the point where her name has often been touted as a vice-presidential prospect for 1996.

Christine Todd Whitman was born Christine Todd on September 26, 1946 in New York State and grew up in Oldwick (Tewksbury Township), in Hunterdon County, New Jersey. Whitman's Republican heritage has deep roots. She is the youngest of the four children of Webster B. Todd, a Republican state chairman and a contractor whose projects included Rockefeller Center and Radio City Music Hall, in New York City, and Eleanor (Schley) Todd, who was vice-chairman of the Republican National Committee, chaired the New Jersey finance committee of George Bush's campaign for the presidential nomination in 1980, and served on the New Jersey Commission on Higher Education. Whitman's brothers, John and Webster Jr., and her sister, Kate Beach, have also served in various elected and appointed offices at the local, state, and federal government levels.

After graduating in 1968 with a bachelor of arts degree in government from Wheaton College in Norton, Massachusetts, Whitman worked for the Republican National Committee, under whose auspices she developed the "Listening Program" to reach out to groups perceived to have been traditionally neglected by the Republican Party. In addition to students and senior citizens, she met with representatives of minority groups, including gang members in the East Ward of Chicago. She also worked for the United States Office of Economic Opportunity. While living in New York in the early 1970s, she taught courses in English as a second language.

Whitman first ran for public office in 1982, when she was elected to the Somerset County Board of Chosen Freeholders, which is similar to a county board of supervisors. Reelected in 1985 with more votes than any other candidate, she served on the board for a total of five years in various capacities, including that of director and deputy director. During her tenure she oversaw construction of a new county courthouse (which was completed on time and under budget), created a countywide open-space program, helped to set up the county's first homeless shelter, and established Somerset County's first halfway house for teenage alcoholic males.

In 1988 Governor Tom Kean appointed Whitman president of the New Jersey Board of Public Utilities, where she instituted a code of ethics and made a favorable impression on unionized workers. "She was the best employer we ever had, bar none," proclaimed the leader of the Communications Workers of America Local 1037, in an interview with Michael Aron, a senior political correspondent for New Jersey Network, the state's public television service. Aron quoted the remark in his book *Governor's Race: A TV Reporter's Chronicle of the 1993 Florio/Whitman Campaign* (1994).

After resigning from the Board of Public Utilities in 1990, Whitman declared her candidacy for the United States Senate. Her attempt to unseat the Democratic incumbent, Bill Bradley, was initially written off by analysts as a political suicide mission, because her name recognition among voters was only 10 percent, compared to Bradley's 98 percent. Compounding the inherent obstacles presented by her relative obscurity were the contents of her coffers, which at first contained just three hundred thousand dollars, a paltry sum by current campaign standards. She began the race by urging her opponent to limit his campaign spending to three million dollars, but he ultimately paid out four times that amount, while she spent only a million dollars, none of it from political action committees, groups that contribute to political campaigns in the hope of advancing certain legislative agendas.

As the campaign wore on, Whitman stepped up her attack on the incumbent. Among other things, she tried to associate her opponent with the savings and loan crisis, a tactic that Bradley's spokesmen claimed was unfair, because the senator had voted against the federal savings and loan bailout plan. Whitman then attempted to prod Bradley into taking a position on Florio's $2.8 billion sales- and income-tax increase, but he repeatedly refused to comment on the governor's highly unpopular move. Although Bradley insisted that because he worked in the nation's capitol he need not have an opinion on a state matter such as Florio's tax hike, his silence didn't wash well with angry voters, many of whom had already adorned their cars with bumper stickers saying "Florio-free in '93." At every opportunity, Whitman said that Bradley's reticence on the issue demonstrated a lack of leadership ability. In the meantime, she said she supported a federal balanced-budget amendment, a line-item veto, and a twelve-year limit on congressional terms of office.

Whitman's efforts to tap into voter dissatisfaction with Florio paid off handsomely at the polls, even though she narrowly lost the election to Bradley. Her defeat notwithstanding, Whitman was heartened by her strong showing (she received 49 percent of the vote), and she resolved to hold on to her newfound name recognition. To that end, she began writing a newspaper column and hosting a biweekly radio talk show on WKXW-FM in Trenton, the capital of New Jersey. In March 1991 she formed the Committee for an Affordable New Jersey, which she billed as a "continuing political committee," to avoid the negative connotations of "political action committee." As its chairman she organized speaking engagements and fund-raising events to support Republican legislative candidates at the local, state, and national levels of government and built a strong political base from which to launch a gubernatorial campaign in 1993.

In the Republican primary elections in June of that year, Whitman triumphed over former state attorney general W. Cary Edwards, who had sought (and failed to obtain) the Republican nomination in 1989, and James H. Wallwork, a former state senator. Whitman's and Edwards's campaigns had gotten off to rocky starts in January, when both candidates disclosed that they had employed illegal aliens as domestic workers and had failed to pay the requisite Social Security and unemployment insurance taxes. The issue faded quickly after each candidate agreed to pay the delinquent taxes. But Whitman committed two gaffes along the way that were later used by the Florio camp to portray her as an out-of-touch patrician with little sympathy for the middle class. In one instance, she rationalized her failure to vote in a local school board election by implying that it was none of her business because her own two children were enrolled at private schools. In another, she responded to a reporter's question about New Jersey's homestead rebate program, which returns up to five hundred dollars to taxpayers, by saying, "Funny as it seems, five hundred dollars is a lot of money to some people." Whitman claimed that the remark, which was widely quoted, had been taken out of context. Despite these blunders, she won 40 percent of the vote to Edwards's 33 percent and Wallwork's 24 percent. Florio ran unopposed in the Democratic primary.

Throughout her campaign against the unpopular but experienced Florio, Whitman was criticized—in ads, speeches, and the press—for her inexperience and her wealth (her 1992 joint tax return revealed that she and her husband had an income of $3.7 million). Most of the attacks were engineered by Florio's consultant James Carville, the political strategist who had helped Bill Clinton win the presidency the year before. Whereas Carville's strategy had worked against a well-established incumbent like George Bush, it backfired when employed against an unknown candidate. The fact that Whitman was both an outsider and an underdog worked to her advantage, because anti-incumbency feelings were still running strong among the overtaxed electorate of New Jersey.

On the defensive for most of the campaign, Whitman deflected allegations that her two farms, for which she had taken tax deductions, were not really working farms by holding a press conference at the larger of the farms, to show that it is indeed a working farm. Due perhaps to inexperience, however, she continued to make occasional public-relations mistakes, which were duly seized upon by her opponents as evidence of her poor judgment. According to most accounts, those mistakes included visiting a gun shop—a politically unwise move given the popularity of Florio's gun-control legislation—and hiring the media consultant Larry McCarthy, apparently unaware that he had been responsible during George Bush's 1988 presidential campaign for the infamous Willie Horton ad, which was widely perceived as racist and beyond the pale of acceptable levels of negative advertising. (McCarthy resigned from the Whitman campaign a day after he was hired, following protests by African-Americans.) Whitman was also taken to task by some Jewish leaders for a remark in which she seemed to compare Florio's proposed welfare restrictions to the ghettoization of Jews by Nazi Germany, a statement that was perceived as trivializing the Holocaust.

Trailing Florio in the polls by twenty points at one time, Whitman managed to close the gap by going on the offensive in the final weeks of the campaign. Promising to cut income taxes by 30 percent over three years, she met with entrenched skepticism until the last few days of the campaign, when her anti-Florio message finally began to hit home. As quoted in *Congressional Quarterly* (November 6, 1993), Congresswoman Marge Roukema, Republican of New Jersey, said that Whitman "began to remind voters how angry, how bitterly angry, they were at Florio. She just rekindled that anger, at the last moment." Although many final polls predicted a Florio victory on November 2, 1993, Whitman squeaked past him by a mere 25,628 ballots out of the 2.5 million cast, winning 49 percent of the vote. After the other two female governors retired at the completion of their terms, in January 1995, Whitman was left the sole female governor in the United States.

Exactly one week after Whitman's narrow victory, the legitimacy of the entire election was thrown into question with an extraordinary admission by Ed Rollins, her campaign manager, who virtually boasted that he had paid half a million dollars to suppress the black vote, by making donations to the favorite charities of black ministers in return for their promises not to rally their congregations and by paying Democratic street workers to "sit and watch television" on Election Day. Whitman denied any wrongdoing and obtained a recantation from Rollins, who said he had exaggerated, as quoted by Michael Aron: "My desire to put a spin on events . . . left the impression of something that was not true and did not occur." A total of five investigations into the legality of the matter found no impropriety, but relations between the Whitman administration and the African-American community remained strained, however, and her transition effort was preoccupied with the issue for some time. In retrospect, most analysts felt that she weathered the political storm as best as she could. In an interview with Dale Russakoff for the *Washington Post* (October 24 1994), Rollins praised Whitman, saying, "She handled that awful crisis I caused her with grace and compassion."

Most of any lingering voter distaste over the Rollins incident was dispelled when Whitman took office in January 1994, because she did not waste any time in implementing her fiscal plans. On January 18, 1994, the day she was sworn in as governor of New Jersey, she proposed a 5 percent tax cut for individuals and businesses, retroactive to January 1. Whereas many inaugural speeches are vague statements of intent, Whitman used the opportunity to enumerate the initiatives she planned to take to create a business-friendly climate. To get her program off the ground, she established an Economic Master Plan Commission with her first executive order, which she signed at the podium. In July 1994, presenting her first budget, she cut another 10 percent from the income tax and simultaneously erased Florio's leftover two billion-dollar budget deficit. The way she performed that "Whitman miracle" generated a squall of a controversy that failed to become a full-blown storm only because of the complexity and dullness of the issue, according to economic and political analysts.

At her inauguration Whitman had pledged not to reduce services or shift to municipalities any financial burden caused by her tax cuts. According to her critics, she instead passed that burden on to future taxpayers, by reducing state contributions to public employees' pension plans by $3.2 billion over four years. Analyzing the governor's 1994–95 budget in an article for the *Washington Post* (September 5, 1994), Malcolm Gladwell noted that because her plan relied on "a complex series of changes in actuarial assumptions and accounting methods," it had for the most part escaped scrutiny by the press and legislators. "At best," Gladwell wrote, "this represents a gamble that the state's economy in the early part of the next century will be stronger than it is today and better able to shoulder pension responsibilities. At worst, according to fiscal experts, Whitman's move represents politics at its most cynical." Gladwell quoted a report by outside consultants hired by the administration as saying, "It appears that the changes are being contemplated primarily to address the state's financial objectives and not to protect retirement funds." Responding directly to Gladwell's article, Whitman's treasurer, Brian W. Clymer, wrote in an Op Ed piece for the *Washington Post* (October 15, 1994), "Unlike the pension raids attempted in other jurisdictions . . . , our funding reforms keep the state's hands off our pensioners' assets."

Perhaps because the pension funds will not have to be replenished for fifteen to twenty years, Whitman's alleged fiddling with the actuarial tables seemed not to perturb most of her constituents. Indeed, she has been among the most popular governors in recent memory. "It's a sad commentary on the public's view of politicians that people get excited because I did what I said I'd do," Whitman told Dale Russakoff. "That should be the norm for a politician." *People* magazine named her among the twenty-five most intriguing people of 1994, and *Newsweek* included her on its list of the six most influential Republicans (the others were Newt Gingrich, the Speaker of the House; Bob Dole, the Senate majority leader; the conservative talk-show host Rush Limbaugh; the Republican strategist William Kristol; and Ralph Reed, the leader of the Christian Coalition).

In 1994 Whitman stumped for twenty-two Republican candidates, for whom she raised $3.5 million. Eighteen of them won, among them George E. Pataki, who was elected governor of New York, and John G. Rowland, who became governor of Connecticut. Crowning the exposure her campaigning gave her with the ultimate sign of party approval, Whitman was chosen by Newt Gingrich in January 1995 to be the first governor to deliver the rebuttal to a presidential State of the Union address. Speaking for all Republicans after President Clinton's speech, Whitman said, "We will keep our word. We will do what you elected us to do." One group whose support she will not have is the 1.5 million-member Christian Coalition, whose leader, Ralph Reed, announced on February 10, 1995 at a Conservative Political Action Conference in Washington, D.C., that "religious conservatives" would not support a Republican presidential candidate who does not oppose abortion rights. "It's when we get into government trying to manage morals and mores that we start to run into trouble," Whitman has said. "But there's room in the party for people who believe differently on those issues."

Having been "recommended" (but not endorsed outright) by the National Organization for Women during her gubernatorial campaign, Whitman has so far compiled a mixed record on women's issues. On January 26, 1995 she signed into law a "checkoff box" on state income-tax forms for residents to donate five dollars, ten dollars, or more to fund breast cancer research. (New Jersey ranks third in the nation in the number of women who die from breast cancer each year.) According to the provisions of her Family Development Program, married couples receiving benefits under the Aid to Families with Dependent Children law will no longer receive 30 percent less than single parents, but benefits will not increase if a welfare recipient has additional children while receiving assistance. On October 31, 1994 Whitman signed a nine-bill package of legislation known as Megan's Law, which, if it survives constitutional challenges, would require that a community be notified if a person convicted of rape, child molestation, or other types of sex crimes moves into the neighborhood.

Whitman's plans for revamping the state's education program generated considerable controversy. Teachers' unions and mayors strongly objected to her fiscal 1995–96 budget, which increased direct financial aid to school districts by only a small amount, most of which would be funneled to thirty of the state's poorest, urban districts. They were especially rankled by Whitman's decision to penalize districts that spend more than 30 percent above the state median on administrative costs. That proposal was intended to direct more aid to classroom instruction, where it is most needed, according to the Whitman administration. Mayors have warned that local property taxes are almost certain to go up to compensate for the coming shortfalls in school budgets.

On June 30, 1995 Whitman signed a sixteen-billion-dollar New Jersey budget for fiscal 1995–96, which included the remaining installment of her promised 30 percent income-tax cut. Although she was widely praised for accomplishing that goal one year earlier than she pledged, she angered many public employees with her veto of legislative efforts to block her plan to privatize the state's Department of Motor Vehicles. Whitman has predicted that privatization, in the process of which hundreds of the state's sixty thousand employees would lose their jobs, would save the state four million dollars in salaries and benefits. Salaries alone have risen 125 percent in the public sector in the last decade, according to the Whitman administration; the equivalent private-sector salaries have increased by only 45.5 percent. Protesting Whitman's budget, workers at the Department of Motor Vehicles walked off the job on June 30, closing seventeen of the affected twenty-three branch offices. On the weekend of the Fourth of July, toll takers on the New Jersey Turnpike and the Garden State parkway also went on strike, but Whitman authorized the use of strike-breaking replacement workers, thereby pacifying holiday travelers. "I am grateful for the work public employees do for New Jersey every day," the governor said in a statement released on July 5. "The importance of their efforts cannot be understated. At the same time, we should not ask taxpayers to subsidize public wages and benefits that are so much greater than what they themselves receive."

Among the boards and commissions on which Whitman has served are the Community Foundation of New Jersey, the National Council on Crime and Delinquency, the New Jersey Advisory Council on Corrections, the Somerset County Board of Social Services, the Somerset County College Board of Trustees, the North Jersey Transportation Coordinating Commission, and the Somerset County Planning Board. In 1994 she was awarded an honorary degree from Rutgers University, in New Brunswick, New Jersey.

Christine Todd Whitman "comes across as a compelling blend of Princess Diana and Margaret Thatcher," according to Lisa Anderson, who interviewed the governor for the *Chicago Tribune* (January 29, 1995): "tall and willowy, with frosty blond hair, intense blue eyes, a faintly upper-crust diction, a soberly tasteful wardrobe, . . . and a don't-mess-with-me attitude." Whitman lives in her hometown of Oldwick with her husband, John R. Whitman, a financial consultant whose paternal grandfather, Charles S. Whitman, was governor of New York from 1915 to 1918, and their teenage children, Kate and Taylor. The Whitmans have two farms: Twenty Springs, a 53.6-acre farm in Far Hills, New Jersey, and Pontefract, a 225-year-old farm covering 237 acres, in Somerset and Hunterdon Counties, on which they raise cows, chickens, and sheep. Whitman bought Pontefract in 1991 from the estate of her mother, who had purchased it in 1933.

Selected Biographical References: Chicago Tribune I p3 Ja 29 '95 por; N Y Times p40 Ja 31 '93 por, A p33+ Ag 23 '93 por; Aron, Michael. Governor's Race: A TV Reporter's Chronicle of the 1993 Florio/Whitman Campaign (1994); Who's Who in America, 1995

Steve Lipovsky/Boston Celtics

Wilkins, Dominique
(dah-mi-NEEK)

Jan. 12, 1960- Basketball player. Address: c/o Boston Celtics, 151 Merrimac St., Boston, MA 02114

One of the most prolific scorers in National Basketball Association history, Dominique Wilkins has been a dazzling run-and-dunk artist since he played at the University of Georgia, where his awesome athleticism earned him the nickname "the Human Highlight Film." Over the course of a subsequent twelve-year stint with the Atlanta Hawks, Wilkins mounted a credible challenge to Michael Jordan's status as the NBA's greatest scorer and most flamboyant specialist in crowd-thrilling dunks. Although he helped transform the Hawks from perennial losers to winners in the mid-1980s, Atlanta invariably seemed to fold in the playoffs, prompting some sports reporters and disgruntled fans to accuse him of pursuing individual accomplishments at the expense of team goals. Consequently, while superstars like Earvin "Magic" Johnson, Larry Bird, and Michael Jordan were mainstays of the United States' men's basketball team at the 1992 Olympics, Wilkins, whose absence from the so-called Dream Team was conspicuous, spent an agonizing off-season attempting to recover from a career-threatening injury.

Staging a remarkable comeback in the 1992–93 season, he silenced critics who had questioned his dedication and once again took his place as one of the league's premier offensive performers. Even though the thirty-four-year-old superstar was playing superb all-around basketball, the Hawks traded him to the Los Angeles Clippers during the 1993–94 campaign, and following the season, he signed a three-year contract with the Boston Celtics. "I'll put myself up there with any of the best [small forwards in the NBA]," Wilkins said in an interview with Glenn Sheeley for *Inside Sports* (December 1990). "It doesn't matter who it is, because I've played on their level and done it. I've accomplished a lot of things they have individually. The only thing I'm missing to be at the top of the NBA is a championship."

The second of the eight children of John and Gertrude Wilkins, Jacques Dominique Wilkins was born on January 12, 1960 in Sorbonne, France, near Paris, where his father, a sergeant in the United States armed services, was stationed. After his parents divorced, when he was about thirteen, Wilkins moved with his mother and his three brothers and four sisters to the small town of Washington, North Carolina. During his childhood, Wilkins's favorite game was, by his own account, marbles ("I was the Larry Bird of marbles," he told Alan Richman, as quoted in the May 2, 1988 issue of *People*), but he soon discovered basketball. By the age of fifteen, he was good enough to challenge older players to one-on-one playground contests for a dollar a game. As a student at Washington High School, he led the Pam Pack basketball squad to back-to-back Triple-A state championships. The then-six-foot-seven-inch Wilkins, nicknamed "Dr. Dunk" by local sportswriters, was selected as a member of *Parade*'s high school All-America team during his senior year, when he averaged 30.0 points and sixteen rebounds per game.

Courted by more than two hundred colleges and aggressively recruited by North Carolina State University, Wilkins was widely touted as the long-awaited successor to David Thompson, the high-scoring state native who had led the North Carolina State Wolfpack to a national championship in the mid-1970s. When he instead chose to attend the University of Georgia, in Athens, a Southeast Conference (SEC) school with a winning football tradition but a mediocre basketball legacy, his family was harassed by irate residents of their hometown, who felt that Dominique had "sold out to another state," as Jack White reported in *Time* (December 24, 1979). The windows in his family's home were broken, paint was splashed on his mother's car, and he and his brothers, all of whom were outstanding basketball players at Washington schools, were reportedly taunted and threatened. In June 1979, following Dominique's graduation from high school, his mother packed up her family and moved to Atlanta, Georgia. "People wanted me to stay in state and go to school," Wilkins explained to Bruce Branch of the *Sporting News* (November 1, 1982). "They didn't care where as long as it was in North Carolina. I was going to go to NC State but everybody kept saying I would be the next David Thompson. I wanted to be the first Dominique Wilkins." He outlined the other factors contributing to his decision when he spoke to Stephen Steiner of *Sport* (February 1982): "I wanted to go to a place where I could play right away, to a school where they weren't winning that much and where I could make my name. [Georgia head coach Hugh Durham] told me if I came [to Georgia] I wouldn't have to live up to anybody else."

When Wilkins arrived on campus in the fall of 1979, he was a skinny, 180-pound forward with exceptional speed and a vertical leap that was said to approach an astonishing four feet, but his basketball skills, while considerable, were unpolished. Over the next year or so, however, he bulked up to 205 pounds, developed a reliable outside jump shot, and became a formidable offensive rebounder. During the 1980–81 season, Wilkins led Georgia to a 19–9 record, the school's best in fifty years, and its first postseason berth, in the National Invitation Tournament (NIT). Having topped the SEC in scoring with an average of 23.6 points a game and been named to the *Sporting News*'s All-America second team, he was tempted to accept when the Detroit Pistons offered him a four-year, $1.6 million pro contract following his sophomore year, but, as he told Stephen Steiner, he "didn't feel comfortable going." "I kept thinking, 'Am I doing the right thing?'" Wilkins explained to Steiner. "But the NBA is a business. In the NBA you get old quick. You've got to have fun while you can."

Returning to the University of Georgia for his junior year, Wilkins again averaged 23.0 points for the Bulldogs, even though Durham tried to reduce the star forward's scoring opportunities by moving him from his outside spot to a more stationary position under the basket. "I went to [Durham] and told him I knew what he was trying to do," Wilkins recalled in his conversation with Bruce Branch. "There were times when minutes would go by and I wouldn't touch the ball. It was obvious he was trying to keep my stats down so I couldn't go pro. But one day I told him, 'No matter what you do, if I have to grab every offensive rebound, I'm going to get mine.'" After spearheading the Bulldogs' drive to a second NIT appearance, Wilkins was a first-team selection on the All-America squads compiled by the NBA coaches, the *Basketball Times*, and *Basketball Weekly*; he also made the Associated Press's All-America second team. In three years, Wilkins had played in seventy-eight games for Georgia, averaging 21.6 points and 7.5 rebounds, but in the spring of 1982 he declared his eligibility for the NBA draft.

The Los Angeles Lakers owned the draft's first pick, and general manager Jerry West was leaning toward selecting the Human Highlight Film because of his acrobatic athleticism and rim-rattling dunks. "Wilkins is one of the most exciting players I've ever seen in my life," West told Fred Mitchell of the *Chicago Tribune* (November 21, 1982). "He's amazing; he's extremely attractive. He sells tickets and gets a team going." But West was unable to persuade the Lakers' coaches and owners, who were said to be concerned about Wilkins's inconsistent outside shooting and rudimentary defensive skills, and the team instead drafted James Worthy, an All-American forward from the University of North Carolina. The San Diego Clippers took DePaul forward Terry Cummings, and the Utah Jazz made Wilkins the third player selected in a draft that was rich in small forwards. Shortly before the start of the 1982–83 season, the financially troubled Jazz organization traded Wilkins to the Atlanta Hawks in exchange for two veteran players and a cash outlay reported to be in the high six figures.

Despite occasional lapses on defense, during his rookie season with the Hawks Wilkins quickly established himself as a crowd pleaser with his soaring, above-the-rim style of play. He was unanimously chosen to the league's 1982–83 All-Rookie first team, and although Hawks coach Kevin Loughery declared that Wilkins was not yet "good enough" to be "another Julius Erving," Phil

Elderkin, writing in the *Christian Science Monitor* (November 16, 1982), observed, "Dominique is part showman and part basketball player. Some of his moves to the basket have already been compared to those of Philadelphia's Julius Erving. Like Dr. J, he can skywalk, he can shoot, and when the lead is big enough he's often as showbiz as the Harlem Globetrotters." In the 1983–84 season, Wilkins broke the twenty-point barrier, averaging a team-high 21.6 points per game. The following year he won the Gatorade slam dunk contest at the NBA's All-Star festivities, besting the Chicago Bulls' high-flying rookie sensation Michael Jordan, and became the chief box-office draw on a team that lost forty-eight times in eighty-two outings.

Although he was consistently among the league's leading scorers, Wilkins was not considered to be one of the NBA's elite forwards until the 1985–86 season, when the Hawks won fifty regular-season games and advanced to the second round of the play-offs for the first time since 1979. Largely because he was an erratic passer and often hoisted ill-advised outside jump shots, Wilkins had been "maligned as a carny act" in some quarters, as Jack McCallum noted in *Sports Illustrated* (April 28, 1986). Before 1986, McCallum wrote, Wilkins was viewed mainly as "a high-jumping, basket-stuffing curiosity and not a Real Player. . . . He peaked in the slam dunk championships on All-Star weekend and was then forgotten, like his Atlanta Hawks, while the prime-time small forwards—the Birds, the Worthys, the Ervings—were trotted out for the play-offs."

Prodded by their demanding young coach, Mike Fratello, the Hawks matured in 1985–86, and, with Michael Jordan sidelined by an injury for most of the season, Wilkins's 30.3-points-per-game average was the best in the league. In one game against the New Jersey Nets on April 10, 1986, he scored a career-high fifty-seven points in just thirty-eight minutes of playing time. Although his five-foot-seven Atlanta teammate Spud Webb dethroned him as the league's slam dunk champion at the annual All-Star weekend, Wilkins was named to the All-NBA first team, and he established single-season career highs for assists, rebounds, steals, and minutes played. "This season I wanted to prove I was a total player," Wilkins told McCallum. "I wanted to change people's opinion of me. It bothered me that I had never made the All-Star team, that people thought all I could do was dunk. Well, I've proved it now. No question about it."

With a strong supporting cast around Wilkins that included center Tree Rollins, power forward Kevin Willis, and Spud Webb and Glenn "Doc" Rivers in the backcourt, the 1986–87 Hawks won fifty-seven regular-season games but failed to advance beyond the second round in the play-offs. Wilkins finished second in scoring, behind Jordan, for the year, and he was the runner-up in the slam dunk contest. That season also saw him surpass the ten-thousand mark in scoring, on April 19, 1987, and equal his career-best total of fifty-seven points, in a game against the Chicago Bulls on December 10, 1986. His efforts earned him a spot on the All-NBA second team.

Over the following season, Wilkins averaged a career-best 30.7 points per game, and his gritty Hawks fought Larry Bird and his fellow Celtics to a standstill in the Eastern Conference play-offs, forcing a series-deciding seventh game at Boston Garden, where Wilkins and Bird, who had been the East team's starting forwards in the All-Star game just a few months earlier, staged "one of the most dramatic shootouts in NBA history," to quote Jack McCallum. After three quarters, the veteran Celtics, clinging to a two-point lead, seemed to be withering under an offensive onslaught by Wilkins, who poured in sixteen of his game-high forty-seven points in the final period. Relatively quiet for most of the game, Bird exploded for twenty fourth-quarter points, finishing the game with thirty-four and pacing Boston to a 118–116 victory. In the view of many sports reporters, what should have been the crowning moment of Wilkins's career to that date was significantly diminished by Bird's clutch performance. "*That* game," Wilkins said to a reporter for *Sport* (February 1994). "I think that's why I've never really been given a lot of attention. Look, I didn't even make the [first] Dream Team. That says it all. I deserved to make the Dream Team, and it hurt deeply that I didn't. Had we won that game in Boston, I think it all might've been different. I think I'd be looked at in a different light."

In the 1988 off-season, Stan Kasten, Atlanta's general manager, attempted to give Fratello's defense-minded Hawks some much-needed offensive punch by replacing Tree Rollins with Moses Malone and acquiring the services of high-scoring swing man Reggie Theus, but the team chemistry seemed to suffer from the loss of Rollins and shooting guard Randy Wittman, who had been traded to make room for Theus, and the Hawks were dispatched in the first round of the 1989 play-offs by the underdog Milwaukee Bucks. Having been the runner-up to the league scoring leader, Michael Jordan, in the 1987–88 season, Wilkins saw his points-per-game average drop to seventh-best in the league in 1988–89. In his interview with Glenn Sheeley, Wilkins attributed the Hawks' decline to unwise personnel changes and the psychological blow of successive play-off losses to the Celtics and the Bucks. "The Boston series took a lot out of us because it's a series we knew we should have won," he remarked. "I think about it a lot. Losing to Milwaukee probably is the one that hurt more than anything because there was no way we should have lost that series. . . . We gave them too much respect in that series—that's why they beat us. Everybody was upset and embarrassed."

In 1990 Wilkins won the slam dunk title on All-Star weekend for the first time in five years (he had placed second two years earlier, in a memorable showdown with Jordan), and he finished the season with the league's fifth-highest scoring average. With his team losing ground in the East to the league champion Detroit Pistons and the up-and-coming Chicago Bulls, Mike Fratello resigned as the Hawks' coach at the end of the 1989–90 season. A temperamental perfectionist who, according to Wilkins, frequently subjected his players to verbal abuse, Fratello advocated a disciplined style of play that was often at odds with Wilkins's free-wheeling, run-and-gun approach, and when Wilkins threw an errant pass or committed an error on defense, Fratello's brittle composure sometimes snapped. "Mike and I always had disagreements—I mean, we argued all the time—but we were able to talk it out and respect each other . . . ," Wilkins told Sheeley. "A couple of times it got personal, but after it was done we sat down and talked to each other. We both apologized and it was over with. It was nothing that lingered on."

Fratello's successor, Bob Weiss, created a tranquil atmosphere at practices and in the locker room that suited Wilkins's easygoing nature and installed an uptempo offense in which the player flourished. "Bobby never says anything negative to us . . . ," Wilkins told Rick Telander of *Sports Illustrated* (March 4, 1991). "He tells us to take the three when it's there. He rests us when we need it. I didn't know basketball was this easy." Wilkins led the Hawks in scoring for the eighth straight time in 1990–91, averaging 25.9 points per game, and he posted career highs in rebounds (almost nine per outing) and assists. Given his statistics, Wilkins was bitterly disappointed when, in September 1991, he was not chosen for the "Dream Team," the elite group of NBA All-Stars who comprised the nucleus of the United States men's basketball team at the 1992 Olympic Games.

Wilkins was well on his way to another stellar season, as if to prove the selection committee was wrong, when, in a game against the Philadelphia 76ers on January 28, 1992, he ruptured his right Achilles tendon—a career-threatening injury from which Wilkins's detractors thought he lacked the dedication to recover. While rehabilitating his foot during the off-season, he entered a new phase of maturity. A carefree, womanizing bachelor who admitted that he was, in his words, "scared to death" after Magic Johnson announced that he had tested positive for the virus that causes AIDS, Wilkins married Nicole Berry on September 26, 1992. Nicole, who had abandoned a promising modeling career to study biology at Georgia State University, was a stabilizing influence on her husband's life. She encouraged Wilkins to maintain a strenuous off-season conditioning program for the first time in his career, and he responded with a newfound determination, strengthening his right leg through a regimen of weight lifting, stationary-bike riding, and jogging.

Without Wilkins in the lineup, Atlanta had dropped twenty-four of its remaining forty games to finish the 1991–92 season with a record of thirty-eight wins and forty-four losses and miss the play-offs, but in 1992–93, with a rejuvenated Wilkins turning in the finest season of his career, the Hawks resumed their winning ways. The league's number-two scorer, behind Jordan, Wilkins averaged 29.9 points and 6.7 rebounds per game, and on February 2, 1993, against the Seattle SuperSonics, he broke Hall-of-Famer Bob Pettit's franchise scoring record when he notched his 20,880th point. Once again he was named to the All-NBA second team and led Atlanta to the playoffs, but the Hawks were eliminated in the first round by the Chicago Bulls, the eventual league champion.

The following season, under a new coach, Lenny Wilkens, Atlanta was challenging Chicago and the New York Knicks for Eastern Conference supremacy when, shortly before the trading deadline, the Hawks shipped Wilkins to the Los Angeles Clippers in exchange for Danny Manning, a twenty-seven-year-old All Star who was perceived to be a better team player. Wilkins, who was averaging 24.4 points at the time and seemed to be adjusting to Lenny Wilkens's strict ball-movement offense, described himself as "bitter and a little bit mad" that he had been cast off just as the Hawks emerged as a championship contender. Nevertheless, he finished the season with a flourish, averaging 26 points and 6.5 rebounds a game for the Clippers, and in the summer of 1994 he played on Dream Team II, the collection of NBA stars who represented the United States at the World Championships in Toronto, Canada.

Having been in the final year of a lucrative contract when he was traded to the woeful Clippers, Wilkins became an unrestricted free agent on July 1, 1994. Although he was courted by the Knicks, a title contender limited to a $1.25 million salary-cap slot, Wilkins instead signed a three-year, $11 million deal with the rebuilding Boston Celtics—a decision that, as Phil Taylor noted in *Sports Illustrated* (August 16, 1994), added "to the widely held impression that Wilkins cares more about individual accomplishments than team goals." "I know how some people see it, but signing with Boston doesn't mean I've given up on winning a championship," Wilkins said in response to Taylor's remarks. "I want a title as badly as anyone. There will definitely be something missing in my career if I never win one. But I couldn't let that be my only consideration. Some teams just couldn't create the space under the salary cap to offer me a reasonable contract. Plus I knew that Boston was serious about bringing in more players. And somehow, the Celtics never stay down for long."

Although Wilkins had a disappointing year with the Celtics, averaging only 17.8 points per game, he managed to become only the ninth player in NBA history to surpass 25,000 points in a career. With the NBA immersed in a bitter labor dispute that threatened the 1995–96 season, Wilkins, who had two years remaining in his contract, abondoned the Celtics and the NBA to play in Greece for Panathinaikos for a reported eight million dollars over two years. Over his NBA career, Wilkins knocked down forty or more points fifty-four times (three times in the play-offs), and he owns the league record for consecutive free throws made in a game.

Dominique Wilkins was described by Jack McCallum of *Sports Illustrated* as "a warm and gentle individual, quick to smile, slow to anger." In his leisure time, he enjoys playing tennis and golf and listening to music, especially jazz. He and his younger brother Gerald, who has played professional basketball with the New York Knicks and the Cleveland Cavaliers, have for some years helped support their mother and their siblings. Wilkins is the father of two children from relationships that ended prior to his marriage to Nicole.

Selected Biographical References: Chicago Tribune IV p3 N 21 '82 por; Inside Sports 12:19+ D '90 pors; People 29:67+ My 2 '88 pors; Sport 73:44+ F '82 pors; Sporting N p24 N 1 '82 pors, p24+ Mr 25 '91 pors, p44 Ap 25 '94 pors; Sports Illus 64:30+ Ap 28 '86 pors, 74:34+ Mr 4 '91 pors, 77:48+ D 7 '92 pors; Time 114:4+ D 24 '79 pors; Who's Who in America, 1995

Block-Korenbrot Public Relations

Woodard, Alfre
(AL-free)

Nov. 8, 1953– Actress. Address: c/o ICM, 8942 Wilshire Blvd., Beverly Hills, CA 90211; c/o Block-Korenbrot Public Relations, 8271 Melrose Ave., Los Angeles, CA 90046

"An actor's actor: chameleonic, idiosyncratic, true . . . ," as Stephen Rebello described her in *Movieline* (May 1994), the prodigiously talented Alfre Woodard is one of the most highly regarded performers in film and television, but outside the entertainment industry she is among the least widely known. For the first nine years of her professional life, the reluctance of show-business executives to cast a woman with distinctly African features thwarted her attempts to build her career. Since being nominated in the early 1980s for an Academy Award for her supporting role in the film *Cross Creek*, however, she has worked steadily, and she has earned enthusiastic praise for such qualities as her strong presence and her extraordinary expressiveness and for what one observer called her "gift for unconditional truth." To date, she has appeared in a dozen feature films, among them *Grand Canyon*, *Passion Fish*, and *Crooklyn*; a dozen made-for-television movies, including *Mandela* and *A Mother's Courage: The Mary Thomas Story*; several television specials; and the series *Tucker's Witch*, *Sara*, and *St. Elsewhere*. Nominated seven times for Emmy Awards, she has won two, for guest performances on the television series *L.A. Law* and *Hill Street Blues*. Woodard has also acted on stage, perhaps most notably in Ntozake Shange's "choreoplay" *For Colored Girls Who Have Considered Suicide/When the Rainbow Is Enuf*.

"For well more than a decade, critics have singled out Woodard as an actress able to make the smallest role significant, able to inject dignity into the most banal film," Stephen Dubner wrote in a profile of her for the *Washington Post* (September 26, 1993). In an earlier *Washington Post* (January 18, 1986) article, Tom Shales described Woodard as "consistently impressive and versatile" and "very, very believable." She "often seems possessed of the world's most honest face (and shows great skill at using it dramatically)," Shales observed. In a cover story for the *Washington Post*'s "TV Week" (September 20, 1987), Jill Nelson wrote that Woodard has "a voice that works the nuances of language like James Brown works a lyric" and "eyes that project, depending on the moment, all the world's joys, sorrows, or lustful feelings." According to the motion picture director and producer Frank Perry, Woodard "combines the saintly and the sexual" and is "a great comedian." "She is truly electric," he told Jean Vallely for *Ms.* (April 1989). "She transcends color, gender almost. When she performs, her color goes out the window and all you see is this blazing talent. She would probably be a huge star right now if she wasn't black."

The youngest of three children, Alfre Woodard was born on November 8, 1953 in Tulsa, Oklahoma to Marion H. Woodard, an interior decorator and entrepreneur in oil-well drilling, and Constance Woodard, a homemaker. She was named by her godmother, who on the night of Alfre's birth saw, in a vision, the name formed in gold letters on a wall. Woodard has said that she was "mothered very fiercely by [her] mom," who was "totally grounded with unconditional love," and she has described her father as "bodacious" and as "the smartest, most wonderful person" she has ever known. Her parents inculcated in Alfre, her sister (who became an assistant principal), and her brother (who is a school counselor) the precept that "if

[you] don't help take care of the people around [you], then [your] life isn't of any real value," in Woodard's words. In her interview with Jean Vallely, Woodard noted that the car trips that her family took every summer to different parts of the United States served as a way of nurturing in her a concern for others; another means was television news broadcasts, which, at her father's insistence, she and her siblings watched daily. "By the time I was twelve I was thinking and talking with an awareness of the world and [the belief] that you don't separate your personal life from the social life around you," she told Vallely.

During her formative years Woodard attended churches of four or five different denominations, and through her godmother she learned the tenets of Christian Science, which she has labeled "a very strong influence" in her life. Another component of her cultural heritage was storytelling, a popular pastime in her close-knit family (which included a grandfather who was part Cree). Her own verbal abilities proved valuable when, at fourteen, she was chosen to address an association of black businessmen. After listening to her speech, which focused on political issues, before the event, her father asked her to add a few lines. "There are repercussions for a guy like me saying certain things, but you can be my mouthpiece," he explained to her, as Michael J. Bandler reported in the *Chicago Tribune* (December 29, 1991). Recalling her reaction to her father's request, Alfre Woodard told Bandler, "I have never felt so proud." In the same year Woodard was elected queen of her school. Overhearing some classmates describe her as the "ugliest queen ever" did not upset her, she maintained to Sheila Benson for *Interview* (May 1994), because she always found herself to be "pretty interesting," and she never wanted to be anyone other than herself. Woodard has credited her parents with instilling in her the idea that she could do whatever she set her mind to.

At Bishop Kelley High School, a Catholic school in Tulsa, a course given by Brother Patrick O'Brien fired Woodard's interest in the dramatic arts. (One of the films he showed—*Intimate Lightning*, by the Czech director Ivan Passer—remains her favorite movie.) Woodard has characterized the intensive drama exercises in which she engaged in the class as both "self-realizing" and "self-releasing." At fifteen, at the urging of Sister Rachel Ann Graham, another teacher, she made her debut as an actor in a student production. The experience proved to be both exhilarating and enlightening, as she revealed to Pamela Johnson for *Essence* (April 1988): "It was as if I had been doing the breaststroke all my life and then somebody put me in the water and I went, 'Ahhh! This is it!'" By the time Woodard graduated from high school, she had discarded her long-held fantasy of becoming a trial lawyer and decided to be an actor. "Acting was the thing I thought I could do every day for the rest of my life—and that people could depend on me to do," she told Jean Vallely.

As a drama major at Boston University, in Massachusetts, Woodard received training in such theatre arts as building sets as well as in acting and in analyzing plays. A class that she especially enjoyed required the students to sing a capella while dressed in bathing suits. "I put on this little yellow striped bikini," Woodard told Pamela Johnson. "My first song was 'It Ain't Necessarily So,' and I was kind of hopping around, being a whale. It was such a fantastic sense of freedom to be looking out onto the snow outside, half-naked, fat, singing and jiggling." Her extracurricular activities included participation in productions of the university's Black Drama Collective. By her own account, Woodard was a "semi-black nationalist" at college—"very into [her] blackness but unable to block other people out because [she] wasn't raised that way." After earning a B.A. degree in about 1974, Woodard acted in two plays (Ron Whyte's *Horatio* and Edward Bond's *Saved*) presented by the Arena Stage, in Washington, D.C. Then, with the aim of furthering her career, she moved to Los Angeles.

During the next six years, Woodard secured acting jobs only about once a year and worked for an average of just three or four weeks annually. In the following three years, she appeared in a total of perhaps six productions. She has attributed her inability to get more roles in those years to her appearance. "I'm a very African-looking woman," she observed during an interview with Aldore Collier for *Ebony* (July 1990). "My look was not in vogue when I started in this business. . . . I was literally told by several agents, 'You're nice,' or 'You were really great . . . but they're looking for an *attractive* young black woman.' . . . I was told that a lot. It could be painful if you believed it, but I had too much else going on around me that did not validate that."

Woodard has told interviewers that her family helped to sustain her both financially and emotionally and that she felt neither discouraged nor anxious during her long fallow periods. "When I set out to do this, I knew that I would be able to do what I wanted to . . . ," she explained to Aldore Collier. "I could be patient. . . . And I believe very strongly in God." In *Essence* (May 1994), Deborah Gregory quoted her as saying that for many black actors, "the tide shifted" in about 1988. "I think that black actors like myself have altered Hollywood's narrow standards of beauty by not going away or even getting angry about it," Woodard said to Gregory. "We just *had* to be hired."

Soon after her arrival in Los Angeles, Woodard joined an improvisation group that performed at the Mark Taper Forum and also for audiences of children in schools. Her work included juggling, tap-dancing, miming, and impersonating animals. In the mid-1970s she played a supporting role in a Mark Taper Forum production of *Me and Bessie*, a musical tribute to the singer Bessie Smith that was presented on Broadway. At around the same time, she appeared in a Los Angeles staging of *For Colored Girls Who Have Considered Sui-*

cide/When the Rainbow Is Enuf, by Ntozake Shange, and she remained with the cast when the show toured Australia. (Years later she delivered a highly praised performance in a PBS presentation of *For Colored Girls*.) Impressed by her work in the Los Angeles production, the director and producer Robert Altman cast her in his film *Health*, which was released in 1982.

Woodard's film career had been launched in 1979, with her portrayal of a salesclerk in Alan Rudolph's *Remember My Name*. In her review of that picture for the *New York Times* (March 11, 1979), Janet Maslin included Woodard's name in a list of cast members that she described as "intrinsically interesting even when their material is not." As with both *Remember My Name* and *Health*, most reviewers panned *Cross Creek* (1983), the third movie in which Woodard appeared, but her performance attracted highly favorable attention. Directed by Martin Ritt from a screenplay by Dalene Young, *Cross Creek* was based on a memoir by Marjorie Kinnan Rawlings, whose novel *The Yearling* won a Pulitzer Prize in 1938. Woodard played Geechee, a local woman who becomes Rawlings's housekeeper after the city-bred writer settles in the scrubland of northern Florida. "Alfre Woodard is remarkably convincing as Geechee, who emerges as the movie's most intriguing character," Kathleen Carroll declared in the New York *Daily News* (September 21, 1983), in a representative assessment of her work in *Cross Creek*. To the surprise of many people in the movie industry—including Woodard herself—the then-little-known performer was nominated for an Academy Award in the category of best supporting actress for her strong portrayal of the spunky servant.

During a conversation with Lynn Hirschberg for *Esquire* (September 1984) soon after the announcement of the Oscar nominations, Woodard mentioned that her next job would probably entail depicting a slave in a Civil War drama, and she then complained, "At some point I hope to get parts where my wardrobe does not consist of rags and a head scarf and where my character has a command of the English language. But the truth is, wonderful offers just aren't pouring in." One strongly desired offer that did not materialize for her was that of the part of Celie, the heroine, in Steven Spielberg's 1985 adaptation of Alice Walker's novel *The Color Purple*.

Woodard's next role of substance turned up not in film but in television. A guest performance on the acclaimed series *Hill Street Blues*, as the grieving mother of a child killed by a police officer, earned her an Emmy Award in 1984. Earlier, she had appeared on the small screen in the made-for-television movies *Freedom Road* (1979), *The Ambush Murders* (1981), and *The Sophisticated Gents* (1981), which were based on books by Howard Fast, Ben Bradlee Jr., and John A. Williams, respectively. In 1984 she was also seen in *The Killing Floor*, a PBS production in which she played the wife of a sharecropper who, after finding work in a Chicago slaughterhouse, gets caught up in the city's race riots of 1919.

Woodard was nominated for an Emmy in 1985, for her work in the PBS production *Words by Heart*, a drama about racial prejudice, and in 1986 and 1988, for her characterization of the doctor Roxanne Turner in *St. Elsewhere*, a television series in which she appeared regularly for three years starting in 1985. Another meaty part (and another Emmy nomination) came Woodard's way when, in 1986, she was cast as Maude DeVictor in John Sayles's fact-based television movie *Unnatural Causes*. As a benefits counselor in the Chicago regional office of the Veterans Administration, DeVictor overcame tremendous obstacles to bring to public attention the apparent links between exposure to Agent Orange, a defoliant used by the United States Army during the Vietnam War, and serious, sometimes fatal, illnesses in many Vietnam veterans. In a New York *Daily News* (November 10, 1986) review of *Unnatural Causes*, Kay Gardella labeled Woodard's acting "nothing short of marvelous." "The movie belongs to the versatile Woodard . . . ," Clifford Terry wrote in the *Chicago Tribune* (November 10, 1986). "Intelligently underplaying what could have been an arm-flailing role, and even affecting a Chicago nasality, she movingly portrays the feisty [DeVictor]." Calling attention to other facets of Woodard's performance, John Leonard reported in the *New York Times* (November 17, 1986) that "as DeVictor, she is deep in cunning, abiding in her somehow sexy stubbornness, her herky-jerky sense of what's fair and what's evil, her tempered steel."

Woodard received her second Emmy Award in 1987, for her portrayal of a terminally ill rape victim on the pilot for the series *L.A. Law*. That year she was also honored with an ACE Award (cable television's version of an Emmy), for her characterization of Winnie Mandela, the wife of the South African political leader Nelson Mandela, in the HBO film *Mandela*. Despite her misgivings about the picture's simplistic rendering of South African history, Woodard accepted the role because, she had discovered, many of her friends knew little or nothing about Mandela and the antiapartheid movement. "I felt a responsibility, saw the film as a place for me to help out, to marry my art and my social conscience," she told Jill Nelson.

In *The Child Saver* (1988), in another performance that attracted the admiring notice of critics, Woodard played an ambitious advertising executive who risks her career in an attempt to rescue a young drug runner from the clutches of a Fagin-like dealer. The telepicture gained "much of its verisimilitude" from Woodard, according to Tom Shales of the *Washington Post* (January 18, 1986). "Even when the script lets her down, Woodard prevails," he wrote. "She has a fervor and a magnetism that obliterate doubt." During a conversation with Michael E. Hill for the *Washington Post* (January 17, 1988), Woodard said that she had been attracted to the opportunities that the script gave her to "run and fall down" and to play someone of a type that she had not previously depicted. "I knew I would have to do my homework to be a businessperson," she explained. "If I've got to figure something out, to do something I'm not used to doing, I am attracted." "It's very difficult to find things to get excited about," she confessed to Hill. "People who want to do things remember what I've done in the past. For me, it's usually too similar to what I've done. Writers don't have the freeness of mind to see a woman—especially a black woman—with humor, sensuality, as someone with any rogue bitchiness, any complexity. . . . I'm looking for writers who don't look upon a character's sex or color as changing the possibilities of what can happen to them . . . who will allow me to be a woman who can get excited about receiving a piece of Wedgwood as easily as a James Brown recording."

Complexity was absent in the characters Woodard portrayed in two feature films—*Extremities* (1986) and *Scrooged* (1988)—in which she appeared before and just after her interview with Michael Hill. Her next two assignments for the silver screen and television provided richer vehicles for her talents. In a role that she has called her favorite and more fun than any of her others, Woodard played a dreamy seamstress named Popeye Jackson in Thomas Schlamme's film *Miss Firecracker* (1989), an adaptation by Beth Henley of one of her plays. In an assessment of *Miss Firecracker* for *New York Newsday* (April 28, 1989), Lynn Darling wrote that Woodard was "a wonder, stealing every scene she's in with her sweetly dizzy charm." Caryn James, on the other hand, declared in the *New York Times* (April 28, 1989) that it was "painful to watch Ms. Woodard, who plays against her ordinarily dignified image, go too far here. Though Popeye is meant to be warm and funny, this is a cruel caricature of a simpleminded person." For her outstanding work as the star of *A Mother's Courage* (1989), a made-for-television movie based on the life of Mary Thomas, the mother of the NBA superstar Isiah Thomas, Woodard was nominated for an Emmy in 1990.

Critics were unanimous in praising Woodard's performance in Lawrence Kasdan's film *Grand Canyon* (1991), in which she played a secretary who becomes the girlfriend of a saintly tow-truck driver (Danny Glover). Woodard "sizzles in her small role," David Ansen declared in a *Newsweek* (December 30, 1991) review, while in the *Christian Science Monitor* (January 3, 1992), David Sterritt called Woodard "marvelously likable." "Among the performers, Ms. Woodard stands out vibrantly despite her underwritten role," Janet Maslin wrote in the *New York Times* (December 25, 1991). As a star of John Sayles's *Passion Fish* (1993), Woodard received similarly enthusiastic reviews. In that film she played Chantelle, a nurse from Chicago who, having lost custody of her daughter because of her addiction to crack, has taken a job as a live-in housekeeper and companion to a bitter accident victim (Mary McDonnell) as a means of proving that she is fit to resume her maternal duties. "Almost everything [Chantelle] says has a touch of acidity or mockery, yet the actress makes you unfailingly aware of the fragility underneath," John Simon observed in a critique of *Passion Fish* for the *National Review* (March 15, 1993). "She has enormous eyes that . . . contain worlds; they speak much more than her mouth and seem always a mite anxious, a couple of jumps ahead of tears. But her tears, like her smiles, are rare and faint; nevertheless, the screen is swamped by them."

In 1993 Woodard also appeared in the movies *Heart and Souls* and *Rich in Love*. *Bopha!* (1993), the actor Morgan Freeman's directorial debut, featured her as the wife of a black South African police officer (Danny Glover). In depicting a woman whose life is shattered by a tangled mix of domestic and political strife, she turned in "a fine, restrained performance that's never allowed to seek easy sympathy," Vincent Canby wrote in the *New York Times* (September 24, 1993). In Spike Lee's semiautobiographical film *Crooklyn* (1994), the screenplay for which was written by Lee, his sister, Joie Lee, and his brother Cinqué Lee, Woodard played a strong, loving mother who sometimes emulates a drill sergeant in her struggle to raise her five children.

"From the beginning of my career, I've been picky about my roles," Woodard told Marla Hart, who interviewed her for the *Chicago Tribune* (December 3, 1989). "That's because acting for me is twenty-four hours a day of physically and emotionally being wrapped up with the character. So I can't bear doing things I don't like." "I turn down things a lot, because I get asked to be a moral prop that makes the writers or filmmakers feel better about themselves," Caryn James quoted her as saying in the *New York Times* (March 28, 1993). Woodard explained to Stephen Rebello, "I have a certain way of looking at the world, certain values. You do what's right, what's honest, what makes you feel good." And she told Deborah Gregory that she asks herself, "Is this something that my mother and father wouldn't be ashamed to watch?"

In tackling any role, Woodard seeks the advice of the actor and screenwriter Roderick Spencer, to whom she has been married since 1983. She explained to Sheila Benson, "I say to Roderick, 'Read this script. Now, who am I? Tell me something.' He can tell me three sentences, and it will be the key to how I approach my character." In breathing life into a role, she first concentrates on various physical aspects of the character. "I start to lean on those things so they become second nature to me," Woodard told Pamela Johnson. "No words, no plot, nothing, because after you've rehearsed it several times, shot it several times, it gets too solid and staid. I leave words for last. Real life happens off the words." "If I could take the essence of Vanessa Redgrave, Mary Alice, and Geraldine Page [and] roll them together, that is what I would like to be as an actor," she confided to Stephen Rebello. She has preserved her thoughts about each of her roles in the daily journal that she has kept for many years.

Among Woodard's other credits are performances, on the stage, in A. R. Gurney's *Love Let-*

ters, Frank Smith's *Two by South*, and New York Shakespeare Festival productions of *A Winter's Tale* and David Hare's *A Map of the World*; in cinema, in *The Gun in Betty Lou's Handbag*; and on television, in the films *Sweet Revenge* and *Blue Bayou*, the series *Tucker's Witch* and *Sara*, and the special *Trial of the Moke*. In 1995 she starred, with Charles Dutton, in a Hallmark Hall of Fame television presentation of August Wilson's play *The Piano Lesson*, giving what Steve Johnson, writing in the *Chicago Tribune* (February 3, 1995), characterized as an "impeccable" preformance as Bernice Charles. On the big screen, she appeared most recently in a supporting role in *How to Make an American Quilt* (1995), an adaptation of a 1991 novel by Whitney Otto, which featured Winona Ryder, Anne Bancroft, and Ellen Burstyn. Woodard believes that the best work she has done to date was in *Pretty Hattie's Baby*, a yet-to-be-released independent film. With the aim of trying her hand at production—and creating what she has called "real movies for real people"—she has recently collaborated with her husband to develop several cinematic projects.

"Even as she picks through a bowl of nuts in the bar of a Manhattan hotel," John Haslett Cuff wrote of Alfre Woodard in the Toronto *Globe and Mail* (November 8, 1986), "her eyes seem to fill the room, to register and reflect a sense of life and conviction that somehow informs even the most mundane act with unexpected nuances. In person and in her art, her eyes seize and seduce." Woodard has characterized herself as "someone who takes her own sense of reality with her." "I can go anywhere and be around anyone, places and people I really object to, and they don't seem to bother me," she explained to Jean Vallely. Interviewers have described her as "straightforward and direct" and "bewitchingly cordial and entertaining." Contrary to the image many people have of her, she has maintained, she is not always serious but likes to "act silly and funny."

Woodard lives in Santa Monica, California with her husband and their three-year-old daughter, Mavis (who was named for Mavis Staples, Woodard's favorite singer), and year-old son, Duncan, both of whom were adopted as infants. A lover of the outdoors, she enjoys skiing, running, jogging, hiking, and bicycling. She was a founding member of Artists for a Free South Africa, and she has participated, in Central America and elsewhere, in activities of the Hollywood Women's Political Committee. Acting, she told one reporter, is her way of "earn[ing] her right to be on Earth." "What I hope to do with my work is to give people a sense of being nurtured, even if it's just a laugh. That's my service."

Selected Biographical References: Chicago Tribune VI p4 D 29 '91 por; Ebony 45:51+ Jl '90 pors; Essence 18:56+ Ap '88 por; Ms. 17:68+ Ap '89 pors; Television and Video Almanac, 1994; Who's Who in America, 1995

Epic Records/Sony Music

Wynette, Tammy

(wie-NET)

May 5, 1942– Singer; songwriter. Address: c/o MCA Records, 60 Music Sq. E., Nashville, TN 37203; c/o Evelyn Shriver Public Relations, 1313 16th Ave. S., Nashville, TN 37212

"The ultimate exponent of the three-hanky ballad," as she has been described, the singer and songwriter Tammy Wynette epitomizes country-and-western music to people the world over. "Wynette's diction, her phrasing, the emotion coursing through her performances and peaking in those eternal instants when her voice breaks the way only her voice can: these elements add up to a symbol as instantly and universally recognizable as the flag of a great nation," Bob Millard declared in *Country Music* (September 1990). Often referred to as the "First Lady of Country Music," Wynette is probably best known for her single "Stand By Your Man," which has aired on the radio more than two million times since its release in 1968. Having done the backbreaking work of picking cotton on the farm where she grew up; raised four children; and experienced five marriages, four divorces, poverty, years of ill health, and an addiction to prescription drugs, Wynette is renowned for the credibility with which she performs the staples of her repertoire: songs that focus on the problems and emotional ups-and-downs with which millions of women grapple every day. "I've lived my songs," she told Dotson Rader, who profiled her for *Parade* (April 9, 1995). A made-for-television film based on Wynette's autobiography, *Stand By Your Man* (1979), was broadcast in 1982.

Under the guidance of the producer and songwriter Billy Sherrill, Wynette leaped to prominence in 1967, when her second single, "Your Good Girl's Gonna Go Bad," became a top-ten country hit, and the next one, "I Don't Wanna Play House," reached the number-one spot and earned her the first of her two Grammy Awards. "Stand By Your Man," which followed "D-I-V-O-R-C-E," another of her signature songs, to the top of the country chart in 1968, quickly became the best-selling single ever recorded by a woman. In 1968, 1969, and 1970 Wynette was named the female vocalist of the year by the Country Music Association. Her celebrity increased exponentially during her six-year marriage to the country-music star George Jones, with whom she collaborated both in the recording studio and in concerts throughout the United States.

After languishing during the 1980s, Wynette's career revived in the early 1990s, with the successes of her album *Best Loved Hits* (1991) and the dance song "Justified & Ancient" (1992), which she recorded with the British pop duo KLF and which became a number-one hit in eighteen countries. Wynette has made more than fifty albums, nearly all on the Epic label, and has had thirty-nine top-ten hits and twenty number-one singles; well over thirty million of her records have been sold to date. *Without Walls* (1994), one of her latest albums, demonstrates the attributes that have made her a country-music legend, as Robert Ross wrote in *Country Weekly* (November 15, 1994): "a rich, flexible, and strong voice, a natural ability to read lyrics, an impeccable musical sense, and a classic knack as a storyteller."

The only child of William Hollice Pugh, a farmer, and Mildred Faye (Russell) Pugh, Tammy Wynette was born Virginia Wynette Pugh on May 5, 1942, in the farmhouse of her maternal grandparents in Itawamba County, Mississippi. (According to some sources, she was born in Red Bay, Alabama.) Her relatives still call her Wynette, a name that her parents chose in honor of a nurse who had ministered to Wynette's father when, five months before her birth, he had undergone surgery for what proved to be an inoperable brain tumor. An untrained musician who played five instruments, Hollice Pugh, as he was known, often performed at local functions. Before he died, when Wynette was nine months old, he reportedly enjoyed sitting at the piano with his daughter on his lap, picking out melodies by guiding her hands on the keys. "The only legacy my father left me was his love of music," she has said. "He made my mother promise him over and over again that she would encourage me to take an interest in music if I had any talent."

Wynette remained in the home of her grandparents, Chester and Flora Russell, when, after her father's death, her mother moved to Memphis, Tennessee to work in a factory. (Mildred Pugh later earned a teaching certificate and became a substitute teacher at the three-room primary school that Wynette attended.) Even after her mother returned to her grandparents' home and, in around 1946, remarried, the Russells continued to raise Wynette virtually as their own daughter. She lived with them until she was thirteen, and during the next few years, because of the frequent quarrels she had with her mother, she repeatedly moved back and forth between their house and that of her mother and her stepfather, Foy Lee, a farmworker. Beginning early in her childhood, Wynette helped with household and farm chores, and, from the age of six or seven until she got married, she picked cotton in her grandfather's fields.

"I loved an audience from the time I could walk," Wynette has said. She sang and learned to harmonize at the local Baptist church, where, after she started taking piano lessons at the age of eight, she also played the piano. When she was twelve an uncle taught her the basics of playing the guitar, and she soon took up the accordion. At Tremont High School she played the flute with the school band, and she often entertained other students in impromptu vocal performances at the piano in the auditorium. In her teens she sang on two local radio shows and in many talent contests (none of which she won). By her own account, she often daydreamed about singing professionally. In one of her favorite fantasies, she has recalled, she would be "standing on a stage singing with her country-music idol, George Jones." She listened to her mother's large collection of George Jones albums so many times that she eventually memorized the words to virtually all his recorded songs.

In 1960, a month or two before her eighteenth birthday and her scheduled high school graduation, Wynette married Euple Byrd, a construction worker who lived nearby. Days afterward, as Mississippi state law required when a student got married, she was expelled from school. In 1961 Wynette gave birth to a daughter, and, the next summer, to another daughter. Practically penniless (Byrd never held a job for long), the couple were then living on her grandfather's property, in a leaky-roofed log house that lacked indoor plumbing, a functioning stove, and airtight walls. During the next three years, she and her husband moved half a dozen times, and Wynette worked briefly as a barmaid, waitress, and receptionist. She also trained in cosmetology and got licenses to practice in Alabama and Mississippi. Meanwhile, Wynette's relationship with her husband had been steadily deteriorating, and she had developed a chronic kidney infection, which worsened after she became pregnant again. In late 1964 or early 1965, she suffered a nervous collapse and, during her subsequent hospitalization, received twelve shock treatments. After her recovery she separated from her husband (they were divorced in 1966) and moved into the Birmingham, Alabama home of some of her paternal relatives. Her third daughter was born soon afterward.

Later in 1965, with the help of an uncle who was the chief engineer at a Birmingham television station, Wynette got a job on *Country Boy Eddie*, a program that aired weekday mornings from 6:00 to 7:00. She earned about thirty-five dollars a week for singing two songs on every show. After finishing up at the station, she would go to her job at a beauty salon, where she worked daily until 7:00 in the evening. A few months after her debut on *Country Boy Eddie*, at the invitation of a Birmingham deejay, she attended the 1965 Disc Jockeys Convention, an event held at the Ryman Auditorium, in Nashville, Tennessee. On her first evening in Nashville, she sang with a country-music band that had stationed themselves right outside the auditorium. "A chill passed all the way through my body when I realized I was actually standing on a stage in *Nashville*," she recalled in her autobiography. "The fact that my 'stage' was a flatbed truck didn't matter. . . . I went home . . . more fired up than I'd ever been about making singing my life's work."

During the next three months, Wynette went periodically to Music Row, in Nashville, to try to get a contract or singing job. Although she made no appointments and had no demonstration tapes, she managed to meet with representatives of several record companies and music publishers. "A few years later I would never have made it past the receptionists, but the attitude along Music Row was looser and more relaxed in 1965, and my ignorance worked for me instead of against me," she has observed. Her interviews failed to generate any offers, but they served to strengthen her determination to pursue a singing career. That determination got a substantial boost when, at the recommendation of staff members of a country-music radio station, the popular country singer Porter Wagoner hired her to open a show that he was giving in Birmingham and then to join him and several other performers on a ten-day concert tour. Wynette loved being on the road. She felt as if she had entered "a very special little clique," in her words. "I knew after the first night that I never wanted to give it up," she recalled in *Stand By Your Man*.

At the beginning of 1966, having resolved to make an all-out effort to get a contract, Wynette moved to Nashville. While her three children waited in her car, she would go for auditions. At the suggestion of Kelso Hurston, who had signed on the singer Billie Jo Spears, she went to see Billy Sherrill, the house producer for Epic Records, a division of CBS (now Sony Music). According to Wynette, Sherrill later told a reporter that she looked like "a pale skinny little blond girl" who appeared to be "at her rope's end." Accompanying herself on Sherrill's guitar, Wynette—whose voice has been described as "a conversational mezzo-soprano with just enough grain to sound vulnerable" and as having a distinctive catch that "sounds like a heartbreak"—sang four songs. Although Sherrill "thought she had a real unique style—like a little teardrop every now and then appears," as Marjorie Rosen quoted him as saying in *People* (December 10, 1990), he expressed no opinion to Wynette about her performance. But to her delight, he told her, "I don't have time to look for material for you, but if you can come up with a good song, I'll record you." A few days later Sherrill himself chose the song "Apartment #9." With Wynette identified on the label as Tammy Wynette (Sherrill had suggested the name change; she "looked like a Tammy," he told her), Epic released her rendition of "Apartment #9" in the fall of 1966. It reached number forty-three or forty-four on the country-music chart.

Knowing that it would be months before she received royalties, Wynette next sought a contract with a booking agency. She got several refusals—one owner told her, "We don't have good luck with girl singers"—before she approached Hubert Long, George Jones's booking agent. "I have three children who need clothes and food," she told him. "I've got to find work." "Years later," she reported in her autobiography, "he told me I was so pitiful, his conscience wouldn't have let him turn me down even if he'd wanted to." Long soon got her a one-week booking at a club in Atlanta, where she did five forty-five-minute shows nightly, alternating between two completely different sets. After that job she began getting regular bookings, and within five or six months her earnings had risen to five hundred dollars a night. (Since she had to pay for her backup instrumentalists, her food and lodging, and other expenses, her net earnings were far less.) Occasionally, she opened shows for George Jones.

"Your Good Girl's Gonna Go Bad" (1967), Wynette's second solo release, reached the top ten on the country-music chart. Her next disk, "My Elusive Dreams," a duet that she recorded with David Houston, shot to the top of the chart, as did her next two singles, "I Don't Wanna Play House" (1967)—for which she won a Grammy Award for best female country-and-western vocal performance—and "Take Me to Your World" (1968). "D-I-V-O-R-C-E" and "Stand By Your Man," both of which were cowritten by Wynette and Sherrill, were number-one country hits in 1968. They also appeared on the pop charts, with "D-I-V-O-R-C-E" reaching number sixty-three, and "Stand By Your Man," number nineteen. ("Stand By Your Man" did even better in the adult/contemporary category, rising to number eleven, and it reached the top spot on the pop chart in England in 1975.) In "D-I-V-O-R-C-E," Wynette voiced the anguish of a young wife whose marriage is about to end. "Our D-I-V-O-R-C-E / Becomes final today . . . ," she sings sorrowfully in one verse, using coded language to avoid alarming her little son. "I know that this will be / Pure H-E-double-L for me / I wish that we could stop this / D-I-V-O-R-C-E." In 1969 Wynette's second, short-lived marriage, to the songwriter Don Chapel, ended in divorce.

Wynette won her second Grammy Award in 1969, for "Stand By Your Man." By her own account, she and Sherrill wrote the song "in about fifteen minutes one afternoon before a recording session." Addressed to women, it begins, "Sometimes it's hard to be a woman / Giving all your love to just one man." It then advises forgiving the man and standing by him ("'cause after all he's just a man"), even when he does things that his female partner "won't understand" and that will cause her to "have bad times." In the *Rolling Stone Album Guide* (1992), Paul Evans observed that Wynette's rendition of the song "set the pattern for the very affecting approach she would later deploy on many of her ballads—she begins singing with a dramatic hesitancy and then builds to a startling intensity." After describing the song as "sentimental and gooey" in a review for *New York Newsday* (May 4, 1989) of a Wynette concert at the Bottom Line, in New York City, Stephen Williams wrote, "It would be laughable in other hands, but Wynette's heartfelt delivery takes it to another plane."

"Stand By Your Man" soon became the best-selling single ever recorded by a female singer. But people supportive of the goals of women's liberation denounced it, because it ostensibly advocated that women remain in demeaning or otherwise unhealthy relationships. In an article entitled "Songs of Non-Liberation" that appeared in *Newsweek* (August 2, 1971) three years after the song's release, a writer expressed the view that "Wynette's music faithfully follows the notion that country music is . . . a salve for the beleaguered housewife who grits her teeth as destiny dumps its slops on her head."

Wynette has insisted that critics of "Stand By Your Man" have distorted its message. "I don't see anything in that song that implies a woman is supposed to sit home and raise babies while a man goes out and raises hell . . . ," she wrote in her autobiography. "To me it means: be supportive of your man; show him you love him and you're proud of him; and be willing to forgive him if he doesn't always live up to your image of what he should be." She reiterated that point in 1992, during then-governor Bill Clinton's presidential campaign, after Hillary Rodham Clinton, in an appearance on *60 Minutes* in which the Clintons discussed their marriage, said, "I'm not sitting here, some little woman, standing by my man like Tammy Wynette." In an angry letter to Hillary Clinton that she also released to many news organizations, Wynette demanded a public apology and declared that the remark was an affront to "all 'little women' in the country who 'stand by their man' and are potential supporters of Governor Clinton." "Where in the song have the lyrics implied that a woman should be . . . the willing recipient of either mental or physical abuse?" she asked. Hillary Clinton apologized to her in a widely publicized telephone call that she made the next day.

"In hindsight," Paul Evans wrote in the 1992 *Rolling Stone Record Guide*, "the perception of Wynette as the country-and-western equivalent of the ultraconservative social activist Phyllis Schlafly . . . seems condescending and facile—while it's true that she parlayed more than her share of long-suffering wife apologias, not only do such songs as 'Your Good Girl's Gonna Go Bad,' 'The Only Time I'm Really Me,' 'I Stayed Long Enough,' and 'Don't Come Home a-Drinkin' (With Lovin' on Your Mind)' counter her perceived submissiveness, but the dismissal of Wynette specifically reads like the more general loathing of white southern life that afflicted many critics of the time. Basically, Wynette . . . embodied the sensitivity of a certain culture. . . . She sang directly from inside the scene, and she gave it authentic, soulful expression." In an impassioned defense of Wynette for the *Village Voice* (March 3, 1992), Doug Simmons advised critics of the singer's "ideology," as they in effect characterized it, to listen to "Stand By Your Man." After describing her "cracking timbre as her voice shifts to the chorus" as "a breathtaking tonal change that launches the lyric's leap of faith," he wrote, "As a testimony of devotion, 'Stand By Your Man' is plainly more an ideal than a reality."

Wynette's work reached audiences far beyond the boundaries of country-music radio and concert halls when, in 1970, the director Bob Rafelson featured "Stand By Your Man" and other of her songs in the soundtrack of the film *Five Easy Pieces*. One of the characters in the film plays Tammy Wynette records nonstop at home and appears to want to *be* Wynette. Indeed, after Wynette and George Jones announced, in 1968, that they had gotten married (in reality they did not exchange vows until 1969), Wynette's life, as depicted in heavy coverage in fan magazines and supermarket tabloids, seemed to have acquired the elements of an American fairy tale. "To outsiders we seemed like the perfect couple," Wynette wrote in *Stand By Your Man*. "*Mr. and Mrs. Country Music!* We had a following of devoted, almost fanatical fans. . . . We were by far the most in-demand duet on the road, and wherever we appeared crowds were so enthusiastic you could feel the waves of affection pouring out from them." She attributed their popularity, in part at least, to what she described as the "special chemistry" that existed between them when they were on stage. "Professionally we brought out the best in each other . . . ," she explained. "Unless Jones was drunk or there had been a bad scene between us, we always had *fun* working together, and it carried from the stage down into the audience and made them have fun, too."

Until their separation at the end of 1974, Wynette and Jones concertized jointly (except at those bookings for which Jones, usually without warning, would fail to show up). A dozen of the duets that they recorded—including some that were released after they were divorced, in 1975—became hits. Prominent among them are "The Ceremony" (1972), "We're Gonna Hold On" (1973), "Golden Ring" and "Near You" (1976), and "Two-Story House" (1980). After she and Jones separated, Wynette started writing songs by herself. When, in 1975, she returned to performing as a soloist, she added an element of intimacy to her act by describing to her audiences the circumstances under which she had written the songs. In a review for the Toronto *Globe & Mail* (January 2, 1985) of a concert in which she apparently used that approach, Liam Lacey wrote, "Wynette is such a downright charming mixture of the cornball, confessional, and aristocratically gracious, there's no doubt about why she holds the reputation she does," and he observed that she "keeps the great spirit of hard-core Nashville alive." "Till I Can Make It On My Own" (1976), an undisguisedly self-referential song that Wynette wrote with Billy Sherrill and George Richey, became another of her number-one country hits as well as another of her signature songs. It was later recorded by many other artists, including Kenny Rogers and Dottie West, whose duet version became a hit in 1979.

In 1978 Wynette married George Richey, who is a country-music producer as well as a songwriter and arranger, and he became her manager. (She and Michael Tomlin, a real-estate executive, had married and divorced in 1976.) Later that year her autobiography, which she wrote with Joan Dew, was published. In a review of the book for *Rolling Stone* (September 6, 1979), Chet Flippo described it as being written in the style of *True Confessions* and observed that her account of her marriage to George Jones "makes words like *stormy* and *tempestuous* inadequate." Two or three months after her marriage to Richey, Wynette was badly beaten and nearly choked to death by a man who abducted her from a shopping-mall parking lot. The abductor was never caught. Also escaping detection by the police were the person or people who, during the previous two years, had broken into her home about fifteen times and once set a fire that destroyed one wing. The break-ins stopped soon after she married Richey. Meanwhile, health problems continued to plague her. Since the 1960s Wynette had undergone major surgery more than a dozen times, as a result of which she became addicted to painkillers and other prescription drugs. She overcame her dependence on them in around 1986, after treatment at the Betty Ford Center.

Wynette has identified her anxieties about her health as one reason for the failure of her career to progress in the decade that began in the late 1970s. She has also said that she "got content with her position in country music," and, as a result, "didn't go looking for material or songwriters." In the last six or seven years, with her physical health markedly improved since she underwent a fifteen-hour abdominal operation at the Mayo Clinic, she has maintained a concert schedule of up to 150 bookings annually. (She suffered temporary setbacks in 1994, when she nearly died from a massive systemic infection, and in 1995, when she had to undergo surgery on her vocal cords.) Her recent albums include *Honky Tonk Angels* (1993), which she recorded with Dolly Parton and Loretta Lynn; *Tears of Fire: The 25th Anniversary Collection* (1993), which showed, according to a reviewer for Q (February 1993), that Wynette "remains one of the definitive country artists because that cry has never left her voice and she still sings every word like she's coming to terms with the terrible heartbreak of everyday life"; and *Without Walls* (1994), in which she sang duets with, among others, Sting, Elton John, Lyle Lovett, Wynonna Judd, and Smokey Robinson.

In 1994, ending a nearly fifteen-year hiatus in their professional relationship, Wynette and George Jones recorded "Golden Ring" for Jones's album *Bradley Barn Sessions*. "It felt like we just stepped out one year and stepped back in the next and never quit," Wynette observed about that joint recording, as quoted by Dick McVey in *Performance* (June 2, 1995). "I seemed to know everything he was going to do vocally. . . . I know when he dips his chin that he's going to go for a lower note, and when he turns his head a certain way that he's going for a high note. . . . It was really a thrill." In 1995 Wynette and Jones worked together again to produce *One*, an album of duets, for MCA Records, which currently represents both singers. "We chose songs that parallel our lives, just like we always did," Wynette said during an interview with Larry Katz for *Entertainment* (August 13, 1995), in reference to such songs on *One* as "It's an Old Love Thing," "What Ever Happened to Us," "Just Look What We've Started Again," and "All I Have to Offer You Is Me." During the extended tour in the United States and Europe that they launched at the Fan Fair celebration in Nashville in mid-1995, Wynette and Jones sandwiched solo performances, with their own bands, between renditions of their signature duets and various songs from *One*. According to a joint profile of the singers by Patrick Carr for *Country Music* (July/August 1995), Wynette "experienced what amounts to a rebirth of her vocal powers" after giving up smoking a year or two ago.

In the April 14, 1973 issue of the *New Yorker*, a writer described Tammy Wynette's manner as affectionate, serene, secure, and dignified; more recently, Bob Millard wrote that she is warm, gracious, and "honest-to-a-fault" and exudes "girlish vulnerability." In the mid-1980s the five-foot three-inch Wynette discarded her trademark hairstyle—highly lacquered, long blonde curls or voluminous wigs—and adopted a shorter, more modern cut. She and George Richey live in Nashville, in a house that once belonged to the legendary country singer Hank Williams. She has four adult daughters (Gwendolyn, Jacquelyn, and Tina, from her marriage to Euple Byrd, and Tamala Georgette, from her marriage to George Jones), several stepchildren, and seven grandchildren. In 1991 she received the TNN/Music City News Living Legend Award. She has been honored sixteen times for her songwriting by BMI (Broadcast Music, Incorporated).

Selected Biographical References: Country Music p42+ Mr/Ap '88 pors, p42+ S '90 pors, p28+ Jl/Ag '95 pors; Parade p4+ Ap 9 '95 pors; People 29:69+ S 29 '86 por, 34:93+ D 10 '90 pors, 44:54+O 2 '95 pors; Washington Post B p1+ O 26 '77 por; Wynette, Tammy and Joan Dew. Stand By Your Man (1979)

Agence France-Presse

Zhirinovsky, Vladimir
(zhee-ri-NOF-skee, VLAD-i-meer)

Apr. 25, 1946- Russian politician; lawyer. Address: c/o Liberal Democratic Party of Russia, Rybnikov per. 1, 103045 Moscow, Russia

Vladimir Volfovich Zhirinovsky emerged from obscurity in June 1991, when he came in third in Russia's first free presidential election, winning nearly 8 percent of the popular vote. The victor, Boris Yeltsin, then the president of the Supreme Soviet (a position comparable to speaker of parliament), and the runner-up, Nikolai I. Ryzhkov, then the Soviet prime minister, among others, were shocked by the results. Zhirinovsky, a lawyer known primarily for his penchant for making extravagant campaign promises and flamboyant threats, had come a long way in the two months since his Liberal Democratic Party (LDP) became the first political group in Soviet history to win official recognition from the ruling Communist Party. Immediately following his victory, he began campaigning for the next election. Pledging to halve the price of vodka, take back Alaska and Finland, blow radioactive waste over the Baltic republics, summarily execute criminals, and expand the territory of Russia to the borders of the former Soviet empire, Zhirinovsky and the LDP captured nearly a quarter of the vote—taking first place—in the parliamentary election of December 1993.

Formerly dismissed by many observers as, variously, a clown, a buffoon, a madman, and a demagogue, Zhirinovsky had suddenly become someone to reckon with, and journalists, rival politicians, and intellectuals scrambled to assess the threat he may pose in the 1996 presidential election. Some downplay Zhirinovsky's stunning 1993 victory as merely the result of a protest vote, an anti-Communist backlash by a downtrodden people faced with surges in crime, unemployment, and inflation, and conclude either that he will self-destruct by virtue of his own outlandish antics—which include brawling with colleagues during sessions of parliament, insulting his foreign hosts while abroad, and allowing himself to be photographed in the nude in bathhouses—or that he will simply fade away. Others reject such predictions as the product of wishful thinking. These observers see disturbing parallels between Weimar Germany, which gave rise to Adolf Hitler, and the society of post-Soviet Russia. Pointing to Russians' widespread despair and uncertainty, which has followed in the wake of drastic economic reforms, they believe Zhirinovsky is a symptom of *bespredel*, an anything-goes climate characterized by rising crime, drug use, child prostitution, general lawlessness, and fear. The likelihood of a Zhirinovsky dictatorship in 1996, some people argue, is increased by the continuing distress of the average Russian.

Portraying himself as one of the people, who, according to his rhetoric, have been "deceived" by false promises and "humiliated" by the loss of Russia's empire status, Zhirinovsky revels in his own past failures at every opportunity. "Life itself forced me to suffer from the very day, the moment, the instant of my birth," Zhirinovsky wrote in his campaign autobiography, *Poslednii brosok na iug* (The Last Dash to the South, 1993). Vladimir Volfovich Zhirinovsky, who likes to point out that his first name is derived from a Russian phrase (*vladet' mirom*) meaning "possessor (or ruler) of the world," was born on April 25, 1946 in Alma-Ata (now Almaty), Kazakhstan, then one of the Soviet republics, in Central Asia. He has frequently complained that the Russians who lived in non-Russian national republics have long been discriminated against in housing, education, and employment, but that situation has developed only recently, after the disintegration of the Soviet Union. Such inequities among nationalities during Zhirinovsky's youth were more often in favor of Russians. Nonetheless, he felt painfully isolated, as he made abundantly clear throughout his autobiography. He grew up in a single room of a communal dwelling with five older half-siblings (three girls and two boys), his mother's children from a previous marriage. Lacking even a bed to call his own, he slept on the couch on Sundays, the one day of the week he spent at home. During the rest of the week, he lived in a twenty-four-hour nursery and, later, day-care center. According to his own testimony in his memoir, he felt an acute sense of rivalry—for his mother's affections and for food—with his stepfather, who was fifteen years younger than his mother.

Given the anti-Semitism of many of Zhirinovsky's followers and the tone of some of his own statements, Zhirinovsky's ethnicity—in particular, the question of whether his biological father was

Jewish—has been the subject of heated debate. The confusion arose at least partly because he was in the habit of saying only that his mother was Russian and that his father was a lawyer. His mother, Aleksandra Pavlovna (Makarova) Zhirinovskaya, a cleaning woman in the cafeteria of a veterinary science institute, was almost certainly Russian; Zhirinovsky's statements and her marriage registration concur on this issue, although he has sometimes described her as Ukrainian in interviews, according to Vladimir Kartsev, the author of *!Zhirinovsky! An Insider's Account of Yeltsin's Chief Rival & "Bespredel"—the New Russian Roulette* (1995). On the other hand, the nationality of Zhirinovsky's father, who worked as a legal consultant for the administration of the Turkestan-Siberian Railroad and died in an auto accident a few months after Zhirinovsky's birth, seems to have been deliberately obfuscated.

In his autobiography, Zhirinovsky claimed that his father's name was Volf (from Wolf, a typical German and/or Jewish name) Andreyevich Zhirinovsky. But the Associated Press reported, as quoted in the *Chicago Tribune* (April 4, 1994), that public records found in Almaty showed that Zhirinovsky was the surname of his mother's first husband, Andrei Vasilyevich, who died of tuberculosis in August 1944, twenty months before Zhirinovsky was born. The archival records, which were photographed by CNN, according to Leyla Boulton of the *Financial Times* (April 5, 1994), included the marriage registration of Aleksandra Pavlovna to Volf Isaakovich Eidelshtein (variously spelled as Eidelstein, Edelshtein, and Edelstein), whose nationality was listed as Jewish. The marriage took place four months before Zhirinovsky's birth. Zhirinovsky's birth certificate said only that his father's name was Volf and that no documents for the father were available.

According to Kartsev, the nationality of a child of parents of differing nationalities in the former Soviet Union was determined by the child, who could claim either one upon reaching the age of majority. Zhirinovsky's birth registration, according to the AP, shows his last name, Eidelshtein, crossed out and, in different handwriting, replaced by Zhirinovsky; the change was dated 1964, the year in which he turned eighteen and applied to the exclusive Institute of Oriental Languages (later renamed the Moscow University Institute of Asian and African Studies), which restricted Jewish enrollment. Zhirinovsky has routinely dismissed evidence of his Jewish heritage as a nothing more than a KGB fabrication. He "was Russian . . . ," he told Wendy Sloane of the *Christian Science Monitor* (December 24, 1993). "I've passed thousands of blood tests. If you have specialists that would be able to find at least 5 percent Jewish blood in me, I would be proud. But there is none."

Previously a below-average student, Zhirinovsky earned A's at the Institute of Oriental Languages, where he specialized in Turkish, hoping to become a diplomat upon graduation. In college he served as secretary of the class trade union and Komsomol organizations. Zhirinovsky's political activities began as early as April 1967, when he wrote to the Central Committee of the Communist Party, suggesting reforms in industry, agriculture, and education. Then, in December 1967, a speech on democracy that he made at a student debate led authorities to brand him as "politically unreliable," and he was denied permission to go on an imminent trip to Turkey.

Zhirinovsky was not allowed to visit that country until April 1969, when he began what was to have been an eight-month internship as an interpreter and translator at Iskenderun Iron and Steel Joint Soviet-Turkish Works, under the auspices of the State Committee for Foreign Economic Affairs. But he was expelled from Turkey before he was able to complete what Vladimir Solovyov and Elena Klepikova, the coauthors of *Zhirinovsky: Russian Fascism and the Making of a Dictator* (1995), have argued may have been an undercover assignment to spy on a nearby American military base for the KGB. Zhirinovsky has insisted that his mistake had been to distribute Soviet pins or badges to Turkish youths, but his biographers contended that he was actually "just getting his feet wet as a spy" and got caught while trying to "satisfy his supervisors' curiosity about the base. . . . He read the situation inaccurately, however," they concluded, "overestimated his opportunities, exceeded his authority, violated instructions, and displayed unnecessary improvisation and zeal." On the other hand, some of Zhirinovsky's former classmates told Lee Hockstader, in interviews for the *Washington Post* (March 6, 1994), that although the KGB may have kept a watchful eye on their activities, they were not agents of the KGB. "I had absolutely no contacts [with the KGB]," Zhirinovsky insisted in his interview with Wendy Sloane. "I wish I had had them."

Despite the Turkish fiasco, Zhirinovsky was allowed to return to the Institute of Oriental Languages and complete his studies, but his career prospects were severely curtailed by his newly acquired status as a "nontraveler," or one who is not allowed abroad. His blunder also precluded acceptance by the Communist Party, further hampering his career. Although he graduated from college with the Red Diploma of excellence in 1970, he was not given a job, as were his fellow alumni, but was instead drafted into the army. He served as an officer in the Transcaucasian Military District from 1970 to 1972, fulfilling an earlier career ambition inspired by his brothers. His marriage in 1971 to a Muscovite, Galina Aleksandrovna Lebedeva, enabled him to live in Moscow after his discharge as a reserve captain. In 1973 Zhirinovsky moved with his wife and infant son, Igor, to Tyoply Stan, a district on the outskirts of the capital city.

From 1972 to 1974 Zhirinovsky performed research as a foreign liaison with the Soviet Peace Committee, which was affiliated with the KGB, according to Solovyov and Klepikova. Still unable to travel, he had to give up the post, which required frequent meetings with foreigners. His next job, as an assistant in the dean's office at the Trade Union Movement Academy, involved advising foreign students. Meanwhile, since 1972 he had been studying law at night at Moscow University, which in 1975 awarded him a law degree. That year he obtained a position with Inyurkollegiya, a state legal agency also known as the International Bar Association, where he was responsible for defending the rights of Soviet citizens who inherited property in other countries. "He was not much of a lawyer," a former associate recalled, as quoted by Kevin Fedarko of *Time* (July 11, 1994). "He disliked responsibilities and shirked any job that might entail them, but he loved to be in the thick of things and loved making public speeches." Other colleagues remembered him as "professionally competent, energetic, and well organized," according to Hockstader.

In 1981 Zhirinovsky asked for a recommendation from his superiors, including Yevgeni Kulichev, his immediate supervisor, for membership in the Communist Party organization at Inyurkollegiya and was rebuffed. "He was very emotional and gratuitously, not constructively, critical," Kulichev explained to Hockstader. "His ideas were disorganized, and he insisted fiercely on them. His character, the remarks he made, the way he related to people—these did not fit the code of Communist behavior." The rejection meant that Zhirinovsky would not be able to obtain a promotion. "He was terribly offended," Kulichev recalled to Kevin Fedarko. "He started writing signed complaints and anonymous denunciations, and he leveled all sorts of accusations at us." Zhirinovsky denied having written more than one letter of complaint, and he has maintained that he did not try to join the Communist Party. (In his campaign speeches he has made much of his status as one of the few Russian politicians who are untainted by a background in the Communist Party.)

Zhirinovsky lost his job at Inyurkollegiya in 1983, after it was alleged that he had received some vacation vouchers from one of his clients, thereby violating a strict rule against accepting improper gifts. Although he returned the vouchers unused, according to Solovyov and Klepikova, his superiors took advantage of the opportunity to let him go. "We offered him the chance to quit quietly, so he did," Kulichev told Fedarko. That version more or less dovetails with Zhirinovsky's memory of the law firm. "When I saw all options were exhausted and there was a pack of wolves against me, what could I do about it?" he asked Hockstader rhetorically. "Such was the regime, the regime that has now collapsed."

Later in 1983 Zhirinovsky landed a job as a legal consultant to Mir Publishing House, in Moscow, where he worked until 1990. Hired to handle copyright issues, he soon demonstrated abilities that led to his transfer to a job as an advocate for employee benefits. Among those he secured were free lunches and free public transportation for commuting. Although he was still not a member of the Communist Party, Zhirinovsky attended its meetings at Mir, where most decisions affecting the company were made, but he was asked to leave before every closed session that was restricted to party members. In 1985 Vladimir Kartsev, who was then the director of Mir, was asked to fire Zhirinovsky by the ideology chief of the local Communist Party branch, who found the lawyer's anti-Communist views irritating, but Kartsev refused, arguing that it was illegal to terminate someone's employment for political reasons.

In 1987 Zhirinovsky tried to run for the district legislature from his base at Mir, but the rules were hastily rewritten to exclude him from the campaign. When he ran for membership in the employees' council in 1988, Kartsev opposed his candidacy on the grounds that Zhirinovsky was "unreasonable and unpredictable and would create more problems than he solved," as Kartsev explained to Hockstader. In 1990 Zhirinovsky ran for director of the publishing house in an attempt to succeed Kartsev, who had taken a job in publishing at the United Nations in New York City. He won only 5 percent of the votes. His only success in any election during that period was in the domestic sphere: he was elected chairman of his building cooperative, as a result of which he was able to move into a better home, in the Sokolniki district of Moscow, eighteen months later.

In the meantime, since 1988 Zhirinovsky had been honing his oratorical skills at political rallies of all stripes, including those sponsored by Pamyat, an ultranationalist, anti-Semitic group, and at meetings of Shalom, a Jewish anti-Zionist organization that discouraged Jews from emigrating. "They were pleased and invited me once more," he told Wendy Sloane, referring to Shalom. "Then I left and forgot about it, because it all took place five years ago." In 1988 he attended the first meeting of Democratic Union, where he met Vladimir Bogachev, a former dissident and political prisoner, who in 1989 invited Zhirinovsky to join his newly created Liberal Democratic Party of the Soviet Union.

On March 16, 1990 the monopoly of the Communist Party was legally ended by the repeal of Article Six of the Constitution of the Soviet Union. Later that month Zhirinovsky was elected chairman of the LDP, and Bogachev was made his deputy. ("I wish I had had an abortion, because I was the one who gave birth to Zhirinovsky," Bogachev later told Kevin Fedarko.) In October 1990 the party tried to expel Zhirinovsky because of his extremist views, but he instead arranged for Bogachev's expulsion. On April 12, 1991, following the establishment of the Russian Federation, Zhirinovsky registered his own party, adopting the LDP's name. The registration of the LDP itself has been the source of some speculation about Zhirinovsky's possible links to the KGB, because he was suddenly allowed to register despite weeks of experiencing difficulty in obtaining the names of the requisite five thousand members. Many of the names he submitted during multiple attempts to register the LDP belonged to children or deceased individuals, which he has acknowledged, blaming the presence of false identities on sabotage attempts. "I'm sure he was created by the KGB, but then he went out of control," Mikhail Lubimov, a retired KGB officer, told Hockstader. "The whole organization was created by the Communist Party in order to show, 'All right, we have a new democracy now and many parties and so on.' Then the situation changed and Zhirinovsky came out on top. In politics, as in life, there is an exchange of places all the time. The leaders become the servants and vice versa."

The campaign for Russia's first free presidential election lasted three weeks. Zhirinovsky's promises of cheap vodka and husbands for all single women were apparently extremely appealing to a relatively impoverished electorate, for on June 12 he won 6.2 million votes, or 7.8 percent of those cast, coming in third behind Boris Yeltsin and Nikolai Ryzhkov. Immediately after his unexpectedly strong showing, Zhirinovsky began campaigning for the next election, not knowing when it would occur. Traveling relentlessly, he met with right-wing political activists in Europe and with Saddam Hussein in Iraq. He founded two newspapers, whose names in English are *Zhirinovsky's Falcon* and *Zhirinovsky's Truth*, and opened a store featuring rock-'n'-roll paraphernalia to attract young converts. The LDP adopted the slogan "Through a pluralism of opinions to the superiority of the law."

Zhirinovsky proved to be undeniably charismatic to people who had never before experienced modern political oratory. "When I first heard him speak on the television, it was a magnetizing effect," Vyacheslav Shishelin, a foreign-policy expert who became Zhirinovsky's press secretary, told Sloane. "He has the gift to talk on two levels—he says the minimum but you understand the maximum. Maybe an hour later, or a day later, you understand the whole message." Although Zhirinovsky had been campaigning for president, he smoothly managed the transition to parliamentary candidate in September 1993, when Yeltsin announced the suspension of the Congress of People's Deputies and the Supreme Soviet and called for new legislative elections and a constitutional referendum in December 1993. On December 13 the constitution was approved by 58.4 percent of the voters, and although Yegor Gaidar's Russia's Choice party won a plurality of seats, Zhirinovsky and the LDP won the largest share in the party preference poll, with 22.8 percent of the vote. The LDP assumed sixty-four seats in the 450-member State Duma, or lower house of parliament, in which Zhirinovsky represents Shchelkovo, a rural industrial town twenty-five miles northeast of Moscow.

Aware that the new constitution, which granted him absolute powers, passed only with Zhirinovsky's support, Yeltsin has moved decidedly rightward in appeasement. For example, he has dropped reformers from his administration, including Gaidar, who told Michael Specter of the *New York Times Magazine* (June 19, 1994) that "Zhirinovsky must be seen as the symbol of something very real, very powerful." As reported in *World Press Review* (July 1994), Otto Latsis, an *Izvestia* commentator, described Zhirinovsky's constituents as primarily aggressive young businessmen who reminded Latsis of the Nazi storm troopers. Joseph Kipp characterized Zhirinovsky's supporters in an article for *Foreign Affairs* (May/June 1994) as "relatively well-educated young males from larger cities, older, less-educated males from smaller cities, disgruntled rural residents, and numerous members of the Russian armed forces."

On April 4, 1994 the 343 delegates to the Fifth Congress of the LDP voted unanimously to give Zhirinovsky dictatorial powers over party affairs for ten years; they also decided not to meet again until 1997. Zhirinovsky continued campaigning, in the process creating a steady stream of both favorable and unfavorable publicity. He has proved to be a master of the political spin, frequently contradicting himself. "If I behave like the good-natured individual I really am, I won't get votes," he told editors of *Time* (July 11, 1994). "It's war out there, and I'm out to win."

During a November 1994 tour of the United States, which included stops in San Francisco and New York City, Zhirinovsky denied that he was an anti-Semite or a fascist, refrained from his usual fist-waving histrionics, and appeared to be a model of decorum. But in an interview with *Time* editors (November 21, 1994), he railed against Jewish influence in the media—in Russia and in the West—and talked of American conspiracies to destroy Russia. He explained his extremism to *Time* editors as being the result of *bespredel*: "It's the sorry state of affairs in this country that forces me to take so tough a stand to avert something even worse. If there were a healthy economy and security for the people, I would lose all the votes I have."

By early 1995 Zhirinovsky-endorsed products had come to include everything from pens and notepads to beer, vodka, cognac, and hard-to-get matchboxes featuring his image and bearing the slogan "We need a great Russia." As his cult of personality flourished—at least within his own party—comparisons to Hitler proliferated. Zhirinovsky rejected the analogy in an interview with Malcolm Gray of *Maclean's* (March 30, 1992), saying, "I much prefer to be compared to Bismarck, the nineteenth-century statesman who united Germany." Some analysts find the Zhirinovsky-as-Hitler analogy irrelevant, contending that any number of would-be dictators are waiting in the wings to use the platform he has created in the event that he should be assassinated.

Zhirinovsky has pledged to shrink the burgeoning ranks of the Russian mob, but they may get to him first. A Russian mafia leader in St. Petersburg was quoted in the London *Sunday Times* (April 7, 1994) as saying, "If he came to power and started interfering in our business, we would make one phone call to Moscow. That's all. And then no more Zhirinovsky." Recognizing the danger, Zhirinovsky travels with his own militia, an elite group of young, armed, uniformed men known as Zhirinovsky's Falcons, and he has at least one body double.

Although Vladimir Zhirinovsky is "an exemplary husband and father," according to Solovyov and Klepikova, he has admitted to having reserved all of his love for his mother. "Probably this son's love for his mother," he wrote in his memoir, "absorbed the entire potential for love, including the potential of a boy's love for a girl. . . . And consequently, for the rest of my whole life, I never met the one beloved woman I so needed. . . . I never had the feeling that I really, truly love my wife; there were normal personal relations, but not self-oblivion in love. Therefore I was able to conserve my efforts for politics." (He was once rumored to have had a second wife named Ludmila Nikolayevna, but reporters have not been able to confirm her existence.) Solovyov and Klepikova speculated that Zhirinovsky, who also has been publicly indifferent to his son, Igor, "may be demonstrating his dislike of his family as a tactical move, trying to keep them safe from attack if he enters the dangerous struggle for the greatest power in Russia."

There have been well-publicized accounts of Zhirinovsky's patronage of striptease clubs and his voyeuristic enjoyment of watching others engage in orgies and ménages-à-trois, which he discussed at length in an interview with Jennifer Gould for *Playboy* (March 1995). Such talk may be intended to quell rumors of homosexuality. The mostly male membership—and exclusively male leadership—of the LDP has led some detractors to label the party Men of Russia, an allusion to its contrast with a parliamentary bloc called Women of Russia. His wife, Galina, a scientist, who calls her husband Voitek, after the hero of a 1960s Soviet romantic melodrama that was showing in local movie theatres when they met, told Kevin Fedarko, "He's complicated, but he's predictable." A geography buff and amateur cartographer of sorts, Zhirinovsky takes pride in redrawing the borders of European countries while explaining his geopolitical plans. He also enjoys volleyball and marksmanship.

Selected Biographical References: Christian Sci Mon p2+ D 23-24 '93 pors; N Y Times A p1+ D 14 '93 por; N Y Times Mag p26+ Je 19 '94 pors; Playboy p47+ Mr '95 pors; Time 144:38+ Jl 11 '94 pors; Washington Post A p1+ Mr 6 '94 pors; Fenomen Zhirinovskogo (1994); Frazer, Graham and George Lancelle. Absolute Zhirinovsky: A Transparent View of the Distinguished Russian Statesman (1994); International Who's Who, 1994-95; Kartsev, Vladimir, with Todd Bludeau. !Zhirinovsky! An Insider's Account of Yeltsin's Chief Rival & "Bespredel"—the New Russian Roulette (1995); McFaul, Michael. Understanding Russia's 1993 Parliamentary Elections: Implications for U.S. Foreign Policy (1994); Solovyov, Vladimir and Elena Klepikova. Zhirinovsky: Russian Fascism and the Making of a Dictator (1995); Zhirinovsky, Vladimir. Poslednii brosok na iug (1993)

OBITUARIES

ABBOTT, GEORGE (FRANCIS) June 25, 1889–Jan. 31, 1995 Theatrical producer; director; playwright; play "doctor"; actor; a towering personage on Broadway for over half a century; during his long prime, was responsible for an average of two productions a season, many cowritten by him; with his artistic judgment and "Abbott touch," could transform even a faulty script into makings of a box-office and critical success; was a meticulous anti-Method director who made his players, in his words, "say their final syllables"; on that stern basis, achieved seamless continuums of movement, dialogue or song, and other elements of stagecraft that were fast-paced and fun in spirit; as actor, was cast in twelve roles on Broadway over approximately a score of years, beginning in 1913; became full-fledged director as well as cowriter with *The Fall Guy* (1925); had first big hit with *Broadway* (1926), a production he first joined as "doctor"; in following years solidified his reputation for rescuing plays found ailing during pre-Broadway tryouts; after coproducing as well as directing and cowriting such plays as *Twentieth Century* (1932), began doing his own solo producing; followed up his first farce, *Three Men on a Horse* (1935), with his first major musical, *On Your Toes* (1936), with *Brother Rat* (1936), and with *Room Service* (1937); directed and wrote book for musical *The Boys from Syracuse* (1938); directed, among other musicals, *Pal Joey* (1940), *Best Foot Forward* (1941), *On the Town* (1944), *High Button Shoes* (1947), *Where's Charley?* (1948), *Call Me Madam* (1950), and *Once Upon a Mattress* (1959); won Tony awards for his direction of musicals *The Pajama Game* (1954), *Damn Yankees* (1955), and *A Funny Thing Happened on the Way to the Forum* (1962); shared Pulitzer Prize for musical *Fiorello!* (1959); later received special Tony for career achievement; during stints in Hollywood between 1928 and 1958, worked on eleven motion pictures, including, as director, film versions of his Broadway productions *Too Many Girls*, *The Pajama Game*, and *Damn Yankees* and, as writer, screen adaptation of *Where's Charley?*; after more than a score of years in retirement, returned to Broadway in 1994 at age 105 to assist in revival of *Damn Yankees*; wrote autobiography, *Mister Abbott* (1963); died at his home in Miami Beach, Florida. See *Current Biography* (October) 1965.

Obituary *N Y Times* B p10 F 2 '95

ARNON, DANIEL I(SRAEL) Nov. 14, 1910–Dec. 20, 1994 Plant physiologist; with his colleagues at University of California at Berkeley, was first to reproduce process of photosynthesis outside a living cell; thus helped, in his words, to bring "nearer the day when man, after mastering the secrets of the process in green cells, will reduce his age-long dependence on crop plants for food and energy by devising his own photosynthetic reactions driven directly by the energy of the sun"; joined Berkeley faculty as instructor in truck crops in 1936; became associate professor of plant nutrition six years later; during his early years at Berkeley, did research in the micronutrients, including such minerals as zinc and manganese, that are essential to plant growth; as army major during and immediately following World War II, applied his expertise to problem of feeding troops in western Pacific; stationed on barren Ascension Island, grew crops in gravel and water enriched with nutrient chemicals; back in Berkeley, as associate and then full professor of plant physiology, began deciphering complex chemistry of photosynthesis; concentrated on study of chloroplasts, extracted from spinach; discovered that photolysis, first step in extracellular photosynthesis, can be accomplished by "photosynthetic phosphorylation" (in which inorganic phosphate is used to form adenosine triphosphate, or ATP, the "energy messenger") in absence of carbon dioxide; announced his team's success in achieving extracellular photosynthesis in 1954; for "his fundamental research into the mechanism of green plant utilization of light to produce chemical energy and oxygen and for contributions to our understanding of plant nutrition," was awarded National Medal of Science in 1973; retired as professor at University of California in 1978; died in Berkeley. See *Current Biography* (June) 1955.

Obituary *N Y Times* A p30 D 23 '94

ASPIN, LES(LIE, JR.) July 21, 1938–May 21, 1995 Democratic U.S. representative from Wisconsin (1971–93); secretary of defense from beginning of administration of President Bill Clinton, in January 1993, until December of that year; was an unlikely Pentagon leader, approaching hot decisions with a scholar's ruminative manner and eye for ambiguities and contradictions; over course of his career, modified his original position as a dovish liberal; while pursuing doctorate in economics in early 1960s, began his political apprenticeship as an aide to Wisconsin senator William Proxmire; between 1966 and 1968 worked as an economist in systems analysis on staff of secretary of defense Robert S. McNamara; subsequently taught economics briefly at Marquette University; won first election to Congress on an anti-Vietnam War platform; in his early years in Congress, gained national attention as a muckraking gadfly, exposing malfeasance and misfeasance, including fraud, mismanagement, and waste, in federal agencies and departments, especially Department of Defense; in time, became highly respected Congressional authority on Pentagon policy, recognized to be not against military but for efficient defense; in 1985 became chairman of powerful House Armed Services Committee; dismayed his party's liberal wing by favoring development of MX missile and defending U.S. support of insurgent army of anticommunist Contras in Nicaragua; to a large extent approved Reagan administration's beefing up of military; argued vociferously, and successfully, for House approval of Bush administration's use of military force against Iraq in 1991; became secretary of defense in time of changing national and international commitments; domestically, was caught between Clinton administration's attempt to liberalize Pentagon's policy regarding homosexuality and resistance of military to that attempt; internationally, was at odds with preference of General Colin L. Powell, then chairman of the Joint Chiefs of Staff, for an all-out, decisive military strategy; rather, favored selective deployment of troops in support of U.S. diplomacy; lost face when his failure to back up small U.S. military presence in Somalia with requested armored vehicles was widely viewed as contributing to situation in which eighteen American soldiers were killed in firefight; on the other hand, fought reduction in military budget proposed by

Office of Management and Budget; died in Washington, D.C. See *Current Biography* (February) 1986.

Obituary *N Y Times* A p1+ My 22 '95

BALLANTINE, IAN (KEITH) Feb. 15, 1916–Mar. 9, 1995 Publisher; with his wife, Betty, was a leader in development of paperback publishing in U.S., thus contributing to mass affordability and accessibility of books; in 1939 organized Penguin U.S.A., American importing branch of Penguin Books, Ltd., British publisher of low-cost paperbound reprints; managed Penguin U.S.A. until 1945, when he and his wife established Bantam Books, Inc., a new publisher of paperback reprints, competitor to Pocket Books in the American market; after seven years as president and director of Bantam Books, left that company in 1952 to found Ballantine Books, where he and his wife concentrated on mass publishing and marketing of paperback originals; made Ballantine Books most distinctive in discovering and introducing to mass market a generation of science fiction, fantasy, western, and mystery novelists; after selling Ballantine Books to Random House in 1974, worked with selected authors at Bantam Books; still jointly with wife, later edited and published under their imprint Rufus Publications (named for Betty Ballantine's dog) illustrated art and fantasy books such as Brian Froud's *Faeries* and James Gurney's *Dinotopia*; died at his home in Bearsville, New York. See *Current Biography* (May) 1954.

Obituary *N Y Times* B p7 Mr 10 '95

BARTON, ROBERT B(ROWN) M(ORISON) Aug. 19, 1903–Feb. 14, 1995 Business executive; lawyer; son-in-law of George S. Parker, founder of Parker Brothers, leading manufacturer of parlor board games (in addition to kindergarten supplies), now owned by Hasbro; after practicing law with his father in Baltimore, joined his father-in-law's then-struggling company in Salem, Massachusetts as assistant treasurer in 1932; succeeded Parker as president in 1933; began Parker Brothers' rise to world dominance in its field with acquisition in 1935 of rights to Monopoly, then a new game that offered Depression-weary players chance to gain imaginary fortunes in real estate; later presided over acquisition of rights to Rook, Risk, Clue, Sorry, Careers, Pit, Flinch, and Mille Bornes, among other games; was personally involved in originating or developing some games, most notably Keyword, a crossword invention introduced in 1953 in answer to a rival firm's Scrabble; retired as president after Parker Brothers was sold to General Mills in 1958; died at his home in Marblehead, Massachusetts. See *Current Biography* (April) 1959.

Obituary *N Y Times* D p15 F 21 '95

BENNETT, JOHN C(OLEMAN) July 22, 1902–Apr. 27, 1995 Clergyman; liberal theologian; applying Christian ethics to contemporary political and social issues, was in advance guard of champions of feminism, ecumenism, civil and economic rights for minorities, and coexistence with Communism; at beginning of World War II, spoke out against American isolationism; a generation later, with Rabbi Abraham Heschel, cofounded Clergy and Laity Concerned about the Vietnam War; with Reinhold Niebuhr, cofounded periodical *Christianity and Crisis*; taught Christian theology at Auburn Theological Seminary from 1930 to 1938, when he became professor at Pacific School of Religion; in 1939 was ordained a Congregational minister; was a leader in merging of Congregational, Evangelical, and Reformed denominations into United Church of Christ, effective 1957; in 1943 joined faculty of interdenominational Union Theological Seminary in New York City, where he became dean of faculty in 1955; during presidential election campaign of 1960, defended candidate John F. Kennedy against Protestant groups who claimed that a Roman Catholic would bring papal influence into the White House; became president of Union Theological Seminary in 1963; as president, brought seminary into extraordinary contractual arrangement with Fordham University, under terms of which Union and the Roman Catholic institution began to pool professors, library resources, and credits in graduate religious studies; was active in World Council of Churches and National Council of Churches from inception of those organizations; wrote some dozen books, including *Christian Ethics and Social Policy* (1946), *Christianity and Communism* (1948), and *Foreign Policy in Christian Perspective* (1966); in the interest of world peace, advocated a less rigid and confrontational attitude toward Communist world; retired as president of Union Theological Seminary in 1970; died in Claremont, California. See *Current Biography* (January) 1961.

Obituary *N Y Times* B p7 My 2 '95

BERNAYS, EDWARD L. Nov. 22, 1891–Mar. 9, 1995 Vienna-born public relations counselor; the preeminent pioneer in his field, which he helped elevate from its once lowly status of mere press agentry; applied principles of social science to engineering of public opinion and public consent; developed use of surveys and polls as well as celebrity endorsements; was consciously influenced by the thought of Sigmund Freud, his uncle; in words of the cultural historian Ann Douglas, orchestrated "the commercialization of a culture"; after working as New York theatrical publicist (1913–17) and U.S. World War I propagandist, opened office in Manhattan in 1919 with Doris E. Fleischman, his future wife and his partner for more than fifty years; as public relations counselor, educated his clients in making news by taking newsworthy actions; first gained national recognition with his promotion in 1929 of Light's Golden Jubilee, celebrating fiftieth anniversary of Edison's invention of electric light; over course of his career, had major clients in fields of government (including every president from Coolidge to Eisenhower), auto manufacturing (General Motors), banking, construction, food, entertainment, radio and television (CBS and NBC), real estate, oil, public utilities, publishing, household products (Proctor and Gamble), transportation, education, race relations (NAACP), and tobacco (American Tobacco Company); in promoting consumption of Lucky Strike cigarettes, made women's smoking in public more acceptable by sponsoring demonstrations in which groups of chic debutantes gathered to light up what were called "torches of freedom"; years later campaigned against tobacco use; wrote a number of books, including *The Engineering of Consent* (1955), the volume of memoirs *Biography of an Idea* (1965), and *The Later Years: Public Relations Insights 1956–1986* (1986), edited by Paul Swift; died at his home in Cambridge, Massachusetts, where he had lived and worked since 1962. See *Current Biography* (September) 1960.

Obituary *N Y Times* B p7 Mr 10 '95

BESTOR, ARTHUR (EUGENE) Sept. 20, 1908–Dec. 13, 1994 Historian; constitutional scholar; professor emeritus of history at University of Washington, where he taught from 1962 until 1976; had previously taught at University of Illinois, among several other universities; at height of his career, was widely known and consulted as expert in constitutional history, especially as it applies to separation of federal powers in such areas as war and peace, impeachment process, and conduct of foreign affairs, including treaty making; earlier had concentrated on history in U.S. of intentional communities, or what he called communitarian societies, going back to sectarian and Owenite phases of communitarian socialism in period from seventeenth century to early nineteenth and Oneida community of Christian communists in mid-nineteenth century; later studied hippie and other alternative communities of 1960s and 1970s; was vociferous critic of American public education; decried "frills" and emphasis on "life adjustment" that he viewed as retardants to educational progress of school children; crusaded against dominant role played by "educationists" in determining public-school curricula and certifying teachers on basis of ability to pass tests on pedagogical method rather than competence in their subjects; wrote *Backwoods Utopias* (1950) and *Educational Wastelands* (1953), among other books; died at his home in Seattle. See *Current Biography* (September) 1958.

Obituary *N Y Times* p24 D 17 '94

BLACKWELL, (SAMUEL) EARL, JR. May 3, 1913–Mar. 1, 1995 Business executive; philanthropist; socialite; celebrity chronicler and promoter; born to Southern gentry, gravitated to famous people from childhood; initially aspiring to acting, landed bit parts in some MGM motion pictures in mid-1930s; subsequently cowrote play *Aries Is Rising*, which flopped on Broadway in 1939; within same year, founded (with a partner, whom he ultimately bought out) Manhattan-based Celebrity Service, Inc., an information and research subscription service used by newspapers, radio and television stations, charitable and civic organizations, government agencies, manufacturers, hotels, stores, other businesses, and individual subscribers, including celebrities themselves; compiled and maintained dossiers on well-known people in all fields of endeavor, with the heaviest concentration in show business; later opened branches of the service in Hollywood, London, Rome, and Paris; several times a week issued to subscribers the *Celebrity Bulletin*; also issued weekly *Theatrical Calendar*, among other publications; with Cleveland Amory, coedited *Celebrity Register: An Irreverent Compendium of American Quotable Notables* (1963); sold Celebrity Service in 1985 but remained active in the business, with title of chairman, until his death; often used his jet-set connections in the cause of various charities, especially scholarship funds and other needs of underprivileged children and young people; sometimes coordinated high-society galas for charitable fund-raising; was a director of Broadway Foundation; died in New York City. See *Current Biography* (November) 1960.

Obituary *N Y Times* p26 Mr 4 '95

BOLT, ROBERT (OXTON) Aug. 15, 1924–Feb. 20, 1995 British playwright; screenwriter; best known for *A Man for All Seasons*, the play and screenplay in which he brilliantly dramatized the crisis of conscience of Sir Thomas More, Lord Chancellor of England under King Henry VIII, who, faced with a conflict of allegiances when Henry broke with Roman Catholic Church, went to martyr's death in 1535 for his refusal to acknowledge king as supreme head of the Church of England; as scenarist, collaborated in making of director David Lean's great screen epics; while teaching English at Millfield School in Somerset in 1950s, wrote plays for broadcast by BBC, including early radio and television versions of *A Man for All Seasons* and radio drama *The Last of the Wine*, which he adapted into his first stage play, a stylized examination of society's helplessness in face of nuclear threat; made his West End (1958) and Broadway (1959) debuts with *Flowering Cherry*, about daydreaming salesman unable to deal with reality; became major figure in British theatre in 1961 with instant success of West End production of *A Man for All Seasons*, which went on to win five Tony Awards on Broadway (1962) and five Oscars for its screen version (1966), including one for Bolt's screenplay; for his scenario for David Lean's *Lawrence of Arabia* (1962), was nominated for Academy Award; received Oscar for screenplay for Lean's *Dr. Zhivago* (1964); also teamed with Lean in making of *Ryan's Daughter* (1970), which starred Sarah Miles, the second of his three wives; was partly paralyzed by severe stroke in 1978; returned to screen one final time with scenario for *The Mission* (1986); died (in presence of Sarah Miles, whom he had remarried) at his home near Petersfield, Hampshire. See *Current Biography* (July) 1963.

Obituary *N Y Times* B p10 F 23 '95

BONSAL, PHILIP WILSON May 22, 1903–June 28, 1995 U.S. career diplomat; as a son of roving correspondent and diplomat Stephen Bonsal, gained cosmopolitan education, including fluency in Spanish, while growing up; beginning in 1926, worked for International Telephone and Telegraph Co. in Cuba, Spain, and Chile for total of nine years; from 1935 to 1937 was telephone expert with Federal Communications Commission; joined Department of State in 1937; received first foreign-service appointment in 1938; over following two decades held such positions as deputy chief of State Department's Office of American Republics, director of its Office of Philippine and Southeastern Affairs, and various consular posts in Madrid, Havana, Paris, and The Hague; as ambassador to Colombia from 1955 to 1957, earned disfavor of dictatorial regime of President Gustavo Rojas Pinilla by his friendly contacts with opposition intellectuals; was ambassador to Bolivia from 1957 to 1959; was named ambassador to Cuba on January 21, 1959, twenty days after leftist revolutionary forces of Fidel Castro had overthrown government of Fulgencio Batista; arrived in Havana the following month with what President Castro described as a "friendly, cordial" attitude; was recalled in October 1960 because of Washington's objection to Castro regime's close economic ties to Soviet Union; opposed American economic sanctions against Castro's Cuba as extreme and counterproductive, more likely than not to drive Castro definitively into the Soviet sphere; in his book *Cuba, Castro, and the United States* (1971), criticized Castro but insisted that "the Cuba of the future must be primarily the creation of Cubans living in Cuba"; died in Washington, D.C. See *Current Biography* (June) 1959.

Obituary *N Y Times* p9 Jl 1 '95

BOTVINNIK, MIKHAIL (MOISSEYEVICH) Aug. 17, 1911–May 5, 1995 Russian grand master of chess; electrical engineer; combined imagination and science in his chess strategy and tactics; with psychological insight and resiliency, would deliberately move into seemingly vulnerable positions, whence to confound his opponents; won first of many Soviet chess championships in 1931; was world chess champion from 1948 to 1957, from 1958 to 1960, and again from 1961 until 1963; retired from international competition in 1965; developed methods of teaching his techniques, which he passed on to new generation of players, including Gary Kasparov and Anatoly Karpov; wrote many books of chess analysis and commentary, including those translated under titles *Championship Chess* (1951) and *One Hundred Selected Games* (1960); died in Moscow. See *Current Biography* (June) 1965.

Obituary *N Y Times* p57 My 7 '95

BRAZZI, ROSSANO Sept. 18, 1916–Dec. 24, 1994 Italian actor; in his middle years, became internationally popular for his romantic screen performances, widely stereotyped as those of a "Latin lover"; made motion-picture debut in *Processo e morte di Socrato* (The Trial and Death of Socrates) in 1939; over next three years, starred in twenty-four films, mostly swashbucklers; in change of pace, had male lead in *Noi vivi* (1942), screen version of Ayn Rand's novel *We the Living*, for which he won Italy's Silver Ribbon; after wartime hiatus in Italian motion-picture industry, returned to screen in derring-do roles without regaining his former popularity, at least in part because of gritty neorealism then newly in vogue in Italian cinema; meanwhile, accrued many stage credits, including leads in Italian productions of Shakespearean and other English-language plays; as husband in *Strange Interlude*, won Italian award for best stage actor for seventh time; was little noticed in nonromantic supporting role of Professor Bhaer in his first American motion picture, *Little Women* (1949); made strong impression as third male lead in *Three Coins in the Fountain* (1954) and stronger yet as impotent Italian count in *The Barefoot Contessa* (1954) and as married Venetian businessman who brings sweet romance, however adulterous and brief, into life of love-starved spinster American tourist in *Summertime* (1955); reached high point of his international popularity in starring role of French planter Émile de Becque in film version of musical *South Pacific* (1958), in which he lip-synched dubbed-in singing; starred as middle-aged Lothario in *A Certain Smile* (1958) and philandering husband in *Count Your Blessings* (1959); appeared in more than two hundred films, including *Furio* (1946), *Vulcano* (1950), *Dark Purpose* (1964), *Krakatoa East of Java* (1969), and *The Great Waltz* (1972); died in Rome. See *Current Biography* (May) 1961.

Obituary *N Y Times* A p15 D 27 '94

BURGER, WARREN E(ARL) Sep. 17, 1907–June 25, 1995 Fifteenth chief justice of U.S. (1969–86); went to U.S. Supreme Court with reputation for law-and-order conservatism; subsequently surprised liberals with many of his opinions, and left behind a court closer to center on social issues than it had been in decades; began career as lawyer in private practice in St. Paul, Minnesota; was assistant attorney general in charge of civil division of U.S. Department of Justice from 1953 to 1956; as judge on U.S. Court of Appeals for District of Columbia from 1956 to 1969, was known for toughness in dealing with criminal defendants; was named to Supreme Court by President Richard Nixon, whose 1968 campaign platform had included a pledge to appoint "strict constructionists" of Constitution and "practitioners of judicial restraint" to change activist course that court had been following under Chief Justice Earl Warren since 1953; spoke for Supreme Court in such decisions as those that validated busing as instrument in desegregation of public schools, provided legal definition of obscenity now in use, bolstered women's protections against sexual discrimination, and affirmed free speech and free press guarantees of First Amendment; participated in court's decision in favor of constitutional right to abortion on basis of privacy; wrote opinion that forced President Nixon to surrender White House tape recordings and papers relating to the Watergate scandal; concerned with reform of judicial and penal systems, was instrumental in founding of several institutions devoted to education and training of personnel in those systems; favored a streamlining of American judicial system based on models of swift justice in Norway, Sweden, Denmark, and the Netherlands, and a transformation of "prison warehouses" into "factories with fences"; after his retirement from Supreme Court, chaired Commission on Bicentennial of the United States Constitution; wrote book *It Is So Ordered* (1995), an account of fourteen landmark constitutional law cases; died in Washington, D.C. See *Current Biography* (November) 1969.

Obituary *N Y Times* A p1+ Je 26 '95

CABOT, THOMAS D(UDLEY) May 1, 1897–June 8, 1995 Business executive; industrialist; banker; philanthropist; scion of Boston Brahman family, the fortune of which was originally rooted in seagoing merchant trading; son of Godfrey Lowell Cabot, who founded a carbon black production company in 1882 and later diversified; joined Godfrey L. Cabot, Inc., controlling company of his father's various enterprises, in 1922; over following four decades, developed company into giant multinational Cabot Corporation, now worth one-and-a-half billion dollars; concurrently, was a director of Carbon Black Export, Inc., United Fruit Company, and several banks and insurance companies, and vice-president and governor of Natural Gas Products Association; served as president of United Fruit Company for a few months in 1948 and 1949; did so, according to his son Louis, in hope of turning company's negative reputation in Central America around, but "the bureaucracy was so entrenched, he was too impatient to wait years for his reforms to work their way through"; was named first director of Office of International Security Affairs in U.S. Department of State in December 1950; in that post, supervised expenditure of six billion dollars in military and nonmilitary foreign aid; after relinquishing active control of Cabot Corporation in 1960, retained various corporate directorships, attended to his many charities, and spent a large portion of his time yachting, skiing, and hiking with his family; died at his home in Weston, Massachusetts. See *Current Biography* (June) 1951.

Obituary *N Y Times* p48 Je 10 '95

CALLENDER, JOHN HANCOCK Jan. 18, 1908–Mar. 30, 1995 Architect; national authority on single family houses; expert on building materials and more efficient and cost-effective construction methods; early proponent of prefabricated housing; as housing researcher with John B. Pierce Foundation in New York City from 1931 to 1943, devised new methods of architectural construction and studied materials with view to lowering housing costs by technical means rather than by government subsidy or manipulation of interest rates; from 1943 to 1945 served with U.S. Army Engineers, Manhattan District; in private practice in New York City beginning in 1945, custom-designed houses for individual affluent clients; concurrently, was consultant to National Housing Agency on veterans' emergency housing during 1946 and 1947, to Quality House Institute (dedicated to persuading speculative and merchant builders of wisdom of employing architects and spending a little more money to make the difference between poor- and good-quality houses) from 1947 to 1953, and to federal Housing and Home Finance Agency on demountable defense housing in 1952; wrote book *Before You Buy a House* (1953); edited standard reference work *Time-Saver Standards for Architectural Design Data* (1947); oversaw subsequent editions of that book through 1982; died in Worcester, Pennsylvania. See *Current Biography* (September) 1955.

Obituary *N Y Times* p32 Ap 8 '95

CALLOWAY, CAB Dec. 25, 1907–Nov. 18, 1994 Orchestra leader; singer; one of last of the great leaders of the Big Band era; the quintessential "hep cat"; as the strutting "king of hi-de-ho," demonstrated with his vaudevillian flair that sophisticated jazz can be given mass appeal; was a major contributor to development of scat singing, the improvising of nonsense lyrics (such as "Hi-de-hi-de-hi-de-ho," his signature refrain); traced beginning of his career to gig as drummer with band on South Side of Chicago; before leaving Chicago, formed his own first, short-lived band; after gaining attention singing "Ain't Misbehavin'" in Broadway revue *Connie's Hot Chocolates*, in 1929 moved with new, successful band into year's engagement alternating with Duke Ellington's orchestra at Harlem's Cotton Club; later played in such prestigious Manhattan venues as Paramount Theater and Cafe Zanzibar; reached wider audience through radio broadcasts of many of his sessions as well as recordings; in beginning, used "St. James Infirmary Blues" as his theme; soon, replaced that with his original trademark song, "Minnie the Moocher," which he cowrote; later added to his repertoire such original compositions as "Jim Jam Jump," "Boog It," "Are You All Reet?," "The Jumpin' Jive," and "Pecka Doodle Doo"; toured and recorded with Cab Calloway and His Orchestra until 1948, when he disbanded orchestra and formed small combo; made musical appearances in numerous films, beginning with *The Big Broadcast* (1932) and including *Stormy Weather* (1943) and *The Blues Brothers* (1980); finally played Sportin' Life (a role originally written by George Gershwin with him in mind) in revival of *Porgy and Bess* that reached Broadway in 1953; returned to Broadway in all-black production of *Hello, Dolly!* in 1967; wrote *Hepster's Dictionary* (1938), a lexicon of "jive language" that he periodically updated; also wrote autobiography, *Of Minnie the Moocher and Me* (1976); died in Hosckessin, Delaware. See *Current Biography* (November) 1945.

Obituary *N Y Times* p59 N 20 '94

CHADWICK, FLORENCE (MAY) Nov. 9, 1918–Mar. 15, 1995 Long-distance swimmer; holder of women's record for swimming English Channel; at ten, became first child to swim San Diego Bay Channel; over next eighteen years won annual two-and-a-half-mile race at La Jolla, California ten times; on August 8, 1950 swam English Channel from Wissant, France to Dover, England in thirteen hours and twenty minutes, breaking record of 14:39:24 set by Gertrude Ederle in 1926; the following year, swam the more arduous England-to-France route across the channel in a record time of 16:22; was first woman swimmer to cross channel in both directions; made a total of four crossings; earned her livelihood by working, for many years, as a stockbroker and, later, as vice-president of First Wall Street Corporation in San Diego, California; died in San Diego. See *Current Biography* (October) 1950.

Obituary *N Y Times* p47 Mr 19 '95

CHAMBERLAIN, JOHN RENSSELAER Oct. 28, 1903–Apr. 9, 1995 Writer; journalist; pundit who tended to view history, politics, and society through the prism of economics, to see democratic political rights as a function of economic rights; with *New York Times* beginning in 1925, held various editing and writing posts, including reporter, Washington correspondent, and daily book reviewer; at various times was also editorially associated with *Scribner's*, *Fortune*, *Barron's*, and *Life* magazines; was editorial page writer for *Wall Street Journal* for ten years, until 1960; from 1960 to 1985 wrote syndicated column on political, social, and economic issues for King Features; in his first book, *Farewell to Reform* (1932), expressed undiluted scorn for efforts of liberal progressives to reform capitalism rather than destroy it; modified his radical leftist view in his second book, *The American Stakes* (1940), renouncing class warfare in favor of "social democracy," or "political pluralism," and a "gradualist" approach to a planned economy; later moved further away from his early Marxism; published six more books, including the collection of essays *The Turnabout Years* (1992); died in New Haven, Connecticut. See *Current Biography* (April) 1940.

Obituary *N Y Times* B p10 Ap 13 '95

CHANDRASEKHAR, SUBRAHMANYAN Oct. 19, 1910–Aug. 21, 1995 Indian-born astrophysicist; professor emeritus, University of Chicago; shared 1983 Nobel Prize for physics for his achievements in stellar research, especially a study of white dwarfs in early 1930s that laid groundwork for discovery of black holes, dying stars that compress indefinitely; had strong grounding in mathematics before turning his attention to astrophysics; published his first scientific research paper, on stellar thermodynamics, at eighteen; in 1930 went on Indian government research scholarship to Cambridge University, in England, where Ralph H. Fowler, building on the studies of Sir Arthur S. Eddington, recognized the common occurrence of white dwarfs, the dense, white-hot balls, approximately the size of Earth, that stars become when their nuclear fuel is exhausted and they undergo gravitational collapse, like spent balloons; applying quantum statistics and special relativity theory to his analysis of the life-and-death cycles of stars at Cambridge, calculated that only low-mass dying stars stabilize into white dwarfs, that stars with a mass more than 1.44 times that of the sun bypass the white-dwarf stage and continue to compress—a conclusion that was derided by traditional astronomers and cosmologists, including Eddington, when Chandrasekhar announced it at a meeting of the Royal Astronomical Society; continued to remain ahead of the field in later theoretical studies in the dynamics of star clusters, hydromagnetics, and radioactive transfer; in 1937 joined faculty of University of Chicago, where he contributed to top-secret atomic-bomb development project conducted there during World War II; from 1952 to 1986 was Morton D. Hull distinguished service professor of astrophysics in astronomy and physics departments and Institute for Nuclear Studies at university; wrote *An Introduction to the Study of Stellar Structure* (1939) and *The Mathematical Theory of Black Holes* (1983), among other books, some of which have been widely used as textbooks; died in Chicago. See *Current Biography* (March) 1986.

Obituary *N Y Times* D p20 Ag 22 '95

CISLER, WALKER (LEE) Oct. 8, 1897–Oct. 18, 1994 Engineer; utilities executive; rose through ranks to become executive vice-president (1948), president (1951), and chairman and chief executive officer (1964) of Detroit Edison Company; supervised reconstruction and expansion of power system that serves southeastern Michigan; an ardent proponent of nuclear energy, was severely disappointed at failure in 1972 of experimental fast-breeder nuclear reactor in Monroe, Michigan that was to have been showpiece of 1974 World Energy Conference; retired in 1975; died at his home in Grosse Pointe, Michigan. See *Current Biography* (September) 1955.

Obituary *N Y Times* A p29 O 21 '94

COLBERT, LESTER L(UM) June 13, 1905–Sep. 15, 1995 President and chairman of Chrysler Corporation, the automobile manufacturer; as teenager in Texas, worked in cotton trading, his father's business; as young lawyer with New York law firm, attracted attention of Walter P. Chrysler, president of Chrysler Corporation, and Chrysler production chief K. T. Keller; joined Chrysler Corporation as resident counsel in Detroit in 1933; subsequently served as vice-president of several of corporation's divisions, including Dodge; during World War II, managed Dodge factory that manufactured B-29 aircraft engines; was president of Dodge division from 1946 to 1950, when he assumed presidency of Chrysler Corporation, then second only to General Motors in manufacture of motor vehicles; later became board chairman as well; after resigning as president and chairman in 1961, chaired a subsidiary, Chrysler Corporation of Canada, Ltd., until 1965; died in Naples, Florida. See *Current Biography* (April) 1951.

Obituary *N Y Times* B p8 S 19 '95

COLEMAN, JAMES S(AMUEL) May 12, 1926–Mar. 25, 1995 Sociologist; professor at University of Chicago since 1973; from his extensive studies of social structures and social relations, developed theories that were widely influential, especially in their effect on course of public education in U.S.; after his "Coleman report" to Congress in 1966, became lightning rod of controversy surrounding political and judicial action aimed at ending de facto segregation of schools; began career as chemical engineer; obtained doctorate in sociology at Columbia University with dissertation that became book on internal politics in a typographical labor union; after stints at University of Chicago and elsewhere, in 1959 joined faculty of Johns Hopkins University; wrote book *Community Conflict* (1957); with two associates, did federally funded study of ten Illinois high schools that resulted in monograph *Social Climates in High Schools* (1961) and books *The Adolescent Society* (1961) and *Adolescents and the Schools* (1965); beginning in 1965, codirected for U.S. Office of Education a major national survey of educational opportunities for minority groups; in 1966 report, concluded that disadvantaged children learned better when integrated into predominantly middle-class school settings; after mandatory busing in school districts across U.S. resulted in "white flight" from the affected areas, in 1975 issued another study recognizing that busing had been a failure—thus setting off an uproar from the political left almost as angry as the one against busing had been from the right; in another study, in 1981, concluded that Catholic and other private schools provided a better education than public schools, but later heavily qualified that conclusion; was professor and department chairman at Johns Hopkins until his return to University of Chicago; wrote thirty books, including *Foundations of Social Theory* (1990), which he considered his most important sociological work; in it, explored role of rational individual choice in the way "natural" communities, such as towns (as opposed to "artificial" corporations, unions, and the like) are structured and run; to end of his life, was engaged with associates in "The High School and Beyond" program, which keeps track of seventy-five thousand people who were high school juniors and seniors in 1980; died in Chicago. See *Current Biography* (October) 1970.

Obituary *N Y Times* B p11 Mr 28 '95

COSELL, HOWARD Mar. 25, 1920–Apr. 23, 1995 Television and radio sportscaster; outspoken sports journalist ("the mouth that roared") who was as well known as any of the athletes he covered; was a self-confessed "frustrated actor" with contentious opinions and a flair for expressing them with rhetorical flourish, in staccato, educated Brooklynese; began career as lawyer; became full-time sports reporter and commentator on ABC network in 1956; while doing world heavyweight championship commentary, beginning in 1959, developed a close public relationship, jocular but mutually respectful, with the boxer Muhammad Ali; emerged into controversial prominence in 1967, when he supported Ali's conscientious refusal to be drafted for Vietnam War and repeatedly vented his outrage over the champion's being punitively stripped of his title and barred from competition; becoming "tired of the hypocrisy and sleaziness of the boxing scene," and disgusted with its brutality, quit covering prizefighting in 1982; reached his widest audience as color commentator on ABC's *Monday Night Football* from 1970 to 1983, when he left the show with the comment that professional football had become "a stagnant bore"; finished his career on ABC television with *SportsBeat* program, which was dropped in 1985 after he severely criticized some of his ABC colleagues in his autobiographical book *I Never Played the Game* (1985); died in New York City. See *Current Biography* (November) 1972.

Obituary *N Y Times* B p11 Ap 24 '95

CRAWFORD, FREDERICK C(OOLIDGE) Mar. 19, 1891–Dec. 9, 1994 Industrialist; as president (1933–53) and chairman (1953–58), led development of Cleveland firm of Thompson Products, Inc. into global titan TRW, Inc., manufacturer of electronic circuits, valves, pumps, and other parts and accessories for auto, aircraft, aerospace, oil-drilling, and defense (especially guided-missile) industries; after taking degree in civil engineering, in 1916 joined Steel Products, Inc., the name of which was changed to Thompson Products ten years later; from entry position of maintenance engineer, worked way up executive ranks; relinquished chairmanship when Thompson Products and Remo-Woolbridge Corporation merged to become TRW; a fiercely conservative Republican, kept photograph of Franklin D. Roosevelt upside down in his office throughout the liberal Democratic president's thirteen years in office; established a strong bond with his employees, who rebuffed every effort of auto workers' union to organize them; died not far from his Cape Cod home, in hospital in Falmouth, Massachusetts. See *Current Biography* (February) 1943.

Obituary *N Y Times* p24 D 17 '94

DEAN, PATRICK (HENRY) Mar. 16, 1909–Nov. 5, 1994 British diplomat; as assistant legal adviser to Foreign Office from 1939 to 1946, helped to negotiate wartime lend-lease agreements with U.S. and participated in Yalta and Potsdam conferences and Nuremberg trials; in postwar years headed German political division of Foreign Office; later was minister to Italy; headed UK's delegation to UN from 1960 to 1964; was ambassador to U.S. from 1965 until his retirement in 1969; later chaired English Speaking Union; died in Kingston, Surrey, in England. See *Current Biography* (May) 1961.

Obituary *N Y Times* D p25 N 16 '94

DESAI, MORARJI (RANCHHODJI) Feb. 29, 1896–Apr. 10, 1995 Former prime minister of India; a puritanical reformer who led conservative faction out of Indian National Congress Party in protest of authoritarian and socialistic policies of Prime Minister Indira Gandhi; under British Raj, worked in Bombay civil service from 1918 until 1930, when he left to devote himself to the national cause and Mohandas K. Gandhi's civil disobedience movement; was arrested and imprisoned repeatedly, beginning in October 1930, after Indian Congress movement was outlawed; in 1931 joined All-India Congress Committee; for many years was secretary of the Congress's committee in his home state of Gujarat, where he was known for his campaigns against political corruption; when British granted provincial autonomy to India in 1937, was elected to Bombay province's legislative assembly and named provincial minister for revenue, cooperation, forests, and agriculture; resigned in 1939 in protest of Britain's peremptory commitment of India as a belligerent in World War II; in 1946 became minister for home and revenue in newly reconstituted Congress Party government in Bombay; continued to serve in that post after India became independent (in 1947), until 1952; outlawed alcohol in Bombay, tried to suppress prostitution, and campaigned against cosmetics, popular music, and public dancing by unmarried couples; as chief minister of Bombay state from 1952 to 1956, introduced far-reaching administrative reforms; in national cabinet of Prime Minister Jawaharlal Nehru was minister of commerce and industry (1956–58) and of finance (1958–63); in government of Prime Minister Indira Gandhi was deputy prime minister and minister of finance from 1967 to 1969, when his opposition to Mrs. Gandhi's policies reached the breaking point; became parliamentary leader of schismatic conservative opposition within Indian National Congress; was arrested and imprisoned when Mrs. Gandhi decreed drastic emergency measures, suspending civil liberties, in 1975; with leaders of other parties, organized the coalition Janata (People's) Party, which swept into power in elections of March 1977; was inaugurated as India's fourth prime minister, and the first from outside the Congress Party, in March 1977; as prime minister, tried to replace Mrs. Gandhi's Moscow-oriented foreign policy with genuine nonalignment; was defeated by Mrs. Gandhi in election of 1979; died in Bombay. See *Current Biography* (June) 1978.

Obituary *N Y Times* B p7 Ap 11 '95

DJILAS, MILOVAN June 12, 1911–Apr. 20, 1995 Montenegrin-born Yugoslav politician; dissident; writer; disillusioned Communist leader and idealogue whose seminal insider's exposure of the ruling Communist elite as a "new class" of "all-powerful masters and exploiters" in the late 1950s made him a vanguard symbol of resistance, three decades ahead of his time; was drawn to clandestine Yugoslav Communist Party in boyhood; became revolutionary leader as student at University of Belgrade; for his political activities against Yugoslavia's dictatorial monarchy, was imprisoned from 1933 to 1935; met Josip Broz, better known by nom de guerre of Tito, secretary-general of Yugoslav Communist Party, in 1937; became member of the party's central committee in 1938 and of its politburo in 1940; during Nazi occupation of Yugoslavia in

World War II, was member of the supreme staff of the guerrilla resistance led by Marshal Tito; as head of military mission to Moscow in 1944, had his first meeting with Josef Stalin, whom he would later describe as "one of those rare terrible dogmatists capable of destroying nine-tenths of the human race to 'make happy' the one-tenth"; in Tito's postwar provisional government (1945-53), held succession of cabinet posts; as one of Tito's closest advisers, was a major contributor to his decision, in 1948, to declare Yugoslavia's independence from the Soviet Union and withdrawal from the Cominform, the international Communist association dominated by Moscow; subsequently criticized the Yugoslav Communist regime itself and, with increasing intensity, called for its liberalization; in January 1954, shortly after he had become president of the national legislature, was ousted from his government and party posts; resigned from the party in April 1954; subsequently—until he received amnesty in 1966—was under police surveillance when not serving prison terms for "hostile propaganda" smuggled out to the West, beginning with his essay "The Storm in Eastern Europe" (1956) and his best-selling book *The New Class* (1957), his indictment of the Communist revolution as hypocritical ("conducted in the name of doing away with classes, it has resulted in the most complete authority of any new class") and of members of the Communist oligarchies as privileged and self-serving elitists; was released from prison in 1961 but imprisoned again after publication in the West of *Conversations with Stalin* (1962); wrote an autobiography in two volumes, *Land without Justice* (1958) and *Memoir of a Revolutionary* (1973); also wrote *The Unperfect Society: Beyond the New Class* (1969), *Parts of a Lifetime* (1975), and a number of other books, some fictional; died in Belgrade. See *Current Biography* (September) 1958.

Obituary *N Y Times* B p7 Ap 21 '95

DREYFUS, PIERRE Nov. 18, 1907-Dec. 25, 1994 French civil servant; industrialist; government official; president of Regie Nationale des Usines Renault (1955-75), Europe's third largest (after Volkswagen and Fiat) automobile manufacturer and France's largest industrial enterprise; following liberation of Paris in World War II, held several posts in French Ministry of Commerce and Industry; in 1947 joined Renault, which had been nationalized two years earlier; became a vice-president in 1948; as president, maintained Renault's relative independence from government control in day-to-day management; made Renault into model state-owned enterprise, with relatively exemplary working conditions, labor relations, efficiency, and productivity; oversaw expansion of company's annual output from 175,000 cars to 1.3 million; was minister of industry under President François Mitterand in 1981; later served as an adviser to Mitterand; died at his home in Paris. See *Current Biography* (July) 1958.

Obituary *N Y Times* D p18 D 28 '94

DUKE, ANGIER BIDDLE Nov. 30, 1915-Apr. 30, 1995 U.S. diplomat; peripatetic public official; Democratic Party officer and fund-raiser; an heir to American Tobacco Company fortune; in 1949 began an erratic career in U.S. foreign service, where his status depended on which party was in power in White House; after serving briefly in Washington, became second secretary and consul at U.S. embassy in Buenos Aires and, in 1951, special assistant to the ambassador in Madrid; was ambassador to El Salvador in 1952 and 1953; in mid-1950s served as official with International Rescue Committee, a private, nonsectarian group doing relief and relocation work with persons displaced by political upheavals in such places as Vietnam, Laos, and Hungary; set up Zellerbach Commission, which surveyed European refugee problem and recommended that U.S. admit fifty thousand refugees in a crash program; campaigned for a more flexible immigration policy; served as vice-president of CARE, the international relief organization, from 1958 to 1960; was chief of protocol at White House and State Department from beginning of Kennedy administration, in 1961, until 1965; in late 1960s was successively ambassador to Spain and to Denmark; in early 1970s served as New York City's Commissioner of City Affairs and Public Events for the salary of one dollar a year; worked in Jimmy Carter's presidential campaign in 1976; retired from U.S. foreign service in 1981; subsequently served as chancellor of Southampton Center of Long Island University, another dollar-a-year post; died in Southampton, New York after being struck by a car while Rollerblading. See *Current Biography* (February) 1962.

Obituary *N Y Times* B p11 My 1 '95

DURRELL, GERALD (MALCOLM) Jan. 7, 1925-Jan. 30, 1995 British naturalist; conservationist; writer; youngest brother of Lawrence Durrell, the novelist; was a world leader in movement to save endangered species from extinction and the pioneer of concept of the zoo as primarily "a reservoir and sanctuary for these harassed creatures"; became interested in natural history and discovered his natural rapport with animals as child on island of Corfu; while working in mid-1940s as a student keeper at Whipsnade Zoological Park, in Bedfordshire, England, began to keep a count of world's animals threatened with extinction; beginning in 1947, made expeditions to collect mammals, reptiles, and birds in British Cameroons, British Guiana, Nigeria, Australia, Paraguay, New Zealand, Mexico, India, and Soviet Union, among other places; in 1958, on thirty-five acres in Trinity on island of Jersey in English Channel, founded Jersey Zoo Park, where he began captive-breeding rare animals for eventual reintroduction into wild; in 1963 set up Jersey Wildlife Preservation Trust to operate the zoo and promote similar efforts internationally; helped found SAFE (Save Animals from Extinction); in 1973, under auspices of SAFE, established Wildlife Preservation Trust International; at Jersey Zoo Park, introduced program for educating students from around world in animal care, field research, and conservation of rare species; in a fluid, easygoing style, recounted his life, travels, and experiences with animals in more than thirty books—including *The Overcrowded Ark* (1953), *My Family and other Animals* (1956), and *Family and Fauna* (1979)—sales of which helped fund his work; also wrote several novels inspired by his experiences; died in St. Helier, Jersey. See *Current Biography* (May) 1985.

Obituary *N Y Times* D p21 F 1 '95

EISENSTAEDT, ALFRED Dec. 6, 1898–Aug. 23, 1995 German-born photographer; a pioneering photojournalist whose work (more published photographs than any other photographer of his time) is marked by humanity and understanding of people; was a master at catching, without trickery, the telling detail in a news story or the revealing expression on a face; exploring new techniques made possible by more advanced photographic equipment, such as the large Ermanox, the first camera capable of taking photos indoors with natural light, and the Leica (which would be his lifelong favorite), the first thirty-five millimeter camera, whose compactness facilitated candid photography, became increasingly well known in Europe in late 1920s and early 1930s as a standard-bearer in development of photojournalism; as a freelance, regularly sold his photographs (of subjects ranging from the meeting of Hitler and Mussolini to teeming street life in Les Halles, Paris) to Associated Press as well as many popular illustrated European magazines; moved to U.S. in 1935; became charter photographer with *Life*, the picture magazine, in 1936; during thirty-six years with *Life*, did more than twenty-five hundred picture stories and fifty cover photographs, the most famous of which is a sailor exuberantly sweeping up a young nurse in a kiss in a celebration of the end of World War II in Times Square on September 2, 1945; remained with *Life* until it ceased regular publication in 1972; was never better than in his sympathetic portraits of people (from George Bernard Shaw and Albert Einstein to Marilyn Monroe and the women of the British royal family), his favorite subject; published several books, including *Witness to Our Time* (1966), a collection of photographs interspersed with text, and *The Eye of Eisenstaedt* (1969), an anecdotal autobiography abundantly illustrated with photographs; died on Martha's Vineyard in Massachusetts. See *Current Biography* (January) 1975.

Obituary *N Y Times* B p7 Ag 25 '95

ELKIN, STANLEY (LAWRENCE) Mar. 11, 1930–May 31, 1995 Writer; university professor; master stylist of darkly humorous fiction; blended wild farce with deep pathos and hard-core everyday reality (including a profound sense of suffering and death) with freewheeling and lyrical fantasy; offered what one critic called "remission and reprieve, a gesture of willingness to . . . laugh in momentary grace at whatever makes life Hell"; at first generally hewed to Bellow-like American-Jewish social realism in linear-plotted short stories (some of which were collected in *Criers and Kibitzers, Kibitzers and Criers*, 1966) whose protagonists are often torn between the view that religious and ethnic tradition is anachronistic and the feeling that assimilation into contemporary American culture is betrayal; began to set his imagination and plot lines free in *Boswell: A Modern Comedy* (1964), in which a latter-day counterpart of Samuel Johnson's biographer seeks to compensate for his mediocrity and assuage his fear of death in bizarre ways, such as surrounding himself with a virtually immortal "club" of celebrities; in his second novel, *A Bad Man* (1967), established himself, in words of one reviewer, as "a bright satirist, a bleak absurdist, and a deadly moralist"; in his third, *The Dick Gibson Show* (1971), told the story of a radio call-in talk-show host who seeks apotheosis as the voice of the people and instead achieves fragmentation and alienation when, with his encouragement, his listeners become their own stars, filling the airwaves with their private obsessions; from 1972 on was progressively crippled by multiple sclerosis, a condition that affected his art as well as his life; published *Searchers and Seizures* (1973), consisting of three novellas, including "The Bailbondsman," which was made into the film *Alex and the Gypsy* (1976); satirized homogenization of American life in his fourth novel, *The Franchiser* (1976); was blasphemously funny, while deadly serious, in three-part work *The Living End* (1979), which might be considered his *Divine Comedy*; subsequently published novels *George Mills* (1982), in which the title Everyman character is replicated through forty generations, *The Magic Kingdom* (1985), in which a group of terminally ill children tour Disney World, *The Rabbi of Lud* (1987), a send-up of New Jersey-vintage Judaism, and *The MacGuffin* (1993), the collection of novellas *Van Gogh's Room at Arles* (1992), and the book of essays *Pieces of Soap* (1992); completed novel *Mrs. Ted Bliss* before his death; joined faculty of Washington University in St. Louis in 1960; as Merle Kling Professor of Modern Letters there since 1983, taught a graduate course in writing each fall; died in St. Louis. See *Current Biography* (July) 1987.

Obituary *N Y Times* A p25 Je 2 '95

ENRIQUE TARANCÓN, VICENTE CARDINAL May 14, 1907–Nov. 28, 1994 Spanish Roman Catholic prelate; a cardinal since 1969; led long overdue modernization of Spanish church; after serving as bishop of Solsona and archbishop of Oviedo, became archbishop of Toledo and primate of Spain in 1969; two years later became archbishop of Madrid-Alcalá, Spain's most important see; in that position, and as head of Spanish national council of bishops (beginning in 1972), helped make Spanish church more open to democratic opposition to dictatorship of Francisco Franco, to which it had been tied from beginning; advocated separation of church and state; following death of Franco in 1975, gave at coronation of King Juan Carlos a sermon that ranks as important document in Spain's transition to constitutional monarchy; after retiring from ecclesiastical duties in 1983, remained a progressive voice in Spanish public life, especially in his criticism of corruption in Prime Minister Felipe González's Socialist government; died in Valencia, Spain. See *Current Biography* (October) 1972.

Obituary *N Y Times* D p21 N 29 '94

FAUBUS, ORVAL E(UGENE) Jan. 7, 1910–Dec. 14, 1994 Former Democratic governor of Arkansas; before becoming governor, was Arkansas state highway commissioner and director of highways; in running for governor in 1954, did so as moderate populist with little interest in race, save for expressing opinion that problem of integrating public schools racially, pursuant to 1954 U.S. Supreme Court decision, "should be solved at the local community level"; was elected in 1954 and reelected in 1956; early in his governorship, brought African-Americans into upper levels of Democratic party in Arkansas and oversaw desegregation of public transportation; did nothing to block voluntary community integration of public schools, which was going on throughout state—with notable exception of Little Rock; in September 1957 sent Arkansas National Guard to block implementation of a federal court's order that all-white Central High School in Little Rock be desegregated; was thwarted in that tactic by President Dwight D. Eisenhower, who nullified his control of the guardsmen by federalizing them and sent in twelve hundred army paratroopers to enforce integration of the school; remaining unbowed, described the action as "the military occupation of Arkansas"; went on to win an unprecedented four additional terms; after retiring from electoral politics, worked in various occupations, including that of bank teller; died at his home in Conway, Arkansas. See *Current Biography* (October) 1956.

Obituary *N Y Times* A p1+ D 15 '94

FOWLER, WILLIAM A(LFRED) Aug. 9, 1911–Mar. 14, 1995 Physicist; Institute professor of physics emeritus, California Institute of Technology; with his colleagues at Cal Tech, founded the new field of nuclear astrophysics, offering a theoretical understanding of how the stars might produce light and heat while synthesizing the chemical elements from light to heavy; began his research in Kellogg Radiation Laboratory at Cal Tech in Pasadena, as graduate student in 1933; joined faculty as research fellow in 1936; became full professor in 1946; pursued research in nuclear physics at Cal Tech for half a century, with interruption during World War II, when he and his colleagues were diverted into U.S. Navy projects; in his nuclear research, worked with his colleagues at the cutting edge of physics and cosmology; arrived at a complete theory explaining how virtually all of the elements in the universe, from carbon to uranium, can be or could have been created inside the stars through nucleosynthesis, beginning with nothing more than the hydrogen and helium produced in the theoretical "Big Bang"; for his work, shared 1983 Nobel Prize in physics with astrophysicist Subrahmanyan Chandrasekhar; was Institute professor of physics at Cal Tech from 1970 until his retirement in 1982; died in Pasadena, California. See *Current Biography* (September) 1974.

Obituary *N Y Times* B p14 Mr 16 '95

FRANCIS, SAM(UEL LEWIS) June 25, 1923–Nov. 4, 1994 Painter; charter member of second generation of American abstract expressionists; strove to use color to make painting itself "a source of light"; created luminous, mural-sized canvases, in some of which gesso white effects bursts of color that gleam like gems; hospitalized after plane crash when he was U.S. Army Air Corps trainee in 1944, was indelibly inspired by what he saw during months flat on his back: the play of light on the ceiling indoors, the skyscapes outdoors; studied at University of California at Berkeley and in Paris; in such early paintings as *Opposites* (1950), an eight-by-six-foot masterpiece of his Berkeley period, showed influence of Mark Rothko's monochromatic paintings in which brush strokes seem to flow into one another while maintaining an elegant pattern of translucent cellular forms; seasoned his abstract expressionism with hints of the color-saturated canvases of such European artists as Klimt, Matisse, Bonnard, and Monet; first gained recognition in Europe, resoundingly, when he was living there during 1950s; also, in late 1950s, found warm appreciation in Japan for his paintings, with their affinity for *haboku*, the Japanese "flowing ink" art style; showed increased receptiveness to Japanese calligraphic and decorative traditions in such paintings as *Round the World* (1958-60); in 1974 established in Santa Monica, California the Litho Shop, where, with master printer George Page, he devoted himself to lithography; died in Santa Monica. See *Current Biography* (October) 1973.

Obituary *N Y Times* B p8 N 8 '94

FRONDIZI, ARTURO Oct.28, 1908–Apr. 18, 1995 Former president of Argentina; lawyer; economist; an eclectic liberal idealogue, sometimes doctrinaire but also pragmatic; as lawyer, was best known for his defense of Communists arrested for political agitation; running on Radical Party ticket, was first elected to federal House of Deputies in 1946; was a leader of the opposition during the regime of dictator Juan Perón, but supported much of Perón's social program; after Perón was ousted in 1955 military coup, was elected president, in 1958, largely because Perón from exile had implicitly authorized his followers to throw their support to him; taking office at a time of national economic crisis, imposed severe austerity measures, including devaluation of the currency, which paved way for an economic recovery but meanwhile created popular unrest; began losing support of military when they learned he had met secretly with Che Guevara, the peripatetic Cuban revolutionary; also alienated military by lifting ban on Perónist candidates, who won a number of congressional elections early in 1962; deprived of military support, was forced to resign presidency in March 1962; later founded Movement for Integration and Development, a small party calling for state promotion and protection of industry; died in Buenos Aires. See *Current Biography* (October) 1958.

Obituary *N Y Times* B p13 Ap 19 '95

FUKUDA, TAKEO Jan. 14, 1905–July 5, 1995 Prime minister of Japan (1976–78); an anti-Communist, pro-American leader of conservative faction of Japan's dominant Liberal Democratic Party; began career as bureaucrat in Ministry of Finance in 1929; by 1947 had risen to post of director of budget; resigned in 1950 under cloud of a bribery scandal; was later acquitted of bribery charges; was first elected to House of Representatives in 1952; became minister of finance in 1965 and was reassigned that portfolio in 1968; as minister of foreign affairs in 1971 and 1972, dealt with trade imbalance dispute with U.S.; as prime minister, in 1977 enunciated "Fukuda doctrine," affirming Japan's renunciation of military ambition and desire for mending relations with other Southeast Asian nations; played important role in signing of first reconciliatory treaty with China since World War II; after leaving office, remained influential as participant in unofficial meetings of former and present world leaders; died in Tokyo. See *Current Biography* (June) 1974.

Obituary *N Y Times* B p10 Jl 6 '95

FULBRIGHT, J(AMES) WILLIAM Apr. 9, 1905–Feb. 9, 1995 U.S. Democratic representative (1943–45) and senator (1945–74) from Arkansas; an internationalist, influential in shaping of foreign policy and promotion of global cooperation and education; while liberal in foreign affairs, leaned to typical Southern conservatism of his generation on such domestic issues as civil rights; at beginning of career, after earning law degree and passing bar, taught law successively at George Washington University and at University of Arkansas, where he was president from 1939 to 1941; in House of Representatives in 1943 introduced bill paving way for creation of United Nations and participation of U.S. therein; in Senate chaired foreign relations committee for fifteen years; in 1945 introduced legislation that resulted in his most conspicuous lasting legacy, the Fulbright fellowships and travel grants for foreign study; throughout Cold War, generally pushed for détente with Soviet Union; wrote bill of particulars in censure of Senator Joseph McCarthy by the Senate in 1954; although dubious about Vietnam War, responded affirmatively and successfully when President Lyndon B. Johnson in 1964 asked his help in gaining Congress's approval of Gulf of Tonkin resolution, giving president carte blanche in waging the war; after learning that Johnson's version of incident in gulf justifying the resolution had been dishonest, was ashamed and furious; became most important government critic of U.S. policy in Vietnam; in his book *The Arrogance of Power* (1966) and in televised hearings in 1966 and 1967, relentlessly argued for withdrawal from Vietnam; influenced President Bill Clinton, who, as a college student, worked in his Senate office; domestically, was proudest of initiating legislation that resulted in creation of John F. Kennedy Center for the Performing Arts; after leaving Senate, practiced law in Washington, D.C.; died at his home in Washington. See *Current Biography* (October) 1955.

Obituary *N Y Times* A p1+ F 10 '95

FURCOLO, (JOHN) FOSTER July 29, 1911–July 5, 1995 Former U.S. representative (1949–52) and governor of Massachusetts (1957–61); moderate Democrat; before entering and after leaving electoral politics, practiced law; resigned his congressional seat in July 1952 to accept appointment as Massachusetts state treasurer and receiver-general; was elected to two-year term in that position in November 1952; as governor, was credited with establishing community college system, expanding University of Massachusetts, sponsoring more generous scholarship and loan programs for underprivileged students, and backing legislation that instituted a tax withholding system, outlawed discrimination in housing, and bolstered programs for the elderly; after leaving office, was indicted on charges of having been involved in bribery conspiracy as governor, charges that were dropped for lack of evidence in 1965; in late 1960s and early 1970s served as assistant district attorney in Middlesex County and taught courses in or relating to law and government at several Massachusetts colleges; under pseudonym John Foster, wrote satirical political novel *Let George Do It!* (1957); also wrote plays and essays; died in Cambridge, Massachusetts. See *Current Biography* (January) 1958.

Obituary *N Y Times* B p10 Jl 6 '95

GABOR, EVA Feb. 11, 1921–July 4, 1995 Actress; youngest of the glamorous and much-married Gabor sisters from Hungary, of whom Zsa Zsa is the campiest and most celebrated; shared in deluge of frothy publicity that gossip columnists and tabloid reporters heaped on her show-business family, but at same time pursued acting career with a professional dedication belying the Gabor reputation for frivolity; in early 1940s began appearing on screen, most typically in secondary roles in low-budget films in which her Hungarian accent passed for French; made television dramatic debut in supporting role of young French woman in *L'Amour the Merrier* (1949); hosted an interview show on television in early 1950s; drew favorable critical attention with her Broadway debut, as Mignonette in *The Happy Time* (1950); later was cast on Broadway as French countess in *Little Glass Clock* (1956) and as one of the girlfriends in revival of *Present Laughter* (1958); starred in many Off-Broadway, stock, and road-company productions; became best known as the socialite Lisa Douglas, the role in which she starred opposite Eddie Albert in TV situation comedy *Green Acres* (1965–71), about a city couple trying to cope with rural living; reprised that role in made-for-television movie *Return to Green Acres* (1990); in Hollywood, accrued supporting credits in such films as *The Last Time I Saw Paris* (1954), *Artists and Models* (1958), *Gigi* (1958), and *Youngblood Hawke* (1964); was voice of Miss Bianca in animated films *The Rescuers* (1977) and *The Rescuers Down Under* (1990); in her later years was owner of very lucrative wig company; was married four times; died in Los Angeles. See *Current Biography* (July) 1968.

Obituary *N Y Times* D p9 Jl 5 '95

GARCIA, JERRY Aug. 1, 1942–Aug. 9, 1995 Musician; lead guitarist, composer, and vocalist of the electric/acoustic band the Grateful Dead, the most idiosyncratic, improvisatory, and durable of the major rock-'n'-roll groups that emerged from San Francisco's psychedelic counterculture in the late 1960s, described by rock critics as "the outlaws of the music industry" and "the ultimate alternative band"; as a composer and performer, was influenced by folk, country, and rhythm and blues, among other idioms; was son of a Spanish-born San Francisco ballroom-jazz musician; learned to play piano as a child and guitar as a teenager; in early 1960s began playing bluegrass banjo in San Francisco coffeehouses; with folk guitarist Bob Weir and others, in 1964 formed Mother McCree's Uptown Jug Champions, which evolved into the psychedelic rock group the Warlocks in 1965 and soon thereafter into the Grateful Dead, who would, in the view of one critic, "provide the soundtrack for the drug experiments of a generation"; with the Dead, as house band for Ken Kesey's "Acid Test" jubilees, was at ground-zero for the psychedelic movement; thereafter proceeded to build the Dead's enduring reputation on long, free-form concerts, begun without a set list and characterized by unpredictable, spontaneous stretches of inspired music; became a beloved cult icon to devoted fans, known as "Deadheads," many of whom followed the band from city to city and, with the band's approval, collected bootleg tapes of live shows; with the Dead, toured the United States and the world regularly; with lyricist Robert Hunter, composed a large proportion of the band's repertoire; with the Dead, recorded numerous studio albums—including *American Beauty*, *Workingman's Dead* (both 1970), and *In the Dark* (1987), which yielded group's only Top Ten single, "Touch of Grey"—and several live albums, none of which, with the possible exception of *Live Dead* (1970), quite captured the magic of their in-person performances; in addition to his playing with the Grateful Dead, had early on appeared on albums by Jefferson Airplane and Crosby, Stills, Nash, and Young, played with bluegrass band Old and in the Way, and produced and played pedal steel on the debut country album of New Riders of the Purple Sage; often collaborated with the mandolin player David Grisman, most recently on an album of music for children, *Not for Kids Only* (1993); also played regularly throughout his career with the more conventional Jerry Garcia Band; one of the most enduring symbols of the spirit of the idealism and joyful communal anarchy of 1967's "Summer of Love," performed his last concert less than two months before his death of a heart attack at Serenity Knolls, a residential drug-treatment facility in Forest Knolls, California. See *Current Biography* (May) 1990.

Obituary *N Y Times* A p1+ Ag 10 95

GERSTACKER, CARL A(LLAN) Aug. 6, 1916–Apr. 23, 1995 Former chairman of Dow Chemical Company, second-largest such corporation in U.S.; was a nephew of James D. Pardee, a major backer of Herbert Henry Dow, founder of the company; after earning a B.A. degree in chemical engineering, joined Dow in 1938 in an accounting position; after service as a supervisor of munitions production with U.S. Army during World War II, rejoined Dow, where he worked his way up through production and purchasing to become treasurer of the company in 1949, a vice-president in 1955, member of the executive committee in 1957, chairman of the finance committee in 1959, and chairman of the board in 1960; as board chairman, had tenure coinciding with Vietnam War, during which Dow, at first the sole supplier to U.S. military of the incendiary jelly called napalm, was target of furious protests, until Dow lost napalm contract in 1970; retired as board chairman in 1976; died in Midland, Michigan. See *Current Biography* (October) 1961.

Obituary *N Y Times* D p25 Ap 26 '95

GLENNAN, T(HOMAS) KEITH Sept. 8, 1905–Apr. ll, 1995 U.S. government official; educator; electrical engineer; first head of National Aeronautics and Space Administration; as electrical engineer, worked in film industry in U.S. and Britain for many years in first stage of his career; during World War II directed U.S. Navy's underwater sound laboratory in New London, Connecticut; after war, briefly directed engineering in Ansco division of General Aniline and Film Corporation; in 1947 was appointed president of Case Institute of Technology (now Case Western Reserve University); was instrumental in developing Case into one of twenty leading technical institutions in U.S.; on leave of absence from Case, served on U.S. Atomic Energy Commission from 1950 to 1952; again on leave, was founding chief of NASA (which would grow larger than he wanted and envisioned) from 1958 until 1961; following retirement from Case in 1966, served as U.S. representative to International Atomic Energy Agency in Vienna; died in Mitchellville, Maryland. See *Current Biography* (October) 1950.

Obituary *N Y Times* B p13 Ap 12 '95

GODUNOV, ALEXANDER Nov. 28, 1949–May 18(?), 1995 Russian-born ballet dancer; film actor; with his tall stature, flowing blond hair, strikingly gaunt face, and dramatic flair, had a magnetic stage presence; danced with dazzling athleticism, soaring in his jumps and moving with extraordinary speed in his pirouettes and *tours à la seconde*; began his training at Riga State Ballet School, where Mikhail Baryshnikov was a fellow student; in 1971 joined Bolshoi Ballet, making his debut as Prince Siegfried in *Swan Lake*; later took on such leading roles as Basil in *Don Quixote*, the Poet in *Les Sylphides*, Prince Florimund in *The Sleeping Beauty*, Count Albrecht in *Giselle*, the title role in *Spartacus*, and Tybalt in *Romeo and Juliet*; defected to West during Bolshoi's 1979 American tour; shortly afterward, like Baryshnikov before him, joined classically oriented American Ballet Theatre (ABT); trying to temper his natural flamboyance and Bolshoi-style theatricality in his first season with that company, seemed to overconcentrate on correctness of his steps; while with ABT, added to his repertoire such roles as Solor in *La Bayadère*, Jean de Brienne in *Raymonda*, and Othello in *The Moor's Pavanne*; in 1982 was abruptly dismissed from ABT by Baryshnikov, artistic director of the troupe since 1980, whose explanation of the dismissal (a conflict in repertoire) did not satisfy puzzled balletomanes; subsequently put together and toured with Alexander Godunov and Stars and made guest appearances with various ballet companies; in film *Witness* (1985), impressed critics with his supporting portrayal of an Amish farmer; was less impressive in subsequent film roles, including villain in action-adventure *Die Hard* (1988); found dead at his home in West Hollywood, California. See *Current Biography* (February) 1983.

Obituary *N Y Times* A p29 My 19 '95

GONZALEZ, PANCHO May 9, 1928–July 3, 1995 Tennis player; a tall and agile player with natural, untrained, and uncoached talent and an intuitive feel for the game; had an extraordinarily powerful right-handed overhead drive and a precise touch in his versatile ground strokes, with his fierce pride, volatile temper, and indomitable spirit, could be a terrifying competitor; in words of two-time Wimbledon champion Don Budge, was "the best player who never won Wimbledon"; won national singles championship in 1948; the following year, held concurrent national championship titles for grass, clay, and indoor courts; with Frank Parker, won doubles at Wimbledon in 1949; after successfully defending his singles title at Forest Hills on Labor Day in 1949, turned professional; dominated pro tour from 1954 to 1962; retired from tour in 1963; in opinion of many of his peers, would in all likelihood have won one or more Wimbledon singles titles if he had not turned professional as early as he had; competing at Wimbledon in the sunset of his career, in 1969, did not win the singles but outlasted Charlie Pasarell in their opening-round match, the longest in Wimbledon history, lasting five hours and twenty-two minutes; died in Las Vegas, Nevada. See *Current Biography* (October) 1949.

Obituary *N Y Times* D p9 Jl 5 '95

GOULD, LAURENCE M(cKINLEY) Aug. 22, 1896–June 20, 1995 Educator; explorer; an expert in polar geology; joined faculty of University of Michigan as geology instructor in 1921; became assistant professor in 1926 and associate professor in 1930; in summer of 1926 was a geologist on an Arctic expedition sponsored by the university; the following summer was the geographer and topographer with the Putnam expedition to Baffin Island in Canadian Pacific; between 1928 and 1930 was second in command of Commander Richard E. Byrd's first Antarctic expedition, devoted to exploring and mapping the South Pole area; wrote book *Cold: The Record of an Antarctic Sledge Journey* (1931); in 1932 left University of Michigan to accept appointment as professor of geology at Carleton College, in Northfield, Minnesota; during World War II headed Arctic section of U.S. Air Force's Arctic, Desert, and Tropics Information Center; became president of Carleton College in 1945; during the 1957-58 International Geophysical Year, returned to Antarctica to supervise U.S. IGY experiments in oceanography, geomagnetism, cosmology, seismology, ionospheric physics, and glaciology; as chairman of Committee on Polar Research of the National Academy of Sciences, testified before U.S. Senate Foreign Relations Committee in favor of treaty dedicating Antarctica as a peaceful international preserve for international scientific cooperation; resigned as president of Carleton College, which he had developed into one of finest small liberal arts colleges in U.S., in 1962; died in Tucson, Arizona. See *Current Biography* (January) 1978.

Obituary *N Y Times* B p6 Je 22 '95

GRACE, J(OSEPH) PETER, JR. May 25, 1913–Apr. 19, 1995 Business executive; presidential consultant; leading Roman Catholic layman; philanthropist; critic of profligate federal spending; represented third generation of his family to head W. R. Grace & Company, century-old shipping, trading, and banking company founded by his grandfather William R. Grace in 1854; as president from 1945 to 1992, transformed company into diversified five billion-dollar conglomerate with interests ranging from specialty chemicals (in which it is world's leader) to consumer goods and specialized health care; gained national prominence when, at request of President Ronald Reagan, he headed from 1982 to 1984 a private-sector study on cost control in federal government, which became known as Grace Commission; in that project, marshaled help of approximately two thousand executives in assiduously compiling host of practical suggestions for rooting out federal inefficiency and waste; warned in 1982, "If this deficit goes to one trillion dollars a year, our freedoms are gone"; in his final years as president of W. R. Grace, turned revamping of company over to J. P. Bolduc, his chief aide on Grace Commission; after Bolduc succeeded him in presidency, remained chairman of board of directors; when Bolduc resigned presidency, was confronted by demands of discontented shareholders for extensive reformation of board of directors; served on several other corporate boards; was generous in his contributions to various charities, especially Grace Institute and others devoted to helping disadvantaged youth in New York City; lived in Manhasset, Long Island; died in hospital in New York City. See *Current Biography* (March) 1960.

Obituary *N Y Times* B p6 Ap 21 '95

GRÈS, MME. (ALIX) Nov. 30, 1903–Nov. 24, 1993 French fashion designer; last survivor of the generation of women, including Elsa Schiaparelli, Madeleine Vionnet, Jeanne Lanvin, and Gabrielle Chanel, who dominated haute couture in France until period following World War II when male designers began their ascendancy; received early training in sculpture, the influence of which would become manifest in her fashion design; served apprenticeship in sketching and cutting; working out of her Paris apartment in early 1930s, began conceiving fashion designs in muslin *toiles* (patterns); was able to realize her conceptions in rich fabrics under auspices of an already established house beginning in 1934; opened her own house in early 1940s; became known for the distinctive classical draping, folds, pleats, and flowing lines of her jersey gowns and other elegant creations; attracted a clientele that included Grace Kelly, Jacqueline Kennedy Onassis, Danielle Mitterand, and the Duchess of Orléans, among other celebrities and socialites; introduced a ready-to-wear line in 1980; in 1984 sold her fashion house to industrialist Bernard Tapie; suffered closure of her Paris atelier for nonpayment of rent in 1987 and sale of rights to professional use of her name to Yagi Tsusho Ltd. in 1988; died at a retirement home in south of France thirteen months before her death became publicly known—a delay apparently explained chiefly by desire of her daughter, Anne Grès, to protect her, in death, from further exploitation. See *Current Biography* (June) 1980.

Obituary *N Y Times* A p1+ D 14 '94

GRISWOLD, ERWIN N(ATHANIEL) July 14, 1904–Nov. 19, 1994 Lawyer; educator; dean of Harvard University Law School (1946-67); U.S. solicitor general (1967-73); as staff attorney in solicitor general's office from 1929 to 1934, argued tax cases before U. S. Supreme Court; began teaching law at Harvard in 1934; as solicitor general in Johnson and Nixon presidential administrations, argued government side of Pentagon Papers case, among others, before Supreme Court; after leaving government, continued arguing cases before Supreme Court as member of private law firm of Jones, Day, Reavis & Pogue; died in Boston. See *Current Biography* (October) 1956.

Obituary *N Y Times* B p10 N 21 '94

GUINAN, MATTHEW Oct. 14, 1910–Mar. 22, 1995 Irish-born trade unionist; former president of AFL-CIO's Transport Workers Union, comprising more than a score of locals, including those representing New York City subway and bus employees, mass transit workers in Philadelphia and several other cities, airline ground service employees, and a variety of other transport personnel, from railroad workers to parking lot attendants; was protégé and designated successor of Michael J. Quill, founder of TWU; immigrated to U.S. in 1929; four years later became trolley-car operator on Kingsbridge (Bronx) line of old Third Avenue Railroad Corporation; as unpaid organizer, led Third Avenue line workers into TWU in 1937; became paid organizer with the national union in 1943; six years later was elected president of Local 100, largest unit within TWU, including eight thousand drivers for private bus lines in New York City and its environs; for those drivers, won five-day, forty-hour work week following twenty-nine-day strike in 1953, one of his proudest achievements; on national level, was elected executive vice-president of TWU in 1952; in addition, became national union's secretary-treasurer in 1956; quit presidency of Local 100 in 1961 to devote himself full time to his duties as closest aide to Quill in TWU; went to jail with Quill for union's defiance of a court order in calling a strike that paralyzed New York City's transit system for twelve days in January 1966; before end of that month, succeeded to presidency of TWU upon Quill's death; as president, oversaw regular renegotiation of twenty-seven local contracts; received most publicity for his biennial wrangling, usually with threats of a strike, with Metropolitan Transit Authority in New York City; led TWU (which reached peak membership of more than 150,000) until his retirement in 1979; died in Lauder Hill, Florida. See *Current Biography* (September) 1974.

Obituary *N Y Times* B p7 Mr 24 '95

HACKETT, ALBERT Feb. 16, 1900–Mar. 16, 1995 Playwright; scenarist; in partnership with his first wife, Frances Goodrich, whom he met when both were stage actors in 1920s, had long and distinguished career in screenwriting; among fewer playwriting efforts with Miss Goodrich, scored singular success with *The Diary of Anne Frank*, which ran for 717 performances on Broadway beginning in October 1955 and won Pulitzer Prize, Tony Award, and New York Drama Critics Circle Award; between 1933 and 1962 wrote thirty screenplays, including those for *The Thin Man* (1934) and two sequels, *Naughty Marietta* (1935), *Ah, Wilderness!* (1935), *Lady in the Dark* (1944), *It's a Wonderful Life* (1946; one of their more original scenarios, inspired by a Christmas card), *Easter Parade* (1948), *Father of the Bride* (1950), *Seven Brides for Seven Brothers* (1954), *Gaby* (1956), and *Five Finger Exercise* (1962), as well as screen adaptation of *The Diary of Anne Frank* (1959); died in New York City. See *Current Biography* (October) 1956.

Obituary *N Y Times* p10 Mr 18 '95

HARDY, PORTER, JR. June 1, 1903–Apr. 19, 1995 Former U.S. representative from Virginia (1947–69); was educated through two years of postgraduate study at School of Business Administration at Harvard University; beginning in 1932, worked his vegetable farm in Churchland, Virginia; also operated an electrical equipment wholesale business; in Congress, was an independent, generally conservative, sometimes unpredictable old-guard Tidewater Democrat; opposed civil rights legislation but did not bow to Virginia Democratic machine of segregationist Senator Harry F. Byrd; refused to support much of the liberal agenda of Democratic administrations but broke with Byrd in voting for public housing and other Johnson administration Great Society programs; in chairing armed services and government operations subcommittees, relentlessly sought out and exposed government fraud and waste; died in Virginia Beach, Virginia. See *Current Biography* (May) 1957.

Obituary *N Y Times* p47 Ap 23 '95

HAUSER, PHILIP M(ORRIS) Sept. 27, 1909–Dec. 13, 1994 Demographer; professor emeritus of urban sociology at University of Chicago, where he began teaching in 1932; went to Washington, D.C., to join U.S. Bureau of the Census as assistant chief statistician in 1938; was promoted to assistant director of bureau in 1942 and deputy director four years later; in late 1940s returned to University of Chicago, where he became full professor and founded Population Research Center; in 1949 and 1950 spent weekdays in Washington serving as acting director of Bureau of the Budget while teaching at University of Chicago on weekends; chaired sociology department at university until 1965; nine years later was named to Lucy Flower Chair of Sociology; until 1979 headed Population Research Center, whose projects had such results as improved methods for estimating size of minority communities often undercounted in censuses; wrote *Social Statistics in Use* (1975) and *World Population and Development* (1979), among other books; with others, contributed to demographic studies on such subjects as racial integration of Chicago's public schools (in which he was closely involved), other racial issues, comparative rates of fertility and mortality, and various aspects of urbanization and overpopulation; died in Chicago. See *Current Biography* (July) 1969.

Obituary *N Y Times* D p20 D16 '94

HAWKINS, ERICK Apr. 23, 1909–Nov. 23, 1994 Choreographer; dancer; founder of Erick Hawkins Dance Company; an idiosyncratic talent whose work was an acquired taste; introduced a generic "free-flow" dance vocabulary, reflecting his Zen philosophy, that was radical departure from specific, codified techniques of traditional modern dance, with their expression of contemporary angst and unresolved psychological conflict and their physical demands; created serene, often soaring dances, including many that were virtually plotless celebrations of human body and its metaphoric relationship to rest of nature; began career as member of George Balanchine's American Ballet Company in mid-1930s; as member of Lincoln Kirstein's Ballet Caravan, choreographed his first ballet, *Show Piece* (1937); gained his early reputation as dance partner of Martha Graham, beginning in 1938; joined Martha Graham Dance Company in 1939; for Graham company, choreographed *John Brown* (1947); married Graham in 1948; while dancing, suffered an injury that led him to believe that prevailing technique, with its agitated percussiveness and tension, forced dancers to move unnaturally; set about developing a new, unforced technique, based on sound knowledge of anatomy; in 1951 left Graham company to experiment independently; was divorced from Graham in 1954; four years later formed his own first full-fledged company, whose dancers he trained in "self-sensing," or becoming aware of how much effort they could expend before a movement became forced; among his early creations for the company were *Early Floating*, a study in liquescence, and the equally plot-free *Here and Now with Watchers*; in 1964 introduced *Geography of Noon*, in which four dancers, symbolizing butterflies, wove patterns around inventive percussion (on boxes and the like) provided by Lucia Dlugoszewski, his second wife and frequent musical collaborator; later created for himself solo dance *Naked Leopard*, "a celebration of animal innocence," *8 Clear Places*, *Black Lake*, and *Plains Daybreak*, an evocation of Native American rituals;

evoked old-fashioned Fourth of July celebration in *Hurrah!*, choreographed in 1975 to Virgil Thomson's Second Symphony; died in New York City. See *Current Biography* (January) 1974.

Obituary *N Y Times* D p19 N 24 '94

HENRY, DAVID D(ODDS) Oct. 21, 1905–Sep. 4, 1995 Public education administrator; university president; professor; while working for graduate degrees in literature at Pennsylvania State University in late 1920s, was supervisor of university's liberal arts extension and instructor in English literature; subsequently held teaching and high administrative posts at Battle Creek (Michigan) College, Wayne State University, and New York University; in 1950s headed committees that contributed to development of educational television in New York area; became president of University of Illinois in 1955; as president, stressed importance of well-rounded liberal arts education and of continuing dialogue between federal government and state educational institutions; oversaw significant expansion of University of Illinois; in 1960 received nationwide publicity by suspending a teacher who had publicly condoned premarital sex for mature students; later found himself again in midst of controversy when he bowed to pressure not to suspend a professor who attributed assassination of President John F. Kennedy to Communist plot; sparked greatest furor in 1968 by setting in motion an overly ambitious affirmative-action program for recruitment of African-American students that overwhelmed university's capacity to accommodate the influx; took an unabashedly hard line against violence by anti-Vietnam War student demonstrators; retired in 1971; died in Naples, Florida. See *Current Biography* (June) 1966.

Obituary *N Y Times* B p17 S 7 '95

HEYNS, ROGER W(ILLIAM) Jan. 27, 1918–Sep. 11, 1995 Educator; university administrator; organization official; psychologist; began teaching psychology at University of Michigan in 1949; became full professor in 1957; simultaneously, was assistant to dean of College of Literature, Science, and Arts with specific responsibility for educational policy and instruction, from 1954 until 1958, when he became dean; in psychology, was chiefly interested in group dynamics, decision-making conferences, measurement of social motives, social conformity and nonconformity, and education of older people; wrote book *The Psychology of Personal Adjustment* (1958); cowrote *An Anatomy for Conformity* (1962); in 1962, while retaining title of professor of psychology at University of Michigan, moved up to position of vice-president of academic affairs; in 1965 was appointed chancellor of University of California at Berkeley, which had been plagued by student and nonstudent strikes, sit-ins, riots, and demonstrations during the preceding year; with his principled judgment and skill in handling campus turbulence, was given much of credit for restoration of order at Berkeley; after leaving Berkeley in 1971, was president of the William and Flora Hewlett Foundation, the charitable organization, until 1993; died while on vacation in Volos, Greece. See *Current Biography* (December) 1968.

Obituary *N Y Times* B p15 S 14 '95

HICKEY, MARGARET A. Mar. 14, 1902–Dec. 7, 1994 Lawyer; women's rights advocate; vocational guidance administrator; public affairs editor of *Ladies Home Journal* since 1946; practiced law until 1933, when she went into personnel training field, opening career school for women secretaries, administrative assistants, and business executives in St. Louis; during World War II chaired Women's Advisory Committee in the federal War Manpower Commission; in that position, was concerned with the most effective use of women in war effort; when women began to lose their jobs at defense plants toward end of war, turned her attention to protecting their rights in workplace; over following years served as top-echelon private and public consultant on such matters; from 1964 to 1966 chaired presidential advisory council on status of women under President Lyndon B. Johnson; died in Tucson, Arizona. See *Current Biography* (December) 1944.

Obituary *N Y Times* p52 D 10 '94

HIGHSMITH, PATRICIA Jan. 19, 1921-Feb. 5, 1995 Expatriate American author; a writer of psychological crime thrillers who was best known in U.S. for her first novel, *Strangers on a Train* (1950), the crisscross, "exchange murders" suspense classic made into 1951 motion picture by Alfred Hitchcock; transcended limitations of crime-fiction genre with her imaginative insertions of subtle psychopathy into civilized circumstances and her chillingly matter-of-fact, value-neutral registering of the results, both ordinary and horrific; as in *Strangers on a Train*, often triggered her plots with fateful intersecting of lives of two radically different characters, "sometimes obviously the good and the evil," as she explained in her nonfiction manual *Plotting and Writing Suspense Fiction* (1966), "sometimes merely mismatched"; was, in the words of Graham Greene, the "poet of apprehension rather than fear," whose tales constituted "a world of her own—a world claustrophobic and irrational which we enter each time with a sense of personal danger"; created, among other antiheroes, the character Tom Ripley, cultured and charming psychopathic criminal who is the protagonist of five of her novels, beginning with *The Talented Mr. Ripley* (1955), made into film *Purple Noon* (1961) by French director René Clement; published total of twenty novels, including *The Cry of the Owl* (1962), adapted for film by director Claude Chabrol in 1988, and *The Tremor of Forgery* (1969), widely regarded as her best, about a culturally disoriented American writer in Tunisia who is unsure whether or not he has killed an intruder; also published seven collections of short stories; in 1963 moved to Europe, where her work was better known and more appreciated than in U.S.; lived first in England, then in France, and finally in Switzerland; died in Locarno, Switzerland. See *Current Biography* (January) 1990.

Obituary *N Y Times* B p8 F 6 '95

HIGINBOTHAM, WILLIAM A(LFRED) Oct. 25, 1910–Nov. 10, 1994 Physicist; was electronics group leader in development of atomic bomb at Los Alamos, New Mexico during World War II; after war, joined with other nuclear scientists in establishing Federation of American Scientists to warn of cataclysmic danger they had unleashed and to promote international control of nuclear weapons; was physicist at Brookhaven National Laboratory on Long Island from 1947 to 1984; died at his home in Gainesville, Georgia. See *Current Biography* (February) 1947.

Obituary *N Y Times* D p29 N 15 '94

HITCH, CHARLES J(OHNSTON) Jan. 9, 1910–Sep. 11, 1995 Economist; university president; government official; efficiency expert; on Rhodes and Medley scholarships, took degrees at Oxford University in 1930s; with time out for desk service in World War II and a year as chief of stabilization controls division of U.S. Office of War Mobilization and Reconversion, held positions of fellow, tutor, and praelector at Queen's College, Oxford from 1935 until 1948, when he joined the Rand Corporation, Santa Monica-based think tank that conducts atomic, space, and defense research for U.S. government, as head of its economics division; in 1960 was named chairman of Rand's research council; cowrote *The Economics of Defense in the Nuclear Age* (1960); in January 1961 joined incoming administration of President John F. Kennedy as assistant secretary of defense in charge of budget; with his systems analysis, was instrumental in changing Pentagon's budgetary procedures and making a temporary dent in its waste and inefficiency; in 1965 left government to become vice-president in charge of finance for nine-campus University of California, largest educational institution in U.S., then beset by staggering financial deficits as well as disruptive student political activism (in which some faculty were complicit); following dismissal of university president Clark Kerr (who was viewed by the incoming California governor, Ronald Reagan, a conservative Republican, as a permissive liberal, soft on campus demonstrators) by state board of regents, was chosen by board to succeed Kerr; as president, beginning in January 1968, took a pragmatic approach to the acrimony and tried to maintain university's autonomy in face of a punitive and budget-slashing governor and legislature; was forced to abandon university's policy of free tuition for state residents, to relinquish to board of regents authority to appoint and promote tenured faculty, and to accept and implement orders from state legislature for disciplining of student disrupters; resigned presidency in 1975, when campus unrest had subsided but finances remained critical, to become president of Resources for the Future, a Washington, D.C., research organization concerned with natural resources; retired in 1978; died in San Leandro, California. See *Current Biography* (November) 1970.

Obituary *N Y Times* D p23 S 12 '95

HOBBY, OVETA CULP Jan. 19, 1905–Aug. 16, 1995 First U.S. secretary of Health, Education, and Welfare; U.S. Army colonel, retired; publisher; communications executive; was parliamentarian of Texas House of Representatives from 1925 to 1931 and from 1939 to 1941; wrote influential book on state parliamentary law, *Mr. Chairman* (1937); in 1931 married William P. Hobby, former governor of Texas and publisher of Houston *Post*, where she had been employed in circulation department; held various editorial and executive positions on *Post* during 1930s; early in World War II went to Washington, D.C., as head of newly formed women's division of War Department's public relations bureau; became director of Women's Auxiliary Army Corps when the corps was formed in May 1942; directed WACs, as the corps became known after the word "Auxiliary" was dropped, until her retirement from active service in July 1945; returned to Houston to work on *Post*; became coeditor and publisher of *Post* in 1952; in meantime, engaged in myriad of civic activities; after having been lifelong Democratic Party activist, backed Republican presidential candidates Thomas E. Dewey, in 1948, and Dwight D. Eisenhower, in 1952; devoted much of her time to successful Eisenhower campaign; became head of Federal Security Agency when Eisenhower took office in January 1953; moved up to cabinet status when agency was transformed into Department of Health, Education, and Welfare in April 1953; resigned in July 1955; after returning to Houston, with title of publisher and editor, assisted her husband in running *Post*, and some of its broadcasting holdings as well; became chairman of board following her husband's death, in 1964; in 1983 sold *Post*, which later ceased operation; was left only with Houston AM radio station KPRC after five television stations owned by H&C Communications, Inc. were sold in 1992; died at her home in Houston. See *Current Biography* (February) 1953.

Obituary *N Y Times* B p13 Ag 17 '95

HOLIFIELD, CHET (CHESTER EARL) Dec. 3, 1903–Feb. 5, 1995 U.S. representative from Los Angeles County, California (1943–73); a liberal Democrat; one of leading Congressional advocates of public power, growth of federal government, and expansion of foreign aid; with his father in Montebello, California in 1920s, established business in manufacturing and selling of men's apparel, which he continued to own after entering Congress; in House of Representatives, was one of few to protest internment of Japanese Americans during World War II; in late 1940s and early 1950s was outspoken adversary of House Committee on Un-American Activities and what he considered its misguided harassing of alleged subversives; as member and chairman of Joint Committee on Atomic Energy, opposed transfer of control of atomic energy to either military or private hands; during 1950s vociferously urged marshaling national preparatory defense against possible Soviet nuclear attack; later managed passage through House of the bill that created Department of Housing and Urban Development and wrote the bill that created Department of Transportation; died in Redlands, California. See *Current Biography* (October) 1955.

Obituary *N Y Times* B p10 F 9 '95

HORGAN, PAUL Aug. 1, 1903–Mar. 8, 1995 Writer; a polymathic and prolific writer of fiction, history, biography, and cultural reportage and commentary reflecting his old-fashioned genteel sensibility and his Catholic-based religious humanism along with, more often than not, his Southwestern regionalism; wrote in a style described as "measured," "Virgilian," and "patrician"; activated his narratives through interaction of finely described characters in evocative settings with painstakingly researched detail; developed his craft as writer while working as librarian at New

Mexico Military Institute, his alma mater; won Harper Prize Novel contest with *The Fault of Angels* (1933); published first of his many Southwestern novels, *No Quarter Given*, in 1935; began to win serious national attention with *The Habit of Empire* (1941), a novel illuminating way in which Catholic missionary triumphalism contributed to imperial psychology of Spanish conquistadors in colonial New Mexico; won two Pulitzers, for his magnum opus, *Great River* (1954), a history of the Rio Grande, and for *Lamy of Santa Fe* (1975), a biography of an antislavery, pro-Indian pioneer archbishop in New Mexico; after four decades of solid but relatively unobtrusive literary distinction, finally achieved best-seller status with novel *Whitewater* (1970), a death-haunted but lyrical evocation of adolescence in a small Southwestern town; over a period of some sixty years published seventeen novels, a novella, four collections of short stories, two plays, three books of verse, and such diverse nonfiction volumes as *Conquistadors in North American History* (1963), *The Heroic Triad: Essays in the Social Energies of Three Southwestern Cultures* (1970), *Encounters with Stravinsky* (1972), and *Approaches to Writing* (1973); taught at several universities, including Wesleyan, with which he was associated continuously from 1959 on and where he directed Center for Advanced Studies during 1960s; became professor emeritus and permanent author in residence at Wesleyan in 1971; died in Middletown, Connecticut. See *Current Biography* (February) 1971.

Obituary *N Y Times* B p13 Mr 9 '95

IVES, BURL (ICLE IVANHOE) June 14, 1909–Apr. 14, 1995 Folk singer; anthologist; actor; often accompanying himself on guitar, put his distinctive stamp, gentle but strong, happy or mournful, on folk standards and children's songs ranging from "Blue Tail Fly" to "Frosty the Snowman"; burly and bearded bear of a man, six feet tall and weighing three hundred pounds, whose most memorable dramatic presence was that of an earthy patriarch in such films as the 1958 releases *Cat on a Hot Tin Roof* and *The Big Country* (for which he won an Academy Award); made his professional acting debut in summer stock in 1938; subsequently had minor roles on Broadway and began performing in nightclubs and on radio, where he had his own show, *The Wayfarin' Stranger*; made his concert debut at Town Hall in New York City in 1945; had supporting role of singing cowboy in his first film, *Smoky* (1946); had leading singing role in Disney musical film *So Dear to My Heart* (1948) and supporting dramatic roles in pictures *Station West* (1948), *Sierra* (1950), *East of Eden* (1955), and *The Power and the Prize* (1956); played Captain Andy in revival of musical *Show Boat* at New York City Center in 1954; created Rabelaisian role of Big Daddy in Tennessee Williams's drama *Cat on a Hot Tin Roof* on Broadway in 1955; accrued total of thirty-two screen credits, including *Desire Under the Elms* (1958) and *Earthbound* (1980); on television, narrated *Rudolph the Red-Nosed Reindeer* (1964) and had a role in series *The Bold Ones* (1970–72); recorded more than one hundred albums, containing such songs as "Big Rock Candy Mountain," "Goober Peas," and "Holly Jolly Christmas"; wrote early autobiography *Wayfarin' Stranger* (1948) and published the collections of folk ballads *The Burl Ives Songbook* (1953) and *Tales of America* (1954); died at his home in Anacortes, Washington. See *Current Biography* (May) 1960.

Obituary *N Y Times* p10 Ap 15 '95

JOBIM, ANTONIO CARLOS Jan. 25, 1927–Dec. 8, 1994 Brazilian composer; songwriter; musician; the individual most responsible for creating and defining the bossa nova, a sophisticated and gently melodious style of popular music in which rhythms of Brazilian samba are subdued by combination with subtle harmonies of cool jazz, along with elements of European pop and echoes of such classical composers as Chopin and Debussy; learned to play piano and guitar when growing up in beach community of Ipanema, near Rio de Janeiro; was grounded in classical piano, but became, in his words, "a surveyor, always with the chords, the chord changes"; as teenager, studied under twelve-tone composer Hans Joachim Koellreutter; was influenced by music of Duke Ellington and other American bandleaders who played in Rio's casinos; later was further influenced by such modern jazz innovators as Miles Davis; in late 1940s began playing his own compositions in local bars and nightclubs; in early 1950s earned his living as an arranger with a Brazilian recording company; later was music director of Odeon Records; in 1956 wrote, with Luis Bonfa, incidental music for play *Orfeu da Conceicao*, which, with the music, was adapted into international award-winning film *Black Orpheus* (1958); wrote music for several subsequent, less successful films, including *Bahia*; crystallized new style of music he had been evolving in his suave and ingratiating composition "Chega de Saudade," recorded as single by guitarist and singer Joao Gilberto in 1958; introduced term "bossa nova" in liner notes to Gilberto's subsequent album; in 1961 reached American ears through Stan Getz and Charlie Byrd's album *Jazz Samba* (1962), which made hits of his "Desafinado" and "Meditation," sparking huge bossa nova fad in U.S.; with Getz and others performed at Carnegie Hall in 1962; reached height of his international success with enormously popular "The Girl from Ipanema," a delicately sensual cut on 1964 album *Getz/Gilberto* with English lyrics by Norman Gimbel sung with caressing intimacy, almost in a whisper, by Astrud Gilberto; between 1967 and 1980 played and sang his own compositions on solo albums *Wave*, *Tide*, *Stone Flower*, *Urubu*, and *Terra Brasilis*; with a quintet, recorded album *Passarim* (1987); gave series of concerts in U.S. in mid- and late 1980s and early 1990s; wrote total of several hundred songs, many of them with lyricists Newton Mendonça and Vinicius de Moraes; maintained homes in New York City and Rio de Janiero; died in New York City. See *Current Biography* (July) 1991.

Obituary *N Y Times* D p20 D 9 '94

JONSSON, JOHN ERIK Sep. 6, 1901–Aug. 31, 1995 Industrialist; mayor of Dallas; helped to develop small manufacturer of devices for oil and gas exploration into electronics giant Texas Instruments, Inc., maker of first integrated circuits using silicon transistors in place of old, cumbersome electronic tubes; in 1930 was hired in Newark, New Jersey to supervise laboratory of Geophysical Service, Inc., first independent company to make reflection seismograph surveys in locating oil fields; in 1934 moved with G.S.I. to Dallas;

was elected secretary of company in 1934, treasurer in 1939, and vice-president in 1942; during World War II, helped G.S.I. obtain lucrative defense contracts; realized that "there was a good, honest living to be made working for the government," and that electronics was a most promising field for the future; during Korean War, when G.S.I. was renamed General Instruments, Inc., obtained Pentagon orders for electronic components contributing significantly to annual sales of more than fifteen million dollars; in December 1951, when company became Texas Instruments (retaining the name Geophysical Service for a subsidiary), assumed presidency; in 1958 was named chairman of board; after assassination of President John F. Kennedy in Dallas, when civic morale was low in the city, reluctantly acquiesced to urging of city's business community that he run for mayor; as mayor, from 1964 to 1971, was "architect and driving force of modern Dallas," in words of Steve Bartlett, one of his successors in mayoralty; retired from board of directors of Texas Instruments in 1977, when company's sales were nearly two billion dollars; died in Dallas. See *Current Biography* (January) 1961.

Obituary *N Y Times* p20 S 4 '95

JOSEPH, KEITH (SINJOHN) Jan. 17, 1918–Dec. 10, 1994 British member of Parliament; a Conservative leader; played major roles in formulation and implementation of Prime Minister Margaret Thatcher's free-market policies between 1979 and 1986; from 1949 to 1960 was fellow at All Souls College, Oxford University; during same period, filled various top executive positions in his family's business, the Bovis group of companies, involved in building construction, civil engineering, and housing and property development in Britain and, to a lesser extent, in several other countries; entered politics in order to pursue his social welfare concerns; associated himself at first with liberal wing of Conservative Party but later became spokesman for traditional Conservative economic and moral values; was elected to House of Commons as member for Leeds North East in 1956; served as minister of housing and local government (1962–64) and secretary of state for social services (1970–74); after Margaret Thatcher took over leadership of Conservative Party in 1975, became one of her closest aides and policy advisers; as secretary of state for industry in Thatcher government from 1979 to 1981 addressed himself to tasks of lessening strength of labor unions and privatizing British industry; succeeded in breaking strike by union workers at British Steel; helped set in motion process that would over next few years bring about sale of many major state-owned companies, including British Telecommunications and British Airways, to private sector; as education and science secretary (1981–86), fought fiercely against efforts of teachers' unions to obtain wage increases; left electoral politics after resigning his cabinet post in 1986; died in London. See *Current Biography* (February) 1975.

Obituary *N Y Times* p66 D 11 '94

JULIA, RAUL Mar. 9, 1940–Oct. 24, 1994 Puerto Rican-born actor; a classically grounded performer who ranged widely in stage and film roles; perhaps best known to general public for his screen performances as Valentin in *Kiss of the Spider Woman* (1985) and, especially, as Gomez, the father, in macabre comedies *The Addams Family* (1991) and *Addams Family Values* (1993); began long association with Joseph Papp's New York Shakespeare Festival in 1966; reached turning point in career playing Proteus in festival's innovative musical production of *Two Gentlemen of Verona* in summer of 1971; the following December moved to Broadway in role of Proteus, for which he won Tony Award nomination; with New York Shakespeare Festival later played range of roles that included title part in *Othello*, Orlando in *As You Like It*, Petruchio in *The Taming of the Shrew*, Mack the Knife in *The Threepenny Opera*, and Lopakhin in *The Cherry Orchard*; in 1978 played title role in road-company production of *Dracula* and replaced Frank Langella in that role on Broadway in 1979; on Broadway in 1980 played Jerry in Harold Pinter's *Betrayal*; was nominated for Tony Award for performance as Guido Contini in Broadway musical *Nine* (1982); on screen, played, among other roles, villains in *The Eyes of Laura Mars* (1978) and *The Escape Artist* (1982), the detective in *Compromising Positions* (1985), the martyred Salvadoran archbishop in *Romero* (1989), and the lawyer Sandy Stern in *Presumed Innocent* (1990); completed filming of "Action Fighter" before his death; on television, starred in 1988 miniseries *Onassis: The Richest Man in the World* and 1994 HBO movie *The Burning Season*, about Brazilian labor leader Chico Mendes; died in Manhasset, New York. See *Current Biography* (September) 1982.

Obituary *N Y Times* B p10 O 25 '94

KAPPEL, FREDERICK R(USSELL) Jan. 14, 1902–Nov. 10, 1994 Communications executive; began career as telephone pole digger at Northwestern Bell Telephone Company, a subsidiary of American Telephone and Telegraph Company, in 1924; working way up ranks, became president of Western Electric Company, AT&T's manufacturing subsidiary, in 1954; was elected president and chief executive officer of AT&T in 1956 and chairman in 1961; retired in 1967; later chaired U.S. Postal Service and a presidential commission on postal organization, among other presidential commissions; was board chairman of International Paper Company and a director of several other corporations; died in Sarasota, Florida. See *Current Biography* (March) 1957.

Obituary *N Y Times* p28 N 12 '94

KATZ, MILTON Nov. 29, 1907–Aug. 9, 1995 Legal educator; public official; as young lawyer, worked in various New Deal agencies in 1930s; began teaching at Harvard University in 1939; on leaves of absence, served with OSS, predecessor of CIA, in World War II and subsequently in a succession of federal positions, including chief delegate to Economic Cooperation Administration (1950–51), better known as Marshall Plan; was director of international legal studies at Harvard from 1954 to 1974 and Henry L. Stimson Professor of Law from 1954 to 1978; was subsequently distinguished professor of law at Suffolk University School of Law, in Boston, until January 1995; wrote and cowrote books on administrative law, international law, and law as related to foundations, the environment, trade and economics, technology, biomedical technologies, and war and peace; died in Brookline, Massachusetts. See *Current Biography* (October) 1950.

Obituary *N Y Times* A p22 Ag 11 '95

KELLY, NANCY Mar. 25, 1921–Jan. 2, 1995 Actress; reached height of her career in mid-1950s as the mother in both stage and screen versions of *The Bad Seed*; appeared in approximately fifty motion pictures as child actress in 1920s; on Broadway, made first appearance in 1931, as one of three leading child characters in *Give Me Yesterday* and first drew major critical attention as adolescent Blossom in *Susan and God* in 1937; meanwhile, was regularly cast in juvenile roles on radio dramatic shows and serials, including *Renfrew of the Mounted, Gangbusters, Myrt and Marge, The Shadow*, and *Aunt Jennie's Real Life Stories*; returned to Hollywood as leading lady in 1938; over next two decades made approximately a score of films, including *Stanley and Livingstone* (1939), *Jesse James* (1939), *To the Shores of Tripoli* (1942), *Women in Bondage* (1944), *Show Business* (1944), *Song of the Sarong* (1945), *The Woman Who Came Back* (1946), and *Crowded Paradise* (1956); resumed Broadway career playing Marion Castle in *The Big Knife* in 1949; during 1950–51 Broadway season took the part of the wife in *Season in the Sun*; the following season, had the starring role in *Twilight Walk*; won Tony Award as best actress of 1954–55 Broadway season for her portrayal in *The Bad Seed* of the mother tormented by the realization that her daughter is a homicidal psychopath, and genetically so; reprised that role in 1956 film of the same name; died at her home in Bel Air, California. See *Current Biography* (June) 1955.

Obituary *N Y Times* p30 Ja 14 '95

KENNEDY, ROSE (FITZGERALD) July 22, 1890–Jan. 22, 1995 Matriarch of an American political dynasty; daughter of John Francis ("Honey Fitz") Fitzgerald, U.S. representative and mayor of Boston; wife of millionaire businessman/ambassador Joseph P. Kennedy Sr., first chairman of federal Securities and Exchange Commission; mother of President John F. Kennedy (assassinated in 1963), Senator Robert F. Kennedy (assassinated in 1968), Senator Edward M. Kennedy, Ambassador Jean Kennedy Smith, and five others; mother-in-law of Jacqueline Kennedy Onassis; grandmother of Kathleen Kennedy Townsend, lieutenant governor of Maryland, Representative Joseph P. Kennedy 2d of Massachusetts, Patrick Kennedy, a state representative in Rhode Island, lawyer John F. Kennedy Jr., and television broadcaster Maria Shriver, among twenty-five other grandchildren; had forty-one great-grandchildren; was a Roman Catholic daily communicant; while peripherally involved in Catholic and other charities and especially interested in helping the mentally handicapped (at least in part because of condition of her eldest daughter, Rosemary, institutionalized since early adulthood), considered her life's work to be motherhood—"a profession that was as fully interesting and challenging as any honorable profession," as she observed in her autobiography, *Times to Remember* (1974); wrote, "What greater aspiration and challenge are there for a mother than the hope of raising a great son or daughter?"; after suffering stroke in 1985, retired to family compound overlooking Nantucket Sound in Hyannisport, Massachusetts; died at the compound. See *Current Biography* (November) 1970.

Obituary *N Y Times* A p1+ Ja 23 '95

KINGSLEY, SIDNEY Oct. 18, 1906–Mar. 20, 1995 Playwright; directed most of his own highly theatrical works, including *Dead End*, and produced several of them; wrote realistic and socially or politically significant plays, some (including prototypes of today's police station and hospital dramas) in contemporary urban settings; captured audiences of his day with his powerful plots, colorful characters, robust dialogue, gritty detail, and melodramatic flair; in his first play, *Men in White*, explored professional/personal conflicts in group of surgeons and nurses; with that work, produced under auspices of avant-garde, Method-oriented Group Theatre in 1933, scored immediate success on Broadway and won Pulitzer Prize; found wider audience for *Men in White* with film version, starring Clark Gable and Myrna Loy released in 1934; in his second Broadway hit, *Dead End* (1935; translated to screen in 1937), set in Manhattan waterfront cul-de-sac where waifs and gangsters live in tenements within view of luxury apartments, effectively dramatized message that social injustice and slum life breed criminals; subsequently wrote, among other plays, the polemics-laden paean to democracy *The Patriots* (1943), *Detective Story* (1949; translated to screen in 1951), his third Broadway hit, *Darkness at Noon* (1951), an adaptation of Arthur Koestler's novel of same name, and *Night Life* (1962); died at his home in Oakland, New Jersey. See *Current Biography* (June) 1943.

Obituary *N Y Times* D p21 Mr 21 '95

KUCHEL, THOMAS H(ENRY) Aug. 15, 1910–Nov. 21, 1994 U. S. senator from California (1953–69); lawyer; described himself early on as "a middle-of-the road Eisenhower Republican" and later as a "progressive Republican"; as Republican Party in general moved to right, was perceived to be a liberal; was state controller of California from 1946 until his appointment to Senate seat vacated by Richard Nixon when Nixon became vice-president of U.S. in January 1953; became deputy to Everett M. Dirksen, the Republican leader in Senate; as Republican whip during Democratic administration of President Lyndon B. Johnson, helped to push to enactment the administration's Great Society programs, including Medicare and the formidable civil rights legislative agenda; left electoral politics after losing primary election in 1968; subsequently was partner in Los Angeles law firm of Wyman, Bautzer, Rothman, Kuchel & Silbert until 1981; died in Beverly Hills, California. See *Current Biography* (February) 1954.

Obituary *N Y Times* D p18 N 24 '94

KUHN, MAGGIE Aug. 3, 1905–Apr. 22, 1995 Social activist; founder and head of Gray Panthers, a coalition of some forty thousand mature adults devoted to fighting age discrimination and other forms of what she viewed as social injustice and stereotyping; for eleven years beginning in late 1920s and extending through Depression of 1930s, worked with YWCA in Cleveland, Philadelphia, and New York in a variety of assignments, including the management of social programs, especially one concerned with helping young working women to organize and unionize, and the editing of YWCA publications; after leaving YWCA, began twenty-five-year professional association with United Presbyterian Church in New York City; with church, served as associate secretary in office of church and society, coordinated programming in division of church and race, wrote for and helped to edit church magazine *Social Progress* (later the *Journal of Church and Society*), and served as alternate Presbyterian observer at UN; in 1970, when she reached mandatory retirement age of sixty-five, met with others in like situation (retiring persons who wanted to remain active in social causes); within a year founded Gray Panthers, first called Consultation of Older and Younger Adults for Social Change, concerned with a variety of social issues (protesting the war in Vietnam had highest priority initially) and with mutual help in meeting economic and social needs of young and old; in 1973 merged Gray Panthers with Ralph Nader's Retired Professional Action Group; organized a number of groups into National Coalition for Nursing Home Reform; two weeks before her death participated in picketing by striking transit workers; wrote the autobiography *No Stone Unturned* (1991); died in home she shared with a group of colleagues in Philadelphia. See *Current Biography* (July) 1978.

Obituary *N Y Times* p41 Ap 23 '95

KUNSTLER, WILLIAM M(OSES) July 7, 1919–Sep. 4, 1995 Attorney; a radical "people's lawyer," committed to championing controversial causes and defending rights of political dissenters, militant poor, and other unpopular clients; was described by David Lerner, director of Center for Constitutional Rights, cofounded by Kunstler, as "a great American hero and a leader in the fight for social justice and against racism in America"; over course of his career had as clients such diverse figures as comedian Lenny Bruce (when he was charged with obscenity), Native American activist Leonard Peltier, black activist Al Sharpton Jr., flag burner Gregory Johnson, and both Malcolm X and—more recently—Malcolm's daughter Qubilah Shabazz; in 1949 became partner with his brother in New York law firm of Kunstler & Kunstler (later Kunstler, Kunstler, Hyman & Goldberg and, since 1992, Kunstler & Kuby); while specializing in marriage, estate, and business law in the 1950s, began taking some American Civil Liberties Union cases pro bono, revealing what he later called his "liberal tendencies" and acquiring "a taste for a certain kind of law where you are dealing with national issues, constitutions, and the rights of individuals"; took another step in becoming "a flaming crusader" when he went to the aid of Martin Luther King Jr. and other civil rights defendants in courtrooms throughout the South in the early 1960s; was "radicalized" during his defense of Chicago Seven, accused of conspiracy to commit violence during 1968 Democratic National Convention; thereafter concentrated on being the legal paladin of "the Movement," the amorphous alignment with which disparate New Left, antiwar, black liberation, and other countercultural groups were then identified; defended, among others, Black Panthers, campus rebels, and the Berrigan brothers and other Catholic peace militants; in 1971 defended prisoners charged in aftermath of rebellion at Attica (New York) Correctional Facility; later defended Wayne Williams, convicted of serial murders of children in Atlanta; despite strong prosecution eyewitness testimony, won acquittal of El Sayyid Nosair on murder charges in slaying of militant Jewish leader Meir Kahane in 1990; was initial defense lawyer for Colin Ferguson, who shot six people to death on Long Island Rail Road train in December 1993; was associate professor of law at New York Law School from 1950 to 1992; wrote eleven books, including *The Case for Courage: The Stories of Ten Famous American Attorneys Who Risked Their Careers in the Cause of Justice* (1962), *Trials and Tribulations* (1985), and *My Life as a Radical Lawyer* (1994); died in New York City. See *Current Biography* (April) 1971.

Obituary *N Y Times* B p6 S 5 '95

KURTZ, EFREM Nov. 7, 1900–June 27, 1995 Russian-born American conductor; had a wide symphonic, operatic, and balletic repertoire, strongly but by no means exclusively Russian; conducted premieres of works by Barber, Copland, Hindemith, Walton, Stravinsky, Khachaturian, and Shostakovich; was director of Stuttgart Philharmonic from 1924 to 1933, when he fled Hitler's then-aborning Third Reich; was musical director of Ballet Russe de Monte Carlo from 1934 to 1943, when he immigrated to U.S. to become conductor of Kansas City (Missouri) Symphony; was music director of Houston Symphony from 1948 to 1954; conducted Liverpool Symphony from 1955 to 1957; thereafter did freelance conducting, chiefly with European orchestras and opera companies, into late 1980s; maintained homes in New York, London, and Monte Carlo; died at his home in London. See *Current Biography* (February) 1946.

Obituary *N Y Times* D p21 Je 29 '95

LAMONT, CORLISS Mar. 28, 1902–Apr. 26, 1995 Socialist activist; secular humanist philosopher; writer; university professor; director of American Civil Liberties Union (1932–54); chairman of National Emergency Civil Liberties Committee for more than thirty years, beginning in 1954; as son of banker Thomas William Lamont, the partner of J. P. Morgan, grew up in privilege; began rebelling against his social class as undergraduate at Harvard; moved further leftward politically as graduate student at Oxford and Columbia Universities; after making his first visit to Soviet Union, published travel diary *Russia Day by Day* (1933) and became active in such organizations as Friends of the Soviet Union and National Council of American-Soviet Friendship; in early 1940s lectured on philosophy at Columbia University and New School for Social Research and on contemporary Soviet life and civilization at Harvard and Cornell Universities; wrote, among other books, *The Illusion of Immortality* (1935), *You Might Like Socialism: A Way of Life for Modern Man* (1939), *The Peoples of the Soviet Union* (1946), and *The Philosophy of Humanism* (1949); in addition, in a myriad of essays, pamphlets, and letters to editors, voiced his opinions on nuclear testing, the conviction of Julius and Ethel Rosenberg on charges of espionage, and other topical issues relating to international peace and understanding; ran unsuccessfully for U.S. Senate on American Labor Party ticket in 1952 and on Independent Socialist Party ticket six years later; in 1953 was cited for contempt of Congress by Communist-hunting Senator Joseph R. McCarthy but won dismissal of the citation in federal court; later won suits against Department of State, which had refused to issue him a passport, and U.S. Postal Service and CIA, which had been opening his mail; for many years continued to teach, chiefly at Columbia University, where he established George Santayana and John Masefield research collections and gave one million dollars for establishment of a chair in civil liberties in the law school; wrote book of memoirs, *Yes to Life* (1981); died at his country home in Ossining, New York. See *Current Biography* (June) 1946.

Obituary *N Y Times* A p31 Ap 28 '95

LANCASTER, BURT Nov. 2, 1913–Oct. 20, 1994 Actor; director; producer; one of the more durable of Hollywood's classic stars; a dedicated and intense craftsman; projected energy, strength, and sure control without having to raise his voice, and moved with cougarlike grace; possessed rugged good looks, strapping six-foot-four-inch physique, and powerful presence that belied a delicate and vulnerable sensibility; although at first typecast as tough guy, soon began breaking from that mold, and in career spanning forty-five years (1945-90) and embracing some seventy films, including a few made for television, demonstrated dramatic range extending to most gentle and even sentimental of interpretations; for more than seven years in 1930s worked in vaudeville, carnivals, and circuses as partner in two-man acrobatic team; as draftee assigned to Special Services in World War II, was relatively menial participant in production of entertainment for U.S Fifth Army in North Africa and Europe; made professional acting debut on stage, as Sergeant Joseph Mooney in *A Sound of Hunting*, which ran on Broadway briefly in 1945; made screen debut as the Swede, innocent thug set up as murder victim, in *The Killers* (1946), first of his several *films noirs*; subsequently starred as savage prison rebel in *Brute Force* (1947), betrayed and bitter ex-convict in *I Walk Alone* (1948), slick thief in *Rope of Sand* (1949), henpecked husband who ambivalently colludes in plot to murder his wife in *Sorry, Wrong Number* (1948), and security guard involved in robbery of his own organization in *Criss Cross* (1949); in his most notable early departure from type, played, with credible earnestness, morally upright son of war profiteer in *All My Sons* (1948); in 1950s capitalized on his athleticism and acrobatic skills in leads in *Jim Thorpe, All-American*, *Trapeze*, and swashbucklers *Ten Tall Men*, *The Flame and the Arrow*, *The Crimson Pirate*, and *His Majesty O'Keefe*; also starred in such action pictures as *Apache*, *Vera Cruz*, *Gunfight at the O.K. Corral* (as Wyatt Earp), and *Run Silent, Run Deep*; alternating his bankable mass-market entertainment ventures with riskier artistic projects, played middle-aged and seedy Doc, failed chiropractor and recovering alcoholic, in *Come Back, Little Sheba* (1952), brawny and lustful truckdriver Alvaro Mangiacavallo in *The Rose Tattoo* (1955), garrulous and prepossessing con man Starbuck in *The Rainmaker* (1956), and merciless Broadway gossip columnist J. J. Hunsecker in *Sweet Smell of Success* (1957); received first of four Oscar nominations for portrayal of tough but compassionate First Sergeant Milton Warden in *From Here to Eternity* (1953); won Academy Award for best actor for his portrayal of eponymous randy charlatan evangelist in *Elmer Gantry* (1960); played conscience-stricken German jurist accused of war crimes in *Judgment at Nuremberg* (1961); ended what he considered high period of his star status—and drew best-actor Oscar nomination—with his poignant portrayal of the prisoner-ornithologist in *Birdman of Alcatraz* (1962); subsequently was outstanding as Sicilian prince in *The Leopard* (1963) and title character in *The Swimmer* (1968); played American general plotting right-wing coup in *Seven Days in May* (1964), old Indian-fighting cavalry scout in *Ulzana's Raid* (1972), CIA agent in *Scorpio* (1972), 1963 Kennedy assassination conspirator in *Executive Action* (1973), and U.S. military adviser in Vietnam in *Go Tell the Spartans* (1978); realized his aim of acting gracefully beyond his prime with more success as over-the-hill numbers runner in touching film *Atlantic City* (1981)—which brought him another Academy Award nomination for best actor—and as patriarch relating to younger generation in *Cattle Annie and Little Britches* (1981) and *Rocket Gibraltar* (1988) than as superannuated train robber in comedy *Tough Guys* (1986); came full circle from his circus days in title role in made-for-television film *Barnum* (1986); died at his home in Century City, California. See *Current Biography* (April) 1986.

Obituary *N Y Times* p12 O 22 '94

LEONARD, BILL Apr. 9, 1916–Oct. 23, 1994 Radio and television journalist; news broadcaster; network executive; a major contributor to development of magazine-format programs; joined Columbia Broadcasting System after his discharge from U.S. Navy in 1945; remained with CBS for thirty-six years, the last four as president of CBS News; during first half of his association with network, was known principally for his local New York City news and feature programs; hosted daily radio magazine show *This Is New York* on CBS's flagship station in Manhattan from 1946 to 1957; moving into television, hosted weekly show *Eye on New York* on WCBS-TV in Manhattan for fifteen years; during 1950s also presented brief daily feature story about New York on local evening news; was CBS News floor reporter at 1952, 1956, and 1960 national political conventions; became full-time CBS News correspondent in 1959; beginning in 1960 spent much of his time helping to produce and reporting and narrating documentaries in award-winning *CBS Reports* series; from 1961 to 1965 led CBS News election unit that worked with I.B.M. and Louis Harris to develop exit-poll method of estimating election results; as a vice-president and senior vice-president, oversaw creation of such long-format news programs as *60 Minutes*; from 1975 to 1979 was vice-president in charge of relations with federal government; as president of CBS News from 1979 to 1982, chose Dan Rather to succeed Walter Cronkite as anchor of *CBS News* and introduced news program *Sunday Morning*, which has been prominent in its time slot ever since; lived in Washington, D.C.; died in hospital in Laurel, Maryland. See *Current Biography* (November) 1960.

Obituary *NY Times* B p12 O 24 '94

LOGAN, HARLAN (DE BAUN) Apr. 30, 1904–Dec. 16, 1994 Publisher; editor; editorial consultant; politician; while teaching English at New York University in early 1930s, began conducting magazine analysis service whose clients included *Life*, *Liberty*, and *Vanity Fair*; as editor of *Scribner's Magazine* from 1936 to 1939, modernized policies, contents, and layout of that old-fashioned literary journal in vain attempt to keep it alive; in 1939 joined staff of *Look*, which he, as assistant to publisher Gardner Cowles, transformed from money-losing sensational picture magazine into respected and profitable family publication; in 1940s rose from managing editor and editor of *Look* to vice-president of magazine's parent company, Cowles Magazines, Inc.; after leaving publishing in 1952, became director of public relations at Corning Glass Works; later was vice-president of General Foods and Republican state representative in New Hampshire; died in Hanover, New Hampshire. See *Current Biography* (January) 1946.

Obituary *N Y Times* B p10 Ja 5 '95

LUPINO, IDA Feb. 4, 1918–Aug. 3, 1995 British-born actress; filmmaker; could be electrifying in her intense screen portrayals of a gallery of gritty characters, from fierce and ruthless villains and shrill neurotics and psychotics to various more fragile, brooding, and poignant personae; was descended from theatrical families, dating back in her father's lineage to Renaissance Italy; studied at Royal Academy of Dramatic Art beginning at age thirteen; began motion picture career at fifteen; after playing in five British films, moved to Hollywood, where over a period of five years she continued to be cast in what she scornfully called "pretty-pretty" ingenue roles; began her breakthrough to a stronger screen presence as Bessie Broke, the vengeful Cockney prostitute in *The Light that Failed* (1939); clinched her hold on heavy and earthy assignments with her bravura performance as Lana Carlsen, the adulterous character driven to murder and madness by unrequited love in *They Drive by Night* (1940); with only rare detours into lighter parts (to which she could, with the power of her eyes alone, lend intimations of giddiness, panic, and other unscripted emotions and states of mind), subsequently had such roles as an escaped convict in *The Sea Wolf*, a loyal gun moll in *High Sierra*, a stolid, homicidal housekeeper in *Ladies in Retirement* (all in 1941), a maniacally ambitious show-business manager who pushes her sister to stardom in *The Hard Way* (1943), an eccentric Emily Brontë in *Devotion* (1946), and a tavern singer who sparks jealousy in the noir melodrama *Road House* (1948); as actress, accrued total of more than fifty screen credits, including Amelia, the vicious warden in *Women's Prison* (1955), and Elvira, the world-weary mother in *Junior Bonner* (1972); as independent producer, director, and cowriter, between 1949 and 1953 addressed with both candor and sensitivity such ugly subjects as rape and psychopathic murder in several successful low-budget feature films, including *The Bigamist*, in which she also acted, and *The Hitch-Hiker* (both 1953); on television during 1950s, directed numerous episodes of such series as *The Untouchables*, *Have Gun, Will Travel*, and *Alfred Hitchcock Presents*; often had roles in dramatic television anthology *Four Star Playhouse*; in 1957 and 1958 produced and played opposite Howard Duff, her third husband, in situation comedy *Mr. Adams and Eve*; returned to television as actress on several occasions in early 1970s; died in Burbank, California. See *Current Biography* (September) 1943.

Obituary *N Y Times* P10 Ag 5 '95

MADIGAN, EDWARD R. Jan. 13, 1936–Dec. 7, 1994 U.S. Republican representative from Illinois (1973–91); secretary of agriculture in administration of President George Bush (1991–93); before going to Washington, D.C., served in Illinois state legislature (1967–73); was a moderate Republican known for his bipartisanship in Congress; as the ranking minority member of House Agriculture Committee, had prominent role in shaping American farm policy during much of 1980s; lived in Lincoln, Illinois; died in Springfield, Illinois. See *Current Biography* (March) 1992.

Obituary *N Y Times* D p20 D 9 '94

MANTLE, MICKEY (CHARLES) Oct. 20, 1931–Aug. 12, 1995 Baseball player; the mightiest switch-hitting slugger in major-league history; had career record of .298 in batting, 536 home runs, and 1,509 runs batted in; hit home runs from both sides of plate in ten games, an American League record; in sequence with Babe Ruth and Joe DiMaggio, symbolized long championship reign of New York Yankees, who won twelve American League pennants and eight World Series during his eighteen years on the team; hit a record total of eighteen home runs in the twelve World Series; began his professional career as a shortstop in minor leagues in 1949; moved to right field when he was called up to New York in 1951; when Joe DiMaggio retired, succeeded DiMaggio in center field, the position he would play for most of his career; beginning in 1952, hit over .300 in ten of his eighteen seasons with Yankees; batting right-handed early in 1953 season, hit the first home run (an estimated 565 feet) ever to clear the left-field wall of Griffith Stadium in Washington, D.C.; was American League leader in home runs in 1955, 1956, 1958, and 1960; in 1956 won baseball's triple crown with a .353 batting average, 52 home runs, and 130 runs batted in; hit 54 home runs in 1961; won Gold Glove for fielding in 1962; was voted American League's most valuable player in 1956, 1957, and 1962; hit three home runs in one game, on May 13, 1965; retired on March 1, 1969, at beginning of spring training; was honored with retirement of his uniform number in ceremonies in Yankee Stadium on June 8, 1969; was inducted into Baseball Hall of Fame in 1974; wrote autobiography, *The Mick*; died in Dallas. See *Current Biography* (July) 1953.

Obituary *N Y Times* p1+ Ag 13, 1995

MASSERMAN, JULES H(OMAN) Mar. 10, 1905–Nov. 6, 1994 Psychiatrist; psychoanalyst; neurologist; educator; author; best known for his theory of "biodynamics," based in part on experiments in behavioral psychology; while accepting basic dynamic formulations of classical Freudian psychoanalytic theory, was innovative and eclectic in his explorations of brief therapies as alternative routes to recovery from neurosis; taught at University of Chicago from 1936 to 1946 and at Northwestern University Medical School from 1946 to 1974; in addition to several hundred papers on psychiatric, neurological, and more general medical topics, wrote a score of books, including *Behavior and Neurosis; An Experimental Psychoanalytic Approach to Psychobiologic Principles* (1943), the textbook *Principles of Dynamic Psychiatry: Including an Integrative Approach to Abnormal and Clinical Psychology* (1946) and its companion volume *Practice of Dynamic Psychiatry* (1955), *The Biodynamic Roots of Human Behavior* (1968), and *A Psychiatric Odyssey: Memoirs of a Maverick Psychiatrist* (1971); beginning in 1961, edited the nineteen volumes of the series *Current Psychiatric Therapies*; late in his career was subject of several malpractice suits (four of which were, by 1992, settled out of court) brought by female patients who claimed that he had drugged and taken sexual advantage of them; died at his home in Chicago. See *Current Biography* (July) 1980.

Obituary *N Y Times* D p29 N 15 '94

MAXWELL, VERA (HUPPÉ) Apr. 22, 1901–Jan. 15, 1995 Fashion designer; "the American Chanel"; a pioneering developer of modern women's sportswear, including casual and comfortable everyday wear intended, in her words, to "live and breathe with the wearer"; created mix-and-match ensembles and other versatile clothes with timeless taste and simplicity; became interested in design while modeling riding habits and other clothes beginning in 1929; accustomed to making her own clothes, began designing, at first for herself, such items as wrap-around blouses and riding and fencing suits; in her first separates creation, inspired by men's Harris tweed jacket/gray flannel trousers outfit, combined gray skirt with russet tweed riding jacket; in subsequent modification, removed jacket's collar; in mid-1930s incorporated collarless jacket into mutable "weekend wardrobe" that also included long skirt, short skirt, and slacks; also created "skirt dress," sheath (combined with jacket or coat) that eliminated problem of blouse pulling out of suit skirt; during World War II, designed clothes using minimum of scarce fabrics and a coverall (prototype of the jumpsuit) for women defense workers; after designing for other sportswear companies, founded her own house, Vera Maxwell, Inc., in Manhattan in 1947; ultimately sold her reasonably priced line in approximately seven hundred stores across U.S.; declined in popularity in 1960s; over the years had such distinguished regular customers as Princess Grace of Monaco (a friend), Lillian Gish, Martha Graham, Patricia Nixon, and Rosalynn Carter; while availing herself of finest natural fabrics, was first American designer to use Ultrasuede; retired in 1985; died in Rincón, Puerto Rico. See *Current Biography* (July) 1977.

Obituary *N Y Times* C p21 Ja 20 '95

MAY, ROLLO (REECE) Apr. 21, 1909–Oct. 22, 1994 Psychologist; a founder of humanistic psychology as a movement distinct from psychoanalysis and behaviorism; in early 1930s attended seminars of Austrian physician and psychologist Alfred Adler, a member of Sigmund Freud's circle, who defected from Freudian "biological determinism" by stressing unique conscious elements in individual psychology; subsequently studied under Paul Tillich at Union Theological Seminary; was also influenced by European existentialism and concepts of Harry Stack Sullivan; as Congregational minister, wrote two theology-oriented books: *The Art of Counseling* (1939) and *Springs of Creative Living* (1941); after two years of pastoral work decided he could do more good as psychologist than as minister; earned doctorate in clinical psychology at Columbia University with an interdisciplinary dissertation published as *The Meaning of Anxiety* (1950); from 1958 to 1975 held several posts, including training and supervisory analyst, at William Alanson White Institute in Manhattan, where programs encompassed humanistic and existential psychotherapy as well as stricter forms of psychoanalysis; lectured at New School for Social Research and several universities; by his faith in human capacity to meet problems, his treatment of anxiety as a positive challenge, and his focus on the desire for self-fulfillment, contributed to growth of human potential movement, beginning in 1960s; popularized his concepts of "the ethic of intention," of recognizing and making positive "the daimonic" in human nature, of personal renewal, and of responsibility (within limitations) for one's choices even in midst of radical change in such books as *Love and Will* (1969), *Power and Innocence* (1972), and *The Courage to Create* (1975); died at his home in Tiburon, California. See *Current Biography* (June) 1973.

Obituary *N Y Times* B p12 O 24 '94

McAFEE, MILDRED H(ELEN) May 12, 1900–Sept. 2, 1994 Educator; military officer; taught economics and sociology at Tusculum College, in Greenville, Tennessee (1923-27); was dean of women and professor of sociology at Centre College in Danville, Kentucky from 1927 to 1932; subsequently held positions at Vassar and Oberlin colleges; was president of Wellesley College from 1936 to 1942, when she took leave of absence to become first director of Women Accepted for Voluntary Emergency Service (WAVES), the U.S. Navy's women's auxiliary in World War II; during her tour of duty, overseeing the women who were filling such positions in navy as flight instructors, truck drivers, weather observers, air-traffic controllers, and maintenance workers, reached rank of captain; returned to her post at Wellesley in 1946; resigned in 1949; served as vice-president of the National Council of Churches and president of American Association of Colleges; in 1945 married the Reverend Douglas Horton, who later became dean of Harvard Divinity School; died in Berlin, New Hampshire. See *Current Biography* (September) 1942.

Obituary *N Y Times* p41 S 4 '94

McCOY, CHARLES B(RELSFORD) Apr. 16, 1909–Jan. 16, 1995 Industrial executive; the second person outside du Pont family to achieve presidency of Delaware-based E. I. du Pont de Nemours & Company, world's largest chemical corporation, which produces agricultural and industrial chemicals, pharmaceuticals, synthetic rubber, and house paints and is perhaps best known for introducing to the world rayon, nylon, and other synthetic fibers as well as various plastics and glues; joined company while still in college; after graduation, in 1932, worked in a variety of positions, rising up through ranks to become general manager of explosives department in 1960, vice-president in 1961, and president in 1967; moved to chairmanship of board of directors in 1971; retired as chairman in 1973 but remained on board until 1987; died in Greenville, Delaware. See *Current Biography* (July) 1970.

Obituary *N Y Times* D p21 Ja 18 '95

McRAE, CARMEN Apr. 8, 1922–Nov. 10, 1994 Singer; a jazz contralto with a distinctive style, marked by exquisite phrasing; was ranked by many of her admirers with Billie Holiday, who most influenced her, and Sarah Vaughan; enthralled audiences with her improvisational skill and sensitive and artful interpretation of lyrics, her first priority; could be by turns or even simultaneously melancholy, wry, cynical, and understatedly passionate; while rooted in jazz, ranged widely in popular song, from Cole Porter through Jule Styne to Billy Joel and Stevie Wonder; included in her repertoire "The Last Time for Love" (her own composition), "Skyliner" (one of her rare commercial hits), "The Music That Makes Me Dance," "Guess Who I Saw Today," "Blame It on My Youth," "Yesterdays," "Mean to Me," "I've Got You Under My Skin," and "Just in Time"; studied piano for five years in childhood, thus gaining the musical knowledge without which she would never have become the adventurous singer that she was, sure of herself on that springboard of improvisation, the interval between the notes; at seventeen, won amateur talent contest at Apollo Theater in Harlem with performance that drew attention of Irene Kitchings, whose husband was the jazz pianist Teddy Wilson; through Wilson, met Billie Holiday, who recorded a song McRae had written, "Dream of Life"; while doing clerical work by day in early 1940s, substituted for singers with bands of Benny Carter, Count Basie, and Earl ("Fatha") Hines; in mid-1940s sang for almost two years with band led by Mercer Ellington, who later observed, "Even then . . . , she sang as a musician would play"; recorded her first singles in late 1940s with jazz accordionist Mat Mathews and his band; soon thereafter began attracting critical notice when singing with Tony Scott at Minton's Playhouse in Harlem; in *Downbeat* magazine's poll of critics in 1954 was voted the "new star" among female singers; tied with Ella Fitzgerald for best female vocalist in *Metronome* magazine's poll in 1955; from then on was in demand as solo performer at Rainbow Grill in Manhattan and other venues in the elite club circuit and at jazz festivals; cut her first solo album in 1954; later recorded phenomenally successful single "Take Five" with Dave Brubeck, who marveled at her "instinctive, intuitive understanding of a lyric," enabling her to "generate an emotional impact seldom found in a popular song"; from 1961 to 1969 sang with her own trio, led by pianist and arranger Norman Simmons, who remarked her mastery of "suspense . . . the drama of the phrasing of the lyrics . . . her romance with words and syllables"; during 1960s cut such LPs as *Bittersweet*, *Woman Talk*, and an album of covers of Billie Holiday classics; in 1970 released the pop sampling *Just a Little Lovin'*; made the charts with *I'm Coming Home* in 1980; recorded a total of nearly two dozen albums, including *The Great American Songbook* and, at end of her career, *Carmen Sings Monk*; retired in 1991, following a performance at Blue Note in Manhattan, when she went into respiratory collapse; in January 1994 received National Endowment for the Arts jazz fellowship award; died at her home in Beverly Hills, California. See *Current Biography* (April) 1983.

Obituary *N Y Times* p29 N 12 '94

MERRILL, JAMES Mar. 3, 1926–Feb. 6, 1995 Poet; was known almost strictly for finely crafted short lyrical poems, generally classified as "New York school" and described by him as "chronicles of love and loss," until he created the epic trilogy brought together in 560-page volume *The Changing Light at Sandover* (1982), an antically visionary work of occult inspiration and cosmological scope; as son of a founder of stock brokerage firm of Merrill, Lynch & Company, was raised in luxury; from age of eleven, had consuming interest in music, especially opera, the influence of which is evident in carefully orchestrated rhythms present in all his lyric poetry; in 1951 published *First Poems*, which was accorded mixed reception; temporarily turned from poetry to prose, including Off-Broadway play *The Immortal Husband* (1953), a retelling of the myth of Tithonus, and novel *The Seraglio* (1957); in view of some critics, found "his own voice" in "brilliant, neurotic, subtly made, and extremely intelligent" poems collected in his second volume, *The Country of a Thousand Years of Peace* (1959); received National Book Award in poetry for *Nights and Days* (1966) and Bolingen Prize in poetry for *Braving the Elements* (1972); won Pulitzer Prize for *Divine Comedies* (1976), two-thirds of which comprised "The Book of Ephraim," beginning of the Sandover trilogy, based on presumed communications from spirits experienced by him and David Jackson, his lifelong companion, in experiments with a Ouija board; won second National Book Award with *Mirabell: Book of Number* (1978), second part of trilogy; completed trilogy with *Scripts for the Pageant* (1980); wrote a memoir of his early life, *A Different Person* (1993); had homes in Stonington, Connecticut and New York City; died in Tucson, Arizona. See *Current Biography* (August) 1981.

Obituary *N Y Times* B p10 F 7 '95

MORGAN, THOMAS E(LLSWORTH) Oct. 13, 1906 July 31, 1995 U.S. Democratic representative from Pennsylvania (1945–77); physician; as chairman of House International Relations Committee from 1958 to 1976, strove to be nonpartisan but opposed President Richard Nixon's Vietnam policy and President Gerald R. Ford's proposal for American assistance to anti-Communist troops in Angola; after retiring from elective politics, resumed his medical practice in Fredericktown, Pennsylvania; died in Waynesberg, Pennsylvania. See *Current Biography* (June) 1959.

Obituary *N Y Times* D p20 Ag 2 '95

NELSON, HARRIET July 18, 1909–Oct. 2, 1994 Actress; singer; under name Harriet Hilliard, began career as actress with her parents' traveling stock company; later performed in vaudeville; in 1935 married Ozzie Nelson, with whose big band she was singing at the time; with Ozzie and, ultimately, their sons, David and Ricky (who died in a plane crash in 1985, after achieving fame as a rock singer), starred in *The Adventures of Ozzie and Harriet*, a situation comedy based on their everyday family life that began on network radio in 1944 and later made transition to network television, where it ran until 1966; on her own beginning in mid-1930s had roles in a number of films, including singing parts in *Follow the Fleet* (1936) and *New Faces of 1937* and starring role in *Life of the Party* (1937); subsequently performed in several musical films with her husband; with entire family starred in *Here Come the Nelsons* (1952); did occasional acting on television; died at her home in Laguna Beach, California. See *Current Biography* (May) 1949.

Obituary *N Y Times* B p8 O 4 '94

NIZER, LOUIS Feb. 6, 1902–Nov. 10, 1994 Attorney; a flamboyant and grandiloquent trial lawyer; senior partner in New York-based firm of Phillips, Nizer, Benjamin, Krim & Ballon; authority on libel, divorce, antitrust, contract, copyright, and plagiarism law; represented such prestigious clients as Occidental Oil Company, film producers and distributors, and a host of celebrities, including the writer Quentin Reynolds (in his successful libel suit against the columnist Westbrook Pegler), Charlie Chaplin, Mae West, Salvador Dali, Eddie Fisher, Alan Jay Lerner, Julius Erving, Governor James A. Rhodes of Ohio, and the blacklisted broadcaster John Henry Faulk (in his successful suit against the ultra-right-wing publication that had accused him of Communist ties); wrote *What to Do with Germany* (1944), best-selling autobiography *My Life in Court* (1962), and other books, on such subjects as public speaking and self-regulation under the motion picture code; died in New York City. See *Current Biography* (November) 1955.

Obituary *N Y Times* B p7 N 11 '94

NU, THAKIN May 25, 1907–Feb. 14, 1995 Former prime minister of Burma (now Myanmar); a moderate socialist who promoted democracy at home and a foreign policy of neutrality in Cold War that existed between Western powers and Communist bloc; as a leader of Anti-Fascist People's Freedom League (a leftist coalition formed during World War II), helped win Burma's independence from Britain; was chosen by British governor to become equivalent of prime minister in 1947, the year before Burma became an autonomous republic; led his party to successive parliamentary majorities in general elections between 1951 and 1960; was a dominant figure at conference of newly emergent nations at Bandung, Indonesia in 1955 and one of five national leaders who subsequently formed the international nonalignment movement; despite his popularity in Burma, was deposed in military coup led by General U Ne Win in 1962; after long periods of imprisonment and house arrest under Ne Win regime, was allowed to leave Burma in 1969; from Thailand, led campaign to oust Ne Win until 1974, when Thai government asked him to leave; lived in India from 1974 until 1980, when he returned to his homeland at invitation of Ne Win, with the stipulation that he abstain from political activity; when massive popular opposition drove Ne Win from power and paralyzed the government in 1988, announced his formation of provisional opposition government and called for free election; in 1989, after military reasserted control, was placed under house arrest, which remained in effect until 1992; died at his home in Yangon (formerly Rangoon). See *Current Biography* (December) 1951.

Obituary *N Y Times* D p21 F 15 '95

ONGANIA, JUAN CARLOS May 17, 1914–June 8, 1995 President of Argentina (1966–70); career Argentine army officer; in rank of brigadier general, was a cavalry commander in late 1950s and early 1960s; in September 1962, following factional strife within army, gained control of high command and, in rank of lieutenant general, was appointed commander in chief of army by José Maria Guido; retained that position after Arturo Illia was elected to succeed Guido in 1963; resigned as army commander in chief in 1965; was installed as president by military junta that overthrew Illia in coup in 1966; after an extraordinarily repressive four-year rule, was himself overthrown by coup; died in Buenos Aires. See *Current Biography* (October) 1968.

Obituary *N Y Times* p48 Je 10 '95

OSBORN, ROBERT C(HESLEY) Oct. 26, 1904–Dec. 20, 1994 Graphic artist; a cartoonist, caricaturist, and illustrator known for his social consciousness, satiric wit, and bold sweep of lines in his pen, pencil, and brush drawings; as student, was art editor of *Yale Record* at Yale University; after graduating, studied painting in Rome and Paris and taught art and Greek philosophy at Hotchkiss School; in late 1930s lived and traveled in Austria, painting landscapes and tutoring; published series of satirical "how-to" books with text and line drawings in 1941 and 1942; in navy during World War II, did some forty thousand drawings for posters and training and safety manuals for aviators; immediately after war, wrote and illustrated humorous book *War Is No Damn Good!*; in late 1940s began to illustrate books and to contribute drawings to such magazines as *Harper's* and *Fortune*; beginning in 1953, did self-sustained satirical cartoon panels on various subjects for *Fortune* and *Look*; became contributor of parodic drawings to *New Republic* in 1956; illustrated such books as C. Northcote Parkinson's *Parkinson's Law* (1957) and Marya Mannes's *Subverse* (1959); did both text and illustrations for *Low & Inside* (1953), *Osborn on Leisure* (1957), and the illustrated autobiography *Osborn on Osborn* (1982); also published *Osborn on Conflict* (1984), containing forty brush drawings; with Herbert Scoville, published *Missile Madness* (1970); in 1987 had art exhibition featuring his drawings of Charles Chaplin; throughout career maintained contact with U.S. Navy by doing cartoon series about wise old navy aviator for *Naval Aviation News*; died at his home in Salisbury, Connecticut. See *Current Biography* (June) 1959.

Obituary *N Y Times* D p19 D 22 '94

OSBORNE, JOHN (JAMES) Dec. 12, 1929–Dec. 24, 1994 Playwright; the original "angry young man" of mid-twentieth-century English drama; with his vitriolic indictments of social institutions and class structure in postwar Britain, especially in his landmark work *Look Back in Anger*, gave voice to a generation of lower-class intellectuals who resented being "beneficiaries" of a welfare state that denied them challenge and upward opportunity in a society that they considered decadent as well as rigged; regarding the family from which he himself came, wrote in his book of memoirs *A Better Class of Person* (1981): "The grudge that was their birthright they pursued with passionate despondency to the grave"; after graduating from secondary school, without going to university, became involved in theatre (even doing some acting) as tutor to touring group of juvenile actors; later managed small theatrical company that played seaside resorts; wrote his first play, *The Devil Inside*, when he was nineteen; in early 1950s cowrote, with Anthony Creighton, *Epitaph for George Dillon*, a play about a penniless aspiring playwright that would not be produced until 1958; by himself wrote "On the Pier at Morecombe," original version of *Look Back in Anger*, whose antihero is, like his creator, a "non-U" intellectual consumed by wrath—one Jimmy Porter, a Midlands street merchant who rails against his dreary life and ruins his marriage (to a middle-class woman) with his self-centered and neurotic emotionalism; after many rejections, found producers for the play, which marked a turning point in contemporary theatre when it was given its debut in London in 1956 and was later adapted to the motion picture screen in two versions; followed that up with *The Entertainer* (1957), a tragicomedy, set in a chintzy seaside resort, about a vulgar music-hall hoofer named Archie Rice who realizes what a self-destructive failure he has been in his life as well as his career; subsequently wrote Tony-winning *Luther* (1961), a Brecht-like historical drama in which the Reformation leader is seen as an angry, relentless rebel influenced by both religious fervor and gastrointestinal problems; among other subsequent plays, wrote *Inadmissible Evidence* (1964), about a barrister whose irascibility alienates all who know him and drives him to brink of nervous breakdown, and *Dejavu* (1992), a sequel to *Look Back in Anger*; as screenwriter, cowrote script for 1960 film version of *The Entertainer*, won Academy Award for his screenplay for *Tom Jones* (1963), and wrote screenplay for 1968 screen adaptation of *Inadmissible Evidence*; in 1991 published second volume of his autobiography, *Almost a Gentleman*; published last book, *Damn You, England*, in 1994; died in Shropshire, where he had lived with his fifth wife since 1986. See *Current Biography* (June) 1959.

Obituary *N Y Times* p15 D 27 '94

PERRY, FRANK Aug. 21, 1930–Aug. 29, 1995 Filmmaker; resisting lure of Hollywood's glamour and financial rewards, helped to establish what he called "personal filmmaking . . . , the picture made by a filmmaker rather than a huge organization"; was concerned with, in his words, themes of human "vulnerability, fallibility, fragility"; although primarily attracted to filmmaking, spent long apprenticeship in theatre, beginning with menial work as a teenager at Westport (Connecticut) Playhouse; spent nine seasons in summer and winter stock at Westport, working as assistant stage manager, production manager, and director; studied directing under Lee Strasberg; was stage manager for 1955 Broadway production of *The Rainmaker*; with an eye toward his filmmaking future, worked for Theatre Guild from 1956 to 1960, cultivating wealthy theatrical investors; on an arduously collected shoestring budget of two hundred thousand dollars and with a screenplay written by the first of his three wives, Eleanor (his scenarist for his earliest films), made his debut as a filmmaker with the blockbuster sleeper *David and Lisa* (1962), sensitive study of two disturbed adolescents in a mental hospital; with less éclat subsequently directed *Ladybug, Ladybug* (1963), about the psychological effect of nuclear holocaust on a group of schoolchildren, and *The Swimmer* (1968), based on a short story by John Cheever; stirred controversy but struck a chord with young audiences with *Last Summer* (1969), about an upper-middle-class teenage girl taunted and sexually molested by peers on Fire Island; in his last collaboration with Eleanor Perry, *Diary of a Mad Housewife* (1970), took a sardonic look at a beleaguered woman in a disintegrating marriage; in revisionist Western *Doc* (1971), debunked heroic Doc Holliday-Wyatt Earp myth; saw his screen version of painful story of late Joan Crawford's adopted daughter Christina, *Mommie Dearest* (1981), become camp classic; changed pace with suburban black comedy *Compromising Positions* (1985); in *On the Bridge* (1993), documented his battle with the prostate cancer that would kill him; made some fifteen films, including *Trilogy* (1969), *Play It as It Lays* (1972), *Man on a Swing* (1974), *Rancho Deluxe* (1975), *Monsignor* (1982), and *Hello Again* (1987); on Broadway, directed *Ladies of the Alamo* in 1977; directed a number of television productions and was host of *Playwright at Work* series on public television; died in New York City. See *Current Biography* (October) 1972.

Obituary *N Y Times* B p15 Ag 31 '95

PINAY, ANTOINE Dec. 30, 1891–Dec. 13, 1994 French statesman; former prime minister; industrialist; in politics, was moderately conservative leader of Republican Independents, best remembered for helping France through some difficult economic times in decades following World War II; ran a leather tannery in St.-Chamond, near Lyons, in the Midi; in 1929 was elected mayor of St.-Chamond, a post he retained until his retirement in 1977; was elected to Chamber of Deputies in 1936 and to Senate two years later; after liberation of France, retreated from national politics under cloud caused by his perceived involvement in regime of Marshal Pétain (who was convicted of treason for cooperating with Germans during wartime occupation); returned to national political scene with election to new national assembly in 1946; between 1948 and 1952 served successively as secretary of state for economic affairs and minister of public works, transportation, and tourism; in dual positions of prime minister and minister of finance from March to December 1952, imposed strict controls to bring postwar inflation under control; subsequently served as minister of foreign affairs (1955–56); as minister of finance and economic affairs (1958–60), again addressed problem of inflation, which he solved by creating the "new franc" (by removing two zeroes from old one); served as first national ombudsman in 1973–74; died at his home in St.-Chamond, France. See *Current Biography* (April) 1952.

Obituary *N Y Times* B p9 D 14 '94

PINEAU, CHRISTIAN (PAUL FRANCIS) Oct. 14, 1904–Apr. 5, 1995 Former French government official; Socialist Party leader; a hero of French Resistance; before entering politics, worked as banker and official of bank employees' union; during Nazi occupation of France, helped found underground newspaper *Libération* and was liaison between Resistance leaders and General Charles de Gaulle's Free French headquarters in London; captured by Gestapo in 1943, was tortured and eventually sent to Buchenwald; after American forces liberated the concentration camp, in April 1945, was appointed minister of food in General de Gaulle's provisional government; was first elected from department of the Sarthe to the national assembly in October 1945; in several successive governments in late 1940s was appointed minister of public works and transportation, minister of finance and economic affairs, and again minister of public works; in early 1950s was twice asked to form a government and twice failed to put together a cabinet; under Prime Minister Guy Mollet, served as foreign minister from 1956 to 1958; directed foreign policy during Suez Canal crisis, which prompted Anglo-French intervention in fall of 1956; sought solutions to France's colonial problems and to question of German reunification; tried to end Cold War by moving from military confrontation with Soviet Union to closer economic ties; died in Paris. See *Current Biography* (July) 1956.

Obituary *N Y Times* B p8 Ap 7 '95

PLEASENCE, DONALD Oct. 5, 1919–Feb. 2, 1995 British character actor; performed with a subtlety and intensity that was often disturbing and could become chilling in his more sinister portrayals; in long and variegated career, had his greatest success on stage, and arguably on screen as well, in title role of Harold Pinter's *The Caretaker* (*The Guest* in its film version); after an apprenticeship with small theatrical companies elsewhere, in 1942 made first of many appearances at Arts Theatre Club in London; performed with Birmingham Repertory Theatre from 1948 until 1950, when he moved on to Bristol Old Vic Company; with a touring troupe, made his first Broadway appearances as the Majordomo in *Caesar and Cleopatra* and Lemprius Euphronius in *Antony and Cleopatra* in 1951; in London during 1950s, played Willie Mossop in *Hobson's Choice*, Huish in his own stage adaptation of Robert Louis Stevenson's short story "Ebb Tide," Leone Gale (his favorite role, because of its challenging transition from the comic to the tragic) in *Rules of the Game*, the Dauphin in *The Lark*, the Cockney clerk in *Misalliance*, and Monsieur Tarde in *Restless Heart*; in 1960 created comic, pathetic, and finally shattering character of Davies the derelict in *The Caretaker*; did so in his wonted manner, by thinking of his character as an animal—in that instance, as an alley cat; after smash opening at Arts Theatre Club, moved with play to West End and thence, in 1961, to similarly triumphal reception on Broadway; later in decade, in West End and on Broadway, starred as Bitos in *Poor Bitos* and Arthur Goldman in *The Man in the Glass Booth*; on screen, reprised his role of Goldman as well as Davies; otherwise ranged from early East Indian and Arab supporting portrayals to later performances as villains, psychotics, or eccentrics in such films as *Dr. Crippen* (1964), *Cul-de-Sac* (1966), *You Only Live Twice* (1967), *Will Penny* (1968), and *The Eagle Has Landed* (1977); played more benign characters in *No Love for Johnnie* (1961), *Lisa* (1962), and *The Great Escape* (1962), among other motion pictures; made more than 120 pictures, including five of those in the Halloween horror series; on television, was seen in numerous dramas, including adaptations of Anthony Trollope's *Barchester Chronicles* and Evelyn Waugh's *Scoop*; returned to London stage in revival of *The Caretaker* in 1991; died at his home in St. Paul de Vence in south of France. See *Current Biography* (June) 1969.

Obituary *N Y Times* D p19 F 3 '95

PONNAMPERUMA, CYRIL (ANDREW) Oct. 16, 1923–Dec. 20, 1994 Chemist; exobiologist; professor of chemistry and director of laboratory of chemical evolution at University of Maryland since 1971; had previously been chief of chemical evolution branch of NASA's Ames Research Center; according to his friend Arthur C. Clarke, was "the leading authority on the origins of life"; exploiting dramatic advances in molecular biology, astrophysics, and micropaleontology, among other disciplines, constructed convincing theory about series of chemical reactions that gave rise to precursors of life on earth; building on work of Harold Urey and Stanley L. Miller, mimicked those reactions in "primordial soup" experiments; wrote book *Origins of Life*; edited journal of same name; and contributed to other professional journals; died in Washington, D.C. See *Current Biography* (April) 1984.

Obituary *N Y Times* p10 D 24 '94

PRICE, DON K(RASHER, JR.) Jan. 23, 1910–July 10, 1995 Political scientist; educator; a pioneer in study of science and technology's impact on political institutions and public policy; with federal Home Owners Loan Corporation in mid-1930s, helped to develop a national housing policy and administrative machinery for implementing that policy; was a major contributor to Social Science Research Council's study *City Manager Government in the United States* (1940); on staff of Public Administration Clearing House between 1939 and 1953, with interruptions, was successively editorial assistant and writer for *Public Administration Review*, assistant director, and associate director; at U.S. Bureau of the Budget in 1945 and 1946, helped draw up legislation for creation of Atomic Energy Commission and National Science Foundation; was associate director (1953–54) and vice-president (1954–58) of Ford Foundation; in 1958 joined faculty of Harvard University as professor of government and dean of Graduate School of Public Administration, which was renamed John Fitzgerald Kennedy School of Government in 1966; from January 1966 to January 1967 served as president of American Academy for the Advancement of Science; in his book *The Scientific Estate* (1965) summed up his reflections on relationship of contemporary science and technology to politics in the American economic and constitutional system; at Harvard, introduced an interdisciplinary graduate seminar in science and public policy; taught at Harvard until his retirement in 1980; died in Wellesley, Massachusetts. See *Current Biography* (February) 1967.

Obituary *N Y Times* D p11 Jl 10 '95

PRIMUS, PEARL Nov. 29, 1919–Oct. 29, 1994 Trinidadian-born dancer; choreographer; teacher; anthropologist; based her dances on primitive African and West Indian music, spirituals and other sources (including folk songs and poetry) relating to slavery and its aftermath in U.S., and jazz, blues, and jitterbug (which she formalized in some of her dances); originally aspired to career in medicine; thwarted in that career prospect by racial barriers after earning premedical degree in 1940, joined federal National Youth Administration dance project; in 1941 won scholarship with New Dance Group, a New York City modern dance school/performing company where she eventually became a faculty member; as choreographer, created in 1943 her dances *Strange Fruit* and *The Negro Speaks of Rivers*; in April 1944 gave her first solo concert, at Manhattan YMHA's Dance Theatre; meanwhile, performed at Cafe Society Downtown, a Greenwich Village jazz nightclub, and its counterpart, Cafe Society Uptown; in Broadway engagement with her own aggregation of dancers, jazz band, drummers, singers, and narrator in fall of 1944, introduced her *Slave Market* and *Rock Daniel*; shortly afterward, at Manhattan's Roxy Theatre, headed her company of dancers in elaborate production of her *African Ceremonial*; later toured with her troupe and with national company in revival of musical *Show Boat*; on Rosenwald Foundation scholarship, visited Africa for first time in 1948; in Trinidad in 1953 met dancer Percival Borde, whom she married and with whom she founded dance school in New York; became director of performing arts center in Monrovia, Liberia in 1959; performed throughout Africa with her husband in early 1960s; received doctorate in anthropology in 1978; performed until 1980; subsequently directed black studies school at State University of New York and taught at other institutions; died at her home in New Rochelle, New York. See *Current Biography* (April) 1944.

Obituary *N Y Times* B p8 O 31 '94

RAPHAEL, CHAIM July 14, 1908–Oct. 10, 1994 British scholar; government economist; popularizer of economics; detective fiction writer; in 1930s lectured in Hebrew at Oxford University, where he held Kennicott Fellowship in Biblical Hebrew; as government liaison officer early in World War II, expedited movement of transmigrant German refugees, many of them Jewish, out of internment camps in Britain and into U.S.; later helped refugees waiting in Canada to obtain visas for entry into U.S.; from 1942 to 1957 was an economist and director of economic information at British Information Services in New York; in information division of Her Majesty's Treasury was deputy director (1957-59) and chief (1959-68); beginning in 1956, under pseudonym Jocelyn Davey, wrote series of crime mysteries—including *A Capitol Offense* and *Murder in Paradise*—the detective hero of which is Ambrose Usher, an Oxford don who often works as a secret agent for the Foreign Office; under his own name wrote fictionalized autobiography, *Memoirs of a Special Case* (1962), and contributed articles and stories to newspapers and magazines, including *Commentary* and *Atlantic Monthly*; died in London. See *Current Biography* (December) 1963.

Obituary *N Y Times* B p15 O 13 '94

RAYE, MARTHA Aug. 27, 1916–Oct. 19, 1994 Comedienne; actress; singer; a zestful knockabout with a voice as big as her elastic mouth; was born into itinerant vaudeville family, whose song-and-dance act she joined when she was three; as a teenager, moved on her own into burlesque stints, musical revues, and nightclub acts; was a seasoned stage veteran when she broke into films as one of the featured musical performers in *Rhythm on the Range* (1936), one of the high points of which was her swinging rendition of "Mr. Paganini" and her portrayal of a drunk; became one of the busiest comediennes in Hollywood, cast in more than thirty films, including *Mountain Music* (1937), *College Swing* (1938), *The Farmer's Daughter* (1940), and *The Boys from Syracuse* (1940); in retrospect, described most of the zany comedies she had made as "mindless"; was perhaps more satisfied with *Four Jills in a Jeep* (1944), a reenactment of her World War II USO tour entertaining troops in England and Africa with three other Hollywood actresses; was justly proudest of her performance as Annabella Bonheur, the indestructible wife in whom the title character, a Parisian Bluebeard (Charlie Chaplin), meets his match in the black comedy *Monsieur Verdoux* (1947); on Broadway in 1940 costarred with Al Jolson in musical revue *Hold On to Your Hats*; was guest on radio shows of Jolson and others; took her buffoonery to television in guest appearances and as star of *Martha Raye Show* on NBC in 1953-54 season; returning to screen, was at her comic and musical best teamed (as on many other occasions) with Jimmy Durante, a longtime friend, in musical circus picture *Jumbo* (1962); in 1967 took her turn as one of a succession of stars in title role in Broadway musical *Hello, Dolly!*; in 1969 won special Academy Award for entertaining troops in Vietnam; died in Los Angeles. See *Current Biography* (July) 1963.

Obituary *N Y Times* B p16 O 20 '94

REYNOLDS, ALLIE Feb. 10, 1919–Dec. 27, 1994 Baseball player; right-handed fastball pitcher; after nearly four full seasons in minor leagues, was called up to Cleveland Indians of American League in September 1942; traded to New York Yankees following 1946 season; as both starting and relief pitcher, helped pitch Yankees to six world championships (including a record five in a row) between 1947 and 1953; set American League record by pitching two no-hitters in one season (1951); led league twice in strikeouts and once in earned-run average (2.06 in 1952, when he won twenty of twenty-eight games); in World Series with Yankees, had seven wins, two losses, four saves, and a 2.79 earned-run average; during thirteen-year major-league career, compiled win-loss record of 182-107, forty-nine saves, thirty-six shutouts, 3.30 earned-run average; after retiring from baseball in 1954, became successful oil businessman in Oklahoma; died in Oklahoma City. See *Current Biography* (June) 1952.

Obituary *N Y Times* D p18 D 28 '94

ROEBLING, MARY G(INDHART) July 29, 1906–Oct. 25, 1994 Banker; first woman to head a major American bank, Trenton (New Jersey) Trust Company; following death of her husband, Siegfried Roebling, took his seat on Trenton Trust's board of directors in 1936 and was elected president in 1937; remained president until 1972, when Trenton Trust was acquired by National State Bank in Elizabeth, New Jersey; chaired the merged institutions until 1984; was first woman to serve as a governor of New York Stock Exchange (1958-62); helped found (1978) and for several years chaired Women's Bank N.A. of Denver, first nationally chartered bank founded by women; died at her home in Trenton, New Jersey. See *Current Biography* (October) 1960.

Obituary *N Y Times* D p24 O 27 '94

ROGERS, GINGER July 16, 1911–Apr. 25, 1995 Actress; a spirited and durable comic and dramatic performer whose grounding was in musical theatre; diverted Depression-weary movie audiences with her graceful dancing in electric partnership with Fred Astaire in string of classy romances, the best of which was probably *Top Hat* (1935); won Academy Award for her melodramatic portrayal of eponymous lovesmitten working girl in the sentimental romance *Kitty Foyle* (1940); demonstrated talent for comedy in such films as *The Major and the Minor* (1942); was groomed for career in show business by her mother, Lela McMath, a writer who did some screenwriting for Fox studios; as teenager began dancing and singing in vaudeville, where she teamed up with Edward Culpepper, first of her five husbands; made Broadway debut as second female lead in musical *Top Speed* in 1929; followed that up with role of Molly Gray in Gershwin musical *Girl Crazy* (1930); meanwhile, had appeared in several short silents; played sassy flappers in her first two feature films, *Young Man of Manhattan* (1930) and *Hat Check Girl* (1932); moved up from B-picture level in such musicals as *Forty-second Street* (1933) and *Gold Diggers of 1933*; launched her dancing partnership with Fred Astaire in *Flying Down to Rio* (1933); was cast in eight subsequent dance musicals with Astaire and later costarred with him in *The Barkleys of Broadway* (1949); made total of some seventy films, including *Lady in the Dark* (1944), *It Had to Be You* (1947), and *Forever Female* (1954) and ending with *Harlow* (1965); in returns to Broadway, starred in comedy *Love and Let Love* (1951) and succeeded Carol Channing in musical *Hello, Dolly!* (1965); played title role in first London production of musical *Mame* (1969); often performed in summer stock; published the autobiography *Ginger: My Story* (1991); died at her home in Rancho Mirage, California. See *Current Biography* (December) 1967.

Obituary *N Y Times* D p24 Ap 26 '95

ROMNEY, GEORGE July 8, 1907–July 26, 1995 Industrialist; liberal Republican governor of Michigan (1963-69); secretary of housing and urban development in cabinet of President Richard Nixon; was Washington lobbyist for Aluminum Corporation of America and Aluminum Wares Association from 1932 to 1938; moved to Detroit as office manager of Automobile Manufacturers Association in 1939; was general manager of association from 1942 until 1948, when he joined Nash-Kelvinator Corporation as special assistant to chairman; after Nash-Kelvinator merged with Hudson Motor Car Company in 1954, became president, chairman, and general manager of the resulting amalgamation, American Motors Corporation, a puny competitor alongside Detroit's "big three" automobile manufacturers, despite its advantage in diversification (chiefly into major appliances); in late 1950s moved American Motors from thirteenth to seventh in auto-production standings by concentrating on production of America's first compact car, the Rambler; resigned in 1962 to run for governor; as governor, promoted civil rights initiatives and turned Michigan's chronic deficit around by introducing several new sets of taxes; was an early, anti-Vietnam war candidate for 1968 Republican presidential nomination, but dropped out of running before first primary; as secretary of housing and urban development, had some success in increasing amount of federally subsidized housing in cities, but not in extending it into suburbs; after leaving cabinet upon Nixon's reelection, in 1972, founded National Center for Voluntary Action, dedicated to encouraging involvement in public affairs; died in Bloomfield Hills, Michigan. See *Current Biography* (June) 1958.

Obituary *N Y Times* D p22 Jl 27 '95

ROOT, OREN June 13, 1911–Jan. 14, 1995 Lawyer; liberal Republican politician; while beginning practice of law in late 1930s, campaigned for election of Fiorello La Guardia as mayor of New York City and Thomas E. Dewey as governor of New York state; was early, major promoter of Wendell L. Willkie for Republican nomination for president in 1940; worked full time as chairman of Associated Willkie Clubs of America during Willkie's unsuccessful run against President Franklin D. Roosevelt; later served as member of New York County Republican Committee and vice-president of New York Young Republican Club; was first president of National Association for Mental Health in early 1950s; in administration of Governor Nelson A. Rockefeller of New York from 1959 to 1964, was successively special assistant for federal and interstate affairs and secretary of banks; for many years practiced law with New York firm of Root Barrett Cohen Knapp & Smith; later was counsel to firm of Lord Day & Lord Barrett Smith until 1994; died in Bedford, New York. See *Current Biography* (July) 1952.

Obituary *N Y Times* B p8 Ja 16 '95

ROSENFELD, HARRY N(ATHAN) Aug. 17, 1911–June 2, 1995 U.S. government official; lawyer; in early 1940s, after working as secretary to commissioner of New York City's board of education, began serving in legal capacities with various federal agencies, including Federal Security Agency's Office of Education; as commissioner of U.S. Displaced Persons Commission for four years beginning in 1948, was responsible for supervising admission to and resettlement in U.S. of refugees who had been displaced by the war in Europe; is credited by Merriam-Webster researchers with making first known use in print of term "baby boom," in his final report to President Harry S. Truman; in 1953, after leaving government service, went into private legal practice in Washington, D.C.; in 1950s was coauthor of multivolume reference work *Immigration Law and Procedure*, which continues to be published in revised editions; died at his home in Washington, D.C. See *Current Biography* (April) 1952.

Obituary *N Y Times* D p10 Je 5 '95

ROSTEN, NORMAN Jan. 1, 1914–Mar. 7, 1995 Poet; playwright; novelist; a Brooklyn-based writer who placed himself outside of "that school which holds to the curious belief that poetry is written for poets and should be as difficult and obscure as possible"; on scholarship at University of Michigan School of Drama in late 1930s, wrote his first play, *Proud Pilgrim-*

age, poetic drama about the Chicago Haymarket riot; subsequently worked with New York Federal Theatre, a WPA project; in 1940 published his first book, *Return Again, Traveler*, a set of poems sentimentally celebrating "our history as we have lived it," from Johnny Appleseed through the building of the Union Pacific Railroad to burlesque dancing on 42d Street, in an American idiom ranging from plain to grandiloquent; in January 1941 saw his first Broadway play, *First Stop to Heaven*, flop; fifteen years later would have slightly greater success on Broadway with *Mister Johnson*; in early 1940s wrote many verse plays and dramatic poems for network radio, the best known of which was *Ballad of Bataan*, a World War II morale booster; in words of one critic, wrote verse collected in *The Fourth Decade* (1943) "in the language, spirit, and mood of a newspaper editorial, with Marxist implications"; dealt with what he called "the drama of roadmaking" in *The Big Road* (1946), book-length narrative poem about building of Alcan Highway; among several novels, had greatest success with *Under the Boardwalk* (1968), about a pubescent Coney Island boy; having known Marilyn Monroe through his friendship with her third husband, Arthur Miller, wrote *Marilyn: An Untold Story* (1973); published *Selected Poems* in 1979; died in Brooklyn, New York. See *Current Biography* (April) 1944.

Obituary *N Y Times* B p13 Mr 9 '95

ROUDEBUSH, RICHARD L(OWELL) Jan. 18, 1918–Jan. 28, 1995 U.S. conservative Republican representative from Indiana (1961–71); former U.S. administrator of veterans affairs; as an enlisted army demolition specialist during World War II, won five battle stars in combat in North Africa and Italy before serious wound led to his medical discharge in 1944; after returning home, was staff member of regional office of Veterans Administration for seven years; at same time, became service officer with Indiana department of Veterans of Foreign Wars; became active in VFW's national rehabilitation program, which assists disabled veterans; rose through ranks of VFW to serve as national commander in chief (1957–58); subsequently concentrated on management of his farm near Noblesville, Indiana and his livestock brokerage business until his campaign for Congress in 1960; in House of Representatives, served on committees on internal security and on science and aeronautics; pushed legislation to benefit veterans, accelerate manned space program, reduce wasteful government spending, promote Americanism, and oppose cooperation with Communist countries; in 1966 received 100 percent rating from conservative Americans for Constitutional Action; at urging of President Richard Nixon, ran for U.S. Senate in 1970; lost bitterly fought campaign against Senator Vance Hartke; headed U.S. Veterans Administration from 1974 to 1977; died in Sarasota, Florida. See *Current Biography* (June) 1976.

Obituary *N Y Times* B p7 Ja 30 '95

RÓZSA, MIKLÓS Apr. 18, 1907–July 27, 1995 Hungarian-born composer; for more than half a century, was towering figure in the two worlds of music and film; began playing violin at five; later learned to play viola and piano as well; as child, was profoundly influenced by culture of Magyar peasants who lived in villages surrounding his family's estate in rural Hungary; became a collector of Palóc folk songs, writing down the music as he heard it; was also influenced by the sometimes dissonant compositions of Bartók and Kódály; studied music and completed his early chamber compositions in Germany until 1931, when he moved to Paris; over following few years became known internationally for his chamber pieces, his music for ballet *Hungaria*, and his orchestral compositions, the best-known of which is the folklike *Theme, Variations, and Finale*; for Sir Alexander Korda's London Films, wrote his earliest scores for films, beginning with *Knight Without Armor* (1937) and including *The Four Feathers* (1939), *The Thief of Baghdad* (1940), *That Hamilton Woman* (1941), and *The Jungle Book* (1942); after becoming freelance composer in Hollywood (where director Billy Wilder was his strongest patron) in early 1940s, scored such pictures as film noir classic *Double Indemnity* (1944), *The Lost Weekend* (1945), *Spellbound* (1945), for which he won his first Academy Award, and *A Double Life* (1948), which brought him his second; adapted *Spellbound*'s love theme into the *Spellbound* Concerto, a light classical piece that became the most recorded of his compositions; at Metro-Goldwyn-Mayer studios, specialized in scoring swashbucklers and historical epics, including *Quo Vadis?* (1951), *Ivanhoe* (1952), and *Julius Caesar* (1953); on leave from MGM, scored the box-office blockbusters *Ben-Hur* (1959) and *El Cid* (1961, regarded by him to be his "last major film score"); during 1960s devoted more time to composing concert pieces, including piano and cello concertos; later scored, among other films, *Providence* (1977), *Time After Time* (1979), for which he was nominated for an Oscar, and *Dead Men Don't Wear Plaid* (1981); wrote autobiography, *Double Life* (1989); died in Los Angeles. See *Current Biography* (February) 1992.

Obituary *N Y Times* p27 Jl 29 '95

RUDOLPH, WILMA (GLODEAN) June 23, 1940–Nov. 12, 1994 Track and field athlete; overcame polio and other childhood diseases to become world champion runner; in Olympics in 1956, won bronze medal in four-hundred-meter relay; in 1960, took three gold medals, winning one hundred meters in 11.0 seconds, setting Olympic record in two hundred meters of 23.2 in the heats (and winning with confirmed final time of 24.0), and anchoring the four-hundred-meter relay, in which she helped set a world record of 44.4 seconds in a heat; in a meet in Louisville, Kentucky in 1961 set new world record of 7.8 seconds in seventy-yard dash; received 1961 Sullivan Award as America's outstanding amateur athlete; later taught school, coached high school basketball, ran a community center, and coached briefly at DePauw University; established Wilma Rudolph Foundation to help bring American heroes to attention of schoolchildren; was inducted into several halls of fame, including National Track and Field Hall of Fame; died at her home in Brentwood, Tennessee. See *Current Biography* (September) 1961.

Obituary *N Y Times* p53 N 13 '94

RUSH, (DAVID) KENNETH Jan. 17, 1910–Dec. 11, 1994 Diplomat; lawyer; corporation executive; in 1934 met Richard Nixon, the future president, at Duke University School of Law, where Rush was a teacher at the time and Nixon a student; after working in legal department of Union Carbide and Carbon Corporation, became a vice-president in 1939 and president in 1966; in 1969 was named ambassador to West Germany by President Nixon; as ambassador, helped negotiate 1971 four-power agreement that brought to an end chronic state of international crisis over Berlin that had existed since the end of World War II; moved to Pentagon as deputy secretary of defense in January 1972 and to Department of State as deputy to secretary of state William P. Rogers in February 1973; briefly served as acting secretary of state in interim between resignation of Rogers and arrival of his successor, Henry A. Kissinger, under whom he remained deputy; in May 1974, as the Watergate scandal was worsening, was brought to White House by Nixon in cabinet-level position of counselor to the president for economic policy; gave strong moral support to Nixon to bitter end of Watergate scandal on August 9, 1974, when the president resigned; the following month was chosen by Nixon's successor, President Gerald R. Ford, to become ambassador to France, effective November 1974; resigned in 1977; died at his home in Delray Beach, Florida. See *Current Biography* (May) 1975.

Obituary *N Y Times* D p22 D 13 '94

RUSK, (DAVID) DEAN Feb. 9, 1909–Dec. 20, 1994 U.S. secretary of state during Kennedy and Johnson administrations (1961–69); during World War II, was deputy chief of staff to General Joseph Stilwell in China-Burma-India theatre of operations and assistant division chief with general staff of Department of War; in 1946 joined Department of State, where he served successively over period of six years in high-level positions concerned with UN affairs, Far Eastern affairs, and establishment of state of Israel; from 1952 to 1960 was president of Rockefeller Foundation; according to Arthur M. Schlesinger Jr., was named secretary of state by President John F. Kennedy over such more likely choices as Chester Bowles and Adlai E. Stevenson (who became Rusk's subordinates) because Kennedy "wanted to be his own secretary of state" and believed that Rusk would be deferential; under Kennedy, usually carried out international missions without being asked for advice; after Lyndon B. Johnson succeeded to the presidency upon Kennedy's assassination, had greater influence in White House, especially when his position regarding American involvement in Vietnam War evolved from skepticism and uncertainty to a commitment matching Johnson's own in its firmness; according to a colleague, "made himself the rock against which crashed the successive waves of dissent" against Johnson's war policy; after leaving government, taught international law at University of Georgia until 1984; wrote book of memoirs, *As I Saw It* (1990); died at his home in Athens, Georgia. See *Current Biography* (July) 1961.

Obituary *NY Times* A p1+ D 22 '94

SALK, JONAS E(DWARD) Oct. 28, 1914–June 23, 1995 Microbiologist; epidemiologist; physician; director of Salk Institute for Biological Studies in La Jolla, California since 1963; became national hero with his perfection, in early 1950s, of "Salk vaccine," which, along with "Sabin vaccine" that superseded it in general use in early 1960s, virtually eradicated epidemic poliomyelitis, or paralytic polio; began bacteriological research under Dr. Thomas Francis, Jr. at New York University College of Medicine; followed Francis to University of Michigan, where, beginning in 1942, they researched influenza virus and developed commercial vaccines against it; in 1947 began seventeen-year tenure as director of virus research laboratory at University of Pittsburgh School of Medicine; there, with help of associates and a technique borrowed from Dr. John F. Enders of Harvard University, devoted himself to finding an inoculum to prevent polio, a crippling viral disease that had been sending waves of public fear across U.S. annually since 1920s; developed an injectable vaccine with formaldehyde-killed virus, unlike Dr. Albert B. Sabin's virus, which would be oral, with a live (although attenuated) virus; until 1975 did his research into such subjects as immunological aspects of multiple sclerosis and cancer in affiliation with University of California at San Diego/La Jolla; during last years of his life was working to find an agent to prevent HIV (human immunodeficiency virus) infection from developing into full-fledged AIDS; died in La Jolla, California. See *Current Biography* (May) 1954.

Obituary *N Y Times* p1+ Je 24 '95

SARTON, MAY May 3, 1912–July 16, 1995 Belgian-born American writer; practiced "the analysis of feeling," especially in women's relationships, in a wide range of literary forms, chiefly the lyric poem, the personal memoir, the novel, and the essay; was underappreciated for four decades, until the feminist movement recognized her as one of its heroines; was the daughter of Mabel (Elwes) Sarton, an artist, and George Sarton, the renowned philosopher and historian of science; apprenticed in acting under Eva La Gallienne in New York City (1929–33); later briefly headed her own theatrical troupe; began supplementing her meager income as struggling young poet and novelist by writing literary reviews and articles about theatre and poetry; supported herself chiefly by teaching creative writing and choral speech at Stuart School in Boston in late 1930s, by writing film scripts for U.S. Office of War Information in early 1940s, and later by lecturing on poetry at colleges and universities; in the sonnets and other formal poems in her first two collections, *Encounter in April* (1937) and *Inner Landscapes* (1939), and in her first novel, *The Single Hound* (1938), began to investigate themes she would continue to pursue throughout her oeuvre, including solitude, the search for self-knowledge, the difference between destructive passionate love and the more genuine love of "positive detachment," the uniqueness of each individual human being, and the artist's need to create order out of the chaos of personal life; for two decades maintained that pursuit discreetly, at a remove, using men as the leading characters, for example, in such novels as *Shadow of a Man* (1950) and *Faithful Are the Wounds* (1955); in later novels with women protagonists, including *The Small Room* (1961) and *Joanna and Ulysses* (1963), anticipated the imminent feminist literary flowering; in her most controversial novel, *Mrs. Stevens Hears the Mermaids Sing* (1965), created a heroine who strives against the grain of her time and place to define herself as an artist and a lesbian;

with the publication of *A Private Mythology* (1966), began to experiment more and more with free verse and irregular rhymes; in later volumes of poetry, shifted easily from free to established poetic forms; although she regarded her journals as minor writings, especially alongside her poems (which she regarded as means of self-communication), began to attract belated critical notice and her greatest popularity through the public diaries in which she recorded and meditated on the details of ordinary life, including *Plant Dreaming Deep* (1968), *The House by the Sea* (1977), and *Journal of Solitude* (1977); in 1983 told an interviewer, "Women have been my muse"; continuing to keep journals into old age, published *At Seventy* (1984), *After the Stroke* (1988), and *Encore: A Journal of the Eightieth Year* (1993); in her 1990 essay "Rewards of a Solitary Life," observed, "Loneliness is most acutely felt with others, . . . even with a lover"; wrote almost a score of novels, including *The Bridge of Years* (1946), *Crucial Conversations* (1975), *A Reckoning* (1978), and *Anger* (1982); published a total of approximately fifty books, including *I Knew a Phoenix: Sketches for an Autobiography* (1959) and her last collection of poems, *Coming into Eighty* (1994); lived by the sea in York, Maine; died in York. See *Current Biography* (May) 1982.

Obituary *N Y Times* B p7 Jl 18 '95

SAWYER, JOHN E(DWARD) May 5, 1917–Feb. 7, 1995 Educator; president of Williams College (1961–73); president of Andrew W. Mellon Foundation (1975–87); from 1949 to 1953 taught courses in development of Western civilization and history of American economic institutions at Harvard University; subsequently taught at Yale University and was a director of interuniversity program of research in American economic history; as president of Williams, guided the small, prestigious liberal arts college in its development of an environmental studies center and a graduate program in art history, its disbanding of fraternities, and its easing the transition to coeducation and a more racially integrated student body; as president of Mellon Foundation, took special interest in conservation and ecology projects and an interdisciplinary studies program, which in his memory the philanthropy recently broadened into the interuniversity John Sawyer Seminars in the Comparative Study of Cultures; died at his home in Woods Hole, Massachusetts. See *Current Biography* (July) 1961.

Obituary *N Y Times* B p8 F 8 '95

SCHILLER, KARL (AUGUST FRITZ) Apr. 24, 1911–Dec. 26, 1994 German political leader; former West German minister of economics and finance; university scholar; in 1946 joined West Germany's reconstituted Social Democratic Party, which he would help turn from doctrinaire Marxism to broad-based liberalism; became professor of economics at University of Hamburg in 1947; as city official, directed post-World War II reconstruction of Hamburg; at request of Willy Brandt, then Social Democratic mayor of West Berlin, took charge of that city's economic affairs during crisis in early 1960s caused by isolation ensuing from construction of Berlin Wall by East German Communist authorities; became chairman of Social Democratic economic policy committee in 1964; was elected to a Berlin seat in Bundestag, lower house of West German parliament, in 1965; became member of his party's presidium the following year; as minister of economics in grand coalition government headed by Chancellor Kurt Kiesinger of Christian Democratic Party from 1966 to 1969, guided West Germany to recovery from a serious recession; when Kiesinger's government was succeeded by new coalition of Social Democrats and Free Democrats under Willy Brandt in 1969, remained in cabinet as minister of economics; took on additional portfolio of finance when Brandt merged economics and finance ministries in 1971; by insisting on sizable cuts in government spending to cope with inflation, had falling out with Brandt; resigned his dual cabinet post in July 1972; left party soon afterward, but rejoined in 1980; died in Hamburg. See *Current Biography* (December) 1971.

Obituary *N Y Times* D p18 D 28 '94

SCHLINK, FREDERICK JOHN Oct. 26, 1891–Jan. 15, 1995 Pioneer consumer advocate; after taking degrees in science and mechanical engineering, worked successively as technical assistant at U.S. Bureau of Standards, physicist in charge of instruments control at Firestone Tire and Rubber Company, mechanical engineer concerned with designing and testing equipment at Western Electric Company, and assistant secretary concerned with specifications at American Standards Association; with Stuart Chase, wrote *Your Money's Worth* (1927); over following two years developed his local consumers club in White Plains, New York into Consumers' Research, Inc., first national organization to test and analyze trademarked products impartially and to publish its findings in bulletins; in bitter labor dispute at his laboratory in Washington, New Jersey in 1935, firmly resisted demands of strikers, who broke off to found much larger and better-known Consumers Union, publisher of *Consumer Reports*; with Arthur Kallet, wrote *One Hundred Million Guinea Pigs* (1933), a plea for federal regulation of food and drugs; also wrote *Eat, Drink and Be Wary* (1935); headed Consumers' Research until 1983; died in Phillipsburg, New Jersey. See *Current Biography* (March) 1941.

Obituary *N Y Times* B p8 Ja 20 '95

SCHOTTLAND, CHARLES I(RWIN) Oct. 29, 1906–June 27, 1995 Commissioner of U.S. Social Security Administration (1954–59); educator; an authority on social welfare; began career as social worker with delinquent boys in Los Angeles in 1927; subsequently worked as administrator with California State Relief Administration and Federation of Jewish Welfare Organizations in Los Angeles; in 1941 went to Washington, D.C., as assistant to chief of children's bureau in U.S. Department of Labor; as a lieutenant colonel on staff of General Dwight D. Eisenhower at Supreme Headquarters Allied Expeditionary Force in Europe during waning years of World War II, was in charge of section dealing with displaced persons, and in 1945 became assistant director of United Nations Relief and Rehabilitation Administration for Germany; played role in repatriation of some five and a half million people; subsequently was, successively, municipal child-welfare administrator in New York City and director of California state department of social welfare; as commissioner of Social Security under President Eisenhower, introduced amendments to 1935 Social Security Act to provide for disabilities coverage and lower minimum age for Social Security eligibility; in 1959 became founding dean of Florence Heller Graduate School for Advanced Studies in Social Welfare at Brandeis University, in Waltham, Massachusetts; was president of Brandeis from 1970 to 1972, when he returned to teaching as a professor; was again dean of Heller School from 1976 to 1979; later taught at Arizona State University and headed Arizona governor's advisory council on aging; published several books in his field; died at his home in Tucson, Arizona. See *Current Biography* (December) 1956.

Obituary *N Y Times* D p17 Je 30 '95

SELDES, GEORGE Nov. 16, 1890–July 2, 1995 Author; journalist; a self-described "progressive" critic of the press who did not mind being called a muckraker; believed, in his words, "in the 'general welfare' as written in the Constitution" and challenged "any publication feeding out of the hand of Big Business to prove by acts that its policy is the same"; was born in short-lived Utopian community founded by his father in Alliance, New Jersey; began career as newspaperman in Pittsburgh; was syndicated correspondent in Europe in World War I; remained in Europe as correspondent for *Chicago Tribune* until 1928; told stories previously suppressed in the European press in his book *You Can't Print That* (1929); during 1930s began to establish his reputation as a scathing critic, increasingly leftist in his point of view, of the American press with his books *Freedom of the Press* (1935) and *Lords of the Press* (1938); in former, argued that press freedom in U.S. was infringed more by influence of business interests and pressure from advertisers than by political censorship or the threat thereof, and called for establishment of a journalistic code of ethics; during same period also wrote, among other books, *Iron, Blood, and Profits* (1934), about the "munitions racket," and *Sawdust Caesar* (1935), about Mussolini; from December 1936 to May 1937 covered Spanish civil war for *New York Post* with a clear anti-Franco bias; extrapolating from his experience in Spain in his book *You Can't Do That* (1938), warned of what he called "the forces attempting, in the name of patriotism, to make a desert of the Bill of Rights" in U.S.; from 1940 to 1950 published *In Fact*, envisioned by him as "a pro-labor, and especially pro-progressive labor" newsletter in which he attempted to "do what Lincoln Steffens did," to publish "the real inside news, the kind newspapers frequently get but dare not print," and to "fight Fascism"; later compiled books *The Great Quotations* (1961) and *The Great Thoughts* (1985); in 1987 published his autobiography, *Witness to a Century*; died in Windsor, Vermont. See *Current Biography* (September) 1941.

Obituary *N Y Times* p46 Jl 3 '95

SHAPP, MILTON J(ERROLD) June 25, 1912–Nov. 24, 1994 Democratic governor of Pennsylvania (1971–79); industrialist; a self-made millionaire turned reformist politician; was trained in electrical engineering; in 1948 founded Jerrold Electronics Corporation, manufacturer and distributor of television cable, master antennae, and signal boosters and pioneer in installation of community-antenna television; was early supporter of and generous financial contributor to presidential candidacy of John F. Kennedy; was credited by some with making suggestion that led to President Kennedy's creation of Peace Corps; in Kennedy administration, was consultant to Peace Corps and Department of Commerce; defying obsolescent Pennsylvania state Democratic Party machine, scored stunning upset over machine's choice, Robert Casey, in gubernatorial primary in 1966 but lost in subsequent general election; in 1970 again defeated Casey and went on to win general election; was reelected in 1974; in his two terms as governor, helped to save Pennsylvania from severe budgetary crisis by winning legislative and judicial approval of state's first income tax; while raising hackles of private insurance and health-care interests, gained respectful national notice for his extraordinary, unrelenting pursuit of consumer protection and advocacy policies; established state-wide lottery, 30 percent of the proceeds of which were tagged for reducing property taxes of poorer older citizens; instituted innovative programs for handicapped as well as elderly; opened state government to light of fullest "sunshine law" in U.S.; introduced strict code of ethics for state employees and full-disclosure requirement for those at executive level; failed in bid for Democratic presidential nomination in 1976; died at hospital in Philadelphia suburb of Wynnewood. See *Current Biography* (July) 1973.

Obituary *N Y Times* p30 N 26 '94

SHELEPIN, ALEKSANDR (NIKOLAEVICH) Aug. 18, 1918–Oct. 24, 1994 Soviet official; a hard-liner in both domestic and foreign affairs; served as first secretary of Komsomol, or Young Communist League, from 1952 to 1958; in struggle for power following death of Stalin in 1953, threw his influence behind Nikita Khrushchev; helped indoctrinate Komsomol members to accept Khrushchev's shocking revelation of Stalin's crimes and denunciation of Stalin's "cult of personality"; as chairman of Committee on State Security (1958-61), better known as KGB, purged secret police agency of last vestiges of its previous notorious terrorism; from 1961 to 1965 was member of Secretariat of Soviet Communist Party's Central Committee; during same period was in charge of new party-state control committee and was deputy chairman of Council of Ministers; was believed to have played key role in deposition of Khrushchev in 1964; served in Communist Party Presidium, or Politburo, from 1964 to 1975. See *Current Biography* (February) 1971.

Obituary *N Y Times* B p9 O 25 '94

SHULMAN, IRVING May 21, 1913–Mar. 23, 1995 Writer; Brooklyn-born novelist and scenarist; began fictional trilogy that was his best-known work with *The Amboy Dukes* (1947), which sold five million copies and was made into 1949 film *City Across the River*; in that melodramatic novel about gang of juvenile delinquents in Brooklyn slum who become involved in a murder, combined "the sociologist's research with the writer's art," as Clifton Fadiman observed; with psychological suspense as well as brutal action, in *Cry Tough!* (1949) and *The Big Brokers* (1951) traced development of the teenaged hoods into full-blown adult organized-crime figures; meanwhile, moved to Hollywood under contract to Warner Brothers as a screenwriter, usually uncredited; in fourth novel, *The Square Trap* (1953), set in Los Angeles' Mexican community, told the story of a young man's efforts to find his way out of poverty through boxing; before publication of that novel, had already written the story's scenario for the film *The Ring* (1952); later wrote novels *Good Deeds Must Be Punished* (1956), about an Italian-American veteran who experiences ethnic prejudice at a small West Virginia college, and *The Velvet Knife* (1959), set in Hollywood; died at his home in Sherman Oaks, California. See *Current Biography* (Yearbook) 1956.

Obituary *N Y Times* A p21 Mr 29 '95

SIMPSON, ADELE Dec. 8, 1903–Aug. 23, 1995 Fashion designer; exemplified finest in American clothing design for women for half a century, turning out affordable yet flattering, tasteful, and functional women's designs; was best known for her smart suits, matching ensembles of jackets and dresses, and classically cut coats in fine fabrics; was at peak of her popularity in the decades following World War II, coinciding with development and mass marketing of American sportswear made possible by new technology; began career in early 1920s as dress designer at Ben Gershel's Seventh Avenue ready-to-wear house, where she soon became head designer; in 1928 moved to Mary Lee Fashions, another Seventh Avenue manufacturing company, owned by Alfred Lasher; there, designed a fashion line with her own label, which attracted a loyal clientele of customers and store buyers; in 1949, bought the company from Lasher and renamed it Adele Simpson, Inc.; built it into the industry's leader in sales volume for the medium-priced field; had outlets for her collections in the finest stores, including B. Altman, Saks Fifth Avenue, and Bonwit Teller; outfitted wives of four U.S. presidents, among other customers; in 1985 retired and turned her company over to relatives, who sold it in 1991; died at her home in Greenwich, Connecticut. See *Current Biography* (November) 1970.

Obituary *N Y Times* D p21 Ag 24 '95

SINCLAIR, JO July 1, 1913–Apr. 4, 1995 Novelist; memoirist; was born to Russian Jewish immigrants in Brooklyn, New York and raised by them in Cleveland, Ohio; based much of her writing on her own background and experiences; during Depression of 1930s, was employed in federal WPA writing and editing projects; beginning in late 1930s, published short fiction and socially significant (fraught with compassion for the unemployed and working poor of the time) nonfiction in late 1930s in such publications as *New Masses, Common Ground*, and *Harper's*; in 1946 won Harper Prize with her first novel, *Wasteland* (1946), about a first-generation American Jew who rejects his roots; in her second novel, *The Changelings* (1955), told a story of the friendship of two teenaged girls, one white and one black, in a racially tense big-city neighborhood; also wrote *Sing at My Wake* (1951), *Anna Teller* (1960), and the memoir *The Seasons: Death and Transfiguration* (1993); died at her home in Jenkintown, Pennsylvania. See *Current Biography* (March) 1946.

Obituary *N Y Times* B p10 Ap 10, 1995

SINGH, GIANI ZAIL May 5, 1916–Dec. 25, 1994 President of India (1982–87); a moderate Sikh, the first of his religion to hold that largely ceremonial but prestigious position in dominantly Hindu India; was protégé of Jawaharlal Nehru, independent India's first prime minister, and loyal confidant of Nehru's daughter, Indira Gandhi; became interested in politics when Indian independence movement under Mohandas K. Gandhi reached his home district of Faridkot in the Punjab, then a province of British India; in 1938 organized branch of Gandhi's All-India Congress Party in Faridkot and founded Praja Mandal movement in Punjab, actions that enraged the ruling rajah of Faridkot; was imprisoned for five years; after India became independent in 1947, held series of posts in Punjab state cabinet; as chief minister, beginning in 1972, was credited with developing the Punjab both agriculturally and industrially; was minister of home affairs, responsible for law enforcement, in India's central government under Prime Minister Indira Gandhi from 1980 until his elevation to presidency; after assassination of Mrs. Gandhi by Sikh bodyguards in 1984, had prickly relationship with her son and successor, Rajiv Gandhi; died in Chandigarh, India. See *Current Biography* (September) 1987.

Obituary *N Y Times* p46 D 26 '94

SINGH, (SARDAR) SWARAN Aug. 19, 1907–Oct. 30, 1994 Indian government official; lawyer; in 1952 entered Rajya Sabha, upper house of India's parliament, and joined Prime Minister Jawaharlal Nehru's government as minister of works, housing, and supply; over the following twenty-three years, served continuously in cabinet in various positions, including minister of steel, mines, and fuel, minister of defense, minister of railroads, minister of food and agriculture, and minister of external affairs; was in last-named post when, in 1971, India's backing of East Pakistani guerrillas fighting for secession from Pakistan precipitated a brief war between India and Pakistan, ending in an Indian victory and creation of a new independent state; addressing UN Security Council, asked for international recognition of "the reality of Bangladesh"; left government of Prime Minister Indira Gandhi in 1975; died in New Delhi. See *Current Biography* (March) 1971.

Obituary *N Y Times* B p8 N 1 '94

SMITH, MARGARET (MADELINE) CHASE Dec. 14, 1897–May 29, 1995 Republican U.S. representative and senator from Maine; in 1930 married Clyde H. Smith, who was elected to U.S. House of Representatives in 1936 and reelected in 1938; after her husband's death, in April 1940, was chosen to fill remainder of his unexpired term in special election; was elected in her own right in September 1940 and reelected in 1942, 1944, and 1946; was first elected to U.S. Senate in 1948; as both congresswoman and senator, hewed to an independent course, supporting much of the liberal legislation sponsored by Democratic administrations, speaking out against conservative Democrats as well as Republicans who voted for perpetuating House Un-American Activities Committee, and joining with six other Republicans in a "declaration of conscience" against Senator Joseph R. McCarthy's inquisitorial hunt for Communists in government;

served on Senate Appropriations Committee and became ranking Republican on Senate Armed Services and Aeronautical and Space Sciences committees; was outspoken advocate of strong national defense policy and firm foreign policy; in 1961 criticized Kennedy administration's apparent lack of will to use nuclear weapons; was nominated for presidency at Republican National Convention in 1964; during Vietnam War, denounced both tactics of radical left and government officials who overreacted to antiwar demonstrators; had perfect Senate attendance record of 2,941 roll calls, unbroken until she was hospitalized for hip surgery; had as her trademark a red rose, fresh daily on her Senate desk; lost her bid for a fifth term in the Senate in the general elections of 1972; died in Skowhegan, Maine. See *Current Biography* (March) 1962.

Obituary *N Y Times* B p6 My 30 '95

SMITH, (CHARLES) PAGE Sept. 6, 1917–Aug. 28, 1995 Historian; professor emeritus of American history, University of California; advisedly departing from the genre of the "scientific" academic monograph, produced by historians for historians, wrote popular books of what he described as "history as biography" in an "old-fashioned" narrative style and including "the spiritual and moral dimension"; viewed his work—based in large measure on serendipitous research in obscure and tangential first-hand contemporary accounts, such as diaries, letters, and newspaper stories—as an experience in "discovery" to be shared with as large an audience as possible; first received critical acclaim with his biography *John Adams* (1962); between 1976 and 1986 published eight-volume *A People's History of the United States*; also wrote, among other books, *The Historian and History* (1964) and *Killing the Spirit* (1990); in the latter, a scathing critique of the current crisis in American higher education, reiterated one of underlying postulates of his oeuvre: "The greatest achievement of the Classical Christian Consciousness, a consciousness characterized by belief in natural law and original sin, was the federal Constitution. After that remarkable accomplishment, the fruit of two thousand years of political speculation, the Classical Christian Consciousness lapsed almost at once into a primarily conservative and reactive mode [the creative residue of which] was what I have called the Protestant passion for redemption [of the U.S. and then the world]"; taught at University of California at Los Angeles from 1953 to 1964; from 1964 to 1970 was founding provost of Cowell College, University of California's extension in Santa Cruz; was professor at Santa Cruz until his resignation in 1973; died in Santa Cruz. See *Current Biography* (September) 1990.

Obituary *N Y Times* B p7 Ag 29 '95

SOMES, MICHAEL (GEORGE) Sept. 28, 1917–Nov. 18, 1994 British ballet dancer; dancing with Sadler's Wells Ballet, as Royal Ballet was then known, first attracted wide acclaim with his interpretation of Young Man in Frederick Ashton's *Horoscope* during company's 1937–38 London season; went on to build his reputation as *danseur noble*, especially in such Ashton ballets as *Dante Sonata*, *The Fairy Queen*, *Cinderella*, and *Daphnis and Chloe* as well as in nineteenth-century classics; began touring U.S. annually with Sadler's Wells in 1949; performed in his own first choreographic effort, *Summer Interlude*, at Sadler's Wells Ballet Theatre in London in 1950; began his famous long-term partnership with Margot Fonteyn in that year; although he was a "self-effacing" partner, "impeccable" in his support of Fonteyn, as many critics noted, still came across, as John Martin observed, as "an artist in his own right . . . visually handsome and noble in carriage and deportment," infusing "the succession of basically wooden princes with humanity and innate gallantry"; retired from classical roles in 1961; subsequently performed in character parts, taught, and helped to stage company's signature productions; was assistant to Frederick Ashton during Ashton's directorship of Royal Ballet, from 1963 to 1970; during visits to New York during following decade, assisted in producing Ashton pieces for Joffrey Ballet; was associated with Royal Ballet until 1984; died in London. See *Current Biography* (December) 1955.

Obituary *N Y Times* p30 N 26 '94

SPEARE, ELIZABETH GEORGE Nov. 21, 1908–Nov. 15, 1994 Author; wrote historical fiction for children; was inspired to write first book, *Calico Captive* (1957), by diary of Susanna Johnson, a New England woman captured during Indian raid and carried off to Canada in late eighteenth century; won her first Newbery Medal for *The Witch of Blackbird Pond* (1958), about a girl from Barbados who migrates to New England in 1687 and is caught up in the witchcraft hysteria of the time; won second Newbery Medal for *The Bronze Bow* (1961) and third for *The Sign of the Beaver* (1983); also wrote *The Prospering* (1967) and *Life in Colonial America* (1954); in 1989 was awarded Laura Ingalls Wilder Medal for her "distinguished, enduring contribution to children's literature"; was cited in that award for her "vitality and energy, grace of writing, historical accuracy, and tremendous feeling for place and character"; died in Tucson, Arizona. See *Current Biography* (Yearbook) 1959.

Obituary *N Y Times* D p24 N 16 '94

SPENDER, STEPHEN (HAROLD) Feb. 28, 1909–July 17, 1995 British writer; probably the most lyrical and compassionate and certainly the most subjective of so-called "Oxford poets," members of the post-Pound/Eliot generation who, beginning in late 1920s, moved English letters from esotericism outward, toward large social and political concerns (summed up in the view that the rise of fascism portended end of an era in Europe) and poetic images and ideas drawn from everyday life; saw himself essentially as "an autobiographer restlessly searching for forms in which to express the stages of my development"; as student at Oxford University's University College, from 1928 to 1931, was member of circle of young intellectuals that included W. H. Auden, Isaiah Berlin, Louis MacNiece, Bernard Spencer, Christopher Isherwood, and C. Day Lewis; in 1929 made first of many visits (often with Isherwood) to Germany; in the fervor and freshness of language of his early poems showed influence of German as well as British Romantic poets; was perhaps at his best in his subtle control in melancholy confessional verse and in such descriptive poems as

"The Landscape Near an Aerodrome"; published *The Destructive Element* (1935), a collection of literary criticism and history; like others in the Oxford group, adopted a Marxist political position, enunciated in his 1937 book *Forward from Liberalism*; witnessing first-hand the Stalinist control of British Communist Party and of International Brigade in Spanish civil war, became disillusioned with Communism early on; wrote anti-Nazi verse drama *Trial of a Judge* (1938); later translated and adapted several works for the stage; coedited literary magazine *Horizon* from 1939 to 1941; as a pacifist, supported British World War II effort by serving as volunteer firefighter during London blitz (1940–41); wrote several powerful poems about air raids, including "Rejoice in the Abyss"; during war, published novel *The Backward Son*, long essay *Life and the Poet*, two new volumes of his poetry, and his translations of Rainer Maria Rilke, Federico García Lorca, Ernst Toller, and Georg Büchner; after spending some time in British-occupied zone in postwar Germany, wrote *European Witness* (1946); published his unusually candid autobiography *World Within World* in 1951; cofounded *Encounter* in 1953; coedited that distinguished anti-Communist intellectual journal until 1966; resigned as contributing editor in 1967, when he learned that the publication had been subsidized in part by funds indirectly supplied by the U.S. Central Intelligence Agency; while editing *Encounter*, published the books of literary criticism and history *The Creative Element*, *The Making of a Poem*, and *The Struggle of the Modern*; later wrote the critical biography *T. S. Eliot* and edited several books of criticism, including tributes to D. H. Lawrence and W. H. Auden, and anthologies of verse; in his *Collected Poems, 1928–53* (1955), presented what he then considered his best 111 poems; reduced that number to 43 (including "I Think Continually of Those Who Are Truly Great," "Elegy for Margaret," "The Pylon," and "The Trance") in his *Selected Poems* (1964); from 1970 to 1977 was professor at University College, London; published memoir *The Thirties and After* in 1978; was knighted in 1983; during 1980s published volume of his journals and one of his letters to Isherwood; after his divorce from Inez Pearn, married Natasha Litvin; in 1993 brought plagiarism suit regarding a novel that, he contended, "closely derived in plot and text from about thirty pages of my autobiography, concerning my relationship with a man I call Jimmy Younger . . . [who before] my marriage to Inez Pearn [was] my friend [and] also my former lover"; won out-of-court settlement in 1994; also in 1994 published volume of recent poetry, *Dolphins*; in addition to his nonfictional prose, published two books of short fiction; died in London. See *Current Biography* (March) 1977.

Obituary *N Y Times* B p6 Jl 18 '95

STENNIS, JOHN C(ORNELIUS) Aug. 3, 1901–Apr. 23, 1995 Democratic U.S. senator from Mississippi (1947–89); lawyer; before his election to Senate, served as state representative, district attorney, and circuit judge in Mississippi; as a member of Armed Services Committee and chairman of Appropriations Committee, wielded unsurpassed influence in military affairs in Senate during 1960s and 1970s; because of his reputation for personal integrity, was often chosen by his colleagues to head such inquiries as the committee investigations that resulted in the censure of Senator Joseph R. McCarthy, in 1954, and the censure of Senator Thomas J. Dodd, along with the drafting of new code of ethics for Senate, in 1967; died in Jackson, Mississippi. See *Current Biography* (January) 1953.

Obituary *N Y Times* B p11 Ap 24 '95

TAGLIAVINI, FERRUCCIO Aug. 14, 1913–Jan. 28, 1995 Italian opera singer; a florid lyric tenor with warm timbre and phrasing, a ravishing pianissimo, and effortless projection; made professional operatic debut as Rodolfo in Puccini's *La bohème* at Teatro Communale in Florence in 1939; in following seasons sang, in addition to Rodolfo, Nemorino in Donizetti's *L'elisir d'amore*, Edgardo in same composer's *Lucia di Lammermoor*, and leading tenor roles in operas by Bellini, Mascagni, and Massenet in major opera houses in Naples, Rome, and Milan as well as Florence; expanded his Puccini repertoire to include Pinkerton in *Madama Butterfly* and Cavaradossi in *Tosca*; after World War II, toured the Americas, moving from Brazil up to Mexico and making his North American debut as Rodolfo in Chicago in October 1946; made his debut at Metropolitan Opera in New York City in same role three months later; making repeated guest appearances, remained a favorite of audiences at Met for several years; beginning in early 1950s, performed almost exclusively in Europe; made last appearance at Met in 1962; returned to New York on several occasions in 1970s, to give recitals, and in 1981, for a concert performance in title role of Mascagni's *Amico Fritz*; performed in several operatic films and a few Italian screen comedies showcasing his voice; died at his home in Reggio Emilia, Italy. See *Current Biography* (June) 1947.

Obituary *N Y Times* B p11 F 2 '95

TAYLOR, PETER (HILLSMAN) Jan. 8, 1917–Nov. 2, 1994 Author; a short-story writer and novelist perhaps fully appreciated only by readers of the *New Yorker* (where many of his short stories were first published), aficionados of southern fiction, and his literary peers, including Anne Tyler, who has called him "the undisputed master of the short-story form"; created fictional memoirs—superficially rambling and digressive but really distilled and compressed—about a circumscribed and genteel world that has all but vanished: that of the middle and upper classes carrying the burden of old manners, mores, and morals with them as they are displaced from country to city in the changing upper South; wrote in realist mode, exact in observation of the minute details of class behavior, yet was gentle, using understatement and, often, ironic humor in communication of the terrible tensions involved in social displacement and family dissolution; in addition to eight collections of short stories, wrote novella *A Woman of Means* (1950), regarded by many as his finest work, an adolescent boy's account of the disintegration of his antagonistic father's second marriage and his sympathetic stepmother's descent into madness; also wrote novels *A Summons to Memphis* (1986) and *In the Tennessee Country* (1994); died in Charlottesville, Virginia. See *Current Biography* (April) 1987.

Obituary *N Y Times* A p33 N 4 '94

TIMMERMAN, GEORGE BELL, JR. Aug. 12, 1912–Nov. 29, 1994 Governor of South Carolina from 1955 to 1959; lawyer; his state's last segregationist chief executive; an untimely defender of states' rights at the historical moment when civil rights was the critical national issue; was lieutenant governor during eight years immediately previous to his governorship; as governor, made unsuccessful effort to oppose federally imposed racial desegregation of South Carolina's transportation facilities, parks, beaches, golf courses, and, the major area, public schools; became circuit judge in 1967; retired in 1988; died at hospital in Columbia, South Carolina. See *Current Biography* (January) 1957.

Obituary *N Y Times* p30 D 3 '94

TOBIN, RICHARD L(ARDNER) Aug. 9, 1910–Sep. 10, 1995 Journalist; joined staff of New York *Herald Tribune* as reporter in 1932; was assistant city editor of *Herald Tribune* from 1935 to 1942; was subsequently assigned to establish and maintain a broadcasting division of newspaper; for two years did daily radio newscasts and early experimental telecasting of news in New York area; wrote book *Invasion Journal* (1944) as a World War II correspondent based in London; later published books *Golden Opinions* (1948), *The Center of the World* (1951), and *Decisions of Destiny* (1961); also wrote *Tobin's English Usage* (1985), based on a monitoring of "intrusive usage battling entrenched diction" among newspaper and magazine editors; left *Herald Tribune* in 1956, after serving as assistant to the publisher; in 1960 joined *Saturday Review* magazine, with which, over a period of sixteen years, he was successively managing editor, executive editor, associate publisher, and senior vice-president; died in Southbury, Connecticut. See *Current Biography* (November) 1944.

Obituary *N Y Times* D p23 S 12 '95

TRUEBLOOD, D(AVID) ELTON Dec. 12, 1900–Dec. 20, 1994 Quaker scholar; theologian; early in career taught at Guilford College and Haverford College; was chaplain and professor of philosophy of religion at Stanford University from 1936 to 1945 and professor of philosophy at Earlham College from 1946 to 1966; at Earlham, founded school of religion and nonsectarian program to train lay leaders; was chief of religious policy at U.S. Information Agency in 1954 and 1955; wrote thirty-three books, including *The Essence of Spiritual Religion* (1936), *Signs of Hope in a Century of Despair* (1950), *The Life We Prize* (1951), *The Recovery of Family Life* (1953), *The Philosophy of Religion* (1957), and *General Philosophy* (1963); died in retirement community near Lansdale, Pennsylvania. See *Current Biography* (January) 1964.

Obituary *N Y Times* A p30 D 23 '94

TURNER, LANA Feb.8, 1920–June 29, 1995 Actress; was "discovered" while still a student at Hollywood High School; first worked as an extra in film *A Star Is Born* (1937); with her central but brief appearance as Mary Clay in social drama *They Won't Forget* (1937), attracted the kind of attention suggested by the sobriquet "the Sweater Girl," with which studio publicists immediately dubbed her; began to demonstrate some depth as an actress in such leading roles as Jane Thomas, the rebellious student in *These Glamour Girls* (1939), Margy Brooks, the struggling young working woman in the populist drama *We Who Are Young* (1940), the shallow title character in *Ziegfeld Girl* (1941), and Elizabeth Cotton, the woman in whom a gambling con man (Clark Gable) meets his match in the comedy/melodrama *Honky Tonk* (1941); during World War II, when she starred in such films as the gangster melodrama *Johnny Eager*, the action film *Somewhere I'll Find You*, and the comedy *Slightly Dangerous*, was ballyhooed as one of the favorite "pinup girls" of American servicemen; gave one of her most credible performances as Cora Smith in *The Postman Always Rings Twice* (1946); during postwar years was cast in such roles as Marianne Patourel in *Green Dolphin Street* (1947), Virginia Marshland in *Cass Timberlane* (1947), and the Countess in *The Three Musketeers* (1948); according to John Houseman, the producer of *The Bad and the Beautiful* (1952), in which she played the alcoholic movie actress Georgia Lorrison, "was capable of brilliant individual scenes but seemed to lack the temperament or the training to sustain a full-length performance . . . [so that] our episodic film [was] just right for her"; was nominated for Academy Award for her performance as Constance MacKenzie in *Peyton Place* (1958); later starred in such films as the tearjerkers *Imitation of Life* (1959), as the career-driven actress Lora Meredith, and *Madame X* (1965), as Holly Anderson, the mother on trial for murder; on television, had roles in prime-time soap opera *The Survivors* (1970) and the serial melodrama *Falcon Crest* (1982–83); before religious conversion in 1980, led a turbulent life, marked by eight marriages and her daughter Cheryl's slaying (declared by a jury to be justifiable homicide) in 1958 of the reputed gangster Johnny Stompanato, Turner's boyfriend at the time; wrote autobiography *Lana: The Lady, the Legend, the Truth* (1982); died in Los Angeles. See *Current Biography* (June) 1943.

Obituary *N Y Times* p9 Jl 1 '95

VOLPE, JOHN A(NTHONY) Dec. 8, 1908–Nov. 11, 1994 Republican governor of Massachusetts; federal official; diplomat; engineer; building contractor; in 1953 became Massachusetts commissioner of public works; in 1956 was appointed interim federal highway administrator in administration of President Dwight D. Eisenhower; in that position, helped inaugurate interstate highway system; was elected to first two-year term as governor in 1960 and to second in 1964; in administration of President Richard Nixon was secretary of transportation (1969-73); was ambassador to Italy from 1973 to 1977; was the publisher of two Massachusetts newspapers, the *Malden News* and the *Medford Daily Mercury*, and an officer of several banks; died in Nahunt, Massachusetts. See *Current Biography* (February) 1962.

Obituary *N Y Times* p53 N 13 '94

WALKER, ERIC A(RTHUR) Apr. 29, 1910–Feb. 17, 1995 President of Pennsylvania State University (1956–70); electrical engineer; after receiving his doctorate at Harvard University, chaired department of engineering at Tufts University until 1940, when he joined faculty of University of Connecticut; two years later, at behest of U.S. Navy, returned to Harvard to help develop in underwater sound laboratory there the homing torpedoes that proved effective against German submarines during World War II; in connection with his work for navy, in 1945 moved to Pennsylvania State University, where he established and served as first director of ordnance research laboratory now known as Applied Research Laboratory; at Penn State headed electrical engineering department from 1945 to 1951 and dean of College of Engineering and Architecture from 1951 until his appointment as president; presided over tripling of enrollment, doubling of faculty, construction of one hundred new buildings, and establishment of Hershey Medical Center; later was vice-president for science and technology of Aluminum Company of America for five years; died at his home in State College, Pennsylvania. See *Current Biography* (March) 1959.

Obituary *N Y Times* p49 F 19 '95

WALTON, ERNEST THOMAS SINTON Oct. 6, 1903–June 25, 1995 Irish nuclear physicist; shared 1951 Nobel Prize in physics with John Douglas Cockcroft for "pioneer work on the transmutation of atomic nuclei by artificially accelerated atomic particles" two decades before; after earning master's degree in classical physics at Trinity College in Dublin in 1926, went to Cambridge University in England for his doctoral work under Ernest Rutherford, who in 1911, using natural radioactivity in form of alpha particles, had achieved first man-made nuclear transformation, converting nitrogen nuclei into oxygen; with his colleague Cockcroft in Cavendish Laboratory at Cambridge, invented powerful little atom smasher, or particle accelerator, what their mentor Rutherford called "a million volts in a shoe box"; using that apparatus, bombarded lithium with artificially accelerated protons and succeeded, in 1932, in demonstrably splitting an atomic nucleus into two helium particles; thus verified Einstein's theory that mass is equivalent to energy; in 1934 returned to Trinity College as a fellow; in 1946 was appointed Erasmus Smith professor of natural and experimental philosophy and chairman of physics department at Trinity College; became chairman of School of Cosmic Physics at Dublin Institute for Advanced Studies in 1952; retired in 1974; died in Belfast, Northern Ireland. See *Current Biography* (March) 1952.

Obituary *N Y Times* B p8 Je 28 '95

WAYNE, DAVID Jan. 30, 1914–Feb. 9, 1995 Actor; a versatile stage, screen, and television performer; obtained his stage training with Eldred Players in Cleveland, Ohio; made Broadway debut in walk-on role in *Escape This Night* in 1938; subsequently played Karl Gunther in *The American Way* (1939), Nish in a revival of *The Merry Widow* (1943), and Mr. Meacham in musical comedy *Park Avenue* (1946); in 1947 achieved stardom, became first recipient of a Tony Award for acting, in role of Og, the leprechaun, in musical fantasy *Finian's Rainbow*; in 1949 took role of Ensign Pulver in long-running comedy *Mr. Roberts*; won second Tony for his performance as Sakini in *The Teahouse of the August Moon* (1953); starred on Broadway in *The Ponder Heart* (1956), *The Loud Red Patrick* (1956), *Say Darling* (1958), and *The Happy Time* (1968); on screen, beginning in 1949, had supporting roles in string of motion pictures, including *Portrait of Jennie* and *Adam's Rib*; starred as the maniacal killer in *M* (1951), Joe in *Up Front* (1951), and the barber in *Wait Till the Sun Shines, Nellie* (1952); had featured roles in motion pictures *How to Marry a Millionaire* (1953), *The Tender Trap* (1955), and *The Three Faces of Eve* (1957); later had roles in films *The Last Angry Man* (1959), *The Andromeda Strain* (1971), and *The Front Page* (1974); on television, played title role of small-town banker in situation comedy *Norby* (1955) and major roles in series *The Good Life* (1971–72) and *The Adventures of Ellery Queen* (1975–76); played Digger Barnes on prime-time soap opera *Dallas* (1978) and Dr. Amos Weatherby on *House Calls* (1980–82); was nominated for Emmy Awards for guest appearances on *Suspicion* and *Gunsmoke*; died at his home in Santa Monica, California. See *Current Biography* (June) 1956.

Obituary *N Y Times* B p6 F 13 '95

WELSH, MATTHEW E(MPSON) Sep. 15, 1912–May 28, 1995 Democratic governor of Indiana (1961–65); lawyer; before his election as governor, practiced law in Vincennes, Indiana and served as U.S. attorney for Southern District of Indiana and as state senator and representative; as governor, succeeded in winning legislative passage of Indiana's first sales tax, part of his program for overhauling state's finances, and reform of the scandal-ridden highway commission; during Democratic presidential primary in Indiana in 1964, intervened to stop the state's fifty-one Democratic delegates from throwing support to George Wallace's candidacy; by law was unable to run for a consecutive term as governor in 1964; lost a second gubernatorial bid in 1968; died at his home in Indianapolis. See *Current Biography* (June) 1962.

Obituary *N Y Times* D p21 My 31 '95

WIESNER, JEROME B(ERT) May 30, 1915–Oct. 21, 1994 Electrical engineer; presidential assistant; educator; began doing experimental work in radio and acoustics in late 1930s; later turned to radiation, radar, and high fidelity sound production; became a specialist in signal identification, an expert on microwave theory, and an analyst of military technology; taught and worked on and off at Massachusetts Institute of Technology beginning in 1942; in 1945 joined staff of University of California's laboratory in Los Alamos, New Mexico; became associate director of M.I.T.'s electronics research laboratory in 1949 and director of the laboratory three years later; in meantime, became full professor at M.I.T., in 1950; directed construction of an additional laboratory at M.I.T. specifically for radar research and development; in 1958 was selected to head steering committee of M.I.T.'s new Center for Communication Sciences; was named special presidential assistant for science and technology by President John F. Kennedy in 1961; among other tasks, did preliminary work on treaty to ban above-ground nuclear tests signed by U.S., Britain, and USSR in 1963; after three years as presidential assistant, returned to M.I.T. as dean of school of science in 1964; became provost at M.I.T. in 1966; after serving briefly in that position, began nine-year term as president; outspoken in his concern about nuclear arms race, was a founding member of International Foundation for the

Survival and Development of Humanity; died at his home in Watertown, Massachusetts. See *Current Biography* (December) 1961.

Obituary *N Y Times* p45 O 23 '94

WIGNER, EUGENE P(AUL) Nov. 17, 1902–Jan. 1, 1995 Theoretical physicist; in apparent chaos among subatomic particles, discovered profound balance and symmetry; while growing up in Budapest, befriended John von Neumann, with whom he later wrote several papers on group theory and quantum mechanics; in Berlin, where he studied chemical engineering and received his Ph.D. in engineering, met fellow Hungarians and quantum physicists Leo Szilard and Edward Teller; published book applying group theory to atomic spectra; after arriving in U.S. in 1930, joined faculty of Princeton University, where he remained, with occasional leaves of absence, until his retirement; fearful, along with others, about what progress Hitler's military nuclear scientists might be making, played important role both in persuading Roosevelt administration to develop atomic bomb during World War II and in working directly in that project; contributed to theoretical bases for world's first controlled chain reaction at University of Chicago, for design of plutonium-making reactors at Hanford, Washington, and for building of first atomic bombs at Los Alamos, New Mexico; as war neared its end, after Allied victory in Europe, along with such colleagues as Albert Einstein and Leo Szilard, petitioned president of U.S. finally to forego use of atomic bomb, in vain; a political conservative and staunch anti-Communist, tended in later polarization among atomic scientists to join Edward Teller on hawkish side, concerned with nuclear defense rather than nuclear disarmament; won Nobel Prize in physics in 1963 for "systematically improving and extending the methods of quantum mechanics and applying them widely"; from 1964 to 1965 was director of civil defense research at Oak Ridge (Tennessee) National Laboratory; retired in 1971; died in Princeton, New Jersey. See *Current Biography* (April) 1953.

Obituary *N Y Times* D p19 Ja 4 '95

WILSON, (JAMES) HAROLD Mar. 11, 1916–May 24, 1995 British politician and statesman; economist; a flexible socialist with the common touch; led Labour Party for thirteen years (1963–76); was prime minister for a total of nearly eight years (1964–70, 1974–76); held his factious party together and kept national social and industrial tensions at bay as he guided Britain through critical period of belated rude awakening to reality of drastic diminution of its influence in the world and its economic strength at home; at Oxford University in late 1930s, was research assistant to Lord Beveridge, the mastermind of Britain's "welfare state"; at Ministry of Fuel and Power during World War II, served in various positions, including director of economics and statistics; wrote *New Deal for Coal* (1945), the book that became basis of Labour Party's plans for nationalization of mines; was member of Parliament from 1945 to 1983; before becoming prime minister, held cabinet posts of parliamentary secretary in Ministry of Works (1945–47) and president of Board of Trade (1947–51); as prime minister, was bedeviled by an inflation rate that rose to 25 percent, by forced devaluation of the pound, by widespread labor unrest, by rebellion against white minority rule in Rhodesia (now Zimbabwe), and by eruption of violence in Northern Ireland; kept British troops out of Vietnam; withdrew troops from Far East; persuaded trade unions to restrain their wage demands; settled coal miners' strike; reduced government spending; imposed limited price controls; won parliamentary enactment of law against capital punishment and of Race Relations Act to prevent discrimination against minorities; obtained voters' approval of national referendum ratifying British membership in Common Market; wrote total of fourteen books, including *War on Want* (1953), *The Relevance of British Socialism* (1964), *The Labour Government (1964–70)* (1971), *The Governance of Britain* (1976), *Final Term: The Labour Government 1974–76* (1979), and two volumes of autobiography; in 1983 was created a life peer with title of Baron Wilson of Rievaulx; died in London. See *Current Biography* (May) 1963.

Obituary *N Y Times* B p15 My 25 '95

WRIGHT, JERAULD June 4, 1898–Apr. 27, 1995 U.S. Navy four-star admiral; ambassador; as ensign just out of U.S. Naval Academy, in World War I did convoy and patrol duty on destroyer U.S.S. *Castine*, based on Gibraltar; between wars, served on executive staff of Naval Academy, as naval aide in White House, and in assignments connected with development of antiaircraft control equipment in the Navy Department's Bureau of Ordnance in addition to doing tours of sea duty; after United States entered World War II, was concerned with planning amphibious operations in office of chief of naval operations; later in World War II participated in planning the Allied amphibious invasions of North Africa, Sicily, and Italian mainland; still later, commanded amphibious assaults in Pacific; after World War II, commanded amphibious forces of U.S. Atlantic fleet; commanded U.S. naval forces in eastern Atlantic and Mediterranean from 1952 to 1954, when he assumed dual duties of commander in chief of U.S. Atlantic fleet and supreme Atlantic commander, NATO; after his retirement from navy, in 1961, was appointed to CIA's Board of Estimates, in 1961; was ambassador to Taiwan from 1963 to 1965; died in Washington, D.C. See *Current Biography* (February) 1955.

Obituary *N Y Times* p29 Ap 29 '95

WRIGHT, PETER (MAURICE) 1916–Apr. 27, 1995 Former British intelligence officer; farmer; author of *Spycatcher* (1987), controversial, best-selling memoir of his twenty-two-year career in MI5, a support branch of the British Security Service's counterintelligence operation; wrote that book in collaboration with filmmaker Charles Greengrass, who had made a documentary on the subject for Granada Television in 1984; as son of pioneering radio engineer Maurice Wright, was an autodidact in electronic surveillance; worked on farm from age of fifteen; in late 1930s studied rural economy at Oxford University; with British Admiralty during and after World War II, was involved in design and development of devices both to detect submarines and to protect submarines from detection; in 1949 became part-time unsalaried adviser to MI5; five years later left Admiralty to work full time as MI5's first salaried scientist; as such, was primarily concerned with creation of technology for spying on Soviet intelligence operations and protection of British operations from Soviet detection; in 1976 retired to ranch in Tasmania, Australia, where he raised sheep and horses; in *Spycatcher*, made damaging and embarrassing revelations of illegality and ineptitude as well as subversion in British Security Service; claimed that Soviet agents had infiltrated the highest echelons of the service, that MI5 director Sir Roger Hollis had been the long unknown "fifth man" in the "ring of five" Soviet double agents that included Guy Burgess, Donald Maclean, Kim Philby, and Sir Anthony Blunt, and that a group of right-wing MI5 agents had tried to launch a misinformation campaign to destabilize government of Prime Minister Harold Wilson in 1974; was accused of violating his personal oath of secrecy as well as Official Secrets Act by British government, which failed in its legal efforts to suppress publication and distribution of *Spycatcher*; died at a hospital in Australia. See *Current Biography* (February) 1988.

Obituary *N Y Times* A p30 Ap 28 '95

ZIM, HERBERT S(PENCER) July 12, 1909–Dec. 5, 1994 Author; educator; wrote approximately one hundred children's science books; published *Mice, Men and Elephants*, his first book, in 1942; soon afterward wrote *Submarines, Parachutes, Air Navigation* and *Man in the Air* and cowrote *Minerals*; became editor of Golden Nature Guides, an inexpensive series for adolescents, in 1947; over following years, in collaboration with others, wrote some of the books in the series, including *Birds, Flowers, Insects, Stars, Trees, Reptiles and Amphibians, Mammals, Seashores*, and *Fishes*; for younger children, in early 1950s wrote *Elephants, What's Inside of Me?*, and *What's Inside of Animals?*; cowrote *Birds of North America* (1966); became associate professor of education at University of Illinois in 1950; was promoted to full professor in 1954; in those positions, in his classes for aspiring teachers, covered such subjects as the teaching of science in elementary school; died in Plantation Key, Florida. See *Current Biography* (September) 1956.

Obituary *N Y Times* B p10 D 12 '94

BIOGRAPHICAL REFERENCES

Africa South of the Sahara, 1995
Almanac of American Politics, 1994
American Art Directory, 1993–94
American Catholic Who's Who (1978)
American Medical Directory (1988)
American Men and Women of Science, 1995–96

Biographical Directory of the United States Congress, 1774–1989 (1992)
Biographical Encyclopedia & Who's Who of the American Theatre (1966)
Biographical Encyclopedia of Scientists (1994)
Burke's Peerage, Baronetage, and Knightage (1980)

Canadian Almanac & Directory, 1994
Canadian Who's Who, 1995
Celebrity Register (1990)
China Yearbook (1982)
Chujoy, A., and Manchester, P. W., eds. Dance Encyclopedia (1967)
Columbia Dictionary of Political Biography (1990)
Concise Oxford Dictionary of Ballet (1982)
Congressional Directory, 1960–1995
Congressional Quarterly Almanac, 1960–1995
Contemporary Artists (1995)
Contemporary Authors (1962–95)
Contemporary Composers (1992)
Contemporary Dramatists (1993)
Contemporary Foreign Language Writers (1989)
Contemporary Literary Criticism, 1973–95
Contemporary Literary Critics (1982)
Contemporary Musicians, 1989–95
Contemporary Novelists (1992)
Contemporary Poets (1991)
Contemporary Poets of the English Language (1970)
Contemporary Theatre, Film, and Television, 1984–95
Contemporary Women Dramatists (1994)
Contemporary World Writers (1993)

Debrett's Peerage and Baronetage (1990)
Dictionary of Contemporary American Artists (1993)
Dictionary of International Biography, 1994–95
Dictionary of Literary Biography, 1978–95
Dictionary of National Biography, 1941–1985 (1986)
Directory of American Scholars (1982)
Directory of British Scientists, 1966–67
Directory of Medical Specialists, 1991–1992

Encyclopedia of Pop, Rock and Soul (1990)
Ewen, D., ed, Composers of Today (1936); Living Musicians (1940; First Supplement 1957); Men and Women Who Make Music (1949); European Composers Today (1954); The New Book of Modern Composers (1961); Composers Since 1900 (1969); Musicians Since 1900 (1978); American Composers (1982); American Songwriters (1987)

Far East and Australasia (1989)
Feather, L. Encyclopedia of Jazz in the Sixties (1967); Encyclopedia of Jazz (1984); Encyclopedia of Jazz in the Seventies (1987)
Filmgoer's Companion (1988)
Football Register, 1992

Gilder, E. The Dictionary of Composers and Their Music (1993)
Grove's Dictionary of Music and Musicians (1955)

International Authors and Writers Who's Who, 1995–96
International Dictionary of Architects and Architecture (1993)
International Dictionary of Ballet (1993)
International Dictionary of Films and Filmmakers (1995)
International Dictionary of Opera (1993)
International Dictionary of Theatre (1992)
International Motion Picture Almanac, 1995
International Television Almanac, 1995
International Who's Who, 1995–96
International Who's Who in Art and Antiques (1976)
International Who's Who in Education (1986)
International Who's Who in Medicine, 1995–96
International Who's Who in Music and Musicians Directory, 1994–95
International Who's Who in Poetry and Poets' Encyclopedia, 1993–94
International Who's Who of the Arab World (1984)
International Who's Who of Women (1992)
International Year Book and Statesmen's Who's Who, 1995–96

Katz, E. Film Encyclopedia (1994)

Martindale-Hubbell Law Directory, 1995
McGraw-Hill Encyclopedia of World Biography (1975)
McGraw-Hill Encyclopedia of World Drama (1984)
McGraw-Hill Modern Scientists and Engineers (1980)
Medical Sciences International Who's Who (1994)
Middle East and North Africa (1994)

National Cyclopaedia of American Biography, 1926–84
New Grove Dictionary of American Music (1986)
New Grove Dictionary of Jazz (1988)
New Grove Dictionary of Music and Musicians (1980)
New Grove Gospel, Blues, and Jazz (1986)
Nobel Prize Winners (1987)
Notable Names in American Theatre (1976)
Notable Women in the American Theatre: A Biographical Dictionary (1989)

Official Catholic Directory, 1996
Oxford Companion to American Theatre (1992)
Oxford Companion to Film (1976)

Oxford Companion to the Theatre (1983)
Oxford Companion to Twentieth-Century Art (1988)
Oxford Guide to British Women Writers (1993)

Political Leaders of the Contemporary Middle East and North Africa (1990)
Political Profiles, 1976-82
Politics in America, 1996
Poor's Register of Corporations, Directors and Executives (1985)

Shestack, M. Country Music Encyclopedia (1974)
Slonimsky, N. Baker's Biographical Dictionary of Musicians (1992)
Something About the Author, 1971-90

Thompson, K. A. Dictionary of Twentieth-Century Composers (1973)
Thompson, O., ed. International Cyclopedia of Music and Musicians (1985)
Thomson, D. Biographical Dictionary of Film (1994)
Twentieth Century Authors (1942; First Supplement, 1955)
Twentieth-Century Children's Writers (1994)
Twentieth-Century Crime and Mystery Writers (1991)
Twentieth-Century Romance and Historical Writers (1994)
Twentieth-Century Science Fiction Writers (1992)
Twentieth-Century Western Writers (1991)

Webster's New Biographical Dictionary (1988)
Wer ist Wer? 1994-95
Who's Who, 1995
Who's Who Among Asian Americans, 1994-95
Who's Who Among Black Americans, 1994-95
Who's Who Among Hispanic Americans, 1994-95
Who's Who in Advertising, 1990-91
Who's Who in Africa, 1992
Who's Who in America, 1996
Who's Who in American Art, 1995-96
Who's Who in American Education, 1994-95
Who's Who in American Film Now (1987)
Who's Who in American Law, 1996-97
Who's Who in American Music: Classical (1985)
Who's Who in American Politics, 1995-96
Who's Who in Art, 1994
Who's Who in Australia and the Far East (1991)
Who's Who in Canada (1995)
Who's Who in Congress, 1995
Who's Who in Economics (1986)
Who's Who in Engineering (1988)
Who's Who in Entertainment, 1992-93
Who's Who in European Politics (1993)
Who's Who in Finance and Industry, 1996-97
Who's Who in France, 1991-92
Who's Who in Germany, 1994
Who's Who in International Affairs (1994)
Who's Who in International Organizations (1992)
Who's Who in Israel, 1985-86
Who's Who in Italy (1994)
Who's Who in Japan, 1991-92
Who's Who in Mexico Today (1993)
Who's Who in Music (1969)
Who's Who in Opera (1976)
Who's Who in Philosophy (1969)
Who's Who in Poetry (1991)
Who's Who in Rock Music (1991)
Who's Who in Russia Today (1993)
Who's Who in Science in Europe (1989)
Who's Who in Space (1993)
Who's Who in Spain, 1994
Who's Who in Switzerland, 1988-89
Who's Who in the Arab World 1995-96
Who's Who in the East, 1995-96
Who's Who in the Midwest, 1994-95
Who's Who in the Motion Picture Industry (1993)
Who's Who in the People's Republic of China (1991)
Who's Who in the South and Southwest, 1995-96
Who's Who in the Soviet Union (1989)
Who's Who in the Theatre (1981)
Who's Who in TV and Cable (1983)
Who's Who in the United Nations (1992)
Who's Who in the West, 1996-97
Who's Who in the World (1995)
Who's Who in U.S. Executives, 1988-89
Who's Who in Western Europe (1991)
Who's Who in World Jewry (1987)
Who's Who in Writers, Editors, & Poets, 1995-96
Who's Who of American Women, 1995-96
Who's Who of British Engineers (1980)
Who's Who of British Scientists, 1980-81
Who's Who of Jazz (1985)
Who's Who of Southern Africa, 1994-95
Who's Who of the Asian Pacific Rim, 1995-96
Who's Who on Television (1990)
World Artists 1950-1980 (1984)
World Artists 1980-1990 (1991)
World Authors 1950-1970 (1975)
World Authors 1970-1975 (1980)
World Authors 1975-1980 (1985)
World Authors 1980-1985 (1991)
World Film Directors 1890-1945 (1987)
World Film Directors 1945-1985 (1988)
World Who's Who in Science (1968)
World's Who's Who of Women, 1995-96
Writers Directory, 1994-96

PERIODICALS AND NEWSPAPERS CONSULTED

Africa Report
Am Artist—American Artist
Am Film—American Film
Am J R—American Journalism Review
Am Record Guide—American Record Guide
Am Scholar—American Scholar
Art & Artists
Artforum
Art in America
ARTnews
Arts
Arts & Arch—Arts & Architecture
Atlantic—Atlantic Monthly
Audubon

Barron's
Book World
Boston Globe
Broadcasting
Bsns W—Business Week

Cable Guide
Chicago Sun-Times
Chicago Tribune
Christian Sci Mon—Christian Science Monitor
Civilization
Classic CD
Columbia J R—Columbia Journalism Review
Commonweal
Cong Digest—Congressional Digest
Cong Q—Congressional Quarterly Weekly Report
Connoisseur (disc.)
Cur Hist—Current History

Dance & Dancers
Dance Mag—Dancemagazine
Details
Discover
Down Beat

Ebony
Economist
Elle
Emerge
Encounter
Entertainment W—Entertainment Weekly
Esquire
Essence

Films & Filming
Financial Times
Foreign Affairs
Foreign Policy Bulletin
Forbes
Fortune

GQ—Gentlemen's Quarterly
German Tribune
Good Housekeeping
Gramophone
Guardian

Harper's
Harper's Bazaar
Hi Fi/Stereo R—Hi/Fi Stereo Review

Inside Sports
International Wildlife
Interview

Ladies Home J—Ladies' Home Journal
Lear's
Le monde
Lib J—Library Journal
Life
London Observer
London R of Bks—London Review of Books
Los Angeles Times

Maclean's
Manchester Guardian W—Manchester Guardian Weekly
McCall's
Mirabella
Modern Maturity
Mother Jones
Ms—Ms.
Mus Am—Musical America (disc.)

N Y Daily News
N Y Newsday
N Y Observer
N Y Post
N Y R of Bks—New York Review of Books
N Y Times
N Y Times Bk R—New York Times Book Review
N Y Times Mag—New York Times Magazine
Nat Geog Mag—National Geographic Magazine
Nat R—National Review
Nation
Nations Bsns—Nation's Business
Natural Hist—Natural History
Nature
New Leader
New Repub—New Republic
New Scientist
New Statesman—New Statesman & Society
New York
New Yorker
Newsweek

Omni
Opera N—Opera News
Ovation

Parade
People
Philadelphia Inquirer
Playbill
Playboy
Plays & Players
Premiere
Pub W—Publishers Weekly

Readers' Digest
Rolling Stone

Sat Eve Post—Saturday Evening Post (disc.)
Sat R—Saturday Review (disc.)
Scala (English edition)
Sci Am—Scientific American
Sci Mo—Scientific Monthly
Sci N L—Science News Letter
Science
Sight & Sound
Smithsonian
Spec—Spectator
Spiegel—Der Spiegel
Spin
Sport
Sporting N—Sporting News
Sports Illus—Sports Illustrated
Stagebill
Stereo R—Stereo Review
Sunday Times—London Sunday Times

Time
Times—London Times
Times Lit Sup—London Times Literary Supplement
Toronto Globe and Mail
TV Guide

USA Today
U S News—U.S. News & World Report

Vanity Fair
Variety
Village Voice
Vogue

Wall St J—Wall Street Journal
Washington M—Washington Monthly
Washington Post
Women's Wear Daily
Working Woman
World Monitor
World Press R—World Press Review

CLASSIFICATION BY PROFESSION—1995

ART
Bennett, Tony
Chihuly, Dale
Chwast, Seymour
Crumb, R.
Danto, Arthur C.
Estes, Richard
Fassett, Kaffe
Kruger, Barbara
Long, Richard
Millet, Kate
Murray, Elizabeth

BUSINESS
Amos, Wally
Ash, Mary Kay
Barad, Jill E.
Branson, Richard
Bronfman, Edgar M., Jr.
Evers-Williams, Myrlie
Garzarelli, Elaine
Hillis, W. Daniel
Huizenga, H. Wayne
Katzenberg, Jeffrey
Lamb, Brian
Magaziner, Ira C.
Malone, John C.
Miller, Nicole
Ovitz, Michael S.
Perry, William J.
Thomas, Dave
Winston, O. Link

CONSERVATION
Galdikas, Biruté M. F.
Leakey, Richard
Payne, Roger S.
Schultes, Richard Evans
Suzuki, David T.

DANCE
Kudelka, James
Perez, Rosie

EDUCATION
Albright, Madeleine Korbel
Armey, Richard K.
Bakker, Robert T.
Bell Burnell, Jocelyn
Chihuly, Dale
Chomsky, Noam
Danto, Arthur C.
Delany, Sadie
Dorris, Michael
Early, Gerald
Edelman, Gerald M.
Hill, Anita
Hooks, Bell
Keen, Sam
King, Mary-Claire
Kruger, Barbara
Perry, William J.
Schopf, J. William
Schultes, Richard Evans
Vermeij, Geerat J.

FASHION
Fassett, Kaffe
Iman
Miller, Nicole

FILM
Allen, Tim
Armstrong, Gillian
Belushi, James
Bronfman, Edgar M., Jr.
Burnett, Charles
Bush, Kate
Carroll, Jim
Franz, Dennis
Gifford, Frank
Goldman, William
Grafton, Sue
Grant, Hugh
Grodin, Charles
Hartley, Hal
Howard, Ron
Ice Cube
Iman
Jones, Tommy Lee
Katzenberg, Jeffrey
Kieślowski, Krzysztof
Knopfler, Mark
Kotto, Yaphet
Loach, Ken
Louis-Dreyfus, Julia
Mary Alice
Mikhalkov, Nikita
Mirren, Helen
Nicholson, Jack
O'Donnell, Rosie
Ovitz, Michael S.
Perez, Rosie
Pop, Iggy
Reeves, Keanu
Reggio, Godfrey
Tarantino, Quentin
Thompson, Emma
Wayans, Keenen Ivory
Woodard, Alfre

GOVERNMENT AND POLITICS, FOREIGN
Albright, Madeleine Korbel
Cédras, Raoul
Havel, Václav
Jiang Zemin
Karadžić, Radovan
Kim Young Sam
Leakey, Richard
Lee Kwan Yew
Mandela, Nelson
Mwinyi, Ali Hassan
Patterson, P. J.
Peres, Shimon
Rabin, Yitzhak
Ramaphosa, Cyril
Zhirinovsky, Vladimir

GOVERNMENT AND POLITICS, U.S.
Albright, Madeleine Korbel
Armey, Richard K.

Iman
King, Mary-Claire
Mandela, Nelson
Millet, Kate
Ramaphosa, Cyril
Sharpton, Al, Jr.
Suzuki, David T.

SOCIAL SCIENCES
Albright, Madeleine Korbel
Armey, Richard K.
Chomsky, Noam
Danto, Arthur C.

SPORTS
Abbott, Jim
Aikman, Troy
Esiason, Boomer
Foreman, George
Gifford, Frank
Huizenga, H. Wayne
Lucas, John
Messier, Mark
Monk, Art
Sanders, Deion
Smith, Bruce
Stockton, John
White, Reggie
Wilkins, Dominique

TELEVISION
Allen, Tim
Belushi, James
Burnett, Charles
Foreman, George
Franz, Dennis
Gifford, Frank
Grafton, Sue
Grant, Hugh
Grodin, Charles
Howard, Ron
Iman
Jones, Tommy Lee
Kinsley, Michael
Kotto, Yaphet
Lamb, Brian
Loach, Ken
Louis-Dreyfus, Julia
Malone, John C.
Mary Alice
Mirren, Helen
Newton, Christopher
Nicholson, Jack
O'Donnell, Rosie
Perez, Rosie
Pop, Iggy
Reeves, Keanu
Rose, Charlie
Shaw, Bernard
Suzuki, David T.
Thompson, Emma
Wayans, Keenen Ivory
Wertheimer, Linda
Woodard, Alfre

THEATRE
Belushi, James
Binchy, Maeve
Busch, Charles
Franz, Dennis
Fraser, Brad
Goldman, William
Grodin, Charles
Havel, Václav
Jones, Tommy Lee
Kotto, Yaphet
Lepage, Robert
Lessing, Doris
Mary Alice
Mirren, Helen
Newton, Christopher
Reeves, Keanu
Thompson, Emma
Woodard, Alfre

CUMULATED INDEX—1991-1995

For the index to the 1940-1990 biographies, see Current Biography Cumulated Index 1940-1990.